Anthropology

The Exploration of Human Diversity

GREENLAND
(Den)
ICELAND
CANADA
UNITED STATES OF AMERICA
ATLANTIC OCEAN
PACIFIC OCEAN
MEXICO
BERMUDA
BAHAMAS
CUBA
DOMINICAN REPUBLIC
JAMAICA
HAITI
PR (U.S.)
ST. KITTS NEVIS
ANTIGUA & BARBUDA
GUADELOUPE (Fr)
DOMINICA
MARTINIQUE (Fr)
ST. LUCIA
ST. VINCENT & GRENADINES
BARB
GRENADA
TRINIDAD & TOBAGO
BELIZE
GUATEMALA
HONDURAS
EL SALVADOR
NICARAGUA
COSTA RICA
PANAMA
VENEZUELA
COLOMBIA
GUYANA
SUR
FR GUI (Fr)
ECUADOR
BRAZIL
PERU
BOLIVIA
CHILE
PARAGUAY
URUGUAY
ARGENTINA
FALKLAND ISLANDS (UK)
NORWAY
SWEDEN
FINLAND
EST
LAT
LITH
DENMARK
IRELAND
UNITED KINGDOM
NETH
BELG
GERMANY
POLAND
BELA
CZECH
SLVK
LUX
FRANCE
SWITZ
AUS
HUN
SLOVE
CRO
BOS HER
YUGO
ROM
ITALY
VATICAN
MAC
BULG
PORTUGAL
SPAIN
ALB
GREECE
GIBRALTAR
MALTA
TUNISIA
MOROCCO
ALGERIA
LIBYA
WESTERN SAHARA
MAURITANIA
MALI
NIGER
CHAD
CAPE VERDE
SENEGAL
GAMBIA
GUINEA-BISSAU
GUINEA
BURKINA FASO
BEN
NIGERIA
SIERRA LEONE
COTE D' IVOIRE
LIBERIA
TOGO
CAR
CAMEROON
EQUATORIAL GUINEA
SAO TOME & PRINCIPE
GABON
REP CONGO
DEM REP CONGO
ANGOLA
NAMIBIA
BOTSWANA
SOUTH AFRICA

CURRENTLY RECOGNIZED SOVEREIGN STATES 1999
uninterrupted independence since:

- 1990–2001
- 1960–1989
- 1940–1959
- 1915–1939
- 1800–1914
- pre–1800
- occupied and dependent territories or other anomalies
- privileged zone: extended economic zone or exclusive fishing zone schematic

Sources: Statesman's Year-Book 1993–94; U.S. State Department; press reports.

A paradox of today's world is that both integration and disintegration are increasing. As new global links have been forged through the media, migration, and advanced information technology, many nation-states have shattered. Since 1990, more than two dozen nation-states have come into being.

Nation-states rise and fall. Only 14 countries can claim an uninterrupted existence exceeding 200 years. Before 1800, states arose on average just once every 175 years. The rate has jumped from one new country every four years in the 19th century, to one every 18 months between 1900 and 1950, and to one every five months since 1950. The world now contains at least 184 internationally recognized nation-states. Some of the newer ones, like Bosnia-Herzogovina, are fragments of older states (Yugoslavia).

Ninth Edition

Anthropology

The Exploration of Human Diversity

Conrad Phillip Kottak
The University of Michigan

Boston Burr Ridge, IL Dubuque, IA Madison, WI New York San Francisco St. Louis
Bangkok Bogotá Caracas Kuala Lumpur Lisbon London Madrid Mexico City
Milan Montreal New Delhi Santiago Seoul Singapore Sydney Taipei Toronto

McGraw-Hill Higher Education
A Division of The **McGraw-Hill** *Companies*

ANTHROPOLOGY: THE EXPLORATION OF HUMAN DIVERSITY

Published by McGraw-Hill, an imprint of The McGraw-Hill Companies, Inc. 1221 Avenue of the Americas, New York, NY, 10020.

This book is printed on acid-free paper.

domestic 1 2 3 4 5 6 7 8 9 0 DOW/DOW 0 9 8 7 6 5 4 3 2 1
international 1 2 3 4 5 6 7 8 9 0 DOW/DOW 0 9 8 7 6 5 4 3 2 1

ISBN 0–07-242652-7

Editorial director: *Phillip A. Butcher*
Senior sponsoring editor: *Carolyn Henderson*
Editorial assistant: *Julie Abodeely*
Marketing manager: *Dan Loch*
Senior project manager: *Christine A. Vaughan*
Production supervisor: *Rose Hepburn*
Media producer: *Shannon Rider*
Director of design: *Keith J. McPherson*
Associate supplement producer: *Joyce J. Chappetto*
Photo research coordinator: *David A. Tietz*
Cover and interior design: *Maureen McCutcheon*
Printer: *R. R. Donnelley & Sons Company*
Typeface: *10/12 Palatino*
Compositor: *Precision Graphics*
Cover image: Children in Doorway, *India Still Picture/Peter Arnold, Inc. #200300*
Interesting Issues icon: Greek Statue, *Antonio M. Rosario/The Image Bank © 2001*
Beyond the Classroom icon: The sarcophagus of Psatemik, Egyptian, *Musee des Beaux Arts, Grenoble, France/Peter Willi/Bridgeman Art Library*
In the News icon: Cycladic female figure, from Island of Amorgo, *© 2000 BC National Archaelogical Museum, Athens, Greece/Bridgeman Art Library*
Table of Contents part images: *Steven Hunt/The Image Bank © 2001*

Library of Congress Cataloging-in-Publication Data

Kottak, Conrad Phillip.
Anthropology : the exploration of human diversity/Conrad Phillip Kottak.—9th ed.
p. cm.
Includes bibliographical references and indexes.
ISBN 0-07-242652-7 (alk. paper)
1. Anthropology I. Title.
GN25 .K67 2002
301—dc21 2001031576

INTERNATIONAL EDITION ISBN 0-07-112116-1

www.mhhe.com

about the author

Conrad Phillip Kottak (A.B. Columbia College, 1963; Ph.D. Columbia University, 1966) is Professor and Chair of the Department of Anthropology at the University of Michigan, where he has taught since 1968. In 1991 he was honored for his teaching by the University and the state of Michigan. In 1992 he received an excellence in teaching award from the College of Literature, Science, and the Arts of the University of Michigan. And in 1999 the American Anthropological Association (AAA) awarded Professor Kottak the AAA/Mayfield Award for Excellence in the Undergraduate Teaching of Anthropology.

Professor Kottak has done field work in cultural anthropology in Brazil (since 1962), Madagascar (since 1966), and the United States. His general interests are in the processes by which local cultures are incorporated—and resist incorporation—into larger systems. This interest links his earlier work on ecology and state formation in Africa and Madagascar to his more recent research on globalization, national and international culture, and the mass media.

The third edition of Kottak's case study *Assault on Paradise: Social Change in a Brazilian Village,* based on his field work in Arembepe, Bahia, Brazil, from 1962 through the present, was published in 1999 by McGraw-Hill. In a project during the 1980s, collaborating with Brazilian and North American researchers, Kottak blended ethnography and survey research in studying "Television's Behavioral Effects in Brazil." That research is the basis of Kottak's book *Prime-Time Society: An Anthropological Analysis of Television and Culture* (Wadsworth 1990)—a comparative study of the nature and impact of television in Brazil and the United States.

Kottak's other books include *The Past in the Present: History, Ecology and Cultural Variation in Highland Madagascar* (1980), *Researching American Culture: A Guide for Student Anthropologists* (1982) (both University of Michigan Press), and *Madagascar: Society and History* (1986) (Carolina Academic Press). The second edition of his *Mirror for Humanity: A Concise Introduction to Cultural Anthropology* was published by McGraw-Hill in 1999. Kottak's newest book, co-authored with Kathryn A. Kozaitis of Georgia State University, is *On Being Different: Diversity and Multiculturalism in the North American Mainstream,* published by McGraw-Hill in 1999.

Conrad Kottak's articles have appeared in academic journals including *American Anthropologist, Journal of Anthropological Research, American Ethnologist, Ethnology, Human Organization,* and *Luso-Brazilian Review.* He also has written for more popular journals, including *Transaction/SOCIETY, Natural History, Psychology Today,* and *General Anthropology.*

In recent research projects, Kottak and his colleagues have investigated the emergence of ecological awareness in Brazil, the social context of deforestation in Madagascar, and popular participation in economic development planning in northeastern Brazil. Since 1999 Professor Kottak has been active in the University of Michigan's Center for the Ethnography of Everyday Life, supported by the Alfred P. Sloan Foundation. In that capacity, for a research project entitled "Media, Family, and Work in a Middle-Class Midwestern Town," Kottak is now investigating how middle-class families draw on various media in planning, managing, and evaluating their choices and solutions with respect to competing demands of work and family.

Conrad Kottak appreciates comments about his textbook from professors and students. He can be readily reached by e-mail at the following Internet address:

ckottak@umich.edu

preface

Since 1968, I've regularly taught Anthropology 101 ("Introduction to Anthropology") to a class of 375 to 550 students. Constant feedback from students, teaching assistants, and my fellow instructors keeps me up to date on the interests, needs, and views of the people for whom this text is written. I continue to believe that effective textbooks are rooted in enthusiasm and enjoyment of one's own teaching experience.

As a college student, I was drawn to anthropology by its breadth and because of what it could tell me about the human condition, present and past. Since then, I've been fortunate in spending my teaching career at a university that values and unites anthropology's four subdisciplines. Although I'm mainly a cultural anthropologist, I have daily contact with members of the other subfields, and as a regular teacher of the four-field introductory anthropology course, I'm happy to keep up with those subfields. I love anthropology's breadth. I believe that anthropology has compiled an impressive body of knowledge about human diversity in time and space, and I'm eager to introduce that knowledge in the pages that follow. I believe strongly in anthropology's capacity to enlighten and inform. Anthropology's subject matter is intrinsically fascinating, and its focus on diversity helps students understand and interact with their fellow human beings in an increasingly interconnected world and an increasingly diverse North America.

I decided to write this book back in 1972, when there were far fewer introductory anthropology texts than there are today. The texts back then tended to be overly encyclopedic. I found them too long and too unfocused for my course and my image of contemporary anthropology. The field of anthropology was changing rapidly. Anthropologists were writing about a "new archaeology" and a "new ethnography." Fresh fossil finds and biochemical studies were challenging our understanding of human and primate evolution. Studies of monkeys and apes in their natural settings were contradicting conclusions that were based on work in zoos. Studies of language as actually used in society were revolutionizing overly formal and static linguistic models. In cultural anthropology, symbolic and interpretive approaches were joining ecological and materialist ones.

I believe strongly that anthropology has a core, which any competent introductory text must explore: anthropology's nature, scope, and roles as a science and as a humanistic field. In *Mirror for Man,* one of the first books I ever read in anthropology, I was impressed by Clyde Kluckhohn's (1944) description of anthropology as "the science of human similarities and differences" (p. 9). Kluckhohn's statement of the need for such a field still stands: "Anthropology provides a scientific basis for dealing with the crucial dilemma of the world today: how can peoples of different appearance, mutually unintelligible languages, and dissimilar ways of life get along peaceably together?" (p. 9).

Part of anthropology's breadth is that it is a humanistic field as well as a science. Bringing a comparative and cross-cultural perspective to forms of creative expression, anthropology influences and is influenced by the humanities. Indeed, anthropology is among the most humanistic of academic fields because of its fundamental respect for human diversity. Anthropologists routinely listen to, record, and attempt to represent voices and perspectives from a multitude of times, places, nations, and cultures.

As I write this preface, more than 25 years after the publication of my first edition in 1974, anthropology hasn't stopped changing. It's been my aim throughout my nine editions to continue to write the most current, timely, and up-to-date textbook available. My approach is to be fair and objective in covering various and sometimes diverging approaches in anthropology, but I make my own views known and write in the first person when it seems appropriate. I've heard colleagues who use other textbooks complain that some authors seem so intent on presenting every conceivable theory about an issue—the origin of agriculture, for example—that students are bewildered by the array of possibilities. Anthropology should not be made so complicated that it is impossible for beginning students to appreciate and understand. So, the textbook author, like the instructor, must be able to guide the student.

Because anthropology, reflecting the world itself, seems to change at an increasing rate, an introductory textbook must not restrict itself to subject matter defined decades ago. Some recent texts present the field more or less as it was a generation ago. They neglect the pervasive changes affecting the peoples, places, and topics that anthropologists have traditionally studied. The organization of my text is intended to cover core concepts and basics while also discussing prominent current issues and interests.

What's New in the Ninth Edition

What are the main content differences between the eighth and ninth editions of *Anthropology: The Exploration of Human Diversity?*

The chapter order has been changed to reflect the way most professors teach the introductory course. Physical anthropology and archaeology now come at the beginning, followed by the cultural/linguistic chapters. Formerly some of the cultural chapters (on culture, language, and ethnicity) had preceded the physical chapters.

All chapters have been updated in terms of their research base, citations, and statistical information. Most chapters, including boxes, have been shortened.

The addition of two new chapters (5 and 10) expands the coverage of physical anthropology and archaeology, to meet the course goals of many instructors.

- Chapter 5 ("Primate Evolution") explores the emergence of the primates, including the latest theories on how they emerged. Its extensive photo program compares fossil primates with their most similar living relatives. The discussion of Miocene apes, based on the latest research, examines several possible common ancestors for humans and the apes.
- Chapter 10 ("The First Cities and States") examines, including theories about, the emergence of towns, cities, chiefdoms, and states. Its examples, enlivened by new photos, maps and tables, include the Middle East, India/Pakistan, China, Mesoamerica, and Peru. Students learn how archaeologists make inferences about ancient societies from contemporary ethnographic studies. This illustrates the text's overall focus on anthropology as a four-field discipline in which findings from one subfield are integral to the others.

All other chapters have been updated, revised, and often shortened. Here are some of the most significant changes:

- In Chapter 2 ("In the Field"), a section on the evolution of ethnography has been added to the text, along with sections on archaeological field work. There is a major new section on "Science, Explanation, and Hypothesis Testing."
- Chapter 3 ("Evolution and Genetics") contains a revised discussion of genes and disease.
- Chapter 4 ("The Primates") presents the most recent information on endangered primates and chimpanzee hunting.
- Based on the most recent discoveries and research on the expansion of early *Homo erectus*, (sometimes known as *H. ergaster*), Chapter 6 ("Early Hominids") describes new fossil finds in Europe.
- Chapter 7 ("Modern Humans") has been updated and shortened and includes the latest on the various theories for the origin of *H. sapiens*.
- Chapter 8 ("Human Diversity and 'Race'") has been reorganized and updated.
- Chapter 12 ("Ethnicity") includes a new section on "Ethnic Markers, Identities, and Statuses."
- New information on BEV, a.k.a. "Ebonics," has been added to Chapter 13 ("Language and Communication"). The section on cyberspace communication includes new information on sociolinguistic dimensions of advanced information technology.
- Chapter 15 ("Families, Kinship, and Descent") has undergone extensive revision, including reorganization and an expanded discussion of extended families. A link to our website provides detailed discussion of all cousin terminologies, for instructors who prefer to teach kinship terminology in greater depth.

- Chapter 18 ("Gender") has been updated and revised, particularly its discussion of gender issues in India.
- New sections on music and dance have been added to Chapter 20 ("The Arts").
- A box on "Preserving Linguistic and Cultural Diversity" has been added to Chapter 23 ("Cultural Exchange and Survival").

Organization

As mentioned, the text has been reorganized between the eighth and ninth editions. The new organization has four parts:

- Part I ("The Basics of Anthropology") introduces anthropology as a four-field, integrated discipline that examines human biological and cultural diversity in time and space. Anthropology is discussed as a global, comparative, and holistic science, with biocultural, historical, and humanistic dimensions. Part I explores links between anthropology and other fields, such as the humanities, history, and other sciences. Field methods in the subfields are discussed, along with research design, hypothesis testing, the ethical aspects of anthropological research, and differences between ethnographic and survey research.
- Part II ("Humankind Evolving") poses and answers several key questions. When did we originate, and how did we become what we are? What role do genes, the environment, society, and culture play in human variation and diversity? What can we tell about our origins and nature from the study of our nearest relatives—nonhuman primates? When and how did the primates originate? What key features of their early adaptations are still basic to our abilities, behavior, and perceptions? How did hominids develop from our primate ancestors? When, where, and how did the first hominids emerge and expand? What about the earliest real humans? How do we explain biological diversity in our own species, *Homo sapiens?* How does such diversity relate to the idea of race? What major transitions have taken place since the emergence of *Homo sapiens?* The origin of food production (the domestication of plants and animals) was a major change in human adaptation, with profound implications for society and culture. The spread and intensification of food production are tied to the appearance of the first towns, cities, and states, and the emergence of social stratification and major inequalities.
- Part III ("Cultural Diversity") begins with a discussion of the culture concept, and the related topic of ethnicity, in relation to race and its social construction. Culture and language are linked through learning, sharing, and reliance on symbolic thought. Throughout Part III, discussions of relevant concepts, theory, and explanations are combined with rich ethnographic examples and case studies. Part III examines how sociocultural diversity is manifest and expressed in such domains as language, economic systems, family and kinship, marriage, political systems, gender, religion, and the arts.
- The organization of this text is intended to cover core concepts and basics, while also discussing prominent current issues. Part IV ("The Modern World") is one of the key differences between this anthropology text and others. Several key questions are addressed in Part IV: How and why did the modern world system emerge? How has world capitalism affected patterns of stratification and inequality within and among nations? What were colonialism and imperialism and their legacies? How do economic development and globalization affect the peoples, cultures, and communities among which anthropologists have traditionally worked? How do people actively interpret and confront the world system and the products of globalization? What is the role of the anthropologist in identifying and solving contemporary social problems in North America and abroad? What factors threaten continued human diversity? How can anthropologists work to ensure the preservation of that diversity?
- Finally, let me point out that this text has three essential chapters not consistently found in other anthropology texts: "Human

Diversity and 'Race'" (8), "Ethnicity" (12), and "Gender" (18). I believe that systematic consideration of race, ethnicity, and gender is vital in an introductory anthropology text. Anthropology's distinctive four-field approach can shed special light on these subjects, and I find it disappointing that some anthropology texts lack chapters on these fundamental topics. Race and gender studies are fields in which anthropology has always taken the lead. I'm convinced that anthropology's special contributions to understanding the biological, social, cultural, and linguistic dimensions of race, ethnicity, and gender should be highlighted in any introductory text. They certainly are highlighted in this one—not just in their special chapters, but throughout the text, starting in Chapter 1.

Pedagogical Aids

Working closely together, the author, editors, and photo researcher have developed a format for this text that supports the goal of a readable, practical, up-to-date, and attractive book. Besides all the changes already mentioned, the number of photographs has been increased in order to make the book even more approachable. Copious tables, figures, and maps highlight and amplify the text coverage.

Here's a summary of the pedagogical features of the ninth edition:

- **Chapter-Opening Vignettes** (new feature)—Fascinating, current "In the News" vignettes now open every chapter, highlighting the relevance of anthropology in today's world.
- **Chapter-Opening Previews**—Succinct chapter-opening outlines and streamlined, more concise overviews help students focus on the chapter's critical concepts and terminology.
- **Plentiful Photographs, Maps, Figures, Charts, and Tables**—A wealth of illustrations and a significantly revised photo program—complete with extended, thought-provoking captions—make chapter material clearer, more understandable, and more inviting than ever before.
- **Unique Student CD-ROM**—This independent study tool—packaged free with every copy of the text—features a chapter-by-chapter electronic study guide with audio, video, text, and web-based review tools, as well as study-break materials and information on how to do better in the course.
- **In-Text Icons**—Useful marginal icons tell students when more information on a particular topic is available on the CD-ROM or Online Learning Center that accompany the text, or where to turn in the text itself for additional information.
- **Intriguing *Interesting Issues* Boxes**—Unique coverage of current issues in anthropology, many with maps and photos, raise students' awareness of some of the more provocative aspects of anthropology today.
- **Timely *In the News* Boxes**—Detailed discussion of the kinds of issues students may be hearing about in the media relates the concepts presented in each chapter back to the real world (maps and photos included).
- **Widely Acclaimed *Beyond the Classroom* Boxes**—Popular thematic boxes highlighting student research in anthropology enable students to read about the work their peers at other schools are doing, further highlighting the relevance of anthropology in the real world.
- **Easy-to-Use End-of-Chapter Reviews**—Clear, concise *numbered* chapter summaries facilitate chapter concept review, while end-of-chapter glossaries enable students to go over the chapter's key terms.
- **Unique Critical Thinking and Internet Exercises**—Chapter-ending exercises challenge students to use their critical thinking skills to apply what they have read about in the chapter and explore chapter concepts in greater detail via web research.
- **Free Online Learning Center**—Accompanying website provides even more review material—self-quizzes (different from those on the CD-ROM), links, flash cards, Internet and critical thinking exercises, PowerPoint lectures, and more.
- **All-New Case Studies**—These case exercises are perfect for those supplementing text reading with *Culture Sketches* (third edition)

by Holly Peters-Golden. These ethnographic cases allow students to link chapter concepts with ethnographic examples in a practical, guided fashion.

- **End-of-Book Glossary**—Brings together all the key terms defined at the end of each chapter, for easy access and review.

Supplements

As a full service publisher of quality educational products, McGraw-Hill does much more than just sell textbooks. We create and publish an extensive array of print, video, and digital supplements for students and instructors. This edition of *Anthropology* boasts an extensive, comprehensive supplements package:

For the Student

- **Student CD-ROM**—this fully interactive student CD-ROM is packaged free of charge with every new textbook and features the following unique tools:
    - *How to Ace This Course:*
        - Animated book walk-through
        - Expert advice on how to succeed in the course (provided on video by the University of Michigan)
        - Learning styles assessment program
        - Study skills primer
        - Internet primer
        - Guide to electronic research
    - *Chapter-by-Chapter Electronic Study Guide:*
        - Video clip from a University of Michigan lecture on the text chapter
        - Interactive map exercise
        - Chapter objectives and outline
        - Key terms with an audio pronunciation guide
        - Self-quizzes (multiple choice, true/false, and short-answer questions with feedback indicating why your answer is correct or incorrect)
        - Critical thinking essay questions
        - Internet exercises
        - Vocabulary flashcards
        - Chapter-related web links
    - *Cool Stuff*
        - Interactive globe
        - Study break links
- **Student's Online Learning Center**—this free web-based student supplement features many of the same tools as the CD-ROM (so students can access these materials either online or on CD, whichever is convenient), but *also* includes:
    - An entirely new self-quiz for each chapter (with feedback, so students can take two pre-tests prior to exams)
    - Career opportunities
    - Additional chapter-related readings
    - Anthropology FAQs
    - PowerPoint lecture notes
    - Monthly updates
    - ***Culture Sketches: Case Studies in Anthropology*, Third Edition by Holly Peters-Golden**—this unique collection of mini-ethnographies is linked to the Kottak textbook via the "Case Study" found at the end of every Kottak chapter, features coverage of 15 anthropologically significant cultures, and provides real-world examples of everything from witchcraft to matriliny to economic development/change. Instructors can package *Culture Sketches* with the Kottak text for a nominal extra charge.
    - ***Through the Looking Glass*, Second Edition** by Cronk/Bryant is a brief, inexpensive collection of readings consisting of current, lively articles from popular magazines and is unique in that its readings span the entire discipline, from race to prehistory to economic development and more.

For the Instructor

- **Instructor's Manual/Testbank**—this indispensable instructor supplement features detailed chapter outlines, key terms, overviews, discussion questions, a complete testbank, and more.

- **Computerized Testbank**—this easy-to-use computerized testing program is available for both Windows and Macintosh computers and makes testing simple. (McGraw-Hill's testing service is also available for instructors who would prefer to have master tests created for them; contact Carolyn_Henderson@mcgraw-hill.com for more information.)
- **PowerPoint Slides**—complete, chapter-by-chapter slideshows featuring text, photos, tables, and illustrations.
- **Instructor's Online Learning Center**—password-protected access to important instructor support materials, downloadable supplements, and additional professional and teaching resources.

Acknowledgments

I'm grateful to many present and past colleagues at McGraw-Hill. Along with the reviewers of the eighth edition, Carolyn Henderson, McGraw-Hill's excellent anthropology editor, helped me conceive, plan, and implement this revision, including the chapter reorganization, the addition of new chapters, and the new features. Carolyn has worked especially hard on planning the supplements package, including the terrific new CD-ROM and the Online Learning Center. It's always a pleasure to work with Phil Butcher, McGraw-Hill's editorial director for the social sciences and humanities. Barbara Salz, my photo researcher since the fourth edition, returned to do her usual excellent job on the photo program for the ninth edition. I enjoyed working with Barbara as we planned, and she located, the photos for the two new chapters. I also thank her for her suggestions about which of the old photos needed replacement, and for constantly being on the alert for photos that best illustrate this text.

Thanks also to Leslie Kraham, McGraw-Hill's former marketing manager for anthropology for her hard work on previous editions of this text, and for her valuable input as we started planning the ninth edition. Let me also thank McGraw-Hill's knowledgeable and dedicated sales representatives for their ongoing feedback, suggestions, hard work, and enthusiasm in getting this book into the proper hands.

I'm grateful to Miriam Beyer for again coordinating the Beyond the Classroom program for the ninth edition, contacting anthropology departments across the country to see if they had undergraduate research projects that might be included in the book. I thank the students and faculty who cooperated with us in preparing these boxes. Limitations of space and the need to choose boxes for particular chapters prevented us from using all the contributions we received.

From the McGraw-Hill office in Burr Ridge, Illinois, Christine Vaughan worked with me as senior project manager for the second time. I thank her for her attentive work in supervising all aspects of production and for keeping everything moving on schedule. Chris Brady of Mapquest.com is responsible for creating the attractive maps that are showcased in our Where in the World graphic program. I also thank Betsy Blumenthal and Sue Nodine for copyediting and proofreading, and Keith McPherson for conceiving and executing the new design and cover.

Christopher Glew, a fifth-year University of Michigan archaeology graduate student, was my research assistant as I wrote the eighth and ninth editions. Chris read the reviews and made various suggestions about ways of responding to comments. He suggested new and revised tables and figures, went to sources to find new and better information, and did the first drafts of many of the tables and figures. Chris also did the map research, locating groups for the Where in the World graphic program and finding sources for other new maps and charts. He and Patrick Livingood wrote the Internet Exercises at the end of each chapter. Chris also wrote the first draft of the section on archaeological methods in Chapter 2. Chris and Patrick are also responsible for the book's web page and CD-ROM integration. Finally, they wrote the Instructor's Manual and Test Bank questions, combining previous work by David Brawn with new writing. Chris has received a teaching award for his work as a graduate student instructor at the University of Michigan. He has also received special training in writing and pedagogy for undergraduates. I am delighted to have had his help on both editions.

I am grateful to the reviewers of the seventh and eighth editions of *Anthropology: The Exploration of Human Diversity*. Their names are as follows:

Reviewers

Julianna Acheson
Green Mountain College

Mohamad Al-Madani
Seattle Central Community College

Robert Bee
University of Connecticut

Daniel Boxberger
Western Washington University

Ned Breschel
Morehead State University

Peter J. Brown
Emory University

Margaret Bruchez
Blinn College

Karen Burns
University of Georgia

Richard Burns
Arkansas State University

Mary Cameron
Auburn University

Dianne Chidester
University of South Dakota

Inne Choi
California Polytechnic State University–San Luis Obispo

Jeffrey Cohen
Penn State University

Barbara Cook
California Polytechnic State University–San Luis Obispo

Norbert Dannhaeuser
Texas A&M University

Michael Davis
Truman State University

Robert Dirks
Illinois State University

Bill Donner
Kutztown University of Pennsylvania

Paul Durrenberger
Pennsylvania State University

George Esber
Miami University of Ohio

Grace Fraser
Plymouth State College

Laurie Godfrey
University of Massachusetts–Amherst

Bob Goodby
Franklin Pierce College

Tom Greaves
Bucknell University

Mark Grey
University of Northern Iowa

Homes Hogue
Mississippi State University

Alice James
Shippensburg University of Pennsylvania

Richard King
Drake University

Eric Lassiter
Ball State University

Jill Leonard
University of Illinois–Urbana–Champaign

David Lipset
University of Minnesota

Jonathan Marks
University of North Carolina–Charlotte

Barbara Miller
George Washington University

John Nass, Jr.
California University of Pennsylvania

Frank Ng
California State University–Fresno

Martin Ottenheimer
Kansas State University

Leonard Plotnicov
University of Pittburgh

Janet Pollak
William Patterson College

Howard Prince
CUNY-Borough of Manhattan Community College

Steven Rubenstein
Ohio University

Mary Scott
San Francisco State University

Brian Siegel
Furman University

Esther Skirboll
Slippery Rock University of Pennsylvania

Gregory Starrett
University of North Carolina–Charlotte

Karl Steinen
State University of Washington–Georgia

Noelle Stout
Last known in Brazil

Susan Trencher
George Mason University

Mark Tromans
Broward Community College

Christina Turner
Virginia Commonwealth University

Donald Tyler
University of Idaho

Daniel Varisco
Hofstra University

Albert Wahrhaftig
Sonoma State University

David Webb
Kutztown University of Pennsylvania

George Westermark
Santa Clara University

Nancy White
University of South Florida

Student Focus Group Participants

James Garron
Drexel University

Mary A. Johnson
Burlington County College

Albert Lee
La Salle University

Matthew J. McGrath
La Salle University

Albert Mori
La Salle University

Ann Marie Nellany
Temple University

Edward Price
La Salle University

Elizabeth C. Robinson
University of Delaware

Edward T. Walker
Drexel University

Alex Welcomb
Drexel University

I thank colleagues and students who have sent me personally, through McGraw-Hill sales reps and via e-mail, their comments, corrections, and suggestions. Anyone—student or instructor—with access to the Internet can contact me at the following address: ckottak@umich.edu.

As usual, my wife, Isabel Wagley Kottak, has offered me understanding and support during the preparation of this edition. I renew my dedication of this book to my mother, Mariana Kottak Roberts, for kindling my interest in the human condition, for reading and commenting on what I write, and for the insights about people and society she continues to provide.

After more than 30 years of teaching, I've benefited from the knowledge, help, and advice of so many friends, colleagues, teaching assistants, and students that I can no longer fit their names into a short preface. I hope they know who they are and will accept my thanks.

Conrad Phillip Kottak

walkthrough

Chapter-Opening Vignettes

Fascinating current "In the News" vignettes now open every chapter, highlighting the relevance of anthropology in today's world.

Chapter-Opening Previews

Succinct chapter-opening outlines and streamlined, more concise overviews help students focus on the chapter's critical concepts and terminology.

Up-to-Date Coverage

Extensive updating of research along with new discussion of such important topics as—to name just a few—ethnography, archaeological fieldwork, genes and disease, race, ethnicity, ebonics, extended families, and applied anthropology—make this the most current book available for the course.

Expanded Coverage

Two all-new chapters, one on "Primate Evolution," one on "The First Cities and States," greatly enhance the book's coverage of physical anthropology and archaeology, critical topics for today's General Anthropology student.

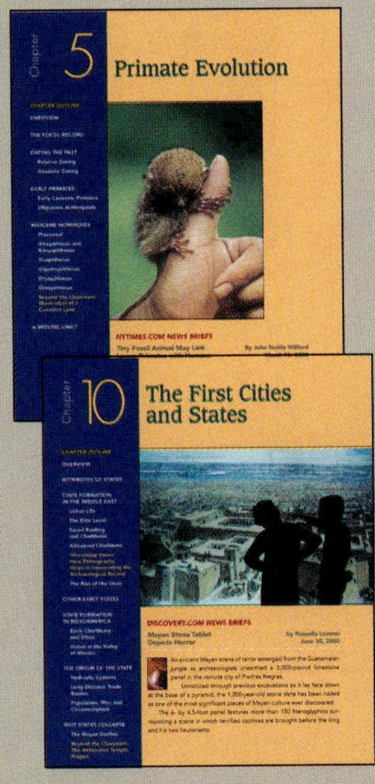

Plentiful Photographs, Charts, and Tables

A wealth of charts and tables and a significantly revised photo program—complete with the extended, thought-provoking captions for which the author is known—make chapter material clearer, more understandable, and more inviting than ever before.

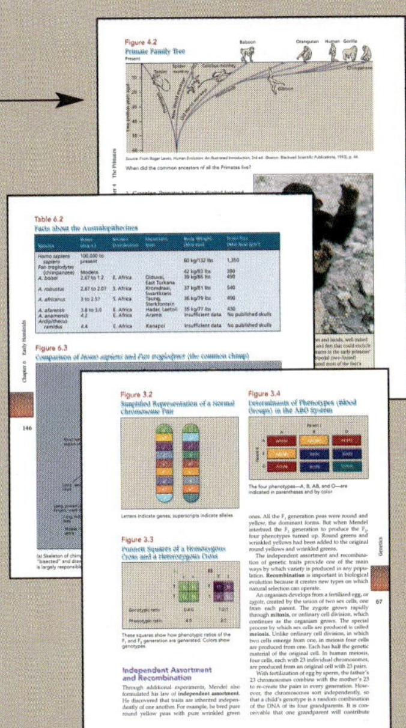

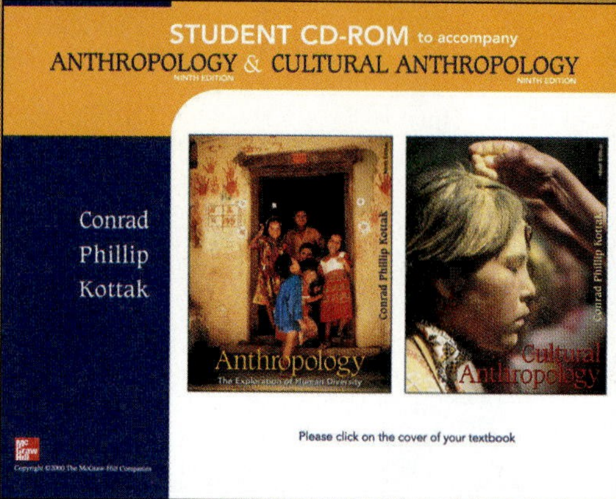

Unique *Exploring Anthropology* Student CD-ROM

This terrific independent study tool—packaged free with every copy of the text—features a chapter-by-chapter electronic study guide with audio, video, text, and web-based review tools as well as study break materials and information on how to do better in the course.

In-Text Icons

Useful marginal icons tell students when more information on a particular topic is available on the CD-ROM or Online Learning Center that accompany the text or where to turn in the text itself for additional information.

Intriguing *Interesting Issues* Boxes

Unique coverage of current issues in anthropology, complete with maps and photos, raise students' awareness of some of the more provocative aspects of anthropology today.

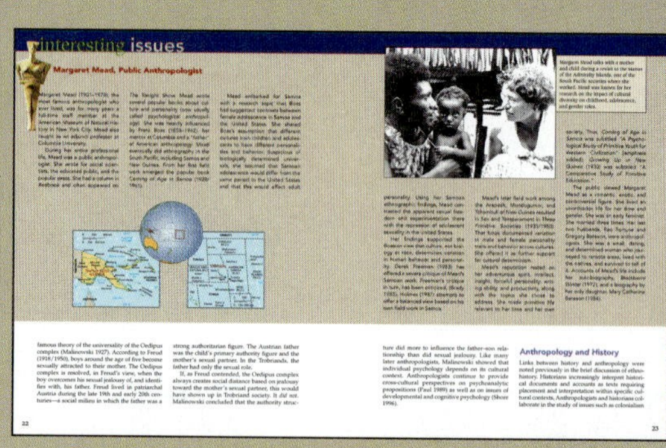

Timely *In the News* Boxes

Detailed discussion of the kinds of issues students may be hearing about in the media relates the concepts presented in each chapter back to the real world (maps and photos included).

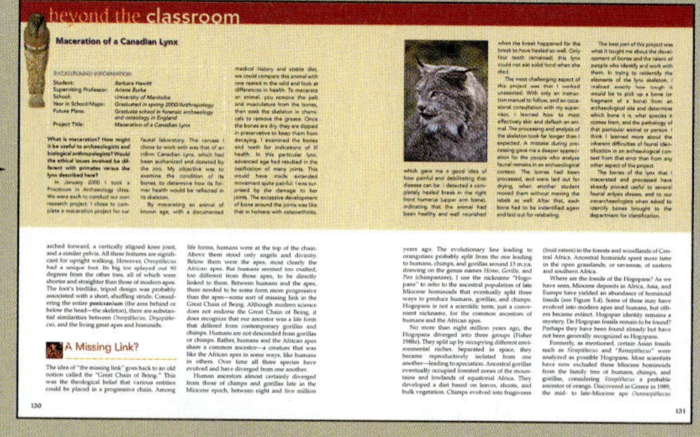

Widely-Acclaimed *Beyond the Classroom* Boxes

Popular thematic boxes highlighting actual student research in anthropology enable students to read about the work that their peers at other schools are doing, further highlighting the relevance of anthropology in the real world.

Easy-to-Use End-of-Chapter Reviews

Clear, concise *numbered* chapter summaries facilitate chapter concept review, while end-of-chapter glossaries enable students to go over the chapter's key terms.

Unique Critical Thinking and Internet Exercises

Chapter-ending exercises challenge students to use their critical thinking skills to apply what they have read about in the chapter and explore chapter concepts in greater detail via web research.

Free Online Learning Center

Accompanying website provides even more review material: self-quizzes (different from those on the CD-ROM), links, flashcards, Internet and critical thinking exercises. PowerPoint lectures, and more.

All-New Case Studies

These case exercises, perfect for those supplementing text reading with the brief ethnographic sketches included in *Culture Sketches* (see Preface), allow students to link chapter concepts with ethnographic examples in a practical, guided fashion.

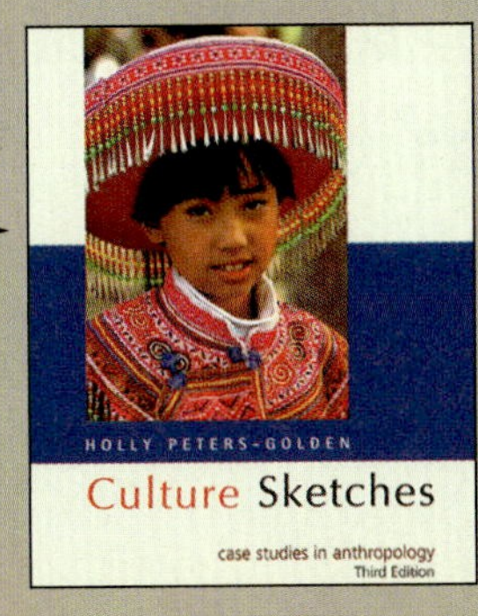

HOLLY PETERS-GOLDEN
Culture Sketches
case studies in anthropology
Third Edition

brief contents

contents

Chapter 14

Chapter 15

Chapter 16

list of boxes

INTERESTING ISSUES

IN THE NEWS

BEYOND THE CLASSROOM

PART I

The Basics of Anthropology

Chapter 1

What Is Anthropology?

CHAPTER OUTLINE

DISCOVERINGARCHAEOLOGY.COM NEWS BRIEFS

Public Opinion Polling Finds Great Support for Archaeology

by Reagan Duplisea
June 20, 2000

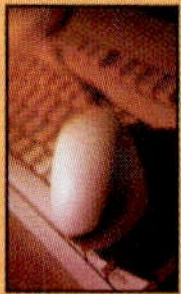

The computer icon appearing beside select text throughout the book indicates there are materials on the book's website that correspond to the indicated text section. The book's website address is **http://www.mhhe.com/kottak9**.

Americans are fascinated by archaeology. In a public opinion survey commissioned by archaeological organizations, 76 percent of those sampled declared a significant interest in archaeology, and a whopping 90 percent think it should be taught in school.

Asked just what attracts them to archaeology, nearly half (43 percent) of those who expressed interest cited learning about how people lived and worked in the past. Others mentioned connecting the past to the present, learning about their ancestors, and the thrill of discovery.

Harris Interactive questioned 1,016 Americans age 18 and older by telephone between August 12 and September 14, 1999. The survey has a margin of error of about plus or minus 3 percent.

Most of those surveyed (56 percent) listed television as a major source of information about archaeology, followed by magazines (33 percent) and newspapers (24 percent). Multiple answers were sought for that question, but very few reported learning about archaeology from groups or events such as public lectures (1 percent), historical and cultural events (1 percent), or participation in an archaeological project (2 percent).

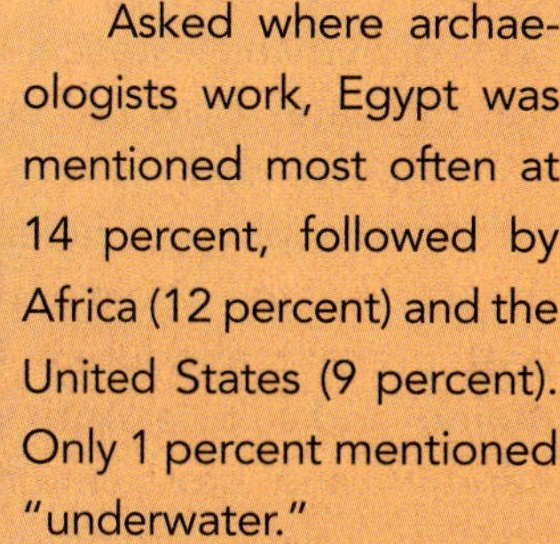

Yet 1 in 10 respondents said they would like to participate in a dig, and only 3 percent said they were not interested in learning about archaeology.

Americans strongly support protecting archaeological resources. The survey found 96 percent of participants agreeing that laws should protect such sites. Eighty-five percent felt laws should prohibit building on the site of a prehistoric Indian village, while 73 percent said construction should be banned on Revolutionary or Civil War battlefields.

The Society for American Archaeology presented a report on the survey, which was sponsored by the Archaeological Conservancy, Archaeological Institute of America, Bureau of Land Management, Fish and Wildlife Service, Forest Service, National Park Service, Society for American Archaeology, and Society for Historical Archaeology.

Other findings:

Asked where archaeologists work, Egypt was mentioned most often at 14 percent, followed by Africa (12 percent) and the United States (9 percent). Only 1 percent mentioned "underwater."

Egypt also topped the survey's list of most important archaeological sites at 38 percent. Latin American sites such as Aztec and Inca ruins were mentioned by 36 percent, while 10 percent cited biblical cities.

Asked for what first comes to mind when they hear the word archaeology, 22 percent said "digging," and another 37 percent cited some variation of that, such as "digging bones."

Interestingly, a surprising 10 percent said their first thought was "dinosaurs," which are studied by paleontologists, not archaeologists. Dinosaur excavations also were listed by 18 percent of participants as the most important archaeological sites.

Source: http://www.discoveringarchaeology.com/articles/062000-survey.shtml

overview

Anthropology includes, but is much broader than, archaeology, yet the two often are confused in everyday talk. Anthropology is the scientific and humanistic study of the human species. It is the exploration of human diversity in time and space. Anthropology confronts basic questions of human existence. Where and when did we originate? How has our species changed? What are we now? Where are we going?

Anthropology is holistic. Holism refers to the study of the whole of the human condition: past, present, and future; biology, society, language, and culture. Anthropology is also comparative and cross-cultural. It systematically compares data from different populations and time periods. Anthropology's four subfields are cultural, archaeological, biological, and linguistic anthropology.

Culture is a key aspect of human adaptability and success. Cultures are traditions and customs, transmitted through learning, that guide the beliefs and behavior of the people exposed to them. Cultural forces constantly mold and shape human biology and behavior. Cultural anthropology examines cultural diversity of the present and recent past. Archaeology reconstructs behavior by studying material remains. Biological anthropologists study human fossils, genetics, and bodily growth. They also study nonhuman primates (monkeys and apes). Linguistic anthropology considers how speech varies with social factors and over time. Anthropology's two dimensions are academic and applied. Applied anthropology uses anthropological knowledge to identify and solve social problems.

Anthropology is related to many other fields, including the sciences and the humanities. There are links to both the natural sciences (e.g., biology) and the social sciences (e.g., sociology). Anthropologists bring their distinctive cross-cultural perspective to the study of economics, politics, psychology, art, music, literature—and society in general.

Human Adaptability

Humans are among the world's most adaptable animals. In the Andes of South America, people wake up in villages 16,000 feet above sea level and then trek 1,500 feet higher to work in tin mines. Tribes in the Australian desert worship animals and discuss philosophy. People survive malaria in the tropics. Men have walked on the moon. The model of the *Starship Enterprise* in Washington's Smithsonian Institution symbolizes the desire to "seek out new life and civilizations, to boldly go where no one has gone before." Wishes to know the unknown, control the uncontrollable, and bring order to chaos find expression among all peoples. Adaptability and flexibility are basic human attributes, and human diversity is the subject matter of anthropology.

Students are often surprised by the breadth of **anthropology,** which is the study of the human species and its immediate ancestors. Anthropology is a uniquely comparative and **holistic** science. Holism refers to the study of the whole of the human condition: past, present, and future; biology, society, language, and culture. Most people think that anthropologists study fossils and nonindustrial, non-Western cultures, and many of them do. But anthropology is much more than the study of nonindustrial peoples: It is a comparative field that examines all societies, ancient and modern, simple and complex. The other social sciences tend to focus on a single society, usually an industrial nation like the United States or Canada. Anthropology, however, offers a unique cross-cultural perspective by constantly comparing the customs of one society with those of others.

People share society—organized life in groups—with other animals, including baboons, wolves, and even ants. Culture, however, is distinctly human. **Cultures** are traditions and customs, transmitted through learning, that govern the beliefs and behavior of the people exposed to them. Children learn such a tradition by growing up in a particular society, through a process called *enculturation.* Cultural traditions include customs and opinions, developed over the generations, about proper and improper behavior. These traditions answer such questions as: How should we do things? How do we make sense of the world? How do we tell right from wrong? What is right, and what is wrong? A culture produces a degree of consistency in behavior and thought among the people who live in a particular society.

The most critical element of cultural traditions is their transmission through learning rather than through biological inheritance. Culture is not itself biological, but it rests on certain features of human biology. For more than a million years, humans have had at least some of the biological capacities on which culture depends. These abilities are to learn, to think symbolically, to use language, and to employ tools and other products in organizing their lives and adapting to their environments.

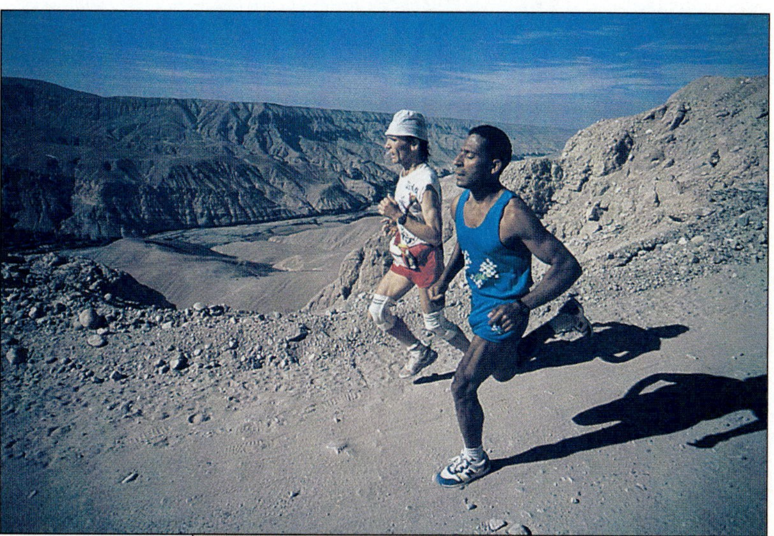

These two men are training in the high Andes for a marathon run from Lima, Peru, through La Paz, Bolivia, ending in Rio de Janeiro, Brazil. Which of the three kinds of high altitude adaptation is going on here? Why do athletes train at high altitudes?

Anthropology confronts and ponders major questions of human existence as it explores human biological and cultural diversity in time and space. By examining ancient bones and tools, we unravel the mysteries of human origins. When did our ancestors separate from those remote great-aunts and great-uncles whose descendants are the apes? Where and when did *Homo sapiens* originate? How has our species changed? What are we now and where are we going? How have changes in culture and society influenced biological change? Our genus, *Homo,* has been changing for more than one million years. Humans continue to adapt and change both biologically and culturally.

Adaptation, Variation, and Change

Adaptation refers to the processes by which organisms cope with environmental forces and stresses. How do organisms change to fit their environments? Like other animals, humans use biological means of adaptation. But humans are unique in also having cultural means of adaptation. For example, consider four ways (one cultural and three biological) in which humans may cope with low oxygen pressure at high altitudes. Illustrating cultural (technological) adaptation would be a pressurized airplane cabin equipped with oxygen masks. There are three ways of adapting biologically to a high altitude: genetic adaptation, long-term physiological adaptation, and short-term physiological adaptation. First, native populations of high altitude areas, such as the Andes of Peru and the Himalayas of Tibet and Nepal, seem to have acquired certain genetic advantages for life at very high altitudes. The tendency to develop a voluminous chest and lungs, for example, probably has a genetic basis. Second, regardless of their genes, people who grow up at a high altitude become physiologically more efficient there than genetically similar people who have grown up at sea level would be. This illustrates long-term physiological adaptation during the body's growth and development. Third, humans also have the capacity for short-term or immediate physiological adaptation. Thus, when lowlanders arrive in the highlands, they immediately increase their breathing and heart rates. Hyperventilation increases the oxygen in their lungs and arteries. As the pulse also increases, blood reaches their tissues more rapidly. All these varied adaptive responses—

Table 1.1

Forms of Cultural and Biological Adaptation (to High Altitude)

Form of Adaptation	Type of Adaptation	Example
Technology	Cultural	Pressurized airplane cabin with oxygen masks
Genetic adaptation (occurs over generations)	Biological	Larger "barrel chests" of native highlanders
Long-term physiological adaptation (occurs during growth and development of the individual organism)	Biological	More efficient respiratory system, to extract oxygen from "thin air"
Short-term physiological adaptation (occurs spontaneously when the individual organism enters a new environment)	Biological	Increased heart rate, hyperventilation

cultural and biological—achieve a single goal: maintaining an adequate supply of oxygen to the body. Table 1.1 summarizes the cultural and biological means that humans use to adapt to high altitudes.

As human history has unfolded, the social and cultural means of adaptation have become increasingly important. In this process, humans have devised diverse ways of coping with the range of environments they have occupied in time and space. The rate of cultural adaptation and change has accelerated, particularly during the past 10,000 years. For millions of years, hunting and gathering of nature's bounty—*foraging*—was the sole basis of human subsistence. However, it took only a few thousand years for **food production** (the cultivation of plants and domestication of animals), which originated some 12,000–10,000 years ago, to replace foraging in most areas.

Between 6000 and 5000 BP (before the present), the first civilizations arose. These were large, powerful, and complex societies, such as ancient Egypt, that conquered and governed large geographic areas. Much more recently, the spread of industrial production has profoundly affected human life. Throughout human history, major innovations have spread at the expense of earlier ones. Each economic revolution has had social and cultural repercussions. Today's global economy and communications link all contemporary people, directly or indirectly, in the modern world system. People must cope with forces generated by progressively larger systems—region, nation, and world. The study of such contemporary adaptations generates new challenges for anthropology: "The cultures of world peoples need to be constantly *re*discovered as these people reinvent them in changing historical circumstances" (Marcus and Fischer 1986, p. 24).

General Anthropology

The academic discipline of anthropology, also known as **general anthropology** or "four-field" anthropology, includes four main subdisciplines or subfields. They are sociocultural, archaeological, biological, and linguistic anthropology. (From here on, the shorter term *cultural anthropology* will be used as a synonym for "sociocultural anthropology.") Of the subfields, cultural anthropology has the largest membership. Most departments of anthropology teach courses in all four subfields.

There are historical reasons for the inclusion of four subfields in a single discipline. American anthropology arose more than a century ago out of concern for the history and cultures of the native peoples of North America. Interest in the origins and diversity of Native Americans brought together studies of customs, social life, language, and physical traits. Anthropologists are still pondering such questions as: Where did Native Americans come from? How many waves of migration brought them to the New World? What are the linguistic, cultural, and biological links among Native Americans and between them and Asia? Another reason for

American anthropology arose out of concern for the history and cultures of Native North Americans. Ely S. Parker, or Ha-sa-no-an-da, was a Seneca Indian who made important contributions to early anthropology. Parker also served as Commissioner of Indian Affairs for the United States.

anthropology's inclusion of four subfields was an interest in the relation between biology (e.g., "race") and culture. More than 50 years ago, the anthropologist Ruth Benedict realized that "In World history, those who have helped to build the same culture are not necessarily of one race, and those of the same race have not all participated in one culture. In scientific language, culture is not a function of race" (Benedict 1940, Ch 2). (Note that a unified four-field anthropology did not develop in Europe, where the subdisciplines tend to exist separately.)

There are also logical reasons for the unity of American anthropology. Each subfield considers variation in time and space (that is, in different geographic areas). Cultural and archaeological anthropologists study (among many other topics) changes in social life and customs. Archaeologists have used studies of living societies and behavior patterns to imagine what life might have been like in the past. Biological anthropologists examine evolutionary changes in physical form, for example, anatomical changes that might have been associated with the origin of language. Linguistic anthropologists may reconstruct the basics of ancient languages by studying modern ones.

The subdisciplines influence each other as anthropologists talk, read books and journals, and associate in professional organizations. General anthropology explores the basics of human biology, society, and culture and considers their interrelations. Anthropologists share certain key assumptions. Perhaps the most fundamental is the idea that sound conclusions about "human nature" cannot be derived from studying a single nation or cultural tradition. A comparative, cross-cultural approach is essential.

We often hear "nature versus nurture" and "genetics versus environment" questions. Consider gender differences. Do male and female capacities, attitudes, and behavior reflect biological or cultural variation? Are there universal emotional and intellectual contrasts between the sexes? Are females less aggressive than males? Is male dominance a human universal? By examining diverse cultures, anthropology shows that many contrasts between men and women reflect cultural training rather than biology.

Cultural Forces Shape Human Biology

Cultural forces constantly mold human biology. For example, culture is a key environmental force determining how human bodies will grow and develop. Cultural traditions promote certain activities and abilities, discourage others, and set standards of physical well-being and attractiveness. Physical activities, including sports, which are influenced by culture, help build the body. For example, North American girls are encouraged to pursue, and therefore do well in, competitive track and field, swimming, diving, and many other sports. Brazilian girls, by contrast, have not fared nearly as well in international athletic competition involving individual sports as have their American and Canadian counterparts. Why are girls encouraged to excel as athletes in some nations but discouraged from physical activities in others? Why don't Brazilian women, and Latin women generally, do better in most athletic categories? Does it have to do with "racial" differences or cultural training?

Cultural standards of attractiveness and propriety influence participation and achievement in sports. Americans run or swim not just to compete but to keep trim and fit. Brazil's beauty standards accept more fat, especially in female

Many differences between the sexes arise not from biology, but from cultural training or economic necessity, as is illustrated by these two scenes from India. Above, male laundry *wallahs* wash clothes at a municipal fountain in Bombay. Below, women shovel rocks at a road construction site. What do you make of the sign "Men at Work" near the women?

buttocks and hips. Brazilian men have had some international success in swimming and running, but Brazil rarely sends female swimmers or runners to the Olympics. One reason Brazilian women avoid competitive swimming in particular is that sport's effects on the body. Years of swimming sculpt a distinctive physique: an enlarged upper torso, a massive neck, and powerful shoulders and back. Successful female swimmers tend to be big, strong, and bulky. The countries that produce them most consistently are the United States, Canada, Australia, Germany, Scandinavia, the Netherlands, and the former Soviet Union, where this body type isn't as stigmatized as it is in Latin countries. Swimmers develop hard bodies, but Brazilian culture says that women should be soft, with big hips and buttocks, not big shoulders. Many young female swimmers in Latin America choose to abandon the sport rather than the "feminine" body ideal.

Culture, not "race," also helps us understand many or most of the differences in the sports success of blacks and whites. Cultural factors help explain why blacks excel in certain sports and whites in others. A key factor is degree of public access to sports facilities. In our public schools, parks, sandlots, and city playgrounds, African-Americans have access to baseball diamonds, basketball courts, football fields, and tracks. However, because of restricted economic opportunities, many black families can't afford to buy hockey gear or ski equipment, take ski vacations, pay for tennis lessons, or belong to clubs with tennis courts, pools, or golf courses. In the United States, mainly white suburban boys (and, increasingly, girls) play soccer, the most popular sport in the world. In Brazil, however, soccer is the national pastime for all males—black and white, rich and poor. There is wide public access. Brazilians play soccer on the beach and in streets, squares, parks, and playgrounds. Many of Brazil's best soccer players, including the world-famous Pelé, have dark skins. When blacks have opportunities to do well in soccer, tennis, golf, or any other sport, they are physically capable of doing as well as whites.

Why does the United States have so many black football and basketball players and so few black swimmers and hockey players? The answer lies mainly in cultural factors, including variable access and opportunities. Many Brazilians prac-

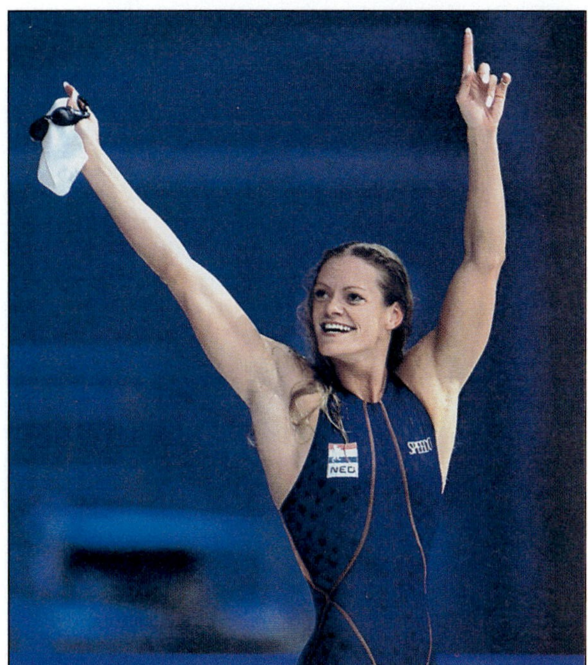

Years of swimming sculpt a distinctive physique: an enlarged upper torso, a massive neck, and powerful shoulders and back. Shown here is the Dutch swimmer Inge de Bruijn, who won multiple medals at the 2000 summer Olympics in Sydney.

tice soccer, hoping to play for money for a professional club. Similarly, American blacks are aware that certain sports have provided career opportunities for African-Americans. They start developing skills in those sports in childhood. The better they do, the more likely they are to persist, and the pattern continues. Culture—specifically differential access to sports resources—has more to do with sports success than "race" does.

Another area in which anthropology's cultural and biological perspectives meet is in examining the purported relation between "race" and IQ. We know of no evidence for biologically based contrasts in intelligence between races, classes, or sexes. Environmental variables, such as educational, economic, and social background, provide much better explanations for performance on intelligence tests by such groups. Standard tests reflect the backgrounds of those who develop and administer them. All tests are to some extent culture-bound and biased.

Prejudice and ignorance guide the mistaken belief that misfortune and poverty result from innate lack of ability. Occasionally, doctrines of inborn superiority are even set forth by scientists, who, after all, often come from privileged backgrounds. One of the best-known examples is Jensenism, named for the educational psychologist Arthur Jensen (Jensen 1969). Jensenism is a highly questionable interpretation of the observation that African-Americans, on average, perform less well on intelligence tests than Euro-Americans do. Jensenism asserts that blacks are hereditarily incapable of doing as well as whites do. Writing with Charles Murray, Richard Hernnstein makes a similar argument in the 1994 book *The Bell Curve,* to which the following critique also applies (see also Jacoby and Glauberman 1995). It should be noted that Jensen, Hernnstein, and Murray have no training or expertise in genetics or human evolution.

Environmental explanations for test scores are much more convincing than are the genetic arguments of Jensen, Herrnstein, and Murray. An environmental explanation does not deny that some people may be smarter than others. In any society, for many reasons, genetic and environmental, the talents of individuals vary. An environmental explanation does deny, however, that these differences can be generalized to whole populations or social groups. Also, even when talking about individuals, we have to decide which of several abilities is the best measure of intelligence.

Psychologists have devised various kinds of tests to measure intelligence, but there are problems with all of them. Early intelligence tests required skill in manipulating words. Such tests do not accurately measure learning ability for several reasons. For example, individuals who have learned two languages as children—bilinguals—don't do as well, on average, on verbal intelligence tests as do those who have learned a single language. It would be absurd to suppose that children who master two languages have inferior intelligence. The explanation seems to be that because bilinguals have vocabularies, concepts, and verbal skills in both languages, their ability to manipulate either one suffers a bit. This would seem to be offset by the advantage of being fluent in two languages.

Tests reflect the experience of the people who devise them, who are usually educated people in Europe and North America. It isn't surprising that middle- and upper-class children do best, because they are more likely to share the test makers' educational expectations and standards. Numerous studies have shown that performance on Scholastic Achievement Tests (SATs) can be improved by coaching and preparation. Parents who can afford to spend hundreds of dollars for an SAT preparation course enhance their kids' chances of getting high scores. Standard college entrance exams are similar to IQ tests in that they have claimed to measure intellectual aptitude. They may do this, but they also measure type and quality of high school education, linguistic and cultural background, and parental wealth. No test is free of bias based on class and culture.

The Brazilian soccer team poses just before the final match of the 1998 World Cup between Brazil and France. Compare the Brazilian soccer team above with the German team on the next page. What contrasts do you notice? How do you explain them?

Links between social, economic, and educational environment and test scores show up in comparisons of American blacks and whites. At the beginning of World War I, intelligence tests were given to approximately one million American army recruits. Blacks from some northern states had higher average scores than did whites from some southern states. At that time, northern blacks got a better public education than many southern whites did, so their superior performance wasn't surprising. The fact that southern whites did better, on average, than southern blacks also was expectable, given the unequal school systems then open to whites and blacks in the South.

Racists tried to dismiss the environmental explanation for the superior performance of northern blacks compared with southerners by suggesting selective migration, that smarter blacks had moved north. However, it was possible to test that idea, which turned out to be false. If smarter blacks had moved north, their superior intelligence should have been evident in their school records while they were still living in the South. It wasn't. Furthermore, studies in New York, Washington, and Philadelphia showed that as length of residence in those cities increased, test scores also rose.

Studies of identical twins raised apart also illustrate the impact of environment on identical heredity. In a study of 19 pairs of twins, IQ scores varied directly with years in school. The average difference in IQ was only 1.5 points for the eight twin pairs with the same amount of schooling. It was 10 points for the 11 pairs with an average of five years' difference. One subject, with 14 years more education than his twin, scored 24 points higher (Bronfenbrenner 1975).

These and similar studies provide overwhelming evidence that test scores measure background and education rather than genetically determined intelligence. For centuries, Europeans and their descendants extended their political and economic control over much of the world. They colonized and occupied environments that they reached in their ships and conquered with their weapons. Even today, most people who live in the world's most powerful and prosperous nations have light skin color. Some people in these currently powerful countries may incorrectly assert and believe that their position rests on innate biological superiority.

We are living in and interpreting the world at a particular time. Archaeology and history teach us that in the past there were far different associations between centers of power and human physical characteristics. When Europeans were simple farmers and herders, advanced civilizations thrived in the Middle East. When Europe was in the Dark Ages, there were civilizations in

The German National Soccer Team warms up during a training session in Nice (France) for the 1998 World Cup.

West Africa, on the East African coast, in Mexico, and in Asia. Before the Industrial Revolution, the ancestors of many white Europeans and North Americans were living more like precolonial Africans than like current members of the American middle class. Do you think that preindustrial Europeans would excel on 20th-century IQ tests?

The Subdisciplines of Anthropology

Cultural Anthropology

Cultural anthropology is the study of human society and culture, the subfield that describes, analyzes, interprets, and explains social and cultural similarities and differences. To study and interpret cultural diversity, cultural anthropologists engage in two kinds of activity: ethnography (based on field work) and ethnology (based on cross-cultural comparison). **Ethnography** provides an account of a particular community, society, or culture. During ethnographic field work, the ethnographer gathers data that he or she organizes, describes, analyzes, and interprets to build and present that account, which may be in the form of a book, article, or film. Traditionally, ethnographers have lived in small communities (such as Arembepe, Brazil—see "Interesting Issues" on the following page) and studied local behavior, beliefs, customs, social life, economic activities, politics, and religion. What kind of experience is ethnography for the ethnographer? The box offers some clues.

The anthropological perspective derived from ethnographic field work often differs radically from that of economics or political science. Those fields focus on national and official organizations and policies and often on elites. However, the groups that anthropologists have traditionally studied usually have been relatively poor and powerless, as are most people in the world today. Ethnographers often observe discriminatory practices directed toward such people, who experience food shortages, dietary deficiencies, and other aspects of poverty. Political scientists tend to study programs that national planners develop, while anthropologists discover how these programs work on the local level.

Cultures are not isolated. As noted by Franz Boas (1940/1966) many years ago, contact between neighboring tribes has always existed and has extended over enormous areas. "Human populations construct their cultures in interaction with one another, and not in isolation" (Wolf 1982, p. ix). Villagers increasingly participate in regional, national, and world events. Exposure to external forces comes through the mass media, migration, and modern transportation. City and nation increasingly invade local communities in the guise of tourists, development agents, government and religious officials, and political candidates. Such linkages are prominent components of regional, national, and international systems of politics, economics, and information. These larger systems increasingly affect the people and places anthropology traditionally has studied. The study of such linkages and systems is part of the subject matter of modern anthropology.

Ethnology examines, interprets, analyzes, and compares the results of ethnography—the data gathered in different societies. It uses such data to compare and contrast and to make generalizations

interesting issues

Even Anthropologists Get Culture Shock

I first lived in Arembepe (Brazil) during the (North American) summer of 1962. That was between my junior and senior years at New York City's Columbia College, where I was majoring in anthropology. I went to Arembepe as a participant in a now defunct program designed to provide undergraduates with experience doing ethnography—firsthand study of an alien society's culture and social life.

Brought up in one culture, intensely curious about others, anthropologists nevertheless experience culture shock, particularly on their first field trip. *Culture shock* refers to the whole set of feelings about being in an alien setting, and the ensuing reactions. It is a chilly, creepy feeling of alienation, of being without some of the most ordinary, trivial (and therefore basic) cues of one's culture of origin.

As I planned my departure for Brazil in 1962, I could not know just how naked I would feel without the cloak of my own language and culture. My sojourn in Arembepe would be my first trip outside the United States. I was an urban boy who had grown up in Atlanta, Georgia, and New York City. I had little experience with rural life in my own country, none with Latin America, and I had received only minimal training in the Portuguese language.

New York City direct to Salvador, Bahia, Brazil. Just a brief stopover in Rio de Janeiro; a longer visit would be a reward at the end of field work. As our prop jet approached tropical Salvador, I couldn't believe the whiteness of the sand. "That's not snow, is it?" I remarked to a fellow field team member . . .

My first impressions of Bahia were of smells—alien odors of ripe and decaying mangoes, bananas, and passion fruit—and of swatting the ubiquitous fruit flies I had never seen before, although I had read extensively about their reproductive behavior in genetics classes. There were strange concoctions of rice, black beans, and gelatinous gobs of unidentifiable

about society and culture. Looking beyond the particular to the more general, ethnologists attempt to identify and explain cultural differences and similarities, to test hypotheses, and to build theory to enhance our understanding of how social and cultural systems work. Ethnology gets its data for comparison not just from ethnography but also from the other subfields, particularly from archaeological anthropology, which reconstructs social systems of the past. (Table 1.2 summarizes the main contrasts between ethnography and ethnology.)

An ethnographer at work. During a 1980 visit, the author, Conrad Kottak, catches up on the news in Arembepe, a coastal community in Bahia state, northeastern Brazil, that he has been studying since 1962. How might culture shock influence one's research?

meats and floating pieces of skin. Coffee was strong and sugar crude, and every tabletop had containers for toothpicks and for manioc (cassava) flour to sprinkle, like Parmesan cheese, on anything one might eat. I remember oatmeal soup and a slimy stew of beef tongue in tomatoes. At one meal a disintegrating fish head, eyes still attached, but barely, stared up at me as the rest of its body floated in a bowl of bright orange palm oil . . .

I only vaguely remember my first day in Arembepe. Unlike ethnographers who have studied remote tribes in the tropical forests of interior South America or the highlands of Papua New Guinea, I did not have to hike or ride a canoe for days to arrive at my field site. Arembepe was not isolated relative to such places, only relative to every other place *I* had ever been . . .

I do recall what happened when we arrived. There was no formal road into the village. Entering through southern Arembepe, vehicles simply threaded their way around coconut trees, following tracks left by automobiles that had passed previously. A crowd of children had heard us coming, and they pursued our car through the village streets until we parked in front of our house, near the central square. Our first few days in Arembepe were spent with children following us everywhere. For weeks we had few moments of privacy. Children watched our every move through our living room window. Occasionally one made an incomprehensible remark. Usually they just stood there . . .

The sounds, sensations, sights, smells, and tastes of life in northeastern Brazil, and in Arembepe, slowly grew familiar . . . I grew accustomed to this world without Kleenex, in which globs of mucus habitually drooped from the noses of village children whenever a cold passed through Arembepe. A world where, seemingly without effort, women . . . carried 18-liter kerosene cans of water on their heads, where boys sailed kites and sported at catching houseflies in their bare hands, where old women smoked pipes, storekeepers offered *cachaça* (common rum) at nine in the morning, and men played dominoes on lazy afternoons when there was no fishing. I was visiting a world where human life was oriented toward water—the sea, where men fished, and the lagoon, where women communally washed clothing, dishes, and their own bodies.

This description is adapted from my ethnographic study *Assault on Paradise: Social Change in a Brazilian Village*, 3rd ed. (New York: McGraw-Hill, 1999).

Archaeological Anthropology

Archaeological anthropology (more simply, "archaeology") reconstructs, describes, and interprets past human behavior and cultural patterns through material remains. At sites where people live or have lived, archaeologists find artifacts, material items that humans have made or modified, such as tools, weapons, camp sites, and buildings. Plant and animal remains and ancient garbage tell stories about consumption and activities. Wild and domesticated grains have different

Table 1.2

Ethnography and Ethnology—Two Dimensions of Cultural Anthropology

Ethnography	Ethnology
Requires field work to collect data	Uses data collected by a series of researchers
Often descriptive	Usually synthetic
Group/community specific	Comparative/cross-cultural

characteristics, which allow archaeologists to distinguish between gathering and cultivation. Examination of animal bones reveals the ages of slaughtered animals and provides other information useful in determining whether species were wild or domesticated.

Analyzing such data, archaeologists answer several questions about ancient economies. Did the group get its meat from hunting, or did it domesticate and breed animals, killing only those of a certain age and sex? Did plant food come from wild plants or from sowing, tending, and harvesting crops? Did the residents make, trade for, or buy particular items? Were raw materials available locally? If not, where did they come from? From such information, archaeologists reconstruct patterns of production, trade, and consumption.

Archaeologists have spent much time studying potsherds, fragments of earthenware. Potsherds are more durable than many other artifacts, such as textiles and wood. The quantity of pottery fragments allows estimates of population size and density. The discovery that potters used materials that were not locally available suggests systems of trade. Similarities in manufacture and decoration at different sites may be proof of cultural connections. Groups with similar pots may be historically related. Perhaps they shared common cultural ancestors, traded with each other, or belonged to the same political system.

Many archaeologists examine paleoecology. Ecology is the study of interrelations among living things in an environment. The organisms and environment together constitute an ecosystem, a patterned arrangement of energy flows and exchanges. Human ecology studies ecosystems that include people, focusing on the ways in which human use "of nature influences and is influenced by social organization and cultural values" (Bennett 1969, pp. 10–11). Paleoecology looks at the ecosystems of the past.

In addition to reconstructing ecological patterns, archaeologists may infer cultural transformations, for example, by observing changes in the size and type of sites and the distance between them. A city develops in a region where only towns, villages, and hamlets existed a few centuries earlier. The number of settlement levels (city, town, village, hamlet) is a measure of social complexity. Buildings offer clues about political and religious features. Temples and pyramids suggest that an ancient society had an authority structure capable of marshaling the labor needed to build such monuments. The presence or absence of certain structures, like the pyramids of ancient Egypt and Mexico, reveals differences in function between settlements. For example, some towns were places where people came to attend ceremonies. Others were burial sites; still others were farming communities.

Archaeologists also reconstruct behavior patterns and life styles of the past by excavating. This involves digging through a succession of levels at a particular site. In a given area, through time, settlements may change in form and purpose, as may the connections between settlements. Excavation can document changes in economic, social, and political activities.

Although archaeologists are best known for studying prehistory, that is, the period before the invention of writing, they also study the cultures of historical and even living peoples. Studying sunken ships off the Florida coast, underwater archaeologists have been able to verify the living conditions on the vessels that brought ancestral African-Americans to the New World as enslaved people. Another, even more contemporary, illustration of archaeology is a research project begun in 1973 in Tucson, Arizona. Archaeologist William Rathje has learned about contemporary life by studying modern garbage. The value of "garbology," as Rathje calls it, is that it provides "evidence of what people did, not what they think

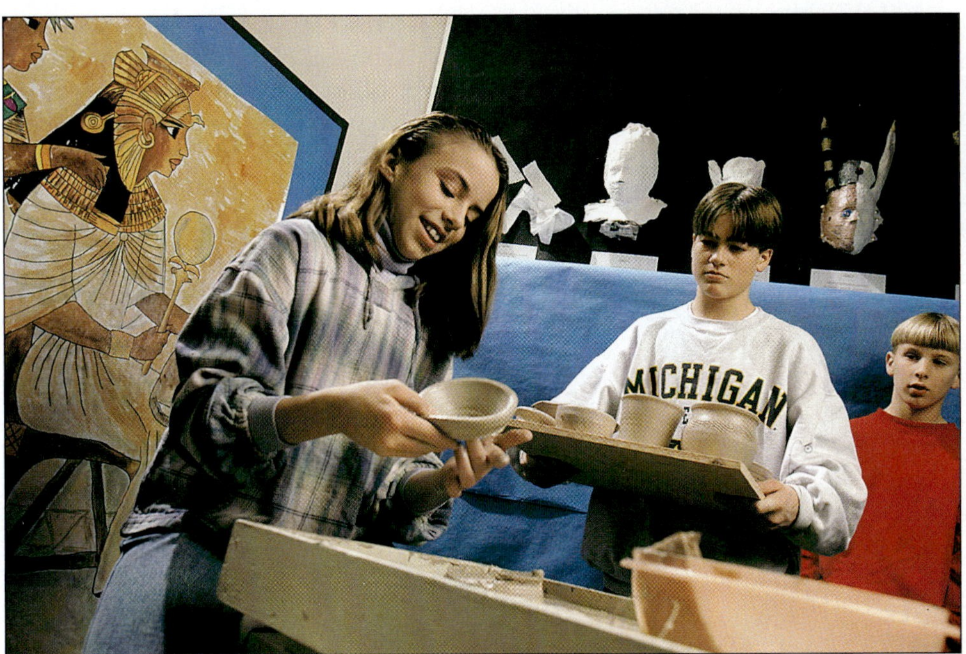

Archaeological anthropology reconstructs, describes, and interprets human behavior through material remains. In Grosse Point Park, Michigan, these high school students have made pottery using online information from an archaeological dig in Egypt.

they did, what they think they should have done, or what the interviewer thinks they should have done" (Harrison, Rathje, and Hughes 1994, p. 108). What people report may contrast strongly with their real behavior as revealed by garbology. For example, the garbologists discovered that the three Tucson neighborhoods that reported the lowest beer consumption actually had the highest number of discarded beer cans per household (Podolefsky and Brown 1992, p. 100)!

Biological, or Physical, Anthropology

The subject matter of **biological,** or **physical, anthropology** is human biological diversity in time and space. The focus on biological variation unites five special interests within biological anthropology:

1. Human evolution as revealed by the fossil record (paleoanthropology).
2. Human genetics.
3. Human growth and development.
4. Human biological plasticity (the body's ability to change as it copes with stresses, such as heat, cold, and altitude).
5. The biology, evolution, behavior, and social life of monkeys, apes, and other nonhuman primates.

These interests link physical anthropology to other fields: biology, zoology, geology, anatomy, physiology, medicine, and public health. Osteology—the study of bones—helps paleoanthropologists, who examine skulls, teeth, and bones, to identify human ancestors and to chart changes in anatomy over time. A paleontologist is a scientist who studies fossils. A paleoanthropologist is one sort of paleontologist, one who studies the fossil record of *human* evolution. Paleoanthropologists often collaborate with archaeologists, who study artifacts, in reconstructing biological and cultural aspects of human evolution. Fossils and tools are often found together. Different types of tools provide information about the habits, customs, and life styles of the ancestral humans who used them.

More than a century ago, Charles Darwin noticed that the variety that exists within any population permits some individuals (those with the favored, or adaptive, characteristics) to do

Paleoanthropologists study the fossil record of human evolution. This photo shows Professor Teuku Jacob with early fossil skulls from Java, Indonesia.

better than others at surviving and reproducing. Genetics, which developed later, enlightens us about the causes and transmission of this variety. However, it isn't just genes that cause variety. During any individual's lifetime, the environment works along with heredity to determine biological features. For example, people with a genetic tendency to be tall will be shorter if they are poorly nourished during childhood. Thus, biological anthropology also investigates the influence of environment on the body as it grows and matures. Among the environmental factors that influence the body as it develops are nutrition, altitude, temperature, and disease, as well as cultural factors, such as the standards of attractiveness we considered previously.

Biological anthropology (along with zoology) also includes primatology. The primates include our closest relatives—apes and monkeys. Primatologists study their biology, evolution, behavior, and social life, often in their natural environments. Primatology assists paleoanthropology, because primate behavior may shed light on early human behavior and human nature.

Linguistic Anthropology

We don't know (and probably never will) when our ancestors acquired the ability to speak, although biological anthropologists have looked to the anatomy of the face and the skull to speculate about the origin of language. And primatologists have described the communication systems of monkeys and apes. We do know that well-developed, grammatically complex languages have existed for thousands of years. Linguistic anthropology offers further illustration of anthropology's interest in comparison, variation, and change. **Linguistic anthropology** studies language in its social and cultural context, across space and over time. Some linguistic anthropologists make inferences about universal features of language, linked perhaps to uniformities in the human brain. Others reconstruct ancient languages by comparing their contemporary descendants and in so doing make discoveries about history. Still others study linguistic differences to discover varied perceptions and patterns of thought in different cultures.

Historical linguistics considers variation in time, such as the changes in sounds, grammar, and vocabulary between Middle English (spoken from approximately AD 1050 to 1550) and modern English. **Sociolinguistics** investigates relationships between social and linguistic variation. No language is a homogeneous system in which everyone speaks just like everyone else. How do different speakers use a given language? How do linguistic features correlate with social factors, including class and gender differences (Tannen 1990)? One reason for variation is geography, as in regional dialects and accents. Linguistic variation also is expressed in the bilingualism of ethnic groups. Linguistic and cultural anthropologists collaborate in studying links between language and many other aspects of culture, such as how people reckon kinship and how they perceive and classify colors.

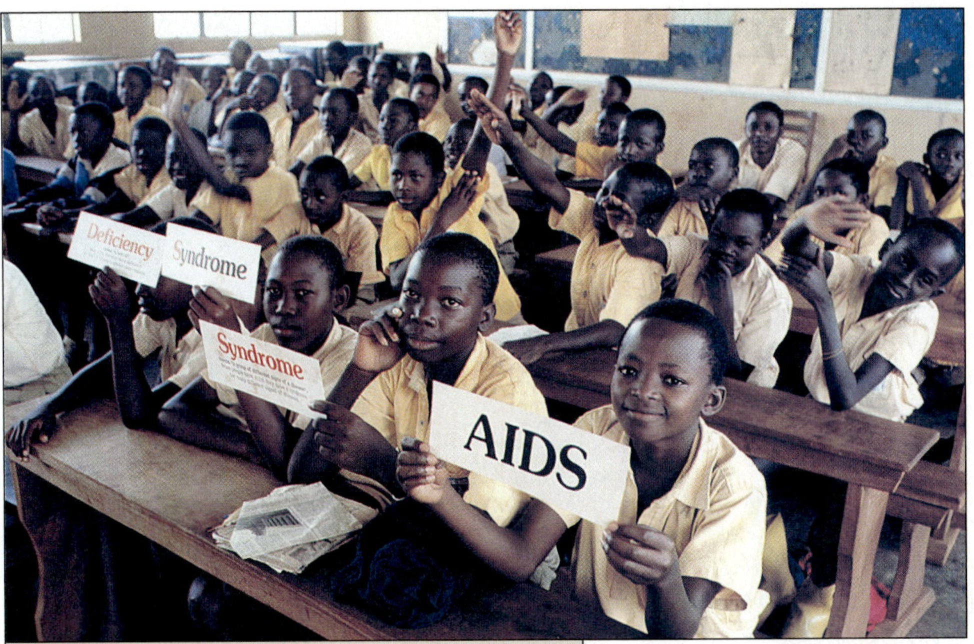

Medical anthropology studies health conditions from a cross-cultural perspective. In Uganda's Mwiri primary school, children are taught about HIV. Can you imagine a similar lesson in the primary school you attended?

Applied Anthropology

Anthropology is not a science of the exotic carried on by quaint scholars in ivory towers. Rather, it is a holistic, comparative, biocultural field with a lot to tell the public. Anthropology's foremost professional organization, the American Anthropological Association, has formally acknowledged a public service role by recognizing that anthropology has two dimensions: (1) theoretical/academic anthropology and (2) practicing or **applied anthropology.** The latter refers to the application of anthropological data, perspectives, theory, and methods to identify, assess, and solve contemporary social problems. More and more anthropologists from the four subfields now work in such "applied" areas as public health, family planning, and economic development.

In its most general sense, applied anthropology includes any use of the knowledge and/or techniques of the four subfields to identify, assess, and solve practical problems. Because of anthropology's breadth, it has many applications. For example, the growing field of medical anthropology considers the sociocultural context and implications of disease and illness. Perceptions of good and bad health, along with actual health threats and problems, differ among cultures. Various societies and ethnic groups recognize different illnesses, symptoms, and causes and have developed different health-care systems and treatment strategies. Medical anthropologists are both biological and cultural, and both theoretical and applied. Applied medical anthropologists, for example, have served as cultural interpreters in public health programs, which must fit into local culture and be accepted by local people.

Other applied anthropologists work for international development agencies, such as the World Bank and USAID (the United States Agency for International Development). The job of such development anthropologists is to assess the social and cultural dimensions of economic development. Anthropologists are experts on local cultures. Working with and drawing on the knowledge of local people, anthropologists can identify specific

Applied anthropology uses anthropological perspectives to identify and solve contemporary problems that affect humans. Deforestation is one such problem. Here children carrying saplings participate in a reforestation project in Sri Lanka.

social conditions and needs that must be addressed and that influence the failure or success of development schemes. Planners in Washington or Paris often know little about, say, the labor necessary for crop cultivation in rural Africa. Development funds are often wasted if an anthropologist is not asked to work with the local people to identify local needs, demands, priorities, and constraints.

Projects routinely fail when planners ignore the cultural dimension of development. Problems arise from lack of attention to, and consequent lack of fit with, existing sociocultural conditions. One example is a very naive and culturally incompatible project in East Africa. The major fallacy was to attempt to convert nomadic herders into farmers. The planners had absolutely no evidence that the herders, on whose land the project was to be implemented, wanted to change their economy. The herders' territory was to be used for new commercial farms, and the herders, converted into small farmers and sharecroppers. The project, whose planners included no anthropologists, totally neglected social issues. The obstacles would have been evident to any anthropologist. The herders were expected readily to give up a generations-old way of life in order to work three times harder growing rice and picking cotton. What could possibly motivate them to give up their freedom and mobility to work as sharecroppers for commercial farmers? Certainly not the meager financial return the project planners estimated for the herders—an average of $300 annually versus more than $10,000 for their new bosses, the commercial farmers.

To avoid such unrealistic projects, and to make development schemes more socially sensitive and culturally appropriate, development organizations now regularly include anthropologists on planning teams. Their team colleagues may include agronomists, economists, veterinarians, geologists, engineers, and health specialists. Applied anthropologists also apply their skills in studying the human dimension of environmental degradation (e.g., deforestation, pollution). Anthropologists examine how the environment influences humans and how human activities affect the biosphere and the earth itself.

Applied anthropologists also work in North America. Garbologists help the Environmental

Table 1.3
The Four Subfields and Two Dimensions of Anthropology

Anthropology's Subfields (General Anthropology)	Examples of Application (Applied Anthropology)
Cultural anthropology	Development anthropology
Archaeological anthropology	Cultural resource management (CRM)
Biological or physical anthropology	Forensic anthropology
Linguistic anthropology	Study of linguistic diversity in classrooms

Protection Agency, the paper industry, and packaging and trade associations. Many archaeologists now work in cultural resource management. They apply their knowledge and skills to interpret, inventory, and preserve historic resources for local, state (provincial), and federal governments. Forensic (physical) anthropologists work with the police, medical examiners, the courts, and international organizations to identify victims of crimes, accidents, wars, and terrorism. From skeletal remains they may determine age, sex, size, race, and number of victims. Applied physical anthropologists link injury patterns to design flaws in aircraft and vehicles.

Ethnographers have influenced social policy by showing that strong kin ties exist in city neighborhoods whose social organization was previously considered "fragmented" or "pathological." Suggestions for improving education emerge from ethnographic studies of classrooms and surrounding communities. Linguistic anthropologists show the influence of dialect differences on classroom learning. In general, applied anthropology aims to find humane and effective ways of helping the people whom anthropologists have traditionally studied. Table 1.3 shows the four subfields and two dimensions of anthropology.

Anthropology and Other Academic Fields

As mentioned previously, one of the main differences between anthropology and the other fields that study people is holism, anthropology's unique blend of biological, social, cultural, linguistic, historical, and contemporary perspectives. Paradoxically, while distinguishing anthropology, this breadth is what also links it to many other disciplines. Techniques used to date fossils and artifacts have come to anthropology from physics, chemistry, and geology. Because plant and animal remains often are found with human bones and artifacts, anthropologists collaborate with botanists, zoologists, and paleontologists.

As a discipline that is both scientific and humanistic, anthropology has links with many other academic fields. Anthropology is a **science**—a "systematic field of study or body of knowledge that aims, through experiment, observation, and deduction, to produce reliable explanations of phenomena, with reference to the material and physical world" (*Webster's New World Encyclopedia* 1993, p. 937). Clyde Kluckhohn (1944, p. 9) called anthropology "the science of human similarities and differences." His statement of the need for such a science still stands: "Anthropology provides a scientific basis for dealing with the crucial dilemma of the world today: how can peoples of different appearance, mutually unintelligible languages, and dissimilar ways of life get along peaceably together?" (p. 9). Anthropology has compiled an impressive body of knowledge that this textbook attempts to encapsulate.

Anthropology also has strong links to the humanities. The humanities include English, comparative literature, classics, folklore, philosophy, and the arts. These fields study languages, texts, philosophies, arts, music, performances, and other forms of creative expression. Ethnomusicology, which studies forms of musical expression on a worldwide basis, is especially closely related to anthropology. Also linked is folklore, the systematic study of tales, myths, and legends from a variety of cultures. One might well argue that anthropology is among the most humanistic of all academic fields because of its fundamental respect for human diversity. Anthropologists listen to, record, and represent voices from a multitude of nations and cultures. Anthropology values local knowledge, diverse worldviews, and alternative philosophies. Cultural and linguistic anthropology in particular bring a comparative and nonelitist perspective to forms of creative expression, including language, art, narratives, music, and dance, viewed in their social and cultural context.

Many anthropologists have studied the arts in cross-cultural perspective and in terms of the social contexts of artists and their works (see the chapter on the arts). Besides ethnomusicology, folklore, and the comparative study of the arts, what are other links between anthropology and the humanities? Interpretive anthropology (Geertz 1973, 1983) approaches cultures as texts whose forms and, especially, meanings must be deciphered in particular cultural and historical contexts. Ethnohistory, yet another area of inquiry within anthropology, is the study of people's accounts of their own histories. Ethnohistorical research also may draw on documents, including archaeological materials, pertaining to that history. Ethnohistorians, like historians, may interpret historical narratives as texts, paying attention to their cultural meaning and the social context of their creation.

Cultural Anthropology and Sociology

Cultural anthropology and sociology share an interest in social relations, organization, and behavior. However, important differences between these disciplines arose from the kinds of societies each traditionally studied. Initially sociologists focused on the industrial West; anthropologists, on nonindustrial societies. Different methods of data collection and analysis emerged to deal with those different kinds of societies. To study large-scale, complex nations, sociologists came to rely on questionnaires and other means of gathering masses of quantifiable data. For many years, sampling and statistical techniques have been basic to sociology, whereas statistical training has been less common in anthropology (although this is changing as anthropologists increasingly work in modern nations).

Traditional ethnographers studied small and nonliterate (without writing) populations and relied on methods appropriate to that context. "Ethnography is a research process in which the anthropologist closely observes, records, and engages in the daily life of another culture—an experience labeled as the fieldwork method—and then writes accounts of this culture, emphasizing descriptive detail" (Marcus and Fischer 1986, p. 18). One key method described in this quote is participant observation—taking part in the events one is observing, describing, and analyzing.

Interdisciplinary collaboration is a hallmark of academic life today, with ready borrowing of ideas and methods between disciplines (Geertz 1980). In many areas and topics, anthropology and sociology are converging. As the modern world system grows, sociologists do research in developing countries and in other places that were once mainly within the anthropological orbit. As industrialization spreads, many anthropologists work in industrial nations, where they study diverse topics, including rural decline, inner-city life, and the role of the mass media in creating national cultural patterns. Anthropologists and sociologists also share an interest in issues of race, ethnicity, social class, gender, and power relations in modern nations, including the United States and Canada.

Anthropology, Political Science, and Economics

Political science and economics developed to investigate particular domains of human behavior. Like sociologists, political scientists and economists have tended to work mainly in modern nations. In the small-scale societies where ethnography grew up, politics and economics usually don't stand out as distinct activities amenable to separate analysis, as they do in a modern society. Rather, they are submerged, or embedded, in the general social order. Thus, there may be no distinctly economic transactions or formal authority figures. People work for and follow orders of their kin rather than formal leaders or bosses. Studying political organization cross-culturally, anthropologists have increased our knowledge of the range and variety of political and legal systems. Legal codes, along with ideas about crime and punishment, vary substantially from culture to culture. Also, anthropologists have studied ways in which conflicts are expressed and resolved in different cultural contexts, especially in societies without formal governments.

The subject matter of economics has been defined as economizing—the rational allocation of scarce means (resources) among alternative ends (uses). How does one use limited resources wisely? What guides decisions about economic transactions? In the West, the goal of maximizing profit—the profit motive—is assumed to guide economic decision making. However, anthropologists know that motivations vary cross-culturally. Motives other than the desire for personal gain guide at least some of the economic decisions that people make in different cultures (as well as within our own). Anthropologists have contributed to the comparative study of economics by showing that principles other than the profit motive propel the economy in other cultures. Through ethnography and cross-cultural comparison, the findings of economists and political scientists, usually based on research in Western nations, can be placed in a broader perspective.

Anthropology and the Humanities

Traditionally, the humanities focused on "highbrow" "fine arts," knowledge of which was considered basic to a "cultured" person. Anthropology has always extended the definition of "cultured" beyond the elitist meaning of cultivated, sophisticated, college-educated, proper, and tasteful. For anthropologists, culture is not confined to elites or to any single social segment. Everyone acquires culture through enculturation, the social process by which culture is learned and transmitted across the generations. All creative expressions, therefore, are of potential interest as cultural products and documents. Growing acceptance of this view has helped broaden the study of the humanities from fine art and elite art to popular and folk art and the creative expressions of the masses and of many cultures.

Anthropology has influenced and is being influenced by the humanities—another example of the interdisciplinary communication and collaboration mentioned earlier. Current approaches in the humanities are shifting the focus more toward "lowbrow," mass, and popular culture and local creative expressions (Jameson 1984, 1988). Another area of convergence between anthropology and the humanities is the view of cultural expressions as patterned texts (Geertz 1973; Ricoeur 1971). Thus, "unwritten behavior, speech, beliefs, oral tradition, and ritual" (Clifford 1988, p. 39) are interpreted in relation to their meaning within a particular cultural context. A final link between anthropology and the humanities is the study of ethnographic accounts as a form of writing (Clifford 1988; Marcus and Fischer 1986).

Anthropology and Psychology

Like sociologists and economists, most psychologists do research in their own society. Anthropology again contributes by providing cross-cultural data. Statements about "human" psychology cannot be based solely on observations made in one society or in a single type of society. The area of cultural anthropology known as psychological anthropology studies cross-cultural variation in psychological traits. Margaret Mead (see "Interesting Issues" on the following page), in her many books (1928/1961, 1930), attempted to show that psychological traits vary widely among cultures. Societies instill different values by training children differently. Adult personalities reflect a culture's child-rearing practices.

Having familiarized yourself with Mead, consider another early contributor to the cross-cultural study of human psychology. Bronislaw Malinowski is famous for his field work among the Trobriand Islanders of the South Pacific. The Trobrianders reckon kinship matrilineally. They consider themselves related to the mother and her relatives, but not to the father. The relative who disciplines the child is not the father but the mother's brother, the maternal uncle. One inherits from the uncle rather than the father. Trobrianders show a marked respect for the uncle, with whom a boy usually has a cool and distant relationship. In contrast, the Trobriand father–son relationship is friendly and affectionate.

Malinowski's work among the Trobrianders suggested modifications in Sigmund Freud's

interesting issues

Margaret Mead, Public Anthropologist

Margaret Mead (1901–1978), the most famous anthropologist who ever lived, was for many years a full-time staff member at the American Museum of Natural History in New York City. Mead also taught as an adjunct professor at Columbia University.

During her entire professional life, Mead was a public anthropologist. She wrote for social scientists, the educated public, and the popular press. She had a column in *Redbook* and often appeared on *The Tonight Show.* Mead wrote several popular books about culture and personality (now usually called *psychological anthropology*). She was heavily influenced by Franz Boas (1858–1942), her mentor at Columbia and a "father" of American anthropology. Mead eventually did ethnography in the South Pacific, including Samoa and New Guinea. From her first field work emerged the popular book *Coming of Age in Samoa* (1928/1961).

Mead embarked for Samoa with a research topic that Boas had suggested: contrasts between female adolescence in Samoa and the United States. She shared Boas's assumption that different cultures train children and adolescents to have different personalities and behavior. Suspicious of biologically determined universals, she assumed that Samoan adolescence would differ from the same period in the United States and that this would affect adult

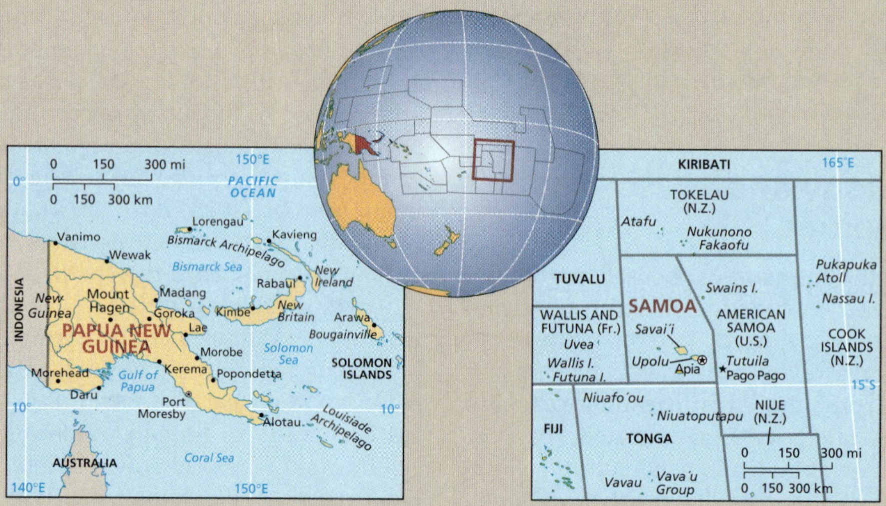

famous theory of the universality of the Oedipus complex (Malinowski 1927). According to Freud (1918/1950), boys around the age of five become sexually attracted to their mother. The Oedipus complex is resolved, in Freud's view, when the boy overcomes his sexual jealousy of, and identifies with, his father. Freud lived in patriarchal Austria during the late 19th and early 20th centuries—a social milieu in which the father was a strong authoritarian figure. The Austrian father was the child's primary authority figure and the mother's sexual partner. In the Trobriands, the father had only the sexual role.

If, as Freud contended, the Oedipus complex always creates social distance based on jealousy toward the mother's sexual partner, this would have shown up in Trobriand society. It *did not.* Malinowski concluded that the authority struc-

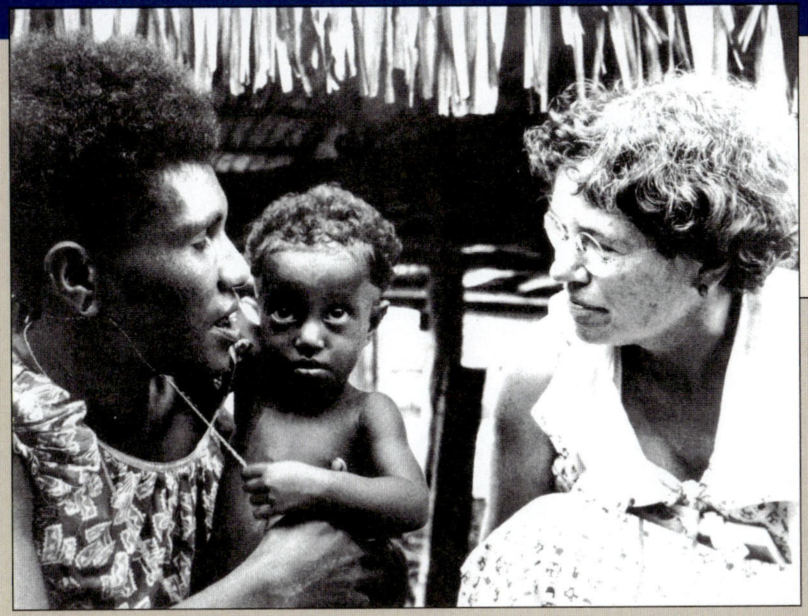

Margaret Mead talks with a mother and child during a revisit to the Manus of the Admiralty Islands, one of the South Pacific societies where she worked. Mead was known for her research on the impact of cultural diversity on childhood, adolescence, and gender roles.

personality. Using her Samoan ethnographic findings, Mead contrasted the apparent sexual freedom and experimentation there with the repression of adolescent sexuality in the United States.

Her findings supported the Boasian view that culture, not biology or race, determines variation in human behavior and personality. Derek Freeman (1983) has offered a severe critique of Mead's Samoan work. Freeman's critique in turn, has been criticized (Brady 1983). Holmes (1987) attempts to offer a balanced view based on his own field work in Samoa.

Mead's later field work among the Arapesh, Mundugumor, and Tchambuli of New Guinea resulted in *Sex and Temperament in Three Primitive Societies* (1935/1950). That book documented variation in male and female personality traits and behavior across cultures. She offered it as further support for cultural determinism.

Mead's reputation rested on her adventurous spirit, intellect, insight, forceful personality, writing ability, and productivity, along with the topics she chose to address. She made primitive life relevant to her time and her own society. Thus, *Coming of Age in Samoa* was subtitled "*A Psychological Study of Primitive Youth* for Western Civilization" [emphasis added]. *Growing Up in New Guinea* (1930) was subtitled "A Comparative Study of Primitive Education."

The public viewed Margaret Mead as a romantic, exotic, and controversial figure. She lived an unorthodox life for her time and gender. She was an early feminist. She married three times. Her last two husbands, Reo Fortune and Gregory Bateson, were anthropologists. She was a small, daring, and determined woman who journeyed to remote areas, lived with the natives, and survived to tell of it. Accounts of Mead's life include her autobiography, *Blackberry Winter* (1972), and a biography by her only daughter, Mary Catherine Bateson (1984).

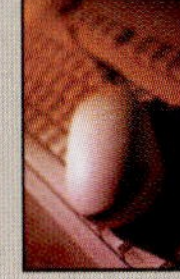

ture did more to influence the father–son relationship than did sexual jealousy. Like many later anthropologists, Malinowski showed that individual psychology depends on its cultural context. Anthropologists continue to provide cross-cultural perspectives on psychoanalytic propositions (Paul 1989) as well as on issues of developmental and cognitive psychology (Shore 1996).

Anthropology and History

Links between history and anthropology were noted previously in the brief discussion of ethnohistory. Historians increasingly interpret historical documents and accounts as texts requiring placement and interpretation within specific cultural contexts. Anthropologists and historians collaborate in the study of issues such as colonialism

beyond the classroom

The Utility of Hand and Foot Bones for Problems in Biological Anthropology

BACKGROUND INFORMATION

Student:	*Alicia Wilbur*
Supervising Professor:	*Della Collins Cook*
School:	*Indiana University*
Year in School/Major:	*Junior and Senior/Anthropology*
Future Plans:	*Ph.D. in Biological Anthropology*
Project Title:	*The Utility of Hand and Foot Bones for Problems in Bioanthropology*

How does this account suggest common problems of interest to more than one subfield of anthropology? Does the research have implications for cultural and applied anthropology as well as for biological and archaeological anthropology?

The large, well-preserved skeletal series from west-central Illinois, housed in the Department of Anthropology at Indiana University, has been the focus of many archaeological and bioanthropological research projects over the years. I became interested in the use of hand and foot bones to determine the stature and sex of the individuals buried in those mounds. This information is important for both archaeological and biological studies of past peoples and their cultures, but is also relevant to modern forensic and mass disaster situations. In both archaeological and modern situations, the human remains recovered may be extremely fragmentary. A single hand or foot can play an important role in identifying modern victims of crime or mass disasters.

Most equations used for estimating adult stature or determining sex from skeletal material are constructed from data on modern Europeans or modern Americans of European or African extraction. Because body proportions differ between populations, applying these equations to skeletal remains of other groups may give inaccurate results. A benefit of my study was that it was constructed on Native American remains and thus could be used for modern Native Americans remains in forensic cases or mass disasters.

I measured femurs (the thigh bone) and hand and foot bones for 410 adult skeletons and used statistical methods to predict the sex of the individuals, with accuracies exceeding 87 percent. Stature esti-

and the development of the modern world system (Cooper and Stoler 1997).

It may be useful to distinguish between change in personnel and change in form as two kinds of historical change affecting people and societies. People enter a particular society through birth and immigration and leave it through death and emigration. There may be such changes in personnel—in individuals—without any significant change in the system's basic form or structure. With the second kind of historical change, the social system changes its structure or form. This may happen because of a sudden, radical, or revolutionary event. Or it may involve the slow accretion of smaller changes as, over the generations, individuals create and innovate so that a change in form takes place gradually.

I have witnessed the two kinds of historical change in the two places I have done my major field work: Brazil and Madagascar. In Madagascar, in the Betsileo village of Ivato, which I originally studied in 1966–67 and revisited in 1981, I observed change in personnel, but no change in the village's basic form. During my 14-year

mation also was found to be possible with hand and foot bones, although the range given was too large to be useful in a court of law. Still, estimates resulting from these equations may be useful for delimiting a range of possible heights for preliminary identification purposes.

The project was published in the *International Journal of Osteoarchaeology* in 1998. While running statistical analyses on the hand and foot data, I noticed a discrepancy in the body proportions of one female adult. Upon carefully examining the rest of her skeleton, I discovered a suite of skeletal anomalies that suggest a rare genetic syndrome called Rubinstein-Taybi Syndrome that affects many organs. Symptoms include delayed growth, mental retardation, and abnormalities of the head and face, including widely spaced eyes and an abnormally large nose. Affected individuals also may have abnormally large big toes and thumbs. There also may be breathing and swallowing difficulties.

It may yet prove possible to analyze DNA from this sample to determine if my diagnosis is correct. If so, it would be the earliest known case of this syndrome. Knowing that this individual lived to mid- to late adulthood with several physical and mental disabilities tells us something about her culture.

These types of studies on skeletal material are important for the information they give us about the past and also for their relevance to modern problems. Future research will focus on genetic and infectious diseases that beset ancient peoples as well as application of this work to modern problems.

absence, individuals were born, died, and moved in and out, but the economy and basic social features of the village did not change. Arembepe, Brazil, by contrast, which I have been studying since 1962, has undergone a major change in form. In a generation, Arembepe was transformed from a fishing village with no social classes and little organized religion into a town with social classes, organized religion, religious diversity, an economy based on tourism, and a dramatic increase in the economic opportunities available to both men and women. Arembepe had experienced change in personnel but also change in form.

There are still historians who focus on individual names and dates without much concern for process or social context. But an increasing number of historians study changes in social form—social transformations. Historians and historically oriented anthropologists are interested in both types of change: small scale and large scale. The growing collaboration of historians and anthropologists has been institutionalized in joint programs in history and anthropology at several universities.

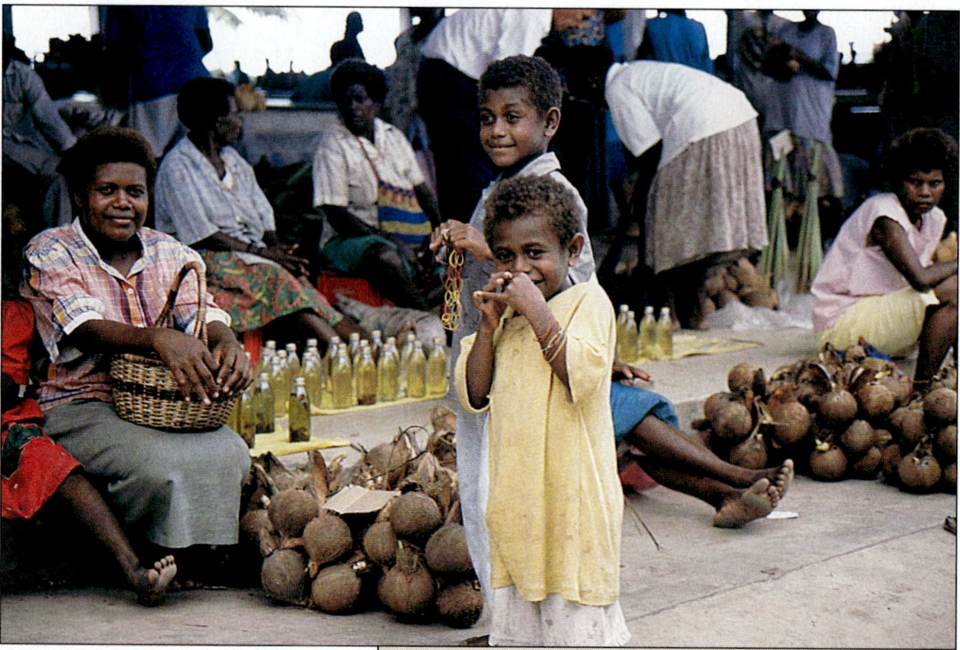

Bronislaw Malinowski is famous for his field work among the matrilineal Trobriand Islanders of the South Pacific. Does this Trobriand market scene suggest anything about the status of Trobriand women?

summary

1. Anthropology is the holistic and comparative study of humanity. It is the systematic exploration of human biological and cultural diversity. Examining the origins of, and changes in, human biology and culture, anthropology provides explanations for similarities and differences. The four subfields of general anthropology are (socio)cultural, archaeological, biological, and linguistic. All consider variation in time and space. Each also examines adaptation—the process by which organisms cope with environmental stresses.
2. Cultural forces mold human biology, including our body types and images. Societies have particular standards of physical attractiveness. They also have specific ideas about what activities, for example, various sports, are appropriate for males and females. Environmental factors, such as educational, economic, and social background, tell us more than genetics does about why various groups perform differently on intelligence tests. Tests reflect the life experiences of the people who develop and administer them. All tests are at least partially culture-bound.
3. Cultural anthropology explores the cultural diversity of the present and the recent past. Archaeology reconstructs cultural patterns, often of prehistoric populations. Biological anthropology documents diversity involving fossils, genetics, growth and development, bodily responses, and nonhuman primates. Linguistic anthropology considers diversity among languages. It also studies how speech changes in social situations and over time. Anthropology has two dimensions: academic and applied. The latter uses anthropological knowledge and methods to identify and solve social problems.
4. Concerns with biology, society, culture, and language link anthropology to many other fields—sciences and humanities. Sociologists traditionally study urban and industrial populations, whereas anthropologists have focused on rural, nonindustrial peoples. Anthropologists bring a comparative perspective to economics and political science. Anthropologists study art, music, and literature across cultures. But their concern is more with the creative expressions of common people that with arts designed for elites. Anthropologists examine creators and products in their social context.
5. Interdisciplinary collaboration has become a hallmark of academic life. Ideas and methods are exchanged among various fields. Such collaboration is especially characteristic of anthropology, given its breadth and its topical diversity. Anthropologists and historians collaborate in placing historical events in their cultural contexts. Psychological anthropology views human psychology in the context of social and cultural variation.

key terms

anthropology The study of the human species and its immediate ancestors.

applied anthropology The application of anthropological data, perspectives, theory, and methods to identify, assess, and solve contemporary social problems.

archaeological anthropology The study of human behavior and cultural patterns and processes through the culture's material remains.

biological anthropology The study of human biological variation in time and space; includes evolution, genetics, growth and development, and primatology.

cultural anthropology The study of human society and culture; describes, analyzes, interprets, and explains social and cultural similarities and differences.

culture Distinctly human; transmitted through learning; traditions and customs that govern behavior and beliefs.

ethnography Field work in a particular culture.

ethnology Cross-cultural comparison; the comparative study of ethnographic data, of society, and of culture.

food production Cultivation of plants and domestication (stockbreeding) of animals; first developed 10,000 to 12,000 years ago.

general anthropology The field of anthropology as a whole, consisting of cultural, archaeological, biological, and linguistic anthropology.

holistic Interested in the whole of the human condition: past, present, and future; biology, society, language, and culture.

linguistic anthropology The descriptive, comparative, and historical study of language and of linguistic similarities and differences in time, space, and society.

physical anthropology See *biological anthropology.*

science A systematic field of study or body of knowledge that aims, through experiment, observation, and deduction, to produce reliable explanations of phenomena, with reference to the material and physical world.

sociolinguistics Investigates relationships between social and linguistic variations.

critical thinking questions

1. Which do you think is more unique about anthropology: its holism or its comparative perspective? Can you think of other fields that are holistic and/or comparative?
2. Besides race and gender, what are some other areas in which anthropology's biocultural, four-field approach might shed light on current issues and debates? Would sexuality be such an area?
3. The author has noted that many other disciplines are limited by their focus on powerful people and elites. How have your professors in other classes tried to justify, or compensate for, such limitations?
4. Besides the examples given in this chapter, think of some other problems or issues in the modern world to which applied anthropology might contribute.

case study

Samoa: This chapter has introduced one of the great debates of modern anthropology, the questions raised by Derek Freeman about Margaret Mead's work in Samoa. Mead hypothesized that the rebellion and turmoil that characterized American teenage years were not a "natural" and universally human consequence of growing into adulthood. In Samoa, she found that adolescents experienced less repression, conflict, and tension and displayed none of the emotional turbulence of "typical" Western teenagers. This supported the view that individuals are very much a product of the environments in which they are nurtured. Freeman took issue with Mead's position, claiming she painted a false picture of Samoa so as to promote her belief in the primacy of "nurture" over "nature." He asserted that Samoa was, in fact, a culture replete with tension and aggression.

In *Culture Sketches,* read Chapter 11, "The Samoans." Using what you've learned about the four subfields of anthropology, and about anthropology's holistic and comparative perspectives, how would you address the Mead–Freeman debate? What might be the consequences, positive and negative, of such a controversy to the field of anthropology? How might the potential for such disagreement influence future field work?

suggested additional readings

Clifford, J.

1988 *The Predicament of Culture: Twentieth-Century Ethnography, Literature, and Art.* Cambridge, MA: Harvard University Press. Literary evaluation of classic and modern anthropologists and discussion of issues of ethnographic authority.

Endicott, K. M., and R. Welsch

2001 *Taking Sides: Clashing Views on Controversial Issues in Anthropology.* Guilford, CT: McGraw-Hill/Dushkin. Thirty-eight anthropologists offer opposing viewpoints on 19 polarizing issues, including ethical dilemmas.

Fagan, B. M.

1999 *Archeology: A Brief Introduction,* 7th ed. New York: Longman. Introduction to archaeological theory, techniques, and approaches, including field survey, excavation, and analysis of materials.

2000 *People of the Earth: An Introduction to World Prehistory,* 10th ed. New York: Longman. Introduction to the archaeological study of prehistoric societies, using examples from all areas.

Geertz, C.

1995 *After the Fact: Two Countries, Four Decades, One Anthropologist.* Cambridge, MA: Harvard University Press. A prominent cultural anthropologist reflects on his work in Morocco and Indonesia.

Harris, M.

1989 *Our Kind: Who We Are, Where We Came From, Where We Are Going.* New York: HarperCollins. Clearly written survey of the origins of humans, culture, and major sociopolitical institutions.

Marcus, G. E., and M. M. J. Fischer

1999 *Anthropology as Cultural Critique: An Experimental Moment in the Human Sciences,* 2nd ed. Chicago: University of Chicago Press. Different types of ethnographic accounts as forms of writing, a vision of modern anthropology, and a consideration of anthropologists' public and professional roles.

Nash, D.

1999 *A Little Anthropology,* 3rd ed. Upper Saddle River, NJ: Prentice Hall. Short introduction to societies and cultures, with comments on developing nations and modern America.

Podolefsky, A., and P. J. Brown, eds.

2001 *Applying Anthropology: An Introductory Reader,* 6th ed. Mountain View, CA: Mayfield. Essays focusing on anthropology's relevance to contemporary life; a readable survey of the current range of activities in applied anthropology.

Wolf, E. R.

1982 *Europe and the People without History,* Berkeley: University of California Press. Influential and award-winning study of the relation between Europe and various nonindustrial populations.

internet exercises

1. News in Anthropology: Look at Texas A&M University's "Anthropology in the News," **http://www.tamu.edu/anthropology/news.html,** which contains links to articles relevant to anthropology.
   a. After reading the chapter in the textbook and reading some recent news articles, do you think anthropology is more or less relevant to your life?
   b. Look at the variety of topics discussed. Are the connections between the articles and anthropology clear to you? Were they clear to you before you read this chapter?
   c. Examine the first 10 articles. Which subfield of anthropology does each article relate to most closely?
   d. Browse the list of article titles. What are some of the current hot topics in the news about anthropology?
2. Careers in Anthropology: Go to the American Anthropological Association's Jobs Page, **http://www.aaanet.org/position.htm,** and Northern Kentucky's list of organizations in their area hiring anthropologists, **http://www.nku.edu/~anthro/careers.html.**
   a. What kinds of organizations are hiring anthropologists?
   b. What kinds of qualifications are those employers looking for? Do they require a graduate degree, or are they seeking people with an undergraduate degree in anthropology?
   c. What subfields are being sought by employers?

Note that these are just two job listing pages on the web, and there are many others. If you have an interest in a field of anthropology that is not listed on these pages, use a web search engine to research what kinds of jobs are available. A good place to start is **http://www.aaanet.org/careers.htm** for more information on careers in anthropology.

See Chapter 1 on your CD-ROM for additional review and interactive exercises. See your McGraw-Hill Online Learning Center for more.

Chapter 2

In the Field

CHAPTER OUTLINE

USATODAY.COM NEWS BRIEFS

Anthropologists Adapt Technology to World's Cultures

by Elizabeth Weise
May 26, 1999

Think anthropologists spend their days hanging out in Pago Pago studying the local culture? Think again. Like everyone else, anthropologists and ethnographers increasingly are finding jobs with high-tech companies, using their highly developed skills as observers to study how people live, work, and use technology.

"This is not *Raiders of the Lost Ark,*" says Susan Squires, incoming president of the 1,000-member National Association for the Practice of Anthropology, which has a website at **www.ameranthassn.org/napa.htm.**

"Anthropology developed methods to understand people who were so different from Europeans that you couldn't just go up and ask questions, so we came up with methods such as participant observation and fieldwork," says Squires, who also works at GVO Inc., a product development company in Palo Alto, California.

The use of those skills in the service of modern technology can be traced to 1979, when the legendary Xerox Palo Alto Research Center hired anthropology graduate student Lucy Suchman. PARC was a center of innovative technological thinking, having created the computer mouse and graphical user interface. Suchman worked in the intelligent systems laboratory, where researchers were trying to build artificial intelligence to help people use complicated copiers.

In a famous film, Suchman showed several people having a terrible time trying to do a copying job. From her research came the realization that features aren't as important as simplicity. That's why Xerox copeirs now, no matter how complex, all include a single green copy button for when you want one uncomplicated copy.

Twenty years later, a hiring boom is going on, plucking newly minted Ph.D.s from anthropology departments across the country, much to the distress of more tradition-bound academics, who think their graduates shouldn't sully the purity of their field by working in industry.

Stanford graduate Genevieve Bell of Hillsboro, Oregon, says that when she left a teaching position at Stanford for a job at Intel, "as far as the faculty was concerned, it was a total sell-out . . ."

Not all schools feel that way. "One of our big problems is that graduate students keep getting snatched up by companies," says Marietta Baba, chairwoman of the anthropology department at Wayne State University in Detroit. It specializes in training cultural anthropology students in rigorous ethnographic methods—the art of observing social interactions to understand the underlying structures of a culture—and teaching them to apply those methods to industry.

She estimates that about 9,000 anthropologists are in academia in the United States and about 2,200 are in applied anthropology positions in industry. "But the proportions are shifting, so you're getting more and more applied ones," she says.

The point of hiring anthropologists is to help companies understand their users and find new products and markets the engineers and marketers never dreamed of . . .

Traditional market research tools are limited by their question-and-answer format, says Andrea Saveri, a director at the Institute for the Future in Menlo Park. She keeps a staff of ethnographers on hand to do research on the consequences of technology.

"In the case of surveys, you're telling the respondent how to answer and you're not giving them any room for anything else." She sees ethnography as an incredibly precise and powerful tool when used properly.

Industry is beginning to catch on, she says. "It's become chic."

Source: http://www.usatoday.com/life/cyber/tech/ctf256.htm

overview

Traditionally, doing anthropology has required field work in another society. The firsthand, personal study of local cultural settings is ethnography. Ethnographers work in natural communities. They form personal relationships with local people as they study their lives. Interview schedules may be used to guide interviews, ensuring that the ethnographer collects comparable information from everyone. Ethnographers work closely with key consultants on particular areas of local life. Life histories document personal experiences with culture and culture change. Genealogical information is particularly important in societies in which principles of kinship, descent, and marriage organize social life. Longitudinal research, often by a team, is the systematic study of an area or field site over time.

Archaeological anthropologists also work in teams and across time and space. Typically, archaeologists combine both local (excavation) and regional (systematic survey) perspectives. Like modern ethnographers, they recognize that sites are not discrete and isolated, but part of larger social systems. Anthroplogists recognize ethical obligations to their scholarly field, to society, and to the human species, other species, and the environment.

Traditionally, anthropologists worked in small-scale societies; sociologists, in modern nations. How does survey research, which typifies sociology, differ from ethnography? With more literate respondents, survey researchers use questionnaires, which research subjects fill out. Sociologists study samples to make inferences about a larger population. The diversity of social life in modern nations requires that even anthropologists adopt some survey procedures. However, anthropologists also retain the intimacy and firsthand investigation characteristic of ethnography.

Anthropology differs from other fields that study human beings because it is comparative, holistic, and global. Anthropologists study biology, language, and culture, past and present, in ancient and modern societies. This chapter compares the field methods of anthropology with those of the other social sciences. Also considered are the ethical dimensions of anthropological research.

Anthropology started to separate from sociology around the turn of the 20th century. Early students of society, such as the French scholar Émile Durkheim, were among the founders of both sociology and anthropology. Theorizing about the organization of simple and complex societies, Durkheim drew on written accounts of the religions of Native Australia (Durkheim 1912/1961) as well as considering mass phenomena (such as suicide rates) in modern nations (Durkheim 1897/1951). Eventually anthropology would specialize in the former, sociology in the latter.

Ethnography

Anthropology developed into a separate field as early scholars worked on Indian (Native American) reservations and traveled to distant lands to study small groups of foragers and cultivators. This type of firsthand personal study of local settings is called *ethnography*. Traditionally, the process of becoming a cultural anthropologist has required a field experience in another society. Early ethnographers lived in small-scale, relatively isolated societies, with simple technologies and economies.

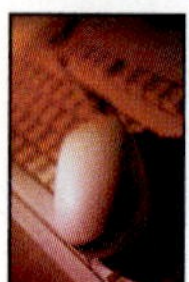

Ethnography thus emerged as a research strategy in societies with greater cultural uniformity and less social differentiation than are found in large, modern, industrial nations. In such nonindustrial settings, ethnographers have needed to consider fewer paths of enculturation to understand social life. Traditionally, ethnographers have tried to understand the whole of a particular culture (or, more realistically, as much as they can, given limitations of time and perception). To pursue this holistic goal, ethnographers adopt a free-ranging strategy for gathering information. In a given society or community, the ethnographer moves from setting to setting, place to place, and subject to subject to discover the totality and interconnectedness of social life.

Ethnography, by expanding our knowledge of the range of human diversity, provides a foundation for generalizations about human behavior and social life. Ethnographers draw on a variety of techniques to piece together a picture of otherwise alien life styles. Anthropologists usually employ several (but rarely all) of the techniques discussed here.

Ethnographic Techniques

The characteristic *field techniques* of the ethnographer include the following:

1. Direct, firsthand observation of daily behavior, including *participant observation.*
2. Conversation with varying degrees of formality, from the daily chitchat that helps maintain rapport and provides knowledge about what is going on to prolonged *interviews,* which can be unstructured or structured. Formal, printed *interview schedules* or questionnaires may be used to ensure that complete, comparable information is available for everyone of interest to the study.
3. The *genealogical method.*
4. Detailed work with *key consultants* about particular areas of community life.
5. In-depth interviewing, often leading to the collection of *life histories* of particular people (narrators).
6. Discovery of local beliefs and perceptions, which may be compared with the ethnographer's own observations and conclusions.
7. Problem-oriented research of many sorts.
8. Longitudinal research—the continuous long-term study of an area or site.
9. Team research—coordinated research by multiple ethnographers.

Observation and Participant Observation

Ethnographers get to know their hosts and usually take an interest in the totality of their lives. Ethnographers must pay attention to hundreds of details of daily life, seasonal events, and unusual happenings. They must observe individual and collective behavior in varied settings. They should record what they see as they see it. Things will never seem quite as strange as they do during the first few days and weeks in the field. The ethnographer eventually gets used to, and accepts as normal, cultural patterns that were initially alien. Ethnographers typically spend more than a year in the field. This permits them to observe the entire annual cycle. Staying a bit more than a year allows the ethnographer to repeat the season of his or her arrival, when certain events and processes may have been missed because of initial unfamiliarity and culture shock.

Many ethnographers record their impressions in a personal *diary,* which is kept separate from more formal *field notes.* Later, this record of early impressions will help point out some of the most basic aspects of cultural diversity. Such aspects include distinctive smells, noises people make, how they cover their mouths when they eat, and how they gaze at others. These patterns, which are so basic as to seem almost trivial, are part of what Bronislaw Malinowski called "the imponderabilia of native life and of typical behavior" (Malinowski 1922/1961, p. 20). These features of culture are so fundamental that local people take them for granted. They are too basic even to talk about, but the unaccustomed eye of the fledgling anthropologist picks them up. Thereafter, becoming familiar, they fade to the edge of consciousness. Initial impressions are valuable and should be recorded. First and foremost, ethnographers should be accurate observers, recorders, and reporters of what they see in the field.

Ethnographers don't study animals in laboratory cages. The experiments that psychologists do with pigeons, chickens, guinea pigs, and rats are very different from ethnographic procedure. Anthropologists don't systematically control subjects' rewards and punishments or their exposure to certain stimuli. Our subjects are not speechless animals but human beings. It is not part of ethnographic procedure to manipulate them, control their environments, or experimentally induce certain behaviors.

Ethnographers strive to establish *rapport*—a good, friendly working relationship based on personal contact—with our hosts. One of ethnography's most characteristic procedures is *participant observation,* which means that we take part in

Ethnographers strive to establish rapport—a friendly relationship based on personal contact—with the people they study. Here anthropologist Nadine Peacock works among the Efe of Congo. What research method does this photo suggest?

community life as we study it. As human beings living among others, we cannot be totally impartial and detached observers. We also must take part in many of the events and processes we are observing and trying to comprehend. By participating, we may learn how and why natives find such events meaningful, as well as see how they are organized and conducted.

To exemplify participant observation, let me describe aspects of my own ethnographic field work in Madagascar, a large island off the southeastern coast of Africa, and in Brazil. During the 14 months I lived in Madagascar in 1966–67, I observed and participated in many occasions in Betsileo life. I helped out at harvest time, joining other people who climbed atop—in order to stomp down on and compact—accumulating stacks of rice stalks. One September, for a reburial ceremony, I bought a silk shroud for a village ancestor. I entered the village tomb and watched people rewrap the bones and decaying flesh of their ancestors. I accompanied Betsileo peasants to town and to market. I observed their dealings with outsiders and sometimes offered help when problems arose.

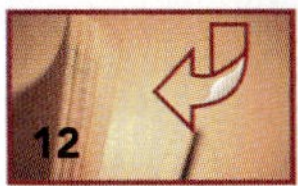

In Arembepe, Brazil (located in the last chapter, p. 12), I learned about fishing by sailing on the Atlantic in simple boats with local fishermen. I gave Jeep rides into the capital to malnourished babies, to pregnant mothers, and once to a teenage girl possessed by a spirit. All those people needed to consult specialists outside the village. I danced on Arembepe's festive occasions, drank libations commemorating new births, and became a godfather to a village girl. Most anthropologists have similar field experiences. The common humanity of the student and the studied, the ethnographer and the research community, makes participant observation inevitable.

Conversation, Interviewing, and Interview Schedules

Participating in local life means that ethnographers constantly talk to people and ask questions about what they observe. As their knowledge of the local language increases, they understand more. There are several stages in learning a field language. First is the naming phase—asking name after name of the objects around us. Later we are able to pose more complex questions and understand the replies. We begin to understand simple conversations between two villagers. If our language expertise proceeds far enough, we eventually become able to comprehend rapid-fire public discussions and group conversations.

One data-gathering technique I have used in both Arembepe and Madagascar involves an ethnographic survey that includes an interview schedule. In 1964, my fellow field-workers and I attempted to complete an interview schedule in each of Arembepe's 160 households. We entered almost every household (fewer than 5 percent refused to participate) to ask a set of questions on a printed form.

Our results provided us with a census and basic information about the village. We wrote down the name, age, and sex of each household member. We gathered data on family type, political party, religion, present and previous jobs, income, expenditures, diet, possessions, and many other items on our eight-page form.

Although we were doing a survey, our approach differed from the survey research design routinely used by sociologists and other social scientists working in large, industrial nations. That survey research, discussed below, involves sampling (choosing a small, manageable study group from a larger population) and impersonal data collection. We did not select a partial sample from the total population. Instead, we tried to interview all households in the community we were studying (that is, to have a total sample). We used an interview schedule rather than a questionnaire. With the **interview schedule,** the ethnographer talks face to face with people, asks the questions, and writes down the answers. **Questionnaire** procedures tend to be more indirect and impersonal; the respondent often fills in the form.

A young interviewer at work on the campus of the University of Southern California (USC). Does this strike you as a formal or an informal interview?

Our goal of getting a total sample allowed us to meet almost everyone in the village and helped us establish rapport. Decades later, Arembepeiros still talk warmly about how we were interested enough in them to visit their homes and ask them questions. We stood in sharp contrast to the other outsiders the villagers had known, who considered them too poor and backward to be taken seriously.

Like other survey research, however, our interview-schedule survey did gather comparable quantifiable information. It gave us a basis for assessing patterns and exceptions in village life. Our schedules included a core set of questions that were posed to everyone. However, some interesting side issues often came up during the interview, which we would pursue then or later.

Anthropologists such as Christie Kiefer typically form personal relationships with their cultural consultants, such as this Guatemalan weaver.

We followed such leads into many dimensions of village life. One woman, for instance, a midwife, became the key cultural consultant we sought out later when we wanted detailed information about local childbirth. Another woman had done an internship in an Afro-Brazilian cult (*candomblé*) in the city. She still went there regularly to study, dance, and get possessed. She became our *candomblé* expert.

Thus, our interview-schedule survey provided a structure that *directed but did not confine* us as researchers. It enabled our ethnography to be both quantitative and qualitative. The quantitative part consisted of the basic information we gathered and later analyzed statistically. The qualitative dimension came from our follow-up questions, open-ended discussions, pauses for gossip, and work with key consultants.

The Genealogical Method

As ordinary people, many of us learn about our own ancestry and relatives by tracing our genealogies. Computer programs such as Brother's Keeper allow us to trace our "family tree" and degrees of relationship. The **genealogical method** is a well-established ethnographic technique. Early ethnographers developed notation and symbols (see the chapter on "Families, Kinship, and Descent") to deal with kinship, descent, and marriage. Genealogy is a prominent building block in the social organization of nonindustrial societies, where people live and work each day with their close kin. Anthropologists need to collect genealogical data to understand current social relations and to reconstruct history. In many nonindustrial societies, kin links are basic to social life. Anthropologists even call such cultures "kin-based societies." Everyone is related to each other and spends most of his or her time with relatives. Rules of behavior attached to particular kin relations are basic to everyday life. Marriage is also crucial in organizing nonindustrial societies because strategic marriages between villages, tribes, and clans create political alliances.

Key Cultural Consultants

Every community has people who by accident, experience, talent, or training can provide the most complete or useful information about particular aspects of life. These people are **key cultural consultants.** In Ivato, the Betsileo village where I spent most of my time, a man named Rakoto was particularly knowledgeable about village history. However, when I asked him to work with me on a genealogy of the 50 to 60 people buried in the village tomb, he called in his cousin Tuesdaysfather, who knew more about this subject. Tuesdaysfather had survived an epidemic of influenza that ravaged Madagascar,

Kinship and descent are vital social building blocks in nonindustrial cultures. Without writing, genealogical information may be preserved in material culture, such as this totem pole being raised in Metlakatla, Alaska. What do you think is the significance of the images on the totem pole?

along with much of the world, around 1919. Immune to the disease himself, Tuesdaysfather had the grim job of burying his kin as they died. He kept track of everyone buried in the tomb. Tuesdaysfather helped me with the tomb genealogy. Rakoto joined him in telling me personal details about the deceased villagers.

Life Histories

In nonindustrial societies as in our own, individual personalities, interests, and abilities vary. Some villagers prove to be more interested in the ethnographer's work and are more helpful, interesting, and pleasant than others. Anthropologists develop likes and dislikes in the field as we do at home. Often, when we find someone unusually interesting, we collect his or her **life history.** This recollection of a lifetime of experiences provides a more intimate and personal cultural portrait than would be possible otherwise. Life histories, which may be recorded or videotaped for later review and analysis, reveal how specific people perceive, react to, and contribute to changes that affect their lives. Such accounts can illustrate diversity, which exists within any community, since the focus is on how different people interpret and deal with some of the same problems.

Local Beliefs and Perceptions, and the Ethnographer's

One goal of ethnography is to discover local views, beliefs, and perceptions, which may be compared with the ethnographer's own observations and conclusions. In the field, ethnographers typically combine two research strategies, the emic (local-oriented) and the etic (scientist-oriented). These terms, derived from linguistics, have been applied to ethnography by various anthropologists. Marvin Harris (1968) has popularized the following meanings of the terms. An **emic** approach investigates how local people think. How do they perceive and categorize the world? What are their rules for behavior? What has meaning for them? How do they imagine and explain things? Operating emically, the ethnographer seeks the "local viewpoint," relying on local people to explain things and to say whether something is significant or not. The term **cultural consultant** refers to individuals the ethnographer gets to know in the field, the people who teach him or her about their culture, who provide the emic perspective.

Ethnographers typically enter the field with a specific topic to investigate. In Oman in 1992, Julie Knight works with Ba'keet, a local sheikh, a key cultural consultant for her investigation of politics and history.

The **etic** (scientist-oriented) approach shifts the focus from local categories, expressions, explanations, and interpretations to those of the anthropologist. The etic approach realizes that members of a culture are often too involved in what they are doing to interpret their cultures impartially. Operating etically, the ethnographer emphasizes what he or she (the observer) notices and considers important. As a trained scientist, the ethnographer should try to bring an objective and comprehensive viewpoint to the study of other cultures. Of course, the ethnographer, like any other scientist, is also a human being with cultural blinders that prevent complete objectivity. As in other sciences, proper training can reduce, but not totally eliminate, the observer's bias. But anthropologists do have special training to compare behavior between different societies.

What are some examples of emic versus etic perspectives? Consider our holidays. For North Americans, Thanksgiving Day has special significance. In our view (emically), it is a unique cultural celebration that commemorates particular historical themes. But a wider, etic, perspective sees Thanksgiving as just one more example of the post-harvest festivals held in many societies. Another example: lay people (including many Americans) may believe that chills and drafts cause colds, which scientists know are caused by germs. In cultures that lack the germ theory of disease, illnesses are emically explained by various causes, ranging from spirits to ancestors to witches. *Illness* refers to a culture's (emic) perception and explanation of bad health, whereas *disease* refers to the scientific—etic—explanation of poor health, involving known pathogens.

A final example is the emics and etics of color terminology, to which we return in the chapter on language. In different cultures, people label colors differently. Some cultures have only two basic color terms—for light and dark—whereas others have all 11 primary color terms, plus a series of additional ones that recognize finer discriminations of shade and hue. Etically, the color spectrum exists everywhere, but emically people interpret and classify it differently in different societies.

Ethnographers typically combine emic and etic strategies in their field work. Local statements, perceptions, categories, and opinions help ethnographers understand how cultures work. Local beliefs are also interesting and valuable in themselves. However, local people often don't admit, or even recognize, certain causes and consequences of their behavior. This is as true of North Americans as it is of people in other societies. To describe and interpret culture, ethnographers should recognize biases that come from their own culture as well as those of the people being studied.

The Evolution of Ethnography

The Polish anthropologist Bronislaw Malinowski (1884–1942), who spent most of his professional life in England, is generally considered the father of ethnography. Like most anthropologists of his time, Malinowski did *salvage ethnography,* in the belief that the ethnographer's job is to study and record cultural diversity threatened by western-

Bronislaw Malinowski (1884–1942), seated with villagers in the Trobriand Islands. A Polish anthropologist who spent most of his professional life in England, Malinowski is generally considered the father of ethnography. Does this photo suggest anything about Malinowski's relationship with the villagers?

ization. Early ethnographic accounts (*ethnographies*), such as Malinowski's classic *Argonauts of the Western Pacific* (1922/1961), were similar to earlier traveler and explorer accounts in describing the writer's discovery of unknown people and places. However, the *scientific* aims of ethnographies set them apart from books by explorers and amateurs.

The style that dominated "classic" ethnographies was *ethnographic realism.* The writer's goal was to present an accurate, objective, scientific account of a different way of life, written by someone who knew it firsthand. This knowledge came from an "ethnographic adventure" involving immersion in an alien language and culture. Ethnographers derived their authority—both as scientists and as voices of "the native" or "the other"—from this personal research experience.

Malinowski's ethnographies were guided by the assumption that aspects of culture are linked and intertwined. Beginning by describing a Trobriand sailing expedition, the ethnographer then follows the links between that entry point and other areas of the culture, such as magic, religion, myths, kinship, and trade. Compared with Malinowski, today's ethnographies tend to be less inclusive and holistic, focusing on particular topics, such as kinship or religion.

According to Malinowski, a primary task of the ethnographer is "to grasp the native's point of view, his relation to life, to realize *his* vision of *his* world" (1922/1961, p. 25—Malinowski's italics). This is a good statement of the need for the emic perspective, as was discussed earlier. Since the 1970s, *interpretive anthropology* has considered the task of describing and interpreting that which is meaningful to natives. Interpretivists such as Clifford Geertz (1973) view cultures as meaningful texts that natives constantly "read" and ethnographers must decipher. According to Geertz, anthropologists may choose anything in a culture that interests them, fill in details, and elaborate to inform their readers about meanings in that culture. Meanings are carried by public symbolic forms, including words, rituals, and customs.

A current trend in ethnographic writing is to question traditional goals, methods, and styles, including ethnographic realism and salvage ethnography (Clifford 1982, 1988; Marcus and Cushman 1982). Marcus and Fischer argue that experimentation in ethnographic writing is necessary because all peoples and cultures have already been "discovered" and must now be "*re*discovered . . . in changing historical circumstances" (1986, p. 24).

In general, experimental anthropologists see ethnographies as works of art as well as works of science. Ethnographic texts may be viewed as literary creations in which the ethnographer, as mediator, communicates information from the "natives" to readers. Some recent experimental ethnographies are "dialogic," presenting ethnography as a dialogue between the anthropologist and one or more native informants (e.g., Dwyer 1982; Behar 1993). These works draw attention to ways in which ethnographers, and by extension their readers, communicate with other cultures. However, some such ethnographies have been criticized for spending too much time talking about the anthropologist and too little time describing the natives and their culture.

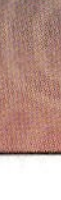

The dialogic ethnography is one genre within a larger experimental category—that is, *reflexive ethnography.* Here the ethnographer-writer puts his or her personal feelings and reactions to the field situation right in the text. Experimental writing strategies are prominent in reflexive accounts. The ethnographer may adopt some of the conventions of the novel, including first-person narration, conversations, dialogues, and humor. Experimental ethnographies, using new ways of showing what it means to be a Samoan or a Brazilian, may convey to the reader a richer and more complex understanding of human experience.

Recent ethnographic writers also have attempted to correct the deficiency of *romanticized timelessness* that is evident in many of the classics. Linked to salvage ethnography was the idea of the *ethnographic present*—the period before westernization, when the "true" native culture flourished. This notion gives classic ethnographies an eternal, timeless quality. Providing the only jarring note in this idealized picture are occasional comments by the author about traders or missionaries, suggesting that in actuality the natives were already part of the world system.

Anthropologists now recognize that the ethnographic present is a rather unrealistic construct. Cultures have been in contact—and have been changing—throughout history. Most native cultures had at least one major foreign encounter before any anthropologist ever came their way. Most of them had already been incorporated in some fashion into nation-states or colonial systems.

Contemporary ethnographies usually recognize that cultures constantly change and that an ethnographic account applies to a particular moment. A current trend in ethnography is to focus on the ways in which cultural ideas serve political and economic interests. Another trend is to describe how various particular "natives" participate in broader historical, political, and economic processes (Shostak 1981).

Problem-Oriented Ethnography

We see, then, a tendency to move away from holistic accounts toward more problem-focused and experimental ethnographies. Although anthropologists are interested in the whole context of human behavior, it is impossible to study everything, and field research usually addresses specific questions. Most ethnographers now enter the field with a specific problem to investigate, and they collect data about variables deemed relevant to that problem. And local people's answers to questions are not the only data source. Anthropologists also gather information on factors such as population density, environmental quality, climate, physical geography, diet, and land use. Sometimes this involves direct measurement—of rainfall, temperature, fields, yields, dietary quantities, or time allocation (Bailey 1990; Johnson 1978). Often it means that we consult government records or archives.

The information of interest to ethnographers is not limited to what local people can and do tell us. In an increasingly interconnected and complicated world, local people lack knowledge about many factors that affect their lives. Our local consultants may be as mystified as we are by the exercise of power from regional, national, and international centers.

Longitudinal Research

Geography limits anthropologists less now than in the past, when it could take months to reach a field site and return visits were rare. New systems of transportation allow anthropologists to widen the area of their research and to return repeatedly. Ethnographic reports now routinely include data from two or more field stays. **Longitudinal research** is the long-term study of a community, region, society, culture, or other unit, usually based on repeated visits. One example of such research is the longitudinal study of Gwembe District, Zambia. This study, planned in 1956 as a longitudinal project by Elizabeth Colson and Thayer Scudder, continues with Colson, Scudder, and their associates of various nationalities. Thus, as is often the case with longitudinal research, the Gwembe study also illustrates team research—coordinated research by multiple ethnographers. The Gwembe research project is both longitudinal (multitime) and multisite (considering several field sites) (Colson and Scudder 1975; Scudder and Colson 1980). Four villages, in different areas, have been followed for five decades. Periodic village censuses provide basic data on population, economy, kinship, and religious behavior. Censused people who have moved are traced and interviewed to see how their lives compare with those of people who have stayed in the villages.

Zambian assistants keep records of local events, as well as diaries of foods bought and eaten. Shifts in preferences for products are documented by shopping lists provided by villagers. Field notes describe attendance at courts, meetings, church services, funerals, and ceremonies. This information is supplemented by interviews with political leaders, officials, traders, technical workers, and foreigners who work for religious missions and *nongovernmental organizations* (NGOs). The anthropologists also consult government archives and other records. Zambian social scientists working in the district also provide insights about the changes taking place.

A series of different research questions have emerged, while basic data on communities and individuals continue to be collected. The first focus of study was the impact of a large hydroelectric dam, which subjected the Gwembe people to forced resettlement. The dam also spurred road building and other activities that brought the people of Gwembe more closely in touch with the rest of Zambia (Colson 1971; Scudder 1982; Scudder and Habarad 1991).

In the late 1960s, education became the research focus. Scudder and Colson (1980) examined how education provided access to new opportunities as it also widened a social gap between people with different educational levels. A third major study then examined a change in brewing and drinking patterns, including a rise in alcoholism, in relation to changing markets, transportation, and exposure to town values (Colson and Scudder 1988).

Team Research

As mentioned, longitudinal research is often team research. My own field site of Arembepe, Brazil, for example, first entered the world of anthropology as a field-team village in the 1960s. It was one of four sites for the now defunct Columbia–Cornell–Harvard–Illinois Summer Field Studies Program in Anthropology. For at least three years, that program sent a total of about 20 undergraduates annually, the author included, to do brief summer research. We were stationed in rural communities in four countries: Brazil, Ecuador, Mexico, and Peru. Since my wife, Isabel Wagley Kottak, and I began studying it in 1962, Arembepe has become a longitudinal field site. There generations of researchers have monitored various aspects of change and development. The community has changed from a village into a town. Its economy, religion, and social life have been transformed.

Brazilian and American researchers worked with us on team research projects during the 1980s (on television's impact) and the 1990s (on ecological awareness and environmental risk perception). Graduate students from the University of Michigan have drawn on our baseline information from the 1960s as they have studied various topics in Arembepe. In 1990, Doug Jones, a Michigan student doing biocultural research, used Arembepe as a field site to investigate standards of physical attractiveness. In 1996–97, Janet Dunn studied family planning and changing female reproductive strategies. Chris O'Leary, who first visited Arembepe in summer 1997, has investigated a striking aspect of

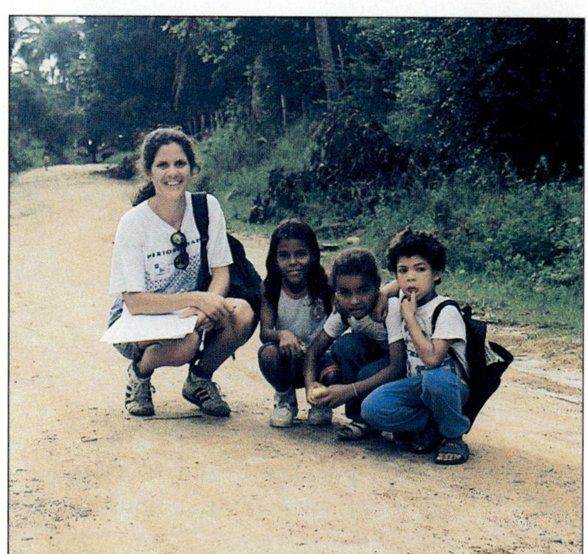

Janet Dunn, one of many anthropologists who have worked in Arembepe. Where is Arembepe, and what kinds of research have been done there?

religious change in Arembepe—the arrival of Protestantism.

Arembepe is thus a site where various fieldworkers have worked as members of a longitudinal team. The more recent researchers have built on prior contacts and findings to increase knowledge about how local people meet and manage new circumstances. I think that scholarship should be a community enterprise. The information we gathered in the past is there for new generations to use. To monitor changing attitudes and to understand the relation between television and family planning, Janet Dunn reinterviewed many of the women we had interviewed in the 1980s. Similarly, Chris O'Leary, who is comparing food habits and nutritional status in Arembepe and another Brazilian town, has access to dietary information from our 1964 interviews.

Contemporary forces of change are too pervasive and complex to be understood fully by a "lone ethnographer"—a researcher who starts from scratch and works alone, for a limited period of time, and who views his or her field site as relatively discrete and isolated. No longer can any ethnographer imagine that his or her field site represents some sort of pristine or autonomous entity. Nor should the ethnographer assume that he or she has exclusive (owner's) rights to the site, or even to the data gathered there. That information, after all, has been produced in friendship, cooperation, and consultation with local people. More and more anthropological field sites, including Malinowski's Trobriand Islands, have been restudied. Ideally, later ethnographers collaborate with and build on the work of their predecessors. Compared with the lone ethnographer model, team work across time (as in Arembepe) and space (as in our comparative studies in various Brazilian towns) produces better understanding of cultural change and social complexity.

Field Work in Archaeological Anthropology

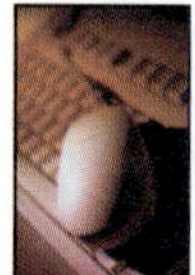

Archaeological anthropologists also work in teams and across time and space. Typically, archaeologists combine both local (excavation) and regional (systematic survey) perspectives. Like modern ethnographers, they recognize that sites are not discrete and isolated, but part of larger social systems. Let's examine some of the main techniques that archaeologists use to study patterns of behavior of past cultures based on their material remains. Archaeologists use varied methods to recover remains from a series of contexts, such as pits, sites, and regions. The archaeologist also integrates information about different social levels of the past, such as the household, the village, and the regional system.

Systematic Survey

Archaeologists use two basic fieldwork strategies: systematic survey and excavation. **Systematic survey** provides a regional perspective on the archaeological record by gathering information on patterns of settlement over a large area. Settlement pattern refers to the distribution of sites within a given region. Regional surveys reconstruct settlement patterns by addressing several questions: Where were sites located? How large were they? What kinds of structures were built at the sites? How old are the sites? Ideally, systematic survey involves walking over the entire survey area and recording the location and size of all sites. On the basis of archaeological materials on the surface, the surveyor also estimates the time period during which each site was occupied. A full coverage survey isn't always possible. The ground cover may be impenetrable (e.g., thick jungle), or certain parts of the survey area may be inaccessible. Permission to survey may be denied by landowners. Survey crews may have to rely on remote sensing (aerial photographs and satellite imagery) to help them locate and map sites.

With regional data, archaeologists can address many questions about the prehistoric communities that lived in a given area. Archaeologists use settlement pattern information to make population estimates and to assess levels of social complexity. Among hunter-gatherers and simple farmers, there are generally low numbers of people living in small campsites or hamlets with very little variation in the architecture. Such sites are scattered fairly evenly across the landscape. With increasing social complexity, the settlement patterns become more elaborate. Population levels rise. Such social factors as trade and warfare have played a more important role in determining the location of sites (on hilltops, waterways, trade routes). In complex societies, a settlement hierarchy of sites emerges. Certain sites are larger, with greater architectural differentiation, than others. Large sites with specialized architecture (elite residences, temples, administrative buildings, meeting areas) are generally interpreted as regional centers that exerted control over the smaller sites with less architectural differentiation.

Excavation

Along with paleontologists and paleoanthropologists, archaeologists also obtain information about the past by excavating sites. During an **excavation,** scientists recover remains by digging through the cultural and natural stratigraphy—the layers of deposits that make up an archaeological site. These layers or strata are used to establish the relative time order of the materials encountered during the dig. This relative chronology is based on the principle of *superposition*: in an undisturbed sequence of strata, the oldest layer is on the bottom. Each successive layer above is younger than the one below. Thus, artifacts from lower strata are

An archaeologist drives in another stake for a large grid at an excavation site in Teotihuacan, Mexico. Such a grid enables the researchers to record the exact location of any artifact or feature found at the site.

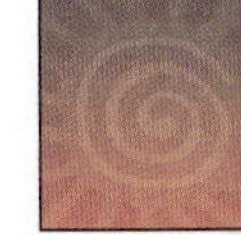

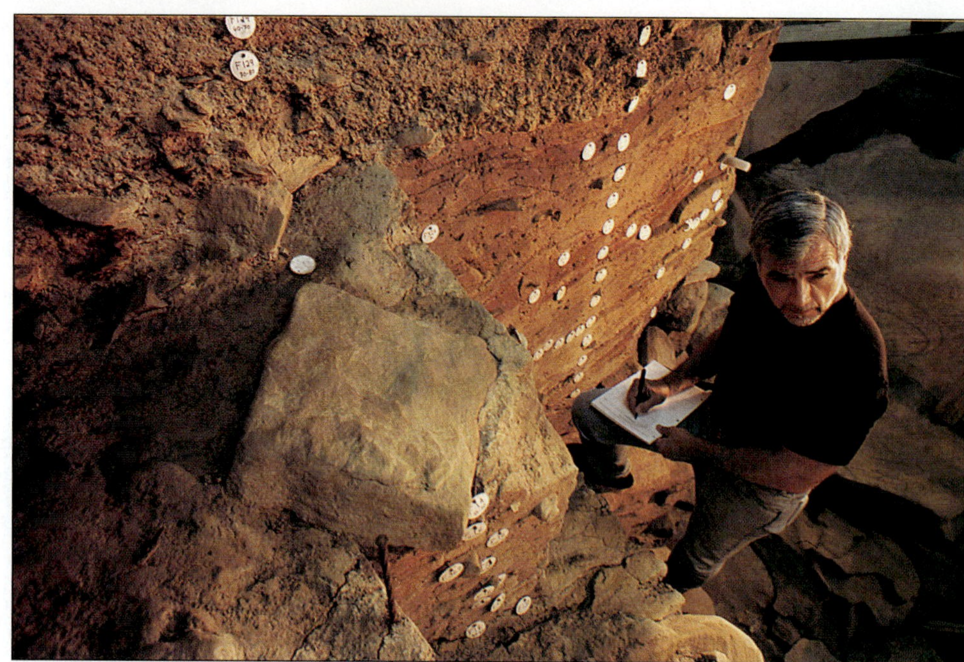

James Adovasio records strata at the Meadowcroft rock shelter site in southwestern Pennsylvania. Over a 25-year period he has excavated thousands of artifacts, some dating back up to 17,000 years. What kinds of remains do you suppose have been found here? See the text for some possibilities.

older than the artifacts recovered from higher strata in the same deposit. This relative time ordering of material remains lies at the heart of archaeological research.

The archaeological and paleontological records are so rich, and excavation is so labor intensive and expensive, that nobody digs a site without a good reason. Sites are excavated because they are in danger of being destroyed or because they address specific research interests. Cultural resource management (CRM), or contract archaeology, focuses on excavating archaeological sites that are threatened by modern development. Many countries require archaeological impact studies before construction can take place. If a site is at risk and the development cannot be stopped, contract archaeologists are called in to salvage what information they can from the site. Another reason a site may be chosen for excavation is because it is well suited to answer specific research questions. (These must be specified in the grant proposal for funding the field work—see the next section.) For example, an archaeologist interested in studying the origins of agriculture would not want to excavate a large, fortified, hilltop city with a series of buildings dating to a period well after the first appearance of farming communities. Rather, he or she would look for a small hamlet-sized site, located on or near good farmland and near a water source. Such a site would have evidence of an early occupation dating to the period during which farming communities first appeared in that region.

Before a site is excavated, it is first mapped and surface collected so that the archaeologist can make an informed decision about where exactly to dig. The collection of surface materials at a given site is similar to what is done over a much larger area in a regional survey. A grid is drawn to represent and subdivide the site. Then collection units, which are equal-sized sections of the grid, are determined and marked off on the actual site. This grid enables the researchers to record the exact location of any artifact or feature found at the site. By examining all the materials on the surface of the site, archaeologists can direct their excavations toward those areas of the site that are most likely to yield information that will address their research interests. Once an area is selected for digging, the excavation proceeds using a one-meter section and either arbitrary levels or the natural stratigraphy of the site. The location of every artifact or feature is recorded in three dimensions.

Digging may be done according to arbitrary levels. Thus, starting from the surface, a consistent amount of soil (usually 10 cm or 20 cm) is removed from the excavation unit so that each level has the same volume. This technique of excavation is a quick way of digging, since everything within a certain depth is removed at once. Digging by arbitrary levels is usually done in test pits, which archaeologists use to determine how deep the deposits of a site go and to establish a rough chronology for that site.

A more labor-intensive and refined method of excavating is to dig through the stratigraphy layer by layer. The layers are separated by differences in color and texture. Each stratum is peeled off one by one. This technique provides more information about the context of the artifacts, fossils, or features because the archaeologist works more slowly and in meaningful layers. A given 10-cm level of deposit may include within it a series of successive house floors, each with artifacts resting on them. If this deposit is excavated according to arbitrary levels, all the artifacts are mixed together. But if it is excavated according to the natural stratigraphy, with each house floor excavated separately, the resulting picture is much more detailed. The procedure here is for the archaeologist to remove and bag all the artifacts from each house floor before proceeding to the level below that one.

Any excavation recovers varied material remains, such as ceramics, stone artifacts (lithics), human and animal bones, and plant remains. Such remains may be small and fragmented. To increase the likelihood that small remains are recovered, all the soil is passed through screens. To recover very small remains such as fish bones and carbonized plant remains, archaeologists use a technique called *flotation*. Soil samples are sorted using water and a series of very fine meshes. When the water dissolves the soil, the carbonized plant remains float to the top. The fish bones and other heavier remains sink to the bottom. Flotation requires considerable time and labor. This makes it inappropriate to use on all the soil that is excavated from a site. Flotation samples are taken from a limited number of deposits, such as house floors, trash pits, and hearths.

Show Me the Money

Anthropologists need funding (research grants) to support their research and to get to the field. Several agencies support research in the various subfields of anthropology. The National Science Foundation (NSF) supports research in all the subfields. The National Institutes of Health (NIH) mainly supports biological anthropology. The Social Science Research Council (SSRC) funds research in cultural anthropology. The Wenner–Gren Foundation for Anthropological Research supports all subfields. For graduate students, the U.S. government's Fulbright IIE and Fulbright–Hays programs mainly fund research in cultural anthropology.

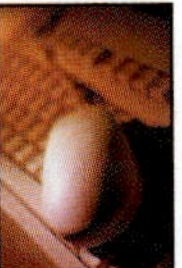

How does one prepare a grant proposal? (College students should review these points if they are planning research beyond the classroom.) The reader of a proposal should know certain things after reading the abstract (summary) and a few pages: What's the topic/problem? What's the research plan? What's going to be tested and how? Why is this research important? Where and when will it happen? Is the person proposing it qualified to do it? How will he or she do it? To obtain funds, which, after all, are limited, any grant proposal should answer four key questions:

1. **Why this topic/problem?** Proposal reviewers determine which research projects are worthy of funding. The grant writer must convince them that the topic is important—more so than other topics being proposed for funding at the same time.
2. **Why this place?** The topic may be important, but why study it in the place proposed? Some topics make sense in certain locales but not others; the grant writer has to show the connection. Remember the discussion, in the last section, of how an archaeologist would choose a site to investigate early farming. Or an example from cultural anthropology: It was easy for me to justify my research on the cultural impact of television in Brazil because that country has the world's most watched commercial television network, with national penetration. On the other hand, it wouldn't have made much sense for me to study television in

Madagascar, where sets and transmissions reach a limited audience—mainly urban.

3. **Why this person?** As the number of anthropologists increases, it is not uncommon to come across two people who want to study similar topics in the same country. Especially in that event, but in any case, it is important to identify the special qualifications of the person who proposes to do this research in this place. Relevant here are such background factors as a history of residing in the country, language training or fluency, pilot (preliminary) research in the proposed project locale, or experience elsewhere with the topic or method.
4. **How will the study be done?** Discussions of the methods to be used and the hypotheses to be tested in the research are important. Books such as *Anthropological Research: The Structure of Inquiry* by Pertti and Gretel Pelto (1978) and especially H. Russell Bernard's *Research Methods in Cultural Anthropology* (1994) have allowed anthropology methods courses to burgeon in colleges and universities. Another recent source is *The Handbook of Methods in Cultural Anthropology* (Bernard 1998). For archaeological methods see *Archaeology: Theories, Methods, and Practice* by Colin Renfrew and Paul Bahn (1996).

Ethics

In writing grant proposals, in conducting research, and in other professional contexts, ethical issues will inevitably arise. Before accepting a research proposal, all federal agencies require a "human subjects review" of the project. There are university panels whose job is to do such a project review before the proposal is submitted. The goal is to ensure that the research will not harm the people to be studied.

In its most recent (1997) Code of Ethics, the American Anthropological Association (AAA) notes that anthropologists have obligations to their scholarly field, to the wider society and culture, and to the human species, other species, and the environment. This Code's aim is to offer guidelines and to promote discussion and education. The AAA does not actually judge claims about unethical behavior.

The Code addresses several contexts in which anthropologists work. Its main points about the ethical dimensions of research may be summarized.

In proposing and conducting research, according to the Code, anthropologists should be open about their purposes, potential impacts, and sources of support.

A. Responsibility to people and animals

1. The primary ethical obligation of the anthropologist is to the people, species, or materials he or she studies. Potential violation of this obligation can lead to decisions not to undertake, or to discontinue, research. This primary ethical obligation entails:

   Avoiding harm or wrong.

   Respecting the well-being of humans and nonhuman primates.

   Working to preserve the archaeological, fossil, and historical records.

   Working to achieve a beneficial working relationship for all parties.
2. Researchers must respect the safety, dignity, and privacy of the people they study. Also, researchers should avoid harm to the safety, psychological well-being, and survival of the animals or species they study.
3. Researchers should determine in advance whether their hosts wish to remain anonymous or receive recognition. They should make every effort to comply with those wishes.
4. Researchers should obtain the informed consent of the people to be studied and of those whose interests may be affected by the research. Informed consent means that the anthropologist should tell people about the goals and procedures of the research, and gain their consent to be participants.
5. Anthropologists who develop close relationships with individuals (e.g., their cultural consultants) must adhere to the obligations of openness and informed consent. They must also carefully and respectfully negotiate the limits of the relationship.
6. Anthropologists may gain personally from their work. But they must not exploit individuals, groups, animals, or cultural or biological materials. They should recognize their debt to

the societies in which they work. They are obliged to reciprocate with the people they study in appropriate ways.

B. Responsibility to scholarship and science

1. Anthropologists should expect to encounter ethical dilemmas during their work.
2. Anthropologists are responsible for the integrity and reputation of their discipline, of scholarship, and of science. They should not deceive or knowingly misrepresent. They should not fabricate evidence, falsify, or plagiarize. Nor should they prevent reporting of misconduct, or obstruct the research of others.
3. Researchers should do all they can to preserve opportunities for future field-workers.
4. To the extent possible, researchers should disseminate their findings to the scientific and scholarly community.
5. Anthropologists should consider reasonable requests for access to their data for purposes of research. They should try to preserve their fieldwork data for use by posterity.

C. Responsibility to the public

1. Researchers should make their results available to sponsors, students, decision makers, and other nonanthropologists. Anthropologists should consider the social and political implications of their work. They should try to ensure that their work is understood, contextualized properly, and used responsibly. And they should be candid about their qualifications and philosophical or political biases.
2. Anthropologists may move beyond disseminating research results to a position of advocacy. This is an individual decision, rather than an ethical responsibility.

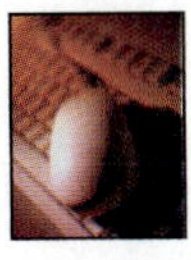

(The full Code of Ethics, which is abbreviated and paraphrased here, is available from the AAA website: **http://www.ameranthassn.org.**)

Survey Research

As anthropologists work increasingly in large-scale societies, they have developed innovative ways of blending ethnography and survey research (Fricke 1994). Before considering such combinations of field methods, I must describe survey research and the main differences between survey research and ethnography as traditionally practiced. Working mainly in large, populous nations, sociologists, political scientists, and economists have developed and refined the **survey research** design, which involves sampling, impersonal data collection, and statistical analysis. Survey research usually draws a **sample** (a manageable study group) from a much larger population. By studying a properly selected and representative sample, social scientists can make accurate inferences about the larger population.

In smaller-scale societies, ethnographers get to know most of the people, but given the greater size and complexity of nations, survey research cannot help being more impersonal. Survey researchers call the people they study *respondents*. These are people who respond to questions during a survey. Sometimes survey researchers personally interview them. Sometimes, after an initial meeting, they ask respondents to fill out a questionnaire. In other cases, researchers mail printed questionnaires to randomly selected sample members or have graduate students interview or telephone them. (In a **random sample,** all members of the population have an equal statistical chance of being chosen for inclusion. A random sample is selected by randomizing procedures, such as tables of random numbers, which are found in many statistics textbooks.) Table 2.1 summarizes the main differences between ethnography and survey research.

Anyone who has grown up recently in the United States or Canada has heard of sampling. Probably the most familiar example is the polling used to predict political races. The media hire agencies to estimate outcomes and do exit polls to find out what kinds of people voted for which candidates. During sampling, researchers gather information about age, gender, religion, occupation, income, and political party preference. These characteristics (**variables**—attributes that vary among members of a sample or population) are known to influence political decisions.

The number of variables influencing social identity and behavior increases with, and can be considered a measure of, social complexity. Many more variables affect social identities, experiences, and activities in a modern nation than is the case in the small communities where ethnography

Table 2.1
Ethnography and Survey Research Contrasted

Ethnography	Survey Research
Studies whole, functioning communities	Studies a small sample of a larger population
Is usually based on firsthand field work, during which information is collected after rapport, based on personal contact, is established between researcher and hosts	Is often conducted with little or no personal contact between study subjects and researchers, as interviews are frequently conducted by assistants over the phone or in printed form
Is generally interested in all aspects of local life (holistic)	Usually focuses on a small number of variables, e.g., factors that influence voting, rather than on the totality of people's lives
Has been traditionally conducted in nonindustrial, small-scale societies, where people often do not read and write	Is normally carried out in modern nations, where most people are literate, permitting respondents to fill in their own questionnaires
Makes little use of statistics, because the communities being studied tend to be small, with little diversity besides that based on age, gender, and individual personality variation	Is heavily dependent on statistical analyses to make inferences regarding a large and diverse population, based on data collected from a small subset of that population

grew up. In contemporary North America, hundreds of factors influence our social behavior and attitudes. These social predictors include our religion; the region of the country in which we grew up; whether we come from a town, suburb, or city; and our parents' professions, ethnic origins, and income levels. Because survey research deals with large and diverse groups and with samples and probability, its results must be analyzed statistically.

Ethnography can be used to supplement and fine-tune survey research. Anthropologists can transfer the personal, firsthand techniques of ethnography to virtually any setting that includes human beings. A combination of survey research and ethnography can provide new perspectives on life in **complex societies** (large and populous societies with social stratification and central governments). Preliminary ethnography also can help develop relevant and culturally appropriate questions for inclusion in surveys.

In my own courses in Ann Arbor, Michigan, undergraduates have done ethnographic research on sororities, fraternities, teams, campus organizations, and the local homeless population. Other students have systematically observed behavior in public places. These include racquetball courts, restaurants, bars, football stadiums, markets, malls, and classrooms. Other "modern anthropology" projects use anthropological techniques to interpret and analyze mass media. Anthropologists have been studying their own cultures for decades, and anthropological research in the

Sociologists and political scientists typically do survey research. Social surveys involve sampling, structured interviews or questionnaires, and statistical analysis. Survey research also is used in political polling and market research. This photo shows poll takers working for the Gallup organization in Mexico City. Do you think the results of survey research are as trustworthy as are those of ethnography?

United States and Canada is booming today. Wherever there is patterned human behavior, there is grist for the anthropological mill.

In any complex society, many predictor variables (*social indicators*) influence behavior and opinions. Because we must be able to detect, measure, and compare the influence of social indicators, many contemporary anthropological studies have a statistical foundation. Even in rural field work, more anthropologists now draw samples, gather quantitative data, and use statistics to interpret them (see Bernard 1994). Quantifiable information may permit a more precise assessment of similarities and differences between communities. Statistical analysis can support and round out an ethnographic account of local social life.

However, in the best studies, the hallmark of ethnography remains: Anthropologists enter the community and get to know the people. They participate in local activities, networks, and associations, in the city or in the countryside. They observe and experience social conditions and problems. They watch the effects of national policies and programs on local life. I believe that the ethnographic method and the emphasis on personal relationships in social research are valuable gifts that cultural anthropology brings to the study of a complex society.

A Brazilian boy forages for valuables in a sidewalk drain outside a restaurant on Copacabana beach, Rio de Janeiro. Anthropologists have studied street children in Brazil and elsewhere. What techniques do you imagine they use for such studies?

Science, Explanation, and Hypothesis Testing

The focus of this chapter so far has been various types of field research—ethnography, excavation, and survey research—in a particular society. Remember, however, that anthropology also has a comparative, cross-cultural dimension. As we saw in Chapter 1, *ethnology* draws on ethnographic (and archaeological) data to compare and contrast, and to make generalizations about, societies and cultures. As a scientific pursuit, ethnology attempts to identify and explain cultural differences and similarities, to test hypotheses, and to build theory to enhance our understanding of how social and cultural systems work.

In their 1996 article "Science in Anthropology," Melvin Ember and Carol R. Ember stress a key feature of science as a way of viewing the world: Science recognizes the tentativeness and uncertainty of our knowledge and understanding. Scientists strive to improve understanding by testing *hypotheses,* which are suggested explanations of things and events. In science, understanding means *explaining*—showing how and why the thing to be understood (the explicandum) is related to other things in some known way. Explanations rely on associations and theories. An association is an observed relationship between two or more measured variables. A theory is more general, suggesting or implying associations and attempting to explain them (Ember and Ember 1996).

A thing or event, for example, water freezing, is explained if it illustrates a general principle or association. The statement that water solidifies at 32 degrees is a statement of an association between two variables: the state of the water (liquid versus solid) and the air temperature. The truth of the principle is confirmed by repeated observations. (In the physical sciences, such relationships are called "laws.") Explanations based on consistent associations allow us to understand the past and predict the future.

beyond the classroom

Stories from Women Domestics of the Yucatán

BACKGROUND INFORMATION

Student:	*Angela C. Stuesse*
Supervising Professor:	*Allan F. Burns*
School:	*University of Florida*
Year in School/Major:	*Senior/Anthropology*
Future Plans:	*Master's in Latin American Studies*
Project Title:	*The* Patrona-Empleada* *Relationship Revealed: Stories from Women Domestics of the Yucatán*

What research techniques are illustrated in this account of undergraduate research? Think about this student's approach in terms of the issues raised in the section on the Evolution of Ethnography.

My fascination with anthropology sprang to life in early 1996, during a semester of study abroad in the Yucatán of Mexico. It was also there that I first came into contact with domestic workers of Latin America. Witness to the daily interactions between my host-family and their servant, I became intrigued by the complex nature of their relationship and decided to return the following year to do research for my honors thesis.

The testimonial of a domestic worker is often the story of both her personal and professional life. This is because she works not in an office, but rather in her *patrona*'s home. Over time, the distinction between employee and family member blurs. The indefinite relationship that results gives rise to many questions: To what extent is the servant influenced by the values and attitudes of her *patrona*? How does the way she perceives her own life compare with the way her *patrona* sees her? Under what conditions does their bond become less work-related and more analogous to family? What causes their association to be hierarchical in nature, and in what ways is this verticality expressed and/or mediated? These themes were the driving force of my investigations.

In the social sciences, associations are usually stated probabilistically: two or more variables *tend to be* related in a predictable way, but there are exceptions (Ember and Ember 1996). For example, in a worldwide sample of societies, the anthropologist John Whiting (1964) found a strong (but not 100 percent) association or correlation between a low-protein diet and a long postpartum sex taboo—a prohibition against sexual intercourse between husband and wife for a year or more following the birth of a child.

Laws and statistical associations explain by relating the explicandum (e.g., the postpartum sex taboo) to one or more other variables (e.g., a low-protein diet). We also want to know *why* such associations or correlations exist. Why do societies with low-protein diets tend to have long postpartum sex taboos? Scientists formulate theories to explain the observed correlations.

A **theory** is an explanatory framework that helps us understand *why* (something exists). Returning to the postpartum sex taboo, why might societies with low-protein diets develop such a taboo? Whiting's theory is that the taboo is adaptive; it helps people survive and reproduce in certain environments. With too little protein in their diets, babies may develop a protein-deficiency disease called kwashiorkor. But if the mother delays her next pregnancy, her current baby, by nursing longer, may have a better chance to survive. Whiting suggests that parents may be unconsciously or consciously aware that having another baby too soon might jeopardize the survival of the first one, so they decide to abstain from intercourse for more than a year after the birth of the first baby.

More complicated than an association, a theory is an explanatory framework containing a

Through personal contacts, I met four domestic workers who agreed to participate in my research. They ranged in age from 17 to 70 years old, and had between 5 and 50 years of experience. Research methods included auto-photography, unstructured and semi-structured interviews, and participant observation. Our conversations were sometimes lighthearted, sometimes very serious, and always key to a deeper understanding of each individual. Apart from listening and discussing, I also learned from these women by watching and doing. I helped them hang the laundry, set the table, sweep the patio, and fill the swimming pool. I visited their pueblos and met their families. We spent hours exchanging thoughts and discussing life. I laughed along with many and I held a hand as one woman cried. It was by participating in simple events like these that I began to understand the profundity and strength of these unique women. By interviewing and getting to know their *patronas* as well, I was able to analyze the nature of their relationships and place them within the context of existing ethnographic literature and theory.

The resulting thesis gives identity to the faceless numbers common in survey and demographic research. Through my writing I have attempted to let these women speak, to give them decision, control, and value. I also have explored the genre known as "narrative ethnography," which, by including first-person experiences, rejects the idea that a valid, professional study must be "objective" and "scientific." My research adds to the growing body of narrative ethnographic, testimonial, and introspective literature about women domestics and change in the Yucatán and Latin America. With each new study we are a few steps closer to a greater cultural understanding.

**Patrona* literally means patron or boss, referring to the female head of the household who oversees the domestic servants.

Empleada literally means employee, here referring to the female domestic servant.

series of statements. An association simply states an observed relationship between two or more known variables. Parts of a theory, by contrast, may be difficult or impossible to observe or to know directly. With Whiting's theory, for example, it would be hard to determine whether people had developed the sex taboo because they recognized it would give babies a better chance to survive. Typically, some elements of a theory are unobservable (at least at present). In contrast, statistical associations are based entirely on observations (Ember and Ember 1996).

If an association is tested and replicated repeatedly, we may consider it proved. Theories, by contrast, are unprovable. Although much evidence may support them, their truth isn't established with certainty. Many of the concepts and ideas in theories aren't directly observable or verifiable. Thus, scientists may try to explain how light behaves by postulating that it consists of "photons," which can't be observed, even with the most powerful microscope. The photon is a "theoretical construct," something that can't be seen or verified directly (Ember and Ember 1996).

Why should we bother with theories if we can't prove them? The Embers suggest that the main value of a theory is to promote new understanding. A theory can suggest patterns, connections, or relationships that may be confirmed by new research. Whiting's theory, for example, suggests hypotheses for future researchers to test. Because the theory proposes that the postpartum taboo is adaptive under certain conditions, one might hypothesize that certain changes would lead the taboo to disappear. By adopting birth control, for instance, families could space births without avoiding intercourse. So, too, might the taboo disappear if babies started receiving protein

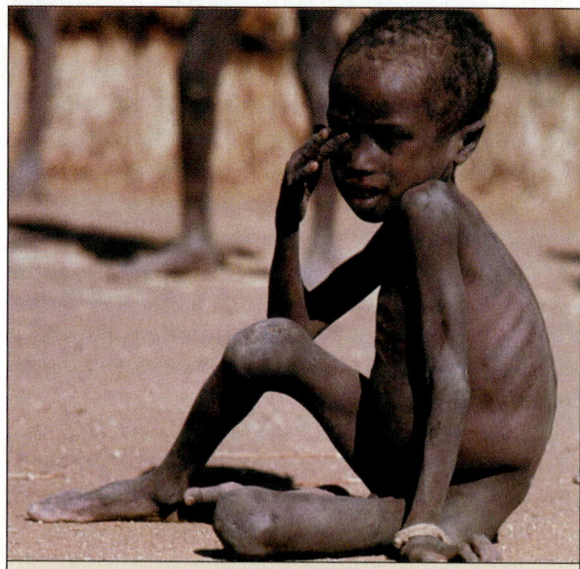

This child's bloated body is due to protein malnutrition. This condition, known as *kwashiorkor*, comes from a West African word meaning "one-two." This refers to the practice in some societies of abruptly weaning one infant when a second one is born. With no mother's milk, the first baby may get no protein at all. What are some cultural ways of fending off kwashiorkor?

supplements, which would reduce the threat of kwashiorkor.

Although theories can't be proved, they can be rejected. The method of *falsification* (showing a theory to be wrong) is our main way of evaluating theories. If a theory is true, certain predictions should stand up to tests designed to disprove them. Theories that haven't been disproved are accepted (for the time being at least) because the available evidence seems to support them.

What is acceptable evidence that an explanation is probably true? Cases that have been personally selected by a researcher (illustrating researcher-biased selection) can't provide an acceptable test of a hypothesis or theory. (Imagine Whiting had combed the ethnographic literature and chosen to cite only those societies that supported his theory.) Ideally, hypothesis testing should be done using a sample of cases that have been randomly selected from some statistical universe. (Whiting did this in choosing his cross-cultural sample.) The relevant variables should be measured reliably, and the strength and significance of the results should be evaluated using legitimate statistical methods (Bernard 1994).

summary

1. Ethnographic methods include observation, rapport building, participant observation, interviewing, genealogies, work with key consultants, life histories, and longitudinal research. Ethnographers do not systematically manipulate their subjects or conduct experiments. Rather, they work in actual communities and form personal relationships with local people as they study their lives.
2. An interview schedule is a form that an ethnographer completes as he or she visits a series of households. The schedule organizes and guides each interview, ensuring that comparable information is collected from everyone. Key consultants teach about particular areas of local life. Life histories dramatize the fact that culture bearers are individuals. Such case studies document personal experiences with culture and culture change. Genealogical information is particularly useful in societies in which principles of kinship and marriage organize social and political life. Emic approaches focus on native perceptions and explanations. Etic approaches give priority to the ethnographer's own observations and conclusions. Longitudinal research is the systematic study of an area or site over time.
3. Anthropological research may be done by teams. Forces of change are often too pervasive and complex to be understood by a lone ethnographer. Archaeological anthropologists also work in teams and across time and space. Typically, archaeologists combine both local (excavation) and regional (systematic survey) perspectives. Like modern ethnographers, they recognize that sites are not discrete and isolated, but part of larger social systems. Archaeologists use settlement pattern information to make population estimates and to assess levels of social complexity. Sites are excavated because they are in danger of being destroyed or because they address specific research interests.

4. Several agencies support research in anthropology. A research proposal should answer certain key questions: What's the topic/problem? What's going to be tested and how? Why is the research important? Where and when will it happen? Is the person proposing it qualified to do it? How will he or she do it? A code of ethics guides anthropologists' research and other professional activities.
5. Traditionally, anthropologists worked in small-scale societies; sociologists, in modern nations. Different techniques were developed to study such different kinds of societies. Social scientists working in complex societies use survey research to sample variation. Anthropologists do their field work in communities and study the totality of social life. Sociologists study samples to make inferences about a larger population. Sociologists often are interested in causal relationships among a very small number of variables. Anthropologists more typically are concerned with the interconnectedness of all aspects of social life.
6. The diversity of social life in modern nations and cities requires social survey procedures. However, anthropologists add the intimacy and direct investigation characteristic of ethnography. Community studies in regions of modern nations provide firsthand, in-depth accounts of cultural variation. Anthropologists may use ethnographic procedures to study urban life. But they also make greater use of survey techniques and analysis of the mass media in their research in contemporary nations.
7. Ethnology attempts to identify and explain cultural differences and similarities, and to build theory about how social and cultural systems work. Scientists strive to improve understanding by testing hypotheses—suggested explanations. Explanations rely on associations and theories. An association is an observed relationship between variables. A theory is more general, suggesting or implying associations and attempting to explain them.

key terms

complex societies Nations; large and populous, with social stratification and central governments.

cultural consultants Subjects in ethnographic research; people the ethnographer gets to know in the field, who teach him or her about their culture.

emic The research strategy that focuses on local explanations and criteria of significance.

etic The research strategy that emphasizes the ethnographer's rather than the locals' explanations, categories, and criteria of significance.

excavation Digging through the layers of deposits that make up an archaeological site.

genealogical method Procedures by which ethnographers discover and record connections of kinship, descent, and marriage, using diagrams and symbols.

interview schedule Ethnographic tool for structuring a formal interview. A prepared form (usually printed or mimeographed) that guides interviews with households or individuals being compared systematically. Contrasts with a *questionnaire* because the researcher has personal contact with the local people and records their answers.

key cultural consultant Person who is an expert on a particular aspect of local life.

life history Of a key consultant or narrator; provides a personal cultural portrait of existence or change in a culture.

longitudinal research Long-term study of a community, region, society, culture, or other unit, usually based on repeated visits.

questionnaire Form (usually printed) used by sociologists to obtain comparable information from respondents. Often mailed to and filled in by research subjects rather than by the researcher.

random sample A sample in which all members of the population have an equal statistical chance of being included.

sample A smaller study group chosen to represent a larger population.

survey research Characteristic research procedure among social scientists other than anthropologists. Studies society through sampling, statistical analysis, and impersonal data collection.

systematic survey Information gathered on patterns of settlement over a large area; provides a regional perspective on the archaeological record.

theory An explanatory framework, containing a series of statements, that helps us understand *why* (something exists); theories suggest patterns, connections, and relationships that may be confirmed by new research.

variables Attributes (e.g., sex, age, height, weight) that differ from one person or case to the next.

critical thinking questions

1. What kinds of problems—practical, personal, and ethical—can you imagine as arising during ethnographic field work?
2. Imagine yourself a foreign ethnographer starting field work in the United States. Where would you locate? What would be some of the imponderabilia of typical life that you'd notice during the first few weeks of your research?
3. If you were an anthropologist planning a field trip, what kinds of preparations would you have to make before and after you plan your research and arrange funding? How would your preparations differ depending on whether you plan to work in an industrial or a nonindustrial society?
4. How might the genealogical method be used in subfields of anthropology other than cultural anthropology?
5. If you were planning to use a life history approach to ethnography and had a year to spend in the field, how many consultants do you think you'd need to interview, and why? What sorts of people would you seek out as key cultural consultants?
6. Using your own society as an example, can you think of additional examples of the emic–etic distinction? What are some folk beliefs for which science has provided more satisfactory explanations? Why do folk beliefs persist if science does such a good job of explaining things?
7. How do you think the subfields of anthropology differ with respect to field work? Are some subfields more likely to use a team approach than others are? What about the equipment needs of the different subfields?
8. What do you see as the strengths and weaknesses of ethnography as compared with survey research? Which provides more accurate data? Might one be better for finding questions, while the other is better for finding answers? Or does it depend on the context of the research?
9. How might ethical issues and concerns differently affect cultural, biological, and archaeological anthropologists?
10. How would you imagine the criteria for grant proposal writing would differ in biological and archaeological anthropology, compared with cultural anthropology? Which of the subfields do you imagine has the largest typical research grant budget, and why?
11. How might the grant proposal guidelines in this chapter help you plan your own field research on campus or nearby?
12. What are some theories, as defined here, that you routinely use to understand the world?

case study

Trobriand Islands: The work of Bronislaw Malinowski was highlighted in this chapter's discussion of ethnographic field work. Malinowski's first trip to New Guinea in 1914 helped establish the ethnographic tradition of living among and building rapport with local people, of field work conducted in the local language and situated in a culture's own context. Some 60 years later, anthropologist Annette Weiner did her own field work in the Trobriands. Her findings both added to Malinowski's earlier work and challenged some of its assumptions. In *Culture Sketches,* read Chapter 13, "The Trobriand Islanders." Considering what you have just learned about field work, how did Malinowski's and Weiner's approaches differ? What are some possible reasons for their different perspectives? What are some challenges that ethnographers face in the 21st century? How might modern technology change the way anthropologists do field work?

suggested additional readings

Agar, M. H.

1996 *The Professional Stranger: An Informal Introduction to Ethnography,* 2nd ed. San Diego: Academic Press. Basics of ethnography, illustrated by the author's field experiences in India and among heroin addicts in the United States.

Berg, B. L.

2001 *Qualitative Research Methods for the Social Sciences,* 4th ed. Boston: Allyn and Bacon. How ethnography and other qualitative procedures may be extended across the range of social sciences; very thorough survey of qualitative methods.

Bernard, H. R.

1994 *Research Methods in Cultural Anthropology,* 2nd ed. Thousand Oaks, CA: Sage. The most complete and up-to-date survey of methods of data collection, organization, and analysis in cultural anthropology.

Bernard, H. R., ed.

1998 *The Handbook of Methods in Cultural Anthropology.* Walnut Creek, CA: Altamira. Various authors describe a series of methods in cultural anthropology.

Chiseri-Strater, E., and B. S. Sunstein

2001 *Fieldworking: Reading and Writing Research,* 2nd ed. Upper Saddle River, NJ: Prentice Hall. Ways of evaluating and presenting research data.

Crane, J. G., and M. V. Angrosino

1992 *Field Projects in Anthropology: A Student Handbook,* 3rd ed. Prospect Heights, IL: Waveland. Methods and key issues in doing field work.

DeVita, P. R., and J. D. Armstrong, eds.

1998 *Distant Mirrors: America as a Foreign Culture,* 2nd ed. Belmont, CA: Wadsworth. The social life, customs, and popular culture of the United States as viewed and interpreted by outsiders.

Kottak, C. P., ed.

1982 *Researching American Culture: A Guide for Student Anthropologists.* Ann Arbor: University of Michigan Press. Advice for college students doing field work in the United States. Includes papers by undergraduates and anthropologists on contemporary American culture.

Kutsche, P.

1998 *Field Ethnography: A Manual for Doing Cultural Anthropology.* Upper Saddle River, NJ: Prentice Hall. Useful guide for fledgling ethnographers.

Michrina, B. P., and C. Richards

1996 *Person to Person: Fieldwork, Dialogue, and the Hermeneutic Method.* Albany, NY: State University of New York Press. Discusses some of the experimental and interpretive ethnographic procedures discussed in this chapter.

Pelto, P. J., and G. H. Pelto

1978 *Anthropological Research: The Structure of Inquiry,* 2nd ed. New York: Cambridge University Press. Discusses data collection and analysis, including the relationship between theory and field work, hypothesis construction, sampling, and statistics.

Renfrew, C., and P. Bahn

2000 *Archaeology: Theories, Methods, and Practice,* 3rd ed. London: Thames and Hudson. Most useful treatment of methods in archaeological anthropology.

Spradley, J. P.

1979 *The Ethnographic Interview.* New York: Harcourt Brace Jovanovich. Discussion of the ethnographic method, with emphasis on discovering native viewpoints.

internet exercises

1. Ethnographic Fieldwork: Look at this collection of papers from the page entitled "Ethnographic Research Done in the Southern Appalachians," **http://www.acs.appstate.edu/dept/anthro/ebooks/ethno97/title.html.**
   a. Read the Preface. What skills were the students able to develop in the field that cannot be taught in a lecture course?
   b. Go to the paper entitled Women's Work in Allegheny County, NC, **http://www.acs.appstate.edu/dept/anthro/ebooks/ethno97/efird.html.** Skim the paper, paying special attention to the introduction, conclusion, and appendices. What did the student learn? How different are the women portrayed in this article from the women in your own community?
   c. Look specifically at the student's appendices. How did she collect the information she needed to make her conclusions? Are there questions you would have added? Why?
   d. Skim at least one other chapter, focusing on the introduction and conclusion. What are the advantages of doing research as a team? If there were only one person doing work on this project in the Appalachians, how do you think the results might be different? Do you think it is possible for a single ethnographer to fully understand a community?
2. Archaeological Fieldwork: Visit the Dust Cave Field School website, **http://www.dustcave.ua.edu/,** and read the History of Dust Cave, **http://www.dustcave.ua.edu/history.htm.**
   a. Watch the video prepared by CNN of the work done at Dust Cave, **http://www.dustcave.ua.edu/dccnn.ram;** the video is in RealPlayer format. (If you do not have a player go to **www.realplayer.com**). Based on the video, is this portrayal of archaeology what you expected? Is there more to conducting field work than just digging? Was it important for the participants to be able to work as a team?
   b. Go to the "Student Research 1999" page, **http://www.dustcave.ua.edu/99/stud99.htm.** These are papers written by undergraduate participants at Dust Cave during the summer of 1999. Read through at least one student paper (by clicking on the photograph of that student). What did the student research? What were the conclusions? How does it contribute to the overall understanding of prehistoric life in Dust Cave?

See Chapter 2 on your CD-ROM for additional review and interactive exercises. See your McGraw-Hill Online Learning Center for more.

Humankind Evolving

PART II

Chapter 3

Evolution and Genetics

CHAPTER OUTLINE

NYTIMES.COM NEWS BRIEFS

Y Chromosome Bears Witness to Story of the Jewish Diaspora

by Nicholas Wade
May 9, 2000

With a new technique based on the male or Y chromosome, biologists have traced the diaspora of Jewish populations from the dispersals that began in 586 BC to the modern communities of Europe and the Middle East.

The analysis provides genetic witness that these communities have, to a remarkable extent, retained their biological identity separate from their host populations, evidence of relatively little intermarriage or conversion into Judaism over the centuries.

Another finding . . . is that by the yardstick of the Y chromosome, the world's Jewish communities closely resemble not only each other but also Palestinians, Syrians, and Lebanese, suggesting that all are descended from a common ancestral population that inhabited the Middle East some four thousand years ago.

Dr. Lawrence H. Schiffman, chairman of the Department of Hebrew and Judaic Studies at New York University, said the study fit with historical evidence that Jews originated in the Near East and with biblical evidence suggesting that there were a variety of families and types in the original population . . .

The study . . . was conducted by Dr. Michael F. Hammer of the University of Arizona with colleagues in the United States, Italy, Israel, England, and South Africa . . .

The analysis . . . is based on the Y chromosome, which is passed unchanged from father to son. Early in human evolution, all but one of the Y chromosomes were lost as their owners had no children or only daughters, so that all Y chromosomes today are descended from that of a single genetic Adam who is estimated to have lived about 140,000 years ago.

In principle, all men therefore should carry the identical sequence of DNA letters on their Y chromosomes, but in fact occasional misspellings have occurred, and because each misspelling is then repeated in subsequent generations, the branching lineages of errors form a family tree rooted in the original Adam.

. . . The type and abundance of the lineages in each population serve as genetic signature by which to compare different populations.

Based on these variations, Dr. Hammer identified 19 variations in the Y chromosome family tree.

The ancestral Middle East population from which both Arabs and Jews are descended was a mixture of men from eight of these lineages.

Among major contributors to the ancestral Arab-Jewish population were men who carried what Dr. Hammer calls the "Med" lineage. This Y chromosome is found all round the Mediterranean and in Europe and may have been spread by the Neolithic inventors of agriculture or perhaps by the voyages of seagoing people like the Phoenicians . . .

The ancestral pattern of lineages is recognizable in today's Arab and Jewish populations, but is distinct from that of European populations and both groups differ widely from sub-Saharan Africans.

Each Arab and Jewish community has its own flavor of the ancestral pattern, reflecting their different genetic histories. Roman Jews have a pattern quite similar to that of Ashkenazis, the Jewish community of Eastern Europe. Dr. Hammer said the finding accorded with the hypothesis that Roman Jews were the ancestors of the Ashkenazis.

Despite the Ashkenazi Jews' long residence in Europe, their Y signature has remained distinct from that of non-Jewish Europeans . . .

Source: http://www.nytimes.com/library/national/science/050900sci-genetics-jews.html

overview

Charles Darwin and Alfred Russel Wallace proposed that natural selection could explain the origin of species, as well as many biological differences and similarities among life forms. For natural selection to work, there needs to be (and there always is) variety within the population undergoing selection.

Darwin didn't know the precise genetic mechanisms that allowed natural selection to work. It was his contemporary Gregor Mendel who discovered that genetic traits are inherited as discrete units, now called chromosomes and genes. Mendel also discovered that hereditary traits may be inherited independently of each other, rather than as a bundle. Such traits may then reunite in new combinations. This genetic recombination supplies some of the variety on which natural selection depends.

The adaptive value of particular traits depends on the environment. If the environment changes, nature can only select from traits that are already present in the population. If there isn't enough variety to permit adaptation to the environmental change, extinction is likely. New types don't appear just because they are needed.

Other evolutionary mechanisms work along with natural selection. Genetic drift operates most obviously in small populations, where pure chance can easily change gene frequencies. Gene flow and interbreeding keep subgroups of the same species connected genetically and thus work against speciation—the formation of new species.

There are links between genetically determined traits, such as hemoglobins in the blood, and selective forces, such as malaria. Selection through differential resistance to disease has influenced the distribution of human blood groups. Natural selection also has operated on facial features, body size and shape, and many other expressions of human biological diversity.

Humans have uniquely varied ways—cultural and biological—of adapting to environmental stresses. Exemplifying cultural adaptation, we manipulate our artifacts and behavior in response to environmental conditions. We turn up thermostats or travel to Florida in the winter. We turn on fire hydrants, swim, or ride in air-conditioned cars from New York City to Maine to escape the summer's heat. Although such reliance on culture has increased during human evolution, people haven't stopped adapting biologically. As in other species, human *populations* adapt genetically in response to environmental forces, and *individuals* react physiologically to stresses. Thus, when we work in the midday sun, sweating occurs spontaneously, cooling the skin and reducing the temperature of subsurface blood vessels.

We are ready now for a more detailed look at the principles that determine human biological adaptation, variation, and change.

Creationism and Evolution

During the 18th century, many scholars became interested in human origins, biological diversity, and our position within the classification of plants and animals. At that time, the commonly accepted explanation for the origin of species came from Genesis, the first book of the Bible: God had created all life during six days of Creation. According to **creationism,** biological similarities and differences originated at the Creation. Characteristics of life forms were seen as immutable; they could not change. Through calculations based on genealogies in the Bible, the biblical scholars James Ussher and John Lightfoot even managed to trace the Creation to a very specific time: October 23, 4004 BC at 9 AM.

Carolus Linnaeus (1707–1778), who accepted the biblical account of Creation, developed the first comprehensive and still influential classification, or taxonomy, of plants and animals. He grouped life forms on the basis of similarities and differences in their physical characteristics. He used traits such as the presence of a backbone to distinguish vertebrates from invertebrates and

According to creationism all life originated during the six days of creation described in the Bible. Catastrophism proposed that fires and floods, including the biblical deluge involving Noah's ark (depicted in this painting by the American artist Edward Hicks), destroyed certain species. How might a creationist account for differences and similarities between fossils and contemporary life forms?

the presence of mammary glands to distinguish mammals from birds. Linnaeus viewed the differences between life forms as part of the Creator's orderly plan. Biological similarities and differences had been established at the time of Creation and had not changed.

Fossil discoveries during the 18th and 19th centuries raised doubts about creationism. Fossils showed that different kinds of life had once existed. If all life had originated at the same time, why weren't ancient species still around? Why weren't contemporary plants and animals found in the fossil record? A modified explanation combining creationism with **catastrophism** replaced the original doctrine. In this view, fires, floods, and other catastrophes, including the biblical flood involving Noah's ark, had destroyed ancient species. After each destructive event, God had created again, leading to contemporary species. How did the catastrophists explain certain clear similarities between fossils and modern animals? They argued that some ancient species had managed to survive in isolated areas. For example, after the biblical flood, the progeny of the animals saved on Noah's ark spread throughout the world.

The alternative to creationism and catastrophism was *transformism,* also called **evolution.** Evolutionists believed that species arose from others through a long and gradual process of transformation, or descent with modification. Charles Darwin became the best known of the evolutionists. However, he was influenced by earlier scholars, including his own grandfather. Erasmus Darwin, in a book called *Zoonomia* published in 1794, had proclaimed the common ancestry of all animal species.

Charles Darwin also was influenced by Sir Charles Lyell, the father of geology. During Darwin's famous voyage to South America aboard the *Beagle,* he read Lyell's influential book *Principles of Geology* (1837/1969), which exposed him to Lyell's principle of **uniformitarianism.** Uniformitarianism states that the present is the key to the past. Explanations for past events should be sought in the long-term action of ordinary forces that still work today. Thus, natural forces (rainfall, soil deposition, earthquakes, and volcanic action) have gradually built and modified geological features such as mountain ranges. The earth's structure has been transformed gradually through natural forces operating for millions of years (see Weiner 1994).

Uniformitarianism was a necessary building block for evolutionary theory. It cast serious doubt on the belief that the world was only 6,000 years old. It would take much longer for such ordinary forces as rain and wind to produce major geological changes. The longer time span also allowed enough time for the biological changes that fossil discoveries were revealing. Darwin applied the ideas of uniformitarianism and long-term transformation through natural

forces to living things. Like other evolutionists, he argued that all life forms are ultimately related. In opposition to the creationists, Darwin argued that the number of species is not immutable but has increased over time. (For more on science, evolution, and creationism, see Futuyma 1995 and Gould 1999.)

Darwin offered natural selection as a principle that could explain the origin of species, biological diversity, and similarities among related life forms. His major contribution was not the theory of evolution, as most people believe, but the idea that natural selection explains evolutionary change. Natural selection wasn't Darwin's unique discovery. Working independently, the naturalist Alfred Russel Wallace had reached a similar conclusion. In a joint paper read to London's Linnaean Society in 1858, Darwin and Wallace made their discovery public. Darwin's book *On the Origin of Species* (1859/1958) offered fuller documentation but created great controversy.

Natural selection is the process by which nature selects the forms most fit to survive and reproduce in a given environment. For natural selection to work on a particular population, there must be variety within that population, as there always is. Natural selection operates when there is competition for *strategic resources* (those necessary for life), such as food and space, between members of the population. Organisms whose attributes render them most fit to survive and reproduce in their environment do so in greater numbers than others do. Over the years, the less fit organisms gradually die out and the favored types survive.

The giraffe's neck can be used to illustrate how natural selection works on variety within a population. In any group of giraffes, there is always variation in neck length. When food is adequate, the animals have no problem feeding themselves with foliage. But in times when there is pressure on strategic resources, so that dietary foliage is not as abundant as usual, giraffes with longer necks have an advantage. They can feed off the higher branches. If this feeding advantage permits longer-necked giraffes to survive and reproduce even slightly more effectively than shorter-necked ones, the trait will be favored by natural selection. The giraffes with longer necks will be more likely to transmit their genetic material to future generations than will giraffes with shorter necks.

An incorrect alternative to this (Darwinian) explanation would be the inheritance of acquired characteristics. That is the idea that in each generation, individual giraffes strain their necks to reach just a bit higher. This straining somehow modifies their genetic material. Over generations of strain, the average neck gradually gets longer through the accumulation of small increments of neck length acquired during the lifetime of each generation of giraffes. This is not how evolution works. If it did work in this way, weight lifters could expect to produce especially muscular babies. Workouts that promise no gain without the pain apply to the physical development of individuals, not species. Instead, evolution works as the process of natural selection takes advantage of the variety that is already present in a population. That's how giraffes got their necks.

The process of natural selection continues as long as the relationship between the population and its environment remains the same. However, if emigration, or some change in the environment, occurs, natural selection will begin to favor types that are more likely to survive and reproduce in the new environment. This new selection will continue until an equilibrium is reached. Environmental change or migration may then occur again. Through such a gradual, branching process, involving adaptation to thousands of environments, natural selection has produced the diverse plants and animals found in the world today.

Genetics

Darwin recognized that for natural selection to operate, there must be variety in the population undergoing selection. Documenting and explaining human variation is a major concern of modern biological anthropology. Genetics, a science that emerged after Darwin, helps us understand the causes of biological variation. We now know that DNA (deoxyribonucleic acid) molecules make up genes and chromosomes, which are the basic hereditary units. Biochemical changes (mutations)

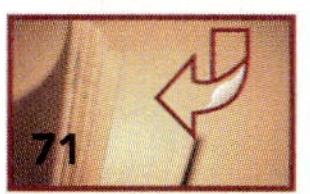

in DNA provide much of the variety on which natural selection operates. (See the section on Mutation on page 71.) Through sexual reproduction, recombination of the genetic traits of mother and father in each generation leads to new arrangements of the hereditary units received from each parent. Such genetic recombination also adds variety on which natural selection may operate.

Mendelian genetics studies the ways in which chromosomes transmit genes across the generations. *Biochemical genetics* examines structure, function, and changes in DNA. (Our website provides additional information on biochemical genetics.) **Population genetics** investigates natural selection and other causes of genetic variation, stability, and change in breeding populations.

Mendel's Experiments

In 1856, in a monastery garden, the Austrian monk Gregor Mendel began a series of experiments that were to reveal the basic principles of genetics. Mendel studied the inheritance of seven contrasting traits in pea plants. For each trait there were only two forms. For example, plants were either tall (6 to 7 feet) or short (9 to 18 inches), with no intermediate forms. Similarly, seeds were either smooth or wrinkled, and pea color was either yellow or green.

Mendel discovered that heredity is determined by discrete particles or units. Although traits could disappear in one generation, they reemerged in their original form in later generations. For example, Mendel crossbred pure strains of tall and short plants. Their offspring were all tall. This was the first descending, or first filial, generation, designated F_1. Mendel then interbred the plants of the F_1 generation to produce a generation of grandchildren, the F_2 generation (Figure 3.1). In this generation, short plants reappeared. Among thousands of plants in the F_2 generation, there was approximately one short plant for every three tall ones.

From similar results with the other six traits, Mendel concluded that although a **dominant** form could mask the other form in *hybrid,* or mixed, individuals, the dominated trait—the **recessive**—was not destroyed; it wasn't even changed. Recessive traits would appear in unaltered form in later generations because genetic traits were inherited as discrete units.

These basic genetic units that Mendel described were factors (now called genes or alleles) located on **chromosomes.** Chromosomes are arranged in matching (homologous) pairs. Humans have 46 chromosomes, arranged in 23 pairs, one in each pair from the father and the other from the mother.

For simplicity, a chromosome may be pictured as a surface (see Figure 3.2) with several positions, to each of which we assign a lowercase letter. Each position is a **gene.** Each gene determines, wholly or partially, a particular biological trait, such as whether one's blood is A, B, or O. **Alleles** (for example, b^1 and b^2 in Figure 3.2) are biochemically different forms of a given gene. In humans, A, B, AB, and O blood types reflect different combinations of alleles of a particular gene.

In Mendel's experiments, the seven contrasting traits were determined by genes located on seven different pairs of chromosomes. The gene for height occurred in one of the seven pairs. When Mendel crossbred pure tall and pure short plants to produce his F_1 generation, each of the offspring received an allele for tallness (T) from one parent and one for shortness (t) from the other. These offspring were mixed, or **heterozygous,** with respect to height; each had two dissimilar alleles of that gene. Their parents, in contrast, had been **homozygous,** possessing two identical alleles of that gene (see Hartl and Jones 1999).

In the next generation (F_2), after the mixed plants were interbred, short plants reappeared in the ratio of one short to three talls. Knowing that shorts only produced shorts, Mendel could assume that they were genetically pure. Another fourth of the F_2 plants produced only talls. The remaining half, like the F_1 generation, were heterozygous; when interbred, they produced three talls for each short. (See Figure 3.3.)

Dominance produces a distinction between **genotype,** or hereditary makeup, and *phenotype,* or expressed physical characteristics. Genotype is what you really are genetically; phenotype is what you appear as. Mendel's peas had three genotypes—TT, Tt, and tt—but only two phenotypes—tall and short. Because of dominance, the

Figure 3.1
Mendel's Second Set of Experiments with Pea Plants

Trait Exhibited by F_1 Hybrids	F_2 Generation (produced by crossbreeding F_1 hybrids)		
	Exhibit Dominant Trait		Exhibit Recessive Trait
Smooth seed shape	Smooth 3	+ :	Wrinkled 1
Yellow seed interior	Yellow 3	+ :	Green 1
Gray seed coat	Gray 3	+ :	White 1
Inflated pod	Inflated 3	+ :	Pinched 1
Green pod	Green 3	+ :	Yellow 1
Axial pod	Axial 3	+ :	Terminal 1
Tall stem	Tall 3	+ :	Short 1
	Offspring exhibit dominant or recessive traits in ratio of 3:1.		

Dominant colors are shown unless otherwise indicated.

heterozygous plants were just as tall as the genetically pure tall ones. How do Mendel's discoveries apply to humans? Although some of our genetic traits follow Mendelian laws, with only two forms—dominant and recessive—other traits are determined differently. For instance, three alleles determine whether our blood type is A, B, AB, or O. People with two alleles for type O have that blood type. However, if they received a gene for either A or B from one parent and one for O from the other, they will have blood type A or B. In other words, A and B are both dominant over O. A and B are said to be *codominant.* If people inherit a gene for A from one parent and one for B from the other, they will have type AB blood, which is chemically different from the other varieties, A, B, and O.

These three alleles produce four phenotypes—A, B, AB, and O—and six different genotypes—OO, AO, BO, AA, BB, and AB (Figure 3.4). There are fewer phenotypes than genotypes because O is recessive to both A and B.

Figure 3.2

Simplified Representation of a Normal Chromosome Pair

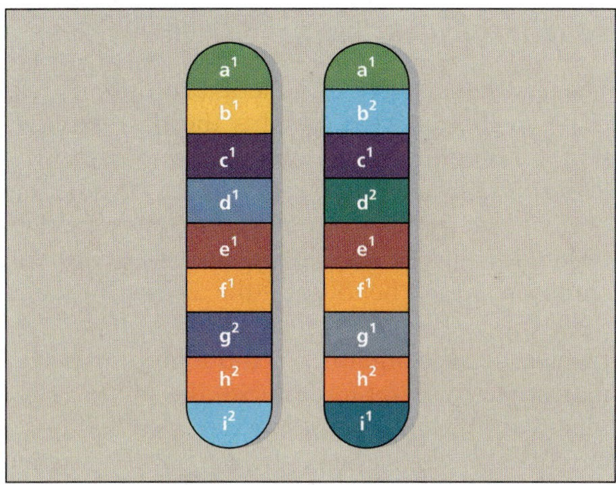

Letters indicate genes; superscripts indicate alleles.

Figure 3.3

Punnett Squares of a Homozygous Cross and a Heterozygous Cross

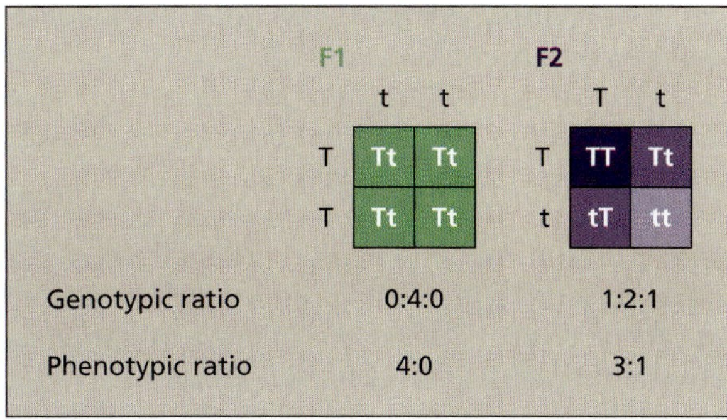

These squares show how phenotypic ratios of the F_1 and F_2 generation are generated. Colors show genotypes.

Independent Assortment and Recombination

Through additional experiments, Mendel also formulated his law of **independent assortment.** He discovered that traits are inherited independently of one another. For example, he bred pure round yellow peas with pure wrinkled green

Figure 3.4

Determinants of Phenotypes (Blood Groups) in the ABO System

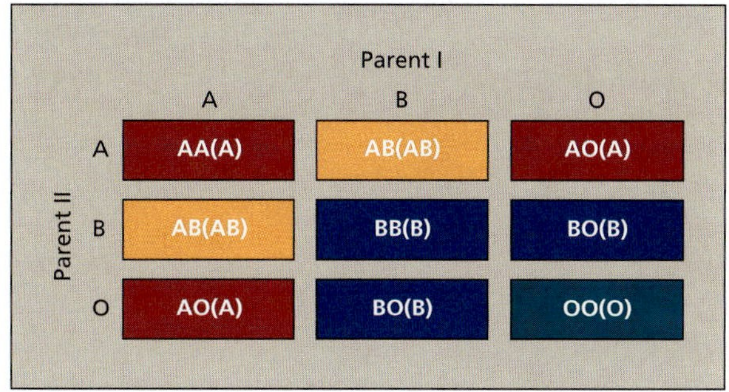

Parent I
A
B
O
Parent II
A
AA(A)
AB(AB)
AO(A)
B
AB(AB)
BB(B)
BO(B)
O
AO(A)
BO(B)
OO(O)

The four phenotypes—A, B, AB, and O—are indicated in parentheses and by color.

ones. All the F_1 generation peas were round and yellow, the dominant forms. But when Mendel interbred the F_1 generation to produce the F_2, four phenotypes turned up. Round greens and wrinkled yellows had been added to the original round yellows and wrinkled greens.

The independent assortment and recombination of genetic traits provide one of the main ways by which variety is produced in any population. **Recombination** is important in biological evolution because it creates new types on which natural selection can operate.

An organism develops from a fertilized egg, or *zygote,* created by the union of two sex cells, one from each parent. The zygote grows rapidly through **mitosis,** or ordinary cell division, which continues as the organism grows. The special process by which sex cells are produced is called **meiosis.** Unlike ordinary cell division, in which two cells emerge from one, in meiosis four cells are produced from one. Each has half the genetic material of the original cell. In human meiosis, four cells, each with 23 individual chromosomes, are produced from an original cell with 23 pairs.

With fertilization of egg by sperm, the father's 23 chromosomes combine with the mother's 23 to re-create the pairs in every generation. However, the chromosomes sort independently, so that a child's genotype is a random combination of the DNA of its four grandparents. It is conceivable that one grandparent will contribute

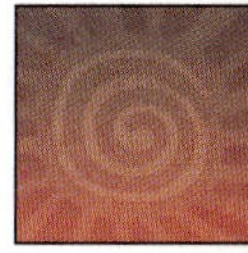

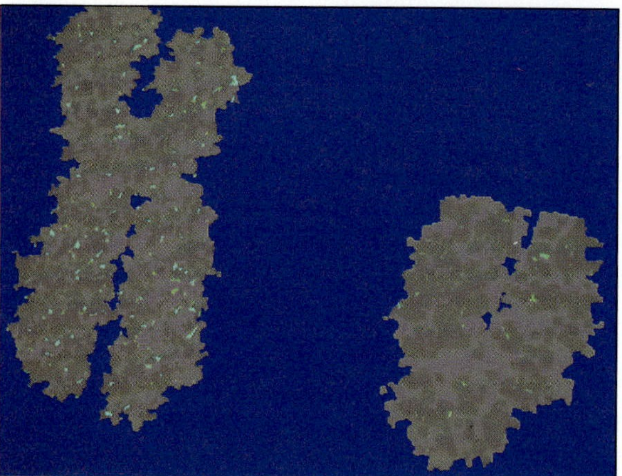

The chromosomes that determine sex in humans. The X chromosome (left) is clearly larger than the Y chromosome (right). What are the genotypes of males and females in terms of these chromosomes?

very little to its grandchild's heredity. Independent assortment of chromosomes is a major source of variety, because the parents' genotypes can be assorted in 2^{23}, or more than 8 million, different ways.

Population Genetics

Population genetics studies stable and changing populations in which most breeding normally takes place (see Gillespie 1998; Hartl 2000). The term **gene pool** refers to all the alleles and genotypes within a breeding population—the "pool" of genetic material available. When population geneticists use the term *evolution,* they have a more specific definition in mind than the one given earlier ("descent with modification over the generations"). For geneticists, **genetic evolution** is defined as change in gene frequency, that is, in the frequency of alleles in a breeding population from generation to generation. Any factor that contributes to such a change can be considered a mechanism of genetic evolution. Those mechanisms include natural selection, mutation, random genetic drift, and gene flow.

Mechanisms of Genetic Evolution

Natural Selection

The first mechanism of genetic evolution is natural selection, which remains the best explanation for evolution. Essential to understanding evolution through natural selection is the distinction between genotype and phenotype. Genotype refers just to hereditary factors—genes and chromosomes. Phenotype—the organism's evident biological characteristics—develops over the years as the organism is influenced by particular environmental forces. (See the photo of the identical twins on the next page. Identical twins have exactly the same genotype, but their actual biology, their phenotypes, may differ as a result of variation in the environments in which they have been raised.) Also, because of dominance, individuals with different genotypes may have identical phenotypes (like Mendel's tall pea plants). Natural selection can operate only on phenotype—on what is exposed, not on what is hidden. For example, a harmful recessive gene can't be eliminated from the gene pool if it is masked by a favored dominant.

Phenotype includes not only outward physical appearance, but also internal organs, tissues, and cells, and physiological processes and systems. Many biological reactions to foods, disease, heat, cold, sunlight, and other environmental factors are not automatic, genetically programmed responses but the product of years of exposure to particular environmental stresses. Human biology is not set at birth but has considerable *plasticity.* That is, it is changeable, being affected by the environmental forces, such as diet and altitude, that we experience as we grow up.

The environment works on the genotype to build the phenotype, and certain phenotypes do better in some environments than other phenotypes do. However, remember that favored phenotypes can be produced by different genotypes. Because natural selection works only on genes that are expressed, maladaptive recessives can be removed only when they occur in homozygous form. When a heterozygote carries a maladaptive recessive, its effects are masked

Twin Wade on the left is bigger and taller than his brother Wyatt. How can this be if they are identical?

by the favored dominant. The process of perfecting the fit between organisms and their environment is gradual.

Directional Selection

After several generations of selection, gene frequencies will change. Adaptation through natural selection will have occurred. Once that happens, those traits that have proved to be the most **adaptive** (favored by natural selection) in that environment will be selected again and again from generation to generation. Given such *directional selection,* or long-term selection of the same trait(s), maladaptive recessive alleles will be removed from the gene pool.

Directional selection will continue as long as environmental forces stay the same. However, if the environment changes, new selective forces start working, favoring different phenotypes. This also happens when part of the population colonizes a new environment. Selection in the changed, or new, environment continues until a new equilibrium is reached. Then there is directional selection until another environmental change or migration takes place. Over millions of years, such a process of successive adaptation to a series of environments has led to biological modification and branching. The process of natural selection has led to the tremendous array of plant and animal forms found in the world today.

It's also important to note that natural selection operates *only* on traits that are present in a population. A favorable mutation *may* occur, but a population doesn't normally come up with a new genotype or phenotype just because one is needed. Many species have become extinct because they weren't sufficiently varied to adapt to environmental shifts.

There are also differences in the amount of environmental stress that organisms' genetic potential enables them to tolerate. Some species are adapted to a narrow range of environments. They are especially endangered by environmental fluctuation. Others—*Homo sapiens* among them—tolerate much more environmental variation because their genetic potential permits many adaptive possibilities. Humans can adapt rapidly to changing conditions by modifying both biological responses and learned behavior. We don't have to delay adaptation until a favorable mutation appears.

Sickle-Cell Anemia

We see that natural selection can *reduce* variety in a population through directional selection—by favoring one allele or trait over another. Selective forces also can work to *maintain* genetic variety by favoring a situation in which the frequencies of two or more alleles of a gene remain constant from generation to generation. This may be because the phenotypes they produce are neutral, equally favored, or equally opposed by selective forces. Sometimes a particular force favors (or opposes) one allele while a different but equally effective force favors (or opposes) the other allele.

One well-studied example involves two alleles, Hb^A and Hb^S, that affect the production of the beta strain (Hb) of human hemoglobin. Hemoglobin, which is located in our red blood cells, carries oxygen from our lungs to the rest of the body via the circulatory system. The allele that

produces normal hemoglobin is Hb^A. Another allele, Hb^S, produces a different hemoglobin. Individuals who are homozygous for Hb^S suffer from *sickle-cell anemia.* Such anemia, in which the red blood cells are shaped like crescents or sickles, is associated with a disease that is usually fatal. This condition interferes with the blood's ability to store oxygen. It increases the heart's burden by clogging the small blood vessels.

Given the fatal disease associated with Hb^S, geneticists were surprised to discover that certain populations in Africa, India, and the Mediterranean had very high frequencies of Hb^S (Figure 3.5). In some West African populations, that frequency is around 20 percent. Researchers eventually discovered that both Hb^A and Hb^S are maintained because selective forces in certain environments favor the heterozygote over either homozygote.

Initially, scientists wondered why, if most Hb^S homozygotes died before they reached reproductive age, the harmful allele hadn't been eliminated. Why was its frequency so high? The answer turned out to lie in the heterozygote's greater fitness. Only people who were homozygous for Hb^S died from sickle-cell anemia. Heterozygotes suffered very mild anemia, if any. On the other hand, although people homozygous for Hb^A did not suffer from anemia, they were much more susceptible to *malaria*—a killer disease that continues to plague *Homo sapiens* in the tropics.

The heterozygote, with one sickle-cell allele and one normal one, was the fittest phenotype for a malarial environment. Heterozygotes have enough abnormal hemoglobin, in which malaria parasites cannot thrive, to protect against malaria. They also have enough normal hemoglobin to fend off sickle-cell anemia. The Hb^S allele has been maintained in these populations because the heterozygotes survived and reproduced in greater numbers than did people with any other phenotype.

The sickle-cell allele spread in the tropics as a result of certain economic and cultural changes—specifically, a shift from hunting and gathering to farming (Livingstone 1958). Many societies in West Africa took up a form of cultivation known as *slash and burn.* With this system, trees were cut down and burned to provide ashes for fertilizing the soil. After the land was farmed for one or two years, yields began to drop, and farmers chose another plot to slash and burn.

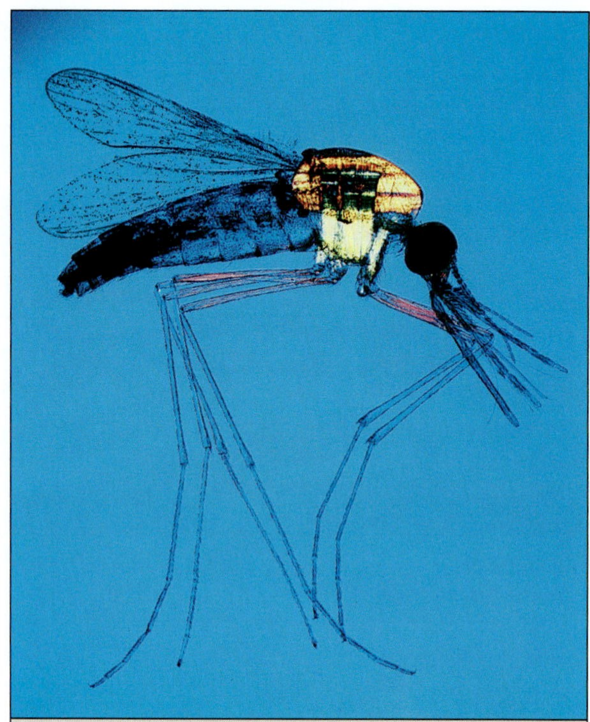

Beware the *Anopheles* mosquito, vector of malaria. An adult female is shown here. What is a genetic antimalarial?

Slash-and-burn cultivation created breeding areas for *Anopheles* mosquitoes, which carry the malarial parasites and transmit them to people. Farming eroded and hardened the topsoil, increasing rain runoff to pools of stagnant water. The destruction of the forest promoted an increase in malarial mosquitoes, which bred more effectively in water exposed to the sun than in shaded areas. Rare in the forest, mosquitoes became common in the new environment.

Simultaneously, the new economy produced more food than the old one had. This fueled population growth. Villages became larger and closer together. Population density increased, providing more hosts for parasites. In this changed environment, the sickle-cell allele began to play an adaptive role.

The example of the sickle-cell allele demonstrates the relativity of evolution through natural selection: Adaptation and fitness are in relation to specific environments. Traits are not adaptive or maladaptive for all times and places. Even harmful alleles can be selected if heterozygotes have

Figure 3.5

Distribution of Sickle-Cell Allele and Falciparum Malaria in the Old World

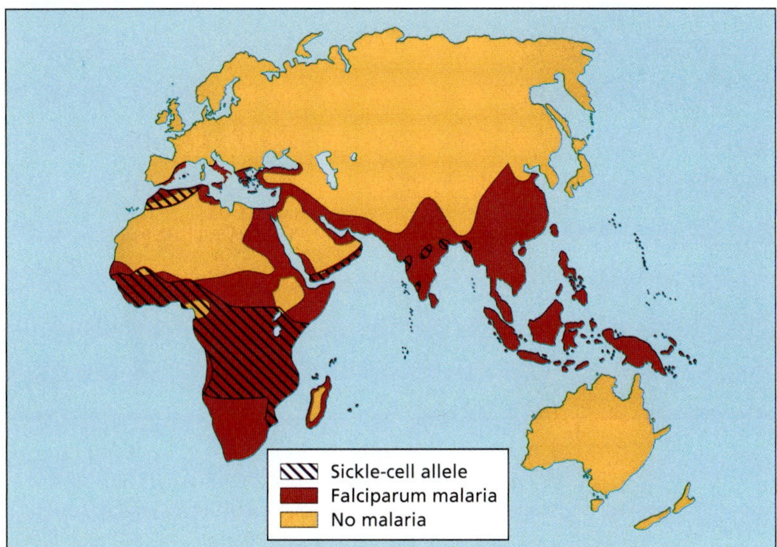

Source: Adapted from *Human Evolution: An Introduction to the New Physical Anthropology* by Joseph B. Birdsell. Copyright © 1975, 1981 by HarperCollins, Publishers, Inc. Reprinted by permission of the publisher.

an advantage. Moreover, as the environment changes, favored phenotypes and gene frequencies can change. In malaria-free environments, normal-hemoglobin homozygotes reproduce more effectively than heterozygotes do. With no malaria, the frequency of Hb^S declines, because Hb^S homozygotes can't compete in survival and reproduction with the other types. This has happened in areas of West Africa where malaria has been reduced through drainage programs and insecticides. Selection against Hb^S also has occurred in the United States among Americans descended from West Africans (Diamond 1997).

Mutation

The second mechanism of genetic evolution is mutation. Mutations, which occur spontaneously and regularly, provide new biochemical forms—variety—on which natural selection may operate. **Mutations** are changes in the DNA molecules of which genes and chromosomes are built. If a mutation occurs in a sex cell that combines with another as a fertilized egg, the new organism will carry the mutation in every cell. This may result in a biochemical difference between the mutant child and the parent. The abnormal protein associated with sickle-cell anemia is caused by just such a difference in a single allele between normal individuals and those with the disease.

Mutations occur in about 5 percent of sex cells. The rate varies from gene to gene. Many geneticists believe that most mutations are neutral, conferring neither advantage nor disadvantage. Others argue that most mutations are harmful and will be weeded out because they deviate from the types that have been selected over the generations. However, if the selective forces affecting a population change, mutations in its gene pool may acquire an adaptive advantage they lacked in the old environment.

Such chemical alterations may provide a population with entirely new phenotypes, which may offer some advantage. Variants produced through mutation can be especially significant if there is a change in selective forces. They may prove to have an advantage they lacked in the old environment. The spread of Hb^S as farming expanded offers one example.

Random Genetic Drift

The third mechanism of genetic evolution is **random genetic drift.** This is a change in allele frequency that results not from natural selection but from chance. Since random genetic drift is most common in small populations, it has probably been important in human evolution, because humans have lived in small groups during much of our history. In a small population, alleles are likely to be lost by chance.

To understand why, compare the sorting of alleles to a game involving a bag of 12 marbles, 6 red and 6 blue. In step 1, you draw six marbles from the bag. Statistically, your chances of drawing three reds and three blues are less than those of getting four of one color and two of the other. Step 2 is to fill a new bag with 12 marbles on the basis of the ratio of marbles you drew in step 1. Assume that you drew four reds and two blues: The new bag will have eight red marbles and four blue ones. Step 3 is to draw six marbles from the new bag. Your chances of drawing blues in step 3 are lower than they were in step 1, and the probability of drawing all reds increases. If you do draw all reds, the next bag (step 4) will have only red marbles.

This game is analogous to random genetic drift operating over the generations. The blue marbles were lost purely by chance. Alleles, too, can be lost by chance rather than because of any disadvantage they confer. Lost alleles can reappear in a gene pool only through mutation.

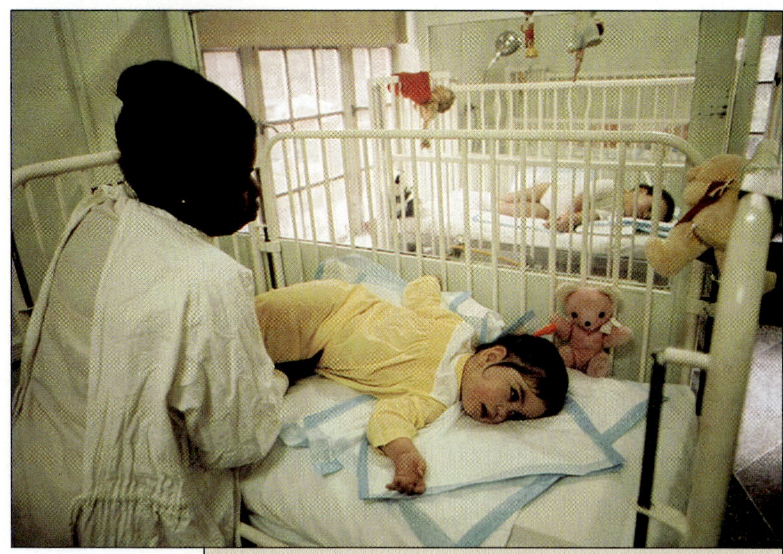

A nurse shifts a baby girl in her crib at New York's Kingsbrook Jewish Medical Center. The girl has Tay-Sachs disease, a fatal genetic disorder in which harmful quantities of a fatty substance accumulate in the nerve cells of the brain. As nerve cells become distended the child becomes blind, deaf, and unable to swallow. Carriers of Tay-Sachs disease can be identified by a simple blood test.

Gene Flow

The fourth mechanism of genetic evolution is **gene flow,** the exchange of genetic material between populations of the same species. Gene flow, like mutation, works in conjunction with natural selection by providing variety on which selection can work. Gene flow may consist of direct interbreeding between formerly separated populations of the same species (e.g., Europeans, Africans, and Native Americans in the United States), or it may be indirect.

Consider the following hypothetical case (Figure 3.6). In a certain part of the world live six local populations of a certain species. P_1 is the westernmost of these populations. P_2, which interbreeds with P_1, is located 50 miles to the east. P_2 also interbreeds with P_3, located 50 miles east of P_2. Assume that each population interbreeds with, and only with, the adjacent populations. P_6 is located 250 miles from P_1 and does not directly interbreed with P_1, but it is tied to P_1 through the chain of interbreeding that ultimately links all six populations.

Assume further that some allele exists in P_1 that isn't particularly advantageous in its environment. Because of gene flow, this allele may be passed on to P_2, by it to P_3, and so on, until it eventually reaches P_6. In P_6 or along the way, the allele may encounter an environment in which it does have a selective advantage. If this happens, it may serve, like a new mutation, as raw material on which natural selection can operate.

Alleles are spread through gene flow even when selection is not operating on the allele. In the long run, natural selection works on the variety within a population, whatever its source: mutation, drift, or gene flow. Selection and gene flow have worked together to spread the Hb^S allele in Central Africa. Frequencies of Hb^S in Africa reflect not only the intensity of malaria but also the length of time gene flow has been going on (Livingstone 1969).

Gene flow is important in the study of the origin of species. A **species** is a group of related organisms whose members can interbreed to produce offspring that can live and reproduce. A species has to be able to reproduce itself through time. We know that horses and donkeys belong to different species because their offspring cannot meet the test of long-term survival. A horse and a donkey may breed to produce a mule, but mules are sterile. So are the offspring of lions with tigers. Gene flow tends to prevent **speciation**—

Figure 3.6
Gene Flow between Local Populations

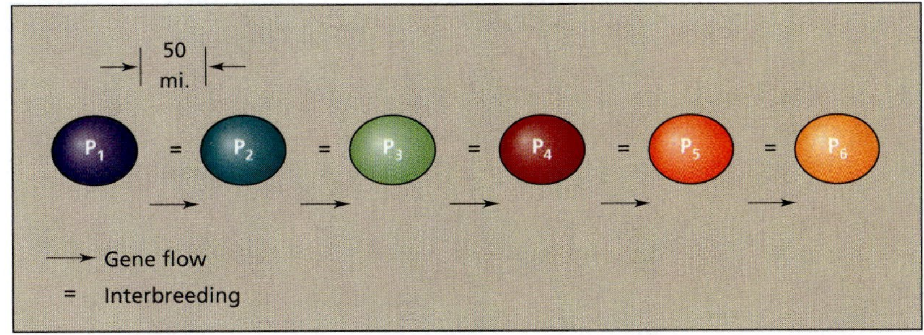

P_1–P_6 are six local populations of the same species. Each interbreeds (=) only with its neighbor(s). Although members of P_6 never interbreed with P_1, P_6 and P_1 are linked through gene flow. Genetic material that originates in P_1 eventually will reach P_6, and vice versa, as it is passed from one neighboring population to the next. Because they share genetic material in this way, P_1–P_6 remain members of the same species. In many species, local populations distributed throughout a larger territory than the 250 miles depicted here are linked through gene flow.

the formation of new species—unless subgroups of the same species are separated for a sufficient length of time.

When gene flow is interrupted, and isolated subgroups are maintained, new species may arise. Imagine that an environmental barrier arises between P_3 and P_4, so that they no longer interbreed. If over time, as a result of isolation, P_1, P_2, and P_3 become incapable of interbreeding with the other three populations, speciation will have occurred.

Human Biological Adaptation

This section considers several examples of human biological diversity that reflect adaptation to environmental stresses, such as disease, diet, and climate. There is abundant evidence for human genetic adaptation and thus for evolution (change in gene frequency) through selection working in specific environments. One example is the adaptive value of the Hb^S heterozygote and its spread in malarial environments. Adaptation and evolution go on in specific environments. There is no generally or ideally adaptive allele and no perfect phenotype. Nor can an allele be assumed to be maladaptive for all times and all places. We have seen that even Hb^S, which produces a lethal anemia, has a selective advantage in the heterozygous form in malarial environments.

Also, alleles that were once maladaptive may lose their disadvantage if the environment shifts. Color blindness (disadvantageous for hunters and forest dwellers) and a form of genetically determined diabetes are examples. Today's environment contains medical techniques that allow people with such conditions to live fairly normal lives. Formerly maladaptive alleles have thus become neutral with respect to selection. With thousands of human genes now known, new genetic traits are discovered almost every day. Such studies tend to focus on genetic abnormalities, because of their medical and treatment implications.

In June 2000 scientists announced completion of a first draft of a map of the human genome—all our genes and chromosomes—some 3 billion genetic letters in human DNA. One of the two main groups behind this discovery is the National Institutes of Health's Human Genome Project, whose website is worth a visit: **http:// www.ornl.gov/hgmis/.**

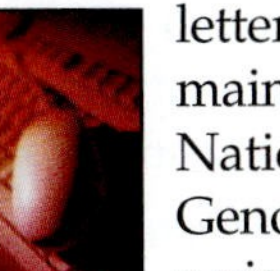

Given current knowledge about genetically transmitted diseases, people with a family history of such a disease can be advised about their children's chances of being affected. Many currently incurable hereditary illnesses are destined to become neutral traits in tomorrow's medical environment. However, genetic testing raises many ethical questions. Given possible discrimination in employment and in obtaining health insurance, some members of the medical community have advised people not to be tested for genetic markers that might indicate a tendency to develop, say, Alzheimer's disease. Laws to forbid genetic discrimination are not yet fully in place. Alzheimer's is likely to become much more prevalent, and costly to treat as a public health problem, as the baby-boomer cohort ages.

In June 2000 scientists announced the completion of a draft map of the human genome—all our genes and chromosomes. Shown here, a member of the Human Genome Project does computer-assisted DNA sequencing at Caltech's Lee Hood Lab.

Genetic discrimination is not new. Some of its most virulent manifestations occurred in Adolph Hitler's Third Reich. More surprisingly, in 1997 it was revealed that, through the 1970s, some 60,000 people were sterilized in Sweden, and 11,000 in Finland, as part of government policies designed to weed out properties like poor eyesight and Gypsy features (Wade 1997). This is an example of **eugenics,** a highly controversial movement aimed at genetic improvement by encouraging the reproduction of individuals with favored features and discouraging that of individuals with features deemed undesirable. Do you think that past crimes committed in the name of eugenics should prevent people from being allowed to choose benefits that genetic engineering may offer in the future? What ethical issues are raised by the cloning of human beings? (See "In The News.")

Genes and Disease

According to the *World Health Report,* published by the World Health Organization (WHO) in Geneva, Switzerland, tropical diseases affect more than 10 percent of the world's population. Malaria, the most widespread of these, afflicts over 400 million people annually. Schistosomiasis (snail fever), a waterborne parasitic disease, affects more than 200 million. Some 120 million people have filariasis, which causes elephantiasis—lymphatic obstruction leading to the enlargement of body parts, particularly the legs and scrotum (check out the website of the World Health Organization at **http://www.who.int/home/**).

The malaria threat is spreading. Brazil had 560,000 cases in 1988, versus 100,000 in 1977. Worldwide, the number of malaria cases rose from 270 million in 1990 to 400 million in 1995 (*New York Times* 1990; World Health Organization 1995). Contributing to this rise is the increasing resistance of parasites to drugs used to treat malaria. However, hundreds of millions of people are genetically resistant. Sickle-cell hemoglobin is the best known of the genetic antimalarials (Diamond 1997).

Microbes have been major selective agents for humans, particularly before the arrival of modern medicine. Some people are genetically more susceptible to certain diseases than others are, and the distribution of human blood types continues to change in response to natural selection.

After food production emerged around 10,000 years ago, infectious diseases posed a mounting risk and eventually became the foremost cause of human mortality. Food production favors infection for several reasons. Cultivation sustains larger, denser populations and a more sedentary life style than does hunting and gathering. People live closer to each other and to their own wastes, making it easier for microbes to survive and to find hosts. Domesticated animals also transmit diseases to people.

Until 1977, when the last case of smallpox was reported, smallpox had been a major threat to humans and a determinant of blood group frequencies (Diamond 1990, 1997). The smallpox virus is a mutation from one of the pox viruses that plague such domesticated animals as cows, sheep, goats, horses, and pigs. Smallpox appeared in human beings after people and animals started living together. Smallpox epidemics have played important roles in world history, often killing one-fourth to one-half of the affected populations. Smallpox contributed to Sparta's defeat of Athens in 430 BC and to the decline of the Roman empire after AD 160.

The ABO blood groups have figured in human resistance to smallpox. Blood is typed according to the protein and sugar compounds on the surface of the red blood cells. Different substances (compounds) distinguish between type A and type B blood. Type A cells trigger the production of *antibodies* in B blood, so that A cells clot in B blood. The different substances work like chemical passwords; they help us distinguish our own cells from invading cells, including microbes, we ought to destroy. The surfaces of some microbes have substances similar to ABO blood group substances. We don't produce antibodies to substances similar to those on our own blood cells. We can think of this as a clever evolutionary trick by the microbes to deceive their hosts, because we don't normally develop antibodies against our own biochemistry.

People with A or AB blood are more susceptible to smallpox than are people with type B or type O. Presumably this is because a substance on the smallpox virus mimics the type A substance, permitting the virus to slip by the defenses of the type A individual. By contrast, type B and type O individuals produce antibodies against smallpox because they recognize it as a foreign substance.

The relation between type A blood and susceptibility to smallpox was first suggested by the low frequencies of the A allele in areas of India and Africa where smallpox had been endemic. A comparative study done in rural India in 1965–66, during a virulent smallpox epidemic, did much to confirm this relationship. Drs. F. Vogel and M. R.

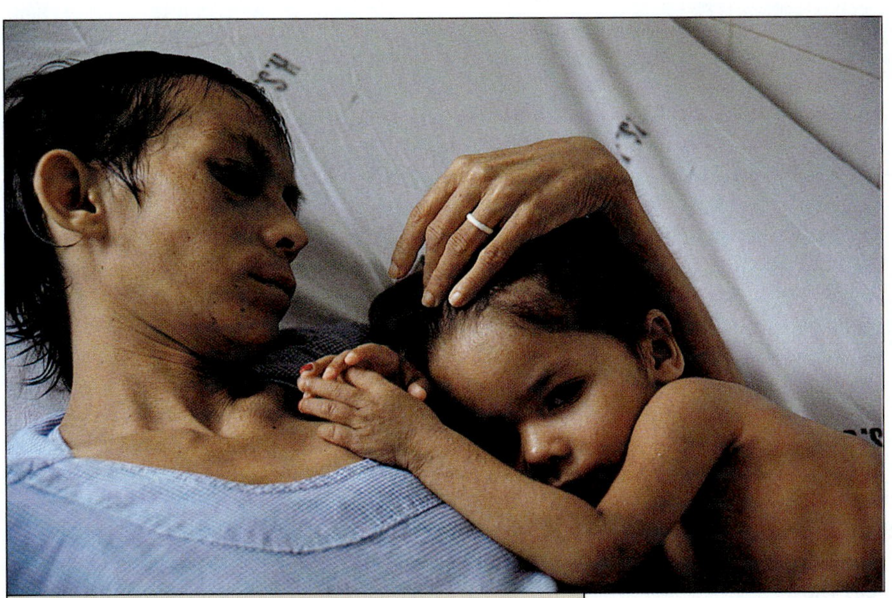

AIDS is widespread in many African nations as well as in the United States, France, Thailand, and Brazil. This Brazilian mother and child, both infected with HIV, have developed AIDS. What would be evidence for genetic variation in susceptibility to the HIV virus?

in the news

Human Cloning: Yesterday's Never Is Today's Why Not?

If life is precious and unique, what kinds of issues are raised by cloning? In 1997 the world first learned of the existence of Dolly, a lamb cloned from the cell of an adult animal. When will the first human be cloned? Human cloning remained legal in most states as of this writing. Legality aside, what ethical questions are raised by human cloning? Who would raise human clones: scientists or families? What will be the legal status of these scientific creations? Will they be people or products? Will they be free human beings or entities designed to satisfy wishes, whims, and medical needs of others? Will they be more or less valuable than their original? Such questions, once explored in the domain of science fiction, are now matters of science fact. Focus on the ethics of cloning as you read this piece.

Dolly the lamb [was] the first animal cloned from a cell taken from an adult . . . In the hubbub that ensued, scientist after scientist and ethicist after ethicist declared that Dolly should not conjure up fears of a Brave New World. There would be no interest in using the technology to clone people, they said.

They are already being proved wrong. There has been an enormous change in attitudes in just a few months; scientists have become sanguine about the notion of cloning and, in particular, cloning a human being . . .

A handful of fertility centers are conducting experiments with human eggs that lay the groundwork for cloning. Moreover, the federal government is supporting new research on the cloning of monkeys, encouraging scientists to perfect techniques that could easily be transferred to humans.

Ultimately, scientists expect cloning to be combined with genetic enhancement, adding genes to give desired traits, which was the fundamental reason cloning was studied in animal research.

"From my perspective, it's just a matter of time before the first human is cloned," said Dr. Steen Willadsen, a cloning pioneer who developed the fundamental methods for cloning animals.

Cloning would be fundamentally different from ordinary reproduction. It would involve taking a cell from a living person, slipping it into an egg cell whose genetic material has been removed and allowing the genetic material of the adult cell to direct the development of a new embryo, then fetus, then person who is the identical twin of the person who provided the initial cell. It would allow a living person to be reborn, in a sense, only at a later time.

Scientists and infertility specialists envision certain specialized circumstances in which it might be acceptable to clone humans. Grieving parents may want to reproduce a terminally ill child. Or a woman may want a child but be infertile. Is it worse somehow for her to clone herself than to obtain an embryo made-to-order with

Chakravartti analyzed blood samples from smallpox victims and their uninfected siblings (Diamond 1990). The researchers found 415 infected children, none ever vaccinated against smallpox. All but 8 of the infected children had an uninfected (also unvaccinated) sibling.

The results of the study were clear: Susceptibility to smallpox varied with ABO type. Of the 415 infected children, 261 had the A allele; 154 lacked it. Among their 407 uninfected siblings, the ratio was reversed. Only 80 had the A allele; 327 lacked it. The researchers calculated that a type A or type AB person had a seven times greater chance of getting smallpox than did an O or B person.

In most human populations, the O allele is more common than A and B combined. A is most common in Europe; B frequencies are highest in Asia. Since smallpox was once widespread in the Old World, we might wonder why natural selection didn't eliminate the A allele entirely. The answer appears to be this: Other diseases spared the type A people and penalized those with other blood groups.

These rabbits were cloned at Russia's Bioengineering Livestock Breeding Center in 1999. In cloning, genetic material from the cell of the animal to be copied is implanted into an egg cell (ovum) from which genetic material has been removed.

donated egg and sperm, the kind that many fertility clinics are already offering the infertile? . . .

But what cloning really accomplishes, experts said, is to make it possible, for the first time, to think seriously about genetically enhancing human beings. Scientists could grow a person's cells in sheets in the laboratory and sprinkle the cells with genes. Only a very few cells would take up the genes, and use them, but it is relatively easy for scientists to find those cells and pluck them out of the mix.

If they then used those cells to make clones, the clones would contain the added genes in every cell of their body. Already, two such experiments have been completed in animals, using cells from fetuses rather than cells from adults. . .

With humans, predicted Dr. Lee Silver, a molecular biologist at Princeton University, the first genetic enhancements might be genes to protect against diseases, like an AIDS resistance gene or a gene to protect against Alzheimer's disease, both of which have already been identified. In a sense, it would be no different morally from vaccinating a child for a disease, Silver said . . .

But some experts said the real question was not whether cloning is ethical but whether it is legal.

"The fact is that, in America, cloning may be bad but telling people how they should reproduce is worse," Willadsen said.

In the end, Willadsen said, "America is not ruled by ethics. It is ruled by law."

Source: Excerpted from Gina Kolata, *New York Times*, December 2, 1997, www.nytimes.com.

For example, type O people seem to be especially susceptible to the bubonic plague—the "Black Death" that killed a third of the population of medieval Europe. Type O people are also more likely to get cholera, which has killed as many people in India as smallpox has. On the other hand, blood group O may increase resistance to syphilis. The ravages of that venereal disease, which may have originated in the New World, may explain the very high frequency of type O blood among the natives of Central and South America. The distribution of human blood groups appears to represent a compromise among the selective effects of many diseases.

Associations between ABO blood type and noninfectious disorders also have been noted. Type O individuals are most susceptible to duodenal and gastric ulcers. Type A individuals seem most prone to stomach and cervical cancer and ovarian tumors. However, since these noninfectious disorders tend to occur after reproduction has ended, their relevance to adaptation and evolution through natural selection is doubtful (see also Weiss 1993).

In the case of diseases for which there are no effective drugs, genetic resistance maintains its significance. There is probably genetic variation in susceptibility to the HIV virus, for example. We know that people exposed to HIV vary in their risk of developing AIDS and in the rate at which the disease progresses. AIDS is widespread in many African nations (and in the United States, France, and Brazil). Particularly in Africa, where treatment strategies now used in the industrial nations are not widely available, the death rate from AIDS could eventually (let us hope it does not) rival that of past epidemics of smallpox and plague. If so, AIDS could cause large shifts in human gene frequencies—again illustrating the ongoing operation of natural selection.

Facial Features

Natural selection also affects facial features. For instance, long noses seem to be adaptive in arid areas (Brace 1964; Weiner 1954), because membranes and blood vessels inside the nose moisten the air as it is breathed in. Long noses are also adaptive in cold environments, because blood vessels warm the air as it is breathed in. This nose form distances the brain, which is sensitive to bitter cold, from raw outer air. These were adaptive biological features for humans who lived in cold climates before the invention of central heating.

The association between nose form and temperature is recognized as **Thomson's nose rule** (Thomson and Buxton 1923), which shows up statistically. In plotting the geographic distribution of nose length among human populations, the average nose does tend to be longer in areas with lower mean annual temperatures.

Other facial features also illustrate adaptation to selective forces. Among contemporary humans, average tooth size is largest among Native Australian hunters and gatherers, for whom large teeth had an adaptive advantage, given a diet based on foods with a considerable amount of sand and grit. People with small teeth—if false teeth and sandfree foods are unavailable—can't feed themselves as effectively as people with more massive dentition can.

Size and Body Build

Certain body builds have adaptive advantages for particular environments. The relation between body weight and temperature is summarized in 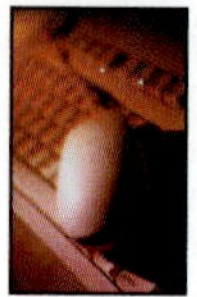 **Bergmann's rule:** The smaller of two bodies similar in shape has more surface area per unit of weight. Therefore, it sheds heat more efficiently. (Heat loss occurs on the body's surface—the skin perspires.) Average body size tends to increase in cold areas and to decrease in hot ones because big bodies hold heat better than small ones do. To be more precise, in a large sample of native populations, average adult male weight increased by 0.66 pound (0.3 kilogram) for every 1 degree Fahrenheit fall in mean annual temperature (Roberts 1953; Steegman 1975). The "pygmies" and the San, who live in hot climates and weigh only 90 pounds on the average, illustrate this relation in reverse.

Body shape differences also reflect adaptation to temperature through natural selection. The relationship between temperature and body shape in animals and birds was first recognized in 1877 by the zoologist J. A. Allen. **Allen's rule** states that the relative size of protruding body parts—ears, tails, bills, fingers, toes, limbs, and so on—increases with temperature. Among humans, slender bodies with long digits and limbs are advantageous in tropical climates. Such bodies increase body surface relative to mass and allow for more efficient heat dissipation. Among the cold-adapted Eskimos, the opposite phenotype is found. Short limbs and stocky bodies serve to conserve heat. Cold area populations tend to have larger chests and shorter arms than do people from warm areas (Roberts 1953).

This discussion of adaptive relationships between climate and body size and shape illustrates that natural selection may achieve the same effect in different ways. East African Nilotes, who live in a hot area, have tall, linear bodies with elongated extremities that increase surface area relative to mass and thus maximize heat dissipation (illustrating Allen's rule). Among the "pygmies," the reduction of body size achieves the same result (illustrating Bergmann's rule). Similarly, the large bodies of northern Europeans and the compact stockiness of the Eskimos serve the same function of heat conservation.

Lactose Tolerance

Many biological traits that illustrate human adaptation are not under simple genetic control. Genetic determination of such traits may be likely but unconfirmed, or several genes may interact to influence the trait in question. Sometimes there is a

This Nilotic man, a Nuer herder from Sudan, has a tall linear body with elongated extremities (note his fingers). Such proportioning increases the surface area relative to mass and thus dissipates heat (Allen's rule). What other body form can achieve the same result?

Cold weather populations tend to have relatively larger chests and shorter arms than do people from warm areas. Among the cold-adapted Inuit, such as this Alaskan woman, short limbs and stocky bodies help to conserve heat. How important is biology to cold adaptation today?

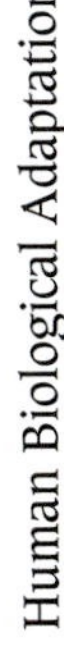

genetic component, but the trait also responds to stresses encountered during growth. We speak of **phenotypical adaptation** when adaptive changes occur during the individual's lifetime. Phenotypical adaptation is made possible by biological plasticity—our ability to change in response to the environments we encounter as we grow (see Frisancho 1993). Recall the discussion of physiological adaptation to high altitude in Chapter 1.

Genes and phenotypical adaptation work together to produce a biochemical difference between human groups in the ability to digest large amounts of milk—an adaptive advantage when other foods are scarce and milk is available, as it is in dairying societies. All milk, whatever its source, contains a complex sugar called *lactose.* The digestion of milk depends on an enzyme called *lactase,* which works in the small intestine. Among all mammals except humans and some of their pets, lactase production ceases after weaning, so that these animals can no longer digest milk.

Lactase production and the ability to tolerate milk vary between populations. About 90 percent of northern Europeans and their descendants are lactose tolerant; they can digest several glasses of milk with no difficulty. Similarly, about 80 percent of two African populations, the Tutsi of Rwanda and Burundi in East Africa, and the Fulani of Nigeria in West Africa, produce lactase and digest milk easily. Both these groups traditionally have been herders. However, such nonherders as the Yoruba and Igbo in Nigeria, the Baganda in Uganda, the Japanese and other Asians, Eskimos, South American Indians, and many Israelis cannot digest lactose (Kretchmer 1972/1975).

Three Japanese women enjoy ice cream cones in Tokyo. Despite the lactose intolerance of many populations, including the Japanese, the consumption of dairy products has spread along with globalization. Lactose tolerance is only partly genetic; it can increase with exposure to dairy products in the diet.

However, the variable human ability to digest milk seems to be a difference of degree. Some populations can tolerate very little or no milk, but others are able to metabolize much greater quantities. Studies show that people who move from no-milk or low-milk diets to high-milk diets increase their lactose tolerance; this suggests some phenotypical adaptation. We can conclude that no simple genetic trait accounts for the ability to digest milk. Lactose tolerance appears to be one of many aspects of human biology governed both by genes and by phenotypical adaptation to environmental conditions.

Human biology is inherently plastic, changing constantly, even without genetic variation. We have considered ways in which humans adapt biologically to their environments, and the effects of such adaptation on human biological diversity. Modern biological anthropology seeks to *explain* specific aspects of human biological variation. The explanatory framework encompasses the same mechanisms—selection, mutation, drift, gene flow, and plasticity—that govern adaptation, variation, and evolution among other life forms (see Futuyma 1998).

summary

1. In the 18th century, Carolus Linnaeus developed biological taxonomy. He viewed differences and similarities among organisms as part of God's orderly plan rather than as evidence for evolution. Charles Darwin and Alfred Russel Wallace proposed that natural selection could explain the origin of species, biological diversity, and similarities among related life forms. Natural selection requires variety in the population undergoing selection.

2. Through breeding experiments with peas in 1856, Gregor Mendel discovered that genetic traits pass on as units. These are now known to be chromosomes, which occur in homologous pairs. Alleles, some dominant, some recessive, are the chemically different forms that occur at a given genetic locus. Mendel also formulated the law of independent assortment. Each of the seven traits he studied in peas was inherited independently of all the others. Independent assortment of

chromosomes and their recombination provide some of the variety needed for natural selection. But the major source of such variety is mutation, a chemical change in the DNA molecules of which genes are made.

3. Population genetics studies gene frequencies in stable and changing populations. Natural selection is the most important mechanism of evolutionary change. Others are mutation, random genetic drift, and gene flow. Given environmental change, nature selects traits already present in the population. If variety is insufficient to permit adaptation to the change, extinction is likely. New types don't appear just because they are needed.

4. One well-documented case of natural selection in contemporary human populations is that of the sickle-cell allele. In homozygous form, the sickle-cell allele, Hb^s, produces an abnormal hemoglobin. This clogs the small blood vessels, impairing the blood's capacity to store oxygen. The result is sickle-cell anemia, which is usually fatal. The distribution of Hb^s has been linked to that of malaria. Homozygotes for normal hemoglobin are susceptible to malaria and die in great numbers. Homozygotes for the sickle-cell allele die from anemia. Heterozygotes get only mild anemia and are resistant to malaria. In a malarial environment, the heterozygote has the advantage. This explains why an apparently maladaptive allele is preserved.

5. Other mechanisms of genetic evolution complement natural selection. Random genetic drift operates most obviously in small populations, where pure chance can easily change allele frequencies. Gene flow and interbreeding keep subgroups of the same species genetically connected and thus impede speciation.

6. Differential resistance to infectious diseases has influenced the distribution of human blood groups. Natural selection also has operated on facial features and body size and shape. Phenotypical adaptation refers to adaptive changes that occur in the individual's lifetime, in response to the environment the organism encounters as it grows. Biological similarities between geographically distant populations may be due to similar but independent genetic changes, rather than to common ancestry. Or they may reflect similar physiological responses to common stresses during growth.

key terms

adaptive Favored by natural selection in a particular environment.

allele A biochemical variant of a particular gene.

Allen's rule Rule stating that the relative size of protruding body parts (such as ears, tails, bills, fingers, toes, and limbs) tends to increase in warmer climates.

Bergmann's rule Rule stating that the smaller of two bodies similar in shape has more surface area per unit of weight and can therefore dissipate heat more efficiently; hence, large bodies tend to be found in colder areas and small bodies in warmer ones.

catastrophism View that extinct species were destroyed by fires, floods, and other catastrophes. After each destructive event, God created again, leading to contemporary species.

chromosomes Basic genetic units, occurring in matching (homologous) pairs; lengths of DNA made up of multiple genes.

creationism Explanation for the origin of species given in Genesis: God created the species during the original six days of Creation.

dominant Allele that masks another allele in a heterozygote.

eugenics Controversial movement aimed at genetic improvement by encouraging the reproduction of individuals with favored features and discouraging that of individuals with features deemed undesirable.

evolution Belief that species arose from others through a long and gradual process of transformation, or descent with modification.

gene Area in a chromosome pair that determines, wholly or partially, a particular biological trait, such as whether one's blood type is A, B, or O.

gene flow Exchange of genetic material between populations of the same species through direct or indirect interbreeding.

gene pool All the alleles and genotypes within a breeding population—the "pool" of genetic material available.

genetic evolution Change in gene frequency within a breeding population.

genotype An organism's hereditary makeup.

heterozygous Having dissimilar alleles of a given gene.

homozygous Possessing identical alleles of a particular gene.

independent assortment Mendel's law of; chromosomes are inherited independently of one another.

meiosis Special process by which sex cells are produced; four cells are produced from one, each with half the genetic material of the original cell.

Mendelian genetics Studies ways in which chromosomes transmit genes across the generations.

mitosis Ordinary cell division; DNA molecules copy themselves, creating two identical cells out of one.

mutation Change in the DNA molecules of which genes and chromosomes are built.

natural selection Originally formulated by Charles Darwin and Alfred Russell Wallace; the process by which nature selects the forms most fit to survive and reproduce in a given environment, such as the tropics.

phenotypical adaptation Adaptive biological changes that occur during the individual's lifetime, made possible by biological plasticity.

population genetics Field that studies causes of genetic variation, maintenance, and change in breeding populations.

random genetic drift Change in gene frequency that results not from natural selection but from chance; most common in small populations.

recessive Genetic trait masked by a dominant trait.

recombination Following independent assortment of chromosomes, new arrangements of hereditary units produced through bisexual reproduction.

speciation Formation of new species; occurs when subgroups of the same species are separated for a sufficient length of time.

species Population whose members can interbreed to produce offspring that can live and reproduce.

Thomson's nose rule Rule stating that the average nose tends to be longer in areas with lower mean annual temperatures; based on the geographic distribution of nose length among human populations.

uniformitarianism Belief that explanations for past events should be sought in ordinary forces that continue to work today.

critical thinking questions

1. If you are (or pretending you are) a creationist, what do you see as the most convincing evidence for evolution?
2. If you are (or pretending you are) an evolutionist, what do you see as the least convincing evidence for evolution?
3. Which of the examples of natural selection mentioned in the book most surprised you? Can you think of examples of natural selection other than those mentioned in the book?
4. Choose five people in your classroom who illustrate a range of phenotypical diversity. Which of their features vary most evidently? How do you explain this variation? Is some of the variation due to culture rather than to biology?
5. Imagine that some of the seven traits that Mendel studied in pea plants were determined by genes on the same chromosome. How might his results have differed?
6. Give three examples of how and why identical genotypes might develop different phenotypes. (Identical twins and clones have identical genotypes.)
7. Is *Homo sapiens* more or less adaptable than other species? What makes us so adaptable? Can you think of some species that are more adaptable than we are?
8. What are two important lessons to be learned from the case of the sickle-cell allele (Hb^S)?
9. Which of the mechanisms of genetic evolution acts to prevent speciation?
10. Did anything stated in this chapter about your ABO blood type give you cause for alarm? Why?
11. How would you design the ideal body for a very cold climate? How about for a very hot one?
12. Besides those mentioned in the book, give an example of a biological trait that depends on physiological adaptation.

suggested additional readings

Cavalli-Sforza, L. L., P. Menozzi, and A. Piazza
1994 *The History and Geography of Human Genes.* Princeton, NJ: Princeton University Press. Comprehensive look at the geographical spread of human genes.

Eiseley, L.
1961 *Darwin's Century.* Garden City, NY: Doubleday, Anchor Books. Discussion of Lyell, Darwin, Wallace, and other major contributors to natural selection and transformation.

Frisancho, A. R.
1993 *Human Adaptation and Accommodation.* Ann Arbor: University of Michigan Press. Influence of the environment on phenotype, particularly during growth and development; a basic text.

Futuyma, D. J.
1995 *Science on Trial,* updated ed. Sunderland, MA: Sinauer Associates. The case of evolution versus creationism—favoring the former.
1998 *Evolutionary Biology.* Sunderland, MA: Sinauer Associates. Basic text.

Gillespie, J. H.
1998 *Population Genetics: A Concise Guide.* Baltimore: The Johns Hopkins University Press. Good introduction to population genetics.

Gould, S. J.
1999 *Rock of Ages: Science and Religion in the Fullness of Life.* New York: Ballantine Books. Evolution, science, and religion by the well-known naturalist and science writer.

Hartl, D. L.
2000 *A Primer of Population Genetics,* 3rd ed. Sunderland, MA: Sinauer Associates. Short introduction to the field.

Hartl, D. L., and E. W. Jones
1999 *Essential Genetics.* Sudbury, MA: Jones and Bartlett. Basic introduction to genetics.

Roberts, D. F.
1986 *Genetic Variation and Its Maintenance: With Particular Reference to Tropical Populations.* New York: Cambridge University Press. Evidence for human genetic evolution, with a focus on tropical populations.

Weiner, J.
1994 *The Beak of the Finch: A Story of Evolution in Our Time.* New York: Alfred A. Knopf. An excellent introduction to Darwin and to evolutionary theory.

Weiss, K. M.
1993 *Genetic Variation and Human Disease: Principles and Evolutionary Approaches.* New York: Cambridge University Press. Selection connected with human diseases.

internet exercises

1. Creationism: Look at the CreationWise cartoon website, **http://members.aol.com/dwr51055/humor.htm.** This site uses cartoons to express the concerns Creationists have about evolution.

   a. What is the Creationist version of the origin of life? What evidence do they use to support their claims? According to these cartoons, what are some of the problems that creationists have with evolution?

   b. What would be the response to these questions from a scientist who studies evolution?

2. Adaptation to Environment: Read Dennis O'Neil's page on "Adapting to Climate Extremes," **http://daphne.palomar.edu/adapt/adapt_2.htm.**

   a. What is Bergmann's Rule? What is Allen's Rule?

   b. How do the !Kung and Australian Aborigines respond to cold differently from the Inuit and groups from Tierra del Fuego? Is there an adaptive reason these groups have different responses to the cold?

   c. What are the advantages of evaporative cooling? What are the disadvantages?

See Chapter 3 on your CD-ROM for additional review and interactive exercises. See your McGraw-Hill Online Learning Center for more.

Chapter 4

The Primates

CHAPTER OUTLINE

NYTIMES.COM NEWS BRIEFS

Saving the Orangutan, Preserving Paradise

by Claudia Dreifus
March 21, 2000

Of the three young women recruited in the 1960s by the paleontologist Louis Leakey to study great apes, Dr. Biruté Galdikas, now 53, is the least known. Dr. Leakey's first disciple, Dr. Jane Goodall, who discovered that chimpanzees made tools, has become an international scientific celebrity, and Dr. Dian Fossey, who lived among the gorillas of Rwanda and was killed there in 1985, was played by Sigourney Weaver in the movie *Gorillas in the Mist.*

But the story of Dr. Galdikas, who quietly devoted herself to the study and preservation of the Indonesian orangutan, remains largely unknown.

"That's because I have a name nobody can pronounce and because I've been in Borneo all these years, tracking an elusive and solitary animal," Dr. Galdikas, whose name is Lithuanian (pronounced bi-ROO-tay GALD-i-kus), said on a recent morning . . .

Still a resident of Borneo, Dr. Galdikas recently became an Indonesian citizen because "the orangutans are Indonesian and because someone in the government suggested it would be helpful." . . .

Q. Give us a report on the state of the world's orangutans?

A. They are poised on the edge of extinction. It's that simple. We're still seeing orangutans in the forest; they are coming into captivity in enormous numbers. You just know that there can't be that many left in the wild.

Q. How did the orangutans come to be so threatened?

A. The main factor was that until 1988, Indonesia had a forestry minister who was a real forester. In 1988, he was replaced by a forestry minister who was an agriculturist, a promoter of plantations. That signaled a shift in government policy from selective logging to clear-cutting of the forest . . . If you selectively log, some animals will survive. But with clear-cutting, the habitat is gone. If that weren't enough, in 1997, there were these horrendous fires that devastated the forests. Moreover, the last three years have been a period of intense political upheaval . . .

After President Suharto stepped down in 1998, there was a vacuum of power in the center. Once people in the provinces understood that, some felt they could do whatever they wanted . . .

At first, only local loggers came in. When nobody stopped them, the bigger commercial loggers followed. Suddenly, there were no more protected parks . . .

We're trying to set up patrols of local men to go out with park rangers so that when they come across illegal loggers, they don't feel totally intimidated. We're working with the Indonesian government to set up new wildlife reserves at expired logging concessions . . .

We have a hospital for 130 orangutans. We have an orphanage for the babies. Eventually, they are released to the wild, though with the fast-disappearing habitat, it's always tough to find a safe place for them.

Q. Tell us what you've learned about orangutans in the nearly 30 years you've been studying them?

A. Well, we've gotten a picture of a very long-lived primate who probably lives 60 to 70 years in the wild. They use a wide variety of foods in the wild, about 400 different kinds, because food is generally scarce for them. The males come and go. They're very, very competitive. Probably very few males are successful at actually impregnating females.

And the females seem to get pregnant about once every eight years. Also, they're very smart. When orangutans have interactions with humans, they use tools at an incredibly rapid pace . . .

Source: http://www.nytimes.com/library/national/science/032100sci-animal-orangutan.html

overview

Humans, apes, monkeys, and prosimians all belong to the zoological order known as primates. The apes are our closest relatives. Humans share more than 98 percent of our DNA with chimpanzees and gorillas.

Early primates, like many contemporary ones, lived in the trees. Reflecting our arboreal heritage, primates share certain anatomical features. These include grasping hands with opposable thumbs, depth and color vision, and use of the fingertip pads as the main organs of touch. With large and complex brains, humans, apes, and monkeys rely extensively on learning. Primates live in social groups and invest considerable time and energy in their offspring and kin.

Gorillas, the least arboreal apes, are vegetarians confined to equatorial Africa. Two species of chimpanzees live in the forests and woodlands of tropical Africa. All the apes and many other primate species are endangered, mainly by deforestation and human hunting. Some important developments in human evolution, such as hunting and tool making, are foreshadowed in other primates, particularly chimpanzees. It is likely that for millions of years sharing and cooperation have been basic features of human social life. Other primates show affection with their kin, but only humans have systems of kinship and marriage that permit us to maintain lifelong ties with relatives in different local groups.

Primatology is the study of nonhuman primates—fossil and living apes, monkeys, and prosimians, including their behavior and social life. Primatology is fascinating in itself, but it also helps anthropologists to make inferences about the early social organization of *hominids* (members of the zoological family that includes fossil and living humans) and to untangle issues of human nature and the origins of culture. Of particular relevance to humans are two kinds of primates:

1. Those whose ecological adaptations are similar to our own: **terrestrial** monkeys and apes—that is, primates that live on the ground rather than in the trees.
2. Those that are most closely related to us: the great apes, specifically the chimpanzees and gorillas.

Our Place among Primates

Similarities between humans and apes are evident in anatomy, brain structure, genetics, and biochemistry. The physical similarities between humans and apes are recognized in zoological **taxonomy**—the assignment of organisms to categories (*taxa;* singular, *taxon*) according to their relationship and resemblance. Many similarities between organisms reflect their common *phylogeny*—their genetic relatedness based on common ancestry. In other words, organisms share features they have inherited from the same ancestor. Humans and apes belong to the same taxonomic superfamily, *Hominoidea* (**hominoids**). Monkeys are placed in two others (Ceboidea and Cercopithecoidea). This means that humans and apes are more closely related to each other than either is to monkeys.

Figure 4.1 summarizes the various levels of classification used in zoological taxonomy. Each lower-level unit belongs to the higher-level unit above it. Thus, looking toward the bottom of Figure 4.1, similar species belong to the same genus (plural, *genera*). Similar genera make up the same family, and so on through the top of Figure 4.1, where similar phyla (plural of *phylum*) are included in the same kingdom.

Compare the human and the gorilla. What similarities do you notice? What differences? Humans, gorillas, and chimps have more than 98 percent of their DNA in common.

Figure 4.1
The Principal Classificatory Units of Zoological Taxonomy

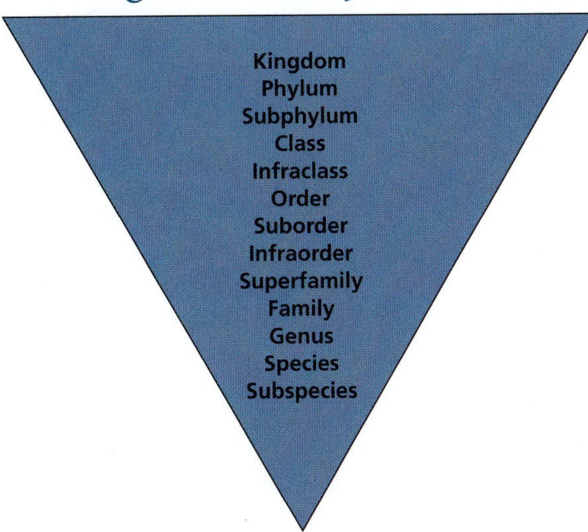

Moving down the figure, the classificatory units become more exclusive, so that "Kingdom" at the top is the most inclusive unit and "Subspecies" at the bottom is the most exclusive.

We see that the highest (most inclusive) taxonomic level is the *kingdom.* At that level, animals are distinguished from plants. The lowest-level taxa are species and subspecies. A *species* is a group of organisms that can mate and give birth to *viable* (capable of living) and *fertile* (capable of reproducing) offspring whose own offspring are viable and fertile. *Speciation* (the formation of a new species) occurs when groups that once belonged to the same species can no longer interbreed. After a sufficiently long period of reproductive isolation, two closely related species assigned to the same genus will have evolved out of one.

At the lowest level of taxonomy, a species may have subspecies. These are its more or less, but not yet totally, isolated subgroups. Subspecies can co-exist in time and space. For example, the Neanderthals, who thrived between 130,000 and 35,000 years ago, often are assigned not to a separate species but merely to a different subspecies of *Homo sapiens.* Just one subspecies of *Homo sapiens* survives today.

The similarities used to assign organisms to the same taxon are called **homologies,** similarities they have jointly inherited from a common ancestor. Table 4.1 summarizes the place of humans in zoological taxonomy. We see in Table 4.1 that we

Table 4.1

The Place of Humans (*Homo sapiens*) in Zoological Taxonomy

Homo sapiens is an Animal, Chordate, Vertebrate, Mammal, Primate, Anthropoid, Catarrhine, Hominoid, and Hominid. (Table 4.2 shows the taxonomic placement of the other primates.)

Taxon	Scientific (Latin) Name	Common (English) Name
Kingdom	Animalia	Animals
Phylum	Chordata	Chordates
Subphylum	Vertebrata	Vertebrates
Class	Mammalia	Mammals
Infraclass	Eutheria	Eutherians
Order	Primates	Primates
Suborder	Anthropoidea	Anthropoids
Infraorder	Catarrhini	Catarrhines
Superfamily	Hominoidea	Hominoids
Family	Hominidae	Hominids
Genus	*Homo*	Humans
Species	*Homo sapiens*	Recent humans
Subspecies	*Homo sapiens sapiens*	Anatomically modern humans

are mammals, members of the *class* Mammalia. This is a major subdivision of the kingdom Animalia. Mammals share certain traits, including mammary glands, that set them apart from other taxa, such as birds, reptiles, amphibians, and insects. Mammalian homologies indicate that all mammals share more recent common ancestry with each other than they do with any bird, reptile, or insect.

Humans are mammals that, at a lower taxonomic level, belong to the *order* Primates. Another mammalian order is Carnivora: the carnivores (dogs, cats, foxes, wolves, badgers, weasels). Rodentia (rats, mice, beavers, squirrels) form yet another mammalian order. The primates share structural and biochemical homologies that distinguish them from other mammals. These resemblances were inherited from their common early primate ancestors after those early primates became reproductively isolated from the ancestors of the other mammals.

Homologies and Analogies

Organisms should be assigned to the same taxon on the basis of homologies. The extensive biochemical homologies between apes and humans confirm our common ancestry and support our traditional joint classification as hominoids. For example, it is estimated that humans, chimpanzees, and gorillas have more than 98 percent of their DNA in common.

However, common ancestry isn't the only reason for similarities between species. Similar traits also can arise if species experience similar selective forces and adapt to them in similar ways. We call such similarities **analogies.** The process by which analogies are produced is called **convergent evolution.** For example, fish and porpoises share many analogies resulting from convergent evolution to life in the water. Like fish, porpoises, which are mammals, have fins. They are also hairless and streamlined for efficient locomotion. Analogies between birds and bats (wings, small size, light bones) illustrate convergent evolution to flying (see Angier 1998).

In theory, only homologies should be used in taxonomy. With reference to the hominoids, there is no doubt that humans, gorillas, and chimpanzees are more closely related to each other than any of the three is to orangutans, which are Asiatic apes (Ciochon 1983). Humans, chimps, and gorillas share a more recent ancestor with each other than they do with orangs. The *Hominidae* family is the zoological family that includes **hominids**—fossil and living humans. Many scientists now also place gorillas and

Table 4.2
Primate Taxonomy

The subdivisions of the two primate suborders: Prosimii (Prosimians) and Anthropoidea (Anthropoids). Humans (see also Table 4.1) are anthropoids who belong to the superfamily Hominoidea (the hominoids), along with the apes.

Suborder	Infraorder	Superfamily	Family	Subfamily
Prosimii (Prosimians)	Lemuriformes	Lemuroidea	Daubentoniidae (Aye-aye) Indridae (Indri) Lemuridae (Lemurs)	
	Lorisiformes	Lorisoidea	Lorisidae	Galaginae (Bushbabies) Lorisinae (Lorises)
	Tarsiiformes	Tarsioidea	Tarsiidae (Tarsiers)	
Anthropoidea (Anthropoids)	Platyrrhini	Ceboidea	Callitrichidae (Tamarins and marmosets)	
			Cebidae	Atelinae (Spider monkeys and woolly monkeys)
	Catarrhini	Cercopithecoidea	Cercopithecidae	Cercopithecinae (Macaques, guenons, and baboons) Colobinae (Colobines)
		Hominoidea	Hylobatidae (Gibbons and siamangs) Pongidae (Orangutans) Hominidae (Gorillas, chimpanzees, and humans)	

Source: Adapted from R. Martin, "Classification of Primates," in S. Jones, R. Martin, and D. Pilbeam, eds., *The Cambridge Encyclopedia of Human Evolution* (Cambridge, England: Cambridge University Press, 1992), pp. 20–21.

chimps in that same family. This leaves the orangutan (genus *Pongo*) as the only member of the pongid family (Pongidae). Table 4.2 and Figure 4.2 illustrate our degree of relatedness to other primates.

Primate Tendencies

Primates are varied because they have adapted to diverse ecological niches. Some primates are active during the day; others at night. Some eat insects; others, fruits; others, shoots, leaves, and bulk vegetation; and others, seeds or roots. Some primates live on the ground, others live in trees, and there are intermediate adaptations. However, because the earliest primates were tree dwellers, modern primates share homologies reflecting their common **arboreal** heritage.

Many trends in primate evolution are best exemplified by the **anthropoids:** monkeys, apes, and humans, which constitute the suborder *Anthropoidea.* The other primate suborder, Prosimii, includes lemurs, lorises, and tarsiers. These **prosimians** are more distant relatives of humans than are monkeys and apes. The primate trends—most developed in the anthropoids—can be summarized briefly. Together they constitute an anthropoid heritage that humans share with monkeys and apes.

Figure 4.2
Primate Family Tree

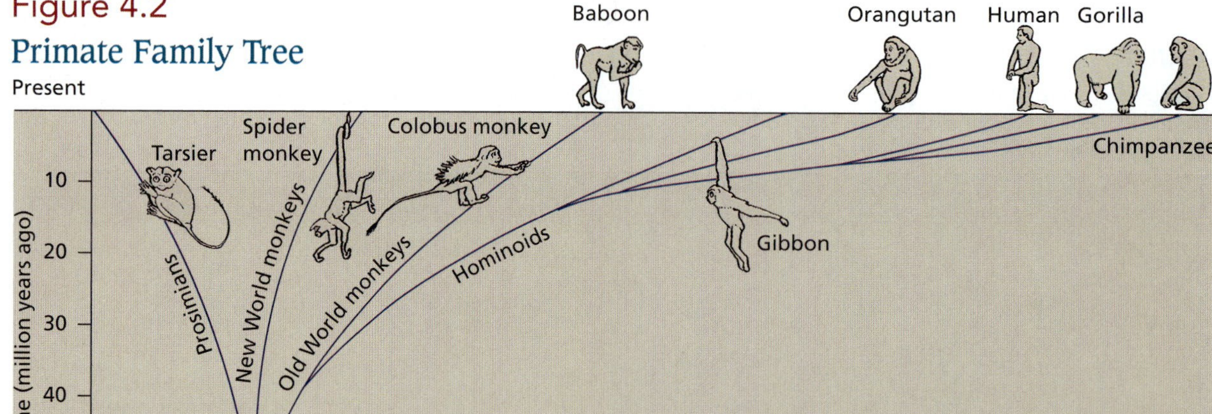

Source: From Roger Lewin, *Human Evolution: An Illustrated Introduction*, 3rd ed. (Boston: Blackwell Scientific Publications, 1993), p. 44.

When did the common ancestors of all the Primates live?

1. **Grasping.** Primates have five-digited feet and hands that are suited for grasping. Certain features of hands and feet that were originally adaptive for arboreal life have been transmitted across the generations to contemporary primates. Flexible hands and feet that could encircle branches were important features in the early primates' arboreal life. Thumb opposability might have been favored by the inclusion of insects in the early primate diet. Manual dexterity makes it easier to catch insects attracted to abundant arboreal flowers and fruits. Humans and many other primates have **opposable thumbs:** The thumb can touch the other fingers. Some primates also have grasping feet. However, in adapting to the **bipedal** (two-footed) locomotion, humans eliminated most of the foot's grasping ability.
2. **Smell to Sight.** Several anatomic changes reflect the shift from smell to sight as the primates' most important means of obtaining information. Monkeys, apes, and humans have excellent *stereoscopic* (able to see in depth) and color vision. The portion of the brain devoted to vision expanded, while the area concerned with smell shrank.
3. **Nose to Hand.** Sensations of touch, conveyed by *tactile* organs, also provide information. The

Primates have five-digited feet and hands, well-suited for grasping. Flexible hands and feet that could encircle branches were important features in the early primates' arboreal life. In adapting to bipedal (two-footed) locomotion, hominids eliminated most of the foot's grasping ability—illustrated here by the chimpanzee.

A crown lemur. Because these prosimians were confined to Madagascar, lemurs had no anthropoid competitors until people colonized that island some 1,500 years ago. Most lemur species are now endangered by human encroachment on their forest habitat.

tactile skin on a dog's or cat's nose transmits information. Cats' tactile hairs, or whiskers, also serve this function. In primates, however, the main touch organ is the hand, specifically the sensitive pads of the "fingerprint" region.

4. **Brain Complexity.** The proportion of brain tissue concerned with memory, thought, and association has increased in primates. The primate ratio of brain size to body size exceeds that of most mammals.
5. **Parental Investment.** Most primates give birth to a single offspring rather than a litter. Because of this, growing primates receive more attention and have more learning opportunities than do other mammals. Learned behavior is an important part of primate adaptation.
6. **Sociality.** Primates tend to be social animals that live with others of their species. The need for longer and more attentive care of offspring places a selective value on support by a social group.

Prosimians

The primate order has two suborders: prosimians and anthropoids. The early history of the primates is limited to prosimian-like animals known through the fossil record. (See Chapter 5.) The first anthropoids, ancestral to monkeys, apes, and humans, appeared more than 40 million years ago. Some prosimians managed to survive in Africa and Asia because they were adapted to nocturnal life. As such, they did not compete with anthropoids, which are active during the day. Prosimians (lemurs) in Madagascar had no anthropoid competitors until people colonized that island some 1,500 years ago.

In their behavior and biology, Madagascar's *lemurs,* with 33 species, show adaptations to an array of environments or ecological niches. Their diets and times of activity differ. Lemurs eat fruits, other plant foods, eggs, and insects. Some are nocturnal; others are active during the day. Some are totally arboreal; others spend some time in the trees and some on the ground. Another kind of prosimian is the *tarsier,* today confined to Indonesia and the Philippines. From the fossil record, we know that 50 million years ago, several genera of tarsier-like prosimians lived in North America and Europe, which were much warmer then than they are now (Boaz 1997). The one genus of tarsier that survived is totally nocturnal. Active at night, tarsiers don't directly compete with anthropoids, which are active during the day. Lorises are other nocturnal prosimians found in Africa and Asia.

Anthropoids

All anthropoids share resemblances that can be considered trends in primate evolution in the sense that these traits are fully developed neither in the fossils of primates that lived prior to 45 million years ago nor among contemporary prosimians.

All anthropoids have overlapping fields of vision, permitting them to see things in depth. With reduction of the snout, anthropoid eyes are placed forward in the skull and look directly ahead. The fields of vision of our eyes overlap. Depth perception, impossible without overlapping visual fields, proved adaptive in the trees. Tree-dwelling primates that could judge distance better because of depth perception survived and reproduced in greater numbers than did those that could not.

The abilities to see in depth and in color may have developed together. Both helped early anthropoids interpret their arboreal world. Superior vision made it easier to distinguish edible insects, fruits, berries, and leaves. Furthermore, having color and depth vision makes it easier to groom—to remove burrs, insects, and other small objects from other primates' hair. Grooming is one way of forming and maintaining social bonds.

Visual and tactile changes have been interrelated. Monkeys, apes, and humans have neither tactile muzzle skin nor "cat's whiskers." Instead, fingers are the main touch organs. The ends of the fingers and toes are sensitive tactile pads. Forward placement of the eyes and depth vision allow anthropoids to pick up small objects, hold them in front of their eyes, and appraise them. Our ability to thread a needle reflects an intricate interplay of hands and eyes that took millions of years to achieve. Manual dexterity, including the opposable thumb, confers a tremendous advantage in examining and manipulating objects and is essential to a major human adaptive capacity: tool making. Among monkeys, thumb opposability is indispensable for feeding and grooming.

Another trend is increased size of the *cranium* (skull) to fit a larger brain. The brain/body size ratio is greater among anthropoids than among prosimians. Even more important, the brain's outer layer—concerned with memory, association, and integration—is relatively larger. Monkeys, apes, and humans store an array of visual images in their memories, which permits them to learn more. The ability to learn from experience and from other group members is a major reason for the success of the anthropoids compared to most other mammals.

Monkeys

The anthropoid suborder has two infraorders: *platyrrhines* (New World monkeys) and *catarrhines* (Old World monkeys, apes, and humans). The catarrhines (sharp-nosed) and platyrrhines (flat-nosed) take their names from Latin terms that describe the placement of the nostrils (Figure 4.3). Old World monkeys, apes, and humans are all catarrhines. Being placed in the same taxon (infraorder in this case) means that monkeys, apes, and humans are more closely related to each other than to New World monkeys. In other words, one kind of monkey (Old World) is more like a human than it is like another kind of monkey (New World). The New World monkeys were reproductively isolated from the catarrhines before the latter diverged into the Old World monkeys, apes, and humans. This is why New World monkeys are assigned to a different infraorder.

All New World monkeys and many Old World monkeys are arboreal. Whether in the trees or on the ground, however, monkeys move differently from apes and humans. Their arms and legs move parallel to one another, as dogs' legs do. This contrasts with the tendency toward *orthograde posture,* the straight and upright stance of apes and humans. Unlike apes, which have longer arms than legs, and humans, who have longer legs than arms, monkeys have arms and legs of about the same length. Most monkeys also have tails, which help them maintain balance in the trees. Apes and humans lack tails. The apes' tendency toward orthograde posture is most evident when they sit down. When they move about, chimps, gorillas, and orangutans habitually use all four limbs.

New World Monkeys

New World monkeys live in the forests of Central and South America. There are interesting parallels between New World monkeys and some

Figure 4.3
Nostril Structure of Catarrhines and Platyrrhines

Above: narrow septum and "sharp nose" of a guenon, a catarrhine (Old World monkey). Below: broad septum and "flat nose" of Humboldt's woolly monkey, a platyrrhine (New World monkey). Which nose is more like your own? What does that similarity suggest?

Figure 4.4
The Prehensile Tail of the Spider Monkey, a New World Monkey

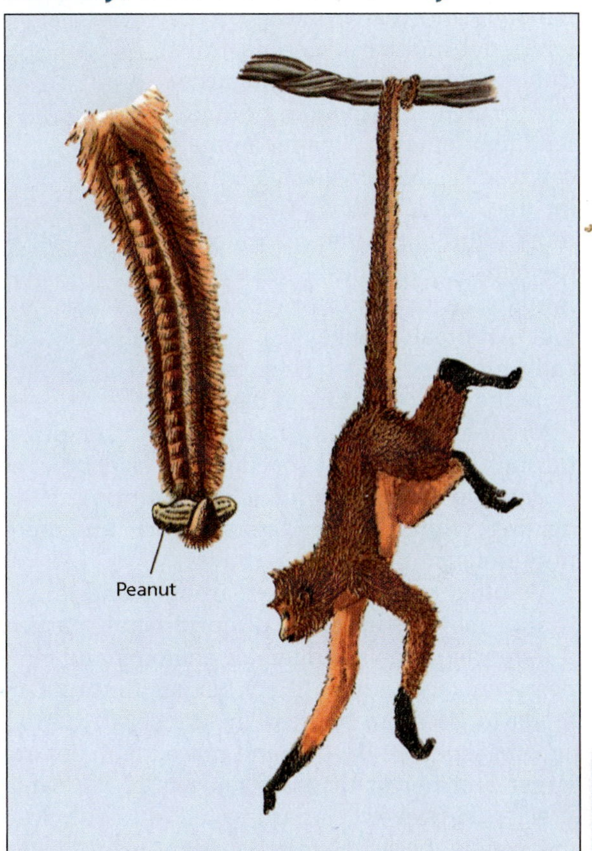

Such a tail can be used to grasp a branch, or to pick up small objects, such as the peanut. Do any of the apes have grasping tails?

arboreal primates of the Old World. These analogies exhibit convergent evolution—that is, they have developed as a result of adaptation to a similar arboreal niche. Like the gibbon, a small Asiatic ape, some New World monkeys have developed **brachiation**—under-the-branch swinging. Most monkeys run and jump from branch to branch, but gibbons and some New World monkeys swing through the trees, using their hands as hooks. Hand over hand, they move from branch to branch, propelled onward by the thrust of their bodies.

Unlike Old World monkeys, many New World monkeys have *prehensile,* or grasping, tails (Figure 4.4). Sometimes the prehensile tail has tactile skin, which permits it to work like a hand, for instance, in conveying food to the mouth. Old World monkeys, however, have developed their own characteristic anatomic specializations. They have rough patches of skin on the buttocks, adapted to sitting on hard rocky ground and rough branches. If the primate you see in the zoo has such patches, it's from the Old World. If it has a prehensile tail, it's a New World monkey.

Old World Monkeys

A hamadryas baboon couple at Germany's Augsburg zoo. How would you describe the sexual dimorphism shown in this photo?

The Old World monkeys have both terrestrial and arboreal species. Baboons and many macaques are terrestrial monkeys. Certain traits differentiate terrestrial and arboreal primates. Arboreal primates tend to be smaller. Smaller animals can reach a greater variety of foods in trees and shrubs, where the most abundant foods are located at the ends of branches. Low weight is adaptive for end-of-branch feeding. Arboreal monkeys are typically lithe and agile. They escape from the few predators in their environment—snakes and monkey-eating eagles—through alertness and speed. Large size, by contrast, is advantageous for terrestrial primates in dealing with their predators, which are more numerous on the ground.

Another contrast between arboreal and terrestrial primates is in **sexual dimorphism**—marked differences in male and female anatomy and temperament (see Fedigan 1992). Sexual dimorphism tends to be more marked in terrestrial than in arboreal species. Baboon and macaque males are larger and fiercer than are females of the same species. However, it's hard to tell, without close inspection, the sex of an arboreal monkey.

Of the terrestrial monkeys, the baboons of Africa and the (mainly Asiatic) macaques have been the subjects of many studies. Why do you think there have been more studies of terrestrial than of arboreal primates? Terrestrial monkeys have specializations in anatomy, psychology, and social behavior that enable them to cope with terrestrial life. Adult male baboons, for example, are fierce-looking animals that can weigh 100 pounds (45 kilograms). They display their long, projecting canines to intimidate predators and when confronting other baboons. Faced with a predator, a male baboon can puff up his ample mane of shoulder hair, so that the would-be aggressor perceives the baboon as larger than he actually is.

Longitudinal field research shows that, near the time of puberty, baboon and macaque males typically leave their home troop for another. Because males move in and out, females form the stable core of the terrestrial monkey troop (Cheney and Seyfarth 1990; Hinde 1983). By contrast, among chimpanzees and gorillas, females are more likely to emigrate and seek mates outside their natal social groups (Rodseth et al. 1991; van Schaik and van Hooff 1983; Wrangham 1980). Among terrestrial monkeys, then, the core group consists of females; among apes it is made up of males.

Apes

The Old World monkeys have their own separate superfamily (Cercopithecoidea), while humans and the apes together compose the hominoid superfamily (Hominoidea). Among the hominoids, the so-called great apes are orangutans, gorillas, and chimpanzees. Humans could be included here, too; we are sometimes called "the third African ape." The lesser (smaller) apes are the gibbons and siamangs of Southeast Asia and Indonesia.

Apes live in forests and woodlands. The light and agile gibbons, which are skilled brachiators, are completely arboreal. The heavier gorillas, chimpanzees, and adult male orangutans spend considerable time on the ground. Nevertheless, ape behavior and anatomy reveal past and present

Figure 4.5
The Limb Ratio of the Arboreal Gibbon and Terrestrial Homo

How does this anatomical difference fit the modes of locomotion used by gibbons and humans?

adaptation to arboreal life. For example, apes still build nests to sleep in trees. Apes have longer arms than legs, which is adaptive for brachiation (see Figure 4.5). The structure of the shoulder and clavicle (collar bone) of the apes and humans suggests that we had a brachiating ancestor. In fact, young apes still do brachiate. Adult apes tend to be too heavy to brachiate safely. Their weight is more than many branches can withstand. Gorillas and chimps now use the long arms they have inherited from their more arboreal ancestors for life on the ground. The terrestrial locomotion of chimps and gorillas is called *knuckle-walking*. In it, long arms and callused knuckles support the trunk as the apes amble around leaning forward.

Gibbons

Gibbons are widespread in the forests of Southeast Asia, especially in Malaysia. Smallest of the apes, male and female gibbons have about the same average height (3 feet, or 1 meter) and weight (12 to 25 pounds, or 5 to 10 kilograms). Gibbons spend most of their time just below the forest canopy (treetops). For efficient brachiation, gibbons have long arms and fingers, with short thumbs. Slenderly built, gibbons are the most agile apes. Unlike knuckle-walkers, they use their long arms for balance when they occasionally walk erect on the ground or along a branch. Gibbons are the preeminent arboreal specialists among the apes. They subsist on a fruit diet. Gibbons and siamangs, their slightly larger relatives, tend to live in *primary groups*, which are composed of a permanently bonded male and female and their preadolescent offspring. Gibbon evolutionary success is confirmed by their numbers and range. Hundreds of thousands of gibbons span a wide area of Southeast Asia.

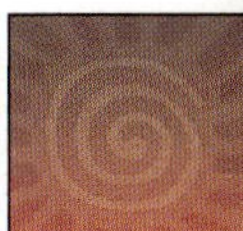

Orangutans

The single orangutan species belongs to the genus *Pongo.* This Asiatic great ape's range once extended into China, but contemporary orangs are confined to two Indonesian islands. Sexual dimorphism is marked, with the adult male weighing more than twice as much as the female. The orangutan male, like his human counterpart, is intermediate in size between chimps and gorillas. Some orang males exceed 200 pounds (90 kilograms). With only half the gorilla's bulk, male orangs can be more arboreal, although they typically climb, rather than swing through, the trees. The smaller size of females and young permits them to make fuller use of

With long arms and fingers, the gibbon is the most agile of the apes. Gibbons occasionally walk upright on the ground, using their long arms as balancers. Shown here, a white-handed gibbon strolls through the forest.

the trees. Orangutans have a varied diet of fruit, bark, leaves, and insects. Because orangutans live in jungles and feed in trees, they are especially difficult to study. However, field reports about orangutans in their natural setting (MacKinnon 1974) have clarified their behavior and social organization. Orangs tend to be solitary animals. Their tightest social units consist of females and preadolescent young. Males forage alone.

Gorillas

With just one species, *Gorilla gorilla,* there are three subspecies of gorillas. The western lowland gorilla is the animal you normally see in zoos. This, the smallest subspecies of gorilla, lives mainly in forests in the Central African Republic, Congo, Cameroon, Gabon, Equatorial Guinea, and Nigeria. The eastern lowland gorilla, of which there are only four in captivity, is slightly larger and lives in eastern Congo. There are no mountain gorillas, the third subspecies, in captivity, and it's estimated that no more than 650 of these animals survive in the wild. These are the largest gorillas with the longest hair (to keep them warm in their mountainous habitat). They are also the rarest gorillas, which Dian Fossey and other scientists have studied in Rwanda, Uganda, and eastern Congo.

Full-grown male gorillas may weigh 400 pounds (180 kilograms) and stand six feet tall (183 centimeters). Like most terrestrial primates, gorillas show marked sexual dimorphism. The average adult female weighs half as much as the male. Gorillas spend little time in the trees. It's particularly cumbersome for an adult male to move his bulk about in a tree. When gorillas sleep in trees, they build nests, which are usually no more than 10 feet (3 meters) off the ground. By contrast, the nests of chimps and female orangs may be 100 feet (30 meters) above the ground.

Most of the gorilla's day is spent feeding. Gorillas move through jungle undergrowth eating ground plants, leaves, bark, fruits, and other vegetation. Like most primates, gorillas live in social groups. The *troop* is a common unit of primate social organization, consisting of multiple males and females and their offspring. Although troops with up to 30 gorillas have been observed, most gorillas live in groups of from 10 to 20. Gorilla troops tend to have fairly stable memberships, with little shifting between troops (Fossey 1983). Each troop has a silver-back male, so designated because of the strip of white hair that extends down his back. This is the physical sign of full maturity among the male gorillas. The silverback is usually the only breeding male in the troop, which is why gorilla troops are sometimes called "one-male groups." However, a few younger, subordinate males may also adhere to such a one-male group (Harcourt et al. 1981; Schaller 1963).

Chimpanzees

Chimpanzees belong to the genus *Pan,* which has two species: *Pan troglodytes* (the common chimpanzee) and *Pan paniscus* (the Bonobo or "pygmy" chimpanzee) (de Waal 1997; Susman

Gorillas, chimpanzees, and male orangutans spend much of their time on the ground. Why? Most of the gorilla's day is spent feeding—on ground plants, leaves, bark, fruits, and other vegetation. Shown here are members of a mountain gorilla troop with primatologist Dian Fossey.

1987). Like humans, chimps are closely related to the gorilla, although there are some obvious differences. Like gorillas, chimps live in tropical Africa, but they range over a larger area and more varied environments than gorillas do (Figure 4.6). The common chimp, *Pan troglodytes,* lives in western central Africa (Gabon, Congo, Cameroon), as well as in western Africa (Sierra Leone, Liberia, The Gambia) and eastern Africa (Congo, Uganda, and Tanzania). Bonobos live in remote and densely forested areas of just one country—the Democratic Republic of Congo. Common chimps live mainly in tropical rain forests but also in woodlands and mixed forest-woodland-grassland areas, such as the Gombe Stream National Park, Tanzania, where Jane Goodall (1996) and other researchers began to study them in 1960.

There are dietary differences between chimps and gorillas. Gorillas eat large quantities of green bulk vegetation, but chimps, like orangutans and gibbons, prefer fruits. Chimps are actually omnivorous, adding animal protein to their diet by capturing small mammals, birds' eggs, and insects.

Chimps are lighter and more arboreal than gorillas are. The adult male's weight—between 100 and 200 pounds (45 to 90 kilograms)—is about a third that of the male gorilla. There is much less sexual dimorphism among chimps than among gorillas. Females approximate 88 percent of the average male height. This is similar to the ratio of sexual dimorphism in *Homo sapiens.*

Several scientists have studied wild chimps, and we know more about the full range of their behavior and social organization than we do about the other apes (see Wrangham et al. 1994). The long-term research of Jane Goodall and others at Gombe provides especially useful information. Approximately 150 chimpanzees range over Gombe's 30 square miles (80 square kilometers). Goodall (1986, 1996) has described communities of about 50 chimps, all of which know one another and interact

Figure 4.6
Geographic Distribution of African Apes

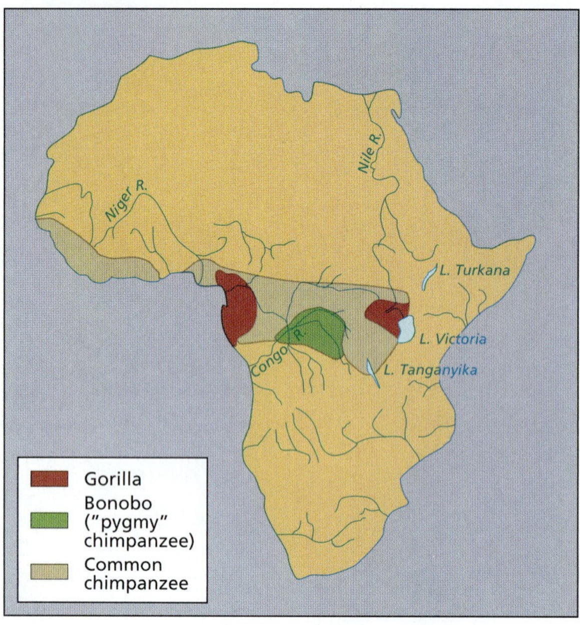

Source: From C. J. Jolly and F. Plog, *Physical Anthropology and Archeology,* 4th ed. (New York: McGraw-Hill, 1986), p. 115.

Chimpanzees and gorillas are primarily rain forest dwellers. However, some chimpanzee populations live in woodland environments. This map shows the ranges of the three species of African apes.

from time to time. Communities regularly split up into smaller groups: a mother and her offspring; a few males; males, females, and young; and occasionally solitary animals. Chimp communities are

semiclosed. The social networks of males are more closed than are those of females, which are more likely to migrate and mate outside their natal group than males are (Wrangham 1994).

When chimps, which are very vocal, meet, they greet one another with gestures, facial expressions, and calls. They hoot to maintain contact during their daily rounds. Like baboons and macaques, chimps exhibit dominance relationships through attacks and displacement. Some adult females outrank younger adult males, although females do not display as strong dominance relationships among themselves as males do. Males occasionally cooperate in hunting parties.

Endangered Primates

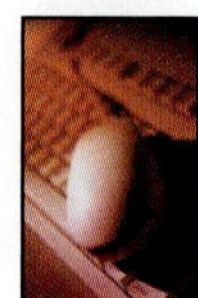

More than half of all plant and animal species live in tropical forests, which are disappearing at the rapid rate of 10 to 20 million hectares per year (the size of the state of New York). This is a serious problem because many people depend on these forests for their livelihood. Deforestation also entails the loss of biological diversity, as the natural habitats of many species disappear.

Consider the Democratic Republic of the Congo (DRC), the country that ranks fourth in the world in terms of greatest biodiversity. Its threatened species include mountain and lowland gorillas, along with bonobos, or pygmy chimpanzees. The major threat to the bonobo, which is found only in the DRC, is forestry and loss of the hardwood forests where most bonobos live (Stern 2000).

Deforestation poses a special risk for the primates, because 90 percent of the 190 living primate species live in tropical forests—in Africa, Asia, South America, and Central America. Figure 4.7 is a map showing the distribution of primates today. As the earth's human population swells, the populations of the nonhuman primates are shrinking. According to the Convention on International Trade in Endangered Species (ratified in 1973), all nonhuman primates are now endangered or soon to be endangered. The apes (gibbons, gorillas, orangutans, and chimps) are in the "most endangered" category. Mountain gorillas, which once ranged widely in the forested mountains of East Africa, are now limited to a small area near the war-ravaged borders of Rwanda, Congo, and Uganda. Other severely threatened species include the golden lion tamarin monkey of southeastern Brazil, the cotton-top tamarin of Colombia, the lion-tailed macaque of southern India, the woolly monkeys of Amazonia, and the orangutan of Southeast Asia.

A combination of forestry and forest fires has been deadly to orangutans in Sumatra and Borneo in Indonesia. Sumatra, which is losing 1,000 orangs a year, has an estimated population of 6,000 left. A road for loggers and miners that penetrated the orangutan range in Sumatra led to contact with humans that proved fatal to hundreds of the animals. Borneo was devastated by

Figure 4.7
Geographic Distribution of Living Primates

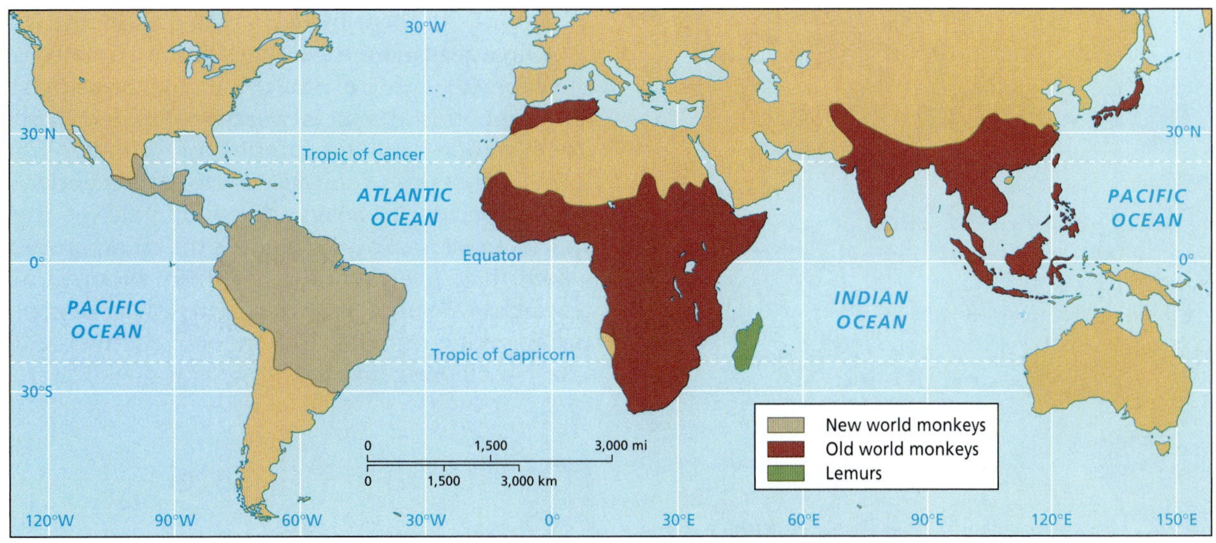

Source: From Roger Lewin, *Human Evolution: An Illustrated Introduction*, 3rd ed. (Boston: Blackwell Scientific Publications, 1993), p. 45.

fires in 1997–98, leaving some 10,000–15,000 orangs, compared with 60,000 in 1980. Habitat destruction and fragmentation can isolate small groups of animals, leaving them vulnerable to extinction due to loss of genetic diversity. Primate populations are slow to recover from such threats. Ape species, for example, are slow reproducers, rarely having more than three to four offspring over a lifetime (Stern 2000).

Although the destruction of their forest habitats is the main reason the primates are disappearing, it isn't the only reason. Another threat is human hunting of primates for bush meat (Viegas 2000). In Amazonia, West Africa, and Central Africa, primates are a major source of food. People kill thousands of monkeys each year. Human hunting is less of a threat to primates in Asia. In India, Hindus avoid monkey meat because the monkey is sacred, while Moslems avoid it because monkeys are considered unclean and not fit for human consumption.

People also hunt primates for their skins and pelts; poachers sell their body parts as trophies and ornaments. Africans use the skins of black-and-white colobus monkeys for cloaks and headdresses, and American and European tourists buy coats and rugs made from colobus pelts. In Amazonia, ocelot and jaguar hunters shoot monkeys to bait the traps they set for the cats.

Poachers pose the greatest threat to the mountain gorillas, of which there were as few as 250 left in the wild when Fossey started studying them (Fossey 1981, 1983). The poachers shoot the apes with high-powered rifles, then decapitate them and cut off their hands. They sell gorilla heads as trophies and turn their hands into grotesque ashtrays. Traps and snares set for antelope and buffalo also endanger gorillas, which sometimes get caught in the traps. Even if they manage to free themselves, they often die from infected wounds. The sad fate (murder and decapitation) of Dian Fossey's favorite gorilla, Digit, is familiar to those who have seen the 1988 film *Gorillas in the Mist,* the story of Fossey, her work with mountain gorillas, and her efforts to save them. Fossey herself was murdered in her cabin at her field site in Rwanda in 1985 (see Roberts 1995). The mystery of her death remains unsolved. The last entry in her diary reads: "When you realize the value of all life, you dwell less on what is past and concentrate on the preservation of the future." Through the efforts of the fund she established, the number of mountain gorillas has increased.

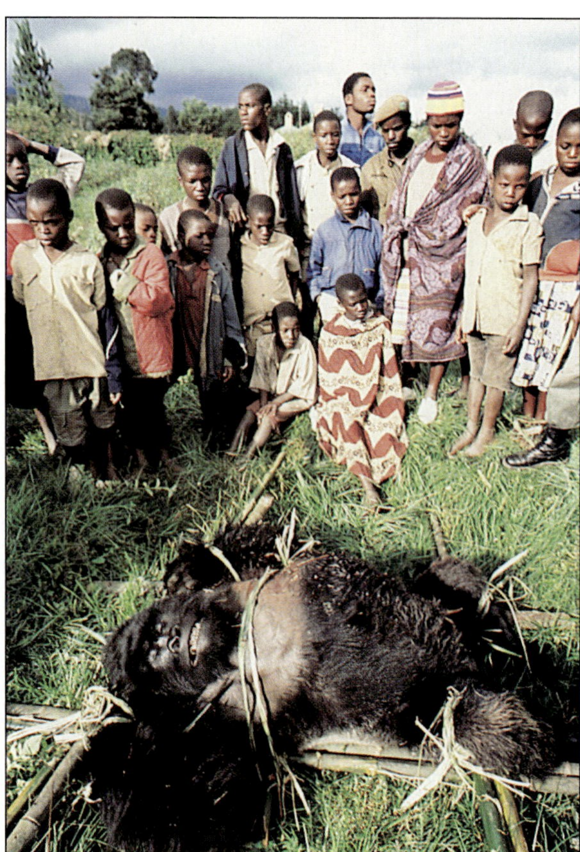

In Africa, poachers shoot apes with high-powered rifles, then decapitate them and cut off their hands. They sell gorilla heads as trophies and turn their hands into grotesque ashtrays. Is killing a gorilla murder?

Chimpanzees are also vulnerable to poachers. One famous chimp, Lucy, raised by an American family and taught to use sign language (see Chapter 13), met a grim fate when she was taken to Africa to live in the wild. In 1986, soon after she had joined an island colony of chimps in The Gambia, Lucy's mutilated corpse was discovered—minus skin, hair, hands, and feet. "We can only speculate that Lucy was killed—probably shot—and skinned. Because of her confidence with humans, she was always the first to confront newcomers to the island. She might have surprised an armed intruder, with fatal consequences" (Carter 1988, p. 47).

Primates also are killed when they are agricultural pests. In some areas of Africa and Asia, baboons and macaques raid the crops on which people depend for subsistence. Between 1947 and 1962, the government of Sierra Leone held annual drives to rid farm areas of monkeys, and between 15,000 and 20,000 primates perished each year.

A final reason for the demise of the primates is the capture of animals for use in labs or as pets. Although this threat is minor compared with deforestation and the hunting of primates for food, it does pose a serious risk to certain endangered species in heavy demand. One of the species most hurt by this trade is the chimpanzee, which has been widely used in biomedical research. One especially destructive way of capturing young primates is to shoot the mother and take her clinging infant.

Human–Primate Similarities

There is a substantial gap between primate society and fully developed human culture. However, studies of primates have revealed many similarities. Scholars used to contend that learned (versus instinctive) behavior separates humans from other animals. We know now that monkeys and apes also rely on learning. Many of the differences between humans and other primates are differences in *degree* rather than in kind. For example, monkeys learn from experiences, but humans learn much more. Another example: Chimpanzees and orangutans make tools for specific tasks, but human reliance on tools is much greater.

Learning

Common to monkeys, apes, and humans is the fact that behavior and social life are not rigidly programmed by the genes. All these animals learn throughout their lives. In several cases, an entire monkey troop has learned from the experiences of some of its members. In one group of Japanese macaques, a three-year-old female monkey started washing dirt off sweet potatoes before she ate them. First her mother, then her age peers, and finally the entire troop began washing sweet potatoes, too. The direction of learning was reversed when members of another macaque troop learned to eat wheat. After the

Learned behavior among wild chimps includes rudimentary tool manufacture. At Tanzania's Gombe Stream National Park, chimps use specially prepared twigs to "fish" for termites.

dominant males had tried the new food, within four hours the practice had spread throughout the troop. Changes in learned behavior seem to spread more quickly from the top down than from the bottom up.

For monkeys as for people, the ability to learn, to profit from experience, confers a tremendous adaptive advantage, permitting them to avoid fatal mistakes. Faced with environmental change, primates don't have to wait for a genetic or physiological response. Learned behavior and social patterns can be modified instead.

Tools

Anthropologists used to distinguish humans from other animals as tool users, and there is no doubt that *Homo* does employ tools much more than any other animal does. However, tool use also turns up among several nonhuman species. For example, in the Galápagos Islands off western South America, there is a "woodpecker finch" that selects twigs to dig out insects and grubs from tree bark. Sea otters use rocks to break open mollusks, which are important in their diet. Beavers are famous for dam construction.

When it became obvious that people weren't the only tool users, anthropologists started contending that only humans make tools with foresight, that is, with a specific purpose in mind. Chimpanzees show that this, too, is debatable. Many researchers, especially Jane Goodall (1996), have increased our knowledge of chimp behavior in natural settings. In 1960, Goodall began observing chimps in Gombe Stream National Park in Tanzania, East Africa. More than any other primate, chimps share the human capacity for deliberate tool manufacture, although in chimps the capacity remains rudimentary. Nevertheless, wild chimps regularly make tools. To get water from places their mouths can't reach, thirsty chimps pick leaves, chew and crumple them, and then dip them into the water. Thus, with a specific purpose in mind, they devise primitive "sponges."

More impressive is "termiting." Chimps make tools to probe termite hills. They choose twigs, which they modify by removing leaves and peeling off bark to expose the sticky surface beneath. They carry the twigs to termite hills, dig holes

with their fingers, and insert the twigs. Finally they pull out the twigs and dine on termites that were attracted to the sticky surface.

Termiting isn't as easy as it might seem. Learning to termite takes time, and many Gombe chimps never master it. Twigs with certain characteristics must be chosen. Furthermore, once the twig is in the hill and the chimp judges that termites are crawling on its surface, the chimp must quickly flip the twig as it pulls it out so that the termites are on top. Otherwise they fall off as the twig comes out of the hole. This is an elaborate skill that neither all chimps nor human observers have been able to master.

Chimps have other abilities essential to culture. When they are trained by humans, their skills flower, as anyone who has ever seen a movie, circus, or zoo chimp knows. Wild chimps and orangs aim and throw objects. The gorilla, our other nearest relative, lacks the chimp's proclivity for tool making. However, gorillas do build nests, and they throw branches, grass, vines, and other objects. Hominids have considerably elaborated the capacity to aim and throw, which is a homology passed down from the common ancestor of humans and apes. Without it we never would have developed projectile technology and weaponry—or baseball.

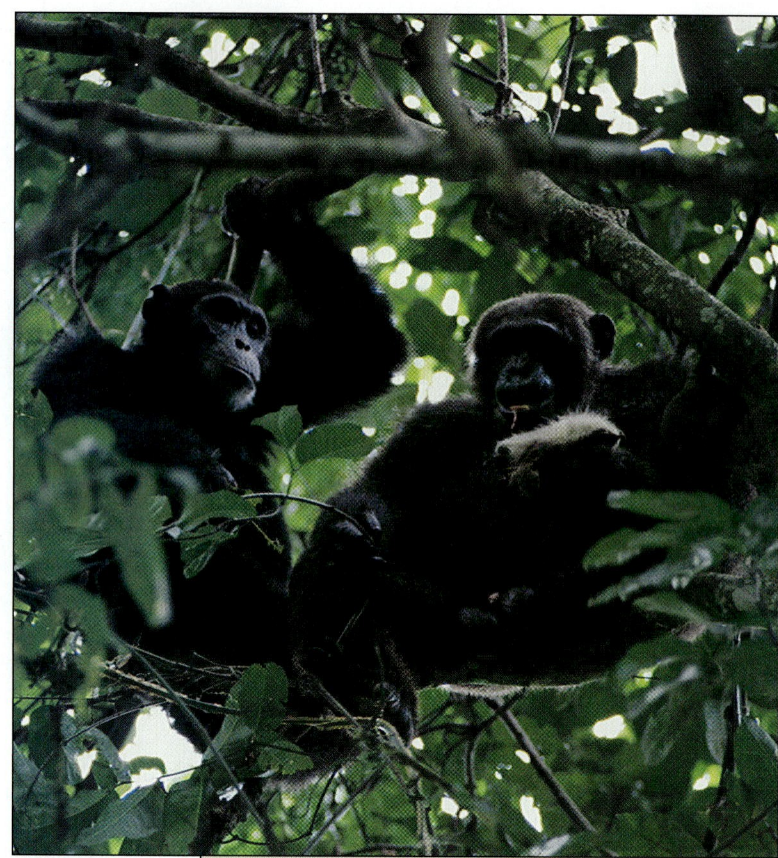

A high-ranking male chimp in Tanzania's Mahale National Park feeds on red colobus monkey while another male looks on. Chimps regularly hunt and eat up to a quarter pound of meat per day. Is hunting a social act?

Predation and Hunting

Like tool making and language, hunting has been cited as a distinctive human activity that is not shared with our ape relatives. Again, however, primate research shows that what was previously thought to be a difference of kind is a difference of degree. The diets of other terrestrial primates are not exclusively vegetarian, as was once thought. Baboons kill and eat young antelopes, and researchers have repeatedly observed hunting by chimpanzees.

For several years John Mitani, David Watts, and other researchers have been observing chimpanzees at Ngogo in Uganda's Kibale National Park. This is the largest chimp community ever described in the wild. In 1998 it consisted of 26 adult males, 40 adult females, 16 adolescent males, 5 adolescent females, and 30 infants and juveniles (Mitani and Watts 1999). (Remember that chimp communities have a more stable male than female core membership—adolescent males tend to stay on while adolescent females tend to leave to join other troops.) The large community size permits the formation of large hunting parties, which contributes to hunting success. Hunting parties at Ngogo included an average of 26 individuals (almost always adult and adolescent males). The average hunting time was 19 minutes, varying from 2 to 91 minutes in 29 observed hunts. Most hunts (78 percent) resulted in at least one prey item being caught—a much higher success rate than that among lions (26 percent), hyenas (34 percent), or cheetahs (30 percent). In most hunts (81 percent) the Ngogo chimps managed to catch multiple prey animals (three on average). The favored prey, at Ngogo as in other chimp communities, was the red colobus monkey.

As described by Mitani and Watts (1999), hunting by chimps is both opportunistic and planned. Opportunistic hunting took place when chimps encountered potential prey as they moved about during the day. Other hunts were organized patrols, in which the chimps became silent and moved together in a single file. They would stop, look up into the trees, scan, and change directions several times. Attentive to any arboreal movement, they would stop and search whenever they detected motion. On spotting a monkey, the chase would begin. Encountering no prey, the chimps would go on patrolling, sometimes for several hours. The Ngogo chimps also collaborate by encircling red colobus groups, blocking potential escape routes, and driving their prey down hill slopes from taller to shorter trees. Chimps may give a specific call, the hunting call, at the start of a hunt, mobilizing hunters into action. Sometimes isolated chimps who encountered a red colobus monkey would give this call, after which other chimps would rush to the site and begin to hunt. As has been reported elsewhere (see "In the News"), reciprocal sharing of prey meat was common among the Ngogo chimps.

Aggression and Resources

The potential for predation and aggression may be generalized in monkeys and apes, but its expression seems to depend on the environment. Jane Goodall specifically linked chimpanzee aggression and predation to human encroachment on their natural habitat. The Gombe chimps are divided into a northern group and a smaller group of southerners. Parties from the north have invaded the southern territory and killed southern chimps. Infant victims were partially eaten by the assailants (Goodall 1986).

John MacKinnon's research (1974) among orangutans on the Indonesian islands of Kalimantan (Borneo) and Sumatra showed that orangutans also have suffered as a result of human encroachment, particularly farming and timbering. On Borneo, in response to nearby human activities, orangs have developed a pattern of extreme sexual antagonism that may further endanger their survival. During MacKinnon's field work, Bornean orangs rarely had sex. Their limited sexual encounters were always brief rapes, often with screaming infants clinging to their mothers throughout the ordeal.

As MacKinnon did his field work, logging operations were forcing orangs whose territory was destroyed into his research area, swelling the population it had to support. The response to this sudden overpopulation was a drastic decline in the local orang birth rate. Primates respond in various ways to encroachment and to population pressure. A change in sexual relationships that reduces the birth rate is one way of easing population pressure on resources.

We see that primate behavior is not rigidly determined by the genes. It is plastic (flexible), capable of varying widely as environmental forces change. Among humans, too, aggression increases when resources are threatened or scarce. What we know about other primates makes it reasonable to assume that early hominids were neither uniformly aggressive nor consistently meek. Their aggression and predation reflected environmental variation (see Silverberg and Gray 1992; Wrangham and Peterson 1996).

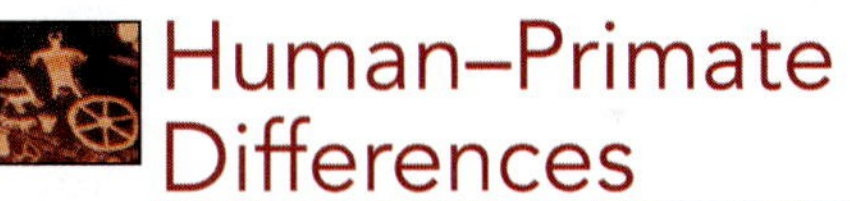

Human–Primate Differences

The preceding sections have emphasized similarities between humans and other primates. *Homo* has elaborated substantially on certain tendencies shared with the apes. A unique concentration and combination of characteristics make humans distinct. However, the savanna or open grassland niche in which early humans evolved also selected certain traits that are not so clearly foreshadowed by the apes.

Sharing and Cooperation

Early humans lived in small social groups called bands, with economies based on hunting and gathering (foraging). Until fairly recently (12,000 to 10,000 years ago), all humans based their subsistence on hunting and gathering and lived in bands. Some such societies even managed to survive into the modern world, and ethnographers

in the news

Carnivorous Chimps

This article describes research confirming the extent to which chimpanzees hunt and eat meat. Surprisingly, chimps eat almost as much meat as some human hunter-gatherers do. Male chimps coordinate their hunting, and they offer meat to females in exchange for sex. They also use meat to cement political alliances, giving meat to their friends but not their enemies. There is seasonal variation in the chimp hunting pattern, with less hunting when more leaves, fruits, and nuts are available.

Researchers studying chimpanzee hunting habits are gaining new insight into the lives of man's closest animal relative. Once thought of as docile vegetarians, these able hunters forage for meat with a passion and motivation not chronicled until recently.

Dr. Craig B. Stanford, an anthropologist at the University of Southern California, . . . found that chimpanzees hunt with such gusto in Gombe National Park in Tanzania that each year they lay waste to one-fifth of their territory's population of the red colobus monkey, their preferred prey. These long-tailed victims, crowned with a thatch of red hair, are plucked with abandon from the trees where they forage near the border with Congo . . .

This level of predation is surprising to many primatologists, but seems less so when compared with the diet of humans, the only other primate known to eat meat regularly. According to Dr. Stanford, chimpanzees can consume up to a quarter-pound of meat a day when they hit their hunting stride, rivaling at times some contemporary tribes of hunter-gatherers . . .

Dr. William C. McGrew, an anthropologist at Miami University of Ohio who studies chimpanzee behavior, said: "You pick up any textbook and it would say that meat eating by chimpanzees is insignificant. This is the first time meat has been shown to be important nutritionally."

Among the first scientists to debunk the myth of chimpanzees as banana-eating vegetarians was Dr. Jane Goodall, a British primatologist, who nearly 30 years ago announced to a startled scientific community that chimpanzees were part-time carnivores. Further research showed that these natives of equatorial Africa kill fellow chimps, use tools and mourn their dead—all behaviors once thought of as uniquely human.

As early as the 1960s, Dr. Geza Teleki, an American primatologist, said after observing male chimps swap meat for sex with females that nutrition was only

have studied them. From those studies we can conclude that in such societies, the strongest and most aggressive members do not dominate, as they do in a troop of terrestrial monkeys. Sharing and curbing of aggression are as basic to technologically simple humans as dominance and threats are to baboons.

Monkeys tend to fend for themselves in the quest for food. However, among human foragers, men generally hunt and women gather. Men and women bring resources back to the camp and share them. Older people who did not engage in the food quest receive food from younger adults. Everyone shares the meat from a large animal. Nourished and protected by younger band members, elders live past the reproductive age and are respected for their knowledge and experience. The amount of information stored in a human band is far greater than that in any other primate society. Sharing, cooperation, and language are intrinsic to information storage.

Among all primates except *Homo,* most food comes from individual foraging, usually for vegetation. The rarity of meat eating and the concentration on vegetation represent a fundamental difference between most apes and humans. Through millions of years of adaptation to an omnivorous diet, hominids have come to rely on one of several reasons chimpanzees ate flesh.

Dr. Stanford builds on this finding, saying that male chimpanzees often hunt as a way to finance their sexual barter when traveling with sexually receptive females. And the more such receptive females are present, the more likely a group of chimpanzees will hunt.

Time after time, Dr. Stanford documented how male chimpanzees dangle a dead red colobus monkey in front of a sexually swollen female, sharing only after first mating. He said that human sexual relationships could have been just as material-based . . .

Female chimpanzees are sexually promiscuous, with or without meat, copulating with more than a dozen males each day. But Dr. Stanford believes the attraction of flesh, consumption of which is shown by Dr. McGrew to be linked to the survival of offspring, could give lower-ranking males a better chance at matings; or that it could be "the difference between getting lots of sex and getting lots and lots of sex.". . .

Most hunting is seasonal at Gombe, Dr. Stanford found. It takes place during the dry summer months, a time when females are generally sexually receptive and when the food supply of fruit, leaves and nuts is scarce. During the winter, however, when sex is not usually an issue and food is more plentiful, chimpanzees can go several weeks without a morsel of monkey, baboon, small antelope or baby bush pig.

But male chimpanzees sometimes hunt at Gombe when no sexually receptive females are nearby, primatologists report. This is when chimpanzee politics comes into play.

Dr. Toshisada Nichida, a Japanese zoologist, described in 1992 a primate patronage system that would be right at home in the back rooms of Capitol Hill. A male [troop] leader in the Mahale Mountains of Tanzania doled out meat portions to allies, while denying the rewards to enemies. At Gombe, Dr. Stanford observed similar politicking at meal time . . .

Archeological evidence indicates that humans hunted at least 2.5 million years ago, based on stone meat-cutting tools found at Olduvai Gorge in Tanzania. But Dr. Stanford said that from what he learned from watching chimpanzees, he believed that humans were avid hunters nearly three million years earlier than remains suggested.

"The amount of meat chimps eat suggests that early hominids, who would have presumably been more intelligent and better able to coordinate their actions and hunt together, were probably eating as much meat as chimps or more," he said . . .

Dr. Stanford said it was unlikely that evidence to support his theory of early hominid hunting would ever be uncovered. To illustrate the point, he held the bone remains of five colobus monkeys (equal to about 60 pounds) in the palm of his hand—leftovers collected after a chimp feast.

"Chimps eat hair, skin, bones—there's nothing left," Dr. Stanford said. "Early hominids probably ate everything and you wouldn't find it in the fossil record."

Source: Verne G. Kopytoff, "Meat Viewed as Staple of Chimp Diet and Mores," *New York Times*, June 27, 1995, pp. B5–B6.

hunting, meat eating, food sharing, and cooperative behavior. These are universal features in human adaptive strategies.

Mating and Kinship

Another difference between humans and other primates has to do with mating. Among baboons and chimpanzees, most sexual intercourse tends to occur when females "go into heat" or enter **estrus,** a period of sexual receptivity. Estrus is signaled by swelling and coloration of the vaginal skin. Receptive females form temporary bonds with males. Among humans, sexual activity occurs throughout the year. Related to this more constant sexuality, all human societies have some form of marriage. Marriage gives mating a reliable basis and grants to each spouse special, though not always exclusive, sexual rights in the other.

Marriage creates another major contrast between humans and nonhumans: exogamy and kinship systems. Most cultures have rules of exogamy requiring marriage outside one's kin or local group. Coupled with the recognition of kinship, exogamy confers adaptive advantages. It creates ties between the spouses' groups of origin. Their children have relatives, and therefore

beyond the classroom

A Behavioral Ecology Study of Two Lemur Species

BACKGROUND INFORMATION

Student 1:	*Jennifer Burns*
Year in School/Major:	*Senior/Anthropology*
Future Plans:	*Field work/graduate school*
Student 2:	*Chris Howard*
Year in School/Major:	*Post-undergraduate/Anthropology*
Future Plans:	*Graduate school*
Supervising Professors:	*Dr. Deborah Overdorff, Dr. Beth Erhart*
Department:	*Anthropology*
School:	*University of Texas at Austin*
Project Title:	*A Behavioral Ecology Study of Two Lemur Species*

Lemurs are endangered prosimians confined to the island of Madagascar. In this and the next account, pay attention to the problems and pitfalls of primatological research. How would the logistics of studying a baboon or gorilla troop differ from the field methods described here?

Simply the word "Madagascar" conjures up brilliant images of an exotic land. Having broken off from Africa approximately 165 million years ago, this magical island mesmerizes the scientific community as 85–90 percent of its flora and fauna is endemic.

Within the heart of southeastern Madagascar, Ranomafana National Park protects 41,600 hectares of montane rain forest. The park was established at the close of the 1980s and has done a remarkable job of integrating the needs of the Malagasy people with *this* segment of rain forests' need for protection from further destruction. A developed infrastructure helps the park to balance local and foreign tourist groups as well as scientific research. With one main research site and two bush camp research sites, many fruitful studies are conducted over a wide variety of flora and fauna.

The aims of our project are to better understand the social dynamics and feeding ecology of two of the twelve species of lemurs living within Ranomafana National Park: the red-fronted lemur, *Eulemur fulvus rufus,* and sifaka species, *Propithecus diadema edwardsi.* For five days each week over a six-month period, behavioral and ecological data were collected on one group from each species. To aid with individual distinction and recognition, the members of each group were fitted with colored identification necklaces, with one collar of each group containing a radio transmitter. This radio-tracking device made it possible to locate the groups each morning. While these classic techniques are tremendously helpful, problems can often occur with the radio equipment. Heavy rainfall can waterlog the gear, and the rugged mountainous terrain adds strong echoes to the signal, making group location more difficult. When the radio fails, finding the groups can be nearly impossible, as they cover a tremendous area and can easily take days, *if* they are found at all.

These two species are of particular interest because of their many contrasts both physically and socially. In trying to more fully define and understand the implications of terms like "dominance," "leadership," "competition," "reproductive stress," and "male versus female roles" within varying lemur species, this study hopes to not only provide new insights, but also open the door to *new* questions.

Through millions of years of adaptation to an omnivorous diet, hominids have come to rely on gathering, hunting, and food sharing. Here, with the help of two boys, a hunter named Kgototxe of the Gwi San group in Botswana, southern Africa, will carry a roasted wild cat back to other members of their band.

allies, in two kin groups rather than just one. The key point here is that ties of affection and mutual support between members of different local groups tend to be absent among primates other than *Homo.* There is a tendency among primates to disperse at adolescence. Among chimps and gorillas, females tend to migrate, seeking mates in other groups. Both male and female gibbons leave home when they become sexually mature. Once they find mates and establish their own territories, ties with their natal groups cease. Among terrestrial monkeys, males leave the troop at puberty, eventually finding places elsewhere. The troop's core members are females. They sometimes form *uterine* groups made up of mothers, sisters, daughters, and sons that have not yet emigrated. This dispersal of males reduces the incidence of incestuous matings. Females mate with males born elsewhere, which join the troop at adolescence. Although kin ties are maintained between female monkeys, no close lifelong links are preserved through males.

Humans choose mates from outside the natal group, and usually at least one spouse moves. However, *humans maintain lifelong ties with sons and daughters.* The systems of kinship and marriage that preserve these links provide a major contrast between humans and other primates.

Sociobiology and Fitness

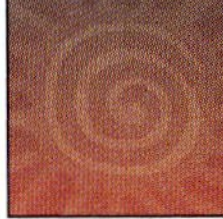

According to evolutionary theory, when the environment changes, natural selection starts to modify the *population*'s pool of genetic material. Natural selection has another key feature: the differential reproductive success of *individuals* within the population. **Sociobiology** studies the evolutionary basis of social behavior. It assumes that the genetic features of any species reflect a long history of differential reproductive success (that is, natural selection). In other words, biological traits of contemporary organisms have been transmitted across the generations because those traits enabled their ancestors to survive and reproduce more effectively than their competition.

Natural selection is based on *differential* reproduction. Members of the same species may compete to maximize their reproductive fitness—their genetic contribution to future generations. *Individual fitness* is measured by the number of direct descendants an individual has. Illustrating a primate strategy that may enhance individual fitness are cases in which male monkeys kill infants after entering a new troop. Destroying the offspring of other males, they clear a place for their own progeny (Hausfater and Hrdy 1984).

Besides competition, one's genetic contribution to future generations also can be enhanced by cooperation, sharing, and other apparently unselfish behavior. This is because of *inclusive fitness*—reproductive success measured by the genes one shares with relatives. By sacrificing for their kin—even if this means limiting their own

Feeding Behavior and Environmental Degradation in Lemurs

BACKGROUND INFORMATION

Student:	*Natalie Cummings*
Supervising Professor:	*Deborah Overdorff*
School:	*University of Texas at Austin*
Year in School/Major:	*Senior/Anthropology*
Future Plans:	*Graduate school*
Project Title:	*Feeding Behavior and Environmental Degradation in Lemurs*

I traveled to Madagascar as a research assistant in order to study the feeding ecology of the eastern gray bamboo lemur (*Hapalemur griseus griseus*). *H. griseus* is one of the three bamboo lemurs, whose diet consists mainly of bamboo. The main focus of the study centered on comparing the feeding habits between groups in a deforested site with groups in a more pristine area within Ranomafana National Park, located in the southeastern region of Madagascar. I became interested in this study for two reasons: (1) limited research has been conducted on this particular species, and therefore little is known about their behavior and ecology; and (2) having both deforested and pristine sites within the same park and the same species existing at each site gives the opportunity to study the effects of deforestation on their feeding ecology. Also, we are able to record if and how feeding behaviors change due to secondary growth.

Collecting accurate and reliable data was the hardest daily obstacle I encountered due to several reasons. First, *H. griseus* is gray and small-bodied, weighing in at 1 kilogram, which makes them difficult to see in a dense rain forest. Second, of the three groups followed, one group was unhabituated. It was therefore impossible to collect data until the habituation process was complete. Finally, the mountainous terrain of Ranomafana, coupled with the frequent treefalls and thick undergrowth, proved to be by far the greatest challenge. I often found myself entangled in the bamboo vines, losing sight of these quick and agile primates. Luckily, I was accompanied by a native guide who was in tune with the local flora and fauna and seldom lost track of our study groups.

One unforeseen aspect of observing *H. griseus* was the use of my auditory sense. Before my experience, I thought I'd be relying mainly on my vision, but after spending a little time chasing these animals I realized listening to them was equally important. For example, I was able to distinguish which part of the bamboo they were eating by listening to the sounds produced.

Although there were difficult times, I found this experience invaluable from a biological, as well as a cultural, experience. Not only did I learn a great deal about this species, but I also gained interest in many of the endemic species of Madagascar.

direct reproduction—individuals actually may increase their genetic contributions (their shared genes) to the future. Inclusive fitness helps us understand why a female might invest in her sister's offspring, or why a male might risk his life to defend his brothers. If self-sacrifice perpetuates more of their genes than direct reproduction does, it makes sense in sociobiological terms. Such a view can help us understand aspects of primate behavior and social organization.

Maternal care always makes sense in terms of reproductive fitness theory because females know their offspring are their own. But it's harder for males to be sure about paternity. Inclusive fitness theory predicts that males will invest most in offspring when they are surest the offspring are theirs. Gibbons, for example, have strict male–female pair bonding, which makes it almost certain that the offspring are those of both members of the pair. Thus we expect male gibbons to offer care and protection to their young, and they do. However, among species and in situations in which a male can't be sure about his paternity, it may make more sense to invest in a sister's offspring than in a mate's because the niece or nephew definitely shares some of that male's genes.

summary

1. Humans, apes, monkeys, and prosimians are primates. The primate order is subdivided into suborders, superfamilies, families, genera, species, and subspecies. Organisms in any subdivision (taxon) of a taxonomy are assumed to share more recent ancestry with each other than they do with organisms in other taxa. But it's sometimes hard to tell the difference between homologies, which reflect common ancestry, and analogies, biological similarities that develop through convergent evolution.

2. Prosimians are the older of the two primate suborders. Some 40 million years ago, anthropoids displaced prosimians from niches their ancestors once occupied. Tarsiers and lorises are prosimians that survived by adapting to nocturnal life. Lemurs survived on the isolated island of Madagascar.

3. Anthropoids include humans, apes, and monkeys. All share fully developed primate trends, such as depth and color vision. Other anthropoid traits include a shift in tactile areas to the fingers. The New World monkeys are all arboreal. Old World monkeys include both terrestrial species (e.g., baboons and macaques) and arboreal ones. The great apes are orangutans, gorillas, and chimpanzees. The lesser apes are gibbons and siamangs.

4. Gibbons and siamangs live in Southeast Asian forests. These apes are slight, arboreal animals whose mode of locomotion is brachiation. Sexual dimorphism, slight among gibbons, is marked among orangutans, which are confined to two Indonesian islands. Sexually dimorphic gorillas, the most terrestrial apes, are vegetarians confined to equatorial Africa. Two species of chimpanzees live in the forests and woodlands of tropical Africa. Chimps are less sexually dimorphic, more numerous, and more omnivorous than gorillas are. Terrestrial monkeys (baboons and macaques) live in troops. Baboon males, the troop's main protectors, are twice the size of females.

5. Deforestation poses a special risk for the primates. Most of the 190 living primate species are in tropical forests—in Africa, Asia, South America, and Central America. Primates also are endangered as humans hunt them for food (bush meat) and capture them for zoos and research.

6. There are significant differences between humans and other primates. But similarities are also extensive, and many differences are of degree rather than of kind. A unique concentration and combination of ingredients make humans distinct. Some of our most important adaptive traits are foreshadowed in other primates, particularly in the African apes. Primate behavior and social organization aren't rigidly programmed by the genes. The ability to learn, which is the basis of culture, is an adaptive advantage available to many nonhuman primates. Chimpanzees make tools for several purposes. They also hunt and share meat.

7. Important differences between humans and other primates remain. Aggression and dominance are characteristic of terrestrial monkeys. Sharing and cooperation are equally significant in human bands. Connected with sharing among humans is a traditional division of subsistence labor by age and gender. Only humans have systems of kinship and marriage that permit us to maintain lifelong ties with relatives in different local groups.

8. From the perspective of sociobiology, individuals in a population compete to increase their genetic contribution to future generations. Maternal care makes sense from this perspective because females can be sure their offspring are their own. Because it's harder for males to be sure about paternity, sociobiological theory predicts they will invest most in offspring when they are surest the offspring are theirs.

key terms

analogies Similarities arising as a result of similar selective forces; traits produced by convergent evolution.

anthropoids Members of Anthropoidea, one of the two suborders of primates; monkeys, apes, and humans are anthropoids.

arboreal Tree-dwelling; arboreal primates include gibbons, New World monkeys, and many Old World monkeys.

bipedal Two-footed; upright bipedalism is the characteristic human mode of locomotion.

brachiation Under-the-branch swinging; characteristic of gibbons, siamangs, and some New World monkeys.

convergent evolution Independent operation of similar selective forces; the process by which analogies are produced.

estrus Period of maximum sexual receptivity in female baboons, chimpanzees, and other primates, signaled by vaginal area swelling and coloration.

gibbons The smallest apes, natives of Asia; arboreal.

hominids Members of the zoological family that includes fossil and living humans; many scientists now include chimpanzees and gorillas in this family.

hominoids Members of the superfamily including humans and all the apes.

homologies Traits that organisms have jointly inherited from a common ancestor.

opposable thumb A thumb that can touch all the other fingers.

primatology The study of fossil and living apes, monkeys, and prosimians, including their behavior and social life.

prosimians The primate suborder that includes lemurs, lorises, and tarsiers.

sexual dimorphism Marked differences in male and female anatomy and temperament.

sociobiology Study of the evolutionary basis of social behavior.

taxonomy Classification scheme; assignment to categories (*taxa;* singular, *taxon*).

terrestrial Ground-dwelling; baboons, macaques, and humans are terrestrial primates; gorillas spend most of their time on the ground.

critical thinking questions

1. Give three examples of homologies between humans and apes. Can you think of behavioral as well as biological homologies?
2. Among the primates, give an example of an analogy produced through convergent evolution. Can you think of analogies involving animals other than primates?
3. What are the main trends in primate evolution? Compare a cat or dog with a monkey, ape, or human. What are the main differences in the sensory organs—those that have to do with vision, smell, and touch, for example?
4. Which seems most similar to human social organization, that of baboons, gorillas, or chimpanzees?
5. What are some examples of ways in which nonhuman primates rely on learning to adapt to their environment?
6. How do tools differ with respect to humans and other animals?
7. What environmental conditions might trigger predatory behavior among primates? How about humans?
8. Give three examples of major behavioral differences between humans and other primates.
9. Why is it significant that among primates, only humans maintain ties of affection and mutual support between different local groups?
10. How do sociobiology and fitness theory help us understand differences between female and male parental investment strategies?

suggested additional readings

Burton, F. D., and M. Eaton

1995 *The Multimedia Guide to Non-Human Primates.* Englewood Cliffs, NJ: Prentice Hall. A CD-ROM combining photos, illustrations, video, sound, and text—presenting over 200 species of nonhuman primates.

De Waal, F. B. M.

1997 *Bonobo: The Forgotten Ape.* Berkeley: University of California Press. Field-based study of rare and remote apes noted for their similarities to humans and their sexual behavior.

1998 *Chimpanzee Politics: Power and Sex among Apes,* rev. ed. Baltimore: Johns Hopkins University Press. Hierarchy, sex, and alliance among apes, mainly based on zoo observations.

Fedigan, L. M.

1992 *Primate Paradigms: Sex Roles and Social Bonds.* Chicago: University of Chicago Press. Focuses on sex roles in primate social organization.

Fossey, D.

1983 *Gorillas in the Mist.* Boston: Houghton Mifflin. Social organization of the mountain gorilla; basis of the popular film.

Goodall, J.

1986 *The Chimpanzees of Gombe: Patterns of Behavior.* Cambridge, MA: Belknap Press of Harvard University Press. Results of decades of research on primate behavior in Tanzania.

1996 *My Life with the Chimpanzees.* New York: Pocket Books. Popular account of the author's life among the chimps.

Hinde, R. A.
1983 *Primate Social Relationships: An Integrated Approach*. Sunderland, MA: Sinaeur Associates. Theoretical implications of aspects of social life among various primates.

Jolly, A.
1985 *The Evolution of Primate Behavior*, 2nd ed. New York: Macmillan. Good introduction.

Montgomery, S.
1991 *Walking with the Great Apes: Jane Goodall, Dian Fossey, Biruté Galdikas*. Boston: Houghton Mifflin. The stories of three primatologists who have worked with, and to preserve, chimpanzees, gorillas, and orangutans.

Morbeck, M. E., A. Galloway, and A. L. Zihlman, eds.
1997 *The Evolving Female: A Life-History Perspective*. Princeton, NJ: Princeton University Press. Primatology and human evolution from a female perspective.

Napier, J. R., and P. H. Napier
1985 *The Natural History of Primates*. Cambridge, MA: The MIT Press. Readable and well-illustrated introduction to the primates.

Roberts, J. L.
1995 *Dian Fossey*. San Diego, CA: Lucent Books. Biography of the gorilla researcher and protector.

Russon, A. E., K. A. Bard, and S. Taylor Parker, eds.
1996 *Reaching into Thought: The Minds of the Great Apes*. New York: Cambridge University Press. Papers examining the intelligence of the apes.

Silverberg, J., and J. P. Gray, eds.
1992 *Aggression and Peacefulness in Humans and Other Primates*. New York: Oxford University Press. Papers on behavior of varied primates, with implications for humans.

Small, M. F.
1993 *Female Choices: Sexual Behavior of Female Primates*. Ithaca, NY: Cornell University Press. Sexual behavior and characteristics of female apes and monkeys.

Small, M. F., ed.
1984 *Female Primates: Studies by Women Primatologists*. New York: Liss. Differences in female strategies in various primate groups.

Smuts, B. B.
1985 *Sex and Friendship in Baboons*. New York: Aldine. Pair bonding, mutual support, and parental investment in baboon social organization, with implications for early human evolution.

Stanford, C. B.
1999 *The Hunting Apes: Meat Eating and the Origins of Human Behavior*. Princeton, NJ: Princeton University Press. The role of meat and hunting in sex and alliance among wild chimps.

Stanford, C. B., and H. T. Bunn, eds.
2001 *Meat-Eating and Human Evolution*. New York: Oxford University Press. Compendium of various recent studies.

Strum, S. C., and L. M. Fedigan, eds.
2000 *Primate Encounters: Models of Science, Gender, and Society*. Chicago: University of Chicago Press. The roles of males and females in primate social organization.

Swindler, D. R.
1998 *Introduction to the Primates*. Seattle: University of Washington Press. Up-to-date survey.

Wrangham, R. W., ed.
1994 *Chimpanzee Cultures*. Cambridge, MA: Harvard University Press.

Wrangham, R. W. and D. Peterson
1996 *Demonic Males: Apes and the Origins of Human Violence*. Boston: Houghton Mifflin. Aggression among the apes and what it says about human tendencies.

internet exercises

1. Primate Conflict: Go to the Living Link's video collection at Emory University's Center for the Advanced Study of Ape and Human Evolution website, **http://www.emory.edu/LIVING_LINKS/a/video.html,** and watch the Chimpanzee Conflict Movie, **http://www.emory.edu/LIVING_LINKS/sounds/ram_text/conflict_28k.ram.**
   a. What different kinds of aggression are presented in the movie?
   b. What are the different responses to aggression? Did these responses tend to escalate or terminate the aggressive behavior?
   c. Is aggressive behavior restricted to adults? Does it take on different forms in juveniles?
   d. Which of these aggressive behaviors and responses do humans share with the chimpanzees? For example, do humans use Bluff Display?

2. Endangered Primates: Go to the Living Link's video collection at Emory University's Center for the Advanced Study of Ape and Human Evolution website, **http://www.emory.edu/LIVING_LINKS/a/video.html,** and watch the African Bushmeat Crisis Movie, **http://www.emory.edu/LIVING_LINKS/sounds/ram_text/bushmeat.ram.**
   a. The filmmakers argue that killing primates is similar to murder. Do you agree?
   b. The filmmakers suggest that the roots of the problem lie in those who hunt gorillas, not in those who buy and consume them. Do you think that if Joseph stopped hunting, people would stop eating gorillas?
   c. What other steps would you suggest to help preserve the mountain gorilla populations in Africa?

See Chapter 4 on your CD-ROM for additional review and interactive exercises. See your McGraw-Hill Online Learning Center for more.

Chapter 5

Primate Evolution

CHAPTER OUTLINE

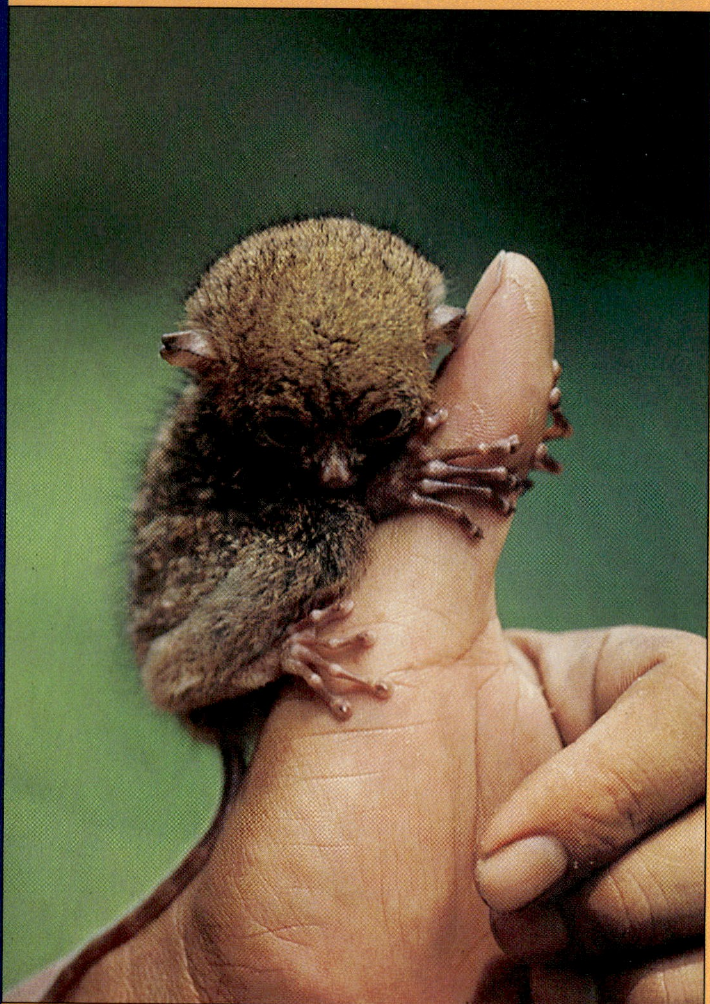

NYTIMES.COM NEWS BRIEFS

Tiny Fossil Animal May Link Lower Primates with Humans

by John Noble Wilford
March 16, 2000

Fossil bones of an animal no bigger than a shrew and weighing less than an ounce have been identified as belonging to the earliest known relative in the primate lineage that led to monkeys, apes and humans. The wee animal lived 45 million years ago in a humid rain forest in what is now China. It was probably nocturnal and solitary, and fed on insects and fruit. If not careful in its usual place up in the trees, this primate often wound up as an owl's midnight feast. In fact, some of the bones in question may well have been regurgitated by an owl after one such repast.

The paleontologists who announced the discovery yesterday said the fossil animals, named *Eosimias* for "dawn monkey," were the best evidence yet for fixing the time and place of one of the more fateful branchings in evolution. *Eosimias* appeared to be a transitional figure when lower primates, known as prosimians, went their separate way, developing into today's lemurs, lorises, bush babies and tarsiers, while the diverging higher primates, anthropoids, evolved into more prepossessing creatures, eventually including human beings.

"We have the first unambiguous evidence that is able to bridge the anatomical gap between lower and higher primates," said Dr. Daniel L. Gebo, a paleontologist at Northern Illinois University in DeKalb who was a member of the discovery team.

A close examination of the tiny ankle and foot bones, some the size of grains of rice, established that *Eosimias* is an extremely primitive member of the anthropoid lineage, Dr. Gebo and other scientists said. The shapes of the bones and structure of joints showed that this fossil species was able to walk on all four limbs on the tops of branches, much like living monkeys.

The lower primates are not built to be quadrupedal walkers. They cling to trees and leap from one to another. As anatomists can readily see, the heel bones of prosimians are longer than those of anthropoids, giving them leverage for their long leaps. All primates, whether lower or higher, are distinguished from other mammals by their larger brains, grasping hands and feet, nails instead of claws and eyes in the front of the skull . . .

The minute size and other primitive characteristics, Dr. Gebo said, "probably means we're getting close to the transition between higher and lower primates."

This was further evidence that, although the more immediate human forebears arose in Africa, their earliest primate ancestors appeared to come from Asia. Somehow primates then migrated to Africa . . .

Working at two sites, one a quarry 100 miles west of Shanghai and the other in Shanxi province along the Yellow River in central China, the American-Chinese expedition was unable to find any complete skeletons, but it found as many as 50 foot bones and many other lower limb bones . . .

"The most interesting aspect of these new foot bones is that they represent a mosaic," Dr. Gebo said in a statement issued by his university. "They possess primitive lower-primate features as well as several advanced or higher-primate characteristics." No other fossil primate at such an early time, he added, "has this interesting combination."

Source: http://www.nytimes.com/library/national/science/031600sci-animal-fossil.htm.

overview

The primate order evolved by exploiting new opportunities that arose at the end of the Mesozoic era. The age of reptiles yielded to the age of mammals—the Cenozoic era, which began some 65 million years ago. Flowering plants proliferated, along with the insects attracted to them and the animals that preyed on those insects. Primate traits like grasping hands and depth perception aided in the capture of insects and were adaptive in an arboreal environment.

By the Eocene epoch, primates had spread and diversified, mainly in Europe and North America, which were connected at that time. Among primates, the Eocene was the age of prosimians. By the end of the Eocene, the anthropoids had emerged; they eventually displaced the prosimians in most places. In the next epoch, the Oligocene, the New World monkeys split off from the catarrhines, the ancestors of Old World monkeys, apes, and humans.

The ensuing Miocene epoch, divided into Early, Middle, and Late, witnessed a fluorescence of proto-apes, an amazing variety unlike anything that survives in the contemporary world. Some 16 million years ago, Africa collided with Eurasia. The new land connection allowed African fauna, including apes, to spread into Europe and Asia, where the apes proliferated. The lines leading to the orangutan, on the one hand, and the African apes, on the other, split during the middle Miocene. The common ancestor of humans, chimps, and gorillas—as yet unidentified—lived during the late Miocene, some five to eight million years ago.

The Fossil Record

The fossil record is not a representative sample of all the species that have lived on earth. Some species and body parts are better represented than others are, for a variety of reasons. Hard parts, like bones and teeth, preserve better than soft parts, like flesh and skin. The chances of fossilization increase when remains are buried in a newly forming sediment, such as silt, gravel, or sand. Good places for bones to be buried in sediments include swamps, flood plains, river deltas, lakes, and caves. The species that inhabit such areas have a better chance to be preserved than do animals that live in other habitats. Fossilization is also favored in areas with volcanic ash, or where rock fragments eroding from rising highlands are accumulating in valleys or lake basins. Once remains do get buried, chemical conditions also must be right for fossilization to occur. If the sediment is too acidic, even bone and teeth will dissolve. The study of the processes that affect the remains of dead animals is called **taphonomy,** from the greek *taphos,* which means "tomb." Such processes include scattering by carnivores and scavengers, distortion by various forces, and the possible fossilization of the remains.

Fossils comprise a very small sample of all the animals that have ever lived. This sample is biased, with some areas and times much better represented than others are. Conditions favoring fossilization open special "time windows" for certain places and times, like western Kenya from 18 to 14 **m.y.a.**—million years ago. Because western Kenya was geologically active then, it has a substantial fossil record. Between 12 and 8 m.y.a., the area was quieter geologically, and there are few fossils. After 8 m.y.a., another time window opens in the Rift Valley area of eastern Kenya. The East African highlands were rising, volcanoes were active, and lake basins were forming and filling with sediments. This time window extends through the present and includes many hominid fossils. Compared with East Africa, West Africa has been more stable geologically and has few time windows (Jolly and White 1995).

The conditions under which fossils are found also influence the fossil record. For example, fossils are more likely to be uncovered through erosion in arid areas than in wet areas. Sparse vegetation allows wind to scour the landscape and to uncover fossils. The fossil record has been accumulating longer and is more extensive in Europe than in Africa because civil engineering projects and fossil hunting have been going on longer in Europe than in Africa. A world map showing where fossils have been found does not indicate the true range of ancient animals. Such a map tells us more about ancient geological activity, modern erosion, or recent human activity—such as paleontological research or road building. In considering the primate fossil record, we'll see that different areas provide more abundant fossil evidence for different time periods. This doesn't necessarily mean that primates were not living elsewhere at the same time. For hominid fossils, for example, the fact that most of the earliest ones come from eastern Africa does not necessarily mean that comparable hominids did not also live in southern Africa then.

A swamp is a good place for bones to be buried in sediments. Here a female mammoth is represented sinking into the La Brea Tarpits in Los Angeles, California. What other locales and conditions favor fossilization?

The discussions of primate and human evolution therefore must be tentative because the fossil record "is woefully limited and spotty. That is why each significant find sets off a new spate of speculations—and often a new barrage of attacks on some previously dug and stoutly held trenches" (Fisher 1988*a*, p. 23). Much is subject to change as knowledge increases. Before considering our fossil ancestors, however, we need to review some techniques used to establish when they lived.

Dating the Past

Paleontology is the study of ancient life through the fossil record, and **paleoanthropology** is the study of ancient humans and their immediate ancestors. These fields have established a time frame, or *chronology,* for the evolution of life, including primates and humans. Scientists use several techniques to date fossils. These methods offer different degrees of precision and are applicable to different periods of the past.

Relative Dating

Chronology is established by assigning dates to geologic layers (strata) and to the material remains, such as fossils and artifacts, within them. Dating may be relative or absolute. **Relative dating** establishes a time frame in relation to other strata or materials, rather than absolute dates in numbers. Many dating methods are based on the geological study of **stratigraphy,** the science that examines the ways in which earth sediments accumulate in layers known as *strata* (singular, *stratum*). In an undisturbed sequence of strata, age increases with depth. Soil that erodes from a hillside into a valley covers, and is younger than, the soil deposited there previously. Stratigraphy permits relative dating. That is, the fossils in a given stratum are younger than those in the layers below and older than those in the layers above. We may not know the exact or absolute dates of the fossils, but we can place them in time relative to remains in other layers. Changing environmental forces, such as lava flows or the alternation of land and sea, cause different materials to be deposited in a given sequence of strata, which allows scientists to distinguish between the strata.

Remains of animals and plants that lived at the same time are found in the same stratum. Based on fossils found in stratigraphic sequences, the history of vertebrate life has been divided into three main eras. The *Paleozoic* was the era of ancient life—fishes, amphibians, and primitive reptiles. The *Mesozoic* was the era of middle life—reptiles, including the dinosaurs. The *Cenozoic* is the era of recent life—birds and mammals. Each era is divided into periods, and the periods are divided into epochs. (See Figure 5.1.)

Anthropologists are concerned with the Cenozoic era, which includes two periods: Tertiary and Quaternary. Each of these periods is subdivided into epochs. The Tertiary had five epochs: Paleocene, Eocene, Oligocene, Miocene, and Pliocene. The Quaternary includes just two epochs: Pleistocene and Holocene, or Recent. Figure 5.1 gives the approximate dates of these epochs. Sediments from the Paleocene epoch (65 to 54 m.y.a.) have yielded fossil remains of diverse small mammals, some possibly ancestral to the primates. Prosimianlike fossils abound in strata dating from the Eocene (54 to 36 m.y.a.). The first anthropoid fossils date to the mid- to late Eocene and early Oligocene (36 to 23 m.y.a.). Hominoids became widespread during the Miocene (23 to 5 m.y.a.), and hominids first appeared in the Pliocene (5 to 2 m.y.a.) (Figure 5.1).

When fossils are found within a stratigraphic sequence, scientists know their dates relative to fossils in other strata; this is relative dating. When fossils are found in a particular stratum, the associated geological features (such as frost patterning) and remains of particular plants and animals offer clues about the climate at the time of deposition.

Besides stratigraphic placement, another technique of relative dating is fluorine absorption analysis. Bones fossilizing in the same ground for the same length of time absorb the same proportion of fluorine from the local groundwater. Fluorine analysis uncovered a famous hoax involving the so-called Piltdown man, once considered an unusual and perplexing human ancestor (Winslow and Meyer 1983). The Piltdown "find," from England, turned out to be the jaw of a young orangutan attached to a *H. sapiens* skull. Fluorine analysis showed the association to be false. The skull had much more fluorine than the jaw—impossible if they had come from the same

Figure 5.1
Geological Time Scales

Era	Period	
Cenozoic	Quaternary	1.8 m.y.a.
	Tertiary	65 m.y.a.
Mesozoic	Cretaceous	146 m.y.a.
	Jurassic	208 m.y.a.
	Triassic	245 m.y.a.
Paleozoic	Permian	286 m.y.a.
	Carboniferous	360 m.y.a.
	Devonian	410 m.y.a.
	Silurian	440 m.y.a.
	Ordovician	505 m.y.a.
	Cambrian	544 m.y.a.
Proterozoic	Neoproterozoic	900 m.y.a.
	Mesoproterozoic	1,600 m.y.a.
	Paleoproterozoic	2,500 m.y.a.
Archaean		3,800 m.y.a.
Hadean		4,500 m.y.a.

The geological time scale, based on stratigraphy. Eras are subdivided into periods, and periods, into epochs. In what era, period, and epoch did *Homo* originate?

Figure 5.1

Geological Time Scales—Concluded

Era	Period	Epoch	Climate and Life Forms
Cenozoic	Quaternary	Holocene 11,000 B.P.	Transition to agriculture; emergence of states
		Pleistocene 1.8 m.y.a.	Climatic fluctuations, glaciation; *Homo, A. boisei*
	Tertiary	Pliocene 5 m.y.a.	*A. robustus, A. africanus, A. afarensis, A. anamensis, Ardipithecus ramidus*
		Miocene 23 m.y.a.	Cooler and drier grasslands spread in middle latitudes; Africa collides with Eurasia (16 m.y.a.); *Afropithecus, Ramapithecus, Sivapithecus*
		Oligocene 38 m.y.a.	Cooler and drier in the north; anthropoids in Africa (Fayum); separation of catarrhines and platyrrhines; separation of hylobatids from pongids and hominids
		Eocene 54 m.y.a.	Warm tropical climates become widespread; modern orders of mammals appear; prosimianlike primates; anthropoids appear by late Eocene
		Paleocene 65 m.y.a.	First major mammal radiation

Periods and Epochs of the Cenozoic Era.

individual and had been deposited in the same place at the same time. Someone had fabricated Piltdown man in an attempt to muddle the interpretation of the fossil record. (The attempt was partially successful—it did fool some scientists.)

Absolute Dating

The previous section reviewed relative dating based on stratigraphy and fluorine absorption analysis. Fossils also can be dated more precisely, with dates in numbers (**absolute dating**), by several methods. For example, the ^{14}C, or carbon-14, technique is used to date organic remains. This is a *radiometric* technique (so called because it measures radioactive decay). ^{14}C is an unstable radioactive isotope of normal carbon, ^{12}C. Cosmic radiation entering the earth's atmosphere produces ^{14}C, and plants take in ^{14}C as they absorb carbon dioxide. ^{14}C moves up the food chain as animals eat plants and as predators eat other animals.

With death, the absorption of ^{14}C stops. This unstable isotope starts to break down into nitrogen (^{14}N). It takes 5,730 years for half the ^{14}C to change to nitrogen; this is the half-life of ^{14}C. After another 5,730 years only one-quarter of the original ^{14}C will remain. After yet another 5,730 years only one-eighth will be left. By measuring the proportion of ^{14}C in organic material, scientists can determine a fossil's date of death, or the date of an ancient campfire. However, because the half-life of ^{14}C is short, this dating technique is less dependable for specimens older than 40,000 years than it is for more recent remains.

Fortunately, other radiometric dating techniques are available for earlier periods. One of the most widely used is the potassium-argon (K/A) technique. ^{40}K is a radioactive isotope of potassium that breaks down into argon-40, a gas. The half-life of ^{40}K is far longer than that of ^{14}C—1.3 *billion* years. With this method, the *older* the specimen, the more reliable the dating. Furthermore, whereas ^{14}C dating can be done only on organic remains, K/A dating can be used only for inorganic substances: rocks and minerals.

^{40}K in rocks gradually breaks down into argon-40. That gas is trapped in the rock until the rock is

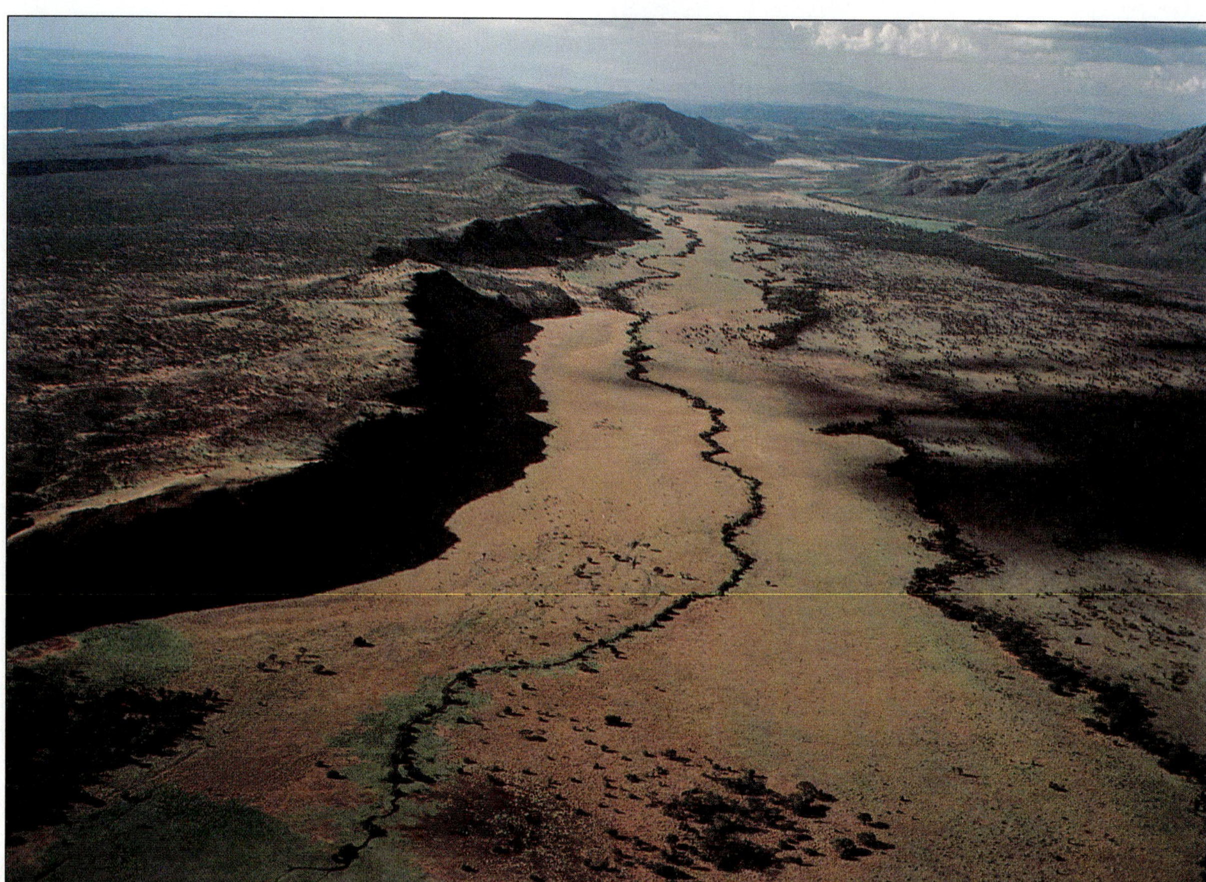

East Africa's Great Rift Valley runs through Ethiopia, Kenya (shown here), and Tanzania. What dating technique(s) can be used in this volcanic region?

intensely heated (as with volcanic activity), at which point it may escape. When the rock cools, the breakdown of potassium into argon resumes. Dating is done by reheating the rock and measuring the escaping gas.

In Africa's Great Rift Valley, which runs down eastern Africa and in which early hominid fossils abound, past volcanic activity permits K/A dating. In studies of strata containing fossils, scientists find out how much argon has accumulated in rocks since they were last heated. They then determine, using the standard ^{40}K deterioration rate, the date of that heating. Considering volcanic rocks at the top of a stratum with fossil remains, scientists establish that the fossils are *older than,* say, 1.8 million years. By dating the volcanic rocks below the fossil remains, they determine that the fossils are *younger than,* say, 2 million years. Thus the age of the fossils and of associated material is set at between 2 million and 1.8 million years. Notice that absolute dating is that in name only; it may give ranges of numbers rather than exact dates.

Many fossils were discovered before the advent of modern stratigraphy. Often we can no longer determine their original stratigraphic placement. Furthermore, fossils aren't always discovered in volcanic layers. Like ^{14}C dating, the K/A technique applies to a limited period of the fossil record. Because the half-life of ^{40}K is so long, the technique cannot be used with materials less than 500,000 years old.

Other radiometric dating techniques can be used to cross-check K/A dates, again by using minerals surrounding the fossils. One such method, *uranium series dating,* measures fission tracks produced during the decay of radioactive

Table 5.1
Absolute Dating Techniques

Technique	Abbreviation	Materials Dated	Effective Time Range
Carbon-14	^{14}C	Organic materials	Up to 40,000 years
Potassium-argon	K/A and ^{40}K	Volcanic rock	Older than 500,000 years
Uranium series	^{238}U	Minerals	Between 1,000 and 1,000,000
Thermoluminescence	TL	Rocks and minerals	Between 5,000 and 1,000,000
Electron spin resonance	ESR	Rocks and minerals	Between 1,000 and 1,000,000

uranium (^{238}U) into lead. Two other radiometric techniques are especially useful for fossils that cannot be dated by ^{14}C (up to 40,000 B.P.) or ^{40}K (more than 500,000 B.P.). These methods are *thermoluminescence* (TL) and *electron spin resonance* (ESR). Both TL and ESR measure the electrons that are constantly being trapped in rocks and minerals (Shreeve 1992). Once a date is obtained for a rock found associated with a fossil, the date also can be applied to that fossil. The time spans for which the various absolute dating techniques are applicable are summarized in Table 5.1.

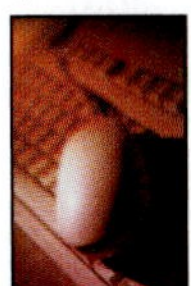

Early Primates

Primates have lived during the past 65 million years, the Cenozoic era, which has seven epochs (see Figure 5.1). When the Mesozoic era ended, and the Cenozoic began, some 65 million years ago, North America was connected to Europe, but not to South America. (The Americas joined some 20 million years ago.) Over millions of years, the continents have "drifted" to their present locations, carried along by the gradually shifting plates of the Earth's surface (Figure 5.2).

During the Cenozoic, most land masses had tropical or subtropical climates. The Mesozoic era had ended with a massive worldwide extinction of plants and animals, including the dinosaurs. Thereafter, mammals replaced reptiles as the dominant large land animals. Trees and flowering plants soon proliferated, supplying arboreal foods for the primates that eventually evolved to fill the new niches.

According to the **arboreal theory,** primates became primates by adapting to arboreal life. The primate traits and trends discussed in the last chapter developed as adaptations to life high up in the trees. A key feature was the importance of sight over smell. Changes in the visual apparatus were adaptive in the trees, where depth perception facilitated leaping. Grasping hands and feet were used to crawl along slender branches. Grasping feet anchored the body as the primate reached for foods at the ends of branches. Early primates probably had omnivorous diets based on foods available in the trees, such as flowers, fruits, berries, gums, leaves, and insects. The early Cenozoic era witnessed a proliferation of flowering plants, attracting insects that were to figure prominently in many primate diets.

Matt Cartmill (1974, 1992) notes that although primate traits work well in the trees, they aren't the only possible adaptations to arboreal life. Squirrels, for example, do just fine with claws and snouts and without binocular vision. Something else must have figured in primate evolution, and Cartmill suggests a **visual predation hypothesis.** This is the idea that binocular vision, grasping hands and feet, and reduced claws developed because they facilitated the capture of insects, which figured prominently in the early primate diet. According to this theory, early primates first adapted to bushy forest undergrowth and low tree branches, where they foraged for fruits and insects. Particularly in pursuing insects, early primates would have relied heavily on vision. Close-set eyes permitted binocular vision and depth perception. Such a visual apparatus would have allowed early primates to judge the distance to their prey without moving their heads. They would have hunted like cats

Figure 5.2
Placement of Continents at the End of the Mesozoic

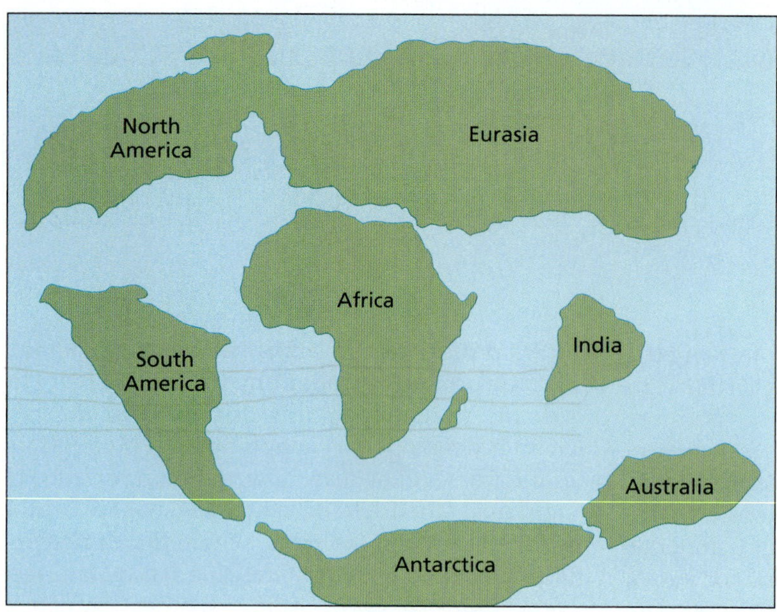

When the Mesozoic era ended, and the Cenozoic began, some 65 million years ago, North America was connected to Europe, but not to South America.

According to one theory, binocular vision and manipulative hands developed among primates because they facilitated the capture of insects. What is this theory called? Here a Colombian squirrel monkey uses its hands and eyes to eat a katydid.

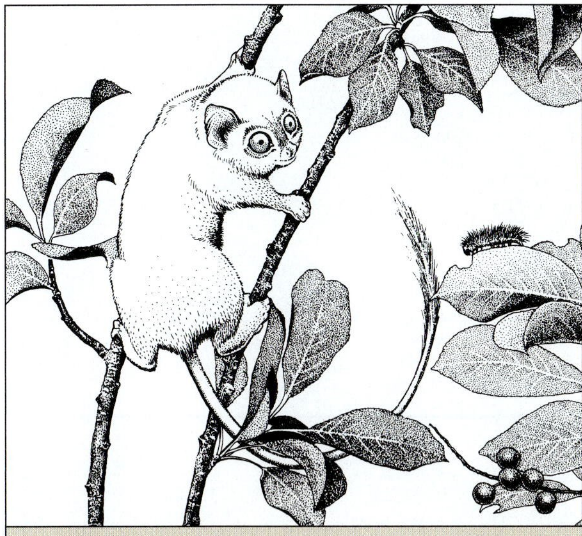

Compare this line drawing reconstruction of *Shoshonius*, a member of the Eocene omomyid family, with a modern tarsier from Mindanao in the Philippines. What similarities and differences do you notice?

and owls. The snout would have been reduced, with a less acute sense of smell, as the eyes came closer together. Early primates would have held on with their grasping feet as they snared their prey with their hands. Several living prosimians retain the small body size and insectivorous diet that may have characterized the first primates. Jurmain (1997) suggests that although key primate traits might have evolved first for life in the lower branches, such traits would have become even more adaptive when bug snatching was done higher up in the trees.

Early Cenozoic Primates

There is considerable fossil evidence that a diversified group of primates lived, mainly in Europe and North America, during the second epoch of the Cenozoic, the Eocene. On that basis it is likely that the earliest primates lived during the first epoch of the Cenozoic, the Paleocene (65–54 m.y.a.). The status of several fossils as possible Paleocene primates has been debated. As there is no consensus on this matter, such fossils are not discussed here.

The first fossil forms clearly identified as primates lived during the Eocene epoch (54–38 m.y.a.) in North America, Europe, Africa, and Asia. They reached Madagascar from Africa late in the Eocene. The ancestral lemurs must have traveled across the Mozambique Channel, which was narrower then than it is now, on thick mats of vegetation. Such naturally formed "rafts" have been observed forming in East African rivers, then floating out to sea.

In primate evolution, the Eocene was the age of the prosimians, with at least 60 genera in two main families (*Adapidae* and *Omomyidae*). The widely distributed **omomyid** family lived in North America, Europe, and Asia. The omomyids were squirrel-sized. But unlike squirrels they had grasping hands and feet, used to manipulate objects and to climb by encircling small branches. Early members of the omomyid family may be ancestral to all anthropoids. Later ones may be ancestral to tarsiers.

The **adapid** family was probably ancestral to the lemur–loris line. The only major difference between the Eocene adapids, such as *Smilodectes*, shown in the photo on page 124, and today's lemurs and lorises is that the latter have a dental comb (see Figure 5.3). This structure is formed from the incisor and canine teeth of the lower jaw.

Sometime during the Eocene, ancestral anthropoids branched off from the prosimians by becoming more diurnal (active during the day) and by strengthening the trend favoring vision over smell. Some Eocene prosimians had larger

Figure 5.3
A Dental Comb

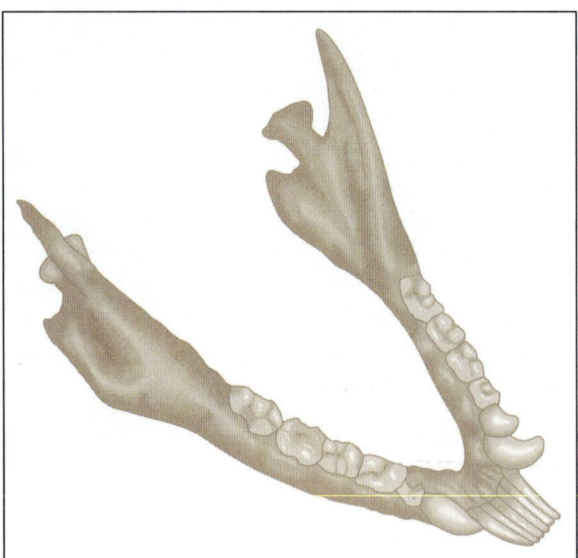

Source: Robert Jurmain and Harry Nelson, *Introduction to Physical Anthropology,* 6th ed. (Minneapolis: West Publishing, 1994), p. 210.

A dental comb is a derived trait present among contemporary lemurs and lorises but absent in Eocene adapids such as *Smilodectes.*)

brains and eyes, and smaller snouts, than others did. These were the ancestors of the anthropoids. Anthropoid eyes are rotated more forward when compared with lemurs and lorises. Also, anthropoids have a fully enclosed bony eye socket, which lemurs and lorises lack. And unlike lemurs and lorises, anthropoids lack a rhinarium, a moist nose continuous with the upper lip. Anthropoids have a dry nose, separate from the upper lip. Another distinguishing anthropoid feature has to do with molar cusps—bumps on the teeth. The primitive number of cusps on mammalian lower molars is six. The anthropoids have lost one or two cusps on their lower molars, so as to have four or five.

The oldest probable anthropoid discovered so far is *Eosimias,* from the Eocene of China (see

Smilodectes was a member of the lemurlike adapid family, which lived during the Eocene. Compare this drawing reconstructing a *Smilodectes* from Wyoming with a modern ring-tailed lemur from Madagascar.

chapter opener). The oldest definite anthropoid is *Catopithecus*, from the late Eocene of Egypt. By the end of the Eocene, many prosimian species had become extinct, reflecting competition from the first anthropoids.

Oligocene Anthropoids

During the Oligocene epoch (38–23 m.y.a.), anthropoids became the most numerous primates. Most of our knowledge of early anthropoids is based on fossils from Egypt's Fayum deposits. This area is a desert today, but 36–31 million years ago it was a tropical rain forest.

The anthropoids of the Fayum lived in trees and ate fruits and seeds. Compared with prosimians, they had fewer teeth, reduced snouts, larger brains, and increasingly forward-looking eyes. Of the Fayum anthropoid fossils, the *parapithecid* family is the more primitive and is perhaps ancestral to the New World monkeys. The parapithecids were very small (two to three pounds), with similarities to living marmosets and tamarins, small South American monkeys. One genus of this group, *Apidium,* is one of the most common fossils in the Fayum beds.

The *propliopithecid* family seems ancestral to the catarrhines—Old World monkeys, apes, and humans. This family includes *Aegyptopithecus,* which at 13–18 pounds, was the size of a large domestic cat. The propliopithecids share with the later catarrhines a distinctive dental formula: 2.1.2.3, meaning two incisors, one canine, two premolars, and three molars. (The formula is based on one-fourth of the mouth, either the right or left side of the upper or lower jaw.) The more primitive primate dental formula is 2.1.3.3. Most other primates, including prosimians and New World monkeys, have the second formula, with three premolars instead of two. Besides the Fayum, Oligocene deposits with primate bones also have been found in North and West Africa, southern Arabia, China, Southeast Asia, and North and South America.

The Oligocene was a time of major geological and climatic change. North America and Europe separated and became distinct continents. The Great Rift Valley system of East Africa formed. India drifted into Asia. A cooling trend began, especially in the Northern Hemisphere, where primates disappeared.

Miocene Hominoids

The earliest hominoid fossils date to the Miocene epoch (23–5 m.y.a.), which is divided into three parts: lower, middle, and upper or late. The early Miocene (23–16 m.y.a.) was a warm and wet period, when forests covered East Africa. Recall from the last chapter that *Hominoidea* is the superfamily that includes fossil and living apes and humans. For simplicity's sake, the earliest hominoids are here called proto-apes, or simply apes. Although some of these may be ancestral to living apes, none is identical, or often even very similar, to modern apes.

Proconsul

The superfamily known as *Pliopithecoidea* includes several species of the genus ***Proconsul.*** The *Proconsul* group represents the most abundant and successful anthropoids of the early Miocene. This group lived in Africa and includes three species: *Proconsul* (*P.*) *africanus, P. nyanzae,* and *P. major.* Possibly descended from the Oligocene propliopithecids, these early Miocene proto-apes had teeth with similarities to those of living apes. But their skeleton below the neck was more monkey-like. Some *Proconsul* species were the size of a small monkey; others, the size of a chimpanzee, usually with marked sexual dimorphism. Their dentition suggests they ate fruits and leaves.

Their skulls were more delicate than those of modern apes, and their legs were longer than their arms—more like monkeys. *Proconsul* probably moved through the trees like a monkey—on four limbs—and lacked the capacity for suspension and brachiation displayed by modern apes. *Proconsul* probably contained the last common ancestor shared by the Old World monkeys and the apes. By the middle Miocene, *Proconsul* had been replaced by Old World monkeys and apes.

Fossils of Miocene monkeys and prosimians are rare; ape fossils are much more common. Like many living apes, those of the Miocene were forest dwellers and fruit eaters. They lived in areas that, as the forests retreated, monkeys would eventually colonize. In the late Miocene, monkeys became the most common anthropoid in the Old World (except for humans, eventually).

Why did the Old World monkeys thrive as the Miocene apes faded? The probable answer was the monkeys' superior ability to eat leaves. Leaves are easier to get than fruits, which are typical ape foods. As the forests retreated at the end of the Miocene, most apes were restricted to the remaining tropical rain forests in areas of (mainly West) Africa and Southeast Asia. Monkeys survived over a wider area. They did so because they could process leaves effectively. Monkey molars developed *lophs:* ridges of enamel that run from side to side between the cusps of the teeth. Old World monkeys have two such lophs, so their molars are called *bilophodont.* Such lophs slice past each other like scissor blades, a good way to shear a leaf.

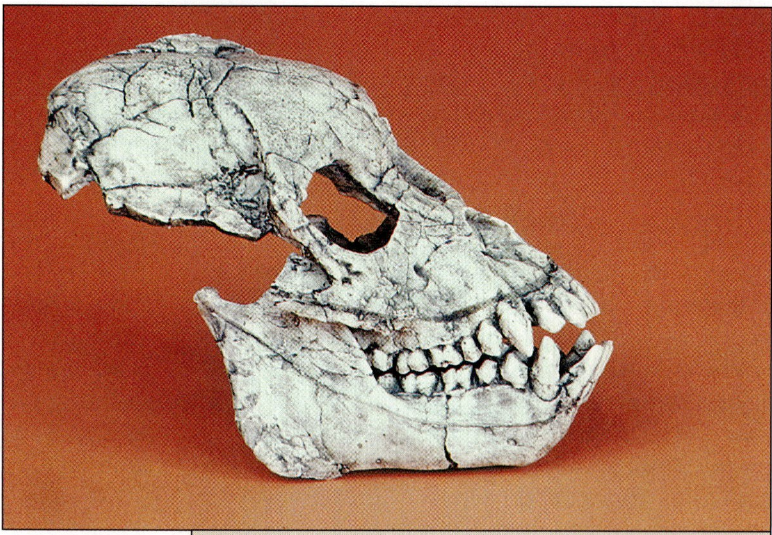

A skull of *Proconsul africanus* from the Kenya National Museum. Why might it be significant that *Proconsul* had all the primitive traits shared by apes and Old World monkeys and none of the derived traits of either?

Some species of *Proconsul* may have been ancestral to the living African apes. *Proconsul* also may be ancestral to the Old World monkeys. *Proconsul* had all the primitive traits shared by apes and Old World monkeys and none of the derived traits of either. *Primitive* traits are those passed on unchanged from an ancestor, such as the five-cusped molars of the apes, which are inherited from an old anthropoid ancestor. *Derived* traits are those that develop in a particular taxon after they split from their common ancestor with another taxon. Examples are bilophodont molars among Old World monkeys. The Old World monkeys have derived bilophodont molars and primitive quadrupedal bodies. The apes have primitive molars and derived brachiating bodies. *Proconsul* had both primitive teeth and a primitive quadrupedal body.

Afropithecus and Kenyapithecus

During the early Miocene, Africa was cut off by water from Europe and Asia. But during the middle Miocene, Afro-Arabia drifted into Eurasia, providing a land connection between the three continents. Migrating both ways—out of and into Africa—after 16 m.y.a. were various animals, including hominoids. Proto-apes were the most common primates of the middle Miocene (16–10 m.y.a.). Over 20 species have been discovered. (See Figure 5.4.) Their teeth retain the primitive anthropoid five-cusped molar pattern.

During the middle Miocene, the hominoids spread widely, in Europe, Asia, and Africa. East African apes of the middle Miocene include *Afropithecus, Equatorius,* and two species of *Kenyapithecus,* one earlier, one later. *Afropithecus* is a large Miocene hominoid from northern Kenya, dated to 18 to 16 m.y.a. (Leakey, Leakey, and Walker 1988). The *Afropithecus* remains consist of skull, jaw, and *postcranial* (below the head) fragments. *Afropithecus* seems to have been a slow-moving arboreal ape, with large projecting front teeth (similar to those of the modern African apes).

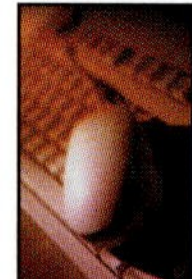

A recent discovery is a 15-million-year-old partial skeleton assigned to a new genus *Equatorius africanus.* The find, from Kenya, consists of upper incisors, a lower jaw with teeth, and bones from the arm, shoulder, collarbone, chest, wrists, fingers, and vertebrae, all belonging to a single male. In its skeleton *Equatorius* is more modern than earlier hominoids, suggesting that it used the ground more frequently than earlier hominoids did.

There are clear similarities between *Equatorius* and the earlier of the two species of *Kenyapithecus.* Based on these similarities, the discoverers of *Equatorius* have suggested that the earlier *Kenyapithecus* species should be reclassified as

Figure 5.4
The Geographic Distribution of Known Miocene Apes

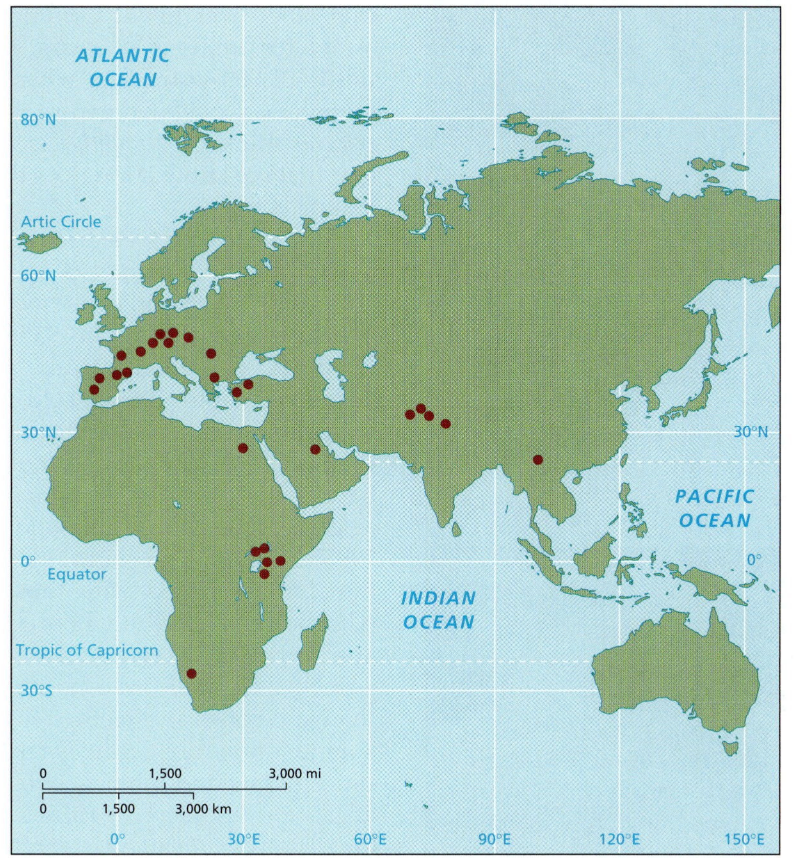

Source: Robert Jurmain and Harry Nelson, *Introduction to Physical Anthropology,* 6th ed. (Minneapolis: West Publishing, 1994), p. 302.

Equatorius. The two *Kenyapithecus* species that have been recognized traditionally are *K. africanus* (earlier) and *K. wickeri* (later). *Equatorius* and *K. africanus* represent an older pattern. *K. wickeri* illustrates a more modern pattern—more like today's great apes. *K. wickeri*'s dental pattern also is found in the teeth of an unnamed ape from a middle Miocene site in Turkey (Ward et al. 1999).

Equatorius and *Afropithecus* are probable *stem hominoids:* species somewhere on the evolutionary line near the origins of the modern ape group. Stem hominoids are considered too primitive to be the direct ancestors of living apes and humans.

Sivapithecus

Middle and late Miocene apes are often grouped in two families: *Ramapithecidae* and *Dryopithecidae.* The ramapithecids lived during the middle and late Miocene in Europe, Asia, and Africa. There are at least two ramapithecid genera: *Sivapithecus* and *Gigantopithecus.*

Sivapithecus fossils were first found in the Siwalik Hills of Pakistan. They include specimens formerly called "*Ramapithecus*" from that region, along with fossil apes from Turkey, China, and Kenya. The earlier forms of *Sivapithecus* that lived in Asia during the middle Miocene may represent the common ancestor of the orangutan and the African apes. A late Miocene find with an almost complete face from Pakistan's Potwar Plateau shows many similarities to the face of the modern orangutan. Because of facial and dental similarities, *Sivapithecus* of the late Miocene is now seen as ancestral to the modern orangutan. The orangutan line appears to have separated from the one leading to the African apes and humans more than 13 million years ago.

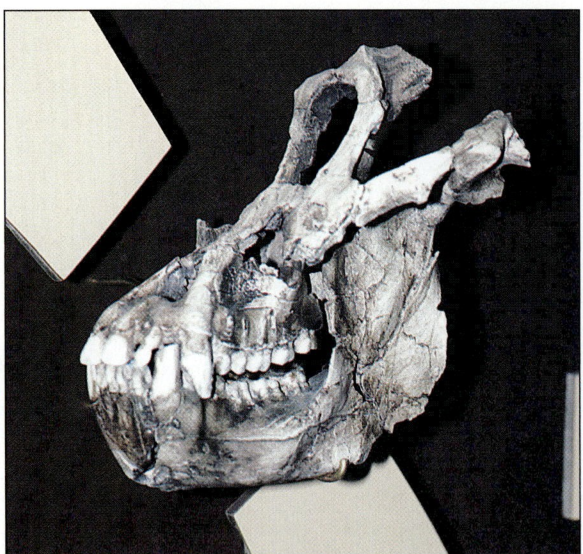

Compare this *Sivapithecus* side view with a contemporary female orangutan.

Hominids undoubtedly originated from a Miocene ape, but it is unclear which one it might be. "*Ramapithecus*" fossils from Asia and Africa were once viewed as a possible hominid ancestor, based on dental similarities with early hominids: thick tooth enamel, broad molars, and robust jaws. But scientists no longer see a close link between "*Ramapithecus*" or *Sivapithecus* and hominids. Their dental and jaw characteristics are widely shared with several other middle and late Miocene hominoids, including *Gigantopithecus.*

Gigantopithecus

Gigantopithecus is almost certainly the largest primate that ever lived. Confined to Asia, it persisted for millions of years, from the Miocene until 400,000 years ago, when it coexisted with members of our own genus, *Homo erectus.* Some people think *Gigantopithecus* is not extinct yet, and that we know it today as the yeti and bigfoot (Sasquatch).

Gigantopithecus was discovered in an unlikely place. In China, druggists sell fossils known as "dragon's" teeth and bones, which are ground up to be used medicinally. In 1935 the anthropologist G. H. R. von Koenigswald recognized that a "dragon's tooth" being sold by a Hong Kong druggist was actually that of an extinct ape. Since then, three jaw bones and more than 1,000 teeth have been recovered, some in drug stores, some at geologic sites in China and Vietnam (Pettifor 1995). Some such sites have *Gigantopithecus* remains associated with those of *Homo erectus* (Ciochon et al. 1990), who may have hunted the ape into extinction.

With a fossil record consisting of nothing more than jaw bones and teeth, it is difficult to say for sure just how big *Gigantopithecus* was. Based on ratios of jaw and tooth size to body size in other apes, various reconstructions have been made. One has *Gigantopithecus* weighing 1,200 pounds and standing 10 feet tall (Ciochon et al. 1990). Another puts the height at 9 feet and cuts the weight in half (Simons and Ettel 1970). All agree, however, that *Gigantopithecus* was the largest ape that ever lived. There have been at least two species of *Gigantopithecus: G. blacki,* the one that coexisted with *H. erectus* in China and Vietnam, and the much earlier (5 m.y.a.) *G. giganteus,* from northern India.

Given its size, *Gigantopithecus* must have been a ground-dwelling ape rather than an arboreal brachiator. Based on its jaw and dental patterns, it probably ate grasses, fruits, seeds, and especially bamboo. Very large animals, including China's giant panda, need an abundant food source such as bamboo. *Gigantopithecus* molars were adapted to a diet demanding cutting, crushing, and grinding of tough, fibrous matter. The molars are massive and flat, with low crowns and thick enamel. The premolars are also broad and flat, resembling molars.

A reconstruction of *Gigantopithecus* by Russell Ciochon and Bill Munns. Munns is shown here with "Giganto." What would be the likely environmental effects of a population of such large apes?

Could it be that *Gigantopithecus* did not go extinct, but survives today as the yeti ("abominable snowman" of the Himalayas) or Sasquatch (reportedly sighted in the Pacific Northwest)? Probably not. These creatures are based on legend, not fact. Survival of a species requires a sufficiently large breeding population. Given its dietary demands, *Gigantopithecus* would surely be detectable and have an observable environmental effect. Never have *Gigantopithecus* fossils or teeth been discovered in the Western Hemisphere. Nor are the areas of yeti and Sasquatch sightings ones in which *Gigantopithecus* would fit adaptively.

Dryopithecus

The **dryopithecids** lived in Europe during the middle and late Miocene. This group probably includes the common ancestor of the lesser apes (gibbons and siamangs) and the great apes. The first fossil member of the *Dryopithecus* group (*Dryopithecus fontani*) was found in France in 1856. The five-cusp and fissure pattern of its molar teeth, known as the Y-5 arrangement, is typical of the dryopithecids and of hominoids in general. Other dryopithecids have been found in Hungary, Spain, and China.

The continental drift that created the land bridge between Africa and Eurasia as the middle Miocene began also triggered mountain building and climatic change. With a cooler, drier climate, forest patches, dry woodlands, and grasslands replaced extensive tropical forests in East Africa and South Asia. The cooling trend continued through the late Miocene (10–5 m.y.a.). As grasslands spread, the stage was set for the divergence of the lines leading to humans, gorillas, and chimps.

Oreopithecus

Is upright bipedalism unique to hominids? A recent reanalysis of the fossil remains of an ancient Italian ape suggests otherwise. *Oreopithecus bambolii,* which lived seven to nine million years ago, apparently spent much of its time standing upright and shuffling short distances to collect fruit and other foods. This mode of locomotion contrasts with those of other fossil and living apes, which climb, brachiate, or knuckle walk. The first *Oreopithecus* fossils were found more than 100 years ago in central Italy. The taxonomic placement and evolutionary significance of *Oreopithecus* have been debated for decades. Similarities have been noted between this Italian ape and both the ramapithecid and the dryopithecid families.

Meike Kohler and Salvador Moya-Sola (1997) recently reanalyzed *Oreopithecus* remains in the Natural History Museum in Basel, Switzerland. These skeletal pieces represented the lower back, pelvis, leg, and foot. The scientists found the creature's lower body to be intermediate between those of apes and early hominids. Like early hominids, *Oreopithecus* had a lower back that

beyond the classroom

Maceration of a Canadian Lynx

BACKGROUND INFORMATION

Student:	*Barbara Hewitt*
Supervising Professor:	*Ariane Burke*
School:	*University of Manitoba*
Year in School/Major:	*Graduated in spring 2000/Anthropology*
Future Plans:	*Graduate school in forensic archaeology and osteology in England*
Project Title:	*Maceration of a Canadian Lynx*

What is maceration? How might it be useful to archaeologists and biological anthropologists? Would the ethical issues involved be different with primates versus the lynx described here?

In January 2000 I took a Practicum in Archaeology class. We were each to conduct our own research project. I chose to complete a maceration project for our faunal laboratory. The carcass I chose to work with was that of an infirm Canadian lynx, which had been euthanized and donated by the zoo. My objective was to examine the condition of its bones, to determine how its former health would be reflected in its skeleton.

By macerating an animal of known age, with a documented medical history and stable diet, we could compare this animal with one reared in the wild and look at differences in health. To macerate an animal, you remove the pelt and musculature from the bones, then soak the skeleton in chemicals to remove the grease. Once the bones are dry, they are dipped in preservative to keep them from decaying. I examined the bones and teeth for indications of ill health. In this particular lynx, advanced age had resulted in the ossification of many joints. This would have made extended movement quite painful. I was surprised by the damage to her joints. The excessive development of bone around the joints was like that in humans with osteoarthritis,

arched forward, a vertically aligned knee joint, and a similar pelvis. All these features are significant for upright walking. However, *Oreopithecus* had a unique foot. Its big toe splayed out 90 degrees from the other toes, all of which were shorter and straighter than those of modern apes. The foot's birdlike, tripod design was probably associated with a short, shuffling stride. Considering the entire **postcranium** (the area behind or below the head—the skeleton), there are substantial similarities between *Oreopithecus, Dryopithecus,* and the living great apes and hominids.

 A Missing Link?

The idea of "the missing link" goes back to an old notion called the "Great Chain of Being." This was the theological belief that various entities could be placed in a progressive chain. Among life forms, humans were at the top of the chain. Above them stood only angels and divinity. Below them were the apes, most clearly the African apes. But humans seemed too exalted, too different from those apes, to be directly linked to them. Between humans and the apes, there needed to be some form more progressive than the apes—some sort of missing link in the Great Chain of Being. Although modern science does not endorse the Great Chain of Being, it does recognize that our ancestor was a life form that differed from contemporary gorillas and chimps. Humans are not descended from gorillas or chimps. Rather, humans and the African apes share a common ancestor—a creature that was like the African apes in some ways, like humans in others. Over time all three species have evolved and have diverged from one another.

Human ancestors almost certainly diverged from those of chimps and gorillas late in the Miocene epoch, between eight and five million

which gave me a good idea of how painful and debilitating that disease can be. I detected a completely healed break in the right front humerus (upper arm bone), indicating that the animal had been healthy and well nourished when the break happened for the break to have healed so well. Only four teeth remained; this lynx could not eat solid food when she died.

The most challenging aspect of this project was that I worked unassisted. With only an instruction manual to follow, and an occasional consultation with my supervisor, I learned how to most effectively skin and deflesh an animal. The processing and analysis of the skeleton took far longer than I expected. A mistake during processing gave me a deeper appreciation for the people who analyze faunal remains in an archaeological context. The bones had been processed, and were laid out for drying, when another student moved them without moving the labels as well. After that, each bone had to be indentified again and laid out for relabeling.

The best part of this project was what it taught me about the development of bones and the talent of people who identify and work with them. In trying to reidentify the elements of the lynx skeleton, I realized exactly how tough it would be to pick up a bone (or fragment of a bone) from an archaeological site and determine which bone it is, what species it comes from, and the pathology of that particular animal or person. I think I learned more about the inherent difficulties of faunal identification in an archaeological context from that error than from any other aspect of the project.

The bones of the lynx that I macerated and processed have already proved useful to several faunal analysis classes, and to our zooarchaeologists when asked to identify bones brought to the department for identification.

years ago. The evolutionary line leading to orangutans probably split from the one leading to humans, chimps, and gorillas around 13 m.y.a. Drawing on the genus names *Homo, Gorilla,* and *Pan* (chimpanzee), I use the nickname "Hogopans" to refer to the ancestral population of late Miocene hominoids that eventually split three ways to produce humans, gorillas, and chimps. Hogopans is not a scientific term, just a convenient nickname, for the common ancestors of humans and the African apes.

No more than eight million years ago, the Hogopans diverged into three groups (Fisher 1988*a*). They split up by occupying different environmental niches. Separated in space, they became reproductively isolated from one another—leading to speciation. Ancestral gorillas eventually occupied forested zones of the mountains and lowlands of equatorial Africa. They developed a diet based on leaves, shoots, and bulk vegetation. Chimps evolved into frugivores (fruit eaters) in the forests and woodlands of Central Africa. Ancestral hominids spent more time in the open grasslands, or savannas, of eastern and southern Africa.

Where are the fossils of the Hogopans? As we have seen, Miocene deposits in Africa, Asia, and Europe have yielded an abundance of hominoid fossils (see Figure 5.4). Some of these may have evolved into modern apes and humans, but others became extinct. Hogopan identity remains a mystery. Do Hogopan fossils remain to be found? Perhaps they have been found already but have not been generally recognized as Hogopans.

Formerly, as mentioned, certain Asian fossils such as *Sivapithecus* and "*Ramapithecus*" were analyzed as possible Hogopans. Most scientists have now excluded these Miocene hominoids from the family tree of humans, chimps, and gorillas, considering *Sivapithecus* a probable ancestor of orangs. Discovered in Greece in 1989, the mid- to late-Miocene ape *Ouranopithecus*

The Great Chain of Being—a powerful visual metaphor for a divinely inspired universal hierarchy ranking all forms of higher and lower life. From Didacus Valades, *Rhetorica Christiana* (1579). What can you tell about the levels in the hierarchy?

lived in Europe some 9–10 m.y.a. This find may be linked to the living African apes and even to hominids (Begun, Ward, and Rose 1997). One trait that *Ouranopithecus* shares with the modern African apes is frontal sinuses.

Because of Miocene finds reported and analyzed during the past decade, some scientists are pondering a new scenario for ape and human evolution. As mentioned, during the middle Miocene, after a land bridge connected Africa and Eurasia, hominoids spread from Africa into Asia and Europe where they diversified into the groups discussed above. At the same time, the apes' forest habitat was shrinking in East Africa, and the number of ape species there along with it. In the middle and late Miocene, there appears to have been much more ape diversity in Europe and Asia than in Africa. During the late Miocene, Old World monkeys took over from the dwindling African apes in many areas they once inhabited. The new hominoid evolutionary scenario, proposed but hardly established, is that the line leading to the African apes and hominids may have emerged in Europe, with a hominoid such as *Ouranopithecus*. Then there would have been a return migration to Africa, where the diversification of the Hogopans actually took place between five and eight million years ago. Continued work by fossil hunters, analysts, and taxonomists may eventually reconcile the main issues involving the Miocene apes in relation to their living successors, to whom we turn in the next chapter.

summary

1. Anthropologists and paleontologists use stratigraphy and radiometric techniques to date fossils. Carbon-14 (^{14}C) dating is most effective with fossils less than 40,000 years old. Potassium-argon (K/A) dating can be used for fossils older than 500,000 years. ^{14}C dating is done on organic matter, whereas the K/A, ^{238}U, TL, and ESR dating techniques are used to analyze minerals that lie below and above fossils.
2. Primates have lived during the past 65 million years, the Cenozoic era, with seven epochs: Paleocene, Eocene, Oligocene, Miocene, Pliocene, Pleistocene, and Recent. The arboreal theory states that primates evolved by adapting to life high up in the trees. The visual predation hypothesis suggests that key primate traits developed because they facilitated the capture of insects.

3. The first fossils clearly identified as primates lived during the Eocene (54–38 m.y.a.), mainly in North America and Europe. The omomyid family may be ancestral to the anthropoids and the tarsier. The adapid family was probably ancestral to the lemur–loris line.
4. During the Oligocene (38–23 m.y.a.), anthropoids became the most numerous primates. The parapithecid family may be ancestral to the New World monkeys. The propliopithecid family, including *Aegyptopithecus,* seems ancestral to the catarrhines—Old World monkeys, apes, and humans.
5. The earliest hominoid fossils are from the Miocene (23–5 m.y.a.). Africa's *Proconsul* group contained the last common ancestor shared by the Old World monkeys and the apes. Since the middle Miocene Africa, Europe, and Asia have been connected. Proto-apes spread beyond Africa and became the most common primates of the middle Miocene (16–10 m.y.a.). East African apes of the middle Miocene include *Afropithecus, Equatorius,* and *Kenyapithecus.* Middle and late Miocene apes are often grouped in two families: *Ramapithecidae* and *Dryopithecidae.* The ramapithecids included at least two genera: *Sivapithecus* and *Gigantopithecus. Sivapithecus* was ancestral to the modern orangutan. Asia's *Gigantopithecus,* the largest primate ever to live, persisted for millions of years, finally coexisting with *Homo erectus.*
6. The dryopithecids, found mainly in Europe, probably include the common ancestor of the lesser apes (gibbons and siamangs) and the great apes. *Oreopithecus bambolii,* which lived 7–9 m.y.a., was an ape that stood upright while collecting fruit and other foods. There are skeletal similarities between *Oreopithecus, Dryopithecus,* and the living great apes and hominids. *Ouranopithecus,* which lived in Europe some 9–10 m.y.a., may be linked to chimps, gorillas, and humans. Anthropologists have yet to identify the fossils of the Hogopans, the common ancestors of humans, gorillas, and chimps. However, biochemical evidence strongly suggests that the Hogopans began to diverge in Africa during the late Miocene.

key terms

absolute dating Dating techniques that establish dates in numbers or ranges of numbers; examples include the radiometric methods of ^{14}C, K/A, ^{238}U, TL, and ESR dating.

adapids Early (Eocene) primate family ancestral to lemurs and lorises.

arboreal theory Theory that the primates evolved by adapting to life high up in the trees, where visual abilities would have been favored over the sense of smell, and grasping hands and feet would have been used for movement along branches.

dryopithecids Zoological ape family living in Europe during the middle and late Miocene; probably includes the common ancestor of the lesser apes (gibbons and siamangs) and the great apes.

m.y.a. Million years ago.

omomyids Early (Eocene) primate family found in North America, Europe, and Asia; early omomyids may be ancestral to all anthropoids; later ones may be ancestral to tarsiers.

Paleoanthropology Study of hominid and human life through the fossil record.

postcranium The area behind or below the head; the skeleton.

Proconsul Early Miocene genus of the pliopithecoid superfamily; the most abundant and successful anthropoids of the early Miocene; the last common ancestor shared by the Old World monkeys and the apes.

relative dating Dating technique, e.g., stratigraphy, that establishes a time frame in relation to other strata or materials, rather than absolute dates in numbers.

Sivapithecus Widespread fossil group first found in Pakistan; includes specimens formerly called "*Ramapithecus*" and fossil apes from Turkey, China, and Kenya; early *Sivapithecus* may contain the common ancestor of the orangutan and the African apes; late *Sivapithecus* is now seen as ancestral to the modern orang.

stratigraphy Science that examines the ways in which earth sediments are deposited in demarcated layers known as *strata* (singular, *stratum*).

taphonomy The study of the processes that affect the remains of dead animals, such as their scattering by carnivores and scavengers, their distortion by various forces, and their possible fossilization.

visual predation theory Theory that the primates evolved in lower branches and undergrowth by developing visual and tactile abilities to aid in hunting and snaring insects.

critical thinking questions

1. What are the pluses and minuses of relying on the fossil record to reconstruct evolution? Besides fossils, what are other lines of evidence for primate and human evolution?
2. What are the strengths and limitations of relative dating? Of absolute dating?
3. What are some unanswered questions about early primate evolution? What kinds of information would help provide answers?
4. Watch a squirrel move about. How do its movements compare with a monkey's movements? With a cat's movements? With your own? What do these observations suggest to you about that animal's ancestral habitat?
5. What is your opinion about the merits of the arboreal theory versus the visual predation theory of primate origins?
6. There have been reported sightings of "bigfoot" in the Pacific Northwest of North America and of the yeti (abominable snowman) in the Himalayas. What facts about apes lead you to question such reports?
7. Who were the Hogopans, when and where did they probably live, and what is the fossil evidence for their existence?

suggested additional readings

Begun, D. R., C. V. Ward, and M. D. Rose
1997 *Description: Function, Phylogeny, and Fossils: Miocene Hominoid Evolution and Adaptations.* New York: Plenum. A collection of very up-to-date scientific articles on the Miocene apes.

Boaz, N. T.
1999 *Essentials of Biological Anthropology.* Upper Saddle River, NJ: Prentice Hall. Basic text in physical anthropology, with information on primate evolution and paleoanthropology.

Ciochon, R. L., J. Olsen, and J. James
1990 *Other Origins: The Search for the Giant Ape in Human Prehistory.* New York: Bantam Books. In search of *Gigantopithecus.*

Eldredge, N.
1997 *Fossils: The Evolution and Extinction of Species.* Princeton, NJ: Princeton University Press. What fossils tell us about the natural history of species.

Fleagle, J. G.
1999 *Primate Adaptation and Evolution,* 2nd ed. San Diego: Academic Press. Excellent introduction to adaptation of past and present primate species.

Hrdy, S. B.
1999 *The Woman That Never Evolved,* rev. ed. Cambridge, MA: Harvard University Press. Revised edition of a well-known contribution to primate and human evolution.

Kemp, T. S.
1999 *Fossils and Evolution.* New York: Oxford University Press. Interpreting the fossil record.

Kimbel, W. H., and L. B. Martin, eds.
1993 *Species, Species Concepts, and Primate Evolution.* New York: Plenum. The evolution of primate species.

MacPhee, R. D. E., ed.

1993 *Primates and Their Relatives in Phylogenetic Perspective.* New York: Plenum. Discussion of the primate family tree and its evolution.

Napier, J. R., and P. H. Napier

1985 *The Natural History of the Primates.* Cambridge, MA: MIT Press. The adaptations of primates, past and present.

Park, M. A.

1999 *Biological Anthropology,* 2nd ed. Mountain View, CA: Mayfield. A concise introduction, with a focus on scientific inquiry.

Wade, N., ed.

1998 *The Science Times Book of Fossils and Evolution.* New York: Lyons Press. Articles on fossils and evolution from the *New York Times.*

internet exercises

1. Dating Techniques: Go to the USGS site on Fossils, Rocks, and Time, **http://pubs.usgs.gov/gip/fossils/contents.html,** and read through all the sections.
   a. How do researchers use the law of superposition to date fossils?
   b. What are isotopes? How are they used by researchers to calculate numeric dates for fossils?
   c. How do relative and absolute/numeric dating techniques complement each other?
2. Bigfoot: Read Lorraine Ahearn's article "Bigfoot Theory: Reality Is What You Make of It," which is a report about a 1999 Bigfoot conference, **http://www.bigfootcentral.com/articlesbc/bf_articles/greens.asp.**
   a. This chapter reported that some people believe that Bigfoot is a living descendant of *Gigantopithicus blackei.* What are the arguments for and against this claim?
   b. What are some other Bigfoot theories presented in this article? How could you go about testing them?
   c. What is your opinion about Bigfoot? How would you go about testing it?

See Chapter 5 on your CD-ROM for additional review and interactive exercises. See your McGraw-Hill Online Learning Center for more.

Chapter 6

Early Hominids

CHAPTER OUTLINE

ABCNEWS.GO.COM NEWS BRIEFS

Walk Like an Ape

by Kenneth Chang
March 22, 2000

When the earliest human ancestors came down from the trees, they likely ambled along on all fours, hunched over like modern-day gorillas and chimpanzees, according to a study of hominid wrists.

The finding, reported in Thursday's issue of the journal *Nature,* would also resolve a long-standing paradox about whether chimpanzees are more closely related to humans or gorillas.

As a gorilla or chimpanzee walks along the ground, it'll swing an arm forward, plant it on the ground and then scoot forward with its weight bearing on the back of the wrist, a type of locomotion called "knuckle walking."

"[Knuckle walking] is a compromise between having long fingers to climb trees while also being able to walk on the ground," says Brian Richmond, a paleoanthropologist at George Washington University in Washington, D.C., and co-author of the *Nature* paper.

Gorillas and chimpanzees are the only creatures known to knuckle walk, and they share other physical characteristics. Modern-day humans walk using feet, of course, and our bones don't show any vestiges of a knuckle-walking past. The fingers of early hominids also lacked the bony ridges of knuckle walkers. That suggested gorillas and chimpanzees are more closely related to each other than to humans.

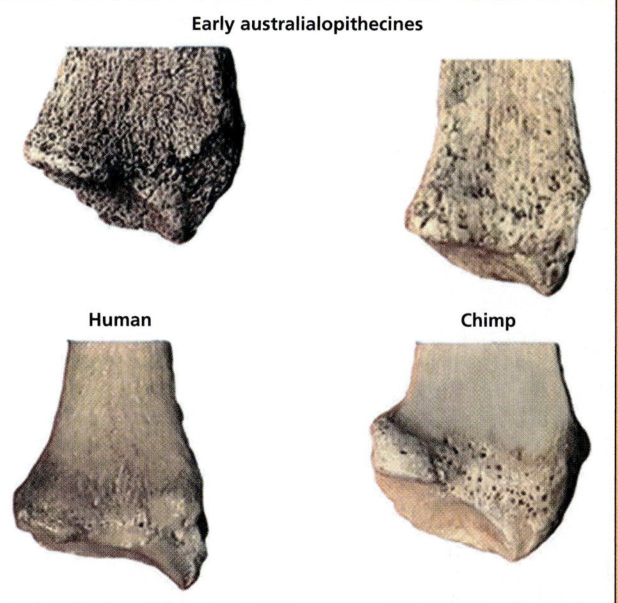

Molecular biologists examining the genes of chimpanzees, gorillas and humans found a different story: that the chimps are more closely related to humans than gorillas.

"This was a conundrum that didn't make a lot of sense," says John Fleagle, a professor of anatomical sciences at the State University of New York at Stony Brook.

Richmond and co-author David Strait, also of George Washington University, believe they solved the conundrum in about 10 seconds.

The two were in the research collection of the Smithsonian Institution, reviewing old articles from the 1960s and 1970s about knuckle-walking primates. Richmond read about a protrusion at the end of the forearm that locks the wrist when weight is put on it. He wondered whether early hominids had similar wrists.

Across the hall was a cast of the famous, well-studied skeleton of Lucy, a hominid of the species *Australopithecus afarensis* who lived about 3.2 million years ago on the grassy plains of Africa.

Richmond and Strait went over, picked up the forearm bone, and "Voila, at the end of the forearm was this projection that is the classic sign of knuckle walking," Richmond says. "We were dumbfounded. We couldn't believe no one had described this feature in early human ancestors before. Within 10 seconds, we went from thinking about the question to knowing the answer. But then it took over a year to do all the hard work of measuring other primates and proving to other scientists that this case was true."

Lucy herself did not knuckle walk, but walked upright like modern people, a conclusion based on her longer legs and other skeletal features. "With longer lower legs, it becomes very clumsy to knuckle walk," Richmond says.

Rather, Richmond and Strait argue, the stiff wrist was just a leftover vestige of an earlier knuckle-walking ancestor. "We're basically inferring about the past from the descendants of the earliest upright walkers," Richmond says. The forearm of an older hominid, *Australopithecus anamensis* of more than 4 million years ago, also had the stiff wrist, while younger hominids have a more modern looking one . . .

Source: http://abcnews.go.com/sections/science/DailyNews/knucklewalk000322.html.

overview

Who were the first hominids? Where did they live? What were they like? Did they have big brains? Did they make tools? Did they walk upright? Did they still seek refuge in the trees? How have hominids changed over several million years?

Hominids have lived during the Pliocene epoch, which began some five million years ago, and the Pleistocene epoch, which began two million years ago. Early hominid remains come from eastern and southern Africa. The australopithecines, members of the hominid genus *Australopithecus*, had evolved by four million years ago. Early australopithecines shared many features with the apes. They had small apelike skulls, slashing front teeth, and marked sexual dimorphism. Yet they walked on two legs. Upright bipedalism is a fundamental human characteristic that goes back more than four million years.

Remains of two groups, *A. africanus* and *A. robustus*, have been found in South Africa. Both had a powerful chewing apparatus, with large back teeth and robust faces, skulls, and muscle markings. The basis of their diet was savanna vegetation, but these early hominids also hunted small animals and scavenged the kills of predators.

By two million years ago, there were two distinct hominid groups: early *Homo* and *A. boisei*, the "hyperrobust" australopithecines, which became extinct a million years ago. Stone tools dating back more than two million years have been found in eastern Africa. Did early *Homo* make them? Or might the australopithecines also have made and used tools? This chapter examines early human evolution through the advent of *Homo* and the extinction of the australopithecines.

Chronology of Hominid Evolution

In terms of the Earth's history, humans haven't been around very long. If we compare Earth's history to a 24-hour day (with one second equaling 50,000 years),

> Earth originates at midnight.
>
> The earliest fossils were deposited at 5:45 A.M.
>
> The first vertebrates appeared at 9:02 P.M.
>
> The earliest mammals, at 10:45 P.M.
>
> The earliest primates, at 11:43 P.M.
>
> The earliest hominids (the australopithecines), at 11:58 P.M.
>
> And *Homo sapiens* arrives 36 seconds before midnight (Wolpoff, 1999, p. 10).

For the study of hominid evolution, the Pliocene (5 to 2 m.y.a.), Pleistocene (2 m.y.a. to 10,000 B.P.), and Recent (10,000 B.P. to the present) epochs are most important. Until the end of the Pliocene, the main hominid genus was *Australopithecus,* which lived in sub-Saharan Africa. By the start of the Pleistocene, *Australopithecus* had evolved into *Homo*.

The **Pleistocene** is traditionally and correctly considered the epoch of human life. Its subdivisions are the Lower Pleistocene (2 to 1 m.y.a.), the Middle Pleistocene (1 m.y.a. to 130,000 B.P.), and the Upper Pleistocene (130,000 to 10,000 B.P.). These subdivisions refer to the placement of geologic strata containing, respectively, older, intermediate, and younger fossils. The Lower Pleistocene extends from the start of the Pleistocene to the advent of the ice ages in the Northern Hemisphere around one million years ago.

Each subdivision of the Pleistocene is associated with a particular group of hominids. Late *Australopithecus* and early *Homo* lived during the Lower Pleistocene. *Homo erectus* spanned most of the Middle Pleistocene. *Homo sapiens* appeared late in the Middle Pleistocene and was the sole hominid of the Upper Pleistocene. We consider the hominids of the Middle and Upper Pleistocene in the next chapter.

During the second million years of the Pleistocene, there were several ice ages, or **glacials,**

Climates that are temperate today were arctic during the glacials. The ice-age tundra in western Europe may have looked like the cold, treeless plain shown here, where Russian Eskimos count on a reindeer herd for their subsistence. Would you expect to find many vegetarians in such an environment?

major advances of continental ice sheets in Europe and North America. These periods were separated by **interglacials,** long warm periods between the major glacials. (Scientists used to think there were four main glacial advances, but the picture has grown more complex.) With each advance, the world climate cooled and continental ice sheets—massive glaciers—covered the northern parts of Europe and North America. Climates that are temperate today were arctic during the glacials.

During the interglacials, the climate warmed up and the *tundra*—the cold, treeless plain—retreated north with the ice sheets. Forests returned to areas, such as southwestern France, that had had tundra vegetation. The ice sheets advanced and receded several times during the last glacial, the *Würm* (75,000 to 12,000 B.P.). Brief periods of relative warmth during the Würm (and other glacials) are called *interstadials,* in contrast to the longer interglacials. Hominid fossils found in association with animals known to occur in cold or warm climates, respectively, permit us to date them to glacial or interglacial (or interstadial) periods.

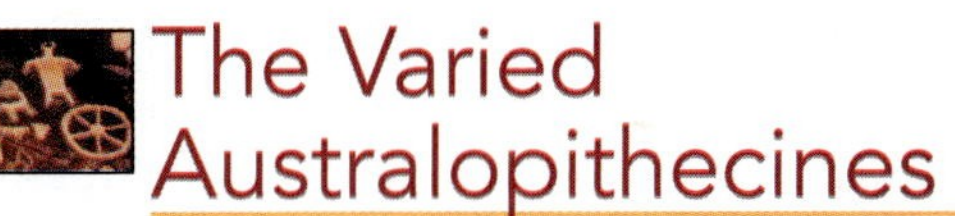

The Varied Australopithecines

Although we still don't know the identity of our Miocene ancestors, we do know that they evolved into a varied group of Pliocene–Pleistocene hominids known as the **australopithecines**—for whom we have an abundant fossil record. This term reflects their former classification as members of a distinct subfamily, the Australopithecinae. Today the distinction between the australopithecines and later hominids is made on the genus level. The australopithecines are assigned to the genus *Australopithecus (A.);* later humans, to *Homo (H.).*

Recent discoveries of fossils and tools have increased our knowledge of early human evolution. Some of the most significant finds come from East Africa—Kenya, Tanzania, and Ethiopia. Speculation about these finds abounds. For

Table 6.1

Dates and Geographic Distribution of the Major Hominoid and Hominid Fossil Groups

Fossil Group	Dates, m.y.a.	Known Distribution
Hominoids		
Afropithecus	18–16	East Africa
"Hogopans"	8–5	East Africa
Hominids		
Ardipithecus ramidus	4.4	Ethiopia
Australopithecines		
A. anamensis	4.2	Kenya
A. afarensis	3.8–3.0	East Africa (Laetoli, Hadar)
Robusts	2.6–1.2	East and South Africa
A. robustus	2.6?–2.0?	South Africa
A. boisei	2.6?–1.2	East Africa
Graciles		
A. africanus	3.0–2.5?	South Africa
Homo		
H. habilis	2.0?–1.6?	East Africa
H. erectus	1.6?–0.3	Africa, Asia, Europe
Homo sapiens	0.3–present	
Archaic *H. sapiens*	0.3–0.035 (300,000–35,000)	Africa, Asia, Europe
H. sapiens neanderthalensis	0.13–0.035 (130,000–35,000)	Europe, Middle East
H. sapiens sapiens	0.1?–present (100,000–present)	Worldwide (after 25,000 B.P.)

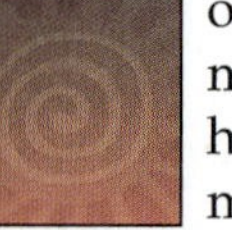

one thing, they come from different places and may be the remains of individuals who lived hundreds of thousands of years apart. Furthermore, geological processes operating over thousands or millions of years inevitably distort fossil remains. Table 6.1 summarizes the major stages of hominid evolution. You should consult it throughout this chapter and the next one.

A fairly recent (1992) find, now assigned to its own genus, *Ardipithecus ramidus,* is considered ancestral to early *Australopithecus* and, ultimately, to *Homo. Ardipithecus ramidus,* discovered at Kanapoi in Ethiopia by Berhane Asfaw, Gen Suwa, and Tim White, dates to 4.4 m.y.a. This fossil group consists of the remains of some 17 individuals, whose cranial, facial, dental, and upper limb bones continue to be analyzed. As of this writing, *Ardipithecus ramidus* is recognized as the earliest known hominid. Presumably, *Ardipithecus ramidus* evolved into *A. anamensis,* a bipedal hominid from Aramis in Kenya, whose fossil remains were first reported by Meave Leakey and Alan Walker in 1995. *A. anamensis* then evolved into *A. afarensis,* which is usually considered ancestral to all the later australopithecines (*africanus, robustus,* and *boisei*) as well as to *Homo* (Figure 6.1).

In the scheme followed here, *Australopithecus* had five species:

1. *A. anamensis* (4.2 m.y.a.)
2. *A. afarensis* (3.8? to 3.0 m.y.a.)
3. *A. africanus* (3.0? to 2.5? m.y.a.)
4. *A. robustus* (2.6? to 2.0 m.y.a.)
5. *A. boisei* (2.6? to 1.2 m.y.a.)

A. anamensis and *A. afarensis* are probably ancestral to all the rest of the *Australopithecus* species, as well as to *Homo,* which appeared (as *H. habilis*) around 2 m.y.a. Early *Homo* then coexisted for almost a million years with *A. boisei,* which became extinct around 1.2 m.y.a. Thereafter *H. erectus,* our direct ancestors—creators of complex tools, cooperative hunters and gatherers—multiplied, expanded, and eventually colonized the world.

The dates given for each species are approximate and somewhat arbitrary because an organism is not a member of one species one day and a

Figure 6.1
Phylogenetic Tree for African Apes and Hominids

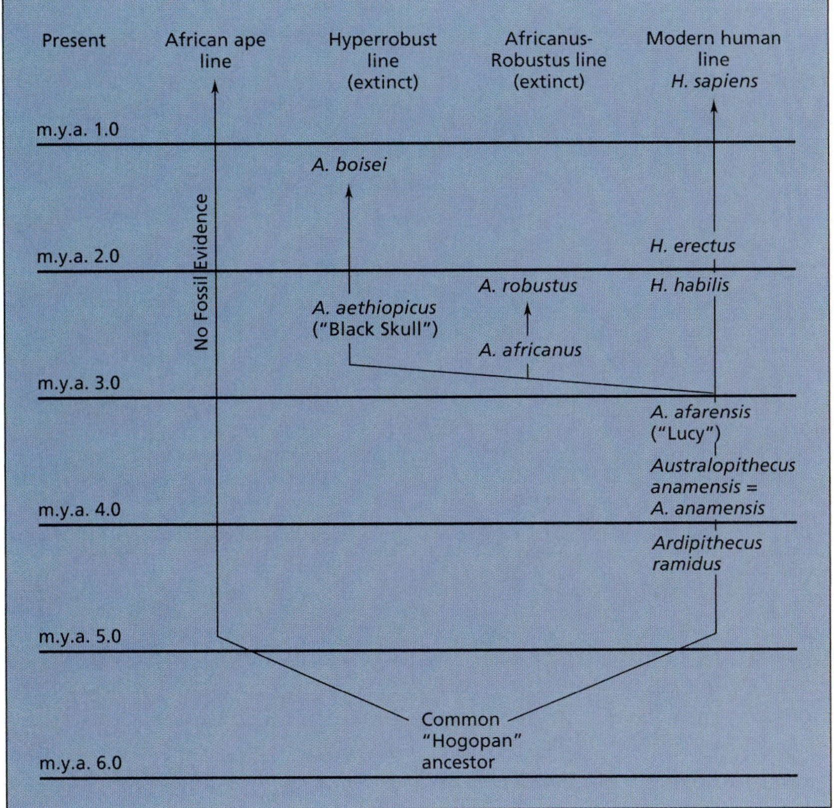

Their presumed divergence date was between 5 and 6 m.y.a. Branching in later hominid evolution is also shown. For more exact dates, see text.

member of another species the next day. Furthermore, accurate dating may be lacking. This is particularly true for the South African australopithecines (*A. africanus* and *A. robustus*), which were discovered in a nonvolcanic area and cannot be radiometrically dated. The hominid fossils from the volcanic regions of East Africa (*A. afarensis, A. boisei, H. habilis,* and *H. erectus*) usually have radiometric dates.

Australopithecus afarensis

The early hominid species known as *A. afarensis* includes fossils found at two sites, Laetoli in northern Tanzania and Hadar in the Afar region of Ethiopia. Laetoli is earlier (3.8 to 3.6 m.y.a.). The Hadar fossils probably date to between 3.3 and 3.0 m.y.a. Thus, based on the current evidence, *A. afarensis* lived between about 3.8 and 3.0 m.y.a. Research directed by Mary Leakey was responsible for the Laetoli finds. The Hadar discoveries resulted from an international expedition directed by D. C. Johanson and M. Taieb. The two sites have yielded significant samples of early hominid fossils. There are two dozen specimens from Laetoli, and the Hadar finds include the remains of between 35 and 65 individuals. The Laetoli remains are mainly teeth and jaw fragments, along with some very informative fossilized footprints. The Hadar sample includes skull fragments and postcranial material, most notably 40 percent of the complete skeleton of a tiny hominid female, dubbed "Lucy," who lived around 3 m.y.a.

Although the hominid remains at Laetoli and Hadar were deposited half a million years apart,

Figure 6.2
Comparison of Dentition in Ape, Human, and *A. afarensis* Palates

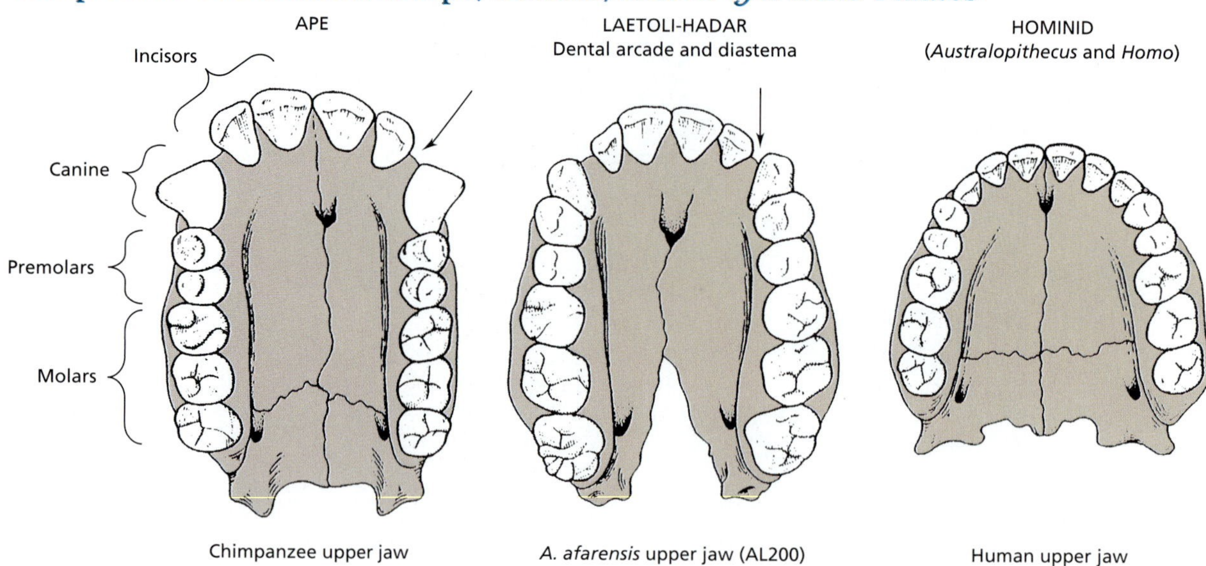

Chimpanzee upper jaw | *A. afarensis* upper jaw (AL200) | Human upper jaw

their many resemblances explain their placement in the same species, *A. afarensis*. These fossils, along with the more recently found *Ardipithecus ramidus* and *A. anamensis*, have forced a reinterpretation of the early hominid fossil record. *A. afarensis*, although clearly a hominid, was so similar in many ways to chimps and gorillas that our common ancestry with the African apes must be very recent, certainly no more than 8 m.y.a. *Ardipithecus ramidus* and *A. anamensis* are even more apelike. These discoveries show that hominids are much closer to the apes than the previously known fossil record had suggested. Studies of the learning abilities and biochemistry of chimps and gorillas have taught a valuable lesson about homologies that the fossil record is now confirming.

The *A. afarensis* finds, which have been more completely described than *Ardipithecus ramidus* and *A. anamensis*, make this clear. The many apelike features are surprising in definite hominids that lived as recently as 3 m.y.a. Discussion of hominid fossils requires a brief review of dentition. Moving from front to back, on either side of the upper or lower jaw, humans (and apes) have two incisors, one canine, two premolars, and three molars. Our dental formula is 2.1.2.3, for a total of eight teeth on each side, upper and lower—32 teeth in all—if we have all our "wisdom teeth" (our third molars). Now back to the australopithecines. Like apes, and unlike modern humans, *A. afarensis* had sharp canine teeth that projected beyond the other teeth. Also like apes, their lower premolar was pointed and projecting to sharpen the upper canine. It had one long cusp and one tiny bump that hints at the bicuspid premolar that eventually developed in hominid evolution.

There is, however, evidence that powerful chewing associated with savanna vegetation was entering the *A. afarensis* feeding pattern. When the coarse, gritty, fibrous vegetation of grasslands and semidesert enters the diet, the back teeth change to accommodate heavy chewing stresses. Massive back teeth, jaws, and facial and cranial structures suggest a diet demanding extensive grinding and powerful crushing. *A. afarensis* molars are large (see Figure 6.2). The lower jaw (mandible) is thick and is buttressed with a bony ridge behind the front teeth. The cheekbones are large and flare out to the side for the attachment of powerful chewing muscles.

The skull of *A. afarensis* contrasts with those of later hominids. The brain case is very small. The cranial capacity of 430 cm^3 (cubic centimeters) barely surpasses the chimp average (390 cm^3). The form of the *A. afarensis* skull is like that of the chimpanzee, but the brain/body size ratio was probably larger.

Below the neck, however—particularly in regard to locomotion—*A. afarensis* was unquestionably human. Early evidence of striding bipedalism comes from Laetoli, where volcanic ash, which can be directly dated by the K/A technique, covered a trail of footprints of two or three hominids walking to a water hole. These prints leave no doubt that a small striding biped lived in Tanzania by 3.6 m.y.a. The structure of the pelvic, hip, leg, and foot bones also confirms that upright bipedalism was *A. afarensis*'s mode of locomotion.

More recent finds show that bipedalism predated *A. afarensis. A. anamensis* (4.2 m.y.a.) was bipedal. Relevant postcranial material from the even older *Ardipithecus ramidus* (4.4 m.y.a.) also suggests a capacity for upright bipedal locomotion. Indeed, it was the shift toward this form of moving around that led to the distinctive hominid way of life. Now check the "In the News" box for several theories about why early hominids became bipedal.

A. afarensis still contrasts in many ways with later homininds. Sexual dimorphism is especially marked. The male–female contrast in jaw size in *A. afarensis* was more marked than in the orangutan. There was a similar contrast in body size. *A. afarensis* females, such as Lucy, stood between three and four feet (91 and 120 centimeters) tall; males might have reached five feet (152 centimeters). *A. afarensis* males weighed perhaps twice as much as the females did (Wolpoff 1999). Table 6.2 (on page 146) summarizes data on the various australopithecines, including mid-sex body weight and brain size. Mid-sex means midway between the male average and the female average.

Lucy and her kind were far from dainty. Lucy's muscle-engraved bones are much more robust than ours are. With only rudimentary tools and weapons, early hominids needed powerful and resistant bones and muscles. Lucy's arms are longer relative to her legs than are those of later hominids. Here again her proportions are more apelike than ours are. Although Lucy neither brachiated nor knuckle-walked, she was probably a much better climber than modern people are, and she spent some of her day in the trees.

The *A. afarensis* fossils show that between 3.8 and 3.0 m.y.a., our ancestors had a mixture of apelike and hominid features. Canines, premolars, and skulls were much more apelike than most scholars had imagined would exist in such a recent ancestor. On the other hand, the molars, chewing apparatus, and cheekbones foreshadowed later hominid trends, and the pelvic and limb bones were indisputably hominid (Figure 6.3 on page 146). The hominid pattern was being built from the ground up.

An ancient trail of hominid footprints fossilized in volcanic ash. Mary Leakey found this 70-meter trail at Laetoli, Tanzania, in 1979. It dates from 3.6 m.y.a. and confirms that *A. afarensis* was a striding biped.

Hominids walk with a striding gait that consists of alternating swing and stance phases for each leg and foot. As one leg is pushed off by the

in the news

From 4 Legs to 2

This article focuses on bipedalism—upright two-legged locomotion—as the key feature differentiating early hominids from the apes. Recent fossil discoveries in Kenya and Ethiopia suggest that hominid bipedalism is more than four million years old. This mode of locomotion is generally considered an adaptation to an open grassland or savanna habitat. Scientists have suggested several advantages of bipedalism in such an environment: the ability to see over long grass, to carry items back to a home base, to move more efficiently in foraging for plant food, and to reduce the body's exposure to solar radiation. The fossil and archaeological records confirm that upright bipedal locomotion preceded tool manufacture and the expansion of the hominid brain. However, although the earliest hominids could move bipedally through the savanna during the day, they also preserved enough of an apelike anatomy to make them good climbers. They could take to the trees to sleep at night or to escape terrestrial predators.

Anthropologists and evolutionary biologists are now agreed that upright posture and two-legged walking—bipedality—was the crucial and probably first major adaptation associated with the divergence of the human lineage from a common ancestor with the African apes . . .

Upright walking required profound changes in anatomy, particularly in the limbs and pelvis, and these were passed on to modern humans. It eventually put limits on the size of infants at birth and thus created the need for longer postnatal nurturing, with sweeping cultural consequences . . . And it certainly opened the way for later toolmaking, some 2.5 million years ago, and probably set the stage for the eventual enlargement of the hominid brain, not before two million years ago . . .

As scientists have learned to reconstruct ancient climate from cores drilled in the ice of Greenland and sediments on the sea floor, one of the favorite explanations for the transition to bipedality has centered on drastic environmental changes that swept Africa more than five million years ago.

big toe and goes into the swing phase, the heel of the other leg is touching the ground and entering the stance phase. Four-footed locomotors such as Old World monkeys are always supported by two limbs. Bipeds, by contrast, are supported by one limb at a time.

The pelvis, the lower spine, the hip joint, and the thigh bone change in accordance with the stresses of bipedal locomotion. Australopithecine pelvises are much more similar (although far from identical) to *Homo*'s than to apes' and show adaptation to bipedalism (Figure 6.4 on page 147). The blades of the australopithecine pelvis (iliac blades) are shorter and broader than are those of the ape. The sacrum, which anchors the pelvis's two side bones, is larger, as in *Homo.* With bipedalism, the pelvis forms a sort of basket that balances the weight of the trunk and supports this weight with less stress. Fossilized spinal bones (vertebrae) show that the australopithecine spine had the lower spine (lumbar) curve characteristic of *Homo.* This curvature helps transmit the weight of the upper body to the pelvis and the legs. Placement of the *foramen magnum* (the "big hole" through which the spinal cord joins the brain) farther forward in *Australopithecus* and *Homo* than in the ape also represents an adaptation to upright bipedalism (Figure 6.5 on page 148).

By that time, Dr. Elisabeth S. Vrba, a paleontologist at Yale University, has pointed out, global climate had become significantly cooler and drier. As it did, grasslands in sub-Sahara Africa expanded and rain forests contracted, shrinking the habitat where tree-dwelling primates lived and foraged.

Another factor possibly upsetting the East African environment at the time was the region's unsteady terrain. Dr. Yves Coppens, a paleontologist at the College of France in Paris, contends that a seismic shift, recognized by geophysicists, deepened the Rift Valley, which cuts through Ethiopia, Kenya and Tanzania. The sinking of the valley produced an upthrust of mountains, leaving the land west of the valley more humid and arboreal, while the east became more arid and dominated by savanna.

As a result, he hypothesizes, the common ancestors of the hominids and the chimpanzees found themselves divided. Those adapting to the humid west evolved into the chimpanzee family. Those left in the east, Dr. Coppens wrote [in 1994] in *Scientific American,* "invented a completely new repertoire in order to adapt to their new life in an open environment."

In any event, according to the hypothesis, at least one type of these primates responded to the environmental crisis by venturing more and more into the open grasslands, looking for food but retreating to nearby trees to escape predators and sleep at night. To move about more efficiently, perhaps also to keep a lookout above the grasses for distant food or predators, these primates began standing up and walking on two legs. Their success presumably improved their chances of surviving and passing on genes favoring this unusual stance and gait, leading eventually to bipedal hominids . . .

If the origin of bipedality was related to prospecting the opening grasslands, Dr. Peter E. Wheeler, a physiologist at Liverpool John Moores University in England, suggests that there may have been another contributing factor. The early hominids, he notes, might have found the heat there especially stressful. Most animals living on savanna can let their body temperature rise during the day without wasting scarce water by sweating. They have built-in ways of protecting the brain from overheating. Not so humans, and presumably their distant ancestors. The only way they can protect the brain is by keeping the whole body cool.

Then perhaps the hominids stood up to keep cool. From his studies with a scale model of the Lucy skeleton, Dr. Wheeler found that a quadrupedal posture would have exposed the body to about 60 percent more solar radiation than a bipedal one. Standing tall thus might result in a substantial reduction in water loss. And the upright body could also catch the cooler breeze above the ground.

Source: John Noble Wilford, "The Transforming Leap, from 4 Legs to 2," *New York Times,* September 5, 1995, p. B5(N)/C1(L).

In apes, the thigh bone (femur) extends straight down from the hip to the knees. In *Australopithecus* and *Homo,* however, the thigh bone angles into the hip, permitting the space between the knees to be narrower than the pelvis during walking. The pelvises of the australopithecines were similar but not identical to those of *Homo.* The most significant contrast is a narrower australopithecine birth canal (Tague and Lovejoy 1986).

Expansion of the birth canal is a trend in hominid evolution. The width of the birth canal is related to the size of the skull and brain. *A. afarensis* had a small cranial capacity. Even in later australopithecines, the average brain size did not exceed 600 cubic centimeters. Undoubtedly, the australopithecine skull grew after birth to accommodate a growing brain, as it does (much more) in *Homo.* However, the brains of the australopithecines expanded less than ours do. In the australopithecines, the cranial sutures (the lines where the bones of the skull eventually come together) fused relatively earlier in life.

Their patterns of molar eruption (Mann 1975) suggest that australopithecine children, like our own, had a slower maturation rate than do the apes. Young australopithecines must have depended on their parents and kin for nurturance and protection. Those years of childhood dependency

Table 6.2
Facts about the Australopithecines

Species	Dates (m.y.a.)	Known Distribution	Important Sites	Body Weight (Mid-sex)	Brain Size (Mid-Sex) (cm³)
Homo sapiens sapiens	100,000 to present			60 kg/132 lbs	1,350
Pan troglodytes (chimpanzee)	Modern			42 kg/93 lbs	390
A. boisei	2.6? to 1.2	E. Africa	Olduvai, East Turkana	39 kg/86 lbs	490
A. robustus	2.6? to 2.0?	S. Africa	Kromdraai, Swartkrans	37 kg/81 lbs	540
A. africanus	3 to 2.5?	S. Africa	Taung, Sterkfontein	36 kg/79 lbs	490
A. afarensis	3.8 to 3.0	E. Africa	Hadar, Laetoli	35 kg/77 lbs	430
A. anamensis	4.2	E. Africa	Aramis	Insufficient data	No published skulls
Ardipithecus ramidus	4.4	E. Africa	Kanapoi	Insufficient data	No published skulls

Figure 6.3
Comparison of *Homo sapiens* and *Pan troglodytes* (the common chimp)

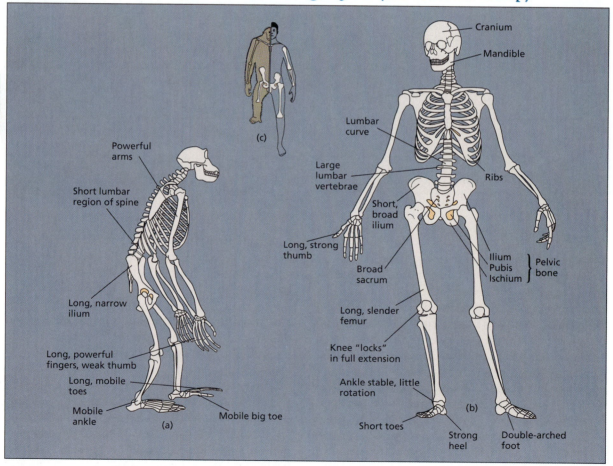

(a) Skeleton of chimpanzee in bipedal position; (b) skeleton of modern human; (c) chimpanzee and human "bisected" and drawn to the same trunk length for comparison of limb proportions. The contrast in leg length is largely responsible for the proportional difference between humans and apes.

Figure 6.4
A Comparison of Human and Chimpanzee Pelvises

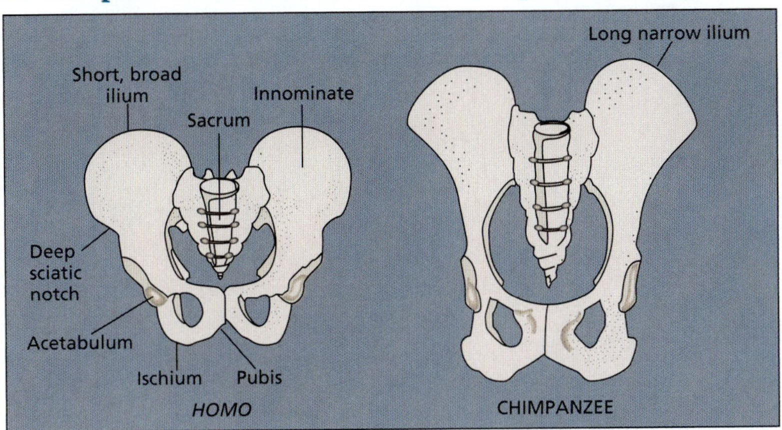

The human pelvis has been modified to meet the demands of upright bipedalism. The blades (*ilia*; singular, *ilium*) of the human pelvis are shorter and broader than those of the ape. The sacrum, which anchors the side bones, is wider. The australopithecine pelvis is far more similar to that of *Homo* than to that of the chimpanzee, as we would expect in an upright biped.

would have provided time for observation, teaching, and learning. This may provide indirect evidence for a rudimentary cultural life.

Gracile and Robust Australopithecines

The fossils of *A. africanus* and *A. robustus* come from South Africa. In 1924, the anatomist Raymond Dart coined *Australopithecus africanus* to describe the first fossil representative of this species, the skull of a juvenile that was found accidentally in a quarry at Taung, South Africa. Radiometric dates are lacking for this nonvolcanic region, but the fossil hominids found at the five main South African sites appear (from stratigraphy) to have lived between 3 and 2 m.y.a.

There were two groups of South African australopithecines: **gracile** (*A. africanus*) and **robust** (*A. robustus*). "Gracile" indicates that members of *A. africanus* were smaller and slighter, less robust, than were members of *A. robustus*. There were also very robust—*hyperrobust*—australopithecines in East Africa. In the classification scheme used here, these have been assigned to *A. boisei*. However, some scholars consider *A. robustus* and *A. boisei* to be regional variants of just one species, usually called *robustus*.

The relationship between the graciles and the robusts has been debated for generations but has not been resolved. Graciles and robusts probably descend from *A. afarensis* or from a South African version of *A. afarensis*. Some scholars have argued that the graciles lived before (3 to 2.5? m.y.a.) and were ancestral to the robusts (2.6? to 2.0? m.y.a.). Others contend that the graciles and the robusts were separate species that may have overlapped in time. (Classifying them as members of different species implies they were reproductively isolated from each other in time or space.) Other paleoanthropologists view the gracile and robust australopithecines as different ends of a continuum of variation in a single *polytypic species*—one with considerable phenotypic variation. The range of *Australopithecus* sites in East and South Africa is shown in Figure 6.6 (on page 149).

The trend toward enlarged back teeth, chewing muscles, and facial buttressing, which is already noticeable in *A. afarensis*, continues in the South African australopithecines. However, the canines are reduced, and the premolars are fully bicuspid. Dental form and function changed as dietary needs shifted from cutting and slashing to chewing and grinding. The mainstay of the australopithecine diet was the vegetation of the savanna.

These early hominids also might have hunted small and slow-moving game. Archaeological analyses of animal remains at australopithecine camps suggest that these hominids scavenged, bringing home parts of kills made by large cats and other carnivores. The campsites of early hominids in East Africa include the remains of small animals and scavenged parts of carnivores' kills. However, the ability to hunt large animals was an achievement of *Homo* and is discussed later.

The skulls, jaws, and teeth of the australopithecines leave no doubt that their diet was mainly vegetarian. Natural selection modifies the teeth to conform to the stresses associated with a particular diet. Massive back teeth, jaws, and

Figure 6.5

A Comparison of the Skull and Dentition (Upper Jaw) of *Homo* and the Chimpanzee

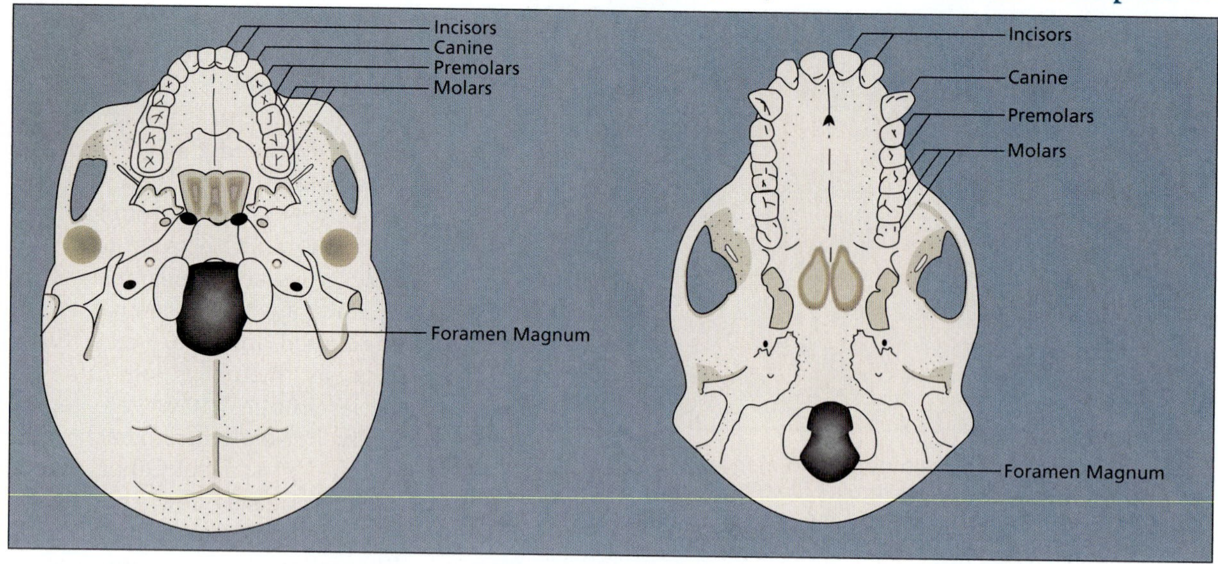

The *foramen magnum*, through which the spinal cord joins the brain, is located farther forward in *Homo* than in the ape. This permits the head to balance atop the spine with upright bipedalism. The molars and premolars of the ape form parallel rows. Human teeth, by contrast, are arranged in rounded, parabolic form. What differences do you note between human and ape canines? Canine reduction has been an important trend in hominid evolution.

associated facial and cranial structures confirm that the australopithecine diet required extensive grinding and powerful crushing.

In the South African australopithecines, both deciduous ("baby") and permanent molars and premolars are massive, with multiple cusps. The later australopithecines had bigger back teeth than did the earlier ones. However, this evolutionary trend ended with early *Homo,* which had much smaller back teeth, reflecting a dietary change that will be described later.

Contrasts with *Homo* in the front teeth are less marked. But they are still of interest because of what they tell us about sexual dimorphism. *A. africanus*'s canines were more pointed, with larger roots, than *Homo*'s are. Still, the *A. africanus* canines were only 75 percent the size of the canines of *A. afarensis.* Despite this canine reduction, there was just as much canine sexual dimorphism in *A. africanus* as there had been in *A. afarensis* (Wolpoff 1999). Sexual dimorphism in general was much more pronounced among the early hominids than it is among *Homo sapiens. A. africanus* females were about four feet (120 centimeters), and males five feet (150 centimeters), tall. The average female probably had no more than 60 percent the weight of the average male (Wolpoff 1980*a*). (That figure contrasts with today's average female/male weight ratio of about 88 percent.)

Teeth, jaw, face, and skull changed to fit a diet based on tough, gritty, fibrous grasslands vegetation. A massive face housed large upper teeth and provided a base for the attachment of powerful chewing muscles. Australopithecine cheekbones were elongated and massive structures (Figure 6.7 on page 150) that anchored large chewing muscles running up the jaw. Another set of robust chewing muscles extended from the back of the jaw to the sides of the skull.

In the more robust australopithecines (*A. robustus* in South Africa and *A. boisei* in East Africa), these muscles were strong enough to produce a *sagittal crest,* a bony ridge on the top of the skull. Such a crest forms as the bone grows. It develops from the pull of the chewing muscles as they meet at the midline of the skull.

Overall robustness, especially in the chewing apparatus, increased through time among the australopithecines. This trend was most striking

Figure 6.6
Australopithecus Sites in Africa

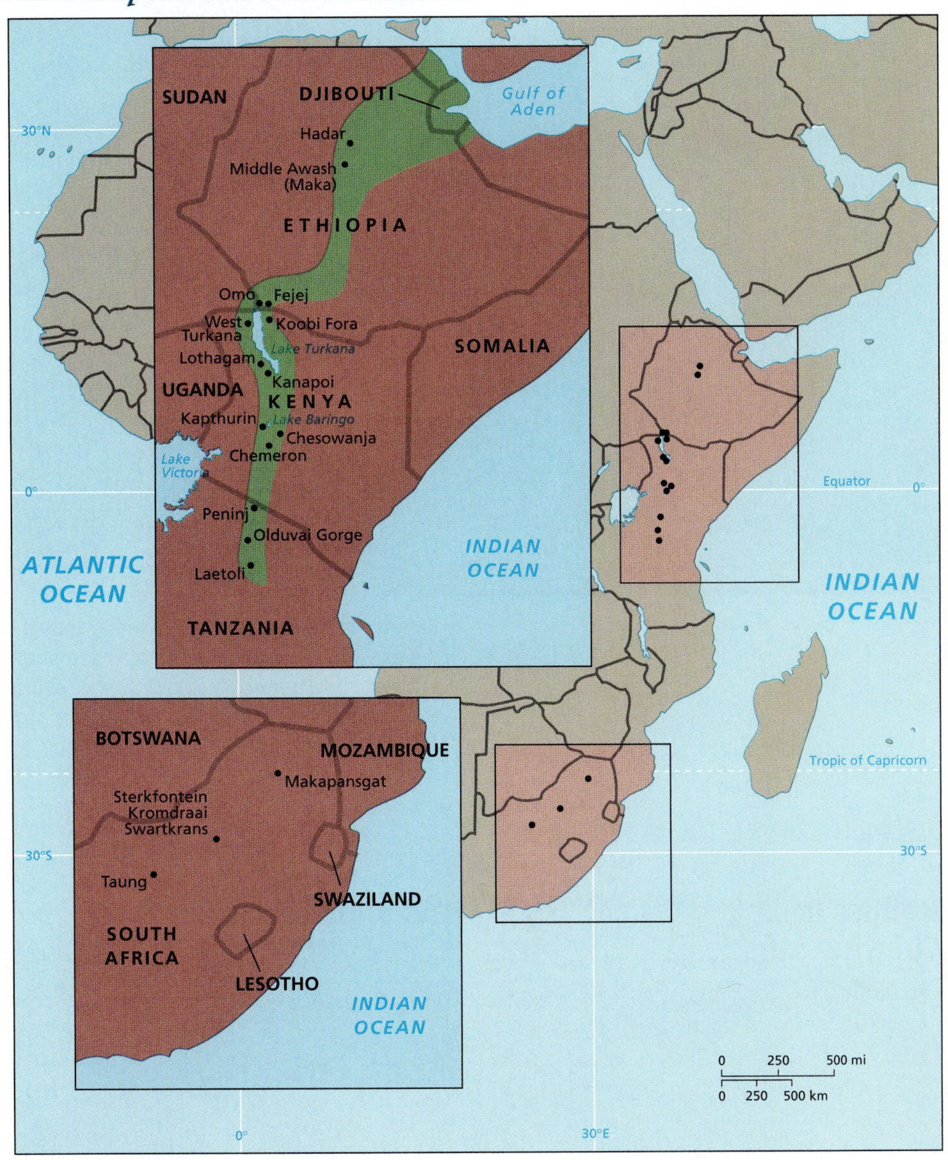

These sites fall into two major clusters: the open, mostly lake bed deposits in and around the East African rift valleys and the limestone cave sites of South Africa.

in *A. boisei,* which survived through 1.2 m.y.a in East Africa. Compared with their predecessors, the later australopithecines tended to have larger overall size, skulls, and back teeth. They also had thicker faces, more prominent crests, and more rugged muscle markings on the skeleton. By contrast, the front teeth stayed the same size.

Brain size (measured as cranial capacity, in cubic centimeters—cm^3) increased only slightly between *A. afarensis* (430 cm^3), *A. africanus* (490 cm^3), and *A. robustus* (540 cm^3) (Wolpoff 1999). These figures can be compared with an average cranial capacity of 1,350 cm^3 in *Homo sapiens*. The modern range goes from less than 1,000 cm^3 to more than 2,000 cm^3 in normal adults. The cranial capacity of chimps (*Pan troglodytes*) averages 390 cm^3 (see Table 6.2). The brains of gorillas (*Gorilla gorilla*) average around 500 cm^3, which is within

Members of an *A. robustus* band brandish limbs to defend their territory. This painting imagines a time of drying, with forests turning to grassland. What was the basis of the *A. robustus* diet? What kind of social organization is suggested by this image?

Figure 6.7

Skulls of Robust (left) and Gracile (right) Australopithecines, Showing Chewing Muscles

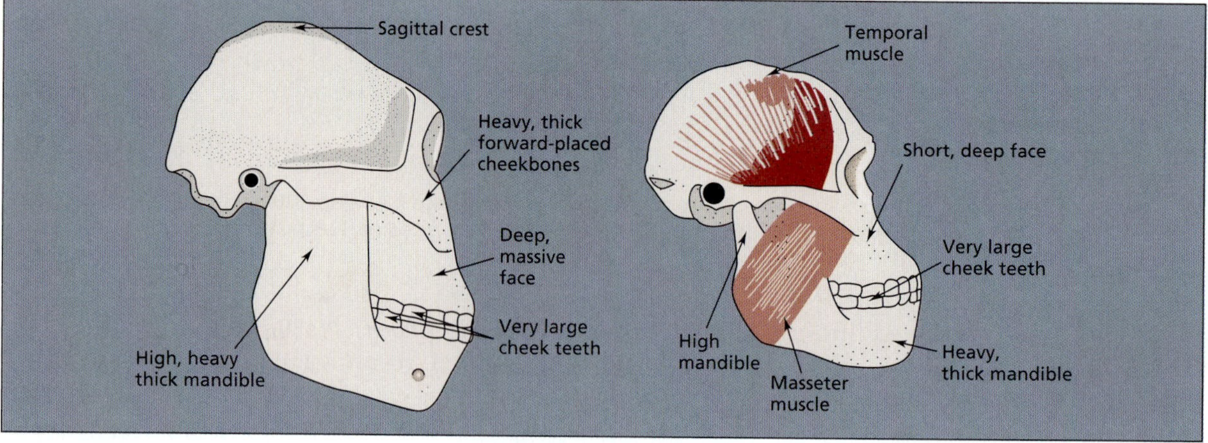

Flaring cheek arches and, in some robusts, a sagittal crest supported this massive musculature. The early hominid diet—coarse, gritty vegetation of the savanna—demanded such structures. These features were most pronounced in *A. boisei.*

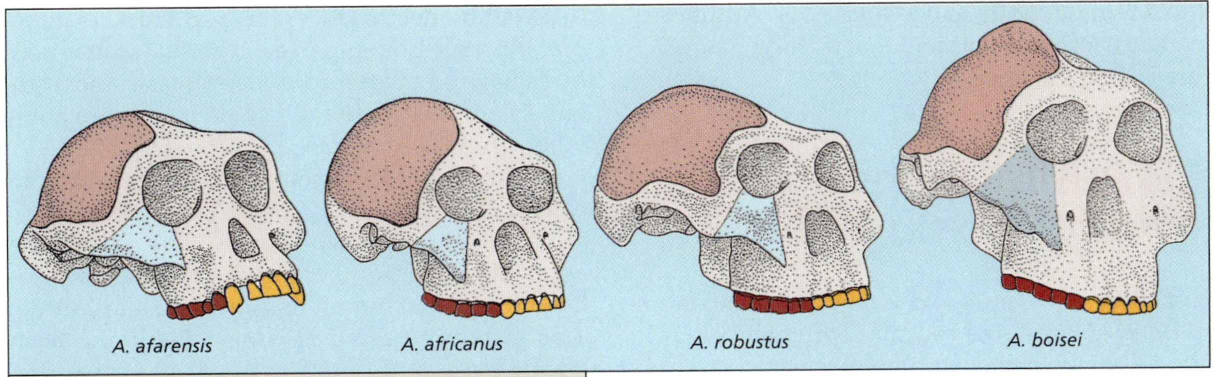

Shown from left to right are *A. afarensis, A. africanus, A. robustus,* and *A. boisei.* What are the main differences you notice among these four types of early hominids?

Palates of *Homo sapiens* (left) and *A. boisei* (right), late, hyperrobust australopithecine. In comparing them, note the australopithecine's huge molars and premolars. What other contrasts do you notice? The large back teeth represent an extreme adaptation to a diet based on coarse, gritty savanna vegetation. Reduction in tooth size during human evolution applied to the back teeth much more than the front.

the australopithecine range, but gorilla body weight is much greater.

Casts of the inside of a skull (endocranial casts) provide information about the brain's size, proportions, and shape, and the areas devoted to particular functions—such as motor activities, speech, memory, sensory integration, and vision. Australopithecine endocranial casts are more human than apelike, as we would expect in an organism that relied more on learning, memory, and intellectual association.

101–102

Given the tool-making abilities of the apes, there is no reason to doubt that the australopithecines relied on rudimentary cultural means of adaptation. Animal bones that are sharpened and scratched, as they might have been if used for digging, were found at one South African australopithecine site. The earliest known stone tools come from East Africa, with radiometric dates of

2 to 2.5 m.y.a. (Jolly and White 1995). Additional evidence for early hominid tool use and manufacture is discussed below.

Australopithecines End, *Homo* Begins

Sometime between 3 and 2 m.y.a., the ancestors of *Homo* split off and became reproductively isolated from the later australopithecines, such as *A. boisei,* which coexisted with *Homo* until around 1.2 m.y.a. The first evidence for speciation is dental. The fossil sample of hominid teeth dated to 2 m.y.a. has two clearly different sizes of teeth. One set is huge, the largest molars and premolars in hominid evolution; these teeth belong to *A. boisei.* The other group of (smaller) teeth belonged to our ancestor, *H. habilis,* the first exemplar of the genus *Homo.*

By 1.6 m.y.a., the difference was even more evident. Two hominid groups occupied different environmental niches in Africa. One of them, *Homo*—by then *Homo erectus*—had a larger brain and a reproportioned skull; it had increased the areas of the brain that regulate higher mental functions. These were our ancestors, hominids with greater capacities for culture than the australopithecines had. *H. erectus* hunted and gathered, made sophisticated tools, and eventually displaced its sole surviving cousin species, *A. boisei.*

A. boisei of East Africa, the hyperrobust australopithecines, had mammoth back teeth. *A. boisei* females had bigger back teeth than did earlier australopithecine males. *A. boisei* became ever more specialized with respect to one part of the traditional australopithecine diet, concentrating on coarse vegetation with a high grit content.

The separation that led to speciation between *A. boisei* and early *Homo* took time. And why, if two new *species* were forming, is one of them assigned to a new genus, *Homo?* This classification is done in retrospect, since we know that one species survived and evolved into a contemporary descendant whereas the other one became extinct. Hindsight shows us their very different lifeways, which suggest their placement in different genera.

We still don't know why, how, and exactly when the split between *Australopithecus* and *Homo* took place. Scholars have defended many different models, or theoretical schemes, to interpret the early hominid fossil record. Because new finds have so often forced reappraisals, most scientists are willing to modify their interpretation when given new evidence.

The model of Johanson and White (1979), who coined the term *A. afarensis,* proposes that *A. afarensis* split into two groups. One group, the ancestors of *Homo,* became reproductively isolated from other hominids between 3 and 2 m.y.a. This group appeared as ***Homo habilis,*** a term coined by L. S. B. and Mary Leakey for the first members of the genus *Homo* and the immediate ancestors of *H. erectus. H. habilis* lived between 2 m.y.a. and about 1.6 m.y.a., by which time it had evolved into *H. erectus.* Other members of *A. afarensis* evolved into the various kinds of australopithecines (*A. africanus, A. robustus,* and hyperrobust *A. boisei,* the last member to become extinct).

In 1985, the paleoanthropologist Alan Walker made a significant find near Lake Turkana in northern Kenya. Called the "black skull" because of the blue-black sheen it bore from the minerals surrounding it, the fossil displayed a "baffling combination of features" (Fisher 1988*a*). The jaw was apelike and the brain was small (as in *A. afarensis*), but there was a massive bony crest atop the skull (as in *A. boisei*). Walker and Richard

The "black skull," dated to 2.6 m.y.a., was discovered by Alan Walker in 1985 near Lake Turkana. It gets its name from the blue-black sheen it acquired from the minerals surrounding it. The jaw is apelike and the brain is small, and there is a massive bony sagittal crest, as in *A. boisei.* Some consider the black skull to be a very early hyperrobust *A. boisei.* Others assign it to its own species, *A. aethiopicus.*

Leakey (Walker's associate on the 1985 expedition) view the black skull (dated to 2.6 m.y.a.) as a very early hyperrobust *A. boisei.* Others (e.g., Jolly and White 1995) assign the "black skull" to its own species, *A. aethiopicus.* The black skull shows that some of the anatomic features of the hyperrobust australopithecines (2.6? to 1.2 m.y.a.) did not change very much during well over one million years.

Regardless of when the split between *Homo* and *Australopithecus* occurred, there is good fossil evidence that *Homo* and *A. boisei* coexisted in East Africa. *A. boisei* seems to have lived in very arid areas, feeding on harder-to-chew vegetation than had any previous hominid. This diet would explain the hyperrobusts' huge back teeth, jaws, and associated areas of the face and skull.

Tools

It may have been *Homo*'s increasing hunting proficiency that forced *A. boisei* into becoming an ever-more-specialized vegetarian. Tool making also might have had something to do with the split. The simplest obviously manufactured tools were discovered in 1931 by L. S. B. and Mary Leakey at Olduvai Gorge. This site gave the tools their name—**Oldowan pebble tools.** The oldest tools from Olduvai are about 1.8 million years old. Richard Leakey also has found tools that old at East Turkana. Still older (2.5 to 2 m.y.a.) tools have been found in Ethiopia, Zaire, and Malawi (Jolly and White 1995; Lemonick and Dorfman 1999).

Oldowan pebble tools (Figure 6.8) are pieces of stone about the size of a tennis ball. Flakes were struck off both sides to form a cutting edge. Stone is more durable than bone, horn, and wood are. Although there were probably early tools made of those materials, these substances are less likely to survive than stone is. Early hominids probably also used tools they did not make, for example, naturally chipped or cracked rocks or flakes. We can tell that early pebble tools were manufactured because their cutting edges are flaked on both sides, whereas rocks that are fractured by natural forces usually have flakes removed from just one side. Other evidence for manufacture is that some tools were made from rocks that were not locally available. They must have been brought to the site from elsewhere (Isaac 1978).

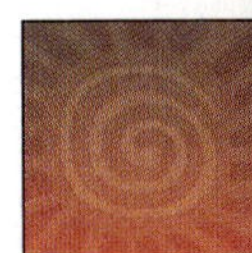

Figure 6.8
Evolution in Tool Making

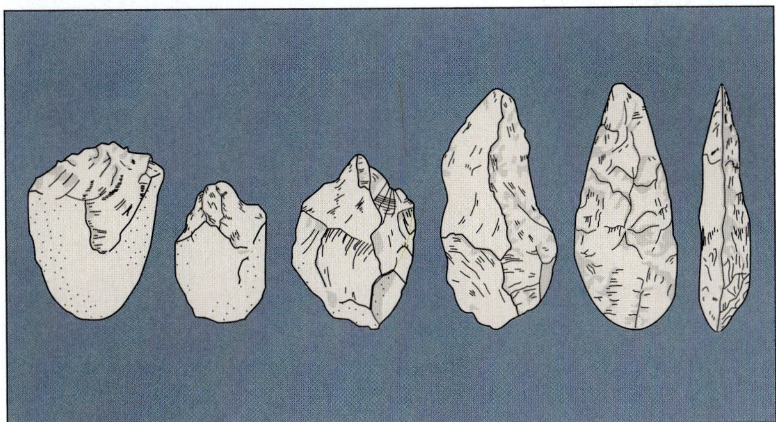

Finds at Olduvai Gorge and elsewhere show how pebble tools (the first tool at the left) evolved into the Acheulian hand ax of *H. erectus.* This drawing begins with an Oldowan pebble tool and moves through crude hand axes to fully developed Acheulian tools. The oldest tools date back to about 2.5 m.y.a. With the split between *Homo* (*habilis,* then *erectus*) and *A. boisei,* stone-tool manufacture rapidly grew more sophisticated. The Acheulian techniques of *H. erectus* are described in the following chapter.

beyond the classroom

Hydrodynamic Sorting of Avian Skeletal Remains

BACKGROUND INFORMATION

Student:	*Josh Trapani*
Supervising Professor:	*Peter Stahl*
School:	*State University of New York at Binghamton*
Year in School/Major:	*Senior/Anthropology*
Future Plans:	*Graduate school*
Project Title:	*Hydrodynamic Sorting of Avian Skeletal Remains*

People have dietary preferences for particular animal parts. Archaeologists typically encounter remains of animals that humans may have hunted and eaten. At a given site, certain kinds of bones may be more common than others are. How can we know whether humans choose some preferred parts to take away, while leaving others, or whether natural processes were responsible? This project examines the effects of water current in sorting avian (bird) bones. Some parts (e.g., skulls) are more likely than others are to have been moved by water, and this helps to determine whether humans played a role in the selection of animal parts at the site.

Taphonomy is the study of the processes that affect preservation of organic remains. Specific taphonomic factors may bias (i.e., alter the preservation, condition, and identifiability of) archaeological and paleontological faunal assemblages in specific ways. It is necessary to understand the taphonomic biases an assemblage has been subjected to so that accurate interpretations about that assemblage can be made.

One important taphonomic agent is sorting by current. Many archaeological sites are located near water, and current action may alter their faunal assemblages. Currents sort bones in the same way they sort sediment: by selectively removing certain bones from a site while leaving others behind. Archaeologists often attribute relative frequencies of different skeletal elements at a site to human agency (e.g., dietary preference for certain parts of an animal over others). But if the assemblage has been subjected to sorting by current (or any of a number of other taphonomic factors), such interpretations may be erroneous.

Previous studies examined the way mammal and turtle bones sort in a current. However, a study with avian material had never been

Scholars still debate the identity of the first tool makers. Some argue for *Homo;* and others, for the australopithecines. A recent *H. habilis* find, tentatively assigned the very early date of 2.4 m.y.a., places *Homo* near the origin of tool making. However, it is possible that the australopithecines also could have made crude tools. A series of anatomic features strongly suggest the existence of australopithecine culture. These include upright locomotion and evidence of a long period of infant and childhood dependency. Upright bipedalism would have permitted the use of tools and weapons against predators and competitors in an open grassland habitat. Bipedal locomotion also allowed early hominids to carry things, such as scavenged parts of carnivore kills. We know that primates have generalized abilities to adapt through learning. It would be amazing if the australopithecines, who are much more closely related to us than the apes are, didn't have even greater cultural abilities than contemporary apes have.

100–101

done before. Bird bones are structurally different from bones of other vertebrates and they often comprise an important component of human diet. I partially and completely skeletonized several domestic pigeons (*Columba livia*) and studied the way their bones sorted in a current.

I conducted the experiments in a flume, which is a large tank that simulates conditions inside a natural channel but allows for control of many variables. The bottom may be lined with sediment, and an adjustable current flows from one end to another. I examined the order that the bones moved in, how they moved, and how likely they were to be buried. I also examined transport of partially skeletonized birds to compare behavior of individual bones with articulated skeletal units. Repeated observations under a number of different flow conditions (e.g., current velocities, bedform types) allowed me to determine a general order in which bones were expected to move.

This "sorting sequence" is useful as a general guide to whether an avian assemblage has been sorted by a current. For example, an assemblage containing skulls (most likely to be moved) and scapulae or shoulder blades (least likely to be moved) was probably not subjected to sorting. However, if an assemblage contains many easily-moved bones and few "lag" bones (or vice versa), it becomes necessary to rule out current sorting before attributing observed relative frequencies to human (or other) agency.

I also attempted to establish correlations between sorting behavior and bone size, shape, and density. Finally, I noted similarities and differences between sorting sequences for the pigeon and already-published sequences for other vertebrates.

Hopefully, this research constitutes a small step in the direction of understanding how current sorting operates as a taphonomic bias. This knowledge may aid our interpretations of site formation and thus allow greater insight into past human behavior and practices.

The position taken here is that the australopithecines probably had a rudimentary capacity for culture and could have made pebble tools. However, cultural abilities developed exponentially with *Homo*'s appearance and evolution. With increasing reliance on hunting, tool making, and other cultural abilities, *Homo erectus* eventually became the most efficient exploiter of the savanna niche. The last surviving members of *A. boisei* may have been forced into ever-more-marginal areas. They eventually became extinct. By 1 m.y.a., a single species of hominid, *H. erectus*, not only had rendered other hominid forms extinct but also had expanded the hominid range to Asia and Europe. An essentially human strategy of adaptation, incorporating hunting as a fundamental ingredient of a generalized foraging economy, had emerged. Despite regional variation, it was to be the basic economy for our genus until 11,000 years ago. We turn now to the fossils, tools, and life patterns of the various forms of *Homo*.

summary

1. Hominids lived during the Pliocene (5 to 2 m.y.a.) and Pleistocene (2 m.y.a. to 10,000 B.P.) epochs. The australopithecines had appeared by 4.2 m.y.a. The five species of *Australopithecus* were *A. anamensis* (4.2 m.y.a.), *A. afarensis* (3.8 to 3.0 m.y.a.), *A. africanus* (3.0 to 2.5 m.y.a.), *A. robustus* (2.5? to 2 m.y.a.), and *A. boisei* (2.6 to 1.0 m.y.a.). The earliest identifiable hominid remains come from Ethiopia and are classified as *Ardipithecus ramidus.* Next comes *A. anamensis,* then a group of fossils from Hadar, Ethiopia, and Laetoli, Tanzania, classified as *A. afarensis.*
2. These early finds suggest that the common ancestor of humans and the African apes lived more recently than had been thought. These earliest hominids shared many primitive features, including slashing canines, elongated premolars, a small apelike skull, and marked sexual dimorphism. Still, *A. afarensis* and its recently discovered predecessors were definite hominids. In *A. afarensis* this is confirmed by large molars and, more important, by skeletal evidence (e.g., in Lucy) for upright bipedalism.
3. Remains of two later groups, *A. africanus* (graciles) and *A. robustus* (robusts), were found in South Africa. Both groups show the australopithecine trend toward a powerful chewing apparatus. They had large molars and premolars and large and robust faces, skulls, and muscle markings. All these features are more pronounced in the robusts than they are in the graciles. The basis of the australopithecine diet was savanna vegetation. These early hominids also hunted small animals and scavenged the kills of predators.
4. Early *Homo, H. habilis* (2? to 1.6 m.y.a.), evolved into *H. erectus* (1.6 m.y.a. to 300,000 B.P.). By 2 m.y.a. there is ample evidence for two distinct hominid groups: early *Homo* and *A. boisei,* the hyperrobust australopithecines. The latter eventually became extinct around 1 m.y.a. *A. boisei* became increasingly specialized, dependent on tough, coarse, gritty, fibrous savanna vegetation. The australopithecine trend toward dental, facial, and cranial robustness continued with *A. boisei,* but these structures were reduced as *H. habilis* evolved into *H. erectus.*
5. Pebble tools dating to between 2.5 and 2 m.y.a. have been found in Ethiopia, Zaire, and Malawi. Scientists disagree about their maker, some arguing that only early *Homo* could have made them. The position taken here is that the australopithecines could have made pebble tools. However, cultural abilities developed exponentially with *Homo's* appearance and evolution.

key terms

australopithecines Varied group of Pliocene–Pleistocene hominids. The term is derived from their former classification as members of a distinct subfamily, the Australopithecinae; now they are distinguished from *Homo* only at the genus level.

glacials The four or five major advances of continental ice sheets in northern Europe and North America.

gracile Opposite of robust; "gracile" indicates that members of *A. africanus* were a bit smaller, and slighter, less robust, than were members of *A. robustus.*

Homo habilis Term coined by L. S. B. and Mary Leakey; immediate ancestor of *H. erectus;* lived from about 2 to 1.7 or 1.6 m.y.a.

interglacials Extended warm periods between such major glacials as Riss and Würm.

Oldowan pebble tools Earliest (2 to 2.5 m.y.a.) stone tools; first discovered in 1931 by L. S. B. and Mary Leakey at Olduvai Gorge.

Pleistocene Epoch of *Homo's* appearance and evolution; began 1.8 million years ago; divided into Lower, Middle, and Upper.

robust Large, strong, sturdy; said of skull, skeleton, muscle, and teeth; opposite of gracile.

critical thinking questions

1. What are some of the unanswered questions about early hominid evolution? What kinds of information would help provide answers?
2. If you found a new hominoid fossil in East Africa, dated to five million years ago, would it most likely be an ape ancestor or a human ancestor? How would you tell the difference?
3. What was the first species of *Australopithecus*? Where and when did it live? What hominid lived before it?
4. What are some different ways of interpreting the relationships among the early hominids, from *Australopithecus* to *Homo*? That is, which were ancestral to *Homo*, and which were sidelines in human evolution?
5. What is the significance of the black skull?
6. Do you think that *Australopithecus* or *Homo* made the first tools? What's the basis of your opinion?

suggested additional readings

Boaz, N. T.
1999 *Essentials of Biological Anthropology.* Upper Saddle River, NJ: Prentice Hall. Basic text in physical anthropology, with information on paleoanthropology.

Bogin, B.
2001 *The Growth of Humanity.* New York: John Wiley. Human growth in relation to human evolution.

Brace, C. L.
1995 *The Stages of Human Evolution,* 5th ed. Englewood Cliffs, NJ: Prentice Hall. Brief introduction to the hominid fossil record.
2000 *Evolution in an Anthropoloical View.* Walnut Creek, CA: AltaMira. Essays on human evolution.

Campbell, B. G.
1998 *Human Evolution: An Introduction to Man's Adaptations,* 4th ed. New York: Aldine de Gruyter. Basic paleoanthropology text.

Campbell, B. G., and J. D. Loy, eds.
2000 *Humankind Emerging,* 8th ed. New York: Longman. Well-illustrated survey of physical anthropology, particularly the fossil record.

Cole, S.
1975 *Leakey's Luck: The Life of Louis Bazett Leakey, 1903–1972.* New York: Harcourt Brace Jovanovich. The personal and professional life of anthropology's greatest fossil finder, written by an archaeologist.

Johanson, D. C., and B. Edgar
1996 *From Lucy to Language.* New York: Simon & Schuster. Popular account of human evolution by a prominent contributor to understanding the fossil record.

Johanson, D. C., and M. Edey
1981 *Lucy: The Origins of Humankind.* New York: Simon & Schuster. Popular account, written for a general audience, of Johanson's Ethiopian research that uncovered *A. afarensis.*

Lewin, R.
1999 . *Human Evolution: An Illustrated Introduction,* 4th ed. Malden, MA: Blackwell Science. Readable and well-illustrated introduction.

Park, M. A.
1999 *Biological Anthropology,* 2nd ed. Mountain View, CA: Mayfield. A concise introduction, with a focus on scientific inquiry.

Poirier, F. E., and J. K. McKee
1999 *Understanding Human Evolution,* 4th ed. Upper Saddle River, NJ : Prentice Hall. Principles of human evolution.

Relethford, J. H.
2000 *The Human Species: An Introduction to Biological Anthropology.* 4th ed. Mountain View, CA: Mayfield. Up-to-date text in biological anthropology.

Wolpoff, M. H.
1999 *Paleoanthropology,* 2nd ed. New York: McGraw-Hill. Thorough introduction to the hominid and pre-hominid fossil record.

internet exercises

1. Early Hominid Skulls: Visit the American Museum of Natural History's Electronic Newspaper page entitle "Fossil Skulls!," **http://www.amnh.org/enews/iskulls.html.**

   a. Click on the *Australopithicus afarensis* skull. This brings up a page where you can use the mouse to rotate the skull and compare it with a modern human skull. What are some of the differences you notice? What do these differences mean about diet, enviornment, and brain size?

   b. Go back and view the *Paranthropus boisei* (equivalent to *Australopithecus boisei* in this text) and the *Australopithecus africanus* skulls. What are the major differences between the two, and what do these differences say about diet, environment, and brain size?

2. Paleoanthropologist Fieldwork in Kenya: Go to the Human Origins Field Projects in Kenya page of the Human Origins Program at the Smithsonian, **http://www.mnh.si.edu/anthro/humanorigins/aop/aop_ken.html.** Explore the pages describing the fieldwork and methods (Press Continue to Next Page).

   a. The site shows pictures of the modern environment of Kenya. How much has the environment changed since early hominids lived there?

   b. Did the fieldwork just involve excavating fossils? What other types of data are researchers gathering to understand early hominids?

   c. Make sure and read the dispatches from the researchers working at Olorgesailie in 1999, **http://www.mnh.si.edu/anthro/humanorigins/aop/Olorgesailie/dispatch/start.html.** Read some of the diary entries. What is a day in the field of a paleoanthropologist like?

See Chapter 6 on your CD-ROM for additional review and interactive exercises. See your McGraw-Hill Online Learning Center for more.

Chapter 7

Modern Humans

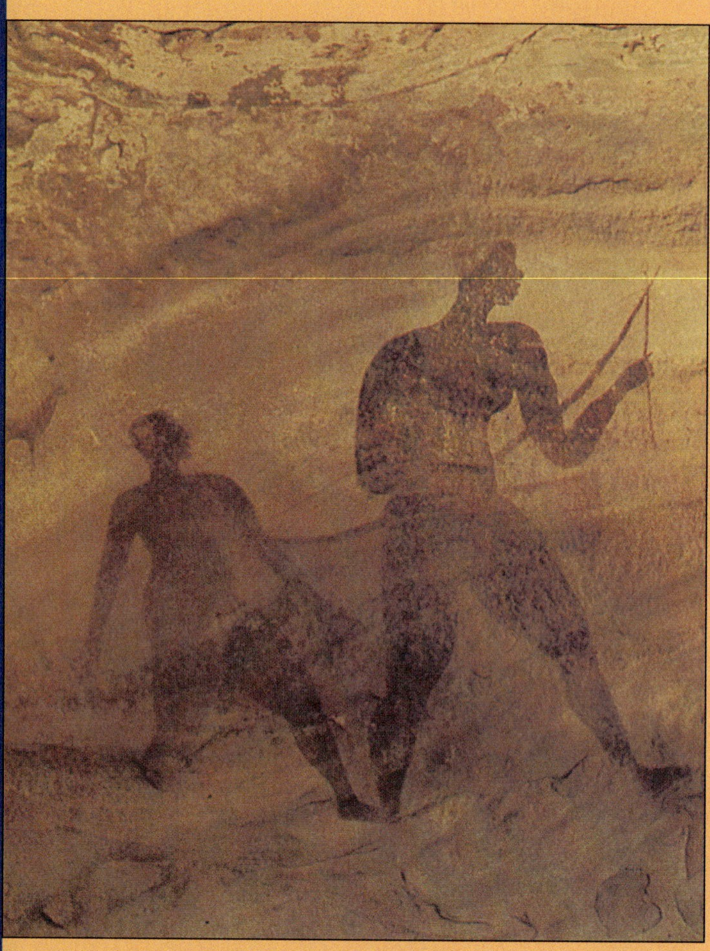

ABCNEWS.GO.COM NEWS BRIEFS

Hominids in Europe: Skulls Probably Represent First Populations to Migrate from Africa

May 12, 2000

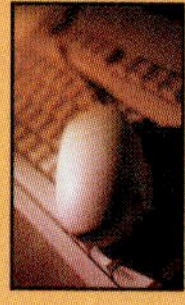

Washington, May 12, 2000—Three skulls dug from under a medieval town in the former Soviet Republic of Georgia and dating back 1.7 million years may represent the first pre-humans who migrated out of Africa and into Europe . . .

The skulls look like those of early humans who lived in East Africa at the same time, and a wealth of tools found at the site look like tools made by the African pre-humans.

This is surprising because archaeologists had believed the species of hominid, called *Homo ergaster*, was too primitive to have made the long and difficult journey from African savanna to the challenging terrain of Europe.

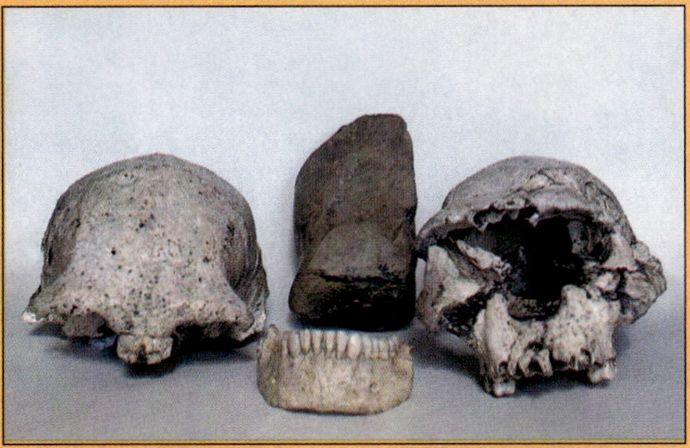

"These constitute the first well-documented humans that came out of Africa," Reid Ferring, a geologist and archaeologist at the University of North Texas at Denton who worked on the study, said in a telephone interview.

"We suggest that these hominids may represent the same species that initially dispersed from Africa and from which the Asian branch of *H. erectus* was derived," the team of U.S., Georgian, French and German scientists wrote in their report . . .

The finding suggests the hominids moved quickly out of Africa across the Levant, what is now Syria and Lebanon, into Turkey and up into Georgia.

Ferring said *Homo ergaster* falls in between the more primitive *Homo habilis* and *Homo erectus*, a robust creature with advanced stone tools that just about everyone thought was the first to move out of Africa to populate Asia and Europe . . .

"In my mind, also, they were advanced in ways that don't show up in their stone tools," he added. This would include the use of wood, but also social development.

The hominids would have had to be organized to survive at 3,000-foot elevations, where it snows heavily in winter . . .

And there would have been lots of them. "It looks like this was a pretty substantial occupation. These people made a lot of tools," Ferring said. "It raises the issue of were these people hunters."

Susan Anton of the University of Florida in Gainesville thinks it is probable.

"The argument that we are making is that during that time in Africa, the savanna is expanding and there is a greater availability of protein on the hoof," she said in a statement.

"With the appearance of *Homo*, we see bigger bodies that require more energy to run, and therefore need these higher-quality sources of protein as fuel." . . .

The site, under a medieval town built on layers of basalt laid down during volcanic activity 1.85 million years ago, offered many clues as to its age. One was provided by the periodic flip-flopping of the Earth's magnetic poles, which leaves a record in the rock.

"We know that 1.78 million years ago the poles shifted from normal to reverse," Ferring said.

The basalt is "normal" but the deposits on top which contain the artifacts and remains are reversed.

This geomagnetic evidence helped them check the other evidence provided by traditional dating of layers and by radiographic dating.

The dates alone would make the hominids the first in Europe.

Source: http://abcnews.go.com/sections/science/DailyNews/hominid_caucasus000512.html.

overview

This chapter begins around two million years ago, with the advent of the genus *Homo.* It ends with the much more recent past, when anatomically modern people were painting artistic masterpieces on cave walls in France and Spain. We focus here on the biological and cultural changes that led from early *Homo,* through intermediate forms, to anatomically modern humans—*Homo sapiens sapiens.*

The earliest member of our genus, *Homo habilis,* evolved into *Homo erectus* between 1.8 and 1.6 million years ago. With *H. erectus,* average cranial capacity doubled, compared with the australopithecines. *H. erectus* extended the human range out of Africa. Complex tools and cooperative hunting suggest a long period of enculturation and learning. Fire permitted expansion into cooler areas, as well as cooking and cave life. *H. erectus* had evolved into archaic *H. sapiens* by 300,000 years ago.

The Neandertals were a form of archaic *H. sapiens* that lived in Western Europe (and elsewhere) early in the last glacial period. Most scientists exclude the Neandertals as ancestors of modern humans. The ancestry of modern humans lies among other archaic *H. sapiens* groups, most probably those in Africa. Modern people had reached Western Europe by 30,000 years ago.

As glacial ice melted, the Western European food quest was generalized to include fish, fowl, and plants, in addition to the diminishing herds of big game. The start of such a diversified economy coincided with an intensification of Upper Paleolithic cave art. On limestone cave walls, prehistoric hunters painted animals important in their lives. Explanations of such cave paintings link them to hunting magic, ceremonies, and initiation rites.

As we saw in Chapter 6, at two million years ago there is evidence for two distinct hominid groups: early *Homo* and *A. boisei,* the hyperrobust australopithecines, which became extinct around 1.2 m.y.a. *A. boisei* became increasingly specialized, dependent on tough, coarse, gritty, fibrous savanna vegetation. The australopithecine trend toward dental, facial, and cranial robustness continued with *A. boisei.* On the other hand, these structures were reduced as late *Homo habilis* evolved into *Homo erectus* between about 1.8 and 1.6 m.y.a. *H. erectus* eventually generalized the subsistence quest to the hunting of large animals to supplement the gathering of vegetation and scavenging.

Early *Homo*

L. S. B. and Mary Leakey gave the name *Homo habilis* to the earliest members of our genus, first found at Olduvai Gorge in Tanzania. Olduvai's oldest layer, Bed I, dates to 1.8 m.y.a. This layer has yielded both small-brained *A. boisei* (average 490 cm^3) fossils and *H. habilis* skulls, with cranial capacities between 600 and 700 cm^3. Richard Leakey uncovered a similarly dated *H. habilis* skull at East Turkana, Kenya. That fossil, known as KNM-ER 1470, has a cranial capacity between 750 and 800 cm^3, which is well outside the australopithecine range of variation.

Another important *habilis* find was made in 1986 by Tim White of the University of California, Berkeley. OH62 (Olduvai Hominid 62) is the partial skeleton of a female *H. habilis* from Olduvai Bed I. This was the first find of a *H. habilis* skull with a significant amount of skeletal material. OH62, dating to 1.8 m.y.a., consists of parts of the skull, the right arm, and both legs. This fossil was surprising because of its small size and its apelike limb bones. Scientists had assumed that *H. habilis* would be taller than Lucy (*A. afarensis*), moving gradually in the direction of *H. erectus.* According to expectations, even a female *H. habilis* should have stood somewhere between Lucy's three feet and the five to six feet of *H. erectus.* However, not only was OH62 just as tiny as Lucy, its arms were longer and more apelike than expected. The limb proportions suggested greater tree-climbing ability than later hominids

Drawing of a *Homo habilis* band, as it might have existed some two million years ago. Besides gathering and hunting small, slow animals, early *Homo* probably scavenged the prey of stronger, faster carnivores such as leopards. What's going on in this photo? Is there any evidence of rudimentary culture?

had. *H. habilis* may still have sought occasional refuge in the trees.

The small size and primitive proportions of *H. habilis* were unexpected given what was already known about early *H. erectus* in East Africa. In deposits near Lake Turkana, Richard Leakey had uncovered two *H. erectus* skulls dating to 1.6 m.y.a. By that date, *H. erectus* had already attained a cranial capacity of 900 cm^3, along with a modern body shape and height. An amazingly complete young male *H. erectus* fossil (WT15,000) found at West Turkana in 1984 by Kimoya Kimeu, a collaborator of the Leakeys, has confirmed this. WT15,000, also known as the Nariokotome boy, was a 12-year-old male who had already reached 168 cm (5 feet 5 inches). He might have grown to 6 feet had he lived. (Some paleoanthropologists use the term *Homo ergaster* to refer to the earliest *H. erectus* fossils in Africa, such as the Nariokotome boy. Here I follow the more traditional scheme of calling them *Homo erectus*.)

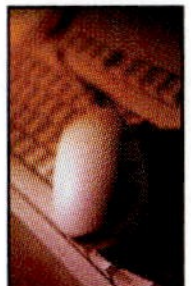

The sharp contrast between the OH62 *H. habilis* (1.8 m.y.a.) and early *H. erectus* (1.6 m.y.a.) suggests an acceleration in hominid evolution during that 200,000-year period. This fossil evidence seems to support a **punctuated equilibrium** model of the early hominid fossil record. In this view, long periods of equilibrium, during which species change little, are interrupted (punctuated) by sudden changes—evolutionary jumps. Apparently hominids changed very little below the neck between Lucy (*A. afarensis*) and *H. habilis*. Then, between 1.8 and 1.6 m.y.a., a profound change—an evolutionary leap—took place. *H. erectus* looks much more human than *H. habilis* does.

THE FAR SIDE By GARY LARSON

"What a find, Williams! The fossilized footprint of a brachiosaurus! . . . And a Homo habilis thrown in to boot!"

What's wrong with this picture?

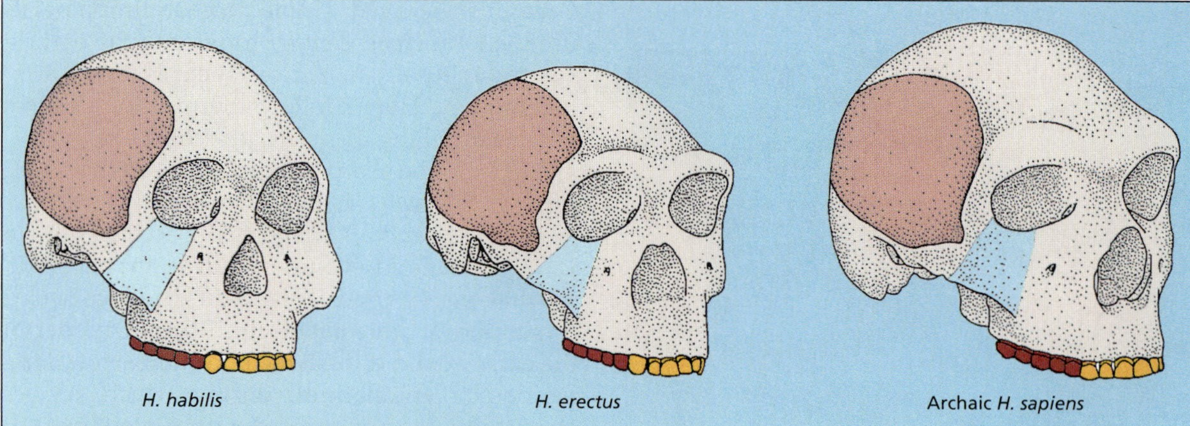

Compare these drawings (left to right) of *H. habilis, H. erectus,* archaic *H. sapiens,* Neandertal, and *H. sapiens sapiens.* What are the main differences you notice? Is the Neandertal more like *H. erectus* or *H. sapiens sapiens*?

This photo shows the early (1.6 m.y.a) *Homo erectus* WT15,000, or Nariokotome boy, found in 1984 near Lake Turkana, Kenya. This is the most complete *Homo erectus* ever found.

Gradual and Rapid Change

Charles Darwin saw life forms as arising from others gradually over time, in a slow and orderly fashion. Small modifications, accumulating over many generations, add up to major changes after thousands of years. Gradualists like Darwin cite intermediate or "mixed-trait" fossils as evidence for their position. They contend we would see even more transitional forms if it weren't for gaps in the fossil record.

Advocates of the punctuated equilibrium model (see Eldredge 1985; Gould 1999) believe that long periods of stasis (stability), when species change little, are interrupted by evolutionary leaps. One reason for such jumps in the fossil record may be extinction followed by invasion by a closely related species. For example, a sea species may die out when a shallow body of water dries up, while a closely related species survives in deeper waters. Later, when the sea reinvades the first locale, the protected species will extend its range to the first area. Another possibility is that when barriers are removed, a group may replace, rather than succeed, a related one because it has a trait that makes it adaptively fitter in the environment they now share.

When there is a sudden environmental change, one possibility is for the pace of evolution to increase. Another possibility is extinction. The earth has witnessed several mass extinctions—worldwide catastrophes affecting multiple species. The biggest one divided the era of "ancient life" (the Paleozoic) from the era of "middle life" (the Mesozoic). This mass

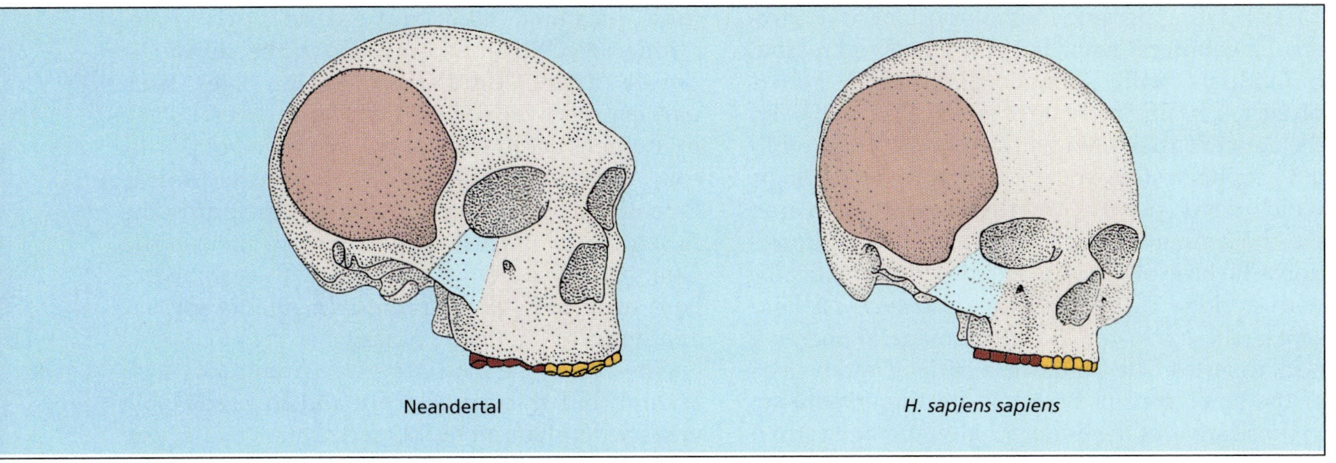

extinction occurred 245 m.y.a., when 4.5 million of the earth's estimated 5 million species (mostly invertebrates) were wiped out. The second biggest extinction, around 65 million years ago, destroyed the dinosaurs. One explanation for the extinction of the dinosaurs is that a massive, long-lasting cloud of gas and dust arose from the impact of a giant meteorite. The cloud blocked solar radiation and therefore photosynthesis, ultimately destroying most plants and the chain of animals that fed on them.

The hominid fossil record exemplifies both gradual and rapid change. Evolution can be slow or fast depending on the rate of environmental change, the speed with which geographic barriers rise or fall, and the effectiveness of the group's adaptive response. Early hominid teeth and skulls show some gradual transitions. For example, some *Homo habilis* fossils combine a larger brain (characteristic of *Homo*) with large back teeth and supportive structures (characteristic of the australopithecines). However, there is no doubt that the pace of hominid evolution sped up around 1.8 m.y.a. This spurt resulted in the emergence (in just 200,000 years) of *H. erectus.* This was followed by a long period of relative stability. One possible key to the rapid emergence of *H. erectus* was a dramatic change in adaptive strategy: greater reliance on hunting through larger body size, along with improved tools and other cultural means of adaptation.

Significant changes in technology occurred during the 200,000-year evolutionary spurt between Bed I (1.8 m.y.a.) and Lower Bed II (1.6 m.y.a) at Olduvai. Tool making got more sophisticated with the advent of *Homo erectus.* Out of the crude tools in Bed I evolved better-made and more varied tools. Edges were straighter, for example, and differences in form suggest functional differentiation—that is, the tools were being made and used for different jobs, such as smashing bones or digging for tubers.

The more sophisticated tools aided in hunting and gathering. With the new tools, *Homo* could obtain meat on a more regular basis and dig and process tubers, roots, nuts, and seeds more efficiently. New tools that could batter, crush, and pulp coarse vegetation also reduced chewing demands.

With changes in the types of foods consumed, the burden on the chewing apparatus eased. Chewing muscles developed less, and supporting structures, like jaws and cranial crests, also were reduced. With less chewing, jaws developed less, and so there was no place to put large teeth. The size of teeth, which form before they erupt, is under stricter genetic control than jaw size and bone size are. Natural selection began to operate against the genes that caused large teeth. In smaller jaws, large teeth now caused dental crowding, impaction, pain, sickness, fever, and sometimes death (there were no dentists).

Some of the main contrasts between *Australopithecus* and early *Homo* are in dentition. *H. erectus* back teeth are smaller; and the front teeth, relatively larger than australopithecine teeth. *H. erectus* used its front teeth to pull, twist, and grip objects. A massive ridge over the eyebrows (a *superorbital torus*) provided buttressing against the forces exerted in these activities.

As hunting became more important to *H. erectus,* encounters with large animals increased. Individuals with stronger skulls had better-protected brains and better survival rates. Given the dangers associated with larger prey, and without sophisticated spear or arrow technology, which developed later, natural selection favored the thickening of certain areas for better protection. The base of the skull expanded dramatically, with a ridge of spongy bone (an *occipital bun*) across the back, for the attachment of massive neck muscles. The frontal and parietal (side) areas of the skull also increased, indicating expansion in those areas of the brain. Finally, average cranial capacity expanded from about 500 cm^3 in the australopithecines to 1,000 cm^3 in *H. erectus,* which is within the modern range of variation.

Out of Africa

Biological and cultural changes enabled *Homo erectus* to exploit a new adaptive strategy—gathering *and* hunting. *H. erectus* pushed the hominid range beyond Africa—to Asia and Europe. Small groups broke off from larger ones and moved a few miles away. They foraged new tracts of edible vegetation and carved out new hunting territories. Through population growth and dispersal, *H. erectus* gradually spread and changed. By 500,000 years ago, hominids were following an essentially human life style based on hunting and gathering. This basic pattern survived until recently in marginal areas of the world, although it is now fading rapidly.

This chapter begins around two million years ago, with the transition to *Homo.* It ends in the less distant past, when anatomically modern humans were painting artistic masterpieces on cave walls in France and Spain. We focus in this chapter on the biological and cultural changes that led from early *Homo,* through intermediate forms, to anatomically modern humans—*Homo sapiens sapiens.*

Paleolithic Tools

The stone-tool-making techniques that evolved out of the Oldowan, or pebble tool, tradition and that lasted until about 15,000 years ago are described by the term **Paleolithic** (from Greek roots meaning "old" and "stone"). The Paleolithic, or Old Stone Age, has three divisions: Lower (early), Middle, and Upper (late). Each part is roughly associated with a particular stage in human evolution. The Lower Paleolithic is roughly associated with *H. erectus;* the Middle Paleolithic with archaic *H. sapiens,* including the Neandertals of Western Europe and the Middle East; and the Upper Paleolithic with early members of our own subspecies, *H. sapiens sapiens,* anatomically modern humans.

The best stone tools are made from rocks such as flint that fracture sharply and in predictable ways when hammered. Quartz, quartzite, chert, and obsidian are also suitable. Each of the three main divisions of the Paleolithic had its typical *tool-making traditions*—coherent patterns of tool manufacture. The main Lower Paleolithic tool-making tradition used by *Homo erectus* was the **Acheulian,** named after the French village of St. Acheul, where it was first identified.

154–155

Like Oldowan tools, the characteristic Acheulian tool, the hand ax, consisted of a modified core of rock. Flakes removed from the core when it was struck with a hammerstone also were used as tools. Flakes, smaller tools with finer cutting edges, became progressively more important later in human evolution, particularly in Middle and Upper Paleolithic tool making.

Acheulian tools were an advance over pebble tools in several ways. Early hominids had made simple tools by picking up pebbles the size of tennis balls and chipping off a few flakes from one end to form a rough and irregular edge. They used these pebble tools (and probably some of the flakes as well) for a variety of purposes, such as smashing animal bones to extract marrow. The Acheulian technique involved chipping the core all over rather than at one end only. The core was converted from a round piece of rock into a flattish oval hand ax about 15 centimeters (6 inches) long. Its cutting edge was far superior to that of the pebble tool.

Hand axes, along with digging sticks made of bone, horn, and wood, were used to dig edible roots and other foods from the ground. Hunters made tools with a sharper cutting edge to skin and cut up their prey. Cleavers—core tools with a straight edge at one end—were used for heavy chopping and hacking at the sinews of larger animals. Flakes were used to make incisions and for

Acheulean hand axes from Olorgesailie, Kenya. Such tools have been found (in Africa) in association with *Homo erectus* fossils dating to 1 million B.P. The characteristic Acheulian tool, the hand ax, was a modified core of rock. Stone flakes also were used as tools.

finer work. The Acheulian tradition illustrates trends in the evolution of technology: greater efficiency, manufacture of tools for specific tasks, and an increasingly complex technology. These trends became even more obvious with the advent of *H. sapiens.*

Adaptive Strategies of *Homo erectus*

Interrelated changes in biology and culture have increased human adaptability—the capacity to live in and modify an ever-wider range of environments. Acheulian tools helped *H. erectus* increase its range. Biological changes also increased hunting efficiency. *H. erectus* had a rugged but essentially modern skeleton that permitted long-distance stalking and endurance during the hunt. The *H. erectus* body was much larger and longer-legged than those of previous hominids, permitting longer-distance hunting of large prey. There is archaeological evidence of *H. erectus*'s success in hunting elephants, horses, rhinos, and giant baboons.

An increase in cranial capacity has been a trend in human evolution. The average *H. erectus* brain (about 1,000 cm^3) doubled the australopithecine average. The capacities of *H. erectus* skulls range from 800 to 1,250 cm^3, well above the *H. sapiens sapiens* minimum.

145

As noted in Chapter 6, larger skulls demand larger birth canals. However, the requirements of upright bipedalism impose limits on the expansion of the pelvic opening. If the opening is too large, the pelvis doesn't provide sufficient support for the trunk. Locomotion suffers, and posture problems develop. If, by contrast, the birth canal is too narrow, mother and child (without the modern option of Caesarean section) may die. Natural selection has struck a balance between the structural demands of upright posture and the tendency toward increased brain size—the birth of immature and dependent children whose brains and skulls grow dramatically after birth.

The interrelation between immature birth, childhood dependency, and social nurturance applies with even greater force to *H. erectus* than it did to the australopithecines. During a long period of dependence, growth, and maturation, children can absorb the traditions and cultural directives of parents and other members of the group. Extended enculturation helps explain increasing complexity in tool manufacture and increasingly efficient coordination of hunting among *H. erectus.*

H. erectus had an essentially modern, though very robust, skeleton with a brain and body closer in size to *H. sapiens* than to *Australopithecus.* Still, several anatomic contrasts, particularly in the cranium, distinguish *H. erectus* from modern humans. Compared with moderns, *H. erectus* had a lower and more sloping forehead accentuated by a large brow ridge above the eyes. Skull bones were thicker, and, as noted, average cranial capacity was smaller. The braincase was lower and flatter than in *H. sapiens,* with spongy bone development at the lower rear of the skull. Seen from behind, the *H. erectus* skull has a broad-based angular shape that has been compared to a half-inflated football (Jolly and White 1995) (Figure 7.1). The *H. erectus* face, teeth, and jaws were larger than those in contemporary humans but smaller than those in *Australopithecus*. The front teeth were especially large, but molar size was well below the australopithecine average. Presumably, this reduction reflected changes in diet or food processing.

Taken together, the *H. erectus* skeleton and chewing apparatus provide biological evidence of a fuller commitment to hunting and gathering, which was *Homo*'s only adaptive strategy until plant cultivation and animal domestication emerged some 10,000 to 12,000 years ago. Archaeologists have found and studied several sites of *H. erectus* activity, including cooperative hunting. At one of these sites, Terra Amata, overlooking Nice in southern France, archaeologists have documented activities of late *H. erectus* (or, possibly, early archaic *H. sapiens*) populations from around 300,000 years ago. Small bands of hunters and gatherers consisting of 15 to 25 people made regular visits during the late spring and early summer to Terra Amata, a sandy cove on the coast of the Mediterranean.

Archaeologists determined the season of occupation by examining fossilized human excrement, which contained pollen from flowers that are known to bloom in late spring. There is evidence for 21 such visits. Four groups camped on a sand bar, six on the beach, and 11 on a sand dune. Archaeologists surmise that the 11 dune sites represent that number of annual visits by the same band (deLumley 1969/1976).

From a camp atop the dune, these people looked down on a river valley where animals were abundant. Bones found at Terra Amata show that their diet included red deer, young elephants, wild boars, wild mountain goats, an extinct variety of rhinoceros, and wild oxen. The Terra Amata people also hunted turtles and birds and collected oysters and mussels. Fish bones also were found at the site.

The arrangement of postholes shows that these people used saplings to support temporary huts. There were hearths—sunken pits and piled stone fireplaces—within the shelters. Stone chips inside the borders of the huts show that tools were made from locally available rocks and beach pebbles. Thus, at Terra Amata, hundreds of thousands of years ago, people were already pursuing an essentially human life style, one that survived in certain coastal regions into the 20th century.

Figure 7.1
Rear Views of Three Skulls of *H. erectus* and One of "Archaic" *Homo sapiens* (a Neandertal)

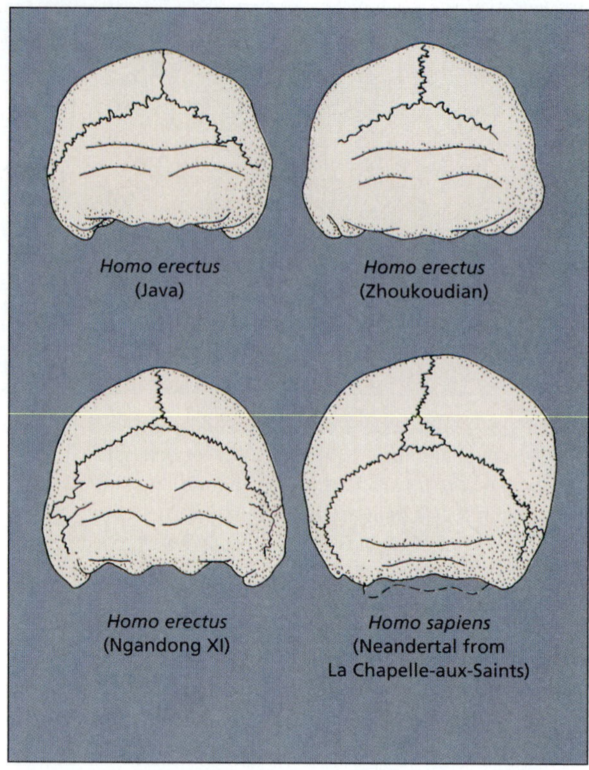

Source: From *Physical Anthropology and Archaeology*, 5th edition, by C. J. Jolly and R. White (New York: McGraw-Hill, 1995), p. 271.

Note the more angular shape of the *H. erectus* skulls, with the maximum breadth low down, near the base.

The hearths at Terra Amata and other sites confirm that fire was part of the human adaptive kit by this time. Fire provided protection against cave bears and saber-toothed tigers. It permitted *H. erectus* to occupy cave sites, including Zhoukoudian, near Beijing in China, which has yielded the remains of more than 40 specimens of *H. erectus*. Fire widened the range of climates open to human colonization. Its warmth enabled people to survive winter cold in temperate regions. Human control over fire offered other advantages, such as cooking, which breaks down vegetable fibers and tenderizes meat. Cooking kills parasites and makes meat more digestible, thus reducing strain on the chewing apparatus.

Could language (fireside chats, perhaps) have been an additional advantage available to *H. erectus?* Archaeological evidence confirms the cooperative hunting of large animals and the manufacture of complicated tools. These activities might have been too complex to have gone on without some kind of language. Speech would have aided coordination, cooperation, and the learning of traditions, including tool making. Words, of course, aren't preserved until the advent of writing. However, given the potential for language-based communication—which even chimps and gorillas share with *H. sapiens*—and given brain size within the low *H. sapiens* range, it seems plausible to assume that *H. erectus* had rudimentary speech. For contrary views, see Binford (1981) and Fisher (1988*b*).

The Evolution and Expansion of *Homo erectus*

The archaeological record of *H. erectus* activities can be combined with the fossil evidence to provide us with a more complete picture of our Lower Paleolithic ancestors. We now consider some of the fossil data, whose geographical distribution is shown in Figure 7.2. Early *H. erectus* remains, found by Richard Leakey's team at East and West Turkana, Kenya, and dated to around 1.6 m.y.a., including the Nariokotome boy, have been discussed previously.

164

Two partial skulls—one of a young adult male (780 cm^3), one of an adolescent female (650 cm^3)—were recently found at the Dmanisi site in the former Soviet Republic of Georgia (see chapter opening vignette). They have been assigned the remarkably early date of 1.7 m.y.a. There are notable similarities between these skulls and that of the Narikotome boy (1.6 m.y.a.) found near Kenya's Lake Turkana. Tools of comparable age associated with the Kenyan and Georgian fossils also are similar. Some paleoanthropologists assign the Nariokotome and Dmanisi finds to a new species, *Homo ergaster,* intermediate between *H. habilis* and *H. erectus.* Others simply consider them early *H. erectus.* The Dmanisi finds suggest a rapid spread, by 1.7 m.y.a., of early *Homo* out of Africa into Europe and eventually into Asia.

Later *H. erectus* remains come from Upper Bed II at Olduvai, Tanzania. Those fossils, about a million years old, were associated with Acheulian tools. Besides Kenya, African *H. erectus* fossils have also been found in Ethiopia, Eritrea, Tanzania, and South Africa. The time span of *H. erectus* in East Africa was long. *H. erectus* fossils also have been found in Bed IV at Olduvai, dating to 500,000 B.P.

In 1891, the Indonesian island of Java yielded the first *H. erectus* fossil find, popularly known as "Java man." Eugene Dubois, a Dutch army surgeon, had gone to Java to discover a transitional form between apes and humans. Of course, we now know that the transition to hominid had taken place much earlier than the *H. erectus* period and occurred in Africa. However, Dubois's good luck did lead him to the most ancient human fossils discovered at that time. Excavating near the village of Trinil, Dubois found parts of a *H. erectus* skull and a thigh bone. During the 1930s and 1940s, excavations in Java uncovered additional remains.

Figure 7.2
The Sites of Discovery of *Homo erectus* and Its Probable Maximum Distribution

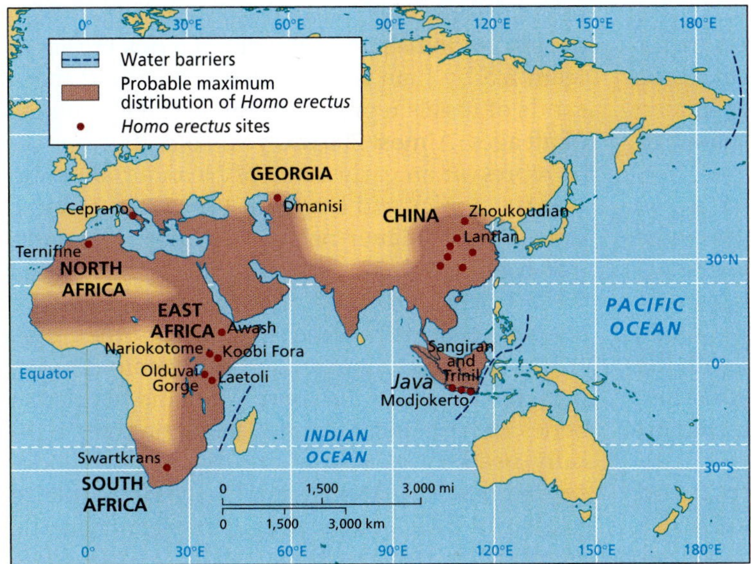

Source: From *Physical Anthropology and Archaeology*, 5th edition, by C. J. Jolly and R. White (New York: McGraw-Hill, 1995), p. 268.

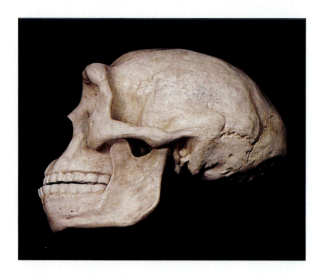

Meet *Homo erectus.* On the left is a reconstruction of one of the *H. erectus* skulls from Zhoukoudian, China. On the right, an attempt to render *H. erectus* in the flesh.

The Indonesian *H. erectus* fossils date back at least 700,000, and maybe more than a million, years. Fragments of a skull and a lower jaw found in northern China at Lantien may be about the same age. Other *H. erectus* remains, of uncertain date, have been found in Algeria and Morocco in North Africa.

The largest group of *H. erectus* fossils was found in the Zhoukoudian cave in China. The Zhoukoudian ("Peking"—now Beijing—"man") site, excavated from the late 1920s to the late 1930s, was a major find for the human fossil record. Zhoukoudian yielded remains of tools, hearths, animal bones, and more than 40 hominids, including five skulls. The analysis of these remains led to the conclusion that the Java and Zhoukoudian fossils were examples of the same broad stage of human evolution. Today they are commonly classified together as *H. erectus.*

The Zhoukoudian individuals lived more recently than did the Javanese *H. erectus,* between 500,000 and 350,000 years ago, when the climate in China was colder and moister than it is today. The inference about the climate has been made on the basis of the animal remains found with the human fossils. The people at Zhoukoudian ate venison, and seed and plant remains suggest they were both gatherers and hunters.

What about Europe? A cranial fragment found at Ceprano, Italy, in 1994, has been assigned a date of 900,000 B.P. Other probable *H. erectus* remains have been found in Europe, but their dates are uncertain. All are later than the Ceprano skull, and they are usually classified as late *H. erectus,* or transitional between *H. erectus* and early *H. sapiens.* There have been recent fossil discoveries at two sites in northern Spain's Atapuerca mountains. The site of Gran Dolina has yielded the remains of 800,000-year-old hominids that Spanish researchers see as a possible common ancestor of *H. sapiens sapiens* and the Neandertals. At the nearby cave of Sima dos Huesos a team led by Juan Luis Arsuaga has found thousands of fossils representing at least 33 hominids of all ages. Almost 300,000 years old, they appear to represent an early stage of Neandertal evolution (Lemonick and Dorfman 1999). A jaw from a gravel pit at Mauer near Heidelberg, Germany, has been assigned a broad time span between 450,000 and 250,000 B.P. Archaeological evidence also suggests the presence of *H. erectus* in Europe. *H. erectus* therefore extended the hominid range from the tropics to the subtropical and temperate zones of Asia and Europe. The stone tools typically used by *H. erectus* are much more widespread than the fossils are. The combination of fossil and archaeological evidence confirms the adaptability of *H. erectus.*

Archaic *Homo sapiens*

Africa, which was center stage during the australopithecine period, is joined by Asia and Europe during the *H. erectus* and *H. sapiens* periods of hominid evolution. European fossils and tools have contributed disproportionately to our knowledge of early (archaic) *H. sapiens.* This doesn't mean that *H. sapiens* evolved in Europe, that most early *H. sapiens* lived in Europe, or that comparable changes in biology and culture were not occurring elsewhere. Indeed, the fossil evidence suggests that parallel physical changes and cultural advances were proceeding in Asia and especially in Africa (Wolpoff 1999). There were probably many more people in the tropics than in Europe during the ice ages. We merely *know more* about recent human evolution in Europe because archaeology and fossil hunting—not human evolution—have been going on longer there than in Africa and Asia.

Recent discoveries, along with reinterpretation of the dating and the anatomic relevance of some earlier finds, are filling in the gap between *H. erectus* and archaic *H. sapiens*. **Archaic *H. sapiens*** (300,000 to 28,000 B.P.) encompasses the earliest members of our species, along with the **Neandertals** (*H. sapiens neanderthalensis*—130,000 to 28,000 B.P.) of Europe and the Middle East and their Neandertal-like contemporaries in Africa and Asia. Brain size in archaic *H. sapiens* was within the modern human range. (The modern average, remember, is about 1,350 cm^3.) (See Table 7.1.) A rounding out of the braincase was associated with the increased brain size. As Jolly and White (1995)

put it, evolution was pumping more brain into the *H. sapiens* cranium—like filling a football with air.

Archaic *H. sapiens* lived during the last part of the *Middle Pleistocene—during* the *Mindel* (second) glacial, the interglacial that followed it, and the following *Riss* (third) glacial. The distribution of the fossils and tools of archaic *H. sapiens,* which have been found in Europe, Africa, and Asia, shows that *Homo*'s tolerance of environmental diversity had increased. For example, the Neandertals and their immediate ancestors managed to survive extreme cold in Europe. Archaic *H. sapiens* occupied the Arago cave in southeastern France at a time when Europe was bitterly cold. The only Riss glacial site with facial material, Arago, was excavated in 1971. It produced a partially intact skull, two jaw bones, and teeth from a dozen individuals. With an apparent date of about 200,000 B.P., the Arago fossils have mixed features that seem transitional between *H. erectus* and the Neandertals.

Table 7.1
Summary of Data on *Homo* Fossil Groups

Fossil representatives of the genus *Homo*, compared with modern humans (*Homo sapiens sapiens*) and chimps (*Pan troglodytes*).

Species	Dates	Known Distribution	Important Sites	Brain Size (in cm^3)
Homo sapiens sapiens	100,000 B.P. to present	Worldwide	Beijing, New York, Paris, Nairobi	1350
Homo sapiens neanderthalensis	130,000 to 28,000 B.P.	Europe, southwestern Asia	La Chapelle-aux-Saints	1430
Archaic *Homo sapiens*	300,000 to 28,000 B.P.	Africa, Europe, Asia	Kabwe, Arago, Dali, Mount Carmel caves	1135
Homo erectus	1.7 m.y.a. to 300,000 B.P.	Africa, Asia, Europe	East + West Turkana, Olduvai, Zhoukoudian, Java, Ceprano	900
Pan troglodytes	Modern	Central Africa	Gombe, Mahale	390

The Neandertals

Neandertals were first discovered in Western Europe. The first one was found in 1856 in a German valley called Neander Valley—*tal* is the German word for valley. Scientists had trouble interpreting the discovery. It was clearly human and similar to modern Europeans in many ways, yet different enough to be considered strange and abnormal. This was, after all, 35 years before Dubois discovered the first *Homo erectus* fossils in Java and almost 70 years before the first australopithecine was found in South Africa. Darwin's *On the Origin of Species,* published in 1859, had not yet appeared to offer a theory of evolution through natural selection. There was no framework for understanding human evolution. Over time, the fossil record filled in, along with evolutionary theory. Subsequent discoveries of Neandertals in Europe and the Middle East and of archaic human fossils with comparable features in Africa and Asia confirmed this stage of human evolution as geographically widespread. With the discovery of earlier and later hominid fossils, the similarities and differences between Neandertals and other members of *Homo sapiens* have become clearer.

Fossils that are not Neandertals but that have similar features (such as large faces and brow ridges) have been found in Africa and Asia. The Kabwe skull from Zambia (130,000 B.P.) is an archaic *H. sapiens* with a Neandertal-like brow ridge. Archaic Chinese fossils with Neandertal-like features have been found at Maba and Dali. Neandertals have been found in Central Europe and the Middle East. For example, Neandertal fossils found at the Shanidar cave in northern Iraq date to around 60,000 B.P., as does a Neandertal skeleton found at Israel's Kebara cave (Shreeve 1992). At the Israeli site of Tabun on Mount Carmel, a Neandertal female skeleton was excavated in 1932. She was a contemporary of the Shanidar Neandertals, and her brow ridges, face, and teeth show typical Neandertal robustness.

Cold-Adapted Neandertals

By 75,000 B.P., after an interglacial interlude, Western Europe's hominids (Neandertals, by then) again faced extreme cold as the Würm glacial began. To deal with this environment, they wore clothes, made more elaborate tools, and hunted reindeer, mammoths, and woolly rhinos.

The Neandertals were stocky, with large trunks relative to limb length—a phenotype that minimizes surface area and thus conserves heat. Another adaptation to extreme cold was the Neandertal face, which has been likened to a *H. erectus* face that has been pulled forward by the nose. This extension increased the distance between outside air and the arteries that carry blood to the brain and was adaptive in a cold climate. The brain is sensitive to temperature changes and must be kept warm. The massive nasal cavities of Neandertal fossils suggest long, broad noses. This would expand the area for warming and moistening air.

Neandertal characteristics also include huge front teeth, broad faces, and large brow ridges, and ruggedness of the skeleton and musculature. What activities were associated with these anatomic traits? Neandertal teeth probably did many jobs later done by tools (Brace 1995; Rak 1986). The front teeth show heavy wear, suggesting that they were used for varied purposes, including chewing animal hides to make soft winter clothing out of them. The massive Neandertal face showed the stresses of constantly using the front teeth for holding and pulling.

Comparison of early and later Neandertals shows a trend toward reduction of their robust features. Neandertal technology, a Middle Paleolithic tradition called **Mousterian,** improved considerably during the Würm glacial. Tools assumed many burdens formerly placed on the anatomy. For example, tools took over jobs once done by the front teeth. Through a still imperfectly understood mechanism, facial muscles and supporting structures developed less. Smaller front teeth—perhaps because of dental crowding—were favored. The projecting face reduced, as did the brow ridge, which had provided buttressing against the forces generated when the large front teeth were used for environmental manipulation.

The Neandertals and Modern People

Scientists disagree about whether the Neandertals were ancestral to modern Western Europeans. The current prevailing view, denying this

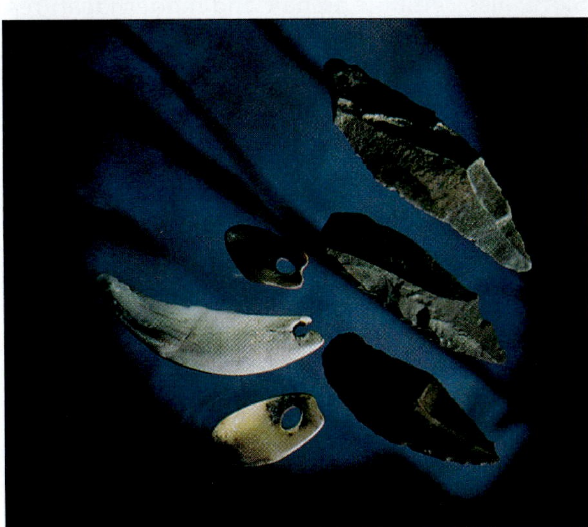

In a wilderness survival school in the mountains of central Spain, Mikel Aguirre flakes a flint knife. Manufactured in four minutes, the razor-sharp blade will be used to butcher a goat. The Neandertals' Mousterian technology improved considerably during the Würm glacial. Shown here, from late Neandertal sites in French rock shelters, come sophisticated flake tools, "backed" to fit the index finger, along with personal decorations, such as elk and wolf teeth.

ancestry, proposes that *H. erectus* split into separate groups, one ancestral to the Neandertals and the other ancestral to *H. sapiens sapiens*—**anatomically modern humans (AMHs)** who appeared in Western Europe after 40,000 B.P. In different versions of this view, modern humans

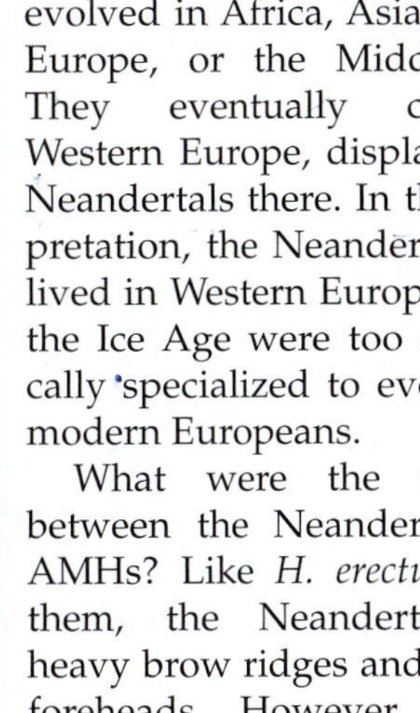

evolved in Africa, Asia, Central Europe, or the Middle East. They eventually colonized Western Europe, displacing the Neandertals there. In this interpretation, the Neandertals who lived in Western Europe during the Ice Age were too anatomically specialized to evolve into modern Europeans.

What were the contrasts between the Neandertals and AMHs? Like *H. erectus* before them, the Neandertals had heavy brow ridges and slanting foreheads. However, average Neandertal cranial capacity (more than 1,400 cm^3) exceeded the modern average. Neandertal jaws were large, providing support for huge front teeth, and their faces were massive. The bones and skull were generally more rugged and had greater sexual dimorphism—particularly in the face and skull—than do those of AMHs. In some Western European fossils, these contrasts between Neandertals and AMHs are accentuated—giving a stereotyped, or *classic Neandertal,* appearance.

Some scientists believe only the classic Neandertals were too different to be ancestors of AMHs. They contend that outside Western Europe, the anatomic differences were fewer and the people who lived there were not really Neandertals but merely Neandertal-like in some respects. Actually, the European Neandertals were variable, and many lacked the "classic" constellation of features.

Doubt about the Neandertal ancestry of Western Europeans is partly due to the history of fossil discoveries. As mentioned, the first Neandertal remains were found in 1856; and the first *H. erectus* ("Java man"), in 1891. The inclusion of "Java man" in the human evolutionary tree was debated for decades. Nor was the first australopithecine skull, uncovered in 1924, immediately accepted as a hominid. Without these earlier hominids, which were much more different from AMHs than the Neandertals were, the differences between Neandertals and moderns stood out and were emphasized.

The interpretation of one fossil contributed most to the scientific rejection of Neandertal ancestry (and to the popular stereotype of the

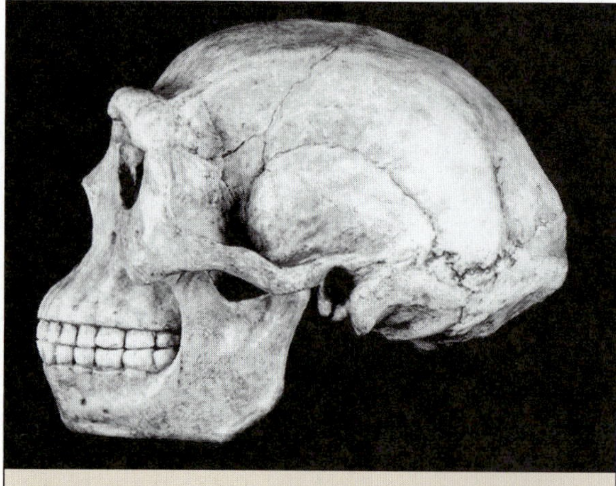

The skull of the classic Neandertal found in 1908 at La Chapelle-aux-Saints. This was the first Neandertal to be discovered with the whole skull, including the face, preserved. Later finds showed that La Chapelle wasn't a typical Neandertal but an extreme form. What was atypical about this fossil?

slouching caveman). This was the complete human skeleton discovered in 1908 at La Chapelle-aux-Saints in southwestern France, in a layer containing the characteristic Mousterian tools made by Neandertals. This was the first Neandertal to be discovered with the whole skull, including the face, preserved.

The skeleton was given for study to the French paleontologist Marcellin Boule. His analysis of the fossil helped create the stereotype of Neandertals as brutes who had trouble walking upright. Boule argued that La Chapelle's brain, although larger than the modern average, was inferior to modern brains. Further, he suggested that the Neandertal head was slung forward like an ape's. To round out the primitive image, Boule proclaimed that the Neandertals were incapable of straightening their legs for fully erect locomotion. However, later fossil finds show that the La Chapelle fossil wasn't a typical Neandertal but an extreme one. Also, this much-publicized "classic" Neandertal turned out to be an aging man whose skeleton had been distorted by osteoarthritis. Hominids, after all, have been erect bipeds for millions of years. European Neandertals were a variable population. Other Neandertal finds lack La Chapelle's combination of extreme features and are more acceptable ancestors for AMHs.

Advocates of the Neandertal ancestry of modern Europeans cite certain fossils to support their view. For example, the Central European site of Mladeč (31,000 to 33,000 B.P.) has yielded remains of several hominids that combine Neandertal robustness with modern features. Wolpoff (1999) also notes modern features in the late Neandertals found at l'Hortus in France and Vindija in Croatia. A recently reported (1999) find of a four-year-old boy in Portugal, dated to 24,000 B.P., also shows mixed Neandertal and modern features.

Fossils from Israel's Mount Carmel site of Skhūl also combine archaic and modern features. But most analyses stress the "modernness" of the Skhūl fossils, which date to 100,000 B.P. Another group of modern-looking and similarly dated (92,000 B.P.) skulls comes from the Israeli site of Qafzeh. The Skhūl and Qafzeh fossils cast serious doubt on the Neandertal ancestry of AMHs in Europe and the Middle East. The skulls from Skhūl (Figure 7.3) and Qafzeh have a modern, rather than a Neandertal, shape and are classified

What images would you have if you heard someone described as "a Neandertal"? The European Neandertals were a variable population, but they have been stereotyped as subhuman brutes. The Neandertal Museum in Erkrath, Germany, near the original fossil discovery site, offers different representations of Neandertals, from a beast to "just a guy in a suit."

Figure 7.3
Skhūl V

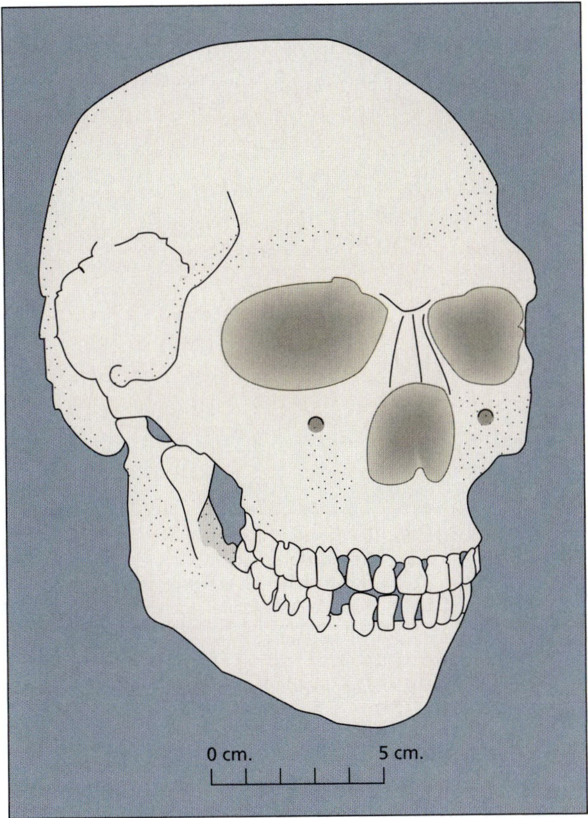

This anatomically modern human with some archaic features was recently redated to 100,000 B.P. This is one of several fossils found at Skhūl, Israel. Formerly dated to 32,000 B.P., this fossil group once seemed transitional between Neandertals and *H. sapiens sapiens.*

as AMHs. Their braincases are higher, shorter, and rounder than Neandertal skulls. There is a more filled-out forehead region, which rises more vertically above the brows. A marked chin is another modern feature. Still, these early AMHs do retain distinct brow ridges, though reduced from their archaic *H. sapiens* ancestor.

Dated to 100,000 and 92,000 B.P., the Skhūl and Qafzeh findings suggest that archaic *H. sapiens* was evolving directly into AMHs in the Middle East more than 50,000 years before the demise of the Western European Neandertals. Neandertals and AMHs, therefore, overlapped in time rather than being ancestor and descendant. AMHs even may have inhabited the Middle East before the Neandertals did. Ofer Bar-Yosef (1987) suggests that during the last (Würm) glacial period, which began around 75,000 B.P., Western European Neandertals spread east and south (and into the Middle East) as part of a general southward expansion of cold-adapted fauna. AMHs, in turn, followed warmer-climate fauna south into Africa, returning to the Middle East once the Würm ended.

Current interpretations of the fossil evidence and dating seem to support the replacement hypothesis, which denies the Neandertal ancestry of AMHs in Western Europe and the Middle East. AMHs seem likely to have evolved from an archaic *H. sapiens* African ancestor. In Africa, as in the Middle East and Asia, the archaic *H. sapiens* fossils generally had flatter, less projecting faces than the Neandertals did. Eventually, AMHs spread to other areas, including Western Europe, where they replaced, or interbred with, the Neandertals, whose robust traits eventually disappeared (Figure 7.4).

About Eve

In 1987 a group of molecular geneticists at the University of California at Berkeley offered support for the idea that *H. sapiens sapiens* (anatomically modern humans or AMHs) arose fairly recently in Africa, then spread out and colonized the world. Rebecca Cann, Mark Stoneking, and Allan C. Wilson (1987) analyzed genetic markers in placentas donated by 147 women whose ancestors came from Africa, Europe, the Middle East, Asia, New Guinea, and Australia.

The researchers focused on mitochondrial DNA (mtDNA). This genetic material is located in the cytoplasm (the outer part—not the nucleus) of cells. Ordinary DNA, which makes up the genes that determine most physical traits, is found in the nucleus and comes from both parents. But only the mother contributes mitochondrial DNA (cloned from her own mtDNA) to the fertilized egg. The father plays no part in mtDNA transmission, just as the mother has nothing to do with the transmission of the Y chromosome, which comes from the father and determines the sex of the child. Because mtDNA is cloned, its genetic pattern is usually an exact replica of the mother's, except when mutations occur.

To establish a "genetic clock," the Berkeley researchers measured the variation in mtDNA in their 147 tissue samples. They cut each sample

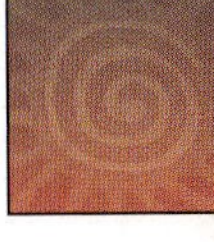

into segments to compare with the others. By estimating the number of mutations that had taken place in each sample since its common origin with the 146 others, the researchers drew an evolutionary tree with the help of a computer.

That tree started in Africa and then branched in two. One group remained in Africa, while the other one split off, carrying its mtDNA to the rest of the world. The variation in mtDNA was greatest among Africans. This suggests that they have been evolving the longest. In fact, some of the earliest dated AMH fossils have been found on the African continent. AMH fossils and associated tools that may date back 100,000 years have been found at two South African cave sites, as well as at Qafzeh and Skhūl, Israel, as described previously.

The Berkeley researchers concluded that everyone alive today descends from a woman (dubbed "Eve") who lived in sub-Saharan Africa around 200,000 years ago. Eve was not the only woman alive then; she was just the only one whose descendants have included a daughter in each generation through the present. Because mtDNA passes exclusively through females, mtDNA lines disappear whenever a woman has no children or has only sons. The details of the Eve theory suggest that her descendants left Africa no more than 135,000 years ago. They eventually displaced the Neandertals in Western Europe and went on to colonize the rest of the world.

Figure 7.4

The Known Distribution of Human Populations Approximately 130,000 to 28,000 B.P.

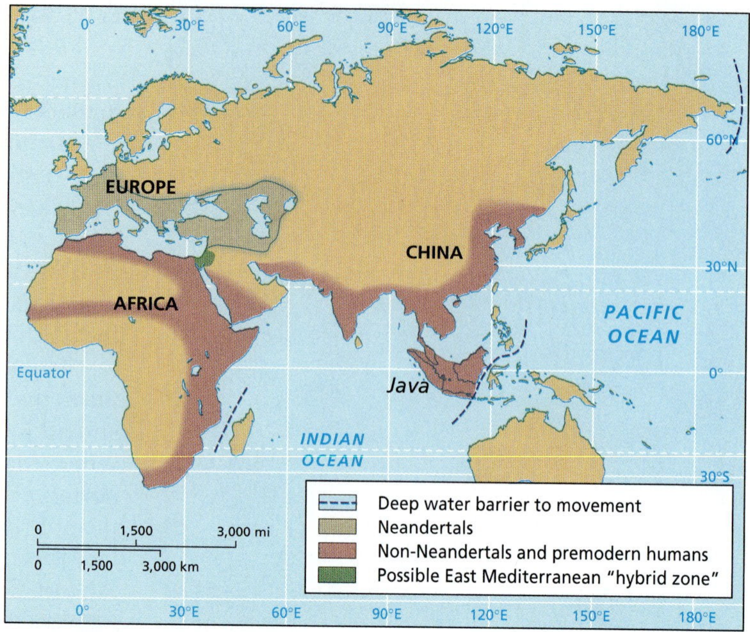

Source: From *Physical Anthropology and Archaeology*, 5th edition, by C. J. Jolly and R. White (New York: McGraw-Hill, 1995), p. 277.

According to some scholars, Neandertals and moderns may have mixed in the East Mediterranean hybrid zone. In your opinion, would that have been possible?

Recent DNA Evidence

Recent DNA evidence strengthens the view that the Neandertals and AMHs were distinct groups, rather than ancestor and descendant. In 1997, ancient DNA was extracted from one of the Neandertal bones originally found in Germany's Neander Valley in 1856. This DNA, from an upper arm bone (humerus), has been compared with the DNA of modern humans. The kinds of matches we would expect in closely related humans did not occur. Thus, there were 27 differences between the Neandertal DNA and a reference sample of modern DNA. By contrast, samples of DNA from modern populations worldwide show only 5 to 8 differences with the reference sample. The differences between the Neandertal and the modern DNA suggest a separation around 550,000 to 690,000 years ago.

This was the first time that DNA of a premodern human had been recovered. The original analysis was done by Svante Pääbo of the University of Munich. The findings were then duplicated by Mark Stoneking and Anne Stone at Pennsylvania State University. The researchers again focused on mitochondrial DNA.

We know that the Neandertals coexisted with modern humans in the Middle East for thousands of years. At certain Israeli sites, modern humans date back 100,000 years. Middle Eastern Neandertals date back 40,000 to 60,000 years. In Western Europe, Neandertals survived perhaps through 28,000 years ago. To what extent did Neandertals and AMHs interact? Did they trade or interbreed? Were the Neandertals out-competed by modern humans or killed off by them? Were they absorbed into the AMH population and genetically swamped?

If the Neandertals did contribute genetically to modern populations, shouldn't there be evident similarities between Neandertal DNA and that of the modern people of Europe, where the Neandertals lasted the longest? Svante Pääbo and his colleagues compared the Neandertal DNA with DNA from five modern populations. Neandertal DNA was no closer to modern Europeans than to the other four groups. While this does not totally rule out the possibility of Neandertal–AMH interbreeding, it does suggest that the Neandertal genetic contribution to modern gene pools, if any, was small (Rose 1997).

Advances in Technology

Early *H. sapiens sapiens* (AMHs) made tools in a variety of traditions, collectively known as **Upper Paleolithic** because of the tools' location in the upper, or more recent, layers of sedimentary deposits. Some cave deposits have Mousterian tools (made by Neandertals) at lower levels and increasing numbers of Upper Paleolithic tools at higher levels.

Although the Neandertals are remembered more for their physiques than for their manufacturing abilities, their tool kits were sophisticated. Mousterian technology included at least 14 categories of tools designed for different jobs. The Neandertals elaborated on a revolutionary technique of flake-tool manufacture invented in southern Africa around 200,000 years ago, which spread widely throughout the Old World. Uniform flakes were chipped off a specially prepared core of rock. Additional work on the flakes produced such special-purpose tools as those shown in Figure 7.5. Scrapers were used to prepare animal hides for clothing. And special tools also were designed for sawing, gouging, and piercing (Binford and Binford 1979).

The Upper Paleolithic traditions of early *H. sapiens sapiens* all emphasized **blade tools.** Blades were hammered off a prepared core, as in Mousterian

Figure 7.5
Middle Paleolithic Tools of the Mousterian Tool-Making Tradition

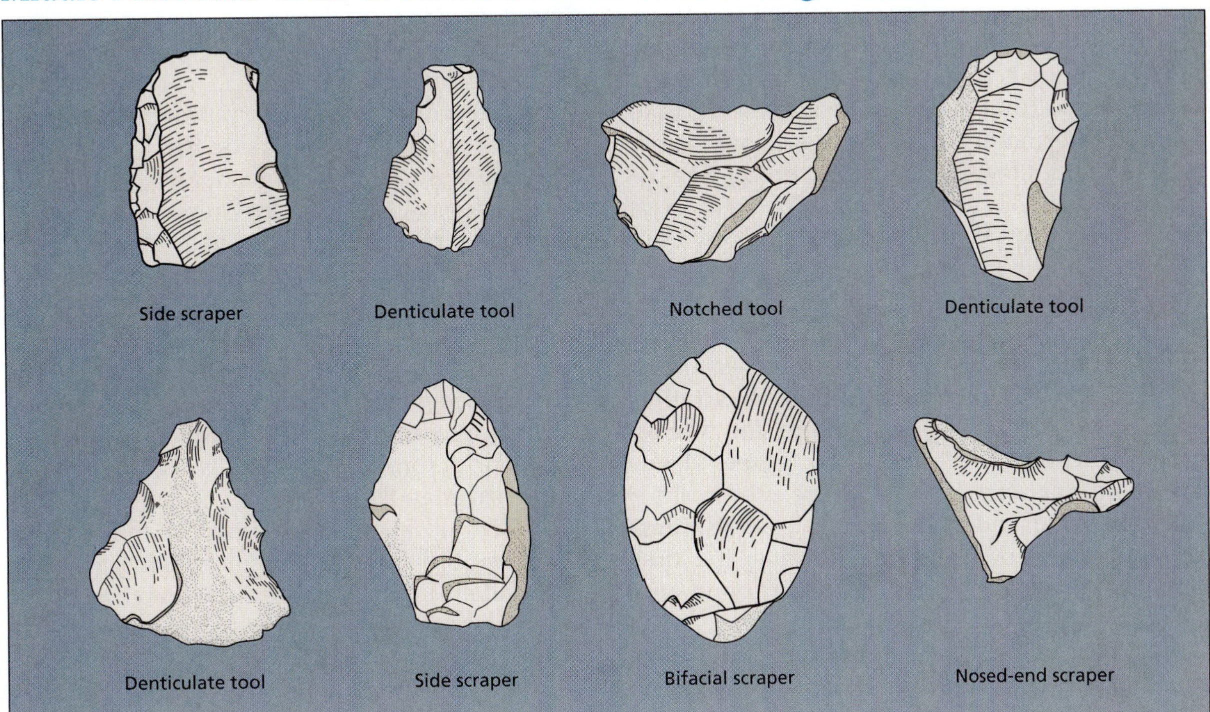

The manufacture of diverse tool types for special purposes confirms Neandertal sophistication.

technology, but a blade is longer than a flake—its length is more than twice its width. Blades were chipped off cores four to six inches high by hitting a punch made of bone or antler with a hammerstone (Figure 7.6). Blades were then modified to produce a variety of special-purpose implements. Some were composite tools that were made by joining reworked blades to other materials.

The blade-core method was faster than the Mousterian and produced 15 times as much cutting edge from the same amount of material. More efficient tool production might have been especially valued by people whose economy depended on cooperative hunting of mammoths, woolly rhinoceroses, bison, wild horses, bears, wild cattle, wild boars, and—principally—reindeer. It has been estimated that approximately 90 percent of the meat eaten by Western Europeans between 25,000 and 15,000 B.P. came from reindeer.

Trends observable throughout the entire archaeological record also mark the changeover from the Mousterian to the Upper Paleolithic. First, the number of distinct tool types increased. This trend reflected functional specialization—the manufacture of special tools for particular jobs. A second trend was increasing standardization in tool manufacture. The form and inventory of tools reflect several factors: the jobs tools are intended to perform, the physical properties of the raw materials from which they are made, and distinctive cultural traditions about how to make tools. Furthermore, accidental or random factors also influenced tool forms and the proportions of particular tool types (Isaac 1972). However, Mousterian and Upper Paleolithic tools were more standardized than those of *H. erectus* were.

Other trends include growth in *Homo*'s total population and geographic range and increasing local cultural diversity as people specialized in particular economic activities. Illustrating increasing economic diversity are the varied special-purpose tools made by Upper Paleolithic populations. Scrapers were used to hollow out wood and bone, scrape animal hides, and remove bark from trees. Burins, the first chisels, were used to make slots in bone and wood and to engrave designs on bone. Awls, which were drills with sharp points, were used to make holes in wood, bone, shell, and skin.

Upper Paleolithic bone tools have survived: knives, pins, needles with eyes, and fishhooks.

Figure 7.6
Upper Paleolithic Blade-Tool Making

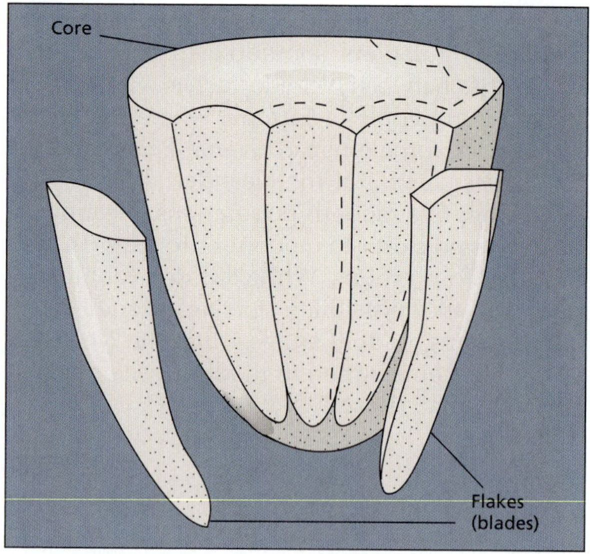

Blades are flakes that are detached from a specially prepared core. A punch (usually a piece of bone or antler) and a hammerstone (not shown here) were used to knock the blade off the core.

The needles suggest that clothes sewn with thread—made from the sinews of animals—were being worn. Fishhooks and harpoons confirm an increased emphasis on fishing.

Different tool types may represent culturally distinct populations who made their tools differently because of different ancestral traditions. Archaeological sites also may represent different activities carried out at different times of the year by a single population. Some sites, for example, are obviously butchering stations, where prehistoric people hunted, made their kills, and carved them up. Others are residential sites, where a wider range of activities was carried out. The major fossils and hominid types found in the Old World through the Upper Paleolithic are summarized in Figure 7.7.

To sum up hominid evolutionary trends: With increasing technological differentiation, specialization, and efficiency, humans have become increasingly adaptable. Through heavy reliance on cultural means of adaptation, *Homo* has become (in numbers and range) the most successful primate by far. The hominid range expanded significantly in Upper Paleolithic times with the colonization of

Figure 7.7

Chronology of Evolution in Human Biology and Tool Making over the Past 4 Million Years

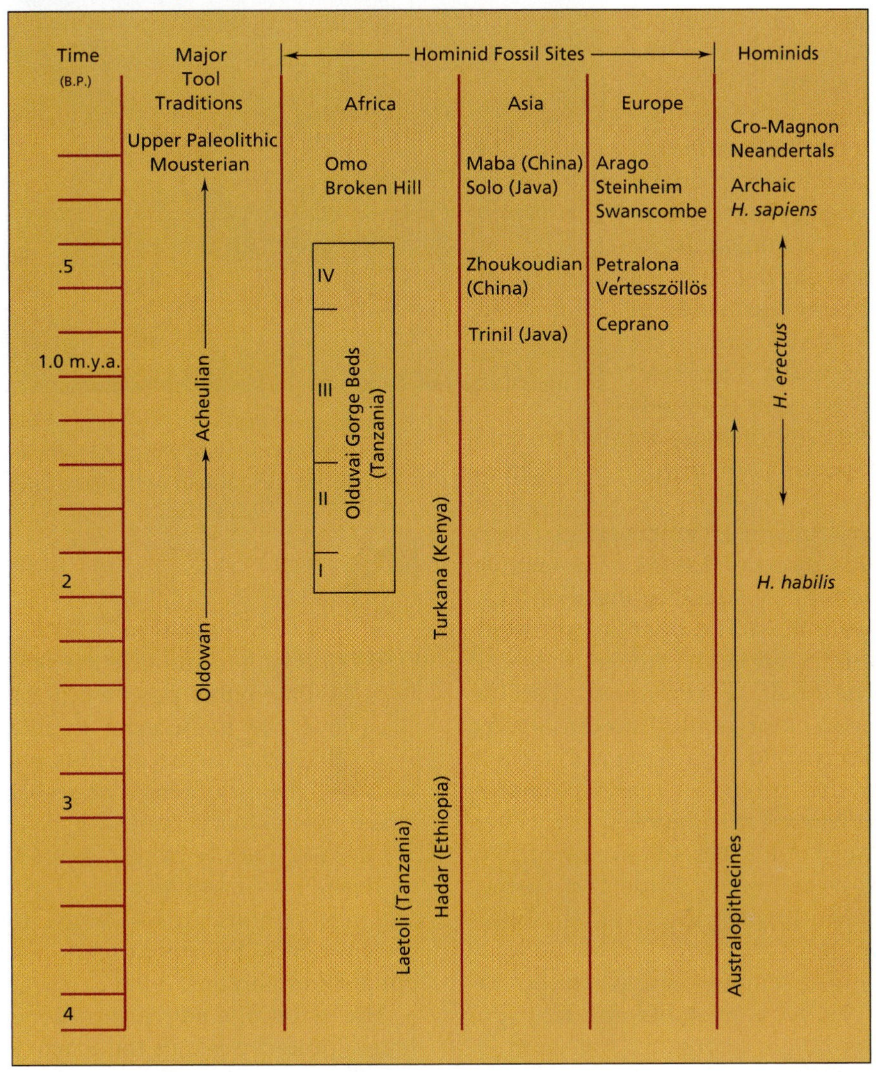

See the text for particular fossils found at the different sites.

two new continents—North America and South America—a story told in Chapter 9. (Australia was colonized by at least 40,000 B.P.)

Glacial Retreat

Consider now one regional example, Western Europe, of the consequences of glacial retreat. The Würm glacial ended in Europe between 17,000 and 12,000 years ago, with the melting of the ice sheet in northern Europe (Scotland, Scandinavia, northern Germany, and Russia). As the ice retreated, the tundra and steppe vegetation grazed by reindeer and other large herbivores gradually moved north. Some people moved north, too, following their prey.

Shrubs, forests, and more solitary animals appeared in southwestern Europe. With most of the big-game animals gone, Western Europeans were forced to use a greater variety of foods. To replace specialized economies based on big game, more generalized adaptations developed during the 5,000 years of glacial retreat.

As water flowed from melting glacial ice, sea levels all over the world started rising. Today, off most coasts, there is a shallow-water zone called the *continental shelf*, over which the sea gradually deepens until the abrupt fall to deep water, which is known as the *continental slope*. During the ice ages, so much water was frozen in glaciers that most continental shelves were exposed. Dry land extended right up to the slope's edge. The waters right offshore were deep, cold, and dark. Few species of marine life could thrive in this environment.

Landscape of the Dordogne region of southwestern France at Beyrac, with limestone cliffs and village below. What is the significance of this area for prehistory?

How did people adapt to the postglacial environment? As seas rose, conditions more encouraging to marine life developed in the shallower, warmer offshore waters. The quantity and variety of edible species increased tremendously in waters over the shelf. Furthermore, because rivers now flowed more gently into the oceans, fish such as salmon could ascend rivers to spawn. Flocks of birds that nested in seaside marshes migrated across Europe during the winter. Even inland Europeans could take advantage of new resources, such as migratory birds and springtime fish runs, which filled the rivers of southwestern France.

Although hunting remained important, southwestern European economies became less specialized. A wider range, or broader spectrum, of plant and animal life was being hunted, gathered, collected, caught, and fished. This was the beginning of what anthropologist Kent Flannery (1969) has called the *broad-spectrum revolution*. It was revolutionary because, in the Middle East, it led to food production—human control over the reproduction of plants and animals. In a mere 10,000 years—after more than a million years during which hominids had subsisted by foraging for natural resources—food production based on plant cultivation and animal domestication replaced hunting and gathering in most areas.

Cave Art

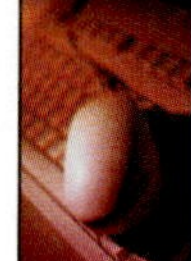

It isn't the tools or the skeletons of Upper Paleolithic people but their art that has made them most familiar to us. Most extraordinary are the cave paintings, the earliest of which dates back some 30,000 years. More than a hundred cave painting sites are known, mainly from a limited area of southwestern France and adjacent northeastern Spain. The most famous site is Lascaux, found in 1940 in southwestern France by a dog and his young human companions.

The paintings adorn limestone walls of true caves located deep in the earth. Over time, the paintings have been absorbed by the limestone and thus preserved. Prehistoric big-game hunters painted their prey: woolly mammoths, wild cattle and horses, deer, and reindeer. The largest animal image is 18 feet long.

Most interpretations associate cave painting with magic and ritual surrounding the hunt. For example, because animals are sometimes depicted with spears in their bodies, the paintings might have been attempts to ensure success in hunting. Artists might have believed that by capturing the animal's image in paint and predicting the kill, they could influence the hunt's outcome.

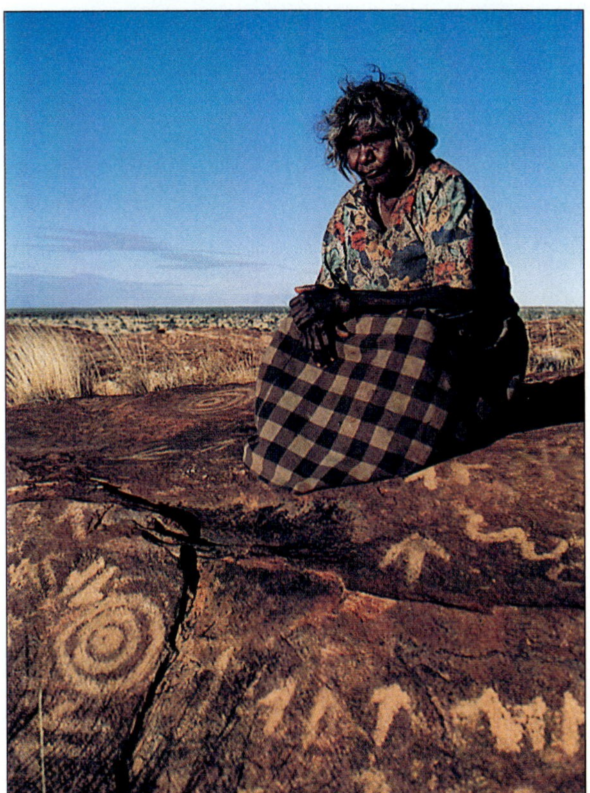

In Australia's Simpson Desert, a woman (Mabel Smith) sits above petroglyphs, carvings on stone. Ms. Smith, a Native Australian, belongs to the Eastern Arrernte group. These are ancient petroglyphs carved by her people.

Another interpretation sees cave painting as a magical human attempt to control animal reproduction. Something analogous was done by Native Australian (Australian aboriginal) hunters and gatherers, who held annual *ceremonies of increase* to honor and to promote, magically, the fertility of the plants and animals that shared their homeland. Australians believed that ceremonies were necessary to perpetuate the species on which humans depended. Similarly, cave paintings might have been part of annual ceremonies of increase. Some of the animals in the cave murals are pregnant, and some are copulating. Did Upper Paleolithic people believe they could influence the sexual behavior or reproduction of their prey by drawing them? Or did they perhaps think that animals would return each year to the place where their souls had been captured pictorially?

Paintings often occur in clusters. In some caves, as many as three paintings have been drawn over the original, yet next to these superimposed paintings stand blank walls never used for painting. It seems reasonable to speculate that an event in the outside world sometimes reinforced a painter's choice of a given spot. Perhaps there was an especially successful hunt soon after the painting had been done. Perhaps members of a social subdivision significant in Upper Paleolithic society customarily used a given area of wall for their drawings.

Cave paintings also might have been a kind of pictorial history. Perhaps Upper Paleolithic people, through their drawings, were reenacting the hunt after it took place, as hunters of the Kalahari Desert in southern Africa still do today. Designs and markings on animal bones may indicate that Upper Paleolithic people had developed a calendar based on the phases of the moon (Marshack 1972). If this is so, it seems possible that late Stone Age hunters, who were certainly as intelligent as we are, would have been interested in recording important events in their lives.

It is worth noting that the *late* Upper Paleolithic, when many of the most spectacular multicolored cave paintings were done and Paleolithic artistic techniques were perfected, coincides with the period of glacial retreat. An intensification of cave painting for any of the reasons connected with hunting magic could have been caused by concern about decreases in herds as the open lands of southwestern Europe were being replaced by forests.

The Mesolithic

The broad-spectrum revolution in Europe includes the late Upper Paleolithic and the **Mesolithic,** which followed it. Again, because of the long history of European archaeology, our knowledge of the Mesolithic (particularly in southwestern Europe and the British Isles) is extensive. According to the traditional typology that distinguishes between Old, Middle, and New Stone Ages, the Middle Stone Age, the Mesolithic, had a characteristic tool type—the *microlith* (Greek for "small stone"). Of interest to

in the news

Prehistoric Art Treasure Is Found in French Cave

This article describes the discovery of a major Upper Paleolithic cave painting site—near Vallon-Pont-d'Arc, a village on the Ardèche River in southern France. This spectacular find rivals such major sites as Lascaux in France and Altamira in Spain. The cave contains more than 300 images of animals and human hands, which seems to be about 20,000 years old.

France has limited tourists' access to such cave sites because human breathing harms the paintings. However, the polychrome majesty of the original Lascaux (now off-limits) has been meticulously reconstructed at Lascaux II, in southwestern France, which is well worth a visit.

Cave paintings were found near Vallon-Pont-d'Arc, France. (From *The New York Times.*)

Paris—In the mountains of southern France, where human beings have habitually hunted, loved and produced art, explorers have discovered an underground cave full of Stone Age paintings, so beautifully made and well preserved that experts are calling it one of the archeological finds of the century.

The enormous underground cavern, which was found on Dec. 18, 1994, in a gorge near the town of Vallon-Pont-d'Arc in the Ardèche region, is studded with more than 300 vivid images of animals and human hands that experts believe were made some 20,000 years ago.

In this great parade of beasts appear woolly-haired rhinos, bears, mammoths, oxen and other images from the end of the Paleolithic era, creatures large and small and variously drawn in yellow ochre, charcoal and hematite. The murals have surprised specialists because they also include a rare image of a red, slouching hyena and the era's first-ever recorded paintings of a panther and several owls. Specialists say this ancient art gallery surpasses in size that of the famous caves of Lascaux and Altamira, which are widely held to be Western Europe's finest collection of Stone Age art.

us is what an abundant inventory of small and delicately shaped stone tools can tell us about the total economy and way of life of the people who made them.

By 12,000 B.P., there were no longer subarctic animals in southwestern Europe. By 10,000 B.P. the glaciers had retreated to such a point that the range of hunting, gathering, and fishing populations in Europe extended to the formerly glaciated British Isles and Scandinavia. The reindeer herds had gradually retreated to the far north, with some human groups following (and ultimately domesticating) them. Europe around 10,000 B.P. was forest rather than treeless steppe and tundra. Europeans were exploiting a wider variety of resources and gearing their lives to the seasonal appearance of particular plants and animals.

People still hunted, but their prey were solitary forest animals, such as the roe deer, the wild ox, and the wild pig, rather than herd species. This led to new hunting techniques: solitary stalking and trapping, similar to more recent practices of many American Indian groups. The coasts and lakes of Europe and the Middle East were fished intensively. Some important Mesolithic sites are Scandinavian shell mounds—the garbage dumps of prehistoric oyster collectors. Microliths were used as fishhooks and in harpoons. Dugout canoes were used for fishing and travel. The process of preserving meat and fish by smoking

Archeologists said they were thrilled not only by the number and the quality of the images but also by the discovery that the great underground site, sealed by fallen debris, appears to have been left undisturbed for thousands of years. They see this as tantamount to finding a time capsule full of hidden treasures.

One remarkable find, they said, was the skull of a bear, placed on a large rock set in the middle of one gallery against a backdrop of bear paintings.

"Is this some kind of altar? Someone placed the skull there for a reason," said Jean Clottes, France's leading rock art specialist. Many other skulls and bones of cave-bears were found in the underground warren, along with bones, flint knives, footprints and remains of fireplaces, all of which archeologists hope will provide important clues to the questions: What was the purpose of these paintings? What did their makers have in mind? . . .

The known part of the cavern consists of four great halls, up to 70 yards long and 40 yards wide, which are connected by smaller galleries roughly five by four yards, according [to] a report issued by the Ministry of Culture. The more than 300 paintings and engravings vary in size between 2 feet and 12 feet long. Some stand alone, while others are clustered in panels or painted with some cohesion, such as two rhinos head-to-head as if in a fight. As Mr. Clottes showed a videotape revealing a panel with four horses' heads close together, drawn in charcoal, he said: "These are one of the great marvels of prehistoric art." The artist or artists, he continued, made use of the natural colors of the rock and of natural stone relief to give form and bulges to the animals.

Archeologists have long believed that the deep prehistoric caves were used not as habitats, because they were too dark, but for religious services or cults about which next to nothing is known. Some specialists believe that initiation rites were held in the caves and that the drawings of the humans' hands from the Paleolithic found here and elsewhere were a token of membership in a cult or community . . .

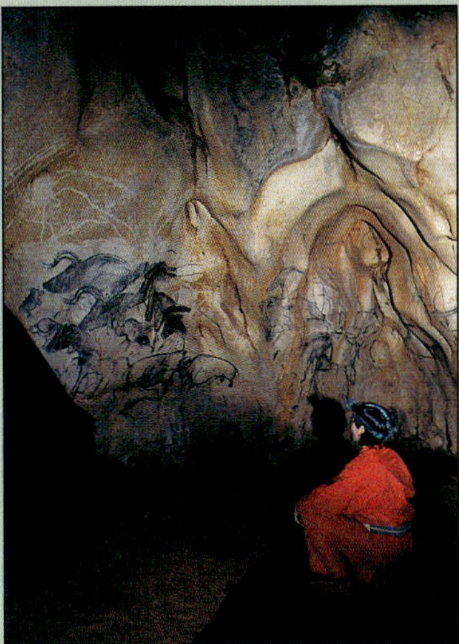

Cave murals dating back 20,000 years at Vallon-Pont-d'Arc in southern France. How would you explain the subject matter and placement of cave paintings?

Source: Marlise Simons, "Prehistoric Art Treasure Is Found in French Cave," *New York Times*, January 19, 1995, pp. A1, A5.

and salting grew increasingly important. (Meat preservation had been less of a problem in a subartic environment since winter snow and ice, often on the ground nine months of the year, offered convenient refrigeration.) The bow and arrow became essential for hunting water fowl in swamps and marshes. Dogs were domesticated, as retrievers, by Mesolithic people (Champion and Gamble 1984). Woodworking was important in the forested environment of northern and Western Europe. Tools used by Mesolithic carpenters appear in the archaeological record: new kinds of axes, chisels, and gouges.

Big-game hunting and, thereafter, Mesolithic hunting and fishing were important in Europe, but other foraging strategies were used by prehistoric humans in Africa and Asia. Among contemporary foragers in the tropics, gathering is the dietary mainstay (Lee 1968/1974). Although herds of big-game animals were more abundant in the tropics in prehistory than they are today, gathering has probably always been at least as important as hunting for tropical foragers (Draper 1975).

Generalized, broad-spectrum economies persisted about 5,000 years longer in Europe than in the Middle East. Whereas Middle Easterners had begun to cultivate plants and breed animals by 10,000 B.P., food production came to Western Europe only around 5000 B.P. (3000 B.C.) and to northern Europe 500 years later. In Chapter 9, we will shift our focus to the Middle East, where the origin of food production took place.

beyond the classroom

Paleolithic Butchering at Verberie

BACKGROUND INFORMATION

Student:	*Kelsey Foster*
Supervising Professor:	*Dr. James G. Enloe*
School:	*University of Iowa*
Year in School/Major:	*Senior/Anthropology*
Future Plans:	*Marine Archaeology Internship/Graduate School*
Project Title:	*Meat and Marrow: Paleolithic Butchering at Verberie*

How can the analysis of animal bones provide evidence for specific kinds of human activity? What kinds of animals were hunted at this Paleolithic site? What kind of eating behavior went on at the site?

The Paleolithic archaeological site of Verberie le Buisson Campin is located along the banks of the Oise River in Northern France. It was the site of repeated occupation by a small band of Paleolithic hunters to mass-kill reindeer, which make up over 98% of the faunal assemblage. Examinations of the faunal material indicate that the reindeer were killed during the fall of the year, which corresponds with the yearly migration of the reindeer herds. Dental analysis and postcranial measurements served to determine that the majority of the reindeer remains were from sub-adult males. This shows great selectivity on the part of the Paleolithic hunters for large, healthy prey.

My research focuses on furthering the existing knowledge of Verberie by attempting to determine the butchering pattern used by the Paleolithic hunters at the site. I examined the faunal remains from the entire upper occupation level (Level II1) for any indication of human modification of bone, which is indicated by the presence of stone tool cut marks and/or impact cones. Stone tool cut marks are produced during the filleting of meat from the bones and during the dismemberment of the carcass. The impact cones are the result of the cracking of bones in order to remove the marrow.

During my research I examined 1,133 specimens of reindeer bone fragments to investigate butchering practices at Verberie. Using Lewis Binford's Meat Utility Index and Marrow Utility Index numbers for the nutritive value of reindeer limb elements, I found that the elements with high marrow index values composed a greater percentage of the assemblage, while the elements with high meat index values were much less represented.

I then compared the numbers and degree of human modification between each element and found that the higher marrow utility elements showed a higher degree of exploitation for marrow cracking than did the lower marrow utility elements. This identified the systematic processing of marrow at Verberie. Conversely, the stone tool cut marks present on the assemblage were predominately the result of dismemberment and not the result of meat removal.

I finally compared the percentages of the elements with a similar ethnoarchaeologic study performed on the remains from a known marrow processing event at a Nunamuit (Alaskan Eskimos, or Inuit) residential site. The extreme similarity between these two assemblages solidified the claim of extensive marrow processing at Verberie.

When all this information is taken together, the butchering sequence at Verberie becomes clear. The butchering practice of Verberie consisted of primary dismemberment of the carcass into smaller units, with intentional snacking on the high marrow utility elements. The lack of filleting marks indicates that minimal, if any, meat exploitation occurred at the hunting camp. Therefore, if the high meat utility elements were not eaten at Verberie, they were transported to a larger residential camp for later consumption.

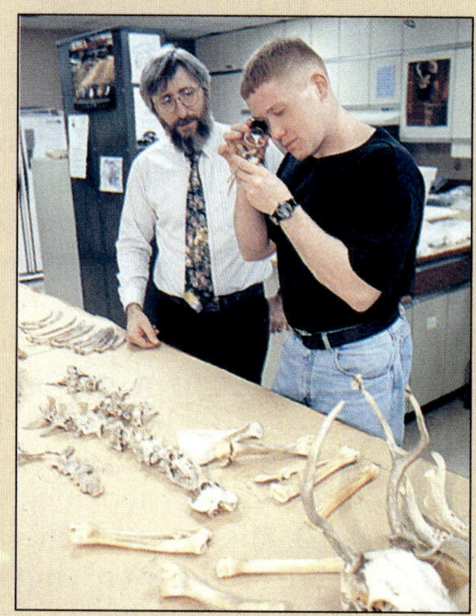

summary

1. Dental, facial, and cranial robustness was reduced as *H. habilis* evolved into *H. erectus,* who extended the hominid food quest to the hunting of large animals. *H. erectus,* with a much larger body, had smaller back teeth but larger front teeth and supporting structures, including a massive eyebrow ridge. The Lower Paleolithic Acheulian tradition provided *H. erectus* with better tools. *H. erectus's* average cranial capacity doubled the australopithecine average. Tool complexity and archaeological evidence for cooperative hunting suggest a long period of enculturation and learning. *H. erectus* extended the hominid range beyond Africa to Asia and Europe.
2. The oldest *H. erectus* skull comes from Kenya and is about 1.7 million years old. At Olduvai Gorge, Tanzania, geological strata spanning more than a million years demonstrate a transition from Oldowan tools to the Archeulian implements of *H. erectus. H. erectus* persisted for more than a million years, evolving into archaic *H. sapiens* by the Middle Pleistocene epoch, some 300,000 years ago. Fire allowed *H. erectus* to expand into cooler areas, to cook, and to live in caves.
3. The classic Neandertals, who inhabited Western Europe during the early part of the Würm glacial, were among the first hominid fossils found. With no examples of *Australopithecus* or *H. erectus* yet discovered, the differences between them and modern humans were accentuated. Even today, most anthropologists exclude the classic Neandertals from the ancestry of Western Europeans. Recent DNA evidence supports this view. The ancestors of AMHs (anatomically modern humans) were other archaic *H. sapiens* groups, most probably those in Africa. AMH fossil finds such as Skhūl (100,000 B.P.) and Qafzeh (92,000 B.P.) support the contention that the Neandertals (130,000 to 28,000 B.P.) and AMHs were contemporaries, rather than ancestor and descendant.
4. The classic Neandertals adapted physically and culturally to bitter cold. Their tool kits were much more complex than those of preceding humans. Their front teeth were among the largest to appear in human evolution. The Neandertals manufactured Mousterian flake tools. *H. sapiens sapiens* made Upper Paleolithic blade tools. The changeover from Neandertal to modern appears to have occurred in Western Europe by 28,000 B.P.
5. As glacial ice melted, foraging patterns were generalized, adding fish, fowl, and plant foods to the diminishing big game supply. The beginning of a broad-spectrum economy in Western Europe coincided with an intensification of Upper Paleolithic cave art. On limestone cave walls, prehistoric hunters painted images of animals important in their lives. Explanations of cave paintings link them to hunting magic, ceremonies of increase, and initiation rites.
6. By 10,000 B.P., people were pursuing broad-spectrum economies in the British Isles and Scandinavia. Tool kits adapted to a forested environment included small, delicately shaped stone tools called microliths. The Mesolithic, or Middle Stone Age, had begun. The broad-spectrum revolution, based on a wide variety of dietary resources, began in the Middle East somewhat earlier than in Europe. As we will see in Chapter 9, it culminated in the first food-producing economies in the Middle East around 10,000 B.P.

key terms

Acheulian Derived from the French village of St. Acheul, where these tools were first identified; Lower Paleolithic tool tradition associated with *H. erectus.*

anatomically modern humans (AMHs) Including the Cro-Magnons of Europe (31,000 B.P.) and the older fossils from Skhūl (100,000) and Qafzeh (92,000); continue through the present; also known as *H. sapiens sapiens.*

archaic *Homo sapiens* Early *H. sapiens,* consisting of the Neandertals of Europe and the Middle East, the Neandertal-like hominids of Africa and Asia, and the immediate ancestors of all these hominids; lived from about 300,000 to 35,000 B.P.

blade tool The basic Upper Paleolithic tool type, hammered off a prepared core.

Mesolithic Middle Stone Age, whose characteristic tool type was the microlith; broad-spectrum economy.

Mousterian Middle Paleolithic tool-making tradition associated with Neandertals.

Neandertals *H. sapiens neanderthalensis,* representing an archaic *H. sapiens* subspecies, lived in Europe and the Middle East between 130,000 and 35,000 B.P.

Paleolithic Old Stone Age (from Greek roots meaning "old" and "stone"); divided into Lower (early), Middle, and Upper (late).

punctuated equilibrium Model of evolution; long periods of equilibrium, during which species change little, are interrupted by sudden changes—evolutionary jumps.

Upper Paleolithic Blade-tool-making traditions associated with early *H. sapiens sapiens;* named from their location in upper, or more recent, layers of sedimentary deposits.

critical thinking questions

1. What were the main differences between the two earliest species of *Homo?* Was *Homo habilis* more like *Homo erectus,* or more like the australopithecines?
2. How do you evaluate the evidence for a punctuated equilibrium model of hominid evolution?
3. How do you evaluate the evidence for a gradualist model of hominid evolution?
4. What were the main trends in the evolution of technology during the Paleolithic? Do these trends continue today?
5. How does the geographic distribution of *H. erectus* differ from that of the australopithecines? What did culture have to do with this difference?
6. Was *Homo erectus* more like *Homo habilis* or more like *Homo sapiens sapiens?* What evidence do you offer for your opinion?
7. Do you think *H. erectus* had language? Why or why not? How about the Neandertals?
8. Do you think that *Homo sapiens sapiens* has Neandertal ancestry? Why? Can you think of ways in which the different theories about the origin of *H. sapiens sapiens* might be reconciled?
9. What cultural changes accompanied glacial retreat in Europe during the late Upper Paleolithic and the Mesolithic? Does anything happening today remind you of the effects of glacial retreat?

suggested additional readings

Cunliffe, B., ed.

1998 *Prehistoric Europe: An Illustrated History.* New York: Oxford University Press. An Oxford illustrated history book.

Dibble, H. L., S. P. McPherron, and B. J. Roth

2000 *Virtual Dig: A Simulated Archaeological Excavation of a Middle Paleolithic Site in France.* Mountain View, CA: Mayfield. Interactive computer excavation of a Middle Paleolithic site.

Fagan, B. M.

1999 *World Prehistory: A Brief Introduction,* 4th ed. New York: Longman. From the Paleolithic to the Neolithic around the world.

2000 *People of the Earth: A Brief Introduction to World Prehistory,* 10th ed. Upper Saddle River:Prentice Hall. Prehistoric peoples and civilizations.

Gamble, C.
1999 *The Palaeolithic Societies of Europe.* New York: Cambridge University Press. Survey mainly of the Middle and Upper Paleolithic in Europe.

Klein, R. G.
1999 *The Human Career: Human Biological and Cultural Origins,* 2nd ed. Chicago: University of Chicago Press. Hominid fossils, origins, and evolution.

Knecht, H., A. Pike-Tay, and R. White, eds.
1993 *Before Lascaux: The Complex Record of the Early Upper Paleolithic.* Boca Raton, FL: CRC Press. Before cave art.

Lieberman, P.
1998 *Eve Spoke: Human Language and Human Evolution.* New York: W. W. Norton. Language and behavior in human evolution.

Oakley, K. P.
1976 *Man the Tool-Maker,* 6th ed. Chicago: University of Chicago Press. Classic, brief introduction to tool making.

Rightmire, G. P.
1990 *The Evolution of* Homo erectus*: Comparative Anatomical Studies of an Extinct Human Species.* New York: Cambridge University Press. Thorough review of the fossil evidence for the *H. erectus* period of human evolution.

Tattersall, Ian
1998 *Becoming Human: Evolution and Human Uniqueness.* New York: Harcourt Brace. Human evolution, including primates, fossil hominids, and social evolution.
1999 *The Last Neandertal: The Rise, Success, and Mysterious Extinction of Our Closest Human Relatives,* rev. ed. Boulder, CO: Westview. One view of what happened to the Neandertals.

Ucko, P., and A. Rosenfeld
1967 *Paleolithic Cave Art.* London: Weidenfeld and Nicolson. A survey, including finds and interpretations.

Wenke, R. J.
1996 *Patterns in Prehistory: Mankind's First Three Million Years,* 4th ed. New York: Oxford University Press. Very thorough survey of fossil and archaeological reconstruction of human evolution.

internet exercises

1. Genetic and Skeletal Techniques in the Study of Hominid Origins: Visit the American Museum of Natural History's Electronic Newspaper page entitled, "Is An African 'Eve' the Mother of Us All?," **www.amnh.org/news/index.html.**
   a. What do geneticists argue about hominid origins? What lines of evidence do they use to support their argument? Based on the analysis they are using, why are they not talking about the African "Adam"?
   b. What do paleontologists say about the African "Eve"?
   c. This website proposes that these two types of analysis should be integrated. Do you think it is possible to effectively combine genetic and paleontological research?

2. Modern Hominid Origins: Visit the American Museum of Natural History's Electronic Newspaper page entitled "Fossil Skulls!," **http://www.amnh.org/enews/iskulls.html.**
   a. Click on the *Homo erectus* skull to compare it with a modern human skull. Use the mouse to rotate the skulls. What are some of the prominent features that differentiate it from a modern human skull? From the image, is it clear who has the bigger brain?
   b. Go back, and look at the *Homo neanderthalensis* skull. Rotate the skulls to look at a profile or side view. Which skull has a large brow ridge; low, elongated skull; and a bun on the back of the skull? From the image, is it clear who has the bigger brain? Some people have argued that modern Europeans descend from Neanderthals. Based on these skulls, do you think this is possible?

See Chapter 7 on your CD-ROM for additional review and interactive exercises. See your McGraw-Hill Online Learning Center for more.

Chapter 8

Human Diversity and "Race"

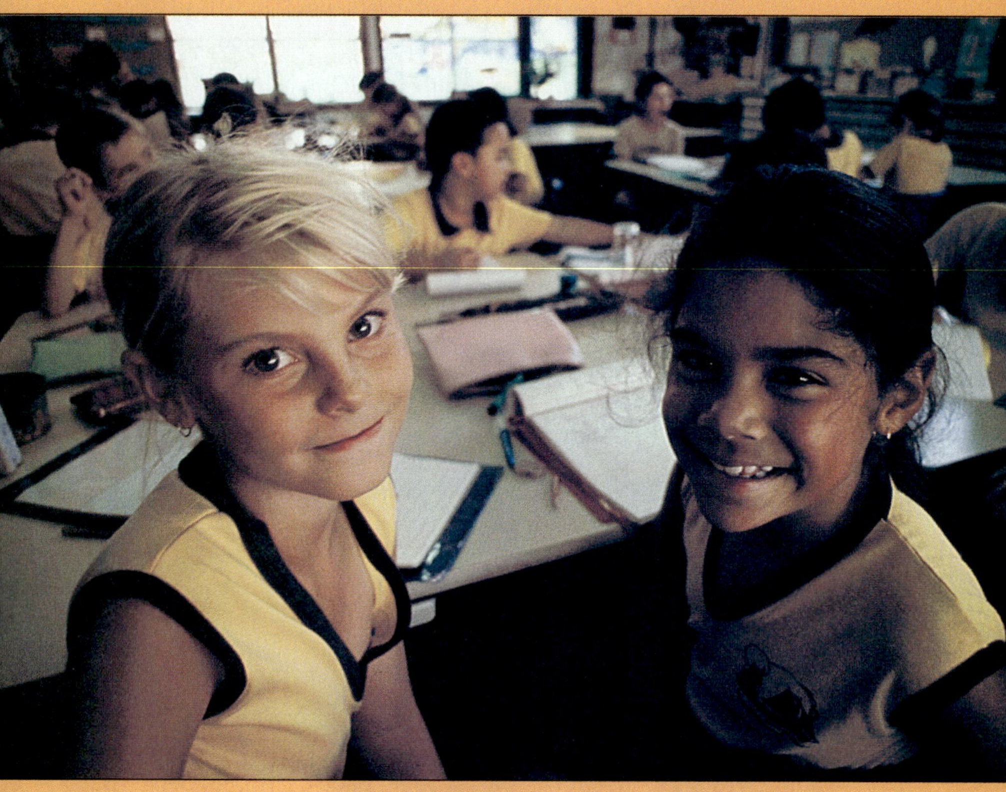

NYTIMES.COM NEWS BRIEFS

No Fare: New York's Cabbies Show How Multi-Colored Racism Can Be

by Thomas J. Lueck
November 7, 1999

It may be the most blatant form of racism in New York City: a cab driver refusing to pick up someone who is black. It happens to blacks all the time. Former Mayor David N. Dinkins says it has even happened to him. And now the actor Danny Glover, who last week went public over what he described as a string of such slights in different areas of Manhattan one night last month.

"I was so angry," Glover told a news conference, recounting how several empty cabs had refused to stop for him, his college-age daughter and her roommate. Later, when one finally did, the driver refused the 6-foot-4 *Lethal Weapon* star access to the front seat even though he has a bad hip and is entitled under taxi industry rules to stretch out in front.

A simple case of traditional American racism? Perhaps. But in New York such incidents often have the distinct flavor of the melting pot: In this case the driver was nonwhite, too—apparently from southern Asia, Glover said.

And so the actor's experience may illustrate not just continuing American racism, but one way its character is subtly changing with demographics: As recent immigrants from Asia, the Middle East and Africa come to dominate the taxi industry, they are bringing with them new strains of bigotry.

Most often, according to people in the taxi industry, racism is perpetuated by cabbies whose attitudes have roots not only in colonial rule and the strict social stratification of their native lands, but also in the more recent distorted images of the global media.

"Racist images flow throughout the world," said Bhairavi Desai, a native of India and the staff director of the Taxi Workers Alliance, a 2,000-member drivers' group. Because of the impact of movies, television and rap music, she said, part of the baggage of some new immigrants is an established, and sometimes deeply flawed, attitude toward race.

Among immigrant cabbies from some nations, including India, she said, "many of the attitudes stem from a history of colonialism, and from a sense of competing for bread crumbs with other poor people." Although no precise breakdown is available, from 60 percent to 70 percent of the city's Yellow Cab drivers are now immigrants from India, Pakistan and Bangladesh . . . Among the other drivers, people born in the United States or western Europe comprise a tiny minority compared with the large number of immigrants from countries like Russia, Korea and the Sudan . . .

"Some drivers really don't want to pick up minorities because they think it will mean ending up in neighborhoods where they won't be able to find another fare," said Edward Rogoff, a Baruch College professor and longtime taxi industry analyst.

And many cabbies, acutely aware of their high vulnerability to robbery and attack, undoubtedly take note of higher rates of crime among lower-income blacks and in certain areas of the city. Still, few seem to doubt the bigotry factor. Industry executives note that they are trying to inculculate racial sensitivity among new immigrant drivers . . .

Acts of racial discrimination by cabbies are illegal, punishable by a fine or the revocation of the offender's taxi-driver license . . .

Source: http://www.nytimes.com (extended search).

overview Scientists have approached the study of human biological diversity in two main ways: racial classification, an approach that has been rejected, and the current explanatory approach. It is not possible to define human races biologically. Because of a range of problems involved in classifying humans into racial categories, biologists now focus on specific biological differences and try to explain them.

Race is a cultural category, not a biological reality. "Races" derive from contrasts perceived in particular societies, rather than from scientific classification. In American culture, one acquires a racial identity at birth. But in the final analysis, race in the United States isn't based on genetics or appearance. Children of mixed unions, no matter what they look like, are usually classified with the minority-group parent. Other cultures have different ways of assigning racial labels, of socially constructing race.

Latin American countries deal with race differently. In Brazil, for example, full siblings may belong to different races if they look different. Brazilians recognize many more races than Americans do. A person's racial identity can change during his or her lifetime. It also varies depending on who is doing the classifying.

Race: A Discredited Concept in Biology

Historically, scientists have approached the study of human biological variation from two main directions: (1) racial classification, an approach that has been rejected; and (2) the current explanatory approach, which focuses on understanding specific differences. I'll briefly review each approach, first considering the problems with racial classification, then providing an example of the explanatory approach to human biological diversity. By the way, to say that the race concept is invalid is not to deny the existence of human biological diversity. Biological differences exist and are apparent to us all. But the current scientific approach is to explain this diversity, rather than trying to pigeonhole humanity into discrete categories called races.

In biological terms, a race would be a geographically isolated subdivision of a species. Such a *subspecies* would be capable of interbreeding with other subspecies of the same species but would not actually do so because of its geographic isolation. If subspecies remained separate long enough, they would eventually develop into different species. Some biologists also use "race" to refer to "breeds," as of dogs or roses. Thus, a pit bull and a chihuahua would be different races of dogs. Such domesticated "races" have been carefully bred by humans for generations. However, human populations have not been isolated enough from one another to develop into discrete races. Nor have humans experienced controlled breeding like that which has created the various kinds of dogs and roses. Humans vary biologically, such as in their genetic attributes, but there are no sharp breaks between human populations of the sort we might associate with discrete subspecies or races. We can observe gradual, rather than abrupt, shifts in gene frequencies between neighboring human populations. Such gradual shifts are called **clines.** We do not, however, find the sharp shifts in genes and other biological features we would associate with discrete races.

Racial classification has fallen out of favor in biology for several reasons. The main reason is that scientists have trouble grouping people into distinct racial units. A race is supposed to reflect

The photos in this chapter illustrate only a small part of the range of human biological diversity. Shown here is a Bai minority woman, from Shapin, in China's Yunnan province.

shared *genetic* material (inherited from a common ancestor), but early scholars used *phenotypical* traits (usually skin color) for racial classification. **Phenotype** refers to an organism's evident traits, its "manifest biology"—anatomy and physiology. There are thousands of evident (detectable) physical traits. They range from skin color, hair form, and eye color (which are visible), to blood type, color blindness, and enzyme production (which become evident through testing).

There are several problems with a phenotypical approach to race. First, which traits should be primary in assigning people to different races? Should races be defined by height, weight, body shape, facial features, teeth, skull form, or skin color? Like their fellow citizens, early European and American scientists gave priority to skin color. The phenotypic features that were most apparent to those early scientists, for example, skin color, were also the very characteristics that had been assigned arbitrary cultural value for purposes of discrimination. Genetic variations (e.g., differences in blood types) that were not directly observable were not used in early racial classification.

Many school books and encyclopedias still proclaim the existence of three great races: the white, the black, and the yellow. This simplistic classification was compatible with the political use of race during the colonial period of the late 19th and early 20th centuries. The tripartite scheme kept white Europeans neatly separate from their African, Asian, and Native American subjects. (See "Interesting Issues" for the "American Anthropological Association (AAA) Statement on 'Race.'") Colonial empires began to break up, and scientists began to question established racial categories, after World War II.

Races Are Not Biologically Distinct

History and politics aside, one obvious problem with "color-based" racial labels is that the terms don't accurately describe skin color. "White" people are more pink, beige, or tan than white. "Black" people are various shades of brown, and "yellow" people are tan or beige. But these terms have also been dignified by more scientific-*sounding* synonyms: Caucasoid, Negroid, and Mongoloid.

Another problem with the tripartite scheme is that many populations don't neatly fit into any one of the three "great races." For example, where would one put the Polynesians? *Polynesia* is a triangle of South Pacific islands formed by Hawaii to the north, Easter Island to the east, and New Zealand to the southwest. Does the "bronze" skin color of Polynesians connect them to the Caucasoids or to the Mongoloids? Some scientists, recognizing this problem, enlarged the original tripartite scheme to include the Polynesian "race." Native Americans presented a similar problem. Were they red or yellow? Some scientists added a fifth race—the "red," or Amerindian—to the major racial groups.

Many people in southern India have dark skins, but scientists have been reluctant to classify them with "black" Africans because of their "Caucasoid" facial features and hair form. Some, therefore, have created a separate race for these people. What about the Australian aborigines, hunters and gatherers native to what has been, throughout human history, the most isolated continent? By skin color, one might place some Native Australians in the same race as tropical Africans. However, similarities to Europeans in hair color (light or reddish) and facial features

interesting issues

American Anthropological Association (AAA) Statement on "Race"

As a result of public confusion about the meaning of "race," claims as to major biological differences among "races" continue to be advanced. Stemming from past AAA actions designed to address public misconceptions on race and intelligence, the need was apparent for a clear AAA statement on the biology and politics of race that would be educational and informational.

The following statement was adopted by the Executive Board of the American Anthropological Association in May 1998, based on a draft prepared by a committee of representative anthropologists. The Association believes that this statement represents the thinking and scholarly positions of most anthropologists.

> In the United States both scholars and the general public have been conditioned to viewing human races as natural and separate divisions within the human species based on visible physical differences. With the vast expansion of scientific knowledge in this century, however, it has become clear that human populations are not unambiguous, clearly demarcated, biologically distinct groups. Evidence from the analysis of genetics (e.g., DNA) indicates that most physical variation, about 94%, lies within so-called racial groups. Conventional geographic "racial" groupings differ from one another only in about 6% of their genes. This means that there is greater variation within "racial" groups than between them. In neighboring populations there is much overlapping of genes and their phenotypic (physical) expressions. Throughout history whenever different groups have come into contact, they have interbred. The continued sharing of genetic materials has maintained all of humankind as a single species.
>
> Physical variations in any given trait tend to occur gradually rather than abruptly over geographic areas. And because physical traits are inherited independently of one another, knowing the range of one trait does not predict the presence of others. For example, skin color varies largely from light in the temperate areas in the north to dark in the tropical areas in the south; its intensity is not related to nose shape or hair texture. Dark skin may be associated with frizzy or kinky hair or curly or wavy or straight hair, all of which are found among different indigenous peoples in tropical regions. These facts render any attempt to establish lines of division among biological populations both arbitrary and subjective.
>
> Historical research has shown that the idea of "race" has always carried more meanings than mere physical differences; indeed, physical variations in the human species have no meaning except the social ones that humans put on them. Today scholars in many fields argue that "race" as it is understood in the United States of America was a social mechanism invented during the 18th century to refer to those populations brought together in colonial America: the English and other European settlers, the conquered Indian peoples, and those peoples of Africa brought in to provide slave labor.
>
> From its inception, this modern concept of "race" was modeled after an ancient theorem of the Great Chain of Being, which posited natural categories on a hierarchy established by God or nature. Thus "race" was a mode of classification linked specifically to peoples in the colonial situation. It subsumed a growing ideology of inequality devised to rationalize European attitudes and treatment of the conquered and enslaved peoples. Proponents of slavery in particular during the 19th century used "race" to justify the retention of slavery. The ideology magnified the differences among Europeans, Africans, and Indians, established a rigid hierarchy of socially exclusive categories, underscored and bolstered unequal rank and status differences, and pro-

vided the rationalization that the inequality was natural or God-given. The different physical traits of African-Americans and Indians became markers or symbols of their status differences.

As they were constructing US society, leaders among European-Americans fabricated the cultural/behavioral characteristics associated with each "race," linking superior traits with Europeans and negative and inferior ones to blacks and Indians. Numerous arbitrary and fictitious beliefs about the different peoples were institutionalized and deeply embedded in American thought . . .

Ultimately "race" as an ideology about human differences was subsequently spread to other areas of the world. It became a strategy for dividing, ranking, and controlling colonized people used by colonial powers everywhere. But it was not limited to the colonial situation. In the latter part of the 19th century it was employed by Europeans to rank one another and to justify social, economic, and political inequalities among their peoples. During World War II, the Nazis under Adolf Hitler enjoined the expanded ideology of "race" and "racial" differences and took them to a logical end: the extermination of 11 million people of "inferior races" (e.g., Jews, Gypsies, Africans, homosexuals, and so forth) and other unspeakable brutalities of the Holocaust.

"Race" thus evolved as a world view, a body of prejudgments that distorts our ideas about human differences and group behavior. Racial beliefs constitute myths about the diversity in the human species and about the abilities and behavior of people homogenized into "racial" categories. The myths fused behavior and physical features together in the public mind, impeding our comprehension of both biological variations and cultural behavior, implying that both are genetically determined. Racial myths bear no relationship to the reality of human capabilities or behavior. Scientists today find that reliance on such folk beliefs about human differences in research has led to countless errors.

At the end of the 20th century, we now understand that human cultural behavior is learned, conditioned into infants beginning at birth, and always subject to modification. No human is born with a built-in culture or language. Our temperaments, dispositions, and personalities, regardless of genetic propensities, are developed within sets of meanings and values that we call "culture." Studies of infant and early childhood learning and behavior attest to the reality of our cultures in forming who we are.

It is a basic tenet of anthropological knowledge that all normal human beings have the capacity to learn any cultural behavior. The American experience with immigrants from hundreds of different language and cultural backgrounds who have acquired some version of American culture traits and behavior is the clearest evidence of this fact. Moreover, people of all physical variations have learned different cultural behaviors and continue to do so as modern transportation moves millions of immigrants around the world.

How people have been accepted and treated within the context of a given society or culture has a direct impact on how they perform in that society. The "racial" world view was invented to assign some groups to perpetual low status, while others were permitted access to privilege, power, and wealth. The tragedy in the United States has been that the policies and practices stemming from this world view succeeded all too well in constructing unequal populations among Europeans, Native Americans, and peoples of African descent. Given what we know about the capacity of normal humans to achieve and function within any culture, we conclude that present-day inequalities between so-called "racial" groups are not consequences of their biological inheritance but products of historical and contemporary social, economic, educational, and political circumstances.

Note: For further information on human biological variations, see the statement prepared and issued by the American Association of Physical Anthropologists, 1996 (*American Journal of Physical Anthropology* 101, pp. 569–70).

A Native American: a Chiquitanos Indian woman from Bolivia.

have led some scientists to classify them as Caucasoids. But there is no evidence that Australians are closer genetically or historically to either of these groups than they are to Asians. Recognizing this problem, scientists often regard Native Australians as a separate race.

Finally, consider the San ("Bushmen") of the Kalahari Desert in southern Africa. Scientists have perceived their skin color as varying from brown to yellow. Some who regard San skin as "yellow" have placed them in the same category as Asians. In theory, people of the same race share more recent common ancestry with each other than they do with any others. But there is no evidence for recent common ancestry between San and Asians. Somewhat more reasonably, some scholars assign the San to the Capoid race (from the Cape of Good Hope), which is seen as being different from other groups inhabiting tropical Africa.

Similar problems arise when any single trait is used as a basis for racial classification. An attempt to use facial features, height, weight, or any other phenotypical trait is fraught with difficulties. For example, consider the *Nilotes,* natives of the upper Nile region of Uganda and Sudan. Nilotes tend to be tall and to have long, narrow noses. Certain Scandinavians are also tall, with similar noses. Given the distance between their homelands, to classify them as members of the same race makes little sense. There is no reason to assume that Nilotes and Scandinavians are more closely related to each other than either is to shorter and nearer populations with different kinds of noses.

Would it be better to base racial classifications on a combination of physical traits? This would avoid some of the problems mentioned above, but others would arise. First, skin color, stature, skull form, and facial features (nose form, eye shape, lip thickness) don't go together as a unit. For example, people with dark skin may be tall or short and have hair ranging from straight to very curly. Dark-haired populations may have light or dark skin, along with various skull forms, facial features, and body sizes and shapes. The number of combinations is very large, and the amount that heredity (versus environment) contributes to such phenotypical traits is often unclear.

There is a final objection to racial classification based on phenotype. The phenotypical characteristics on which races are based supposedly reflect genetic material that is shared and that has stayed the same for long time periods. But phenotypical similarities and differences don't necessarily have a genetic basis. Because of changes in the environment that affect individuals during growth and development, the range of phenotypes characteristic of a population may change

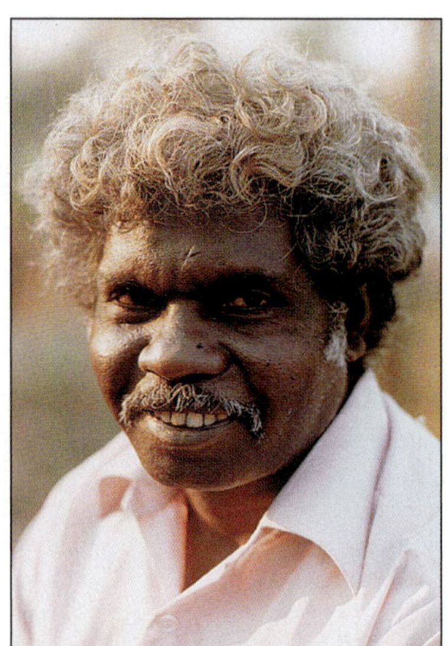

A Native Australian.

A man from Jaibur, India.

without any genetic change. There are several examples. In the early 20th century, the anthropologist Franz Boas (1940/1966) described changes in skull form (e.g., toward rounder heads) among the children of Europeans who had migrated to North America. The reason for this was not a change in genes, for the European immigrants tended to marry among themselves. Also, some of their children had been born in Europe and merely raised in the United States. Something in the environment, probably in the diet, was producing this change. We know now that changes in average height and weight produced by dietary differences in a few generations are common and may have nothing to do with race or genetics.

Explaining Skin Color

Traditional racial classification assumed that biological characteristics were determined by heredity and that they were stable (immutable) over long periods of time. We now know that a biological similarity doesn't necessarily indicate recent common ancestry. Dark skin color, for example, can be shared by tropical Africans and Native Australians for reasons other than common ancestry. It is not possible to *define races* biologically. Still, scientists have made much progress in *explaining* variation in human skin color, along with many other expressions of human biological diversity. We shift now from classification to *explanation,* in which natural selection plays a key role.

As recognized by Charles Darwin and Alfred Russell Wallace, **natural selection** is the process by which nature selects the forms most fit to survive and reproduce in a given environment—such as the tropics. Over the years, the less fit organisms die out, and the favored types survive by producing more offspring. The role of natural selection in producing variation in skin color will illustrate the explanatory approach to human biological diversity. Comparable explanations have been provided for many other aspects of human biological variation.

Skin color is a complex biological trait. That means it is influenced by several genes. Just how many isn't known. **Melanin,** the primary determinant of human skin color, is a chemical substance manufactured in the epidermis, or outer skin layer. The melanin cells of darker-skinned people produce more and larger granules of melanin than do those of lighter-skinned people. By screening out ultraviolet radiation from the sun, melanin offers protection against a variety of maladies, including sunburn and skin cancer.

Before the 16th century, almost all the very dark skinned populations of the world lived in the tropics, as does this Samburu woman from Kenya.

Figure 8.1
The Distribution of Human Skin Color before A.D. 1400

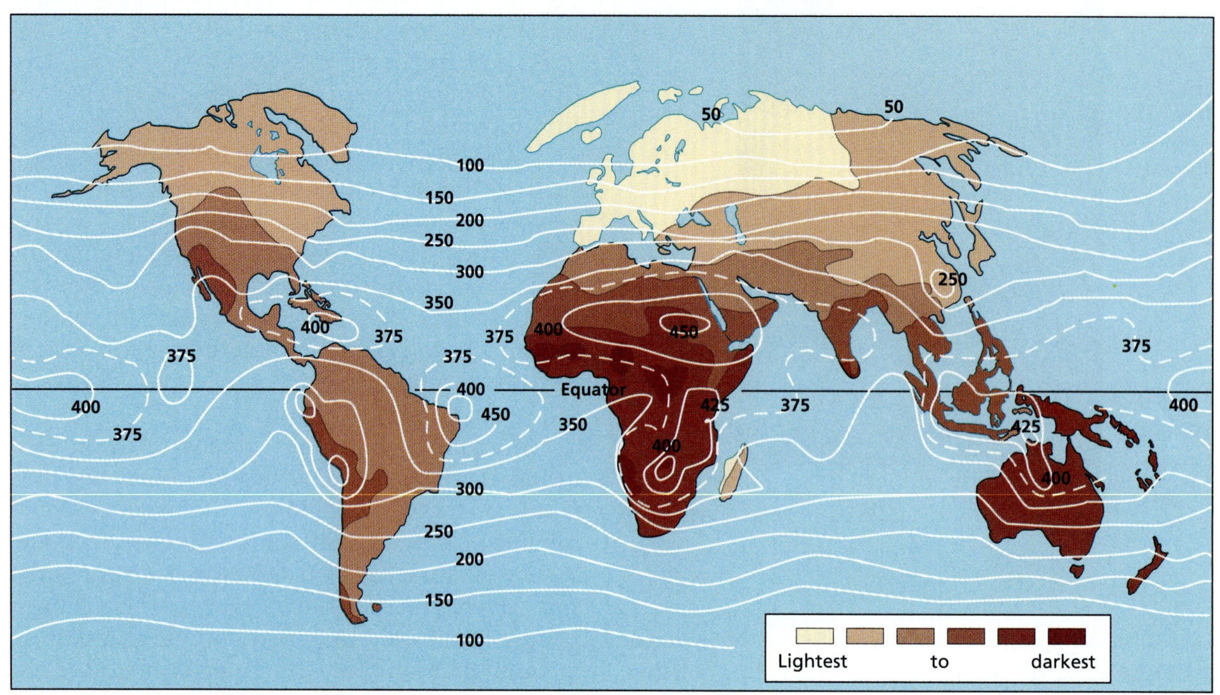

Source: Figure from *Evolution and Human Origins* by B.J. Williams. Copyright © 1979 by B.J. Williams. Reprinted by permission of HarperCollins, Publishers, Inc.

Also shown is the average amount of ultraviolet radiation in watt-seconds per square centimeter.

Before the 16th century, most of the world's very dark-skinned peoples lived in the **tropics,** a belt extending about 23 degrees north and south of the equator, between the Tropic of Cancer and the Tropic of Capricorn. The association between dark skin color and a tropical habitat existed throughout the Old World, where humans and their ancestors have lived for millions of years. The darkest populations of Africa evolved not in shady equatorial forests but in sunny open grassland, or savanna, country.

Outside the tropics, skin color tends to be lighter. Moving north in Africa, for example, there is a gradual transition from dark brown to medium brown. Average skin color continues to lighten as one moves through the Middle East, into southern Europe, through central Europe, and to the north. South of the tropics skin color is also lighter (Figure 8.1). In the Americas, by contrast, tropical populations do not have very dark skin. This is because the settlement of the New World, by light-skinned Asian ancestors of Native Americans, was relatively recent, probably dating back no more than 20,000 years.

How, aside from migrations, can we explain the geographic distribution of skin color? Natural selection provides an answer. In the tropics, there is intense ultraviolet radiation from the sun. Unprotected humans there face the threat of severe sunburn, which can increase susceptibility to disease. This confers a selective *dis*advantage (i.e., less success in surviving and reproducing) on lighter-skinned people in the tropics (unless they stay indoors or use cultural products, like umbrellas or lotions, to screen sunlight). Sunburn also impairs the body's ability to sweat. This is a second reason why light skin color, given tropical heat, can diminish the human ability to live and work in equatorial climates. A third disadvantage of having light skin color in the tropics is that exposure to ultraviolet radiation can cause skin cancer (Blum 1961).

A fourth factor affecting the geographic distribution of skin color is vitamin D production by the body. W. F. Loomis (1967) focused on the role of ultraviolet radiation in stimulating the manufacture of vitamin D by the human body. The unclothed human body can produce its own vitamin D when exposed to sufficient sunlight. But in a cloudy environment that is also so cold that people have to dress themselves much of the year (such as northern Europe, where very light skin color evolved), clothing interferes with the body's manufacture of vitamin D. The ensuing shortage of vitamin D diminishes the absorption of calcium in the intestines. A nutritional disease known as **rickets,** which softens and deforms the bones, may develop. In women, deformation of the pelvic bones from rickets can interfere with childbirth. During northern winters, light skin color maximizes the absorption of ultraviolet radiation and the manufacture of vitamin D by the few parts of the body that are exposed to direct sunlight. There has been selection against dark skin color in northern areas because melanin screens out ultraviolet radiation.

Considering vitamin D production, light skin is an advantage in the cloudy north, but a disadvantage in the sunny tropics. Loomis suggested that in the tropics, dark skin color protects the body against an *overproduction* of vitamin D by screening out ultraviolet radiation. Too much vitamin D can lead to a potentially fatal condition (**hypervitaminosis D**), in which calcium deposits build up in the body's soft tissues. The kidneys may fail. Gallstones, joint problems, and circulation problems are other symptoms of hypervitaminosis D.

Very light skin color, illustrated in this photo of a blond, blue-eyed North Sea German fisherman, maximizes absorption of ultraviolet radiation by those few parts of the body exposed to direct sunlight during northern winters. This helps prevent rickets.

This discussion of skin color shows that common ancestry, the presumed basis of race, is not the only reason for biological similarities. We see that natural selection has made a major contribution to our understanding of human biological differences and similarities.

Social Race

Medical studies often report on different health risks and conditions of blacks and whites. Next time you see such a study, think about how the results might have differed if people had been grouped, say, as light-skinned versus dark-skinned, or assessed along a continuum of skin color, rather than simply classified as black or white. Do you imagine that blue-eyed people and brown-eyed people are prone to different health risks and medical conditions? Do they belong to different races?

We have seen that it is not possible to define races biologically. Only cultural constructions of race are possible—even though the average citizen conceptualizes "race" in biological terms. The belief that races exist and are important is much more common among the public than it is among biologists and anthropologists. Most Americans, for example, believe that their population includes biologically based "races" to which various labels have been applied. These labels include "white," "black," "yellow," "red," "Caucasoid," "Negroid," "Mongoloid," "Amerindian," "Asian-American," "African-American," "Euro-American," and "Native American."

The races we hear about every day are culturally constructed categories that may have little to do with actual biological differences. In Charles Wagley's terms (Wagley 1959/1968), they are **social races** (groups assumed to have a biological basis but actually defined in a culturally arbitrary, rather than a scientific manner). Many Americans mistakenly assume that "whites" and "blacks," for example, are biologically distinct and that these terms stand for discrete races. But these labels, like racial terms used in other societies, really designate culturally defined and perceived, rather than biologically based, groups.

Hypodescent: Race in the United States

How is race culturally constructed in the United States? In American culture, one acquires his or her racial identity at birth, but race isn't based on biology or on simple ancestry. Take the case of the child of a "racially mixed" marriage involving one black and one white parent. We know that 50 percent of the child's genes come from one parent and 50 percent from the other. Still, American culture overlooks heredity and classifies this child as black. This rule is arbitrary. From *genotype* (genetic composition), it would be just as logical to classify the child as white.

American rules for assigning racial status can be even more arbitrary. In some states, anyone known to have any black ancestor, no matter how remote, is classified as a member of the black race. This is a rule of **descent** (it assigns social identity on the basis of ancestry), but of a sort that is rare outside the contemporary United States. It is called **hypodescent** (Harris and Kottak 1963) (hypo means "lower") because it automatically places the children of a union or mating between members of different groups in the minority group. Hypodescent helps divide American society into groups that have been unequal in their access to wealth, power, and prestige.

Millions of Americans have faced discrimination because one or more of their ancestors happened to belong to a minority group. The following case from Louisiana is an excellent illustration of the arbitrariness of the hypodescent rule. It also illustrates the role that governments (federal, or state in this case) play in legalizing, inventing, or eradicating race and ethnicity (Williams 1989). Susie Guillory Phipps, a light-skinned woman with "Caucasian" features and straight black hair, discovered as an adult that she was "black." When Phipps ordered a copy of her birth certificate, she found her race listed as "colored." Since she had been "brought up white and married white twice," Phipps challenged a 1970 Louisiana law declaring anyone with at least one-thirty-second "Negro blood" to be legally black. In other words, having one "Negro" great-great-great grandparent out of 32 is sufficient to make one black. Although the state's lawyer admitted that Phipps "looks like a white person," the state of Louisiana insisted that her racial classification was proper (Yetman 1991, pp. 3–4).

Cases like Phipps's are rare, because "racial" and ethnic identities are usually ascribed at birth and usually don't change. The rule of hypodescent affects blacks, Asians, Native Americans, and Hispanics differently. It's easier to negotiate Indian or Hispanic identity than black identity. The ascription rule isn't as definite, and the assumption of a biological basis isn't as strong.

To be considered "Native American," one ancestor out of eight (great-grandparents) or four (grandparents) may suffice. This depends on whether the assignment is by federal or state law or an Indian tribal council. The child of a Hispanic may (or may not, depending on context) claim Hispanic identity. Many Americans with an Indian or Latino grandparent consider themselves "white" and lay no claim to minority group status.

The controversy that erupted in 1990–91 over the casting of the Broadway production of the musical *Miss Saigon* also illustrates the cultural construction of race in the United States. The musical had opened a few years earlier in London, where the Filipina actress Lea Salonga had played Kim, a young Vietnamese woman. Another major role is that of the Eurasian (half-French, half-Vietnamese) pimp known as the "Engineer." For the New York production, the producer wanted Salonga to play Kim and the English actor Jonathan Pryce, who had originated the part in London, to play the Engineer. Actors' Equity must approve the casting of foreign stars in New York productions. The union initially ruled that Pryce, a "Caucasian," could not play a Eurasian. The part had to go to an "Asian" instead. (Actors' Equity eventually reconsidered its position and allowed Pryce to open in the musical.)

In this case the American hypodescent rule was being extended from the offspring of black–white unions to "Eurasians" (in this case French-Vietnamese). Again, the cultural construction of

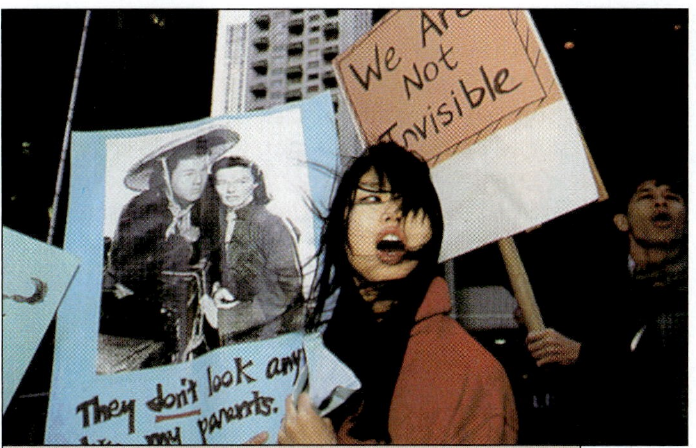

The protest over the casting of *Miss Saigon* illustrates that what has been used against a group also can be used to promote the interests of that group. What cultural rule underlies the notion that an Asian is more appropriate to play a Eurasian than a "Caucasian" is?

race is that children get their identity from the minority parent—Asian rather than European. This notion also assumes that all Asians (e.g., Vietnamese, Chinese, and Filipinos) are equivalent. Thus it's okay for someone from the Philippines to play a Vietnamese (or even a Eurasian), but an Englishman can't play a half-French Eurasian.

The culturally arbitrary rule of hypodescent is behind the idea that an Asian is more appropriate to play a Eurasian than a "Caucasian" is. Hypodescent governs racial and ethnic ascription in the United States. This rule of descent channels discrimination against offspring of mixed unions, who are assigned minority status. But, as the case of *Miss Saigon* illustrates, a cultural rule that has been used against a group also can be used to promote the interests of that group. There has been a shortage of parts for Asian and Asian American actors. In this case, the hypodescent rule was used to stake a claim for Asians and Asian Americans to have prime access to "Eurasian" as well as "Asian" parts.

Interracial, Biracial, and Multiracial Identity

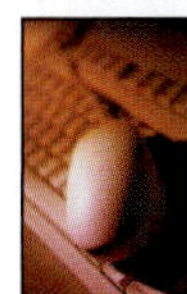

The U.S. Census Bureau has gathered data by race since 1790. Initially this was done because the Constitution specified that a slave counted as three-fifths of a white person and because Indians were not taxed. The racial categories specified in the U.S. census include White, Black or Negro, Indian (Native American), Eskimo, Aleut or Pacific Islander, and Other. A separate question asks about Spanish-Hispanic heritage. An attempt by social scientists and interested citizens to add a "multiracial" census category has been opposed by the NAACP and the National Council of La Raza. As the *Miss Saigon* incident demonstrates, racial classification is a political issue. It involves access to resources, including parts, jobs, voting districts, and federal funding of programs aimed at minorities. The hypodescent rule results in all the population growth being attributed to the minority category. Minorities fear their political clout will decline if their numbers go down.

But things are changing. Choice of the "Other" category in the U.S. Census grew 45 percent from 1980 (7 million) to 1990 (10 million)—suggesting imprecision in and dissatisfaction with the existing categories (Mar 1997). The number of interracial marriages and children is

A biracial American family. What's the race of the father? The mother? The child?

In this 1997 photo, Tiger Woods tees off at Ponte Vedra Beach, Florida. The number of interracial marriages and children is increasing, which has implications for the traditional American system of racial classification.

increasing, with implications for the traditional system of American racial classification. "Interracial," "biracial," or "multiracial" kids who grow up with both parents undoubtedly identify with particular qualities of either parent. It is troubling for many of them to have so important an identity as race dictated by the arbitrary rule of hypodescent. It may be especially discordant when racial identity doesn't parallel gender identity, for example, for boys with a white father and a black mother, or girls with a white mother and a black father. Children tend to use the parent of the same sex as a social role model.

As the number of Americans with mixed parentage grows, more and more people are confronting issues of identification and identity. From 1960 to 1980, the number of interracial couples in the United States rose by 535 percent, to almost 2 percent of all married couples. By 1990 the figure was 2.7 percent. Mixed race children now constitute 3.2 percent of American births annually.

Some 6 percent of black men, but only 2 percent of black women, marry outside their racial category. Asians and Hispanics (especially Cubans) have the highest intermarriage rates with whites. The rate of interethnic and interracial marriages tends to rise with income and educational level (Mar 1997).

Not Us: Race in Japan

American culture ignores considerable diversity in biology, language, and geographic origin as it socially constructs race within the United States. North Americans also overlook diversity by seeing Japan as a nation that is homogeneous in race, ethnicity, language, and culture—an image the Japanese themselves cultivate. Thus in 1986, former Prime Minister Nakasone created an international furor by contrasting his country's supposed homogeneity (responsible, he suggested, for Japan's success in international business) with the ethnically mixed United States. To describe Japanese society, Nakasone used *tan'itsu minzoku,* an expression connoting a single ethnic-racial group (Robertson 1992).

Japan is hardly the uniform entity Nakasone described. Some dialects of the Japanese language are mutually unintelligible. Scholars estimate that 10 percent of Japan's population are minorities of various sorts. These include aboriginal Ainu, annexed Okinawans, outcast *burakumin,* children of mixed marriages, and immigrant nationalities, especially Koreans, who number more than 700,000 (De Vos et al. 1983).

Americans tend to see Japanese and Koreans as alike, but the Japanese stress the difference between themselves and Koreans. To describe racial attitudes in Japan, Jennifer Robertson (1992) uses Kwame Anthony Appiah's (1990) term *intrinsic racism*—the belief that a (perceived) racial difference is a sufficient reason to value one person less than another.

In Japan, the valued group is majority ("pure") Japanese, who are believed to share "the same blood." Thus, the caption to a printed photo of a Japanese-American model reads: "She was born in Japan but raised in Hawaii. Her nationality is American but no foreign blood flows in her veins" (Robertson 1992, p. 5). Something like hypodescent also operates in Japan, but less precisely than in the United States, where mixed offspring automatically become members of the minority group. The children of mixed marriages between majority Japanese and others (including Euro-Americans) may not get the same "racial" label as their minority parent, but they are still stigmatized for their non-Japanese ancestry (De Vos and Wagatsuma 1966).

How is race culturally constructed in Japan? The (majority) Japanese define themselves by opposition to others, whether minority groups in their own nation or outsiders—anyone who is "not us." Aspects of *phenotype* (detectable physical traits, such as perceived body odor) are considered part of being *racially different by opposition.* Other races don't smell as "we" do. The Japanese stigmatize Koreans by saying they smell different (as Europeans also do). Japanese also stereotype their minorities with behavioral and psychological traits. Koreans are stereotyped as underachievers, crime-prone, and working class. They are placed in opposition to dominant Japanese, who are positively stereotyped as harmonious, hard-working, and middle class (Robertson 1992).

The "not us" should stay that way; assimilation is generally discouraged. Cultural mechanisms, especially residential segregation and taboos on "interracial" marriage, work to keep minorities "in their place." (Still, many marriages between minorities and majority Japanese do occur.) However, perhaps to give the appearance of homogeneity, people (e.g., Koreans) who become Japanese citizens are expected to take Japanese-sounding names (Robertson 1992; De Vos et al. 1983).

In its construction of race, Japanese culture regards certain ethnic groups as having a biological basis, when there is no evidence that they do. The best example is the *burakumin,* a stigmatized group of at least four million outcasts. They are sometimes compared to India's untouchables. The *burakumin* are physically and genetically indistinguishable from other Japanese. Many of them "pass" as (and marry) majority Japanese, but a deceptive marriage can end in divorce if *burakumin* identity is discovered (Aoki and Dardess 1981).

Burakumin are perceived as standing apart from the majority Japanese lineage. Through ancestry and descent (and thus, it is assumed, "blood," or genetics), *burakumin* are "not us." Majority Japanese try to keep their lineage pure by discouraging mixing. The *burakumin* are residentially segregated in neighborhoods (rural or urban) called *buraku,* from which the racial label is derived. Compared with majority Japanese, the *burakumin* are less likely to attend high school and college. When *burakumin* attend the same schools as majority Japanese, they face discrimination. Majority children and teachers may refuse to eat with them because *burakumin* are considered unclean.

In applying for university admission or a job, and in dealing with the government, Japanese must list their address, which becomes part of a household or family registry. This list makes residence in a *buraku,* and likely *burakumin* social status, evident. Schools and companies use this information to discriminate. (The best way to pass is to move so often that the *buraku* address eventually disappears from the registry.) Majority Japanese also limit "race" mixture by hiring marriage mediators to check out the family histories of prospective spouses. They are especially careful to check for *burakumin* ancestry (De Vos et al. 1983).

The origin of the *burakumin* lies in a historic system of stratification (from the Tokugawa period: 1603–1868). The top four ranked categories were warrior-administrators (*samurai*), farmers, artisans, and merchants. The ancestors of the *burakumin* were below this hierarchy. An outcast group, they did unclean jobs, like animal slaughter and disposal of the dead. *Burakumin* still do related jobs, including work with animal products, like leather. The *burakumin* are more likely than majority Japanese to do manual labor (including farm work) and to belong to the national lower class. *Burakumin* and other Japanese minorities are also more likely to have careers in crime, prostitution, entertainment, and sports (De Vos et al. 1983).

Like blacks in the United States, the *burakumin* are class-stratified. Because certain jobs are reserved for the *burakumin,* people who are successful in those occupations (e.g., shoe factory owners) can be wealthy. *Burakumin* also have found jobs as government bureaucrats. Financially successful *burakumin* can temporarily escape their stigmatized status by travel, including foreign travel.

Japan's stigmatized *burakumin* are physically and genetically indistinguishable from other Japanese. In response to *burakumin* political mobilization, Japan has dismantled the legal structure of discrimination against *burakumin.* This Sports Day for *burakumin* children is one kind of mobilization.

Today, most discrimination against the *burakumin* is *de facto* rather than *de jure.* It is strikingly like the discrimination that blacks have faced in the United States. The *burakumin* often live in villages and neighborhoods with poor housing and sanitation. They have limited access to education, jobs, amenities, and health facilities. In response to *burakumin* political mobilization, Japan has dismantled the legal structure of discrimination against *burakumin* and has worked to improve conditions in the *buraku.* Still, Japan has not instituted American-style affirmative action programs for education and jobs. Discrimination against nonmajority Japanese is still the rule in companies. Some employers say that hiring *burakumin* would give their company an unclean image and thus create a disadvantage in competing with other businesses (De Vos et al. 1983).

Burakumin are citizens of Japan. Most Japanese Koreans, who form one of the nation's largest minorities (about 750,000 people), are not. As resident aliens, Koreans in Japan face discrimination in education and jobs. They lack citizens' health-care and social-service benefits. Government and company jobs don't usually go to non-Japanese.

Koreans started arriving in Japan, mainly as manual laborers, after Japan conquered Korea in 1910 and ruled it through 1945. During World War II, there were more than two million Koreans in Japan. They were recruited to replace Japanese farm workers who left the fields for the imperial army. Some Koreans were women (numbering from 70,000 to 200,000) forced to serve as prostitutes ("comfort women") for Japanese troops. By 1952, most Japanese Koreans had been repatriated to a divided Korea. Those who stayed in Japan were denied citizenship. They became "resident aliens," forced, like Japanese criminals, to carry an ID card, which resentful Koreans call a "dog tag." Unlike most nations, Japan doesn't grant automatic citizenship to people born in the country. One can become Japanese by having one parent born in Japan and living there three successive years (Robertson 1992).

Like the *burakumin,* many Koreans (who by now include third and fourth generations) fit physically and linguistically into the Japanese population. Most Koreans speak Japanese as their primary language. Many of them pass as majority Japanese. Still, they tend to be segregated residentially. Often they live in the same neighborhoods as *burakumin,* with whom they sometimes intermarry. Koreans maintain strong kin ties and a sense of ethnic identity with other Koreans, especially in their neighborhoods. Most Japanese Koreans who qualify for citizenship choose not to take it because of Japan's policy of forced assimilation. Anyone who naturalizes is strongly encouraged to take a Japanese name. Many Koreans feel that to do so would cut them off from their kin and ethnic identity. Knowing they can never become majority Japanese, they choose not to become "not us" twice.

Phenotype and Fluidity: Race in Brazil

There are more flexible, less exclusionary ways of constructing social race than those used in the United States and Japan. Along with the rest of Latin America, Brazil has less exclusionary categories, which permit individuals to change their racial classification. Brazil shares a history of slavery with the United States, but it lacks the hypodescent rule. Nor does Brazil have racial aversion of the sort found in Japan. The history of Brazilian slavery dates back to the 16th century, when Africans were brought as slaves to work on sugar plantations in northeastern Brazil. Later, Brazilians used slave labor in mines and on coffee plantations. The contributions of Africans to Brazilian culture have been as great as they have been to North American culture. Today, especially in areas of Brazil where slaves were most numerous, African ancestry is evident.

The system that Brazilians use to classify biological differences contrasts with those used in the United States and Japan. First, Brazilians use many more racial labels (over 500 have been reported [Harris 1970]) than North Americans or Japanese do. In northeastern Brazil, I found 40 different racial terms in use in Arembepe, a village of only 750 people (Kottak 1999). Through their classification system, Brazilians recognize and attempt to describe the physical variation that exists in their population. The system used in the United States, by recognizing only three or four races, blinds North Americans to an equivalent range of evident physical contrasts. Japanese races, remember, don't even originate in physical contrasts. *Burakumin* are physically indistinguishable from other Japanese but are considered to be biologically different.

The system that Brazilians use to construct social race has other special features. In the United States, one's race is assigned automatically at birth by hypodescent and doesn't usually change. In Japan, race also is ascribed at birth, but it can change when, say, a *burakumin* or a naturalized Korean passes as a majority Japanese. In Brazil, racial identity is less automatic and more flexible. Brazilian racial classification pays attention to phenotype. A Brazilian's phenotype, and racial label, may change due to environmental factors, such as the tanning rays of the sun.

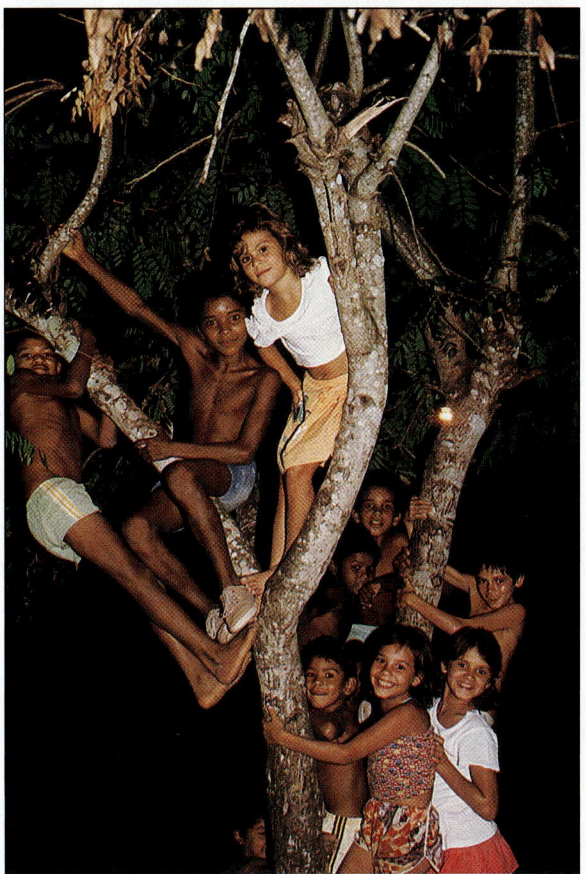

Families migrate to the Amazon from many parts of Brazil. Notice the phenotypical diversity in this photo. How might it be reflected in racial classification?

For historical reasons, darker-skinned Brazilians tend to be poorer than lighter-skinned Brazilians are. When Brazil abolished slavery in 1889, the freed men and women received no land or other reparations. They took what jobs were available. For example, the freed slaves who founded the village of Arembepe, which I have been studying since 1962, turned to fishing. Many Brazilians (including slave descendants) are poor because they lack a family history of

beyond the classroom

Skin Pigmentation in Papua New Guinea

BACKGROUND INFORMATION

Student:	*Heather Norton*
Suppervising Professors:	*Jonathan Friedlaender, Temple University; Andy Merriwether, University of Michigan; and Mark Shriver, Pennsylvania State University*
School:	*Pennsylvania State University*
Year in School:/Major:	*Graduated in spring 2000 with a BA in anthropology*
Future Plans:	*Field work in Melanesia (the Solomon Islands) tentatively in spring 2001.*
Project Title:	*Skin Pigmentation in Papua New Guinea.*

What aspects of human biological variation are addressed in this study? Are they genotypic or phenotypic?

In summer 2000, following my senior year at Penn State, I spent five weeks in Papua New Guinea studying variation in skin pigmentation. I was part of a larger research effort led by Dr. Jonathan Friedlaender and Dr. Andy Merriwether. The goal was to examine variation in mitochondrial and Y-chromosome DNA sequences in an attempt to identify patterns of migration to the islands of Melanesia. Skin pigmentation is a phenotypic trait that shows extensive variation around the world.

Skin color is primarily determined by the pigment melanin, although others, such as hemoglobin, may also contribute. One way to measure skin pigmentation is to use reflectometry, the controlled illumination of an object and the precise measurement of the light that is reflected from it. The narrow-band spectrophotometer that I used estimates the concentration of hemoglobin and melanin by taking reflectance readings. The resulting measurements are known as the melanin index (M), and the erythema index (E). The more darkly pigmented an individual, the greater their M-index measurement. I took multiple measurements on both of the

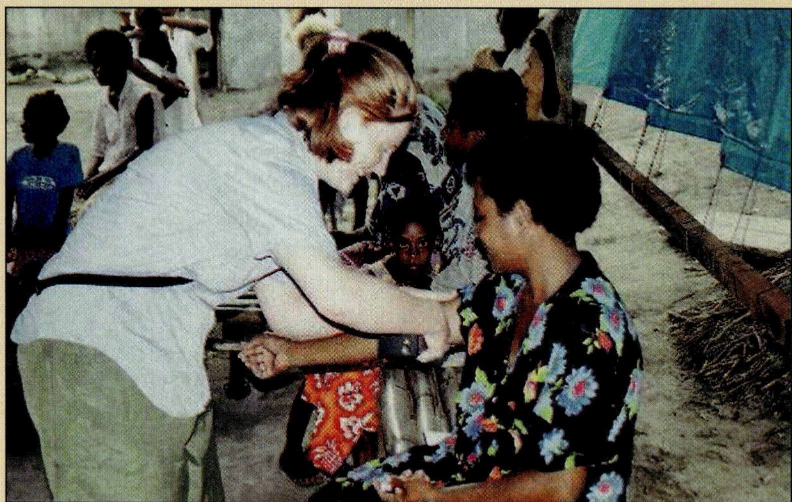

access to land or commercial wealth and because upward social mobility is difficult. Continuing today, especially in cities, it is poor, dark-skinned Brazilians, on average, who face the most intense discrimination.

Given the correlation between poverty and dark skin, one's class status affects one's racial classification in Brazil. Thus, someone who has light skin and is poor will be perceived and classified as darker than a comparably colored person who is rich. The racial term applied to a wealthy person with dark skin will tend to "lighten" his or her skin color. This gives rise to the Brazilian expression "money whitens." In the

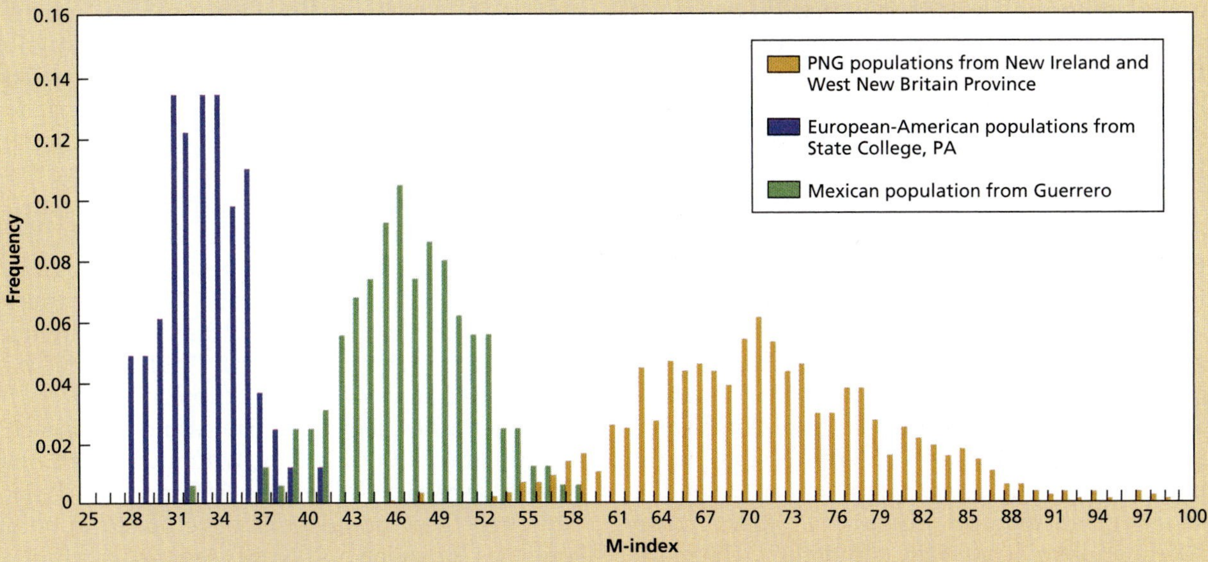

inner arms of each subject, as well as measurements of their hair color.

I chose to study pigmentation in Melanesia because of its variability among individuals there. In two weeks I was able to obtain samples from Bougainvillians, whose skin contains large amounts of melanin, as well as from lighter-skinned individuals from the Sepik region of Papua New Guinea. This area of the world is also interesting from a pigmentation perspective in terms of hair color. Individuals from Papua New Guinea and other Melanesian islands, as well as Australian aborigines, display a trait known as blondism. This refers to very blond hair, similar to someone of European descent, with darkly pigmented skin. This histogram shows the wide range of pigmentation found on the two islands—individuals at the upper end of the scale are from Bougainville, while those at the lower end are from areas such as the Sepik.

I am currently doing statistical analyses to see if differences in skin color are associated in any way with language. Although close to 1,000 languages are spoken in Papua New Guinea, they belong to two main groups, Austronesian and non-Austronesian. The non-Austronesian speakers appear to have migrated to New Guinea first, followed by a second wave of Austronesian-speaking groups. Current mitochondrial DNA evidence supports this theory. If significant skin color differences between the two groups can be shown, it may help lend support to that argument. I hope to return to Melanesia in the spring of 2001 to continue my study of pigmentation variation, this time in the neighboring Solomon Islands.

United States, by contrast, race and class are correlated, but racial classification isn't changed by class. Because of hypodescent, racial identity in the United States is fixed and lifelong, regardless of phenotype or economic status. One illustration of the absence of hypodescent in Brazil is the fact that (unlike the United States) full siblings there may belong to different races (if they are phenotypically different).

Arembepe has a mixed and physically diverse population, reflecting generations of immigration and intermarriage between its founders and outsiders. Some villagers have dark, others, light, skin color. Facial features, eye and hair color, and hair type also vary. Although physically heterogeneous, until recently Arembepe was economically homogeneous: local residents had not risen out of the national lower class. Given such economic uniformity, wealth contrasts do not affect racial classification, which Arembepeiros base on the physical differences they perceive between individuals. As physical characteristics change (sunlight alters skin color, humidity affects hair form), so do racial terms. Furthermore, racial differences have been so insignificant in structuring community life that people often forget the terms they have applied to others. Sometimes they even forget the ones they've used for themselves. To reach this conclusion, I made it a habit to ask the same person on different days to tell me the races of others in the village (and my own). In the United States, I am always "white" or "Euro-American," but in Arembepe I got lots of terms besides *branco* ("white"). I could be *claro* ("light"), *louro* ("blond"), *sarará* ("light-skinned redhead"), *mulato claro* ("light mulatto"), or *mulato* ("mulatto"). The racial term used to describe me or anyone else varied from person to person, week to week, even day to day. My best local friend, a man with very dark skin color, changed the term he used for himself all the time—from *escuro* ("dark") to *preto* ("black") to *moreno escuro* ("dark brunet").

The North American and Japanese racial systems are creations of particular cultures. They are not scientific—or even accurate—descriptions of human biological differences. Brazilian racial classification is also a cultural construction. However, Brazilians have devised a way of describing human biological diversity that is more detailed, fluid, and flexible than the systems used in most cultures. Brazil lacks Japan's racial aversion. It also lacks a rule of descent like that which ascribes racial status in the United States (Degler 1970; Harris 1964).

The operation of the hypodescent rule helps us understand why the populations labeled "black" and "Indian" (Native American) are growing in the United States but shrinking in Brazil. North American culture places all "mixed" children in the minority category, which therefore gets all the resultant population increase. Brazil, by contrast, assigns the offspring of mixed marriages to intermediate categories, using a larger set of ethnic and racial labels. A Brazilian with a "white" (*branco*) parent and a "black" (*preto*) parent will almost never be called *branco* or *preto* but instead by some intermediate term (of which dozens are available). The United States lacks fully functional intermediate categories, but it is those categories that are swelling in Brazil. Brazil's assimilated Indians are called *cabôclos* (rather than *indíos,* or a specific tribal name, like Kayapó or Yanomami). With hypodescent, by contrast, someone may have just one of four or eight Indian grandparents or great-grandparents and still "feel Indian," be so classified, and even have a tribal identity.

For centuries, the United States and Brazil each has had mixed populations, with ancestors from Native America, Europe, Africa, and Asia. Although these populations have mixed in both countries, Brazilian and North American cultures have constructed the results differently. The historic reasons for this contrast lie mainly in the different characteristics of the settlers of the two countries. The mainly English early settlers of the United States came as women, men, and families. Brazil's Portuguese colonizers, by contrast, were mainly men—merchants and adventurers. Many of these Portuguese men married Native American women and recognized their "racially mixed" children as their heirs. Like their North American counterparts, Brazilian plantation owners had sexual relations with their slaves. But the Brazilian landlords more often freed the children that resulted—for demographic and economic reasons. (Sometimes these were their only children.) Freed offspring of master and slave became plantation overseers and foremen and filled many intermediate positions in the emerging Brazilian economy. They were not classed with the slaves, but allowed to join a new intermediate category. No hypodescent rule ever developed in Brazil to ensure that whites and blacks remained separate (see Degler 1970; Harris 1964).

summary

1. How do scientists approach the study of human biological diversity? Because of a range of problems involved in classifying humans into racial categories, contemporary biologists focus on specific differences and try to explain them. Biological similarities between groups may reflect—rather than common ancestry—similar but independent adaptation to similar natural selective forces.
2. Race is a cultural category, not a biological reality. "Races" derive from contrasts perceived in particular societies, rather than from scientific classifications based on common genes. In the United Statess, "racial" labels like "white" and "black" designate social races—categories defined by American culture. In American culture, one acquires his or her racial identity at birth. But American racial classification, governed by the rule of hypodescent, is based on neither phenotype nor genes. Children of mixed unions, no matter what their appearance, are classified with the minority group parent.
3. Ten percent of Japan's people are minorities: Ainu, Okinawans, *burakumin,* children of mixed marriages, and immigrant nationalities, especially Koreans. Racial attitudes in Japan illustrate "intrinsic racism"—the belief that a perceived racial difference is a sufficient reason to value one person less than another. The valued group is majority ("pure") Japanese, who are believed to share "the same blood." Majority Japanese define themselves by opposition to others. These may be minority groups in Japan or outsiders—anyone who is "not us." Residential segregation and taboos on "interracial" marriage work against minorities. Japanese culture regards certain ethnic groups as having a biological basis when there is no evidence that they do. The *burakumin* are physically and genetically indistinguishable from other Japanese, but they still face discrimination as a social race.
4. Such exclusionary racial systems are not inevitable. Although Brazil shares a history of slavery with the United States, it lacks the hypodescent rule. Full siblings who are phenotypically different can belong to different races. Brazilian racial identity is more of an achieved status. It can change during someone's lifetime, reflecting phenotypical changes. Given the correlation between poverty and dark skin, the class structure affects Brazilian racial classification. Someone with light skin who is poor will be classified as darker than a comparably colored person who is rich.

key terms

cline A gradual shift in gene frequencies between neighboring populations.

descent Rule assigning social identity on the basis of some aspect of one's ancestry.

hypervitaminosis D Condition caused by an excess of vitamin D; calcium deposits build up in the body's soft tissues and the kidneys may fail; symptoms include gallstones and joint and circulation problems; may affect unprotected light-skinned individuals in the tropics.

hypodescent Rule that automatically places the children of a union or mating between members of different socioeconomic groups in the less-privileged group.

melanin Substance manufactured in specialized cells in the lower layers of the epidermis (outer skin layer); melanin cells in dark skin produce more melanin than do those in light skin.

natural selection As formulated by Charles Darwin and Alfred Russell Wallace, the process by which nature selects the forms most fit to survive and reproduce in a given environment.

phenotype An organism's evident traits, its "manifest biology"—anatomy and physiology.

rickets Nutritional disease caused by a shortage of vitamin D; interferes with the absorption of calcium and causes softening and deformation of the bones.

social race A group assumed to have a biological basis but actually perceived and defined in a social context, by a particular culture rather than by scientific criteria.

tropics Geographic belt extending about 23 degrees north and south of the equator, between the Tropic of Cancer (north) and the Tropic of Capricorn (south).

critical thinking questions

1. If race is a discredited term in biology, what has replaced it?
2. What are the main problems with racial classification based on phenotype?
3. Besides those given in the text, can you think of other reasons why "race" is problematic?
4. What does racism mean if race has no biological basis?
5. What are three examples of ways in which the hypodescent rule affects American racial classification?
6. What are the main physical differences between majority Japanese, on the one hand, and *burakumin*, on the other?
7. What kind of racial classification system operates in the community where you grew up or now live? Does it differ from the racial classification system described for American culture in this chapter?
8. What is the difference between race and skin color in contemporary American culture? Are the social identities of Americans and discrimination against some Americans based on one or both of these attributes?
9. When medical studies find differences between blacks and whites, are those differences best explained by sociocultural or biological factors? Could such studies be more accurate if they abandoned the labels "black" and "white" in favor of other measures of biological variation, such as actual skin color or body fat?
10. If you had to devise an ideal system of racial categories, would it be more like the North American, the Japanese, or the Brazilian system? Why?

suggested additional readings

Cohen, M.

1998 *Culture of Intolerance: Chauvinism, Class, and Racism.* New Haven: Yale University Press. Various forms of intolerance, prejudice, and discrimination are examined.

Crosby, A. W., Jr.

1986 *Ecological Imperialism: The Biological Expansion of Europe, 900–1900.* New York: Cambridge University Press. The expansion of people, plants, animals, and microorganisms.

Degler, C.

1970 *Neither Black nor White: Slavery and Race Relations in Brazil and the United States.* New York: Macmillan. The main contrasts between Brazilian and North American race relations and the historic, economic, and demographic reasons for them.

De Vos, G. A., and H. Wagatsuma

1966 *Japan's Invisible Race: Caste in Culture and Personality.* Berkeley: University of California Press. Considers many aspects of the *burakumin* (and other minorities) and their place in Japanese society and culture, including psychological factors.

Diamond, J. M.

1997 *Guns, Germs, and Steel: The Fates of Human Societies.* New York: W.W. Norton. An ecological approach to expansion and conquest in world history by a non-anthropologist.

Goldberg, D. T.

1997 *Racial Subjects: Writing on Race in America.* New York: Routledge. Survey of treatments of race in the United States.

Goldberg, D. T., ed.

1990 *Anatomy of Racism.* Minneapolis: University of Minnesota Press. Collection of articles on race and racism.

Harris, M.

1964 *Patterns of Race in the Americas.* New York: Walker. Reasons for different racial and ethnic relations in North and South America and the Caribbean.

Jurmain, R.

2000 *Introduction to Physical Anthropology,* 8th ed. Belmont, CA: Wadsworth. This basic text discusses aspects of human biological diversity.

Molnar, S.

1998 *Human Variation: Races, Types, and Ethnic Groups.* Upper Saddle River, NJ: Prentice Hall. Links between biological and social diversity.

Montagu, A.

1981 *Statement on Race: An Annotated Elaboration and Exposition of the Four Statements on Race Issued by the United Nations Educational, Scientific, and Cultural Organization.* Westport, CT: Greenwood. United Nations positions on race analyzed.

Montagu, A., ed.

1997 *Man's Most Dangerous Myth: The Fallacy of Race.* Walnut Creek, CA: AltaMira. Revision of classic book.

Shanklin, E.

1994 *Anthropology and Race.* Belmont, CA: Wadsworth. A concise introduction to the race concept from the perspective of anthropology.

internet exercises

1. Ethnic Groups in the US: Go to the US Census page entitled "Race and Hispanic Origin Population Density of the United States in 1990," **http://www.census.gov/geo/www/mapGallery/RHOriginPD-1990.html.**

a. Examine all four maps showing the proportion of specific ethnic groups by county in the US. Try to explain the historical processes that brought about the patterns of high and low density.

b. Click on the first map, which shows the density of the American Indian, Eskimo, and Aleut people in every county in the US. What is the closest county to you with a high proportion of Native Americans?

c. Examine the map of African-American population density. Why are there so many African Americans clustered in the southeastern part of the US?

d. Examine the map of the Hispanic population in the US. How do you explain the pockets of high concentrations of Hispanics in the Pacific northwest, Midwest, and east coast?

e. Where do you find the highest concentrations of Asian Americans? Why are the concentrations of Asian Americans so different from other ethnic groups?

2. Race and the Census: Read Gregory Rodriguez's article in *Salon* magazine entitled "Do the Multiracial Count?," **http://www.salon.com/news/feature/2000/02/15/census/index.html.**

a. What was the problem that some people had with the original census? How does this reflect American notions of race as described in this chapter?

b. What was the compromise that the Clinton administration presented? What are its ramifications?

c. In this case what role does the federal government play in our society's notions of race? Is the federal government merely responding to changing conceptions of race of the American people, or is it trying to shape the way the American public thinks about race?

d. Based on this chapter, how do you think this kind of question on the census form would be handled in Brazil? In Japan?

See Chapter 8 on your CD-ROM for additional review and interactive exercises. See your McGraw-Hill Online Learning Center for more.

Chapter 9

The First Farmers

CHAPTER OUTLINE

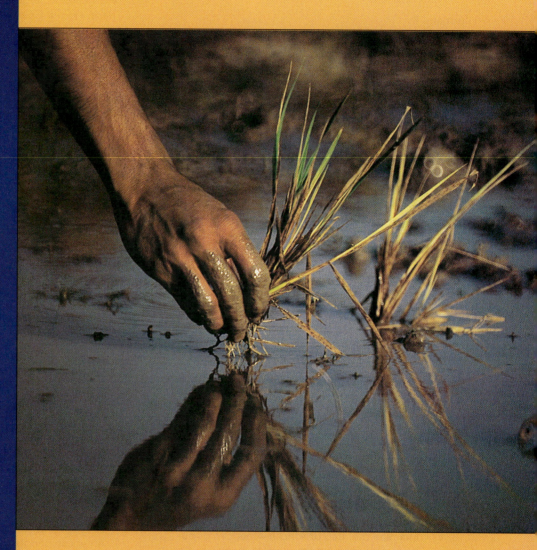

ABCNEWS.GO.COM NEWS BRIEFS

Western Hemisphere Inhabited at Least 15,000 Years Ago

by Ron Todt
April 7, 2000

Philadelphia—New research on an early human settlement in Virginia suggests that the Western Hemisphere was settled at least 15,000 years ago—far earlier than previously believed.

Don't expect the findings to settle the debate.

"I think it's enough to begin a resolution. I don't think it's going to end it," said Yale paleobotanist Lucinda McWeeney, who helped date the findings to be presented today at a conference of the Society for American Archaeology. "It means . . . we need to keep an open mind, because some people did come here earlier."

Researchers studied material from an early human settlement on a sandy slope called Cactus Hill, 45 miles south of Richmond.

Their findings may finally force anthropologists to rethink the longstanding image of a wave of skin-clad, spear-carrying humans trudging over a land bridge from Siberia after the last ice age.

"The significant thing today is that we're very sure the site exists, that the older level really is there," said archaeologist Joseph M. McAvoy, leader of the research team.

Researchers generally agree humans evolved several hundred thousand years ago . . . in Africa, then spread across Europe and Asia. In the 1930s, a dig near Clovis, N.M., revealed a "Clovis culture," characterized by distinctive spear points and dating back 10,900 to 11,500 years. The culture quickly spread throughout North America.

In 1997, a site in Chile called Monte Verde was found to have been occupied 12,500 years ago—1,000 years earlier than Clovis. McAvoy has worked since 1989 at Cactus Hill, about 100 yards from the Nottoway River, where Clovis tools had been found. But beneath the Clovis-era site, they found tools of a different material that dated back 15,000 to 17,000 years.

Soils scientist James Baker of Virginia Tech, with the help of laser dating, provided evidence that older areas of the site had not been polluted by the younger eras. The sand from the site was examined for evidence of disturbance by living material.

McWeeney used two methods to show that remains of white pine trees matched the time sequence provided by other evidence. Charred bone fragments were identified and believed to have been burned in a hearth rather than a forest fire.

The results prove humans occupied the site far earlier than the Clovis era, McAvoy said.

McAvoy said the earlier residents were hunter-gatherers and may have eaten the Eastern mud turtles and whitetail deer, burned remains of which were found. Their presence means the Americas were not populated by a single mass migration, he said.

"The Western Hemisphere was probably populated in spurts, probably starting more than 20,000 years ago, by small groups of nomadic hunters that just came in at various periods of time like opening and shutting the faucet of a sink," McAvoy said. "It wasn't a long, significant migration probably until much later."

Source: http://abcnews.go.com/sections/science/DailyNews/first_americans000407.html.

overview

Food production encompasses the domestication of plants and animals and the farming and herding economies that result. This new economy developed out of foraging, as people gradually added domesticates to the broad spectrum of resources used for subsistence. By 10,000 B.P. ancient Middle Easterners, the first farmers, were cultivating wheat and barley and influencing the reproduction of goats and sheep. It took a few thousand years, however, for them to become full-time food producers.

There were seven independent inventions of food production: in the Middle East, sub-Saharan Africa, northern and southern China, Mesoamerica, the south central Andes, and the eastern United States. They occurred at different times and were based on different sets of crops. In Mesoamerica between 7000 and 4000 B.P., maize and other domesticates were gradually added to a broad-spectrum foraging economy. The first permanent farming communities arose in the lowlands and in a few frost-free areas of the highlands. In the Valley of Mexico, quick-growing maize eventually made year-round village life possible. This paved the way for the emergence of the state and city life at Teotihuacan (A.D. 100 to A.D. 700) and Tenochtitlan, the Aztec capital (1325 to 1520).

Food production and the social and political systems it supported brought advantages and disadvantages. The advantages included many discoveries and inventions. The disadvantages included harder work, poorer health, crime, war, social inequality, and environmental degradation.

In Chapter 7, we considered the economic implications of the end of the Ice Age in Europe. With glacial retreat, foragers pursued a more generalized economy, focusing less on large animals. This was the beginning of what Kent Flannery (1969) has called the **broad-spectrum revolution.** This refers to the period beginning around 15,000 B.P. in the Middle East and 12,000 B.P. in Europe, during which a wider range, or broader spectrum, of plant and animal life was hunted, gathered, collected, caught, and fished. It was revolutionary because, in the Middle East, it led to **food production**—human control over the reproduction of plants and animals.

After 15,000 B.P., throughout the inhabited world, as the big-game supply diminished, foragers had to pursue new resources. Human attention shifted from large-bodied, slow reproducers (such as mammoths) to species such as fish, mollusks, and rabbits that reproduce quickly and prolifically (Hayden 1981).

For example, archaeologist David Lubell and his colleagues have reconstructed a pattern of intensive snail collecting at Kef Zoura, eastern Algeria. Dozens of sites in and around the Kef Zoura valley were occupied between 10,000 and 7,000 years ago by members of the Capsian culture. The *Capsians* were a Mesolithic people who based much of their subsistence on land snails, including the modern species the French call *escargot.* The Kef Zoura site has yielded millions of snail shells. The Capsians were nomadic, shifting campsites after depleting the local snail supply. They also ate plants, including various grasses, acorns, pine nuts, and pistachio nuts (Bower and Lubell 1988).

Spirit Cave in northwestern Thailand has yielded the earliest plant remains from Southeast Asia (Gorman 1969). Between about 9200 and about 8600 B.P., the people at Spirit Cave ate wild nuts, gourds, water chestnuts, black pepper, and cucumbers. Although these plants were not yet domesticated, their association at the same site does indicate a diverse diet and a broad-spectrum pattern that eventually led to food production.

The Japanese site of Nittano (Akazawa 1980), on an inlet near Tokyo, offers additional evidence for the widespread importance of broad-spectrum foraging. Nittano was occupied several times between 6000 and 5000 B.P. by members of the *Jomon* culture, for which 30,000 sites are known in Japan. The Jomon people hunted deer, pigs, bears, and antelope. They also ate fish, shellfish, and plants. Jomon sites have yielded the remains of 300 species of shellfish and 180 species of edible plants (including berries, nuts, and tubers) (Akazawa and Aikens 1986).

Early experiments in food production illustrate another, and the most significant form of intensified resource use in the post–Ice Age world. By 10,000 B.P., a major economic shift was under way in the Middle East (Turkey, Iraq, Iran, Syria, Jordan, and Israel). People started intervening in the reproductive cycles of plants and animals their ancestors had foraged for generations. Middle Easterners eventually became the world's first farmers and herders (Moore 1985). No longer simply harvesting nature's bounty, they grew their own food and modified the biological characteristics of the plants and animals in their diet. By 10,000 B.P., domesticated plants and animals were part of the broad spectrum of resources used by Middle Easterners. By 7500 B.P., most Middle Easterners were moving away from a broad-spectrum foraging pattern toward more specialized economies based on fewer species, which were domesticates.

Kent Flannery (1969) has proposed a series of eras during which the Middle Eastern transition to farming and herding took place (Table 9.1). The era of seminomadic hunting and gathering (12,000 to 10,000 B.P.) encompasses the last stages of broad-spectrum foraging. This was the period just before the first domesticated plants (wheat and barley) and animals (goats and sheep) were added to the diet. Next came the era of early dry farming (of wheat and barley) and caprine domestication (10,000 to 7500 B.P.). *Dry farming* refers to farming without irrigation; such farming depended on rainfall. *Caprine* (from *capra*, Latin for "goat") refers to goats and sheep, which were domesticated during this era.

During the era of increasing specialization in food production (7500 to 5500 B.P.), new crops were added to the diet, along with more productive varieties of wheat and barley. Cattle and pigs were domesticated. By 5500 B.P., agriculture extended to the alluvial plain of the Tigris and Euphrates rivers (Figure 9.1), where early Mesopotamians lived in walled towns, some of which grew into

Table 9.1
The Transition to Food Production in the Middle East

Era	Dates (B.P.)
Origin of state (Sumer)	5500
Increasing specialization in food production	7500–5500
Early dry farming and caprine domestication	10,000–7500
Seminomadic hunting and gathering (e.g., Natufians)	12,000–10,000

"Neolithic" was coined to refer to techniques of grinding and polishing stone tools, like these axes and hammers from Austria, Hungary, and the Czech Republic. Was the new tool-making style the most significant thing about the Neolithic?

cities. Metallurgy and the wheel were invented. After two million years of stone-tool making, *H. sapiens* was living in the Bronze Age.

The archaeologist V. Gordon Childe (1951) used the term *Neolithic Revolution* to describe the origin and impact of **food production**—plant cultivation and animal domestication. **Neolithic,** which means "New Stone Age," was coined to refer to techniques of grinding and polishing stone tools. However, the main significance of the Neolithic was the new total economy rather than just the tool-making techniques. *Neolithic* now refers to the first cultural period in a given region in which the first signs of domestication are present. The Neolithic economy based on food production produced substantial changes in human life styles. The pace of social and cultural change increased enormously.

The First Farmers and Herders in the Middle East

Middle Eastern food production arose in the context of four environmental zones. From highest to lowest, they are plateau (5,000 feet, or 1,500 meters), Hilly Flanks, steppe (treeless plain), and alluvial plain of the Tigris and Euphrates rivers (100 to 500 feet, or 30 to 150 meters). The **Hilly Flanks** is a subtropical woodland zone that flanks those rivers to the north (Figures 9.1 and 9.2).

It was once thought that food production began in oases in the alluvial plain. (*Alluvial* describes rich, fertile soil deposited by rivers and streams.) This arid region was where Meso-

Figure 9.1

The Ancestors of Wheat and Barley Grew Wild in the Subtropical Woodland Zone

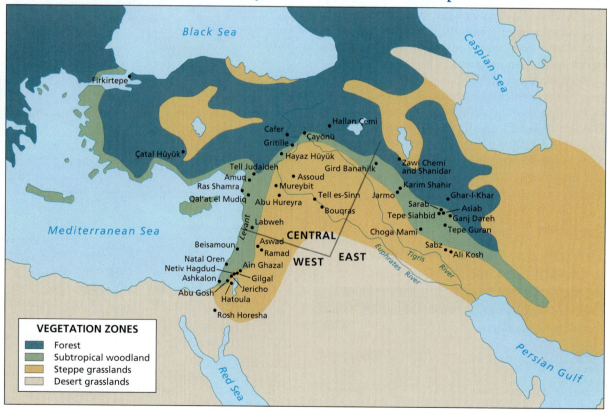

Food production emerged on the margins of the subtropical woodland zone, at places such as Ali Kosh, rather than within it, at places such as Jarmo. Food production did not reach the alluvial desert lowlands near the Tigris and Euphrates rivers (see Figure 9.2), where Mesopotamian civilization arose around 5500 B.P., until irrigation was invented, much later.

potamian civilization arose later. Today, we know that although the world's first civilization (Mesopotamian) did indeed develop in this zone, irrigation, a late (7000 B.P.) invention, was necessary to farm the alluvial river plain, a desert area. Plant cultivation and animal domestication started not in the arid river zone but in areas of reliable rainfall.

The archaeologist Robert J. Braidwood (1975) proposed instead that food production started in the Hilly Flanks, or subtropical woodland, zone, where wild wheat and barley would have been most abundant (see Figures 9.1 and 9.2). In 1948, a team headed by Braidwood started excavations at Jarmo, an early food-producing village inhabited between 9000 and 8500 B.P., located in the Hilly Flanks. We now know, however, that there were farming villages earlier than Jarmo (Figure 9.1) in zones adjacent to the Hilly Flanks. One example is Ali Kosh (Figure 9.1), a village in the foothills (piedmont steppe) of the Zagros mountains. By 9000 B.P., the people of Ali Kosh were herding goats, intensively collecting various wild plants, and harvesting wheat during the late winter and early spring (Hole, Flannery, and Neely 1969).

Figure 9.2
The Vertical Economy of the Ancient Middle East

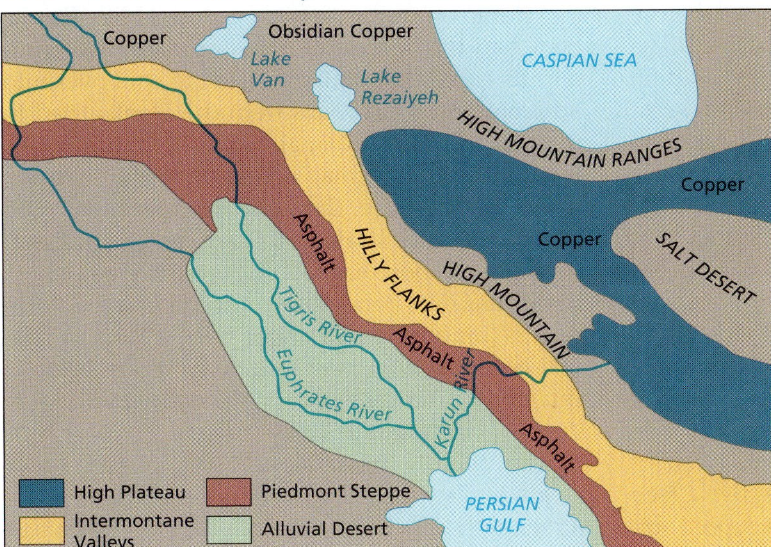

Geographically close but contrasting environments were linked by seasonal movements and trade patterns of broad-spectrum foragers. Traded resources included copper, obsidian, and asphalt, located in particular zones. As people traveled and traded, they removed plants from the zones where they grew wild in the Hilly Flanks into adjacent zones where humans became agents of selection.

Climate change played a role in the origin of food production (Smith 1995). The end of the Ice Age brought greater regional and local variation in climatic conditions. Lewis Binford (1968) proposed that in certain areas of the Middle East (such as the Hilly Flanks), local environments were so rich in resources that foragers could adopt **sedentism**—sedentary (settled) life in villages. Binford's prime example is the widespread Natufian culture (12,500 to 10,500 B.P.), based on broad-spectrum foraging. The **Natufians,** who collected wild cereals and hunted gazelles, had year-round villages. They were able to stay in the same place (early villages) because they could harvest nearby wild cereals for six months.

Donald Henry (1989, 1995) documented a climate change toward warmer, more humid conditions just before the Natufian period. This expanded the altitude range of wild wheat and barley, thus enlarging the available foraging area and allowing a longer harvest season. Wheat and barley ripened in the spring at low altitudes, in the summer at middle altitudes, and in the fall at high altitudes. As locations for their villages, the Natufians chose places where they could harvest wild cereals in all three zones.

Around 11,000 B.P., this favorable foraging pattern was threatened by a second climate change—to drier conditions. As many wild cereal habitats dried up, the optimal zone for foraging shrank. Natufian villages were now restricted to areas with permanent water. As population continued to grow, some Natufians attempted to maintain productivity by transferring wild cereals to these well-watered areas, where they started cultivating.

In the view of many scholars, the people most likely to adopt a new subsistence strategy, such as food production, would be those having the most trouble in following their traditional subsistence strategy (Binford 1968; Flannery 1973; Wenke 1996). Thus, those ancient Middle Easterners living outside the area where wild foods were most abundant would be the most likely to experiment and to adopt new subsistence strategies. This would have been especially true as the climate dried up. Recent archaeological finds support this hypothesis that food production began in *marginal areas,* such as the piedmont steppe, rather than in the optimal zones, such as the Hilly Flanks, where traditional foods were most abundant.

Some 12,000 to 10,000 years ago, ancient Middle Easterners migrated seasonally. They followed the availability of plants and animals, from lower to higher zones. With domestication, this pattern evolved into nomadic herding (pastoralism). Contemporary Middle Eastern herders, like this Bedouin boy in Jordan, still take their flocks to grazing areas at different elevations.

Even today, wild wheat grows so densely in the Hilly Flanks that one person working just an hour with Neolithic tools can easily harvest a kilogram of wheat (Harlan and Zohary 1966). People would have had no reason to invent cultivation when wild grain was ample to feed them. Wild wheat ripens rapidly and can be harvested over a three-week period. According to Flannery, over that time period, a family of experienced plant collectors could harvest enough grain—2,200 pounds (1,000 kilograms)—to feed themselves for a year. But after harvesting all that wheat, they'd need a place to put it. They could no longer maintain a nomadic lifestyle, since they'd need to stay close to their wheat.

Sedentary village life thus developed before farming and herding in the Middle East. The Natufians and other Hilly Flanks foragers had no choice but to build villages near the densest stands of wild grains. They needed a place to keep their grain. Furthermore, sheep and goats came to graze on the stubble that remained after humans had harvested the grain. The fact that basic plants and animals were available in the same area also favored village life. Hilly Flanks foragers built houses, dug storage pits for grain, and made ovens to roast it.

Natufian settlements, occupied year-round, show permanent architectural features and evidence for the processing and storage of wild grains. One such site is Abu Hureyra, Syria (see Figure 9.1), which was initially occupied by Natufians around 11,000 to 10,500 B.P. Then it was abandoned—to be reoccupied later by food producers, between 9500 and 8000 B.P. From the Natufian period, Abu Hureyra has yielded the remains of grinding stones, wild plants, and 50,000 gazelle bones, which represent 80 percent of all the bones recovered at the site (Jolly and White 1995).

Prior to domestication, the favored Hilly Flanks zone had the densest human population. Eventually, its excess population started to spill over into adjacent areas. Colonists from the Flanks tried to maintain their traditional broad-spectrum foraging in these marginal zones. But with sparser resources available, they had to experiment with new subsistence strategies. Eventually, population pressure on more limited resources forced people in the marginal zones to become the first food producers (Binford 1968; Flannery 1969). *Early cultivation began as an attempt to copy, in a less favorable environment, the dense stands of wheat and barley that grew wild in the Hilly Flanks.*

The Middle East, along with certain other world areas where food production originated, is a region that for thousands of years has had a *vertical economy.* (Other examples include Peru and **Mesoamerica**—Middle America, including Mexico, Guatemala, and Belize.) A vertical economy exploits environmental zones that, although close together in space, contrast with one another in altitude, rainfall, overall climate, and vegetation

(Figure 9.2). Such a close juxtaposition of varied environments allowed broad-spectrum foragers to use different resources in different seasons.

Early seminomadic foragers in the Middle East had followed game from zone to zone. In winter they hunted in the piedmont steppe region, which had winter rains rather than snow and provided winter pasture for game animals 12,000 years ago. (Indeed it is still used for winter grazing by herders today.) When winter ended, the steppe dried up. Game moved up to the Hilly Flanks and high plateau country as the snow melted. Pasture land became available at higher elevations. Foragers gathered as they climbed, harvesting wild grains that ripened later at higher altitudes. Sheep and goats followed the stubble in the wheat and barley fields after people had harvested the grain.

The four Middle Eastern environmental zones shown in Figure 9.2 also were tied together through trade. Certain resources were confined to specific zones. Asphalt, used as an adhesive in the manufacture of sickles, came from the steppe. Copper and turquoise sources were located in the high plateau. Contrasting environments were therefore linked in two ways: by foragers' seasonal migration and by trade.

The movement of people, animals, and products between zones—plus population increase supported by highly productive broad-spectrum foraging—was a precondition for the emergence of food production. As they traveled between zones, people carried seeds into new habitats. Mutations, genetic recombinations, and human selection led to new kinds of wheat and barley. Some of the new varieties were better adapted to the steppe and, eventually, the alluvial plain than the wild forms had been.

Genetic Changes and Domestication

What are the main differences between wild and domesticated plants? The seeds of domesticated cereals, and often the entire plant, are larger. Compared with wild plants, crops produce a higher yield per unit of area. Domesticated plants also lose their natural seed dispersal mechanisms. Cultivated beans, for example, have pods that hold together, rather than shattering as they do in the wild. Domesticated cereals have tougher connective tissue holding the seedpods to the stem.

Grains of wheat, barley, and other cereals occur in bunches at the end of a stalk (Figure 9.3). The grains are attached to the stalk by an *axis.* In wild cereals, this axis is brittle. Sections of the axis break off one by one, and a seed attached to each section falls to the ground. This is how wild cereals spread their seeds and propagate their species. But a brittle axis is a problem for people. Imagine the annoyance experienced by broad-spectrum foragers as they tried to harvest wild wheat, only to have the grain fall off or be blown away.

In very dry weather, wild wheat and barley ripen—their axes totally disintegrating—in just three days (Flannery 1973). The brittle axis must have been even more irritating to people who planted the seeds and waited for the harvest. But fortunately, certain stalks of wild wheat and barley happened to have tough axes. These were the ones whose seeds people saved to plant the following year.

Another problem with wild cereals is that the edible portion is enclosed in a tough husk. This

Figure 9.3
A Head of Wheat or Barley

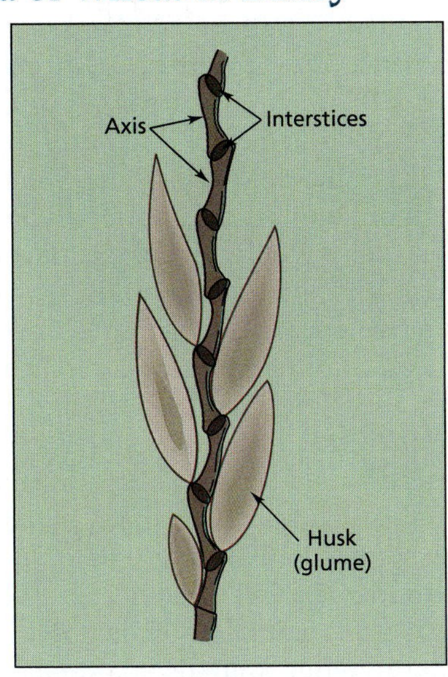

In the wild, the axis comes apart as its parts fall off one by one. The connecting parts (interstices) are tough and don't come apart in domesticated grains. In wild grains, the husks are hard. In domestic plants, they are brittle, which permits easy access to the grain. How did people deal with hard husks before domestication?

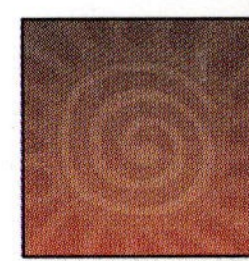

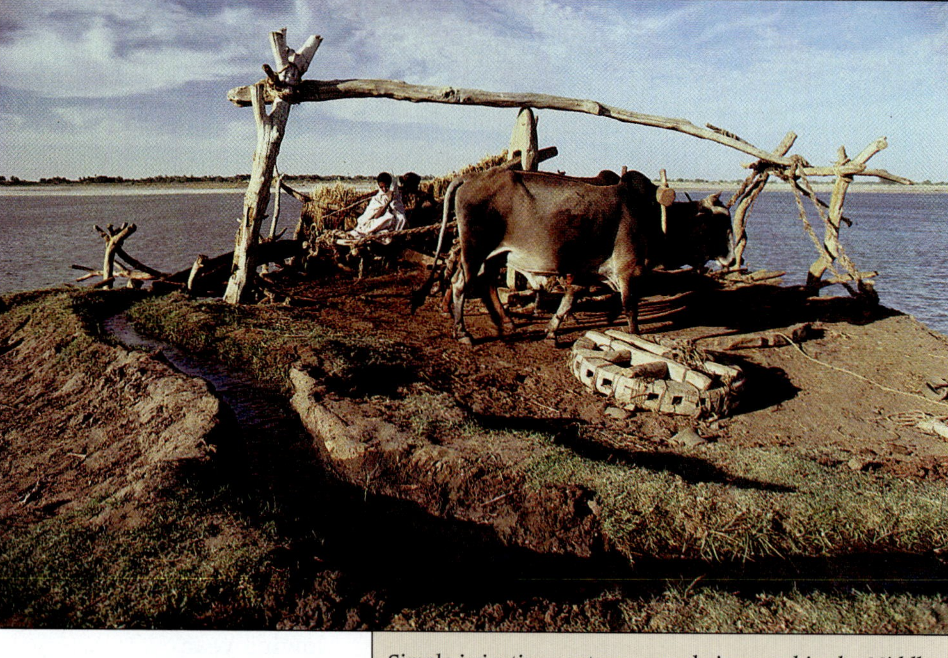

Simple irrigation systems were being used in the Middle East by 7000 B.P. By 6000 B.P., complex irrigation techniques made agriculture possible in the arid lowlands of southern Mesopotamia. Here in Sudan, we see a fairly simple, ox-powered irrigation system.

husk was too tough to remove with a pounding stone. Foragers had to roast the grain to make the husk brittle enough to come off. However, some wild plants happened to have genes for brittle husks. Humans chose the seeds of these plants (which would have germinated prematurely in nature) because they could be more effectively prepared for eating.

People also selected certain features in animals (Smith 1995). Some time after sheep were domesticated, advantageous new phenotypes arose. Wild sheep aren't woolly; wool coats were products of domestication. Although it's hard to imagine, a wool coat offers protection against extreme heat. Skin temperatures of sheep living in very hot areas are much lower than temperatures on the surface of their wool. Woolly sheep, but not their wild ancestors, could survive in hot, dry alluvial lowlands. Wool had an additional advantage: its use for clothing.

What are some of the differences between wild and domesticated animals? Plants got larger with domestication, while animals got smaller, probably because smaller animals are easier to control. Middle Eastern sites document changes in the horns of domesticated goats. Such change may have been genetically linked to some other desirable trait that has left no skeletal evidence behind.

Food Production and the State

The shift from foraging to food production was gradual. The knowledge of how to grow crops and breed livestock didn't immediately convert Middle Easterners into full-time farmers and herders. Domesticated plants and animals began as minor parts of a broad-spectrum economy. Foraging for fruits, nuts, grasses, grains, snails, and insects continued.

Over time, Middle Eastern economies grew more specialized, geared more exclusively toward crops and herds. The former marginal zones became centers of the new economy and of population increase and emigration. Some of the increasing population spilled back into the Hilly Flanks, where people eventually had to intensify production by cultivating. Domesticated crops could now provide a bigger harvest than could the grains that grew wild there. Thus, in the Hilly Flanks, too, farming eventually replaced foraging as the economic mainstay.

Farming colonies spread down into drier areas. By 7000 B.P., simple irrigation systems had developed, tapping springs in the foothills. By 6000 B.P., more complex irrigation techniques made agriculture possible in the arid lowlands of southern Mesopotamia. In the alluvial desert plain of the Tigris and Euphrates rivers, a new economy based on irrigation and trade fueled the growth of an entirely new form of society. This was the *state,* a social and political unit featuring a central government, extreme contrasts of wealth, and social classes.

We now understand why the first farmers lived neither in the alluvial lowlands, where the Mesopotamian state arose around 5500 B.P., nor in the Hilly Flanks, where wild plants and animals abounded. Food production began in marginal zones, such as the piedmont steppe, where people experimented at reproducing, artificially, the dense grain stands that grew wild in the Hilly Flanks. As seeds were taken to new environments, new phenotypes were favored by a combination of natural and human selection. The spread of cereal grains outside their natural habitats was part of a system of migration and trade between zones, which had developed in the Middle East during the broad-spectrum period. Food production also owed its origin to the need to intensify production to feed an increasing human population—the legacy of thousands of years of productive foraging.

Other Old World Farmers

The path from foraging to farming was one that people followed independently in at least seven world areas. As we'll see later, three were in the Americas. Four were in the Old World, including the very first farmers and herders in the Middle East. In each of these seven centers, people independently invented domestication—albeit of different sets of crops and animals. Food production also spread out from the Middle East and other centers of domestication. This happened through trade, through diffusion of products and information, and through the actual migration of farmers, who in some cases displaced native foragers. Probably, though, trade and the exchange of ideas did more to spread crops and livestock than did actual migration of food producers. The crops and livestock that were originally domesticated in the Middle East spread westward to northern Africa, including Egypt's Nile Valley, and into Europe (Price 2000). Trade also extended eastward from the Middle East to India and Pakistan. In Egypt, an agricultural economy based on plants and animals originally domesticated in the Middle East led to a pharaonic civilization. Another early civilization eventually arose in western Pakistan. Around 8,000 B.P., communities on Europe's Mediterranean shores, in Greece, Italy, and France, started shifting from foraging to farming, using imported species. By 7000 B.P., there were fully sedentary farming villages in Greece and Italy. By 6000 B.P., there were thousands of farming villages as far east as Russia and as far west as northern France. By chance, we can even meet a man from one of those European Neolithic villages. The "Iceman" discovered in Austria in 1991 (see "In the News") came from a village of farmers who raised wheat, barley, sheep, and goats.

Compared with the Middle East, less is known about early farmers in such Old World areas as sub-Saharan Africa, South and Southeast Asia, and China. Partly this reflects the poorer preservation of archaeological remains in hot, moist habitats. Mostly it reflects the need for more archaeological research in such areas. In Pakistan's Indus River Valley, ancient cities (Harappa and Mohenjo-daro) emerged slightly later than did the first Mesopotamian city-states. Domestication and state formation in the Indus Valley were probably influenced by developments in, and trade with, the Middle East. Still, archaeological research confirms the early (8000 B.P.) presence of domesticated goats, sheep, cattle, wheat, and barley in Pakistan (Meadow 1991).

China was also one of the first world areas to develop farming, based on millet and rice. Millet is a tall, coarse cereal grass still grown in northern China. This grain, which today feeds a third of the world's population, is used in contemporary North America mainly as bird seed. By 7500 B.P., two varieties of millet supported early farming communities in northern China, along the Yellow River. Millet cultivation paved the way for widespread village life and eventually for Shang dynasty civilization, based on irrigated agriculture,

The Iceman

This item describes the discovery and subsequent identification of the glacially preserved "Iceman" as a Neolithic Alpine European who lived around 5300 B.P. The find is significant because of its age, its state of preservation, and its combination of a human cadaver with clothing and possessions, including stone and metal (copper) tools. The Iceman probably came from an Alpine farming village. He was on an autumn hunting trip when he was killed and eventually frozen. The Neolithic, which began some 10,000 years ago in the Middle East, had spread to Western Europe by 6500 B.P.

The "Iceman," who scientists now know lived about 5,300 years ago, had been in the ice 1,000 years when the Egyptians built the pyramids at Giza, more than 3,000 years when Jesus was born. Yet he was found with a remarkable array of clothing, weapons and equipment, including some mysterious objects of types never seen before.

Some—including the man's fur hat, the oldest known in Europe—were found just last summer in a new expedition to the normally ice-bound site on the Austrian–Italian border.

Archaeologists are excited, because the man's body was found not in a grave, the usual source of ancient remains, but at a campsite he made during a sojourn in the mountains, and because snow and ice covered him and his things, preserving them almost perfectly.

His perishable belongings—items made of wood, leather, grass, and apparently even food and medicines—have come out of the ice virtually intact, providing scientists with the most intimate picture ever seen of the daily life of a prehistoric man.

For example, his ax, which has a copper head, looks and feels as new and dangerous as on the fall day in about 3300 BC [5,300 B.P.], when the man leaned it against a rock before bedding down for his last night. It is among the oldest copper axes known and one of the best made, dating from the dawn of the use of metals.

Archaeologists know that fateful night was in the autumn, because frozen with him was a ripe blackthorn fruit, the plumlike berry also called sloe, which grows at lower altitudes and ripens in the fall.

The man's body is startlingly well preserved—by far the most lifelike from prehistoric times—and is being kept in a high-security freezer at the University of Innsbruck medical school.

The body was naturally freeze-dried and is in such good condition that pores in the skin look normal. Even his eyeballs can still be seen behind lids frozen open, and CT scans show the brain and other internal organs in place.

"We have never had a prehistoric discovery as complete as this," said Andreas Lippert, a University of Vienna archaeologist who led the expedition to the site last summer. The group found more than 400 objects, most of them parts of the man's clothing.

Yet several key questions remain. What was he doing so high in the mountains? How did he die? And, most intriguing to archaeologists, did he come from one of the known prehistoric cultures of the region, or does he represent something entirely new?

What is clear is that he lived during one of the more critical transitions in the development of human culture, when stone tools were beginning to give way to metal.

Farming, which began in the Middle East about 5,000 years earlier, had spread to much of Eurasia by 5,300 years ago. The man probably came from a village of farmers who raised wheat, barley and oats and herded sheep and goats.

The man in the ice was discovered Sept. 19, 1991, by Helmut and Erika Simon, a German couple hiking in the Alps. Near the 10,500-foot-high ridge that defines the Austrian–Italian border they were tramping over the snow and ice of a commonly used pass when they saw a human head and shoulders sticking out of the ice. The body was lying face down, its skin a tawny color and the head hairless. The Simons reported it to police in the Italian state of South Tirol.

The local Carabinieri, Italian police familiar with the common problem of retrieving bodies of modern climbers, insisted that this

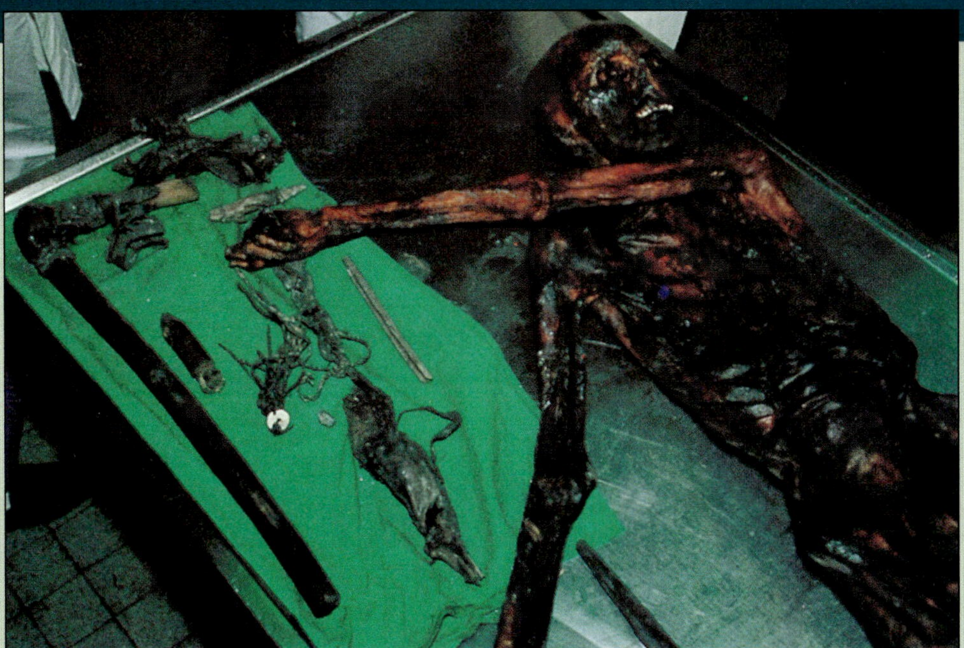

Meet the Iceman. Since his frozen body emerged from a glacier in the Italian Alps in 1991, scientists have come to realize he is the closest we may ever come to meeting a real person from the Stone Age. How would you evaluate his state of preservation?

time the site was in Austria and not their problem.

Two days later the Austrian police from north Tirol arrived with a helicopter and—not realizing the site's importance—used an air hammer to hack the body out of the ice. They accidentally cut into the man's hip, but his legs stayed stuck. Forensic officials spotted the copperbladed ax on a nearby rock and, presuming foul play in the man's death, took it as "evidence."

Bad weather forced a temporary retreat. But word of the find encouraged curious hikers to trek to the body, and several tried to chop it free.

On Sept. 23, four days after the find, a forensic team from the University of Innsbruck helicoptered to the site, found that meltwater had refrozen around the body and began again to chop. When they pulled out the prone body, it was later realized, the man's penis remained embedded in the ice.

Workers also gathered up some pieces of fur and leather clothing, string, a leather bag and a flint dagger. A long stick, apparently a bow, was still partly embedded in ice, so workers broke off part and took that, too.

Hikers and skiers had been lost in the Alps many times, but they usually emerged a few decades later when the flow of the glaciers transported them to lower altitudes where they melted out. Moreover, these "young" bodies were usually horribly transformed into misshapen blobs of "fat wax." This man in the ice, though dried and somewhat shriveled like a mummy, looked too good to be very old.

A team of glaciologists soon resolved the question with another visit to the site. They found that the body had lain at the bottom of a narrow ravine. Snow could have filled the 6-to-10-foot-deep crevice, but the resulting ice was trapped.

The glaciologists also found evidence to support the man's antiquity—his quiver, which contained 14 arrows, two of them fitted with flint arrowheads, hardly the choice of any bowman who lived since the Iron Age swept Eurasia more than 3,000 years ago.

And the glaciologists explained why the body had only just emerged. Earlier in 1991 great storms had blown dust from North Africa into the Alps, darkening the snow cover. The dust absorbed solar heat, causing more than the usual amount of snow to melt during the summer of 1991, exposing the body.

Source: Boyce Rensberger, "A Man Who Lived 5,300 Years Ago," *The Washington Post*, November 26, 1992, p. E1.

between 3600 and 3100 B.P. (See Chapter 10.) The northern Chinese also had domesticated dogs, pigs, and possibly cattle, goats, and sheep by 7000 B.P. (Chang 1977).

Recent discoveries by Chinese archaeologists suggest that rice was domesticated in the Yangtze River corridor of southern China as early as 8400 B.P. (Smith 1995). Other early rice comes from the 7,000-year-old site Hemudu, on Lake Dongting in southern China. The people of Hemudu used both wild and domesticated rice, along with domesticated water buffalo, dogs, and pigs. They also hunted wild game (Jolly and White 1995).

Millet, being harvested here on a Chinese plateau, was grown in the Hwang-Ho (Yellow River) Valley by 7000 B.P. This grain supported early farming communities in northern China. What was being grown in southern China at the same time?

China seems to have been the scene of two independent transitions to food production, based on different crops grown in strikingly different climates. Southern Chinese farming was rice aquaculture in rich subtropical wetlands. Southern winters were mild; and summer rains, reliable. Northern China, by contrast, had harsh winters, with unreliable rainfall during the summer growing season. This was an area of grasslands and temperate forests. Still, in both areas by 7500 B.P., food production supported large and stable villages. Based on the archaeological evidence, early Chinese villagers had architectural expertise. They lived in substantial houses, made elaborate ceramic vessels, and had rich burials.

At Nok Nok Tha in central Thailand, pottery made more than 5,000 years ago has imprints of husks and grains of domesticated rice (Solheim 1972/1976). Animal bones show that the people of Nok Nok Tha also had humped zebu cattle similar to those of contemporary India. Rice might have been cultivated at about the same time in the Indus River Valley of Pakistan and adjacent western India.

It appears that food production arose independently as many as seven times in different world areas. Figure 9.4 is a map highlighting those seven areas: the Middle East, north China, south China, sub-Saharan Africa, central Mexico, the south central Andes, and the eastern United States. A different set of major foods was domesticated, at different times, in each area, as we see in Table 9.2. Some grains, such as millet and rice, were domesticated more than once. Millet grows wild in China and Africa, where it became an important food crop, as well as in Mexico, where it did not. Indigenous African rice, grown only in West Africa, belongs to the same genus as Asian rice. Pigs and possibly cattle were independently domesticated in the Middle East, China, and sub-Saharan Africa. Independent domestication of the dog was virtually a worldwide phenomenon, including the western hemisphere. We turn now to archaeological sequences in the Americas.

The First American Farmers

Homo did not, of course, originate in the western hemisphere. Never have fossils of Neandertals or earlier hominids been found in North or South America. The settlement of the Americas was one of the major achievements of *H. sapiens sapiens*. This colonization continued the trends toward population increase and expansion of geographic range that have marked human evolution generally.

Figure 9.4
Seven World Areas Where Food Production Was Independently Invented

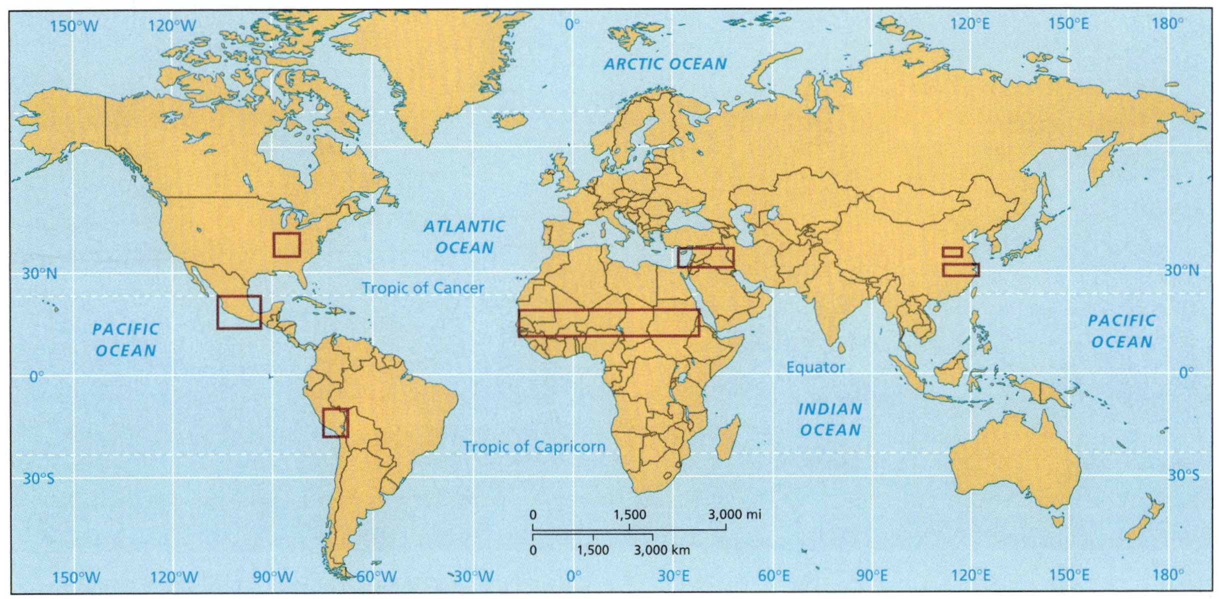

Source: B. D. Smith, *The Emergence of Agriculture* (New York: Scientific American Library, W. H. Freeman, 1995), p. 12.

Do any of these areas surprise you?

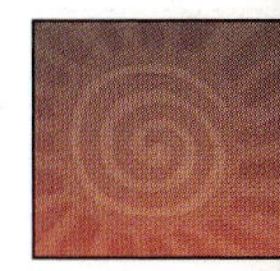

Table 9.2
Seven World Areas Where Food Production Was Independently Invented

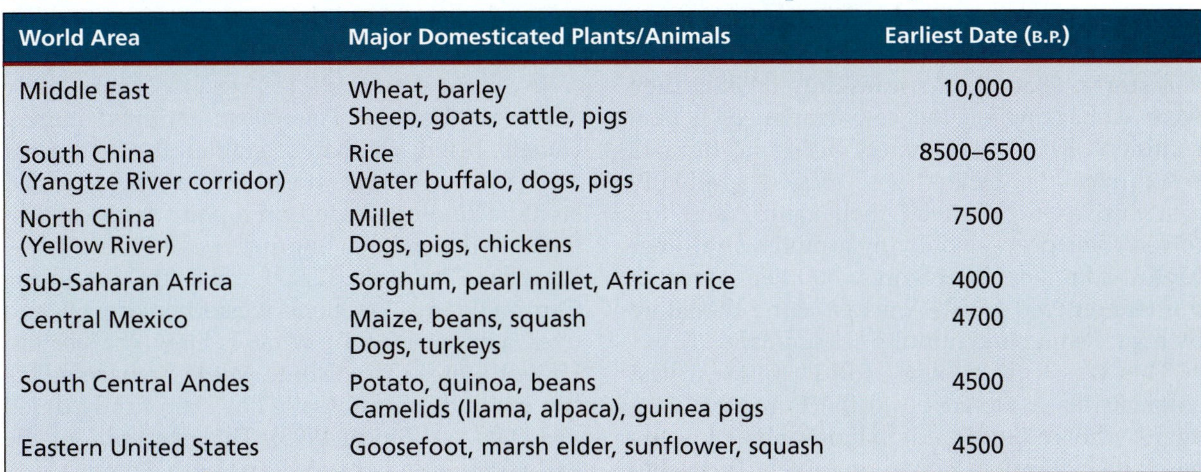

World Area	Major Domesticated Plants/Animals	Earliest Date (B.P.)
Middle East	Wheat, barley Sheep, goats, cattle, pigs	10,000
South China (Yangtze River corridor)	Rice Water buffalo, dogs, pigs	8500–6500
North China (Yellow River)	Millet Dogs, pigs, chickens	7500
Sub-Saharan Africa	Sorghum, pearl millet, African rice	4000
Central Mexico	Maize, beans, squash Dogs, turkeys	4700
South Central Andes	Potato, quinoa, beans Camelids (llama, alpaca), guinea pigs	4500
Eastern United States	Goosefoot, marsh elder, sunflower, squash	4500

Source: Data compiled from B. D. Smith, *The Emergence of Agriculture* (New York: Scientific American Library, W. H. Freeman, 1995).

Overland migrations from Asia ended when rising sea levels flooded Beringia, leaving a landscape of ice, ocean, and jagged peaks. How might later Asian migrants have entered North America? How might archaeologists find out more about the people who lived in Beringia?

America's First Immigrants

The original settlers of the Americas came from Northeast Asia. They were the ancestors of American Indians. They entered North America via the Bering land bridge, *Beringia,* which connected North America and Siberia several times during the ice ages. Beringia, which today lies under the Bering Sea, was a dry land area several hundred miles wide, exposed during the glacial advances (Figure 9.5).

Living in Beringia thousands of years ago, the ancestors of Native Americans didn't realize they were embarking on the colonization of a new continent. They were merely big-game hunters who, over the generations, moved gradually eastward as they spread their camps and followed their prey—woolly mammoths and other tundra-adapted herbivores. Other ancient hunters entered North America along the shore by boat, fishing and hunting sea animals.

This was truly a "new world" to its earliest colonists, as it would be to the European voyagers who rediscovered it thousands of years later. Its natural resources, particularly its big game, had never before been exploited by humans. Early bands followed the game south. Although ice sheets covered most of what is now Canada, colonization gradually penetrated the heartland of what is now the United States. Successive generations of hunters followed game through unglaciated corridors, breaks in the continental ice sheets. Others spread by boat down the Pacific coast.

In North America's rolling grasslands, early American Indians, *Paleoindians,* hunted horses, camels, bison, elephants, mammoths, and giant sloths. The **Clovis tradition**—a sophisticated stone technology based on a point that was fastened to the end of a hunting spear (Figure 9.6)—flourished between 12,000 and 11,000 B.P. in the Central Plains, on their western margins, and over a large area of what is now the eastern United States. The Monte Verde archaeological site in south central Chile has been firmly dated to 12,000 B.P. (Smith 1995). This evidence for the early occupation of southern South America suggests that the first migration of humans into the Americas may date back between 15,000 and 20,000 years.

Figure 9.5

The Ancestors of Native Americans Came to North America as Migrants from Asia

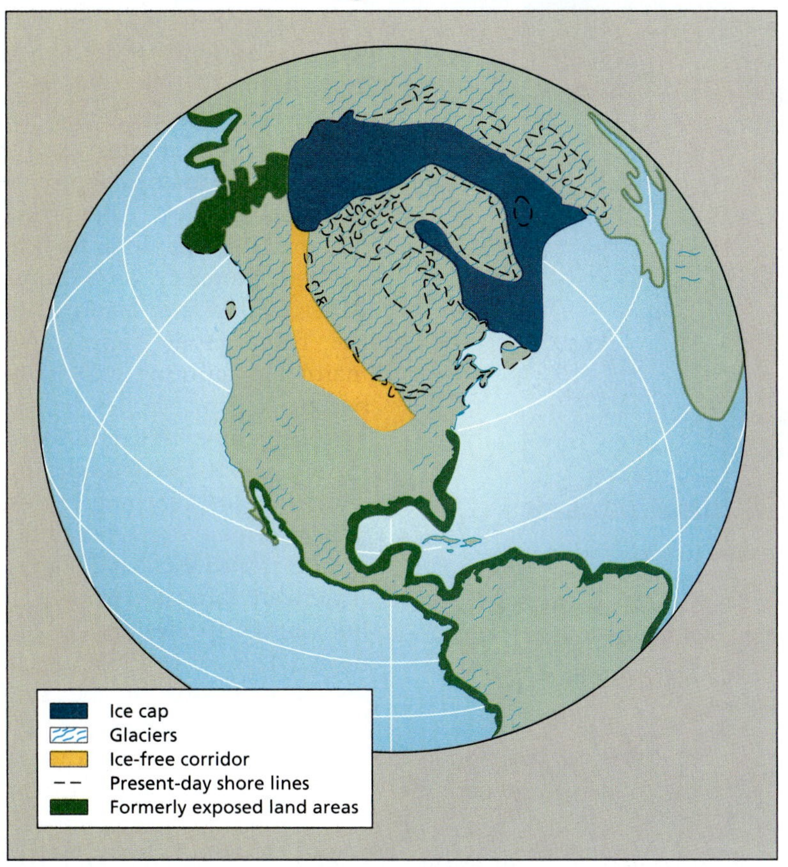

They followed big-game herds across Beringia, an immense stretch of land exposed during the ice ages. Was their settlement of the Americas intentional? When did it probably happen? Other migrants reached North America along the shore by boat, fishing and hunting sea animals.

The Foundations of Food Production

As hunters benefiting from the abundance of big game, bands of foragers gradually spread through the Americas. As they moved, these early Americans learned to cope with a great diversity of environments. Thousands of years later, their descendants independently invented food production, paving the way for the emergence of states based on agriculture and trade in Mexico and Peru. New World food production emerged 3,000 to 4,000 years later than in the Middle East, as did the first states.

The most significant contrast between Old and New World food production involved animal domestication, which was much more important in the Old World than in the New World. The animals that had been hunted during the early American big-game tradition either became extinct before people could domesticate them or were not domesticable. The largest animal ever domesticated in the New World (in Peru, around 4,500 B.P.) was the llama. Early Peruvians and Bolivians ate llama meat and used that animal as a beast of burden (Flannery, Marcus, and Reynolds 1989). They bred the llama's relative, the alpaca, for its wool. (Llamas and alpacas are

Figure 9.6
A Clovis Spear Point

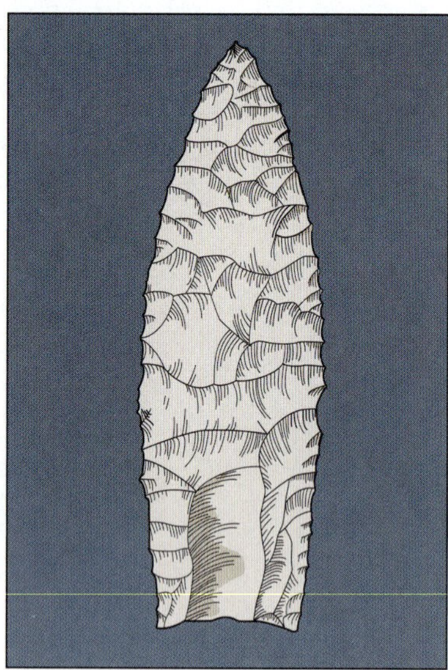

Such points were attached to spears used by Paleoindians of the North American plains between 12,000 and 11,000 B.P. Are there sites with comparable ages in South America?

members of the *camelid* family.) Peruvians added animal protein to their diet by raising and eating guinea pigs and ducks.

The turkey was domesticated in Mesoamerica and in the southwestern United States. Lowland South Americans domesticated a type of duck. The dog is the only animal that was domesticated throughout the New World. There were no cattle, sheep, or goats in the areas where food production arose. As a result, neither herding nor the kinds of relationships that developed between herders and farmers in many parts of the Middle East, Europe, Asia, and Africa emerged in the precolonial Americas. The New World crops were different, although staples as nutritious as those of the Old World were domesticated from native wild plants.

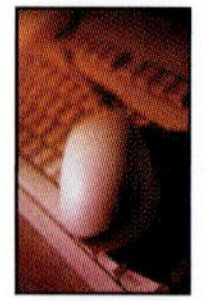

Three *caloric staples,* major sources of carbohydrates, were domesticated by Native American farmers. **Maize,** or corn, first domesticated in highland Mexico, became the caloric staple in Mesoamerica and Central America; it eventually spread to coastal Peru. The other two staples were root crops: white ("Irish") potatoes, first domesticated in the Andes, and **manioc,** or cassava, a tuber first cultivated in the South American lowlands. Other crops added variety to New World diets and made them nutritious. Beans and squash, for example, provided essential proteins, vitamins, and minerals. The "three sisters" of maize, beans, and squash were the basis of the Mesoamerican diet.

Food production was independently invented in three areas of the Americas: Mesoamerica, the eastern United States, and the south central Andes. Mesoamerica is discussed in detail in the next section. Food plants known as goosefoot and marsh elder, along with the sunflower and a species of squash, were domesticated by Native Americans in the eastern United States by 4500 B.P. These crops supplemented a diet based mainly on hunting and gathering. They never became caloric staples like maize, wheat, rice, millet, manioc, and potatoes. Eventually maize diffused from Mesoamerica into what is now the United States, reaching both the Southwest and the eastern area just mentioned. Maize provided a more reliable caloric staple for Native North American farming. In what is now Peru and Bolivia, six species appear to have been domesticated more or less together in the highland valleys and basins of the south central Andes between 5000 and 4000 B.P. These domesticates were the potato, quinoa (a cereal grain), beans, llamas, alpacas, and guinea pigs (Smith 1995).

Early Farming in the Mexican Highlands

Long before Mexican highlanders developed a taste for maize, beans, and squash, they hunted as part of a pattern of broad-spectrum foraging. Mammoth remains dated to 11,000 B.P. have been found along with spear points in the basin that surrounds Mexico City. However, small animals were more important than big game, as were the grains, pods, fruits, and leaves of wild plants.

In the *Valley of Oaxaca,* in Mexico's southern highlands, between 10,000 and 4000 B.P., foragers concentrated on certain wild animals—deer and rabbits—and plants—cactus leaves and fruits, and tree pods, especially mesquite (Flannery 1986). Those early Oaxacans dispersed to hunt and gather in fall and winter. But they came together in late spring and summer, forming larger groups to harvest seasonally available plants. Cactus fruits appeared in the spring. Since summer rains would reduce the fruits to mush and since birds, bats, and rodents competed for them, cactus collection

Early Peruvians and Bolivians ate llama meat, harnessed llamas as beasts of burden (as is shown here), and used llama dung to fertilize their fields. What was the largest animal domesticated in the New World?

By diffusion, manioc or cassava, originally domesticated in lowland South America, has become a caloric staple in the tropics worldwide. This young Thai farmer displays his manioc crop.

required hard work by large groups of people. The edible pods of the mesquite, available in June, also required intensive gathering.

In fall, these early Oaxacan foragers gathered a wild grass known as **teocentli,** or *teosinte,* the wild ancestor of maize. Sometime between 7000 and 4000 B.P., teocentli-maize underwent a series of genetic changes like those described earlier

217–218

for Middle Eastern wheat and barley. These changes included increases in the number of kernels per cob, cob size, and the number of cobs per stalk (Flannery 1973). Such steps toward domestication made it increasingly profitable to collect wild maize and eventually to plant maize.

Undoubtedly, some of the mutations necessary for domesticated maize had occurred in wild teocentli before people started growing it. However, since teocentli was well adapted to its natural niche, the mutations offered no advantage and didn't spread. But once people started harvesting wild maize intensively, they became selective agents. As foragers wandered during the year, they carried teocentli to environments different from its natural habitat.

Furthermore, as people harvested teocentli, they took back to camp a greater proportion of plants with tough axes and stalks. These were the plants most likely to hold together during harvesting and least likely to disintegrate on the way back home. Now teocentli depended on humans for its survival, since it lacked the natural means of dispersal—a brittle axis or stalk. If humans chose plants with tough axes inadvertently, their selection of plants with soft husks must have been intentional. Their selection of corn ears with larger cobs, more kernels per cob, and more cobs per plant was also intentional.

Eventually, people started planting maize in the alluvial soils of valley floors. This was the zone where foragers had traditionally congregated for the annual summer harvest of mesquite pods. By 4000 B.P., a type of maize had been developed that provided more food than the mesquite pods did. Once that happened, people started cutting down mesquite trees and replacing them with corn fields.

Farming triggered a population explosion and adaptive radiation throughout Mesoamerica. Yet

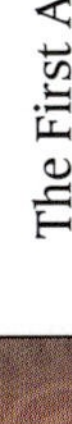

again, changes were gradual. In the Middle East, thousands of years intervened between the first experiments in domestication and the appearance of the state. The same was true in Mesoamerica.

From Early Farming to the State

Eventually, food production led to the *early village farming community.* Permanent villages sustained by farming were occupied year-round. The earliest such settlements in Mesoamerica developed around 3500 B.P., in two kinds of environment. One was humid lowlands, along the Gulf Coast of Mexico and the Pacific Coast of Mexico and Guatemala. Here, maize farming in rich soils was combined with gathering and hunting of several species of wild plants and animals.

Early village farming communities also emerged in one part of the Mexican highlands. In the Valley of Oaxaca in southern Mexico, winter frosts are absent, and simple irrigation permitted the establishment of early permanent villages based on maize farming. Water close to the surface allowed early farmers to dig wells right in their corn fields. Using pots, they dipped water out of these wells and poured it on their growing plants, a technique known as *pot irrigation.* The earliest year-round Mesoamerican farming depended on reliable rainfall, pot irrigation, or access to humid river bottomlands.

The subsequent spread of maize farming resulted in further genetic changes, higher yields, higher human populations, and more intensive farming. Pressures to intensify cultivation led to improvements in early water-control systems. New varieties of fast-growing maize eventually appeared, expanding the range of areas that could be cultivated. Increasing population and irrigation also helped spread maize farming.

The gradual transformation of broad-spectrum foraging into intensive cultivation laid the foundation for the emergence of the state in Mesoamerica—some 3,000 years later than in the Middle East (Table 9.3). A *state* is a form of social and political organization that has a formal, central government and a division of society into classes. Chiefdoms are precursors to states; they have privileged and effective leaders—chiefs—but they lack the sharp class divisions that characterize states. Evidence of what archaeologists call the *elite level,* indicating a chiefdom or a state, appears around 3500 B.P. An early example comes from Mexico's Gulf Coast, where, between 3200 and 2500 B.P., the *Olmecs* (a chiefdom) built several ritual centers. Large earthen mounds, presumably dedicated to religion, document the ability of Olmec elites to marshal labor. The Olmecs also sculpted massive stone heads, which may be representations of their chiefs.

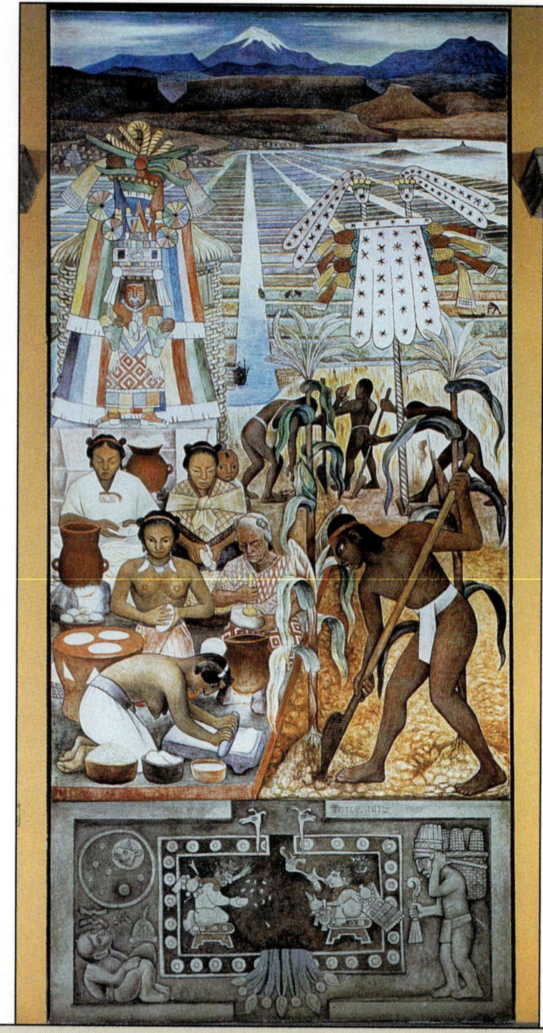

As maize cultivation spread, genetic changes led to higher yields and more productive farming. Pressures to intensify cultivation helped improve water-control systems, such as the canal irrigation shown in this mural by Diego Rivera.

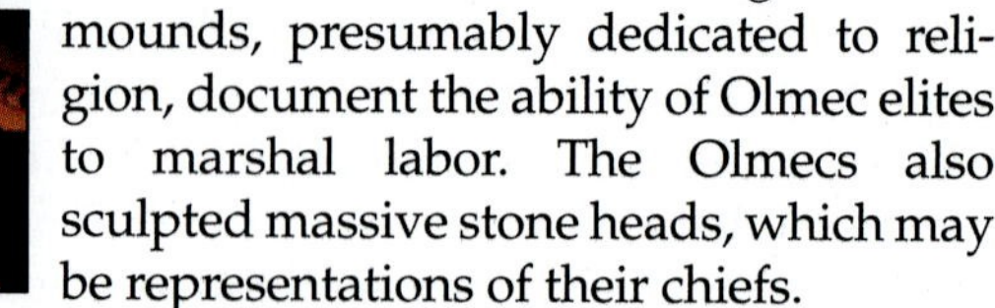

By 2500 B.P., Olmec culture had dimmed, but the elite level was spreading throughout Meso-

Table 9.3

The Rise of Food Production and the State in Mesoamerica

These developments, from early corn domestication to the fall of the Aztec state, are organized here according to period names. Elite-level societies (beginning with the Olmecs, through the Spanish conquest of the Aztecs) are described as Preclassic (Olmecs and Oaxaca). Next come Classic (Oaxaca continues, along with Teotihuacan and the Maya area) and Postclassic (Toltecs and Aztecs).

Period	Date (B.P.)	Area/Sites	Settlement Types	Ranking/Stratification System
Conquest (Cortez)	AD 1521	Mexico	Colony of Spain	Spanish domination; world system
Postclassic	1150–500 (AD 900–1200) (AD 1325–1521)	Toltec Aztec	Cities, social unrest Increased militarism More secular rule Expanded trade	State Empire Empire
Classic	1750–1150	Teotihuacan Oaxaca Maya	Cities Trade, crafts expand	Stratification, states
Preclassic (Formative)	3500–1750	Olmec Oaxaca	Ceremonial centers Writing (by end)	Ranking, chiefdoms Stratification (by end)
Early food production	4000–3500	Oaxaca Pacific Coast Gulf Coast	Village farming community	Ranking
Earliest domestication	5000	Tehuacan Oaxaca	Seminomadic bands	Egalitarian

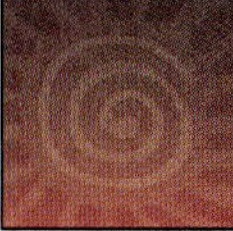

america. By AD 1 (2000 B.P.), the highlands, particularly the Valley of Mexico, moved to center stage in the Mesoamerican transformation. It was in the Valley of Mexico that the city and state of Teotihuacan flourished between 1900 and 1300 B.P. (AD 100 and AD 700). The Aztec state, which lasted until the Spanish conquest in 1521, arose in the valley around 1325. (The Classic Maya state thrived in Mexico's Yucatan peninsula and in neighboring areas of what are now Guatemala and Belize from AD 200 to 900.)

Costs and Benefits

Food production brought advantages and disadvantages. Among the advantages were discoveries and inventions. People learned to spin and weave; to make pottery, bricks, and arched masonry; and to smelt and cast metals. They developed trade and commerce by land and sea. By 5500 B.P., Middle Easterners were living in vibrant cities with markets, streets, temples, and palaces. They created sculpture, mural art, writing systems, weights, measures, mathematics, and new forms of political and social organization (Jolly and White 1995).

Because it increased economic production and led to new social, scientific, and creative forms, food production is often considered an evolutionary advance. But the new economy also brought hardships. For example, food producers typically work harder than foragers do—and for a less adequate diet. Because of their extensive leisure time, foragers have been characterized as living in "the original affluent society" (Sahlins 1972). As we'll see in Chapter 14, certain foragers have survived into recent times and have been studied by anthropologists. Among foragers living in the Kalahari Desert of southern Africa, only part of the group needed to hunt and gather, maybe 20 hours a week, to provide an adequate diet for the entire group. Women gathered, and adult men hunted. Their labor supported older people and children. Early retirement from the food quest was possible, and forced child labor was unknown.

interesting issues

Pseudo-Archaeology

The 1998 film *The X-Files* opens with a scene purportedly dating to 35,000 BC. Two prehistoric men trek across a glacial landscape in North Texas. Soon they have an alien encounter. Who's more likely to have been in Texas back then: the humans or the aliens? The study of prehistory has spawned popular-culture creations, including movies, TV programs, and books. In these fictional works, the anthropologists (and the natives as well) usually don't bear much resemblance to their real-life counterparts. Unlike Indiana Jones, normal and reputable archaeologists don't have nonstop adventures—fighting Nazis, lashing whips, or rescuing antiquities. The archaeologist's profession isn't a matter of raiding lost arks or of going on crusades but of reconstructing lifeways through the analysis of material remains, in order to understand culture and human behavior.

Much of the popular nonfiction dealing with prehistory is also suspect. Through books and the mass media, we have been exposed to the ideas of popular writers such as Thor Heyerdahl and Erich von Daniken. Heyerdahl, a well-known diffusionist, believes that developments in one world area are usually based on ideas borrowed from another. Von Daniken carries diffusionism one step further, proposing that major human achievements have been borrowed from beings from space who have visited us at various periods of our past. Heyerdahl and von Daniken seem to share (with some science-fiction writers) a certain contempt for human inventiveness and originality. They take the position that major changes in ancient human life styles were the results of outside instruction or interference rather than the achievements of the natives of the places where the changes took place.

In *The Ra Expeditions* (Heyerdahl 1971), for example, world traveler and adventurer Heyerdahl argued that his voyage in a papyrus boat from the Mediterranean to the Caribbean demonstrates that ancient Egyptians could have navigated to the New World. (The boat was modeled on an ancient Egyptian vessel, but Heyerdahl and his crew took along such modern conveniences as a radio and canned goods.) Heyerdahl maintained that given the possibility of ancient transatlantic voyages, Old World people could have influenced the emergence of civilization in the Americas.

What is the scientific evaluation of Heyerdahl's contention? Even if Old World ancients had reached the New World, they couldn't have done much to propel Native Americans toward state organization because the New World wasn't yet ready for food production and the state. When Egypt became a major power capable of sending scouts across the seas, around 5,000 years ago, Mexicans were broad-spectrum foragers. Had they even started cultivating corn? (See the text for the answer.) The gradual nature of the Mesoamerican transition from foraging to food production is clearly demonstrated by archaeological sequences in such sites as Oaxaca and the Valley of Mexico. Had foreign inputs been important, they would have shown up in the material remains that constitute the archaeological record.

Beginning some 2,000 years ago, states fully comparable to those of Mesopotamia and Egypt began to rise and fall in the Mexican highlands. This occurred more than 1,000 years after the height

With food production, yields are more reliable, but people work much harder. Herds, fields, and irrigation systems need care. Weeding can require hours of arduous bending. No one has to worry about where to keep a giraffe or a gazelle, but pens and corrals are built and maintained for livestock. Trade takes men, and sometimes women, away from home, leaving burdens for those who stay behind. For several reasons, food producers tend to have more children than foragers do. This means greater child care demands, but child labor also tends to be more needed and valued than it is among foragers. Many tasks in farming and herding can be done by children.

How much does Indiana Jones tell us about real archaeologists? The photo is from *Indiana Jones and the Temple of Doom.*

of ancient Egyptian influence, between 3600 and 3400 B.P. Had Egypt or any other ancient Old World state contributed to the rise or the fall of Mesoamerican civilization, we would expect this influence to have been exerted during Egypt's heyday as an ancient power—not 1,500 years later.

There is abundant archaeological evidence for the gradual, evolutionary emergence of food production and the state in the Middle East, in Mesoamerica, and in Peru. This evidence effectively counters the diffusionist theories about how and why human achievements, including farming and the state, began. Popular theories to the contrary, changes, advances, and setbacks in ancient American social life were the products of the ideas and activities of the Native Americans themselves.

There are certain unresolved issues, to be sure, in explaining why Mesoamerican civilizations rose and fell. Archaeologists are still unraveling the causes of the collapse around AD 900 of the Mayan culture of Mexico and Guatemala. However, there is simply no valid evidence for Old World interference before the European Age of Discovery, which began late in the 15th century. Francisco Pizzaro conquered Peru's Inca state in 1532, 11 years after its Mesoamerican counterpart, Tenochtitlan, the Aztec capital, fell to Spanish conquistadores in 1521. (We do have abundant archaeological, as well as written, evidence for this recent, historically known contact between Europeans and Native Americans.)

The archaeological record also casts doubt on contentions that the advances of earthlings came with extraterrestrial help, as Erich von Daniken argued in his book *Chariots of the Gods* (1971), and as Discovery-type TV sometimes suggests. Abundant, well-analyzed archaeological data from the Middle East, Mesoamerica, and Peru tell a clear story. Plant and animal domestication, the state, and city life were not brilliant discoveries, inventions, or secrets that humans needed to borrow from extraterrestrials. They were long-term, gradual processes, developments with down-to-earth causes and effects. They required thousands of years of orderly change, not some chance meeting in the high Andes between an ancient Inca chief and a beneficent Johnny Appleseed from Aldebaran.

This is not to deny, by the way, that intelligent life and civilizations at a variety of technological levels—some more, some less advanced than earth—may exist throughout the galaxy or even that extraterrestrials may have occasionally ventured into this relatively isolated outer spiral arm of the Milky Way galaxy and even visited earth itself. However, even if extraterrestrials have been on earth, archaeological evidence suggests that their starship commanders observed a prime directive of noninterference in the affairs of less-advanced planets. There is no scientifically valid evidence for the rapid kind of changes that sustained extraterrestrial intervention would have produced. What would constitute such evidence?

The division of economic labor grows more complex, so that children and older people have assigned economic roles.

Not only does the new economy require hard work, so do the social and political systems supported by food production (See Chapter 10). States may have mathematicians, artists, astronomers, priests, and kings, but ordinary people have to sweat in the fields to grow food for the elites and specialists. Unlike foragers, food producers have bosses. The elites conscript labor to build temples and pyramids, to move stone for enduring monuments. In states, people have to pay taxes and get drafted for work or war. It is a myth that leisure

The labor demands of food production far exceed those associated with foraging. Here, in India's Andra Pradesh, these Banjara women are pounding grain. Such processing of food is just one step in getting the grain from the fields into people's mouths. What are some of the other steps?

time increases with civilization. For some, there is leisure and privilege; for most, there is work and obligation.

And public health declines. Diets based on crops and dairy products tend to be less varied, less nutritious, and less healthful than foragers' diets, which are usually higher in proteins and lower in fats and carbohydrates. With the shift to food production, the physical well-being of the population often declines. Communicable diseases, protein deficiency, and dental caries increase (Cohen and Armelagos 1984). Greater exposure to pathogens comes with food production.

Compared with a seminomadic foraging band, food producers tend to be sedentary. Their populations are denser, which makes it easier to transmit and maintain diseases. We saw in Chapter 3

that malaria and sickle-cell anemia spread along with food production. Population concentrations, especially cities, are breeding grounds for epidemic diseases. People live nearer other people and animals and their wastes, which also affect public health (Diamond 1997). Compared with farmers, herders, and city dwellers, foragers were relatively disease-free, stress-free, and well-nourished.

Other hardships and stresses accompanied food production and the state. Social inequality and poverty increased. Elaborate systems of social stratification eventually replaced the egalitarianism of the past. Resources were no longer common goods, open to all, as they tend to be among foragers. Property distinctions proliferated. Slavery and other forms of human bondage were invented. Crime, war, and human sacrifice became widespread.

The rate at which human beings degraded their environments also increased with food production. The environmental degradation in today's world, including air and water pollution and deforestation, is on a much larger scale, compared with early villages and cities, but modern trends are foreshadowed. After food production, population increase and the need to expand farming led to deforestation in the Middle East. Even today, many farmers think of trees as giant weeds to be cut down to make way for productive fields. Previously, we

saw how early Mesoamerican farmers cut down mesquite trees for maize cultivation in the Valley of Oaxaca.

Many farmers and herders burn trees, brush, and pasture. Farmers burn to remove weeds; they also use the ashes for fertilizer. Herders burn to promote the growth of new tender shoots for their livestock. But such practices do have environmental costs, including air pollution. Smelting and other chemical processes basic to the manufacture of metal tools also have environmental costs. As modern industrial pollution has harmful effluents, early chemical processes had by-products that polluted air, soils, and waters. Salts, chemicals, and microorganisms accumulate in irrigated fields. These and other pathogens and pollutants, which were by-and-large nonissues during the Paleolithic, endanger growing human populations. To be sure, food production had benefits. But its costs are just as evident. We see that progress is much too optimistic a word to describe food production, the state, and many other aspects of the evolution of society.

Late Postclassic Economy in Northern Belize

BACKGROUND INFORMATION

Student:	*Maxine H. Oland*
Supervising Professor:	*Marilyn A. Masson*
School:	*State University of New York–Albany*
Year in School/Major:	*Senior/Anthropology*
Future Plans:	*Graduate school in anthropology*
Project Title:	*Late Postclassic Economy in Northern Belize: Stone Tools and Raw Materials from the Freshwater Creek Drainage*

What techniques were used to distinguish between locally made and imported tools? Does it surprise you that a food-producing state-level society such as the Maya would be using stone tools?

Laguna de On is a small archaeological site located on an island in Honey Camp Lagoon in Northern Belize. The Maya village site dates to the Postclassic Period (AD 900–1500). In order to better understand the economy of the region during this epoch, I sought to define patterns of local exchange regarding stone tools and raw materials. The project was funded by the National Science Foundation Research Experience for Undergraduates Award. It was completed during a field school run by the University at Albany.

It was already known that many of the tools at Laguna de On were made at Colha, a specialized lithic (stone tool) manufacturing center only 10 km away. Archaeological data at Colha indicate mass production of uniform stone tools made of highly distinctive chert. My project was concerned with the extent to which the inhabitants of Laguna de On were using local stone resources, and for what purposes.

In order to recognize those raw materials immediately available to the residents of Laguna de On, a survey was conducted of the region surrounding the lagoon. Various coarse cherts, chalcedonies, and quartz-blend materials were found outcropping naturally in sugar cane fields, road-cuts, and back yards. Every locality from which samples were collected was plotted on a map of Belize with the use of a global positioning system. The survey was purely geological, although one archaeological quarry was discovered in the process. This locality showed a surprising variety of fine chalcedonies in a concentrated area, as well as ample evidence for human modification of the materials.

In the field laboratory small samples were made of each material, using a geologist's hammer to create flakes from each nodule. These samples were labeled by locality and type (A, B, C, etc.) within the locality. They were then photographed to provide a visual record.

In the archaeology labs of the University at Albany a separate analysis of the stone tools was completed, classifying each artifact by raw material and tool type. Of the 417 stone tools examined in the study, 42 percent were made from Colha chert, which implies a heavy reliance on tools from Colha. Locally available materials made up the remaining 58 percent. An examination of tool type showed that formal tools (oval bifaces, stemmed blades) were almost exclusively acquired from Colha, while local resources were used for expedient (immediate use) tools (flakes, hammerstones).

Future work will build upon this research by comparing these findings to other nearby Postclassic sites of Northern Belize. A continuation of the raw material survey is planned, as the identification of more outcrops is essential to truly understanding procurement systems.

summary

1. After 15,000 B.P., as the big game supply diminished, foragers sought out new foods. By 10,000 B.P., domesticated plants and animals were part of a broad spectrum of resources used by Middle Easterners. By 7500 B.P., most Middle Easterners were moving away from broad-spectrum foraging toward more specialized food producing economies. *Neolithic* refers to the period when the first signs of domestication appeared.
2. Braidwood proposed that food production started in the Hilly Flanks zone, where wheat and barley grew wild. Others questioned this: The wild grain supply in that zone already provided an excellent diet for the Natufians and other ancient Middle Easterners. There would have been no incentive to domesticate. Other scholars view the origin of food production in the context of increasing population and climate changes.
3. Ancient Middle Eastern foragers migrated seasonally in pursuit of game. They also collected wild plant foods as they ripened at different altitudes. As they moved about, these foragers took grains from the Hilly Flanks zone, where they grew wild, to adjacent areas. Humans became agents of selection, preferring plants with certain attributes. Population spilled over from the Hilly Flanks into adjacent areas like the piedmont steppe. In such marginal zones people started cultivating plants. They were trying to duplicate the dense wild grains of the Hilly Flanks.
4. After the harvest, sheep and goats fed off the stubble of these wild plants. Animal domestication occurred as people started selecting certain features and behavior and guiding the reproduction of goats, sheep, cattle, and pigs. Gradually, food production spread into the Hilly Flanks. Later, with irrigation it spread down into Mesopotamia's alluvial desert, where the first cities, states, and civilizations developed by 5500 B.P. Food production then spread west from the Middle East into North Africa and Europe and east to India and Pakistan.
5. There were seven independent inventions of food production: in the Middle East, sub-Saharan Africa, northern and southern China, Mesoamerica, the south central Andes, and the eastern United States. Millet was domesticated by 7000 B.P. in northern China; and rice, by 8000 B.P. in southern China.
6. The transition to food production took place thousands of years later in the New World. Humans entered the Americas between 15,000 and 20,000 years ago. Pursuing big game, they gradually moved into North America. Adapting to different environments, Native Americans developed a variety of cultures. Some continued to rely on big game. Others became broad-spectrum foragers.
7. In the New World the most important domesticates were maize, potatoes, and manioc. The llama of the central Andes was the largest animal domesticated in the New World, where herding traditions analogous to those of the Old World did not develop. Economic similarities between the hemispheres must be sought in foraging and farming.
8. The earliest New World farming was in Mesoamerica. At Oaxaca, in Mexico's southern highlands, maize was gradually added to a broad-spectrum diet between 7000 and 4000 B.P. The first permanent villages, supported by maize cultivation, arose in the lowlands and in a few frost-free areas of the highlands. In the Valley of Mexico, quick-growing maize made year-round village life possible and paved the way for the emergence of civilization and city life.
9. Food production and the social and political system it supported brought advantages and disadvantages. The advantages included discoveries and inventions. The disadvantages included harder work, poorer health, crime, war, social inequality, and environmental degradation.

key terms

broad-spectrum revolution Period beginning around 15,000 B.P. in the Middle East and 12,000 B.P. in Europe, during which a wider range, or broader spectrum, of plant and animal life was hunted, gathered, collected, caught, and fished; revolutionary because it led to food production.

Clovis tradition Stone technology based on a projectile point that was fastened to the end of a hunting spear; it flourished between 12,000 and 11,000 B.P. in North America.

food production Human control over the reproduction of plants and animals.

Hilly Flanks Woodland zone that flanks the Tigris and Euphrates rivers to the north; zone of wild wheat and barley and of sedentism (settled, nonmigratory life) preceding food production.

maize Corn; domesticated in highland Mexico.

manioc Cassava; a tuber domesticated in the South American lowlands.

Mesoamerica Middle America, including Mexico, Guatemala, and Belize.

Natufians Widespread Middle Eastern culture, dated to between 12,500 and 10,500 B.P.; subsisted on intensive wild cereal collecting and gazelle hunting and had year-round villages.

Neolithic "New Stone Age," coined to describe techniques of grinding and polishing stone tools; the first cultural period in a region in which the first signs of domestication are present.

sedentism Settled (sedentary) life; preceded food production in the Old World and followed it in the New World.

teocentli Or *teosinte*, a wild grass; apparent ancestor of maize.

critical thinking questions

1. How would you explain the origin of food production? Would your explanation for the first farming in the Middle East also apply to Mesoamerica?
2. What environmental and demographic conditions contributed to the origin of food production in the Middle East? Did they also apply in Mesoamerica?
3. Is your own diet more like that of a forager or an early farmer? How so?
4. What were the main similarities and differences between early food production in the Middle East and in Mesoamerica?
5. For the Old World, name four caloric staples. Name three for the New World. Where was each domesticated? For each staple, is it part of your diet? What's the most important caloric staple in your diet?
6. What evidence supports the statement that transitions to food production were gradual and evolutionary?
7. Do you think it's likely that food production originated independently in south China and north China? Why?
8. From an anthropological perspective, what's most wrong with *The X-Files* movie? Can you think of other glaring errors in how anthropological subjects are treated in a movie, book, or TV program?
9. Was the origin of food production good or bad? Why?

suggested additional readings

Ashmore, W., and R. Sharer
2000 *Discovering Our Past: A Brief Introduction to Archaeology,* 3rd ed. Mountain View, CA: Mayfield. Good introduction.

Cohen, M. N., and G. J. Armelagos, eds.
1984 *Paleopathology at the Origins of Agriculture.* New York: Academic Press. Some of the negative consequences of food production for human health.

Diamond, J. M.
1997 *Guns, Germs, and Steel: The Fates of Human Societies.* New York: W. W. Norton. Disease, tools, and environmental forces and effects throughout human history.

Fagan, B. M.
1999 *World Prehistory: A Brief Introduction,* 4th ed. New York: Longman. Major events in human prehistory, including the emergence of food production and the state in various locales.
2000 *Ancient Lives: An Introduction to Method and Theory in Archaeology.* Upper Saddle River, NJ: Prentice Hall. How archaeologists do what they do.

Feinman, G. M. and T. D. Price
2001 *Archaeology at the Millennium: A Sourcebook.* New York: Kluwer Academic/Plenum. Prospects and new directions in archaeology.

Gamble, C.
2000 *Archaeology, the Basics.* New York: Routledge. The title says it all.

Henry, D. O.
1995 *Prehistoric Cultural Ecology and Evolution: Insights from Southern Jordan.* New York: Plenum Press. The origin of food production in the Middle East, with reference to environmental factors.

Kent, S., ed.
1998 *Gender in African Prehistory.* Walnut Creek, CA: AltaMira Press. Women and men in the African past.

Price, T. D., ed.
2000 *Europe's First Farmers.* New York: Cambridge University Press. The expansion of farming into Europe.

Price, T. D., and G. M. Feinman
1997 *Images of the Past,* 2nd ed. Mountain View, CA: Mayfield. Introduction to prehistory, including the origin of food production.

Price, T. D. and A. B. Gebauer, eds.
1995 *Last Hunters, First Farmers: New Perspectives on the Prehistoric Transition to Agriculture.* Santa Fe, NM: School of American Research Press. Recent ideas on the origin of food production.

Renfrew, C., and P. Bahn
2000 *Archaeology: Theories, Methods, and Practives,* 3rd ed. New York: Thames and Hudson. *Basic methods text.*

Smith, B. D.
1995 *The Emergence of Agriculture.* New York: Scientific American Library, W. H. Freeman. The first farmers and herders in several world areas.

Staeck, J.
2001 *Back to Earth: An Introduction to Archaeology.* Mountain View, CA: Mayfield. Introduction to the field.

Wenke, R.
1996 *Patterns in Prehistory: Humankind's First Three Million Years,* 4th ed. New York: Oxford University Press. Rise of food production and the state throughout the world; thorough, useful text.

internet exercises

1. What We Ate Before Farming: Read the article by Jack Chellum in *The Nutrition Science News* entitled "Paleolithic Nutrition: Your Future Is in Your Dietary Past," **http://www.healthwellexchange.com/nutritionsciencenews/nsn_backs/Apr_97/paleolithic.cfm.**
   a. What kinds of foods typified the Paleolithic diet? What kinds of food typify the modern American diet?
   b. What changes have occurred to the numbers and kinds of foods consumed by humans? Why are our foods higher in saturated fats? What changes have occurred in vitamin intake?
   c. Despite the fact that humans may not be completely adapted to an agricultural diet, what are the physical and cultural advantages of agriculture?

2. The Domestication of Maize: Read the "History of Maize," extracted from *A Historical Dictionary of the World's Plant Foods,* **http://uk.cambridge.org/history/features/food_history/samples/live_maize.htm.**
   a. When and where was maize domesticated?
   b. Maize is a very important source of carbohydrates and is one of the top three cereal crops in the world (along with rice and wheat). However, what are its nutritional deficiencies? How did Native Americans respond to this deficiency?
   c. When did maize first arrive in Europe? How was it carried there? Where else did it spread?

See Chapter 9 on your CD-ROM for additional review and interactive exercises. See your McGraw-Hill Online Learning Center for more.

Chapter 10

The First Cities and States

CHAPTER OUTLINE

DISCOVERY.COM NEWS BRIEFS

Mayan Stone Tablet Depicts Horror

by Rossella Lorenzi
June 30, 2000

An ancient Mayan scene of terror emerged from the Guatemalan jungle as archaeologists unearthed a 3,000-pound limestone panel in the remote city of Piedras Negras.

Unnoticed through previous excavations as it lay face down at the base of a pyramid, the 1,200-year-old stone slate has been hailed as one of the most significant pieces of Mayan culture ever discovered.

The 6- by 4.5-foot panel features more than 150 hieroglyphics surrounding a scene in which terrified captives are brought before the king and his two lieutenants.

"You can see them moaning and screaming, clutching themselves in terror. With this panel the Maya have begun to experiment with showing emotion, something that had not been present before," said Brigham Young University archaeologist Stephen Houston, announcing the discovery last week.

The captives had plenty of reasons to worry about their fate. Houston describes the Late Classical Maya as "brutally warlike" people who did not think twice about sacrificing humans by throwing them down 100-foot pyramid stairs. But the Maya were also the only pre-Columbian Americans to have developed a sophisticated writing system, ample evidence of which decorates their buildings.

Piedras Negras, one of the Maya's greatest cities, represents a "milestone" with cracking the Maya writing: in 1960, scholar Tatiana Proskouriakoff demonstrated that the texts on its carved stones dealt with real people and not myth. Houston's discovery is a confirmation. "The panel tells of a Mayan king, Itzamk'anahk K'in Ajaw. He came to the throne when only 13 years old—rather like Louis XIV. Much like that French king, he reigned for an exceptionally long time," said Houston.

The stone panel tells that Itzamk'anahk was born May 25, 626 and became king April 15, 639. The first 25 years of his reign were peaceful. But a battle on December 3, 664, initiated a riotous time marked by two other wars in 668 and 669.

The king survived the tumultuous period, as he was buried in a pyramid 17 years after the last war. Itzamk'anahk's son, named Yo'nalahk, commissioned and erected the panel at the top of the pyramid. To him, the contrast between the frightened faces of the captives and the utter lack of emotion of the king was the best way to honor his father.

"Houston's find adds a piece of the puzzle to our overall understanding of the complex political history of the Late Classic Maya," says Arlen F. Chase, Professor of Anthropology at the University of Central Florida, an authority on the Maya.

Source: http://www.discovery.com/news/briefs/20000630/aw_maya.html.

overview

In the last chapter we saw that the spread and intensification of food production paved the way for state formation. The first states developed in Mesopotamia by 5500 B.P. and in Mesoamerica some 3000 years later. Chiefdoms were precursors to states, with privileged and effective leaders—chiefs—but lacking the sharp class divisions that characterize states. By 7000 B.P. in the Middle East and 3200 B.P. in Mesoamerica, there is evidence for what archaeologists call the *elite level,* indicating a chiefdom or a state. Chapter 9 cited the first Mesoamerican example of the elite level, the Olmec chiefdom that thrived between 3200 and 2500 B.P. on Mexico's Gulf Coast.

Like food production, states developed in several world areas. The very first states arose in Mesopotamia (between the Tigris and Euphrates rivers) by 5500 B.P. and in the Nile Valley by 5250 B.P. Another state flourished between 4,600 and 3,900 years ago in the Indus River Valley of Pakistan and western India. The Shang dynasty state arose in the Huang He (Yellow) River valley of northern China around 3,750 years ago. By 2000 B.P., the process of state formation had accelerated in Mesoamerica and the Andes.

Attributes of States

A **state** is a society with a formal, central government and a division of society into classes. Certain attributes distinguish states from earlier forms of society:

1. A state controls a specific regional territory, such as the Nile Valley or the Valley of Mexico. The regional expanse of a state contrasts with the much smaller territories controlled by kin groups and villages in prestate societies.
2. Early states had productive farming economies, supporting dense populations, often in cities. The agricultural economies of early states usually involved some form of water control or irrigation.
3. Early states used tribute and taxation to accumulate, at a central place, resources needed to support hundreds, or thousands, of specialists.
4. States are stratified into social classes. In the first states, the non-food-producing population consisted of a tiny elite, plus artisans, officials, priests, and other specialists. Most people were commoners. Slaves and prisoners comprised the lowest rung of the social ladder. Rulers stayed in power by combining personal ability, religious authority, economic control, and force.
5. Early states had imposing public buildings and monumental architecture, including temples, palaces, and storehouses.
6. Early states developed some form of record-keeping system, usually a written script (Fagan 1996).

State Formation in the Middle East

In the last chapter we saw that food production arose in the ancient Middle East around 10,000 B.P. In the ensuing process of change, the center of population growth shifted from the zone where wheat and barley grew wild (Hilly Flanks) to

Figure 10.1
Sites in Middle Eastern State Formation

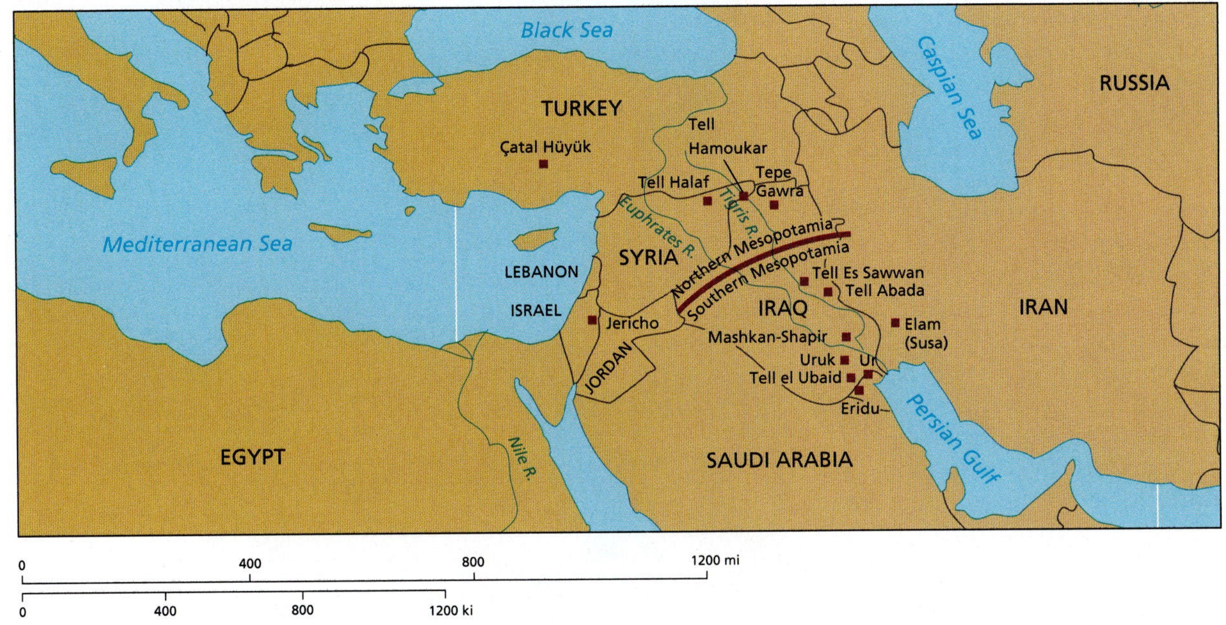

adjacent areas (steppe) where those grains were first domesticated. By 6000 B.P., population was increasing most rapidly in the alluvial plain of southern Mesopotamia. (**Mesopotamia** refers to the area between the Tigris and Euphrates rivers in what is now southern Iraq and southwestern Iran.) This growing population supported itself through irrigation and intensive river valley agriculture. By 5500 B.P. towns had grown into cities. The earliest city-states were Sumer (southern Iraq) and Elam (southwestern Iran), with their capitals at Uruk (Warka) and Susa, respectively.

Urban Life

The first towns arose around 10,000 years ago in the Middle East. Over the generations houses of mud brick were built and rebuilt in the same place. Substantial tells or mounds arose from the debris of a succession of such houses. The Middle East and Asia have hundreds or thousands of such mounds, only a few of which have been excavated. These sites have yielded remains of ancient community life, including streets, buildings, terraces, courtyards, wells, and other artifacts.

The earliest known town was Jericho, located in what is now Israel, below sea level at a well-watered oasis a few miles northwest of the Dead Sea (Figure 10.1). From the lowest (oldest) level, we know that around 11,000 years ago, Jericho

was first settled by Natufian foragers. Occupation continued thereafter, through and beyond biblical times, when "Joshua fit the battle of Jericho, and the walls came tumbling down."

During the phase just after the Natufians, the earliest known town appeared. It was an unplanned, densely populated settlement with round houses and some 2,000 people. At this time, well before the invention of pottery, Jericho was surrounded by a sturdy wall, with a massive tower. The wall may have been built initially as a flood barrier rather than for defense. Around 9000 B.P. Jericho was destroyed, to be rebuilt later. The new occupants lived in square houses with finished

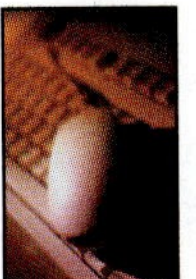

plaster floors. They buried their dead beneath their homes, a pattern seen at other sites, such as Çatal Hüyük in Turkey (see below). Pottery reached Jericho around 8000 B.P. (Gowlett 1993).

Long-distance trade, especially of obsidian, a volcanic glass used to make tools and ornaments, became important in the Middle East between 9500 and 7000 B.P. One town that prospered from this trade was Çatal Hüyük in Anatolia, Turkey (DeMarco 1997). A grassy mound 65 feet high holds the remains of this 9,000-year-old town, probably the largest settlement of the Neolithic age. Çatal Hüyük was located on a river, which deposited rich soil for crops, created a lush environment for animals, and was harnessed for irrigation by 7000 B.P. Over the mound's 32 acres (12.9 hectares), up to 10,000 people once lived in crowded mudbrick houses packed so tight that residents entered from their roofs.

The world's earliest known town was Jericho, located in what is now Israel. Jericho was first settled by Natufian foragers around 11,000 B.P. This round tower dates back 8,000 years.

Shielded by a defensive wall, Çatal Hüyük flourished between 8000 and 7000 B.P. Its individual mud-brick dwellings, rarely larger than a suburban American bedroom, had separate areas reserved for ritual and secular uses. In a given house, the ritual images were placed along the walls that faced north, east, or west, but never south. That area was reserved for cooking and other domestic tasks. The ritual areas were originally identified as shrines, but ritual appears now to have been organized at the household level rather than by religious specialists. Priests appeared later in Middle Eastern history.

The ritual spaces were decorated with wall paintings, sculpted ox heads, bull horns, and relief models of bulls and rams. The paintings showed bulls surrounded by stick figures running, dancing, and sometimes throwing stones. Vultures attacked headless humans. One frieze had human hand prints painted below mounted bull horns. These images and their placement are reminiscent of Paleolithic cave art. The dwellings at Çatal Hüyük were entered through the roof, and people had to crawl through holes from room to room, somewhat like moving between chambers of a cave. The deeper down one went, the richer the art became. The town's spiritual life seems to have revolved around a preoccupation with animals, danger, and death, perhaps related to the site's recent hunter-gatherer past.

180–181

Two or three generations of a family were buried beneath their homes. In one dwelling, archaeologists found remains of 17 individuals, mostly children. After two or three generations of family burials, the ritual art was removed; and the dwelling, burned. The site was then covered with fine dirt, and a floor laid for a new dwelling.

Çatal Hüyük's residents, though living in a town, acted independently in family groups without any apparent control by a priestly or political elite. The town never became a full-fledged city with centralized organization. Just as it lacked priests, Çatal Hüyük never had leaders who controlled or managed trade and production (Fagan 1996). Food was not stored and processed collectively, but on a smaller, domestic, scale (DeMarco 1997).

The Elite Level

The first pottery (ceramics) dates back a bit more than 8,000 years, when it first reached Jericho. Before that date, the Neolithic is called the prepottery Neolithic. By 7000 B.P., pottery had become widespread in the Middle East. Archaeologists consider pottery shape, finishing, decoration, and type of clay as features used for dating.

The geographic distribution of a given pottery style may indicate trade or alliance spanning a large area at a particular time.

An early and widespread pottery style, the **Halafian,** was first found at Tell Halaf in the mountains of northern Syria. Halafian (7500–6500 B.P.) refers to a delicate ceramic style. It also describes the period during which the elite level and the first chiefdoms emerged. The low number of Halafian ceramics suggests they were luxury goods associated with a social hierarchy.

By 7000 B.P. ranked chiefdoms had emerged in the Middle East. The Ubaid period (7000–6000 B.P.) is named for a southern Mesopotamian pottery type first discovered at a small site, Tell el-Ubaid, located near the major city of Ur in southern Iraq. Similar pottery has been discovered in the deep levels of the Mesopotamian cities of Ur, Uruk, and Eridu. Ubaid pottery is associated with advanced chiefdoms and perhaps the earliest states. It diffused rapidly over a large area, becoming more widespread than earlier ceramic styles such as the Halafian.

Social Ranking and Chiefdoms

It is easy for archaeologists to identify early states. Evidence for state organization includes monumental architecture, central storehouses, irrigation systems, and written records. In Mesoamerica, even chiefdoms are easy to detect archaeologically. Ancient Mexican chiefdoms left behind stone works, such as temple complexes and the huge carved Olmec heads. Mesoamericans also had a penchant for marking their elites with durable ornaments and prestige goods, including those buried with chiefs and their families. Early Middle Eastern chiefs were less ostentatious in their use of material markers of prestige, making their chiefdoms somewhat harder to detect archaeologically (Flannery 1999).

On the basis of the kinds of status distinctions within society, the anthropologist Morton Fried (1959) divided societies into three types: egalitarian, ranked, and stratified (Table 10.1). An **egalitarian society,** most typically found among foragers, lacks status distinctions except for those

Table 10.1
Egalitarian, Ranked, and Stratified Societies

Kind of Status Distinction	Nature of Status	Common Form of Subsistence Economy	Common Forms of Social Organization	Examples
Egalitarian	Status differences are not inherited. All status is based on age, gender, and on individual qualities, talents, and achievements.	Foraging	Bands and tribes	Inuit, Ju/'hoansi San, and Yanomami
Ranked	Status differences are inherited and distributed along a continuum from the highest ranking member (chief) to the lowest without any breaks.	Horticulture, pastoralism, and some foraging groups	Chiefdoms and some tribes	Native American groups of the Pacific Northwest (for example, Salish and Kwakiutl), Natchez, Halaf and Ubaid Period polities, Olmec
Stratified	Status differences are inherited and divided sharply between distinct noble and commoner classes.	Agriculture	States	Teotihuacan, Uruk Period states, Inca, Shang dynasty, Rome, U.S., Great Britian

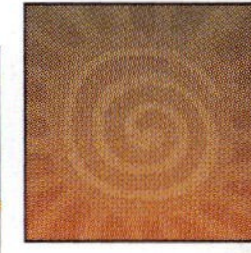

based on age, gender, and individual qualities, talents, and achievements. Thus, depending on the society, adult men, elder women, talented musicians, or ritual specialists might receive special respect for their activities or knowledge. In egalitarian societies, status distinctions are not usually inherited. The child of a respected person will not receive special recognition because of his or her parent, but must earn such respect.

Ranked societies, in contrast, do have hereditary inequality. But they lack **stratification** (sharp social divisions—*strata*—based on unequal access to wealth and power) into noble and commoner classes. In ranked societies, individuals tend to be ranked in terms of their genealogical distance from the chief. Closer relatives of the chief have higher rank or social status than more distant ones do. But there is a continuum of status, with many individuals and kin groups ranked about equally, which can lead to competition for positions of leadership.

Not all ranked societies are chiefdoms. Robert Carneiro (1991) has distinguished between two kinds of ranked societies, only the second of which is a chiefdom. In the first type, exemplified by some Indians of North America's Pacific Northwest, there were hereditary differences in rank, but villages were independent of one another. Exemplifying the second type were the Cauca of Colombia and the Natchez of the eastern United States. These ranked societies had become **chiefdoms,** societies in which relations among villages as well as among individuals were unequal. The smaller villages had lost their autonomy and were under the authority of leaders who lived at larger villages. According to Kent Flannery (1999), *only those ranked societies with such loss of village autonomy should be called chiefdoms.* In chiefdoms, there is always inequality—differences in rank—among both individuals and communities.

Unlike states, such as Britain, whose princes Charles, William, and Harry are shown here, egalitarian societies lack inherited wealth and status and succession to political office. How are inherited status distinctions marked in Great Britain? In the United States?

In Mesopotamia, Mesoamerica, and Peru, chiefdoms were precursors to **primary states** (states that arose on their own, and not through contact with other state societies—see Wright 1994). Primary states emerged from competition among chiefdoms, as one chiefdom managed to conquer its neighbors and to make them part of a larger political unit (Flannery 1995).

Archaeological evidence for chiefdoms in Mesoamerica, where several states arose between 2,500 and 1,600 years ago, dates back more than 3,000 years. Mesoamerican chiefdoms are easy to detect archaeologically because they were flamboyant in the way they marked their aristocracy. High-status families deformed the heads of their infants and buried them with special symbols and grave goods. In burials, prestige goods show a continuum from graves with many, to less, to none, of precious materials, such as jade and turquoise (Flannery 1999).

The first Middle Eastern states developed between 6000 and 5500 B.P. The first societies based on rank, including the first chiefdoms, emerged during the preceding 1,500 years. In the Middle East, the archaeological record of the period after 7300 B.P. reveals behavior typical of

This funerary chamber from Sipan, Peru (a Moche site) contains gold jewelry, pottery, and other artifacts. In chiefdoms and states, high-status families often bury their dead with distinctive symbols and grave goods.

chiefdoms, including exotic goods used as markers of status, along with raiding and political instability. Early Middle Eastern chiefdoms included both the Halafian culture of northern Iraq and the Ubaid culture of southern Iraq, which eventually spread north.

As in Mesoamerica, ancient Middle Eastern chiefdoms had cemeteries where chiefly relatives were buried with distinctive items: vessels, statuettes, necklaces, and high-quality ceramics. Such goods were buried with children too young to have earned prestige on their own, but who happened to be born into elite families. In the ancient village of Tell es-Sawwan, infant graves show a continuum of richness from six statuettes, to three statuettes, to one statuette, to none. Such signs of slight gradations in social status are exactly what one expects in ranked societies (Flannery 1999).

Such burials convince Flannery (1999) that hereditary status differences were present in the Middle East by 7000 B.P. But had the leaders of large villages extended their authority to the smaller villages nearby? Is there evidence for the loss of village autonomy, converting simple ranked societies into chiefdoms? One clue that villages were linked in political units is the use of a common canal to irrigate several villages. This suggests a way of resolving disputes among farmers over access to water, for example, by appeal to a strong leader. By later Halafian times in northern Mesopotamia, there is evidence for such multivillage alliances (Flannery 1999). Another clue to the loss of village autonomy is the emergence of a two-tier settlement hierarchy, with small villages clustering around a large village, especially one with public buildings. There is evidence for this pattern in northern Mesopotamia during the Halafian (Watson 1983).

Advanced Chiefdoms

In northeastern Syria, near the border with Iraq, archaeologists have been excavating an ancient settlement that once lay on a major trade route. This large site, Tell Hamoukar, dates back more than 5,500 years (Wilford 2000). Its remains suggest that advanced chiefdoms arose in northern areas of the Middle East independently of the better-known city-states of southern Mesopotamia, in southern Iraq (Wilford 2000).

The oldest layer yet uncovered at Tell Hamoukar contains traces of villages dating back 6,000 years. By 5700 B.P. the settlement was a prosperous town of 32 acres, enclosed by a defensive wall 10 feet high and 13 feet wide. The site had fine pottery and large ovens—evidence of food preparation on an institutional scale. The site has yielded pieces of large cooking pots, animal bones, and traces of wheat, barley, and oats for baking and brewing. The archaeologist McGuire Gibson, one of the excavators, believes that food preparation on this scale is evidence of a rank society in which elites were organizing people and resources (Wilford 2000). Most likely they were hosting and entertaining in a chiefly manner (as discussed in "Interesting Issues").

Also providing evidence for social ranking are the seals used to mark containers of food and other goods. Some of the seals are small, with only simple incisions or cross-hatching. Others

interesting issues

How Ethnography Helps in Interpreting the Archaeological Record

When they excavate sites, how do archaeologists know whether they've found a chiefdom, or some less complex form of society? Grave goods and settlement hierarchy offer clues, as discussed in the text. Also, studying ethnography helps archaeologists interpret the past.

Thus, to infer the archeological characteristics of ancient Middle Eastern chiefdoms, Kent Flannery (1999) looks to recent chiefdoms that have been studied ethnographically in that region. One example is the Basseri, a population of 16,000 migratory herders in Iran (Barth 1964). The Basseri had a large grazing territory, but some of their chiefly families also owned farming villages and city homes. Leading the Basseri was a chief, whose brothers, cousins, uncles, and nephews vied for leadership during "periods of confusion" (Barth 1964). Such political rivalry among close kin is typical of chiefdoms worldwide.

Using the Basseri as an ethnographic analogy, Flannery (1999) suggests likely characteristics of an ancient Middle Eastern chiefdom. Such an ancient confederacy of several thousand people would have had a hereditary aristocracy, but no capital city. There would have been no palace, no temples, no clear territorial boundaries. Its thousands of tents would barely leave a trace archaeologically. But by analogy with the Basseri, we might find remains of a few chiefly houses in mud-walled cities.

According to Barth (1964), a Basseri chief's home was large—to entertain visitors. The chief gave substantial gifts to his prominent subjects, who were expected to reciprocate. The chief's close kinsmen were almost as privileged as he was. By analogy, Flannery (1999) suggests, to identify an ancient Middle Eastern chiefdom, archaeologists should look not for one unique residence but also for the nearby houses of chiefly kin. Such homes would be large enough to entertain many visitors (perhaps with a spacious central court). They might have a large kitchen and storerooms for food staples and craft products used as gifts. Indeed, prehistoric houses fitting this description have been found (Jasim 1985).

According to Robert Carneiro (1991), raiding is especially common in chiefdoms. Illustrating such raiding, early chiefdoms in Mexico and Peru had public art featuring enemy corpses, mutilated prisoners, and trophy heads (Marcus 1992). Middle Eastern chiefdoms lacked this kind of art. But their sites did have defensive walls, ditches, and watchtowers comparable to those of Mesoamerica. Political alliance also offered some protection against raiding.

Despite their defenses and alliances, prehistoric chiefdoms were still raided. There is archaeological evidence that large houses, belonging to community leaders, were sacked and burned during raids in the Halafian and Ubaid periods. Consider Tepe Gawra, a site dating to the late Ubaid period (Tobler 1950). This densely packed town was defended by its position atop a mound, and by a watchtower. Its largest residence had an inner court that illustrates the kind of large, elegant reception space Flannery (1999) expects to find in the home of a chief who hosted many subordinates and visitors. There was also a large kitchen.

On the same street was a slightly less impressive residence, supporting the belief that archaeologists should look for multiple elite houses in chiefly neighborhoods. This town had been raided and partly burned. At least four victims—a baby and three youths—were left unburied in the ruins. The building hardest hit was that with the largest inner court, confirming that, as is usual, the chiefly family was the raid's main target.

From such clues—archaeological and ethnographic—we infer that chiefly families and a pattern of raiding one's rivals were present in the Middle East between 7300 and 5800 B.P.

are larger and more elaborate, presumably for higher officials to stamp more valuable goods. Gibson suspects the larger seals with figurative scenes were held by the few people who had greater authority. The smaller, simply incised seals were used by many more people with less authority (Wilford 2000).

The Rise of the State

In southern Mesopotamia at this time (5700 B.P.), an expanding population and increased food production from irrigation were changing the social landscape even more drastically than in the north. Irrigation had allowed Ubaid communities to spread along the Euphrates River. Travel and trade were expanding, with water serving as the highway system. Such raw materials as hardwood and stone, which southern Mesopotamia lacked, were imported via river routes. Population density increased as new settlements appeared. Social and economic networks now linked communities on the rivers in the south and in the foothills to the north. Settlements spread north into what is now Syria. Social differentials also increased. Priests and political leaders joined expert potters and other specialists. These non-food-producers were supported by the larger population of farmers and herders (Gilmore-Lehne 2000).

Economies were being managed by central leadership. Agricultural villages had grown into cities, some of which were ruled by local kings. The Uruk period (6000–5200 B.P.), which succeeded the Ubaid period, takes it name from a prominent southern city-state located more than 400 miles south of Tell Hamoukar (Table 10.2). The Uruk period established Mesopotamia as "the cradle of civilization" (see Pollock 1999).

There is no evidence of Uruk influence at Tell Hamoukar until 5200 B.P., when some Uruk pottery showed up. When southern Mesopotamians expanded north, they found advanced chiefdoms, which were not yet states. The fact that writing originated in Sumer, in southern Mesopotamia, indicates a more advanced, state-organized society there. The first writing presumably developed to handle record-keeping for a centralized economy.

Writing was initially used to keep accounts, reflecting the needs of trade. Rulers, nobles, priests, and merchants were the first to benefit from it. Writing spread from Mesopotamia to Egypt by 5000 B.P. The earliest writing was pictographic, for example, with pictorial symbols of horses used to represent them.

Early Mesopotamian scribes used a stylus (writing implement) to scrawl symbols on raw clay. This writing left a wedge-shaped impression on the clay, called **cuneiform** writing, from the Latin word for wedge. Both the Sumerian (southern Mesopotamia) and Akkadian (northern Mesopotamia) languages were written in cuneiform (Gowlett 1993).

Table 10.2
Archaeological Periods in Middle Eastern State Formation

Dates	Period	Age
3000–2539 B.P.	Neo-Babylonian	Iron Age
3600–3000 B.P.	Kassite	
4000–3600 B.P.	Old Babylonian	Bronze Age
4150–4000 B.P.	Third Dynasty of Ur	
4350–4150 B.P.	Akkadian	
4600–4350 B.P.	Early Dynastic III	
4750–4600 B.P.	Early Dynastic II	
5000–4750 B.P.	Early Dynastic I	
5200–5000 B.P.	Jemdet Nasr	
6000–5200 B.P.	Uruk	Chalcolithic
7500–6000 B.P.	Ubaid (southern Mesopotamia)–Halaf (northern Mesopotamia)	
10,000–7000 B.P.		Neolithic

Illustrating pictographic writing is this limestone tablet from the proto-urban period of lower Mesopotamia. This Sumerian script records proper names, including that of a landowner—symbolized by the hand—who commissioned the tablet.

Early Mesopotamian scribes used a stylus to scrawl symbols on raw clay. This writing, called *cuneiform*, left a wedge-shaped impression on the clay. What languages were written in cuneiform?

Writing and temples played key roles in the Mesopotamian economy. For the historic period after 5600 B.P., when writing was invented, there are temple records of economic activities. States can exist without writing, but literacy facilitates the flow and storage of information. We know that Mesopotamian priests managed herding, farming, manufacture, and trade. Temple officials allotted fodder and pasture land for cattle and donkeys, which were used as plow and cart animals. As the economy expanded, trade, manufacture, and grain storage were centrally managed. Temples collected and distributed meat, dairy products, crops, fish, clothing, tools, and trade items. Potters, metal workers, weavers, sculptors, and other artisans perfected their crafts.

Prior to the invention of **metallurgy** (knowledge of the properties of metals, including their extraction and processing and the manufacture of metal tools), raw copper was shaped by hammering. If copper is hammered too long it hardens and becomes brittle, with a risk of cracking. But once heated (annealed) in a fire, copper becomes malleable again. Such annealing of copper was an early form of metallurgy. A vital step for metallurgy was the discovery of **smelting,** the high-temperature process by which pure metal is produced from an ore. Ores, including copper ore, have a much wider distribution than does native copper, which was initially traded as a luxury good because of its rarity (Gowlett 1993).

When and how smelting was discovered is unknown. But after 5000 B.P., metallurgy evolved rapidly. The Bronze Age began when alloys of arsenic and copper, or tin and copper (in both cases known as **bronze**), became common and greatly extended the use of metals. Bronze flows more easily than copper does when heated to a similar temperature, so bronze was more convenient for metal casting. Early molds were carved in stone, as shaped depressions to be filled with molten metal. A copper axe cast from such a mold has been found in northern Mesopotamia and predates 5000 B.P. Thereafter, other metals came into common use. By 4500 B.P. golden objects were found in royal burials at Ur.

This ziggurat, or temple tower, at Ur, Iraq, dates back to 4100 B.P. [2100 BC]. Temples and their officials played key roles in the Mesopotamian economy. Who handles such duties in our own society?

The Bronze Age began when bronze—an alloy of arsenic and copper, or of tin and copper—became common. This Bronze Age kettle from Iran is displayed at the Ashmolean Museum in Oxford, England.

Iron ore is distributed more widely than is copper ore. Iron, when smelted, can be used on its own; there is no need for tin or arsenic to make a metal alloy (bronze). The Iron Age began once high-temperature iron smelting was mastered. In the Old World after 3200 B.P., iron spread rapidly. Formerly valued as highly as gold, iron crashed in value when it became plentiful (Gowlett 1993).

The Mesopotamian economy, based on craft production, trade, and intensive agriculture, spurred population growth and an increase in urbanism. Sumerian cities were protected by a fortress wall and surrounded by a farming area. By 4800 B.P., Uruk, the largest early Mesopotamian city, had a population of 50,000. As irrigation and the population expanded, communities fought over water. People sought protection in the fortified cities (Adams 1981), which defended themselves when neighbors or invaders threatened.

By 4600 B.P., secular authority had replaced temple rule. The office of military coordinator developed into kingship. This change shows up architecturally in palaces and royal tombs. The palace raised armies and supplied them with armor, chariots, and metal armaments. At Ur's royal cemetery,

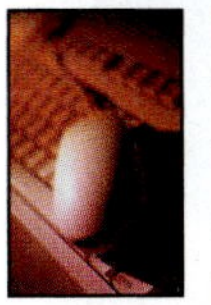

by 4600 B.P. monarchs were being buried with soldiers, charioteers, and ladies in waiting. These subordinates were killed at the time of royal burial to accompany the monarch to the afterworld.

Agricultural intensification made it possible for the number of people supported by a given area to increase. Population pressure on irrigated fields helped create a stratified society. Land became scarce private property that was bought and sold. Some people amassed large estates, and their wealth set them off from ordinary farmers. These landlords joined the urban elite, while sharecroppers and serfs toiled in the fields. By 4600 B.P., Mesopotamia had a well-defined class structure, with complex stratification into nobles, commoners, and slaves.

Other Early States

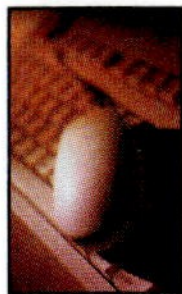

In northwestern India and Pakistan, the Indus River Valley (or *Harappan*) state, with major cities at Harappa and Mohenjo-daro, takes its name from the river valley along which it extended. (Figure 10.2 maps the four great early river valley states of the Old World: Mesopotamia, Egypt,

The creator of this sculpture, entitled "Ram Caught in a Thicket," used gold, silver, lapis lazuli, copper, shell, red limestone, and bitumen to make it. It is one of the treasures from the Royal Tombs of Ur.

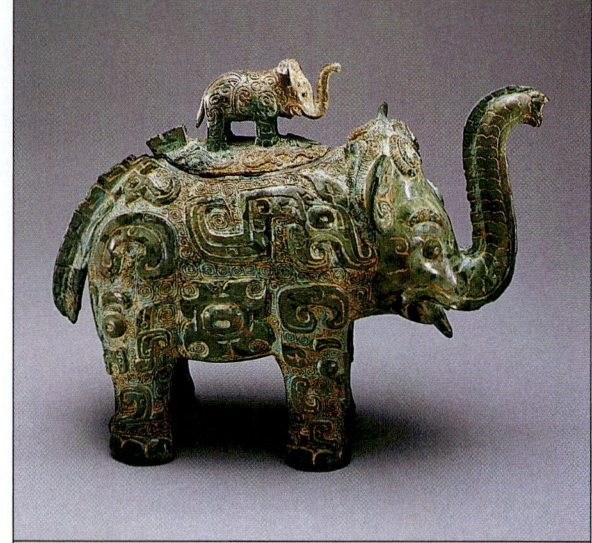

This bronze vessel was commissioned during China's Shang dynasty. The small elephant on top forms the handle of the lid. Wine was poured through the spout formed by the big elephant's trunk. Three notable features of the Shang dynasty were bronze, writing, and social stratification.

India/Pakistan, and northern China.) Trade and the spread of writing from Mesopotamia may have played a role in the emergence of the Harappan state around 4600 B.P. Located in Pakistan's Punjab Province, the ruins of Harappa were the first to be identified as part of the Indus River Valley civilization. At its peak, the Indus River Valley state incorporated 1,000 cities, towns, and villages, spanning 280,000 square miles (725,000 square kilometers). This state flourished between 4600 and 3900 B.P. It displayed such features of state organization as urban planning, social stratification, and an early writing system, which remains undeciphered. The Harappans maintained a uniform system of weights, and their cites had carefully planned residential areas with wastewater systems. An array of products from sophisticated craft industries included ceramic vessels made on potter's wheels (Meadow and Kenoyer 2000).

The Indus River Valley state collapsed, apparently through warfare, around 3900 B.P. Its cities became largely depopulated. Skeletons of massacre victims have been found in the streets of Mohenjo-daro. Harappa continued to be occupied, but on a much smaller scale than previously (Meadow and Kenoyer 2000).

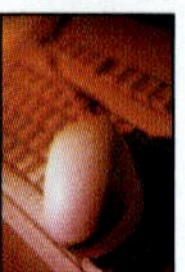

(For more on the ongoing Harappa Archaeological Research Project, visit www.harappa.com.)

The first Chinese state, dating to 3750 B.P., was that of the Shang dynasty. It arose in the Huang He (Yellow) River area of northern China, where wheat, rather than rice, was the dietary staple. This state was characterized by urbanism, palatial (as well as domestic) architecture, human sacrifice, and a sharp division between social classes. Burials of the aristocracy were marked by ornaments of stone, including jade. The Shang had bronze metallurgy and an elaborate writing system. In warfare they used chariots and took prisoners (Gowlett 1993).

Like Mesopotamia and China, many early civilizations came to rely on metallurgy. At Nok Nok

Figure 10.2
The Four Great Early River Valley States of the Old World

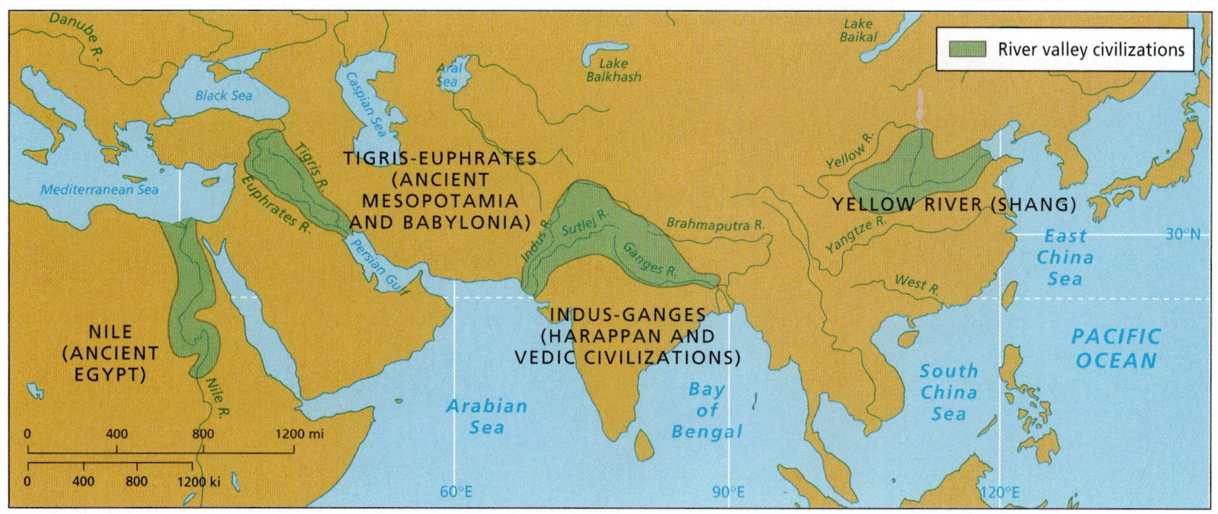

Source: Based on Map 1-1, Chapter 1, "Birth of Civilization." In Albert M. Craig, *The Heritage of World Civilizations*, Volume I, *to 1650*, 4th ed. Upper Saddle River, NJ: Prentice Hall, 1997.

By approximately 4,000 B.P. urban life had been established along the Tigris and Euphrates rivers in Mesopotamia, the Nile River in Egypt, the Indus and Ganges rivers in India/Pakistan, and the Yellow River in China.

Tha in northern Thailand, metal working goes back 6,000 years. In Peru's Andes metal working appeared around 4000 B.P. The ancient inhabitants of the Andes were skilled workers of bronze, copper, and gold. They are also well known for their techniques of pottery manufacture. Their arts, crafts, and agricultural knowledge compared well with those of Mesoamerica at its height, to which we now turn. Note that both Mesoamerican and Andean state formation were truncated by Spanish conquest. The Aztecs of Mexico were conquered in AD 1519; and the Inca of Peru, in 1532.

State Formation in Mesoamerica

In the last chapter we examined the independent inventions of farming in the Middle East and Mesoamerica. The processes of state formation that took place in these areas were also comparable, beginning with ranked societies and chiefdoms, and ending with fully formed states and empires.

The first monumental buildings (temple complexes) in the Western Hemisphere were constructed by Mesoamerican chiefdoms in three areas: the Olmec lowlands, the Oaxaca Valley (southern Mexico), and the Valley of Mexico in the highlands. These chiefdoms influenced one another as they traded fine materials, such as obsidian, shells, and pottery. (Figure 10.3 maps major sites in the emergence of Mesoamerican food production, chiefdoms, and states. See Table 9.3 on p. 229 of Chapter 9 for a chronology of Mesoamerican state formation.)

Early Chiefdoms and Elites

The Olmecs built a series of ritual centers on Mexico's southern Gulf Coast between 3,200 and 2,500 years ago. Three of these, each from a different century, have been especially well excavated. Earthen mounds were grouped into plaza complexes, presumably for religious use. Such centers show that Olmec chiefs could marshal human labor to construct monumental buildings. The Olmecs were also master sculptors; they carved massive stone heads, perhaps in the image of their chiefs.

Figure 10.3

Major Sites in the Emergence of Food Production and the State in Mesoamerica

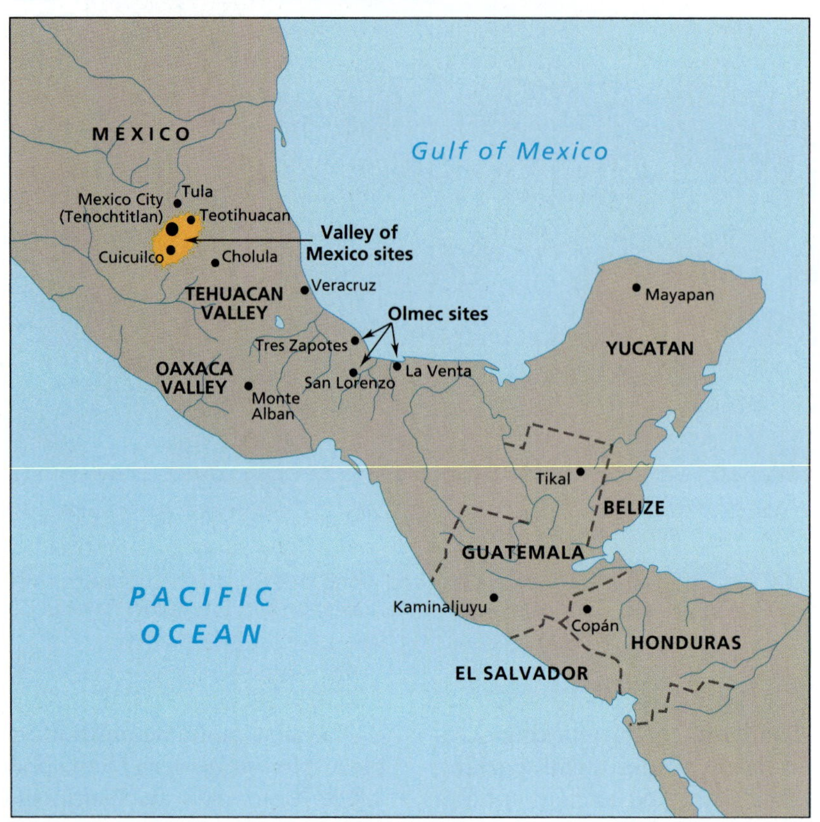

Source: From *Physical Anthropology and Archaeology*, 4th ed., by C. J. Jolly and F. Plog (New York: McGraw-Hill, 1986), p. 115.

There is evidence, too, that trade routes linked the Olmecs with other parts of Mesoamerica, such as the Valley of Oaxaca in the southern highlands and the Valley of Mexico. By 3000 B.P. a ruling elite had emerged in Oaxaca. The items traded at that time between Oaxaca and the Olmecs were for elite consumption. High-status Oaxacans wore ornaments made of mussel shells from the coast. In return, the Olmec elite imported mirrors made by Oaxacan artisans.

By 2500 B.P. Olmec influence had diminished. Oaxaca and other highland areas now overshadowed the Olmec area and the lowlands in general. By 2500 B.P. Oaxaca had developed a distinctive art style, perfected at the city of Monte Alban. Until the Spanish conquest, Oaxaca was the site of a major Mesoamerica state (see Blanton 1999).

As the Olmec chiefdoms were declining, the elite level was spreading throughout Mesoamerica. By AD 1 (2000 B.P.), the Valley of Mexico, located in the highlands where Mexico City now stands, came to prominence in Mesoamerican state formation. In this large valley **Teotihuacan** flourished between 1900 and 1300 B.P. (AD 100 and 700).

States in the Valley of Mexico

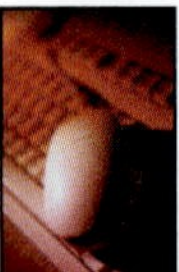

The Valley of Mexico is a large basin surrounded by mountains. The valley has rich volcanic soils, but rainfall isn't always reliable. The northern part of the valley, where the huge city and state of Teotihuacan eventually arose, is colder and drier than the south. Frosts there limited farming until

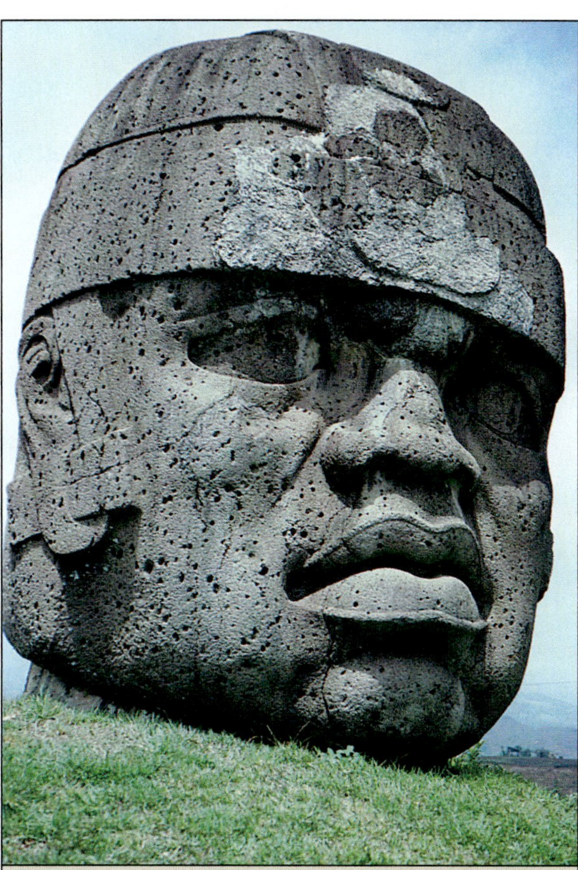

An Olmec head from San Lorenzo, Mexico. What is the significance of such a massive artifact?

quick-growing varieties of maize were developed. Until 2500 B.P., most people lived in the warmer and wetter southern part of the valley, where rainfall made farming possible. After 2500 B.P., new maize varieties and small-scale irrigation appeared. Population increased and began to spread north.

By AD 1 Teotihuacan was a town of 10,000 people. It governed a territory of a few thousand square kilometers and perhaps 50,000 people (Parsons 1974). Teotihuacan's growth reflected its agricultural potential. Perpetual springs permitted irrigation of a large alluvial plain. Rural farmers supplied food for the growing urban population.

By this time, a clear **settlement hierarchy** had emerged. This is a ranked series of communities that differ in size, function, and building types. The settlements at the top of the hierarchy were political and religious centers. Those at the bottom were rural villages. Such a three-level settlement hierarchy (capital city, smaller urban centers, and rural villages) provides archaeological evidence of state organization (Wright and Johnson 1975). How many levels indicate a chiefdom?

Along with state organization went large-scale irrigation, status differentiation, and complex architecture. Teotihuacan thrived between AD 100 and 700. It grew as a planned city built on a grid pattern, with the Pyramid of the Sun at its center. By AD 500, the population of Teotihuacan had reached 130,000, making it larger than imperial Rome. Farmers were one of its diverse specialized groups, along with artisans, merchants, and political, religious, and military personnel.

After AD 700 Teotihuacan declined in size and power. By AD 900 its population had shrunk to 30,000. Between AD 900 and 1200, the Toltec period, the population scattered, and small cities and towns sprang up throughout the valley. People also left the Valley of Mexico to live in larger cities—like Tula, the Toltec capital—on its edge (see Figure 10.3).

Population increase (including immigration by the ancestors of the Aztecs) and urban growth returned to the Valley of Mexico between AD 1200 and 1520. During the **Aztec** period (AD 1325 to 1520) there were several cities, the largest of which—Tenochtitlan, the capital—may have surpassed Teotihuacan at its height. A dozen Aztec towns had more than 10,000 people. Fueling this population growth was intensification of agriculture, particularly in the southern part of the valley, where the drainage of lake bottoms and swamps added new cultivable land (Parsons 1976).

Another factor in the renaissance of the Valley of Mexico was trade. Local manufacture created products for a series of markets. The major towns and markets were located on the lake shores, with easy access to canoe traffic. The Aztec capital stood on an island in the lake. In Tenochtitlan, the production of luxury goods was more prestigious and more highly organized than that of pottery, basket making, and weaving. Luxury producers, such as stone workers, feather workers, and gold- and silversmiths, occupied a special position in Aztec society. The manufacture of luxury goods for export was an important part of the economy of the Aztec capital (Hassig 1985; Santley 1985).

The Pyramid of the Sun, Teotihuacan's largest structure, is shown in the upper part of the photo. At its height around AD 500, Teotihuacan was larger than imperial Rome. The mobilization of manual labor to build such structures is one of the costs of state organization.

The Aztecs played the board game of patolli, as represented here in the Codex Magliabecchiano, housed in the National Library in Florence Italy.

The Origin of the State

How and why did states originate? The state develops to handle regulatory problems encountered as the population grows and/or the economy increases in scale and diversity. Anthropologists and historians have identified the causes of state formation and have reconstructed the rise of several states. Many factors always contribute to state formation, with the effects of one magnifying those of the others. Although some contributing factors appear again and again, no single one is always present. In other words, state formation has generalized rather than universal causes.

Furthermore, because state formation may take centuries, people experiencing the process at any time rarely perceive the significance of the long-term changes. Later generations find themselves dependent on government institutions that took generations to develop.

Hydraulic Systems

One suggested cause of state formation is the need to regulate *hydraulic* (water-based) agricultural economies (Wittfogel 1957). In certain arid areas, states have emerged to manage systems of irrigation, drainage, and flood control. However, hydraulic agriculture is neither a sufficient nor a necessary condition for the rise of the state. That is, many societies with irrigation never experienced state formation, and states have developed without hydraulic systems.

But hydraulic agriculture does have certain implications for state formation. Water control increases production in arid lands, such as ancient Mesopotamia and Egypt. Because of its labor demands and its ability to feed more people, irrigated agriculture fuels population growth. This in turn leads to enlargement of the system. The expanding hydraulic system supports larger and denser concentrations of people. Interpersonal problems increase, and conflicts over access to water and irrigated land become more frequent. Political systems may arise to regulate interpersonal relations and the means of production.

Large hydraulic works can sustain towns and cities and become essential to their subsistence. Regulators protect the economy by mobilizing crews to maintain and repair the hydraulic system. These life-and-death functions enhance the authority of state officials. Thus, growth in hydraulic systems is often (as in Mesopotamia, Egypt, and the Valley of Mexico), but not always, associated with state formation.

Long-Distance Trade Routes

Another theory is that states develop at strategic locations in regional trade networks. These sites include points of supply or exchange, such as crossroads of caravan routes, and places (e.g., mountain passes and river narrows) situated so as to threaten or halt trade between centers. Here again, however, the cause is generalized but neither necessary nor sufficient. Long-distance trade has been important in the evolution of many states, including Mesopotamia and Mesoamerica. Such exchange does eventually develop in all states, but it can follow rather than precede state formation. Furthermore, long-distance trade

One theory for state formation is that states develop at key locations, such as crossroads, in regional trade networks. One such ancient route extended to Samarkand, Uzbekistan, depicted here, with caravan traders and their camels. What impact on politics does trade have today?

An oasis, such as the one shown here in Africa's Sudan, is circumscribed. It is surrounded by a desert. When such a place is conquered, the losers often have no place else to go. They have to submit and work harder in order to pay tribute to the victors. What are some other examples of environmental circumscription?

also occurs in societies such as those of Papua New Guinea, where no states developed.

Population, War, and Circumscription

Carneiro (1970) proposed a theory that incorporates three factors working together instead of a single cause of state formation. (We call a theory involving multiple factors or variables a **multivariate** theory.) Wherever and whenever *environmental circumscription* (or *resource concentration*), *increasing population,* and *warfare* exist, says Carneiro, state formation will begin. Environmental circumscription may be physical or social. Physically circumscribed environments include small islands and, in arid areas, river plains, oases, and valleys with streams. Social circumscription exists when neighboring societies block expansion, emigration, or access to resources. When strategic resources are concentrated in limited areas—even when no obstacles to migration exist—the effects are similar to those of circumscription.

Coastal Peru, one of the world's most arid areas, illustrates the interaction of environmental circumscription, warfare, and population increase. Early cultivation was limited to valleys with springs. Each valley was circumscribed by the Andes Mountains to the east, the Pacific Ocean to the west, and desert regions to the north and south. The transition from foraging to food production triggered population increase (Figure 10.4). In each valley, villages got bigger. Colonists split off from the old villages and founded new ones. Rivalries and raiding developed between villages in the same valley. As villages proliferated and the valley population grew, a scarcity of land developed.

Population pressure and land shortages were developing in all the valleys. Because the valleys were circumscribed, when one village conquered another, the losers had to submit to the winners—they had nowhere else to go. Conquered villagers could keep their land only if they agreed to pay tribute to their conquerors. To do this, they had to intensify production, using new techniques to produce more food. By working harder, they managed to pay tribute while meeting their own subsistence needs. Villagers brought new

Figure 10.4

Carneiro's Multivariate Approach to the Origin of the State as Applied to Coastal Peru

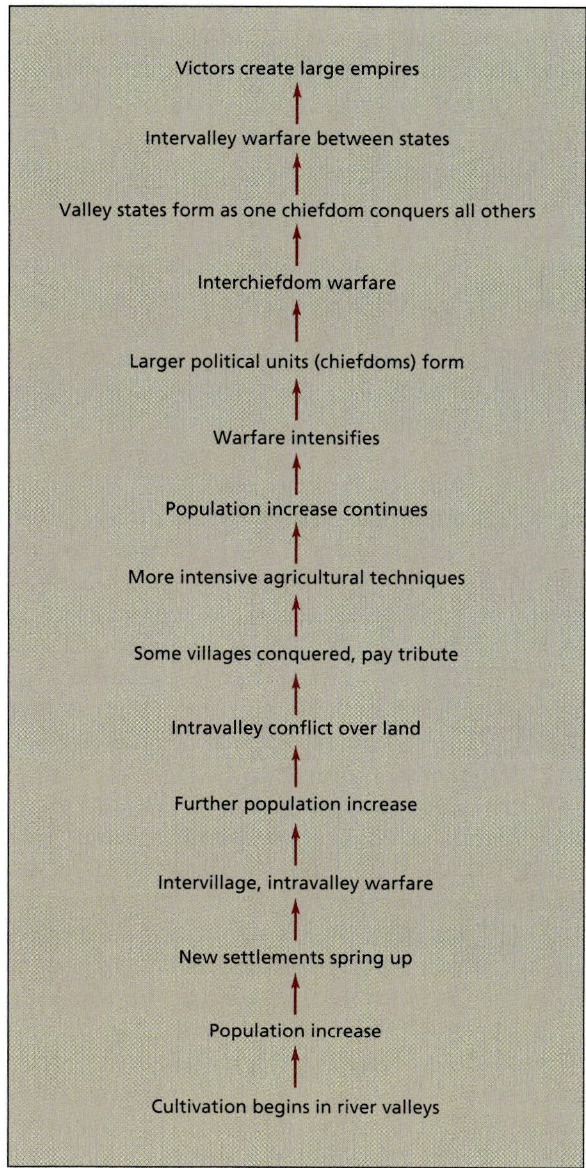

In this very arid area, food production developed in narrow river valleys where water for cultivation was available (resource concentration). With cultivation, the population increased. Population pressure on land led to warfare, and some villages conquered others. Physical circumscription meant that the losers had no way to escape. The process accelerated as the population grew and as warfare and cultivation intensified. Chiefdoms, states, and empires eventually developed.

areas under cultivation by means of irrigation and terracing.

Those early inhabitants of the Andes didn't work harder because they chose to do so. They were *forced* to pay tribute, accept political domination, and intensify production by factors beyond their control. Once established, all these trends accelerated. Population grew, warfare intensified, and villages were eventually united in chiefdoms. The first states developed when one chiefdom in a valley conquered the others (Carneiro 1990). Eventually, different valleys began to fight. The winners brought the losers into growing states and empires, which eventually expanded from the coast to the highlands. By the 16th century, from their capital, Cuzco, in the high Andes, the Inca ruled one of the major empires of the tropics.

Carneiro's theory is very useful, but again, the association between population density and state organization is generalized rather than universal. States do tend to have large and dense populations (Stevenson 1968). However, population increase and warfare within a circumscribed environment did not trigger state formation in highland Papua New Guinea. Certain valleys there are socially or physically circumscribed and have population densities similar to those of many states. Warfare also was present, but no states emerged. Again we are dealing with an important theory that explains many but not all cases of state formation.

Early states arose in different areas for many reasons. In each case, interacting causes (often comparable ones) magnified each other's effects. To explain any instance of state formation, we must search for the specific changes in access to resources and in regulatory problems that fostered stratification and state machinery. The opposite of state formation is state decline.

Why States Collapse

Early states were vulnerable to outsiders who had no reason to respect their order and stability. Various factors could threaten their economies and political institutions. Invasion, disease, famine, or prolonged drought could upset the balance. A state's citizens might harm the environment, usually with economic costs. For example, farmers and smelters might cut down trees. Such deforestation promotes erosion and leads to a decline in the water supply. Overuse of land may deplete the soil of nutrients needed to grow crops.

We've just considered theories for the origin of the state. If factors such as irrigation help create states to begin with, does their decline or failure explain the fall of the state? Irrigation does have costs as well as benefits. In ancient Mesopotamia, irrigation water came from the Tigris and Euphrates rivers. Because sediment (silt) had accumulated in those rivers, their beds were higher than the alluvial plain and fields they irrigated. Canals channeled river water as it flowed down into the fields by gravity. As the water evaporated, water-borne mineral salts remained in the fields, eventually creating a poisonous environment for plants.

One of the worst droughts of the past 10,000 years, perhaps global in scale, began around 4300 B.P. and lasted three centuries. According to Richard Kerr (1998), this long dry spell contributed to the fall of northern Mesopotamia's Akkadian empire. By 4200 B.P., overall agricultural production in Mesopotamia had fallen to a fraction of what it once had been. Many fields were abandoned as useless. The drought probably played a role. So did the buildup of mineral salts in the irrigated fields.

Mashkan-shapir was a Mesopotamian city located about 20 miles from the Tigris, to which it was connected by a network of canals. This city was abandoned just 20 years after it was settled. Destruction of its fields by mineral salts seems to have been a prime factor in its collapse (see Annenberg/CPB Exhibits at http://www.learner.org/exhibits/collapse/mesopotamia.html).

One key role of the state is regulation, whether of the economy or of relations between individuals and groups. Subsistence needs must be met, and chiefdoms and states may offer greater food security than do less centralized forms of society. Political leaders often maintain storehouses or central supplies of food and other goods, which may be distributed to the people in times of need. For example, tribute collected by Mexico's Aztec rulers was used for several purposes: (1) to appease troublesome nobles and otherwise to reward the elite establishment, (2) to support royal craftsmen, and (3) to be stored in royal granaries for distribution to the urban population in times of acute food stress (Santley 1985).

States may collapse when they fail to do what they are supposed to do, such as maintain social order, protect themselves against outsiders, and allow their people to meet subsistence needs. As the economy collapses, the political structure is likely to disintegrate as well. When a state declines, basic skills typically survive, but more refined levels of knowledge, shared by fewer people, tend to be lost (Gowlett 1993).

The Mayan Decline

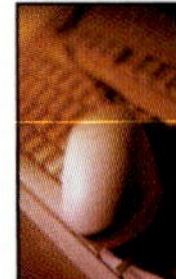

Generations of scholars have debated the decline of classic Mayan civilization around AD 900 (1700–1100 B.P.). Most think the state structure collapsed because its economy could no longer support its population, especially its division into elites and commoners. Classic Mayan culture, featuring several competing states, flourished between AD 300 and 900 in parts of what are now Mexico, Honduras, El Salvador, Guatemala, and Belize. The ancient Maya are known for their monuments (temples and pyramids), calendars, mathematics, and hieroglyphic writing.

238–239

Archaeological clues to Mayan decline have been found at Copán, in western Honduras. This classic Maya royal center, the largest site in the southeastern part of the Maya area, covered 29 acres. It was built on an artificial terrace overlooking the Copán river. Its rulers inscribed their monuments with accounts of their coronation, their lineage history, and reports of important battles. The Maya dated their monuments with the names of kings and when they reigned. One monument at Copán was intended to be the ruler's throne platform. But only one side had been finished. The monument bears a date, AD 822, in a section of unfinished text. Copán has no monuments with later dates.

Copán's collapse seems to have been linked to erosion and soil exhaustion due to overpopulation and overfarming. About as many people (25,000) live in the Copán valley today as did so in AD 822. Like the ancient Maya, their subsistence rests on maize farming. Today's farmers cultivate the land year after year, with no fallow or resting period, and they complain of declining harvests. That yields are falling suggests the land could use fallow time to recoup the nutrients needed for successful farming.

A spider monkey strolls through Copán, a classic Maya royal center in western Honduras.

Food stress and malnutrition were clearly present at Copán, where 80 percent of the buried skeletons display signs of anemia, due to iron deficiency. One skull shows anemia severe enough to have been the cause of death. Even the nobility were malnourished. One noble skull, known to be such from its carved teeth and cosmetic deformation, also has telltale signs of anemia: spongy areas at its rear (Annenberg/CPB Exhibits).

Subsistence farming in the Copán valley did not end when the center collapsed but continued for a few centuries thereafter. However, by AD 1250 (as evidenced by mahogany pollen), a forest cover had returned, suggesting less intense farming. Previously, overfarming had caused deforestation and erosion. Hillside farm houses in particular had debris from erosion—probably caused by overfarming the hillsides. This erosion began around AD 750 and continued for generations, until such farm sites were abandoned, with some eventually buried by erosion debris.

The people of Copán used numerous cutting blades made of obsidian, which have been dated to AD 500 to 1000. Thereafter, the number of blades falls, suggesting a reduced population, which allowed the forest to return (Annenberg/CPB Exhibits). For the classic Maya in general, William Sanders (1972, 1973) has attributed state decline to overfarming, which resulted in environmental degradation through grass invasion and erosion. Overfarming was due to population growth. Social decay, crisis, and the Mayan collapse were the products of stress on land, food, and other resources.

Just as the origins of states, and their causes, are diverse, so are the reasons for state decline. For a discussion of threats to state organization in the contemporary world, see our website, where a section called "The Challenge to the State" can be found.

The Akhenaten Temple Project

BACKGROUND INFORMATION

Student:	*Jerusha Achterberg*
Supervising Professor:	*Donald Redford*
School:	*The Pennsylvania State University*
Year in School/Major:	*Senior/Anthropology*
Minors:	*Mathematics/Education Policy Studies Future*
Plans:	*Graduate school*
Project Title:	*The Akhenaten Temple Project*

What is the nature of the student work described here? How independent was this research?

My first archaeological fieldwork experience was in Egypt, where I worked as a site supervisor on the 10th round of excavations at Mendes (Tel er-Rub'a), on Middle Kingdom levels of that site in summer 2000. As a newcomer to the field, many techniques were unfamiliar to me. But the most difficult things for me to adapt to were the working conditions. Egyptian weather in July was not what my body was used to, and I was unprepared for what it would be like to work primarily with a team of native workers with whom I shared very little language. I was assigned a dig site, and a team of Egyptian workers including a Kufdi, who essentially guided the team, two pickmen and four basket-girls who removed the dirt after excavation. Rather than my primary job being the digging, as site supervisor, I recorded, measured, and mapped all our finds and loci. I was also responsible for making on-the-spot decisions about the course of our progress.

Because I had done no hands-on archeology before my arrival in Egypt, I was surprised by how quickly I learned the techniques we used. I kept constant records of every find in my site, as well as of the soil type. For those who have not worked in Egypt, it is hard to imagine the shear volume of pottery that is found at the sites. Every piece had to be sorted and catalogued following excavation. As a result, after excavating from 6 A.M.–1 P.M., we spent the afternoons sorting and washing pottery. On occasion I was able to participate in the more specialized tasks, such as tracing the stance of representative pottery fragments and sorting through the small finds collection.

One job in which I found particular skill was rebuilding pottery vessels from the excavated fragments. This job is important, although too tedious for most people's patience. I found the repetitiveness of the work relaxing compared to the excavation work of the morning. Also, because of my past work in mathematics I found I was good at profiling the excavation site stratigraphy, and drawing spatial representations of the architecture and finds. This work was usually done with a partner. One person called out measurements from a baseline, while the other plotted the information on a grid. This was later fleshed out with information about the materials involved, orientation, and presence of particular features. Prior to going to Egypt, I was concerned about handling human remains. I had never had a problem considering the idea while sitting in a classroom, but I worried that the hands-on work might be different. Recalling this worry was humorous after several hours of cleaning off a human skull. I had become so involved with the work and the satisfaction of slowly revealing the fragile bone, it hadn't occurred to me to be concerned about handling the remains. In fact, it seemed as though the care I was granting the skull was more respectful that leaving it in the ground to weather further. My reaction, or lack thereof, came as a surprise to me, but a welcome one. Overall, I'm very proud of the work I did in Egypt and the help I provided to the ongoing work at Mendes.

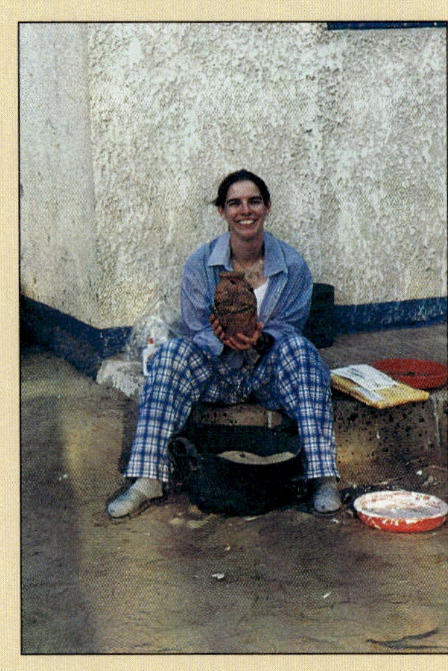

summary

1. A state is a society with a formal, central government and a division of society into classes. The first cities and states, supported by irrigated farming, developed in southern Mesopotamia between 6000 and 5500 B.P. Evidence for early state organization includes monumental architecture, central storehouses, irrigation systems, and written records.
2. Towns predate pottery in the Middle East. The first towns grew up 10,000 to 9,000 years ago. The first pottery dates back just over 8,000 years. Halafian (7500–6500 B.P.) refers to a pottery style and to the period when the first chiefdoms emerged. Ubaid pottery (7000–6000 B.P.) is associated with advanced chiefdoms and perhaps the earliest states. Most state formation occurred during the Uruk period (6100–5100 B.P.)
3. Based on the status distinctions they include, societies may be divided into egalitarian, ranked, and stratified. In egalitarian societies, status distinctions are not usually inherited. Ranked societies have hereditary inequality, but they lack stratification. Stratified societies have sharp social divisions—social classes or *strata*—based on unequal access to wealth and power. Ranked societies with loss of village autonomy are chiefdoms. The first chiefdoms appeared between 7,300 and 5,800 years ago. Chiefdoms feature political instability, raiding, and exotic goods used to mark status.
4. Mesopotamia's economy was based on craft production, trade, and intensive agriculture. Writing, invented by 5600 B.P., was first used to keep accounts for trade. With the invention of smelting, the Bronze Age began just after 5000 B.P.
5. In northwestern India and Pakistan, the Indus River Valley state flourished from 4600 to 3900 B.P. The first Chinese state, dating to 3750 B.P., was that of the Shang dynasty in northern China. The major early states of the Western Hemisphere were in Mesoamerica and Peru.
6. States arose between 2500 and 1600 B.P. (500 BC and AD 400) in Mesoamerica. Previously, Olmec chiefdoms had built ritual centers on Mexico's southern Gulf Coast between 3,200 and 2,500 years ago. By AD 1 (2000 B.P.), the Valley of Mexico had come to prominence. In this large valley in the highlands, Teotihuacan thrived between AD 100 and 700. Tenochtitlan, the capital of the Aztec state (AD 1325 to 1520), may have surpassed Teotihuacan at its height.
7. States develop to handle regulatory problems as the population grows and the economy gets more complex. Multiple factors contribute to state formation. Some appear repeatedly, but no single factor is always present. Among the most important factors are irrigation and long-distance trade. Coastal Peru, a very arid area, illustrates how environmental circumscription, population growth, and warfare may contribute to state formation.
8. Early states faced various threats: invasion, disease, famine, drought, soil exhaustion, erosion, and the buildup of irrigation salts. States may collapse when they fail to keep social and economic order or to protect themselves against outsiders. The Mayan state fell when its economy could no longer support its population, especially its division into elites and commoners.

key terms

Aztec Last independent state in the Valley of Mexico; capital was Tenochtitlan. Thrived between AD 1325 and the Spanish conquest in 1520.

bronze An alloy of arsenic and copper or of tin and copper.

chiefdom A ranked society in which relations among villages as well as among individuals are unequal, with smaller villages under the authority of leaders in larger villages; has a two-level settlement hierarchy.

cuneiform Early Mesopotamian writing that used a stylus (writing implement) to write wedge-shaped impressions on raw clay; from the Latin word for wedge.

egalitarian society A type of society, most typically found among hunter-gatherers, that lacks status distinctions except for those based on age, gender, and individual qualities, talents, and achievements.

Halafian An early (7500–6500 B.P.) and widespread pottery style, first found in northern Syria; refers to a delicate ceramic style and to the period when the first chiefdoms emerged.

Mesopotamia The area between the Tigris and Euphrates rivers in what is now southern Iraq and southwestern Iran; location of the first cities and states.

metallurgy Knowledge of the properties of metals, including their extraction and processing and the manufacture of metal tools.

multivariate Involving multiple factors, causes, or variables.

primary states States that arise on their own (through competition among chiefdoms), and not through contact with other state societies.

ranked society A type of society with hereditary inequality but not social stratification; individuals are ranked in terms of their genealogical closeness to the chief, but there is a continuum of status, with many individuals and kin groups ranked about equally.

settlement hierarchy A ranked series of communities differing in size, function, and type of building; a three-level settlement hierarchy indicates state organization.

smelting The high-temperature process by which pure metal is produced from an ore.

state A form of social and political organization with a formal, central government and a division of society into classes.

stratification A stratified society has sharp social divisions—*strata*—based on unequal access to wealth and power, e.g., into noble and commoner classes.

Teotihuacan AD 100 to 700; first state in the Valley of Mexico and earliest major Mesoamerican empire.

critical thinking questions

1. What were the main similarities and differences in the processes of state formation in the Middle East and in Mesoamerica?
2. Was the origin of the state good or bad? Why?
3. Can you think of three reasons to build walls around a town or a city? What is probably the most common reason? Does Çatal Hüyük remind you of an Upper Paleolithic cave site? Why and why not?
4. Imagine yourself transported back in time to an early chiefdom of your choice. Would it be in the Middle East or Mesoamerica? Why?
5. What would be the advantages and disadvantages of being an early chief in the Middle East? Would you rather be the chief or a chief's close relative?
6. Imagine yourself an archaeologist trying to identify ancient chiefdoms in the Middle East after excavating Mesoamerican chiefdom sites. What similar and different lines of evidence for ranking and political alliance might you find in the two hemispheres?
7. Imagine yourself transported back in time to an early state of your choice. Where would it be and why?
8. Would you feel more secure in an ancient chiefdom or an ancient state? How about those societies compared with the more egalitarian societies of prehistoric hunters and gatherers?
9. Is it harder to tell the difference between a chiefdom and a state in the ancient Middle East or in Mesoamerica. Why?
10. What kind of economic roles were available in early states, as compared with the earliest food-producing societies?
11. Why do you think the earliest states developed about 3,000 years later in Mesoamerica than in the Middle East? Imagine what might have happened if those states had developed at the same time.

12. Compare the origin of the United States or Canada with the origin of ancient states. Do any of the theories for the origin of the state apply to your country?

13. If our own state declined, what would be the most likely cause(s)? Do you view our government as stronger or weaker than it was a generation ago? How about a century ago? What is the likely reason for this strength or weakness?

14. Do you view our government as stronger or weaker than those of ancient states? What are the main reasons for this strength or weakness?

suggested additional readings

Blanton, R. E.
1999 *Ancient Oaxaca: The Monte Alban State.* New York: Cambridge University Press. The story of an early—and enduring—area of Mesoamerican state formation.

Blanton, R. E., S. A. Kowalewski, G. M. Feinman, and L. M. Finsten, eds.
1993 *Ancient Mesoamerica: A Comparison of Change in Three Regions,* 2nd ed. New York: Cambridge University Press. This book synthesizes research on three well-studied regions of Mesoamerica: the Valley of Oaxaca, the Valley of Mexico, and the Maya lowlands.

Diamond, J. M.
1997 *Guns, Germs, and Steel: The Fates of Human Societies.* New York: W.W. Norton. Disease, tools, and environmental forces and effects throughout human history.

Fagan, B. M.
1999 *World Prehistory: A Brief Introduction,* 4th ed. New York: Longman. Major events in human prehistory, including the emergence of the state in various locales.

Feinman, G. M., and J. Marcus, eds.
1998 *Archaic States.* Santa Fe, NM: School of American Research Press. Features of early states, in general and in particular world areas.

Joyce, R. A.
2000 *Gender and Power in Prehispanic Mesoamerica.* Austin, TX: University of Texas Press. Issues of gender and power in Mesoamerica before the Spanish conquest.

Pollock, S.
1999 *Ancient Mesopotamia: The Eden That Never Was.* Cambridge: Cambridge University Press. Mesopotamia state formation—a new synthesis.

Smith, M. E., and M. A. Masson, eds.
2000 *The Ancient Civilizations of Mesoamerica: A Reader.* Malpen, MA: Blackwell. Explore the diversity of Mesoamerican chiefdoms and states.

Trigger, B. G.
1995 *Early Civilizations: Ancient Egypt in Context.* New York: Columbia University Press. Considers the Incas (Inka); the Shang and western Chou of China; the Aztecs and Mayas of Mesoamerica; the Yoruba and Benin of West Africa; Mesopotamia; and ancient Egypt.

Wenke, R.
1996 *Patterns in Prehistory: Humankind's First Three Million Years,* 4th ed. New York: Oxford University Press. Rise of food production and the state throughout the world; thorough, useful text.

internet exercises

1. Early Cities in Mesoamerica: Read *Archaeology Magazine's* article on the New Tomb Found at Teotihuacan, **http://www.archaeology.org/online/features/mexico/index.html.**

   a. Where was the tomb found at Teotihuacan, and how old is it? Was the tomb created early or late in the history of this city? How does the tomb help us to understand the history of Teotihuacan?

   b. What was found in the tomb? What do they signify?

   c. As an example of a state, what are some of the institutions that you think may have existed at Teotihuacan? For example, do you think they had military and professional religion practitioners?

2. Indus Valley Civilization: Go to Mark Kenyoyer's "Around the Indus in 90 Slides" presentation, **http://www.harappa.com/indus/indus0.html,** and read his Essay about the Indus civilization, **http://www.harappa.com/indus/indus1.html.**

   a. Where is the Indus? When did its first cities arise? What are the names of some of the cities?

   b. What are some of the characteristics of Indus cities? Are those characteristic of a state?

   c. What are some of the common misconceptions about the origins of Indus civilization?

   d. The Indus had a form of writing. What did they write on? What are some of the common images and motifs associated with the inscriptions?

See Chapter 10 on your CD-ROM for additional review and interactive exercises. See your McGraw-Hill Online Learning Center for more.

PART III

Cultural Diversity

Chapter 11

Culture

SEATTLEP-I.NWSOURCE.COM NEWS BRIEFS

In Modern Japan, Personal Expression Often Frowned Upon

by Howard W. French
May 22, 2000

TOKYO—Ever since Japanese started to live in the West and travel there in large numbers in the 1970s, people have been predicting dramatic changes for one of the world's most insular societies. But in a country already famous for keeping foreigners at arm's length, returning Japanese say that the taint of other cultures is often enough for them to be regarded as somehow no longer fully Japanese.

This phenomenon, experienced by many Japanese expatriates, is perhaps the most dramatic measure of the challenge this . . . nation faces as it struggles to come to terms with the pressures of globalization.

In a reaction that sociologists call the "U-turn phenomenon," Japanese who are frustrated by their reception back home and are no longer willing to put up with the society's many strictures are often going back overseas as fast as possible.

The problems they encounter, many say, go far beyond the simple use of language, encompassing the whole range of human relations, from the rhythms of daily life and workplace politics to a mechanical educational system and affairs of the heart.

Strikingly, many overseas Japanese say the adjustment required to fit back into their society is often more traumatic than the adaptations required in moving abroad.

School-age returnees, for example, say they are often taunted as "gaijin," a mildly derogatory word for foreigner, by their schoolmates. Many young people also say they feel saddened and empty by the emotional reserve that is the norm here: Eye contact is rare in Japan, hugging and touching are far less common than in Western cultures, and simple gestures such as smiling or holding the door for strangers are almost unheard of.

Companies hiring new recruits often frown on Japanese with foreign high school or college educations as insufficiently socialized into the ways of Japan, which place an emphasis on outright acceptance of directives from above and preserving group harmony.

And even managers sent overseas by their own companies are routinely assigned to back-office jobs until their superiors can be sure that their foreign ways have dissipated. . .

With its population dwindling rapidly, Japan has recently begun to debate the extent to which it will need to attract workers from other countries. The experiences of expatriate Japanese suggest, however, that even before it comes to terms with new immigrants, this country will first have to learn how to better accommodate its own citizens who have lived abroad.

"The kind of assimilation pressure here is very strong," said Kazuhiro Ebuchi, a professor of cultural anthropology at the University of the Air, in Tokyo. "Even people who speak good English are teased here because Japanese should speak English in the Japanese way. Japanese people like to say that we appreciate cultural differences, but this is only lip service. In fact, there is not much place for difference here. "

Source: http://www.seattlep-i.nwsource.com/national/pac223.shtml.

overview

Culture is learned, and is passed from one generation to the next, through the process of enculturation. Only humans have cultural learning, which depends on symbols. Symbols have a particular meaning and value for people who share the same culture. Experiences, memories, values, and beliefs are shared as a result of common enculturation. Cultural traditions take natural phenomena, including biologically based urges, and channel them in particular directions. Everyone is cultured, not just people with elite educations. Societies are integrated and patterned through their dominant economic forces, social patterns, key symbols, and core values. Cultural rules don't always dictate behavior. There is room for creativity, flexibility, diversity, and disagreement within societies. Cultural means of adaptation have been crucial in human evolution. However, aspects of culture also can be maladaptive.

There are different levels of cultural systems. Diffusion and migration carry the same cultural traits and patterns to different areas. Such features are therefore shared across national boundaries. Nations also have internal cultural diversity associated with ethnicity, region, and social class. Some cultural features are universal. Others are widespread or generalized. Still others are unique and distinctive to particular societies. Mechanisms of cultural change include diffusion, acculturation, and independent invention. Globalization describes a series of processes that promote change in a world whose nations and people are increasingly linked.

The concept of culture has long been basic to anthropology. More than a century ago, in his book *Primitive Culture,* the British anthropologist Edward Tylor proposed that cultures, systems of human behavior and thought, obey natural laws and therefore can be studied scientifically. Tylor's definition of culture still offers an overview of the subject matter of anthropology and is widely quoted.

"Culture . . . is that complex whole which includes knowledge, belief, arts, morals, law, custom, and any other capabilities and habits acquired by man as a member of society" (Tylor 1871/1958, p.1). The crucial phrase here is "acquired by man as a member of society." Tylor's definition focuses on attributes that people acquire not through biological inheritance but by growing up in a particular society where they are exposed to a specific cultural tradition. **Enculturation** is the process by which a child *learns* his or her culture.

What Is Culture?

Culture Is Learned

The ease with which children absorb any cultural tradition rests on the uniquely elaborated human capacity to learn. Other animals may learn from experience; for example, they avoid fire after discovering that it hurts. Social animals also learn from other members of their group. Wolves, for instance, learn hunting strategies from other pack members. Such social learning is particularly important among monkeys and apes, our closest biological relatives. But our own *cultural learning* depends on the uniquely developed human capacity to use **symbols,** signs that have no necessary or natural connection to the things they signify or for which they stand.

On the basis of cultural learning, people create, remember, and deal with ideas. They grasp and apply specific systems of symbolic meaning. Anthropologist Clifford Geertz defines culture as ideas based on cultural learning and symbols. Cultures have been characterized as sets of "control mechanisms—plans, recipes, rules, instructions, what computer engineers call programs for the governing of behavior" (Geertz 1973, p. 44). These programs are absorbed by people through enculturation in particular traditions. People gradually internalize a previously established system of meanings and symbols. They use this cultural system to define their world, express their feelings, and make their judgments. This system helps guide their behavior and perceptions throughout their lives.

Every person begins immediately, through a process of conscious and unconscious learning and interaction with others, to internalize, or incorporate, a cultural tradition through the process of enculturation. Sometimes culture is taught directly, as when parents tell their children to say "thank you" when someone gives them something or does them a favor.

Culture also is transmitted through observation. Children pay attention to the things that go on around them. They modify their behavior not just because other people tell them to but as a result of their own observations and growing awareness of what their culture considers right and wrong. Culture also is absorbed unconsciously. North Americans acquire their culture's notions about how far apart people should stand when they talk (see "Interesting Issues" on pages 270 and 271) not by being directly told to maintain a certain distance but through a gradual process of observation, experience, and conscious and unconscious behavior modification. No one tells Latins to stand closer together than North Americans do, but they learn to do so anyway as part of their cultural tradition.

Anthropologists agree that cultural learning is uniquely elaborated among humans and that all humans have culture. Anthropologists also accept a doctrine named in the 19th century as "the psychic unity of man." This means that although *individuals* differ in their emotional and intellectual tendencies and capacities, all human *populations* have equivalent capacities for culture. Regardless of their genes or their physical appearance, people can learn *any* cultural tradition.

To understand this point, consider that contemporary Americans and Canadians are the genetically mixed descendants of people from all over the world. Our ancestors were biologically varied, lived in different countries and continents, and participated in hundreds of cultural traditions. However, early colonists, later immigrants, and their descendants have all become active participants in American and Canadian life. All now share a national culture.

Culture Is Shared

Culture is an attribute not of individuals per se but of individuals as members of *groups*. Culture is transmitted in society. Don't we learn our culture by observing, listening, talking, and interacting with many other people? Shared beliefs, values, memories, and expectations link people who grow up in the same culture. Enculturation unifies people by providing us with common experiences.

People in the United States sometimes have trouble understanding the power of culture because of the value that American culture places on the idea of the individual. Americans are fond of saying that everyone is unique and special in some way. However, in American culture, individualism itself is a distinctive shared value. Individualism is transmitted through hundreds of statements and settings in our daily lives. From daytime TV's Mr. Rogers to "real-life" parents, grandparents, and teachers, our enculturative agents insist that we are all "someone special."

Today's parents were yesterday's children. If they grew up in North America, they absorbed certain values and beliefs transmitted over the generations. People become agents in the enculturation of their children, just as their parents were for them. Although a culture constantly changes, certain fundamental beliefs, values, worldviews, and child-rearing practices endure. Consider a simple American example of enduring shared enculturation. As children, when we didn't finish a meal, our parents reminded us of starving children in some foreign country, just as our grandparents had done a generation earlier. The specific country changes (China, India, Bangladesh, Ethiopia, Somalia, Rwanda—what was it in your home?). Still, American culture goes on transmitting the idea that by eating all our brussels sprouts or broccoli, we can justify our own good fortune, compared to a hungry Third World child.

Despite characteristic American notions that people should "make up their own minds" and

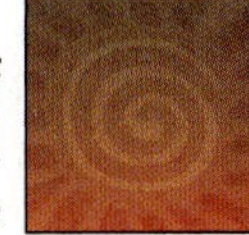

interesting issues

Touching, Affection, Love, and Sex

Comparing the United States to Brazil—or virtually any Latin nation—we can see a striking cultural contrast between a culture that tends to discourage physical contact and demonstrations of affection and one in which the contrary is true.

"Don't touch me." "Take your hands off me." Such statements are not uncommon in North America, but they are virtually never heard in Brazil, the Western Hemisphere's second most populous country. Brazilians like to be touched (and kissed) more than North Americans do. The world's cultures have strikingly different notions about displays of affection and about matters of personal space. When North Americans talk, walk, and dance, they maintain a certain distance from others—their personal space. Brazilians, who maintain less physical distance, interpret this as a sign of coldness. When conversing with a North American, the Brazilian characteristically moves in as the North American "instinctively" retreats. In these body movements, neither Brazilian nor North American is trying consciously to be especially friendly or unfriendly. Each is merely executing a program written on the self by years of exposure to a particular cultural tradition. Because of different ideas about proper social space, cocktail parties in international meeting places such as the United Nations can resemble an elaborate insect mating ritual as diplomats from different cultures advance, withdraw, and sidestep.

One easily evident difference between Brazil and the United States involves kissing, hugging, and touching. Middle-class Brazilians teach their kids—both boys and girls—to kiss (on the cheek, two or three times, coming and going) every adult relative they ever see. Given the size of Brazilian extended families, this can mean hundreds of people. Females continue kissing throughout their lives. They kiss male and female kin, friends, relatives of friends, friends of relatives, friends of friends, and, when it seems appropriate, more casual acquaintances. Males go on kissing their female relatives and friends. Until they are adolescents, boys also kiss adult male relatives. Brazilian men typically greet each other with hearty handshakes and a traditional male hug (*abraço*). The closer the relationship, the tighter and longer-lasting the embrace. These comments apply to brothers, cousins, uncles, and friends. Many Brazilian men keep on kissing their fathers and uncles throughout their lives. Could it be that homophobia (fear of homosexuality) prevents American men from engaging in such displays of affection with other men? Are American women more likely to show affection with each other than American men are?

Like other North Americans who spend time in a Latin culture, I miss the numerous kisses and handshakes when I get back to the United States. After several months in Brazil, I find North Americans

"have a right to their opinion," little of what we think is original or unique. We share our opinions and beliefs with many other people. Illustrating the power of shared cultural background, we are most likely to agree with and feel comfortable with people who are socially, economically, and culturally similar to ourselves. This is one reason why Americans abroad tend to socialize with each other, just as French and British colonials did in their overseas empires. Birds of a feather flock together, but for people, the familiar plumage is culture.

Culture Is Symbolic

Symbolic thought is unique and crucial to humans and to cultural learning. Anthropologist Leslie White defined culture as

> dependent upon symbolling . . . Culture consists of tools, implements, utensils, clothing, ornaments, customs, institutions, beliefs, rituals, games, works of art, language, etc. (White 1959, p. 3)

For White, culture originated when our ancestors acquired the ability to use symbols, that is, to

Cultures have strikingly different standards of personal space, such as how far apart people should stand in normal encounters and interactions. Contrast the distance between the American businessmen and the closeness (including touching) of the two rabbis in Jerusalem. Have you noticed such differences in your own interactions with others?

rather cold and impersonal. Many Brazilians share this opinion. I have heard similar feelings expressed by Italian-Americans as they describe North Americans with different ethnic backgrounds.

Question: *Ethnocentrism* is the tendency to view one's own culture as superior and to apply one's own cultural values in judging the behavior and beliefs of people from other cultures (see page 276). Do you have an ethnocentric position on the matter of displays of affection?

According to clinical psychologist David E. Klimek, who has written about intimacy and marriage in the United States, "in American society, if we go much beyond simple touching, our behavior takes on a minor sexual twist" (Slade 1984). North Americans define demonstrations of affection between males and females with reference to marriage. Love and affection are supposed to unite the married pair, and they blend into sex. When a wife asks her husband for "a little affection," she may mean, or he may think she means, sex.

A certain lack of clarity in North American definitions of love, affection, and sex is evident on Valentine's Day, which used to be just for lovers. Valentines used to be sent to wives, husbands, girlfriends, and boyfriends. Now, after years of promotion by the greeting card industry, they also go to mothers, fathers, sons, daughters, aunts, and uncles. There is a blurring of sexual and nonsexual affection. In Brazil, Lovers' Day retains its autonomy. Mother, father, and children have their own separate days of recognition.

It's true, of course, that in a good marriage love and affection exist alongside sex. Nevertheless, affection does not necessarily imply sex. The Brazilian culture shows that there can be rampant kissing, hugging, and touching without sex—or fears of improper sexuality. In Brazilian culture, physical demonstrations help cement many kinds of close personal relationships that have no sexual component.

originate and bestow meaning on a thing or event, and, correspondingly, to grasp and appreciate such meanings (White 1959, p. 3)

A symbol is something verbal or nonverbal, within a particular language or culture, that comes to stand for something else. There is no obvious, natural, or necessary connection between the symbol and what it symbolizes. A pet that barks is no more naturally a *dog* than a *chien, Hund,* or *mbwa,* to use the words for the animal we call "dog" in French, German, and Swahili. Language is one of the distinctive possessions of *Homo sapiens.* No other animal has developed anything approaching the complexity of language.

Symbols are usually linguistic. But there are also nonverbal symbols, such as flags, that stand for countries, as arches do for hamburger chains. Holy water is a potent symbol in Roman Catholicism. As is true of all symbols, the association between a symbol (water) and what is symbolized (holiness) is arbitrary and conventional. Water is not intrinsically holier than milk, blood, or other natural liquids. Nor is holy water chemically different from ordinary water. Holy water is a symbol within Roman Catholicism, which is part of an international cultural system. A natural thing has been arbitrarily associated with a particular meaning for Catholics, who share common beliefs and experiences that are based on learning and that are transmitted across the generations.

For hundreds of thousands of years, humans have shared the abilities on which culture rests. These abilities are to learn, to think symbolically, to manipulate language, and to use tools and other cultural products in organizing their lives and coping with their environments. Every contemporary human population has the ability to use symbols and thus to create and maintain culture. Our nearest relatives—chimpanzees and gorillas—have rudimentary cultural abilities. However, no other animal has elaborated cultural abilities—to learn, to communicate, and to store, process, and use information—to the extent that *Homo* has.

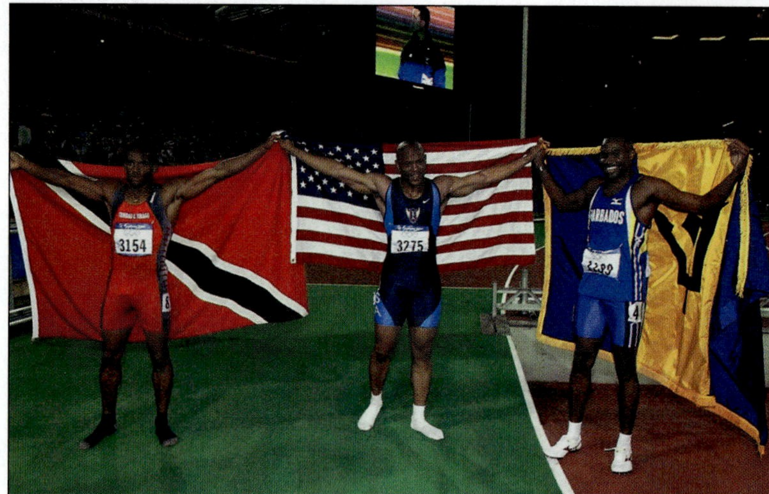

Three winners of the men's 100-meter sprint at the 2000 Sydney Olympics. American gold medalist Maurice Greene is at the center, silver medalist Ato Bolden of Trinidad and Tobago is on the left, and bronze medalist Obadele Thompson of Barbados stands to the right. What are the symbols in this photo and caption?

Culture and Nature

Culture takes the natural biological urges we share with other animals and teaches us how to express them in particular ways. People have to eat, but culture teaches us what, when, and how. In many cultures people have their main meal at noon, but most North Americans prefer a large dinner. English people may eat fish for breakfast, while North Americans may prefer hot cakes and cold cereals. Brazilians put hot milk into strong coffee, whereas North Americans pour cold milk into a weaker brew. Midwesterners dine at 5 or 6 PM, Spaniards at 10 PM.

Cultural habits, perceptions, and inventions mold "human nature" in many directions. People have to eliminate wastes from their bodies. But some cultures teach people to defecate squatting, while others tell them to do it sitting down. A generation ago, in Paris and other French cities, it was customary for men to urinate almost publicly, and seemingly without embarrassment, in barely shielded *pissoirs* located on city streets. Our "bathroom" habits, including waste elimination, bathing, and dental care, are parts of cultural traditions that have converted natural acts into cultural customs.

Our culture—and cultural changes—affect the ways in which we perceive nature, human nature, and "the natural." Through science, invention, and discovery, cultural advances have overcome many "natural" limitations. We prevent and cure diseases such as polio and smallpox that felled our ancestors. We use Viagra to restore sexual potency. Through cloning, scientists have altered the way we think about biological identity and the meaning of life itself. Culture, of course, has not freed us from natural threats. Hurricanes, floods, earthquakes, and other natural forces regularly challenge our wishes to modify the environment through building, development, and expansion. Can you think of other ways in which nature strikes back at people and their products?

Culture Is All-Encompassing

For anthropologists, culture includes much more than refinement, taste, sophistication, education, and appreciation of the fine arts. Not only college graduates but all people are "cultured." The most interesting and significant cultural forces are those that affect people every day of their lives, particularly those that influence children during enculturation. *Culture,* as defined anthropologi-

Cultures are integrated systems. When one behavior pattern changes, others also change. During the 1950s most American women expected to have domestic careers. But as more and more women have entered the work force, attitudes toward work and family have changed. Contrast the "fifties Mom" with a modern career woman. The twice-elected U.S. Senator Patty Murray of Washington State originally ran as a "mom in tennis shoes." Which of these women is more like your mother?

cally, encompasses features that are sometimes regarded as trivial or unworthy of serious study, such as "popular" culture (see the appendix). To understand contemporary North American culture, we must consider television, fast-food restaurants, sports, and games. As a cultural manifestation, a rock star may be as interesting as a symphony conductor, a comic book as significant as a book-award winner.

Culture Is Integrated

Cultures are not haphazard collections of customs and beliefs. Cultures are integrated, patterned systems. If one part of the system (e.g., the economy) changes, other parts change as well. For example, during the 1950s, most American women planned domestic careers as homemakers and mothers. Most of today's college women, by contrast, expect to get paid jobs when they graduate.

What are some of the social repercussions of the economic change? Attitudes and behavior regarding marriage, family, and children have changed. Late marriage, "living together," and divorce have become more common. The average age at first marriage for American women rose from 20 in 1955 to almost 25 in 1996 (Lugaila 1998; Saluter 1996). The comparable figures for men were 23 and 27 (Lugaila 1998; *World Almanac* 1992, p. 943). The number of currently divorced Americans quadrupled from 4 million in 1970 to more than 19 million in 1998 (Lugaila 1999). Work competes with marriage and family responsibilities and reduces the time available to invest in child care.

Cultures are integrated not simply by their dominant economic activities and related social patterns but also by sets of values, ideas, symbols, and judgments. Cultures train their individual members to share certain personality traits. A set of characteristic central or **core values** (key, basic, or central values) integrates each culture and helps distinguish it from others. For instance, the work ethic and individualism are core values that have integrated American culture for generations. Different sets of dominant values influence the patterns of other cultures.

People Use Culture Actively

Although cultural rules tell us what to do and how to do it, people don't always do what the rules say should be done. People use their culture actively and creatively, rather than blindly following its dictates. We are not passive beings who are doomed to follow our cultural traditions like programmed robots. Instead, people can

learn, interpret, and manipulate the same rule in different ways. Also, culture is contested. That is, different groups in society often struggle with one another over whose ideas, values, and beliefs will prevail. Even common symbols may have radically different *meanings* to different people and groups in the same culture. Golden arches may cause one person to salivate while another plots a vegetarian protest. The flag is a national symbol for the United States, but its meaning varies radically among Americans.

Even if they agree about what should and shouldn't be done, people don't always do as their culture directs or as other people expect. Many rules are violated, some very often (for example, automobile speed limits). Some anthropologists find it useful to distinguish between ideal and real culture. The *ideal culture* consists of what people say they should do and what they say they do. *Real culture* refers to their actual behavior as observed by the anthropologist. This contrast is like the emic–etic contrast discussion in Chapter 2.

39–40

Culture is both public and individual, both in the world and in people's minds. Anthropologists are interested not only in public and collective behavior but also in how *individuals* think, feel, and act. The individual and culture are linked because human social life is a process in which individuals internalize the meanings of *public* (i.e., cultural) messages. Then, alone and in groups, people influence culture by converting their private understandings into public expressions (D'Andrade 1984).

Culture Can Be Adaptive and Maladaptive

As we saw in Chapter 1, humans have both biological and cultural ways of coping with environmental stresses. Besides our biological means of adaptation, we also use "cultural adaptive kits," which contain customary activities and tools. Although humans continue to adapt biologically, reliance on social and cultural means of adaptation has increased during human evolution.

Sometimes, adaptive behavior that offers short-term benefits to particular individuals may harm the environment and threaten the group's long-term survival. Economic growth may benefit some people while it also depletes resources needed for society at large or for future generations (Bennett 1969, p. 19). Despite the crucial role of cultural adaptation in human evolution, cultural traits, patterns, and inventions also can be *maladaptive,* threatening the group's continued existence (survival and reproduction). Air conditioners help us deal with heat, as fires and furnaces protect us against the cold. Automobiles permit us to make a living by getting us from home to workplace. But the by-products of such "beneficial" technology often create new problems. Chemical emissions increase air pollution, deplete the ozone layer, and contribute to global warming. Many cultural patterns, such as overconsumption and pollution, appear to be maladaptive in the long run.

Levels of Culture

Of increasing importance in today's world are the distinctions between different levels of culture: national, international, and subcultural. **National culture** refers to the beliefs, learned behavior patterns, values, and institutions shared by citizens of the same nation. **International culture** is the term for cultural traditions that extend beyond and across national boundaries. Because culture is transmitted through learning rather than genetically, cultural traits can spread through borrowing or *diffusion* from one group to another.

Because of borrowing, migration, and multinational organizations, many cultural traits and patterns have international scope. For example, Roman Catholics in many different countries share beliefs, symbols, experiences, and values transmitted by their church. The contemporary United States, Canada, Great Britain, and Australia share cultural traits they have inherited from their common linguistic and cultural ancestors in Great Britain. The World Cup has become an international cultural event, as people in many countries know the rules of, play, and follow soccer.

Cultures also can be smaller than nations. Although people who live in the same country share a national cultural tradition, all cultures also contain diversity. Individuals, families, communities, regions, classes, and other groups within a culture have different learning experiences as well as shared ones. **Subcultures** are different symbol-based patterns and traditions

Illustrating the international level of culture, Roman Catholics in different nations share knowledge, symbols, beliefs, and values transmitted by their church. Here we see a prayer vigil in Seoul, Korea. In addition to religious conversion, what other forces work to spread international culture?

associated with particular groups in the same complex society. In a large nation like the United States or Canada, subcultures originate in region, ethnicity, language, class, and religion. The religious backgrounds of Jews, Baptists, and Roman Catholics create subcultural differences between them. While sharing a common national culture, U.S. northerners and southerners also differ in aspects of their beliefs, values, and customary behavior as a result of regional variation. French-speaking Canadians contrast with English-speaking people in the same country. Italian Americans have ethnic traditions different from those of Irish, Polish, and African-Americans. Using sports and foods, Table 11.1 gives some examples of international, national, and subculture. Soccer and basketball are played internationally. Monster-truck rallies are held throughout the United States. Bocci is a bowling-like sport from Italy still played in some Italian-American neighborhoods.

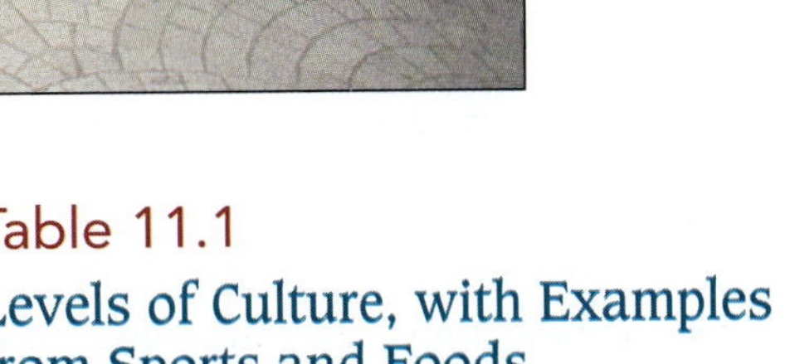

Table 11.1
Levels of Culture, with Examples from Sports and Foods

Level of Culture	Sports Examples	Food Examples
International	Soccer, basketball	Pizza
National	Monster-truck rallies	Apple pie
Subculture	Bocci	Big Joe Pork Barbeque (South Carolina)

Nowadays, many anthropologists are reluctant to use the term *subculture*. They feel that the prefix "sub-" is offensive because it means "below." "Subcultures" may thus be perceived as "less than" or somehow inferior to a dominant, elite, or national culture. In this discussion of levels of culture, I intend no such implication. My point is simply that nations may contain many different culturally defined groups. As mentioned earlier, culture is contested. Various groups may strive to promote the correctness and value of their own practices, values, and beliefs in comparison with those of other groups, or the nation as a whole.

Ethnocentrism, Cultural Relativism, and Human Rights

Ethnocentrism is the tendency to view one's own culture as superior and to apply one's own cultural values in judging the behavior and beliefs of people raised in other cultures. Ethnocentrism is a cultural universal. It contributes to social solidarity, a sense of value and community, among people who share a cultural tradition. People everywhere think that their familiar explanations, opinions, and customs are true, right, proper, and moral. They regard different behavior as strange, immoral, or savage. The tribal names that appear in anthropology books often come from the native word for *people.* "What are you called?" asks the anthropologist. "Mugmug," reply informants. *Mugmug* may turn out to be synonymous with *people,* but it also may be the only word the natives have for themselves. Other tribes are not considered fully human. The not-quite-people in neighboring groups are not classified as *Mugmug.* They are given different names that symbolize their inferior humanity. Neighboring tribes may be ridiculed and insulted because of their customs and preferences. They may be castigated as cannibals, thieves, or people who do not bury their dead.

In the Trans-Fly region of Papua New Guinea live several tribes in which homosexual activities are valued over heterosexual ones (see the chapter on gender). Men who grow up in the Etoro tribe (Kelly 1976) favor oral sex between men, while their neighbors, the Marind-anim, encourage men to engage in anal sex. (In both groups, heterosexual coitus is stigmatized and allowed only for reproduction.) Etoro men consider Marind-anim anal sex to be disgusting, while seeing nothing abnormal about their own oral practices.

Opposing ethnocentrism is **cultural relativism,** the argument that behavior in one culture should not be judged by the standards of another culture. This position also can present problems. At its most extreme, cultural relativism argues that there is no superior, international, or universal morality, that the moral and ethical rules of all cultures deserve equal respect. In the extreme relativist view, Nazi Germany would be evaluated as nonjudgmentally as Athenian Greece.

In today's world, human rights advocates challenge many of the tenets of cultural relativism.

For example, several cultures in Africa and the Middle East have traditions of female genital modification. *Clitoridectomy* is the removal of a girl's clitoris. *Infibulation* involves sewing the lips (labia) of the vagina so as to constrict the vaginal opening. Both procedures reduce female sexual pleasure, and, it is believed in some cultures, the likelihood of adultery. One or both of the procedures have been traditional in several societies, but such practices, characterized as female genital mutilation, have been opposed by human rights advocates, especially women's rights groups. The idea is that the tradition infringes on a basic human right: disposition over one's body and one's sexuality. Although such practices continue in certain areas, they are fading as a result of worldwide attention to the problem and changing sex-gender roles. Some African countries have banned or otherwise discouraged the procedures, as have Western nations that receive immigration from such cultures. (See the chapter on gender.) Similar issues arise with circumcision and other male genital operations. Is it right for a baby boy to be circumcised without his knowledge and permission, as has been routinely done in the United States? Is it proper to require adolescent boys to undergo collective circumcision to fulfill cultural tradition, as is done traditionally in parts of Africa and Australia?

The idea of **human rights** challenges cultural relativism by invoking a realm of justice and morality beyond and superior to particular countries, cultures, and religions. Human rights, usually seen as vested in individuals, include the right to speak freely, to hold religious beliefs without persecution, and to not be murdered, injured, enslaved, or imprisoned without charge. These rights are not ordinary laws that particular governments make and enforce. Human rights are seen as *inalienable* (nations cannot abridge or terminate them) and international (larger than and superior to individual nations and cultures). Four United Nations documents describe nearly all the human rights that have been internationally recognized. Those documents are the UN Charter; the Universal Declaration of Human Rights; the Covenant on Economic, Social and Cultural Rights; and the Covenant on Civil and Political Rights.

Alongside the human rights movement has arisen an awareness of the need to preserve cul-

The notion of indigenous intellectual property rights (IPR) has arisen in an attempt to conserve each society's cultural base, which may have commercial value. One example is ethnomedicine—traditional medical knowledge and techniques, including the use of medicinal plants, such as Madagascar's rosy periwinkle. Can you think of another example of IPR?

tural rights. Unlike human rights, **cultural rights** are vested not in individuals but in *groups,* such as religious and ethnic minorities and indigenous societies. Cultural rights include a group's ability to preserve its culture, to raise its children in the ways of its forebears, to continue its language, and not to be deprived of its economic base by the nation in which it is located (Greaves 1995). Many countries have signed pacts endorsing, for cultural minorities within nations, such rights as self-determination; some degree of home rule; and the right to practice the group's religion, culture, and language. The related notion of indigenous  intellectual property rights (**IPR**) has arisen in an attempt to conserve each society's cultural base—its core beliefs and principles. IPR are claimed as a cultural right, allowing indigenous groups to control who may know and use their collective knowledge and its applications. Much traditional cultural knowledge has commercial value. Examples include ethnomedicine (traditional medical knowledge and techniques), cosmetics, cultivated plants, foods, folklore, arts, crafts, songs, dances, costumes, and rituals. According to the IPR concept, a particular group may determine how indigenous knowledge and its products may be used and distributed, and the level of compensation required.

The notion of cultural rights is related to the idea of cultural relativism, and the problem discussed previously arises again. What does one do about cultural rights that interfere with human rights? I believe that anthropology's main job is to present accurate accounts and explanations of cultural phenomena. The anthropologist doesn't have to approve customs such as infanticide, cannibalism, and torture to record their existence and determine their causes. However, each anthropologist has a choice about where he or she will do field work. Some anthropologists choose not to study a particular culture because they discover in advance or early in field work that behavior they consider morally repugnant is practiced there. Anthropologists respect human diversity. Most ethnographers try to be objective, accurate, and sensitive in their accounts of other cultures. However, objectivity, sensitivity, and a cross-cultural perspective don't mean that anthropologists have to ignore international standards of justice and morality. What do you think?

Universality, Generality, and Particularity

In studying human diversity in time and space, anthropologists distinguish among the universal, the generalized, and the particular. Certain biological, psychological, social, and cultural features are **universal,** found in every culture. Others are merely **generalities,** common to several but not all human groups. Still other traits are **particularities,** unique to certain cultural traditions.

Universality

Universal traits are the ones that more or less distinguish *Homo sapiens* from other species (see Brown 1991). Biologically based universals include a long period of infant dependency, year-round (rather than seasonal) sexuality, and a complex brain that enables us to use symbols, languages, and tools. Psychological universals involve common ways in which humans think, feel, and process information. Most such universals probably reflect human biological universals, e.g., the structure of the human brain or certain physical differences between men and women, or children and adults.

Among the social universals is life in groups and in some kind of family. In all human societies, culture organizes social life and depends on social interactions for its expression and continuation. Family living and food sharing are universals. Among the most significant cultural universals are exogamy and the *incest taboo* (prohibition against marrying or mating with a close relative). All cultures consider some people (various cultures differ about *which* people) too closely related to mate or marry. The violation of this taboo is *incest,* which is discouraged and punished in a variety of ways in different cultures. If incest is prohibited, *exogamy*—marriage outside one's group—is inevitable. Because it links human groups together into larger networks, exogamy has been crucial in human evolution. Exogamy elaborates on tendencies observed among other primates. Recent studies of monkeys and apes show that these animals also avoid mating with close kin and often mate outside their native groups.

Generality

Between universals and uniqueness (see the next section) is a middle ground that consists of cultural generalities. These are regularities that occur in different times and places but not in all cultures. One reason for generalities is diffusion. Societies can share the same beliefs and customs because of borrowing or through (cultural) inheritance from a common cultural ancestor. Speaking English is a generality shared by North Americans and Australians because both countries had English settlers. English also has spread through diffusion to many countries, as it has become the world's foremost language for business and travel. Cultural generalities also can arise through independent invention of the same cultural trait or pattern in two or more different cultures. For example, farming arose through independent invention in the Eastern (e.g., the Middle East) and Western (e.g., Mexico) Hemispheres. Similar needs and circumstances have led people in different lands to innovate in parallel ways. They have independently come up with the same cultural solution to a common problem.

One cultural generality that is present in many but not all societies is the *nuclear family,* a kinship group consisting of parents and children. Although many middle-class Americans ethnocentrically view the nuclear family as a proper and "natural" group, it is not universal. It is absent, for example, among the Nayars, who live on the Malabar Coast of India. The Nayars live in female-headed households, and husbands and wives do not live together. In many other societies, the nuclear family is submerged in larger kin groups, such as extended families, lineages, and clans. However, the nuclear family is prominent in many of the technologically simple societies that live by hunting and gathering. It is also a significant kin group among contemporary middle-class North Americans and Western Europeans. Later, an explanation of the nuclear family as a basic kinship unit in specific types of society will be given.

Particularity

Many cultural traits are widely shared because of diffusion and independent invention and as cultural universals. Nevertheless, different cultures emphasize different things. Cultures are integrated and patterned differently and display tremendous variation and diversity. Uniqueness and particularity stand at the opposite extreme from universality.

Unusual and exotic beliefs and practices lend distinctiveness to particular cultural traditions. Many cultures ritually observe such universal life-cycle events as birth, puberty, marriage, parenthood, and death. However, cultures vary in just which event merits special celebration. Americans regard expensive weddings as more socially appropriate than lavish funerals. However, the Betsileo of Madagascar take the opposite view. The marriage ceremony is a minor event that brings

Cultures use rituals to mark such universal life-cycle events as birth, puberty, marriage, parenthood, and death. But particular cultures differ as to which event merits special celebration. Compare the lavish traditional wedding party of these Bai Chinese with the colorful and well-attended funeral at Quetzaltenango in the western highlands of Guatemala. What event merits the most elaborate celebration in your culture?

beyond the classroom

Folklore Reveals Ethos of Heating Plant Workers

BACKGROUND INFORMATION

Student:	*Mark Dennis*
Supervising Professor:	*Usher Fleising*
School:	*University of Calgary*
Year in School/Major:	*Fifth-Year Senior/Social Anthropology*
Future Plans:	*Graduate school, traveling*
Project Title:	*Folklore Reveals Ethos of Heating Plant Workers*

What role does folklore play among the workers described in this account? What functions do common tales serve in enabling workers to adapt to their work setting? What attributes of culture are represented here?

At the periphery of the University of Calgary campus exists a place, ironically called the central heating and cooling plant. Housed within its four walls and three levels are the industrial machinery and a tangle of pipes that snake through an eight-mile tunnel system in the bowels of the earth, bringing heat and cooling to a campus of 21,000.

Folklore is an oral form of knowledge shared by a cultural group. The objective of my research was to reveal the social and cultural manifestations of folklore among the University Central Heating and Cooling Plant (CHCP) employees. In an isolated control room, a fieldworker finds plant employees engaged in a social atmosphere filled with storytelling and humor. Accustomed to the mental and physical distance from the rest of the university, the men of the CHCP were glad to share their knowledge and folklore with me.

In addition to simple observations and document analysis, my research method consisted primarily of unstructured interviews. Using this technique I was able to control the direction of the conversation while still giving the informants (cultural consultants, community members) freedom to express themselves.

Folklore at the CHCP was passed on between employees during their shifts or during shift changes. Most stories were known by all employees. The themes included slapstick humor, disaster stories, tales about eccentric char-

together just the couple and a few close relatives. However, a funeral is a measure of the deceased person's social position and lifetime achievement, and it may attract a thousand people. Why use money on a house, the Betsileo say, when one can use it on the tomb where one will spend eternity in the company of dead relatives? How different from contemporary Americans' growing preference for quick and inexpensive funerals and cremation, which would horrify the Betsileo, whose ancestral bones and relics are important ritual objects.

What are some of the particularities of modern American culture? Although the mass media and a consumers' culture are spreading (diffusing) globally, these trends are most advanced in contemporary North America. They pervade all aspects of our culture. The fact that TVs outnumber toilets in American households is a significant cultural fact that anthropologists can't afford to ignore. My own research on Michigan college students is probably generalizable to other young Americans. They visit fast-food restaurants more often than they visit houses of worship. Almost all have seen a Walt Disney movie and have attended rock concerts and football games. Such shared experiences are major features of American enculturation patterns. Certainly any extraterrestrial anthropologist doing field work in the United States would stress them as prominent patterns of contemporary American national culture.

Cultures vary tremendously in their beliefs, practices, integration, and patterning. By focus-

acters, practical jokes, and stories about complaints. The folklore was based entirely on oral history, with no written documentation ever produced.

During the course of fieldwork, I found that folklore functioned as an organic mechanism adapting to the needs of the employees by providing stress relief. Folklore helped them to deal constructively with job frustrations, and it created social cohesion among employees.

The last six years at the CHCP have been turbulent because of a management change. Conflicting working methods and rapid changes in technology made it hard for many employees to adapt. In this context the humor that folklore provided not only lightened the mood, but it also brought back fond memories of the easy-going past.

The CHCP has a unique working environment. At its worst, days can be filled with isolation and mundane activity, leaving the employees feeling that no one cares about the important work they do. Folklore is a healthy way of dealing with the isolation and ignorance of others. Workers share stories of the prestigious visitors, like university presidents, who have visited the plant over the years. By telling these stories the plant workers can see that there is hope for educating people about what they do. Such stories affirm that their jobs are very important.

Finally, folklore is a cohesive force whereby plant workers both old and new can celebrate the shared knowledge and unique work environment that surrounds them, leading to a happier and more productive work environment. Folklore is an interesting starting point from which to analyze subcultures and their social relations. The study of the Central Heating and Cooling Plant at the University of Calgary was one application of folklore as a theoretical basis for social analysis.

ing on and trying to explain alternative customs, anthropology forces us to reappraise our familiar ways of thinking. In a world full of cultural diversity, contemporary American culture is just one cultural variant, more powerful perhaps, but no more natural, than the others.

Mechanisms of Cultural Change

Why and how do cultures change? One way is **diffusion,** or borrowing of traits between cultures. Such exchange of information and products has gone on throughout human history because cultures have never been truly isolated. Contact between neighboring groups has always existed and has extended over vast areas (Boas 1940/1966). Diffusion is *direct* when two cultures trade, intermarry, or wage war on one another. Diffusion is *forced* when one culture subjugates another and imposes its customs on the dominated group. Diffusion is *indirect* when items move from group A to group C via group B without any firsthand contact between A and C. In this case, group B might consist of traders or merchants who take products from a variety of places to new markets. Or group B might be geographically situated between A and C, so that what it gets from A eventually winds up in C, and vice versa. In today's world, much transnational diffusion is

Within and between nations, the Internet spreads information about products, rights, and life styles. Shown here, a coffee shop in Cairo, Egypt, with men, laptop computer, and hookahs (pipes). For what purposes do you think these men use the computer?

due to the spread of the mass media and advanced information technology.

Acculturation, a second mechanism of cultural change, is the exchange of cultural features that results when groups have continuous firsthand contact. The cultures of either or both groups may be changed by this contact (Redfield, Linton, and Herskovits 1936). With acculturation, parts of the cultures change, but each group remains distinct. One example of acculturation is a *pidgin,* a mixed language that develops to ease communication between members of different cultures in contact. This usually happens in situations of trade or colonialism. Pidgin English, for example, is a simplified form of English. It blends English grammar with the grammar of a native language. Pidgin English was first used for commerce in Chinese ports. Similar pidgins developed later in Papua New Guinea and West Africa. In situations of continuous contact, cultures also have exchanged and blended foods, recipes, music, dances, clothing, tools, and technologies.

Independent invention—the process by which humans innovate, creatively finding solutions to problems—is a third mechanism of cultural change. Faced with comparable problems and challenges, people in different societies have innovated and changed in similar ways, which is one reason cultural generalities exist. One example is the independent invention of agriculture in the Middle East and Mexico. Over the course of human history, major innovations have spread at the expense of earlier ones. Often a major invention, such as agriculture, triggers a series of subsequent interrelated changes. These economic revolutions have social and cultural repercussions. Thus, in both Mexico and the Middle East, agriculture led to many social, political, and legal changes, including notions of property and distinctions in wealth, class, and power.

 Globalization

The term **globalization** encompasses a series of processes, including diffusion and acculturation, working to promote change in a world in which nations and people are increasingly interlinked and mutually dependent. Promoting such linkages are economic and political forces, along with modern systems of transportation and communication. The forces of globalization include international commerce, travel and tourism, transnational migration, the media, and various high-tech information flows. During the Cold War, which ended with the fall of the Soviet Union, the basis of international alliance was political, ideological, and military. Now, international pacts tend to focus on trade and economic issues. Multinational mergers are in the news daily. New economic unions have been created through NAFTA (the North American Free Trade Agreement), GATT (the General Agreement on Trade and Tariffs), and EEC (the European Economic Community).

Long-distance communication is easier, faster, and cheaper than ever and extends to remote areas. The mass media help propel a globally spreading culture of consumption, stimulating participation in the world cash economy. Within nations and across their borders, the media spread information about products, services, rights, institutions, and life styles. Emigrants transmit information and resources transnationally as they maintain their ties with home (phoning, faxing, e-mailing, making visits, sending money). In a sense, such people live multilocally—in different places and cultures at once. They learn to play various social roles and to change behavior and identity depending on the situation.

Local people must increasingly cope with forces generated by progressively larger systems—region, nation, and world. An army of alien actors and agents now intrudes on people everywhere. Tourism has become the world's number one industry. Economic development agents and the media promote the idea that work should be for cash rather than mainly for subsistence. Indigenous peoples and traditional cultures have devised various strategies to deal with threats to their autonomy, identity, and livelihood. New forms of political mobilization and cultural expression, including the rights movements discussed previously, are emerging from the interplay of local, regional, national, and international cultural forces.

summary

1. Culture, which is distinctive to humanity, refers to customary behavior and beliefs that are passed on through enculturation. Culture rests on the human capacity for cultural learning. Culture encompasses rules for conduct internalized in human beings, which lead them to think and act in characteristic ways.
2. Although other animals learn, only humans have cultural learning, dependent on symbols. Humans think symbolically—arbitrarily bestowing meaning on things and events. By convention, a symbol stands for something with which it has no necessary or natural relation. Symbols have special meaning for people who share memories, values, and beliefs because of common enculturation. People absorb cultural lessons consciously and unconsciously.
3. Cultural traditions mold biologically based desires and needs in particular directions. Everyone is cultured, not just people with elite educations. Cultures may be integrated and patterned through economic and social forces, key symbols, and core values. Cultural rules don't rigidly dictate our behavior. There is room for creativity, flexibility, diversity, and disagreement within societies. Cultural means of adaptation have been crucial in human evolution. Aspects of culture also can be maladaptive.
4. There are levels of culture, which can be larger or smaller than a nation. Diffusion and migration carry cultural traits and patterns to different areas. Such traits are shared across national boundaries. Nations also include cultural differences associated with ethnicity, region, and social class.
5. Using a comparative perspective, anthropology examines biological, psychological, social, and cultural universals and generalities. There are also unique and distinctive aspects of the human condition. North American cultural traditions are no more natural than any others. Mechanisms of cultural change include diffustion, acculturation, and independent invention. Globalization describes a series of processes that promote change in a world in which nations and people are interlinked and mutually dependent.

key terms

acculturation The exchange of cultural features that results when groups come into continuous firsthand contact; the cultural patterns of either or both groups may be changed, but the groups remain distinct.

core values Key, basic, or central values that integrate a culture and help distinguish it from others.

cultural relativism The position that the values and standards of cultures differ and deserve respect. Extreme relativism argues that cultures should be judged solely by their own standards.

cultural rights Doctrine that certain rights are vested in identifiable groups, such as religious and ethnic minorities and indigenous societies. Cultural rights include a group's ability to preserve its culture, to raise its children in the ways of its forebears, to continue its language, and not to be deprived of its economic base by the nation-state in which it is located.

diffusion Borrowing of cultural traits between societies, either directly or through intermediaries.

enculturation The social process by which culture is learned and transmitted across the generations.

ethnocentrism The tendency to view one's own culture as best and to judge the behavior and beliefs of culturally different people by one's own standards.

generality Culture pattern or trait that exists in some but not all societies.

globalization The accelerating interdependence of nations in a world system linked economically and through mass media and modern transportation systems.

human rights Doctrine that invokes a realm of justice and morality beyond and superior to particular countries, cultures, and religions. Human rights, usually seen as vested in individuals, would include the right to speak freely, to hold religious beliefs without persecution, and to not be murdered, injured, enslaved, or imprisoned without charge.

independent invention Development of the same cultural trait or pattern in separate cultures as a result of comparable needs, circumstances, and solutions.

international culture Cultural traditions that extend beyond national boundaries.

IPR Intellectual property rights, consisting of each society's cultural base—its core beliefs and principles. IPR are claimed as a group right—a cultural right, allowing indigenous groups to control who may know and use their collective knowledge and its applications.

national culture Cultural experiences, beliefs, learned behavior patterns, and values shared by citizens of the same nation.

particularity Distinctive or unique culture trait, pattern, or integration.

subcultures Different cultural traditions associated with subgroups in the same complex society.

symbol Something, verbal or nonverbal, that arbitrarily and by convention stands for something else, with which it has no necessary or natural connection.

universal Something that exists in every culture.

critical thinking questions

1. How does human learning differ from animal learning? What and how much can you teach a cat? A dog? An ape? A child?
2. What cultural symbols have the most meaning for you? For your family? For your nation?
3. What are some cultural features that you share just with members of your hometown?
4. What are the key symbols and values that work to unite your religious group or other organization to which you belong?
5. Give some examples of cultural practices that are adaptive in the short run but probably maladaptive in the long run.

6. To how many cultures do you belong? Do you participate in an international culture and a subculture in addition to a national culture?
7. Do you feel you have multiple cultural identities? If so, how do you handle them?
8. What are some issues about which you find it hard to be culturally relativistic?
9. What are some issues about which you find it easy to be culturally relativistic?
10. Besides the examples discussed in the text, what are some other cultural universals? Is religion a cultural universal?
11. Besides the ones discussed in the text, are there other particularities in contemporary American (or Canadian) culture?
12. Think of three ways in which globalization has affected you in the past week.

case study

Aztec: Most people regard the Aztecs as part of a civilization that was lost long ago. However, in Mexico today there are indigenous social movements that seek to link the present directly with an Aztec past. In *Culture Sketches* by Holly Peters-Golden, read the chapter on the Aztec: Ancient Legacy, Modern Pride. Think about the uses and meanings of culture you've read about in this textbook. What might motivate contemporary Nahua peoples and others in Mexico to embrace Aztec culture? What is the significance of the ways in which they have chosen to recognize the Aztec heritage? Is this phenomenon something you recognize as happening among other groups? In other nations?

suggested additional readings

Archer, M. S.

1996 *Culture and Agency: The Place of Culture in Social Theory,* rev. ed. Cambridge: Cambridge University Press. Examines interrelations among individual action, social structure, culture, and social integration.

Bohannan, P.

1995 *How Culture Works.* New York: Free Press. A consideration of the nature of culture.

Brown, D.

1991 *Human Universals.* New York: McGraw-Hill. Surveys the evidence for "human nature" and explores the roles of culture and biology in human variation.

Geertz, C.

1973 *The Interpretation of Cultures.* New York: Basic Books. Essays about culture viewed as a system of symbols and meaning.

Hall, E. T.

1990 *Understanding Cultural Differences.* Yarmouth, ME: Intercultural Press. Focusing on business and industrial management, this book examines the role of national cultural contrasts among France, Germany, and the United States.

1992 *An Anthropology of Everyday Life: An Autobiography.* New York: Doubleday. A prominent student of language and culture examines his own life in the context of intercultural communication.

Kroeber, A. L., and C. Kluckhohn
1963 *Culture: A Critical Review of Concepts and Definitions.* New York: Vintage. Discusses and categorizes more than a hundred definitions of culture.

Lindholm, C.
2001 *Culture and Identity: The History, Theory, and Practice of Psychological Anthropology.* New York: McGraw-Hill. An introduction to psychological anthropology, with special attention to the roles of culture and the individual.

Naylor, L. L.
1996 *Culture and Change: An Introduction.* Westport, CT: Bergin and Garvey. Anthropology, culture, and change.

Scholte, J. A.
2000 *Globalization: A Critical Introduction.* New York: St. Martin's. International relations, culture contact, and change in the era of globalization.

Van der Elst, D., and P. Bohannan
1999 *Culture as Given, Culture as Choice.* Prospect Heights, IL: Waveland. Culture and individual choices.

Wagner, R.
1981 *The Invention of Culture,* rev. ed. Chicago: University of Chicago Press. Culture, creativity, society, and the self.

Wilson, R., ed.
1996 *Human Rights: Culture and Context: Anthropological Perspectives.* Chicago: Pluto. Issues of cultural relativism and cross-cultural studies of human rights issues.

internet exercises

1. *Acculturation:* Go and read Cyndi Patee's article on "Pidgins and Creoles," **http://logos.uoregon.edu/explore/socioling/pidgin.html.**
   a. What are pidgins and creoles? How are they examples of acculturation?
   b. What role did colonialism play in the development of pidgins and creoles?
   c. Take the quiz at the end of the page. Which sentences were easiest for you to read? Which were hardest? Look at the answers. Does the substrate language explain your ability or inability to understand?

2. *The Kiss:* Read Washington State University's page on "The Kiss," **http://www.wsu.edu:8001/vcwsu/commons/topics/culture/behaviors/kissing/kissing-essay.html.**
   a. Is kissing an instinctive human display of affection? Or is it learned?
   b. What is the history of the kiss?
   c. Is there a single, universal meaning for a kiss? How and why can the meanings change by culture and situation?

See Chapter 11 on your CD-ROM for additional review and interactive exercises. See your McGraw-Hill Online Learning Center for more.

Chapter 12

Ethnicity

CHAPTER OUTLINE

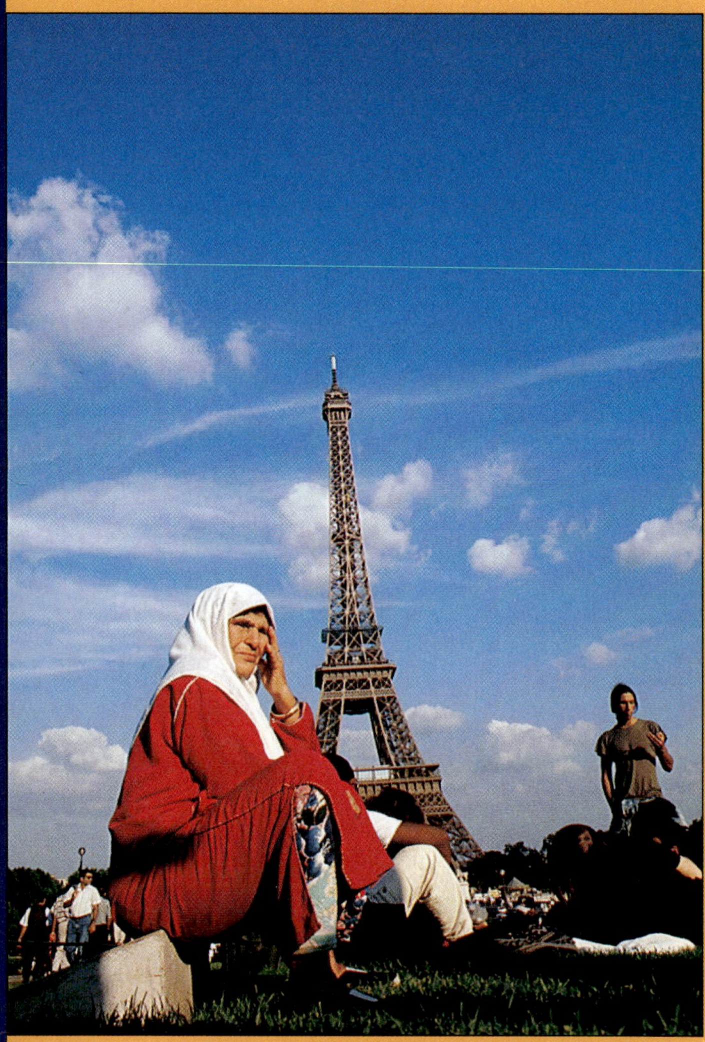

NYTIMES.COM NEWS BRIEFS

Encyclopedia Raises Veil on Ancient Saudi Culture

by Judith Miller
June 30, 2000

. . . The "Encyclopedia of Folklore of the Kingdom of Saudi Arabia," a 12-volume, Arabic-language compendium of a vanishing way of life, has just been printed in Belgium. Its authors say that the series, which includes 5,000 drawings, illustrations and graphs, is the largest body of secular scholarship ever produced in Saudi Arabia. It includes separate volumes on topics like historical and archaeological sites, traditional medicine, geography, even children's games. And there is an entire volume devoted to the camel . . .

Thanks to oil wealth, lifestyles have changed faster and more dramatically in Saudi Arabia than in almost any other country. Fifty-year-old Saudis can recall baked-mud hovels, with neither electricity nor running water, in which most of them were raised, but young Saudis today can barely imagine life without the Internet, cellular telephones, vacations abroad, air-conditioned suburban homes, sport utility vehicles and fancy shopping malls. Few have ever even ridden a camel.

Yet Saudi contributors to the volumes say that a work of this nature could probably not have been undertaken as long as tribal and regional divisions continued to plague the kingdom. "Oil wealth has helped unify Saudis politically and culturally," said Sa'ad al-Sowayan, an anthropologist with a doctorate from the University of California at Berkeley and the encyclopedia's chief editor. "Until Saudis spoke the same Arabic dialect and tribal and regional cultural differences diminished, a project examining the country's heritage would have been too contentious to be approved by the censors."

In addition, he observed, until recently many Saudi scholars viewed folk culture as academically dubious. They believed that attention to traditional ways of life emphasized backwardness. But after the gulf war, Mr. Sowayan said, "people realized that our old civilization was dying out, and that we had a limited window to capture what was being lost, mostly through memory. It gave us a renewed sense of urgency."

Some 75 leading Saudi scholars and writers contributed to the encyclopedia. Their texts were then vetted by older, often uneducated Saudis who still remembered many of the nearly extinct customs.

Consider the 547-page volume on the camel. The volume notes that it was the domestication of this amazingly adaptive, aggressive, often crotchety creature that made Bedouin nomadic life possible. Saudis rarely tired of extolling the camel's endurance, forbearance, fortitude and other virtues in chants, conversation, lore and song . . .

Ultimately, the volume asserts, the camel was superseded as the major symbol of Arabia by the palm tree, the emblem of the sedentary farmers, merchants and traders who were the Muslim prophet Muhammad's first and most enduring followers.

This community, which loathed and feared the warring Bedouins, imposed its written, settled culture on nomadic culture, said Abdulaziz Fahad, a lawyer and an early champion of the project. As a result, Saudi society remains deeply ambivalent about the desert and the traditional Bedouin life . . .

"This work will not only help us preserve our vanishing past, but by examining the past, will emphasize our new cultural and political unity," Mr. Sowayan said. "In that sense, it is a truly nationalist project."

Source: http://www.nytimes.com/library/books/070100saudi-encyclopedia.html.

overview

To say there is ethnic diversity in a nation is to say there are different cultures, or cultural traditions, within it. The global scale of modern migration introduces unparalleled ethnic variety to host nations. "Ethnic group" describes a particular culture in a nation or region that contains others. Ethnicity is based on cultural similarities (among members of the same ethnic group) and differences (between that group and others). Ethnic distinctions can arise from language, religion, history, geography, kinship, or "race." A race is an ethnic group assumed to have a biological basis.

Because of migration, conquest, and colonialism, most nation-states are not ethnically homogeneous. Assimilation is a process an ethnic group may experience when it moves to a country where another culture dominates. By assimilating, the minority adopts the patterns and norms of its host culture. Multiculturalism contrasts with assimilation, in which minorities are expected to abandon their cultural traditions. A multicultural society socializes individuals not only into the dominant (national) culture but also into an ethnic culture.

Ethnicity can be expressed in peaceful multiculturalism, or in discrimination or violent confrontation. Ethnic conflict often arises in relation to prejudice (attitudes and judgments) or discrimination (action). A dominant group may try to destroy certain ethnic practices (ethnocide). Or it may attempt to force ethnic group members to adopt the dominant culture (forced assimilation).

We know from the last chapter that culture is learned, shared, symbolic, integrated, and all-encompassing, and that it can be adaptive or maladaptive. Now we consider the relation between culture and ethnicity. Ethnicity is based on cultural similarities and differences in a nation or region. The similarities are with members of the same ethnic group; the differences are between that group and others.

Ethnic Groups and Ethnicity

How does an ethnic group differ from a culture? An ethnic group is almost synonymous with a culture. We use the term "ethnic group" when we are describing a particular culture in a nation or region that contains others. To say that there are different ethnic groups in the same nation is to say there are different cultures, or cultural traditions, within that society. Ethnic groups must deal with other such groups in the nation or region they inhabit, so that interethnic relations are important in the study of that nation or region.

Ethnicity and Race

Members of an ethnic group may define themselves—and/or be defined by others—as different and special because of their language, religion, geography, history, ancestry, or physical traits. When an ethnic group is assumed to have a biological basis (shared "blood" or genetic material), it is called a *race.*

We hear the words *ethnicity* and *race* frequently, but American culture doesn't draw a very clear line between them. As an illustration, consider two articles in *The New York Times* of May 29, 1992. One, discussing the changing ethnic composition of the United States, states (correctly) that Hispanics "can be of any race" (Barringer 1992, p. A12). In other words, "Hispanic" is an ethnic category that crosscuts "racial" contrasts such as that between "black" and "white." The other article reports that during the Los Angeles riots of spring 1992, "hundreds of Hispanic residents were interrogated about their immigration status on the basis of their *race* alone [emphasis added]" (Mydans 1992*a*, p. A8). Use of "race" here seems inappropriate because "Hispanic" is usually perceived as referring to a lin-

"Hispanic" and "Latino" are ethnic categories that crosscut "racial" contrasts such as that between "black" and "white." Note the physical diversity exemplified by these Latina teenagers.

guistically based (Spanish-speaking) ethnic group, rather than a biologically based race. Since these Los Angeles residents were being interrogated because they were Hispanic, the article is actually reporting on ethnic, not racial, discrimination. However, given the lack of a precise distinction between race and ethnicity, it is probably better to use the term "ethnic group" instead of "race" to describe *any* such social group, for example, African-Americans, Asian-Americans, Irish-Americans, Anglo-Americans, of Hispanics. (Table 12.1 lists American ethnic groups, as given in the 2000 census.)

Now read the "In the News" box. Is there any confusion in the box about race and ethnicity, especially with reference to Hispanics?

Today, some people think that "ethnic group" and "ethnicity" are just politically correct ways of talking about race. That's not so. Ethnicity is based on common cultural traditions—not mainly on biological features, as race is. The complex issues of race is discussed further in the chapter on human diversity and race.

Ethnic Markers, Identities, and Statuses

As with any culture, members of an **ethnic group** *share* certain beliefs, values, customs, and norms because of their common background. They define themselves as special and different from other such groups because of cultural features. Members of a given ethnic group may speak a common language, practice the same religion, and share historical experience. Markers of an ethnic group may include a collective name, belief in common ancestry, a sense of solidarity, and an association with a specific territory, such as a homeland, that the group may or may not hold (Ryan 1990, pp. xiii, xiv).

Ethnicity means identifying with, and feeling part of, an ethnic group. Ethnicity also means being excluded from other groups because of one's ethnic identity. Ethnic feeling varies in intensity within ethnic groups and countries and over time. A change in the importance attached to an ethnic identity may reflect a political change. For example, with the fall of the Soviet Union, ethnic feeling rose in many areas of the former U.S.S.R. where ethnic expression had previously been discouraged. The importance of an ethnic identity also may change during the individual life cycle. For example, young people may relinquish, or old people reclaim, an ethnic background.

Ethnic differences have been around for a long time. Archaeologists find evidence that different ethnic groups participated in the same social system thousands of years ago. For example, some 1,500 years ago, traders from different regions

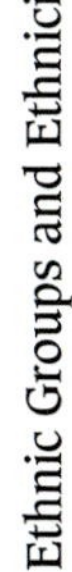

Table 12.1

Racial/Ethnic Identification in the United States, 2000 Census

Claimed Identity	Millions of People
African-Americans	34.7
Asians and Pacific Islanders	10.6
American Indians, Eskimos, and Aleuts	2.5
Hispanics (any "race")	35.3
Two or more "races"	6.8
Non-Hispanic whites	176.1
Others	15.4
Total population	281.4

Source: Census 2000, www.census.gov.

in the news

Sosa vs. McGwire: It's a Race, but Is It Also about Race?

Racial, ethnic, and national identities affected the way different Americans rooted for Mark McGwire or Sammy Sosa during their 1998 home run race. This box, excerpted from a *New York Times* story by Bull Dedman, reports on fan reaction as the contest was nearing its close. How did you feel when McGwire won the race, with 70 home runs? Do you think that the fans who rooted for one or the other because of his race, ethnicity, or national origin were prejudiced? What is Sammy Sosa's race? What's his ethnicity? What's his national origin? What's his nationality? How about Mark McGwire?

All across the country, Americans are talking baseball and home runs. Or more specifically, Mark McGwire and Sammy Sosa. Take a seat at the bar in Denver, or at a hamburger joint in Los Angeles. The questions are simple: Who are you rooting for in the home run race? And why?

The answers are not so simple. It does not take long for the vexing issues of race and national origin to creep onto the field. In Atlanta or Boston, in Houston or Miami, awkward pauses and disagreements renew the long, uncomfortable relationship between the national pastime and the national enigma.

With only one week to go in the Home Run Derby of 1998, with two players already past Roger Maris's record of 61 home runs in a season, the overwhelming reaction of sports fans and nonfans has been delight at the simple joy of the competition. McGwire of the St. Louis Cardinals, who had 64 home runs going into yesterday's games, and Sosa of the Chicago Cubs, who had 63, are seen as embodiments of power, sportsmanship and grace.

And yet a fact remains, mentioned frequently by fans: one of the sluggers, McGwire, happens to be a white, red-headed Californian, a European American. The other, Sosa, is a dark-skinned, Spanish-speaking Dominican, a Latin American.

In dozens of conversations in 10 cities in recent days, the complexities of race emerged from the simplest questions about the home run race. The answers raise more questions, unsettled and unsettling: If it is a matter of pride for Latinos to root for Sosa, why would many consider it racist for whites to root for McGwire because he is white? And how precise are the racial labels anyway? Which group may claim Sosa as a hero? And what of citizenship? Will an immigrant, an American citizen, be considered by everyone an American hero if he wins? . . .

For those who are picking a champion, race often seems to play a role. Latinos, whites and blacks speak of choosing "one of our own" of "someone like us."

and ethnic groups regularly visited the monumental Mexican site of Teotihuacan to sell their products in its markets. Variation in material remains such as pottery, ornaments, statuary, and building styles can point to ethnic differences in an ancient city.

We saw in the last chapter that people participate in various levels of culture. Groups within the same society (including ethnic groups in a nation) have different learning experiences as well as shared ones. Subcultures may originate in ethnicity, class, region, or religion. Individuals often have more than one group identity. Depending on circumstances, people may identify with their neighborhood, school, town, state or province, region, nation, continent, religion, ethnic group, gender, profession, or interest group. In a complex society like the United States or Canada, people constantly negotiate their social identities. All of us "wear different hats," presenting ourselves sometimes as one thing, sometimes as another.

In St. Louis, Missouri, on August 7, 1998, Mark McGwire, the eventual winner of the 1998 home run derby, greets his rival, Sammy Sosa.

This allegiance causes some to flinch, and fills others with pride.

In Latino neighborhoods across the country, Dominican flags are flying, and Latinos of every origin are soaping Sosa's name and uniform No. 21 onto windows. In South Florida, Cuban radio stations have been preaching that all Hispanics should support Sosa . . .

In San Diego last week, 12-year-old Armando Flores 3d went to a Padres–Cubs game to see Sosa. "I've never hit a home run, so I like to look up to Sammy and see how he does it, how he feels hitting a home run," said Flores, a Mexican-American. "My team won the district, and I'm a shortstop, and I want to be a major league player.

"I think because he is the same color of skin as me, I like that . . ."

Sometimes the racial labels are hard to keep straight. In Atlanta, with a large African-American population, Sosa is often considered a black man. In Miami and Los Angeles, with larger Hispanic populations, he is a Latino man, and the black label is rejected as robbing Hispanics of a hero.

And in all precincts, nationality is up for grabs. McGwire is often referred to as "the American," and Sosa as "the foreigner." Hardly anyone seems to know that Sosa has been an American citizen for three years.

"Personally, I pull for McGwire because he's an American," said Ethon Vivion, 27, a black man, director of health and fitness for a Boys Club in Atlanta. "Sosa's a brother, and I'm a brother. But McGwire's an American." . . .

Source: Copyright 1998 The New York Times Company, September 20, 1998. By Bill Dedman (excerpted).

In daily conversation, we hear the term "status" used as a synonym for prestige. In this context, "He's got a lot of status" means he's got a lot of prestige; people look up to him. Among social scientists, that's not the primary meaning of "status." Social scientists use *status* more neutrally—for any position, no matter what the prestige, that someone occupies in society. In this sense, **status** encompasses the various positions that people occupy in society. Parent is a social status. So are professor, student, factory worker, Democrat, shoe salesperson, homeless person, labor leader, ethnic group member, and thousands of others. People always occupy multiple statuses (e.g., Hispanic, Catholic, infant, brother). Among the statuses we occupy, particular ones dominate in particular settings, such as son or daughter at home and student in the classroom.

Some statuses are **ascribed:** People have little or no choice about occupying them. Age is an ascribed status; we can't choose not to age. Race and ethnicity are

Figure 12.1
Social Statuses

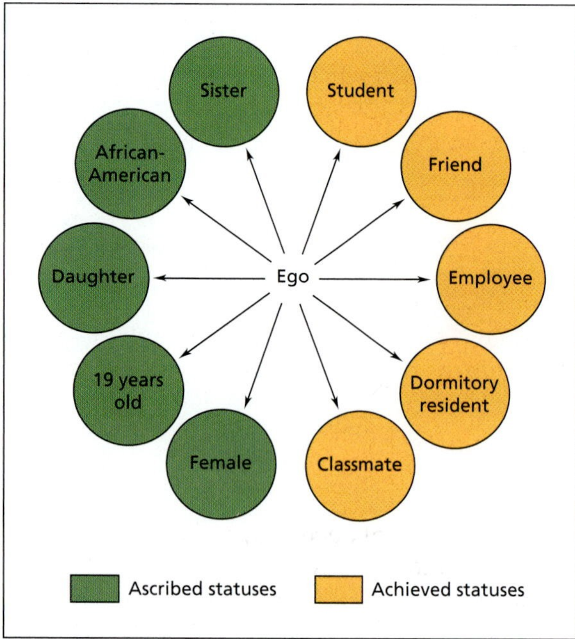

The person in this figure—"ego," or "I"—occupies many social statuses. The green circles indicate ascribed statuses; the yellow circles represent achieved statuses.

usually ascribed; people are born members of a certain group and remain so all their lives. **Achieved statuses,** by contrast, are not automatic but come through talents, choices, actions, efforts, and accomplishments (Figure 12.1). Examples of achieved statuses include physician, senator, salesperson, union member, father, and college student. Our kinship statuses are partly ascribed, partly achieved. As we'll see in the chapter "Families, Kinship, and Descent," most of us are born into a *family of orientation,* consisting of our parents and siblings. Those relatives who came before us will be our kin forever. Our relationship to them is an ascribed status. But we choose to marry or not, and to have children or not, so that our status as spouse or parent is achieved.

An ascribed status may be associated with a position in a social or political hierarchy. Certain groups, called *minority groups,* are subordinate. That means they have less power and less secure access to resources than do *majority groups* (which are superordinate or dominant). Minorities need not have fewer members than the majority group does. Women in the United States and blacks in South Africa have been numerical majorities but minorities in terms of income, authority, and power. Often, ethnic groups are minorities.

Status Shifting

Sometimes statuses, especially ascribed ones, are mutually exclusive. It's hard to bridge the gap between black and white, or male and female (although some rock stars seem to be trying to do so). Sometimes, assuming a status or joining a group requires a conversion experience. One acquires a new and meaningful identity, such as "coming out" as gay or becoming a "born again" Christian.

Some statuses are not mutually exclusive, but contextual. People can be both black and Hispanic, or both a mother and a senator. One identity is used in certain contexts or settings, another in different ones. This is called the *situational negotiation of social identity.* When ethnic identity is flexible and situational (Moerman 1965), it becomes an achieved status.

Hispanics, for example, may shift ethnic affiliations as they negotiate their identities. "Hispanic" is an ethnic category based mainly on language. It includes whites, blacks, and "racially" mixed Spanish speakers and their ethnically conscious descendants. (There are also "Native American," and even "Asian," Hispanics). "Hispanic" lumps together millions of people of diverse geographic origin. Hispanic locales include Puerto Rico, Mexico, Cuba, El Salvador, Guatemala, the Dominican Republic, and other Spanish-speaking countries of Central and South America and the Caribbean. "Latino" is a broader category, which also can include Brazilians (who speak Portuguese).

Mexican Americans (Chicanos), Cuban Americans, and Puerto Ricans may join together to promote general Hispanic issues (e.g., opposition to "English-only" laws), but act as three separate interest groups in other contexts. Cuban Americans are richer on average than Chicanos and Puerto Ricans are, and their class interests and voting patterns differ. Cubans often vote Republican. Puerto Ricans and Chicanos tend to favor Democrats. Some Mexican Americans whose families have lived in the United States for generations have little in common with new Hispanic immigrants, such as those from Central America. Many Americans (especially those who are fluent in English) claim Hispanic ethnicity in some contexts but shift to a general "American" identity in others. As discussed in the chapter "Language and Communication," bilingual people may manage an ethnic identity while also participating in a national culture.

Ethnic Groups, Nations, and Nationalities

What's the relation between an ethnic group and a nation? The term **nation** was once synonymous with "tribe" or "ethnic group"—what today we would call a culture. All these terms have been used to refer to a single culture sharing a single language, religion, history, territory, ancestry, and kinship. Thus, one could speak interchangeably of the Seneca (American Indian) nation, tribe, ethnic group, or culture. Now, in our everyday language, *nation* has come to mean a **state**—an independent, centrally organized political unit—a government. *Nation* and *state* have become synonymous. Combined in **nation-state,** they refer to an autonomous political entity, a "country"—like the United States, "one nation, indivisible."

Because of migration, conquest, and colonialism (see below), most nation-states are not ethnically homogeneous. Of 132 nation-states existing in 1971, Connor (1972) found only 12 (9 percent) to be ethnically homogeneous. In another 25 countries (19 percent), a single ethnic group accounted for more than 90 percent of the population. Forty percent of the countries had more than five significant ethnic groups. In a later study, Nielsson (1985) found that in only 45 of 164 states (27 percent) did a single ethnic group have more than 95 percent of the population.

Nationalities and Imagined Communities

Ethnic groups that once had, or that wish to have or regain, autonomous political status (their own country) are called **nationalities.** In the words of Benedict Anderson (1991), nationalities are "imagined communities." They can only imagine they all participate in the same group. Even when they become nation-states, they remain imagined communities, because most of their members, though feeling strong comradeship, will never meet (Anderson 1991, pp. 6–10).

Anderson traces Western European nationalism, which arose in imperial powers like England, France, and Spain, back to the 18th century. He stresses that language and print played a crucial role in the growth of European national consciousness. (See "Interesting Issues" on pages 296–297 for a modern illustration.) The novel and the newspaper were "two forms of imagining" communities that flowered in the 18th century (Anderson 1991, pp. 24–25). Such communities consisted of people who read the same sources and thus witnessed the same events.

World War I split the Kurds, who form a majority in no state. They are a minority group in Turkey, Iran, Iraq, and Syria. This is an April 1991 photo of a Kurdish woman and baby near the Iran/Iraq border. There was an exodus of Kurd refugees from Iraq during the Gulf War.

Making a similar point, Terry Eagleton (1983, p. 25) describes the role of the novel in promoting English national consciousness and identity. The

Ethnic Nationalism Runs Wild

The Socialist Federal Republic of Yugoslavia was a nonaligned country outside the former Soviet Union (U.S.S.R.). Like the U.S.S.R., Yugoslavia fell apart, mainly along ethnic and religious lines, in the early 1990s. Among Yugoslavia's ethnic groups were Roman Catholic Croats, Eastern Orthodox Serbs, Muslim Slavs, and ethnic Albanians. Citing ethnic and religious differences, several republics broke away from Yugoslavia in 1991–92. These included Slovenia, Croatia, and Bosnia-Herzegovina (see Figure 12.2). Serbia and Montenegro are the two remaining republics within Yugoslavia. In Kosovo, which is a province in Serbia, but whose population is 90 percent ethnic Albanian, there has been a strong movement for independence, led by the Kosovo Liberation Army.

Much of the ethnic differentiation in Yugoslavia has been based on religion, culture, political and military history, and some differences involving language. Serbo-Croatian is a Slavic language spoken, with dialect variation, by Serbs, Croats, and Muslim Slavs alike. (Albanian is a separate language.) Croats and Serbs use different alphabets. The Croats have adopted our Roman alphabet, but the Serbs use the Cyrillic alphabet, which they share with Russia and Bulgaria. The two alphabets help promote ethnic differentiation and nationalism. Serbs and Croats, who share speech, are divided by writing—by literature, newsprint, and political manifestos.

The Yugoslav Serbs reacted violently—with military intervention—after a 1992 vote for the independence of Muslim-led Bosnia-Herzegovina, whose population is one-third Serbian. In Bosnia, the Serbs initiated a policy of forced expulsion—"ethnic purification"—against Croats, but mainly against Muslim Slavs. Serbs in Yugoslavia, who controlled the National Army, lent their support to the Bosnian Serbs in their "ethnic-cleansing" campaign.

Backed by the Yugoslav army, Bosnian Serb militias rounded up Bosnian Muslims, killed groups of them, and burned and looted their homes. Thousands of Slavs fled. Hundreds of thousands of Muslims became involuntary refugees in tent camps, school gyms, and parks.

The Serbs had no use for the ethnic coexistence that the previous Yugoslav socialist government

Figure 12.2

Former Yugoslavia, with Province and Republics

The former Yugoslavia, although a socialist nation, was a nonaligned country outside the former Soviet Union. Like the U.S.S.R., Yugoslavia disintegrated in the early 1990s. The breakaway portions included Slovenia, Croatia, and Bosnia-Herzegovina.

In 1999 thousands of refugees returned to a ravaged Kosovo. On June 16, 1999, Zeline Mucolli (right), accompanied by her aunt, returned to discover her ruined home, where her family was killed.

had encouraged. The Serbs also wished to avenge historic affronts by Muslims and Croats. In the 15th century, Muslim Turks had overthrown a Serbian ruler, persecuted the Serbs, and—eventually—converted many local people to Islam during their centuries of rule in this area. Bosnian Serbs still resent Muslims—including the descendants of the converts—for the Turkish conquest.

Bosnian Serbs claimed to be fighting to resist the Muslim-dominated government of Bosnia-Herzegovina. They feared that a policy of Islamic fundamentalism might arise and threaten the Serbian Orthodox Church and other expressions of Serbian identity. The Serbs' goal was to carve up Bosnia along ethnic lines, and they wanted two-thirds of it for themselves. A stated aim of Bosnia's ethnic purification was to ensure that the Serbs would never again be dominated by another ethnic group (Burns 1992*a*).

Although the Croats and the Muslim Slavs also carried out forced deportations in other parts of the former Yugoslavia, the Serbian campaign in Bosnia was the widest and the most systematic. More than 200,000 people were killed during the Bosnian conflict (Cohen 1995). With Bosnia's capital, the multiethnic city of Sarajevo, under siege, the conflict was suspended following a December 1995 peace settlement signed in Dayton, Ohio.

In spring 1999 NATO began a 78-day bombing campaign against Yugoslavia in retaliation for Serbian atrocities against ethnic Albanians in the separatist province of Kosovo. In May 1999 then Yugoslav President Slobodan Milosevic was indicted for abuses against the Kosovar Albanian population by the war crimes tribunal in The Hague, Netherlands. By June 1999, accords ending 78 days of NATO bombing placed Kosovo under international control, enforced by NATO peacekeepers, who remian there as of this writing (January 2001). In the year 2000 Yugoslavia itself took several steps toward democracy. In September 2000, Milosevic was voted out of office and replaced by a new president, Vajislav Kostinica. Parliamentary elections in December 2000 removed the last vestiges of power that Milosevic had built up during the previous decade.

How can we explain Yugoslavia's ethnic conflict? According to Fredrik Barth (see pages 299–300), ethnic differences are most secure and enduring where the groups occupy different ecological niches: They make their living in different ways or places, don't compete, and are mutually dependent. In Bosnia, the Serbs, the Croats, and the Muslim Slavs were more mixed than in any other former Yugoslav republic (Burns 1992*b*). Is it possible that the boundaries among the three groups were not sharp enough to keep them together by keeping them apart?

novel gave the English "a pride in their national language and literature; if scanty education and extensive hours of labor prevented them personally from producing a literary masterpiece, they could take pleasure in the thought that others of their kind—English people—had done so."

German, Italian, Japanese, Middle Eastern, and Eastern European immigrants have assimilated, culturally and linguistically, to a common Brazilian culture. Here, a Japanese-Brazilian woman reminds her grandson of his heritage by teaching him Japanese script. Does this photo suggest assimilation or multiculturalism?

Over time, political upheavals and wars have divided many imagined national communities. The German and Korean homelands were artificially divided after wars, and according to socialist and capitalist ideologies. World War I split the Kurds, who remain only an imagined community. Kurds form a majority in no state. They are a minority group in Turkey, Iran, Iraq, and Syria. Similarly, Azerbaijanis, who are related to Turks, were a minority in the former Soviet Union, as they still are in Iran. Twentieth century Jews imagined the modern nation of Israel long before its creation.

Migration is another reason certain ethnic groups live in different nation-states. Massive migration in the decades before and after 1900 brought Germans, Poles, and Italians to Brazil, Canada, and the United States. Chinese, Senegalese, Lebanese, and Jews have spread all over the world. Some such people (e.g., descendants of Germans in Brazil and the United States) have assimilated to their host nations and no longer feel part of the imagined community of their origin. Such dispersed populations, which have spread out, voluntarily or not, from a common center or homeland, are called *diasporas.* The African diaspora, for example, encompasses descendants of Africans worldwide, such as in the United States, the Caribbean, and Brazil.

In creating multiethnic states, former colonial powers such as France and England often erected boundaries that corresponded poorly with preexisting cultural divisions. **Colonialism** refers to the political, social, economic, and cultural domination of a territory and its people by a foreign power for an extended time. Often, the colonial powers followed a "divide and rule" policy. They split up an ethnic group between colonies to dilute its strength in numbers. Or they stirred up rivalries among different ethnic groups in the same colony so as to strengthen allegiance to the colonial power. Still, interethnic contacts fostered by colonial institutions also helped create new "imagined communities" beyond nations. One example is the idea of ***négritude*** ("black association and identity"). This concept was developed by dark-skinned intellectuals from the Francophone (French-speaking) colonies of West Africa and the Caribbean.

Peaceful Coexistence

Ethnic diversity may be associated with positive group interaction and coexistence or with conflict—which is discussed in the next section. In many nations, multiple cultural groups live together in reasonable harmony. Three ways of realizing such peaceful coexistence are assimilation, the plural society, and multiculturalism.

Assimilation

Assimilation describes the process of change that a minority ethnic group may experience when it moves to a country where another cul-

Table 12.2
Selected Ethnic Origins—Canada, Quebec, and Ontario, 1991

	Canada	Quebec	Ontario
Total population	26,994,045	6,810,300	9,977,050
Single origins	19,199,790	6,237,905	6,698,995
French	6,129,680	5,068,450	527,005
English	3,958,405	159,260	1,813,105
German	911,560	31,345	289,420
Scottish	893,125	42,910	390,285
Canadian	765,095	20,025	525,240
Italian	750,055	74,530	486,765
Irish	725,660	82,790	318,700
Chinese	586,645	36,820	273,870
Ukranian	406,645	11,450	104,995
North American Indian	365,375	49,880	65,710
Dutch	358,180	7,100	179,760
East Indian, not included elsewhere	324,840	17,460	172,960
Polish	272,810	23,695	154,155
Portuguese	246,890	37,165	176,300
Jewish	245,840	77,600	132,110
Black	214,265	39,065	144,720
Filipino	157,250	9,920	78,550
Greek	151,150	49,890	83,780
Hungarian	100,725	8,990	53,055
Vietnamese	84,005	19,980	34,335
Metis	75,150	8,670	4,680
Inuit	30,085	6,850	620
Other single origins	1,446,355	254,060	688,875
Multiple origins	7,794,250	572,395	3,278,055

Source: *Statistics Canada,* Catalog no. 93–315. http://www.statcan.ca/English/Pgdb/People/Population/demo28b.htm.

ture dominates. By assimilating, the minority adopts the patterns and norms of its host culture. It is incorporated into the dominant culture to the point that it no longer exists as a separate cultural unit. This is the "melting pot" model; ethnic groups give up their own cultural traditions as they blend into a common national stew. Some countries, such as Brazil, are more assimilationist than others are. Germans, Italians, Japanese, Middle Easterners, and East Europeans started migrating to Brazil late in the 19th century. These immigrants have assimilated to a common Brazilian culture, which has Portuguese, African, and Native American roots. The descendants of these immigrants speak the national language (Portuguese) and participate in national culture. (During World War II, Brazil, which was on the Allied side, forced assimilation by banning instruction in any language other than Portuguese—especially in German.)

Brazil has been more of a melting pot than have the United States and Canada, in which ethnic groups retain more distinctiveness and self-identity (see Table 12.2). I remember my first visit to the southern Brazilian city of Porto Alegre, the site of mass migration by Germans, Poles, and Italians. Transferring an expectation derived from my North American culture to Porto Alegre, I asked my tour guide to show me his city's ethnic neighborhoods. He couldn't understand what I was talking about. Except for a Japanese-Brazilian neighborhood in the city of São Paulo, the idea of an ethnic neighborhood is alien to Brazil.

The Plural Society

Assimilation isn't inevitable, and there can be ethnic harmony without it. Ethnic distinctions can be maintained, rather than assimilated, despite decades, or even generations, of interethnic contact. Through a study of three ethnic groups in Swat, Pakistan, Fredrik Barth (1958/1968) challenged an old idea that interaction always leads to assimilation. He showed that

In the United States and Canada, multiculturalism is of growing importance. Especially in large cities like Toronto (shown here), people of diverse backgrounds attend ethnic fairs and festivals and feast on ethnic foods. What are some other expressions of multiculturalism in your society?

ethnic groups can be in contact for generations without assimilating and that they can live in peaceful coexistence.

Barth (1958/1968, p. 324) defines **plural society** as a society combining ethnic contrasts, ecological specialization (that is, use of different environmental resources by each ethnic group), and the economic interdependence of those groups. Consider his description of the Middle East (in the 1950s): "The 'environment' of any one ethnic group is not only defined by natural conditions, but also by the presence and activities of the other ethnic groups on which it depends. Each group exploits only part of the total environment, and leaves large parts of it open for other groups to exploit."

In Barth's view, ethnic boundaries are most stable and enduring when the groups occupy different ecological niches. That is, they make their living in different ways and don't compete. Ideally, they should depend on each other's activities and exchange with one another. Under such conditions, ethnic diversity can be maintained, although the specific cultural features of each group may change. By shifting the analytic focus from specific cultural practices and values to the *relations* between ethnic groups, Barth (1958/1968 and 1969) has made important contributions to ethnic studies.

Multiculturalism

Multiculturalism views cultural diversity in a country as something desirable and to be encouraged. The multicultural model contrasts sharply with the assimilationist model, in which minorities are expected to abandon their traditions, replacing them with those of the majority population. Multiculturalism encourages the practice of many ethnic traditions. A multicultural society socializes individuals not only into the dominant (national) culture but also into an ethnic culture. Thus, in the United States, millions of people speak both English and another language. They eat both "American" foods (apple pie, steak, hamburgers) and "ethnic" cuisine (e.g., Chinese, Cambodian, Armenian). They celebrate both national (July 4, Thanksgiving) and ethnic-religious holidays. And they study both national and ethnic group histories. Multiculturalism works best in a society whose political system promotes free expression and in which there are many and diverse ethnic groups.

Figure 12.3
Ethic Composition of the United States

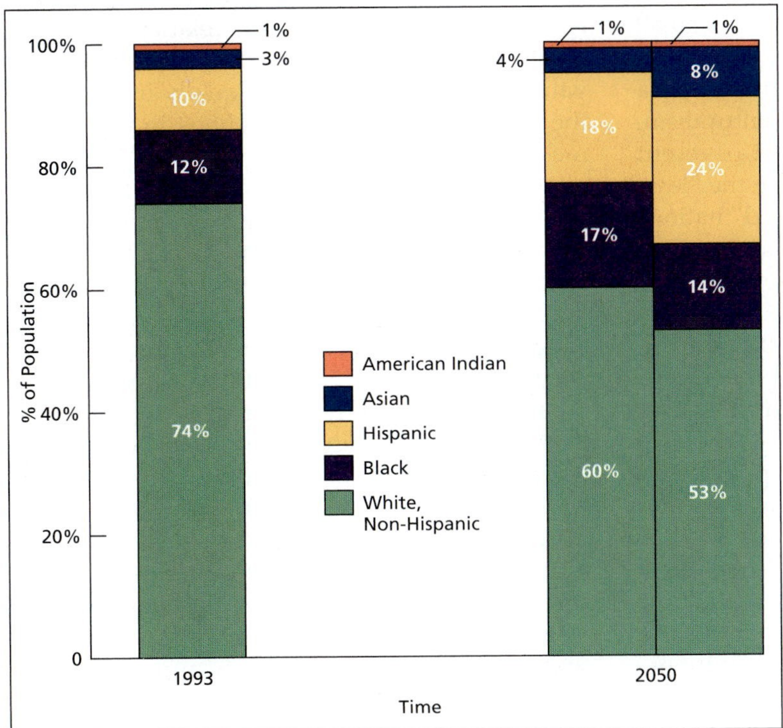

Source: Martin and Midgley 1994, p. 9.

The proportion of the American population that is white and non-Hispanic is declining. Consider two projections of the ethnic composition of the United States in AD 2050. The first assumes an annual immigration rate of zero; the second assumes continuation of the current level of immigration—about 880,000 immigrants per year. With either projection, the non-Hispanic white proportion of the population declines dramatically.

In the United States and Canada, multiculturalism is of growing importance. This reflects awareness that the number and size of ethnic groups have grown dramatically in recent years. If this trend continues, the ethnic composition of the United States will change dramatically. See Figure 12.3.

Because of immigration and differential population growth, whites are now outnumbered by minorities in many urban areas. For example, of the 8,008,278 residents of New York City in 2000, 27 percent were black, 27 percent Hispanic, 10 percent Asian, and 36 percent other—including non-Hispanic whites. The comparable figures for Los Angeles (3,694,820 people) were 11 percent black, 47 percent Hispanic, 9 percent Asian, and 33 percent other—including non-Hispanic whites (Census 2000, www.census.gov).

One response to ethnic diversity and awareness has been for whites to claim or reclaim ethnic identities (Italian, Albanian, Serbian, Lithuanian, etc.) and to join ethnic associations (clubs, gangs). Some such groups are new. Others have existed for decades, although they lost members during the assimilationist years of the 1920s through the 1950s. Even "whiteness" has entered the domain of ethnicity. Today's political and academic environments include particular ethnic movements and studies, such as the Latino movement and Latino studies. In this context, there has emerged an increasing debate—as yet far from resolved—about what it means to be white. Relevant questions include: What kinds of people are considered white today versus a century ago? What kind of identity is conferred by the simple label "white"? What is the range of variation among people who are classified as "white"? How is the label related to cultural practices?

Multiculturalism seeks ways for people to understand and interact that don't depend on sameness but on respect for diversity. Multiculturalism assumes that each group has something to offer and to learn from the others. We see evidence of multiculturalism all around us. Seated near you in the classroom (perhaps in your chair!) are students whose parents were born in other countries. Islamic mosques have joined synagogues and churches in American cities. To help in exam scheduling, colleges inform professors about the main holidays of many religions. You can attend ethnic fairs and festivals, watch ethnically costumed dancers on TV, eat ethnic foods, and buy such foods at your supermarket. Some foods (e.g., bagels, pasta, tacos) have become so familiar that their ethnic origin has faded from our memories. (From the perspective of other countries, the United States has its own ethnic foods. Hamburgers, hot dogs, fried chicken, and apple pies are foods that are considered typical of American meals. These have been diffused widely by international chains such as McDonald's, Burger

King, and KFC.) Popular shrines celebrate the union of ethnic diversity and globalization: At Disneyland and Walt Disney World, a chorus of ethnically costumed dolls drone on that "it's a small world after all."

Several forces have propelled North America away from assimilation toward multiculturalism. First, multiculturalism reflects the fact of recent large-scale migration, particularly from the "less-developed countries" to the "developed" nations of North America and Western Europe. The global scale of modern migration introduces unparalleled ethnic variety to host nations. People use modern means of transportation to migrate to nations whose life styles they learn about through the media and from tourists who increasingly visit their countries.

Migration also is fueled by rapid population growth, coupled with insufficient jobs, in the less-developed countries. As traditional rural economies decline or mechanize, displaced farmers move to cities, where they and their children are often unable to find jobs. As people in the less-developed countries get better educations, they seek more skilled employment. They hope to partake in an international culture of consumption that includes such modern amenities as refrigerators, televisions, and automobiles.

Contrary to popular belief, many of the people who migrate to the United States or to Canada are not poor and unskilled but middle-class and fairly well educated. Educated people migrate for several reasons. Often they can't find jobs to match their skills in their countries of origin (Grasmuck and Pessar 1991; Margolis 1994). Also, they are knowledgeable enough to deal with international rules and regulations. Arriving in North America or Western Europe, immigrants find themselves in democracies whose citizens are allowed, even encouraged, to organize for a "fair share" of resources, political influence, and cultural respect. Educated immigrants often become political organizers and particularly effective advocates of multiculturalism.

Often, people claim and express ethnic identities for political and economic reasons. Michel Laguerre's (1984) study of Haitian immigrants in New York City shows that they mobilize to deal with discrimination against black people, such as themselves, in American society. Ethnicity (their common Haitian Creole language and cultural background) is an evident basis for their mobilization. Haitian ethnicity then helps distinguish them from African-Americans and other ethnic groups who may be competing for the same resources. In studying ethnic relations, it is not enough to look just at the cultural practices and values of the ethnic group. Equally important is the political and economic context in which ethnic diversity exists.

Much of the world is experiencing an "ethnic revival." A new assertiveness by long-resident ethnic groups is seen among the Basques and Catalans in Spain, the Bretons and Corsicans in France, and the Welsh and Scots in the United Kingdom. The United States and Canada have become increasingly multicultural, focusing on their internal diversity. "Melting pots" no longer, they are better described as ethnic "salads" (each ingredient remains distinct, although in the same bowl, with the same dressing).

A document of the University of Michigan Program in American Culture offers a good exposition of the multicultural model. It recognizes "the multiplicity of American cultures." It presents multiculturalism as a new approach to the central question in American studies: What does it mean to be an American? The document suggests a shift from the study of core myths and values (see the appendix), and people's relationships to them as generalized Americans, to "recognizing that 'America' includes people of differing community, ethnic, and cultural histories, different points of view and degrees of empowerment." Such a perspective spurs studies of specific ethnic groups rather than the country as a whole (Internal Review document of the Program in American Culture of the University of Michigan—March 12, 1992).

Roots of Ethnic Conflict

Ethnicity can be expressed in peaceful multiculturalism, or in discrimination or violent interethnic confrontation. Culture is both adaptive and maladaptive (see the last chapter). The perception of cultural differences can have disastrous effects on social interaction. The roots of ethnic conflict can be political, economic, religious, linguistic, cultural, or "racial." Why do ethnic differences often lead to conflict and violence? The causes include a sense of injustice

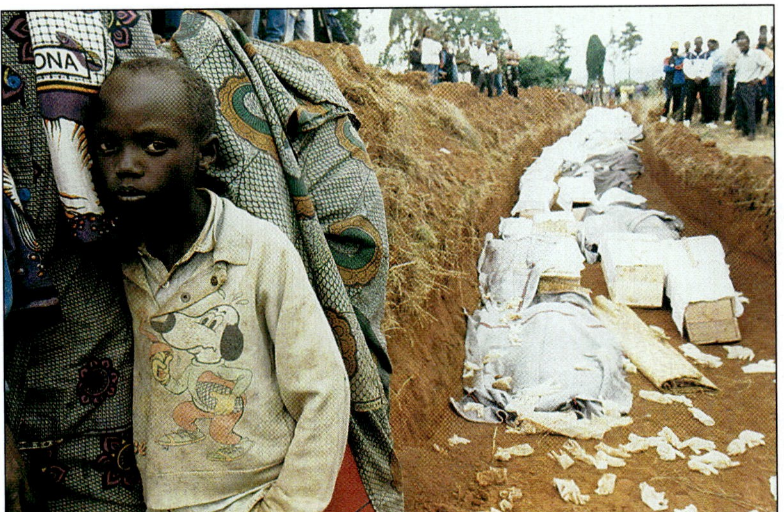

Genocide is the deliberate elimination of a group through mass murder. In Burundi, on July 20, 1996, 312 Tutsi living in a refugee camp at Bugendana were murdered by Hutu rebels. Here the victims are buried at that camp.

because of resource distribution, economic or political competition, and reaction to prejudice or discrimination (Ryan 1990, p. xxvii).

Prejudice and Discrimination

Ethnic conflict may arise in the context of prejudice (attitudes and judgments) and/or discrimination (action). **Prejudice** means devaluing (looking down on) a group because of its assumed behavior, values, abilities, or attributes. People are prejudiced when they hold stereotypes about groups and apply them to individuals. (*Stereotypes* are fixed ideas—often unfavorable—about what the members of a group are like.) Prejudiced people assume that members of the group will act as they are "supposed to act," according to the stereotype. They interpret a wide range of individual behaviors as evidence of the stereotype. They use this behavior to confirm their stereotype (and low opinion) of the group.

Discrimination refers to policies and practices that harm a group and its members. Discrimination may be *de facto* (practiced, but not legally sanctioned) or *de jure* (part of the law). An example of *de facto* discrimination is the harsher treatment that American minorities tend to get from the police and the judicial system. Such unequal treatment isn't legal, but it happens anyway. Segregation in the southern United States and *apartheid* in South Africa provide two examples of *de jure* discrimination, which are no longer in existence. In the United States, *de jure* segregation has been illegal since the 1960s. The South African *apartheid* system was abandoned in 1991. In both systems, by law, blacks and whites had different rights and privileges. Their social interaction ("mixing") was legally curtailed. Slavery is the most extreme form of legalized inequality; people are treated as property.

We also can distinguish between attitudinal and institutional discrimination. With *attitudinal discrimination*, people discriminate against members of a group because they are prejudiced against that group. For example, in the United States, members of the Ku Klux Klan have expressed their prejudice against blacks, Jews, and Catholics through verbal, physical, and psychological harassment.

The most extreme form of ethnic discrimination is genocide, the deliberate elimination of a group through mass murder. The United Nations defines

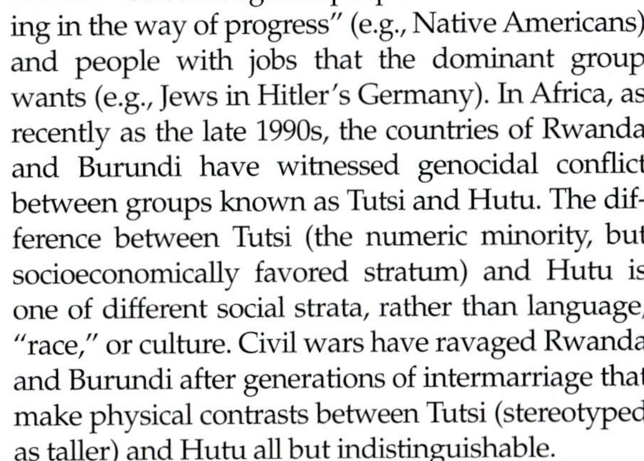

genocide as acts "committed with intent to destroy, in whole or in part, a national, ethnical, racial, or religious group, as such" (Ryan 1990, p. 11). Genocide has been directed against people viewed as "standing in the way of progress" (e.g., Native Americans) and people with jobs that the dominant group wants (e.g., Jews in Hitler's Germany). In Africa, as recently as the late 1990s, the countries of Rwanda and Burundi have witnessed genocidal conflict between groups known as Tutsi and Hutu. The difference between Tutsi (the numeric minority, but socioeconomically favored stratum) and Hutu is one of different social strata, rather than language, "race," or culture. Civil wars have ravaged Rwanda and Burundi after generations of intermarriage that make physical contrasts between Tutsi (stereotyped as taller) and Hutu all but indistinguishable.

Institutional discrimination refers to laws, policies, and arrangements that deny equal rights to, or differentially harm, members of particular groups. Historical examples, already mentioned, include South African *apartheid* and segregationist

"Environmental racism" refers to policy decisions that locate a disproportionate share of environmental hazards in minority communities. Here in Norco, Louisiana, neighborhood residents play basketball at a park across from a Shell oil refinery. Why, in your opinion, do poor neighborhoods have a higher concentration of hazards than richer ones do?

policies in the American South. Both those forms of institutional discrimination treated blacks as lesser citizens with fewer rights and protection under the law than whites enjoyed. Another, less formal, example of institutional discrimination is what Bunyan Bryant and Paul Mohai (1991, p. 4) call *environmental racism:* "the systematic use of institutionally based power . . . to formulate policy decisions that will lead to the disproportionate burden of environmental hazards in minority communities." Thus, toxic waste dumps tend to be located in areas with nonwhite populations.

Environmental racism is discriminatory but not always intentional. Sometimes, toxic wastes *are* deliberately dumped in areas whose residents are considered unlikely to protest because they are poor, "disorganized," or "uneducated." In other cases, property values fall after toxic waste sites are located in an area. The wealthier people move out. Poorer people, often minorities, move in, to suffer the consequences of living in a hazardous environment.

Chips in the Multicultural Mosaic

Although multiculturalism is increasingly prominent in North America, ethnic competition and conflict also are evident. Enmity may develop between new arrivals, such as Central Americans and Koreans, and long-established ethnic groups, such as African-Americans. Ethnic antagonism flared in South-Central Los Angeles in spring 1992. Rioting followed the acquittal of four white police officers who had been tried for the videotaped beating of an African-American motorist, Rodney King.

Angry blacks attacked whites, Koreans, and Hispanics. This violence expressed the frustration of African-Americans about their prospects in an increasingly multicultural society. A *New York Times*/CBS News poll conducted just after the Los Angeles riots found that blacks had a bleaker outlook than whites did about the effects of immigration on their lives. Only 23 percent of the blacks felt they had more opportunities than recent immigrants, compared with twice that many whites (Toner 1992).

South-Central Los Angeles, where the 1992 rioting took place, is an ethnically mixed area. It used to be mainly African-American. As blacks have moved out, there has been an influx of

A policy of expulsion may create refugees—people who have been forced (involuntary refugees) or who have chosen (voluntary refugees) to flee a country to escape persecution or war. In this 1996 photo, some 350,000 Hutu refugees return to Rwanda from Congo (then Zaire).

Mexicans and Central Americans. The Hispanic population of South-Central Los Angeles increased by 119 percent in a decade, while the number of blacks there declined by 17 percent. By 1992, the neighborhood had become 45 percent Hispanic and 48 percent black. Also, many store owners in South-Central Los Angeles are Korean immigrants (see Abelmann and Lie 1995).

Korean stores were hard hit during the 1992 riots, and more than a third of the businesses destroyed were Hispanic-owned. A third of those who died in the riots were Hispanics. These mainly recent migrants lacked deep roots to the neighborhood and, as Spanish speakers, faced language barriers (Newman 1992). Many Koreans also had trouble with English.

Koreans interviewed on ABC's *Nightline* on May 6, 1992, recognized that blacks resented them and considered them unfriendly. One man explained, "It's not part of our culture to smile." African-Americans interviewed for the same program complained about Korean unfriendliness. "They come into our neighborhoods and treat us like dirt." These comments suggest a shortcoming of the multicultural perspective: Ethnic groups (blacks here) expect other ethnic groups in the same nation to assimilate to some extent to a shared (national) culture. The African-Americans' comments invoked a general American value system that includes friendliness, openness, mutual respect, community participation, and "fair play." Los Angeles blacks wanted their Korean neighbors to act more like generalized Americans, and good neighbors.

One way in which Koreans in cities like New York and Los Angeles have succeeded economically is through family enterprise. Family members work together in small grocery stores, like those in South-Central Los Angeles. They pool their labor and their wealth. In our high-tech society, good jobs demand education beyond high school. Korean "family values" and support systems encourage children to study and work hard, with eventual careers in mind. These values also fit certain general American ideals. Work, achievement, and the need to save for a college education were American values that the Korean-Americans being interviewed invoked to explain their practice of using family labor, rather than hiring people from the neighborhood. The Koreans said they couldn't succeed financially if they had to hire nonrelatives. (Family solidarity is also a general American value, but the specific meaning of "family" varies between groups.) Note that both African-Americans and Korean-Americans appealed to a national set of values as they discussed reasons for their behavior and attitude toward other groups.

Aftermaths of Oppression

Among the factors that fuel ethnic conflict are forced assimilation, ethnocide, and cultural colonialism. A dominant group may try to destroy the cultures of certain ethnic groups (*ethnocide*) or force them to adopt the dominant culture (*forced assimilation*). Many countries have penalized or banned the language and customs of an ethnic group (including its religious observances). One example of forced assimilation is the anti-Basque campaign that the dictator Francisco Franco (who ruled between 1939 and 1975) waged in Spain. Franco banned Basque books, journals, newspapers, signs, sermons, and tombstones. He imposed fines for using the Basque language in schools. His policies led to the formation of a Basque terrorist group and spurred strong nationalist sentiment in the Basque region (Ryan 1995).

A policy of ethnic expulsion aims at removing groups who are culturally different from a country. Recent examples include Bosnia-Herzegovina and Kosovo in the 1990s (see "Interesting Issues," pages 296–297). Uganda expelled 74,000 Asians in 1972. The neofascist parties of contemporary Western Europe advocate repatriation (expulsion) of immigrant workers (West Indians in England, Algerians in France, and Turks in Germany) (Ryan 1995). A policy of expulsion may create *refugees*—people who have been forced (involuntary refugees) or who have chosen (voluntary refugees) to flee a country, to escape persecution or war.

Colonialism, another form of oppression, is the domination of a territory and its people by a foreign power for an extended time (Bell 1981). The British and French colonial empires are familiar examples of colonialism. The United States has been like a colonial power with respect to Native Americans. We also can extend the term to the former Soviet empire, formerly known as "the Second World."

Using the labels "First World," "Second World," and "Third World" is a common, although clearly ethnocentric, way of categorizing nations. The *First World* refers to the "democratic West"—traditionally conceived in opposition to a "Second World" ruled by "communism." The First World includes Canada, the United States, Western Europe, Japan, Australia, and New Zealand. The *Second World* refers to the Warsaw Pact nations, including the former Soviet Union and the Socialist and once-Socialist countries of Eastern Europe and Asia. Proceeding with this classification, the "less-developed countries" or "developing nations" make up the *Third World.* See Figure 12.4.

Figure 12.4
"First," "Second," and "Third" Worlds

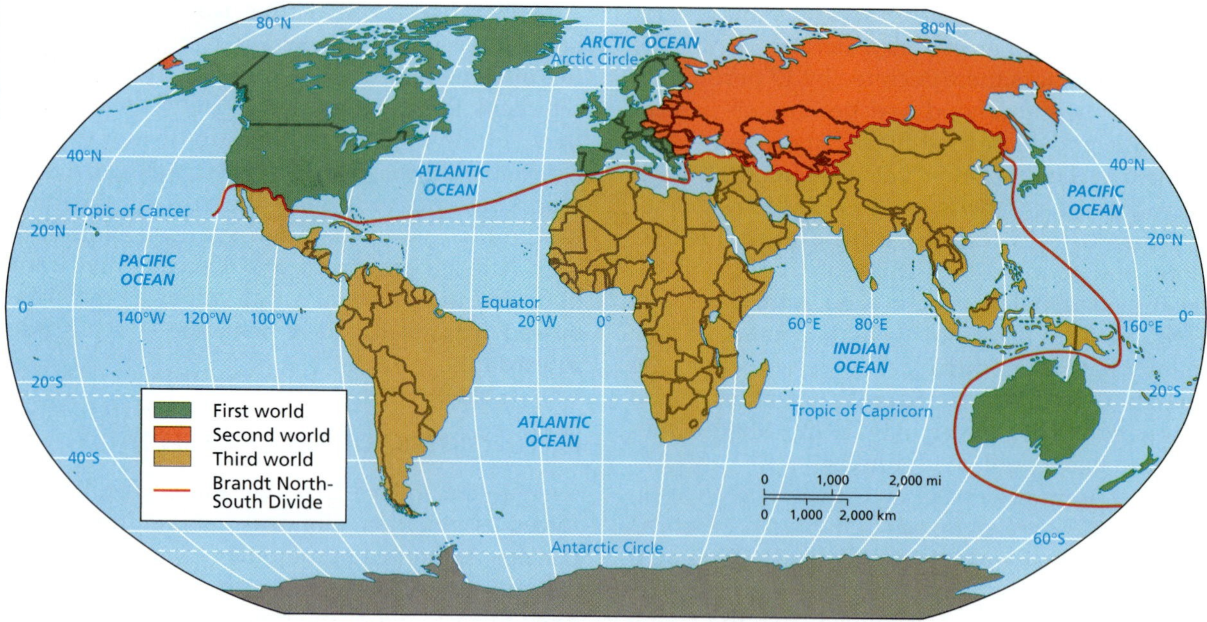

Use of "First World," "Second World," and "Third World" is a common, albeit ethnocentric, way of categorizing nations. "First World" refers to the "democratic West"—traditionally conceived in opposition to a "Second World" ruled by "communism." The "less-developed countries" or "developing nations" make up the "Third World." Another way of viewing the world in terms of differential economic and political influence is the Brandt North–South divide. This division classifies Australia and New Zealand as northern nations even though they are in the southern hemisphere. The map shows both divisions.

An example of cultural colonialism was the domination of the former Soviet empire by Russian people, language, and culture. Ethnic minorities had very limited self-rule in republics and regions controlled by Moscow. These Siberian children are trained to be model Soviet (Russian) citizens. Can you think of examples of cultural colonialism in your own country?

The frontiers imposed by colonialism were not usually based on, and often didn't reflect, preexisting cultural units. In many countries, colonial nation-building left ethnic strife in its wake. Thus, over a million Hindus and Moslems were killed in the violence that accompanied the division of the Indian subcontinent into India and Pakistan. Problems between Arabs and Jews in Palestine began during the British mandate period, before the creation of the independent state of Israel. Ethnic conflicts in the less-developed countries have proliferated since the early 1960s, when decolonization (the end of colonialism and the rise of independence) reached its height. There have been bitter ethnic conflicts in Congo, Nigeria, Bangladesh, Sudan, India, Sri Lanka, Ethiopia, Uganda, Lebanon, and Cyprus. Many of these remain unresolved.

Multiculturalism may be growing in the United States and Canada, but the opposite is happening in the disintegrating Second World, where ethnic groups (nationalities) want their own nation-states. The rise of ethnic feeling and conflict as the Soviet empire disintegrated illustrates that years of political repression and ideology provide insufficient "common ground" for lasting unity.

Cultural colonialism refers to internal domination—by one group and its culture/ideology over others. One example is the domination over the former Soviet empire by Russian people, language, and culture, and by socialist ideology. The dominant culture makes itself the official culture. This is reflected in schools, the media, and public interaction. Under Soviet rule, ethnic minorities had limited self-rule in republics and regions controlled by Moscow. All the republics and their peoples were to be united by the oneness of "socialist internationalism."

One common technique in cultural colonialism is to flood ethnic areas with members of the dominant ethnic group. Thus, in the former Soviet Union, ethnic Russian colonists were sent to many areas, such as Tajikistan (see Figure 12.5), to diminish the cohesion and clout of the local people. Tajikistan is a small, poor state (and former Soviet republic) in central Asia, near Afghanistan, with 5.1 million people. In Tajikistan, as in central Asia generally, most people are Muslims. Today, Islam, as an alternative way of ordering spiritual and social life, is replacing socialist ideology. This comes after more than 70 years of official atheism and suppression of religion. The Soviets destroyed mosques and discouraged religious practice by

Figure 12.5
Former Soviet Socialist Republics of Central Asia, Including Tajikistan

the young, while allowing it for old people. Still, Islam was taught at home, around the kitchen table, so it has been called "kitchen Islam."

Now, as the Russians leave Tajikistan, the force of Russian culture and language is receding. Islamic influence is growing. Women have started covering their arms, legs, and hair. More and more people speak and pray in Tajik, a language related to Persian (which is spoken in Iran) (Erlanger 1992).

"The Commonwealth of Independent States" is all that remains of the former Soviet Union. In this group of new nations, ethnic groups (nationalities) like the Tajiks and Chechens are seeking to establish separate and viable nation-states based on cultural boundaries. This celebration of ethnic autonomy is a reaction to the Soviet Union's decades of suppressing diversity: historic, national, linguistic, ethnic, cultural, and religious. It is part of an ethnic florescence that—as surely as globalization—is a trend at the new millennium.

summary

1. An "ethnic group" refers to a particular culture in a nation or region that contains others. Ethnicity is based on cultural similarities (among members of the same ethnic group) and differences (between that group and others). Ethnic distinctions can be based on language, religion, history, geography, kinship, or "race." A race is an ethnic group assumed to have a biological basis. Usually race and ethnicity are ascribed statuses; people are born members of a group and remain so all their lives.

2. The term *nation* was once synonymous with "ethnic group." Now *nation* has come to mean a state—a centrally organized political unit. *Nation* and *state* have become synonymous. Combined in *nation-state,* they refer to such a political entity, a "country." Because of migration, conquest, and colonialism, most nation-states are not ethnically homogeneous. Ethnic diversity may be associated with harmony or conflict. In creating multitribal and multiethnic states, colonial regimes often erected boundaries that corresponded poorly with preexisting cultural divisions. Ethnic groups that seek autonomous political status (their own country) are *nationalities.* Political upheavals, wars, and migrations have divided many imagined national communities.

3. *Assimilation* describes the process of change an ethnic group may experience when it moves to a country where another culture dominates. By assimilating, the minority adopts the patterns and norms of its host culture. Assimilation isn't inevitable, and there can be ethnic harmony without it. A plural society combines ethnic contrasts and economic interdependence between ethnic groups. The view of cultural diversity in a nation-state as good and desirable is multiculturalism. A multicultural society socializes individuals not only into the dominant (national) culture but also into an ethnic one.

4. Ethnicity can be expressed in peaceful multiculturalism, or in discrimination or violent confrontation. Ethnic conflict often arises in reaction to prejudice (attitudes and judgments) or discrimination (action). *Prejudice* means devaluing (looking down on) a group because of its assumed attributes. *Discrimination* refers to policies that harm a group and its members. Discrimination may be *de facto* (practiced, but not legally sanctioned or *de jure* (part of the law). The most extreme form of anti-ethnic discrimination is genocide, the deliberate elimination of a group through mass murder.

5. A dominant group may try to destroy certain ethnic practices (ethnocide) or to force ethnic group members to adopt the dominant culture (forced assimilation). A policy of ethnic explusion may create refugees. *Colonialism* refers to the political, social, economic, and cultural domination of a territory and its people by a foreign power for an extended time. *Cultural colonialism* refers to internal domination—by one group and its culture and/or ideology over others. One example is the domination of the former Soviet empire by the Russian people, language, and culture.

key terms

achieved status Social status that comes through talents, choices, actions, and accomplishments, rather than ascription.

ascribed status Social status (e.g., race or gender) that people have little or no choice about occupying.

assimilation The process of change that a minority group may experience when it moves to a country where another culture dominates; the minority is incorporated into the dominant culture to the point that it no longer exists as a separate cultural unit.

colonialism The political, social, economic, and cultural domination of a territory and its people by a foreign power for an extended time.

discrimination Policies and practices that harm a group and its members.

ethnic group Group distinguished by cultural similarities (shared among members of that group) and differences (between that group and others); ethnic group members share beliefs, customs, and norms, and, often, a common language, religion, history, geography, and kinship.

ethnicity Identification with, and feeling part of, an ethnic group, and exclusion from certain other groups because of this affiliation.

multiculturalism The view of cultural diversity in a country as something good and desirable; a multicultural society socializes individuals not only into the dominant (national) culture but also into an ethnic culture.

nation Once a synonym for "ethnic group," designating a single culture sharing a language, religion, history, territory, ancestry, and kinship; now usually a synonym for *state* or *nation-state.*

nationalities Ethnic groups that once had, or wish to have or regain, autonomous political status (their own country).

nation-state An autonomous political entity; a country like the United States or Canada.

négritude Black association and identity—an idea developed by dark-skinned intellectuals in Francophone (French-speaking) West Africa and the Caribbean.

plural society A society that combines ethnic contrasts and economic interdependence of the ethnic groups.

prejudice Devaluing (looking down on) a group because of its assumed behavior, values, abilities, or other attributes.

state An independent, centrally organized political unit; a government.

status Any social position that someone occupies; may be ascribed or achieved.

critical thinking questions

1. What's the difference between a culture and an ethnic group? In what culture(s) do you participate? To what ethnic group(s) do you belong? What is the basis of your primary cultural identity?
2. Name five social statuses you currently occupy. Which of those statuses are ascribed, and which ones are achieved?
3. Are your ascribed statuses more important to you than your achieved statuses, or vice versa?
4. Is ethnicity ever an achieved status? If so, give an example.
5. What is a minority group? Must it be a numerical minority? What are some minority groups in contemporary North America?
6. What are some of the forces that help forge and maintain imagined communities in the world today?
7. Do linguistic and cultural similarities between ethnic groups tend to produce ethnic harmony or conflict?
8. How does multiculturalism differ from assimilation? Which process do you favor for your country?
9. How does prejudice differ from discrimination? Give three examples of each.
10. Give a few examples of "ethnic florescence" in today's world.

case study

Hmong: This chapter discussed ethnic pride, along with ethnic discrimination and violence. The Hmong are a tribal people who traditionally have lived in remote mountain villages throughout China, Laos, Thailand, and Vietnam. Their history is one of struggle, rebellion, and perseverance. For centuries, Hmong have suffered persecution by many groups, while fiercely defending their ethnic heritage. Despite war and resettlement, they continue to strive to maintain their traditions. In *Culture Sketches* by Holly Peters-Golden, read the chapter on the Hmong: Struggle and Perseverance. Hmong in the United States have been criticized as unwilling to assimilate. Why might they be viewed this way? How might their long history of ethnic discrimination influence the way they think about themselves and their cultural heritage? How might you account for the clashes described in their adjustment to life in the United States?

suggested additional readings

Abelmann, N., and J. Lie

1995 *Blue Dreams: Korean Americans and the Los Angeles Riots.* Cambridge, MA: Harvard University Press. Some of the roots of ethnic conflict in Los Angeles today.

Anderson, B.

1991 *Imagined Communities: Reflections on the Origin and Spread of Nationalism,* rev. ed. London: Verso. The origins of nationalism in Europe and its colonies, with special attention to the role of print, language, and schools.

1998 *The Spectre of Comparisons: Nationalism, Southeast Asia, and the World.* New York: Verso. A regional and international focus on nationalism.

Barth, F.

1969 *Ethnic Groups and Boundaries: The Social Organization of Cultural Difference.* London: Allyn and Unwin. Classic discussion of the prominence of differentiation and boundaries (versus cultural features per se) in interethnic relations.

Delamont, S.

1995 *Appetites and Identities: An Introduction to the Social Anthropology of Western Europe.* London: Routledge. An anthropological account of national cultures and ethnic variation in Western Europe.

Fox, R. G., ed.

1990 *Nationalist Ideologies and the Production of National Cultures.* American Ethnological Society Monograph Series, no. 2. Washington, DC: American Anthropological Association. A series of papers about ethnicity and nationalism in Israel, Romania, India, Guatemala, Guyana, Burundi, and Tanzania.

Friedman, J.

1994 *Cultural Identity and Global Process.* Thousand Oaks, CA: Sage. Issues of ethnic and cultural identity in the face of globalization.

Gellner, E.

1983 *Nations and Nationalism.* Ithaca, NY: Cornell University Press. Industrialism and nation-building.

1997 *Nationalism.* New York: New York University Press. Up-to-date comments from a longtime anthropological student of nationalism.

Hastings, A.

1997 *The Construction of Nationhood : Ethnicity, Religion, and Nationalism.* New York: Cambridge University Press. Beliefs, identities, and nation-building.

Hobsbawm, E. J.

1992 *Nations and Nationalism since 1780: Programme, Myth, Reality,* 2nd ed. New York: Cambridge University Press. The making of modern nation-states.

Kottak, C. P., and K. A. Kozaitis

1999 *On Being Different: Diversity and Multiculturalism in the North American Mainstream.* New York: McGraw-Hill. Aspects of diversity in the United States and Canada, plus an original theory of multiculturalism.

Laguerre, M. S.

1998 *Diasporic Citizenship: Haitian Americans in Transnational America.* New York: St. Martin's Press. Haitians in today's America.

Ryan, S.

1995 *Ethnic Conflict and International Relations,* 2nd ed. Brookfield, MA: Dartmouth. Cross-national review of the roots of ethnic conflict.

Yetman, N., ed.

1999 *Majority and Minority: The Dynamics of Race and Ethnicity in American Life,* 6th ed. Boston: Allyn and Bacon. A wide-ranging anthology focusing on the United States.

internet exercises

1. *Ethnicity on the Border:* Read Gregory Rodriguez's article entitled "We're Patriotic Americans because We're Mexican" in *Salon Magazine,* **http://www.salon.com/news/feature/2000/02/24/laredo/index.html?CP=SAL&DN=110.**
   a. Who is participating in the celebration of George Washington's Birthday?
   b. How does this celebration reflect the influence of Mexican and American cultures? Since it is a mixture, is this celebration any less "pure"?
   c. Do you think a multiethnic identity is incompatible with a single national identity?
   d. What factors would cause a border community to invest so much energy in recognizing a day such as Washington's Birthday that so many other Americans ignore? Do you think it is more important for communities living on the border to assert their nationality than for communities living in the heartland?

2. *The Marketing of Ethnicity:* Read Marilyn Halter's article in the *Washington Post* entitled "Ethnicity for Sale," **http://washingtonpost.com/wp-dyn/print/sunday/outlook/inside/A48082-2000Jul15.html.**
   a. In the past what were the predominant American attitudes toward ethnic minorities? How have they changed?
   b. How are these new attitudes toward ethnic minorities reflected in American business? What are some examples?
   c. How has the "Roots" phenomenon influenced the St. Patrick's Day celebration?
   d. How do you predict America's attitude toward ethnic minorities will change in the future?

See Chapter 12 on your CD-ROM for additional review and interactive exercises. See your McGraw-Hill Online Learning Center for more.

Chapter 13

Language and Communication

CHAPTER OUTLINE

CBSNEWS.CBS.COM NEWS BRIEFS

Children without Language So They Invent One of Their Own

by Scott Pelley
May 14, 2000

(CBS) . . . No one had ever put together a successful program to educate the deaf children of Nicaragua. In 1979, after the Sandinista revolution, the government set up two schools in Managua and brought in deaf kids from all around the country. But the kids had never been exposed to language in their lives, so they couldn't understand what the teachers were saying and the teachers couldn't understand them.

Then, something extraordinary happened. The children began comparing the signs that they had been using at home, and added to them and modified them. Soon, even though the teachers still didn't know what was going on, the children were talking to each other in a new language.

Mystified, the Nicaraguans called in Judy Kegl, an American linguist who studies language and the brain.

As Kegl recorded their conversations she began to understand that this was no jumble of gestures, but a true language with precise rules and order. They did it on their own.

Kegl believes their case proves that the brain has an instinct for communication.

"It's like a rocket going off in your head," says Adrian Perez, one of the children liberated by the invented language. "It's just an understanding that soars."

Today Perez teaches the new language, known simply as Nicaraguan Sign Language. He lost his hearing to a fever when he was a toddler. He was born into a happy family, but as a deaf boy in Nicaragua, he couldn't share in their happiness.

"You can't express your feelings," he says of being without language. "Your thoughts may be there but you can't get them out. And you can't get new thoughts in."

Kegl wondered if she could find other Nicaraguans trapped without language. She's an authority on how the brain creates language. If she could find people who had not been reached by the new sign language—people with no language—she might learn about how language evolved in the first place.

Kegl thought that her work in Nicaragua would last a few weeks. That was 15 years ago. Today she is still traveling the rain forests of Nicaragua's Mosquito Coast finding what no linguist believed could ever be found—humans without language.

Kegl's research suggests the brain is open to language until the age of 12 or 13, then the opportunity begins to close. So far, Kegl has found about 300 people who have missed this window. They are invaluable to research—among the only people on Earth who can provide clues to the beginnings of human communication.

But over time Kegl couldn't get over the tragedy of these people. Five years ago, Kegl decided to start teaching as well as studying. She and her husband James started a one room school on the Mosquito Coast to teach the new sign language . . .

"When I was little, I would look at books in my house," signs Daphne Rodriguez, one of 30 students in the school. "I would look at them but I didn't know what they said."

Now, with language, the students are filled with questions, and they have the tools to ask them.

"I'm convinced that language is in the brain," Kegl says. "But I'm also convinced that language needs a trigger.". . .

Source: http://cbsnews.cbs.com/now/story/0,1597,188527-412,00.shtml.

overview

Linguistic anthropology shares the field's general interest in diversity in time and space. Linguistic anthropology examines language structure and use, linguistic change, and relations among language, society, and culture.

In the wild, nonhuman primates use limited call systems to communicate. The call systems of our hominid ancestors eventually grew too complicated for genetic transmission. They began to rely on learning and the call systems evolved into language, our main system of communication. But humans also continue to use nonverbal communication, such as facial expressions and gestures. No language includes all the sounds the human vocal apparatus can make. Phonology, the study of speech sounds, focuses on sounds that make a difference in a given language.

Sociolinguistics investigates relationships between social and linguistic variation. How do different kinds of people use language? Do men and women speak differently? How about classes, professions, and ethnic groups? People vary their speech on different occasions, shifting styles, dialects, even languages.

Historical linguistics is useful for anthropologists interested in historical relationships. Linguistic clues can suggest past contacts between cultures. Relationships between languages don't necessarily mean there are biological ties between their speakers, because people can learn new languages.

The world navigable via computer is part of a global, high-tech communications environment—access to which remains unequal both within and among nations. New communicative and linguistic practices develop for different media, including the Internet and cyberspace.

Language, spoken (*speech*) and written (*writing*—which has existed for about 6,000 years), is our primary means of communication. Like culture in general, of which language is a part, language is transmitted through learning, as part of enculturation. Language is based on arbitrary, learned associations between words and the things for which they stand. Unlike the communication systems of other animals, language allows us to discuss the past and future, share our experiences with others, and benefit from their experiences.

Anthropologists study language in its social and cultural context. Linguistic anthropology illustrates anthropology's characteristic interest in comparison, variation, and change. Some linguistic anthropologists reconstruct ancient languages by comparing their contemporary descendants and in so doing make discoveries about history. Others study linguistic differences to discover the varied world views and patterns of thought in a multitude of cultures. Sociolinguists examine dialects and styles in a single language to show how speech reflects social differences (Fasold 1990; Labov 1972*a, b*). Linguistic anthropologists also explore the role of language in colonization and in the expansion of the world economy (Geis 1987).

Animal Communication

Call Systems

Only humans speak. No other animal has anything approaching the complexity of language. The natural communication systems of other primates (monkeys and apes) are **call systems.** These vocal systems consist of a limited number of sounds—*calls*—that are produced only when particular environmental stimuli are encountered. Such calls may be varied in intensity and duration, but they are much less flexible than language because they are automatic and can't be combined. When primates encounter food and danger simultaneously, they can make only one call. They can't combine the calls for food and danger into a single utterance, indicating that both are present. At some point in human evolution, however, our ancestors began to combine calls and to understand the combinations. The number of calls also expanded, eventually

Apes, such as these Congo chimpanzees, use call systems to communicate in the wild. Their vocal systems consist of a limited number of sounds—*calls*—that are produced only when particular environmental stimuli are encountered.

becoming too great to be transmitted even partly through the genes. Communication came to rely almost totally on learning.

Although wild primates use call systems, the vocal tract of apes is not suitable for speech. Until the 1960s, attempts to teach spoken language to apes suggested that they lack linguistic abilities. In the 1950s, a couple raised a chimpanzee, Viki, as a member of their family and systematically tried to teach her to speak. However, Viki learned only four words ("mama," "papa," "up," and "cup").

Sign Language

More recent experiments have shown that apes can learn to use, if not speak, true language (Miles 1983). Several apes have learned to con-

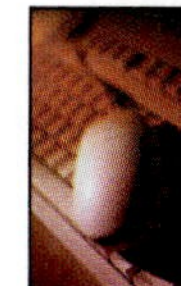

verse with people through means other than speech. One such communication system is American Sign Language, or ASL, which is widely used by deaf and mute Americans. ASL employs a limited number of basic gesture units that are analogous to sounds in spoken language. These units combine to form words and larger units of meaning.

The first chimpanzee to learn ASL was Washoe, a female. Captured in West Africa, Washoe was acquired by R. Allen Gardner and Beatrice Gardner, scientists at the University of Nevada in Reno, in 1966, when she was a year old. Four years later, she moved to Norman, Oklahoma, to a converted farm that had become the Institute for Primate Studies. Washoe revolutionized the discussion of the language-learning abilities of apes. At first she lived in a trailer and heard no spoken language. The researchers always used ASL to communicate with each other in her presence. The chimp gradually acquired a vocabulary of more than 100 signs representing English words (Gardner, Gardner, and Van Cantfort 1989). At the age of two, Washoe began to combine as many as five signs into rudimentary sentences such as "you, me, go out, hurry."

The second chimp to learn ASL was Lucy, Washoe's junior by one year. Lucy died, or was murdered by poachers, in 1986, after having been introduced to "the wild" in Africa in 1979 (Carter 1988). From her second day of life until her move to Africa, Lucy lived with a family in Norman, Oklahoma. Roger Fouts, a researcher from the nearby Institute for Primate Studies, came two days a week to test and improve Lucy's knowledge of ASL. During the rest of the week, Lucy used ASL to converse with her foster parents. After acquiring language, Washoe and Lucy expressed several human traits: swearing, joking, telling lies, and trying to teach language to others (Fouts 1997).

When irritated, Washoe has called her monkey neighbors at the institute "dirty monkeys." Lucy insulted her "dirty cat." On arrival at Lucy's place, Fouts once found a pile of excrement on the floor. When he asked the chimp what it was, she replied, "dirty, dirty," her expression for feces. Asked whose "dirty, dirty" it was, Lucy named Fouts's coworker, Sue. When Fouts refused to believe her about Sue, the chimp blamed the excrement on Fouts himself.

Cultural transmission of a communication system through learning is a fundamental attribute of language. Washoe, Lucy, and other chimps have tried to teach ASL to other animals, including their own offspring. Washoe has taught gestures to other institute chimps, including her son Sequoia, who died in infancy (Fouts, Fouts, and Van Cantfort 1989).

Because of their size and strength as adults, gorillas are less likely subjects than chimps for such experiments. Lean adult male gorillas in the wild weigh 400 pounds (180 kilograms), and full-grown females can easily reach 250 pounds (110 kilograms). Because of this, psychologist Penny Patterson's work with gorillas at Stanford University seems more daring than the chimp experiments. Patterson raised her now full-grown female gorilla, Koko, in a trailer next to a Stanford museum. Koko's vocabulary surpasses that of any chimp. She regularly employs 400 ASL signs and has used about 700 at least once.

Koko and the chimps also show that apes share still another linguistic ability with humans: **productivity.** Speakers routinely use the rules of their language to produce entirely new expressions that are comprehensible to other native speakers. I can, for example, create "baboonlet" to refer to a baboon infant. I do this by analogy with English words in which the suffix *-let* designates the young of a species. Anyone who speaks English immediately understands the meaning of my new word. Koko, Washoe, Lucy, and others have shown that apes also are able to use language productively. Lucy used gestures she already knew to create "drinkfruit" for watermelon. Washoe, seeing a swan for the first time, coined "waterbird." Koko, who knew the gestures for "finger" and "bracelet," formed "finger bracelet" when she was given a ring.

Chimps and gorillas have a rudimentary capacity for language. They may never have invented a meaningful gesture system in the wild. However, given such a system, they show many humanlike abilities in learning and using it. Of course, language use by apes is a product of human intervention and teaching. The experiments mentioned here do not suggest that apes can invent language (nor are human children ever faced with that task). However, young apes have managed to learn the basics of gestural language. They can employ it productively and creatively, although not with the sophistication of human ASL users.

(Cartoon by Sidney Harris)

Apes, like humans, also may try to teach their language to others. Lucy, not fully realizing the difference between primate hands and feline paws, once tried to mold her pet cat's paw into ASL signs. Koko taught gestures to Michael, a male gorilla six years her junior.

Apes also have demonstrated linguistic **displacement.** Absent in call systems, this is a key ingredient in language. Normally, each call is tied to an environmental stimulus such as food. Calls are uttered only when that stimulus is present. Displacement means that humans can talk about things that are not present. We don't have to see the objects before we say the words. Human conversations are not limited by place. We can discuss the past and future, share our experiences with others, and benefit from theirs.

Patterson has described several examples of Koko's capacity for displacement (Patterson 1978). The gorilla once expressed sorrow about having bitten Penny three days earlier. Koko has used the sign "later" to postpone doing things she doesn't want to do. Table 13.1 summarizes the contrasts between language, whether sign or spoken, and the call systems that primates use in the wild.

Certain scholars still doubt the linguistic abilities of chimps and gorillas (Sebeok and Umiker-Sebeok 1980; Terrace 1979). These people contend

Table 13.1
Language Contrasted with Call Systems

Human Language	Primate Call Systems
Has the capacity to speak of things and events that are not present (displacement).	Are stimuli-dependent; the food call will only be made in the presence of food; it cannot be faked.
Has the capacity to generate new expressions by combining other expressions (productivity).	Consist of a limited number of calls that cannot be combined to produce new calls.
Is group specific in that all humans have the capacity for language, but each linguistic community has its own language, which is culturally transmitted.	Tend to be species specific, with little variation among communities of the same species for each call.

that Koko and the chimps are comparable to trained circus animals and don't really have linguistic ability. However, in defense of Patterson and the other researchers (Hill 1978; Van Cantfort and Rimpau 1982), only one of their critics has worked with an ape. This was Herbert Terrace, whose experience teaching a chimp sign language lacked the continuity and personal involvement that have contributed so much to Patterson's success with Koko.

No one denies the huge difference between human language and gorilla signs. There is a major gap between the ability to write a book or say a prayer and the few hundred gestures employed by a well-trained chimp. Apes aren't people, but they aren't just animals either. Let Koko express it: When asked by a reporter whether she was a person or an animal, Koko chose neither. Instead, she signed "fine animal gorilla" (Patterson 1978).

The Origin of Language

The capacity to remember and combine linguistic expressions seems to be latent in the apes (Miles 1983). In human evolution, the same ability flowered into language. Language did not appear miraculously at a certain moment in human history. It developed over hundreds of thousands of years, as our ancestors' call systems were gradually transformed. Language offered a tremendous adaptive advantage to *Homo*. Language permits the information stored by a human society to exceed by far that of any nonhuman group. Language is a uniquely effective vehicle for learning. Because we can speak of things we have never experienced, we can anticipate responses before we encounter the stimuli. Adaptation can occur more rapidly in *Homo* than in the other primates because our adaptive means are more flexible.

Nonverbal Communication

Language is our principal means of communicating, but it isn't the only one we use. We communicate when we transmit information about ourselves to others and receive such information from them. Our facial expressions, bodily stances, gestures, and movements, even if unconscious, convey information and are part of our communication styles. Deborah Tannen (1990) discusses differences in the communication styles of American men and women, and her comments go beyond language. She notes that girls and women tend to look directly at each other when they talk, whereas boys and men do not. Males are more likely to look straight ahead rather than to turn and make eye contact with someone, especially another man, seated beside them. Also, in conversational groups, men tend to relax and sprawl out. Women may adopt a similar relaxed posture in all-female groups, but when they are with men, they tend to draw in their limbs and adopt a tighter stance.

Kinesics is the study of communication through body movements, stances, gestures, and facial expressions. Related to kinesics is the

Men and women differ in their phonology, grammar, and vocabulary, and in the body stances and movements that accompany speech. What differences do you note in the communication styles of the two women in the foreground, compared with the several men in the background?

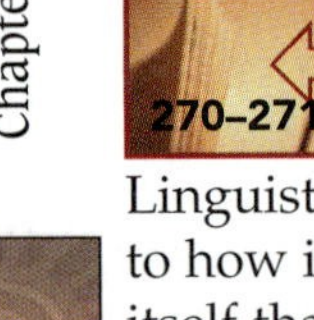

examination of cultural differences in personal space and displays of affection in the chapter "Culture." Linguists pay attention not only to what is said but to how it is said, and to features besides language itself that convey meaning. We use gestures, such as a jab of the hand, for emphasis. A speaker's enthusiasm is conveyed not only through words, but also through facial expressions, gestures, and other signs of animation. We use verbal and nonverbal ways of communicating our moods: enthusiasm, sadness, joy, regret. We vary our intonation and the pitch or loudness of our voice (see "In the News" on pp. 330–331 for a Japanese example). We communicate through strategic pauses, and even by being silent. An effective communication strategy may be to alter pitch, voice level, and grammatical forms, such as declaratives ("I am. . ."), imperatives ("Go forth. . ."), and questions ("Are you. . . ?"). Culture teaches us that certain manners and styles should accompany certain kinds of speech. Our demeanor, verbal and nonverbal, when our favorite team is winning would be out of place at a funeral, or when a somber subject is being discussed.

Some of our facial expressions reflect our primate heritage. We can see them in monkeys and especially in the apes. How "natural" and universal are the meanings conveyed by facial expressions? Throughout the world, smiles, laughs, frowns, and tears tend to have similar meanings, but culture does intervene. In some cultures, people smile less than in others. In a given culture, men may smile less than women; and adults, less than children. A lifetime of smiling and frowning marks the face, so that smile lines and frown furrows develop. In North America, smile lines may be more marked in women than men. Margaret Mead focused on kinesics in her studies of infant care in different cultures. She noted differences in mother–child interactions, finding that patterns of holding, releasing, and playing varied from culture to culture. In some cultures, babies were held more securely than in others. Mead thought that patterns of infant and child care played an important role in forming adult personality.

Culture always plays a role in shaping the "natural." Animals communicate through odors, using scent to mark territories, a chemical means of communication. Among modern North Americans, the perfume, mouthwash, and deodorant industries are based on the idea that the sense of smell plays a role in communication and social interaction. But different cultures are more tolerant of "natural" odors than ours is. Cross-culturally, nodding does not always mean affirmative, nor does head shaking from side to side always mean negative. Brazilians wag a finger to mean no. Americans say "uh huh" to affirm, whereas in Madagascar a similar sound is made to deny. Americans point with their fingers; the people of Madagascar point with their lips. Patterns of "lounging around" vary, too. Outside, when resting, some people may sit or lie on the ground; others squat; others lean against a tree.

Body movements communicate social differences. Lower-class Brazilians, especially women, offer limp handshakes to their social superiors. In many cultures, men have firmer handshakes than women do. In Japan, bowing is a regular part of social interaction, but different bows are used depending on the social status of the people who are interacting. In Madagascar and Polynesia, people of lower status should not hold their heads above those of people of higher status. When one approaches someone older or of higher status, one bends one's knees and lowers one's head as a sign of respect. In Madagascar, one always does this, for politeness, when passing between two people. Although our gestures, facial expressions, and body stances have roots in our primate heritage, and can be seen in the monkeys and the apes, they have not escaped the cultural shaping described in previous chapters. Language, which is so highly dependent on the use of symbols, is the domain of communication, in which culture plays the strongest role.

The Structure of Language

The scientific study of a spoken language (*descriptive linguistics*) involves several interrelated areas of analysis: phonology, morphology, lexicon, and syntax. **Phonology,** the study of speech sounds, considers which sounds are present and significant in a given language. **Morphology** studies the forms in which sounds combine to form *morphemes*—words and their meaningful parts. Thus, the word *cats* would be analyzed as containing two morphemes: *cat,* the name for a kind of animal, and *-s,* a morpheme indicating plurality. A language's **lexicon** is a dictionary containing all its morphemes and their meanings. **Syntax** refers to the arrangement and order of words in phrases and sentences. Syntactic questions include whether nouns usually come before or after verbs, or whether adjectives normally precede or follow the nouns they modify.

Speech Sounds

From the movies and TV, and from actually meeting foreigners, we know something about foreign accents and mispronunciations. We know that someone with a marked French accent doesn't pronounce *r* like an American does. But at least someone from France can distinguish between "craw" and "claw," which someone from Japan may not be able to do. The difference between *r* and *l* makes a difference in English and in French, but it doesn't in Japanese. In linguistics, we say that the difference between *r* and *l* is *phonemic* in English and French but not in Japanese; that is, *r* and *l* are phonemes in English and French but not in Japanese. A **phoneme** is a sound contrast that makes a difference, that differentiates meaning.

We find the phonemes in a given language by comparing *minimal pairs,* words that resemble each other in all but one sound. The words have totally different meanings, but they differ in just one sound. The contrasting sounds are therefore phonemes in that language. An example in English is the minimal pair *pit/bit.* These two words are distinguished by a single sound contrast between /p/ and /b/ (we enclose phonemes in slashes). Thus /p/ and /b/ are phonemes in English. Another example is the different vowel sound of *bit* and *beat* (see Figure 13.1). This contrast serves to distinguish these two words and the two vowel phonemes written /I/ and /i/ in English.

Standard (American) English (SE), the "region-free" dialect of TV network newscasters, has about 35 phonemes: at least 11 vowels and 24 consonants. The number of phonemes varies from language to language—from 15 to 60, averaging between 30 and 40. The number of phonemes also varies between dialects of a given language. In

Figure 13.1

Vowel Phonemes in Standard American English

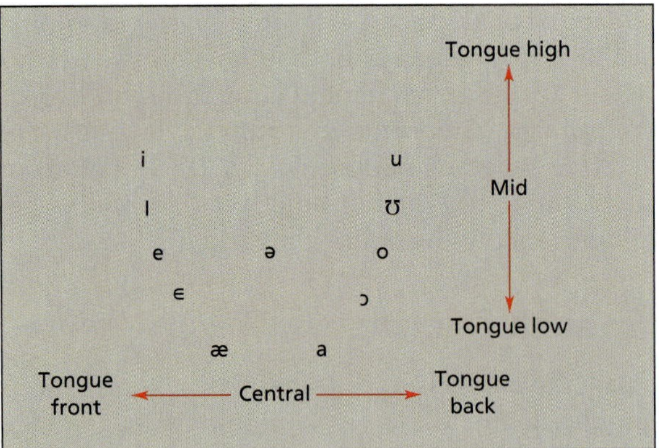

High front (spread)	[i]	as in *beat*
Lower high front (spread)	[I]	as in *bit*
Mid front (spread)	[e]	as in *bait*
Lower mid front (spread)	[ɛ]	as in *bet*
Low front	[æ]	as in *bat*
Central	[ə]	as in *butt*
Low back	[a]	as in *pot*
Lower mid back (rounded)	[ɔ]	as in *bought*
Mid back (rounded)	[o]	as in *boat*
Lower high back (rounded)	[ʊ]	as in *put*
High back (rounded)	[u]	as in *boot*

Source: Adaptation of excerpt and figure 2–1 from *Aspects of Language*, third edition, by Dwight Bollinger and Donald Sears, copyright © 1981 by Harcourt Brace Jovanovich, Inc., reprinted by permission of the publisher..

The phonemes are shown according to height of tongue and tongue position at front, center, or back of mouth. Phonetic symbols are identified by English words that include them; note that most are minimal pairs.

American English, for example, vowel phonemes vary noticeably from dialect to dialect (see "Interesting Issues" on page 323). Readers should pronounce the words in Figure 13.1, paying attention to (or asking someone else) whether they distinguish each of the vowel sounds. Most Americans don't pronounce them all.

Phonetics is the study of speech sounds in general, what people actually say in various languages, like the differences in vowel pronunciation described in "Interesting Issues." **Phonemics** studies only the *significant* sound contrasts (phonemes) of a given language. In English, like /r/ and /l/ (remember *craw* and *claw*), /b/ and /v/ are also phonemes, occurring in minimal pairs like *bat* and *vat*. In Spanish, however, the contrast between [b] and [v] doesn't distinguish meaning, and they are therefore not phonemes (we enclose sounds that are not phonemic in brackets). Spanish speakers normally use the [b] sound to pronounce words spelled with either *b* or *v*.

In any language, a given phoneme extends over a phonetic range. In English, the phoneme /p/ ignores the phonetic contrast between the [p^h] in *pin* and the [p] in *spin*. Most English speakers don't even notice that there is a phonetic difference. [p^h] is aspirated, so that a puff of air follows the [p]. The [p] in *spin* is not. (To see the difference, light a match, hold it in front of your mouth, and watch the flame as you pronounce the two words.) The contrast between [p^h] and [p] is phonemic in some languages, such as Hindi (spoken in India). That is, there are words whose meaning is distinguished only by the contrast between an aspirated and an unaspirated [p].

Native speakers vary in their pronunciation of certain phonemes, such as the /e/ phoneme discussed in "Interesting Issues." This variation is important in the evolution of language. With no shifts in pronunciation, there can be no linguistic change. The section on sociolinguistics below considers phonetic variation and its relationship to social divisions and the evolution of language.

Language, Thought, and Culture

The well-known linguist Noam Chomsky (1955) has argued that the human brain contains a limited set of rules for organizing language, so that all languages have a common structural basis. (Chomsky calls this set of rules *universal grammar.*) The fact that people can learn foreign languages and that words and ideas can be translated from one language into another tends to support Chomsky's position that all humans have similar linguistic abilities and thought processes. Another line of support comes from creole languages. Such languages develop from pidgins, languages that form in situations of acculturation, when different societies come into

Do Midwesterners Have Accents?

Depending on where we live, Americans have certain stereotypes about how people in other regions talk. Some stereotypes, spread by the mass media, are more generalized than others. Most Americans think they can imitate a "southern accent." We also have nationwide stereotypes about speech in New York City (the pronunciation of *coffee*, for example) and Boston ("I pahked the kah in Hahvahd Yahd").

Many Americans also believe that midwesterners don't have accents. This belief stems from the fact that midwestern dialects don't have many stigmatized linguistic variants—speech patterns that people in other regions recognize and look down on, such as *r*lessness and *dem, dese,* and *dere* (instead of *them, these,* and *there*).

Actually, regional patterns influence the way all Americans speak. Midwesterners do have detectable accents. College students from out of state easily recognize that their in-state classmates speak differently. In-state students, however, have difficulty hearing their own speech peculiarities, because they are accustomed to them and view them as normal.

Far from having no accents, midwesterners, even in the same high school, exhibit linguistic variation (see Eckert 1989, 2000). Furthermore, dialect differences are immediately obvious to people, like myself, who come from other parts of the country. One of the best examples of variable midwestern pronunciation, involving vowels, is the /e/ phoneme, which occurs in words like *ten, rent, French, section, lecture, effect, best,* and *test.* In southeastern Michigan, where I live and teach, there are four different ways of pronouncing this phoneme. Speakers of Black English and immigrants from Appalachia often pronounce *ten* as *tin,* just as southerners habitually do. Some Michiganders say *ten,* the correct pronunciation in Standard English. However, two other pronunciations are more common. Instead of *ten,* many Michiganders say *tan,* or *tun* (as though they were using the word *ton,* a unit of weight).

My students often astound me with their pronunciation. One day I met one of my Michigan-raised teaching assistants in the hall. She was deliriously happy. When I asked why, she replied, "I've just had the best suction."

"What?" I said.

"I've just had a wonderful suction," she repeated.

"What?" I still wasn't understanding.

She finally spoke more precisely. "I've just had the best saction." She considered this a clearer pronunciation of the word *section.*

Another TA complimented me, "You luctured to great effuct today." After an exam, a student lamented that she hadn't been able to do her "bust on the tust." Once I lectured about uniformity in the fast-food restaurant chains. One of my students had just vacationed in Hawaii, where, she told me, hamburger prices were higher than they were on the mainland. It was, she said, because of the runt. Who, I wondered, was this runt? The very puny owner of Honolulu's McDonald's franchise? Perhaps he advertised on television, "Come have a hamburger with the runt." Eventually I figured out that she was talking about the high cost of *rent* on those densely packed islands.

contact and must devise a system of communication. As mentioned in the "Culture" chapter, pidgins based on English and native languages developed in the context of trade and colonialism in China, Papua New Guinea, and West Africa. Eventually, after generations of being spoken, pidgins may develop into *creole languages.* These are more mature languages, with developed grammatical rules and native speakers (that is, people who learn the language as their primary means of communication during enculturation). Creoles are spoken in several Caribbean societies. Gullah, which is spoken by African-Americans on coastal islands in South

Carolina and Georgia, is also a creole language. Supporting the idea that creoles are based on universal grammar is the fact that such languages all share certain features. Syntactically, all use particles (e.g., will, was) to form future and past tenses and multiple negation to deny or negate (e.g., he don't got none). Also, all form questions by changing inflection rather than by changing word order. For example, "You're going home for the holidays?" (with a rising tone at the end) rather than "Are you going home for the holidays?"

Shown here in 1995 is Leigh Jenkins, who was or is Director of Cultural Preservation for the Hopi tribal council. Would the Hopi language have to distinguish between *was* and *is* in that sentence?

The Sapir-Whorf Hypothesis

Other linguists and anthropologists take a different approach to the relation between language and thought. Rather than seeking universal linguistic structures and processes, they believe that different languages produce different ways of thinking. This position is sometimes known as the **Sapir-Whorf hypothesis** after Edward Sapir (1931) and his student Benjamin Lee Whorf (1956), its prominent early advocates. Sapir and Whorf argued that the grammatical categories of different languages lead their speakers to think about things in particular ways. For example, the third-person singular pronouns of English (*he, she; him, her; his, hers*) distinguish gender, whereas those of the Palaung, a small tribe in Burma, do not (Burling 1970). Gender exists in English, although a fully developed noun-gender and adjective-agreement system, as in French and other Romance languages (*la belle fille, le beau fils*), does not. The Sapir-Whorf hypothesis therefore might suggest that English speakers can't help paying more attention to differences between males and females than do the Palaung and less than do French or Spanish speakers.

English divides time into past, present, and future. Hopi, a language of the Pueblo region of the Native American Southwest, does not. Rather, Hopi distinguishes between events that exist or have existed (what we use present and past to discuss) and those that don't or don't yet (our future events, along with imaginary and hypothetical events). Whorf argued that this difference leads Hopi speakers to think about time and reality in different ways than English speakers do. A similar example comes from Portuguese, which employs a future subjunctive verb form, introducing a degree of uncertainty into discussions of the future. In English, we routinely use the future tense to talk about something we think will happen. We don't feel the need to qualify "The sun'll come out tomorrow," by adding "if it doesn't go supernova." We don't hesitate to proclaim "I'll see you next year," even when we can't be absolutely sure we will. The Portuguese future subjunctive qualifies the future event, recognizing that the future can't be certain. Our way of expressing the future as certain is so ingrained that we don't even think about it, just as the Hopi don't see the need to distinguish between present and past, both of which are real, while the future remains hypothetical. It would seem, however, that language does not tightly restrict thought, because cultural changes can produce changes in thought and in language, as we shall see in the next section.

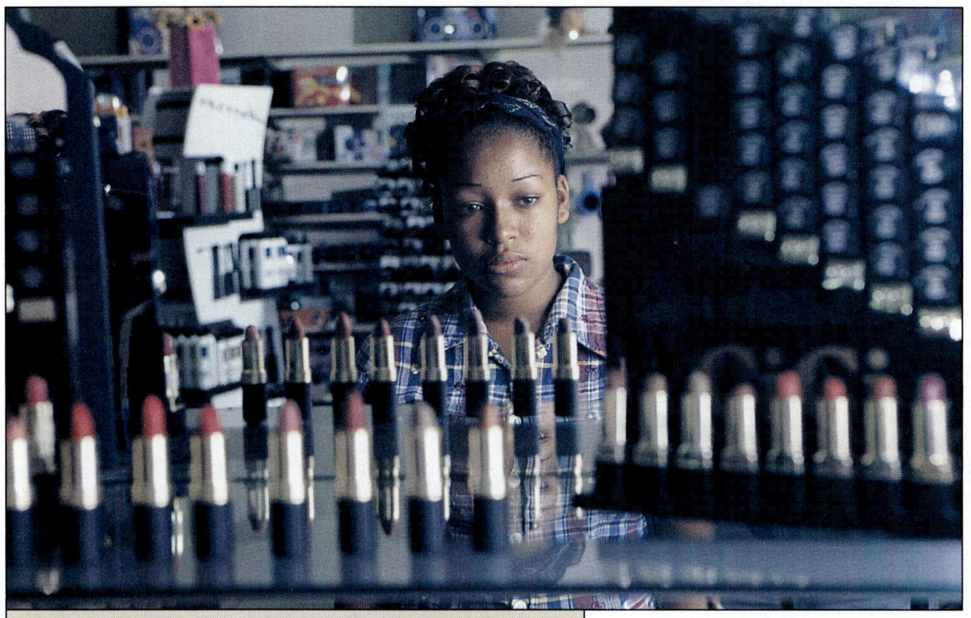

Color terms and distinctions have increased with the growth of the fashion and cosmetic industries. Here a women contemplates a display of lipsticks at a cosmetics counter. How many colors do you see among the lipsticks in this photo?

Focal Vocabulary

A lexicon (or vocabulary) is a language's dictionary, its set of names for things, events, and ideas. Lexicon influences perception. Thus, Eskimos have several distinct words for different types of snow that in English are all called *snow.* Most English speakers never notice the differences between these types of snow and might have trouble seeing them even if someone pointed them out. Eskimos recognize and think about differences in snow that English speakers don't see because our language provides us with just one word.

Similarly, the Nuer of Sudan have an elaborate vocabulary to describe cattle. Eskimos have several words for snow and Nuer have dozens for cattle because of their particular histories, economies, and environments (Brown 1958; Eastman 1975). When the need arises, English speakers also can elaborate their snow and cattle vocabularies. For example, skiers name varieties of snow with words that are missing from the lexicons of Florida retirees. Similarly, the cattle vocabulary of a Texas rancher is much more ample than that of a salesperson in a New York City department store. Such specialized sets of terms and distinctions that are particularly important to certain groups (those with particular *foci* of experience or activity) are known as **focal vocabulary.**

Vocabulary is the area of language that changes most readily. New words and distinctions, when needed, appear and spread. For example, who would have "faxed" anything a generation ago? Names for items get simpler as they become common and important. A television has become a *TV,* an automobile a *car,* and a videocassette recorder a *VCR.*

Language, culture, and thought are interrelated. However, and in opposition to the Sapir-Whorf hypothesis, it would be more reasonable to say that changes in culture produce changes in language and thought than the reverse. Consider differences between female and male Americans in regard to the color terms they use (Lakoff 1975). Distinctions implied by such terms as *salmon, rust, peach, beige, teal, mauve, cranberry,* and *dusky orange* aren't in the vocabularies of most American men. However, many of

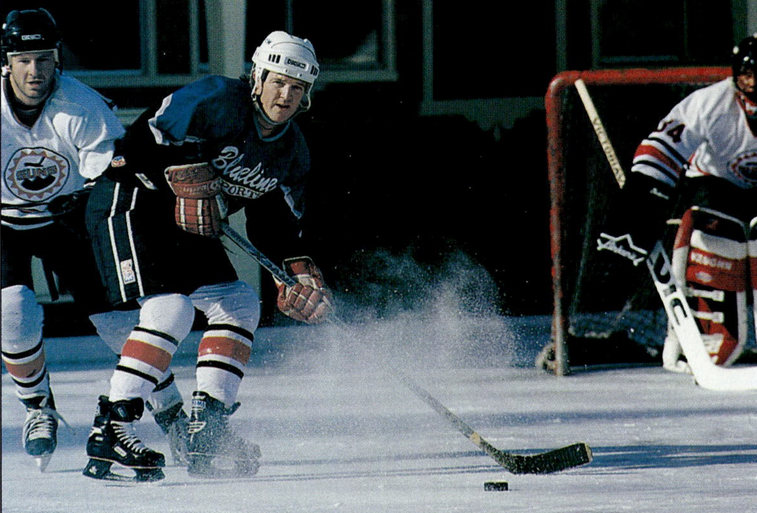

How would a hockey insider use focal vocabulary to describe the items shown in this photo? How would you describe them?

them weren't even in American women's lexicons 50 years ago. These changes reflect changes in American economy, society, and culture. Color terms and distinctions have increased with the growth of the fashion and cosmetic industries. A similar contrast (and growth) in Americans' lexicons shows up in football, basketball, and hockey vocabularies. Sports fans, more often males than females, use more terms in reference to, and make more elaborate distinctions between, the games they watch, such as hockey (see Table 13.2). Thus, cultural contrasts and changes affect lexical distinctions (for instance, *peach* versus *salmon*) within semantic domains (for instance, color terminology). **Semantics** refers to a language's meaning system.

Table 13.2

Focal Vocabulary for Hockey

Insiders have special terms for the major elements of the game.

Elements of Hockey	Insiders' Term
puck	biscuit
goal/net	pipes
penalty box	sin bin
hockey stick	twig
helmet	bucket
space between a goalie's leg pads	five hole

Meaning

Speakers of particular languages use sets of terms to organize, or categorize, their experiences and perceptions. Linguistic terms and contrasts encode (embody) differences in meaning that people perceive. **Ethnosemantics** studies such classification systems in various languages. Well-studied ethnosemantic *domains* (sets of related things, perceptions, or concepts named in a language) include kinship terminology and color terminology. When we study such domains, we are examining how those people perceive and distinguish between kin relationships or colors. Other such domains include ethnomedicine—the terminology for the causes, symptoms, and cures of disease (Frake 1961); ethnobotany—native classification of plant life (Berlin, Breedlove, and Raven 1974; Conklin 1954); and ethnoastronomy (Goodenough 1953).

The ways in which people divide up the world—the contrasts they perceive as meaningful or significant—reflect their experiences. Anthropologists have discovered that certain lexical domains and vocabulary items evolve in a determined order. For example, after studying color terminology in more than 100 languages, Berlin and Kay (1991/1999) discovered 10 basic color terms: *white, black, red, yellow, blue, green, brown, pink, orange,* and *purple* (they evolved in more or less that order). The number of terms varied with cultural complexity. Representing one extreme were Papua New Guinea cultivators and Australian hunters and gatherers, who used only two basic terms, which translate as *black* and *white* or *dark* and *light.* At the other end of the continuum were European and Asian languages with all the color terms. Color terminology was most developed in areas with a history of using dyes and artificial coloring.

Sociolinguistics

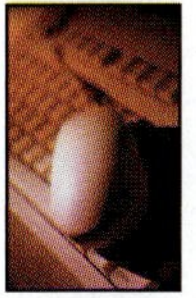

No language is a uniform system in which everyone talks just like everyone else. Linguistic *performance* (what people actually say) is the concern of sociolinguists. The field of **sociolinguistics** investigates relationships between social and linguistic variation, or language in its social context (Eckert and Rickford 2001). How do different speakers use a given language? How do linguistic features correlate with social stratification, including class, ethnic, and gender differences (Tannen 1990, 1993)? How is language used to express, reinforce, or resist power (Geis 1987; Thomas 1999)?

Sociolinguists don't deny that the people who speak a given language share knowledge of its basic rules. Such common knowledge is the basis of mutually intelligible communication. However, sociolinguists focus on features that vary systematically with social position and situation. To study variation, sociolinguists must do field work. They must observe, define, and measure variable use of language in real-world situations. To show that linguistic features correlate with social, economic, and political differences, the social attributes of speakers also must be measured and related to speech (Fasold 1990; Labov 1972*a*).

Variation within a language at a given time is historical change in progress. The same forces that, working gradually, have produced large-scale linguistic change over the centuries are still at work today. Linguistic change doesn't occur in a vacuum but in society. When new ways of speaking are associated with social factors, they are imitated, and they spread. In this way, a language changes.

Linguistic Diversity

As an illustration of the linguistic variation that is encountered in all nations, consider the contemporary United States. Ethnic diversity is revealed by the fact that millions of Americans learn first languages other than English. Spanish is the most common. Most of those people eventually become bilinguals, adding English as a second language. In many multilingual (including colonized) nations, people use two languages on different occasions: one in the home, for example, and the other on the job or in public.

Whether bilingual or not, we all vary our speech in different contexts; we engage in **style shifts.** In certain parts of Europe, people regularly switch dialects. This phenomenon, known as **diglossia,** applies to "high" and "low" variants of the same language, for example, in German and Flemish (spoken in Belgium). People employ the "high" variant at universities and in writing, professions, and the mass media. They use the "low" variant for ordinary conversation with family members and friends.

Just as social situations influence our speech, so do geographical, cultural, and socioeconomic differences. Many dialects coexist in the United States with Standard (American) English (SE). SE itself is a dialect that differs, say, from "BBC English," which is the preferred dialect in Great Britain. According to the principle of *linguistic relativity,* all dialects are equally effective as systems of communication, which is language's main job. Our tendency to think of particular dialects as cruder or more sophisticated than others is a social rather than a linguistic judgment. We rank certain speech patterns as better or worse because we recognize that they are used by groups that we also rank. People who say *dese, dem,* and *dere* instead of *these, them,* and *there* communicate perfectly well with anyone who recognizes that the *d* sound systematically replaces the *th* sound in their speech. However, this form of speech has become an indicator of low social rank. We call it, like the use of *ain't,* "uneducated speech." The use of *dem, dese,* and *dere* is one of many phonological differences that Americans recognize and look down on.

Gender Speech Contrasts

Comparing men and women, there are differences in phonology, grammar, and vocabulary, as well as in the body stances and movements that accompany speech (Tannen 1990). In phonology, American women tend to pronounce their vowels more peripherally ("rant," "rint"), whereas men tend to pronounce theirs more centrally ("runt"—in all cases when saying the word "rent"). In public contexts, Japanese women tend to adopt an artificially high voice, for the sake of politeness,

according to their traditional culture (see "In the News," pages 330–331). In North America and Great Britain, women's speech tends to be more similar to the standard dialect than men's is. Consider the data in Table 13.3, gathered in Detroit. In all social classes, but particularly in the working class, men were more apt to use double negatives (e.g., "I don't want none"). Women tend to be more careful about "uneducated speech." This trend shows up in both the United States and England. Men may adopt working-class speech because they associate it with masculinity. Perhaps women pay more attention to the media, where standard dialects are employed.

Certain dialects are stigmatized, not because of actual linguistic deficiencies, but because of a symbolic association between a certain way of talking and low social status. In this scene from *My Fair Lady,* Professor Henry Higgins (Rex Harrison) encounters Eliza Doolittle (Audrey Hepburn), a Cockney flower girl. Higgins will teach Doolittle how to speak like an English aristocrat.

According to Robin Lakoff (1975), the use of certain types of words and expressions has been associated with women's traditional lesser power in American society (see also Coates 1986; Tannen 1990). For example, *Oh dear, Oh fudge,* and *Goodness!* are less forceful than *Hell* and *Damn.* Men's customary use of "forceful" words reflects their traditional public power and presence. Watch the lips of a disgruntled athlete in a televised competition, such as a football game. What's the likelihood he's saying "Phooey on you"? Women, by contrast, are more likely to use such adjectives as *adorable, charming, sweet, cute, lovely,* and *divine* than men are.

Let's return to the previously discussed domains of sports and color terminology for additional illustration of differences in lexical (vocabulary) distinctions that men and women make. Men typically know more terms related to sports, make more distinctions among them (e.g., runs versus points), and try to use the terms more precisely than women do. Correspondingly, influenced more by the fashion and cosmetics industries than men are, women use more color terms and attempt to use them more specifically than men do. Thus, when I lecture on

Table 13.3
Multiple Negation ("I don't want none") According to Gender and Class (in Percentages)

	Upper Middle Class	Lower Middle Class	Upper Working Class	Lower Working Class
Male	6.3	32.4	40.0	90.1
Female	0.0	1.4	35.6	58.9

Source: From *Sociolinguistics: An Introduction to Language and Society* by Peter Trudgill (London: Pelican Books, 1974, revised edition 1983), p. 85, copyright © Peter Trudgill, 1974, 1983. Reproduced by permission of Penguin Books Ltd.

sociolinguistics, and to make this point, I bring an off-purple shirt to class. Holding it up, I first ask women to say aloud what color the shirt is. The women rarely answer with a uniform voice, as they try to distinguish the actual shade (mauve, lavender, wisteria, or some other purplish hue). I then ask the men, who consistently answer as one, "PURPLE." Rare is the man who on the spur of the moment can imagine the difference between *fuchsia* and *magenta*.

Whether it's fair or not, people judge you by the way you speak. "Proper language" becomes a strategic resource, correlated with wealth, prestige, and power. Linguistic stratification can reflect both class and ethnic contrasts. In Guatemala, a Spanish-speaking elite couple enjoy a garden breakfast served by an Indian maid. Can you think of ways in which speech habits help determine access to employment?

Differences in the linguistic strategies and behavior of men and women are examined in several books by the well-known sociolinguist Deborah Tannen (1990, 1993). Tannen (1990) uses the terms "rapport" and "report" to contrast women's and men's overall linguistic styles. Women, says Tannen, typically use language and the body movements that accompany it to build rapport, social connections with others. Men, on the other hand, tend to make reports, reciting information that serves to establish a place for themselves in a hierarchy, as they also attempt to determine the relative ranks of their conversation mates.

Stratification

We use and evaluate speech in the context of *extralinguistic* forces—social, political, and economic. Mainstream Americans evaluate the speech of low-status groups negatively, calling it "uneducated." This is not because these ways of speaking are bad in themselves but because they have come to symbolize low status. Consider variation in the pronunciation of *r*. In some parts of the United States, *r* is regularly pronounced, and in other (*r*less) areas, it is not. Originally, American *r*less speech was modeled on the fashionable speech of England. Because of its prestige, *r*lessness was adopted in many areas and continues as the norm around Boston and in the South.

New Yorkers sought prestige by dropping their *r*'s in the 19th century, after having pronounced them in the 18th. However, contemporary New Yorkers are going back to the 18th-century pattern of pronouncing *r*'s. What matters, and what governs linguistic change, is not the reverberation of a strong midwestern *r* but *social* evaluation, whether *r*'s happen to be "in" or "out."

Studies of *r* pronunciation in New York City have clarified the mechanisms of phonological change. William Labov (1972*b*) focused on whether *r* was pronounced after vowels in such words as *car, floor, card,* and *fourth.* To get data on how this linguistic variation correlated with social class, he used a series of rapid encounters with employees in three New York City department stores, each of whose prices and locations attracted a different socioeconomic group. Saks Fifth Avenue (68 encounters) catered to the upper middle class, Macy's (125) attracted middle-class shoppers, and S. Klein's (71) had predominantly lower-middle-class and working-class customers. The class origins of store personnel tended to reflect those of their customers.

Having already determined that a certain department was on the fourth floor, Labov approached ground-floor salespeople and asked where that department was. After the salesperson had answered, "Fourth floor," Labov repeated his "Where?" in order to get a second response. The

in the news

Japan's Feminine Falsetto Falls Right Out of Favor

Gender differences in speech may show up in grammar, vocabulary, phonology, or intonation, and they may be accentuated by style shifting in certain social contexts. Japanese women tend to adopt a very high-pitched voice when speaking in public. However, this linguistic standard of politeness is fading today, as a result of familiarity with gender roles in other cultures and exposure to the mass media (where female announcers now use lower voices).

Smiling beatifically at the restless shoppers, more like a saint than an elevator operator, Hiromi Saito opened her mouth to do her duty.

"I thank you from the bottom of my heart for favoring us by paying an honorable visit to our store," she said in The Voice. "I will stop at the floor your honorable self is kind enough to use, and then I will go to the top floor."

The Voice is as fawning as her demeanor, as sweet as syrup, and as high as a dog whistle. Any higher, and it would shatter the crystal on the seventh floor.

Most Japanese women cannot muster the Mount Fuji–like heights of Miss Saito's voice, but their voices regularly skirt the foothills. For a quick gauge of the status of women in Japan, just cock your ear and listen to Japanese women speak—or squeak.

European women no longer rearrange their bodies with corsets, and Chinese no longer cripple their daughters by binding their feet. But many Japanese women speak well above their natural pitch, especially in formal settings, on the phone or when dealing with customers . . .

Yet . . . women's voices in Japan are dropping significantly. Japan still has many squeakers, but a growing number of women speak in natural voices . . .

One standard-bearer of the changing times is Miyuki Morita, who was rejected when she first tried to enter broadcasting, as a disk jockey. "They said my voice was too somber, and they wouldn't hire me," Ms. Morita recalled. She eventually found a job with a television station in northern Japan, and she tried to imitate other female journalists who spoke in high voices.

"Then when I saw a video of myself, I saw my face, but it wasn't my voice," she said. "It didn't sound convincing. So I settled back to my voice."

That voice is now among the best known in Japan. Ms. Morita is the evening anchor of NHK News, the most popular television news program in the country . . .

second reply was more formal and emphatic, the salesperson presumably thinking that Labov hadn't heard or understood the first answer. For each salesperson, therefore, Labov had two samples of /r/ pronunciation in two words.

Labov calculated the percentages of workers who pronounced /r/ at least once during the interview. These were 62 percent at Saks, 51 percent at Macy's, but only 20 percent at S. Klein's. He also found that personnel on upper floors, where he asked "What floor is this?" (and where more expensive items were sold), pronounced /r/ more often than groundfloor salespeople did.

In Labov's study, summarized in Table 13.4, *r* pronunciation was clearly associated with prestige. Certainly the job interviewers who had hired the salespeople never counted *r*'s before offering employment. However, they did use speech evaluations to make judgments about how effective certain people would be in selling particular kinds of merchandise. In other words, they practiced sociolinguistic discrimination, using linguistic features in deciding who got certain jobs.

Our speech habits help determine our access to employment and other material resources. Because of this, "proper language" itself becomes

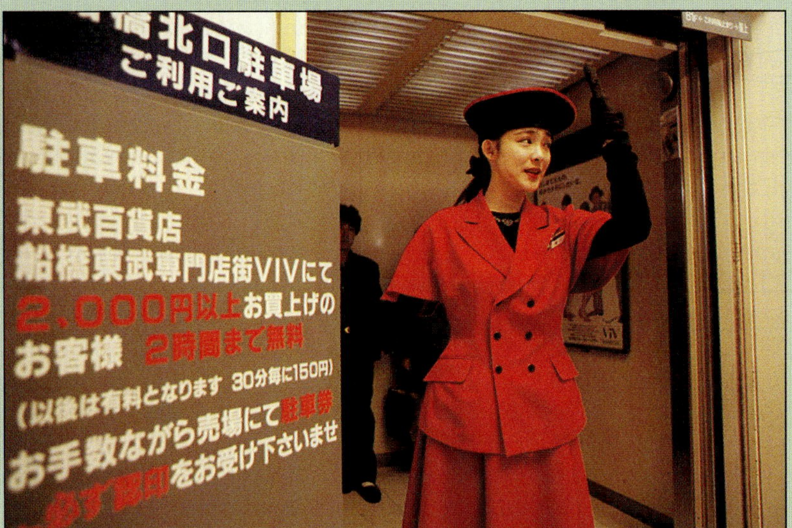

Japanese women, like this department store elevator operator, traditionally use a high-pitched voice for public speaking. In your society, do men and women have different public speaking strategies?

The pitch of female singers is also falling. Tadahiro Murao, professor of music at Aichi University of Education, has analyzed the frequency of 200 songs dating from the 1950's, and found a clear trend. "From the late 1980's, the pitch of female songs has dropped dramatically," Professor Murao said . . .

Almost everyone agrees that high pitch is wrapped up in the Japanese preoccupation with courtesy. In polite conversation in Japan, people routinely denigrate themselves and try to sound unsure even about things they are certain of.

One technique women use to sound tentative, and therefore polite, is to raise their pitch and let their sentences trail off, the way Americans sometimes ask questions.

"A lower voice sounds too bullying, too aggressive, too manly," said Julie Saito, a reporter at Asahi Shimbun.

Ms. Saito said Japanese men seem attracted by high voices and girlish behavior, which some Japanese women then emulate. The attraction to young girls is known here as the Loli-con—short for Lolita Complex—and it is a Japanese phenomenon, the basis for endless psychoanalyses of the Japanese mind and libido.

"A high voice sounds more cute, more like a girlish image of women," Ms. Saito said. "In the United States I project more confidence, while in Japan I find I act in a more cute way.". . .

Source: Nicholas D. Kristof, "Japan's Feminine Falsetto Falls Right Out of Favor," *New York Times*, December 13, 1995, pp. A1, A4.

Table 13.4
Pronunciation of *r* in New York City Department Stores

Store	Number of Encounters	% *r* Pronunciation
Saks Fifth Avenue	68	62
Macy's	125	51
S. Klein's	71	20

a strategic resource—and a path to wealth, prestige, and power (Gal 1989). Illustrating this, many ethnographers have described the importance of verbal skill and oratory in politics (Beeman 1986; Bloch, 1975; Brenneis 1988; Geis 1987). Ronald Reagan, known as a "great communicator," dominated American society in the 1980s as a two-term president. Another twice-elected president, Bill Clinton, despite his Southern accent, was known for his verbal skills in certain contexts (e.g., televised debates and town-hall meetings). Communications flaws may have helped doom the presidencies of Gerald Ford, Jimmy Carter, and George Bush (the elder) ("Couldn't do that; wouldn't be prudent.").

The French anthropologist Pierre Bourdieu views linguistic practices as *symbolic capital* that properly trained people may convert into economic and social capital. The value of a dialect—its standing in a "linguistic market"—depends on the extent to which it provides access to desired positions in the labor market. In turn, this reflects its legitimation by formal institutions: educational institutions state, church, and prestige media. Even people who don't use the prestige dialect accept its authority and correctness, its "symbolic domination" (Bourdieu 1982, 1984). Thus, linguistic forms, which lack power in themselves, take on the power of the groups they symbolize. The education system, however (defending its own worth), denies this, misrepresenting prestige speech as being inherently better. The linguistic insecurity often felt by lower-class and minority speakers is a result of this symbolic domination.

Black English Vernacular (BEV), a.k.a. "Ebonics"

No one pays much attention when someone says "runt" instead of "rent." But some nonstandard speech carries more of a stigma. Sometimes stigmatized speech is linked to region, class, or educational background; sometimes it is associated with ethnicity or "race."

A national debate involving language, race, and education was triggered by a vote on December 18, 1996, by the Oakland, California, school board. The board unanimously declared that many black students did not speak Standard English but instead spoke a distinct language called "ebonics" (from "ebony" and "phonics"), with roots in West African languages. Soon disputing this claim were the poet Maya Angelou, the Reverend Jesse Jackson, and the Clinton administration, along with virtually all professional linguists, who see ebonics as a dialect of English rather than a separate language. Linguists call ebonics BEV (Black English Vernacular) or AAEV (African-American English Vernacular).

Some saw the Oakland resolution as a ploy designed to permit the school district to increase its access to federal funds available for bilingual programs for Hispanic and Asian students. According to federal law, black English is not a separate language eligible for Title 7 funds. Funds for bilingual education (itself a controversial issue, especially in California politics) have been available to support the education of immigrant students (Golden 1997). Some educators have argued that similar support should be available to blacks. If ebonics were accepted as a foreign language, teachers could receive merit pay for studying black English and for using their knowledge of it in their lessons (Applebome 1996).

Early in 1997, responding to the widespread negative reaction to its original resolution, the Oakland educational task force proposed a new resolution. This one required only the recognition of language differences among black students, in order to improve their proficiency in English. School officials emphasized that they had never intended to teach black students in ebonics. They just sought to employ some of the same tools used with students brought up speaking a foreign language to help black students improve their English-language skills. The Oakland school board planned to expand its 10-year-old pilot program for black students, which taught the phonetic and grammatical differences between Standard English and what the students spoke outside the classroom (Golden 1997).

Linguists view ebonics as a dialect rather than a separate language, and they more often trace its roots to southern English than to Africa. Still, most linguists see nothing wrong with the Oakland schools' goal of understanding the speech patterns of black students and respecting that speech while teaching Standard English. Indeed, this is policy and teaching strategy in many American school districts. The Linguistic Society of America (LSA) considers ebonics or Black English to be "systematic and rule-governed" (Appleborne 1997).

What about ebonics as a linguistic system? William Labov and several associates, both white and black, have conducted detailed studies of what they call **Black English Vernacular (BEV).** (*Vernacular* means ordinary, casual speech.) BEV is the "relatively uniform dialect spoken by the majority of black youth in most parts of the United States today, especially in the inner city areas of New York, Boston, Detroit, Philadelphia, Washington, Cleveland, . . . and other urban cen-

Rap and hip-hop music weave BEV into musical expression. Here we see Ghostface Killa, a member of the Wu Tang Clan singing group.

ters. It is also spoken in most rural areas and used in the casual, intimate speech of many adults" (Labov 1972*a*, p. xiii).

BEV isn't an ungrammatical hodgepodge. Rather, BEV is a complex linguistic system with its own rules, which linguists have described. The phonology and syntax of BEV are similar to those of southern dialects. This reflects generations of contact between southern whites and blacks, with mutual influence on each other's speech patterns. Many features that distinguish BEV from SE (Standard English) also show up in southern white speech, but less frequently than in BEV.

Linguists disagree about exactly how BEV originated (Rickford 1997). Smitherman (1977) calls it an Africanized form of English reflecting both an African heritage and the conditions of servitude, oppression, and life in America. She notes certain structural similarities between West African languages and BEV. African linguistic backgrounds no doubt influenced how early African-Americans learned English. Did they restructure English to fit African linguistic patterns? Or did they quickly learn English from whites, with little continuing influence from the African linguistic heritage? Or, possibly, in acquiring English, did African slaves fuse English with African languages to make a pidgin or creole, which influenced the subsequent development of BEV? Creole speech may have been brought to the American colonies by the many slaves who were imported from the Caribbean during the 17th and 18th centuries. Some slaves may even have learned, while still in Africa, the pidgins or creoles spoken in West African trading forts (Rickford 1997).

Origins aside, there are phonological and grammatical differences between BEV and SE. One phonological difference between BEV and SE is that BEV speakers are less likely to pronounce *r* than SE speakers are. Actually, many SE speakers don't pronounce *r*'s that come right before a consonant (ca*r*d) or at the end of a word (car). But SE speakers do usually pronounce an *r* that comes right before a vowel, either at the end of a word (fou*r* o'clock) or within a word (Ca*r*ol). BEV speakers, by contrast, are much more likely to omit such intervocalic (between vowels) *r*'s. The result is that speakers of the two dialects have different *homonyms* (words that sound the same but have different meanings). BEV speakers who don't pronounce intervocalic *r*'s have the following homonyms: Carol/Cal; Paris/pass.

Observing different phonological rules, BEV speakers pronounce certain words differently than SE speakers do. Particularly in the elementary school context, where the furor over ebonics has raged, the homonyms of BEV-speaking students typically differ from those of their SE-speaking teachers. To evaluate reading accuracy, teachers should determine whether students are recognizing the different meanings of such BEV homonyms as *passed, past,* and *pass.* Teachers need to make sure students understand what they are reading, which is probably more important than whether they are pronouncing words correctly according to the SE norm.

The phonological contrasts between BEV and SE speakers often have grammatical consequences.

One of these is *copula deletion,* which means the absence of SE forms of the copula—the verb *to be.* For example, SE and BEV may contrast as follows:

SE	SE Contraction	BEV
you are tired	you're tired	you tired
he is tired	he's tired	he tired
we are tired	we're tired	we tired
they are tired	they're tired	they tired

In its deletion of the present tense of the verb *to be,* BEV is similar to many languages, including Russian, Hungarian, and Hebrew. BEV's copula deletion is simply a grammatical result of its phonological rules. Notice that BEV deletes the copula where SE has contractions. BEV's phonological rules dictate that *r*'s (as in *you're, we're,* and *they're*) and word-final *s*'s (as in *he's*) be dropped. However, BEV speakers do pronounce *m,* so that the BEV first-person singular is "I'm tired," just as in SE. Thus, when BEV omits the copula, it merely carries contraction one step further, as a result of its phonological rules.

Also, phonological rules may lead BEV speakers to omit *-ed* as a past-tense marker and *-s* as a marker of plurality. However, other speech contexts demonstrate that BEV speakers do understand the difference between past and present verbs, and between singular and plural nouns. Confirming this are irregular verbs (e.g., *tell, told*) and irregular plurals (e.g., *child, children*), in which BEV works the same as SE.

SE is not superior to BEV as a linguistic system, but it does happen to be the prestige dialect—the one used in the mass media, in writing, and in most public and professional contexts. SE is the dialect that has the most "symbolic capital." In areas of Germany where there is diglossia, speakers of Plattdeusch (Low German) learn the High German dialect to communicate appropriately in the national context. Similarly, upwardly mobile BEV-speaking students learn SE.

Historical Linguistics

Sociolinguists study contemporary variation in speech—language change in progress. **Historical linguistics** deals with longer-term change. Historical linguists can reconstruct many features of past languages by studying contemporary **daughter languages.** These are languages that descend from the same parent language and that have been changing separately for hundreds or even thousands of years. We call the original language from which they diverge the **protolanguage.** Romance languages such as French and Spanish, for example, are daughter languages of Latin, their common protolanguage. German, English, Dutch, and the Scandinavian languages are daughter languages of proto-Germanic. The Romance languages and the Germanic languages all belong to the Indo-European language family. Their common protolanguage is called PIE, Proto-Indo-European. Historical linguists classify languages according to their degree of relationship (see Figure 13.2).

Language changes over time. It evolves—varies, spreads, divides into **subgroups** (languages within a taxonomy of related languages that are most closely related). Dialects of a single parent language become distinct daughter languages, especially if they are isolated from one another. Some of them split, and new "granddaughter" languages develop. If people remain in the ancestral homeland, their speech patterns also change. The evolving speech in the ancestral homeland should be considered a daughter language like the others.

A close relationship between languages does not necessarily mean that their speakers are closely related biologically or culturally, because people can adopt new languages. In the equatorial forests of Africa, "pygmy" hunters have discarded their ancestral languages and now speak those of the cultivators who have migrated to the area. Immigrants to the United States spoke many different languages on arrival, but their descendants now speak fluent English.

Knowledge of linguistic relationships is often valuable to anthropologists interested in history, particularly events during the past 5,000 years. Cultural features may (or may not) correlate with the distribution of language families. Groups that speak related languages may (or may not) be more culturally similar to each other than they are to groups whose speech derives from different linguistic ancestors. Of course, cultural similarities aren't limited to speakers of related languages. Even groups whose members speak unrelated languages have contact through trade, intermarriage, and warfare. Ideas and inventions

Figure 13.2

PIE Family Tree

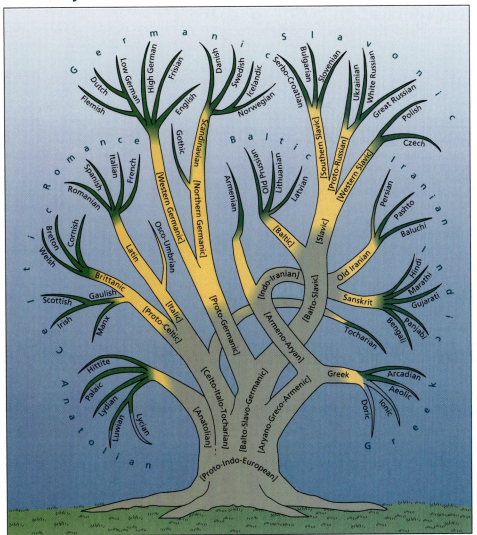

This is a family tree of the Indo-European languages. All can be traced back to a protolanguage, Proto-Indo-European (PIE), spoken more than 6,000 years ago. PIE split into dialects that eventually evolved into separate languages, which, in turn, evolved into languages such as Latin and proto-Germanic, which are ancestral to dozens of modern daughter languages. To what branch—Germanic, Romance, Slavonic—does your parents' native language(s) belong? How about English? What are the closest linguistic relatives of English (i.e., its sister languages)?

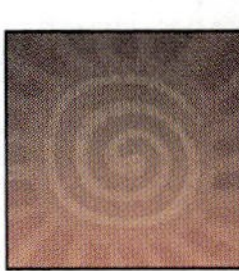

diffuse widely among human groups. Many items of vocabulary in contemporary English come from French. Even without written documentation of France's influence after the Norman Conquest of England in 1066, linguistic evidence in contemporary English would reveal a long period of important firsthand contact with France. Similarly, linguistic evidence may confirm cultural contact and borrowing when written history is lacking. By considering which words have been borrowed, we also can make inferences about the nature of the contact.

beyond the classroom

Cybercommunication in Collegespace

BACKGROUND INFORMATION

Student:	*Jason A. DeCaro*
Supervising Professor:	*Robert Herbert*
School:	*State University of New York at Binghamton*
Year in School/Major:	*Senior/Anthropology and Biochemistry dual major*
Future Plans:	*Ph.D. in Biological Anthropology; career in academics or public health*
Project Title:	*Cybercommunication in Collegespace: The Electronic/Personal Juncture in a Campus Living Community*

How is online communication related to face-to-face communication and to social interaction? On the basis of this research and the discussion below, is electronic communication good or bad for community formation?

Why do people who live in face-to-face proximity communicate using their computers? What is the interaction between their social lives "on-" and "off-line"? How does this affect their sense of community? I conducted research to address these questions through an anthropological case study.

The Internet has been interpreted as personalizing or depersonalizing, as highly democratic or merely chaotic, and as vitalizing or damaging to American "community." Some theorists suppose that electronic communication extends the pool of individuals with whom one maintains contact. However, others suggest that this merely creates an electronic "pseudocommunity" with shifting membership and superficial social ties. If this "pseudocommunity" competes for members' time and energy, it may be detrimental to their face-to-face interaction. Despite the active theoretical debate, very few studies have examined the interaction between electronic and face-to-face community in a geographically local group of individuals.

I observed a group of students of mixed gender who live in close proximity on a college campus. These students chose their living arrangement on the basis of com-

Cyberspace: A New Realm of Communication

The world navigable via computer—cyberspace—is part of a larger high-tech communications environment, which may be called advanced information technology (AIT). Other elements of this environment include computer hardware and software, modems, advanced telephone systems, cable TV, satellite dishes, and faxing capability. One of the key features of AIT is its international scope. Along with modern transportation systems, AIT plays a key role in connecting people worldwide.

AIT links people in networks both narrow (focused in a common interest) and wide (global in scope). Many of us regularly use targeted forums, such as e-mail groups and chatrooms. Cyber groups may be based on common work, activities, or attributes. Such *affinity groups* link people with common interests and/or characteristics (Harvey 1996). These include members of a single organization, branches of that organization, or similar professionals—for example, ENT (ear, nose, and throat) physicians all over the world. *Transecting groups* create direct communication channels between groups that previously

mon interest in computers, robotics, and engineering. Not all are computer scientists; some pursue majors such as creative writing and chemistry. Roughly a dozen alumni, some of whom no longer live in the local area, remain integral to the organization.

I am an alumnus; thus, I have a personal as well as a professional interest. One of my most challenging jobs was to avoid unintentional manipulation—even distancing myself from the group would have changed it! Yet, by remaining an "insider," I received tremendous access, and had a great deal of fun.

Members maintain face-to-face social activity and a busy electronic mailing list. The "real" and "virtual" communities thus created have overlapping but nonidentical membership. Most members who communicate exclusively within the "virtual" electronic domain are alumni. Students vary with respect to the form of communication that they favor. A few shun the electronic medium entirely and thereby opt out of the "virtual" community.

I distributed questionnaires, analyzed one year's mailing list traffic, and remained a participant in face-to-face social life. I found that conversations sometimes flow on and off the mailing list, and members do organize face-to-face social activities on-line. However, most people segregate the electronic and face-to-face domains, and most messages serve no explicit organizational purpose. Messages in this latter category allow contact between people who are not local, or strengthen bonds between individuals who see each other regularly.

Those who dedicate considerable time and energy to the virtual community put the mailing list to its widest range of uses. However, there is little evidence that electronic communication detracts from face-to-face interaction. Most people who are highly social on-line are highly social off-line as well. I suspect that individuals supplement, rather than replace, their face-to-face social lives with electronic communication. This is particularly valuable to those who do not live locally, or are less than comfortable with face-to-face communication. Thus, on the whole, members are integrated far more than they are alienated by the mailing list.

had, or otherwise have, trouble communicating—for example, physicians and patients.

Although AIT links the world, access to its riches is unequal both among and within nations. The "developing" nations have poorer access than do North America, Western Europe, Japan, Australia, and New Zealand. Even within a "developed" nation such as the United States or Canada, socioeconomic, demographic, and cultural factors affect access to and use of cyberspace. Not everyone has been integrated equally. There is privileged access to AIT by class, race, ethnicity, gender, education, profession, age, and family background. Young people tend to be more comfortable with AIT than old people are (see Table 13.5).

Class affects access to and use of AIT. Families with higher incomes tend to have better access to the whole range of high-tech items. Members of such families also tend to have and get better educations and to participate in the information-processing professions and settings in which AIT is used most regularly. Groups with more restricted access to AIT include minorities, the poor, females, older people, and developing nations. Computers and associated AIT are concentrated in affluent school districts. There is some evidence that communication via cyberspace can break down barriers between differentially privileged members of a physical community (a town or city). Michaelson (1996) describes

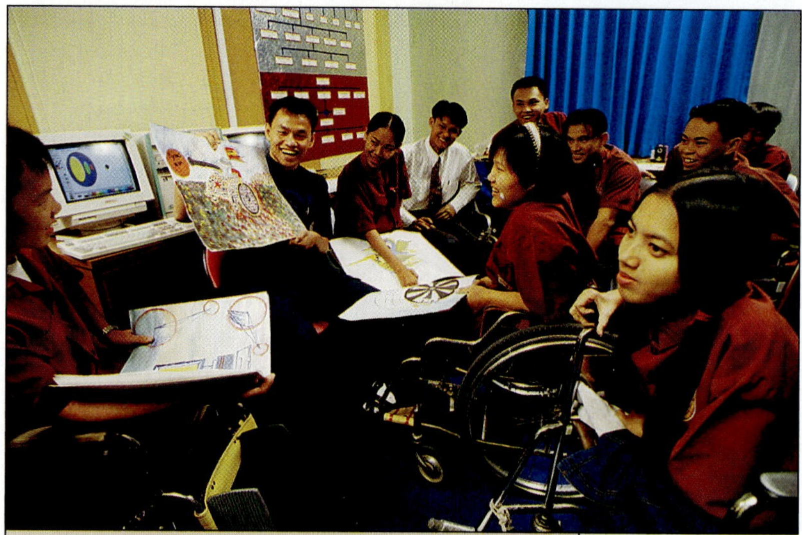

Among its many roles, advanced information technology (AIT) links *affinity groups*—groups of user-participants with common interests and/or characteristics, such as these Thai youths. How do you imagine they use the Internet?

communication networks linking homeless people using public library computers and middle-class people using computers in homes, jobs, and schools, and similar connectivity between children and elderly.

Communication via AIT has not banished class bias, despite several democratizing features of cyberspace communication. One equalizing feature of *cyberspeak* (the range of styles and conventions people use when they write messages in cyberspace) is its informality compared with print. Specific communicative and linguistic practices develop in different media. Language is neither as fixed nor as precise in cyberspace as it is in writing for print. Cyberwriters aren't as concerned with typos as are writers for print. Writing exclusively in capital letters (using the Caps Lock key) is bad form ("shouting"). Some people hardly use capital letters at all. Others are more attentive to the canons of print, and this—along with vocabulary and punctuation—is a way in which training and education show up. Class anonymity is not fully possible. Nor, probably, is gender. Using expletives or beginning a message with the salutation "Dude" suggest male identity. And female use of cyberspace shows some of the sociolinguistic strategies that have been noted in other contexts (Lakoff 1975; Tannen 1990), with women more likely to end their messages with softening disclaimers, such as "But that's just my opinion."

Social scientists are still investigating how the use of cyberspace is related to the use of other media and to participation in face-to-face groups

Table 13.5
Internet Access and Social Diversity

Social Category (selected)	Estimated December 31, 2000, Percent	Projected December 31, 2005, Percent
By income:		
High (above $75,000)	75	93
Low (below $15,000)	21	45
By ethnic group:		
Asian-American	69	84
White	54	76
Latino	41	68
African-American	36	64
By age:		
Young adults (19–35)	57	80
Older adults (50–64)	41	66
Kids (2–12)	32	62
Seniors (65+)	16	48

Source: Based on Likpe 2000.

and communities. One unresolved question is how participation in on-line forums affects participation in face-to-face ("real time") groups based on the same issue (e.g., alcohol abuse). There is no a priori reason to assume that one form of participation will diminish the other. For example, my own research in Brazil revealed television's role in promoting a general media-hunger (Kottak 1990*a*). The more people watched TV, the more they were likely to use all available media. The number of media-hungry people is increasing worldwide. If not yet there, they will surely be attracted to cyberspace. And the growth of real-life support groups has been correlated with their appearance on various media (print, radio, TV, and cyberspace).

Despite certain utopian visions of the potential role of virtual networks in integrating physical communities (e.g., Kling 1996), it is doubtful that AIT will play much of a role in strengthening whole local communities—towns and cities. It is more likely that AIT will be used mainly to facilitate communication among affinity groups: relatives; friends; people with common identities, experiences, and interests, especially work and business interests. AIT will be used especially for immediate communication within groups of coworkers and members of an organization. Its main role, however, will be to establish and maintain links between physically dispersed people who have, and come to have, more in common.

summary

1. Wild primates use call systems to communicate. Environmental stimuli trigger calls, which cannot be combined when multiple stimuli are present. Contrasts between language and call systems include displacement, productivity, and cultural transmission. Over time, our ancestral call systems grew too complex for genetic transmission, and hominid communication began to rely on learning. Humans still use nonverbal communication, such as facial expressions, gestures, and body stances and movements. But language is the main system humans use to communicate. Chimps and gorillas can understand and manipulate nonverbal symbols based on language.
2. No language uses all the sounds the human vocal tract can make. Phonology—the study of speech sounds—focuses on sound contrasts (phonemes) that distinguish meaning. The grammars and lexicons of particular languages can lead their speakers to perceive and think in certain ways. Studies of domains such as kinship, color terminologies, and pronouns show that speakers of different languages categorize their experiences differently.
3. Linguistic anthropologists share anthropology's general interest in diversity in time and space. Sociolinguistics investigates relationships between social and linguistic variation by focusing on the actual use of language. Only when features of speech acquire social meaning are they imitated. If they are valued, they will spread. People vary their speech, shifting styles, dialects, and languages. As linguistic systems, all languages and dialects are equally complex, rule-governed, and effective for communication. However, speech is used, is evaluated, and changes in the context of political, economic, and social forces. Often the linguistic traits of a low-status group are negatively evaluated. This devaluation is not because of *linguistic* features per se. Rather, it reflects the association of such features with low *social* status. One dialect, supported by the dominant institutions of the state, exercises symbolic domination over the others.
4. Historical linguistics is useful for anthropologists interested in historical relationships among populations. Cultural similarities and differences often correlate with linguistic ones. Linguistic clues can suggest past contacts between cultures. Related languages—members of the same language family—descend from an original protolanguage. Relationships between languages don't necessarily mean that there are biological ties between their speakers, because people can learn new languages.
5. The world navigable via computer—cyberspace—is part of a larger, global, high-tech communications environment, advanced information technology (AIT). AIT connects people in both wider and narrower networks. The narrower groups are based on affinity, homogeneous groups of user-participants. AIT also can open communication channels between people who otherwise might have trouble communicating. Access to AIT is unequal both among and within nations. There is privileged access by class, race, ethnicity, gender, education, profession, age, and family background.

key terms

Black English Vernacular (BEV) A rule-governed dialect of American English with roots in southern English. BEV is spoken by African-American youth and by many adults in their casual, intimate speech—sometimes called "ebonics."

call systems Systems of communication among non-human primates, composed of a limited number of sounds that vary in intensity and duration. Tied to environmental stimuli.

cultural transmission A basic feature of language; transmission through learning.

daughter languages Languages developing out of the same parent language; for example, French and Spanish are daughter languages of Latin.

diglossia The existence of "high" (formal) and "low" (informal, familial) dialects of a single language, such as German.

displacement A basic feature of language; the ability to speak of things and events that are not present.

ethnosemantics The study of lexical (vocabulary) contrasts and classifications in various languages.

focal vocabulary A set of words and distinctions that are particularly important to certain groups (those with particular foci of experience or activity), such as types of snow to Eskimos or skiers.

historical linguistics Subdivision of linguistics that studies languages over time.

kinesics The study of communication through body movements, stances, gestures, and facial expressions.

language Human beings' primary means of communication; may be spoken or written; features productivity and displacement and is culturally transmitted.

lexicon Vocabulary; a dictionary containing all the morphemes in a language and their meanings.

morphology The study of form; used in linguistics (the study of morphemes and word construction) and for form in general—for example, biomorphology relates to physical form.

phoneme Significant sound contrast in a language that serves to distinguish meaning, as in minimal pairs.

phonemics The study of the sound contrasts (phonemes) of a particular language.

phonetics The study of speech sounds in general; what people actually say in various languages.

phonology The study of sounds used in speech.

productivity A basic feature of language; the ability to use the rules of one's language to create new expressions comprehensible to other speakers.

protolanguage Language ancestral to several daughter languages.

Sapir-Whorf hypothesis Theory that different languages produce different ways of thinking.

semantics A language's meaning system.

sociolinguistics Study of relationships between social and linguistic variation; study of language (performance) in its social context.

style shifts Variations in speech in different contexts.

subgroups Languages within a taxonomy of related languages that are most closely related.

syntax The arrangement and order of words in phrases and sentences.

critical thinking questions

1. Based on your own knowledge of one or more languages, can you think of additional examples of ways in which language can influence perception and thought?
2. Give some additional examples of nonverbal communication. Check out your classmates during a discussion and see what examples you notice.

3. During a class discussion, what examples do you notice of sociolinguistic variation—say between men and women, the professor and students, and so forth?

4. List some stereotypes about how different sorts of people speak. Are those real differences, or just stereotypes? Are the stereotypes positive or negative? Why do you think those stereotypes exist?

5. Based on your own experience and observations, list five ways in which young children and adults differ in their communication styles. Now classify these differences as kinesic, phonological, grammatical, lexical—or other.

6. Based on your own experience and observations, list five ways in which men and women differ in their use of language. Now classify these differences as kinesic, phonological, grammatical, lexical—or other.

7. What can historical linguistics tell us about history?

8. Do you agree with the principle of linguistic relativity? If not, why not? What dialects and languages do you speak? Do you tend to use different dialects, languages, or speech styles in different contexts? Why?

9. How do you use cyberspace? Jot down and try to categorize the places you visit via computer in a given week. Does use of the computer make you feel less or more isolated from other people?

10. How many identities have you used recently in cyberspace? Why have you used various "handles"? Has the contrast between a cyberspace identity and a real-life identity ever created problems for you or for someone you know?

suggested additional readings

Baron, D.
1986 *Grammar and Gender.* New Haven, CT: Yale University Press. Differences in grammatical patterns and strategies of men and women.

Bonvillain, N.
2000 *Language, Culture, and Communication: The Meaning of Messages,* 3rd ed. Upper Saddle River, NJ: Prentice Hall. Up-to-date text on language and communication in cultural context.

Downes, W.
1998 *Language and Society,* 2nd ed. New York: Cambridge University Press.

Eckert, P.
2000 *Linguistic Variation as Social Practice: The Linguistic Construction of Identity in Belten High.* Malden, MA: Blackwell. How speech correlates with high school social networks and cliques.

Fasold, R. W.
1990 *The Sociolinguistics of Language.* Oxford: Basil Blackwell. Recent text with up-to-date examples.

Foley, W. A.
1997 *Anthroplogical Linguistics: An Introduction.* Cambridge, MA: Blackwell Publishers. Language, society, and culture.

Fouts, R.
1997 *Next of Kin: What Chimpanzees Have Taught Me about Who We Are.* New York, William Morrow. A teacher of Washoe, Lucy, and other signing chimps tells what he's learned from them.

Geis, M. L.
1987 *The Language of Politics.* New York: Springer-Verlag. Thorough examination of political uses of speech and oratory and the manipulation of language in power relations.

Gumperz, J., and S. C. Levinson, eds.
1996 *Rethinking Linguistic Relativity.* New York: Cambridge University Press. Essays on thought and thinking, language and culture.

Hanks, W. F.
1996 *Language and Communicative Practices.* Boulder, CO: Westview. The nature and role of language in communication and society.

Lakoff, R.

1975 *Language and Woman's Place.* New York: Harper & Row. Influential nontechnical discussion of how women use and are treated in Standard American English.

2000 *The Language War.* Berkeley: University of California Press. Politics and language in the United States today.

Rickford, J. R.

1999 *African American Vernacular English: Features, Evolution, Educational Implications.* Malden, MA: Blackwell. An introduction to BEV and its social significance.

Rickford, J. R., and R. J. Rickford

2000 *Spoken Soul: The Story of Black English.* New York: John Wiley & Sons. Readable account of the history and social meaning of BEV.

Romaine, S.

1999 *Communicating Gender.* Mahwah, NJ: L. Erlbaum Associates, 1999. Gender and language.

2000 *Language in Society: An Introduction to Sociolinguistics,* 2nd ed. New York: Oxford University Press. An introduction to sociolinguistics.

Salzmann, Z.

1998 *Language, Culture, and Society: An Introduction to Linguistic Anthropology,* 2nd ed. Boulder, CO: Westview. The function of language in culture and society.

Tannen, D.

1990 *You Just Don't Understand: Women and Men in Conversation.* New York: Ballantine. Popular book on gender differences in speech and conversational styles.

Tannen, D., ed.

1993 *Gender and Conversational Interaction.* New York: Oxford University Press. Twelve papers about conversational interaction illustrate the complexity of the relation between gender and language use.

Thomas, L.

1999 *Language, Society and Power.* New York: Routledge. Political dimensions and use of language.

Trudgill, P.

1995 *Sociolinguistics: An Introduction to Language and Society,* 3rd rev. ed. New York: Penguin. Readable short introduction to the role and use of language in society.

internet exercises

1. *Politeness Strategies:* Go and read Cyndi Patee's article on "Linguistic Politeness Strategies," **http://logos.uoregon.edu/explore/socioling/politeness.html.**
   a. What kind of strategy do you most often use? Do your strategies change when you are talking to different people (i.e., your friend, your parent, your professor)?
   b. What kind of politeness strategy do you like other people to use with you? Would you prefer people to sacrifice politeness for directness?
   c. Pay attention to what politeness strategies are being used around you in class, at home, and with friends. Can you identify any patterns in the way people select politeness strategies?

2. *Urban Legends:* Read the Urban Legends information page at About.com, **http://urbanlegends.about.com/science/urbanlegends/library/weekly/aa082497.htm.** Make sure and read some of the examples of urban legends that are provided.
   a. What constitutes an urban legend?
   b. Why are urban legends so popular? Many of them are not true, so why do they continue to be shared?
   c. What role does the Internet play in propagating urban legends?
   d. After reading this page, are you going to be more or less skeptical the next time a friend relates a story to you?

See Chapter 13 on your CD-ROM for additional review and interactive exercises. See your McGraw-Hill Online Learning Center for more.

Chapter 14

Making a Living

CHAPTER OUTLINE

NGNEWS.COM NEWS BRIEFS

Traditional Knowledge Brings Bloom Back to India

by Pallava Bagla
May 31, 2000

A large, green oasis has been created by illiterate farmers in the midst of a barren, desolate, and devastated landscape of western India. A slow and steady transformation has been going on in the . . . Alwar district of Rajasthan, a region—which until about a decade ago faced chronic, severe water shortages . . .

While most parts of Rajasthan suffer from the worst drought in a century, this small cluster of about 750 villages continues to enjoy adequate supplies of water simply because the local population decided to regenerate their lost traditions of water "harvesting.". . .

There are 750 villages where [a] non-governmental organization has built some 3,500 water-harvesting structures with absolutely no financial support from the Indian government . . . The villagers are bearing more than three-fourths of the costs themselves . . .

The structures have been built utilizing people's traditional know-how. In tandem with appropriate forest conservation practices, they have replenished ground water supplies and boosted the water table, enabling five small rivers . . . to flow perennially once again . . .

The main livelihood . . . in this semi-arid region is a combination of rain-dependent cultivation and animal husbandry. Water conservation has traditionally involved trapping water where it falls during the short rainy months by constructing a series of small dams and tanks locally called "johads."

Johads . . . require regular maintenance by way of removing silt that accumulates with rain water. These small structures not only provide surface water but also help to recharge precious ground water.

. . . It is important that the slopes of hills or other catchment surfaces remain forested to avoid soil erosion, which in turn would cause silting and choking the storage capacity of the ponds. Forests also act like sponges, retaining water when it rains heavily and then slowly releasing it over a period of time. Following India's independence some 53 years ago, overdependence of the Indian state on irrigation engineering resulted in villagers ignoring the regular maintenance of their johads, which was really the beginning of trouble. Simultaneously, excessive deforestation in the hilly areas not only stripped the area of ground cover but also increased soil erosion and choked the johads with silt. This double whammy led to large-scale harvest failures and starvation and subsequent migration of locals to urban areas.

. . . The region was classified by the government as a "dark zone," a place where there was insufficient potable water to sustain the populace. However, after the villagers adopted traditional water harvesting . . . in 1994, the government was able to re-classify the area as a "white zone," bringing much needed relief to about half a million people.

Not only has the area seen an increase in food production but even its green mantle has increased rapidly. Tree regeneration has taken place over large tracts and, with that, a slow revival of some wild animal populations has also been seen.

Recently, wild herbivores such as blue bulls and sambar have bounced back from near local extinction, and villagers report the occasional presence of two leopards in this first people's sanctuary of India. A migrant tiger has also been spotted in the sprouting forests . . . Swati Shrestha, a researcher from . . . New Delhi . . . says ". . . village elders welcome the presence of carnivores, claiming that the disappearance of . . . predators . . . was the reason behind depletion of forests." . . . The locals maintain that "the presence of predators will inhibit people from going into the forest unless absolutely necessary."

Source: http://www.ngnews.com/news/2000/05/05312000/india_2757.asp. *National Geographic* 2000.

overview

Four basic economic types are found in nonindustrial societies: foraging, horticulture, agriculture, and pastoralism. Food production eventually supplanted foraging in most world areas. Among foragers the band is a basic social unit. Ties of kinship and marriage link its members. Men usually hunt and fish. Women usually gather.

Horticulture and agriculture are two forms of farming, representing different ends of a continuum based on land and labor use. Horticulture always has a fallow period, but agriculturalists farm the same land year after year. Agriculturalists also use labor intensively, in irrigation and terracing, and by maintaining domesticated animals. The mixed nature of pastoralism, based on herding, is evident. Nomadic pastoralists trade with farmers. Among transhumant pastoralists, part of the population farms, while another part takes the herds to pasture.

Economic anthropologists study systems of production, distribution (exchange), and consumption. Economics has been defined as the science that studies the allocation of scarce means to alternative ends. Western economists assume the idea of scarcity is universal—which it isn't—and that in making choices, people strive to maximize personal profit. However, people may and do maximize values other than individual profit.

There are three forms of exchange. Market exchange is based on impersonal purchase and sale, motivated by profit. With redistribution, goods are collected at a central place, with some eventually given back to the people. Reciprocity governs exchanges between social equals. Reciprocity, redistribution, and the market principle may coexist in the same society. The primary exchange mode in a society is the one that allocates the means of production.

Adaptive Strategies

In today's world, communities and societies are being incorporated, at an accelerating rate, into larger systems. The origin and spread of food production (plant cultivation and animal domestication) led to the formation of larger social and political systems, such as states. Food production led to major changes in human life. The pace of cultural transformation increased enormously. This chapter provides a framework for understanding a variety of human adaptive strategies and economic systems.

The anthropologist Yehudi Cohen (1974*b*) used the term *adaptive strategy* to describe a group's system of economic production. Cohen argued that the most important reason for similarities between two (or more) unrelated societies is their possession of a similar adaptive strategy. For example, there are clear similarities among societies that have a foraging (hunting and gathering) strategy. Cohen developed a typology of societies based on correlations between their economies and their social features. His typology includes these five adaptive strategies: foraging, horticulture, agriculture, pastoralism, and industrialism. Industrialism is discussed in the chapter "The Modern World System." The present chapter focuses on the first four adaptive strategies.

Foraging

Until 10,000 years ago, people everywhere were foragers, also known as hunter-gatherers. However, environmental differences did create contrasts among the world's foragers. Some, such as the people who lived in Europe during the ice ages, were big-game hunters. Today, hunters in the Arctic still focus on large animals and herd animals; they have much less vegetation and variety in their diets than do tropical foragers. In general, as one moves from colder to warmer areas, there is an increase in the number of species. The tropics contain tremendous biodiversity, a great variety of plant and animal species, many of which have been used by human foragers. Tropical foragers typically hunt and gather a wide range of plant and animal life.

Figure 14.1
Worldwide Distribution of Recent Hunter-Gatherers

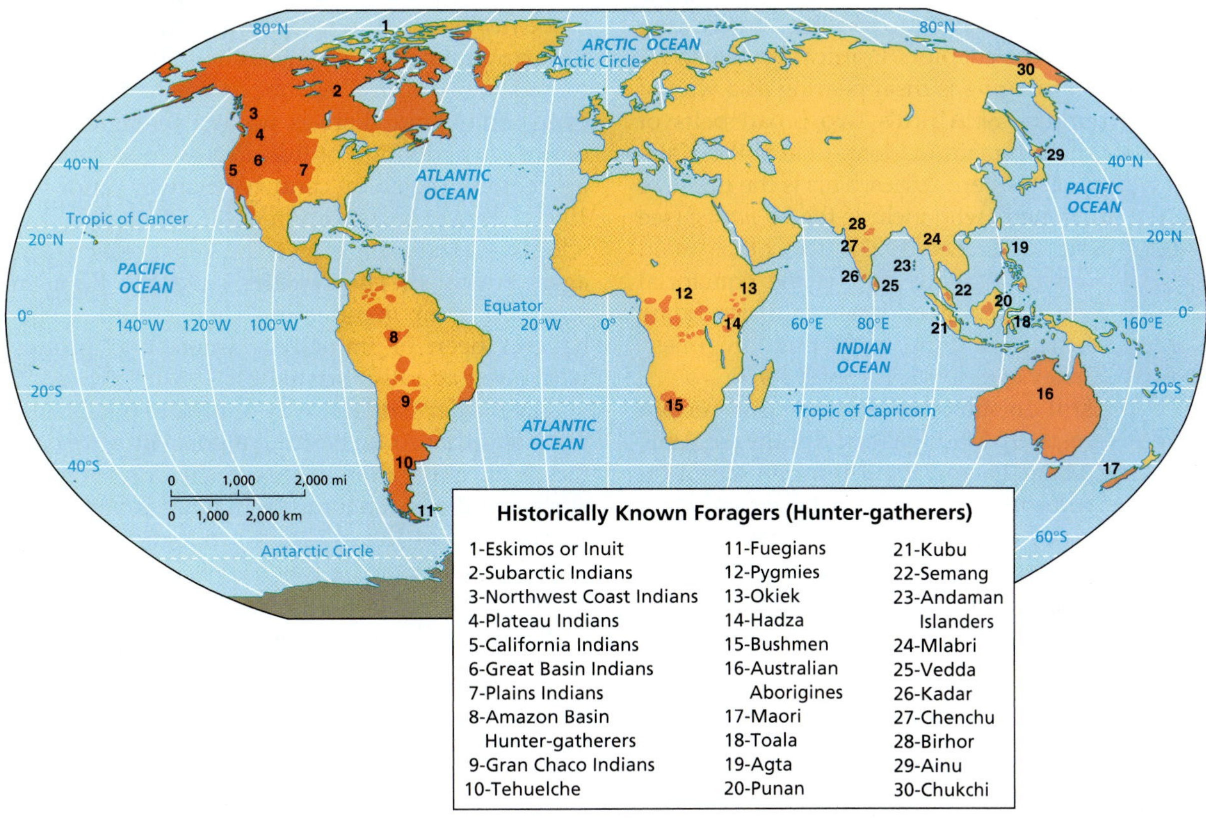

Source: Gäran Burenhult, ed., *People of the Stone Age: Hunters and Gatherers and Early Farmers* (San Francisco: HarperCollins, 1993).

The same may be true in temperate areas, such as the North Pacific Coast of North America, where Native American foragers could draw on a variety of land and sea resources, including salmon, other fish species, berries, mountain goats, seals, and sea mammals. Nevertheless, despite differences due to environmental variation, all foraging economies have shared one essential feature: People rely on nature to make their living.

Animal domestication (initially of sheep and goats) and plant cultivation (of wheat and barley) began 10,000 to 12,000 years ago in the Middle East. Cultivation based on different crops, such as maize, manioc (cassava), and potatoes, arose independently some 3,000 to 4,000 years later in the Americas. In both hemispheres the new economy spread rapidly. Most foragers eventually turned to food production. Today, almost all foragers have at least some dependence on food production or on food producers (Kent 1992).

The foraging way of life survived in certain environments (see Figure 14.1), including a few islands and forests, along with deserts and very cold areas—places where food production was not practicable with simple technology (see Lee and Daly 1999). In many areas, foragers had been exposed to the "idea" of food production but never adopted it because their own economies provided a perfectly adequate and nutritious diet—with a lot less work. In some areas, people reverted to foraging after trying food production and abandoning it. In most areas where hunter-gatherers did survive, foraging should be described as "recent" rather than "contemporary." All modern foragers live in nation-states, depend to some extent on government assistance, and have contacts with food-producing neighbors, as well as missionaries and other outsiders. We should not view contemporary foragers as isolated or pristine survivors of the

Stone Age. Modern foragers are influenced by regional forces (e.g., trade and war), national and international policies, and political and economic events in the world system. (See the "Interesting Issues" box in the chapter "Political Systems.")

Although foraging is disappearing as a way of life, the outlines of Africa's two broad belts of recent foraging remain evident. One is the Kalahari Desert of southern Africa. This is the home of the *San* (Bushmen), who include the *Ju/'hoansi* (see

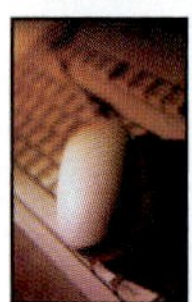

Kent 1996; Lee 1993). The other main African foraging area is the equatorial forest of central and eastern Africa, home of the Mbuti, Efe, and other "pygmies" (Bailey et al. 1989; Turnbull 1965).

People still do subsistence foraging in certain remote forests in Madagascar; Southeast Asia, including Malaysia and the Philippines; and on certain islands off the Indian coast (Lee and Daly 1999). Some of the best-known recent foragers are the aborigines of Australia. Those Native Australians lived on their island continent for more than 40,000 years without developing food production.

The Western Hemisphere also had recent foragers. The Eskimos, or Inuit, of Alaska and Canada are well-known hunters. These (and other) northern foragers now use modern technology, including rifles and snowmobiles, in their subsistence activities (Pelto 1973). The native populations of California, Oregon, Washington, British Columbia, and Alaska were all foragers, as were those of inland subarctic Canada and the Great Lakes. For many Native Americans, fishing, hunting, and gathering remain important subsistence (and sometimes commercial) activities.

Coastal foragers also lived near the southern tip of South America, in Patagonia. On the grassy plains of Argentina, southern Brazil, Uruguay, and Paraguay, there were other hunter-gatherers. The contemporary Aché of Paraguay are usually called "hunter-gatherers" even though they get just a third of their livelihood from foraging. The Aché also grow crops, have domesticated animals, and live in or near mission posts, where they receive food from missionaries (Hawkes et al. 1982; Hill et al. 1987).

Throughout the world, foraging survived mainly in environments that posed major obstacles to food production. (Some foragers took refuge in such areas after the rise of food production, the state, colonialism, or the modern world system.) The difficulties of cultivating at the North Pole are obvious. In southern Africa, the Dobe Ju/'hoansi San area studied by Richard Lee is surrounded by a waterless belt 70 to 200 kilometers in breadth. The Dobe area is hard to reach even today, and there is no archaeological evidence of occupation of this area by food producers before the 20th century (Solway and Lee 1990). However, environmental limits to other adaptive strategies aren't the only reason foragers survived. Their niches have one thing in common: their marginality. Their environments haven't been of immediate interest to groups with other adaptive strategies.

The hunter-gatherer way of life did persist in a few areas that could be cultivated, even after contact with cultivators. Those tenacious foragers, such as indigenous foragers in what is now California, did not turn to food production because they were supporting themselves adequately by hunting and gathering. As the modern world system spreads, the number of foragers continues to decline.

Correlates of Foraging

Typologies, such as Cohen's adaptive strategies, are useful because they suggest **correlations**—that is, association or covariation between two or more variables. (Correlated variables are factors that are linked and interrelated, such as food intake and body weight, such that when one increases or decreases, the other tends to change, too.) Ethnographic studies in hundreds of societies have revealed many correlations between the economy and social life. Associated (correlated) with each adaptive strategy is a bundle of particular cultural features. Correlations, however, are rarely perfect. Some foragers lack cultural features usually associated with foraging, and some of those features are found in groups with other adaptive strategies.

What, then, are the usual correlates of foraging? People who subsist by hunting, gathering, and fishing often live in band-organized societies. Their basic social unit, the **band,** is a small group of fewer than a hundred people, all related by kinship or marriage. Band size varies between cultures and often from one season to the next in a given culture. In some foraging societies, band

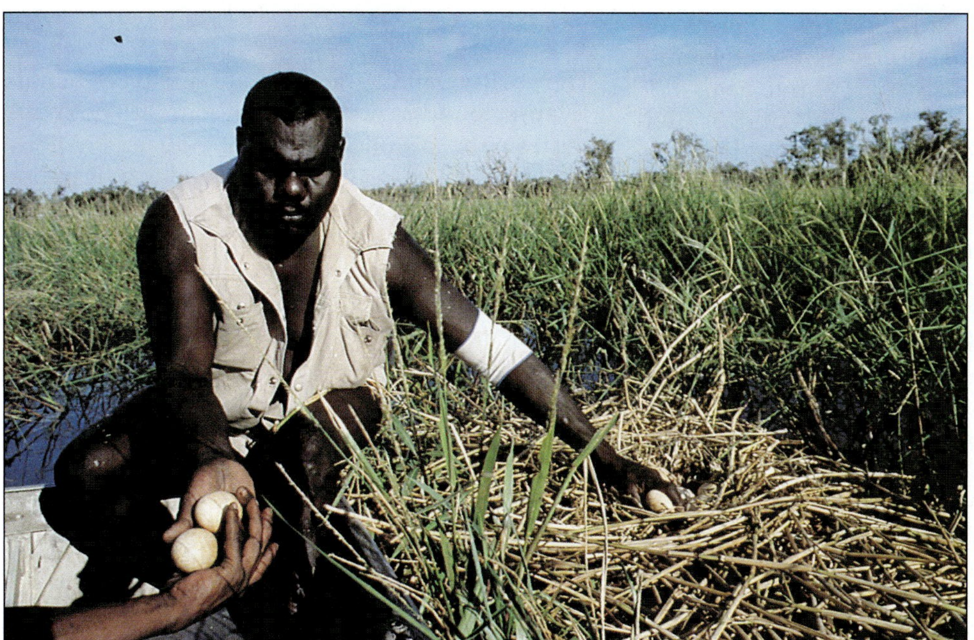

A contemporary forager from Australia's Cape York peninsula collects eggs from the nest of a magpie goose. Such hunter-gatherers are not isolated survivors of the Stone Age, but contemporary people who live in nation-states and have contact with outsiders. In what forms does foraging survive in our own society?

size stays about the same year-round. In others, the band splits up for part of the year. Families leave to gather resources that are better exploited by just a few people. Later, they regroup for cooperative work and ceremonies.

Several examples of seasonal splits and reunions are known from ethnography and archaeology. In southern Africa, some San aggregate around water holes in the dry season and split up in the wet season, whereas other bands disperse in the dry season (Barnard 1979; Kent 1992). This reflects environmental variation. San who lack permanent water must disperse and forage widely for moisture-filled plants. In ancient Oaxaca, Mexico, before the advent of plant cultivation there around 4,000 years ago, foragers assembled in large bands in summer. They collectively harvested tree pods and cactus fruits. Then in fall, they split into much smaller family groups to hunt deer and gather grasses and plants that were effectively foraged by small teams.

One typical characteristic of the foraging life is mobility. In many San groups, as among the Mbuti of Congo, people shift band membership several times in a lifetime. One may be born, for example, in a band where one's mother has kin. Later, one's family may move to a band where the father has relatives. Because bands are exogamous (people marry outside their own band), one's parents come from two different bands, and one's grandparents may come from four. People may join any band to which they have kinship or marriage links. A couple may live in, or shift between, the husband's and the wife's band.

One also may affiliate with a band through *fictive kinship*—personal relationships modeled on kinship, such as that between godparents and godchildren. San, for example, have a limited number of personal names. People with the same name have a special relationship; they treat each other like siblings. San expect the same hospitality in bands where they have *namesakes* as they do in a band in which a real sibling lives. Namesakes share a strong identity. They call everyone in a namesake's band by the kin terms the namesake uses. Those people reply as if they were addressing a real relative. Kinship, marriage, and fictive kinship permit San to join several bands, and nomadic (regularly on-the-move) foragers do change bands often. Band membership therefore can change tremendously from year to year.

All human societies have some kind of division of labor based on gender. Among foragers, men typically hunt and fish while women gather and collect, but the specific nature of the work varies among cultures. Sometimes women's work contributes most to the diet. Sometimes male hunting and fishing predominate. Among foragers in tropical and semitropical areas, gathering tends to contribute more to the diet than hunting and fishing do—even though the labor costs of gathering tend to be much higher than those of hunting and fishing.

All foragers make social distinctions based on age. Often old people receive great respect as guardians of myths, legends, stories, and traditions. Younger people value the elders' special knowledge of ritual and practical matters. Most foraging societies are *egalitarian.* This means that contrasts in prestige are minor and are based on age and gender.

When considering issues of "human nature," we should remember that the egalitarian band was a basic form of human social life for most of our history. Food production has existed less than 1 percent of the time *Homo* has spent on earth. However, it has produced huge social differences. We now consider the main economic features of food-producing strategies.

Cultivation

In Cohen's typology, the three adaptive strategies based on food production in nonindustrial societies are horticulture, agriculture, and pastoralism. In non-Western cultures, as is also true in modern nations, people carry out a variety of economic activities. Each adaptive strategy refers to the main economic activity. Pastoralists (herders), for example, consume milk, butter, blood, and meat from their animals as mainstays of their diet. However, they also add grain to the diet by doing some cultivating or by trading with neighbors. Food producers also may hunt or gather to supplement a diet based on domesticated species.

Horticulture

Horticulture and agriculture are two types of cultivation found in nonindustrial societies. Both differ from the farming systems of industrial nations like the United States and Canada, which use large land areas, machinery, and petrochemicals. According to Cohen, **horticulture** is cultivation that makes intensive use of *none* of the factors of production: land, labor, capital, and machinery. Horticulturalists use simple tools such as hoes and digging sticks to grow their crops. Their fields are not permanently cultivated and lie fallow for varying lengths of time.

In slash-and-burn horticulture, the land is cleared by cutting down (slashing) and burning trees and bush, using simple technology. After such clearing this woman uses a digging stick to plant mountain rice in Madagascar. What might be the environmental effects of slash-and-burn cultivation?

Horticulture often involves *slash-and-burn* techniques. Here, horticulturalists clear land by cutting down (slashing) and burning forest or bush or by setting fire to the grass covering the plot. The vegetation is broken down, pests are killed, and the ashes remain to fertilize the soil. Crops are then sown, tended, and harvested. Use of the plot is not continuous. Often it is cultivated for only a year. This depends, however, on soil fertility and weeds, which compete with cultivated plants for nutrients.

Domesticated animals may serve as "tools" for agricultural production. These Burmese farmers harness oxen to plow their rice fields in Arakan state. What's the main use of domesticated animals in your society?

When horticulturalists abandon a plot because of soil exhaustion or a thick weed cover, they clear another piece of land, and the original plot reverts to forest. After several years of fallowing (the duration varies in different societies), the cultivator returns to farm the original plot again. Horticulture is also called *shifting cultivation.* Such shifts from plot to plot do not mean that whole villages must move when plots are abandoned. Horticulture can support large permanent villages. Among the Kuikuru of the South American tropical forest, for example, one village of 150 people remained in the same place for 90 years (Carneiro 1956). Kuikuru houses are large and well made. Because the work involved in building them is great, the Kuikuru would rather walk farther to their fields than construct a new village. They shift their plots rather than their settlements. On the other hand, horticulturalists in the montaña (Andean foothills) of Peru live in small villages of about 30 people (Carneiro 1961/1968). Their houses are small and simple. After a few years in one place, these people build new villages near virgin land. Because their houses are so simple, they prefer rebuilding to walking even a half mile to their fields.

Agriculture

Agriculture is cultivation that requires more labor than horticulture does, because it uses land intensively and continuously. The greater labor demands associated with agriculture reflect its common use of domesticated animals, irrigation, or terracing.

Domesticated Animals

Many agriculturalists use animals as means of production—for transport, as cultivating machines, and for their manure. Asian farmers typically incorporate cattle and/or water buffalo into agricultural economies based on rice production. Rice farmers may use cattle to trample pretilled flooded fields, thus mixing soil and water, prior to transplanting. Many agriculturalists attach animals to plows and harrows for field preparation before planting or transplanting. Also, agriculturalists typically collect manure from their animals, using it to fertilize their plots, thus increasing yields. Animals are attached to carts for transport, as well as to implements of cultivation.

Irrigation

While horticulturalists must await the rainy season, agriculturalists can schedule their planting in advance, because they control water. Like other irrigation experts in the Philippines, the Ifugao irrigate their fields with canals from rivers, streams, springs, and ponds. Irrigation makes it possible to cultivate a plot year after year. Irrigation enriches

the soil because the irrigated field is a unique ecosystem with several species of plants and animals, many of them minute organisms, whose wastes fertilize the land.

An irrigated field is a capital investment that usually increases in value. It takes time for a field to start yielding; it reaches full productivity only after several years of cultivation. The Ifugao, like other irrigators, have farmed the same fields for generations. In some agricultural areas, including the Middle East, however, salts carried in the irrigation water can make fields unusable after 50 or 60 years.

Terracing

Terracing is another agricultural technique the Ifugao have mastered. Their homeland has small valleys separated by steep hillsides. Because the population is dense, people need to farm the hills. However, if they simply planted on the steep hillsides, fertile soil and crops would be washed away during the rainy season. To prevent this, the Ifugao cut into the hillside and build stage after stage of terraced fields rising above the valley floor. Springs located above the terraces supply their irrigation water. The labor necessary to build and maintain a system of terraces is great. Terrace walls crumble each year and must be partially rebuilt. The canals that bring water down through the terraces also demand attention.

Costs and Benefits of Agriculture

Agriculture requires human labor to build and maintain irrigation systems, terraces, and other works. People must feed, water, and care for their animals. Given sufficient labor input and management, agricultural land can yield one or two crops annually for years or even generations. An agricultural field does not necessarily produce a higher single-year yield than does a horticultural plot. The first crop grown by horticulturalists on long-idle land may be larger than that from an agricultural plot of the same size. Furthermore, because agriculturalists work harder than horticulturalists do, agriculture's yield relative to labor is also lower. Agriculture's main advantage is that the long-term yield per area is far greater and more dependable. Because a single field sustains its owners year after year, there is no need to maintain a reserve of uncultivated land as horticulturalists do. This is why agricultural societies tend to be more densely populated than are horticultural ones.

The Cultivation Continuum

Because nonindustrial economies can have features of both horticulture and agriculture, it is useful to discuss cultivators as being arranged along a **cultivation continuum.** Horticultural systems stand at one end—the "low-labor, shifting-plot" end. Agriculturalists are at the other—the "labor-intensive, permanent-plot" end.

We speak of a continuum because there are today intermediate economies, combining horticultural and agricultural features—more intensive than annually shifting horticulture but less intensive than agriculture. These recall the intermediate economies revealed by archaeological sequences leading from horticulture to agriculture in the Middle East, Mexico, and other areas of early food production. Unlike nonintensive horticulturalists, who farm a plot just once before fallowing it, the South American Kuikuru grow two or three crops of *manioc,* or cassava— an edible tuber—before abandoning their plots. Cultivation is even more intense in certain densely populated areas of Papua New Guinea, where plots are planted for two or three years, allowed to rest for three to five, and then recultivated.

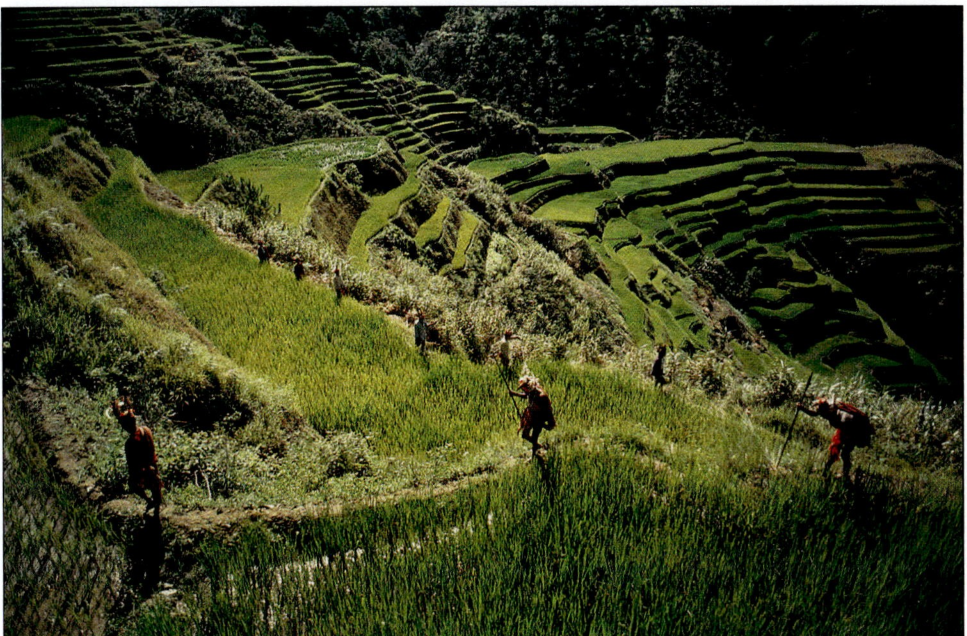

Agriculture requires more labor than horticulture does and uses land intensively and continuously. Labor demands associated with agriculture reflect its use of domesticated animals, irrigation, and terracing. The rice farmers of Luzon in the Philippines, such as the Ifugao, are famous for their irrigated and terraced fields.

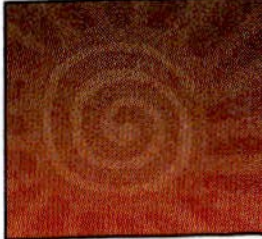

After several of these cycles, the plots are abandoned for a longer fallow period. Such a pattern is called *sectorial fallowing* (Wolf 1966). Besides Papua New Guinea, such systems occur in places as distant as West Africa and highland Mexico. Sectorial fallowing is associated with denser populations than is simple horticulture. The simpler system is the norm in tropical forests, where weed invasion and delicate soils prevent more intensive cultivation.

The key difference between horticulture and agriculture is that horticulture always uses a fallow period whereas agriculture does not. The earliest cultivators in the Middle East and in Mexico were rainfall-dependent horticulturalists. Until recently, horticulture was the main form of cultivation in several areas, including parts of Africa, Southeast Asia, the Pacific islands, Mexico, Central America, and the South American tropical forest.

Intensification: People and the Environment

The range of environments available for food production has widened as people have increased their control over nature. For example, in arid areas of California, where Native Americans once foraged, modern irrigation technology now sustains rich agricultural estates. Agriculturalists live in many areas that are too arid for nonirrigators or too hilly for nonterracers. Many ancient civilizations in arid lands arose on an agricultural base. Increasing labor intensity and permanent land use have major demographic, social, political, and environmental consequences.

Thus, because of their permanent fields, intensive cultivators are sedentary. People live in larger and more permanent communities located closer to other settlements. Growth in population size and density increases contact between individuals and groups. There is more need to regulate interpersonal relations, including conflicts of interest. Economies that support more people usually require more coordination in the use of land, labor, and other resources.

Intensive agriculture has significant environmental effects. Irrigation ditches and paddies (fields with irrigated rice) become repositories for organic wastes, chemicals (such as salts), and disease microorganisms. Intensive agriculture typically spreads at the expense of trees and forests, which are cut down to be replaced by fields. Accompanying such deforestation is loss of environmental diversity. Agricultural economies grow increasingly specialized—focusing on one or a few caloric staples, such as rice, and on the animals that are raised and tended to aid the agricultural economy. Because tropical horticulturalists typically cultivate dozens of plant species simultaneously, a horticultural plot tends to mirror the botanical diversity that is found in a tropical forest. Agricultural plots, by contrast, reduce ecological diversity by cutting down trees and concentrating on just a few staple foods. Such crop specialization is true of agriculturalists both in the tropics (e.g., Indonesian paddy farmers) and outside the tropics (e.g., Middle Eastern irrigated farmers).

At least in the tropics, the diets of both foragers and horticulturalists are typically more diverse, although under less secure human control, than the diets of agriculturalists. Agriculturists attempt to reduce risk in production by favoring stability in the form of a reliable annual harvest and long-term production. Tropical foragers and horticulturalists, by contrast, attempt to reduce risk by relying on multiple species and benefiting from ecological diversity. The agricultural strategy is to put all one's eggs in one big and very dependable basket. Of course, even with agriculture, there is a possibility that the single staple crop may fail, and famine may result. The strategy of tropical foragers and horticulturalists is to have several smaller baskets, a few of which may fail without endangering subsistence. The agricultural strategy makes sense when there are lots of children to raise and adults to be fed. Foraging and horticulture, of course, are associated with smaller, sparser, and more mobile populations.

Agricultural economies also pose a series of regulatory problems—which central governments often have arisen to solve. How is water to be managed—along with disputes about access to and distribution of water? With more people living closer together on more valuable land, agriculturalists are more likely to come into conflict than foragers and horticulturalists are. Agriculture paved the way, for the origin of the state, and most agriculturalists live in *states:* complex sociopolitical systems that administer a territory and populace with substantial contrasts in occupation, wealth, prestige, and power. In such societies, cultivators play their role as one part of a differentiated, functionally specialized, and tightly integrated sociopolitical system. The social and political implications of food production and intensification are examined more fully in the chapter "Political Systems."

Pastoralism

Pastoralists live in North Africa, the Middle East, Europe, Asia, and sub-Saharan Africa. These herders are people whose activities focus on such domesticated animals as cattle, sheep, goats, camels, and yak. East African pastoralists, like many others, live in symbiosis with their herds. (*Symbiosis* is an obligatory interaction between groups—here humans and animals—that is beneficial to each.) Herders attempt to protect their animals and to ensure their reproduction in return for food and other products, such as leather. Herds provide dairy products, meat, and blood. Animals are killed at ceremonies, which occur throughout the year, and so beef is available regularly.

People use livestock in a variety of ways. Natives of North America's Great Plains, for example, didn't eat, but only rode, their horses. (Europeans reintroduced horses to the Western Hemisphere; the native American horse had become extinct thousands of years earlier.) For Plains Indians, horses served as "tools of the trade," means of production used to hunt buffalo, a main target of their economies. So the Plains Indians were not true pastoralists but *hunters* who used horses—as many agriculturalists use animals—as means of production.

Unlike the use of animals merely as productive machines, pastoralists typically make direct use of their herds for food. They consume their meat, blood, and milk, from which they make yogurt, butter, and cheese. Although some pastoralists rely on their herds more completely than others do, it is impossible to base subsistence solely on animals. Most pastoralists therefore supplement their diet by hunting, gathering, fish-

Pastoralists may be nomadic or transhumant, but they don't typically live off their herds alone. They either trade or cultivate. The photo at the top shows a female pastoralist who is a member of the Kirghiz ethnic group in Xinjiang Province, China. The photo at the bottom shows an Alpine shepherd in Germany. This man accompanies his flocks to highland meadows each year.

ing, cultivating, or trading. To get crops, pastoralists either trade with cultivators or do some cultivating or gathering themselves.

Unlike foraging and cultivation, which existed throughout the world before the Industrial Revolution, pastoralism was almost totally confined to the Old World. Before European conquest, the only pastoralists in the Americas lived in the Andean region of South America. They used their llamas and alpacas for food and wool and in agriculture and transport. Much more recently, Navajo of the southwestern United States developed a pastoral economy based on sheep, which were brought to North America by Europeans. The populous Navajo are now the major pastoral population in the Western Hemisphere.

Two patterns of movement occur with pastoralism: nomadism and transhumance. Both are based on the fact that herds must move to use pasture available in particular places in different seasons. In **pastoral nomadism,** the entire group—women, men, and children—moves with the animals throughout the year. The Middle East and North Africa provide numerous examples of pastoral nomads. In Iran, for example, the Basseri and the Qashqai ethnic groups traditionally followed a nomadic route more than 300 miles (480 kilometers) long. Starting each year near the coast, they took their animals to grazing land 17,000 feet (5,400 meters) above sea level.

With **transhumance,** part of the group moves with the herds, but most people stay in the home village. There are examples from Europe and Africa. In Europe's Alps, it is just the shepherds and goatherds—not the whole village—who accompany the flocks to highland meadows in summer. Among the Turkana of Uganda, men and boys accompany the herds to distant pastures, while much of the village stays put and does some horticultural farming. Villages tend to be located in the best-watered areas, which have the longest pasture season. This

Table 14.1
Yehudi Cohen's Adaptive Strategies (Economic Typology) Summarized

Adaptive Strategy	Also Known as	Key Features/Varieties
Foraging	Hunting-gathering	Mobility, use of nature's resources
Horticulture	Slash-and-burn, shifting cultivation, swiddening, dry farming	Fallow period
Agriculture	Intensive farming	Continuous use of land, intensive use of labor
Pastoralism	Herding	Nomadism and transhumance
Industrialism	Industrial production	Factory production, capitalism, socialist production

permits the village population to stay together during a large chunk of the year.

During their annual trek, pastoral nomads trade for crops and other products with more sedentary people. Transhumants don't have to trade for crops. Because only part of the population accompanies the herds, transhumants can maintain year-round villages and grow their own crops. Table 14.1 summarizes the main features of Cohen's adaptive strategies.

Modes of Production

An **economy** is a system of production, distribution, and consumption of resources; *economics* is the study of such systems. Economists tend to focus on modern nations and capitalist systems, while anthropologists have broadened understanding of economic principles by gathering data on nonindustrial economies. Economic anthropology studies economics in a comparative perspective (see Gudeman 1999; Plattner 1989; Wilk 1996).

A **mode of production** is a way of organizing production—"a set of social relations through which labor is deployed to wrest energy from nature by means of tools, skills, organization, and knowledge" (Wolf 1982, p. 75). In the capitalist mode of production, money buys labor power, and there is a social gap between the people (bosses and workers) involved in the production process. By contrast, in nonindustrial societies, labor is not usually bought but is given as a social obligation. In such a *kin-based* mode of production, mutual aid in production is one among many expressions of a larger web of social relations.

Societies representing each of the adaptive strategies just discussed (e.g., foraging) tend to have a similar mode of production. Differences in the mode of production within a given strategy may reflect the differences in environments, target resources, or cultural traditions. Thus, a foraging mode of production may be based on individual hunters or teams, depending on whether the game is a solitary or a herd animal. Gathering is usually more individualistic than hunting, although collecting teams may assemble when abundant resources ripen and must be harvested quickly. Fishing may be done alone (as in ice or spear fishing) or in crews (as with open sea fishing and hunting of sea mammals).

Production in Nonindustrial Societies

Although some kind of division of economic labor related to age and gender is a cultural universal, the specific tasks assigned to each sex and to people of different ages vary. Many horticultural societies assign a major productive role to women, but some make men's work primary. Similarly, among pastoralists, men generally tend large animals, but in some cultures women do the milking. Jobs accomplished through teamwork in some cultivating societies are done by smaller groups or individuals working over a longer period of time in others.

The cultivation of rice, one of the world's most important food crops, illustrates a division of labor by age and gender. These young women are transplanting rice seedlings in Sulawesi, Indonesia, and these men are threshing rice, to separate the grains from the stem, in Bangladesh.

The Betsileo of Madagascar have two stages of teamwork in rice cultivation: transplanting and harvesting. Team size varies with the size of the field. Both transplanting and harvesting feature a traditional division of labor by age and gender that is well known to all Betsileo and is repeated across the generations. The first job in transplanting is the trampling of a previously tilled flooded field by young men driving cattle, in order to mix earth and water. They bring cattle to trample the fields just before transplanting. The young men yell at and beat the cattle, striving to drive them into a frenzy so that they will trample the fields properly. Trampling breaks up clumps of earth and mixes irrigation water with soil to form a smooth mud into which women transplant seedlings. Once the tramplers leave the field, older men arrive. With their spades, they break up the clumps that the cattle missed. Meanwhile, the owner and other adults uproot rice seedlings and bring them to the field.

At harvest time, four or five months later, young men cut the rice off the stalks. Young women carry it to the clearing above the field. Older women arrange and stack it. The oldest men and women then stand on the stack, stomping and compacting it. Three days later, young men thresh the rice, beating the stalks against a rock to remove the grain. Older men then attack the stalks with sticks to make sure all the grains have fallen off.

Most of the other tasks in Betsileo rice cultivation are done by individual owners and their immediate families. All household members help weed the rice field. It's a man's job to till the fields with a spade or a plow. Individual men repair the irrigation and drainage systems and the earth walls that separate one plot from the next. Among other agriculturalists, however, repairing the irrigation system is a task involving teamwork and communal labor.

Means of Production

In nonindustrial societies, there is a more intimate relationship between the worker and the means of production than there is in industrial nations. **Means, or factors, of production** include land (territory), labor, and technology.

Land

Among foragers, ties between people and land are less permanent than they are among food producers. Although many bands have territories, the boundaries are not usually marked, and there is no way they can be enforced. The hunter's stake in an animal that is being stalked or has been hit with a poisoned arrow is more important than where the animal finally dies. A person acquires the rights to use a band's territory by being born in the band or by joining it through a tie of kinship, marriage, or fictive kinship. In Botswana in southern Africa, Ju/'hoansi San women, whose work provides over half the food, habitually use specific tracts of berry-bearing trees. However, when a woman changes bands, she immediately acquires a new gathering area.

Among food producers, rights to the means of production also come through kinship and marriage. Descent groups (groups whose members claim common ancestry) are common among nonindustrial food producers, and those who descend from the founder share the group's territory and resources. If the adaptive strategy is horticulture, the estate includes garden and fallow land for shifting cultivation. As members of a descent group, pastoralists have access to animals to start their own herds, to grazing land, to garden land, and to other means of production.

Labor, Tools, and Specialization

Like land, labor is a means of production. In nonindustrial societies, access to both land and labor comes through social links such as kinship, marriage, and descent. Mutual aid in production is merely one aspect of ongoing social relations that are expressed on many other occasions.

Nonindustrial societies contrast with industrial nations in regard to another means of production: technology. In bands and tribes, manufacturing is often linked to age and gender. Women may weave and men may make pottery or vice versa. Most people of a particular age and gender share the technical knowledge associated with that age and gender. If married women customarily make baskets, all or most married women know how to make baskets. Neither technology nor technical knowledge is as specialized as it is in states.

However, some tribal societies do promote specialization. Among the Yanomami of Venezuela and Brazil, for instance, certain villages manufacture clay pots and others make hammocks. They don't specialize, as one might suppose, because certain raw materials happen to be available near particular villages. Clay suitable for pots is widely available. Everyone knows how to make pots, but not everybody does so. Craft specialization reflects the social and political environment rather than the natural environment. Such specialization promotes trade, which is the first step in creating an alliance with enemy villages (Chagnon 1997). Specialization contributes to keeping the peace, although it has not prevented intervillage warfare.

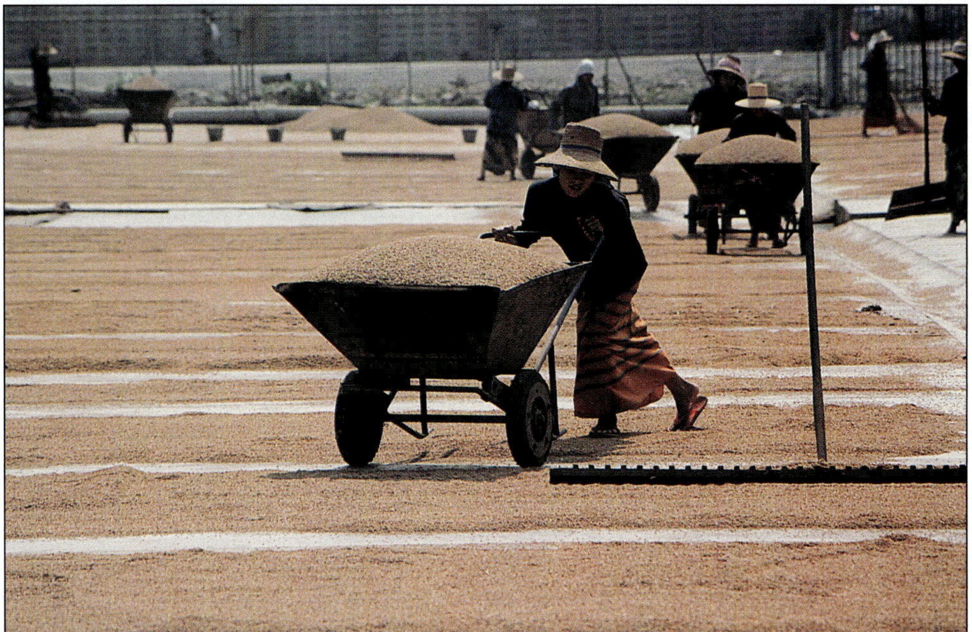

Not just factory work, but agricultural production may be industrialized, so that workers feel alienated from their product. This scene shows not a family farm but the mass production of rice in Thailand. Is alienation an issue in your own work?

Alienation in Industrial Economies

There are some significant contrasts between industrial and nonindustrial economies. When factory workers produce for sale and for their employer's profit, rather than for their own use, they may be alienated from the items they make. Such alienation means they don't feel strong pride in or personal identification with their products. They see their product as belonging to someone else, not to the man or woman whose labor actually produced it. In nonindustrial societies, by contrast, people usually see their work through from start to finish and have a sense of accomplishment in the product. The fruits of their labor are their own, rather than someone else's.

In nonindustrial societies, the economic relation between coworkers is just one aspect of a more general social relation. They aren't just coworkers but kin, in-laws, or celebrants in the same ritual. In industrial nations, people don't usually work with relatives and neighbors. If coworkers are friends, the personal relationship usually develops out of their common employment rather than being based on a previous association.

Thus, industrial workers have impersonal relations with their products, coworkers, and employers. People sell their labor for cash, and the economic domain stands apart from ordinary social life. In nonindustrial societies, however, the relations of production, distribution, and consumption are *social relations with economic aspects*. Economy is not a separate entity but is *embedded* in the society.

Economizing and Maximization

Economic anthropologists have been concerned with two main questions:

1. How are production, distribution, and consumption organized in different societies? This question focuses on *systems* of human behavior and their organization.

2. What motivates people in different cultures to produce, distribute or exchange, and consume? Here the focus is not on systems of behavior but on the motives of the *individuals* who participate in those systems.

Anthropologists view both economic systems and motivations in a cross-cultural perspective. Motivation is a concern of psychologists, but it also has been, implicitly or explicitly, a concern of economists and anthropologists. Economists tend to assume that producers and distributors make decisions rationally using the *profit motive,* as do consumers when they shop around for the best value. Although anthropologists know that the profit motive is not universal, the assumption that individuals try to maximize profits is basic to the capitalist world economy and to much of Western economic theory. In fact, the subject matter of economics is often defined as **economizing,** or the rational allocation of scarce means (or resources) to alternative ends (or uses). What does that mean? Classical economic theory assumes that our wants are infinite and that our means are limited. Since means are limited, people must make choices about how to use their scarce resources: their time, labor, money, and capital. (The "Interesting Issues" on "Scarcity and the Betsileo" disputes the idea that people always make economic choices based on scarcity.) Economists assume that when confronted with choices and decisions, people tend to make the one that maximizes profit. This is assumed to be the most rational (reasonable) choice.

The idea that individuals choose to maximize profits was a basic assumption of the classical economists of the 19th century and one that is held by many contemporary economists. However, certain economists now recognize that individuals in Western cultures, as in others, may be motivated by many other goals. Depending on the society and the situation, people may try to maximize profit, wealth, prestige, pleasure, comfort, or social harmony. Individuals may want to realize their personal or family ambitions or those of another group to which they belong.

Alternative Ends

To what uses do people in various societies put their scarce resources? Throughout the world, people devote some of their time and energy to building up a *subsistence fund* (Wolf 1966). In other words, they have to work to eat, to replace the calories they use in their daily activity. People also must invest in a *replacement fund.* They must maintain their technology and other items essential to production. If a hoe or plow breaks, they must repair or replace it. They also must obtain and replace items that are essential not to production but to everyday life, such as clothing and shelter.

People also have to invest in a *social fund.* They have to help their friends, relatives, in-laws, and neighbors. It is useful to distinguish between a social fund and a *ceremonial fund.* The latter term refers to expenditures on ceremonies or rituals. To prepare a festival honoring one's ancestors, for example, requires time and the outlay of wealth.

Citizens of nonindustrial states also must allocate scarce resources to a *rent fund.* We think of rent as payment for the use of property. However, rent fund has a wider meaning. It refers to resources that people must render to an individual or agency that is superior politically or economically. Tenant farmers and sharecroppers, for example, either pay rent or give some of their produce to their landlords, as peasants did under feudalism.

Peasants are small-scale agriculturalists who live in nonindustrial states and have rent fund obligations (see Kearney 1996). They produce to feed themselves, to sell their produce, and to pay rent. All peasants have two things in common:

1. They live in state-organized societies.
2. They produce food without the elaborate technology—chemical fertilizers, tractors, airplanes to spray crops, and so on—of modern farming or agribusiness.

In addition to paying rent to landlords, peasants must satisfy government obligations, paying taxes in the form of money, produce, or labor. The rent fund is not simply an *additional* obligation for peasants. Often it becomes their foremost and unavoidable duty. Sometimes, to meet the obligation to pay rent, their own diets suffer. The demands of paying rent may divert resources from subsistence, replacement, social, and ceremonial funds.

Motivations vary from society to society, and people often lack freedom of choice in allocating their resources. Because of obligations to pay rent, peasants may allocate their scarce means toward

interesting issues

Scarcity and the Betsileo

From October 1966 through December 1967, my wife and I lived among the Betsileo people of Madagascar, studying their economy and social life (Kottak 1980). Soon after our arrival, we met two well-educated schoolteachers who were interested in our research. The woman's father was a congressman who became a cabinet minister during our stay. Our schoolteacher friends told us that their family came from a historically important and typical Betsileo village called Ivato, which they invited us to visit with them.

We had traveled to many other villages, where we were often displeased with our reception. As we drove up, children would run away screaming. Women would hurry inside. Men would retreat to doorways, where they lurked bashfully. Eventually someone would summon the courage to ask what we wanted. This behavior expressed the Betsileo's great fear of the *mpakafo*. Believed to cut out and devour his victim's heart and liver, the *mpakafo* is the Malagasy vampire. These cannibals are said to have fair skin and to be very tall. Because I have light skin and stand six feet four inches tall, I was a natural suspect. The fact that such creatures were not known to travel with their wives helped convince the Betsileo that I wasn't really a *mpakafo*.

When we visited Ivato, we found that its people were different. They were friendly and hospitable. Our very first day there, we did a brief census and found out who lived in which households. We learned people's names and their relationships to our schoolteacher friends and to each other. We met an excellent informant who knew all about the local history. In a few afternoons, I learned much more than I had in the other villages in several sessions.

Ivatans were willing to talk because I had powerful sponsors, village natives who had made it in the outside world, people the Ivatans knew would protect them. The schoolteachers vouched for us, but even more significant was the cabinet minister, who was like a grandfather and benefactor to everyone in town. The Ivatans had no reason to fear me because their more influential native son had asked them to answer my questions.

Once we moved to Ivato, the elders established a pattern of visiting us every evening. They came to talk, attracted by the inquisitive foreigners but also by the wine, cigarettes, and food we offered. I asked questions about their customs and beliefs. I eventually developed interview schedules about various subjects, including rice production. I mimeographed these forms to use in Ivato and in two other villages I was studying less intensively. Never have I interviewed as easily as I did in Ivato. So enthusiastic were the Ivatans about my questions that even people from neighboring villages came to join the study. Since these people knew nothing about the social scientist's techniques, I couldn't discourage them by saying that they weren't in my sample. Instead, I agreed to visit each village, where I filled out the interview schedule in just one house. Then I told the other villagers that the household head had done such a good job of teaching me about their village I wouldn't need to ask questions in the other households.

As our stay drew to an end, the elders of Ivato began to lament, saying, "We'll miss you. When you leave, there won't be any more cigarettes, any more wine, or any more questions." They wondered what it would be like for us back in the United States. They knew that I had an automobile and that I regularly purchased things, including the wine, cigarettes, and food I shared with them. I could afford to buy products they would never have. They commented, "When you go back to your country, you'll need a lot of money for things like cars, clothes, and food. We don't need to buy those things. We make almost everything we use. We don't need as much money as you, because we produce for ourselves."

The Betsileo are not unusual among people whom anthropologists have studied. Strange as it may seem to an American consumer, who may believe that he or she can never have enough money, some rice farmers actually believe that *they have all they need*. The lesson from the Betsileo is that scarcity, which economists view as universal, is variable. Although shortages do arise in nonindustrial societies, the concept of scarcity (insufficient means) is much less developed in stable subsistence-oriented societies than in the societies characterized by industrialism, particularly as the reliance on consumer goods increases.

ends that are not their own but those of government officials. Thus, even in societies where there is a profit motive, people are often prevented from rationally maximizing self-interest by factors beyond their control.

 Distribution, Exchange

The economist Karl Polanyi (1968) stimulated the comparative study of exchange, and several anthropologists followed his lead. To study exchange cross-culturally, Polanyi defined three principles orienting exchanges: the market principle, redistribution, and reciprocity. These principles can all be present in the same society, but in that case they govern different kinds of transactions. In any society, one of them usually dominates. The principle of exchange that dominates in a given society is the one that allocates the means of production.

The Market Principle

In today's world capitalist economy, the **market principle** dominates. It governs the distribution of the means of production: land, labor, natural resources, technology, and capital. "Market exchange refers to the organizational process of purchase and sale at money price" (Dalton 1967). With market exchange, items are bought and sold, using money, with an eye to maximizing profit, and value is determined by the *law of supply and demand* (things cost more the scarcer they are and the more people want them).

Bargaining is characteristic of market-principle exchanges. The buyer and seller strive to maximize—to get their "money's worth." In bargaining, buyers and sellers don't need to meet personally. But their offers and counteroffers do need to be open for negotiation over a fairly short time period.

Redistribution

Redistribution operates when goods, services, or their equivalent move from the local level to a center. The center may be a capital, a regional collection point, or a storehouse near a chief's residence. Products often move through a hierarchy of officials for storage at the center. Along the way, officials and their dependents may consume some of them, but the exchange principle here is *re*distribution. The flow of goods eventually reverses direction—out from the center, down through the hierarchy, and back to the common people.

One example of a redistributive system comes from the Cherokee, the original owners of the Tennessee Valley. Productive farmers who subsisted on maize, beans, and squash, supplemented by hunting and fishing, the Cherokee had chiefs. Each of their main villages had a central plaza, where meetings of the chief's council took place, and where redistributive feasts were held. According to Cherokee custom, each family farm had an area where the family, if they wished, could set aside a portion of their annual harvest for the chief. This supply of corn was used to feed the needy, as well as travelers and warriors journeying through friendly territory. This store of food was available to all who needed it, with the understanding that it "belonged" to the chief and was dispersed through his generosity. The chief also hosted the redistributive feasts held in the main settlements (Harris 1978).

Reciprocity

Reciprocity is exchange between social equals, who are normally related by kinship, marriage, or another close personal tie. Because it occurs between social equals, it is dominant in the more egalitarian societies—among foragers, cultivators, and pastoralists. There are three degrees of reciprocity: generalized, balanced, and negative (Sahlins 1968, 1972; Service 1966). These may be imagined as areas of a continuum defined by these questions:

1. How closely related are the parties to the exchange?
2. How quickly and unselfishly are gifts reciprocated?

Generalized reciprocity, the purest form of reciprocity, is characteristic of exchanges between closely related people. In *balanced reciprocity,* social distance increases, as does the need to reciprocate. In *negative reciprocity,* social distance is greatest and reciprocation is most calculated.

Sharing the fruits of production, a keystone of many nonindustrial societies, also has been a goal of socialist nations, such as China. These workers in Yunnan province strive for an equal distribution of meat.

With **generalized reciprocity,** someone gives to another person and expects nothing concrete or immediate in return. Such exchanges (including parental gift giving in contemporary North America) are not primarily economic transactions but expressions of personal relationships. Most parents don't keep accounts of every penny they spend on their children. They merely hope that the children will respect their culture's customs involving love, honor, loyalty, and other obligations to parents.

Among foragers, generalized reciprocity tends to govern exchanges. People routinely share with other band members (Bird-David 1992; Kent 1992). A study of the Ju/'hoansi San found that 40 percent of the population contributed little to the food supply (Lee 1968/1974). Children, teenagers, and people over 60 depended on other people for their food. Despite the high proportion of dependents, the average worker hunted or gathered less than half as much (12 to 19 hours a week) as the average American works. Nonetheless, there was always food because different people worked on different days.

So strong is the ethic of reciprocal sharing that most foragers lack an expression for "thank you." To offer thanks would be impolite because it would imply that a particular act of sharing, which is the keystone of egalitarian society, was unusual. Among the Semai, foragers of central Malaysia (Dentan 1979), to express gratitude would suggest surprise at the hunter's generosity or success (Harris 1974).

Balanced reciprocity applies to exchanges between people who are more distantly related than are members of the same band or household. In a horticultural society, for example, a man presents a gift to someone in another village. The recipient may be a cousin, a trading partner, or a brother's fictive kinsman. The giver expects something in return. This may not come immediately, but the social relationship will be strained if there is no reciprocation.

Exchanges in nonindustrial societies also may illustrate **negative reciprocity,** mainly in dealing with people outside or on the fringes of their social systems. To people who live in a world of close personal relations, exchanges with outsiders are full of ambiguity and distrust. Exchange is one way of establishing friendly relations with outsiders, but especially when trade begins, the relationship is still tentative. Often,

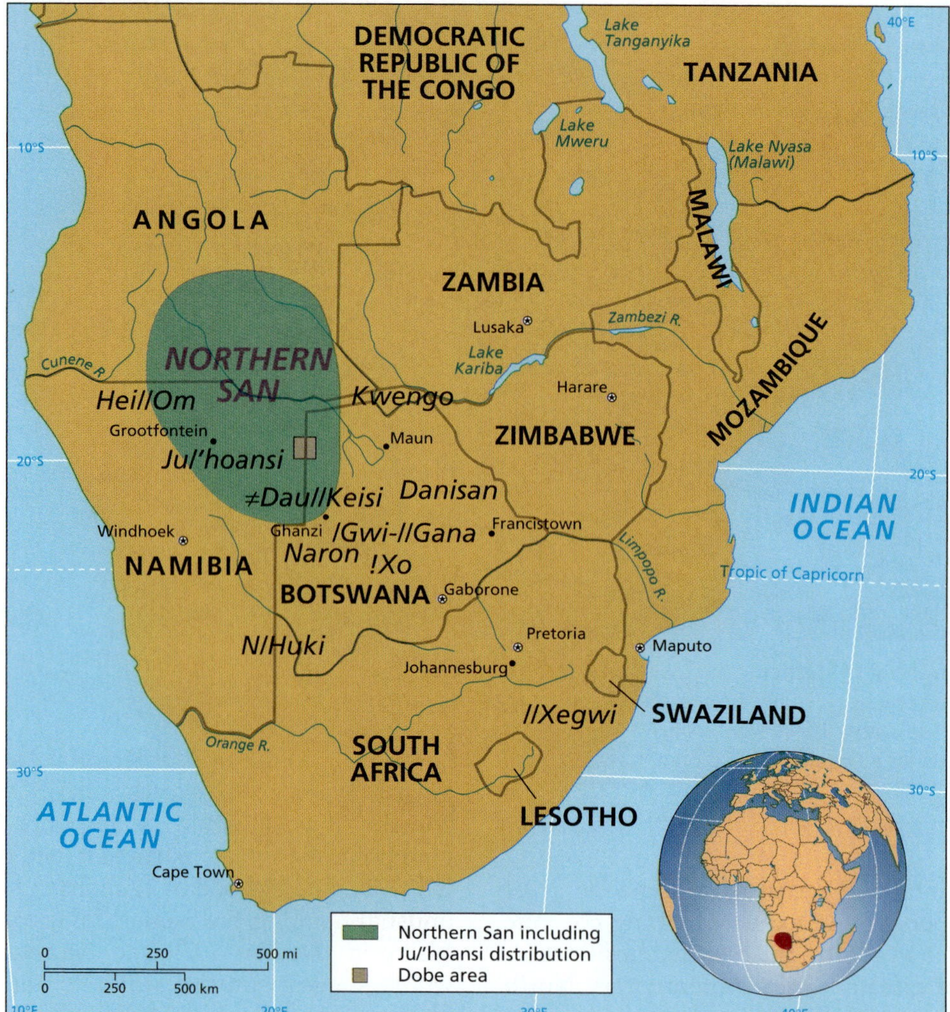

the initial exchange is close to being purely economic; people want to get something back immediately. Just as in market economies, but without using money, they try to get the best possible immediate return for their investment.

Generalized and balanced reciprocity are based on trust and a social tie. But negative reciprocity involves the attempt to get something for as little as possible, even if it means being cagey or deceitful or cheating. Among the most extreme and "negative" examples of negative reciprocity was 19th century horse thievery by North American Plains Indians. Men would sneak into camps and villages of neighboring tribes to steal horses. A similar pattern of cattle raiding continues today in East Africa, among tribes like the Kuria (Fleisher 2000). In these cases, the party that starts the raiding can expect reciprocity—a raid on their own village—or worse. The Kuria hunt down cattle thieves and kill them. It's still reciprocity, governed by "Do unto others as they have done unto you."

One way of reducing the tension in situations of potential negative reciprocity is to engage in "silent trade." One example is the silent trade of the Mbuti "pygmy" foragers of the African equatorial forest and their neighboring horticultural villagers. There is no personal contact during their exchanges. A Mbuti hunter leaves game, honey, or another forest product at a customary site. Villagers collect it and leave crops in exchange. Often the parties bargain silently. If one feels the return is insufficient, he or she simply leaves it at the trading site. If the other party wants to continue trade, it will be increased.

Coexistence of Exchange Principles

In today's North America, the market principle governs most exchanges, from the sale of the means of production to the sale of consumer goods. We also have redistribution. Some of our tax money goes to support the government, but some of it also comes back to us in the form of social services, education, health care, and road building. We also have reciprocal exchanges. Generalized reciprocity characterizes the relationship between parents and children. However, even here the dominant market mentality surfaces in comments about the high cost of raising children and in the stereotypical statement of the disappointed parent: "We gave you everything money could buy."

Exchanges of gifts, cards, and invitations exemplify reciprocity, usually balanced. Everyone has heard remarks like "They invited us to their daughter's wedding, so when ours gets married, we'll have to invite them" and "They've been here for dinner three times and haven't invited us yet. I don't think we should ask them back until they do." Such precise balancing of reciprocity would be out of place in a foraging band, where resources are communal (common to all) and daily sharing based on generalized reciprocity is an essential ingredient of social life and survival.

Potlatching

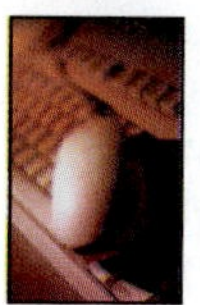

One of the most thoroughly studied cultural practices known to ethnography is the **potlatch,** a festive event within a regional exchange system among tribes of the North Pacific Coast of North America, including the Salish and Kwakiutl of Washington and British Columbia and the Tsimshian of Alaska. Some tribes still practice the potlatch, sometimes as a memorial to the dead (Kan 1986, 1989). At each such event, assisted by members of their communities, potlatch sponsors traditionally gave away food, blankets, pieces of copper, or other items. In return for this, they got prestige. To give a potlatch enhanced one's reputation. Prestige increased with the lavishness of the potlatch, the value of the goods given away in it.

The potlatching tribes were foragers, but atypical ones. They were sedentary and had chiefs. And unlike the environments of most other recent foragers, theirs was not marginal. They had access to a wide variety of land and sea resources. Among their most important foods were salmon, herring, candlefish, berries, mountain goats, seals, and porpoises (Piddocke 1969).

If classical economic theory is correct that the profit motive is universal, with the goal of maximizing material benefits, then how does one explain the potlatch, in which wealth is given away? Many scholars once cited the potlatch as a classic case of economically wasteful behavior. In this view, potlatching was based on an economically irrational drive for prestige. This interpretation stressed the lavishness and supposed wastefulness, especially of the Kwakiutl displays, to support the contention that in some societies people strive to maximize prestige at the expense of their material well being. This interpretation has been challenged.

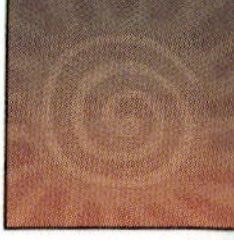

Ecological anthropology, also known as *cultural ecology,* is a theoretical school in anthropology that attempts to interpret cultural practices, such as the potlatch, in terms of their long-term role in helping humans adapt to their environments. A different interpretation of the potlatch has been offered by the ecological anthropologists Wayne Suttles (1960) and Andrew Vayda (1961/1968). These scholars see potlatching not in terms of its apparent wastefulness, but in terms of its long-term role as a cultural adaptive mechanism. This view not only helps us understand potlatching, it also has comparative value because it helps us understand similar patterns of lavish feasting in many other parts of the world. Here is the ecological interpretation: Customs like the potlatch are cultural adaptations to alternating periods of local abundance and shortage.

How does this work? The overall natural environment of the North Pacific Coast is favorable, but resources fluctuate from year to year and place to place. Salmon and herring aren't equally abundant every year in a given locality. One village can have a good year while another is experiencing a bad one. Later their fortunes reverse. In this context, the potlatch cycle of the Kwakiutl and Salish had adaptive value, and the potlatch was not a competitive display that brought no material benefit.

A village enjoying an especially good year had a surplus of subsistence items, which it could trade for more durable wealth items, like blankets, canoes, or pieces of copper. Wealth, in turn, by being distributed, could be converted into prestige. Members of several villages were invited to any potlatch and got to take home the resources that were given away. In this way, potlatching linked villages together in a regional economy—an exchange system that distributed food and wealth from wealthy to needy communities. In return, the potlatch sponsors and their villages got prestige. The decision to potlatch was determined by the health of the local economy. If there had been subsistence surpluses, and thus a buildup of wealth over several good years, a village could afford a potlatch to convert its food and wealth into prestige.

The long-term adaptive value of intercommunity feasting becomes clear when we consider what happened when a formerly prosperous village had a run of bad luck. Its people started accepting invitations to potlatches in villages that were doing better. The tables were turned as the temporarily rich became temporarily poor and vice versa. The newly needy accepted food and wealth items. They were willing to receive rather than bestow gifts and thus to relinquish some of their stored-up prestige. They hoped their luck would eventually improve so that resources could be recouped and prestige regained.

The historic photo (above) shows Tlingit clan members attending a potlatch at Sitka, Alaska, in 1904. Such ancestral headdresses have been repatriated recently from museums back to Tlingit clans. The photo below shows a modern potlatch, lasting four days, celebrated by Alaska's Tsimshian Indians. The gifts to be distributed are piled at the center of the large room where the event is taking place. Have you ever partaken in anything like a potlatch?

The potlatch linked local groups along the North Pacific Coast into a regional alliance and exchange network. Potlatching and intervillage exchange had adaptive functions, regardless of the motivations of the individual participants. The anthropologists who stressed rivalry for prestige were not wrong. They were merely emphasizing motivations at the expense of an analysis of economic and ecological systems.

The use of feasts to enhance individual and community reputations and to redistribute wealth is not peculiar to populations of the North Pacific Coast. Competitive feasting is widely characteristic of nonindustrial food producers. But among most foragers, who live, remember, in

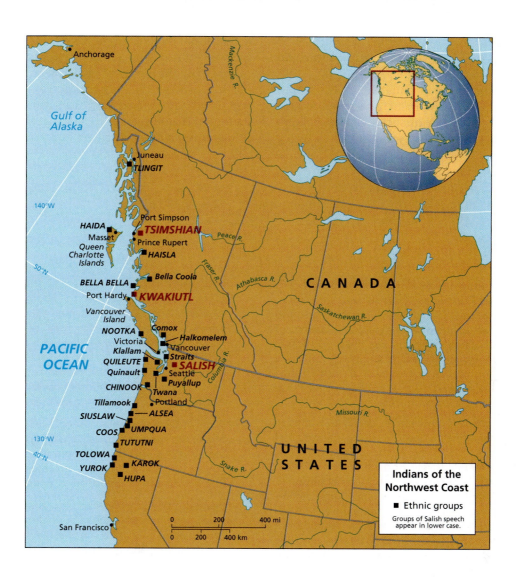

Indians of the Northwest Coast

■ Ethnic groups

Groups of Salish speech appear in lower case.

marginal areas, resources are too meager to support feasting on such a level. In such societies, sharing rather than competition prevails.

Like many other cultural practices that have attracted considerable anthropological attention, the potlatch does not, and did not, exist apart from larger world events. For example, within the spreading world capitalist economy of the 19th century, the potlatching tribes, particularly the Kwakiutl, began to trade with Europeans (fur for blankets, for example). Their wealth increased as a result. Simultaneously, a huge proportion of the Kwakiutl population died from previously unknown diseases brought by the Europeans. As a result, the increased wealth from trade flowed into a drastically reduced population. With many of the traditional sponsors dead (such as chiefs and their families), the Kwakiutl extended the right to give a potlatch to the entire population. This stimulated very intense competition for prestige. Given trade, increased wealth, and a decreased population, the Kwakiutl also started converting wealth into prestige by destroying wealth items such as blankets, pieces of copper, and houses (Vayda 1961/1968). Blankets and houses could be burned, and coppers could be buried at sea. Here, with dramatically increased wealth and a drastically reduced population, Kwakiutl potlatching changed its nature. It became much more destructive than it had been previously and than potlatching continued to be among tribes that were less affected by trade and disease.

In any case, note that potlatching also served to prevent the development of socioeconomic stratification, a system of social classes. Wealth relinquished or destroyed was converted into a nonmaterial item: prestige. Under capitalism, we reinvest our profits (rather than burning our cash), with the hope of making an additional profit. However, the potlatching tribes were content to relinquish their surpluses rather than use them to widen the social distance between themselves and their fellow tribe members.

summary

1. Cohen's adaptive strategies include foraging (hunting and gathering), horticulture, agriculture, pastoralism, and industrialism. Foraging was the only human adaptive strategy until the advent of food production (farming and herding) 10,000 years ago. Food production eventually replaced foraging in most places. Almost all modern foragers have at least some dependence on food production or food producers.
2. Horticulture and agriculture stand at opposite ends of a continuum based on labor intensity and continuity and land use. Horticulture doesn't use land or labor intensively. Horticulturalists cultivate a plot for one or two years and then abandon it. Further along the continuum, horticulture becomes more intensive, but there is always a fallow period. Agriculturalists farm the same plot of land continuously and use labor intensively. They use one or more of the following: irrigation, terracing, domesticated animals as means of production, and manuring.
3. The pastoral strategy is mixed. Nomadic pastoralists trade with cultivators. Part of a transhumant pastoral population cultivates while another part takes the herds to pasture. Except for some Peruvians and the Navajo, who are recent herders, the New World lacks native pastoralists.
4. Economic anthropology is the cross-cultural study of systems of production, distribution, and consumption. In nonindustrial societies, a kin-based mode of production prevails. One acquires rights to resources and labor through membership in social groups, not impersonally through purchase and sale. Work is just one aspect of social relations expressed in varied contexts.
5. Economics has been defined as the science of allocating scarce means to alternative ends. Western economists assume the notion of scarcity is universal—which it isn't—and that in making choices, people strive to maximize personal profit. In nonindustrial societies, indeed as in our own, people often maximize values other than individual profit. Furthermore, people may lack free choice in allocating their resources.
6. In nonindustrial societies, people invest in subsistence, replacement, social, and ceremonial funds. States add a rent fund: People must share their output with social superiors. In states, the obligation to pay rent often becomes primary.
7. Besides production, economic anthropologists study and compare exchange systems. The three principles of exchange are the market principle, redistribution, and reciprocity. The market principle, based on supply and demand and the profit motive, dominates in states. With redistribution, goods are collected at a central place, but some of them are eventually given back, or redistributed, to the people. Reciprocity governs exchanges between social equals. It is the characteristic mode of exchange among foragers and horticulturists. Reciprocity, redistribution, and the market principle may coexist in a society, but the primary exchange mode is the one that allocates the means of production. Patterns of feasting and exchanges of wealth among villages are common among nonindustrial food producers, as among the potlatching cultures of North America's North Pacific Coast. Such systems help even out the availability of resources over time.

key terms

agriculture Nonindustrial systems of plant cultivation characterized by continuous and intensive use of land and labor.

balanced reciprocity See *generalized reciprocity.*

band Basic unit of social organization among foragers. A band includes fewer than 100 people; it often splits up seasonally.

correlation An association between two or more variables such that when one changes (varies), the other(s) also change(s) (covaries); for example, temperature and sweating.

cultivation continuum A continuum based on the comparative study of nonindustrial cultivating societies in which labor intensity increases and fallowing decreases.

economizing The rational allocation of scarce means (or resources) to alternative ends (or uses); often considered the subject matter of economics.

economy A population's system of production, distribution, and consumption of resources.

generalized reciprocity Principle that characterizes exchanges between closely related individuals. As social distance increases, reciprocity becomes balanced and finally negative.

horticulture Nonindustrial system of plant cultivation in which plots lie fallow for varying lengths of time.

market principle Profit-oriented principle of exchange that dominates in states, particularly industrial states. Goods and services are bought and sold, and values are determined by supply and demand.

means (or factors) of production Land, labor, technology, and capital—major productive resources.

mode of production Way of organizing production—a set of social relations through which labor is deployed to wrest energy from nature by means of tools, skills, and knowledge.

negative reciprocity See *generalized reciprocity.*

nomadism, pastoral Movement throughout the year by the whole pastoral group (men, women, and children) with their animals; more generally, such constant movement in pursuit of strategic resources.

pastoralists People who use a food-producing strategy of adaptation based on care of herds of domesticated animals.

peasant Small-scale agriculturalist living in a state with rent fund obligations.

potlatch Competitive feast among Indians on the North Pacific Coast of North America.

reciprocity One of the three principles of exchange; governs exchange between social equals; major exchange mode in band and tribal societies.

redistribution Major exchange mode of chiefdoms, many archaic states, and some states with managed economies.

transhumance One of two variants of pastoralism; part of the population moves seasonally with the herds while the other part remains in home villages.

critical thinking questions

1. What are some of the main advantages and disadvantages of living in a foraging society? How about horticulture? Agriculture? Pastoralism? In which one would you want to live, and why?
2. If you had to spend the rest of your life in a foraging society, how would you go about becoming a member of that society?
3. What do you see as the main differences and similarities between ancient and modern hunter-gatherers?
4. What are the benefits and costs, including the environmental costs, of horticulture compared with irrigated agriculture?

5. What are your scarce means? How do you make decisions about allocating them?
6. What do you attempt to maximize? Does that vary depending on the situation?
7. Does anything (or many things) about living in a nonindustrial society strike you as attractive?
8. Give examples from your own exchanges of reciprocity, redistribution, and the market principle.
9. Give examples from your own exchanges of different degrees of reciprocity.

case study

Basseri: This chapter has examined systems of production, distribution, and consumption among societies with various adaptive strategies. In *Culture Sketches* by Holly Peters-Golden, read the chapter on the "Basseri: Pastoral Nomads on the il-Rah." What are some ways in which the Basseri's adaptive strategy, pastoral nomadism, influences their other social institutions and relationships? How might Basseri life change with increasing sedentism?

suggested additional readings

Bates, D. G.
2001 *Human Adaptive Strategies: Ecology, Culture, and Politics.* 2nd ed. Boston: Allyn and Bacon. Recent discussion of the different adaptive strategies and their political correlates.

Chatty, D.
1996 *Mobile Pastoralists: Development Planning and Social Change in Oman.* New York: Columbia University Press. Based on 10 years of research in a nomadic Middle Eastern community, this study examines forces of "modernization," including a shift from herding to cash employment and the changing role of women.

Cohen, Y.
1974 *Man in Adaptation: The Cultural Present,* 2nd ed. Chicago: Aldine. Presents Cohen's economic typology of adaptive strategies and uses it to organize a valuable set of essays on culture and adaptation.

Gudeman, S., ed.
1999 *Economic Anthropology.* Northhampton, MA: E. Elgar. Reference essays in economic anthropology.

Ingold, T., D. Riches, and J. Woodburn
1991 *Hunters and Gatherers.* New York: Berg (St. Martin's). Volume I examines history and social change among foragers. Volume II looks at their property, ideology, and power relations. These broad regional surveys illuminate current issues and debates.

Kearney, M.
1996 *Reconceptualizing the Peasantry: Anthropology in Global Perspective.* Boulder, CO: Westview. How peasants live today, in post–Cold War nation-states.

Kent, S.
1996 *Cultural Diversity among Twentieth-Century Foragers: An African Perspective.* New York: Cambridge University Press. Africa's hunter-gatherers, their adaptations, social life, and variety.

Lee, R. B.
1993 *The Dobe Ju/'hoansi,* 2nd ed. Fort Worth: Harcourt Brace. Account of well-known San foragers, by one of their principal ethnographers.

Lee, R. B., and R. H. Daly
1999 *The Cambridge Encyclopedia of Hunters and Gatherers.* New York: Cambridge University Press. Indispensable reference work on foragers.

Plattner, S., ed.
1989 *Economic Anthropology.* Stanford, CA: Stanford University Press. Articles on economic features of foraging, tribal, peasant, state, and industrial societies.

Salzman, P. C., and J. G. Galaty, eds.
1990 *Nomads in a Changing World.* Naples: Istituto Universitario Orientale. Pastoral nomads in varied contemporary settings.

Srivastava, J., N. J. H. Smith, and D. A. Forno
1998 *Integrating Biodiversity in Agricultural Intensification: Toward Sound Practices.* Washington, DC: World Bank. Environmentally and socially sustainable agriculture in today's world.

Wilk, R. R.
1996 *Economies and Cultures: An Introduction to Economic Anthropology.* Boulder, CO: Westview. An up-to-date introduction to economic anthropology.

Wilmsen, R.
1989 *Land Filled with Flies: A Political Economy of the Kalahari.* Chicago: University of Chicago Press. A revisionist view of the San, in the context of colonialism and the world system.

Young, W. C.
1996 *The Rashaayada Bedouin: Arab Pastoralists of Eastern Sudan.* Fort Worth: Harcourt Brace. This examination of a pastoral economy also weaves in information on gender and "race."

internet exercises

1. *Reciprocity:* Go to the Living Link's video collection at Emory University's Center for the Advanced Study of Ape and Human Evolution web page, **http://www.emory.edu/LIVING_LINKS/a/video.html,** and watch the Chimpanzee Food Sharing Movie, **http://www.emory.edu/LIVING_LINKS/sounds/ram_text/food_sharing28k.ram.**
   a. What is an example in this film of generalized reciprocity?
   b. What is an example of balanced reciprocity?
   c. What is an example of negative reciprocity?
   d. What inferences can be made from the observation that humans and chimpanzees exhibit similar capacities for reciprocity? Even when humans and chimpanzees enact similar behaviors (i.e., generalized reciprocity), are there important differences?
2. *Subsistence and Settlement:* Go to the Ethnographic Atlas Cross-tabulations page, **http://lucy.ukc.ac.uk/cgi-bin/uncgi/Ethnoatlas/atlas.vopts.** This site has compiled ethnographic information on many different groups, and you can use the tools provided to cross-tabulate the prevalence of certain traits. Go to the site, under "Select Row Category" choose "subsistence economy," and under "Select Column Category" select "settlement patterns." Press the Submit Query button. The table that appears shows the frequency with which groups of different subsistence systems use certain mobility strategies.
   a. Notice that a high number of groups with agriculture use "Compact and relatively permanent settlements." Is this what you would expect?
   b. What kinds of subsistence strategies are used by groups that are the most mobile (have "Migratory or nomadic," "Seminomadic," or "Semisedentary" settlement patterns)?
   c. Now let's focus on the groups that are exceptional and do not combine subsistence and settlement strategies in the most usual or common way. There is a single group that uses intensive agriculture and is seminomadic. Click on the number at that location. What is the name of that group and where are they found?
   d. There are a few groups that are in permanent settlements and use hunting, gathering, or fishing. What region of the world are most of these groups from?
   e. Feel free to explore many of the other variables listed in the table. We suggest you check "mean size of local communities," "settlement patterns," and "subsistence economy" against each other. What patterns do you see?

See Chapter 14 on your CD-ROM for additional review and interactive exercises. See your McGraw-Hill Online Learning Center for more.

Chapter 15

Families, Kinship, and Descent

CHAPTER OUTLINE

FOXNEWS.COM NEWS BRIEFS

Anthropologists Turn to Exotic New Type of Human: The American Middle Class

by Matt Crenson
July 9, 2000

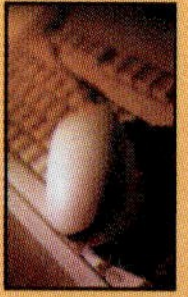

TRAVERSE CITY, Mich—After dedicating their careers to studying exotic cultures in faraway lands, a few anthropologists are coming home. They're taking research techniques they once used in African shantytowns and Himalayan villages to Knights of Columbus halls, corporate office buildings and suburban shopping centers.

The idea is to study American culture with fresh eyes unclouded by preconceived notions—to study "us" the way anthropologists used to look at "them."

"I've seen a line coming out of that Dairy Queen that goes down the block," Conrad Kottak says.

He's cruising a Michigan suburb, pointing out cultural landmarks. The high school. A satellite dish. Fast food joints. Video rental stores. Newspaper boxes that indicate which residents are reading what.

Kottak, the chairman of the University of Michigan anthropology department, works with research fellow Lara Descartes on a project titled "The Relationship of Media to Work and Family Issues Among the Middle Class." They interview people about their viewing habits, and spend evenings watching television in suburban homes . . .

Traditionally, American anthropologists have been reluctant to study their own cultures. They've preferred remote subjects not yet gripped by Hollywood, pop music and the other tentacles of Western culture.

Even when they do work in the United States, most anthropologists concentrate on subcultures: drug addicts, streetwalkers, transvestites.

Rebecca Upton recently completed a classic anthropology Ph.D. in Botswana. Now she does much of her research at an Ann Arbor, Mich., playground.

Upton introduces herself to parents and interviews them about their lives for a project on young families that have just had or are considering a second child.

"There's all this study about what happens at the first child," Upton says. "There's nothing about what happens with the second." In Africa, Upton could start from scratch, learning about the culture as if she were a child. In Ann Arbor, the first thing she has to do is forget everything she thought she knew. "Suddenly I'm questioning my observations and assumptions about everything," Upton says.

"Something dramatic is happening here. Something is changing," says University of Michigan anthropologist Tom Fricke. America, he says, is going through the most profound social upheaval since the Industrial Revolution, when a rural nation of farmers became a country of factory towns and cities. Dual-career families, single parenthood and divorce are supplanting the traditional model of family. Factory work has given way to high-tech jobs that require college and graduate degrees. The mass media saturate our lives. Everybody knows all this is happening, but there has been little research on how these changes affect the way Americans think about their lives.

To that end, the Alfred P. Sloan Foundation has funded two research centers to do anthropological studies of the relationship between work and family life in middle-class America. Fricke heads the Center for the Ethnography of Everyday Life, based at the University of Michigan. The other one, based at Emory University in Atlanta, is called the Center for Myth and Ritual in American Life. Anthropologists at the centers study American families the same way they would Polynesian cargo cults or Mongolian nomads—by inserting themselves into the daily lives of their subjects . . .

Source: http://www.foxnews.com/etcetera/070900/everyday_life.sml.

overview

Especially in nonindustrial societies, kinship, descent, and marriage are basic social building blocks, linking otherwise separate groups in a common social system. Kin groups, such as families and descent groups, are social units whose members can be identified and whose residence patterns and activities can be observed. A nuclear family, for instance, consists of a married couple and their children, living together. Although nuclear families are widespread among the world's societies, other social forms, such as extended families and descent groups, can complement or even replace the nuclear family.

In the United States and Canada, the nuclear family has long been a basic kin group, especially for the middle class. Among the poor, expanded family households and sharing with extended kin occur more frequently; resources may be pooled to deal with poverty. Also, in contemporary North America, the nuclear family household is declining both in frequency and as a cultural norm. We observe more diversity in family, household, and living arrangements.

Unlike families, descent groups have perpetuity—they last for generations. There are several kinds of descent groups, such as lineages and clans. Some descent groups are patrilineal; they reckon descent through males only. Some are matrilineal; they trace descent exclusively through females.

Kinship terminologies are ways of classifying one's relatives based on perceived differences and similarities. Comparative research has made it clear that the number of systems of kinship terminology is limited. For the parental generation, there are four basic ways of classifying kin. There are six basic ways of classifying relatives in one's own generation, which includes siblings and cousins.

Families

The kinds of societies that anthropologists have traditionally studied have stimulated a strong interest in families, along with larger systems of kinship, descent, and marriage. Kinship—as vitally important in daily life in nonindustrial societies as work outside the home is in our own— has become an essential part of anthropology because of its importance to the people we study. We are ready to take a closer look at the systems of kinship and descent that have organized human life for much of our history.

Ethnographers quickly recognize social divisions, groups, within any society they study. During field work, they learn about significant groups by observing their activities and composition. People often live in the same village or neighborhood or work, pray, or celebrate together because they are related in some way. To understand the social structure, an ethnographer must investigate such kin ties. For example, the most significant local groups may consist of descendants of the same grandfather. These people may live in neighboring houses, farm adjoining fields, and help each other in everyday tasks. Other sorts of groups, based on other kin links, get together less often.

The nuclear family is one kind of kin group that is widespread in human societies. Other kin groups include extended families (families consisting of three or more generations) and descent groups—lineages and clans. Descent groups, which are composed of people claiming common ancestry, are basic units in the social organization of nonindustrial food producers.

Nuclear and Extended Families

A nuclear family lasts only as long as the parents and children remain together. Most people belong to at least two nuclear families at different times in their lives. They are born into a family consisting of their parents and siblings. When they reach adulthood, they may marry and establish a nuclear family that includes the spouse and eventually the children. Since most societies permit divorce, some people establish more than one family through marriage.

In many cultures siblings play important roles in child rearing, as in this Mexico City slum. Are siblings part of your family of orientation or family of procreation?

Anthropologists distinguish between the **family of orientation** (the family in which one is born and grows up) and the **family of procreation** (formed when one marries and has children). From the individual's point of view, the critical relationships are with parents and siblings in the family of orientation and with spouse and children in the family of procreation.

Nuclear family organization is widespread but not universal. In certain societies, the nuclear family is rare or nonexistent. In other cultures, the nuclear family has no special role in social life. Other social units—most notably descent groups and extended families—can assume most or all of the functions otherwise associated with the nuclear family. In other words, there are many alternatives to nuclear family organization.

Consider an example from the former Yugoslavia. Traditionally, among the Muslims of western Bosnia (Lockwood 1975), nuclear families lacked autonomy. Several such families were embedded in an extended-family household called a *zadruga*. The *zadruga* was headed by a male household head and his wife, the senior woman. It also included married sons and their wives and children, and unmarried sons and daughters. Each nuclear family had a sleeping room, decorated and partly furnished from the bride's trousseau. However, possessions—even clothing items—were freely shared by *zadruga* members. Even trousseau items were appropriated for use elsewhere. Such a residential unit is known as a *patrilocal* extended family, because each couple resides in the husband's father's household after marriage.

296

The *zadruga* took precedence over its component units. Social interaction was more usual among women, men, or children than between spouses or between parents and children. Larger households ate at three successive settings: for men, women, and children. Traditionally, all children over 12 slept together in boys' or girls' rooms. When a woman wished to visit another village, she sought the permission of the male *zadruga* head. Although men usually felt closer to their own children than to those of their brothers, they were obliged to treat them equally. Children were disciplined by any adult in the household. When a nuclear family broke up, children under seven went with the mother. Older children could choose between their

parents. Children were considered part of the household where they were born even if their mother left. One widow who remarried had to leave her five children, all over seven, in their father's *zadruga,* now headed by his brother.

Among herders living in the steppe region of the Mongolian People's Republic, patrilocal extended families often span four generations. Is the family shown here more like a *zadruga* or a *tarawad?*

Another example of an alternative to the nuclear family is provided by the Nayars (or Nair), a large and powerful caste on the Malabar Coast of southern India (Gough 1959; Shivaram 1996). Their traditional kinship system was matrilineal (descent traced only through females). Nayar lived in matrilineal extended family compounds called *tarawads.* The *tarawad* was a residential complex with several buildings, its own temple, granary, water well, orchards, gardens, and land holdings. Headed by a senior woman, assisted by her brother, the *tarawad* housed her siblings, sisters' children, and other matrikin—matrilineal relatives.

Traditional Nayar marriage seems to have been hardly more than a formality—a kind of coming of age ritual. A young woman would go through a marriage ceremony with a man, after which they might spend a few days together at her *tarawad.* Then the man would return to his own *tarawad,* where he lived with his sisters, aunts, and other matrikin. Nayar men belonged to a warrior class, who left home regularly for military expeditions, returning permanently to their *tarawad* on retirement. Nayar women could have multiple sexual partners. Children became members of the mother's *tarawad;* they were not considered to be relatives of their biological father. Indeed, many Nayar children didn't even know who their genitor was. Child care was the responsibility of the *tarawad.* Nayar society therefore reproduced itself biologically without the nuclear family.

Industrialism and Family Organization

For many Americans and Canadians, the nuclear family is the only well-defined kin group. Family isolation arises from geographic mobility, which is associated with industrialism, so that a nuclear family focus is characteristic of

The Nayars live throughout Kerala state in southwestern India.

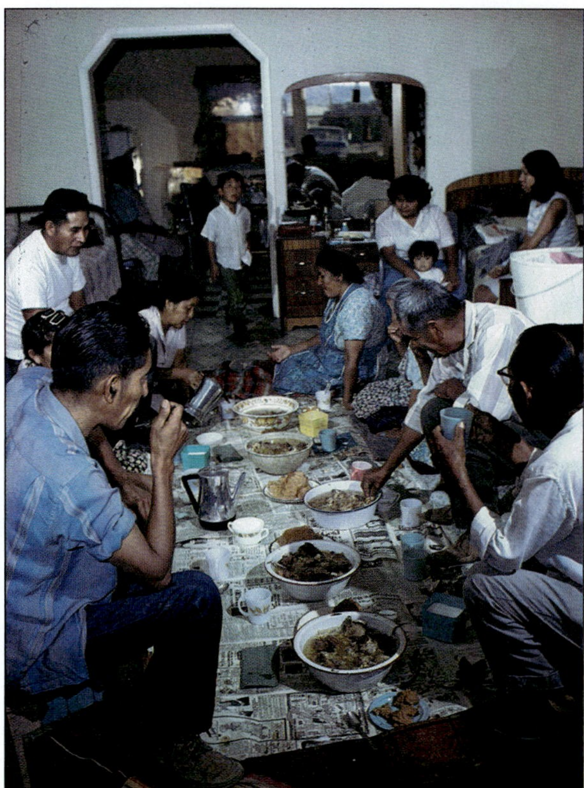

Many Native Americans live in expanded family households. This reflects a combination of cultural values and economic need. If they find it difficult to survive economically as nuclear families, relatives may pool their resources in an expanded family household. Here, in Arizona, Hopi Indians assemble in such a household to celebrate an infant-naming ceremony.

many modern nations. Born into a family of orientation, North Americans leave home for work or college, and the break with parents is underway. Eventually most North Americans marry and start a family of procreation. Because less than 3 percent of the U.S. population now farms, most people aren't tied to the land. Selling our labor on the market, we often move to places where jobs are available.

Many married couples live hundreds of miles from their parents. Their jobs have determined where they live. Such a postmarital residence pattern is called **neolocality:** Married couples are expected to establish a new place of residence—a "home of their own." Among middle-class North Americans, neolocal residence is both a cultural preference and a statistical norm. Most middle-class Americans eventually establish households and nuclear families of their own.

Within stratified nations, value systems vary to some extent from class to class, and so does kinship. There are significant differences between middle-class and poorer North Americans. For example, in the lower class the incidence of *expanded family households* (those that include nonnuclear relatives) is greater than it is in the middle class. When an expanded family household includes three or more generations, it is an **extended family.** Another type of expanded family is the *collateral household,* which includes siblings and their spouses and children.

The higher proportion of expanded family households among poorer Americans has been explained as an adaptation to poverty (Stack 1975). Unable to survive economically as nuclear family units, relatives band together in an expanded household and pool their resources. Adaptation to poverty causes kinship values and attitudes to diverge from middle-class norms. Thus, when North Americans raised in poverty achieve financial success, they often feel obligated to provide financial help to a wide circle of less fortunate relatives.

Changes in North American Kinship

Although the nuclear family remains a cultural ideal for many Americans, Table 15.1 shows that nuclear families accounted for just 25 percent of American households in 1998. Nonnuclear family arrangements now outnumber the "traditional" American household three to one. There are several reasons for the changing household composition documented in Table 15.1. Americans leave home to work, often in a different community. Women are increasingly joining men in the work force. This often removes them from their family of orientation while making it economically feasible to delay marriage. Furthermore, job demands compete with romantic attachments. According to the U.S. Census Bureau, the average age at first marriage for American women rose from 20 years in 1955 to almost 25 in 1998 (Lugaila 1998*a;* Saluter 1996). The comparable figures for men were 23 and 27 (Lugaila 1998*a; World Almanac 1992,* p. 943).

Table 15.2 summarizes changes in the marital status of Americans, along with their living

Table 15.1
Changes in Family and Household Organization in the United States: 1970 vs. 1998

1970	1998
Married couples with children made up 40 percent of households	Married couples with children made up 25 percent of households
3.1 people per household	2.6 people per household
20 percent of households with five or more people	10 percent of households with five or more people
People living alone made up 17 percent of households	People living alone made up 26 percent of households
5.6 million families maintained by women with no husband present	12.7 million families maintained by women with no husband present
1.2 million families maintained by men with no wife present	3.9 million families maintained by men with no wife present
44 percent of families with no own children under 18 at home	51 percent of families with no own children under 18 at home

Source: From Bryson 1996; Casper and Bryson 1998.

Table 15.2
Marital Status of Americans and Selected Living Arrangements

	1970	1998
Currently divorced (number)	4.3 million	19.4 million
Never married (number)	21.4 million	46.6 million
Women living alone (number)	7.3 million	15.3 million
Men living alone (number)	3.5 million	11.0 million
Unmarried as percent of all households	28	40
Married as percent of all households	72	60
Percent of children living with only one parent	12	28
Percent of children living with two parents	85	68

Source: Based on data in Lugaila 1998*b*; Saluter 1996; and U.S. Census Bureau 1998.

arrangements, between 1970 and 1998. The numbers in Table 15.2 suggest that life is growing increasingly lonely for many North Americans. The disappearance of extended families reflects the mobility of industrialism. However, even nuclear families are breaking up. The divorce rate has risen, with the number of divorced Americans more than quadrupling from 4.3 million to 19.4 million in 1998. Single-parent families also have increased. In 1970, 85 percent of American kids lived with two parents, but this had fallen to 68 percent in 1998. Kids in fatherless households tripled from 8 percent in 1960 to 23 percent in 1998. The percentage in motherless households increased from 1 percent in 1960 to 4 percent in 1998. The currently unmarried as a percentage of all adults increased from 28 percent to 40 percent between 1970 and 1998. The never-married adult population rose from 21 million to almost 47 million. To be sure, contemporary Americans maintain social lives through work, friendship, sports, clubs, religion, and organized social activities. However, the isolation from kin that these figures suggest is unprecedented in human history.

In contemporary North America, single-parent families are increasing at a rapid rate. In 1960, 88 percent of American children lived with both parents, compared with 68 percent today. This divorced mom, Valerie Jones, is enjoying a candlelight dinner with her kids. What do you see as the main differences between nuclear families and single-parent families?

Our changing household organization has been reflected in the mass media. During the 1950s and early 1960s, such television sitcoms as *Father Knows Best, The Adventures of Ozzie and Harriet*, and *Leave It to Beaver* portrayed "traditional" nuclear families. The incidence of *blended families* (kin units formed when parents remarry and bring their children into a new household) has risen, as represented in programs such as *The Brady Bunch* (see Interesting Issues box on pp. 380–381). Three-quarters of divorced Americans remarry. Television programs and other media presentations now routinely feature coresident friends, roommates, unmarried couples, singles, single parents, unrelated retirees or "survivors," nannies, hired male housekeepers, and working mothers.

The idealized middle-class and upper-middle-class TV families of the 1950s and 1960s survived through the 1980s and 1990s, as portrayed on *Family Ties* and *The Cosby Show.* But changes in family dynamics and in the roles of parents and kids have evolved in the media and in "real life." In particular, TV fathers have become much less omniscient. More recently TV has brought us working-class families like that of *Roseanne* (sometimes an expanded family household) and the often dysfunctional families of *Married with Children* and *The Simpsons.* It would be hard to accuse Homer Simpson of knowing best most of the time. Changes in life styles are reflected by the media, which in turn help promote further modifications in our values concerning kinship, marriage, and living arrangements (Kottak 1990*a*, Kottak and Kozaitis 1999).

The entire range of kin attachments is narrower for North Americans, particularly those in the middle class, than it is for nonindustrial peoples. Although we recognize ties to grandparents, uncles, aunts, and cousins, we have less contact with, and depend less on, those relatives than people in other cultures do. We see this when we answer a few questions: Do we know exactly how we are related to all our cousins? How much do we know about our ancestors, such as their full names and where they lived? How many of the people with whom we associate regularly are our relatives?

Table 15.3

Household and Family Size in the United States and Canada, 1975 versus 1998

	1975	1998
Average family size:		
United States	3.4	3.2
Canada	3.5	3.1
Average household size:		
United States	2.9	2.6
Canada	2.9	2.6

Source: U.S. Census Bureau, *Statistical Abstract of the United States, 1998;* Statistics Canada, Catalogue no. 91-213, http://www.StatCan.CA/english/Pgdb/People/Famili.htm#fam.

Table 15.3 documents similar changes in family and household size in the United States and Canada between 1975 and 1998. Those figures confirm a general trend toward smaller families and living units in North America. This trend is also detectable in Western Europe and other industrial nations.

interesting issues

Brady Bunch Nirvana

One teaching technique I started using several years ago, taking advantage of students' familiarity with television, is to demonstrate changes in American kinship and marriage patterns by contrasting the TV programs of the 50s with more recent ones. (Students know about the history of sitcom families from syndicated reruns, especially on the cable channel Nickelodeon.) In the 1950s, the usual TV family was a nuclear family consisting of employed dad, homemaker mom, and kids. Examples include *Father Knows Best*, *Ozzie and Harriet*, and *Leave It to Beaver*. These programs, appropriate for the 1950s market, are dramatically out of sync with today's social and economic realities. Only 16 million American women worked outside the home in 1950, compared with three times that number today. Today less than 7 percent of American households fit the former ideal: breadwinner father, homemaker mother, and two children.

Most of my students (even at the millennium) have watched reruns of the 1960s family series *The Brady Bunch*, whose social organization offers an instructive contrast with 1950s programs. Here a new, blended, family forms when a widow with three daughters marries a widower with three sons. Blended families have been increasing in American society because of more frequent divorce and remarriage. When *The Brady Bunch* first aired, divorce was too controversial to give rise to a prime-time TV family. Widow(er)hood had to be the basis of the blended family, as it was in *The Brady Bunch*.

The Brady husband-father was a successful architect. The Bradys were wealthy enough to employ a housekeeper, Alice. Mirroring American culture when the program was made, the wife's career was part-time and subsidiary. Women lucky enough to find wealthy husbands didn't compete with other women—even professional housekeepers—in the work force.

Each time I begin my kinship lecture using sitcom material, a few people in the class immediately recognize (from reruns) the nuclear families of the 1950s, especially the Beaver Cleaver family. And when I start diagraming the Bradys, students start shouting out their names: "Jan," "Bobby," "Greg," "Cindy," "Marsha," "Peter," "Mike," "Carol," "Alice." As the cast of characters nears completion, my class, filled with TV-enculturated natives, is usually shouting out in unison names made almost as familiar as their parents' through exposure to TV reruns. My students almost seem to find nirvana (a feeling of religious ecstasy) through their collective remembrance of the

Differences in the answers to these questions by people from industrial and those from nonindustrial societies confirm the declining importance of kinship in contemporary nations. Immigrants are often shocked by what they perceive as weak kinship bonds and lack of proper respect for family in contemporary North America. In fact, most of the people whom middle-class North Americans see every day are either nonrelatives or members of the nuclear family. On the other hand, Stack's (1975) study of welfare-dependent families in a ghetto area of a Midwestern city shows that sharing with nonnuclear relatives is an important strategy that the urban poor use to adapt to poverty.

One of the most striking contrasts between the United States and Brazil, the two most populous nations of the Western Hemisphere, is in the meaning and role of the family. Contemporary North American adults usually define their families as consisting of their husbands or wives and their children. However, when middle-class Brazilians talk about their families, they mean their parents, siblings, aunts, uncles, grandparents, and cousins. Later they add their children, but rarely the husband or wife, who has his or her own family. The

Bradys and in the ritual-like incantation of their names.

Given its massive penetration of the modern home (at least 98 percent of all households), television's effects on our socialization and enculturation can hardly be trivial. Indeed, the common information and knowledge we acquire by watching the same TV programs is indisputably culture in the anthropological sense. Culture is collective, shared, meaningful. It is transmitted by conscious and unconscious learning experiences acquired by humans, not through their genes but as a result of growing up in a particular society. Of the hundreds of culture bearers who have passed through the Anthropology 101 classroom over the past decade, many have been unable to recall the full names of their parents' first cousins. Some have forgotten their grandmother's maiden name. But most have absolutely no trouble identifying names and relationships in a family that exists only in television land.

How might *The Brady Bunch* have differed if this blended family had been created after divorce, rather than after the deaths of two former spouses?

children are shared by the two families. Because middle-class Americans lack an extended family support system, marriage assumes more importance. The husband–wife relationship is supposed to take precedence over either spouse's relationship with his or her own parents. This places a significant strain on North American marriages.

Living in a less mobile society, Brazilians stay in closer contact with their relatives, including members of the extended family, than North Americans do. Residents of Rio de Janeiro and São Paulo, two of South America's largest cities, are reluctant to leave those urban centers to live away from family and friends. Brazilians find it hard to imagine, and unpleasant to live in, social worlds without relatives. Contrast this with a characteristic American theme: learning to live with strangers.

The Family among Foragers

Populations with foraging economies are far removed from industrial societies in terms of social complexity. Here again, however, the nuclear family is often the most significant kin group, although in no foraging society is the nuclear family the only group based on kinship.

The two basic social units of traditional foraging societies are the nuclear family and the band.

Unlike middle-class couples in industrial nations, foragers don't usually reside neolocally. Instead, they join a band in which either the husband or the wife has relatives. However, couples and families may move from one band to another several times. Although nuclear families are ultimately as impermanent among foragers as they are in any other society, they are usually more stable than bands are.

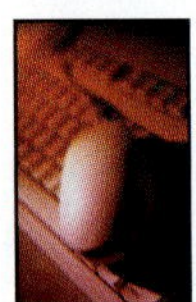

Many foraging societies lacked year-round band organization. The Native American Shoshone of the Great Basin in Utah and Nevada provide an example. The resources available to the Shoshone were so meager that for most of the year families traveled alone through the countryside hunting and gathering. In certain seasons families assembled to hunt cooperatively as a band; after just a few months together they dispersed.

Industrial and foraging economies do have something in common. In neither type are people tied permanently to the land. The mobility and the emphasis on small, economically self-sufficient family units promote the nuclear family as a basic kin group in both types of societies.

Friends: Ross (David Schwimmer), Joey (Matt LeBlanc), and Chandler (Matthew Perry) during the 7th season of the NBC show. How are family relations depicted on *Friends?*

Descent

We've seen that the nuclear family is important in industrial nations and among foragers. The analogous group among nonindustrial food producers is the descent group. A **descent group** is a permanent social unit whose members say they have ancestors in common. Descent group members believe they share, and descend from, those common ancestors. The group endures even though its membership changes, as members are born and die, move in and move out. Often, descent-group membership is determined at birth and is lifelong. In this case, it is an ascribed status.

Descent Groups

Descent groups frequently are exogamous (members must seek their mates from other descent groups). Two common rules serve to admit certain people as descent-group members while excluding others. With a rule of **matrilineal descent,** people join the mother's group automatically at birth and stay members throughout life. Matrilineal descent groups therefore include only the children of the group's women. With **patrilineal descent,** people automatically have lifetime membership in the father's group. The children of all the group's men join the group, but the children of the female members of that group are excluded. (In Figures 15.1 and 15.2, which show matrilineal and patrilineal descent groups respectively, the pyramids stand for males and the circles for females.) Matrilineal and patrilineal descent are types of **unilineal descent.** This means the descent rule uses one line only, either the male or the female line. Patrilineal descent is much more common than is matrilineal descent. In a sample of 564 societies (Murdock 1957), about three times as many were found to be patrilineal (247 to 84).

Descent groups may be **lineages** or **clans.** Common to both is the belief that members

Figure 15.1
A Matrilineage Five Generations Deep

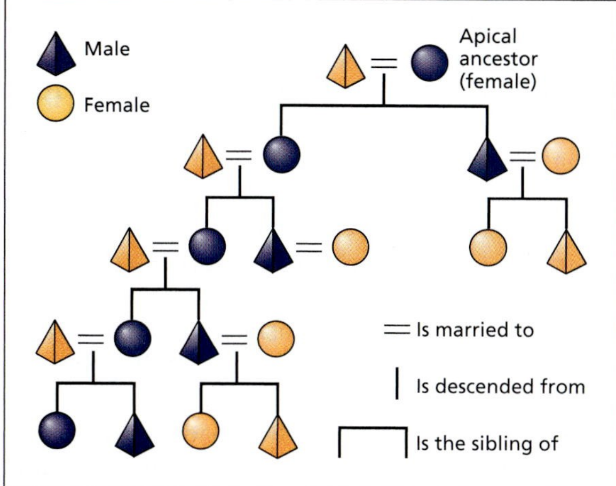

Matrilineages are based on demonstrated descent from a female ancestor. Only the children of the group's women (blue) belong to the matrilineage. The children of the group's men are excluded; they belong to their mother's matrilineage.

descend from the same *apical ancestor.* That person stands at the apex, or top, of the common genealogy. For example, Adam and Eve are the apical ancestors of the biblical Jews, and, according to the Bible, of all humanity. Since Eve is said to have come from Adam's rib, Adam stands as the original apical ancestor for the patrilineal genealogy laid out in the Bible.

How do lineages and clans differ? A lineage uses *demonstrated descent.* Members can recite the names of their forebears in each generation from the apical ancestor through the present. (This doesn't mean their recitations are accurate, only that lineage members think they are.) In the Bible the litany of men who "begat" other men is a demonstration of genealogical descent for a large patrilineage that ultimately includes Jews and Arabs (who share Abraham as their last common apical ancestor).

Unlike lineages, clans use *stipulated descent.* Clan members merely say they descend from the apical ancestor. They don't try to trace the actual genealogical links between themselves and that ancestor. The Betsileo of Madagascar have both clans and lineages. Descent may be demonstrated for the most recent 8 to 10 generations, then stipulated for the more remote past—sometimes with mermaids and vaguely defined foreign royalty mentioned among the founders (Kottak 1980). Like the Betsileo, many societies have both lineages and clans. In such a case, clans have more members and cover a larger geographical area than lineages do. Sometimes a clan's apical ancestor is not a human at all but an animal or plant (called a *totem*). Whether human or not, the ancestor symbolizes the social unity and identity of the members, distinguishing them from other groups.

Figure 15.2

A Patrilineage Five Generations Deep

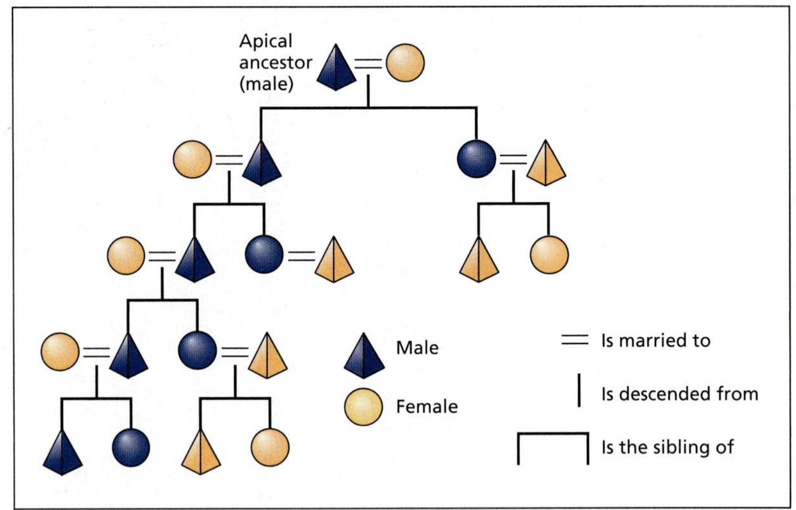

Lineages are based on demonstrated descent from a common ancestor. With patrilineal descent, children of the group's men (blue) are included as descent-group members. Children of the group's female members are excluded; they belong to their father's patrilineage. Also notice lineage exogamy.

The economic types that usually have descent group organization are horticulture, pastoralism, and agriculture, as discussed in the last chapter. Such societies tend to have several descent groups. Any one of them may be confined to a single village, but they usually span more than one village. Any branch of a descent group that lives in one place is a *local descent group.* Two or more local branches of different descent groups may live in the same village. Descent groups in the same village or different villages may establish alliances through frequent intermarriage.

Lineages, Clans, and Residence Rules

As we've seen, descent groups, unlike nuclear families, are permanent and enduring units, with new members added in every generation. Members have access to the lineage estate, where some of them must live, in order to benefit from and manage that estate across the generations. To endure, descent groups need to keep at least some of their members at home, on the ancestral estate. An easy way to do this is to have a rule about who belongs to the descent group and where they should live after they get married. Patrilineal and matrilineal descent, and the postmarital residence rules that usually accompany them, ensure that about half the people born in each generation will live out their lives on the ancestral estate. Neolocal residence, which is the rule for most middle-class Americans, isn't very common outside modern North America, Western Europe, and the European-derived cultures of Latin America.

Much more common is **patrilocality:** When a couple marries, it moves to the husband's community, so that their children will grow up in their father's village. Patrilocality is associated with patrilineal descent. This makes sense. If the group's male members are expected to exercise their rights in the ancestral estate, it's a good idea to raise them on that estate and to keep them there after they marry. This can be done by having wives move to the husband's village, rather than vice versa.

A less common postmarital residence rule, often associated with matrilineal descent, is **matrilocality:** Married couples live in the wife's community, and their children grow up in the mother's village. This rule keeps related women together. Together, patrilocality and matrilocality are known as *unilocal* rules of postmarital residence.

Ambilineal Descent

The descent rules examined so far admit certain people as members while excluding others. A unilineal rule uses one line only, either the female or the male. Besides the unilineal rules, there is another descent rule called nonunilineal or **ambilineal** descent. As in any descent group, membership comes through descent from a common ancestor. However, ambilineal groups differ from unilineal groups in that they do not *automatically* exclude either the children of sons or those of daughters. People can choose the descent group they join (for example, that of their father's father, father's mother, mother's father, or mother's mother). People also can change their descent-group membership, or belong to two or more groups at the same time.

294

Unilineal descent is a matter of ascribed status; ambilineal descent illustrates achieved status. With unilineal descent, membership is automatic; no choice is permitted. People are born members of their father's group in a patrilineal society or of their mother's group in a matrilineal society. They are members of that group for life. Ambilineal descent permits more flexibility in descent-group affiliation.

Before 1950, descent groups were generally described simply as patrilineal or matrilineal. If the society tended toward patrilineality, the anthropologist classified it as a patrilineal rather than an ambilineal group. The treatment of ambilineal descent as a separate category was a formal recognition that many descent systems are flexible—some more so than others.

Most societies have a prevailing opinion about where a couple should live after they marry; this is called a postmarital residence rule. A common rule is patrilocality: the couple lives with the husband's relatives, so that children grow up in their father's community. On the top, a traditional Korean wedding. The residence change takes place via a spousal utility vehicle with four-person drive. On the bottom, in Lendak, Slovakia, women transport part of the bride's dowry to the groom's house.

Kinship Calculation

In addition to studying kin groups, anthropologists also are interested in **kinship calculation:** the system by which people in a society reckon kin relationships. To study kinship calculation,

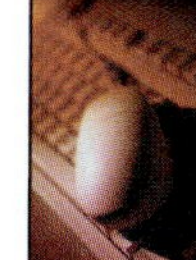

an ethnographer must first determine the word or words for different types of "relatives" used in a particular language and then ask questions such as, "Who are your relatives?" Kinship, like race and gender (discussed in other chapters), is culturally constructed. This means that some genealogical kin are considered to be relatives whereas others are not. Through questioning, the ethnographer discovers the specific genealogical relationships between "relatives" and the person who has named them—the **ego.** By posing the same questions to several local people, the ethnographer learns about the extent and direction of kinship calculation in that society. The ethnographer also begins to understand the relationship between kinship calculation and kin groups: how people use kinship to create and maintain personal ties and to join social groups. In the kinship charts that follow, the black cube labeled "ego" (Latin for *I*) identifies the person whose kinship calculation is being examined.

Genealogical Kin Types and Kin Terms

At this point, we may distinguish between *kin terms* (the words used for different relatives in a particular language) and *genealogical kin types.* We designate genealogical kin types with the letters and symbols shown in Figure 15.3. *Genealogical kin type* refers to an actual genealogical relationship (e.g., father's brother) as opposed to a kin term (e.g., *uncle*).

Kin terms reflect the social construction of kinship in a given culture. A kin term may (and usually does) lump together several genealogical relationships. In English, for instance, we use *father* primarily for one kin type: the genealogical father. However, *father* can be extended to an adoptive father or stepfather—and even to a priest. *Grandfather* includes mother's father and father's father. The term *cousin* lumps together several kin types. Even the more specific *first cousin* includes mother's brother's son (MBS), mother's brother's daughter (MBD), mother's sister's son (MZS), mother's sister's daughter (MZD), father's brother's son (FBS), father's brother's daughter (FBD), father's sister's son (FZS), and father's sister's daughter (FZD). *First cousin* thus lumps together at least eight genealogical kin types.

Uncle encompasses mother's and father's brothers, and *aunt* includes mother's and father's sisters. We also used *uncle* and *aunt* for the spouses of our "blood" aunts and uncles. We use the term for mother's brother and father's brother because we perceive them as being the same sort of relative. Calling them *uncles,* we distinguish between them and another kin type, F, whom we call *Father, Dad,* or *Pop.* In many societies, however, it is common to call a father and a father's brother by the same term. Later we'll see why.

In the United States and Canada, the nuclear family continues to be the most important group based on kinship. This is true despite an increased incidence of single parenthood, divorce, and remarriage. The nuclear family's relative isolation from other kin groups in modern nations reflects geographical mobility within an industrial economy with sale of labor for cash.

It's reasonable for North Americans to distinguish between relatives who belong to their

Figure 15.3
Kinship Symbols and Genealogical Kin Type Notation

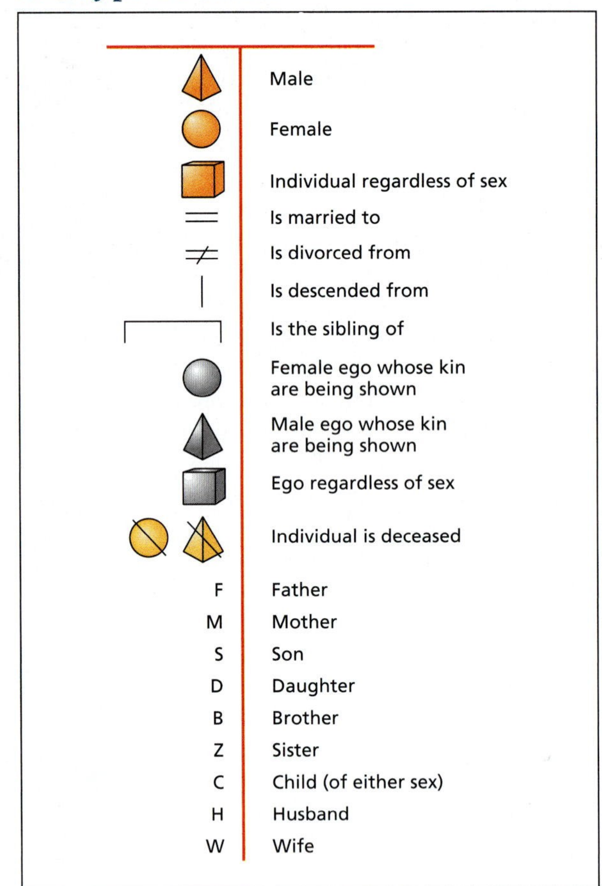

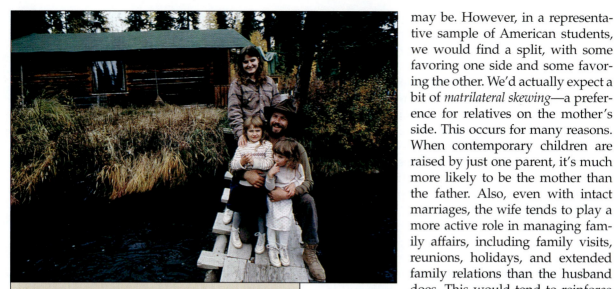

A Canadian nuclear family—Richard and Jenny Dix and their two daughters. The Dixes are one of Canada's westernmost nuclear families. They live in Yukon territory just miles from the Alaska border. Nuclear family organization is associated with geographical mobility.

nuclear families and those who don't. We are more likely to grow up with our parents than with our aunts and uncles. We tend to see our parents more often than we see our uncles and aunts, who may live in different towns and cities. We often inherit from our parents, but our cousins have first claim to inherit from our aunts and uncles. If our marriage is stable, we see our children daily as long as they remain at home. They are our heirs. We feel closer to them than to our nieces and nephews.

American kinship calculation and kin terminology reflect these social features. Thus, the term *uncle* distinguishes between the kin types MB and FB on the one hand and the kin type F on the other. However, this term also lumps kin types together. We use the same term for MB and FB, two different kin types. We do this because American kinship calculation is **bilateral**—traced equally through males and females, for example, father and mother. Both kinds of uncle are brothers of one of our parents. We think of both as roughly the same kind of relative.

"No," you may object, "I'm closer to my mother's brother than to my father's brother." That may be. However, in a representative sample of American students, we would find a split, with some favoring one side and some favoring the other. We'd actually expect a bit of *matrilateral skewing*—a preference for relatives on the mother's side. This occurs for many reasons. When contemporary children are raised by just one parent, it's much more likely to be the mother than the father. Also, even with intact marriages, the wife tends to play a more active role in managing family affairs, including family visits, reunions, holidays, and extended family relations than the husband does. This would tend to reinforce her kin network over his and thus favor matrilateral skewing.

Bilateral kinship means that people tend to perceive kin links through males and females as being similar or equivalent. This bilaterality is expressed in interaction with, living with or near, and rights to inherit from relatives. We don't usually inherit from uncles, but if we do, there's about as much chance that we'll inherit from the father's brother as from the mother's brother. We don't usually live with either aunt, but if we do, the chances are about the same that it will be the father's sister as the mother's sister.

Kinship Terminology

People perceive and define kin relations differently in different cultures. In any culture, kinship terminology is a classification system, a taxonomy or typology. It is a *native taxonomy*, developed over generations by the people who live in a particular society. A native classification system is based on how people perceive similarities and differences in the things being classified.

However, anthropologists have discovered that there are a limited number of patterns in which people classify their kin. People who speak very different languages may use exactly the same system of kinship terminology. This section examines the four main ways of classifying kin on the parental generation: lineal, bifurcate merging, generational, and bifurcate collateral. We also consider the social correlates of these classification systems. (Note that each of the systems described here applies to the parental generation. There are also differences in kin terminology on ego's generation. These involve the classification of siblings and cousins. There are six such systems, called Eskimo, Iroquois, Hawaiian, Crow, Omaha, and Sudanese cousin terminology, after societies that traditionally used them. You can see them diagrammed and discussed on our website.)

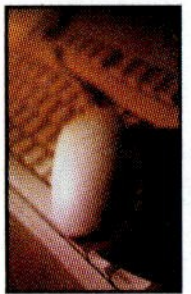

A **functional explanation** will be offered for each system of kinship terminology, such as lineal, bifurcate merging, and generational terminology. Functional explanations attempt to relate particular customs (such as use of kin terms) to other features of a society, such as rules of descent and postmarital residence. Certain aspects of a culture are so closely related that when one of them changes, the others inevitably change too. For certain terminologies, the social correlates are very clear.

Kinship terms provide useful information about social patterns. If two relatives are designated by the same term, we can assume that they are perceived as sharing socially significant attributes. Several factors influence the way people interact with, perceive, and classify relatives. For instance, do certain kinds of relatives customarily live together or apart? How far apart? What benefits do they derive from each other, and what are their obligations? Are they members of the same descent group or of different descent groups? With these questions in mind, let's examine systems of kinship terminology.

Lineal Terminology

Our own system of kinship classification is called the *lineal system* (Figure 15.4). The number 3 and the color green stand for the term *uncle,* which we apply both to FB and to MB. **Lineal kinship terminology** is found in societies such as the United States and Canada in which the nuclear family is the most important group based on kinship.

Lineal kinship terminology distinguishes lineal relatives from collateral relatives. A **lineal relative** is an ancestor or descendant, anyone on the direct line of descent that leads to and from ego (Figure 15.5). Thus, lineal relatives are one's parents, grandparents, great-grandparents, and other direct forebears. Lineal relatives also include children, grandchildren, and great-grandchildren. **Collateral relatives** are all other kin. They include siblings, nieces and nephews, aunts and uncles, and cousins (Figure 15.5). **Affinals** are relatives by marriage, whether of lineals (e.g., son's wife) or collaterals (sister's husband).

Figure 15.4

Lineal Kinship Terminology

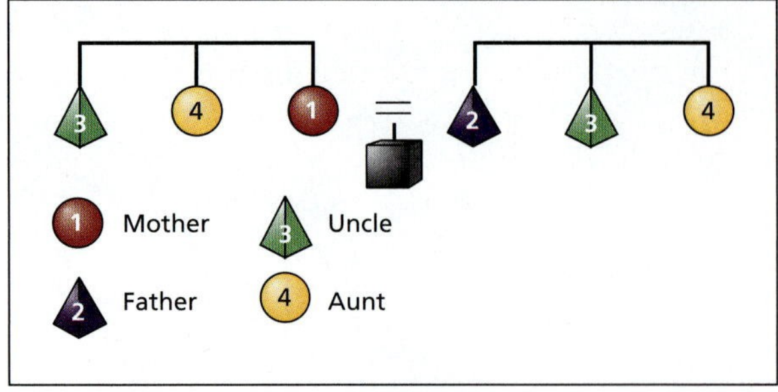

Bifurcate Merging Terminology

Bifurcate merging kinship terminology (Figure 15.6) bifurcates, or splits, the mother's side and the father's side. But it also merges same-sex siblings of each parent. Thus, mother and mother's sister are merged under the same term (1), while father and father's brother also get a common term (2). There are different terms for mother's brother (3) and father's sister (4).

People use this system in societies with unilineal (patrilineal and matrilineal) descent rules and unilocal (patrilocal and matrilocal) postmarital residence rules. When the society is unilineal and unilocal, the logic of bifurcate merging terminology is fairly clear. In a patrilineal society, for example, father and father's brother belong to the same descent group, gender, and generation. Since patrilineal societies usually have patrilocal residence, the father and his brother live in the same local group. Because they share so many attributes that are socially relevant, ego regards them as social equivalents and calls them by the same kinship term—2. However, the mother's brother belongs to a different descent group, lives elsewhere, and has a different kin term—3.

What about mother and mother's sister in a patrilineal society? They belong to the same descent group, the same gender, and the same generation. Often they marry men from the same village and go to live there. These social similarities help explain the use of the same term—1—for both.

Similar observations apply to matrilineal societies. Consider a society with two matrilineal clans, the Ravens and the Wolves. Ego is a member of his mother's clan, the Raven clan. Ego's father is a member of the Wolf clan. His mother and her sister are female Ravens of the same generation. If there is matrilocal residence, as there often is in matrilineal societies, they will live in the same village. Because they are so similar socially, ego calls them by the same kin term—1.

Figure 15.5

The Distinctions among Lineals, Collaterals, and Affinals as Perceived by Ego

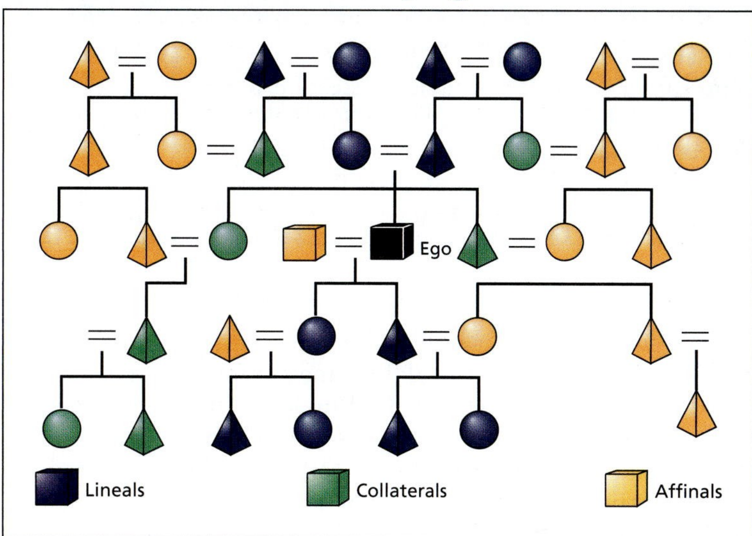

The father's sister, however, belongs to a different group, the Wolves; lives elsewhere; and have a different kin term—4. Ego's father and father's brother are male Wolves of the same generation. If they marry women of the same clan and live in the same village, this creates additional social similarities that reinforce this usage.

Figure 15.6

Bifurcate Merging Kinship Terminology

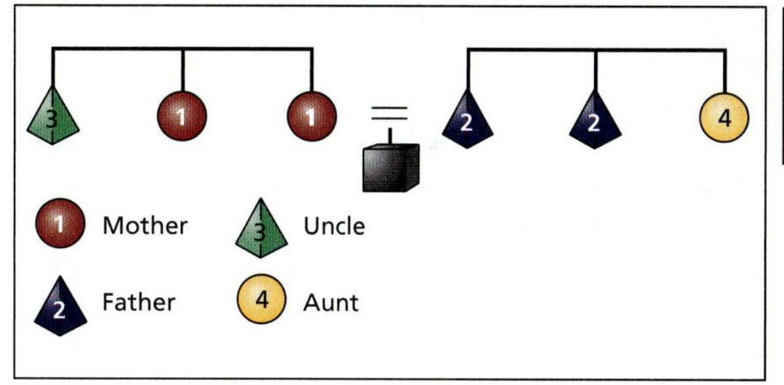

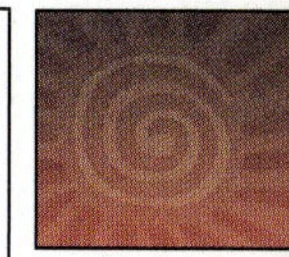

Generational Terminology

Like bifurcate merging kinship terminology, **generational kinship terminology** uses the same term for parents and their siblings, but the lumping is more complete (Figure 15.7). With generational terminology, there are only two terms for the parental generation. We may translate them as "father" and "mother," but more accurate translations would be "male member of the parental generation" and "female member of the parental generation."

Generational kinship terminology does not distinguish between the mother's and father's sides. It does not bifurcate, but it certainly does merge. It uses just one term for father, father's brother, and mother's brother. In a unilineal society, these three kin types would never belong to the same descent group. Generational kinship terminology also uses a single term for mother, mother's sister, and

Figure 15.7

Generational Kinship Terminology

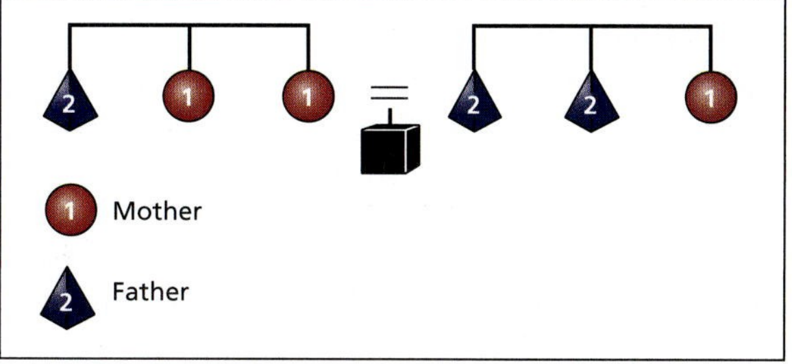

Table 15.4
The Four Systems of Kinship Terminology, with Their Social and Economic Correlates

Kinship Terminology	Kin Group	Residence Rule	Economy
Lineal	Nuclear family	Neolocal	Industrialism, foraging
Bifurcate merging	Unilineal descent group—patrilineal or matrilineal	Unilocal—patrilocal or matrilocal	Horticulture, pastoralism, agriculture
Generational	Ambilineal descent group, band	Ambilocal	Agriculture, horticulture, foraging
Bifurcate collateral	Varies	Varies	Varies

father's sister. Nor, in a unilineal society, would these three ever be members of the same group.

Nevertheless, generational terminology suggests closeness between ego and his or her aunts and uncles—much more closeness than exists between Americans and these kin types. How likely would you be to call your uncle "Dad" or your aunt "Mom"? We'd expect to find generational terminology in cultures in which kinship is much more important than it is in our own but in which there is no rigid distinction between the father's side and the mother's side.

385

It's logical, then, that generational kin terminology is typical of societies with ambilineal descent. In such contexts, descent-group membership is not automatic. People may choose the group they join, change their descent-group membership, or belong to two or more descent groups simultaneously. Generational terminology fits these conditions. The use of intimate kin terms signals that people have close personal relations with all their relatives on the parental generation. People exhibit similar behavior toward their aunts, uncles, and parents. Someday they'll have to choose a descent group to join. Furthermore, in ambilineal societies, postmarital residence is usually ambilocal. This means that the married couple can live with either the husband's or the wife's group.

Significantly, generational terminology also characterizes certain foraging bands, including Kalahari San groups and several native societies of North America. Use of this terminology reflects certain similarities between foraging bands and ambilineal descent groups. In both societies, people have a choice about their kin-group affiliation. Foragers always live with kin, but they often shift band affiliation and so may be members of several different bands during their lifetimes. Just as in food-producing societies with ambilineal descent, generational terminology among foragers helps maintain close personal relationships with several parental-generation relatives whom ego may eventually use as a point of entry into different groups. Table 15.4 summarizes the types of kin group, the postmarital residence rule, and the economy associated with the four types of kinship terminology.

Bifurcate Collateral Terminology

Of the four kin classification systems, **bifurcate collateral kinship terminology** is the most specific. It has separate terms for each of the six kin types on the parental generation (Figure 15.8). Bifurcate collateral terminology isn't as common as the other types. Many of the societies that use it are in North Africa, and the Middle East, and many of them are offshoots of the same ancestral group.

Bifurcate collateral terminology also may be used when a child has parents of different ethnic backgrounds and uses terms for aunts and uncles derived from different languages. Thus, if you have a mother who is Latina and a father who is Anglo, you may call your aunts and uncles on your mother's side "tia" and "tio," while calling those on your father's side "aunt" and "uncle." And your mother and father may be "Mom" and "Pop." That's a modern form of bifurcate collateral kinship terminology.

Figure 15.8
Bifurcate Collateral Kinship Terminology

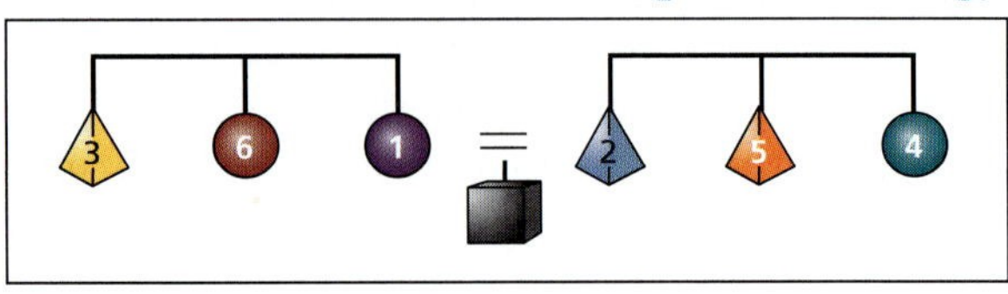

summary

1. In nonindustrial societies, kinship, descent, and marriage organize social and political life. In studying kinship, we must distinguish between kin groups, whose composition and activities can be observed, and kinship calculation—how people identify and designate their relatives.
2. One widespread kin group is the nuclear family, consisting of a married couple and their children. There are functional alternatives to the nuclear family. That is, other groups may assume functions usually associated with the nuclear family. Nuclear families tend to be especially important in foraging and industrial societies. Among farmers and herders, other kinds of kin groups often overshadow the nuclear family.
3. In contemporary North America, the nuclear family is the characteristic kin group for the middle class. Expanded households and sharing with extended family kin occur more frequently among the poor, who may pool their resources in dealing with poverty. Today, however, even in the American middle class, nuclear family households are declining as single-person households and other domestic arrangements increase.
4. The descent group is a basic kin group among nonindustrial food producers (farmers and herders). Unlike families, descent groups have perpetuity—they last for generations. Descent-group members share and manage a common estate; land, animals, and other resources. There are several kinds of descent groups. Lineages are based on demonstrated descent; clans, on stipulated descent. Descent rules may be unilineal or ambilineal. Unilineal (patrilineal and matrilineal) descent is associated with unilocal (respectively, patrilocal and matrilocal) postmarital residence.
5. A kinship terminology is a classification of relatives based on perceived differences and similarities. Comparative research has revealed a limited number of ways of classifying kin. Because there are correlations between kinship terminology and other social practices, we often can predict kinship terminology from other aspects of culture. The four basic kinship terminologies for the parental generation are lineal, bifurcate merging, generational, and bifurcate collateral. Many foraging and industrial societies use lineal terminology, which is associated with nuclear family organization. Cultures with unilocal residence and unilineal descent tend to have bifurcate merging terminology. Generational terminology correlates with ambilineal descent and ambilocal residence.

key terms

affinals Relatives by marriage, whether of lineals (e.g., son's wife) or collaterals (e.g., sister's husband).

ambilineal Principle of descent that does not automatically exclude the children of either sons or daughters.

bifurcate collateral kinship terminology Kinship terminology employing separate terms for M, F, MB, MZ, FB, and FZ.

bifurcate merging kinship terminology Kinship terminology in which M and MZ are called by the same term, F and FB are called by the same term, and MB and FZ are called by different terms.

bilateral kinship calculation A system in which kinship ties are calculated equally through both sexes: mother and father, sister and brother, daughter and son, and so on.

clan Unilneal descent group based on stipulated descent.

collateral relative A genealogical realtive who is not in ego's direct line, such as B, Z, FB, or MZ.

descent group A permanent social unit whose members claim common ancestry; fundamental to tribal society.

ego Latin for *I*. In kinship charts, the point from which one views an egocentric genealogy.

extended family Expanded household including three or more generations.

family of orientation Nuclear family in which one is born and grows up.

family of procreation Nuclear family established when one marries and has children.

functional explanation Explanation that establishes a correlation or interrelationship between social customs. When customs are functionally interrelated, if one changes, the others also change.

generational kinship terminology Kinship terminology with only two terms for the parental generation, one designating M, MZ, and FZ and the other designating F, FB, and MB.

kinship calculation The system by which people in a particular society reckon kin relationships.

lineage Unilineal descent group based on demonstrated descent.

lineal kinship terminology Parental generation kin terminology with four terms: one for M, one for F, one for FB and MB, and one for MZ and FZ.

lineal relative Any of ego's ancestors or descendants (e.g., parents, grandparents, children, grandchildren); on the direct line of descent that leads to and from ego.

matrilineal descent Unilineal descent rule in which people join the mother's group automatically at birth and stay members throughout life.

matrilocality Customary residence with the wife's relatives after marriage, so that children grow up in their mother's community.

neolocality Postmarital residence pattern in which a couple establishes a new place of residence rather than living with or near either set of parents.

patrilineal descent Unilineal descent rule in which people join the father's group automatically at birth and stay members throughout life.

patrilocality Customary residence with the husband's relatives after marriage, so that children grow up in their father's community.

unilineal descent Matrilineal or patrilineal descent.

critical thinking questions

1. Why is kinship so important to anthropologists? How might the study of kinship be useful for research in fields of anthropology other than cultural anthropology?
2. To what sorts of family or families do you belong? Have you belonged to other kinds of families? When you were growing up, how did you feel about your family compared with those of your friends?
3. Choose two of your friends who have families of orientation that differ from your own. How do they differ?
4. How might a society reproduce itself biologically without the nuclear family?
5. What residence choices have you made during your lifetime? What factors do you think will determine your future residence choices?
6. Do you belong to any kin group that has lasted or will last for more than one generation?
7. What do "family" and "family values" mean to you?
8. Based on your experience, do you agree with the discussion of changing portrayals of families on North American TV? What other changes have you noticed? Has TV actually caused any of those changes?
9. Besides industrial societies, where else are nuclear families important, and why?
10. How do the kin terms you use compare with the four classification systems discussed in this chapter? What's the strangest use of kin terms you've ever heard (among your friends or acquaintances)?

case study

Nuer: Traditionally, Nuer political organization was based on segmentary lineage organization (SLO—see the text chapter "Political Systems"). SLO offered an effective way of resolving disputes and of mobilizing support among kin groups. In the 1990s, however, civil war in Sudan led to widespread resettlement. Many Nuer took refuge in camps in Ethiopia and elsewhere, with many thousands of Nuer eventually settling in the United States. In *Culture Sketches* by Holly Peters-Golden, read the chapter on the "Nuer: Cattle and Kinship in Sudan." This chapter and the chapter "Political Systems" demonstrate the potential political significance of kinship alliances. For Nuer emigrants, what might be some challenges in creating social ties without the political ties and village links that underlie traditional Nuer solidarity?

suggested additional readings

Buchler, I. R., and H. A. Selby
1968 *Kinship and Social Organization: An Introduction to Theory and Method.* New York: Macmillan. Introduction to comparative social organization; includes several chapters on interpretations of kinship classification systems.

Cigno, A.
1994 *Economics of the Family.* New York: Oxford University Press. How economists explain changes in birth rates and divorce rates and other features of family organization and functioning.

Collier, J. F., and S. J. Yangisako, eds.
1987 *Gender and Kinship: Essays toward a Unified Analysis.* Stanford, CA: Stanford University Press. Consideration of kinship in the context of gender issues.

Finkler, K.
2000 *Experiencing the New Genetics: Family and Kinship on the Medical Frontier.* Philadelphia: University of Pennsylvania Press. Examines some medical and genetic aspects of kinship, along with social dimensions of contemporary medical/genetics debates.

Graburn, N., ed.
1971 *Readings in Kinship and Social Structure.* New York: Harper & Row. Several important articles on kinship terminology.

Hansen, K. V., and A. I. Garey, eds.
1998 *Families in the U.S.: Kinship and Domestic Politics.* Philadelphia: Temple University Press. Families, family policy, and diversity in the contemporary United States.

Netting, R. M. C., R. R. Wilk, and E. J. Arnould, eds.
1984 *Households: Comparative and Historical Studies of the Domestic Groups.* Berkeley, CA: University of California Press. Excellent collection of articles on household research.

Parkin, R.
1997 *Kinship: An Introduction to Basic Concepts.* Cambridge, MA: Blackwell. The basics of kinship study.

Pasternak, B., C. R. Ember, and M. Ember
1997 *Sex, Gender, and Kinship: A Cross-cultural Perspective.* Upper Saddle River, NJ: Prentice Hall. Sex roles, kinship, and marriage in comparative perspective.

Radcliff-Brown, A. R., and D. Forde, eds.
1994 *African Systems of Kinship and Marriage.* New York: Columbia University Press. Reissue of a classic work, indispensable to understand kinship, descent, and marriage.

Stacey, J.
1998 *Brave New Families: Stories of Domestic Upheaval in Late Twentieth Century America.* Berkeley, CA: University of California Press. Contemporary family life in the United States, based on field work in California's Silicon Valley.

Stone, L.
2000 *Kinship and Gender: An Introduction,* 2nd ed. Boulder, CO: Westview. Kinship, gender roles, and gender identity.

2000 *New Directions in Anthropological Kinship.* Lanham, MD; Rowman and Littlefield. How contemporary anthropologists think about kinship.

Scheffler, H. W.
2000 *Filiation and Affiliation.* Boulder, CO: Westview. How does one recognize his or her kin if unilineal descent excludes some very close relatives?

Weston, K.
1991 *Families We Choose: Lesbians, Gays, Kinship.* New York: Columbia University Press. Kinship and family issues affecting gays and lesbians.

internet exercises

1. *Kinship and Conflict:* Go to the Yanamamo Interactive: Understanding the Ax Fight web page, **http://www.anth.ucsb.edu/projects/axfight/index.html,** and go to the web version of the CD-ROM, **http://www.anth.ucsb.edu/projects/axfight/prep.html.** View the film of the Ax Fight and read the text entitled "Chagnon's Voice-Over Narration from the 1975 *The Ax Fight.*" The questions below ask you to interpret the fight, and it may be necessary to view the film or read the text more than once to understand it.

   a. What is the cause of the fight?

   b. Who are the aggressors? Who are they attacking?

   c. As the fight escalates, more people join in. What is their relationship to the people who start the fight? Why is that important?

   d. How is kinship important for understanding this conflict? Can you think of examples from your own society where kinship served to escalate or diffuse conflict?

2. *Descent and Subsistence:* Go to the Ethnographic Atlas Cross-tabulations page, **http://lucy.ukc.ac.uk/cgi-bin/uncgi/Ethnoatlas/atlas.vopts.** This site has compiled ethnographic information on many different groups and you can use the tools provided to cross-tabulate the prevalence of certain traits. Go to the site. Under "Select Row Category" choose "region," and under "Select Column Category" select "descent." Press the Submit Query button. The table that appears shows the frequency of descent patterns from regions around the world.

   a. Look at the total row for descent. Which forms of descent are most common worldwide? What is the *most* common? Is that the system with which you are most familiar in your own society?

   b. Where are most of the patrilineal societies found? Where are most of the bilateral societies found? In the Insular Pacific, is any one descent system predominant?

c. Now go back to the Ethnographic Atlas Cross-tabulations page and change the "Select Row Category" from "region" to "subsistence economy" and press the Submit Query button. What kind of subsistence economy do most patrilineal societies practice? Are matrilineal societies more likely to use hunting, gathering, or fishing or to use agriculture? Is the pattern as strong as with patrilineal groups? Are there any strong patterns for the type of subsistence economy practiced by bilateral groups?

3. *Kinship Terminologies:* Go to the website created by Professor Brian Schwimmer of the Department of Anthropology at the University of Manitoba, **http://www.umanitoba.ca/faculties/arts/anthropology/kintitle.html.** Click on "Begin Tutorial." Next click on topic 3—Kinship Terminology. Press "Continue" at the bottom left of the next two pages until you reach a page titled "Systematic Kinship Terminologies." Scroll down the page to the diagram labeled "Eskimo Kin Terms."

   a. To what parental generation kin terminology discussed in the book (lineal, bifurcate merging, generational, or bifurcate collateral) do the Eskimo cousin terms correspond?

   b. Answer the same question for Iroquois, Hawaiian, and Sudanese terms.

   c. Do you see any logic in the relation between the terms used on the parental generation (for parents, aunts, and uncles) and those used on ego's own generation (for siblings and cousins)?

   d. How do these associated sets of kin terms fit with particular kinds of kin groups, for example, the nuclear family, a unilineal descent group, an ambilineal descent group?

   e. At the bottom of the web page, can you see how Omaha kin terms might fit with patrilineal descent and Crow terms, with matrilineal descent?

See Chapter 15 on your CD-ROM for additional review and interactive exercises. See your McGraw-Hill Online Learning Center for more.

Chapter 16

Marriage

CHAPTER OUTLINE

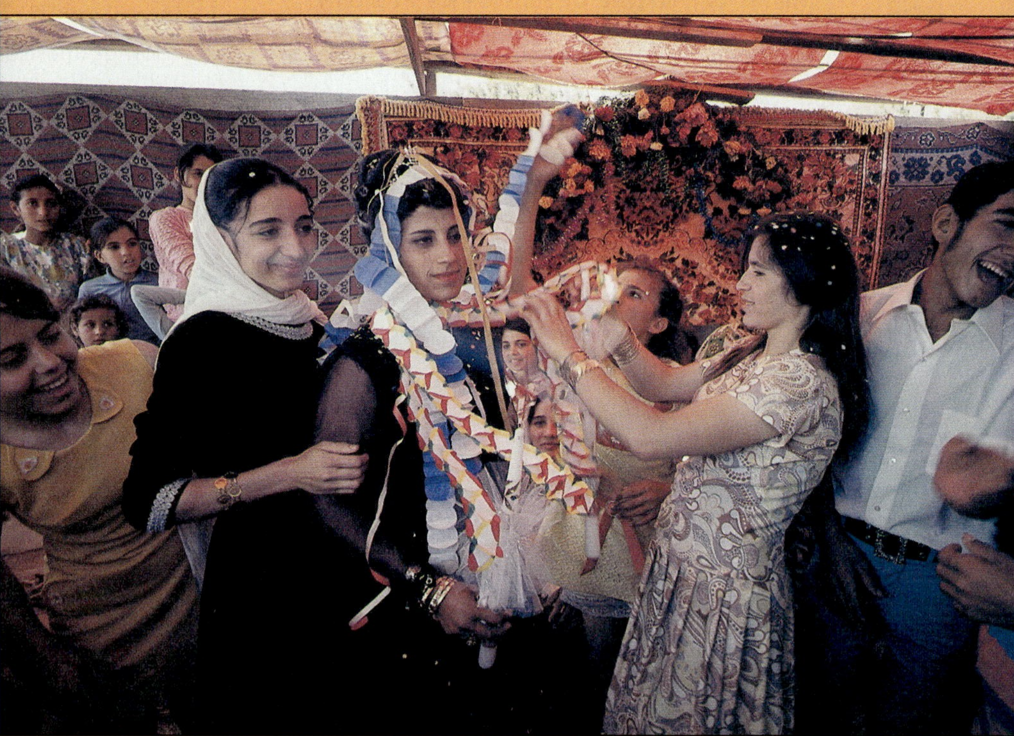

NYTIMES.COM NEWS BRIEF

Young Man Decides to Wive It Wealthily in Uganda

by Ian Fisher
July 5, 2000

OBULENZI, Uganda—Ahamadah Ntale has a vision for a new compact between men and women in Uganda, starting with him. A few weeks ago, he walked into the local office of one of Uganda's national newspapers and left the reporter with a story that ran with this headline: "Man hunts old woman to marry."

He is 25, a scooter taxi driver. He said he wanted a woman between 35 and 45, loving and free of AIDS. Most important, she would have to defy Uganda's tradition of men paying a dowry [bridewealth] for their brides. The bride-to-be must cough it up to HIS parents.

The first call came at 7 A.M. the day the article was published, from a 38-year-old businesswoman in the capital, Kampala. By nightfall, there were 193 phone calls, he said, and in the next week more than 400. One woman promised 10 cows if he chose her and gave up the search.

The question is, why are women so interested in this obscure taxi driver from a small town? One answer is: because they can be. In the last decade, women in Uganda have made major strides politically and economically, more so than in many African nations.

Literacy rates have shot up, and Kampala swims with middle-class working women, chatting on mobile phones and making money. The vice president of Uganda is a woman, as are several leading opposition members . . .

"In Uganda, people are saying we are now equal," said Zebia Namugera, a 31-year-old youth counselor here. She also owns a successful shop, selling cosmetics and handbags, something she said would have been difficult even a decade ago. "Men are now tired of doing everything," she said. "We have joined them."

Mr. Ntale was standing in front of her, after a stroll where he was cheered on by men and women alike as something of a local hero. "As you can see," said Ms. Namugera, who is married, "in fact he is handsome. That is also why women are coming." In a nice yellow shirt and belt with a dubious Gucci label, he looked perfectly acceptable. But his offer seems the intriguing thing. Based on a few hours talking with him here, that offer combines two passions in his life: women, particularly older ones, and money . . . He said, however, he is on a crusade for all men in Uganda . . .

"I want to see if women could support me, as men have always supported women after we have married them," he added. "I want to experience the way they treat us after marrying us." . . .

A local Muslim elder, Ahamadah Matovu, said he thought Mr. Ntale's initiative was excellent, though he must love her and the marriage must be strictly religious.

"The woman must be willing to have only one man," he said. Asked if Mr. Ntale would have to confine himself to only one woman, Mr. Matovu gave a practical answer, though not in line with the current thinking about sex equality: "He is limited by his finances. I don't think he has much money."

Source: http://www.nytimes.com/library/world/africa/070500uganda-marriage.html.

overview

We know, or think we know, what marriage is in our own society. But marriage, which is usually a form of domestic partnership, is notoriously difficult to define. How does marriage vary around the world? What does religion have to do with marriage? What rights and obligations are created by marriage? Should someone marry one person or several? Can men ever marry men and women marry women? Does society tell us whom to marry and whom to avoid? Do people have to mate inside certain groups and outside others? How is marriage related to sex? Should wedlock be an exclusive sexual arrangement? Must people always avoid their biological relatives when they mate and marry? What's the explanation for the incest taboo?

How does marriage in nonindustrial societies differ from marriage in our own? What kind of property is passed on when a marriage takes place? How do wealth transfers correlate with the social status of the bride and groom? What treatment can wives and husbands expect after they marry? Why are marriages arranged? Is marriage only an individual matter? Is the connection between romantic love and marriage a cultural universal? Why do men marry more than one woman, and women team up with more than one man? What makes marriage stable or unstable? Why do we have such a high divorce rate? This chapter attempts to answer these and other questions as it explores human diversity as revealed in marital customs, forms, and functions.

No definition of marriage is broad enough to apply easily to all societies and situations. A commonly quoted definition comes from *Notes and Queries on Anthropology:*

> Marriage is a union between a man and a woman such that the children born to the woman are recognized as legitimate offspring of both partners. (Royal Anthropological Institute 1951, p. 111)

This definition isn't universally valid for several reasons. For example, some societies recognize same-sex marriages. Also, in many societies, marriages unite more than two spouses. Here we speak of *plural marriages,* as when a woman weds a group of brothers—an arrangement called *fraternal polyandry* that is characteristic of certain Himalayan cultures. In the Brazilian community of Arembepe, people can choose among various forms of marital union. Most people live in long-term "common-law" domestic partnerships that are not legally sanctioned. Some have civil marriages, which are licensed and legalized by a justice of the peace. Still others go through religious ceremonies, so they are united in "holy matrimony," although not legally. And some have both civil and religious ties. The different forms of union permit someone to have multiple spouses (e.g., one common-law, one civil, one religious) without ever getting divorced.

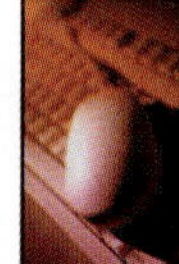

In Sudan, a Nuer woman can marry a woman if her father has only daughters but no male heirs, who are necessary if his patrilineage is to survive. He may ask his daughter to stand as a son in order to take a bride. This is a symbolic and social relationship rather than a sexual one. The "wife" has sex with a man or men (whom her female "husband" must approve) until she gets pregnant. The children born to the wife are accepted as the offspring of both the female husband and the wife. Although the female husband is not the actual **genitor,** the biological father, of the children, he is their **pater,** or socially recognized father. What's important in this Nuer case is *social* rather than *biological paternity.* We see again how kinship is socially constructed. The bride's children are considered the legitimate offspring of her female "husband," who is biologically a woman but socially a man, and the descent line continues.

The British anthropologist Edmund Leach (1955) despaired of ever arriving at a universal definition of marriage. Instead, he suggested that depending on the society, several different kinds of rights are allocated by institutions classified as marriage. These rights vary from one culture to another, and no single one is widespread enough to provide a basis for defining marriage.

According to Leach, marriage can, but doesn't always, accomplish the following:

1. Establish the legal father of a woman's children and the legal mother of a man's.
2. Give either or both spouses a monopoly in the sexuality of the other.
3. Give either or both spouses rights to the labor of the other.
4. Give either or both spouses rights over the other's property.
5. Establish a joint fund of property—a partnership—for the benefit of the children.
6. Establish a socially significant "relationship of affinity" between spouses and their relatives.

Marriage conveys certain rights, obligations, and benefits. Here we see one of several same-sex couples who were "married" in 1993 at a demonstration in front of the Internal Revenue Service. This Saturday event, at which clergy officiated, was part of a giant 1993 march on Washington for lesbian and gay civil rights, including equal treatment by the IRS.

Same-Sex Marriage

Increasingly, we hear discussions of same-sex marriage. Gay men and lesbians are the strongest supporters of the idea, while religious conservatives are its strongest opponents. This section on same-sex marriage will serve to illustrate the six rights just listed, by seeing what happens in their absence. What if same-sex marriages, which are by and large illegal in the United States, were legal? Could a same-sex marriage establish legal parentage of children born to one or both partners after the partnership is formed? In the case of a different-sex marriage, children born to the wife after the marriage takes place usually are legally defined as her husband's regardless of whether or not he is the genitor.

Nowadays, of course, DNA testing makes it possible to establish paternity, just as modern reproductive technology makes it possible for a lesbian couple to have one or both partners artificially inseminated. If same-sex marriages were legal, the social construction of kinship could easily make both partners parents (as in the controversial children's book *Heather's Two Mommies*, which pops into the news from time to time as the target of a book banning). If a Nuer woman married to a woman can be the pater of a child she did not father, why can't two lesbians be the **maters** (socially recognized mothers) of a child one of them did not father? And if a married different-sex couple can adopt a child and have it be theirs through the social and legal construction of kinship, the same logic could be applied to a gay male or lesbian couple.

Continuing with Leach's list of the rights transmitted by marriage, same-sex marriage could certainly give each spouse rights to the sexuality of the other. Unable to marry legally, gay men and lesbians use various devices, such as the mock wedding shown in the photo, to declare their commitment and desire for a monogamous sexual relationship. In April 2000, Vermont passed a bill allowing same-sex couples to unite legally, with virtually all the benefits of marriage.

Same-sex marriages, as forms of monogamous commitment, have been endorsed by representatives of many religions, including Unitarians and Quakers (the Society of Friends). Among Quakers, such issues are decided by local congregations, which have sanctioned thousands of same-sex marriages. In 1993, the General Assembly of the Union of American Hebrew Congregations (reform Jewish synagogues) passed a resolution advocating legal recognition of same-sex unions (Eskridge 1996). According to Eskridge (1996), a 1990 survey of several thousand gay men and lesbians found that 75 percent of the lesbians and 60 percent of the gay men were living in long-term domestic partnerships.

If they were legal, same-sex marriages could easily give each spouse rights to the other spouse's labor and its products. Some societies do allow marriage between members of the same biological sex. Several Native American groups had figures known as *berdaches*. These were biological men who assumed many of the mannerisms, behavior patterns, and tasks of women. Sometimes *berdaches* married men, who shared the products of their labor from hunting and traditional male roles, as the *berdache* fulfilled the traditional wifely role. Also, in some Native American cultures, a marriage of a "manly-hearted women" to another woman brought the traditional male–female division of labor to their household. The manly woman hunted and did other male tasks, while the wife played the traditional female role.

There's no logical reason why same-sex marriage could not give spouses rights over the other's property. But in the United States, the same inheritance rights that apply to male–female couples do not apply to same-sex couples. For instance, even in the absence of a will, property can pass to a widow or a widower without going through probate. The wife or husband pays no inheritance tax. This benefit is not available to gay men and lesbians. Nor, in most cities, can rights to rent-controlled apartments be passed on to a same-sex heir. They can be to a wife or a husband. Many other legal rights that apply to male–female marriages are missing for same-sex partners. What happens when a same-sex partner is in a nursing home, prison, or hospital? The other partner may not have the same visiting rights as would a husband, wife, or biological relative. With same-sex marriage illegal, couples may even find themselves unable in some places to share accommodations that require roommates or housemates to be related by blood or marriage (Weston 1991).

What about Leach's fifth right—to establish a joint fund of property—to benefit the children? Here again, gay and lesbian couples are at a disadvantage. As mentioned previously, same-sex couples cannot count on the inheritance laws that apply to different-sex couples. If there are children, property is separately, rather than jointly, transmitted. Nor, usually, can gay and lesbian couples and their children benefit from family discounts available to traditional families. Some organizations do make staff benefits, such as health and dental insurance, available to same-sex domestic partners. Typically, this requires some official sworn statement that such a partnership exists.

Finally, there is the matter of establishing a socially significant "relationship of affinity" between spouses and their relatives. As we'll see later in this chapter, in many societies, one of the main roles of marriage is to establish an alliance between groups, in addition to the individual bond. As we saw in the chapter "Families, Kinship and Descent," affinals are relatives through marriage, such as a brother-in-law or mother-in-law. Only married people have these official relationships. I remember a Brazilian man who had lived with the same woman for more than 20 years. Their "marriage" was an unofficial domestic partnership of a sort that is common in the village of Arembepe, Bahia. Although his wife had given birth to 13 of his children, and although they ran a successful business together, he insisted she was his "woman" rather than his "wife." An official marriage requires a license and a service performed by a justice of the peace. They had chosen to have neither. According to Brazilian inheritance law, children receive at least half of any estate, with the legal spouse getting the other half. Neither my informant nor his wife could inherit from each other. Their children, who were officially registered in the names of both parents, could and would inherit from each. Nor could he or she receive a pension from the other. Finally, neither had affinals. He recognized no brothers- or sisters-in-law, mother-in-law, or

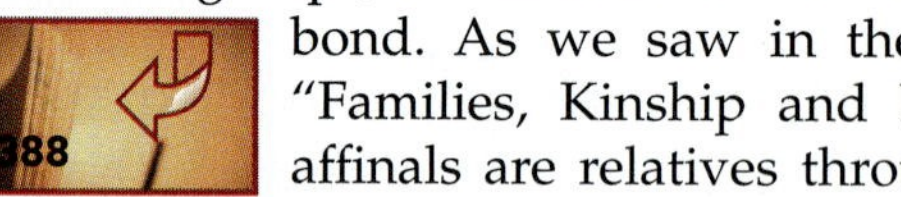

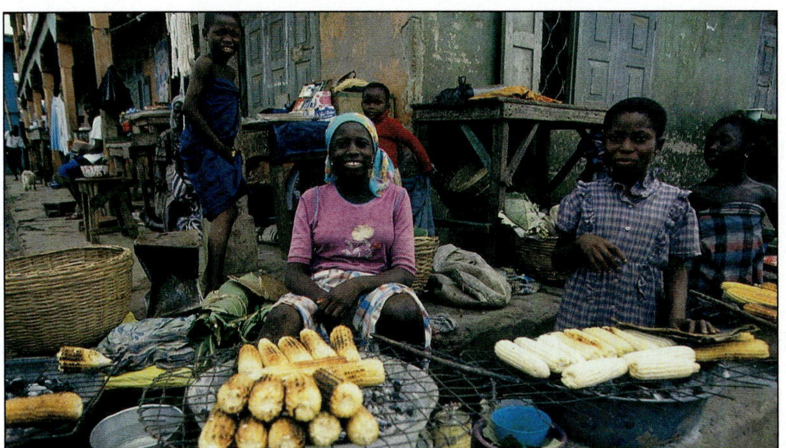

In parts of Nigeria, shown here, prominent market women may take a wife. Such marriage allows wealthy women to strengthen their social status and the economic importance of their households.

father-in-law, nor did she. Such arrangements are typical of Arembepe, where estates are generally meager and there is no social pressure to marry formally (Kottak 1999).

For same-sex couples in contemporary North America, affinal relations are problematic. In an unofficial union, terms like "daughter-in-law" and "mother-in-law" may sound strange. Despite the existence of organizations like PFLAG, Parents and Friends of Lesbians and Gays, many parents are suspicious of their children's sexuality and life-style choices. As long as same-sex marriage is illegal, parents retain certain rights with respect to their adult children, for example, to make medical decisions that a legal spouse would otherwise make. Consider also the case of a woman who divorces a man for another woman, or whose husband dies, after which she forms a lesbian domestic partnership. There are legal cases in the United States in which custody of her children has been awarded to her former husband's parents, or to her own, rather than to her—because of her life-style choice. Ties of "blood" and formal marriage take legal precedence in the United States, as in many countries.

This discussion of same-sex marriage has been intended to illustrate the different kinds of rights that typically accompany marriage, by seeing what may happen when there is a permanent pair bond without legal sanction. In all 50 United States, with the fleeting exception of Hawaii, which flirted with the legalization of same-sex marriage, and Vermont, as mentioned previously, such unions are illegal. As we have seen, same-sex marriages have been recognized in different historical and cultural settings. In certain African cultures, including the Igbo of Nigeria and the Lovedu of South Africa, women may marry other women. In situations in which women, such as prominent market women in West Africa, are able to amass property and other forms of wealth, they may take a wife. Such marriage allows the prominent woman to strengthen her social status and the economic importance of her household (Amadiume 1987).

One of the most famous examples of same-sex marriage is that of the Azande of Sudan, where male warriors took younger male brides, who served them sexually and by performing domestic duties. The warriors paid "bride price" (discussed later in this chapter) for their male "brides," which established an affinal relationship with the young man's lineage. When Azande warriors retired from that role, they gave up their male bride and sometimes married the sister of the former male bride. The former male brides, in turn, moved into the warrior grade and took their own younger male brides. The Azande, flexible in their sexuality, had no trouble shifting from homosexual acts to heterosexual acts (see Murray and Roscoe 1998).

 Incest and Exogamy

In many nonindustrial societies, a person's social world includes two main categories: kin and strangers. Strangers are potential or actual enemies. Marriage is one of the primary ways of converting strangers into kin, of creating and maintaining personal and political alliances, relationships of affinity. **Exogamy,** the practice of seeking a husband or wife outside one's own group, has adaptive value because it links people into a wider social network that nurtures, helps, and protects them in times of need.

Incest refers to sexual relations with someone considered to be a close relative. All cultures have taboos against it. However, although the taboo is a cultural universal, cultures define incest differently. As an illustration, consider some implications of the distinction between two kinds of first cousins: cross cousins and parallel cousins.

The children of two brothers or two sisters are **parallel cousins.** The children of a brother and a sister are **cross cousins.** Your mother's sister's children and your father's brother's children are your parallel cousins. Your father's sister's children and your mother's brother's children are your cross cousins.

The American kin term *cousin* doesn't distinguish between cross and parallel cousins, but in many societies, especially those with unilineal descent, the distinction is essential. As an example, consider a community with only two descent groups. This exemplifies what is known as *moiety* organization—from the French *moitié*, which means "half." Descent bifurcates the community so that everyone belongs to one half or the other. Some societies have patrilineal moieties; others have matrilineal moieties.

In Figures 16.1 and 16.2, notice that cross cousins are always members of the opposite moiety and parallel cousins always belong to your (ego's) own moiety. With patrilineal descent (Figure 16.1), people take the father's descent-group affiliation; in a matrilineal society (Figure 16.2), they take the mother's affiliation. You can see from these diagrams that your mother's sister's children (MZC) and your father's brother's children (FBC) belong to your group. Your cross cousins—that is, FZC and MBC—belong to the other moiety.

Parallel cousins therefore belong to the same generation and the same descent group as ego does, and they are like ego's brothers and sisters. They are called by the same kin terms as brother and sister are. Defined as close relatives, parallel cousins are tabooed as sex or marriage partners. They fall within the incest taboo, but cross cousins don't.

In societies with unilineal moieties, cross cousins belong to the opposite group. Sex with cross cousins isn't incestuous, because they aren't considered forbidden relatives. In fact, in many unilineal societies, people must marry either a cross cousin or someone from the same descent group as a cross cousin. A unilineal descent rule ensures that the cross cousin's descent group is

Figure 16.1
Parallel and Cross Cousins and Patrilineal Moiety Organization

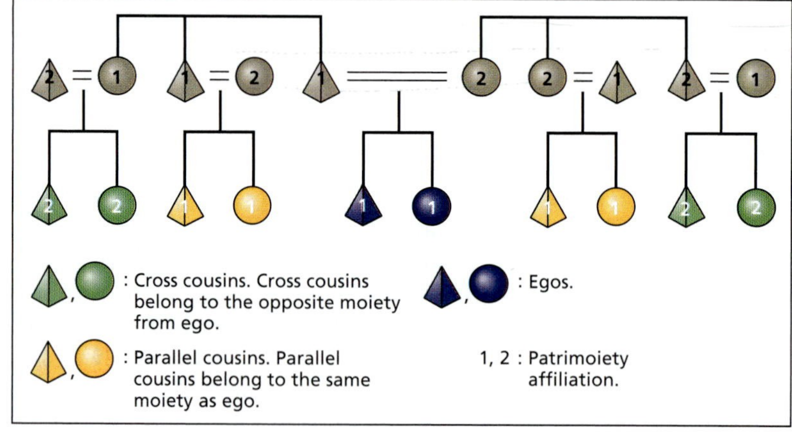
: Cross cousins. Cross cousins belong to the opposite moiety from ego.
: Parallel cousins. Parallel cousins belong to the same moiety as ego.
: Egos.
1, 2 : Patrimoiety affiliation.

Figure 16.2
Matrilineal Moiety Organization

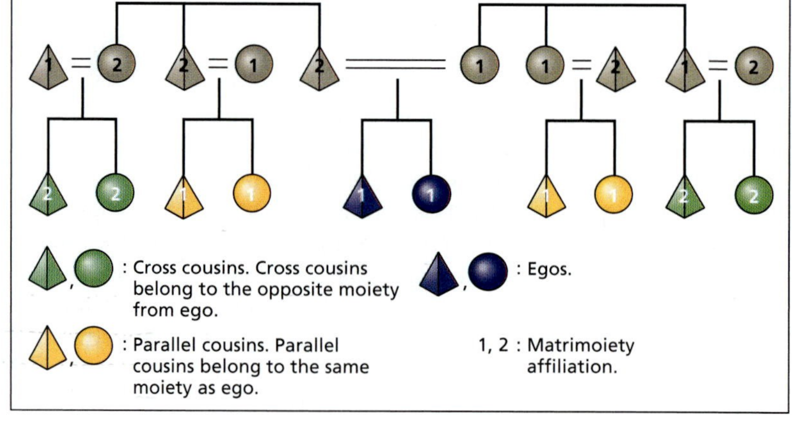
: Cross cousins. Cross cousins belong to the opposite moiety from ego.
: Parallel cousins. Parallel cousins belong to the same moiety as ego.
: Egos.
1, 2 : Matrimoiety affiliation.

Among the Yanomami of Brazil and Venezuela (shown here), sex with (and marriage to) cross cousins is proper, but sex with parallel cousins is considered incestuous. With unilineal descent, sex with cross cousins isn't incestuous because cross cousins never belong to ego's descent group.

never one's own. With moiety exogamy, spouses must belong to different moieties.

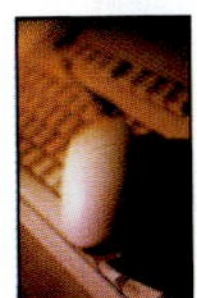

Among the Yanomami of Venezuela and Brazil (Chagnon 1997), men anticipate eventual marriage to a cross cousin by calling her "wife." They call their male cross cousins "brother-in-law." Yanomami women call their male cross cousins "husband" and their female cross cousins "sister-in-law." Among the Yanomami, as in many societies with unilineal descent, sex with cross cousins is proper but sex with parallel cousins is considered incestuous.

A custom that is much rarer than cross-cousin marriage also illustrates that people define their kin, and thus incest, differently in different societies. When unilineal descent is very strongly developed, the parent who does not belong to one's own descent group isn't considered a relative. Thus, with strict patrilineality, the mother is not a relative but a kind of in-law who has married a member of ego's group—ego's father. With strict matrilineality, the father isn't a relative, because he belongs to a different descent group.

The Lakher of Southeast Asia are strictly patrilineal (Leach 1961). Using the male ego in Figure 16.3, let's suppose that ego's father and mother get divorced. Each remarries and has a daughter by a second marriage. A Lakher always belongs to his or her father's group, all the members of which (one's *agnates,* or patrikin) are considered too closely related to marry because they are members of the same patrilineal descent group. Therefore, ego can't marry his father's daughter by the second marriage, just as in contemporary North America it's illegal for half-siblings to marry.

However, in contrast to our society, where all half-siblings are tabooed, the Lakher permit ego to marry his mother's daughter by a different father. She is not a forbidden relative because she belongs to her own father's descent group rather than ego's. The Lakher illustrate clearly that definitions of forbidden relatives, and therefore of incest, vary from culture to culture.

We can extend these observations to strict matrilineal societies. If a man's parents divorce and his father remarries, ego may marry his paternal half-sister. By contrast, if his mother remarries and has a daughter, the daughter is

Figure 16.3
Patrilineal Descent-Group Identity and Incest among the Lakher

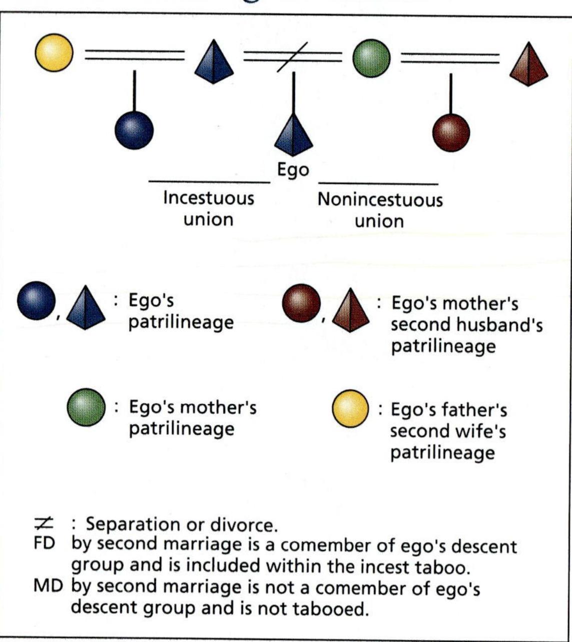

considered ego's sister, and sex between them is taboo. Cultures therefore have different definitions and expectations of relationships that are biologically or genetically equivalent.

Explaining the Taboo

Instinctive Horror

There is no simple or universally accepted explanation for the fact that all cultures ban incest. Do primate studies offer any clues? Research with primates does show that adolescent males (among monkeys) or females (among apes) often move away from the group in which they were born (Rodseth et al. 1991). This emigration helps reduce the frequency of incestuous unions. The human avoidance of mating with close relatives may therefore express a generalized primate tendency.

One argument (Hobhouse 1915; Lowie 1920/1961) is that the incest taboo is universal because

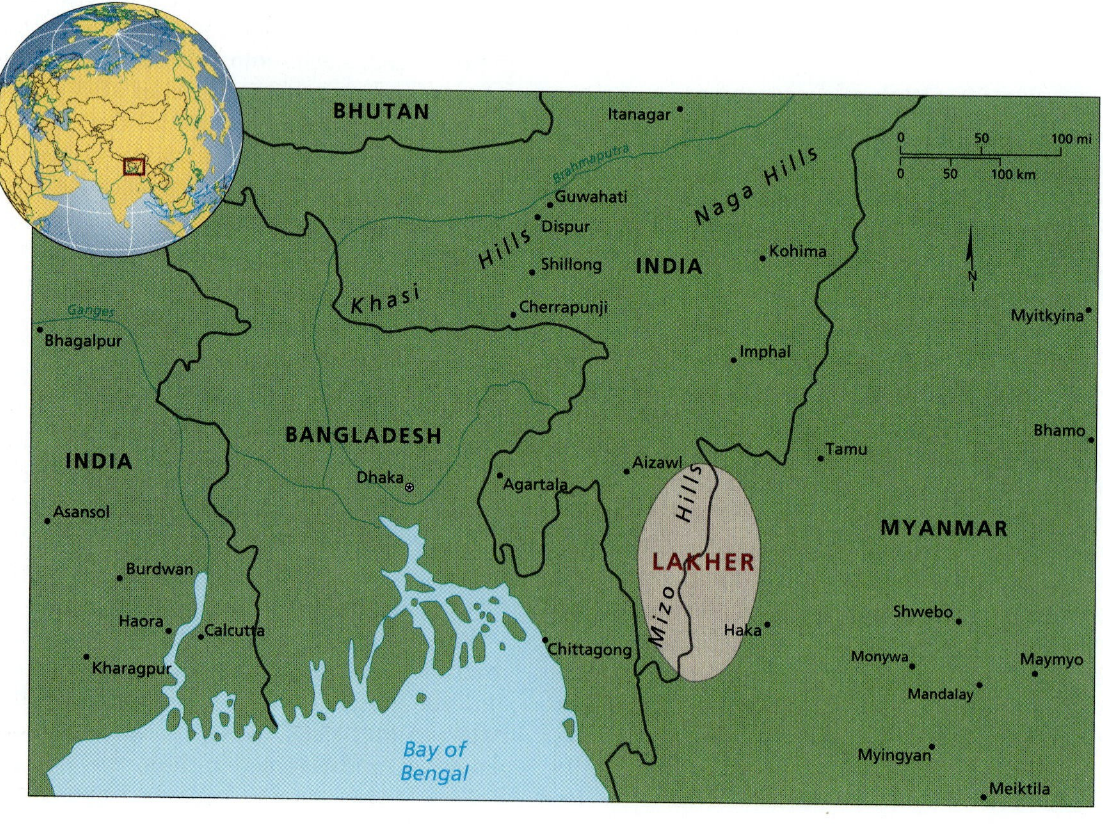

incest horror is instinctive: *Homo sapiens* has a genetically programmed disgust toward incest. Because of this feeling, early humans banned it. However, cultural universality doesn't necessarily entail an instinctual basis. Fire making, for example, is a cultural universal, but it certainly is not an ability transmitted by the genes. Furthermore, if people really did have an instinctive horror of mating with blood relatives, a formal incest taboo would be unnecessary. No one would ever do it. However, as social workers, judges, psychiatrists, and psychologists know, incest is not as uncommon as we might suppose.

A final objection to the instinctive horror theory is that it can't explain why in some societies people can marry their cross cousins but not their parallel cousins. Nor does it tell us why the Lakher can marry their maternal, but not their paternal, half-siblings. No known instinct can distinguish between parallel and cross cousins.

The specific kin types included within the incest taboo—and the taboo itself—have a cultural rather than a biological basis. Even among nonhuman primates, there is no definite evidence for an instinct against incest. Adolescent dispersal does not prevent—but merely limits the frequency of—incestuous unions. Among humans, cultural traditions determine the specific relatives with whom sex is considered incestuous. They also deal with the people who violate prohibited relationships in different ways. Banishment, imprisonment, death, and threats of supernatural retaliation are some of the punishments imposed.

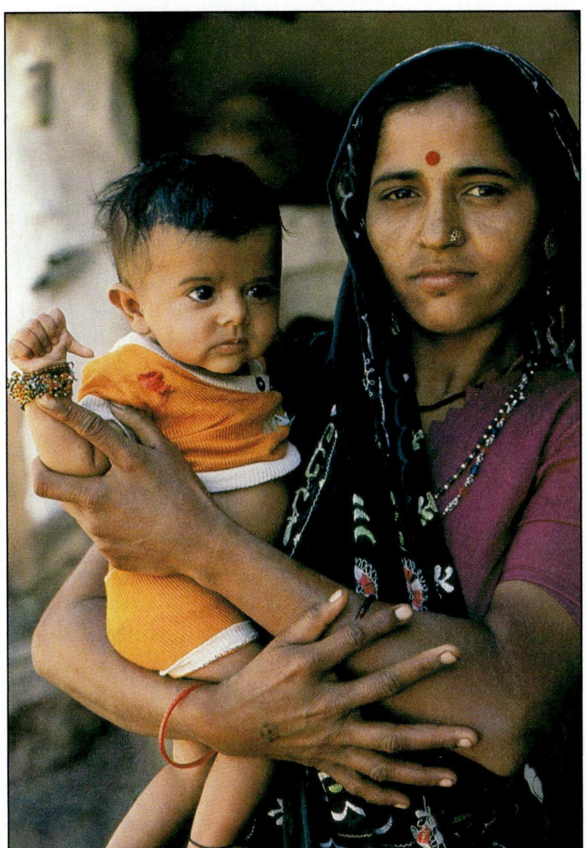

How many fingers do this Indian woman and her child have? Such genetically determined traits as polydactylism (extra fingers) may show up when there is high incidence of endogamy. Despite the biological effects of inbreeding, marriage preferences and prohibitions are based on specific cultural beliefs rather than universal concerns about future biological degeneration.

Biological Degeneration

Another theory is that the taboo emerged because early *Homo* noticed that abnormal offspring were born from incestuous unions (Morgan 1877/1963). To prevent this, our ancestors banned incest. The human stock produced after the taboo originated was so successful that it spread everywhere.

What is the evidence for this theory? Laboratory experiments with animals that reproduce faster than humans do (such as mice and fruit flies) have been used to investigate the effects of inbreeding: A decline in survival and fertility does accompany brother–sister mating across several generations. However, despite the potentially harmful biological results of systematic inbreeding, human marriage patterns are based on specific cultural beliefs rather than universal concerns about biological degeneration several generations in the future. Neither instinctive horror nor fear of biological degeneration explains the very widespread custom of marrying cross cousins. Nor can fears about degeneration explain why breeding with parallel cousins but not cross cousins is so often tabooed.

Attempt and Contempt

Sigmund Freud is the most famous advocate of the theory that children have sexual feelings toward their parents, which they eventually repress or resolve. Other scholars have looked to the dynamics of growing up for an explanation of the incest taboo. Bronislaw Malinowski believed that children would naturally seek to express their sexual feelings, particularly as they increased in adolescence, with members of their nuclear family, because of preexisting intimacy and affection. Yet, he thought, sex was too powerful a force to unleash in the family. It would threaten existing family roles and ties; it could destroy the family. Malinowski proposed that the incest taboo originated to direct sexual feeling outside, so as to avoid disruption of existing family structure and relations.

The opposite theory is that children are not likely to be sexually attracted to those with whom they have grown up (Westermarck 1894). This is related to the idea of instinctive horror, but without assuming a biological (instinctual) basis. The notion here is that a lifetime of living together in particular, nonsexual relationships would make the idea of sex with a family member less desirable. The two opposed theories are sometimes characterized as "familiarity breeds attempt" versus "familiarity breeds contempt." One bit of evidence to support the contempt theory comes from Joseph Shepher's (1983) study of Israeli *kibbutzim.* He found that unrelated people who had been raised in the same *kibbutz* (domestic community) avoided intermarriage. They tended to choose their mates from outside—not because they were related, but because their prior residential histories and roles made sex and marriage unappealing. Again, there is no final answer to the question of whether people who grow up together, related or unrelated, are likely to be sexually attracted to one another. Usually they aren't; sometimes they are. Incest is universally tabooed, but it does happen.

Marry Out or Die Out

One of the most accepted explanations for the incest taboo is that it arose in order to ensure exogamy, to force people to marry outside their kin groups (Lévi-Strauss 1949/1969; Tylor 1889; White 1959). In this view, the taboo originated early in human evolution because it was adaptively advantageous. Marrying a close relative, with whom one is already on peaceful terms, would be counterproductive. There is more to gain by extending peaceful relations to a wider network of groups.

This view emphasizes the role of marriage in creating and maintaining alliances. By forcing members to marry out, a group increases its allies. Marriage within the group, by contrast, would isolate that group from its neighbors and their resources and social networks, and might ultimately lead to the group's extinction. Exogamy and the incest taboo that propels it help explain human adaptive success. Besides the sociopolitical function, exogamy ensures genetic mixture between groups and thus maintains a successful human species.

 Endogamy

The practice of exogamy pushes social organization outward, establishing and preserving alliances among groups. In contrast, rules of **endogamy** dictate mating or marriage within a group to which one belongs. Formal endogamic rules are less common but are still familiar to anthropologists. Indeed, most societies *are* endogamous units, although they usually do not need a formal rule requiring people to marry someone from their own society. In our own society, classes and ethnic groups are quasi-endogamous groups. Members of an ethnic or religious group often want their children to marry within that group, although many of them do not do so. The outmarriage rate varies among such groups, with some more committed to endogamy than others are.

Homogamy means to marry someone similar, as when members of the same social class intermarry. There's a correlation between socioeconomic status (SES) and education. People with similar SES tend to have similar educational aspirations, to attend similar schools, and to aim at similar careers. For example, people who meet at an elite private university are likely to have similar backgrounds and career prospects. Homogamous marriage may work to concentrate wealth in social classes and to reinforce the system of social stratification. In the United States, for example, the rise in female employment, especially in professional careers, when coupled with homogamy, has dramatically increased household incomes in the upper classes. This pattern has been one factor in sharpening the contrast in household income between the richest and poorest quintiles (top and bottom 20 percent) of Americans.

Caste

An extreme example of endogamy is India's caste system, which was formally abolished in 1949, although its structure and effects linger. Castes are stratified groups in which membership is ascribed at birth and is lifelong. Indian castes are grouped into five major categories, or *varna*. Each is ranked relative to the other four, and these categories extend throughout India. Each *varna* includes a large number of subcastes (*jati*), each of which includes people within a region who may intermarry. All the *jati* in a single *varna* in a given region are ranked, just as the *varna* themselves are ranked.

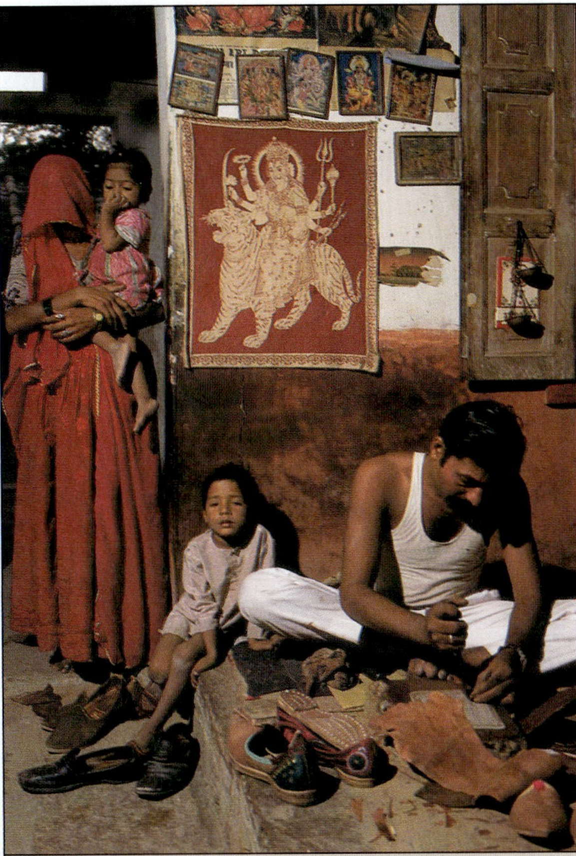

An extreme example of endogamy is India's caste system, which was formally abolished in 1949, although its structure and effects linger. In Gadwada village, cobblers still make shoes in a traditional style. Here, Devi-Lal sits with his child as his wife looks on. In the traditional caste system, such cobblers had a higher status than did sweepers and tanners, whose work is considered so smelly and dirty that they live at the far end of the village.

Occupational specialization often sets off one caste from another. A community may include castes of agricultural workers, merchants, artisans, priests, and sweepers. The untouchable *varna*, found throughout India, includes subcastes whose ancestry, ritual status, and occupations are considered so impure that higher-caste people consider even casual contact with untouchables to be defiling.

The belief that intercaste sexual unions lead to ritual impurity for the higher-caste partner has been important in maintaining endogamy. A man who has sex with a lower-caste woman can restore his purity with a bath and a prayer. However, a woman who has intercourse with a man of a lower caste has no such recourse. Her defilement cannot be undone. Because the women have the babies, these differences protect the purity of the caste line, ensuring the pure ancestry of high-caste children. Although Indian castes are endogamous groups, many of them are internally subdivided into exogamous lineages. Traditionally this meant that Indians had to marry a member of another descent group from the same caste.

Royal Incest

Royal incest is similar to caste endogamy. The best-known examples come from Inca Peru, ancient Egypt, and traditional Hawaii. Those cultures allowed royal brother–sister marriages. In Peru and Hawaii, privileged endogamy, a violation of the incest taboo that applied to commoners in those societies, was a means of differentiating between rulers and subjects.

Manifest and Latent Functions

To understand royal brother–sister marriage, it is useful to distinguish between the manifest and latent functions of behavior. The *manifest function* of a custom refers to the reasons natives give for it. Its *latent function* is an effect the custom has on the society that the native people don't mention or may not even recognize.

Royal incest illustrates this distinction. Hawaiians and other Polynesians believed in an impersonal force called *mana*. Mana could exist in things or people, in the latter case marking them off from other people and making them divine. The Hawaiians believed that no one had as much mana as the ruler. Mana depended on genealogy. The person whose own mana was exceeded only by the king's was his sibling. The most appropriate wife for a king was his own full sister. Notice that the brother–sister marriage also meant that royal heirs would be as manaful, or divine, as possible. The manifest function of royal incest in ancient Hawaii was part of that culture's beliefs about mana and divinity.

Royal incest also had latent functions—political repercussions. The ruler and his spouse had the same parents. Since mana was believed to be inherited, they were almost equally divine. When the king and his sister married, their children indisputably had the most mana in the land. No one could question their right to rule. However, if the king had taken a wife with less mana than his sister, his sister's children with someone else might eventually cause problems. Both sets of children could assert their divinity and right to rule. Royal sibling marriage therefore limited conflicts about succession because it reduced the number of people with claims to rule. The same result would be true in ancient Egypt and Peru as in ancient Hawaii. Other kingdoms have solved this problem differently. Some succession rules, for instance, specify that only the oldest child (usually the son) of the reigning monarch can succeed; this custom is called *primogeniture*. Commonly, rulers have banished or killed claimants who rival the chosen heir.

Royal incest also had a latent economic function. If the king and his sister had rights to inherit the ancestral estate, their marriage to each other, again by limiting the number of heirs, kept it intact. Power often rests on wealth, and royal incest tended to ensure that royal wealth remained concentrated in the same line.

Marriage as Group Alliance

Outside industrial societies, marriage is often more a relationship between groups than one between individuals. We think of marriage as an individual matter. Although the bride and groom usually seek their parents' approval, the final choice (to live together, to marry, to divorce) lies with the couple. The idea of romantic love symbolizes this individual relationship.

In nonindustrial societies, although there can be romantic love, as we see in "In the News (on page 410)," marriage is a group concern. People

Gift-giving customs are associated with marriage throughout the world. In this photo, guests bring presents in baskets to a wedding in Wenjiang, China.

In this photo of an elaborate royal wedding, plates of money are presented at the marriage of an Indian maharajah. How does marriage vary with social status in your society?

don't just take a spouse; they assume obligations to a group of in-laws. When residence is patrilocal, for example, a woman often must leave the community where she was born. She faces the prospect of spending the rest of her life in her husband's village, with his relatives. She may even have to transfer her major allegiance from her own group to her husband's.

Bridewealth

In societies with descent groups, people enter marriage not alone but with the help of the descent group. Descent-group members often have to contribute to the **bridewealth,** a customary gift before, at, or after the marriage from the husband and his kin to the wife and her kin. Another word for bridewealth is *brideprice,* but this term is inaccurate because people with the custom don't usually regard the exchange as a sale. They don't think of marriage as a commercial relationship between a man and an object that can be bought and sold.

Bridewealth compensates the bride's group for the loss of her companionship and labor. More important, it makes the children born to the woman full members of her husband's descent group. For this reason, the institution is also called **progeny price.** Rather than the woman herself, it is her children who are permanently transferred to the husband's group. Whatever we call it, such a transfer of wealth at marriage is common in patrilineal groups. In matrilineal societies, children are members of the mother's group, and there is no reason to pay a progeny price.

Dowry is a marital exchange in which the wife's group provides substantial gifts to the husband's family. Dowry, best known from India, correlates with low female status. Women are perceived as burdens. When husbands and their families take a wife, they expect to be compensated for the added responsibility.

Although India passed a law in 1961 against compulsory dowry, the practice continues. When the dowry is considered insufficient, the bride may be harassed and abused. Domestic violence can escalate to the point where the husband or his family burn the bride, often by pouring kerosene on her and lighting it, usually killing her. It should be pointed out that dowry doesn't necessarily lead to domestic abuse. In fact, Indian dowry murders seem to be a fairly recent phenomenon. It also has been estimated that the rate of spousal murders in the contemporary United States may rival the incidence of India's dowry murders (Narayan 1997).

Sati is the practice through which widows are burned alive, voluntarily or forcibly, on their husband's funeral pyre (Hawley 1993). Although it

in the news

Love and Marriage

Love and marriage, the song says, go together like a horse and carriage. But the link between love and marriage, like the horse–carriage combination, isn't a cultural universal. This news item describes a cross-cultural survey, published in the anthropological journal *Ethnology,* that found romantic ardor to be widespread, perhaps universal. Previously, anthropologists had tended to ignore evidence for romantic love in other cultures, probably because arranged marriages were so common. Today, diffusion, mainly via the mass media, of Western ideas about the importance of love for marriage appears to be influencing marital decisions in other cultures.

Some influential Western social historians have argued that romance was a product of European medieval culture that spread only recently to other cultures. They dismissed romantic tales from other cultures as representing the behavior of just the elites. Under the sway of this view, Western anthropologists did not even look for romantic love among the peoples they studied. But they are now beginning to think that romantic love is universal . . .

"For decades anthropologists and other scholars have assumed romantic love was unique to the modern West," said Dr. Leonard Plotnicov, an anthropologist at the University of Pittsburgh and editor of the journal *Ethnology.* "Anthropologists came across it in their field work, but they rarely mentioned it because it wasn't supposed to happen."

"Why has something so central to our culture been so ignored by anthropology?" asked Dr. William Jankowiak, an anthropologist at the University of Nevada.

The reason, in the view of Dr. Jankowiak and others, is a scholarly bias throughout the social sciences that viewed romantic love as a luxury in human life, one that could be indulged only by people in Westernized cultures or among the educated elites of other societies. For example, it was assumed in societies where life is hard that romantic love has less chance to blossom, because higher economic standards and more leisure time create more opportunity for dalliance. That also contributed to the belief that romance was for the ruling class, not the peasants.

But, said Dr. Jankowiak, "There is romantic love in cultures around the world." Last year Dr. Jankowiak, with Dr. Edward Fischer, an anthropologist at Tulane University, published in *Ethnology* the first cross-cultural study, systematically comparing romantic love in many cultures.

In the survey of ethnographies from 166 cultures, they found what they considered clear evidence that romantic love was known in 147 of them—89 percent. And in the other 19 cultures, Dr. Jankowiak said, the absence of conclusive evidence seemed due more to anthropologists' oversight than to a lack of romance.

Some of the evidence came from tales about lovers, or folklore that offered love potions or other advice on making someone fall in love.

Another source was accounts by informants to anthropologists. For example, Nisa, a !Kung woman among the Bushmen of the Kala-

has become well-known, *sati* was mainly practiced in a particular area of northern India by a few small castes. It was banned in 1829, but the practice has recurred. India had to ban *sati* again as recently as 1987 (Kantor 1996). Dowry murders and *sati* are flagrant examples of *patriarchy,* a political system ruled by men in which women have inferior social and political status, including basic human rights.

Bridewealth exists in many more cultures than dowry does, but the nature and quantity of transferred items differ. In many African societies, cathari, made a clear distinction between the affection she felt for her husband, and that she felt for her lovers, which was "passionate and exciting," though fleeting. Of these extramarital affairs, she said: "When two people come together their hearts are on fire and their passion is very great. After a while the fire cools and that's how it stays." . . .

While finding that romantic love appears to be a human universal, Dr. Jankowiak allows that it is still an alien idea in many cultures that such infatuation has anything to do with the choice of a spouse.

"What's new in many cultures is the idea that romantic love should be the reason to marry someone," said Dr. Jankowiak. "Some cultures see being in love as a state to be pitied. One tribe in the mountains of Iran ridicules people who marry for love."

Of course, even in arranged marriages, partners may grow to feel romantic love for each other. For example, among villagers in the Kangra valley of northern India, "people's romantic longings and yearnings ideally would become focused on the person they're matched with by their families," said Dr. Kirin Narayan, an anthropologist at the University of Wisconsin.

But that has begun to change, Dr. Narayan is finding, under the influence of popular songs and movies. "In these villages the elders are worried that the younger men and women are getting a different idea of romantic love, one where you choose a partner yourself," said Dr. Narayan. "There are starting to be elopements, which are absolutely scandalous."

The same trend toward love matches, rather than arranged marriages, is being noted by anthropologists in many other cultures. Among aborigines in Australia's Outback, for example, marriages had for centuries been arranged when children were very young.

That pattern was disrupted earlier in this century by missionaries, who urged that marriage not occur until children reached adolescence. Dr. Victoria Burbank, an anthropologist at the University of California at Davis, said that in premissionary days, the average age of a girl at marriage was always before menarche, sometimes as young as 9 years. Today the average age at marriage is 17; girls are more independent by the time their parents try to arrange a marriage for them.

"More and more adolescent girls are breaking away from arranged marriages," said Dr. Burbank. "They prefer to go off into the bush for a 'date' with someone they like, get pregnant, and use that pregnancy to get parental approval for the match."

Even so, parents sometimes are adamant that the young people should not get married. They prefer, instead, that the girls follow the traditional pattern of having their mothers choose a husband for them.

"Traditionally among these people, you can't choose just any son-in-law," said Dr. Burbank. "Ideally, the mother wants to find a boy who is her maternal grandmother's brother's son, a pattern that insures partners are in the proper kin group."

Dr. Burbank added: "These groups have critical ritual functions. A marriage based on romantic love, which ignores what's a proper partner, undermines the system of kinship, ritual, and obligation."

Nevertheless, the rules for marriage are weakening. "In the grandmothers' generation, all marriages were arranged. Romantic love had no place, though there were a few stories of a young man and woman in love running off together. But in the group I studied, in only one recent case did the girl marry the man selected for her. All the rest are love matches."

Source: Daniel Goleman, "Anthropology Goes Looking in All the Old Places," *New York Times*, November 24, 1992, p. B1.

tle constitute bridewealth, but the number of cattle given varies from society to society. *As the value of bridewealth increases, marriages become more stable.* Bridewealth is insurance against divorce.

Imagine a patrilineal society in which a marriage requires the transfer of about 25 cattle from the groom's descent group to the bride's. Michael, a member of descent group A, marries Sarah from group B. His relatives help him assemble the bridewealth. He gets the most help from his close agnates: his older brother, father, father's brother, and closest patrilineal cousins.

The distribution of the cattle once they reach Sarah's group mirrors the manner in which they were assembled. Sarah's father, or her oldest brother if the father is dead, receives her bridewealth. He keeps most of the cattle to use as bridewealth for his sons' marriages. However, a share also goes to everyone who will be expected to help when Sarah's brothers marry.

When Sarah's brother David gets married, many of the cattle go to a third group: C, which is David's wife's group. Thereafter, they may serve as bridewealth to still other groups. Men constantly use their sisters' bridewealth cattle to acquire their own wives. In a decade, the cattle given when Michael married Sarah will have been exchanged widely.

In such societies, marriage entails an agreement between descent groups. If Sarah and Michael try to make their marriage succeed but fail to do so, both groups may conclude that the marriage can't last. Here it becomes especially obvious that such marriages are relationships between groups as well as between individuals. If Sarah has a younger sister or niece (her older brother's daughter, for example), the concerned parties may agree to Sarah's replacement by a kinswoman.

However, incompatibility isn't the main problem that threatens marriage in societies with bridewealth. Infertility is a more important concern. If Sarah has no children, she and her group have not fulfilled their part of the marriage agreement. If the relationship is to endure, Sarah's group must furnish another woman, perhaps her younger sister, who can have children. If this happens, Sarah may choose to stay with her husband. Perhaps she will someday have a child. If she does stay on, her husband will have established a plural marriage.

Most nonindustrial food-producing societies, unlike most foraging societies and industrial nations, allow **plural marriages,** or *polygamy.* There are two varieties; one is common and the other is very rare. The more common variant is **polygyny,** in which a man has more than one wife. The rare variant is **polyandry,** in which a woman has more than one husband. If the infertile wife remains married to her husband after he has taken a substitute wife provided by her descent group, this is polygyny. Reasons for polygyny other than infertility will be discussed shortly.

Durable Alliances

It is possible to exemplify the group-alliance nature of marriage by examining still another common practice: continuation of marital alliances when one spouse dies.

Sororate

What happens if Sarah dies young? Michael's group will ask Sarah's group for a substitute, often her sister. This custom is known as the **sororate** (Figure 16.4). If Sarah has no sister or if all her sisters are already married, another woman from her group may be available. Michael marries her, there is no need to return the bridewealth, and the alliance continues. The sororate exists in both matrilineal and patrilineal societies. In a matrilineal society with matrilocal postmarital residence, a widower may remain with his wife's group by marrying her sister or another female member of her matrilineage (Figure 16.4).

Levirate

What happens if the husband dies? In many societies, the widow may marry his brother. This custom is known as the **levirate** (Figure 16.4). Like the sororate, it is a continuation marriage that

Figure 16.4
Sororate and Levirate

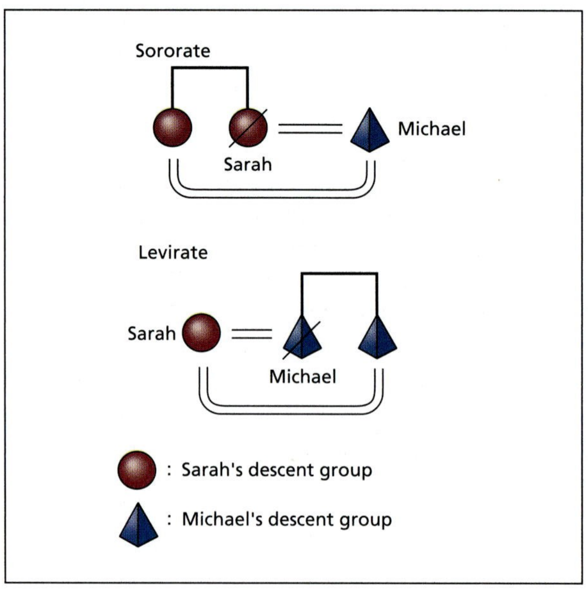

maintains the alliance between descent groups, in this case by replacing the husband with another member of his group. The implications of the levirate vary with age. A recent study found that in African societies, the levirate, though widely permitted, rarely involves cohabitation of the widow and her new husband. Furthermore, widows don't automatically marry the husband's brother just because they are allowed to. Often, they prefer to make other arrangements (Potash 1986).

Divorce

Ease of divorce varies across cultures. What factors work for and against divorce? As we've seen, marriages that are political alliances between groups are more difficult to dissolve than are marriages that are more individual affairs, of concern mainly to the married couple and their children. We've seen that substantial bridewealth may decrease the divorce rate for individuals and that replacement marriages (levirate and sororate) also work to preserve group alliances. Divorce tends to be more common in matrilineal than in patrilineal societies. When residence is matrilocal (in the wife's place), the wife may simply send off a man with whom she's incompatible. Divorce is harder in a patrilineal society, especially when substantial bridewealth would have to be reassembled and repaid if the marriage failed. A woman residing patrilocally (in her husband's household and community) might be reluctant to leave him. Their children, after all, would need to stay with their father, as members of his patrilineage.

Political and economic factors complicate the divorce process. Among foragers, different factors tend to favor and oppose divorce. What factors work against durable marriages? Since foragers tend to lack descent groups, the political alliance functions of marriage are less important to them than they are to food producers. Foragers also tend to have minimal material possessions. The process of dissolving a joint fund of property is less complicated when spouses do not hold substantial resources in common. What factors favor marital stability among foragers? In societies where the family is an important year-round unit with a gender-based division of labor, ties between spouses tend to be durable. Also, sparse populations mean few alternative spouses if a marriage doesn't work out. But in band-organized societies, foragers can always find a band to join or rejoin if a marriage doesn't work. And food producers can always draw on their descent-group estate if a marriage fails. With patriliny, a woman often can return home, albeit without her children, and with matriliny, a man can do the same. Descent-group estates are not transferred through marriages, although moveable resources such as bridewealth cattle certainly are.

In our own society, the more substantial the joint property, the more complicated the divorce process. The increasing importance of prenuptial agreements shows that in our own culture some aspects of marriage involve more than romantic love, especially when the financial/material stakes are high. And, of course, we have divorce specialists, lawyers, who are absent in nonindustrial societies. In those settings, the specialist comes before the marriage, rather than at its end. It's up to the matchmakers who arrange marriages to do as good a job as possible so the union doesn't end in divorce.

In contemporary Western societies, we do stress the idea that romantic love is necessary for a good marriage (see "In the News," page 410). When romance fails, so may the marriage. Or it may not fail, if the other rights associated with marriage, as discussed previously in this chapter, are compelling. Economic ties and obligations to kids, along with other factors, such as concern about public opinion, or simple inertia, may keep marriages intact after sex, romance, and/or companionship fade. Also, even in modern societies, royalty, leaders, and other elites may have political marriages similar to the arranged marriages of nonindustrial societies.

Divorce is more common now than it was a generation ago or a century ago. In the United States, divorce figures have been kept since 1860, with a fairly steady increase since then in the divorce rate. Divorces tend to increase after wars and to decrease when times are bad economically. But with more women working outside the home, economic dependence on the husband as breadwinner is weaker, which no doubt facilitates a decision to divorce when a marriage has major problems.

Table 16.1

Changing Divorce Rates (Number per Year) in the United States, 1940 through 1999

Year	Divorce Rate per 1,000 Population	Divorce Rate per 1,000 Women Aged 15 and Older
1940	2.0	8.8
1950	2.6	10.3
1960	2.2	9.2
1970	3.5	14.9
1980	5.2	22.6
1990	4.7	20.9
1999	4.1	19.5

Sources: Clarke 1995; Hughes 1996; National Vital Statistics Reports 2000.

Table 16.1 is based on two measures of the divorce rate (Hughes 1996). The left column shows the rate per 1,000 people per year in the overall population. The right column shows the annual rate per 1,000 married women over the age of 15, which is the best measure of divorce. In either case, comparing 1999 with 1960, the divorce rate more than doubled. Note that the rate rose slightly after World War II (1950), then declined a decade later (1960). The most notable rate rise occurred between 1960 and 1980. The rate actually has been falling since 1980.

The United States has one of the world's highest divorce rates. There are several probable causes: economic, cultural, and religious among them. Economically, the United States has a larger percentage of gainfully employed women than most nations. Work outside the home provides a cash basis for independence, as it also places strains on marriage and social life for both partners. Culturally, Americans tend to value independence and its modern form, self-actualization. Also, Protestantism (in its various guises) is the most common form of religion in the United States. Of the two major religions in the United States and Canada (where Catholicism predominates), Protestantism has been less stringent in denouncing divorce than has Catholicism. Also, notions of salvation in traditional Protestantism focus more on the individual than on the household or family (Weber 1904/1958).

Cherlin (1992) has done a study of changing patterns of American marriage, divorce, and remarriage, using four generations of American women, the first born 1908–1912, the last born in 1970. Although there was little change in the first marriage rate across the generations, the likelihood of divorce changed strikingly. Likelihood for the first generation was 22 percent, versus its double, 44 percent, for women born in 1970. The chance of remarriage and redivorce also increased across the generations. The likelihood of a second divorce was 2 percent for the oldest generation, versus 16 percent for women born in 1970. The changing rate of divorce has obvious implications for family life and child care, some of which were discussed in the last chapter.

378

Plural Marriages

In contemporary North America, where divorce is fairly easy and common, polygamy (marriage to more than one spouse at the same time) is against the law. Marriage in industrial nations joins individuals, and relationships between individuals can be severed more easily than can those between groups. As divorce grows more common, North Americans practice *serial monogamy:* Individuals have more than one spouse but never, legally, more than one at the same time. As stated earlier, the two forms of polygamy are polygyny and polyandry. Polyandry is practiced in only a few cultures, notably among certain groups in Tibet, Nepal, and India. Polygyny is much more common.

Polygyny

We must distinguish between the social approval of plural marriage and its actual frequency in a particular society. Many cultures approve of a man having more than one wife. However, even when polygyny is encouraged, most men are monogamous, and polygyny characterizes only a fraction of the marriages. Why is this true?

One reason is equal sex ratios. In the United States, about 105 males are born for every 100 females. In adulthood, the ratio of men to women equalizes, and eventually it reverses. The average North American woman outlives the average man. In many nonindustrial societies as well, the

In Cameroon, a man (front left) with five of his six wives and 20 of his 36 children. Why do people marry polygynously?

The Kanuri live in Nigeria's Bornu province.

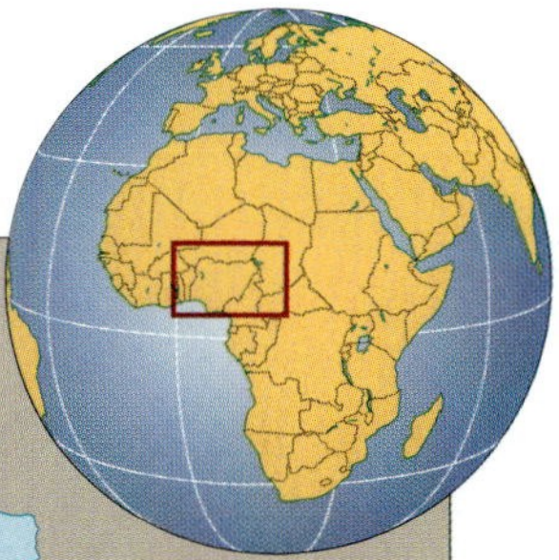

male-biased sex ratio among children reverses in adulthood.

The custom of men marrying later than women promotes polygyny. Among the Kanuri people of Bornu, Nigeria (Cohen 1967), men get married between the ages of 18 and 30; women, between 12 and 14. The age difference between spouses means that there are more widows than widowers. Most of the widows remarry, some in polygynous unions. Among the Kanuri of Bornu and in other polygynous societies, widows make up a large number of the women involved in

There's no single explanation for polygyny, illustrated by this Utah man (Tom Green) and his three wives (from left to right, June, Shirley, and Linda) and children. In 1988, when this photo was taken, Mr. Green had a total of 4 wives and 14 children. Some religious sects in the United States have encouraged polygyny, despite laws against it.

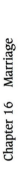

plural marriages (Hart, Pilling, and Goodale 1988). In many societies, including the Kanuri, the number of wives is an indicator of a man's household productivity, prestige, and social position. The more wives, the more workers. Increased productivity means more wealth. This wealth in turn attracts additional wives to the household. Wealth and wives bring greater prestige to the household and head.

If a plural marriage is to work, there needs to be some agreement among the existing spouses when another one is to be added, especially if they are to share the same household. In certain societies, the first wife requests a second wife to help with household chores. The second wife's status is lower than that of the first; they are senior and junior wives. The senior wife sometimes chooses the junior one from among her close kinswomen. Among the Betsileo of Madagascar, the different wives always lived in different villages. A man's first and senior wife, called "Big Wife," lived in the village where he cultivated his best rice field and spent most of his time. High-status men with several rice fields and multiple wives had households near each field. They spent most of their time with the senior wife but visited the others occasionally throughout the year.

Plural wives can play important political roles in nonindustrial states. The king of the Merina, a society with more than one million people in the highlands of Madagascar, had palaces for each of his 12 wives in different provinces. He stayed with them when he traveled through the kingdom. They were his local agents, overseeing and reporting on provincial matters. The king of Buganda, the major precolonial state of Uganda, took hundreds of wives, representing all the clans in his nation. Everyone in the kingdom became the king's in-law, and all the clans had a chance to provide the next ruler. This was a way of giving the common people a stake in the government.

These examples show that there is no single explanation for polygyny. Its context and function vary from society to society and even within the same society. Some men are polygynous because they have inherited a widow from a brother (the levirate). Others have plural wives

because they seek prestige or want to increase household productivity. Still others use marriage as a political tool or a means of economic advancement. Men and women with political and economic ambitions cultivate marital alliances that serve their aims. In many societies, including the Betsileo of Madagascar and the Igbo of Nigeria, women arrange the marriages.

Polyandry

Polyandry is rare and is practiced under very specific conditions. Most of the world's polyandrous peoples live in South Asia: Tibet, Nepal, India, and Sri Lanka. India's polyandrous groups inhabit the lower ranges of the Himalayas, in northern India. They are known as Paharis, which means "people of the mountains." Gerald Berreman (1962, 1975) did a comparative study of two Pahari groups, one in the foothills of the western Himalayas and the other in the central foothills.

The western and central Paharis are historically and genetically related to each other and speak dialects of the same language. Polyandry exists among the western, but not the central, Paharis. Because there are so many other cultural and social similarities between the western and central Paharis, including caste stratification and patrilineal clans, Berreman wondered why one group practiced polyandry and the other did not.

Pahari marriage customs turned out to correlate with demographic contrasts. Sex ratios were different in the two areas. In the polyandrous west, there was a shortage of females (789 per 1,000 males). Although female infanticide was not documented in the area, neglect of girls (*covert* female infanticide) helped explain the shortage of women (Levine 1988). In some parts of the Himalayas, the practice of sending girls to Buddhist nunneries also contributes to a shortage of marriageable women. Among the western Paharis, the polyandry was always *fraternal:*

Polyandry in northwest Nepal. The seated young woman is Terribal, age 15. She holds her youngest husband, age 5. Left of Terribal is another husband, age 12. Standing directly behind her is her third husband, age 9. The two older standing men are brothers who are married to the same woman, standing to the right. These are Terribal's "fathers" and mother.

Husbands were brothers. The oldest brother arranged the marriage, which made all the brothers legal husbands of the wife. Subsequently, they could marry additional women. All these women were joint wives and sexual partners of the brothers. Children born to any wife called all the brothers "father."

Nevertheless, there was considerable variation in the actual marriage arrangements in western Pahari households (Berreman 1975). In one village, only 9 percent of the households were polyandrous, 25 percent were polygynous, and 34 percent were monogamous. The others had mixed marriage types, such as polyandrous-polygynous (see below). Variation in the marriage type and household composition reflected household wealth, the age of the brothers, and divorce. Household composition went through a developmental cycle. For example, one group of three brothers took their first wife in 1910. In 1915, they added a second wife. This changed simple fraternal polyandry into a polyandrous-polygynous household. A few years later, they added a third wife, and later they added a fourth. By a decade later, one of the brothers had died and two of the wives had divorced and remarried elsewhere. By 1955, the household had become monogamous, as only one husband and one wife survived.

This flexible marriage system was adaptive because it allowed the western Paharis to spread people and labor out over the land. The number of working adults in a western Pahari household was proportional to the amount of farmland it owned. Because women did as much agricultural work as men, given the same amount of land, two brothers might require and support three or four wives whereas three or four brothers might have only one or two. Plural marriages were uncommon in landless households, whose resources and labor needs were lowest. Landless people were more monogamous (43 percent) than were landowners (26 percent).

Among the nonpolyandrous central Paharis, by contrast, there were more women than men.

Most (85 percent) marriages were monogamous. Only 15 percent were plural—polygynous. Despite the absence of a formal polyandry here, it was customary for brothers to contribute to each other's bridewealth, and they could have sex with each other's wives. The major difference was that central Pahari children recognized only one father. However, because brothers had common sexual rights, socially recognized fathers were not necessarily the true genitors.

Polyandry in other parts of South Asia seems to be a cultural adaptation to mobility associated with customary male travel for trade, commerce, and military operations. Polyandry ensures that there will be at least one man at home to accomplish male activities within a gender-based division of labor. Fraternal polyandry is also an effective strategy when resources are scarce. Brothers with limited resources (in land) pool their resources in expanded (polyandrous) households. They take just one wife. Polyandry restricts the number of wives and heirs. Less competition among heirs means that land can be transmitted with minimal fragmentation.

summary

1. Marriage, which is usually a form of domestic partnership, is hard to define. The discussion of same-sex marriage, which, by and large, is illegal in contemporary North America, illustrates the various rights that go along with different-sex marriages. Marriage establishes the legal parents of children. It gives spouses rights to the sexuality, labor, and property of the other. And it establishes a socially significant "relationship of affinity" between spouses and each other's relatives. Some of these rights may be established by same-sex domestic partnerships.
2. All societies have some kind of incest taboo. The following are some of the explanations that have been offered for this universal taboo: (1) It codifies instinctive horror of incest, (2) it expresses concern about the biological effects of incestuous unions, (3) it reflects feelings of attraction or aversion that develop as one grows up in a household, and (4) it has an adaptive advantage because it promotes exogamy, thereby increasing networks of friends and allies.
3. Exogamy extends social and political ties outward. This is confirmed by a consideration of endogamy—marriage within the group. Endogamic rules are common in stratified societies. One extreme example is India, where castes are the endogamous units. Castes are subdivided into exogamous descent groups. The same culture can therefore have both endogamic and exogamic rules. Certain ancient kingdoms encouraged royal incest while condemning incest by commoners.
4. In societies with descent groups, marriages are relationships between groups as well as between spouses. With the custom of bridewealth, the groom and his relatives transfer wealth to the bride and her relatives. As the bridewealth's value increases, the divorce rate declines. Bridewealth customs show that marriages among nonindustrial food producers create and maintain group alliances. So do the sororate, by which a man marries the sister of his deceased wife, and the levirate, by which a woman marries the brother of her deceased husband.
5. The ease and frequency of divorce vary across cultures. Political, economic, social, cultural, and religious factors affect the divorce rate. When marriage is a matter of intergroup alliance, as is typically true in societies with descent groups, divorce is less common. A large fund of joint property also complicates divorce.
6. Many societies permit plural marriages. The two kinds of polygamy are polygyny and polyandry. The former involves multiple wives; the latter, multiple husbands. Polygyny is much more common than is polyandry.

key terms

bridewealth See *progeny price.*

cross cousins Children of a brother and a sister.

dowry A marital exchange in which the wife's group provides substantial gifts to the husband's family.

endogamy Rule or practice of marriage between people of the same social group.

exogamy Rule requiring people to marry outside their own group.

genitor Biological father of a child.

incest Forbidden sexual relations with a close relative.

levirate Custom by which a widow marries the brother of her deceased husband.

mater Socially recognized mother of a child.

parallel cousins Children of two brothers or two sisters.

pater Socially recognized father of a child; not necessarily the genitor.

plural marriage Any marriage with more than two spouses, a.k.a. *polygamy.*

polyandry Variety of plural marriage in which a woman has more than one husband.

polygyny Variety of plural marriage in which a man has more than one wife.

progeny price A gift from the husband and his kin to the wife and her kin before, at, or after marriage; legitimizes children born to the woman as members of the husband's descent group.

sororate Custom by which a widower marries the sister of the deceased wife.

critical thinking questions

1. Try to come up with a definition of marriage that fits all the cases examined in this chapter. What problems do you encounter in doing this?
2. When advocates argue for same-sex marriage, are they asking for special rights?
3. What explanations have been offered for the universality of the incest taboo? Which do you prefer, and why? What, if any, are the problems with the explanation you prefer?
4. What are your views about traditional marriage in India after reading this chapter? Is that an ethnocentric opinion? Review the discussions of ethnocentrism and human rights in the chapter "Culture."
5. What is bridewealth? What else is it called, and why? Do we have anything like it in our own society? Why or why not?
6. What is the difference between sororate and levirate? What do they have in common? Do these customs make sense to you?
7. How would you explain the high rate of divorce in contemporary North America?
8. If you had to live in a society with plural marriage, would you prefer polygyny or polyandry? Why?
9. What general conclusions do you draw about the differences between marriage in your society and in nonindustrial societies?

case study

Tiwi: A tradition, no longer practiced, that all Tiwi females had to be married led to the betrothal of baby girls and the mandatory remarriage of all widows. This practice served several social ends. In *Culture Sketches* by Holly Peters-Golden, read the chapter on the "Tiwi: Tradition in Australia." How do Tiwi marriage customs illustrate the social functions of marriage, as discussed in this text chapter? How do Tiwi customs compare with the rules and functions of marriage in your own society? Have those changed over time? If so, what might be the reason?

suggested additional readings

Chagnon, N.
1997 *Yanomamö,* 5th ed. Fort Worth: Harcourt Brace. Latest edition of well-known case study of marital alliances and politics in a nonindustrial society—now in the context of genocide and habitat destruction.

Collier, J. F., ed.
1988 *Marriage and Inequality in Classless Societies.* Stanford, CA: Stanford University Press. Marriage and issues of gender stratification in bands and tribes.

Fox, R.
1985 *Kinship and Marriage.* New York: Viking Penguin. Well-written survey of kinship and marriage systems and theories about them.

Goody, J., and S. T. Tambiah
1973 *Bridewealth and Dowry.* Cambridge: Cambridge University Press. Marital exchanges in comparative perspective.

Hart, C. W. M., A. R. Pilling, and J. C. Goodale
1988 *The Tiwi of North Australia,* 3rd ed. Fort Worth: Harcourt Brace. Latest edition of classic case study of Tiwi marriage arrangements, including polygyny, and social change over 60 years of anthropological study.

Hawley, J. S., ed.
1993 *Sati, the Blessing and the Curse: The Burning of Wives in India.* New York: Oxford University Press. A collection of essays on sati and a celebrated case from India.

Ingraham, C.
1999 *White Weddings: Romancing Heterosexuality in Popular Culture.* New York: Routledge. Love and marriage, including the ceremony, in today's United Sates.

Levine, N. E.
1988 *The Dynamics of Polyandry: Kinship, Domesticity, and Population in the Tibetan Border.* Chicago: University of Chicago Press. Case study of fraternal polyandry and household organization in northwestern Nepal.

Malinowski, B.
1985 (orig. 1927) *Sex and Repression in Savage Society.* Chicago: University of Chicago Press. Classic study of sex, marriage, and kinship among the matrilineal Trobrianders.

Murray, S. O., and W. Roscoe, eds.
1998 *Boy-Wives and Female Husbands: Studies in African Homosexualities.* New York: St. Martin's. Same-sex sex and marriage in Africa.

Radcliffe-Brown, A. R., and D. Forde, eds.

1994 *African Systems of Kinship and Marriage.* New York: Columbia University Press. Reissue of a classic work, indispensable to understand kinship, descent, and marriage.

Shepher, J.

1983 *Incest, a Biosocial View.* New York: Academic Press. A view from Israel, based on a case study in the kibbutz.

Shostak, M.

1981 *Nisa, the Life and Words of a !Kung Woman.* New York: Vintage Books. An insider's account of social life, including marriage, love, and sex from a Ju/'hoansi San woman.

2000 *Return to Nisa.* Cambridge, MA: Harvard University Press. A revisit to the !Kung woman immortalized in Shostak's earlier book, *Nisa.*

Simpson, B.

1998 *Changing Families: An Ethnographic Approach to Divorce and Separation.* New York: Berg. Current marriage and divorce trends in Great Britain.

internet exercises

1. *Weddings:* Here are some websites that sell wedding supplies for couples from different nationalities and traditions. Pick three of these websites and answer the questions below: Indian, **http://www.weddingsutra.com/**; Jewish, **http://www.mazornet.com/jewishcl/jewishwd.htm;** African-American, **http://melanet.com/awg/;** Mormon, **http://www.ldsweddings.com/;** Myanmar, **http://www.marriage.com.my/english/index.htm;** Eastern Orthodox, **http://www.askginka.com/religions/eastern_orthodox.htm.**
   a. What kind of clothes are worn by the bride and the groom? To what degree are the clothes dictated by tradition or modern style? How much choice do the wedding planners have in the clothing that is worn?
   b. What kind of locations are popular for the weddings?
   c. What aspects of each of these weddings is most different from your own? What aspects are similar?
   d. Why do you think wedding traditions vary so much by culture and religion?
2. *Descent and Postmarital Residence Rules:* Go to the Ethnographic Atlas Cross-tabulations page, **http://lucy.ukc.ac.uk/cgi-bin/uncgi/Ethnoatlas/atlas.vopts.** This site has compiled ethnographic information on many different groups, and you can use the tools provided to cross-tabulate the prevalence of certain traits. Go to the site; under "Select Row Category" choose "descent," and under "Select Column Category" select "transfer of residence at marriage: prevalent form." Press the Submit Query button. The table that appears shows the frequency of postmarital residence rules for groups with different descent systems.
   a. What postmarital residence rules are most common for patrilineal groups? For matrilineal groups? Is this what you would expect?
   b. Based on your observations in section *a,* what postmarital residence practice would you least expect to find in patrilineal societies? How many groups in this chart practice such a pattern? Click on the number at that location to find out which groups those are and where they are located. What postmarital residence pattern would you least expect to find in matrilineal societies? Which groups practice that pattern?
   c. What is the most common form of descent for groups with an "Optional for couple" (ambilocal) postmarital residence pattern? Does this make sense?

See Chapter 16 on your CD-ROM for additional review and interactive exercises. See your McGraw-Hill Online Learning Center for more.

Chapter 17

Political Systems

CHAPTER OUTLINE

NGNEWS.COM NEWS BRIEFS

Chat Rooms, Bedouin Style

by Ilene R. Prusher
April 28, 2000

In the historical fabric of Kuwait, diwaniyas have been men-only political salons—a local equivalent of neighborhood pub and town-hall meeting combined. They serve not only as parlors for chit-chats, but governance, too. Diwaniyas are so integral to Kuwaiti culture that during election season, candidates don't go door to door, but diwaniya to diwaniya. This is where business deals are made and marriages arranged . . .

Traditionally, most men have an open invitation to attend a diwaniya on any given night, and wealthy families have a large, long room adjacent to their homes expressly for their diwaniya. Some neighborhoods have a common diwaniya, much like a community center.

At a typical men-only diwaniya . . . the attendees lounge among the partitions of a never-ending couch that follow the contours of the room in one giant U. They usually gather once a week, starting at 8 in the evening and sometimes going past midnight.

As they discuss issues . . . they twirl smoothly polished beads around their fingers and worry aloud whether change has come to Kuwait too fast. The presence of malls and movies, they fret, is breaking down social norms like the taboo against premarital dating . . .

At the Al-Fanar Center, with its bevy of Body Shops and Benettons, teenage boys say they also have no interest in chattering the night away when they could be flirting. "We like to follow around girls without hijab [veil]," says teenager Abdul Rahman Al-Tarket, roaming the mall with his two friends . . .

Mixed [male and female] diwaniyas are still anomaly. "For me, the diwaniya is a very comfortable place to have people come and see me," says artist Thoraya al-Baqsami, who co-hosts one mixed gathering. "I know many people don't like it, but we are in the 21st century now," she says as she gives a tour of her adjacent gallery . . .

Many women here say they're happy to leave the diwaniya to the domain of men. But more problematic is that it is the diwaniya at which much of the country's decision-making and networking takes place. It is also a forum where a constituent can meet his parliamentary representative and consult him about major problems or minor potholes.

The importance of diwaniyas to Kuwaiti society cannot be understated. Kuwait's parliament emerged from a 1921 proposal by diwaniyas. And Sheik Jaber al-Sabah, who dissolved the assembly in 1986, restored it in 1992 following pressure from diwaniyas.

And since that is a male-only world, even liberal-minded youth say they can't see allowing a woman to represent them in office. A bill to give women the right to vote and to run for parliament lost by a narrow vote of 32 to 20 last November.

"I was stopped for driving without a license, and a friend of my father's got me released," says one teenager. "If we elected a woman, what would she do? She can't come to the diwaniya and she can't have those kinds of contacts, so she can't represent us."

Some here say they wouldn't mind seeing the decline of the diwaniya. Says Kuwait University political scientist Shamlan El-Issa: "The positive aspects are that it helps democracy—men meet every day and talk and complain for two or three hours. The negative is that it replaces the family—men go to work and diwaniya, and never see their wives."

Source: http://www.ngnews.com/news/2000/04/04282000/kuwait_12448.asp. © 2000 The Christian Science Publishing Society.

overview

Some people make a career of politics, also known as "leadership" or "public service." Holding office, our politicians lead and manage affairs of public policy. They make decisions and try to implement them. Anthropologists have wondered whether societies with neither politicans nor permanent political offices can have politics.

Political anthropology is the cross-cultural study of political systems, of formal and informal political institutions. A related field is legal anthropology, the comparative study of legal systems or law. Although not all societies have law, in the sense of a formal legal code, judiciary, and enforcement, all societies do have some means of social control. Their members don't live in total anarchy. Surveying many societies, we see a range of political systems. Some have informal or temporary leaders with limited authority, exercised only at the local level. Others have strong and permanent political institutions that prevail over entire regions.

The terms *band*, *tribe*, *chiefdom*, and *state* describe different forms of social and political organization, with different degrees of political authority and power. Bands are small, mobile, kin-based groups with little differential power. Tribes have villages and/or descent groups but lack a formal government. Chiefdoms, intermediate between tribes and states, are kin-based, but they have differential access to resources and a permanent political structure. The state is an autonomous political unit encompassing many communities. Its government has the power to collect taxes, to draft people for work or war, and to decree and enforce laws. The state is defined as a form of political organization based on central government and socioeconomic stratification—a division of society into classes.

Anthropologists and political scientists share an interest in political systems and organization, but the anthropological approach is global and comparative. Anthropological data reveal substantial variations in power, authority, and legal systems in different cultures. (Power is the ability to exercise one's will over others; authority is the socially approved use of power.)

Decades ago, the anthropologist Elman Service (1962) listed four types, or levels, of political organization: band, tribe, chiefdom, and state. Bands, as we have seen, are small *kin-based* groups (all members of the group are related to each other by kinship or marriage ties) found among foragers. **Tribes** are associated with nonintensive food production (horticulture and pastoralism). They have villages and/or descent groups, but they lack a formal government and social classes (socioeconomic stratification). In a tribe, there is no reliable means of enforcing political decisions. The **chiefdom** is a form of sociopolitical organization that is intermediate between the tribe and the state. In chiefdoms, social relations are mainly based on kinship, marriage, descent, age, generation, and gender—just as they are in bands and tribes. Although chiefdoms are kin-based, they feature differential access to resources (some people have more wealth, prestige, and power than others do) and a permanent political structure. The **state** is a form of sociopolitical organization based on a formal government structure and socioeconomic stratification.

Many anthropologists have criticized Service's typology as being too neat and simple, because it condenses a wide range of political complexity into just four categories. Indeed, in the discussion that follows, we'll see that the four labels are too simple to account for the full range of political complexity we examine. We'll see, for instance, that tribes vary widely in their political systems and institutions. Nevertheless, Service's typology does offer a handy set of labels for highlighting some major contrasts in political organization. For example, in bands and tribes, unlike states, the political order, or *polity*, is not a separate entity that stands out from the total social order. In bands and tribes, it is difficult to characterize an act or event as political rather than merely social.

Recognizing that political organization is sometimes just an aspect of social organization, Morton Fried offered this definition:

> Political organization comprises those portions of social organization that specifically relate to the individuals or groups that manage the affairs of *public policy* or seek to control the appointment or activities of those individuals or groups. (Fried 1967, pp. 20–21, emphasis added)

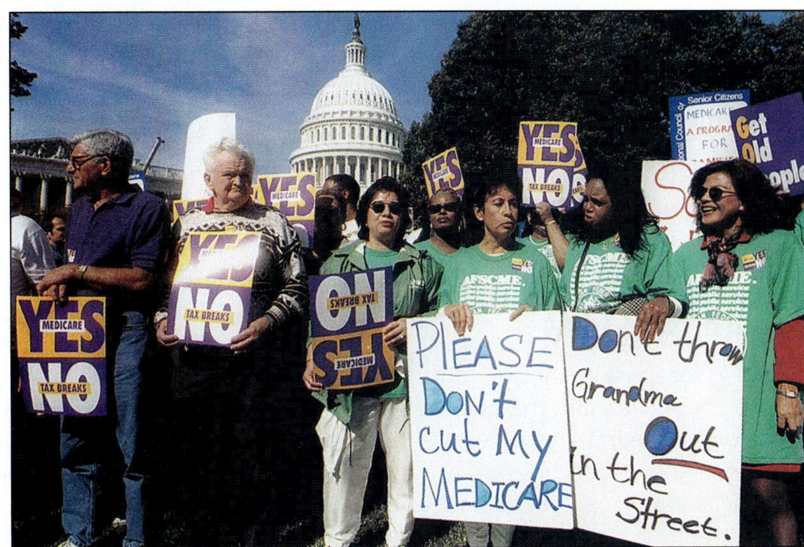

Citizens often use collective action to influence public policy. Politicians are well aware that the elderly are the most reliable of all voters. Shown here, a 1995 Washington, D.C., protest against Medicare cuts. Have your actions ever influenced public policy?

This definition certainly fits contemporary North America. Under "individuals or groups that manage the affairs of public policy" come federal, state (provincial), and local (municipal) governments. Those who seek to control the activities of the groups that manage public policy include such interest groups as political parties, unions, corporations, consumers, activists, action committees, and religious groups.

Fried's definition is much less applicable to bands and tribes, where it is often difficult to detect any "public policy." For this reason, I prefer to speak of *socio*political organization in discussing the regulation or management of interrelations among groups and their representatives. In a general sense, *regulation* is the process that ensures that variables stay within their normal ranges, corrects deviations from the norm, and thus maintains a system's integrity. In the case of *political* regulation, this includes such things as decision making and conflict resolution. The study of political regulation draws our attention to those who make decisions and resolve conflicts (are there formal leaders?).

Types and Trends

Ethnographic and archaeological studies in hundreds of places have revealed many correlations between economy and social and political organization. Band, tribe, chiefdom, and state are categories or types in a system of *sociopolitical typology*. These types are correlated with the adaptive strategies (*economic typology*) discussed in the chapter "Making a Living." Thus, foragers (an economic type) tend to have band organization (a sociopolitical type). Similarly, many horticulturalists and pastoralists live in tribal societies (or, more simply, tribes). The economies of chiefdoms tend to be based on productive horticulture or agriculture, but some pastoralists also participate in chiefdoms. Nonindustrial states usually have an agricultural base.

Food producers tend to have larger, denser populations and more complex economies than foragers do. These features create new regulatory problems, which give rise to more complex relations and linkages. Many sociopolitical trends reflect the increased regulatory demands associated with food production. Archaeologists have studied these trends through time, and cultural anthropologists have observed them among contemporary groups.

Bands and Tribes

This chapter examines a series of societies with different political systems. A common set of questions will be addressed for each. What kinds of social groups does the society have? How do people affiliate with those groups? How do the groups link up with larger ones? How do the groups represent themselves to each other? How are their internal and external relations regulated? To answer these questions, we begin with bands and tribes, then move on to chiefdoms and states.

Foraging Bands

In most foraging societies, only two kinds of groups are significant: the nuclear family and the band. Unlike sedentary villages (which appear in tribal societies), bands are impermanent. They form seasonally as component nuclear families come together. The particular combination of families in a band may vary from year to year. In such settings, the main social building blocks are the personal relationships of individuals. For example, marriage and kinship create ties between members of different bands. Because one's parents and grandparents come from different bands, a person has relatives in several of these groups. Trade and visiting also link local groups, as does fictive kinship, such as the San namesake system described in the chapter "Making a Living." Similarly, Inuit men traditionally had trade partners, whom they treated almost like brothers, in different bands.

Foraging bands are fairly egalitarian in terms of power and authority, although particular talents do lead to special respect. For example, someone can sing or dance well, is an especially good storyteller, or can go into a trance and communicate with spirits. Band leaders are leaders in name only. They are first among equals. Sometimes they give advice or make decisions, but they have no way to enforce their decisions.

Foragers lack formal **law** in the sense of a legal code that includes trial and enforcement. But they do have methods of social control and dispute settlement. The absence of law doesn't mean total anarchy. The aboriginal Inuit (Hoebel 1954, 1954/1968) provide a good example of methods of settling disputes in stateless societies. As described by E. A. Hoebel (1954) in a study of Inuit conflict resolution, a sparse population of some 20,000 Inuit spanned 9,500 kilometers (6,000 miles) of the Arctic region. The most significant social groups were the nuclear family and the band. Personal relationships linked the families and bands. Some bands had headmen. There were also shamans (part-time religious specialists). However, these positions conferred little power on those who occupied them.

Hunting and fishing by men were the primary Inuit subsistence activities. The diverse and abundant plant foods available in warmer areas, where female labor in gathering is important, were absent in the Arctic. Traveling on land and sea in a bitter environment, Inuit men faced more dangers than women did. The traditional male role took its toll in lives. Adult women would have outnumbered men substantially without occasional female *infanticide* (killing of a baby), which Inuit culture permitted.

Despite this crude (and to us unthinkable) means of population regulation, there were still more adult women than men. This permitted some men to have two or three wives. The ability to support more than one wife conferred a certain amount of prestige, but it also encouraged envy. (**Prestige** is esteem, respect, or approval for culturally valued acts or qualities.) If a man seemed to be taking additional wives just to enhance his reputation, a rival was likely to steal one of them. Most disputes were between men and originated over women, caused by wife stealing or adultery. If a man discovered that his wife had been having sexual relations without his permission, he considered himself wronged.

Although public opinion would not let the husband ignore the matter, he had several options. He could try to kill the wife stealer. However, if he succeeded, one of his rival's kinsmen would surely try to kill him in retaliation. One dispute could escalate into several deaths as relatives avenged a succession of murders. No government existed to intervene and stop such a *blood feud* (a murderous feud between families). However, one also could challenge a rival to a song battle. In a public setting, contestants made up insulting songs about each other. At the end of the match, the audience judged one of them the winner. However, if a man whose wife had been stolen won, there was no guarantee she would return. Often she would decide to stay with her abductor.

Several acts of killing that are crimes in contemporary North America were not considered

criminal by the Inuit. Infanticide has already been mentioned. Furthermore, people who felt that, because of age or infirmity, they were no longer useful might kill themselves or ask others to kill them. Old people or invalids who wished to die would ask a close relative, such as a son, to end their lives. It was necessary to ask a close relative in order to ensure that the kin of the deceased did not take revenge on the killer.

Thefts are common in societies with marked property differentials, like our own, but thefts are uncommon among foragers. Each Inuit had access to the resources needed to sustain life. Every man could hunt, fish, and make the tools necessary for subsistence. Every woman could obtain the materials needed to make clothing, prepare food, and do domestic work. Inuit men could even hunt and fish in territories of other local groups. There was no notion of private ownership of territory or animals. However, certain minor personal items were associated with a specific person. In various societies, such items include things like arrows, a tobacco pouch, clothing, and personal ornaments. One of the most basic Inuit beliefs was that "all natural resources are free or common goods" (Hoebel 1954/1968). Band-organized societies usually lack differential access to strategic resources. If people want something from someone else, they ask for it, and it is usually given.

Tribal Cultivators

Tribes usually have a horticultural or pastoral economy and are organized by village life and/or descent-group membership. Socioeconomic stratification (i.e., a class structure) and a formal government are absent. Many tribes have small-scale warfare, often in the form of intervillage raiding. Tribes have more effective regulatory mechanisms interesting issues

The Great Forager Debate

How representative are modern hunter-gatherers of Stone Age peoples, all of whom were foragers? G. P. Murdock (1934) described living hunter-gatherers as "our primitive contemporaries." This label gave an image of foragers as living fossils—frozen, primitive, unchanging social forms that had managed to hang on in remote areas.

Later, many anthropologists followed the prolific ethnographer Richard Lee (1984) in using the San ("Bushmen") of the Kalahari Desert of southern Africa to represent the hunting-gathering way of life. But critics increasingly wonder about how much modern foragers can tell us about the economic and social relations that characterized humanity before food production. Modern foragers, after all, live in nation-states and an increasingly interlinked world.

For generations, the pygmies of Congo have traded with their neighbors who are cultivators. They exchange forest products (e.g., honey and meat) for crops (e.g., bananas and manioc). The San speakers of southern Africa have been influenced by Bantu speakers (farmers and herders) for 2,000 years and by Europeans for centuries. All foragers now trade with food producers, and most rely on governments and on missionaries for at least part of what they consume. The Aché of Paraguay get food from missionaries, grow crops, and have domesticated animals (Hawkes et al. 1982; Hill et al. 1987). They spend only a third of their subsistence time foraging.

There is a debate in hunter-gatherer studies between "traditionalists" (e.g., Richard Lee) and "revisionists" (e.g., Edwin Wilmsen). Reconsideration of the status of contemporary foragers is related to the reaction against the ethnographic present discussed in Chapter 2. Anthropologists have rejected the old tendency to depict societies as uniform and frozen in time and space. Attempts to capture the ethnographic present often ignored internal variation, change, and the influence of the world system.

The debate over foragers has focused on the San, whom the traditionalists view as autonomous foragers with a cultural identity different from that of their neighbors who are herders and cultivators (Lee 1979; Silberbauer 1981; Tanaka 1980). These scholars depict most San as egalitarian band-organized people who until recently were nomadic or seminomadic. Traditionalists recognize contact between the San and food producers, but they don't think this contact has destroyed San culture.

The revisionists claim the San tell us little about the ancient world in which all humans were foragers. They argue that the San have been linked to food producers for generations, and that this contact has changed the basis of their culture. For Edwin Wilmsen (1989), the San are far from being isolated survivors of a pristine era. They are a rural underclass in a larger political and economic system dominated by Europeans and Bantu food producers. Many San now tend cattle for wealthier Bantu, rather than foraging independently. Wilmsen also argues that many San descend from herders who were pushed into the desert by poverty or oppression.

The isolation and autonomy of foragers also have been questioned for African pygmies (Bailey et al. 1989) and for foragers in the Philippines (Headland and Reid 1989). The Mikea of southwest Madagascar may have moved into their remote forest habitat to escape a nearby state. Eventually, the Mikea became an economically specialized group of hunter-gatherers on the fringes of that state. The Tasaday of the Philippines maintain ties with food producers and probably descend from cultivating ancestors. This is true despite the initial "Lost Tribe" media accounts. The reports that followed the "discovery" of the Tasaday portrayed them as survivors of the Stone Age, hermetically sealed in a pristine world all their own. Many scholars now question the authenticity of the Tasaday as a separate cultural group (Headland, 1992).

The debate about foragers raises a larger question: Why do the ethnographic accounts and interpretations vary? The reasons include variation in space and time in the society, and different

Among tropical foragers, gathering (for example, of edible roots like the ones shown here) typically contributes more to the diet than hunting and fishing do. Women make an important economic contribution through gathering, as is true among the San shown here in Botswana. What evidence do you see in the photo that contemporary foragers participate in the modern world system?

assumptions by ethnographers. Susan Kent (1992, 1996) notes a tendency to stereotype foragers, to treat them as all alike. Foragers used to be stereotyped as isolated, primitive survivors of the Stone Age. A new stereotype sees them as culturally deprived people forced by states, colonialism, or world events into marginal environments. This view is probably more accurate, although often exaggerated. All modern foragers have links with external systems, including food producers and nation-states. Because of this, they differ substantially from Stone Age hunter-gatherers.

In challenging both stereotypes, Kent (1996) stresses the variation among foragers. She focuses on diversity in time and space among the San. The traditionalist–revisionist debate, suggests Kent, is largely based on failure to recognize the extent of diversity among the San. Researchers on both sides may be correct, depending on the group of San being described and the time period of the research.

San economic adaptations range from hunting and gathering to fishing, farming, herding, and wage work. Solway and Lee (1990) describe environmental degradation caused by herding and population increase. These factors are depleting game and forcing more and more San to give up foraging. Even traditionalists recognize that all San are being drawn inexorably into the modern world system. (Many of us remember the Coke bottle that fell from the sky into a San band in the movie *The Gods Must Be Crazy*—a film filled with many stereotypes.)

The nature of San life has changed appreciably since the 1950s and 1960s, when a series of anthropologists from Harvard University, including Richard Lee, embarked on a systematic study of life in the Kalahari. Lee and others have documented many of the changes in various publications. Such longitudinal research monitors variation in time, while field work in many San areas has revealed variation in space. One of the most important contrasts is between settled (sedentary) and nomadic groups (Kent and Vierich 1989). Sedentism is increasing, but some San groups (along rivers) have been sedentary, or have traded with outsiders, for generations. Others, including Lee's Dobe Ju/'hoansi San and Kent's Kutse San, have been more cut off and have retained more of the hunter-gatherer life style.

Modern foragers are not Stone Age relics, living fossils, lost tribes, or noble savages. Still, to the extent that foraging is the basis of subsistence, modern hunter-gatherers can illustrate links between a foraging economy and other aspects of culture. For example, San groups that are still mobile, or that were so until recently, emphasize social, political, and gender equality. Social relations that stress kinship, reciprocity, and sharing work well in an economy with limited resources and few people. The nomadic pursuit of wild plants and animals tends to discourage permanent settlements, accumulation of wealth, and status distinctions. People have to share meat when they get it; otherwise it rots. Kent (1996) suggests that by studying diversity among the San, we can better understand foraging and how it is influenced by sedentism and other factors. Such study will enhance our knowledge of past, present, and future small-scale societies.

than foragers do, but tribal societies have no sure means of enforcing political decisions. The main regulatory officials are village heads, "big men," descent-group leaders, village councils, and leaders of pantribal associations. All these figures and groups have limited authority.

Like foragers, horticulturalists tend to be egalitarian, although some have marked *gender stratification:* an unequal distribution of resources, power, prestige, and personal freedom between men and women. Horticultural villages are usually small, with low population density and open access to strategic resources. Age, gender, and personal traits determine how much respect people receive and how much support they get from others. Egalitarianism diminishes, however, as village size and population density increase. Horticultural villages usually have headmen—rarely, if ever, headwomen.

Yanomami village heads represent their communities in dealings with outsiders. Davi Kopenawa, a leader of the Brazilian Yanomami, has become involved in international protests against Amazonian deforestation.

The Village Head

The Yanomami (Chagnon 1997) are Native Americans who live in southern Venezuela and adjacent Brazil. Their tribal society has about 20,000 people living in 200 to 250 widely scattered villages, each with a population between 40 and 250. The Yanomami are horticulturalists who also hunt and gather. Their staple crops are bananas and plantains (a bananalike crop). There are more significant social groups among the Yanomami than exist in a foraging society. The Yanomami have nuclear families, villages, and descent groups. Their descent groups are patrilineal and exogamous and span more than one village. However, local branches of two different descent groups may live in the same village and intermarry.

As in many village-based tribal societies, the only leadership position among the Yanomami is that of **village head** (always a man). His authority, like that of the foraging band leader, is severely limited. If a headman wants something done, he must lead by example and persuasion. The headman lacks the right to issue orders. He can only persuade, harangue, and try to influence public opinion. For example, if he wants people to clean up the central plaza in preparation for a feast, he must start sweeping it himself, hoping that his covillagers will take the hint and relieve him.

When conflict erupts within the village, the headman may be called on as a mediator who listens to both sides. He will give an opinion and advice. If a disputant is unsatisfied, the headman can do nothing. He has no power to back his decisions and no way to impose punishments. Like the band leader, he is first among equals.

A Yanomami village headman also must lead in generosity. Because he must be more generous than any other villager, he cultivates more land. His garden provides much of the food consumed when his village holds a feast for another village. The headman represents the village in its dealings with outsiders. Sometimes he visits other villages to invite people to a feast.

The way a person acts as headman depends on his personal traits and the number of supporters he can muster. One village headman, Kaobawa, intervened in a dispute between a husband and wife and kept him from killing her (Chagnon 1983/1992). He also guaranteed safety to a delegation from a village with which a covillager of his wanted to start a war. Kaobawa was a particularly effective headman. He had demonstrated his fierceness in battle, but he also knew how to use diplomacy to avoid offending other villagers. No one in the village had a better personality for the headmanship. Nor (because Kaobawa had many brothers) did anyone have more supporters. Among the Yanomami, when a group is dissatisfied with a village headman, its members can leave and found a new village; this is done from time to time.

Yanomami society, with its many villages and descent groups, is more complex than a band-organized society. The Yanomami also face more regulatory problems. A headman can sometimes prevent a specific violent act, but there is no government to maintain order. In fact, intervillage raiding in which men are killed and women are captured has been a feature of some areas of Yanomami territory, particularly those studied by Chagnon (1997).

We also must stress that the Yanomami are not isolated from outside events (although there are still uncontacted villages). The Yanomami live in two nation-states, Venezuela and Brazil, and external warfare waged by Brazilian ranchers and miners has increasingly threatened them (Chagnon 1997; *Cultural Survival Quarterly* 1989; Ferguson 1995). During a Brazilian gold rush between 1987 and 1991, one Yanomami died each day, on average, from external attacks (including biological warfare—introduced diseases to which the Indians lack resistance). By 1991, there were some 40,000 Brazilian miners in the Yanomami homeland. Some Indians were killed outright. The miners introduced new diseases, and the swollen population ensured that old diseases became epidemic. In 1991, a commission of the American Anthropological Association reported on the plight of the Yanomami (*Anthropology Newsletter,* September 1991). Brazilian Yanomami were dying at a rate of 10 percent annually, and their fertility rate had dropped to zero. Since then, both the Brazilian and the Venezuelan governments have intervened to protect the Yanomami. The Brazilian president declared a huge Yanomami territory off-limits to outsiders. Unfortunately, by mid-1992, local politicians, miners, and ranchers were increasingly evading the ban. The future of the Yanomami remains uncertain.

The "Big Man"

In many areas of the South Pacific, particularly the Melanesian Islands and Papua New Guinea, native cultures have a kind of political leader that we call the big man. The **big man** (almost always a male) is an elaborate version of the village head, but there is one very significant difference. The village head's leadership is within one village; the big man has supporters in several villages. He is therefore a regulator of regional political organization. Here we see the trend toward expansion in the scale of sociopolitical regulation—from village to region.

The Kapauku Papuans live in Irian Jaya, Indonesia (which is on the island of New Guinea). Anthropologist Leopold Pospisil (1963) studied the Kapauku (45,000 people), who grow

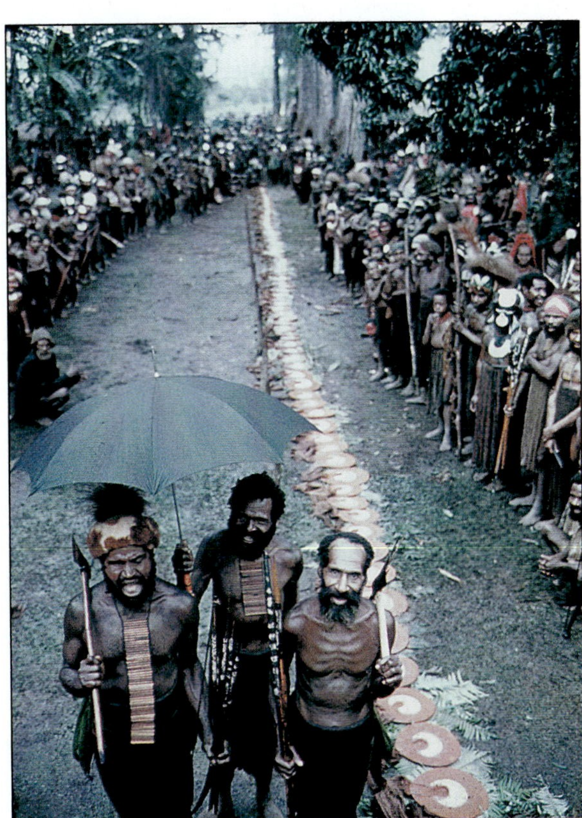

The "big man" persuades people to organize feasts, which distribute pork and wealth. Shown here is such a regional event, drawing on several villages, in Papua New Guinea. Big men owe their status to their individual personalities rather than to inherited wealth or position. Does our society have equivalents of big men?

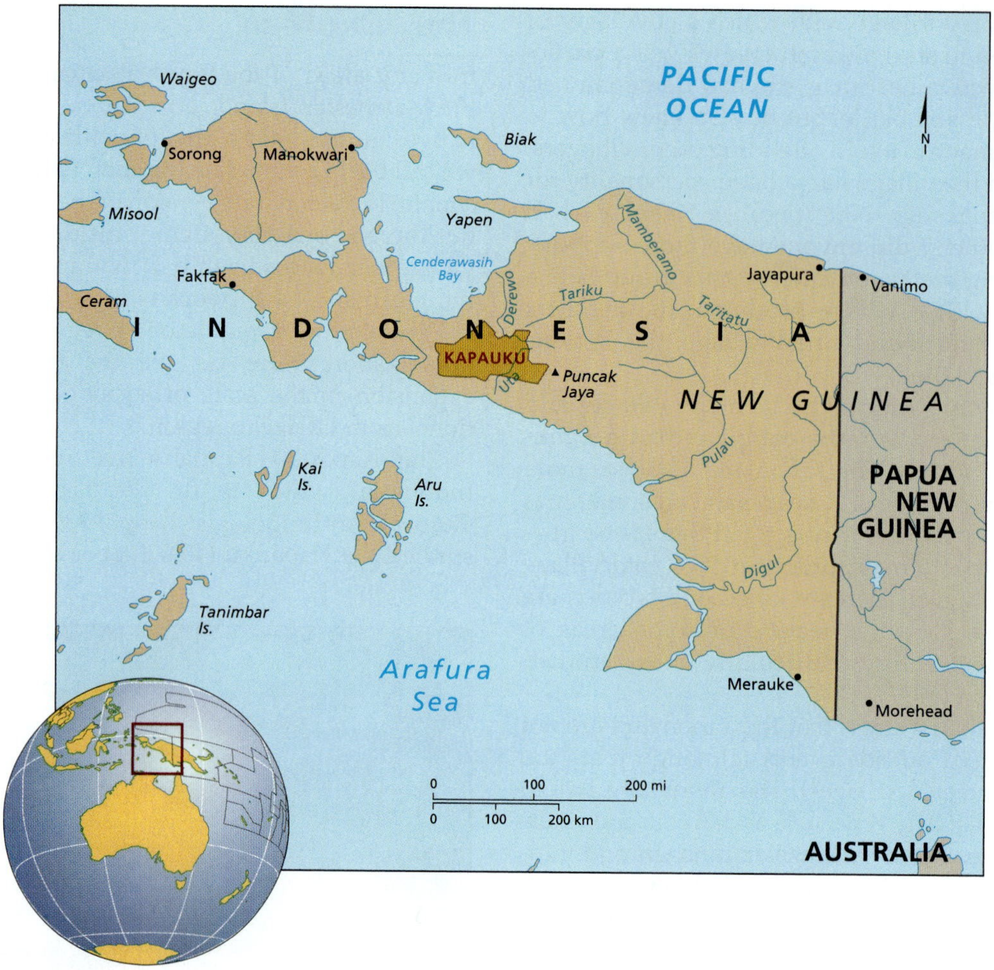

crops (with the sweet potato as their staple) and raise pigs. Their economy is too complex to be described as simple horticulture. Beyond the household, the only political figure among the Kapauku is the big man, known as a *tonowi.* A *tonowi* achieves his status through hard work, amassing wealth in the form of pigs and other native riches. Characteristics that can distinguish a big man from his fellows include wealth, generosity, eloquence, physical fitness, bravery, and supernatural powers. Big men are what they are because they have certain personalities. They amass their resources during their lifetimes, rather than inheriting their wealth or position.

Any man who is determined enough can become a big man, because people create their own wealth through hard work and good judgment. Wealth depends on successful pig breeding and trading. As a man's pig herd and prestige grow, he attracts supporters. He sponsors ceremonial pig feasts in which pigs are slaughtered and their meat is distributed to guests.

The big man has some advantages that the Yanomami village head lacks. His wealth exceeds that of his fellows. His primary supporters, in recognition of past favors and anticipation of future rewards, recognize him as a leader and accept his decisions as binding. He is an important regulator of regional events in Kapauku life. He helps determine the dates for feasts and markets. He persuades people to sponsor feasts, which distribute pork and wealth. He initiates economic projects that require the cooperation of a regional community.

The Kapauku big man again exemplifies a generalization about leadership in tribal societies: If people achieve wealth and widespread respect and support, they must be generous.

The big man works hard not to hoard wealth but to be able to give away the fruits of his labor, to convert wealth into prestige and gratitude. If a big man is stingy, he loses his supporters, and his reputation plummets. The Kapauku take even more extreme measures against big men who hoard. Selfish and greedy rich men may be murdered by their fellows.

Political figures such as the big man emerge as regulators both of demographic growth and of economic complexity. Kapauku cultivation uses varied techniques for specific kinds of land. Labor-intensive cultivation in valleys involves mutual aid in turning the soil before planting. The digging of long drainage ditches is even more complex. Kapauku plant cultivation supports a larger and denser population than does the simpler horticulture of the Yanomami. Kapauku society could not survive in its present form without collective cultivation and political regulation of the more complex economic tasks.

Segmentary Lineage Organization

The big man is a temporary regional regulator. Big men can mobilize supporters in several villages for produce and labor on specific occasions. Another temporary form of regional political organization is **segmentary lineage organization (SLO).** This means that the descent-group structure (usually patrilineal) has several levels or segments. The largest segments are maximal lineages, whose common ancestor lived long ago, and whose membership is spread out over a large territory. The smallest segments are minimal lineages, whose common ancestor lived fairly recently—no more than four generations ago. Members of the minimal lineage live in the same village.

The Nuer of Sudan provide a classic example of SLO. The Nuer all claim to share a common (patrilineal) ancestry separate and distinct from

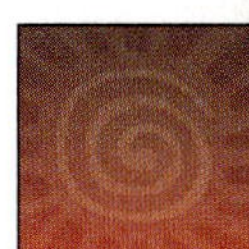

that of their neighbors. One of several *Nilotic populations* (populations that inhabit the Upper Nile region of eastern Africa), the Nuer (Evans-Pritchard 1940; Hutchinson 1996; Kelly 1985), numbering more than 200,000, live in Sudan. Cattle pastoralism was fundamental to their traditional mixed economy, which also included horticulture. The Nuer had many institutions that are typical of tribal societies, including patrilineal descent groups arranged into a segmentary structure. Their political organization was based on descent rules and genealogical reckoning.

Brothers are very close in such societies, especially when the father is alive. When he dies, the brothers usually keep on living in the same village, but one may take his share of the herds and start a settlement of his own. However, his brothers are still his closest allies. He will live as close as he can to them. Even if the brothers all stay in the same village, some of the grandchildren will move away in search of new pastures. However, each will try to remain as close to the home village as possible, settling nearest his brothers and nearer to his first cousins than to more distant relatives.

With SLO, the basic principle of solidarity is that the closer the relationship in terms of patrilineal descent, the greater the mutual support. The more distant the shared ancestor, the greater the potential for hostility. Segmentary descent regulates disputes and their resolution. If a fight breaks out between men who share a living patrilineal ancestor, he intervenes to settle it. As head of the minimal descent group that includes the disputants, he backs his authority with the threat of banishment. However, when there is no common living ancestor, a blood feud may develop.

Disputes among the Nuer did not arise over land, which a person acquired as a member of a minimal descent group. A frequent cause of quarrels was adultery, and if a person injured or killed someone, a feud might develop. The best alternative to the blood feud was for the disputants to consult the leopard-skin man, so called because he customarily wore a leopard skin over his shoulders. Leopard-skin men conducted rituals, but their most important role was to mediate disputes. For instance, elders might ask a leopard-skin man to persuade a murder victim's kin to accept a certain number of cattle in recompense.

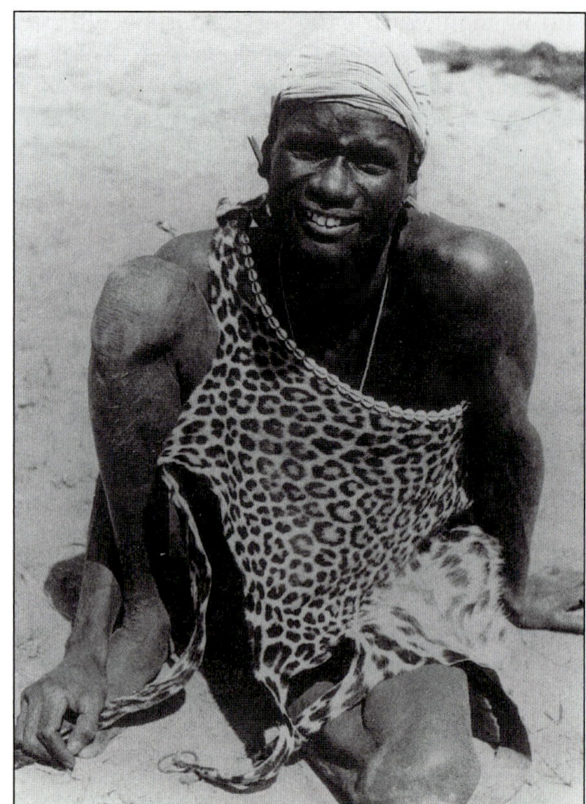

A leopard-skin man, traditional mediator among the Nuer. Think of a mediator in your own society. How does the authority of that mediator compare with that of the leopard-skin man?

The leopard-skin man relied on persuasion and avoided blaming either side. He could not enforce his decisions, but in theory he could use the threat of supernatural punishment. If one of the disputing groups was adamant, he might, in disgust, threaten to curse it. If, after seeking mediation, the disputants refused to agree, the leopard-skin man might withdraw.

Negotiations involved the disputants, their elders, and other close kin. There was full and free discussion before a settlement was reached. The disputants might gradually come to accept the collective opinion of the mediator and the elders. However, although the peace-making abilities of the leopard-skin man were greater than anything found among the Yanomami and Inuit, blood feuds still existed among the stateless Nuer.

With SLO, no individual has a constant group of allies. One's allies change from one dispute to the next, depending on the genealogical distance. Still, the belief in common descent, and the ability to trace it way back, did allow the Nuer to mobilize effectively, if temporarily, to fight their neighbors who lacked such a descent system. When the need arose, the Nuer could present a common front against outsiders: people with different genealogical and ethnic identities (Sahlins 1961). When the outside threat went away, the Nuer could revert to their usual pattern of local social organization, with occasional disputes between minimal lineages.

Like the Nuer, Arabs claim to demonstrate their segmentary descent patrilineally from the biblical Ishmael. There is an Arab adage, "I and my brother against my cousin [father's brother's son]. I, my brother, and my cousin against all other Arabs. I, my brother, my cousin, and all other Arabs against all the world" (Murphy and Kasdan 1959, p. 20). Jews believe themselves to be descended from Isaac, half-brother of Ishmael. The Jews and Arabs share a common ancestor, Abraham, the father of both Ishmael and Isaac. In the modern world, of course, political mechanisms other than SLO, including national governments and regional alliances, work to determine relations between Arabs and Jews. And Nuer social organization has been disrupted in the modern world by fighting between the Sudanese Liberation Army, which has Nuer members, and the Sudanese central government, based in the North.

Pantribal Sodalities and Age Grades

We have seen that events initiated by big men temporarily unite people from different villages. Segmentary lineage organization permits short-term mobilization of an entire society against an outside threat. There are many other kinds of sociopolitical linkages between local groups in a region. Clans, for example, often span several villages.

Kinship and descent provide important social linkages in tribal societies. Principles other than kinship also may link local groups. In a modern nation, a labor union, national sorority or fraternity, political party, or religious denomination may provide such a nonkin-based link. In tribes, nonkin groups called associations or *sodalities* may serve the same linking function. Often, sodalities are based on common age or gender, with all-male sodalities more common than all-female ones.

Pantribal sodalities (those that extend across the whole tribe, spanning several villages) tend to be found in areas where two or more different cultures come into regular contact. They are especially likely to develop when there is warfare between tribes. Since pantribal sodalities draw their members from different villages of the same tribe, they can mobilize men in many local groups for attack or retaliation against another tribe.

In the cross-cultural study of nonkin groups, we must distinguish between those that are confined to a single village and those that span several local groups. Only the latter, the pantribal groups, are important in general military mobilization and regional political organization. Localized men's houses and clubs, limited to particular villages, are found in many horticultural societies in tropical South America, Melanesia, and Papua New Guinea. These groups may organize village activities and even intervillage raiding, but their leaders are similar to village heads and their political scope is mainly local. The following discussion, which continues our examination of the growth in scale of regional sociopolitical organization, concerns pantribal groups.

The best examples of pantribal sodalities come from the Central Plains of North America and from tropical Africa. During the 18th and 19th centuries, native populations of the Great Plains of the United States and Canada experienced a rapid growth of pantribal sodalities. This development reflected an economic change that followed the spread of horses, which had been reintroduced to the Americas by the Spanish, to the states between the Rocky Mountains and the Mississippi River. Many Plains Indian societies changed their adaptive strategies because of the horse. At first, they had been foragers who hunted bison (buffalo) on foot. Later, they adopted a mixed economy based on hunting, gathering, and horticulture. Finally, they changed to a much more specialized economy based on horseback hunting of bison (eventually with rifles).

Natives of the Great Plains of North America originally hunted bison (buffalo) on foot, using the bow and arrow. The introduction of horses and rifles fueled a pattern of horse raiding and warfare. How far had the change gone, as depicted in this painting?

As the Plains tribes were undergoing these changes, other Indians also adopted horseback hunting and moved into the Plains. Attempting to occupy the same area, groups came into conflict. A pattern of warfare developed in which the members of one tribe raided another, usually for horses. The new economy demanded that people follow the movement of the bison herds. During the winter, when the bison dispersed, a tribe fragmented into small bands and families. In the summer, as huge herds assembled on the Plains, members of the tribe reunited. They camped together for social, political, and religious activities, but mainly for communal bison hunting.

Only two activities in the new adaptive strategy demanded strong leadership: organizing and carrying out raids on enemy camps (to capture horses) and managing the summer bison hunt. All the Plains cultures developed pantribal sodalities, and leadership roles within them, to police the summer hunt. Leaders coordinated hunting efforts, making sure that people did not cause a stampede with an early shot or an ill-advised action. Leaders imposed severe penalties, including seizure of a culprit's wealth, for disobedience.

Some of the Plains sodalities were **age sets** of increasing rank. Each set included all the men—from that tribe's component bands—born during a certain time span. Each set had its distinctive dance, songs, possessions, and privileges. Members of each set had to pool their wealth to buy admission to the next higher level as they moved up the age hierarchy. Most Plains societies had pantribal warrior associations whose rituals celebrated militarism. As noted previously, the leaders of these associations organized bison hunting and raiding. They also arbitrated disputes during the summer, when large numbers of people came together.

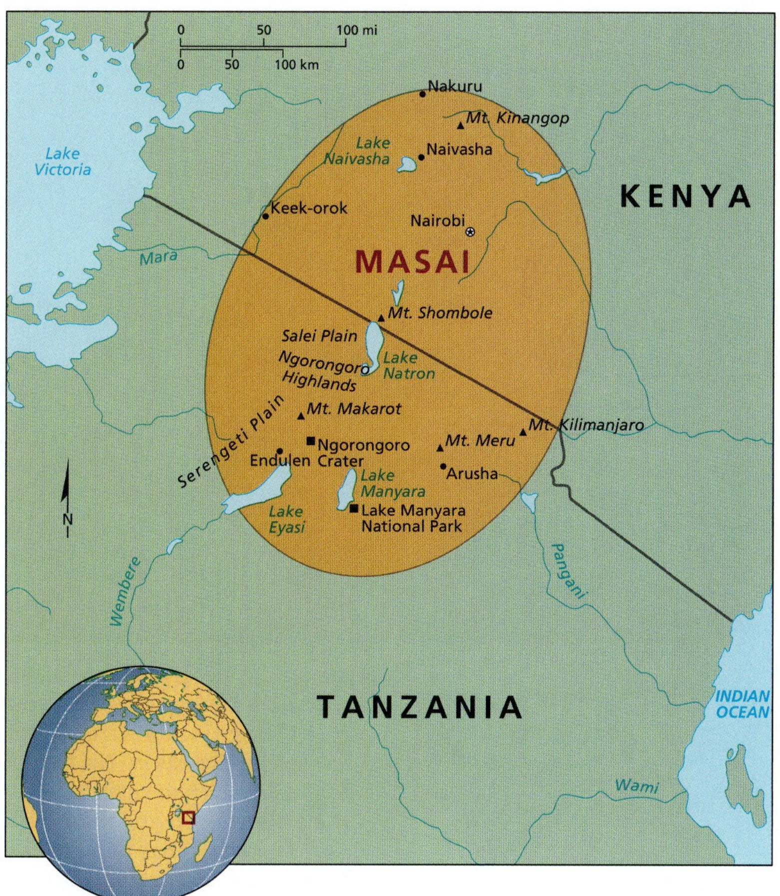

Many of the tribes that adopted this Plains strategy of adaptation had once been foragers for whom hunting and gathering had been individual or small-group affairs. They had never come together previously as a single social unit. Age and gender were available as social principles that could quickly and efficiently forge unrelated people into pantribal groups.

Raiding of one tribe by another, this time for cattle rather than horses, also was common in eastern and southeastern Africa, where pantribal sodalities, including age sets, also developed. Among the pastoral Masai of Kenya, men born during the same four-year period were circumcised together and belonged to the same named group, an age set, throughout their lives. The sets moved through grades, the most important of which was the warrior grade. Members of the set who wished to enter the warrior grade were at first discouraged by its current occupants, who eventually vacated the warrior grade and married. Members of a set felt a strong allegiance to one another and eventually had sexual rights to each other's wives. Masai women lacked comparable set organization, but they also passed through culturally recognized age grades: the initiate, the married woman, and the postmenopausal woman.

To understand the difference between an age set and an age grade, think of a college class, the Class of 2005, for example, and its progress through the university. The age set would be the group of people constituting the Class of 2005, while the first ("freshman"), sophomore, junior, and senior years would represent the age grades.

Not all cultures with age grades also have age sets. When there are no sets, men can enter or leave a particular grade individually or collectively, often by going through a predetermined ritual. The grades most commonly recognized in Africa are these:

Among the Masai of Kenya, men born during the same four-year period were circumcised together. They belonged to the same named group, an age set, throughout their lives. The sets moved through grades, of which the most important was the warrior grade. Here we see the warrior (*ilmurran*) age grade dancing with a group of girls of a lower age grade (*intoyie*). Do we have any equivalents of age sets or grades in our own society?

1. Recently initiated youths.
2. Warriors.
3. One or more grades of mature men who play important roles in pantribal government.
4. Elders, who may have special ritual responsibilities.

In certain parts of West Africa and Central Africa, the pantribal sodalities are *secret societies,* made up exclusively of men or women. Like our college fraternities and sororities, these associations have secret initiation ceremonies. Among the Mende of Sierra Leone, men's and women's secret societies are very influential. The men's group, the Poro, trains boys in social conduct, ethics, and religion and supervises political and economic activities. Leadership roles in the Poro often overshadow village headship and play an important part in social control, dispute management, and tribal political regulation. Like descent, then, age, gender, and ritual can link members of different local groups into a single social collectivity in tribal society and thus create a sense of ethnic identity, of belonging to the same cultural tradition.

Nomadic Politics

Although many pastoralists, such as the Nuer and the Masai, live in tribes, a range of demographic and sociopolitical diversity occurs with pastoralism. A comparison of pastoralists shows that as regulatory problems increase, political hierarchies become more complex. Political organization becomes less personal, more formal, and less kinship-oriented. The pastoral strategy of adaptation does not dictate any particular political organization. A range of authority structures manage regulatory problems associated with specific environments. Some pastoralists have traditionally existed as well-defined ethnic groups in nation-states. This reflects pastoralists' need to interact with other populations—a need that is less characteristic of the other adaptive strategies.

The scope of political authority among pastoralists expands considerably as regulatory problems increase in densely populated regions. Consider two Iranian pastoral nomadic tribes: the Basseri and the Qashqai (Salzman 1974). Starting each year from a plateau near the coast, these groups took their animals to grazing land 5,400 meters (17,000 feet) above sea level. The Basseri and the Qashqai shared this route with one another and with several other ethnic groups.

Use of the same pasture land at different times was carefully scheduled. Ethnic-group movements were tightly coordinated. Expressing this schedule is *il-rah,* a concept common to all Iranian nomads. A group's *il-rah* is its customary path in time and space. It is the schedule, different for each group, of when specific areas can be used in the annual trek.

Each tribe had its own leader, known as the *khan* or *il-khan.* The Basseri *khan,* because he dealt with a smaller population, faced fewer problems

Political organization is well-developed among the Qashqai, who share their nomadic route and strategic resources with several other tribes. Here, Qashqai nomads cross a river in Iran's Fars province.

in coordinating its movements than did the leaders of the Qashqai. Correspondingly, his rights, privileges, duties, and authority were weaker. Nevertheless, his authority exceeded that of any political figure we have discussed so far. However, the *khan*'s authority still came from his personal traits rather than from his office. That is, the Basseri followed a particular *khan* not because of a political position he happened to fill but because of their personal allegiance and loyalty to him as a man. The *khan* relied on the support of the heads of the descent groups into which Basseri society was divided, following a rough segmentary lineage model.

In Qashqai society, however, allegiance shifts from the person to the office. The Qashqai had multiple levels of authority and more powerful chiefs or *khans*. Managing 400,000 people required a complex hierarchy. Heading it was the *il-khan*, helped by a deputy, under whom were the heads of constituent tribes, under each of whom were descent-group heads.

A case illustrates just how developed the Qashqai authority structure was. A hailstorm prevented some nomads from joining the annual migration at the appointed time. Although everyone recognized that they were not responsible for their delay, the *il-khan* assigned them less favorable grazing land, for that year only, in place of their usual pasture. The tardy herders and other Qashqai considered the judgment fair and didn't question it. Thus, Qashqai authorities regulated the annual migration. They also adjudicated disputes between people, tribes, and descent groups.

These Iranian cases illustrate the fact that pastoralism is often just one among many specialized economic activities within complex nation-states and regional systems. As part of a larger whole, pastoral tribes are constantly pitted against other ethnic groups. In these nations, the state becomes a final authority, a higher-level regulator that attempts to limit conflict between ethnic groups. State organization arose not just to manage agricultural economies but also to regulate the activities of ethnic groups within expanding social and economic systems.

Chiefdoms

Having looked at bands and tribes, we turn to more complex forms of sociopolitical organization: chiefdoms and states. The first states emerged in the Old World about 5,500 years ago. The first chiefdoms developed perhaps a thousand years earlier, but few survive today. The chiefdom was a transitional form of organization that emerged during the evolution of tribes into states. State formation began in Mesopotamia (currently Iran and Iraq). It next occurred in Egypt, the Indus Valley of Pakistan and India, and northern China. A few thousand years later, states also arose in two parts of the Western Hemisphere: Mesoamerica (Mexico, Guatemala, Belize) and the central Andes (Peru and Bolivia). Early states are known as *archaic states,* or nonindustrial states, in contrast to modern industrial nation-states. Robert Carneiro defines the state as "an autonomous political unit encompassing many communities within its territory, having a centralized government with the power to collect taxes, draft men for work or war, and decree and enforce laws" (Carneiro 1970, p. 733).

Chiefdoms created the megalithic cultures of Europe, such as the one that built Stonehenge—shown here—over 5,000 years ago. Between the emergence and spread of food production and the expansion of the Roman empire, much of Europe was organized at the chiefdom level, to which it reverted after the fall of Rome.

The chiefdom and the state, like many categories used by social scientists, are *ideal types.* That is, they are labels that make social contrasts seem sharper than they really are. In reality, there is a continuum from tribe to chiefdom to state. Some societies have many attributes of chiefdoms but retain tribal features. Some advanced chiefdoms have many attributes of archaic states and thus are difficult to assign to either category. Recognizing this "continuous change" (Johnson and Earle 2000), some anthropologists speak of "complex chiefdoms" (Earle 1987), which are almost states.

Political and Economic Systems in Chiefdoms

State formation remained incomplete and only chiefdoms emerged in several areas, including the circum-Caribbean (e.g., Caribbean islands, Panama, Colombia), lowland Amazonia, what is now the southeastern United States, and Polynesia. Between the emergence and spread of food production and the expansion of the Roman empire, much of Europe was organized at the chiefdom level, to which it reverted for centuries after the fall of Rome in the fifth century AD. Chiefdoms created the megalithic cultures of Europe, such as the one that built Stonehenge.

Much of our ethnographic knowledge about chiefdoms comes from Polynesia (Kirch 2000), shaded khaki in the map on the next page, where they were common at the time of European exploration. In chiefdoms, social relations are mainly based on kinship, marriage, descent, age, generation, and gender—as they are in bands and tribes. This is a basic difference between chiefdoms and states. States bring nonrelatives together and oblige them to pledge allegiance to a government.

Unlike bands and tribes, however, chiefdoms are characterized by *permanent political regulation* of the territory they administer. Chiefdoms may include thousands of people living in many villages and/or hamlets. Regulation is carried out by the chief and his or her assistants, who occupy

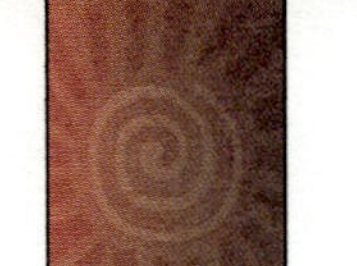

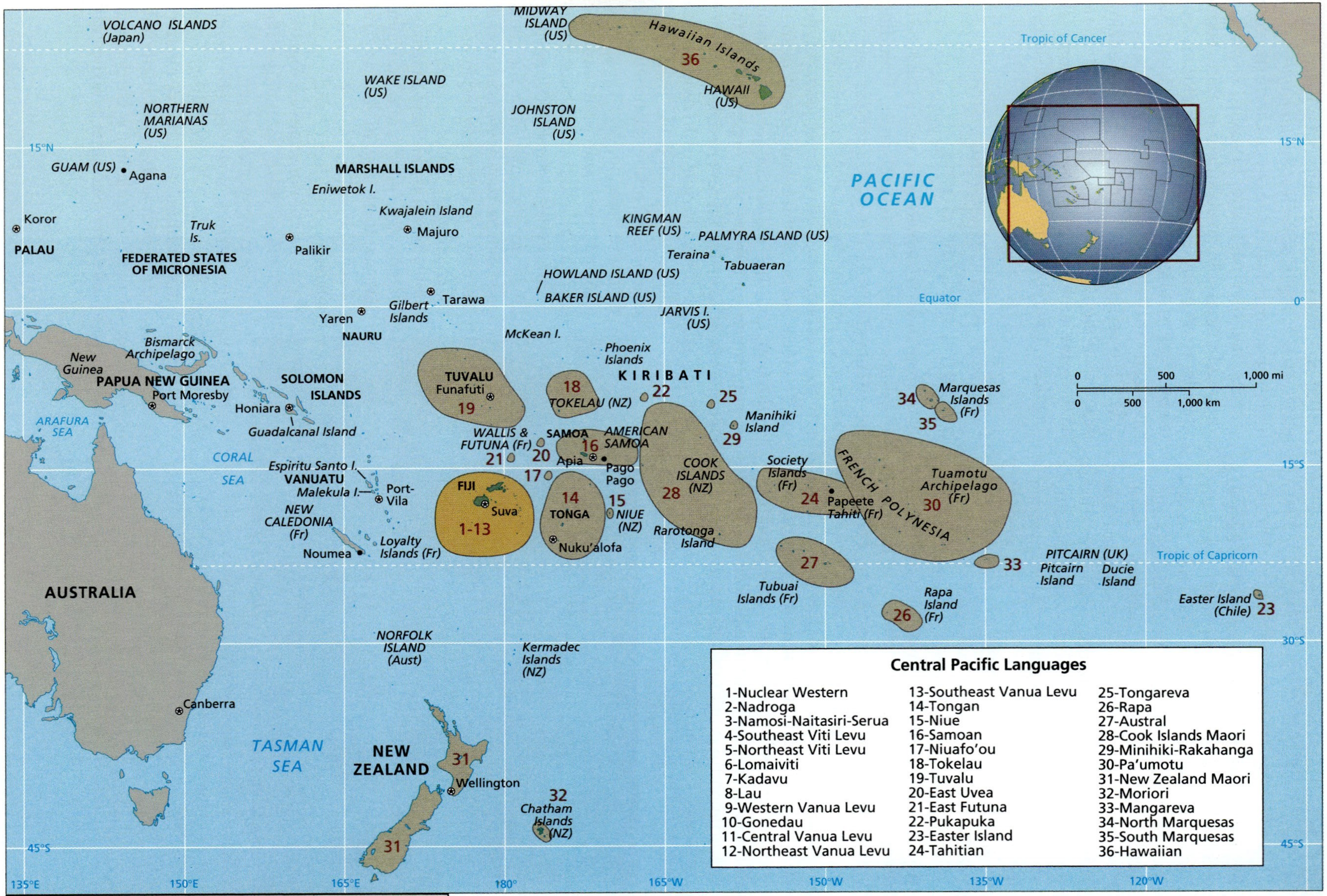

Central Pacific Languages
1-Nuclear Western
2-Nadroga
3-Namosi-Naitasiri-Serua
4-Southeast Viti Levu
5-Northeast Viti Levu
6-Lomaiviti
7-Kadavu
8-Lau
9-Western Vanua Levu
10-Gonedau
11-Central Vanua Levu
12-Northeast Vanua Levu
13-Southeast Vanua Levu
14-Tongan
15-Niue
16-Samoan
17-Niuafo'ou
18-Tokelau
19-Tuvalu
20-East Uvea
21-East Futuna
22-Pukapuka
23-Easter Island
24-Tahitian
25-Tongareva
26-Rapa
27-Austral
28-Cook Islands Maori
29-Minihiki-Rakahanga
30-Pa'umotu
31-New Zealand Maori
32-Moriori
33-Mangareva
34-North Marquesas
35-South Marquesas
36-Hawaiian
PACIFIC OCEAN
AUSTRALIA
NEW ZEALAND
TASMAN SEA
CORAL SEA
ARAFURA SEA
PAPUA NEW GUINEA
SOLOMON ISLANDS
FEDERATED STATES OF MICRONESIA
MARSHALL ISLANDS
KIRIBATI
FRENCH POLYNESIA
TUVALU
FIJI
TONGA
SAMOA
AMERICAN SAMOA
COOK ISLANDS (NZ)
Hawaiian Islands
Tropic of Cancer
Equator
Tropic of Capricorn
0 500 1,000 mi
0 500 1,000 km

Polynesian islands are shaded khaki. Other Central Pacific languages outside of Polynesia are spoken in the area shaded orange, which includes Fiji.

political offices. An **office** is a permanent position, which must be refilled when it is vacated by death or retirement. Because offices are systematically refilled, the structure of a chiefdom endures across the generations, ensuring permanent political regulation.

In the Polynesian chiefdoms, the chiefs were full-time political specialists in charge of regulating the economy—production, distribution, and consumption. Polynesian chiefs relied on religion to buttress their authority. They regulated production by commanding or prohibiting (using religious taboos) the cultivation of certain lands and crops. Chiefs also regulated distribution and consumption. At certain seasons—often on a ritual occasion such as a first-fruit ceremony—people would offer part of their harvest to the chief through his or her representatives. Products moved up the hierarchy, eventually reaching the chief. Conversely, illustrating obligatory sharing with kin, chiefs sponsored feasts at which they gave back much of what they had received.

Such a flow of resources to and then from a central office is known as *chiefly redistribution.* Redistribution offers economic advantages. If the different areas specialized in particular crops, goods, or services, chiefly redistribution made those products available to the whole society. Chiefly redistribution also played a role in risk management. It stimulated production beyond the immediate subsistence level and provided a central storehouse for goods that might become scarce at times of famine (Earle 1987, 1991). Chiefdoms and archaic states had similar economies, often based on intensive cultivation, and both administered systems of regional trade or exchange.

Social Status in Chiefdoms

Social status in chiefdoms was based on seniority of descent. Because rank, power, prestige, and resources came through kinship and descent, Polynesian chiefs kept extremely long genealogies. Some chiefs (without writing) managed to trace their ancestry back 50 generations. All the people in the chiefdom were thought to be related to each other. Presumably, all were descended from a group of founding ancestors.

The chief (usually a man) had to demonstrate seniority in descent. Degrees of seniority were calculated so intricately on some islands that there were as many ranks as people. For example, the third son would rank below the second, who in turn would rank below the first. The children of an eldest brother, however, would all rank above the children of the next brother, whose children would in turn outrank those of younger brothers. However, even the lowest-ranking person in a chiefdom was still the chief's relative. In such a kin-based context, everyone, even a chief, had to share with his or her relatives.

Because everyone had a slightly different status, it was difficult to draw a line between elites and common people. Although other chiefdoms calculated seniority differently and had shorter genealogies than did those in Polynesia, the concern for genealogy and seniority and the absence of sharp gaps between elites and commoners are features of all chiefdoms.

Status Systems in Chiefdoms and States

The status systems of chiefdoms and states are similar in that both are based on **differential access** to resources. This means that some men and women had privileged access to power, prestige, and wealth. They controlled strategic resources such as land, water, and other means of production. Earle characterizes chiefs as "an incipient aristocracy with advantages in wealth and lifestyle" (1987, p. 290). Nevertheless, differential access in chiefdoms was still very much tied to kinship. The people with privileged access were generally chiefs and their nearest relatives and assistants.

Compared with chiefdoms, archaic states drew a much firmer line between elites and masses, distinguishing at least between nobles and commoners. Kinship ties did not extend from the nobles to the commoners because of *stratum endogamy*—marriage within one's own group. Commoners married commoners; elites married elites.

Such a division of society into socioeconomic strata contrasts strongly with bands and tribes, whose status systems are based on prestige, rather than on differential access to resources. The prestige differentials that do exist in bands reflect special qualities and abilities. Good hunters get respect from their fellows as long as

Social status in chiefdoms is based on seniority of descent. In the modern world system, seniority may still confer prestige, but the differences in wealth and power between chiefs and their juniors are often minor. Shown here is a contemporary chief (center) in the Marquesas Islands, Polynesia. How does the status of chief compare with the status of king or queen in today's world?

they are generous. So does a skilled curer, dancer, storyteller—or anyone else with a talent or skill that others appreciate.

In tribes, some prestige goes to descent-group leaders, to village heads, and especially to the big man, a regional figure who commands the loyalty and labor of others. However, all these figures must be generous. If they accumulate more resources—that is, property or food—than others in the village, they must share them with the others. Since strategic resources are available to everyone, social classes based on the possession of unequal amounts of resources can never exist.

In many tribes, particularly those with patrilineal descent, men have much greater prestige and power than women do. The gender contrast in rights may diminish in chiefdoms, where prestige and access to resources are based on seniority of descent, so that some women are senior to some men. Unlike big men, chiefs are exempt from ordinary work and have rights and privileges that are unavailable to the masses. However, like big men, they still return much of the wealth they take in.

The status system in chiefdoms, although based on differential access, differed from the status system in states because the privileged few were always relatives and assistants of the chief. However, this type of status system didn't last very long. Chiefs would start acting like kings and try to erode the kinship basis of the chiefdom. In Madagascar, they would do this by demoting their more distant relatives to commoner status and banning marriage between nobles and commoners (Kottak 1980). Such moves, *if accepted by the society,* created separate social strata—*unrelated* groups that differ in their access to wealth, prestige, and power. (A *stratum* is one of two or more groups that contrast in regard to social status and access to strategic resources. Each stratum includes people of both sexes and all ages.) The creation of separate social strata is called **stratification,** and its emergence signified the transition from chiefdom to state. *The presence and acceptance of stratification is one of the key distinguishing features of a state.*

The influential sociologist Max Weber (1922/1968) defined three related dimensions of social

This employee of the Chirping Chicken fast-food store, shown with her coworkers, just won $22,500,000 in the New York State lottery. Wealth and prestige are not always correlated. Do you imagine the winner's eating habits will change? Will her prestige rise?

stratification: (1) Economic status, or **wealth,** encompasses all a person's material assets, including income, land, and other types of property (Schaefer and Lamm 1992). (2) **Power,** the ability to exercise one's will over others—to do what one wants—is the basis of political status. (3) **Prestige**—the basis of social status—refers to esteem, respect, or approval for acts, deeds, or qualities considered exemplary. Prestige, or "cultural capital" (Bourdieu 1984), provides people with a sense of worth and respect, which they may often convert into economic and political advantage (Table 17.1).

These Weberian dimensions of stratification are present to varying degrees in chiefdoms. However, chiefdoms lack the sharp division into classes that characterize states. Wealth, power, and prestige in chiefdoms are all tied to kinship factors.

In archaic states—for the first time in human evolution—there were contrasts in wealth, power, and prestige between entire groups (social strata) of men and women. Each stratum included people of both sexes and all ages. The **superordinate** (the higher or elite) stratum had privileged access to wealth, power, and other valued resources. Access to resources by members of the **subordinate** (lower or underprivileged) stratum was limited by the privileged group.

Socioeconomic stratification continues as a defining feature of all states, archaic or industrial. The elites control a significant part of the means of production, for example, land, herds, water, capital, farms, or factories. Those born at the bottom of the hierarchy have reduced chances of social mobility. Because of elite ownership rights, ordinary people lack free access to resources. Only in states do the elites get to keep their differential wealth. Unlike big men and chiefs, they don't have to give it back to the people whose labor has built and increased it.

Table 17.1
Max Weber's Three Dimensions of Stratification

wealth	=>	economic status
power	=>	political status
prestige	=>	social status

States

Table 17.2 summarizes the information presented so far on bands, tribes, chiefdoms, and states. States, remember, are autonomous political units with social classes and a formal government, based on law. States tend to be large and populous, as compared to bands, tribes, and chiefdoms. Certain statuses, systems, and subsystems with specialized functions are found in all states. They include the following:

1. *Population control:* fixing of boundaries, establishment of citizenship categories, and the taking of a census.
2. *Judiciary:* laws, legal procedure, and judges.
3. *Enforcement:* permanent military and police forces.
4. *Fiscal:* taxation.

In archaic states, these subsystems were integrated by a ruling system or government composed of civil, military, and religious officials (Fried 1960).

Population Control

To know whom they govern, all states conduct censuses. States demarcate boundaries that separate them from other societies. Customs agents, immigration officers, navies, and coast guards patrol frontiers. Even nonindustrial states have boundary-maintenance forces. In Buganda, an archaic state on the shores of Lake Victoria in Uganda, the king rewarded military officers with estates in outlying provinces. They became his guardians against foreign intrusion.

States also control population through administrative subdivision: provinces, districts, "states," counties, subcounties, and parishes. Lower-level officials manage the populations and territories of the subdivisions.

In nonstates, people work and relax with their relatives, in-laws, fictive kin, and age mates—people with whom they have a personal relationship. Such a personal social life existed throughout most of human history, but food production spelled its eventual decline. After millions of years of human evolution, it took a mere 4,000 years for the population increase and regulatory problems spawned by food production to lead from tribe to chiefdom to state. With state organization, kinship's pervasive role diminished. Descent groups may continue as kin groups within archaic states, but their importance in political organization declines.

States foster geographic mobility and resettlement, severing long-standing ties among people, land, and kin. Population displacements have increased in the modern world. War, famine, and job seeking across national boundaries churn up migratory currents. People in states come to identify themselves by new statuses, both ascribed and achieved, including ethnic background, place of birth or residence, occupation, party, religion, and team or club affiliation, rather than only as members of a descent group or extended family.

Table 17.2
Economic Basis of and Political Regulation in Bands, Tribes, Chiefdoms, and States

Sociopolitical Type	Economic Type	Examples	Type of Regulation
Band	Foraging	Inuit, San	Local
Tribe	Horticulture, pastoralism	Yanomami, Nuer, Kapauku	Local, temporary regional
Chiefdom	Productive horticulture, pastoral nomadism, agriculture	Qashqai, Polynesia, Cherokee	Permanent regional
State	Agriculture, industrialism	Ancient Mesopotamia, contemporary United States and Canada	Permanent regional

To handle disputes and crimes, all states, including Bermuda, shown here, have courts and judges. Does this photo say anything about cultural diffusion?

States also manage their populations by granting different rights and obligations to citizens and noncitizens. Status distinctions among citizens are also common. Many archaic states granted different rights to nobles, commoners, and slaves. Unequal rights within state-organized societies persist in today's world. In recent American history, before the Emancipation Proclamation, there were different laws for slaves and free people. In European colonies, separate courts judged cases involving only natives and those that involved Europeans. In contemporary America, a military code of justice and court system continue to coexist alongside the civil judiciary.

Judiciary

States have *laws* based on precedent and legislative proclamations. Without writing, laws may be preserved in oral tradition, with justices, elders, and other specialists responsible for remembering them. Oral traditions as repositories of legal wisdom have continued in some nations with writing, such as Great Britain. Laws regulate relations between individuals and groups.

Crimes are violations of the legal code, with specified types of punishment. However, a given act, such as killing someone, may be legally defined in different ways (e.g., as manslaughter, justifiable homicide, or first-degree murder). Furthermore, even in contemporary North America, where justice is supposed to be "blind" to social distinctions, the poor are prosecuted more often and more severely than are the rich.

To handle disputes and crimes, all states have courts and judges. Precolonial African states had subcounty, county, and district courts, plus a high court formed by the king or queen and his or her advisers. Most states allow appeals to higher courts, although people are encouraged to solve problems locally.

A striking contrast between states and nonstates is intervention in family affairs. In states, aspects of parenting and marriage enter the domain of public law. Governments step in to halt blood feuds and regulate previously private disputes. States attempt to curb *internal* conflict, but they aren't always successful. About 85 percent of the world's armed conflicts since 1945 have begun within states—in efforts to overthrow a ruling regime or as disputes over tribal, religious, and ethnic minority issues. Only 15 percent have been fights across national borders (Barnaby, 1984). Rebellion, resistance, repression, terrorism, and warfare continue. Indeed, recent states have perpetrated some of history's bloodiest deeds.

Enforcement

All states have agents to enforce judicial decisions. Confinement requires jailers, and a death penalty calls for executioners. Agents of the state collect fines and confiscate property. These officials wield power that is much more effective than the curse of the Nuer leopard-skin man.

A major concern of government is to defend hierarchy, property, and the power of the law. The government suppresses internal disorder (with police) and guards the nation against external threats (with the military). As a relatively new form of sociopolitical organization, states have

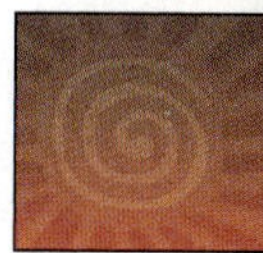

beyond the classroom

Perspectives on Group Membership

BACKGROUND INFORMATION

Student:	*Abigail Dreibelbis*
Supervising Professor:	*Miriam Chaiken*
School:	*Indiana University of Pennsylvania*
Year in School/Major:	*Senior/Anthropology*
Future Plans:	*Seeking positions in resource management and environmental protection*
Project Title:	*Delta, Delta, Delta, Can I Help Ya, Help Ya, Help Ya*

This research examines reasons why college women do or don't join sororities. Does the achieved status of sorority membership differ significantly from the mainly ascribed group memberships discussed in this chapter? Do you think that men join fraternities for the same reasons women join sororities? What relation do you see between the Greek system on college campuses and politics?

There is a human need for belonging, for affiliation. Identification with a group that has common norms and roles helps fulfill this need for security and creates social bonds that establish and assure companionship and personal identification.

This understanding has come from the study I did on members and nonmembers of social sororities at Indiana University of Pennsylvania. Since I started college, I had noticed a dichotomy between these two groups. I wanted to find out the real and perceived differences between them. My hypothesis was that there was a higher level of need for group identity and involvement in sorority members, and conversely more independence in nonmembers. I formed a survey for both groups, with questions about demographics and activities and I used open-ended questions to elicit their views and followed up with in-depth interviews to get a more personal response.

I found that participation in high school student government had been three times higher for members of sororities. This showed the great importance of social identity for Greeks, as student government members have prestige as a minority segment of the student body. Membership is competitive and based on peer acceptance. Conversely, activity in the arts was twice as high in the independent (nonsorority) group. This is a more aes-

competed successfully with less-complex societies throughout the world. Military organization helps states subdue neighboring nonstates, but this is not the only reason for the spread of state organization. Although states impose hardships, they also offer advantages. More obviously, they provide protection from outsiders and preserve internal order. They curb the feuding that has plagued tribes such as the Yanomami and the Nuer. By promoting internal peace, states enhance production. Their economies support massive, dense populations, which supply armies and colonists to promote expansion.

Fiscal Systems

A financial or **fiscal** system is needed in states to support rulers, nobles, officials, judges, military personnel, and thousands of other specialists. As in the chiefdom, the state intervenes in production, distribution, and consumption. The state may decree that a certain area will produce certain things or forbid certain activities in particular places. Although, like chiefdoms, states also have redistribution (through taxation), generosity and sharing are played down. A smaller proportion of what comes in flows back to the people.

thetic, personal activity, done for the act itself (singing or performing) rather than to gain the acceptance of peers.

The affinity for group identity is reflected in the expressed reasons for joining a sorority. Members found a "sense of belonging" and "self-confidence." Independents cited these same as reasons for joining, yet they saw this need as negative, and leading to a "group identity [that] is their identity." They did not like the "controlling" qualities of the sorority. The sorority member acknowledges the search for social and personal identification in a group as well as the resulting gratification in joining.

It has been hypothesized that the eldest child is the most independent. I found that twice as many nonsorority women were the oldest siblings in their family. Independents "just weren't the type" for a sorority. Nonmembers seem to find identity or belonging through other groups (volunteering, sports, honors societies) more for personal interest than social merit. This statistic seemed to support the idea that women who join sororities have a higher value of social involvement and acceptance for security and identity.

Everyone finds support and identity in groups. Groups provide safety along with a sense of personal worth and common identity with at least a few people in this vast world. Through my research I found that this need varies in degree among individuals. Those with a higher level of need find fulfillment in a social group such as a sorority. Non-Greeks do not value and are less dependent on such a social identity. These personality differences may create a sense of separation between the two groups and result in the dichotomy observed on campus.

It was fulfilling to challenge my hypothesis through questions of my own making and to come to an understanding of how and why people function. By gaining these insights on aspects of personality that underlie culture, I have developed a broader view of the intangible differences that affect our daily interactions.

In nonstates, people customarily share with relatives, but residents of states face added obligations to bureaucrats and officials. Citizens must turn over a substantial portion of what they produce to the state. Of the resources that the state collects, it reallocates part for the general good and uses another part (often larger) for the elite.

The state does not bring more freedom or leisure to the common people, who usually work harder than do the people in nonstates. They may be called on to build monumental public works. Some of these projects, such as dams and irrigation systems, may be economically necessary. However, people also build temples, palaces, and tombs for the elites.

Monument building began in chiefdoms, where "ceremonies of place" were associated with the creation of a "sacred landscape" through constructions such as (stone) henges of Europe, the mounds of the southeastern United States, and the temples of Hawaii (Earle 1987, 1991). Like chiefs, state officials may use religion to buttress their authority. Archaeology shows that temples abounded in early states. Even in mature states, rulers may link themselves to godhood through divine right or claim to be deities or their earthly representatives. Rulers convoke peons or slaves to build magnificent castles or tombs, cementing the ruler's place in history or status in the afterlife. Monumental architecture survives as an enduring reminder of the exalted prestige of priests and kings.

Markets and trade are usually under at least some state control, with officials overseeing distribution and exchange, standardizing weights and measures, and collecting taxes on goods passing into or through the state. Taxes support government and the ruling class, which is clearly separated from the common people in regard to activities, privileges, rights, and obligations. Taxes also support the many specialists: administrators, tax collectors, judges, lawmakers, generals, scholars, and priests. As the state matures, the segment of the population freed from direct concern with subsistence grows.

The elites of archaic states revel in the consumption of *sumptuary goods:* jewelry, exotic food and drink, and stylish clothing reserved for, or affordable only by, the rich. Peasants' diets suffer as they struggle to meet government demands. Commoners perish in territorial wars that have little relevance to their own needs.

summary

1. Many anthropologists make use of a sociopolitical typology that classifies societies as bands, tribes, chiefdoms, and states. Foragers tend to live in egalitarian band-organized societies. Personal networks link individuals, families, and bands. Band leaders are first among equals, with no sure way to enforce decisions. Disputes rarely arise over strategic resources, which are open to all. Political authority and power tend to increase along with population and the scale of regulatory problems. More people mean more relations among individuals and groups to regulate. Increasingly complex economies pose further regulatory problems.
2. Heads of horticultural villages are local leaders with limited authority. They lead by example and persuasion. Big men have support and authority beyond a single village. They are regional regulators, but temporary ones. In organizing a feast, they mobilize labor from several villages. Sponsoring such events leaves them with little wealth but with prestige and a reputation for generosity.
3. Another form of temporary regional organization is segmentary lineage organization (SLO). In societies with SLO, alliance is relative and based on genealogical distance. People support the disputant with whom they share the closest patrilineal ancestor. Disputes can mobilize the entire segmentary lineage—that is, the entire society—against outsiders.
4. Age and gender also can be used for regional political integration. Among North America's Plains Indians, men's associations (pantribal sodalities) organized raiding and buffalo hunting. Such men's associations tend to emphasize the warrior grade. They serve for offense and defense when there is intertribal raiding for animals. Among pastoralists, the degree of authority and political organization reflects population size and density, interethnic relations, and pressure on resources.
5. The state is an autonomous political unit that encompasses many communities. Its government collects taxes, drafts people for work and war, and decrees and enforces laws. The state is defined as a form of sociopolitical organization based on central government and social stratification—a division of society into classes. Early states are known as archaic, or nonindustrial, states, in contrast to modern industrial nation-states.
6. Unlike tribes, but like states, chiefdoms have permanent regional regulation and differential access to resources. But chiefdoms lack stratification. Unlike states, but like bands and tribes, chiefdoms are organized by kinship, descent, and marriage. State formation remained incomplete, and only chiefdoms emerged in several areas, including the circum-Caribbean, lowland Amazonia, the southeastern United States, and Polynesia.

7. Weber's three dimensions of stratification are wealth, power, and prestige. In early states—for the first time in human history—contrasts in wealth, power, and prestige between entire groups of men and women came into being. A socioeconomic stratum includes people of both sexes and all ages. The superordinate—higher or elite—stratum enjoys privileged access to resources.

8. Certain systems are found in all states: population control, judiciary, enforcement, and fiscal. These are integrated by a ruling system or government composed of civil, military, and religious officials. States conduct censuses and demarcate boundaries. Laws are based on precedent and legislative proclamations. Courts and judges handle disputes and crimes. A police force maintains internal order, and a military defends against external threats. A financial or fiscal system supports rulers, officials, judges, and other specialists.

key terms

age set Group uniting all men or women born during a certain time span; this group controls property and often has political and military functions.

big man Regional figure often found among tribal horticulturalists and pastoralists. The big man occupies no office but creates his reputation through entrepreneurship and generosity to others. Neither his wealth nor his position passes to his heirs.

chiefdom Form of sociopolitical organization intermediate between the tribe and the state; kin-based with differential access to resources and a permanent political structure.

differential access Unequal access to resources; basic attribute of chiefdoms and states. Superordinates have favored access to such resources, while the access of subordinates is limited by superordinates.

fiscal Pertaining to finances and taxation.

head, village A local leader in a tribal society who has limited authority, leads by example and persuasion, and must be generous.

law A legal code, including trial and enforcement; characteristic of state-organized societies.

office Permanent political position.

power The ability to exercise one's will over others—to do what one wants; the basis of political status.

prestige Esteem, respect, or approval for acts, deeds, or qualities considered exemplary.

segmentary lineage organization (SLO) Political organization based on descent, usually patrilineal, with multiple descent segments that form at different genealogical levels and function in different contexts.

sodality, pantribal A non-kin-based group that exists throughout a tribe, spanning several villages.

state Sociopolitical organization based on central government and socioeconomic stratification—a division of society into classes.

stratification Characteristic of a system with socioeconomic strata—groups that contrast in regard to social status and access to strategic resources. Each stratum includes people of both sexes and all ages.

subordinate The lower, or underprivileged, group in a stratified system.

superordinate The upper, or privileged, group in a stratified system.

tribe Form of sociopolitical organization usually based on horticulture or pastoralism. Socioeconomic stratification and centralized rule are absent in tribes, and there is no means of enforcing political decisions.

wealth All a person's material assets, including income, land, and other types of property; the basis of economic status.

critical thinking questions

1. What's the rationale for using the term "socio-political organization" instead of "political organization"?
2. Classify the Inuit, Yanomami, and Nuer according to Service's sociopolitical typology and according to Cohen's typology of adaptive strategies (see the chapter "Making a Living").
3. What is law? Does the absence of law entail social disorder?
4. What kinds of authority figures exist in bands? Compare them with Yanomami village heads. Do any authority figures in your own society remind you of such people in band and tribal society?
5. How do the political roles of village head and big man differ? Does your own society have figures comparable to big men?
6. How is segmentary lineage organization (SLO) similar to a big man system?
7. What are sodalities? Does your society have them? Do you belong to any?
8. What conclusions do you draw from this chapter about the relationship between population density and political hierarchy?
9. What are the main similarities and differences between chiefdoms and tribes? In which would you like to live and why?
10. What are the main similarities and differences between chiefdoms and states? In which would you prefer to live and why?
11. In your opinion, how does redistribution differ from taxation?
12. Give examples from your own society of the four special-purpose subsystems found in all states.
13. What are the advantages and disadvantages of the state from the ordinary citizen's perspective?

case study

Kapauku: This chapter has discussed the formal and informal leadership roles found in various societies, among them that of the "big man." In *Culture Sketches* by Holly Peters-Golden, read the chapter on the "Kapauku: New Guinea 'Capitalists.'" An important role in Kapauku society is the *tonowi*, a "big man." How is this leadership role related to the other key features of Kapauku society, such as individualism and economics?

suggested additional readings

Arnold, B., and B. Gibson, eds.

1995 *Celtic Chiefdom, Celtic State.* New York: Cambridge University Press. This collection of articles examines the structure and development of Europe's prehistoric Celtic societies and debates whether they were chiefdoms or states.

Borneman, J.

1998 *Subversions of International Order: Studies in the Political Anthropology of Culture.* Albany: State University of New York Press. Political culture, international relations, world politics, and national characteristics.

Chagnon, N.

1997 *Yanomamö*, 5th ed. Fort Worth: Harcourt Brace. Most recent revision of a well-known account of the Yanomami, including their social organization, politics, warfare, cultural change, and the crisis they now confront.

Cheater, A. P., ed.

1999 *The Anthropology of Power: Empowerment and Disempowerment in Changing Structures*. New York: Routledge. Overcoming social marginality through participation and political mobilization in today's world.

Cohen, R., and E. R. Service, eds.

1978 *Origins of the State: The Anthropology of Political Evolution*. Philadelphia: Institute for the Study of Human Issues. Several articles on state formation in many areas.

Earle, T. K.

1997 *How Chiefs Come to Power: The Political Economy in Prehistory*. Stanford, CA: Stanford University Press. Political succession and the economic basis of power in chiefdoms.

Ferguson, R. B.

1995 *Yanomami Warfare: A Political History*. Santa Fe, NM: School of American Research. From village raiding to incursions from nation-states.

Heider, K. G.

1997 *Grand Valley Dani: Peaceful Warriors*, 3rd ed. Fort Worth: Harcourt Brace. Comprehensive and readable account of a tribal group on the island of New Guinea, now under Indonesian rule.

Johnson, A. W., and T. K. Earle

2000 *The Evolution of Human Societies: From Foraging Group to Agrarian State*, 2nd ed. Stanford, CA: Stanford University Press. Recent revision of important study of human social evolution.

Kelly, R. C.

2000 *Warless Societies and the Origin of War*. Ann Arbor, MI: University of Michigan Press. An anthropologist looks at stateless societies in Papua New Guinea to reconstruct the origins of warfare.

Kirch, P. V.

1984 *The Evolution of the Polynesian Chiefdoms*. Cambridge: Cambridge University Press. Diversity and sociopolitical complexity in native Oceania.

2000 *On the Road of the Winds: An Archaeological History of the Pacific Islands before European Contact*. Berkeley, CA: University of California Press. The settling and development of island societies where chiefdoms arose.

Kurtz, D. V.

2001 *Political Anthropology: Power and Paradigms*. Boulder, CO: Westview. Up-to-date treatment of the field of political anthropology.

Saitoti, T. O.

1988 *The Worlds of a Masai Warrior: An Autobiography*. Berkeley: University of California Press. The autobiography of a former warrior from Kenya.

Wolf, E. R., with S. Silverman

2001 *Pathways of Power: Building an Anthropology of the Modern World*. Berkeley, CA: University of California Press. Political and social identity and power in the modern world.

internet exercises

1. *Subsistence and Status:* Go to the Ethnographic Atlas Cross-tabulations page, **http://lucy.ukc.ac.uk/cgi-bin/uncgi/Ethnoatlas/atlas.vopts.** This site has compiled ethnographic information on many different groups, and you can use the tools provided to cross-tabulate the prevalence of certain traits. Go to the site; under "Select Row Category" choose "subsistence economy," and under "Select Column Category" select "class stratification, prevailing type." Press the Submit Query button. This table shows the frequency of class stratification among groups with different subsistence strategies.
   a. What kinds of subsistence strategies are most common among groups with "Complex" class stratification? Do any of these groups use hunting, gathering, or fishing as the primary means of feeding themselves?

b. Is any one subsistence strategy predominant among groups with "Absence among freemen" class stratification (egalitarian)?

c. Looking at the table, which of the following statements is (are) true: All societies with complex class stratification are agriculturalists; All agriculturalists have complex class stratification; No societies that practice hunting, fishing, and gathering have complex class stratification; All hunting, fishing, and gathering societies have class stratification absent among freemen (egalitarian).

2. Read the Mesa Community College page on "A Look at Bigman: Bougainville," **http:/www.mc.maricopa.edu/academic/cult_sci/anthro/lost_tribes/bigman/mumi.html** and their "Rules for a Bigman," **http://www.mc.maricopa.edu/academic/cult_sci/anthro/lost_tribes/bigman/rules.html.**

   a. Where is Bougainville? What is the environment like? What are the main sources of food?

   b. What is a *mumi?* How does one become a *mumi?* What role do feasts play in determining who is a *mumi?* How important are friends and family for an aspiring *mumi?*

   c. What other statuses exist in Bougainville society for men?

   d. After reading the rules for a bigman, does the life of a bigman appear to be a life of leisure or does it involve a lot of work?

3. In the year 2000, the field of anthropology was jolted by the announcement of the publication of a book called *Darkness in El Dorado* by the journalist Patrick Tierney (New York: W. W. Norton, 2000). The book contained accusations of inappropriate, unethical, and perhaps even criminal behavior by scientists who had studied the Yanomami Indians of Brazil and Venezuela since the late 1960s.

   a. For a brief account of the controversy, check out **www.salon.com/books/feature/2000/09/ 28/yanomamo/index.html.**

   b. For the author's main arguments and response to his critics, go to the book's official website: **http://darknessineldorado.com.**

   c. Now visit various sites that document the history of the controversy, offer critiques of Tierney's account, and rebut the changes in his book: **http://www.anth.uconn.edu/gradstudents/dhume/index.htm; http://www.anth.ucsb/edu/chagnon.html; http://www.umich.edu/~urel/darkness.html; http://www.umich.edu/~idpah/.**

   d. What do you make of the controversy? Is it possible to choose sides from the information you have examined?

   e. What are the larger ethical issues raised by the furor surrounding Tierney's book?

See Chapter 17 on your CD-ROM for additional review and interactive exercises. See your McGraw-Hill Online Learning Center for more.

Chapter 18

Gender

CHAPTER OUTLINE

NYTIMES.COM NEWS BRIEFS

A Conversation with Dr. Nawal M. Nour: A Life Devoted to Stopping the Suffering of Mutilation

by Claudia Dreifus
July 11, 2000

BOSTON . . . There is nothing quite like the African Women's Health Practice of the obstetrics and gynecology department at Brigham and Women's Hospital here. . . This unusual clinic is the brainchild of Dr. Nawal M. Nour, 34, a Sudanese-born, Harvard-trained gynecologist whose 1988 Brown University undergraduate thesis was "The Emancipation of the Egyptian Woman."

A crusader against female circumcision, Dr. Nour founded the clinic to help women who had been mutilated and to give her a platform to organize doctors and other professionals against the ritual. . .

Q. When did you first become aware of female circumcision?

A. Early. I grew up in the Sudan, Egypt and Great Britain, and so, for as long as I can remember, I was aware of it . . . At school, I remember the girls saying: "I was circumcised. Have you been?" I remember one girl saying she'd been circumcised and that it hurt, but it was a good thing because now she was a woman . . .

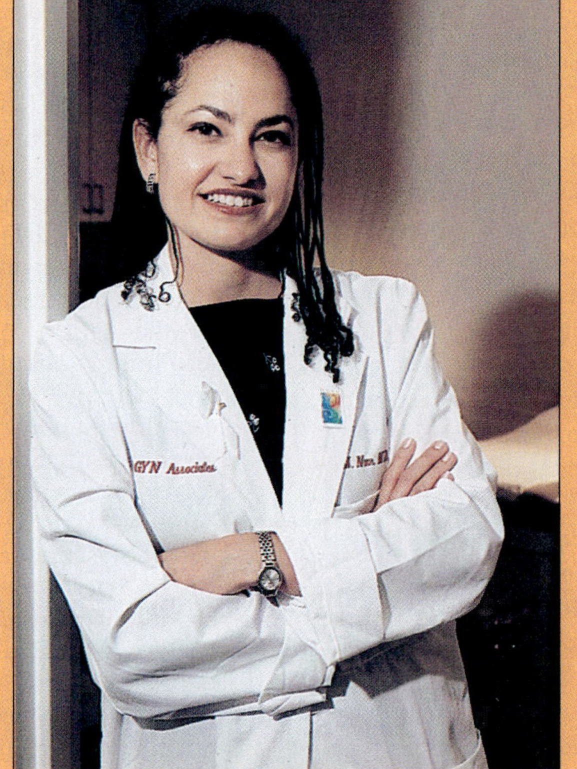

As a child, I couldn't understand why people would do something that wasn't good for them. I think I became a physician so that I could find an effective way to attack it . . .

Q. How did this African women's clinic begin?

A. In 1995 . . . I started attracting patients from the Sudan, Ethiopia, Somalia and West Africa. I became known in the immigrant community around Boston as that "African woman doctor." . . . Most of these women who came to me, obviously, had undergone female circumcision. So eventually, I went to people from the immigrant community and asked, "Would you like for me to open an African clinic for Africans?" People were very excited . . .

Q. What kinds of clinical problems do your circumcised patients bring to you?

A. The major complications are seen on women who have undergone Type 3 circumcision. Type 1 removes the clitoris—this is common in Ethiopia. Type 2 excises the clitoris and the inner vaginal lips, which may end up fusing together. Type 3 is removing the clitoris, the inner lips, the outer lips, then sewing everything together, leaving only a very small opening for urination and menses.

This is mainly done among Somalis and Sudanese and in parts of West Africa . . . The women who've undergone Type 3 can have scarring problems and problems with their menses.

Some of them have terrible trouble having sex with their husbands . . . I saw a woman the other week who was pregnant and had a pencil-sized opening . . . If a patient is considering getting pregnant and she has a very small opening as a result of the circumcision, I encourage her to be opened up. If she is coming in with chronic urinary tract infections, pain on intercourse or pain in menses, I often suggest it, too.

Q. . . . Have you gained any insight on why female cicumcision persists?

A. . . . People do it because of a deeply ingrained belief that they are protecting their daughters. This is not done to be hurtful, but out of love. The parents do it because they think this is necessary to ensure that their daughters will get married. They love their children. These are the same parents who in time of war of famine will give up their food so that the children will be fed.

Source: http://www.nytimes.com/library/national/science/health/071100hth-conversation-nour.html.

overview

Gender refers to the cultural construction of sexual differences. Male and female are biological sexes that differ in their X and Y chromosomes. Culture takes that biological difference and associates it with certain activities, behavior, and ideas. Some cultures recognize more than two genders.

Gender roles are the activities a culture assigns to each sex. Gender stratification describes an unequal distribution of resources between men and women. Sometimes, a distinction between women's domestic work and men's extradomestic "productive" labor can reinforce a contrast between men as public and valuable and women as domestic and less valuable. Gender stratification varies with the economy, political system, rule of descent, and postmarital residence pattern. Matrilineal and bilateral societies tend to have less gender stratification than patrilineal-patrilocal societies do.

Anthropological evidence casts some doubt on the idea that sexual orientation is fixed. To some extent at least, erotic expression is learned and malleable. Despite individual variation in sexual orientation within a society, culture always plays a role in molding individual sexual urges toward a collective norm. Sexual norms vary widely from culture to culture.

Patriarchy describes a political system in which women have inferior social and political status, including basic human rights. Although anthropologists know of no matriarchies, women in many societies do wield power and lead.

Economic forces have contributed to recent changes in gender roles and stratification. In North America, female cash labor has increased, promoting greater economic and social autonomy of many women. But also increasing, globally, is the feminization of poverty, the rise in the percentages of female-headed households and of poor families headed by women.

Because anthropologists study biology, society, and culture, they are in a unique position to comment on nature (biological predispositions) and nurture (environment) as determinants of human behavior. Human attitudes, values, and behavior are limited not only by our genetic predispositions—which are often difficult to identify—but also by our experiences during enculturation. Our attributes as adults are determined both by our genes and by our environment during growth and development.

Debate about the effects of nature and nurture proceeds today in scientific and public arenas. **Biological determinists** assume that some—they differ about how much—of human behavior and social organization is biologically determined. **Cultural determinists** find most attempts to link behavior to genes unconvincing. They assume that human evolutionary success rests on flexibility, or the ability to adapt in various ways. Because human adaptation relies so strongly on cultural learning, we can change our behavior more readily than members of other species can.

The nature–nurture debate emerges in the discussion of human sex-gender roles and sexuality. Men and women differ genetically. Women have two X chromosomes, and men have an X and a Y. The father determines a baby's sex because only he has the Y chromosome to transmit. The mother always provides an X chromosome.

The chromosomal difference is expressed in hormonal and physiological contrasts. Humans are sexually dimorphic, more so than some primates, such as gibbons (small tree-living Asiatic apes), less so than others, such as gorillas and orangutans. **Sexual dimorphism** refers to differences in male and female biology besides the contrasts in breasts and genitals. Women and men differ not just in primary (genitalia and reproductive organs) and secondary (breasts, voice, hair distribution) sexual characteristics but in average weight, height, strength, and longevity. Women tend to live longer than men and have excellent endurance capabilities. In a given population, men tend to be taller and to weigh more than women do. Of course, there is a considerable overlap between the sexes in terms of height, weight, and physical strength, and there has been a pronounced reduction in sexual dimorphism during human biological evolution.

The realm of cultural diversity contains richly different social constructions and expressions of gender roles, as is illustrated by these Bororo male dancers. For what reasons do men decorate their bodies in our society?

Just how far, however, do such genetically and physiologically determined differences go? What effects do they have on the way men and women act and are treated in different cultures? On the cultural determinist side, anthropologists have discovered substantial variability in the roles of men and women in different cultures. The anthropological position on sex-gender roles and biology may be stated as follows:

> The biological nature of men and women [should be seen] not as a narrow enclosure limiting the human organism, but rather as a broad base upon which a variety of structures can be built. (Friedl 1975, p.6)

Although in most cultures men tend to be somewhat more aggressive than women, many of the behavioral and attitudinal differences between the sexes emerge from culture rather than biology. *Sex* differences are biological, but *gender* encompasses all the traits that a culture assigns to and inculcates in males and females. "Gender," in other words, refers to the cultural construction of male and female characteristics (Rosaldo 1980*b*).

Given the "rich and various constructions of gender" within the realm of cultural diversity, Susan Bourque and Kay Warren (1987) note that the same images of masculinity and femininity do not always apply. Margaret Mead did an early ethnographic study of variation in gender roles. Her book *Sex and Temperament in Three Primitive Societies* (1935/1950) was based on field work in three societies in Papua New Guinea: Arapesh, Mundugumor, and Tchambuli. The extent of personality variation in men and women in these three societies on the same island amazed Mead. She found that Arapesh men and women both acted as Americans have traditionally expected women to act: in a mild, parental, responsive way. Mundugumor men and women both, in contrast, acted as she believed we expect men to act: fiercely and aggressively. Tchambuli men were "catty," wore curls, and went shopping, but Tchambuli women were energetic and managerial and placed less emphasis on personal adornment than did the men. [Drawing on their recent case study of the Tchambuli, whom they call the Chambri, Errington and Gewertz (1987), while recognizing gender malleability, have disputed the specifics of Mead's account.]

There is a well-established field of feminist scholarship within anthropology (di Leonardo 1991; Nash and Safa 1986; Rosaldo 1980*b*; Strathern 1988). Anthropologists have gathered systematic ethnographic data about gender in many cultural settings (Bonvillain 2001; Morgen 1989; Mukhopadhyay and Higgins 1988; Peplau 1999; Ward 1996). We can see that the gender roles vary with environment, economy, adaptive strategy, and type of political system. Before we examine the cross-cultural data, some definitions are in order.

Gender roles are the tasks and activities that a culture assigns to the sexes. Related to gender roles are **gender stereotypes,** which are oversimplified but strongly held ideas about the characteristics of males and females. **Gender stratification** describes an unequal distribution of rewards (socially valued resources, power, prestige, and personal freedom) between men and women, reflecting their different positions in a social hierarchy. According to Ann Stoler (1977), the "economic determinants of female status" include freedom or autonomy (in disposing of one's labor and its fruits) and social power (control over the lives, labor, and produce of others).

In stateless societies, gender stratification is often more obvious in regard to prestige than it is in regard to wealth. In her study of the Ilongots of northern Luzon in the Philippines, Michelle Rosaldo (1980*a*) described gender differences related to the positive cultural value placed on adventure, travel, and knowledge of the external world. More often than women, Ilongot men, as headhunters, visited distant places. They acquired knowledge of the external world, amassed experiences there, and returned to express their knowledge, adventures, and feelings in public oratory. They received acclaim as a result. Ilongot women had inferior prestige because they lacked external experiences on which to base knowledge and dramatic expression. On the basis of Rosaldo's study and findings in other stateless societies, Ong (1989) argues that we must distinguish between prestige systems and actual power in a given society. High male prestige may not entail economic or political power held by men over their families.

Gender among Foragers

Several studies have shown that economic roles affect gender stratification. In one cross-cultural study, Peggy Sanday (1974) found that gender stratification decreased when men and women made roughly equal contributions to subsistence. She found that gender stratification was *greatest* when the women contributed either *much more* or *much less* than the men did.

This finding applied mainly to food producers, not to foragers. In foraging societies, gender stratification was most marked when men contributed much *more* to the diet than women did. This was true among the Inuit and other northern hunters and fishers. Among tropical and semitropical foragers, by contrast, gathering usually supplies more food than hunting and fishing do. Gathering is generally women's work. Men usually hunt and fish, but women also do some fishing and may hunt small animals. When gathering is prominent, gender status tends to be more equal than it is when hunting and fishing are the main subsistence activities.

Gender status is also more equal when the domestic and public spheres aren't sharply sepa-

Among foragers, gender stratification tends to increase when men contribute much more to the diet than women do—as has been true among the Inuit and other northern hunters and fishers. Shown here, unable to bring a whale ashore for butchering, these Inuit are taking its *muktuk* (skin and blubber).

rated. (*Domestic* means within or pertaining to the home.) Strong differentiation between the home and the outside world is called the **domestic–public dichotomy** or the *private–public contrast.* The outside world can include politics, trade, warfare, or work. Often when domestic and public spheres are clearly separated, public activities have greater prestige than domestic ones do. This can promote gender stratification, because men are more likely to be active in the public domain than women are. Cross-culturally, women's activities tend to be closer to home than men's are. Thus, another reason hunter-gatherers have less gender stratification than food producers do is that the domestic–public dichotomy is more developed among food producers.

A division of labor linked to gender has been found in all cultures. However, the particular tasks assigned to men and women vary from society to society. Food producers often assign the arduous tasks of carrying water and firewood and pounding grain to women. In 1967 in the Soviet Union, women filled 47 percent of the factory positions, including many unmechanized jobs requiring hard physical labor. Most Soviet sanitation workers, physicians, and nurses were women (Martin and Voorhies 1975). Many jobs that men do in some societies are done by women in others, and vice versa.

Certain roles are more sex-linked than others. Men are the usual hunters and warriors. Given such weapons as spears, knives, and bows, men make better fighters because they are bigger and stronger on the average than are women in the same population (Divale and Harris 1976). The male hunter-fighter role also reflects a tendency toward greater male mobility.

In foraging societies, women are either pregnant or lactating during most of their childbearing period. Late in pregnancy and after childbirth, carrying a baby limits a woman's movements, even her gathering. However, among the Agta of the Philippines (Griffin and Estioko-Griffin, eds. 1985) women not only gather, they also hunt with dogs while carrying their babies with them. Still, given the effects of pregnancy and lactation on mobility, it is rarely feasible for women to be the primary hunters (Friedl 1975). Warfare, which also requires mobility, is not found in most foraging societies, nor is interregional trade well developed. Warfare and trade are two public arenas that contribute to status inequality of males and females among food producers.

The Ju/'hoansi San illustrate the extent to which the activities and spheres of influence of men and women may overlap among foragers (Draper 1975). Traditional Ju/'hoansi gender roles were interdependent. During gathering, women discovered information about game animals, which they passed on to the men. Men and women spent about the same amount of time away from the camp, but neither worked more than three days a week. Between one-third and one-half of the band stayed home while the others worked.

The Ju/'hoansi saw nothing wrong in doing the work of the other gender. Men often gathered food and collected water. A general sharing ethos dictated that men distribute meat and that women share the fruits of gathering. Boys and girls of all ages played together. Fathers took an active role in raising children. Resources were adequate, and competition and aggression were discouraged. Exchangeability and interdependence of roles are adaptive in small groups.

Patricia Draper's field work among the Ju/'hoansi is especially useful in showing the relationships between economy, gender roles, and stratification because she studied both foragers and a group of former foragers who had become sedentary. Just a few thousand Ju/'hoansi continue their culture's traditional foraging pattern. Most are now sedentary, living near food producers or ranchers (see Kent 1992; Solway and Lee 1990; Wilmsen 1989).

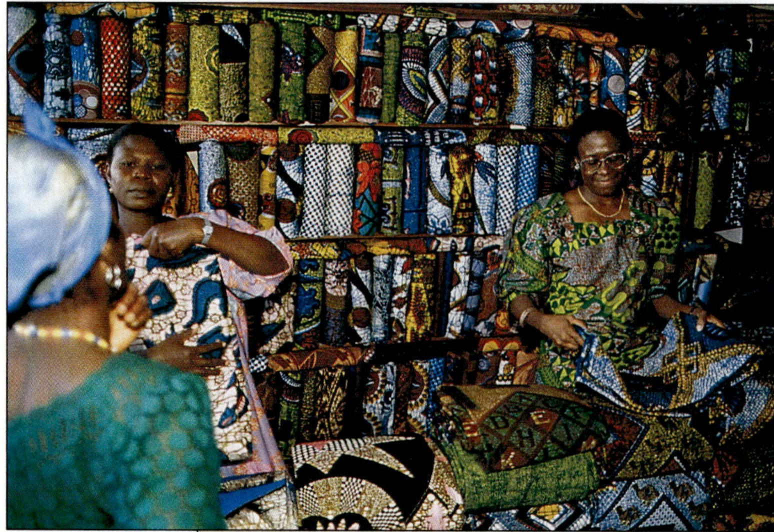

Many jobs that men do in some societies are done by women in others, and vice versa. In West Africa, women play a prominent role in trade and marketing. In Togo, shown here, women dominate textile sales. Is there a textile shop near you? Who runs it?

Draper studied sedentary Ju/'hoansi at Mahopa, a village where they herded, grew crops, worked for wages, and did a small amount of gathering. Their gender roles were becoming more rigidly defined. A domestic–public dichotomy was developing as men traveled farther than women did. With less gathering, women were confined more to the home. Boys could gain mobility through herding, but girls' movements were more limited. The equal and communal world of the bush was yielding to the social features of sedentary life. A differential ranking of men according to their herds, houses, and sons began to replace sharing. Males came to be seen as the most valuable producers.

If there is some degree of male dominance in every contemporary society, it may be because of changes such as those that have drawn the Ju/'hoansi into wage work, market sales, and thus the world capitalist economy. A historical interplay between local, national, and international forces influences systems of gender stratification (Ong 1989). In traditional foraging cultures, however, egalitarianism extended to the relations between the sexes. The social spheres, activities, rights, and obligations of men and women overlapped. Foragers' kinship systems tend to be bilateral (calculated equally through males and females) rather than favoring either the mother's side or the father's side. Foragers may live with either the husband's or the wife's kin and often shift between one group and the other.

One last observation about foragers: It is among them that the public and private spheres are least separate, hierarchy is least marked, aggression and competition are most discouraged, and the rights, activities, and spheres of influence of men and women overlap the most. Our ancestors lived entirely by foraging until 10,000 years ago. If there is any most "natural" form of human society, it is best, although imperfectly, represented by foragers. Despite the popular stereotype of the club-wielding caveman dragging his mate by the hair, relative gender equality is a much more likely ancestral pattern.

Gender among Horticulturalists

Gender roles and stratification among cultivators vary widely, depending on specific features of the economy and social structure. Demonstrating this, Martin and Voorhies (1975) studied a sample

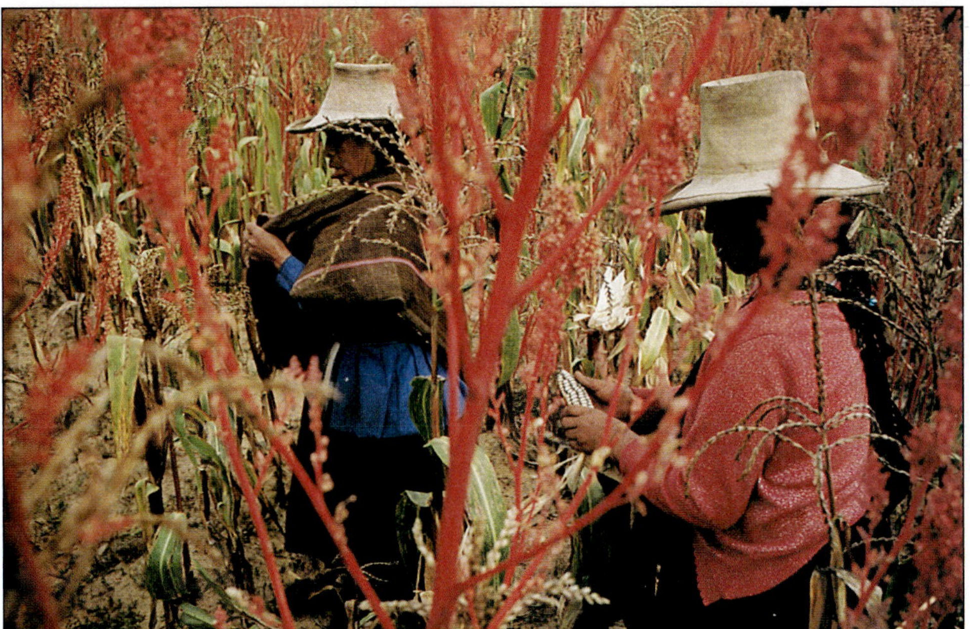

Women are the main producers in horticultural societies. Women like these South American corn farmers do most of the cultivating in such societies. What kinds of roles do women play in contemporary North American farming?

of 515 horticultural societies, representing all parts of the world. They looked at several variables, including descent and postmarital residence, the percentage of the diet derived from cultivation, and the productivity of men and women.

Women were found to be the main producers in horticultural societies. In 50 percent of those societies, women did most of the cultivating. In 33 percent, contributions to cultivation by men and women were equal. In only 17 percent did men do most of the work. Women tended to do a bit more cultivating in matrilineal compared with patrilineal societies. They dominated horticulture in 64 percent of the matrilineal societies versus 50 percent of the patrilineal ones.

Reduced Gender Stratification—Matrilineal, Matrilocal Societies

Cross-cultural variation in gender status is related to rules of descent and postmarital residence (Friedl 1975; Martin and Voorhies 1975). Among horticulturalists with matrilineal descent and *matrilocality* (residence after marriage with the wife's relatives, so that children grow up in their mother's village), female status tends to be high. Matriliny and matrilocality disperse related males, rather than consolidating them. By contrast, patriliny and *patrilocality* (residence after marriage with the husband's kin) keep male relatives together, an advantage given warfare. Matrilineal-matrilocal systems tend to occur in societies where population pressure on strategic resources is minimal and warfare is infrequent.

Women tend to have high status in matrilineal, matrilocal societies for several reasons. Descent-group membership, succession to political positions, allocation of land, and overall social identity all come through female links. In Negeri Sembilan, Malaysia (Peletz 1988), matriliny gave women sole inheritance of ancestral rice fields. Matrilocality created solidarity clusters of female kin. Women had considerable influence beyond the household (Swift 1963). In such matrilineal contexts, women are the basis of the entire social structure. Although public authority may be (or may appear to be) assigned to the men, much of the power and decision making may actually belong to the senior women.

Anthropologists have never discovered a **matriarchy,** a society ruled by women. Still, some matrilineal societies, including the *Iroquois* (Brown 1975), a confederation of tribes in aboriginal New York, show that women's political and ritual influence can rival that of the men.

Women generally have high status in matrilineal, matrilocal societies. Descent-group membership, succession to office and land, and overall social identity come through female links. In Negeri Sembilan, Malaysia, matriliny lets women inherit rice fields and enables clusters of female kin to live their lives together. Do we have customs or institutions that promote the solidarity of female kin?

We saw that among foragers, gender status was most equal when there was no sharp separation of male and female activities and of public and domestic spheres. However, gender stratification also can be reduced by roles that remove men from the local community. We now refine our generalizations: It is the sharp contrast between male and female roles *within the local community* that promotes gender stratification. Gender stratification may be reduced when women play prominent local roles, while men pursue activities in a wider, regional system. Iroquois women, for example, played a major subsistence role, while men left home for long periods. As is usual in matrilineal societies, *internal* warfare was uncommon. Iroquois men waged war only on distant groups; this could keep them away for years.

Iroquois men hunted and fished, but women controlled the local economy. Women did some fishing and occasional hunting, but their major productive role was in horticulture. Women owned the land, which they inherited from matrilineal kinswomen. Women controlled the production and distribution of food.

Iroquois women lived with their husbands and children in the family compartments of a communal longhouse. Women born in a longhouse remained there for life. Senior women, or *matrons,* decided which men could join the longhouse as husbands, and they could evict incompatible men. Women therefore controlled alliances between descent groups, an important political job in tribal society.

Iroquois women thus managed production and distribution. Social identity, succession to office and titles, and property all came through the female line, and women were prominent in ritual and politics. Related tribes made up a confederacy, the League of the Iroquois, with chiefs and councils.

A council of male chiefs managed military operations, but chiefly succession was matrilineal. The matrons of each longhouse nominated a man as their representative. If the council rejected their first nominee, the women proposed others until one was accepted. Matrons constantly monitored the chiefs and could impeach them. Women could veto war declarations, withhold provisions for war, and initiate peace efforts. In religion, too, women shared power. Half the tribe's religious practitioners were women, and the matrons helped select the others.

Reduced Gender Stratification—Matrifocal Societies

Nancy Tanner (1974) also found that the combination of male travel and a prominent female economic role reduced gender stratification and promoted high female status. She based this finding on a survey of the **matrifocal** (mother-

Historic territory of the Iroquois.

centered, often with no resident husband-father) organization of certain societies in Indonesia, West Africa, and the Caribbean. Matrifocal societies are not necessarily matrilineal. A few are even patrilineal.

For example, Tanner (1974) found matrifocality among the Igbo of eastern Nigeria, who are patrilineal, patrilocal, and polygynous (men have multiple wives). Each wife had her own house, where she lived with her children. Women planted crops next to their houses and traded surpluses. Women's associations ran the local markets, while men did the long-distance trading.

In a case study of the Igbo, Ifi Amadiume (1987) noted that either sex could fill male gender roles. Before Christian influence, successful Igbo women and men used wealth to take titles and acquire wives. Wives freed husbands (male and female) from domestic work and helped them accumulate wealth. Female husbands were not considered masculine but preserved their femininity. Igbo women asserted themselves in women's groups, including those of lineage daughters, lineage wives, and a community-wide women's council led by titled women. The high status and influence of Igbo women rested on the separation of males from local subsistence and on a marketing system that encouraged women to leave home and gain prominence in distribution and—through these accomplishments—in politics.

Increased Gender Stratification—Patrilineal-Patrilocal Societies

The Igbo are unusual among patrilineal-patrilocal societies, many of which have marked gender stratification. Martin and Voorhies (1975) link the decline of matriliny and the spread of the

A significant number of female-centered, or matrifocal, households characterize many Caribbean societies, such as the Bahamas, shown here. As men travel, women pursue such economic activities as handicraft production and sales. This Cat Island beach scene shows a female-run basketry shop.

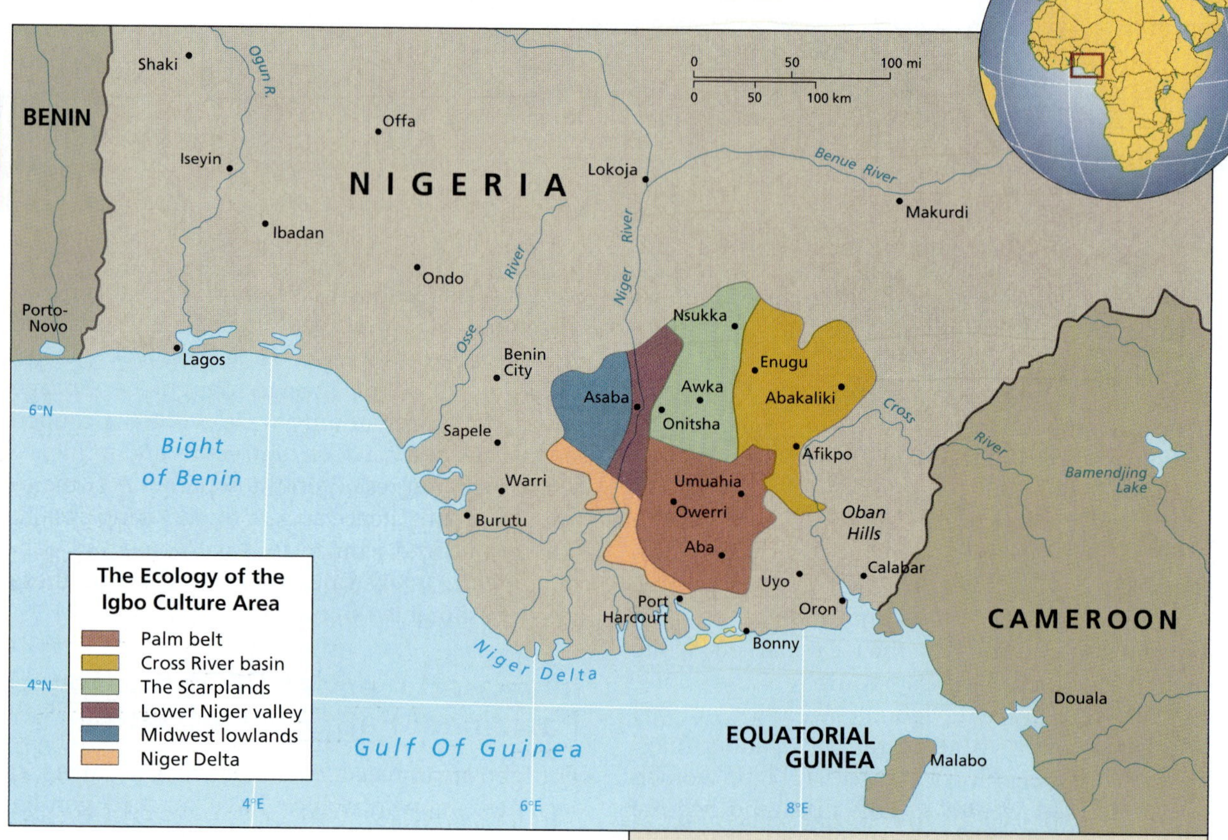

The Igbo cultural area in Nigeria, with its ecological subdivisions.

patrilineal-patrilocal complex (consisting of patrilineality, patrilocality, warfare, and male supremacy) to pressure on resources. Faced with scarce resources, patrilineal-patrilocal cultivators such as the Yanomami often wage warfare against other villages. This favors patrilocality and patriliny, customs that keep related men together in the same village, where they make strong allies in battle. Such societies tend to have a sharp domestic–public dichotomy, and men tend to dominate the prestige hierarchy. Men may use their public roles in warfare and trade and their greater prestige to symbolize and reinforce the devaluation or oppression of women.

The patrilineal-patrilocal complex characterizes many societies in highland Papua New Guinea. Women work hard growing and processing subsistence crops, raising and tending pigs (the main domesticated animal and a favorite food), and doing domestic cooking, but they are isolated from the public domain, which men control. Men grow and distribute prestige crops, prepare food for feasts, and arrange marriages. The men even get to trade the pigs and control their use in ritual.

In densely populated areas of the Papua New Guinea highlands, male–female avoidance is associated with strong pressure on resources (Lindenbaum 1972). Men fear all female contacts, including sex. They think that sexual contact with women will weaken them. Indeed, men see everything female as dangerous and polluting. They segregate themselves in men's houses and hide their precious ritual objects from women. They delay marriage, and some never marry.

By contrast, the sparsely populated areas of Papua New Guinea, such as recently settled areas, lack taboos on male–female contacts. The image of woman as polluter fades, heterosexual intercourse is valued, men and women live together, and reproductive rates are high.

In some parts of Papua New Guinea, the patrilineal-patrilocal complex has extreme social repercussions. Regarding females as dangerous and polluting, men may segregate themselves in men's houses (such as this one, located near the Sepik River), where they hide their precious ritual objects from women. Are there places like this in your society?

Homosexual Behavior among the Etoro

One of the most extreme examples of male–female sexual antagonism in Papua New Guinea comes from the *Etoro* (Kelly 1976), a group of 400 people who subsist by hunting and horticulture in the Trans-Fly region. The Etoro also illustrate the power of culture in molding human sexuality. The following account applies only to Etoro males and their beliefs. Etoro cultural norms prevented the male anthropologist who studied them from gathering comparable information about female attitudes. Etoro opinions about sexuality are linked to their beliefs about the cycle of birth, physical growth, maturity, old age, and death.

Etoro men believe that semen is necessary to give life force to a fetus, which is said to be placed within a woman by an ancestral spirit. Because men are believed to have a limited supply of semen, sexuality saps male vitality. The birth of children, nurtured by semen, symbolizes a necessary (and unpleasant) sacrifice that will lead to the husband's eventual death. Heterosexual intercourse, which is required only for reproduction, is discouraged. Women who want too much sex are viewed as witches, hazardous to their husbands' health. Etoro culture permits heterosexual intercourse only about 100 days a year. The rest of the time it is tabooed. Seasonal birth clustering shows that the taboo is respected.

So objectionable is heterosexuality that it is removed from community life. It can occur neither in sleeping quarters nor in the fields. Coitus can happen only in the woods, where it is risky because poisonous snakes, the Etoro say, are attracted by the sounds and smells of sex.

Although coitus is discouraged, homosexual acts are viewed as essential. Etoro believe that boys cannot produce semen on their own. To grow into men and eventually give life force to their children, boys must acquire semen orally from older men. From the age of 10 until adulthood, boys are inseminated by older men. No taboos are attached to this. Homosexual activity can go on in the sleeping area or garden. Every three years, a group of boys around the age of 20 are formally initiated into manhood. They go to a secluded mountain lodge, where they are visited and inseminated by several older men.

Etoro homosexuality is governed by a code of propriety. Although homosexual relations between older and younger males are culturally essential, those between boys of the same age are discouraged. A boy who gets semen from other youths is believed to be sapping their life force and stunting their growth. When a boy develops very rapidly, this suggests that he is ingesting semen from other boys. Like a sex-hungry wife, he is shunned as a witch.

Etoro homosexuality rests not on hormones or genes but on cultural traditions. The Etoro represent one extreme of a male–female avoidance pattern that is widespread in Papua New Guinea and in patrilineal-patrilocal societies.

Sexualities and Gender

The Etoro share a pattern, which Gilbert Herdt (1984) has characterized as ritualized homosexuality, with about 50 other tribes in Papua New Guinea, especially in that country's Trans-Fly region. These tribes illustrate cultural determinism by showing the extent to which culture can influence basic biological forces, such as sexual urges. Etoro culture regards male–female sex as unpleasant, although necessary for reproduction.

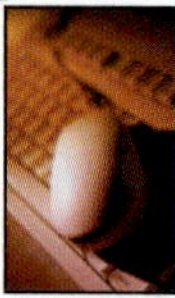

The taboos that apply to heterosexual coitus do not apply to male–male sex, which also is seen as necessary for reproduction, but which is viewed much more positively. For cultural reasons, Etoro men are freer to enjoy the sex they have with other men than they are to enjoy the sex they have with their wives.

Do the taboos that have surrounded homosexuality in our own society remind you of Etoro taboos? Homosexual activity has been stigmatized in Western industrial societies. Indeed, sodomy laws continue to make it illegal in many U.S. states. Among the Etoro, male–female sex is banned from the social center and moved to the fringes or margins of society (the woods, filled with dangerous snakes). In our own society, homosexual activity has traditionally been hidden, furtive, and secretive—also moved to the margins of society rather than its valued center. Imagine what our own sex lives would be like if we had been raised with Etoro beliefs and taboos.

Recently in the United States, there has been a tendency to see sexual orientation as fixed and probably biologically based. There is not enough information at this time to say for sure that sexual orientation is based on biology. What we can say is that to some extent at least, all human activities and preferences, including erotic expression, are learned and malleable. **Sexual orientation** stands for a person's habitual sexual attraction to, and activities with: persons of the opposite sex, *heterosexuality;* the same sex, *homosexuality;* or both sexes, *bisexuality. Asexuality,* indifference toward, or lack of attraction to, either sex, is also a sexual orientation. All four of these forms are found in contemporary North America, and throughout the world. But each type of desire and experience holds different meanings for individuals and groups. For example, an asexual disposition may be acceptable in some places but may be perceived as a character flaw in others. Bisexuality may be a private orientation in Mexico, rather than socially sanctioned and encouraged as among the Sambia of Papua New Guinea (see Kottak and Kozaitis 1999, Chapter 10).

In any culture, individuals will differ in the nature, range, and intensity of their sexual interests and urges. No one knows for sure why such individual sexual differences exist. Part of the answer may be biological, reflecting genes or hormones. Another part may have to do with experiences during growth and development. But whatever the reasons for individual variation, culture always plays a role in molding individual sexual urges toward a collective norm. And such sexual norms vary from culture to culture.

The western part of the island of New Guinea is part of Indonesia. The eastern part of the island is the independent nation of Papua New Guinea, home of the Etoro, Kaluli, and Sambia.

Since people differ within any culture, there'll always be some people who are more comfortable with the norm than others are. Some will follow the pack; some will trail, resist, or experiment with alternatives. Sometimes society will be tolerant of such experimentation; sometimes it won't. Often, as in our own society, sexual norms and mores will be hotly contested, with some people claiming to know what's right, and others bitterly disputing that claim. Sex then enters the world of politics. Part of the liberal/conservative split in evaluating the Clinton presidency rested on strongly different ideas about proper sex and the proper treatment of forms of sex viewed as illicit. The Clinton presidency began with a political dispute over "gays in the military." It drew to an end with disagreement about what would be proper punishment for "sex, lies, and videotape." (For more on the politics of sexual orientation, see Kottak and Kozaitis 1999, Chapter 10.)

What do we know about variation in sexual norms from culture to culture, and over time? A classic cross-cultural study (Ford and Beach 1951) found wide variation in attitudes about masturbation, bestiality (sex with animals), and homosexuality. Even in a single culture, such as the United States, attitudes about sex differ with socioeconomic status, region, and rural versus urban residence. However, even in the 1950s, prior to the "age of sexual permissiveness" (the pre-HIV period from the mid-1960s through the 1970s), research showed that almost all American men (92 percent) and more than half of American women (54 percent) admitted to masturbation. Between 40 and 50 percent of American farm boys had sex with animals. In the famous Kinsey report (Kinsey, Pomeroy, and Martin 1948), 37 percent of the men surveyed admitted having had at least one homosexual experience leading to orgasm. In a later study of 1,200 unmarried women, 26 percent reported same-sex sexual activities.

Attitudes toward homosexuality, masturbation, and bestiality in other cultures differ strikingly, as I find when I contrast the cultures I know best: the United States, urban and rural Brazil, and Madagascar. During my first stay in Arembepe, Brazil, when I was 19 years old and unmarried, young men told me details of their experience with prostitutes in the city. In Arembepe, a rural community, sex with animals was common. Targets of the male sex drive included cattle, horses, sheep, goats, and turkeys. Arembepe's women were also more open about their sex lives than North American women were at that time.

Arembepeiros talked about sex so willingly that I wasn't prepared for the silence and avoidance of sexual subjects that I encountered in Madagascar. My wife's and my discreet attempts to get the Betsileo to tell us at least the basics of their culture's sexual practices led nowhere. I did discover from city folk that, as in many non-Western cultures, traditional ceremonies were times of ritual license, when normal taboos lapsed and Betsileo men and women engaged in what Christian missionaries described as "wanton" sexuality. Only during my last week in Madagascar did a young man in the village of Ivato, where I had spent a year, take me aside and offer to write down the words for genitals and sexual intercourse. He could not say these tabooed words, but he wanted me to know them so that my knowledge of Betsileo culture would be as complete as possible.

I have never worked in a culture with institutionalized homosexuality of the sort that exists among several tribes in Papua New Guinea, such as Etoro, Kaluli (Schieffelin 1976), or Sambia (Herdt 1981, 1986). The Kaluli believe that semen has a magical quality that promotes knowledge and growth. Before traveling into alien territory, boys must eat a mixture of semen, ginger, and salt to enhance their ability to learn a foreign language. At age 11 or 12, a Kaluli boy forms a sexual relationship with an older man chosen by his father. (This man cannot be a relative, because that would violate their incest taboo.) The older man has anal intercourse with the boy. The Kaluli cite the boy's peach-fuzz beard, which appears thereafter, as evidence that semen is promoting growth. The young Kaluli men also have homosexual intercourse at the hunting lodges, where they spend an extended period learning the lore of the forest and the hunt from older bachelors.

Homosexual activities were absent, rare, or secret in only 37 percent of 76 societies for which data were available (Ford and Beach 1951). In the others, various forms of homosexuality were considered normal and acceptable. Sometimes sexual relations between people of the same sex involved transvestism on the part of one of the partners, like the *berdaches* discussed in the chapter "Marriage." See "Interesting Issues" for other examples of transvestism and men who have sex with men.

401

Transvestism did not characterize male–male sex among the Sudanese Azande, who valued the warrior role (Evans-Pritchard 1970). Prospective warriors—boys aged 12 to 20— left their families and shared quarters with adult fighting men, who paid bridewealth for, and had sex with, them. During this apprenticeship, the young men did the domestic duties of women. Upon reaching warrior status, those young men took their own younger male brides. Later, retiring from the warrior role, Azande men married women. Flexible in their sexual expression, Azande males had no difficulty shifting from sex with older men (as male brides), to sex with younger men (as warriors), to sex with women (as husbands).

There appears to be greater cross-cultural acceptance of homosexuality than of bestiality or masturbation. Most societies in the Ford and Beach (1951) study discouraged masturbation. Only five allowed human–animal sex. However, these figures measure only the social approval of sexual practices, not their actual frequency. As in our own society, socially disapproved sex acts are more widespread than people admit.

Flexibility in human sexual expression seems to be an aspect of our primate heritage. Both masturbation and homosexual behavior exist among chimpanzees and other primates. Male bonobos (pygmy chimps) regularly engage in a form of mutual masturbation known as "penis fencing." Female bonobos get sexual pleasure from rubbing their genitals against those of other females (De Waal 1997). Our primate sexual potential is molded by culture, the environment, and reproductive necessity. Heterosexuality is practiced in all human societies—which, after all, must reproduce themselves—but alternatives are also widespread (Davis and Whitten 1987; Rathus, Nevid, and Fichner-Rathus 2000). The sexual component of human personality—just how we express our "natural" sexual urges—is a matter that culture and environment determine and limit.

Gender among Agriculturalists

As horticulture developed into agriculture, women lost their role as primary cultivators. Certain agricultural techniques, particularly plowing, were assigned to men because of their greater average size and strength (Martin and Voorhies 1975). Except when irrigation was used, plowing eliminated the need for constant weeding, an activity usually done by women.

Cross-cultural data illustrate these changes in productive roles. Women were the main workers in 50 percent of the horticultural societies surveyed but in only 15 percent of the agricultural groups. Male subsistence labor dominated 81 percent of the agricultural societies but only 17 percent of the horticultural ones (Martin and Voorhies 1975) (see Table 18.1).

With agriculture, women were cut off from production for the first time in human history. Perhaps this reflected the need for women to stay closer to home to care for the larger numbers of children that typify agriculture, compared with less labor-intensive economies. Belief systems started contrasting men's valuable extradomestic labor with women's domestic role, now viewed as inferior. (**Extradomestic** means outside the home; within or pertaining to the public domain.) Changes in kinship and postmarital residence patterns also hurt women. Descent groups and polygyny declined with agriculture, and the nuclear family became more common. Living with her husband and children, a woman was isolated from her kinswomen and cowives. Female sexuality is carefully supervised in agricultural economies; men have easier access to divorce and extramarital sex, reflecting a "double standard."

Still, female status in agricultural societies is not inevitably bleak. Gender stratification is associated with plow agriculture rather than with intensive cultivation per se. Studies of peasant gender roles and stratification in France and Spain (Harding 1975; Reiter 1975), which have plow agriculture, show that people think of the house as the female sphere and the fields as the male domain. However, such a dichotomy is not inevitable, as my own research among Betsileo agriculturalists in Madagascar shows.

Betsileo women play a prominent role in agriculture, contributing a third of the hours invested in rice production. They have their customary tasks in the division of labor, but their work is more seasonal than men's is.

No one has much to do during the ceremonial season, between mid-June and mid-September. Men work in the rice fields almost daily the rest of the year. Women's cooperative work occurs during transplanting (mid-September through November) and harvesting (mid-March through early May). Along with other members of the household, women do daily weeding in December and January. After the harvest, all family members work together winnowing the rice and then transporting it to the granary.

If we consider the strenuous daily task of husking rice by pounding (a part of food preparation rather than production per se), women

Table 18.1
Male and Female Contributions to Production in Cultivating Societies

	Horticulture (Percentage of 104 Societies)	Agriculture (Percentage of 93 Societies)
Women are primary cultivators	50	15
Men are primary cultivators	17	81
Equal contributions to cultivation	33	3

Source: Martin and Voorhies 1975, p. 283.

interesting issues

Hidden Women, Public Men—Public Women, Hidden Men

For several years, one of Brazil's top sex symbols has been Roberta Close, whom I first saw in a furniture commercial. Roberta, whose looks reminded me of those of the young Natalie Wood, ended her pitch with an admonition to prospective furniture buyers to accept no substitute for the advertised product. "Things," she warned, "are not always what they seem."

Nor was Roberta. This petite and incredibly feminine creature was actually a man. Nevertheless, despite the fact that he—or she (speaking as Brazilians do)—is a man posing as a woman, Roberta has won a secure place in Brazilian mass culture. Her photos have decorated magazines. She has been a panelist on a TV variety show and has starred in a stage play in Rio with an actor known for his super-macho image. Roberta even inspired a well-known, and apparently heterosexual, pop singer to make a "video" honoring her. In it, she pranced around Rio's Ipanema Beach in a bikini, showing off her ample hips and buttocks.

The video depicted the widespread male appreciation of Roberta's beauty. As confirmation, one heterosexual man told me that he had recently been on the same plane as Roberta and had been struck by her looks. Another man said he wanted to have sex with her. These comments, it seemed to me, illustrated striking cultural contrasts about gender and sexuality. In Brazil, a Latin American country noted for its *machismo,* heterosexual men do not feel that attraction toward a transvestite blemishes their masculine identities.

Roberta Close exists in relation to a gender-identity scale that jumps from extreme femininity to extreme masculinity, with little in between. Masculinity is stereotyped as active and public, femininity as passive and domestic. The male–female contrast in rights and behavior is much stronger in Brazil than it is in North America. Brazilians confront a more rigidly defined masculine role than North Americans do.

The active–passive dichotomy also provides a stereotypical model for male–male sexual relations. One man is supposed to be the active, masculine (inserting) partner, whereas the other is the passive, effeminate one. The latter man is derided as a *bicha* (intestinal worm), but little stigma attaches to the inserter. Indeed, many "active" (and married) Brazilian men like to have sex with transvestite prostitutes, who are biological males.

If a Brazilian man is unhappy pursuing either active masculinity or passive effeminacy, there is one other choice—active femininity. For Roberta Close and others like her, the cultural demand of ultramasculinity has yielded to a performance of ultrafemininity. These men-women form a third gender in relation to Brazil's polarized male–female identity scale.

Transvestites like Roberta are particularly prominent in Rio de Janeiro's annual Carnaval, when an ambience of inversion rules the city. In the culturally accurate words of the American popular novelist Gregory McDonald, who sets one of his books in Brazil at Carnaval time:

> Everything goes topsy-turvy... Men become women; women become men; grown-ups become children; rich people pretend they're poor; poor people, rich; sober people become drunkards; thieves

actually contribute slightly more than 50 percent of the labor devoted to producing and preparing rice before cooking.

Not just women's prominent economic role but traditional social organization enhances female status among the Betsileo. Although postmarital residence is mainly patrilocal, descent rules permit married women to keep membership in and a strong allegiance to their own descent groups. Kinship is broadly and bilaterally calculated (on both sides—as in contemporary North America). The Betsileo exemplify Aihwa Ong's (1989) generalization that bilateral (and matrilineal) kinship systems, combined

At Carnaval time in Rio de Janeiro, Brazil, transvestites compete in beauty and costume contests. Have you recently seen any men dressed as women, or vice versa? If so, what was the context?

become generous. Very topsy-turvy. (McDonald 1984, p. 154)

Most notable in this costumed inversion (DaMatta 1991), men dress as women. Carnaval reveals and expresses normally hidden tensions and conflicts as social life is turned upside down. Reality is illuminated through a dramatic presentation of its opposite.

This is the final key to Roberta's cultural meaning. She emerged in a setting in which male–female inversion is part of the year's most popular festival. Transvestites are the pièces de résistance at Rio's Carnaval balls, where they dress as scantily as the real women do. They wear postage-stamp bikinis, sometimes with no tops. Photos of real women and transformed ones vie for space in the magazines. It is often impossible to tell the born women from the hidden men. Roberta Close is a permanent incarnation of Carnaval—a year-round reminder of the spirit of Carnavals past, present, and yet to come.

Roberta emerges from a Latin culture whose gender roles contrast strongly with those of the United States. From small village to massive city, Brazilian males are public and Brazilian females are private creatures. Streets, beaches, and bars belong to the men. Although bikinis adorn Rio's beaches on weekends and holidays, there are many more men than women there on weekdays. The men revel in their ostentatiously sexual displays. As they sun themselves and play soccer and volleyball, they regularly stroke their genitals to keep them firm. They are living publicly, assertively, and sexually in a world of men.

Brazilian men must work hard at this public image, constantly acting out their culture's definition of masculine behavior. Public life is a play whose strong roles go to men. Roberta Close, of course, is a public figure. Given that Brazilian culture defines the public world as male, we can perhaps better understand now why the nation's number one sex symbol has been a man who excels at performing in public as a woman.

with subsistence economies in which the sexes have complementary roles in food production and distribution, are characterized by reduced gender stratification. Such societies are common among South Asian peasants (Ong 1989).

Betsileo men do not have exclusive control over the means of production. Women can inherit rice fields, but most women, on marrying, relinquish their shares to their brothers. Sometimes a woman and her husband cultivate her field, eventually passing it on to their children.

Traditionally, Betsileo men participate more in politics, but the women also hold political office. Women sell their produce and products

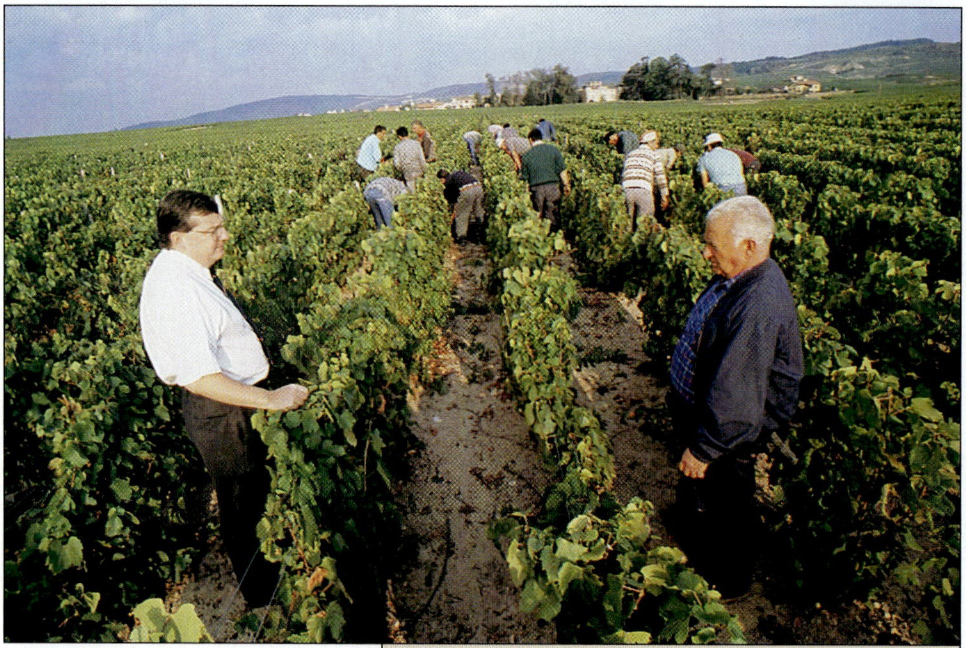

Studies of peasant gender roles in France and Spain, which have plow agriculture, show that people think of the house as the female sphere and the fields as the male domain.

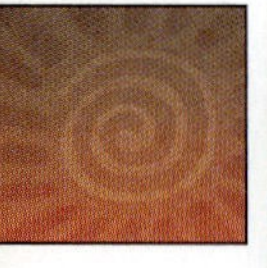

Bilateral kinship systems, combined with subsistence economies in which the sexes have complementary roles in food production and distribution, have reduced gender stratification. Such features are common among Asian rice cultivators, such as the Ifugao of the Philippines (shown here).

in markets, invest in cattle, sponsor ceremonials, and are mentioned during offerings to ancestors. Arranging marriages, an important extradomestic activity, is more women's concern than men's. Sometimes Betsileo women seek their own kinswomen as wives for their sons, reinforcing their own prominence in village life and continuing kin-based female solidarity in the village.

The Betsileo illustrate the idea that intensive cultivation does not necessarily entail sharp gender stratification. We can see that gender roles and stratification reflect not just the type of adaptive strategy but also specific environmental variables and cultural attributes. Betsileo women continue to play a significant role in their society's major economic activity, rice production.

We have seen that patrilocality is usually associated with gender stratification. However, some cultures with these institutions, including the Betsileo and the matrifocal Igbo of eastern Nigeria, offer contrasts to the generalization. The Igbo and Betsileo are not alone in having female traders. Many patrilineal, polygynous societies in West Africa also include women with careers in commerce. Polygyny may even help an aspiring woman trader, who can leave her children with her cowives while she pursues a business career. She repays them with cash and other forms of assistance.

Patriarchy and Violence

In the chapter "Marriage," dowry murders and *sati* (widow burning) in India were cited as blatant examples of **patriarchy.** This term describes a political system ruled by men in which women

have inferior social and political status, including basic human rights. Barbara Miller (1997), in a study of systematic neglect of females, describes women in rural northern India as "the endangered sex." Societies that feature a full-fledged patrilineal-patrilocal complex, replete with warfare and intervillage raiding, also typify patriarchy. Chagnon (1968) has described Yanomami males as "fierce" warriors, who exalt the male role in warfare and devalue females in relation to males. In such settings, women may be captured, raped, or murdered in intervillage raiding. Since such societies value the male war role, they tend to prefer sons over daughters. This may be expressed in female infanticide. For example, if a first child is a girl, she may be killed. But a first-born son is allowed to survive. Such practices as dowry murders, *sati,* female infanticide, and clitoridectomy illustrate patriarchy, which extends from tribal societies like the Yanomami to state societies like India, Pakistan, and even contemporary Western societies.

Although more prevalent in certain social settings than in others, family violence and domestic abuse of women are worldwide problems. We've seen that gender stratification is typically reduced in matrilineal, matrifocal, and bilateral societies in which women have prominent roles in the economy and social life. When a woman lives in her own village, she has kin nearby to look after and protect her interests. Even in patrilocal polygynous settings, women often count on the support of their cowives and sons in disputes with potentially abusive husbands. However, such settings, which tend to provide a safe haven for women, are retracting rather than expanding in today's world. Isolated families and patrilineal social forms have spread at the expense of matrilineality. Many nations have declared polygyny illegal. More and

more women, and men, find themselves cut off from extended kin and families of orientation.

Domestic violence is often associated with a woman's isolation from supportive kin ties. This happens in patrilineal-patrilocal settings ranging from the Yanomami to India, Pakistan, Afghanistan, and substantial chunks of Central Asia and North Africa. In Pakistan, for example, 50 percent of all murders are those of a woman by her husband (Kantor 1996). Domestic violence also occurs in neolocal–nuclear family settings, such as Canada and the United States. In Canada, 62 percent of murdered women are killed by their husband or domestic partner (Kantor 1996). Cities, with their impersonality and isolation from extended kin networks, are breeding groups for domestic violence.

Domestic violence is one of a series of often-interconnected manifestations of patriarchy. It is in patrilineal-patrilocal societies that anthropologists most typically find forced female (and male) genital operations, intervillage raiding, preference for males, female infanticide, dowry, and oppression of women by their in-laws. With the spread of the women's rights movement and the human rights movement, attention to domestic violence and abuse of women has increased. Laws have been passed; and mediating institutions established. Brazil's female-run police stations for battered women provide an example, as do shelters for victims of domestic abuse in the United States and Canada. But patriarchal institutions clearly do persist in what should be a more enlightened world.

Gender and Industrialism

The domestic–public dichotomy, which is developed most fully among patrilineal-patrilocal food producers and plow agriculturalists, also has affected gender stratification in industrial societies, including the United States and Canada. However, gender roles have been changing rapidly in North America. The "traditional" idea that "a woman's place is in the home" developed among middle- and upper-class Americans as industrialism spread after 1900. Earlier, pioneer women in the Midwest and West had been recognized as fully productive workers in farming and home industry. Under industrialism, attitudes about gendered work came to vary with class and region. In early industrial Europe, men, women, and children had flocked to factories as wage laborers. American slaves of both sexes had done grueling work in cotton fields. After abolition, southern African-American women continued working as field hands and domestics. Poor white women labored in the South's early cotton mills. In the 1890s, more than one million American women held menial, repetitious, and unskilled factory positions (Margolis 1984, 2000; Martin and Voorhies 1975). Poor, immigrant, and African-American women continued to work throughout the 20th century.

After 1900, European immigration produced a male labor force willing to work for wages lower than those of American-born men. Those immigrant men moved into factory jobs that previously had gone to women. As machine tools and mass production further reduced the need for female labor, the notion that women were biologically unfit for factory work began to gain ground (Martin and Voorhies 1975).

Maxine Margolis (1984, 2000) has shown how gendered work, attitudes, and beliefs have varied in response to American economic needs. For example, wartime shortages of men have promoted the idea that work outside the home is women's patriotic duty. During the world wars, the notion that women are biologically unfit for hard physical labor faded. Inflation and the culture of consumption have also spurred female employment. When prices and/or demand rises, multiple paychecks help maintain family living standards.

The steady increase in female paid employment since World War II also reflects the baby boom and industrial expansion. American culture has traditionally defined clerical work, teaching, and nursing as female occupations. With rapid

During the world wars, the notion that women were biologically unfit for hard physical labor faded. Shown here is World War II's famous Rosie the Riveter. Is there a comparable poster woman today? What does her image say about modern gender roles?

population growth and business expansion after World War II, the demand for women to fill such jobs grew steadily. Employers also found that they could increase their profits by paying women lower wages than they would have to pay returning male war veterans.

Woman's role in the home has been stressed during periods of high unemployment, although when wages fall or inflation occurs simultaneously, female employment may still be accepted. Margolis (1984, 2000) contends that changes in the economy lead to changes in attitudes toward and about women. Economic changes paved the way for the contemporary woman's movement, which also was spurred by the publication of Betty Friedan's book *The Feminine Mystique* in 1963 and the founding of NOW, the National Organization of Women, in 1966. The movement in turn promoted expanded work opportunities for women, including the goal of equal pay for equal work. Between 1970 and 1998, the female percentage of the American work force rose from 38 to more than 46 percent. In other words, almost half of all Americans who work outside the home are women. Almost 64 million women now have paid jobs, compared with 74 million men. Women now fill more than half (53 percent) of all professional jobs (*Statistical Abstract of the United States* 1999, pp. 411, 424). And it's not mainly single women working, as once was the case. Table 18.2 presents figures on the ever-increasing cash employment of American wives and mothers.

Note in Table 18.2 that the cash employment of American married men has been falling while that of American married women has been rising. There has been a dramatic change in behavior and attitudes since 1960, when 89 percent of all married men worked, compared with just 32 percent of married women. The comparable figures in 1998 were 77 percent and 61 percent. Ideas about the gender roles of males and females have changed. Compare your grandparents and your parents. Chances are you have a working mother, but your grandmother was more likely a stay-home mom. Your grandfather is more likely than your father to have worked in manufacturing and to have belonged to a union. Your father is more likely than your grandfather to have shared child care and domestic responsibilities. Age at marriage has been delayed for both men and women. College educations and professional degrees have increased. What other changes do you associate with the increase in female employment outside the home?

Table 18.3 details employment in the United States in 1997 by gender, income, and job type. Notice that the income gap between women and men was widest in sales, where women averaged 60 percent the male salary. Overall, the ratio rose from 68 percent in 1989 to 74 percent in 1997.

Today's jobs aren't especially demanding in terms of physical labor. With machines to do the heavy work, the smaller average body size and lesser average strength of women are no longer impediments to blue-collar employment. The

Table 18.2

Cash Employment of American Mothers, Wives, and Husbands, 1960–1998*

Year	Percentage of Married Women, Husband Present with Children under 6	Percentage of All Married Women[a]	Percentage of All Married Men[b]
1960	19	32	89
1970	30	40	86
1980	45	50	81
1990	59	58	79
1998	64	61	77

*Civilian population 16 years of age and older.

[a]Husband present.

[b]Wife present.

Source: *Statistical Abstract of the United States* 1999, pp. 416–417.

main reason we don't see more modern-day Rosies working alongside male riveters is that the U.S. work force itself is abandoning heavy-goods manufacture. In the 1950s, two-thirds of American jobs were blue-collar, compared with less than 15 percent today. The location of those jobs has shifted within the world capitalist economy. Third World countries with cheaper labor produce steel, automobiles, and other heavy goods less expensively than the United States can, but the United States excels at services. The American mass education system has many inadequacies, but it does train millions of people for service- and information-oriented jobs, from sales clerks to computer operators.

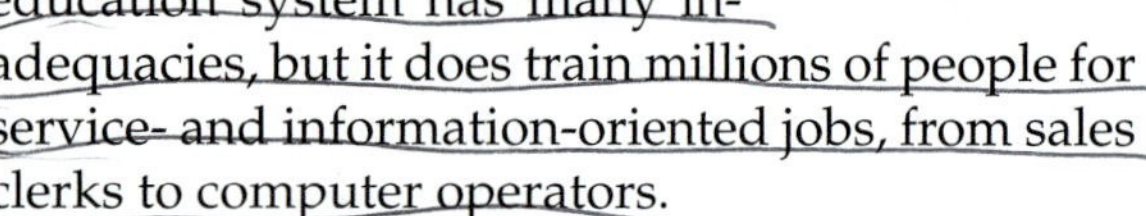

In the United States, women now fill more than half of all professional jobs. The number of professional women also is increasing in Canada and Western Europe.

The Feminization of Poverty

Alongside the economic gains of many American women stands an opposite extreme: the feminization of poverty. This refers to the increasing representation of women (and their children) among America's poorest people. Women head over half of U.S. households with incomes below the poverty line. Feminine poverty has been a trend in the United States since World War II, but it has accelerated recently. In 1959, female-headed households accounted for just one-fourth of the American poor. Since then, that figure has more than doubled. About half the female poor are "in transition." These are women who are confronting a temporary economic crisis caused by the departure, disability, or death of a husband. The other half are more permanently dependent on the welfare system or on friends or relatives who live nearby (Schaefer and Lamm 1994). The feminization of poverty and its consequences in

Table 18.3

Earnings in the United States (1997) by Gender and Job Type for Year-Round Full-Time Workers*

	MEDIAN ANNUAL SALARY		RATIO OF EARNINGS FEMALE/MALE	
	Women	Men	1997	1989
Median earnings	$24,973	$33,674	74	68
By Job Type				
Executive/administrative/managerial	$33,037	$50,149	66	61
Professional	35,417	50,402	70	71
Sales	21,392	35,655	60	54
Service	15,964	22,335	71	62

*By occupation of longest job held.

Source: *Statistical Abstract of the United States*, 1999, p. 446, Table 703.

Table 18.4

Median Annual Income of U.S. Households, by Household Type, 1997

	Number of Households (1000s)	Median Annual Income (Dollars)	Percentage of Mean Earnings Compared with Married-Couple Households
All households	102,528	$37,005	72
Family households:	70,880	45,347	88
Married-couple families	54,317	51,681	100
Male earner, no wife	3,911	36,634	71
Female earner, no husband	12,652	23,040	45
Nonfamily households:	31,648	21,705	42
Single male	11,010	23,871	46
Single female	15,317	15,530	30

Source: Based on data from the *Statistical Abstract of the United States* 1999, Table 747, p. 477.

regard to living standards and health are widespread even among wage earners. Many American women continue to work part time for low wages and meager benefits.

Married couples are much more secure economically than single mothers are. The data in Table 18.4 demonstrate that the average income for married-couple families is more than twice that of families maintained by a woman. The average one-earner family maintained by a woman had an annual income of $15,530 in 1997. This was less than one-third the mean income ($51,681) of a married-couple household.

The feminization of poverty isn't just a North America trend. The percentage of female-headed households has been increasing worldwide. In Western Europe, for example, it rose from 24 percent in 1980 to 31 percent in 1990. The figure ranges from below 20 percent in certain South Asian and Southeast Asian countries to almost 50 percent in certain African countries and the Caribbean (Buvinic 1995).

Why must so many women be solo household heads? Where are the men going, and why are they leaving? Among the causes are male migration, civil strife (men off fighting), divorce, abandonment, widowhood, unwed adolescent parenthood, and, more generally, the idea that children are women's responsibility.

Globally, households headed by women tend to be poorer than are those headed by men. In one study, the percentage of single-parent families considered poor was 18 percent in Britain, 20 percent in Italy, 25 percent in Switzerland, 40 percent in Ireland, 52 percent in Canada, and 63 percent in the United States. Poverty, of course, has health consequences. Studies in Brazil, Zambia, and the Philippines show the survival rates of children from female-headed households to be inferior to those of other children (Buvinic 1995).

In the United States, the feminization of poverty is a concern of the National Organization of Women. NOW still exists, alongside many newer women's organizations. The women's movement has become international in scope and membership. And its priorities have shifted from mainly job-oriented to more broadly social issues. These include poverty, homelessness, women's health care, day care, domestic violence, sexual assault, and reproductive rights (Calhoun, Light, and Keller 1997). These issues and others that particularly affect women in the developing countries were addressed at the United Nations' Fourth World Conference on Women held in 1995 in Beijing. In attendance were women's groups from all over the world. Many of these were national and international NGOs (nongovernmental organizations), which work with women at the local level to augment productivity and improve access to credit.

It is widely believed that one way to improve the situation of poor women is to encourage them to organize. New women's groups can in some cases revive or replace traditional forms of social organization that have been disrupted. Membership in a group can help women to mobilize resources, to rationalize production, and to reduce the risks and costs associated with credit. Organization also allows women to develop self-confidence and to decrease dependence on others. Through such organization, poor women throughout the world are working to determine their own needs and priorities, and to change things so as to improve their social and economic situation (Buvinic 1995).

What Determines Gender Variation?

We see that gender roles and stratification have varied widely across cultures and through history. Among many foragers and matrilineal cultivators, there is little gender stratification. Competition for resources leads to warfare and the intensification of production. These conditions favor patriliny and patrilocality. To the extent that women lose their productive roles in agricultural societies, the domestic–public dichotomy is accentuated and gender stratification is sharpened. With industrialism, attitudes about gender vary in the context of female extradomestic employment. Gender is flexible and varies with cultural, social, political, and economic factors. The variability of gender in time and space suggests that it will continue to change. The biology of the sexes is not a narrow enclosure limiting humans but a broad base upon which a variety of structures can be built (Friedl 1975).

summary

1. Gender roles and gender stratification vary with environment, economy, adaptive strategy, level of social complexity, and degree of participation in the world economy. *Gender roles* are the tasks and activities that a culture assigns to each sex. *Gender stereotypes* are oversimplified ideas about attributes of males and females. *Gender stratification* describes an unequal distribution of rewards by gender, reflecting different positions in a social hierarchy.
2. When gathering is prominent, gender status is more equal than it is when hunting or fishing dominates the foraging economy. Gender status is more equal when the domestic and public spheres aren't sharply separated. Foragers lack two public arenas that contribute to higher male status among food producers: warfare and organized interregional trade.
3. Gender stratification also is linked to descent and residence. Women's status in matrilineal societies tends to be high because descent-group membership, political succession, land allocation, and overall social identity come through female links. Although there are no matriarchies, women in many societies wield power and make decisions. Scarcity of resources promotes intervillage warfare, patriliny, and patrilocality. The localization of related males is adaptive for military solidarity. Men may use their warrior role to symbolize and reinforce the social devaluation and oppression of women.
4. There has been a recent tendency to see sexual orientation as fixed and biologically based. But to some extent, at least, all human activities and preferences, including erotic expression, are influenced by culture. Sexual orientation stands for a person's habitual sexual attraction to, and activities with: persons of the opposite sex, *heterosexuality;* the same sex, *homosexuality;* or both sexes, *bisexuality.* Sexual norms vary widely from culture to culture.
5. With the advent of plow agriculture, women were removed from production. The distinction between women's domestic work and men's "productive" labor reinforced the contrast between men as public and valuable and women as homebound and inferior. Patriarchy describes a political system ruled by men in which women have inferior social and political status, including basic human rights. Some expressions of patriarchy include female infanticide, dowry murders, widow burning, domestic abuse, and forced genital operations.
6. Americans' attitudes toward gender vary with class and region. When the need for female labor declines, the idea that women are unfit for many jobs increases, and vice versa. Factors such as war, falling wages, and inflation help explain female cash employment and Americans' attitudes toward it. Countering the economic gains of many American women is the feminization of poverty. This has become a global phenomenon, as impoverished female-headed households have increased worldwide.

key terms

biological determinists Those who argue that human behavior and social organization are biologically determined.

cultural determinists Those who relate behavior and social organization to cultural or environmental factors. This view focuses on variation rather than universals and stresses learning and the role of culture in human adaptation.

domestic–public dichotomy Contrast between women's role in the home and men's role in public life, with a corresponding social devaluation of women's work and worth.

extradomestic Outside the home; within or pertaining to the public domain.

gender roles The tasks and activities that a culture assigns to each sex.

gender stereotypes Oversimplified but strongly held ideas about the characteristics of males and females.

gender stratification Unequal distribution of rewards (socially valued resources, power, prestige, and personal freedom) between men and women, reflecting their different positions in a social hierarchy.

matriarchy A society ruled by women; unknown to ethnography.

matrifocal Mother-centered; often refers to a household with no resident husband-father.

patriarchy Political system ruled by men in which women have inferior social and political status, including basic human rights.

patrilineal-patrilocal complex An interrelated constellation of patrilineality, patrilocality, warfare, and male supremacy.

sexual dimorphism Marked differences in male and female biology besides the contrasts in breasts and genitals.

sexual orientation A person's habitual sexual attraction to, and activities with: persons of the opposite sex, *heterosexuality;* the same sex, *homosexuality;* or both sexes, *bisexuality.*

critical thinking questions

1. Is anatomy destiny? What characteristics of men and women do you see as most directly linked to biological differences between the sexes? What kinds of characteristics are most influenced by culture?
2. Using your own society, give an example of a gender role, a gender stereotype, and gender stratification.
3. How do gender roles among northern foragers compare with those in U.S. or Canadian society?
4. Would you prefer to live in a society that is matrilineal and matrilocal or in one that is patrilineal and patrilocal? Why?
5. What lessons about human sexuality do you draw from the Etoro? How fixed is human sexual orientation, in your opinion?
6. Would you rather live in an agricultural or a horticultural society? Why?
7. What do you see as the main factor that has changed North American gender roles since World War II? How do you expect gender roles to change in the next generation?
8. If you had to pick three factors that play a role in determining cross-cultural variation in gender roles, what would they be?

case study

Minangkabau: This chapter has discussed the influences of matrilineality and matrilocality on gender roles. In *Culture Sketches* by Holly Peters-Golden, read the chapter on the "Minangkabau: Merantau and Matriliny." What are some ways in which matrilineality influences, and is reflected in, other aspects of Minangkabau life?

suggested additional readings

Behar, R., and D. A. Gordon, eds.
1995 *Women Writing Culture*. Berkeley: University of California Press. Feminist scholars reflect on identity and difference.

Blackwood, E.
2000 *Webs of Power: Women, Kin, and Community in a Sumatran Village*. Lanham, MD: Rowman and Littlefield. Women, sex-gender roles, and social conditions in a matrilineal society: the Minangkabau.

Blackwood, E. and S. Wieringa, eds.
1999 *Female Desires: Same-Sex Relations and Transgender Practices across Cultures*. New York: Columbia University Press. Lesbianism and male homosexuality in cross-cultural perspective.

Bonvillain, N.
2001 *Women and Men: Cultural Constructions of Gender*, 3rd ed. Upper Saddle River, NJ: Prentice Hall. A cross-cultural study of gender roles and relationships, from bands to industrial societies.

Carver, T.
1996 *Gender Is Not a Synonym for Women*. Boulder, CO: Lynne Reinner. Gender in relation to class, race, ethnicity, sex, and sexuality.

Connell, R. W.
1995 *Masculinities*. Berkeley: University of California Press. Changing notions of masculinity in the context of a global economy.

Dahlberg, F., ed.
1981 *Woman the Gatherer*. New Haven, CT: Yale University Press. Female roles and activities among prehistoric and contemporary foragers.

Gilchrist, R.
1999 *Gender and Archaeology: Contesting the Past*. New York: Routledge. Feminist perspectives in archaeology.

Gilmore, D.
1991 *Manhood in the Making: Cultural Concepts of Masculinity*. New Haven, CT: Yale University Press. Cross-cultural study of manhood as an achieved status.

Kimmel, M. S., and M. A. Messner, eds.
2001 *Men's Lives*, 5th ed. Boston: Allyn & Bacon. The study of men in society and concepts of masculinity in the United States.

Lamphere, L., H. Ragone, and P. Zavella, eds.
1997 *Situated Lives: Gender and Culture in Everyday Life*. New York: Routledge. Essays on gender and culture as illustrated by everyday social interaction.

Lancaster, R. N., and M. Di Leonardo, eds.
1997 *The Gender/Sexuality Reader: Culture, History, Political Economy*. New York: Routledge. Gender and sexuality in history and in the modern social context.

Miller, B. D., ed.
1993 *Sex and Gender Hierarchies.* New York: Cambridge University Press. A series of articles, including several essays on human gender hierarchies, as well as those of nonhuman primates.

Peplau, L. A., ed.
1999 *Gender, Culture, and Ethnicity: Current Research about Women and Men.* Mountain View, CA: Mayfield. Gender in relation to ethnic issues.

Pollard, T. M., and S. B. Hyatt
1999 *Sex, Gender, and Health.* New York: Cambridge University Press. This study in medical anthropology relates health conditions and gender cross-culturally.

Rathus, S. A., J. S. Nevid, and J. Fichner-Rathus
2000 *Human Sexuality in a World of Diversity,* 4th ed. Boston: Allyn & Bacon. Multicultural and ethnic perspectives.

Reiter, R., ed.
1975 *Toward an Anthropology of Women.* New York: Monthly Review Press. Classic anthology, with a particular focus on peasant societies.

Rosaldo, M. Z., and L. Lamphere, eds.
1974 *Woman, Culture, and Society.* Stanford, CA: Stanford University Press. Another classic anthology, covering many areas of the world.

Ward, M. C.
1999 *A World Full of Women.* 2nd ed. Boston: Allyn & Bacon. A global and comparative approach to the study of women.

internet exercises

1. *Gender in the Classroom:* Read the article "Student Ratings of Professors Are Not Gender Blind" by Susan Basow, **http://eserver.org/feminism/workplace/fces-not-gender-blind.txt.**
   a. How much difference is there between male and female students who are rating a male professor? How much difference is there between male and female students in rating a female professor?
   b. What are the added expectations students have for female professors? What do you think is the source of those expectations? Do you think the expectations discussed in this article hold true for female teachers all over the world?
   c. Do you think the findings of this study are consistent with the way you and your friends rate professors?

2. *Gender on the Internet:* Read the paper by Amy Bruckman entitled "Gender Swapping on the Internet," **http://www.inform.umd.edu/EdRes/Topic/WomensStudies/Computing/Articles+ResearchPapers/gender-swapping.**
   a. Do gender roles exist on the Internet, such as in the MUDs described in this article, or in chat rooms, or e-mail? Do gender roles belong on the Internet? Would it be possible for people to remain gender-neutral on the Internet indefinitely?
   b. Imagine you are using a MUD. You encounter a character with a gender-neutral name (like Pat) and description. What clues would you use to identify the gender of Pat and Pat's user? Do you think this detective work would be more or less difficult if Pat's user was also from a different culture than your own?
   c. Do the cases described in this paper say more about the person swapping genders or about the other users?

See Chapter 18 on your CD-ROM for additional review and interactive exercises. See your McGraw-Hill Online Learning Center for more.

Chapter 19

Religion

CHAPTER OUTLINE

JSONLINE.COM NEWS BRIEFS

For Native American Church, Peyote Is Sacred

by Karen Lincoln Michel
Dec. 17, 1999

All his life, Tommy Billy has faced ridicule for practicing a religious belief as old as the red canyon rocks near his home on the Navajo Reservation in northern Arizona.

He is a follower of an ancient religion that uses the peyote cactus—classified as a hallucinogenic drug in this country—in the manner that Catholics use sacramental wine.

He has come to accept that mainstream America misunderstands his way of worship, the Native American Church, which claims about 250,000 members, 30,000 among the Navajo. But there is another kind of disregard toward his belief that worries him. This time, it is the people on his own reservation who are the perpetrators.

Non-believers, mainly Navajo teens, reportedly have been using peyote in the way some people take recreational drugs. The active ingredient in the cactus is mescaline, a mind-altering stimulant that the federal Drug Enforcement Administration has placed in the same category as heroin and LSD. A federal law, however, exempts church members from prosecution when peyote is used in religious ceremonies.

The Navajo Nation government is holding public hearings around the reservation to discuss stricter tribal laws that will crack down on illegal use of peyote without obstructing the religious freedom of bona fide church members . . .

It hurts Billy that his own people would abuse something he considers a holy medicine. And it hurts me, too . . .

I was born into the church and baptized in the Half-Moon Fireplace of the Native American Church of Wisconsin. The principles of the Wisconsin chapter are built on the belief in the Father, Son and Holy Spirit.

We sit on the ground and worship the triune God in all-night prayer services. We listen to sermons, sing praises to the Creator, offer prayers and foster fellowship among the congregation.

We also partake of the sacrament, a sacred rite that opens our souls and senses to fully receive the Creator. That's the part non-believers have difficulty understanding.

There are people outside the church, however, who accept and support our beliefs. A Catholic priest once told me that many Christians hear the word of God, but few allow the Holy Spirit to enter and connect on a divine spiritual plane. After hearing me talk about my religious beliefs, the priest said it sounded as though sacramental use of peyote was a conduit to reaching that spiritual level. Well put . . .

Most Americans believe the First Amendment has protected the right of all organized religions to practice their faith. But after the federal government listed peyote as a hallucinogen nearly 30 years ago, the cactus was outlawed in 22 states. It wasn't until the American Indian Religious Freedom Act was amended in 1994 that religious use of peyote by Native American Church members was legalized nationwide . . .

Billy doesn't have much faith in the media helping to educate the public about this issue. He criticized a recent Associated Press article that said seeing "visions" is part of the spiritual experience when peyote is ingested. He said that's how misconceptions get formed about his way of worship.

I agree. It's hard to understand beliefs of another culture when society views them through Euro-centric and Judeo-Christian eyes . . .

Source: http://www.jsonline.com/news/editorials/dec99/michel19121799.asp.

overview

Religion is a cultural universal. It consists of beliefs and behavior concerned with supernatural beings, powers, and forces. Cross-cultural studies have revealed many expressions and functions of religion. These include explanatory, emotional, social, and ecological functions.

People may use magic to try to influence outcomes over which they have no technical or rational control. Religion can provide comfort and psychological security at times of crisis. But rites also can create anxiety. Rituals are formal, invariant, earnest acts that require people to join actively in a social collectivity. Rites of passage may mark any change in social status, age, place, or social condition. Collective rituals often are cemented by communitas, a feeling of intense fellowship and solidarity.

Religion establishes and maintains social control. It does this through a series of moral and ethical beliefs, along with real and imagined rewards and punishments, internalized in individuals. Religion also achieves social control by mobilizing its members for collective action. Although it maintains social order, religion also can promote change. Religious movements aimed at the revitalization of society have helped people cope with changing conditions.

A growing religious diversity in the United States and Canada is related to age, region, and congregation. Contemporary religious trends include both rising secularism and a resurgence of religious fundamentalism. Some of today's new religions are inspired by science and technology; others, by spiritualism. Rituals can be secular as well as religious.

The anthropologist Anthony F. C. Wallace has defined **religion** as "belief and ritual concerned with supernatural beings, powers, and forces" (1966, p. 5). Like ethnicity or language, religion may be associated with social divisions within and between societies and nations. Religious behavior and beliefs both unite and divide. Participation in common rites may affirm, and thus maintain, the social solidarity of a religion's adherents. On the other hand, religious differences may be associated with bitter enmity.

In studying religion cross-culturally, anthropologists pay attention not only to the social roles of religion but also to the content and nature of religious acts, events, processes, settings, practitioners, and organizations. We also consider such verbal manifestations of religious beliefs as prayers, chants, myths, texts, and statements about ethics and morality.

The supernatural is the extraordinary realm outside (but believed to impinge on) the observable world. It is nonempirical, mysterious, and inexplicable in ordinary terms. It must be accepted "on faith." Supernatural beings—gods and goddesses, ghosts, and souls—are not of the material world. Nor are supernatural forces, some of which are wielded by beings. Other sacred forces are impersonal; they simply exist. In many societies, however, people believe they can benefit from, become imbued with, or manipulate supernatural forces.

Religion, as defined here, exists in all human societies. It is a cultural universal. However, we'll see that it isn't always easy to distinguish the supernatural from the natural and that different cultures conceptualize supernatural entities very differently.

Origins, Functions, and Expressions of Religion

When did religion begin? No one knows for sure. There are suggestions of religion in Neandertal burials and on European cave walls, where painted stick figures may represent shamans, early religious specialists. Nevertheless, any statement about when, where, why, and how religion arose, or any description of its original nature, can only be speculative. However, although such speculations are inconclusive, many have revealed important functions and effects of religious behavior. Several theories will be examined now.

Ancient Greek polytheism is illustrated by this image of Apollo, with a lyre, and Artemis, sacrificing over an altar fire. The red-figured terra cotta vessel dates to 490–480 BCE.

Animism

The founder of the anthropology of religion was the Englishman Sir Edward Burnett Tylor (1871/1958). Religion was born, Tylor thought, as people tried to understand conditions and events they could not explain by reference to daily experience. Tylor believed that our ancestors—and contemporary nonindustrial peoples—were particularly intrigued with death, dreaming, and trance. In dreams and trances, people see images they may remember when they wake up or come out of the trance state.

Tylor concluded that attempts to explain dreams and trances led early humans to believe that two entities inhabit the body: one active during the day and the other—a double or soul—active during sleep and trance states. Although they never meet, they are vital to each other. When the double permanently leaves the body, the person dies. Death is departure of the soul. From the Latin for soul, *anima,* Tylor named this belief animism. The soul was one sort of spiritual entity; people remembered various images from their dreams and trances—other spirits. For Tylor, **animism,** the earliest form of religion, was a belief in spiritual beings.

Tylor proposed that religion evolved through stages, beginning with animism. *Polytheism* (the belief in multiple gods) and then *monotheism* (the belief in a single, all-powerful deity) developed later. Because religion originated to explain things people didn't understand, Tylor thought it would decline as science offered better explanations. To an extent, he was right. We now have scientific explanations for many things that religion once elucidated. Nevertheless, because religion persists, it must do something more than explain the mysterious. It must, and does, have other functions and meanings.

Mana and Taboo

Besides animism—and sometimes coexisting with it in the same society—is a view of the supernatural as a domain of raw impersonal power, or *force,* that people can control under certain conditions. (You'd be right to think of *Star Wars.*) Such a conception of the supernatural is particularly prominent in Melanesia, the area of the South Pacific that includes Papua New Guinea and adjacent islands. Melanesians believed in **mana,** a sacred impersonal force existing in the universe. Mana can reside in people, animals, plants, and objects.

Melanesian mana was similar to our notion of efficacy or luck. Melanesians attributed success to mana, which people could acquire or manipulate in different ways, such as through magic. Objects with mana could change someone's luck. For example, a charm or amulet belonging to a successful hunter might transmit the hunter's mana to the next person who held or wore it. A woman might put a rock in her garden, see her yields improve dramatically, and attribute the change to the force contained in the rock.

Beliefs in mana—a supernatural force or power, which people may manipulate for their own ends—are widespread. Mana can reside in people, animals, plants, and objects, such as the skull held here by a member of the headhunting Iban tribe of Malaysia. Do you own anything that contains mana?

Beliefs in manalike forces are widespread, although the specifics of the religious doctrines vary. Consider the contrast between mana in Melanesia and Polynesia (the islands included in a triangular area marked by Hawaii to the north, Easter Island to the east, and New Zealand to the southwest). In Melanesia, one could acquire mana by chance, or by working hard to get it. In Polynesia, however, mana wasn't potentially available to everyone but was attached to political offices. Chiefs and nobles had more mana than ordinary people did.

So charged with mana were the highest chiefs that contact with them was dangerous to the commoners. The mana of chiefs flowed out of their bodies wherever they went. It could infect the ground, making it dangerous for others to walk in the chief's footsteps. It could permeate the containers and utensils chiefs used in eating. Contact between chief and commoners was dangerous because mana could have an effect like an electric shock. Because high chiefs had so much mana, their bodies and possessions were **taboo** (set apart as sacred and off-limits to ordinary people). Contact between a high chief and commoners was forbidden. Because ordinary people couldn't bear as much sacred current as royalty could, when commoners were accidentally exposed, purification rites were necessary.

One role of religion is to explain (see Horton 1993). A belief in souls explains what happens in sleep, trance, and death. Melanesian mana explains differential success that people can't understand in ordinary, natural terms. People fail at hunting, war, or gardening not because they are lazy, stupid, or inept but because success comes—or doesn't come—from the supernatural world.

The beliefs in spiritual beings (e.g., animism) and supernatural forces (e.g., mana) fit within the definition of religion given at the beginning of this chapter. Most religions include both spirits and impersonal forces. Likewise, the supernatural beliefs of contemporary North Americans include beings (gods, saints, souls, demons) and forces (charms, talismans, crystals, and sacred objects).

Magic and Religion

Magic refers to supernatural techniques intended to accomplish specific aims. These techniques include spells, formulas, and incantations used with deities or with impersonal forces. Magicians use *imitative magic* to produce a desired effect by imitating it. If magicians wish to injure or kill someone, they may imitate that effect on an image of the victim. Sticking pins in "voodoo dolls" is an example. With *contagious magic,* whatever is done to an object is believed to affect a person who once had contact with it. Sometimes practitioners of contagious magic use body products from prospective victims—their nails or hair, for example. The spell performed on the body product is believed to reach the person eventually and work the desired result.

We find magic in cultures with diverse religious beliefs. It can be associated with animism, mana, polytheism, or monotheism. Magic is neither simpler nor more primitive than animism or the belief in mana.

Anxiety, Control, Solace

Religion and magic don't just explain things and help people accomplish goals. They also enter the realm of human feelings. In other words, they serve emotional needs as well as cognitive (e.g., explanatory) ones. For example, supernatural beliefs and practices can help reduce anxiety. Magical techniques can dispel doubts that arise when outcomes are beyond human control. Similarly, religion helps people face death and endure life crises.

Although all societies have techniques to deal with everyday matters, there are certain aspects of people's lives over which they lack control. When people face uncertainty and danger, according to Malinowski, they turn to magic.

> [H]owever much knowledge and science help man in allowing him to obtain what he wants, they are unable completely to control chance, to eliminate accidents, to foresee the unexpected turn of natural events, or to make human handiwork reliable and adequate to all practical requirements. (Malinowski 1931/1978, p. 39)

Malinowski found that the Trobriand Islanders used magic when sailing, a hazardous activity. He proposed that because people can't control matters such as wind, weather, and the fish supply, they turn to magic. People may call on magic when they come to a gap in their knowledge or powers of practical control yet have to continue in a pursuit (Malinowski 1931/1978).

According to Malinowski, magic is used to establish control, but religion "is born out of . . . the real tragedies of human life" (1931/1978, p. 45). Religion offers emotional comfort, particularly when people face a crisis. Malinowski saw tribal religions as concerned mainly with organizing, commemorating, and helping people get through such life events as birth, puberty, marriage, and death.

Rituals

Several features distinguish **rituals** from other kinds of behavior (Rappaport 1974). Rituals are formal—stylized, repetitive, and stereotyped. People perform them in special (sacred) places and at set times. Rituals include *liturgical orders*—sequences of words and actions invented prior to the current performance of the ritual in which they occur.

These features link rituals to plays, but there are important differences. Plays have audiences rather than participants. Actors merely *portray* something, but ritual performers—who make up congregations—are *in earnest.* Rituals convey information about the participants and their traditions. Repeated year after year, generation after generation, rituals translate enduring messages, values, and sentiments into action.

Rituals are *social* acts. Inevitably, some participants are more committed than others are to the beliefs that lie behind the rites. However, just by taking part in a joint public act, the performers signal that they accept a common social and moral order, one that transcends their status as individuals.

Rites of Passage

Magic and religion, as Malinowski noted, can reduce anxiety and allay fears. Ironically, beliefs and rituals also can *create* anxiety and a sense of insecurity and danger (Radcliffe-Brown 1962/1965). Anxiety may arise *because* a rite exists. Indeed, participation in a collective ritual may build up stress, whose common reduction, through the completion of the ritual, enhances the solidarity of the participants.

Rites of passage, for example, the collective circumcision of teenagers, can be very stressful. The traditional vision quests of Native Americans, particularly the Plains Indians, illustrate **rites of passage** (customs associated with the transition from one place or stage of life to another), which are found throughout the world. Among the Plains Indians, to move from boyhood to manhood, a youth temporarily separated from his community. After a period of isolation in the wilderness, often featuring fasting and drug consumption, the young man would see a vision, which would become his guardian spirit. He would then return to his community as an adult.

The rites of passage of contemporary cultures include confirmations, baptisms, bar and bat mitzvah, and fraternity hazing. Passage rites involve changes in social status, such as from boyhood to manhood and from nonmember to sorority sister. There are also rites and rituals in our business and corporate lives. Examples include promotion and retirement parties. More generally, a rite of passage may mark any change in place, condition, social position, or age.

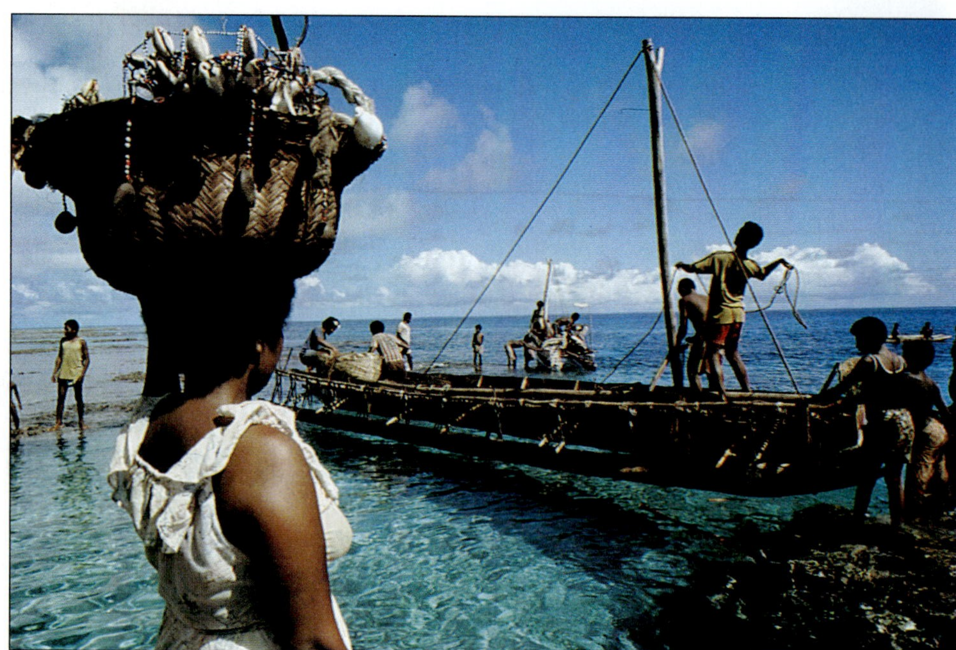

Trobriand Islanders prepare a traditional trading canoe for use in the Kula, which is a regional exchange system. The woman's basket contains trade goods, while the men prepare the long canoe to set sail. Magic is often associated with uncertainty, such as sailing in unpredictable waters.

All rites of passage have three phases: separation, liminality, and incorporation. In the first phase, people withdraw from the group and begin moving from one place or status to another. In the third phase, they reenter society, having completed the rite. The *liminal* phase is the most interesting. It is the period between states, the limbo during which people have left one place or state but haven't yet entered or joined the next (Turner 1974).

Liminality always has certain characteristics. Liminal people occupy ambiguous social positions. They exist apart from ordinary distinctions and expectations, living in a time out of time. They are cut off from normal social contacts. A variety of contrasts may demarcate liminality from regular social life. For example, among the Ndembu of Zambia, a chief underwent a rite of passage before taking office. During the liminal period, his past and future positions in society were ignored, even reversed. He was subjected to a variety of insults, orders, and humiliations.

Unlike the vision quest and the Ndembu initiation, which are individual experiences, passage rites are often collective. Several individuals—boys being circumcised, fraternity or sorority initiates, men at military boot camps, football players in summer training camps, women becoming nuns—pass through the rites together as a group. Table 19.1 summarizes the contrasts or oppositions between liminality and normal social life.

Most notable is a social aspect of *collective liminality* called **communitas** (Turner 1969), an intense community spirit, a feeling of great social solidarity, equality, and togetherness. People experiencing liminality together form a community of equals. The social distinctions that have existed before or will exist afterward are temporarily forgotten. Liminal people experience the same treatment and conditions and must act alike. Liminality may be marked ritually and symbolically by *reversals* of ordinary behavior. For example, sexual taboos may be intensified, or, conversely, sexual excess may be encouraged.

Liminality is basic to every passage rite. Furthermore, in certain societies, including our own, liminal symbols may be used to set off one (religious) group from another, and from society as a whole. Such "permanent liminal groups" (e.g., sects, brotherhoods, and cults) are found most

Liminal people, like these Mandji girls in Gabon, West Africa, who are temporarily confined to a menstrual hut, exist apart from ordinary expectations. They live in a time out of time, cut off from normal social contacts. A variety of contrasts, such as their body paint, may demarcate liminality from regular social life. What was your last liminal experience?

characteristically in complex societies—nation-states. Such liminal features as humility, poverty, equality, obedience, sexual abstinence, and silence may be required for all sect or cult members. Those who join such a group agree to its rules. As if they were undergoing a passage rite—but in this case a never-ending one—they may rid themselves of their previous possessions and cut themselves off from former social links, including those with family members.

Identity as a member of the group is expected to transcend individuality. Cult members often wear uniform clothing. They may try to reduce distinctions based on age and gender by using a common hair style (shaved head, short hair, or long hair). The Heaven's Gate cult, whose mass suicide garnered headlines in 1997, even used castration to increase *androgyny*

Table 19.1
Oppositions between Liminality and Normal Social Life

Liminality	Normal Social Structure
Transition	State
Homogeneity	Heterogeneity
Communitas	Structure
Equality	Inequality
Anonymity	Names
Absence of property	Property
Absence of status	Status
Nakedness or uniform dress	Dress distinctions
Sexual continence or excess	Sexuality
Minimization of sex distinctions	Maximization of sex distinctions
Absence of rank	Rank
Humility	Pride
Disregard of personal appearance	Care for personal appearance
Unselfishness	Selfishness
Total obedience	Obedience only to superior rank
Sacredness	Secularity
Sacred instruction	Technical knowledge
Silence	Speech
Simplicity	Complexity
Acceptance of pain and suffering	Avoidance of pain and suffering

Source: Adapted from Victor W. Turner, *The Ritual Process*. Copyright © 1969 by Victor W. Turner. By permission of Aldine de Gruyter, New York.

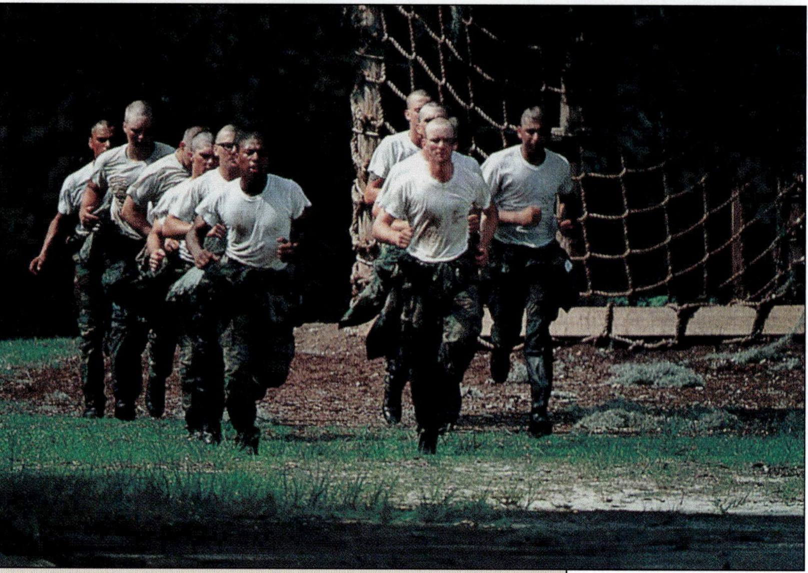

Passage rites are often collective. A group—such as these initiates in Togo or these Marine recruits in South Carolina—passes through the rites as a unit. Such liminal people experience the same treatment and conditions and must act alike. They share communitas, an intense community spirit, a feeling of great social solidarity or togetherness.

(similarity between males and females). With such cults, the individual, so important in American culture, is submerged in the collective. This is one reason Americans are so fearful and suspicious of "cults." In a variety of contexts, liminal features signal the distinctiveness or sacredness of groups, persons, settings, and events. Liminal symbols mark entities and circumstances as extraordinary—outside and beyond ordinary social space and routine social events.

Totemism

Rituals serve the social function of creating temporary or permanent solidarity among people—forming a social community. We see this also in practices known as totemism. Totemism has been important in the religions of the Native Australians. *Totems* can be animals, plants, or geographical features. In each tribe, groups of people have particular totems. Members of each totemic group believe themselves to be descendants of their totem. Traditionally they customarily neither killed nor ate a totemic animal, but this taboo was lifted once a year, when people assembled for ceremonies dedicated to the totem. These annual rites were believed to be necessary for the totem's survival and reproduction.

Totemism uses nature as a model for society. The totems are usually animals and plants, which are part of nature. People relate to nature through their totemic association with natural species. Because each group has a different totem, social differences mirror natural contrasts. Diversity in the natural order becomes a model for diversity in the social order. However, although totemic plants and animals occupy different niches in nature, on another level they are united because they all are part of nature. The unity of the human social order is enhanced by symbolic association with and imitation of the natural order (Durkheim 1912/1961; Lévi-Strauss 1963; Radcliffe-Brown 1962/1965).

One role of religious rites and beliefs is to affirm, and thus maintain, the solidarity of a religion's adherents. Totems are sacred emblems symbolizing common identity. This is true not just among Native Australians, but also among Native American groups of the North Pacific coast of North America, whose totem poles are well known. Their totemic carvings, which commemorate, and tell visual stories about, ancestors, animals, and spirits, also are associated with ceremonies. In totemic rites, people gather together to honor their totem. In so doing, they use ritual to maintain the social oneness that the totem symbolizes.

Religion and Cultural Ecology

Another domain in which religion plays a prominent role is cultural ecology. Behavior motivated by beliefs in supernatural beings, powers, and forces may help people survive in their material environment. In this section, we will see how beliefs and rituals may function as part of a group's cultural adaptation to its environment.

Sacred Cattle in India

The people of India worship zebu cattle, which are protected by the Hindu doctrine of *ahimsa,* a principle of nonviolence that forbids the killing of animals generally. Western economic development experts occasionally (and erroneously) cite the Hindu cattle taboo to illustrate the idea that religious beliefs can stand in the way of rational economic decisions. Hindus seem to be irrationally ignoring a valuable food (beef) because of their cultural or religious traditions. The economic developers also comment that Indians don't know how to raise proper cattle. They point to the scraggly zebus that wander about town and country. Western techniques of animal husbandry grow bigger cattle that produce more beef and milk. Western planners lament that Hindus are set in their ways. Bound by culture and tradition, they refuse to develop rationally.

However, these assumptions are both ethnocentric and wrong. Sacred cattle actually play an important adaptive role in an Indian ecosystem that has evolved over thousands of years (Harris 1974, 1978). Peasants' use of cattle to pull plows and carts is part of the technology of Indian agriculture. Indian peasants have no need for large, hungry cattle of the sort that economic developers, beef marketers, and North American cattle ranchers prefer. Scrawny animals pull plows and carts well enough but don't eat their owners out of house and home. How could peasants with limited land and marginal diets feed supersteers without taking food away from themselves?

Indians use cattle manure to fertilize their fields. Not all the manure is collected, because peasants don't spend much time watching their cattle, which wander and graze at will during certain seasons. In the rainy season, some of the manure that cattle deposit on the hillsides washes down to the fields. In this way, cattle also fertilize the fields indirectly. Furthermore, in a country where fossil fuels are scarce, dry cattle dung, which burns slowly and evenly, is a basic cooking fuel.

Far from being useless, as the development experts contend, sacred cattle are essential to Indian cultural adaptation. Biologically adapted to poor pasture land and a marginal environment, the scraggly zebu provides fertilizer and fuel, is indispensable in farming, and is affordable for peasants. The Hindu doctrine of *ahimsa* puts the

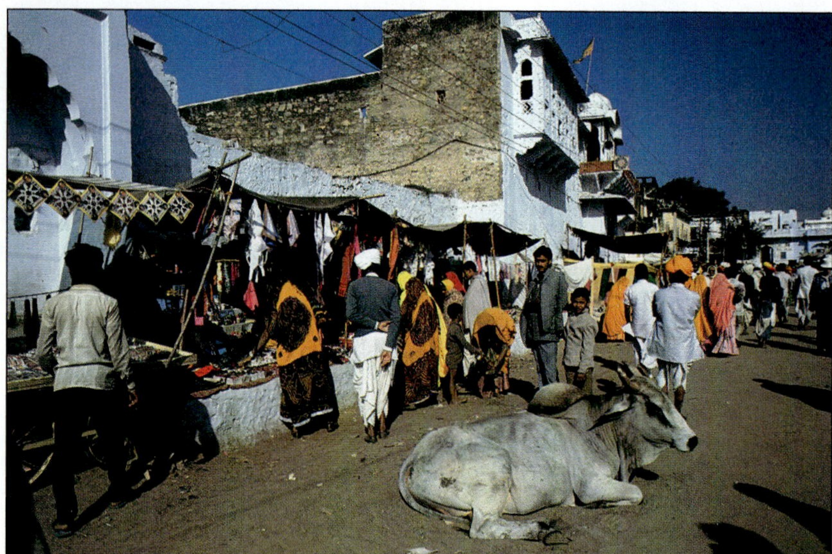

India's zebu cattle are protected by the doctrine of *ahimsa,* a principle of nonviolence that forbids the killing of animals generally. This Hindu doctrine puts the full power of organized religion behind the command not to destroy a valuable resource even in times of extreme need. What kinds of animal avoidance taboos do you observe? Is their origin religious or secular?

full power of organized religion behind the command not to destroy a valuable resource even in times of extreme need.

 Social Control

Cross-cultural research has documented richly varied images of, ideas about, and expressions and functions of religion. Religion has meaning to individuals. It helps them cope with adversity and tragedy and provides hope that things will get better. Lives can be transformed through spiritual healing or rebirth. Sinners can repent and be saved, or they can go on sinning and be damned. If the faithful truly internalize a system of religious rewards and punishments, their religion becomes a powerful means of controlling their beliefs, behavior, and what they teach their children.

Many people engage in religious activity because they believe it works. Prayers get answered. Faith healers heal. Sometimes it doesn't take much to convince the faithful that religious actions are efficacious. Many American Indian people in southwestern Oklahoma use faith healers at high monetary costs, not just because it makes them feel better about the uncertain, but because they are convinced that faith healing works (Lassiter 1998). Each year, legions of Brazilians visit a church, Nosso Senhor do Bomfim, in the city of Salvador, Bahia. They vow to repay "Our Lord" (Nosso Senhor) if healing happens. Showing that the vows are seen as having worked, and are repaid, are the thousands of *ex votos,* plastic impressions of every conceivable body part, that adorn the church, along with photos of people who have been cured.

Religion works through sacred force. It also works by getting inside people and mobilizing their emotions: their joy, their wrath, their righteousness. Émile Durkheim (1912/1961), a prominent French social theorist and scholar of religion, described the collective "effervescence" that can develop in religious contexts. Intense emotion bubbles up. People feel a deep sense of shared joy, meaning, experience, communion, belonging, and commitment to their religion.

The power of religion affects action. When religions meet, they can coexist peacefully, or their differences can be a basis for enmity and disharmony, even battle. Religious fervor has inspired Christians on crusades against the infidel (non-Christian) and has led Muslims to wage jihads,

holy wars against non-Islamic peoples. Throughout history, political leaders have used religion to promote and justify their views and policies.

Religion also has been used to mobilize society, or segments of society, against particular groups. Discrimination on the basis of religion is a familiar theme in national and world history. How may religious leaders mobilize communities and, in so doing, gain support for their own policies? One way is by persuasion; another is by instilling hatred or fear. Consider witchcraft accusations. Witch hunts can be powerful means of social control by creating a climate of danger and insecurity that affects everyone, not just the people who are likely targets. No one wants to seem deviant, to be accused of being a witch. In state societies, witch hunts often take aim at people who can be accused and punished with least chance of retaliation. During the great European witch craze, during the 15th, 16th, and 17th centuries (Harris 1974), most accusations and convictions were against poor women with little social support.

Witchcraft accusations are often directed at socially marginal or anomalous individuals. Among the Betsileo of Madagascar, for example, who prefer patrilocal postmarital residence, men living in their wife's or their mother's village violate a cultural norm. Linked to their anomalous social position, just a bit of unusual behavior (e.g., staying up late at night) on their part is sufficient for them to be called witches and avoided

Religion and Social Control in Afghanistan

This article describes an extreme form of religion and social control. The Taliban Islamic movement in Afghanistan has installed "the world's harshest form of Islamic rule." What issues of cultural relativism, ethnocentrism, and human rights are raised by this article?

KABUL, Afghanistan—Nearly a year after the Taliban Islamic movement cemented its position as the dominant power in this country by seizing Kabul, the Afghan capital is a place of deepening frustration and fear.

The white flags that the Taliban raised over Kabul's rooftops on Sept. 27, 1996, signaled the advent of the world's harshest form of Islamic rule. Led by Muslim clerics . . . , the Taliban announced their intention to create "a pure Islamic society" modeled on the teachings of the Koran.

Women were barred from work and girls from schools. Any female past puberty was barred from even talking to men unless they were blood relatives. Any woman venturing from her house had to have an approved reason, like going to the bazaar for food.

Men were required to grow bushy beards and also came in for a bewildering array of restraints, including taboos on popular pastimes like playing cards, listening to music, keeping pigeons and flying kites.

To impose their decrees, the Taliban unleashed an army of armed enforcers who scoured Kabul and other parts of Afghanistan, conducting "beard checks" and other controls on behalf of a religious police force known as the General Department for the Preservation of Virtue and the Elimination of Vice . . .

In the bazaars, an old Persian word, *wahshat,* meaning a paralyzing sense of fear, occurs regularly in conversations. Many people seem caught between this fear and an urge to speak out, but they quickly plunge back into something approaching panic.

"God help me if the Taliban come to know that I spoke to you," said a man working in a tiny tailor's shop in the city center. "They would call me a traitor to Islam."

One Afghan working for a Western aid organization erupted in anger after a morning visiting war orphans, widows and others who receive little or no attention from the Taliban, except for "inspections" to check that no edicts have been breached.

"I'll tell you this, and as a Muslim I never thought I could say such a thing," the man said. "I think we'd be better off under almost any kind of rulers—Hindu, Sikh, Jewish, even Christian—than under these fanatics. Most days, I wake up thinking we'd all be better off dead."

The Taliban have responded to the backlash by saying that the

as a result. In tribes and peasant communities, people who stand out economically, especially if they seem to be benefitting at the expense of others, often face witchcraft accusations, leading to social ostracism or punishment. In this case, witchcraft accusation becomes a **leveling mechanism,** a custom or social action that operates to reduce differences in wealth and thus to bring standouts in line with community norms—another form of social control.

To ensure proper behavior, religions offer rewards, for example, the fellowship of the religious community, and punishments, for example, the threat of being cast out or excommunicated. "The Lord giveth and the Lord taketh away." Many religions promise rewards for the good life and punishment for the bad. Your physical, mental, moral, and spiritual health, now and forever, may depend on your beliefs and behavior. For example, the Betsileo of Madagascar believe that if you don't pay enough attention to the ancestors, they may snatch your children from you.

Religions, especially the formal organized ones typically found in state societies, often pre-

A recent scene in Afghanistan. Before the Taliban, in the town of Mazar i Sharif, shown here, wedding shops were common.

most controversial aspect of their rule, the exclusion of women from work and girls from school, will be reviewed once the security situation improves . . .

In interviews, several powerful mullahs repeated earlier pledges to give "a positive response" to their opponents' pleas for moderation once their enemies in the north, who control 10 of Afghanistan's 32 provinces, have been defeated. But they quickly reasserted the basis for the restrictions on women, saying they were necessary to prevent Afghanistan's falling into the pit of "evil and corruption" that women's emancipation has brought to the West.

Sher Mohammed Abbas Stanakzai, the acting foreign minister, offered a view he said was reinforced by a visit he made last year to Washington . . .

In each day's newspaper, he said, he read of Americans' "intoxication with sexuality" and of its effects, including charges of sexual harassment and rape against Army instructors.

Stanakzai, 38, speaking English learned in college in India, contrasted this with life for women under the Taliban, which he said respected their "human rights," as well as their nature.

"In Western countries, women come out of their houses almost naked, they go freely to nightclubs, they drink and they dance all night," he said. "And when our society says you cannot do such things, a woman's role is to marry a well-respected gentleman, have children and stay at home, you say we are taking people back to the old ages." . . .

Source: Copyright 1997 The New York Times Company. Abridged from www.nytimes.com, "A Year of Harsh Islamic Rule Weighs Heavily for Afghans," by John F. Burns, September 24, 1997.

scribe a code of ethics and morality to guide behavior. The Judaic Ten Commandments lay down a set of prohibitions against killing, stealing, adultery, and other misdeeds. Sins are breaches of religious strictures, as crimes are breaches of secular laws. Some rules (e.g., the Ten Commandments) proscribe or prohibit behavior; others prescribe behavior. The Golden Rule, for instance, is a religious guide to do unto others as you would have them do unto you. Moral codes are ways of maintaining order and stability. Codes of morality and ethics are constantly repeated in religious sermons, catechisms, and the like. They become internalized psychologically. They guide behavior and produce regret, guilt, shame, and the need for forgiveness, expiation, and absolution when they are not followed.

Religions also maintain social control by stressing the temporary and fleeting nature of this life. They promise rewards (and/or punishment) in an afterlife (Christianity) or reincarnation (Hinduism and Buddhism). Such beliefs serve to reinforce the status quo. People can accept what they have now, knowing they can expect something better in the afterlife or the next life, if they follow religious guidelines. Under slavery in the American South, the masters taught portions of the Bible, such as the story of Job, that stressed compliance. The slaves, however, seized on the story of Moses, the promised land, and deliverance.

Kinds of Religion

Religion is a cultural universal. But religions are parts of particular cultures, and cultural differences show up systematically in religious beliefs and practices. For example, the religions of stratified, state societies differ from those of cultures with less marked social contrasts and power differentials.

Considering several cultures, Wallace (1966) identified four types of religion: shamanic, communal, Olympian, and monotheistic (Table 19.2). Unlike priests, the **shamans** of a shamanic religion aren't full-time religious officials but part-time religious figures who mediate between people and supernatural beings and forces. All cultures have medico-magico-religious specialists. *Shaman* is the general term encompassing curers ("witch doctors"), mediums, spiritualists, astrologers, palm readers, and other diviners. Wallace found shamanic religions to be most characteristic of foraging societies, particularly those found in the northern latitudes, such as the Inuit and the native peoples of Siberia.

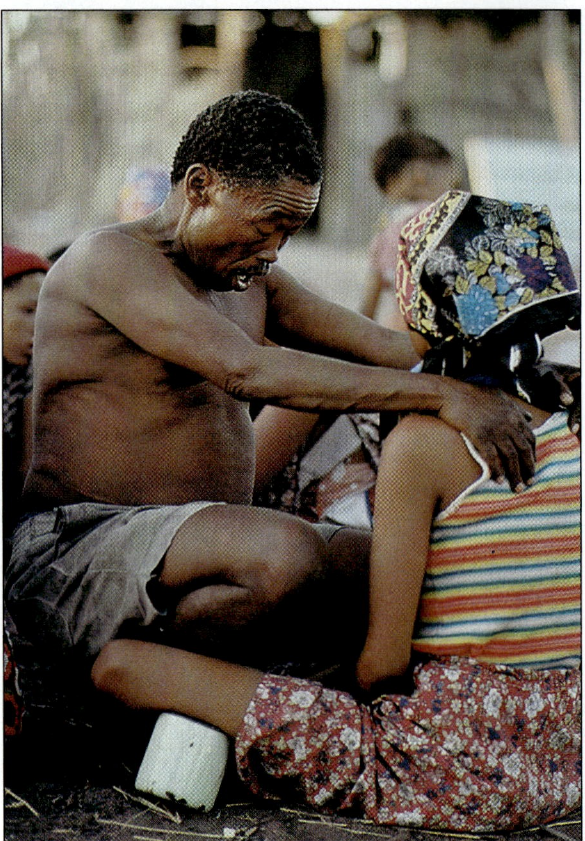

What are the world's oldest professions? Shaman is one. Shamanic religions are typically found among foragers, such as the San (shown here). This San shaman (left) falls into a trance as he heals.

Table 19.2
Anthony F. C. Wallace's Typology of Religions

Type of Religion (Wallace)	Type of Practitioner	Conception of Supernatural	Type of Society
Monotheistic	Priests, ministers, etc.	Supreme being	States
Olympian	Priesthood	Hierarchical pantheon with powerful deities	Chiefdoms and archaic states
Communal	Part-time specialists; occasional community-sponsored events, including rites of passage	Several deities with some control over nature	Food-producing tribes
Shamanic	Shaman = part-time practitioner	Zoomorphic (plants and animals)	Foraging bands

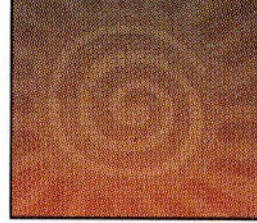

Although they are only part-time specialists, shamans often set themselves off symbolically from ordinary people by assuming a different or ambiguous sex or gender role. (In nation-states, priests, nuns, and vestal virgins do something similar by taking vows of celibacy and chastity.) Transvestism is one way of being sexually ambiguous. Among the Chukchee of Siberia (Bogoras 1904), where coastal populations fished and interior groups hunted, male shamans copied the dress, speech, hair arrangements, and life styles of women. These shamans took other men as husbands and sex partners and received respect for their supernatural and curative expertise. Female shamans could join a fourth gender, copying men and taking wives.

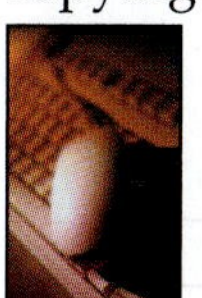

Among the Crow of the North American Plains, certain ritual duties were reserved for *berdaches,* men who rejected the male role of bison hunter, raider, and warrior and joined a third gender. The fact that certain key rituals could be conducted

400

only by *berdaches* indicates their regular and normal place in Crow social life (Lowie 1935).

Communal religions have, in addition to shamans, community rituals such as harvest ceremonies and rites of passage. Although communal religions lack *full-time* religious specialists, they believe in several deities (**polytheism**) who control aspects of nature. Although some hunter-gatherers, including Australian totemites, have communal religions, these religions are more typical of farming societies.

Olympian religions, which arose with state organization and marked social stratification, add full-time religious specialists—professional *priesthoods.* Like the state itself, the priesthood is hierarchically and bureaucratically organized. The term *Olympian* comes from Mount Olympus, home of the classical Greek gods. Olympian religions are polytheistic. They include powerful anthropomorphic gods with specialized functions, for example, gods of love, war, the sea, and death.

Olympian *pantheons* (collections of supernatural beings) were prominent in the religions of many nonindustrial nation-states, including the Aztecs of Mexico, several African and Asian kingdoms, and classical Greece and Rome. Wallace's fourth type—**monotheism**—also has priesthoods and notions of divine power, but it views the supernatural differently. In monotheism, all supernatural phenomena are manifestations of, or are under the control of, a single eternal, omniscient, omnipotent, and omnipresent supreme being.

 Religion in States

Robert Bellah (1978) coined the term "world-rejecting religion" to describe most forms of Christianity, including Protestantism. The first world-rejecting religions arose in ancient civilizations, along with literacy and a specialized priesthood. These religions are so named because of their tendency to reject the natural (mundane, ordinary, material, secular) world and to focus instead on a higher (sacred, transcendent) realm of reality. The divine is a domain of exalted morality to which humans can only aspire. Salvation through fusion with the supernatural is the main goal of such religions.

Christian Values

Notions of salvation and the afterlife dominate Christian ideologies. However, most varieties of Protestantism lack the hierarchical structure of earlier monotheistic religions, including Roman Catholicism. With a diminished role for the priest (minister), salvation is directly available to individuals. Regardless of their social status, Protestants have unmediated access to the supernatural. The individualistic focus of Protestantism offers a close fit with capitalism and with American culture.

In his influential book *The Protestant Ethic and the Spirit of Capitalism* (1904/1958), the social theorist Max Weber linked the spread of capitalism to the values preached by early Protestant leaders. Weber saw European Protestants (and eventually their American descendants) as more successful financially than Catholics. He attributed this difference to the values stressed by their religions. Weber saw Catholics as more concerned with immediate happiness and security. Protestants were more ascetic, entrepreneurial, and future-oriented, he thought.

Capitalism, said Weber, required that the traditional attitudes of Catholic peasants be replaced by values fitting an industrial economy based on capital accumulation. Protestantism placed a premium on hard work, an ascetic life, and profit seeking. Early Protestants saw success on earth as a sign of divine favor and probable salvation. According to some Protestant credos, individuals could gain favor with God through good works. Other sects stressed predestination, the idea that only a few mortals have been selected for eternal life and that people could not change their fates. However, material success, achieved through hard work, could be a strong clue that someone is predestined to be saved.

Weber also argued that rational business organization required the removal of industrial production from the home, its setting in peasant societies. Protestantism made such a separation possible by emphasizing individualism: individuals, not families or households, would be saved or not. Interestingly, given the connection that is usually made with morality and religion in contemporary American discourse about family values, the family was a secondary matter for Weber's early Protestants. God and the individual reigned supreme.

Today, of course, in North America as throughout the world, people of many religions and with diverse world views are successful capitalists. Furthermore, the old Protestant emphasis on honesty and hard work often has little to do with today's economic maneuvering. Still, there is no denying that the individualistic focus of Protestantism was compatible with the severance of ties to land and kin that industrialism demanded. These values remain prominent in the religious background of many of the people of the United States.

Religion in North America Today

Protestantism remains the predominant religion in the United States. The American Protestant population has declined somewhat, from 67 percent in 1967 to 59 percent in 1998 (Table 19.3). But in both years, the number of Protestants substantially

Table 19.3
Religious Composition (in Percentages) of the Populations of the United States, 1967 and 1998, and Canada, 1981 and 1991

	UNITED STATES		CANADA	
	1967	1998	1981	1991
Protestant	67	59	41	36
Catholic	25	27	47	46
Jewish	3	2	1	1
Other	3	5	3	4
None given	2	7	7	12

Source: U.S. Census Bureau, *Statistical Abstract of the United States*, 1999, p. 71, Table 89; Census of Canada, www.StatCan.ca, 1991.

Table 19.4
U.S. Church, Synagogue (etc.) Membership (in Percentages) by Age Group and Region, 1997

	Percent
Age Group:	
18–29	63
30–49	66
50 and older	73
Region:	
North	70
Midwest	73
South	73
West	51

Source: U.S. Census Bureau, *Statistical Abstract of the United States*, 1999, p. 71, Table 89.

exceeded that of Catholics, who comprise about a quarter of the population. In Canada, by contrast, Catholics outnumber Protestants. In both countries, reflecting immigration, especially from Asia, membership in the "other" religious category has increased—to 5 percent in the United States in 1998, versus just 2 percent in 1967.

The organized religions and churches represented in the United States and Canada include, but are not limited to, Christianity, Judaism, Islam, Hinduism, and Buddhism. Christianity dominates in both countries, with more than 80 percent of the population. In order, Canada's other major organized religions are Eastern Orthodox (1.4 percent), Judaism (1.2), Islam (0.9), Buddhism (0.6), Hinduism (0.6), and Sikh (0.5). In the United States, equivalent figures were not available, but the order of membership is Judaism, Eastern Orthodox, Islam, Buddhism, Hinduism, and Sikh.

Both countries have marked regional variation in religious affiliation and church membership. In Canada, the province of Quebec has the largest concentration of Roman Catholics. In the United States, the Jewish population, only 2 percent nationally, is significantly larger in New York State (9 percent) and City. Southerners and Midwesterners (73 percent) are more likely to belong to a church or temple than are Westerners (51 percent) (Table 19.4). However, the rate of actual church attendance is similar throughout the country. The most Christian states are Utah, whose population is almost 80 percent Christian, with the nation's largest concentration of Mormons, and North Dakota (almost 76 percent Christian). The least religious state is Nevada. Less than a third of the population there belongs to a congregation.

Religious affiliation also varies with age (Table 19.4). Older people are more likely to belong to a congregation than younger people are. The proportion of affiliated people is 63 percent among those 18–29 years old, rising to 73 percent among Americans over 50. This is probably both a generation effect and an age effect. That is, older people tend to be more religious both because they grew up at a more religious time in American history and because there is a tendency to seek religious consolation and think about the afterlife as the end of life draws nearer.

Religion and Change

Fundamentalists seek order based on strict adherence to purportedly traditional standards, beliefs, rules, and customs. Christian and Islamic fundamentalists recognize, decry, and attempt to redress change, yet they also contribute to change. In a worldwide process, new religions challenge established churches. In the United States, conservative Christian TV hosts have

become influential broadcasters and opinion shapers. In Latin America, evangelical Protestantism is winning millions of converts from Roman Catholicism.

Religion helps maintain social order, but it also can be an instrument not just of change, but also of revolution. As a response to conquest or foreign domination, for example, religious leaders often undertake to alter or revitalize a society. In an "Islamic Revolution," Iranian ayatollahs marshaled religious fervor to create national solidarity and radical change. We call such movements nativistic movements (Linton 1943) or revitalization movements (Wallace 1956).

Revitalization Movements

Revitalization movements are social movements that occur in times of change, in which religious leaders emerge and undertake to alter or revitalize a society. Christianity originated as a revitalization movement. Jesus was one of several prophets who preached new religious doctrines while the Middle East was under Roman rule. It was a time of social unrest, when a foreign power ruled the land. Jesus inspired a new, enduring, and major religion. His contemporaries were not so successful.

The Handsome Lake religion arose around 1800 among the Iroquois of New York State (Wallace 1970). Handsome Lake, the founder of this revitalization movement, was a leader of one of the Iroquois tribes. The Iroquois had suffered because of their support of the British against the American colonials (and for other reasons). After the colonial victory and a wave of immigration to their homeland, the Iroquois were dispersed on small reservations. Unable to pursue traditional horticulture and hunting in their homeland, they became heavy drinkers and quarreled among themselves.

466–467

Handsome Lake was a heavy drinker who started having visions from heavenly messengers. The spirits warned him that unless the Iroquois changed their ways, they would be destroyed. His visions offered a plan for coping with the new order. Witchcraft, quarreling, and drinking would end. The Iroquois would copy European farming techniques, which, unlike traditional Iroquois horticulture, stressed male rather than female labor. Handsome Lake preached that the Iroquois should also abandon their communal long houses and matrilineal descent groups for more permanent marriages and individual family households. The teachings of Handsome Lake produced a new church and religion, one that still has members in New York and Ontario. This revitalization movement helped the Iroquois adapt to and survive in a modified environment. They eventually gained a reputation among their non-Indian neighbors as sober family farmers.

Syncretisms

281–282

Especially in today's world, religious expressions emerge from the interplay of local, regional, national, and international cultural forces. **Syncretisms** are cultural mixes, including religious blends, that emerge from acculturation—the exchange of cultural features when cultures come into continuous firsthand contact. One example of religious syncretism is the mixture of African, Native American, and Roman Catholic saints and deities in Caribbean vodun, or "voodoo," cults. This blend also is present in Cuban *santeria* and in *candomblé*, an "Afro-Brazilian" cult. Another syncretism is the blend of Melanesian and Christian beliefs in cargo cults.

Like the Handsome Lake religion just discussed, cargo cults are revitalization movements. Such movements may emerge when natives have regular contact with industrial societies but lack their wealth, technology, and living standards. Some such movements attempt to *explain* European domination and wealth and to achieve similar success magically by mimicking European behavior and manipulating symbols of the desired life style. The syncretic **cargo cults** of Melanesia and Papua New Guinea weave Christian doctrine with aboriginal beliefs. They take their name from their focus on cargo: European goods of the sort natives have seen unloaded from the cargo holds of ships and airplanes.

In one early cult, members believed that the spirits of the dead would arrive in a ship. These ghosts would bring manufactured goods for the natives and would kill all the whites. More recent cults replaced ships with airplanes (Worsley 1959/1985). Many cults have used elements of European culture as sacred objects. The rationale

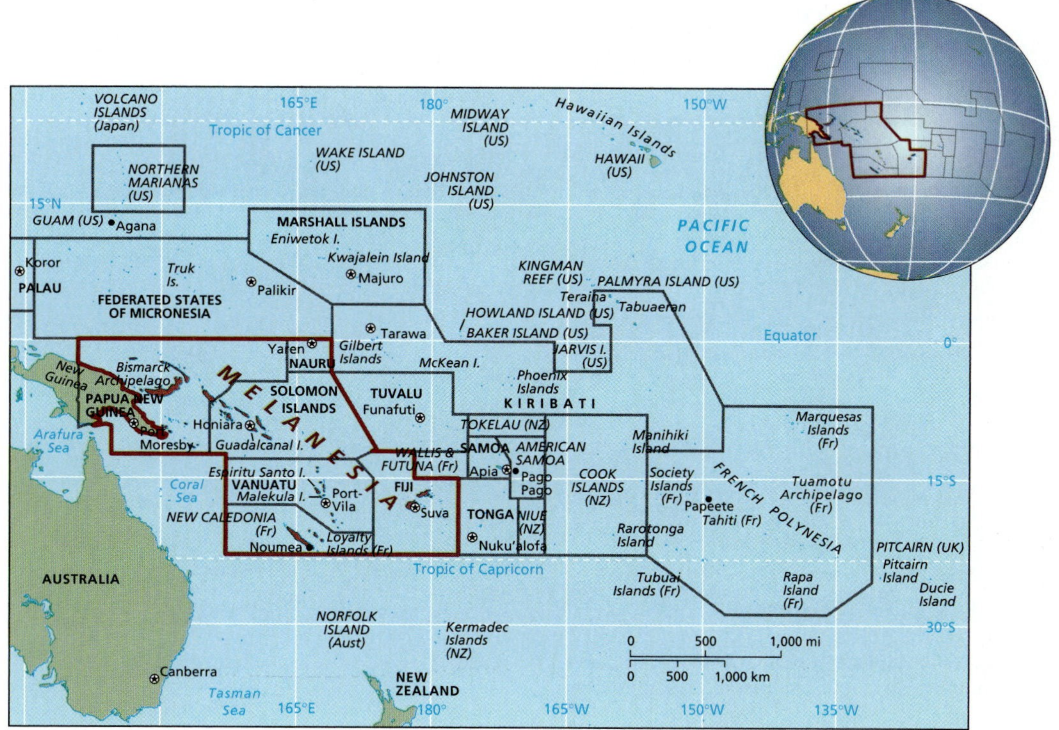

Religion and Change

is that Europeans use these objects, have wealth, and therefore must know the "secret of cargo." By mimicking how Europeans use or treat objects, natives hope also to come upon the secret knowledge needed to gain cargo.

For example, having seen Europeans' reverent treatment of flags and flagpoles, the members of one cult began to worship flagpoles. They believed the flagpoles were sacred towers that could transmit messages between the living and the dead. Other natives built airstrips to entice planes bearing canned goods, portable radios, clothing, wristwatches, and motorcycles. Near the airstrips they made effigies of towers, airplanes, and radios. They talked into the cans in a magical attempt to establish radio contact with the gods.

Some cargo cult prophets proclaimed that success would come through a reversal of European domination and native subjugation. The day was near, they preached, when natives, aided by God, Jesus, or native ancestors, would turn the tables. Native skins would turn white, and those of Europeans would turn brown; Europeans would die or be killed.

As syncretisms, cargo cults blend aboriginal and Christian beliefs. Melanesian myths told of ancestors shedding their skins and changing into powerful beings and of dead people returning to life. Christian missionaries, who had been in Melanesia since the late 19th century, also spoke of resurrection. The cults' preoccupation with cargo is related to traditional Melanesian big-man systems. In the chapter "Political Systems," we saw that a Melanesian big man had to be generous. People worked for the big man, helping him amass wealth, but eventually he had to give a feast and give away all that wealth.

433–435

Because of their experience with big-man systems, Melanesians believed that all wealthy people eventually had to give their wealth away. For decades, they had attended Christian missions and worked on plantations. All the while they expected Europeans to return the fruits of their labor as their own big men did. When the Europeans refused to distribute the wealth or even to let natives know the secret of its production and distribution, cargo cults developed.

A cargo cult in Vanuatu. Boys and men march with spears, imitating British colonial soldiers. Does anything in your own society remind you of a cargo cult?

Like arrogant big men, Europeans would be leveled, by death if necessary. However, natives lacked the physical means of doing what their traditions said they should do. Thwarted by well-armed colonial forces, natives resorted to magical leveling. They called on supernatural beings to intercede, to kill or otherwise deflate the European big men and redistribute their wealth.

Cargo cults are religious responses to the expansion of the world capitalist economy. However, this religious mobilization had political and economic results. Cult participation gave Melanesians a basis for common interests and activities and thus helped pave the way for political parties and economic interest organizations. Previously separated by geography, language, and customs, Melanesians started forming larger groups as members of the same cults and followers of the same prophets. The cargo cults paved the way for political action through which the indigenous peoples eventually regained their autonomy.

A New Age

Among the changes involving religion in contemporary North America is a certain decline in formal organized religions and a rise of secularism. Between 1967 and 1998, the number of Americans giving no religious preference grew from 2 to 7 percent. The comparable Canadian figure was a rise from 7 to 12 percent between 1981 and 1991 (Table 19.3). Atheists and "secular humanists" are not just bugaboos for religious conservatives. They really do exist, and they, too, are organized. Like members of religious groups, they use varied media, including print and the Internet, to communicate among themselves. Just as Buddhists can peruse *Tricycle: The Buddhist Review,* secular humanists can find their views validated in *Free Inquiry,* a quarterly identifying itself as "the international secular humanist magazine." Secular humanists speak out against organized religion and its "dogmatic pronouncements" and "supernatural or spiritual agendas" and the "obscurantist views" of religious leaders who presume "to inform us of God's views" by appealing to sacred texts (Steinfels 1997).

Even as our society appears to be growing more secular, some middle-class people have also turned to spiritualism, in search of the meaning of life. Spiritual orientations serve as the basis of new social movements. Some white people have appropriated the symbols, settings, and purported religious practices of Native Americans and, in Australia, of Native Australians, for New Age religions. Many natives have strongly protested the use of their sacred property and places by such groups.

New religious movements have varied origins. Some have been influenced by Christianity, others by Eastern (Asian) religions, still others by mysticism and spiritualism. Religion also evolves in tandem with science and technology. For example, the Raelian Movement, a religious group centered in Switzerland and Montreal, promotes cloning as a way of achieving "eternal life." Raelians believe that extraterrestrials called "Elohim" artificially created all life on earth. The group has established a company called Valiant Venture Ltd., which offers infertile and homosexual couples the opportunity to have a child cloned from one of the spouses (Ontario Consultants on Religious Tolerance 1996).

In the United States, the official recognition of a religion entitles it to a modicum of respect, and certain benefits, such as exemption from taxation on its income and property (as long as it does not engage in political activity). Not all would-be religions receive official recognition. For example, Scientology is recognized as a Church in the United States but not in Germany. In 1997, United States government officials spoke out against Germany's persecution of Scientologists as a form of "human rights abuse." Germans protested vehemently, calling Scientology a dangerous nonreligious political movement, with between 30,000 and 70,000 German members.

Secular Rituals

In concluding this discussion of religion, we may recognize some problems with the definition of religion given at the beginning of this chapter. The first problem: If we define religion with reference to supernatural beings, powers, and forces, how

do we classify ritual-like behavior that occurs in secular contexts? Some anthropologists believe there are both sacred and secular rituals. Secular rituals include formal, invariant, stereotyped, earnest, repetitive behavior and rites of passage that take place in nonreligious settings.

A second problem: If the distinction between the supernatural and the natural is not consistently made in a society, how can we tell what is religion and what isn't? The Betsileo of Madagascar, for example, view witches and dead ancestors as real people who play roles in ordinary life. However, their occult powers are not empirically demonstrable.

A third problem: The behavior considered appropriate for religious occasions varies tremendously from culture to culture. One society may consider drunken frenzy the surest sign of faith, whereas another may inculcate quiet reverence. Who is to say which is "more religious"?

A Pilgrimage to Walt Disney World

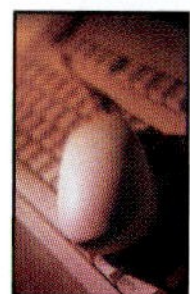

This final section will illustrate some of the approaches that anthropologists use to analyze and interpret religious behavior, with reference to a familiar and apparently nonreligious example. Secular behavior may exhibit clear parallels to religious behavior. We can see this by considering how a visit to Walt Disney World takes on some of the attributes of a religious pilgrimage. Florida's Walt Disney World, along with California's Disneyland, is one of two Disney "shrines" in the United States. These centers of mass visitation owe their success not just to the amusement they offer but to years of preprogramming that have influenced Americans for well over half a century. Disney's creations—movies, television programs, cable TV channels, Broadway musicals, cartoons, comics, toys, stores, and theme parks—are important forces in American enculturation.

The religions of many cultures focus on sacred sites and shrines. Infertile women in Madagascar seek fecundity by spilling the blood of a rooster in front of phallic stones. Australian totems are associated with holy sites where, in mythology, totemic beings first emerged from the ground.

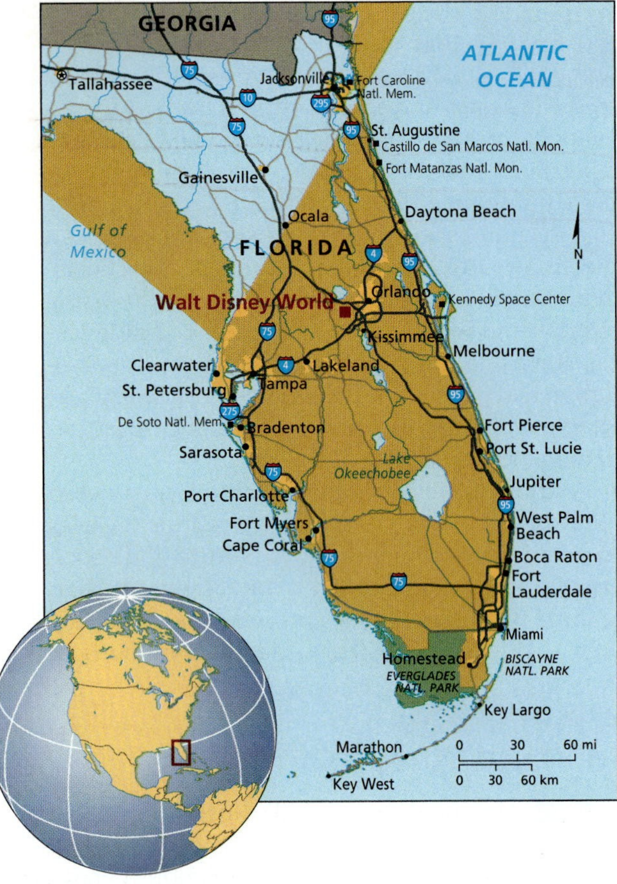

Sacred groves provide symbolic unity for dispersed clans among the Jie of Uganda (Gulliver 1965/1974). Pilgrims seek miraculous cures at shrines such as Lourdes, in France, and Fátima, in Portugal, which are associated with Roman Catholicism. In the arid *sertão* of northeastern Brazil, thousands of pilgrims journey each August 6 to fulfill their vows to a wooden statue in a cave—Bom Jesus de Lapa. Similarly, but virtually every day of the year, thousands of American families travel long distances and invest significant amounts of time, effort, and money to experience Disneyland and Walt Disney World.

A conversation with the anthropologist Alexander Moore, now of the University of Southern California, then of the University of Florida, first prompted me to think of Walt Disney World as analogous to religious pilgrimage centers. Moore pointed out that like other shrines, Walt Disney World has an inner, sacred center and an outer, more secular domain. At Walt Disney World, appropriately enough, the inner, sacred area is known as "the Magic Kingdom."

Motels, restaurants, and campgrounds dot the approach to Walt Disney World, becoming increasingly concentrated near the resort. You enter Walt Disney World on "World Drive." You can choose between the Magic Kingdom or turnoffs to Epcot, Disney's Animal Kingdom Theme Park, or the Disney–MGM Studios. The following analysis applies only to the Magic Kingdom.

Travelers enter a mammoth parking lot by driving through a structure like a turnpike toll booth. Sections of the parking lot have totemlike designations—Minnie, Goofy, Pluto, and Chip 'n' Dale—each with numbered rows. Uniformed attendants direct motorists to parking places, making sure every space is filled in order. As visitors emerge from their cars, they are directed to open-air trams. Lest they forget where their cars are parked, they are told as they board the tram to "remember" Minnie, Pluto, or whichever mythological figure has become the temporary guardian of their vehicle. Many travelers spend the first minute of the tram ride reciting "Minnie 30, Minnie 30," memorizing the automobile's row number. Leaving the tram, visitors hurry to booths where they purchase entrance to the Magic Kingdom and its attractions ("adventures"). They then pass through turnstiles behind the ticket sales booths and prepare to be transported, usually by "express" monorail, to the Magic Kingdom itself.

On that monorail, which bridges the opposition between the outer, secular, areas and the Magic Kingdom, similarities between Disney pilgrims and participants in rites of passage are especially obvious. (Rites of passage may be transitions in space, age, or social status.) Disney pilgrims on the monorail exhibit, as one might expect in a transition from secular to sacred space (a magic kingdom), many liminal attributes. Like liminal periods in other passage rites, aboard the monorail all prohibitions that apply everywhere else in Walt Disney World are intensified. In the outer, secular, areas and in the Magic Kingdom itself, people may smoke and eat, and in the secular areas they can consume alcohol and go shoeless, but all these things are taboo on the monorail. Like ritual passengers, monorail riders temporarily relinquish control over their destinies. Herded like cattle into the monorail, passengers move out of ordinary space and into a time out of time. Social distinctions disappear; everyone is reduced to a common level. As the monorail departs, a disembodied voice prepares the pilgrims for what is to come, enculturating them in the lore and standards of Walt Disney World.

Symbols of rebirth at the end of liminality are typical of liminal periods. Rebirth symbolism is an aspect of the monorail ride. As the monorail speeds through the Contemporary Resort Hotel, travelers facing forward observe and pass through an enormous tiled mural that covers an entire wall. Just before the monorail reaches the hotel, but much more clearly after it emerges, travelers see Walt Disney World's primary symbol: Cinderella castle. The sudden emergence from the mural into full view of the Magic Kingdom can be seen as a simulation of rebirth.

Within the Magic Kingdom

Once the monorail pulls into the Magic Kingdom station, the transition is complete. Passengers are now on their own. Soon they are in the Magic Kingdom, walking down "Main Street, U.S.A." The Magic Kingdom itself invites comparison with shrines and rites. Pilgrims agree implicitly to constitute a temporary community, to spend a few hours or days observing the same rules, sharing experiences, and behaving alike. They share a common social status as pilgrims, waiting for hours in line and partaking in the same "adventures." As we have seen, several anthropologists contend that a major social function of rituals is to reaffirm, and thus to maintain, solidarity among members of a congregation. Victor Turner (1974) suggested that certain rituals among the Ndembu of Zambia serve a mnemonic function (they make people remember). Women's belief that they can be made ill by the spirits of their deceased matrilineal kinswomen leads them to take part in rites that remind them of their ancestors.

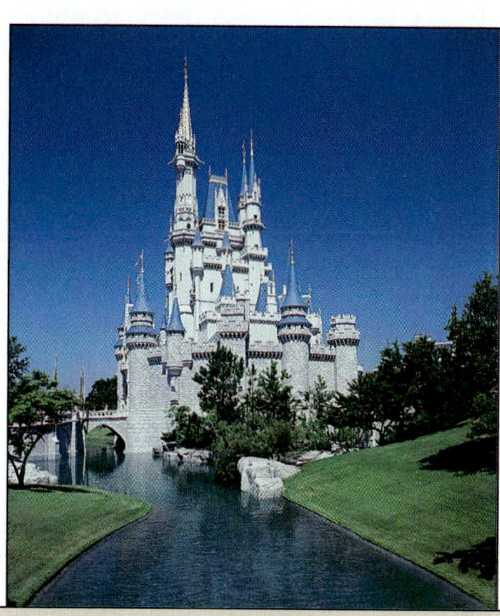

At Florida's Walt Disney World Resort, what is the role and function of Cinderella castle? Have you ever visited such a place? Do you think of your journey there as a pilgrimage?

Similar observations can be made about Walt Disney World: Frontierland; Liberty Square; Main Street, U.S.A.; Tomorrowland; Fantasyland; and Mickey's Toontown Fair—the major sections of the Magic Kingdom—make us remember departed presidents (our national ancestors) and American history. They also juxtapose and link together the past, present, and future; childhood and adulthood; the real and the unreal. Many of the adventures, or rides, particularly the roller coasters, can be compared to anxiety-producing rites. Anxiety is dispelled when the pilgrims realize they have survived simulated speeds of 90 miles an hour.

One might wonder how a visitor from a nonindustrial society would view Walt Disney World adventures, particularly those based on fantasy. In many nonindustrial societies, witches are actual people—part of reality rather than fantasy. Peasants in many countries believe in witches, werewolves, and nefarious creatures of the night. Such a visitor might find it hard to understand why Americans voluntarily take rides designed to produce uncertainty and fright.

The structure and attractions of the Magic Kingdom are meant to represent, recall, and reaffirm a set of American memories and values. In Liberty Square's Hall of Presidents, pilgrims silently and reverently view moving, talking, lifelike dummies. Like Tanzanian rites, the Magic Kingdom makes us remember not just presidents and history but characters in children's literature, such as Tom Sawyer. And, of course, we meet the cartoon characters who, in the person of costumed humans, walk around the Magic Kingdom, posing for photographs with children.

The juxtaposition of past, present, future, and fantasy symbolizes eternity. It argues that our nation, our people, our technological expertise, our beliefs, myths, and values will endure. Disney propaganda uses Walt Disney World itself to illustrate what American creativity joined with technical know-how can accomplish. Students in American history are told how our ancestors carved a new land out of wilderness. Similarly, Walt Disney is presented as a mythic figure, creator of cosmos out of chaos—a structured world from the undeveloped chaos of Florida's central interior.

A few other links between Walt Disney World and religious and quasi-religious symbols and shrines should be examined. Walt Disney World's most potent symbol is Cinderella castle, complete with a moat where pilgrims throw coins and make wishes. On my first visit, I was surprised to discover that the castle has a largely symbolic function as a trademark or logo for Walt Disney World. The castle has little utilitarian value. A few shops on the ground floor and a restaurant on the second floor were open to the public, but the rest of the building was off limits. In interpreting Cinderella castle, I recalled a lecture given in 1976 by British anthropologist Sir Edmund Leach. In describing the ritual surrounding his dubbing as a knight, Leach noted that Queen Elizabeth stood in front of the British throne and did not, in accordance with our stereotype of monarchs, sit on it. Leach surmised that the primary value of the throne is to represent, to make concrete, something enduring but abstract—the British sovereign's right to rule. Similarly, the most important thing about Cinderella castle is its symbolism. It offers concrete testimony to the eternal aspects of Disney creations.

Recognizing Religion

Some anthropologists think that rituals are distinguished from other behavior by special emotions, nonutilitarian intentions, and supernatural entities. However, other anthropologists define ritual more broadly. Writing about football, W. Arens (1981) pointed out that behavior can simultaneously have sacred and secular aspects. On one level, football is "simply a sport"; on another, it is a public ritual. Similarly, Walt Disney World, an amusement park, is on one level a mundane, secular place, but, on another, it assumes some of the attributes of a sacred place.

In the context of comparative religion, this isn't surprising. The French sociologist/anthropologist Émile Durkheim (1912/1961) pointed out long ago that almost everything from the sublime to the ridiculous has in some societies been treated as sacred. The distinction between sacred and profane doesn't depend on the intrinsic qualities of the sacred symbol. In Australian totemism, for example, sacred beings include such humble creatures as ducks, frogs, rabbits, and grubs, whose inherent qualities could hardly have given rise to the religious sentiment they inspire. If frogs and grubs can be elevated to a sacred level, why not the products of popular and commercial culture?

Many Americans believe that recreation and religion are separate domains. From my field work in Brazil and Madagascar and my reading about other societies, I believe that this separation is both ethnocentric and false. Madagascar's tomb-centered ceremonies are times when the living and the dead are joyously reunited, when people get drunk, gorge themselves, and enjoy sexual license. Perhaps the gray, sober, ascetic, and moralistic aspects of many religious events in the United States, in taking the "fun" out of religion, force us to find our religion in fun. Many Americans seek in such apparently secular contexts as amusement parks, rock concerts, and sporting events what other people find in religious rites, beliefs, and ceremonies.

summary

1. Religion, a cultural universal, consists of belief and behavior concerned with supernatural beings, powers, and forces. Religion also encompasses the feelings and meanings associated with such beliefs and behavior. Anthropological studies have revealed many aspects and functions of religion.
2. Tylor considered animism—the belief in spirits or souls—to be religion's earliest and most basic form. He focused on religion's explanatory role, arguing that religion would eventually disappear as science provided better explanations. Besides animism, yet another view of the supernatural also occurs in nonindustrial societies. This sees the supernatural as a domain of raw, impersonal power or force (called *mana* in Polynesia and Melanesia). People can manipulate and control mana under certain conditions.
3. When ordinary technical and rational means of doing things fail, people may turn to magic. Often they use magic when they lack control over outcomes. Religion offers comfort and psychological security at times of crisis. However, rites also can create anxiety. Rituals are formal, invariant, stylized, earnest acts in which people subordinate their particular beliefs to a social collectivity. Rites of passage have three stages: separation, liminality, and incorporation. Such rites can mark any change in social status, age, place, or social condition. Collective rites often are cemented by communitas, a feeling of intense solidarity.
4. Besides their psychological and social functions, religious beliefs and practices play a role in the adaptation of human populations to their environments. The Hindu doctrine of *ahimsa,* which prohibits harm to living things, makes cattle sacred and beef a tabooed food. The taboo's force stops peasants from killing their draft cattle even in times of extreme need.
5. Religion establishes and maintains social control through a series of moral and ethical beliefs, and real and imagined rewards and punishments, internalized in individuals. Religion also achieves social control by mobilizing its members for collective action.
6. Wallace defines four types of religion: shamanic, communal, Olympian, and monotheistic. Each has its characteristic ceremonies and practitioners. Religion helps maintain social order, but it also can promote change. Revitalization movements blend old and new beliefs and have helped people adapt to changing conditions.
7. Protestant values have been important in the United States, as they were in the rise and spread of capitalism in Europe. There is growing religious diversity in the United States and Canada. Religious trends in contemporary North America include rising secularism and new religions, some inspired by science and technology, some by spiritism. There are secular as well as religious rituals.

key terms

animism Belief in souls or doubles.

cargo cults Postcolonial, acculturative religious movements, common in Melanesia, that attempt to explain European domination and wealth and to achieve similar success magically by mimicking European behavior.

communal religions In Wallace's typology, these religions have, in addition to shamanic cults, communal cults in which people organize community rituals such as harvest ceremonies and rites of passage.

communitas Intense community spirit, a feeling of great social solidarity, equality, and togetherness; characteristic of people experiencing liminality together.

leveling mechanism A custom or social action that operates to reduce differences in wealth and thus to bring standouts in line with community norms.

liminality The critically important marginal or in-between phase of a rite of passage.

magic Use of supernatural techniques to accomplish specific aims.

mana Sacred impersonal force in Melanesian and Polynesian religions.

monotheism Worship of an eternal, omniscient, omnipotent, and omnipresent supreme being.

Olympian religions In Wallace's typology, develop with state organization; have full-time religious specialists—professional priesthoods.

polytheism Belief in several deities who control aspects of nature.

religion Belief and ritual concerned with supernatural beings, powers, and forces.

revitalization movements Movements that occur in times of change, in which religious leaders emerge and undertake to alter or revitalize a society.

rites of passage Culturally defined activities associated with the transition from one place or stage of life to another.

ritual Behavior that is formal, stylized, repetitive, and stereotyped, performed earnestly as a social act; rituals are held at set times and places and have liturgical orders.

shaman A part-time religious practitioner who mediates between ordinary people and supernatural beings and forces.

syncretisms Cultural mixes, including religious blends, that emerge from acculturation—the exchange of cultural features when cultures come into continuous firsthand contact.

taboo Set apart as sacred and off-limits to ordinary people; prohibition backed by supernatural sanctions.

critical thinking questions

1. What are the problems with the definition of religion given at the beginning of this chapter?
2. What are some of the explanatory, emotional, and social functions of religion? Do you see any problem in talking about religion in terms of its functions?
3. What's an example of a religious ritual in which you've engaged? How about a nonreligious ritual?
4. Describe a rite of passage you, or a friend, have been through. How did it fit the three-stage model given in the text?
5. Name three rites of passage that take place in your own society.
6. Can you think of additional ways in which religion has ecological functions?
7. What are two ways in which religion establishes and maintains social control?
8. From the news or your own knowledge, can you provide additional examples of revitalization movements, new religions, or liminal cults?
9. How are shamans similar to and different from priests? Are there shamans in your society? Who are they?
10. Have you participated in a secular ritual of the sort described at the end of the chapter?

case study

Azande: This chapter has discussed ways in which religious beliefs may serve to establish social control and to provide comfort and answers in times of crisis. In *Culture Sketches* by Holly Peters-Golden, read the chapter on the "Azande: Witchcraft and Oracles in Africa." Witchcraft among the Azande traditionally served as an effective means of social control. What are the major institutions and beliefs in your own culture that function similarly? Think about the ways in which members of your society are compelled to behave in socially acceptable ways. Is religion among them? There is a "logic" to the Azande belief in witchcraft and the causality of misfortune. Do you employ logic that is similar or different, when explaining negative events? Are there several different "systems of logic" that may be invoked, depending on the circumstances?

suggested additional readings

Brown, K. M.

1991 *Mama Lola: A Vodou Priestess in Brooklyn*. Berkeley: University of California Press. Ethnographic study of a religious community and its leader.

Child, A. B., and I. L. Child

1993 *Religion and Magic in the Lives of Traditional Peoples*. Englewood Cliffs, NJ: Prentice Hall. A cross-cultural study.

Harris, M.

1974 *Cows, Pigs, Wars, and Witches: The Riddles of Culture*. New York: Vintage. The cultural ecology of religion, taboos, and witchcraft.

Hicks, D., ed.

1999 *Ritual and Belief: Readings in the Anthropology of Religion*. New York: McGraw-Hill. Up-to-date reader, with useful annotation.

Horton, R.

1993 *Patterns of Thought in Africa and the West: Essays on Magic, Religion and Science*. New York: Cambridge University Press. Essays address issues involving religion and explanation.

Klass, M.

1995 *Ordered Universes: Approaches to the Anthropology of Religion*. Boulder, CO: Westview. Wide-ranging overview of key issues in the anthropology of religion.

Klass, M., and M. Weisgrau, eds.

1999 *Across the Boundaries of Belief: Contemporary Issues in the Anthropology of Religion*. Boulder CO: Westview. Up-to-date collection of articles.

Lehmann, A. C., and J. E. Meyers, eds.

2000 *Magic, Witchcraft, and Religion: An Anthropological Study of the Supernatural*, 5th ed. Mountain View, CA: Mayfield. A comparative reader covering Western and non-Western cultures.

Lessa, W. A., and E. Z. Vogt, eds.

1978 *Reader in Comparative Religion: An Anthropological Approach*, 4th ed. New York: Harper & Row. Excellent collection of major articles on the origins, functions, and expressions of religion in comparative perspective.

Rappaport, R. A.

1999 *Holiness and Humanity: Ritual in the Making of Religious Life*. New York: Cambridge University Press. The nature, meaning, and functions of ritual in religion.

Turner, V. W.

1995 (orig. 1969) *The Ritual Process*. Hawthorne, NY: Aldine de Gruyter. Liminality among the Ndembu discussed in a comparative perspective.

Wallace, A. F. C.

1966 *Religion: An Anthropological View*. New York: Random House. Survey of anthropological approaches to religion.

1970 *The Death and Rebirth of the Seneca*. New York: Knopf. The story of the Handsome Lake religion.

internet exercises

1. *Boot Camp:* Go to the Parris Island home page of the U.S. Marines and read the page on "The Transformation Process" in basic training, **http://www.parrisisland.com/transfor.htm.**

   a. In your textbook, basic training is presented as an example of a communal rite of passage. After reading this page, do you agree?

   b. If this is a rite of passage, we should be able to identify the phases: separation, liminality, and incorporation. Can you do so?

   c. Do recruits experience communitas while at Parris Island?

   d. Can you think of a rite of passage that you have experienced? For instance, joining a club or a team, being confirmed in the Catholic Church, celebrating your bar/bat mitzvah? In what ways are these experiences similar to basic training? In what ways are they different?

2. *Cargo Cults:* Go and read the article by Ted Daniels entitled "Jon Frum: Cargo and Catastrophe," **http://www.channel1.com/mpr/Articles/63-frum.html.**

   a. When did the Jon Frum Cargo Cult develop? What role did World War II play in its origins?

   b. How did the presence of Westerners (like missionaries) in Vanuatu influence the development of the Jon Frum Cargo Cult?

   c. What are some of the threats to the existence of the Jon Frum Cargo Cult? What are some of the steps its practitioners have taken to perpetuate its practices?

See Chapter 19 on your CD-ROM for additional review and interactive exercises. See your McGraw-Hill Online Learning Center for more.

Chapter 20

The Arts

CHAPTER OUTLINE

FOXNEWS.COM NEWS BRIEFS

Is There a Music Gene? Scholars Mull Music's Roots

by Matt Crenson
July 17, 2000

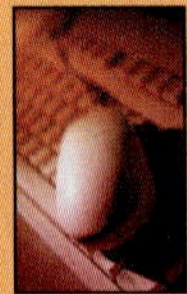

NEW YORK— . . . Some scientists have recently proposed that music may have been an evolutionary adaptation, like upright walking or spoken language, that arose early in human history and helped the species survive.

"Of course it's utter speculation," says David Huron, a professor of music at The Ohio State University in Columbus.

Most experts still assume music was a cultural invention, like cave painting or writing, that humans invented to make their lives easier or more pleasant.

Yet Huron and many of his colleagues wonder if music might have biological roots. The "music gene" would have arisen tens or hundreds of thousands of years ago, and conferred an evolutionary advantage on those who possessed it. Natural selection would have nurtured the gift of music, favoring those who possessed it with more offspring who were themselves more likely to reproduce . . .

That music is everywhere suggests it arose early in the history of the species, before humans scattered across the globe and developed manifold cultures. In fact, concrete evidence of music's antiquity exists in the form of a carved bone flute found recently in a cave in Slovenia. The "Divje babe flute," as musicologists call it, is the oldest known musical instrument. It dates back 40,000 years, to a time when Europe and much of North America were mantled in ice, and humans lived side by side with Neanderthals . . .

Sandra Trehub of the University of Toronto . . . travels the globe, studying mothers as they sing to their children. No matter where she goes, people sing to their infants the same way, at a high pitch, in a slow tempo and in a distinctive tone. Every culture has lullabies. They are so similar that you could never mistake them for anything else . . .

Music would have been adaptive because mothers who were better musicians had an easier time calming their babies, Trehub suggests. A happy baby who fell asleep easily and rarely made a fuss was much more likely to survive to adulthood especially in primitive societies. Their cries would not attract predators; they and their mothers would get more rest; they would be less likely to be mistreated.

So if a genetic predisposition to music appeared early in human history, those who had it would have produced more healthy offspring who themselves reproduced. The most musical of those children would have the same advantage, and they would pass the music genes to their children, and so on, each generation benefitting from the gift of music . . .

Perhaps music is something that pulls us together into groups. As individuals we are slow, clawless and hairless—easy prey for all manner of vicious beast. But in groups, *Homo sapiens* has conquered the globe.

Music is all about groups—choirs, symphonies, ensembles, and bands. Maybe people with a biological penchant for music lived more effectively in societies . . .

Source: http://www.foxnews.com/science/071700/music.sml.

overview

Is art, like religion, a cultural universal? People in all cultures do seem to associate an aesthetic experience with certain objects and events. Experiencing art involves feelings as well as appreciation of form. The arts, sometimes called "expressive culture," include the visual arts, literature, music, and theater arts.

Students of non-Western art have been criticized for ignoring individual artists, and for focusing too much on the social nature and context of art. Many non-Western societies do recognize the achievements of individual artists. Community standards judge the completeness and mastery displayed in a work of art. Standards may be maintained informally in society, or by specialists, such as art critics.

Folk art, music, and lore refer to the expressive culture of ordinary, usually rural, people. The arts are part of culture, and aesthetic judgments depend, at least to an extent, on cultural background. Growing acceptance of the anthropological definition of culture has helped broaden the study of the humanities from fine art and elite art to popular and folk art and the creative expressions of the masses and of many peoples. Myths, legends, tales, and storytelling play important roles in transmitting culture and preserving traditions.

The arts go on changing, although certain art forms have survived for thousands of years. In today's world, a huge "arts and leisure" industry links Western and non-Western art forms in an international network with both aesthetic and commercial dimensions.

What Is Art?

Many cultures lack a word for "art." Yet even without such a word, people everywhere do associate an aesthetic experience—a sense of beauty, appreciation, harmony, pleasure—with objects and events having certain qualities. The Bamana people of Mali have a word (like "art") for something that attracts your attention, catches your eye, and directs your thoughts (Ezra 1986). Among the Yoruba of Nigeria, the word for art, *ona,* encompasses the designs made on objects, the art objects themselves, and the profession of the creators of such patterns and works. For two Yoruba lineages of leather workers, Otunisona and Osiisona, the suffix *-ona* in their names denotes art (Adepegba 1991).

A dictionary defines **art** as "the quality, production, expression, or realm of what is beautiful or of more than ordinary significance; the class of objects subject to aesthetic criteria" (*The Random House College Dictionary* 1982, p. 76). Drawing on the same dictionary, **aesthetics** involves ". . . the qualities perceived in works of art . . . ; the . . . mind and emotions in relation to the sense of beauty" (p. 22). However, it is possible for a work of art to attract our attention, direct our thoughts, and have more than ordinary significance without being judged as beautiful by most people who experience that work. Pablo Picasso's *Guernica,* a famous painting of the Spanish Civil War, comes to mind as a scene that, while not beautiful, is indisputably moving, and thus a work of art.

George Mills (1971) notes that, in many cultures, the role of art lover lacks definition because art is not viewed as a separate activity. But this doesn't stop individuals from being moved by objects and events in a way that we would call aesthetic. Our own society does provide a fairly well-defined role for the connoisseur and collector of the arts, as well as a sanctuary, the museum, into which such people may occasionally retreat with their refined tastes.

"The **arts**" include the visual arts, literature (written and oral), music, and theater arts. These manifestations of human creativity are sometimes called **expressive culture.** People express themselves creatively in dance, music, song, painting, sculpture, pottery, cloth, storytelling, verse, prose, drama, and comedy.

This chapter will not attempt to do a systematic survey of all the arts, or even their major subdivisions. Rather, the approach will be to examine topics and issues that apply to expressive culture generally. "Art" will be used to encompass all the arts, not just the visual ones. In other words, the observations to be made about "art" are generally intended to apply to music and narratives as well as to painting and sculpture.

That which is aesthetically pleasing is perceived with the senses. Usually, when we think of art, we have in mind something that can be seen or heard. But others might define art more broadly to include things that can be smelled (scents, fragrances), tasted (recipes), or touched (cloth textures). How enduring must art be? Visual works and written works, including musical compositions, may last for centuries. Can a single noteworthy event, such as a feast, which is not in the least eternal, except in memory, be a work of art?

Art and Religion

Some of the issues raised in the discussion of religion also apply to art. Definitions of both art and religion mention the "more than ordinary" or the "extraordinary." Religious scholars may distinguish between the sacred (religious) and the profane (secular). Similarly, art scholars may distinguish between the artistic and the ordinary.

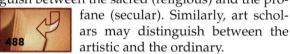

488

If we adopt a special attitude or demeanor when confronting a sacred object, do we display something similar when experiencing a work of art? According to the anthropologist Jacques Maquet (1986), an artwork is something that stimulates and sustains contemplation. It compels attention and reflection. Maquet stresses the importance of the object's form in producing such artistic contemplation. But other scholars stress feeling and meaning in addition to form. The experience of art involves feeling, such as being moved, as well as appreciation of form, such as balance or harmony.

Such an artistic attitude can be combined with and used to bolster a religious attitude. Much art has been done in association with religion. Many of the high points of Western art and music had religious inspiration, or were done in the service of religion, as a visit to a church or a large museum will surely illustrate. Bach and Handel are as well known for their church music as Michelangelo is for his religious painting and sculpture. The buildings (churches and cathedrals) in which religious music is played and in which visual art is displayed may themselves be works of art. Some of the major architectural achievements of Western art are religious structures. Examples include the Amiens, Chartres, and Notre Dame cathedrals in France.

Art may be created, performed, or displayed outdoors in public, or in special indoor settings, such as a theater, concert hall, or museum. Just as churches demarcate religion, museums and theaters set art off from the ordinary world, making it special, while inviting spectators in. Buildings dedicated to the arts help create the artistic atmosphere. Architecture may accentuate the setting as a place for works of art to be presented.

The settings of rites and ceremonies, and of art, may be temporary or permanent. State societies have permanent religious structures: churches and temples. So, too, may state societies have buildings and structures dedicated to the arts. Nonstate societies tend to lack such permanently demarcated settings. Both art and religion are more "out there" in society. Still, in bands and tribes, religious settings can be created without churches. Similarly, an artistic atmosphere can be created without museums. At particular times of the year, ordinary space can be set aside for a visual art display or a musical performance. Such special occasions parallel the times set aside for religious ceremonies. In fact, in tribal performances, the arts and religion often mix. For example, masked and costumed performers may imitate spirits. Rites of passage often feature special music, dance, song, bodily adornment, and other manifestations of expressive culture.

365–368

In the chapter "Making a Living," we looked at the potlatching tribes of the North Pacific Coast of North America. Erna Gunther (1971) shows how various art forms combined among those tribes to create the visual aspects of ceremonialism. During the winter, spirits were believed to pervade the atmosphere. Masked and costumed dancers represented the spirits. They dramatically re-enacted spirit encounters with human beings, which are part of the origin myths of villages, clans, and lineages. In some areas, dancers

This photo was taken in Phnom Penh, Cambodia, in 1988. On the grounds of a Buddhist temple, artisans make religious artifacts. We see a young man carving a Buddha, along with several completed Buddha statues.

devised intricate patterns of choreography. Their esteem was measured by the number of people who followed them when they danced.

In any society, art is produced for its aesthetic value as well as for religious purposes. According to Schildkrout and Keim (1990), non-Western art is usually, but wrongly, assumed to have some kind of connection to ritual. Non-Western art may be, but isn't always, linked with religion. Westerners have trouble accepting the idea that non-Western societies have art for arts' sake just as Western societies do. There has been a tendency for Westerners to ignore the individuality of non-Western artists and their interest in creative expression. According to Isidore Okpewho (1977), an oral literature specialist, scholars have tended to see religion in all traditional African arts. Even when acting in the service of religion, there is room for individual creative expression. In the oral arts, for example, the audience is much more interested in the delivery and performance of the artist than in the particular god for whom the performer may be speaking.

Locating Art

Aesthetic value is one way of distinguishing art. Another way is to consider placement. The special places where we find art include museums, concert halls, opera houses, and theaters. If something is displayed in a museum, or in another socially accepted artistic setting, someone at least must think it's art. But decisions about what to admit as a work of art may be political and controversial. In our own society, museums often have to balance concern over community standards with a wish to be as creative and innovative as the artists and works they display. Although tribal societies typically lack museums, they may maintain special areas where artistic expression takes place. One example, discussed below, is the separate space in which ornamental burial poles are manufactured among the Tiwi of North Australia.

Will we know art if we see it? Art has been defined as involving that which is beautiful and of more than ordinary significance. But isn't beauty in the eye of the beholder? Don't reactions to art differ among spectators? And, if there can be secular ritual, can there also be ordinary art? The boundary between what's art and what's not is blurred. The American artist Andy Warhol is famous for transforming Campbell's soup cans, Brillo pads, and images of Marilyn Monroe into

This photo, taken in Berlin, Germany, illustrates art within art. In the background, the experimental artist Christo has wrapped the Reichstag, a German parliament building. In the foreground, visitors pose for souvenir photos. One man has wrapped himself in gold and stands on a box wrapped in green. The man and Christo's wrapped Reichstag are being incorporated as new art in the photo being taken. Do you think this is art?

art. Many recent artists, such as Christo (see the photo above) have tried to erase the distinction between art and ordinary life by converting the everyday into a work of art.

If something is mass produced or industrially modified, can it be art? Prints made as part of a series may certainly be considered art. Sculptures that are created in clay, then fired with molten metal, such as bronze, at a foundry, are also art. But how does one know if a film is art? Is *Star Wars* art? How about *Citizen Kane?* When a book wins a National Book Award, is it immediately elevated to the status of art? What kinds of prizes make art? Objects never intended as art, such as an Olivetti typewriter, may be transformed into art by being placed in a museum, such as New York's Museum of Modern Art. Jacques Maquet (1986) distinguishes such "art by transformation" from art created and intended to be art, which he calls "art by destination."

In state societies, we have come to rely on critics, judges, and experts to tell us what's art and what isn't. A recent play titled *Art* is about conflict that arises among three friends when one of them buys an all-white painting. They disagree, as people often do, about the definition and value of a work of art. Such variation in art appreciation is especially common in contemporary society, with its professional artists and critics and great cultural diversity. We'd expect more uniform standards and agreement in less-diverse, less-stratified societies.

276

To be culturally relativistic, we need to avoid applying our own standards about what art is to the products of other cultures. Sculpture is art, right? Not necessarily. Previously, we challenged the view that non-Western art always has some kind of connection to religion. The Kalabari case to be discussed now makes the opposite point: that religious sculpture is not always art.

Among the Kalabari of southern Nigeria, wooden sculptures are not carved for aesthetic reasons, but to serve as "houses" for spirits (Horton 1963). These sculptures are used to control the spirits of Kalabari religion. The Kalabari place such a carving, and thus localize a spirit, in a cult house into which the spirit is invited. Here, sculpture

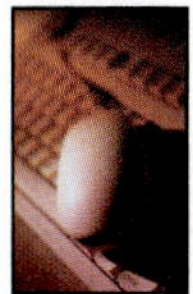

is done not for art's sake but as a means of manipulating spiritual forces. The Kalabari do have standards for the carvings, but beauty isn't one of them. A sculpture must be sufficiently complete to represent its spirit. Carvings judged too crude are rejected by cult members. Also, carvers must base their work on past models. Particular spirits have particular images associated with them. It's considered dangerous to produce a carving that deviates too much from a previous image of the spirit or that resembles another spirit. Offended spirits may retaliate. As long as they observe these standards of completeness and established images, carvers are free to express themselves. But these images are considered repulsive rather than beautiful. And they are not manufactured for artistic but for religious reasons. For these reasons, they probably should not be classified as art.

Art and Individuality

Those who work with non-Western art have been criticized for ignoring the individual and focusing too much on the social nature and context of art. When art objects from Africa or Papua New Guinea are displayed in museums, generally only the name of the tribe and of the Western donor are given, rather than that of the individual artist. It's as though skilled individuals don't exist in non-Western societies. The impression is that art is collectively produced. Sometimes it is; sometimes it isn't.

To some extent, there *is* more collective production in non-Western societies than in the United States and Canada. According to Hackett (1996), African artworks (sculpted figures, textiles, paintings, or pots) are generally enjoyed, critiqued, and used by communities or groups, rather than being the prerogative of the individual alone. The artist may receive more feedback during the creative process than the individual artist typically encounters in our own society. Here, the feedback often comes too late, after the product is complete, rather than during production, when it can still be changed.

During his field work among Nigeria's Tiv people, Paul Bohannan (1971) concluded that the proper study of art there should pay less attention to artists and more attention to art critics and products. There were few skilled Tiv artists, and such people avoided doing their art publicly. However, mediocre artists would work in public, where they routinely got comments from onlookers (critics). Based on critical suggestions, an artist often changed a design, such as a carving, in progress. There was yet another way in which Tiv artists worked socially rather than individually. Sometimes, when an artist put his work aside, someone else would pick it up and start working on it. The Tiv clearly didn't recognize the same kind of connection between individuals and their art that we do. According to Bohannan, every Tiv was free to know what he liked and to try to make it if he could. If not, one or more of his fellows might help him out.

In Western societies, artists of many sorts (e.g., painters, sculptors, actors, classical and rock musicians) have reputations for being iconoclastic and antisocial. Social acceptance may be more important in the societies anthropologists have traditionally studied. Still, there are well-known individual artists in non-Western societies. They are recognized as such by other community members and perhaps by outsiders as well. Their artistic labor may even be conscripted for special displays and performances, including ceremonies, or palace arts and events.

To what extent can a work of art stand apart from its artist? Philosophers of art commonly regard works of art as autonomous entities, independent of their creators (Haapala 1998). Haapala argues the contrary, that artists and their works are inseparable. "By creating works of art a person creates an artistic identity for himself. He creates himself quite literally into the pieces he puts into his art. He exists in the works he has created." In this view, Picasso created many Picassos, and exists in and through those works of art.

Sometimes little is known or recognized about the individual artist responsible for an enduring art work. We are more likely to know the name of the recording artist than of the writer of the songs we most commonly remember and perhaps sing. Sometimes we fail to acknowledge art individually because the artwork was collectively created. To whom should we attribute a pyramid or a cathedral? Should it be the architect, the ruler or leader who commissioned the work, or the master builder who implemented the design? A thing of beauty may be a joy forever even if and when we do not credit its creator(s).

The Work of Art

Some may see art as a form of expressive freedom, as giving free range to the imagination and the human need to create or to be playful. But consider the word *opera.* It is the plural of *opus,* which means a work. For the artist, at least, art is work, albeit creative work. In nonstate societies, artists may have to hunt, gather, herd, fish, or farm in order to eat, but they still manage to find time to work on their art. In state societies, at least, artists have been defined as specialists—professionals who have chosen careers as artists, musicians, writers, or actors. If they manage to support themselves from their art, they may be full-time professionals. If not, they do their art part time, while earning a living from another activity. Sometimes artists associate in professional groups such as medieval guilds or contemporary unions. Actors Equity in New York, a labor union, is a modern guild, designed to protect the interests of its artist members.

Just how much work is needed to make a work of art? In the early days of French impressionism, many experts viewed the paintings of Claude Monet and his colleagues as too sketchy and spontaneous to be true art. Established artists and critics were accustomed to more formal and classic studio styles. The French impressionists got their name from their sketches—*impressions*—of natural and social settings. They took advantage of technological innovations, particularly the availability of oil paints in tubes, to take their palettes, easels, and canvases into the field. There they captured the images of changing light and color that hang today in so many museums, where they are now fully recognized as art. But before Impressionism became an officially recognized "school" of art, its works were perceived by its critics as crude and unfinished. In terms of community standards, the first impressionist paintings were evaluated as harshly as were the overly crude and incomplete Kalibari wood carvings of spirits, as discussed previously.

521–522

To what extent does the artist—or society—make the decision about completeness? For familiar genres, such as painting or music, societies tend to have standards by which they judge whether an art work is complete or fully realized. Most people would doubt, for instance, that an all-white painting could be a work of art. Standards may be maintained informally in society, or by specialists, such as art critics. It may be difficult for unorthodox or renegade artists to innovate. But, like the impressionists, they may eventually succeed. Some societies tend to reward conformity, an artist's skill with traditional models and techniques. Others encourage breaks with the past, innovation.

Art, Society, and Culture

Art goes back at least 30,000 years, to the Upper Paleolithic period in Western Europe (see Conkey et al. 1997). Cave paintings, the best-known examples of Upper Paleolithic art, were, in fact, separated from ordinary life and everyday social space. Those images were painted in true caves, located deep in the bowels of the earth. They may have been painted as part of some kind of rite of passage, involving retreat from society. Portable art objects carved in bone and ivory, along with musical whistles and flutes, also confirm artistic expression during the Upper Paleolithic.

Art is usually more public than the cave paintings. Typically, it is exhibited, evaluated, performed, and appreciated in society. It has spectators or audiences. It isn't just for the artist.

Ethnomusicology is the comparative study of the musics of the world and of music as an aspect of culture and society. The field of ethnomusicology thus unites music and anthropology. The music side involves the study and analysis of the music itself and the instruments used to create it. The anthropology side views music as a way to explore a culture, to determine the role—historic and contemporary—that music plays in that society, and the specific social and cultural features that influence how music is created and performed.

Ethnomusicology studies non-Western music, traditional and folk music, even contemporary popular music from a cultural perspective. To do this there has to be field work—firsthand study of particular forms of music, their social functions and cultural meanings, within particular societies. Ethnomusicologists talk with local musicians, make recordings in the field, and learn about the place of musical instruments, performances, and performers in a given society (Kirman 1997). Nowadays, given globalization, diverse cultures and musical styles easily meet and mix. Music that draws on a wide range of cultural instruments and styles is called World Fusion, World Beat, or World Music—another topic within contemporary ethnomusicology

Music, which is often performed in groups, would seem to be among the most social of the arts. Even master pianists and violinists are frequently accompanied by orchestras or singers. Alan Merriam (1971) describes how the Basongye people of the Kasai province of Congo use three features to distinguish between music and other sounds, which are classified as "noise." First, music always involves humans. Sounds emanating from nonhuman creatures, such as birds and animals, are not music. Second, musical sounds must be organized. A single tap on the drum isn't music, but drummers playing together in a pattern is. Third, music must continue. Even if several drums are struck together simultaneously, it isn't music. They must go on playing to establish some kind of sound pattern. For the Basongye, then, music is inherently cultural (distinctly human) and social (dependent on cooperation).

Originally coined for European peasants, **"folk"** art, music, and lore refer to the expressive culture of ordinary people, as contrasted with the "high" art or "classic" art of the European elites. When European folk music is performed (see top photo on page 526), the combination of costumes, music, and often song and dance is supposed to say something about local culture and about tradition. Tourists and other outsiders often perceive rural and "folk" life mainly in terms of such performances. And community residents themselves often use such performances to display and enact their local culture and traditions for outsiders.

Art says something about continuity and change. Art can stand for tradition, even when traditional art is removed from its original (rural) context. As will be seen in the chapter "Cultural Exchange and Survival," the creative products and images of folk, rural, and non-Western cultures are increasingly spread—and commercialized—by the media and tourism. A result is that many Westerners have come to think of "culture" in terms of colorful customs, music, dancing, and adornments—clothing, jewelry, and hairstyles.

A bias toward the arts and religion, rather than more mundane, less photogenic, economic and social tasks, shows up on TV's Discovery Channel, and even in many anthropological films.

Many ethnographic films start off with music, often drum beats: "Bonga, bonga, bonga, bonga. Here in (supply place name), the people are very religious." We see in such presentations the previously critiqued assumption that the arts of nonindustrial societies usually have a link with religion. The (usually unintended) message is that non-Western peoples spend much of their time wearing colorful clothes, singing, dancing, and practicing religious rituals. Taken to an extreme, such images portray culture as recreational and ultimately unserious, rather than as something that ordinary people live every day of their lives—not just when they have festivals.

Art also functions in society as a form of communication between artist and community or audience. Sometimes, however, there are intermediaries between the artist and the audience. Actors, for example, are artists who translate the works and ideas of other artists (writers and directors) into the performances that audiences see and appreciate. Musicians play compositions of other people along with music they themselves have composed. Using music written by others, choreographers plan and direct patterns of dance, which dancers then execute for audiences.

How does art communicate? We need to know what the artist intends to communicate and how the audience reacts. Often, the audience communicates right back to the artist. Live performers, for instance, get immediate feedback, as may writers and directors by viewing a performance

Musicians in folk outfits play violins in a town square in Ljubljana, Slovenia. For whose pleasure do you suppose this performance is being given? Nowadays, such performances attract tourists as well as local people.

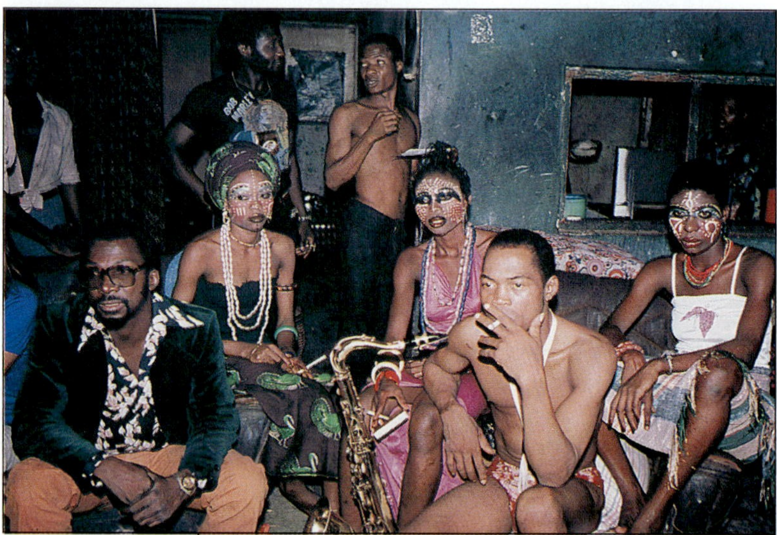

When it creates a significant national following, music can play a role in nation building. Nigeria's immensely popular singer Fela Kuti is shown here with three of his many wives, and fans in Lagos. What kind of music helps define your society?

This photo, taken on October 13, 1996, shows the Names Project Memorial AIDS Quilt display, in Washington, D.C. Quilts with the names of AIDS victims are displayed on Washington Mall. What functions of art are illustrated in this photo?

of their own work. Artists expect at least some variation in reception. In contemporary societies, with increasing diversity in the audience, uniform reactions are rare. Contemporary artists, like businesspeople, are well aware that they have target audiences. Certain segments of the population are more likely to appreciate certain forms of art than other segments are.

Art can transmit several kinds of messages. It can convey a moral lesson or tell a cautionary tale. It can teach lessons the artist, or society, wants told. Like the rites that induce, then dispel, anxiety, the tension and resolution of drama can lead to **catharsis,** intense emotional release, in the audience. Art can move emotions, make us laugh, cry, feel up or down. Art appeals to the intellect as well as to the emotions. We may delight in a well-constructed, nicely balanced, well-realized work of art.

Art can be self-consciously prosocial. It can express community sentiment, with political goals, used to call attention to social issues. Often, art is meant to commemorate and to last. Like a ceremony, art may serve a mnemonic function, making people remember. Art, such as the quilt display shown in the photo above, may be designed to make people remember either individuals or events, such as the AIDS epidemic that has proved so lethal in many world areas.

What is art's social role? To what extent should art serve society? Should the arts reflect, or question, community standards? We've seen that art has entered the political arena. Today, no museum director can mount an exhibit without worrying that it will offend some politically organized segment of society. The United States has an ongoing battle between liberals and conservatives involving the National Endowment for the Arts. Artists have been criticized as aloof from society, as creating only for themselves and for elites, as out of touch with conventional and traditional aesthetic values, even as mocking the values of ordinary people.

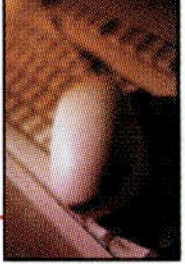

The Cultural Transmission of the Arts

Because art is part of culture, appreciation of the arts depends on cultural background. Watch Japanese tourists in a Western art museum trying to interpret what they are seeing. Conversely, the

Appreciation for the arts must be learned. Here, three American boys seem intrigued by the painting "Paris on a Rainy Day" at the Chicago Art Institute. How does the placement of art in museums affect art appreciation?

form and meaning of a Japanese tea ceremony, or a demonstration of origami (Japanese paper folding), will be alien to a foreign observer. Appreciation for the arts must be learned. It is part of enculturation, as well as of more formal education. Robert Layton (1991) suggests that whatever universal principles of artistic expression may exist, they have been put into effect in a diversity of ways in different cultures.

What is aesthetically pleasing depends to some extent on culture. Based on familiarity, music with certain tonalities and rhythm patterns will please some people and alienate others. In a study of Navajo music, McAllester (1954) found that it reflected the overall culture of that time in three main ways: First, individualism is a key Navajo cultural value. Thus, it's up to the individual to decide what to do with his or her property—whether it be physical property, knowledge, ideas, or songs. Second, McAllester found that a general Navajo conservatism also extended to music. The Navajo saw foreign music as dangerous and rejected it as not part of their culture. (This second point is no longer true; there are now Navajo rock bands.) Third, a general stress on proper form applied to music. There is, in Navajo belief, a right way to sing every kind of song.

People learn to listen to certain kinds of music and to appreciate particular art forms, just as they learn to hear and decipher a foreign language. Unlike Londoners and New Yorkers, Parisians don't flock to musicals. Despite its multiple French origins, even the musical *Les Miserables,* a huge hit in London, New York, and dozens of cities worldwide, bombed in Paris. Humor, too, a form of verbal art, depends on cultural background and setting. What's funny in one culture may not translate as funny in another. When a joke doesn't work, an American may say, "Well, you had to be there at the time." Jokes, like aesthetic judgments, depend on context.

274–275

At a smaller level of culture, certain artistic traditions may be transmitted in families. In Bali, for example, there are families of carvers, musicians, dancers, and mask makers. Among the Yoruba of Nigeria, two lineages of leather workers are entrusted with important bead embroidery works, such as for the king's crown and the bags and bracelets of priests. The arts, like other professions,

This photo was taken on St. Paul Island, on the Bering Sea coast of Alaska. A traditional Aleut storyteller uses a drum to tell his tale to young Aleut people. Who are the storytellers of your society? How do their narrative techniques and styles differ from the one shown here?

interesting issues

I'll Get You, My Pretty, and Your Little R2

Myths, legends, and tales express cultural beliefs and values. Sometimes they offer hope, adventure, and pleasure. Sometimes, as cautionary tales, they warn against certain kinds of behavior. They also teach lessons that society wants taught. On encountering the word *myth,* most people probably think of stories about Greek, Roman, or Norse gods and heroes. However, all societies have myths. Their central characters need not be unreal, superhuman, or physically immortal. Such tales may be rooted in actual historical events.

> The popular notion that a "myth" is . . . "untrue"—indeed that its untruth is its defining characteristic—is not only naive but shows misunderstanding of its very nature. Its "scientific truth" or otherwise is irrelevant. A myth is a statement about society and man's place in it and the surrounding universe. (Middleton 1967, p. x)

Myths are hallowed stories that express fundamental cultural values. They are widely and recurrently told among, and have special meaning to, people who grow up in a particular culture. Myths may be set in the past, present, or future or in "fantasyland." Whether set in "real time" or fictional time, myths are always at least partly fictionalized.

Techniques that anthropologists have used to analyze myths and tales can be extended to two fantasy films that most of you have seen. *The Wizard of Oz* has been telecast annually for decades. The original *Star Wars* remains one of the most popular films of all time. Both are familiar and significant cultural products with obvious mythic qualities. The contributions of the French structuralist anthropologist Claude Lévi-Strauss (1967) and the neo-Freudian psychoanalyst Bruno Bettelheim (1975) to the study of myths and fairy tales permit the following analysis of visual fairy tales that contemporary Americans know well.

Examining the myths and tales of different cultures, Lévi-Strauss determined that one tale could be converted into another through a series of simple operations, for example, by doing the following:

1. Converting the positive element of a myth into its negative.
2. Reversing the order of the elements.
3. Replacing a male hero with a female hero.
4. Preserving or repeating certain key elements.

Through such operations, two apparently dissimilar myths can be shown to be variations on a common structure, that is, to be transformations of each other.

We'll see now that *Star Wars* is a systematic structural transformation of *The Wizard of Oz.* We may speculate about how many of the resemblances were conscious and how many simply reflect a process of enculturation that *Star Wars* writer and director George Lucas shares with other Americans.

The Wizard of Oz and *Star Wars* both begin in arid country, the first in Kansas and the second on the desert planet Tatooine (Table 20.1). *Star Wars* converts *The Wizard*'s female hero into a boy, Luke Skywalker. Fairy-tale heroes usually have short, common first names and second names that describe their origin or activity. Thus Luke, who travels aboard spaceships, is a Skywalker, while Dorothy Gale is swept off to Oz by a cyclone (a gale of wind). Dorothy leaves home with her dog, Toto, who is pursued by and has managed to escape from a woman who in Oz becomes the Wicked Witch of the West. Luke follows his "Two-Two" (R2D2), who is fleeing Darth Vader, the witch's structural equivalent.

Dorothy and Luke each starts out living with an uncle and an aunt. However, because of the gender change of the hero, the primary relationship is reversed and inverted. Thus, Dorothy's relationship with her aunt is primary, warm, and loving, whereas Luke's relationship with his uncle, though primary, is strained and distant. Aunt and uncle are in the tales for the same reason. They represent home (the nuclear family of orientation), which children (according to American culture norms) must eventually leave to make it on their own. As Bettelheim (1975) points out, fairy tales often dis-

Table 20.1
Star Wars as a Structural Transformation of *The Wizard of Oz*

Star Wars	The Wizard of Oz
Male hero (Luke Skywalker)	Female hero (Dorothy Gale)
Arid Tatooine	Arid Kansas
Luke follows R2D2:	Dorothy follows Toto:
R2D2 flees Vader	Toto flees witch
Luke lives with uncle and aunt:	Dorothy lives with uncle and aunt:
Primary relationship with uncle (same sex as hero)	Primary relationship with aunt (same sex as hero)
Strained, distant relationship with uncle	Warm, close relationship with aunt
Tripartite division of same-sex parent:	Tripartite division of same-sex parent:
2 parts good, 1 part bad father	2 parts bad, 1 part good mother
Good father dead at beginning	Bad mother dead at beginning
Good father dead (?) at end	Bad mother dead at end
Bad father survives	Good mother survives
Relationship with parent of opposite sex (Princess Leia Organa):	Relationship with parent of opposite sex (Wizard of Oz):
Princess is unwilling captive	Wizard makes impossible demands
Needle	Broomstick
Princess is freed	Wizard turns out to be sham
Trio of companions:	Trio of companions:
Han Solo, C3PO, Chewbacca	Scarecrow, Tin Woodman, Cowardly Lion
Minor characters:	Minor characters:
Jawas	Munchkins
Sand People	Apple Trees
Stormtroopers	Flying Monkeys
Settings:	Settings:
Death Star	Witch's castle
Verdant Tikal (rebel base)	Emerald City
Conclusion:	Conclusion:
Luke uses magic to accomplish goal (destroy Death Star)	Dorothy uses magic to accomplish goal (return to Kansas)

guise parents as uncle and aunt, and this establishes social distance. The child can deal with the hero's separation (in *The Wizard of Oz*) or the aunt's and uncle's deaths (in *Star Wars*) more easily than with the death of or separation from real parents. Furthermore, this permits the child's strong feelings toward his or her real parents to be represented in different, more central characters, such as the Wicked Witch of the West and Darth Vader.

Both films focus on the child's relationship with the parent of the same sex, dividing that parent into three parts. In *The Wizard,* the mother is split into two parts bad and one part good. They are the Wicked Witch of the East, dead at the beginning of the movie; the Wicked Witch of the West, dead at the end; and Glinda, the good mother, who survives. The original *Star Wars* reversed the proportion of good and bad, giving Luke a good father (his own), the Jedi knight who is proclaimed dead at the film's beginning. There is another good father, Ben Kenobi, who is ambiguously dead when the movie ends. Third is the evil father figure, Darth Vader. As the good-mother third survives *The Wizard of Oz,* the bad-father third lives on after *Star Wars,* to strike back in the sequel.

The child's relationship with the parent of the opposite sex also is represented in the two

(continued)

films. Dorothy's father figure is the Wizard of Oz, an initially terrifying figure who later is proved to be a fake. Bettelheim notes that the typical fairy-tale father is disguised as a monster or giant. Or else, when preserved as a human, he is weak, distant, or ineffective. Dorothy counts on the wizard to save her but finds that he makes seemingly impossible demands and in the end is just an ordinary man. She succeeds on her own, no longer relying on a father who offers no more than she herself possesses.

In *Star Wars* (although emphatically not in the later films), Luke's mother figure is Princess Leia. Bettelheim notes that boys commonly fantasize their mothers to be unwilling captives of their fathers. Fairy tales often disguise mothers as princesses whose freedom the boy-hero must obtain. In graphic Freudian imagery, Darth Vader threatens Princess Leia with a needle the size of the witch's broomstick. By the end of the film, Luke has freed Leia and defeated Vader.

There are other striking parallels in the structure of the two films. Fairy-tale heroes often are accompanied on their adventures by secondary characters who personify the virtues needed in a successful quest. Such characters often come in threes. Dorothy takes along wisdom (the Scarecrow), love (the Tin Woodman), and courage (the Lion). *Star Wars* includes a structurally equivalent trio—Han Solo, C3PO, and Chewbacca—but their association with particular qualities isn't as precise. The minor characters are also structurally parallel: Munchkins and Jawas, Apple Trees and Sand People, Flying Monkeys and Stormtroopers. And compare settings—the witch's castle and the Death Star, the Emerald City and the rebel base. The endings are also parallel. Luke accomplishes his objective on his own, using the Force (mana, magical power). Dorothy's goal is to return to Kansas. She does that by tapping her shoes together and drawing on the Force in her ruby slippers.

All successful cultural products blend old and new, drawing on familiar themes. They may rearrange them in novel ways and thus win a lasting place in the imaginations of the culture that creates or accepts them. *Star Wars* successfully used old cultural themes in novel ways. It did that by drawing on *the* American fairy tale, one that had been available in book form since the turn of the 20th century.

often "run" in families. The Bachs, for example, produced not only Johann Sebastian, but several other noted composers and musicians.

In Chapter 1, anthropology's approach to the arts was contrasted with a traditional humanities focus on "fine arts" and elite expressions. Anthropology has extended the definition of "cultured" well beyond the elitist meaning of "high" art and culture. For anthropologists, everyone acquires culture through enculturation. In academia, growing acceptance of the anthropological definition of culture has helped broaden the study of the humanities from fine art and elite art to popular and folk art and the creative expressions of the masses and of many cultures.

In many societies, myths, legends, tales, and the art of storytelling play important roles in the transmission of culture and the preservation of tradition. In the absence of writing, oral traditions may preserve details of history and genealogy, as in many parts of West Africa. Art forms often go together. For example, music and storytelling may be combined for drama and emphasis (see the photo on page 529), much as they are in films and theater.

At what age do children start learning the arts? In some cultures, they start early. Contrast the photo of the Korean violin class with the photo of the Native Australian man playing the didgeridoo. The Korean scene shows formal instruction. The teachers take the lead in showing the kids how to play the violin. The Australian photo shows a more informal local scene in which children are observing, rather than being taught, about performing. Presumably, the Korean children are learning the arts because their parents want them to, not necessarily because they have an artistic temperament that they need or wish to express. Sometimes children's participation in

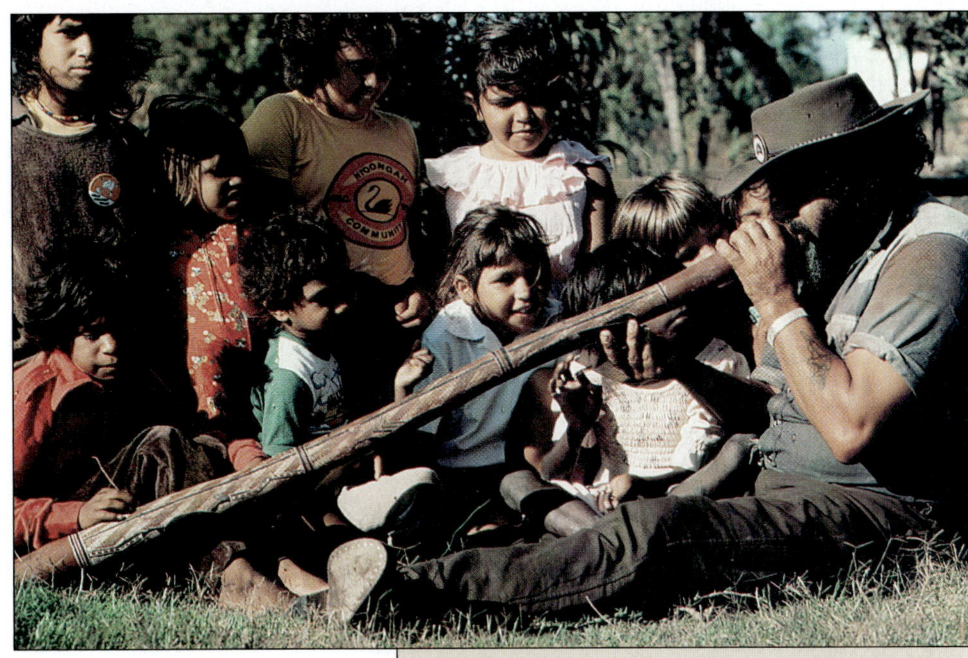

A Native Australian man blows into a didgeridoo, a traditional Australian wind instrument, as several children look on. This musical art is not set off from society. Making and playing the instrument are traditional skills.

A violin class for a large group of four-year-old children at a Korean music school.

arts or performance, including sports, exemplifies forced enculturation. It may be pushed by parents rather than by kids themselves. In the United States, performance, usually associated with schools, has a strong social, and usually competitive, component. Kids perform with their peers. In the process, they learn to compete, whether for a first place finish in a sports event or a first chair in the school orchestra or band.

The Artistic Career

In nonindustrial societies, artists tend to be part-time specialists. In states, there are more ways for artists to practice their craft full time. The number of positions in "arts and leisure" has mushroomed in contemporary societies, especially in North America. Many non-Western societies also offer career tracks in the arts: For example, a child born into a particular family or lineage may discover that he or she is destined for a career in leather working or weaving. Some societies are noted for particular arts, such as dance, wood carving, or weaving.

An artistic career also may involve some kind of a calling. Individuals may discover they have a particular talent and find an environment in which that talent is nourished. Separate career paths for artists usually involve special training and apprenticeship. Such paths are more likely in a complex society, where there are many separate career tracks, than in band or tribal societies, where expressive culture is less formally separated from daily life.

Artists need support if they are to devote full time to creative activity. They find support in their families or lineages if there is specialization in the arts involving kin groups. State societies often have patrons of the arts. Usually members of the elite class, patrons offer various kinds of support to aspiring and talented artists, such as court and palace painters, musicians, or sculptors. In some cases, an artistic career may entail a lifetime of dedication to religious art.

Goodal and Koss (1971) describe the manufacture of ornamental burial poles among the Tiwi of North Australia. Temporary separation and detachment from other social roles allowed burial pole artists to devote themselves to their work. The pole artists were ceremonially commissioned as such after a death. They were granted temporary freedom from the daily food quest. Other community members agreed to serve as their patrons. They supplied the artists with hard-to-get materials needed for their work. The burial pole artists were sequestered in a work area near the grave. That area was taboo to everyone else.

The arts are usually defined as neither practical nor ordinary. They rely on talent, which is individual, but which must be channeled and shaped in socially approved directions. Inevitably, artistic talent and production pull the artist away from the practical need to make a living. The issue of how to support artists and the arts arises again and again. We've all heard the phrase "struggling artist." But how should society support the arts? If there is state or religious support, something is typically expected in return. There is inevitably some limitation of the artist's "free" expression. Patronage and sponsorship also may result in the creation of art works that are removed from public display. Art commissioned for elites is often displayed only in their homes, perhaps finding its way into museums after their deaths. Church-commissioned art may be closer to the people. Artistic expressions of popular culture, intended for public rather than elite consumption, are discussed further in the chapter "Cultural Exchange and Survival."

Continuity and Change

The arts go on changing, although certain art forms have survived for thousands of years. The Upper Paleolithic cave art that has survived 30,000 years was itself a highly developed manifestation of human creativity and symbolism, with an undoubtedly long evolutionary history. Monumental architecture along with sculpture, reliefs, ornamental pottery, and written music, literature, and drama have survived from early civilizations.

Countries and cultures are known for particular contributions, including art. The Balinese are known for dance; the Navajo for sand paintings, jewelry, and weaving; and the French for making cuisine an art form. We still read Greek tragedies and comedies in college, as we also read Shakespeare and Milton, and view the works of Michelangelo. Greek theater is among the most enduring of the arts. The words of Aeschylus, Sophocles, Euripides, and Aristophanes have

In Athens, Greece, ancient Greek theater is being staged for a contemporary audience. Theater is typically a multimedia experience, with visual, aural, and often musical attributes.

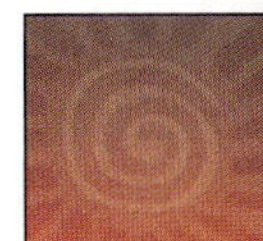

A synthesis of new and old theater techniques, including puppetry, is used in the Broadway production of Disney's *The Lion King.* What artistic influences have inspired the images shown in this photo?

beyond the classroom

Capoeira: The Afro-Brazilian Art of Unity and Survival

BACKGROUND INFORMATION

Student:	*Anne Haggerson*
Supervising Professor:	*Rudi Colloredo-Mansfeld*
School:	*University of Iowa*
Year in School/Major:	*Senior/Anthropology and Spanish*
Future Plans:	*Internship in Washington, D.C.; Ph.D.*
Project Title:	*Capoeira: The Afro-Brazilian Art of Unity and Survival*

Which of the features and functions of art are illustrated by this account? Can you think of parallels to *capoeira* in form and/or function in your own society?

For two months, I lived in a small, concrete apartment in Mangueira, an inner-city shantytown constructed over trash and swamps in Salvador, Bahia. I was doing a fieldwork project for my senior thesis while working as an English teacher for GRUCON (Grupo de União e Consciência Negra), the local black consciousness movement that had been actively involved in community mobilization and youth-based consciousness raising projects for 30 years. My research focused on institutions that helped children and families overcome the forces of poverty, unemployment, racism, and failing schools. Thus, I set out to investigate *capoeira*, an Afro-Brazilian martial art that assumes metaphors of slavery, liberation, and survival. The *capoeira* academy in the neighborhood was a subset of GRUCON and was grounded in a shared historical identity, fighting against economic oppression and political exclusion through music, dance, and African pride.

To prepare for this work, I researched problems of street children, took advanced Portuguese language courses, and worked out a research design that included interviews and participant observation. I trained formally with a local *capoeira* group for five months before going to Brazil, familiarizing myself with the key movements and game etiquette. Joining a *capoeira* academy in Brazil was one of the most challenging aspects of my research since I was a white, American woman participating in an activity dominated by Afro-Brazilian men. However, my active participation in the art was a crucial part of my fieldwork, allowing me to enter into the physical and

been captured in writing and live on. Who knows how many great preliterate creations and performances have been lost?

Classic Greek theater survives throughout the world. It is read in college courses, seen in the movies, and performed live on stages from Athens to New York. In today's world, the dramatic arts are part of a huge "arts and leisure" industry, which links Western and non-Western art forms in an international network that has both aesthetic and commercial dimensions (see Marcus and Myers 1995; Root 1996). For example, non-Western musical traditions and instruments, including the Australian didgeridoo shown in the photo on page 533, don't function apart from the modern world system. We've seen that local musicians perform for outsiders, including tourists who increasingly visit their villages. And "tribal" instruments such as didgeridoos are now exported worldwide. At least one store in Amsterdam, the Netherlands, specializes in didgeridoos, the only item it carries. Dozens of stores in any world capital hawk "traditional" arts, including musical instruments, from a hundred Third World countries. The commodification of non-Western art and the contemporary use of the arts to forge and re-

psychological space of my informants, experience the power of symbolic movement, and access the sense of friendship, unity, and commitment among the players.

The practices were held in a small, humble concrete room and were administered with a high level of discipline and seriousness. The *mestre* served as the teacher, role model, and mediator of the 40 team members and created meaning and stability in their lives, encouraging them to pass physical limits, harness leadership roles on the team, proudly display their skills in the *roda* or performance circle, and research the history of *capoeira* in their free time.

Beyond participant observation, I also recorded important events and interviewed participants. I witnessed a spectacular annual community event called a *batizado* or baptism, where the students graduate to a higher-level *capoeira* belt. By observing and photographing this yearly initiation, it became clear that *capoeira* was much more than a pastime; it was a survival strategy, an educational tool, and a microcosmic social hierarchy that was maintained by a complex web of community political leaders and organizers.

Associated with rich memories of embarrassment and accomplishment, I proudly wear the *capoeira* warrior name the *mestre* gave me, "Serpente" or Snake, which, to me, is a symbolic tattoo that represents the dynamic beauty of doing anthropological fieldwork at the base level of urban society and thereby unleashing important insight on the resilient spirit of a vital civil society and the importance of building robust community institutions that spark political change and cultural solidarity.

define group identities are discussed further in the chapter "Cultural Exchange and Survival."

We've seen that the arts typically draw in multiple media. Given the richness of today's media world, multimedia are even more marked. As ingredients and flavors from all over the world are combined in modern cuisine, so, too, are elements from many cultures and epochs woven into contemporary art and performance.

Our culture values change, experimentation, innovation, and novelty. But creativity also may be based on tradition. The Navajo, remember, can be at once individualistic, conservative, and attentive to proper form. In some cases and cultures, it's not necessary for artists to be innovative as they are being creative. Creativity can be expressed in variations on a traditional form. We see an example of this in "Interesting Issues" on pages 530–532, in which *Star Wars,* despite its specific story and innovative special effects, is shown to share its narrative structure with a previous film and fairy tale. It isn't always necessary for artists, in their work, to make a statement separating themselves from the past. Often, artists pay fealty to the past, associating with and building on, rather than rejecting, the work of their predecessors.

summary

1. Even if they lack a word for "art," people everywhere do associate an aesthetic experience with objects and events having certain qualities. The arts, sometimes called "expressive culture," include the visual arts, literature (written and oral), music, and theater arts. Some issues raised about religion also apply to art. If we adopt a special attitude or demeanor when confronting a sacred object, do we display something similar with art? Much art has been done in association with religion. In tribal performances, the arts and religion often mix. But non-Western art isn't always linked to religion.
2. The special places where we find art include museums, concert halls, opera houses, and theaters. However, the boundary between what's art and what's not may be blurred. Variation in art appreciation is especially common in contemporary society, with its professional artists and critics and great cultural diversity.
3. Those who work with non-Western art have been criticized for ignoring individual artists and for focusing too much on the social context and collective artistic production. Art is work, albeit creative work. In state societies, some people manage to support themselves as full-time artists. In nonstates artists are normally part time. Community standards judge the mastery and completion displayed in a work of art. Typically, the arts are exhibited, evaluated, performed, and appreciated in society. Music, which is often performed in groups, is among the most social of the arts. "Folk" art, music, and lore refer to the expressive culture of ordinary, usually rural, people.
4. Art can stand for tradition, even when traditional art is removed from its original context. Art can express community sentiment, with political goals, used to call attention to social issues. Often, art is meant to commemorate and to last. Growing acceptance of the anthropological definition of culture has guided the humanities beyond fine art, elite art, and Western art to the creative expressions of the masses and of many cultures. Myths, legends, tales, and the art of storytelling often play important roles in the transmission of culture. Many societies offer career tracks in the arts; a child born into a particular family or lineage may discover that he or she is destined for a career in leather working or weaving.
5. The arts go on changing, although certain art forms have survived for thousands of years. Countries and cultures are known for particular contributions. Today, a huge "arts and leisure" industry links Western and non-Western art forms in an international network with both aesthetic and commercial dimensions.

key terms

aesthetics Appreciation of the qualities perceived in works of art; the mind and emotions in relation to a sense of beauty.

art An object or event that evokes an aesthetic reaction—a sense of beauty, appreciation, harmony, and/or pleasure; the quality, production, expression, or realm of what is beautiful or of more than ordinary significance; the class of objects subject to aesthetic criteria.

arts The arts include the visual arts, literature (written and oral), music, and theater arts.

catharsis Intense emotional release.

ethnomusicology The comparative study of the musics of the world and of music as an aspect of culture and society.

expressive culture The arts; people express themselves creatively in dance, music, song, painting, sculpture, pottery, cloth, storytelling, verse, prose, drama, and comedy.

folk Of the people; originally coined for European peasants; refers to the art, music, and lore of ordinary people, as contrasted with the "high" art or "classic" art of the European elites.

critical thinking questions

1. Think of something visual that you consider to be art, but whose status as art is debatable. How would you convince someone else that it is art? What kinds of arguments against your position would you expect to hear?
2. Think of a musical composition or performance you consider to be art, but whose status as such is debatable. How would you convince someone else that it is art? What kinds of arguments against your position would you expect to hear?
3. Where did you last witness art? In what kind of a setting was it? Did people go there to appreciate the arts, or for some other reason?
4. Is *Star Wars* art? If so, what kind of art? How would you analyze it as art?
5. Based on your own experience, how may the arts be used to buttress religion?
6. Can you think of a political dispute involving art or the arts? What were the different positions being debated?
7. Should society support the arts? Why or why not? If so, how?

case study

Kaluli: This chapter has discussed the uses and places of arts in social life, describing music as one of the most social forms of expressive culture. In *Culture Sketches* by Holly Peters-Golden, read the chapter on the "Kaluli: Story, Song, and Ceremony." How does Kaluli music reflect central cultural ideas? What aspects of Kaluli life and society are represented in their music? How is the Kaluli relationship to music similar to, or different from, your own society's relationship to music? Several American and European musicians have joined to produce a recording of Bosavi music, "Voices of the Rainforest" (see "Interesting Issues" in the text chapter "Cultural Exchange and Survival"). Profits from its sale benefit the Bosavi People's Fund, set up to provide financial aid to maintain Kaluli cultural survival in the face of threats to their rainforest environment. Why might it be music, in particular, that was chosen to raise money for the Kaluli?

suggested additional readings

Anderson, R.

1989 *Art in Small-Scale Societies.* Upper Saddle River, NJ: Prentice Hall. Introduction to non-Western art, with a focus on the visual arts.

1990 *Calliope's Sisters: A Comparative Study of Philosophies of Art.* Upper Saddle River, NJ: Prentice Hall. A comparative study of aesthetics in 10 cultures.

2000 *American Muse: Anthropological Excursions into Art and Aesthetics.* Upper Saddle River, NJ: Prentice Hall. Bringing an anthropological perspective to bear on arts in America.

Anderson, R., and K. Field, eds.

1993 *Art in Small-Scale Societies: Contemporary Readings.* Upper Saddle River, NJ: Prentice Hall. An anthology of studies of non-Western art, with a focus on the visual arts.

Conkey, M., O. Soffer, D. Stratmann, and N. Jablonski
1997 *Beyond Art: Pleistocene Image and Symbol.* San Francisco: Memoirs of the California Academy of Sciences, no. 23. A consideration of the symbolic basis and nature of prehistoric art.

Coote, J., and A. Shelton, eds.
1992 *Anthropology, Art, and Aesthetics.* New York: Oxford University Press. Useful collection of essays.

Hatcher, E. P.
1999 *Art as Culture: An Introduction to the Anthropology of Art,* 2nd ed. Westport, CT: Bergin & Garvey. Up-to-date introduction.

Layton, R.
1991 *The Anthropology of Art,* 2nd ed. New York: Cambridge University Press. Survey of the major issues, with a focus on visual art.

Marcus, G. E., and F. R. Myers, eds.
1995 *The Traffic in Culture: Refiguring Art and Anthropology.* Berkeley, CA: University of California Press. Art, society, and the marketing of culture in global perspective.

Mirzoeff, N.
1999 *An Introduction to Visual Culture.* New York: Routledge. Popular culture, art, and society.

Napier, A. D.
1992 *Foreign Bodies: Performance, Art, and Symbolic Anthropology.* Berkeley, CA: University of California Press. Focuses on the performing arts and symbols of society.

Otten, C. M., ed.
1971 *Anthropology and Art; Readings in Cross-Cultural Aesthetics.* Garden City, NY: American Museum of Natural History. Classic anthology.

Root, D.
1996 *Cannibal Culture: Art, Appropriation, and the Commodification of Difference.* Boulder, CO: Westview. How Western art and commerce classify, co-opt, and commodify "native" experiences, creations, and products.

Rushing, W. Jackson, ed.
1999 *Native American Art in the Twentieth Century.* New York: Routledge. Themes, motifs, and collections of Indian art.

internet exercises

1. *Body Art:* Visit the National Museum of Natural History's online exhibit of "Canela body adornment," **http://www.nmnh.si.edu/naa/canela/canela1.htm.** Read all three pages of the exhibit and answer the questions below:

   a. In this example, how interrelated are art and world view? How is art being used by the Canela?

   b. What individuals among the Canela get their ears pierced, and what does it signify? Who participates in the piercing? How does this practice compare to ear piercing in Western society?

   c. Cultures can change through time. What kinds of changes have occurred in the Canela practices of ear piercing since the 1950s? In the same way, what kinds of changes have occurred in ear piercing practices in Western society? What do these changes signify?

2. *Comparing Art:* Go to the Metropolitan Museum of Art's Collection page, **http://www.metmuseum.org/collections/index.asp** and browse their collections of Egyptian Art, **http://www.metmuseum.org/collections/department.asp?dep=10,** European Paintings, **http://www.metmuseum.org/collections/department.asp?dep=11,** and Modern Art, **http://www.metmuseum.org/collections/department.asp?dep=21.** For each of these collections, address the following questions:

   a. By whom is this art produced, and for whom is it produced?

   b. For what purpose is this art being produced (e.g., religious, aesthetic, political, monetary)?

   c. What themes and subjects are portrayed in the art?

   d. By just looking at the art, what can you learn about the culture that produced it?

See Chapter 20 on your CD-ROM for additional review and interactive exercises. See your McGraw-Hill Online Learning Center for more.

PART IV
The Modern World

Chapter 21

The Modern World System

CHAPTER OUTLINE

NGNEWS.COM NEWS BRIEFS

Global Warming Melts Inuit's Arctic Lifestyle

by Lisa Krause
July 12, 2000

WASHINGTON—Traditionally, the 130 members of the Inuit community of Sachs Harbor, located on the western tip of Banks Island in the Canadian Arctic, supported themselves through age-old patterns of hunting, trapping, and fishing. Recently, however, members of the community have taken on a new role: climate-change observers.

Here, 400 miles (640 kilometers) north of the Arctic Circle, global warming is not a theory that is debated among scientists, but a reality of everyday life. Sea ice is thinning, and disappearing. Indigenous animals are moving farther north. And melting permafrost has loosened the ground enough to weaken foundations and cause homes to lean. This, plus rising sea levels, threatens to displace an entire community.

Surrounded by signs of change, in 1998 the residents of Sachs Harbor devised a plan to document the changes affecting their homes and bring attention to the very obvious signs of global warming.

Led by Rosemarie Kupatana, a Sachs Harbor resident, Inuit Observations on Climate Change is a community-based project developed in cooperation with the International Institute for Sustainable Development. Aided by project scientists, community members are working to produce a video that will record the changes threatening their home.

Among the most alarming changes is the disappearance of native species. Caribou, long a staple of Inuit diet, are falling through once-solid sea ice. Polar bears are moving farther north, as are seals, who need the shelter of pack ice to give birth to their young.

As traditional Arctic species move north, new species are moving in. Grizzly bears have been spotted in territory once dominated by polar bears. Salmon, never before caught this far north, are making appearances in fishermen's nets.

The changes make hunting and fishing very difficult. "Even with generations of indigenous knowledge available to the hunters and trappers of Sachs Harbor they are having a difficult time predicting when once-predictable seasonal migrations will occur," says Jennifer Castleden, project officer for the International Institute of Sustainable Development.

Physical changes to the land include rising water and softening permafrost, which threaten to ruin house foundations and the one road that leads to the tiny community. Slumping, the collapse of land under the weight of newly thawed permafrost, is also altering the look of the land along the coast.

Scientists and other project team members have traveled to Sachs Harbor four times in the past year to document climate changes recorded by the community. The result of their labor is a 42-minute video, narrated entirely by Sachs Harbor community members, detailing the drastic changes affecting this Arctic outpost.

In addition to the video, which will be released in November, project scientists will compile a detailed report on the value of traditional knowledge and local observations in documenting climate change.

"As far as we know, this is the only project of its kind in the Arctic," said Castleden, who noted that news reports from eastern Arctic communities indicated similar patterns. Perhaps, she notes, this project will raise awareness of the need to document climate change in other parts of the Arctic.

"Climate change is a reality, not a distant threat," says Castleden. "This community is the 'canary in the coal mine' of climate change."

Source: http://www.ngnews.com/news/2000/07/07132000/inuitclimatechange_2837.asp.

overview

Local societies increasingly participate in wider systems, which are regional, national, and global in scale. The modern world system refers to a global system in which nations are economically and politically interdependent.

The world economy is based on production for sale, guided by the profit motive. This capitalist world economy has political and economic specialization based on three positions: core, semiperiphery, and periphery. These positions have existed since the 16th century, although the particular countries filling them have changed.

After 1760 industrialization increased production in farming and manufacturing. The work force moved from homes to factories, from rural areas to industrial cities. Today's world system maintains the distinction between those who own the means of production and those who don't. But the division is now worldwide. And a middle class of skilled and professional workers has been added to the class structure.

There is a marked contrast between capitalists and workers in the core nations and workers on the periphery. Several forces have worked to remove people from the land, as even peripheral nations have begun to industrialize. One effect of industrialization has been the destruction of indigenous economies, ecologies, cultures, and peoples. For the past 500 years, the main forces influencing cultural interaction have been commercial expansion, industrial capitalism, and the differential power of core nations.

Although field work in small communities is anthropology's hallmark, isolated groups are impossible to find today. Truly isolated cultures probably have never existed. For thousands of years, human groups have been in contact with one another. Local societies have always participated in a larger system, which today has global dimensions. We call it the *modern world system,* by which we mean a world in which nations are economically and politically interdependent.

City, nation, and world increasingly invade local communities. Today, if anthropologists want to study a fairly isolated society, they must journey to the highlands of Papua New Guinea or the tropical forests of South America. Even in those places, they will probably encounter missionaries or prospectors. In contemporary Australia, sheep owned by people who speak English graze where totemic ceremonies once were held. Farther in the outback, some descendants of those totemites may be working in a movie crew making *Crocodile Dundee IV.* A Hilton hotel stands in the capital of faraway Madagascar, and a paved highway now has an exit for Arembepe, the Brazilian fishing village I have been studying since 1962. When and how did the modern world system begin?

The world system and the relations among the countries within that system are shaped by the world capitalist economy. World-system theory can be traced to the French social historian Fernand Braudel. In his three-volume work *Civilization and Capitalism, 15th–18th Century* (1981, 1982, 1992), Braudel argues that society consists of parts assembled into an interrelated system. Societies are subsystems of bigger systems, with the world system as the largest.

The Emergence of the World System

As Europeans took to ships, developing a transoceanic trade-oriented economy, people throughout the world entered Europe's sphere of influence. In the 15th century, Europe established regular contact with Asia, Africa, and eventually the New World (the Caribbean and the Americas). Christopher Columbus's first voyage from Spain

The modern world system rests on the world capitalist economy. Shown here is a Honda motorcycle plant, the world's largest such plant, in Bangkok, Thailand. Is Honda a Thai firm? Where do you imagine such motorcycles are sold?

to the Bahamas and the Caribbean in 1492 was soon followed by additional voyages. These journeys opened the way for a major exchange of people, resources, diseases, and ideas, as the Old and New Worlds were forever linked (Crosby 1972, 1986; Diamond 1997; Viola and Margolis 1991). Led by Spain and Portugal, Europeans extracted silver and gold, conquered the natives (taking some as slaves), and colonized their lands.

Previously in Europe as throughout the world, rural people had produced mainly for their own needs, growing their own food and making clothing, furniture, and tools from local products. Production beyond immediate needs was undertaken to pay taxes and purchase trade items such as salt and iron. As late as 1650, the English diet, like diets in most of the world today, was based on locally grown starches (Mintz 1985). However, in the 200 years that followed, the English became extraordinary consumers of imported goods. One of the earliest and most popular of those goods was sugar (Mintz 1985).

Sugarcane was originally domesticated in Papua New Guinea, and sugar was first processed in India. Reaching Europe via the Middle East and the eastern Mediterranean, it was carried to the New World by Columbus (Mintz 1985). The climate of Brazil and the Caribbean proved ideal for growing sugarcane, and Europeans built plantations there to supply the growing demand for sugar. This led to the development in the 17th century of a plantation economy based on a single cash crop—a system known as monocrop production.

The demand for sugar in a growing international market spurred the development of the transatlantic slave trade and New World plantation economies based on slave labor. By the 18th century, an increased English demand for raw cotton led to rapid settlement of what is now the southeastern United States and the emergence there of another slave-based monocrop production system. Like sugar, cotton was a key trade item that fueled the growth of the world system.

The increasing dominance of trade led to the **capitalist world economy** (Wallerstein 1982), a single world system committed to production for sale or exchange, with the object of maximizing profits rather than supplying domestic needs. **Capital** refers to wealth or resources invested in business, with the intent of producing a profit; the defining attribute of capitalism is economic orientation to the world market for profit.

The key claim of world-system theory is that an identifiable social system, based on wealth and power differentials, extends beyond individual states and nations. That system is formed by a set of economic and political relations that have characterized much of the globe since the 16th century, when the Old World established regular contact with the New World.

According to Wallerstein (1982), the nations within the world system occupy three different positions of economic and political power: core, periphery, and semiperiphery. There is a geographic center or **core,** the dominant position in the world system, consisting of the strongest and most powerful nations. In core nations, "the complexity of economic activities and the level

From producer to consumer, in the modern world system. The top photo, taken in the Caribbean nation of Dominica, shows the hard labor required to extract sugar using a manual press. In the bottom photo, an English middle-class family enjoys afternoon tea, sweetened with imported sugar. Which of the ingredients in your breakfast today were imported?

of capital accumulation is [sic] the greatest" (Thompson 1983, p. 12). With its sophisticated technologies and mechanized means of production, the core produces capital-intensive high-technology goods. Most of those products flow to other core nations, but some also go to the periphery and semiperiphery. According to Arrighi (1994), the core monopolizes the most profitable activities, especially the control of world finance.

306

Semiperiphery and **periphery** nations, which roughly correspond to what is usually called the Third World, have less power, wealth, and influence. The semiperiphery is intermediate between the core and the periphery. Contemporary nations of the semiperiphery are industrialized. Like core nations, they export both industrial goods and commodities, but they lack the power and economic dominance of core nations. Thus Brazil, a semiperiphery nation, exports automobiles to Nigeria and auto engines, orange juice extract, and coffee to the United States.

Economic activities in the periphery are less mechanized and use human labor more intensively than do those in the semiperiphery. The periphery produces raw materials and agricultural commodities for export to the core and the semiperiphery. However, in the modern world, industrialization has reached even peripheral nations. The relationship between the core and the periphery is fundamentally exploitative. Trade and other forms of economic relations between core and periphery tend to benefit capitalists in the core at the expense of the periphery (Shannon 1996).

Industrialization

By the 18th century, the stage had been set for the **Industrial Revolution**—the historical transformation (in Europe, after 1750) of "traditional" into "modern" societies through industrialization of the economy. Industrialization required capital for investment. The established system of transoceanic trade and commerce supplied this capital from the enormous profits it generated. Wealthy people sought investment opportunities and eventually found them in machines and engines to drive machines. Industrialization increased production in both farming and manufacturing, as capital and scientific innovation fueled invention.

European industrialization developed from (and eventually replaced) the *domestic system* (cottage industry or home-handicraft system) of manufacture. In this system, an organizer-entrepreneur supplied the raw materials to workers in their homes and collected the finished products from them. The entrepreneur, whose sphere of operations might span several villages, owned the materials, paid for the work, and arranged the marketing.

Causes of the Industrial Revolution

The Industrial Revolution began in the cotton products, iron, and pottery trades. These were widely used goods whose manufacture could be broken down into simple routine motions that machines could perform. When manufacturing moved from home to factory, where machinery replaced handwork, agrarian societies evolved into industrial ones. As factories produced cheap staple goods, the Industrial Revolution led to a dramatic increase in production. Industrialization fueled urban growth and created a new kind of city, with factories crowded together in places where coal and labor were cheap.

The Industrial Revolution began in England rather than in France. Why? Unlike the English, the French didn't have to transform their domestic manufacturing system by industrializing. Faced with an increased need for products, with a late-18th-century population twice that of Great Britain, France could simply extend its domestic system of production by drawing in new homes. The French were able to increase production *without innovating*—they could enlarge the existing system rather than adopt a new one. However, to meet mounting demand for staples—at home and in the colonies—England, with fewer workers, had to industrialize.

Britain's population doubled during the 18th century (particularly after 1750) and did so again between 1800 and 1850. This demographic explosion fueled consumption, but British entrepreneurs couldn't meet the increased demand with

the traditional production methods. This spurred experimentation, innovation, and rapid technological change.

In the home-handicraft, or domestic, system of production, an organizer supplied raw materials to workers in their homes and collected their products. Family life and work were intertwined, as in this English scene. Is there a modern equivalent to the domestic system of production?

English industrialization drew on national advantages in natural resources. Great Britain was rich in coal and iron ore and had navigable waterways and easily negotiated coasts. It was a seafaring island-nation located at the crossroads of international trade. These features gave Britain a favored position for importing raw materials and exporting manufactured goods. Another factor in England's industrial growth was the fact that much of its 18th-century colonial empire was occupied by English settler families who looked to the mother country as they tried to replicate European civilization in the New World. These colonies bought large quantities of English staples.

It also has been argued that particular cultural values and religion contributed to industrialization. Thus, many members of the emerging English middle class were Protestant nonconformists. Their beliefs and values encouraged industry, thrift, the dissemination of new knowledge, inventiveness, and willingness to accept change (Weber 1904/1958). Weber's ideas about Protestant values and capitalism were discussed in the chapter "Religion."

Stratification

The socioeconomic effects of industrialization were mixed. English national income tripled between 1700 and 1815 and increased 30 times more by 1939. Standards of comfort rose, but prosperity was uneven. At first, factory workers got wages higher than those available in the domestic system. Later, owners started recruiting labor in places where living standards were low and labor (including that of women and children) was cheap.

Social ills increased with the growth of factory towns and industrial cities, with conditions like those Charles Dickens described in *Hard Times.* Filth and smoke polluted the 19th-century cities. Housing was crowded and unsanitary, with insufficient water and sewage disposal facilities and rising disease and death rates. This was the world of Ebenezer Scrooge, Bob Cratchit, Tiny Tim—and Karl Marx.

Industrial Stratification

The social theorists Karl Marx and Max Weber focused on the stratification systems associated with industrialization. From his observations in England and his analysis of 19th-century industrial capitalism, Marx (Marx and Engels 1848/1976) saw socioeconomic stratification as a sharp and simple division between two opposed classes: the bourgeoisie (capitalists) and the proletariat (propertyless workers). The bourgeoisie traced its origins to overseas ventures and the world capitalist economy, which had transformed the social structure of northwestern Europe, creating a wealthy commercial class.

Industrialization shifted production from farms and cottages to mills and factories, where mechanical power was available and where workers could be assembled to operate heavy machinery.

The **bourgeoisie** were the owners of the factories, mines, large farms, and other means of production. The **working class,** or proletariat, was made up of people who had to sell their labor to survive. With the decline of subsistence production and with the rise of urban migration and the possibility of unemployment, the bourgeoisie came to stand between workers and the means of production.

Industrialization hastened the process of *proletarianization*—the separation of workers from the means of production. The bourgeoisie also came to dominate the means of communication, the schools, and other key institutions. Marx viewed the nation-state as an instrument of oppression and religion as a method of diverting and controlling the masses.

Class consciousness (recognition of collective interests and personal identification with one's economic group) was a vital part of Marx's view of class. He saw bourgeoisie and proletariat as socioeconomic divisions with radically opposed interests. Marx viewed classes as powerful collective forces that could mobilize human energies to influence the course of history. Finding strength through common experience, workers would develop organizations to protect their interests and increase their share of industrial profits.

And so they did. During the 19th century, trade unions and socialist parties emerged to express a rising anticapitalist spirit. The concerns of the English labor movement were to remove young children from factories and limit the hours during which women and children could work. The profile of stratification in industrial core nations gradually took shape. Capitalists controlled production, but labor was organizing for better wages and working conditions. By 1900, many governments had factory legislation and social-welfare programs. Mass living standards in core nations rose as population grew.

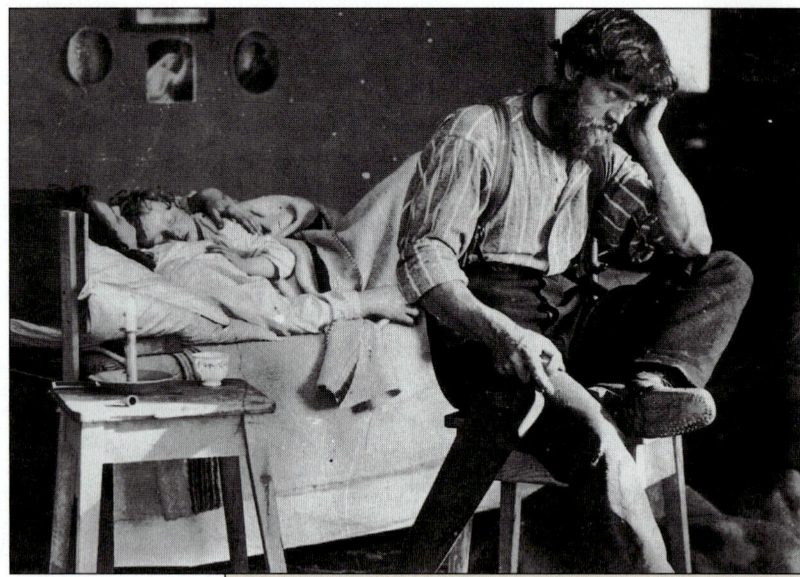

In several books, including *Hard Times*, Charles Dickens described the social ills that plagued English industrial cities. This photo, taken in 1859 by O. G. Rejlauder, is also entitled "Hard Times." It shows a dejected laborer sitting in front of the bed in which his family is sleeping. What kinds of social ills did Dickens describe? Do cities still have such problems?

The modern capitalist world system maintains the distinction between those who own the means of production and those who don't. The class division into capitalists and propertyless workers is now worldwide. Nevertheless, modern stratification systems aren't simple and dichotomous. They include (particularly in core and semiperiphery nations) a middle class of skilled and professional workers. Gerhard Lenski (1966) argues that social equality tends to increase in advanced industrial societies. The masses improve their access to economic benefits and political power. In Lenski's scheme, the shift of political power to the masses reflects the growth of the middle class, which reduces the polarization between owning and working classes. The proliferation of middle-class occupations creates opportunities for social mobility. The stratification system grows more complex (Giddens 1973).

Faulting Marx for an overly simple and exclusively economic view of stratification, Weber (1922/1968) defined three dimensions of social stratification: wealth (economic status), power (political status), and prestige (social status). Although, as Weber showed, wealth, power, and prestige are separate components of social ranking, they do tend to be correlated. Weber also believed that social identities based on ethnicity, religion, race, nationality, and other attributes could take priority over class (social identity based on economic status). In addition to class contrasts, the modern world system is cross-cut by status groups, such as ethnic and religious groups and nations (Shannon 1996). Class conflicts tend to occur within nations, and nationalism has prevented global class solidarity, particularly of proletarians.

Although the capitalist class dominates politically in most countries, the leaders of core nations have found it to be in their interest to allow proletarians to organize and make demands. Growing wealth has made it easier for core nations to grant higher wages (Hopkins and Wallerstein 1982). However, the improvement in core workers' living standards wouldn't have occurred without the world system. The added surplus that comes from the periphery allows core capitalists to maintain their profits while satisfying the demands of core workers. In the periphery, wages and living standards are much lower. The current *world stratification system* features a substantial contrast between both capitalists and workers in the core nations and workers on the periphery.

Karl Marx (1818–1883), shown in 1860.

Max Weber (1864–1920). Did Weber improve on Marx's view of stratification?

Poverty on the Periphery

With the expansion of the world capitalist economy, people on the periphery have been removed from the land by large landowners and agribusiness interests. One result is increased poverty, including food shortages. Displaced people can't earn enough to buy the food they can no longer grow.

Bangladesh illustrates some of the causes of Third World poverty and food shortages. Climate, soils, and water availability in Bangladesh are favorable for a productive agriculture. Indeed, before the arrival of the British in the 18th century, Bangladesh (then called Bengal) had a prosperous local cotton industry. There was some stratification, but peasants had enough land to provide an adequate diet. Land was neither privately owned nor part of the market economy. Things changed under British colonial rule. The British encouraged cash-crop farming for export and converted land into a commodity that could be bought and sold.

Increased stratification was a result of colonialism and tighter linkage with the world capitalist economy. The peasantry of Bangladesh gradually lost its land. A study done in 1977 (Bodley 2000) showed that a small group of wealthy people owned most of the land. One-third of the households owned no land at all. Poverty was expressed in food shortages. Many landless people worked as sharecroppers, with landowners claiming at least half the crop. The peasants were underpaid for their crops and overcharged for the commodities they needed.

Malaysian Factory Women

Successive waves of integration into the world system have washed Malaysia, another former British colony. The Malays have witnessed sea

trade, conquest, the influx of British and Chinese capital, and immigration from China and India. For centuries, Malaysia has been part of the world system. Recently, the Malaysian government has promoted export-oriented industry to bring rural Malays into the capitalist system. This has been done in response to rural discontent over poverty and landlessness as some 10,000 families per year are pushed off the land. Transnational companies have been installing labor-intensive manufacturing operations in rural Malaysia.

The industrialization of Malaysia is part of a global strategy. To escape the mounting labor costs in the core, corporations headquartered in Japan, Western Europe, and the United States have been moving labor-intensive factories to the periphery. Malaysia now has hundreds of Japanese and American subsidiaries, which mainly produce garments, foodstuffs, and electronics components. In electronics plants in rural Malaysia, thousands of young women from peasant families now assemble microchips and microcomponents for transistors and capacitors. Aihwa Ong (1987) did a study of electronics assembly workers in an area where 85 percent of the workers were young unmarried females from nearby villages.

Ong found that factory discipline and social relations contrasted strongly with traditional com-

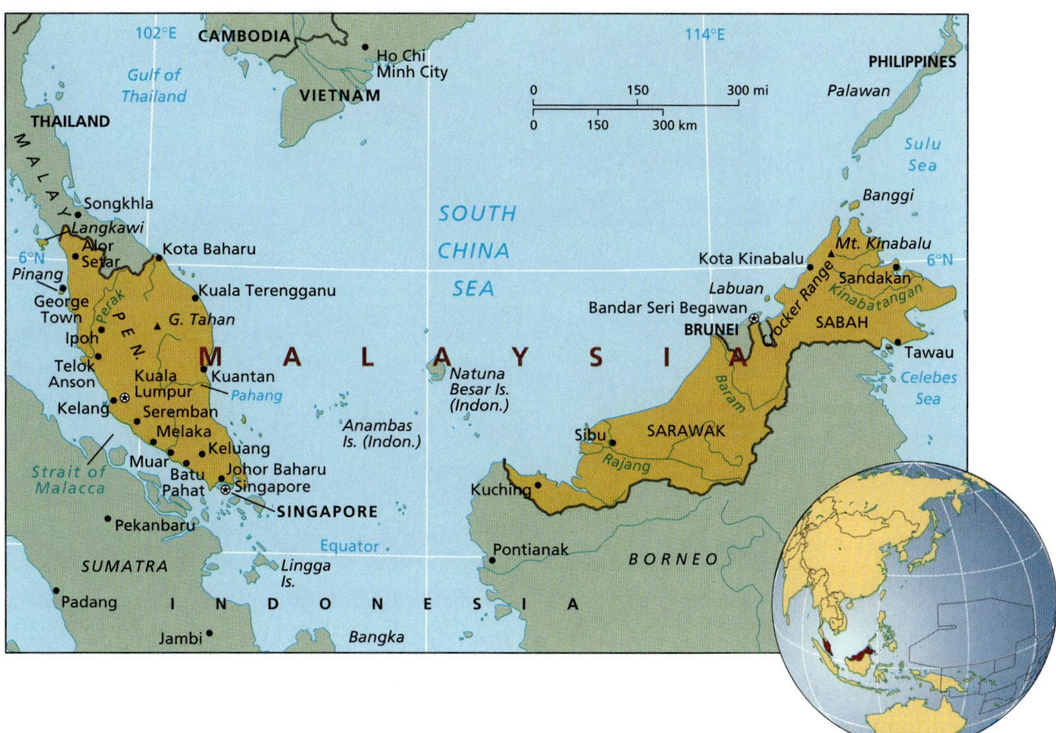

munity life. Previously, agricultural cycles and daily Islamic prayers, rather than production quotas and work shifts, had framed the rural economy and social life. Villagers had planned and done their own work, without bosses. In factories, however, village women had to cope with a rigid work routine and constant supervision by men.

Factory relations of production featured a hierarchy, pay scale, and division of labor based on ethnicity and gender. Japanese men filled top management, while Chinese men were the engineers and production supervisors. The Malay men also worked as supervisors of the factory work force, which consisted of nonunion female semiskilled workers from poor Malay peasant families.

The Japanese firms in rural Malaysia were paternalistic. Managers assured village parents that they would care for their daughters as though they were their own. Unlike the American firms, the Japanese subsidiaries worked hard at maintaining good relations with rural elders. Management gave money for village events, visited workers' home communities, and invited parents to the plant for receptions. In return, village elders accorded high status to the Japanese managers. The elders colluded with the managers to urge young women to accept and stay with factory work.

The discipline, diligence, and obedience that factories value is learned in local schools, where uniforms help prepare girls for the factory dress code. Peasant women wear loose, flowing tunics, sarongs, and sandals, but factory workers must don tight overalls and heavy rubber gloves, in which they feel constrained and controlled.

Assembling electronics components requires precise, concentrated labor. Demanding, exhausting, depleting, and dehumanizing, labor in these factories illustrates the separation of intellectual and manual activity that Marx considered the defining feature of industrial work. One woman said about her bosses, "They exhaust us very much, as if they do not think that we too are human beings" (Ong 1987, p. 202). Nor does factory work bring women a substantial financial reward, given low wages, job uncertainty, and family claims on wages. Young women typically work just a few years. Production quotas, three daily shifts, overtime, and surveillance take their toll in mental and physical exhaustion.

One response to factory discipline and relations of production is spirit possession, which

India's rural division of labor is based on caste and gender. This northern Indian woman is piling up cow dung cakes, to be burned for cooking. At every caste level, Indian women tend to do more menial labor than men of the same caste. The word for caste, *jati*, means kind or sort. Many Indians say there are only two *jati:* men and women. They recognize that gender stratification exists alongside caste stratification.

Ong interprets as an unconscious protest against labor discipline and male control of the industrial setting. Sometimes possession takes the form of mass hysteria. The spirits have simultaneously invaded as many as 120 factory workers. Weretigers (the Malay equivalent of the werewolf) arrive to avenge the construction of a factory on local burial grounds. Disturbed earth and grave spirits swarm on the shop floor. First the women see the spirits, then their bodies are invaded. The women become violent and scream abuses. The vengeful weretigers send the women into sobbing, laughing, and shrieking fits. To deal with possession, factories employ local medicine men, who sacrifice chickens and goats to fend off the spirits. This solution works only some of the time; possession still goes on. Factory women continue to act as vehicles to express the anger of avenging ghosts and their own frustrations.

Ong argues that spirit possession expresses anguish caused by, and resistance to, capitalist relations of production. However, she also notes that by engaging in this form of rebellion, factory women avoid a direct confrontation with the source of their distress. Ong concludes that spirit possession, while expressing repressed resentment, doesn't do much to modify factory conditions. (Other tactics, such as unionization, would do more—see "Interesting Issues: Troubles in Swooshland.") Spirit possession may even help maintain the current conditions of inequality and dehumanization by operating as a safety valve for accumulated tensions.

Open and Closed Class Systems

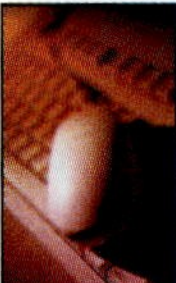

Inequalities, which are built into the structure of state societies, tend to persist across the generations. The extent to which they do or don't is a measure of the openness of the stratification system, the ease of social mobility it permits. Within the world capitalist economy, stratification has taken many forms, including caste, slavery, and class systems.

Caste systems are closed, hereditary systems of stratification that often are dictated by religion. Hierarchical social status is ascribed at birth, so that people are locked into their parents' social position. Caste lines are clearly defined, and legal and religious sanctions are applied against those who seek to cross them.

407

The world's best-known caste system is associated with Hinduism in traditional India. As described by Gargan (1992), despite the formal abolition of the caste system in 1949, caste-based stratification remains important in modern India. An estimated 5 million adults and 10 million children are bonded laborers. These people live in complete servitude, working to repay real or imagined debts. Most of them are untouchables, impoverished and powerless people at the bottom of the caste hierarchy. Some families have been bonded for generations; people are born into servitude because their parents or grandparents were sold previously. Bonded workers toil unpaid in stone quarries, brick kilns, and rice paddies.

Once indentured, it is difficult to escape. Bonded labor is against Indian law, but it persists despite court rulings and efforts to stop it. Social workers obtain court orders to release bonded workers, but local officials and police often ignore them. Agents for quarries and kilns continue to entice untouchables into bonded labor with deceptive promises. Others enter bondage seeking to repay loans that can never be fully repaid. In this way, the caste system continues to form a highly restrictive system of social and economic stratification in India.

Another castelike system, *apartheid,* existed until recently in South Africa. In that legally maintained hierarchy, blacks, whites, and Asians had their own separate (and unequal) neighborhoods, schools, laws, and punishments.

In **slavery,** the most inhumane and degrading form of stratification, people are treated as property. In the Atlantic slave trade, millions of human beings were treated as commodities. The plantation systems of the Caribbean, the southeastern United States, and Brazil were based on forced slave labor. Slaves lacked control over the means of production. They were like proletarians in this respect. But proletarians at least are legally free. Unlike slaves, they have some control over where they work, how much they work, for whom they work, and what they do with their wages. Slaves, in contrast, were forced to live and work at their master's whim. Defined as lesser human beings, slaves lacked legal rights. They could be sold and resold; their families, split apart. Slaves had nothing to sell—not even their own labor (Mintz 1985). Slavery is the most extreme, coercive, and abusive form of legalized inequality.

Slavery is the most extreme, coercive, and abusive form of legalized inequality. Although proletarians, such as these "white slaves of England," also lacked control over the means of production, they did have some control over where they worked. In what other ways do proletarians differ from slaves?

Vertical mobility is an upward or downward change in a person's social status. A truly **open class system** would facilitate mobility. Individual achievement and personal merit would determine social rank. Hierarchical social statuses would be achieved on the basis of people's efforts. Ascribed statuses (family background, ethnicity, gender, religion) would be less important. Open class systems would have blurred class lines and a wide range of status positions.

293–294

interesting issues

Troubles in Swooshland

Famous for its Swoosh, Nike is the world's leading manufacturer of athletic shoes. Asian labor plays a prominent role in shoe making, which Nike subcontracts to factories in Vietnam, Indonesia, China, Thailand, and Pakistan. Most of the 530,000 workers in these factories are women between the ages of 15 and 28.

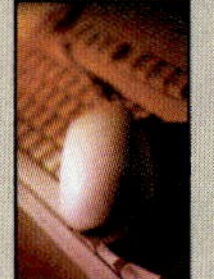

In 1996, the CBS program *48 Hours* ran a segment critical of work conditions at Nike factories in Vietnam. The practices of Nike's Asian subcontractors, and of Nike itself, were questioned by international media, labor, and human rights groups. Publicity centered on the fact that the shoes were being produced by very cheap Asian labor, then being sold in North America for up to $100 a pair. Nike also was faulted for celebrity endorsements featuring such highly paid sports figures as Michael Jordan and Tiger Woods, when Asian workers were making less than $2.00 a day. Disturbed by the CBS report, a group of Vietnamese Americans organized to form a new NGO, Vietnam Labor Watch. With the company's cooperation, this group carried out a study of Nike's Vietnamese operations.

They confirmed that wages and working conditions were problematic. Across Asia, the wages paid to Nike workers averaged $1.84 per day. In Vietnam's Ho Chi Minh City, where the cost of three simple meals was $2.10 per day, Nike factory workers made only $1.60 per day. Health was also a concern, as was factory safety. Salaries were too low to ensure adequate nutrition. According to law, factory doors must be kept open during operating hours, a precaution against fire. In fact, doors were often closed. Workers also had to endure overheated factories with bad air, filled with chemical smells of paint and glue.

Nike's young female workers, like those in the Malaysian electronics factories described in the text, had to wear uniforms. Adding to their regimentation was a military boot camp atmosphere. Workers were bullied, insulted, and subjected to harsh discipline. Workers were allowed only one toilet break and two chances to drink per eight hours. There were complaints of physical abuse and sexual harassment by male supervisors and insults by foreign supervisors (Koreans).

Prior to 1996, Nike already had a Code of Conduct, but the company had no effective way of ensuring that its contractors would abide by the code. In theory, the Vietnamese workers should have been protected both by Nike's Code of Conduct and by Vietnam's labor standards and laws. But the study by Vietnam Labor Watch (1997) found that many labor laws were being broken. Some women were working 11 hours a day, six days a week, sometimes also on Sunday. By law, but not consistently in practice, overtime work should have a higher rate of compensation. Nor should workers have to work more than 200 overtime hours annually. In fact, the Nike workers in Ho Chi Minh City weren't receiving proper overtime pay, and many were working well over the 200-hour limit. Workers were threatened with punishment or firing if they refused requests to work overtime. The factory needed to keep working to meet production quotas.

After more than a year of negative publicity and accusations by human rights and labor groups, Nike announced a new policy on May 12, 1998. Nike chairman and CEO Philip Knight proposed "major changes" to Nike's overseas operations. The new policy would institute a minimal age of 18 for shoe workers and 16 for workers in Nike's apparel and athletic equipment (e.g., soccer ball) factories. The previous minimum age for shoes had been 16, but younger women had sometimes been hired.

The new policy also would improve factory safety by implementing U.S. standards. Nike committed to "adopting U.S. Occupational Safety and Health Administration (OSHA) indoor air quality standards for all footwear factories" (http://www.corpwatch.

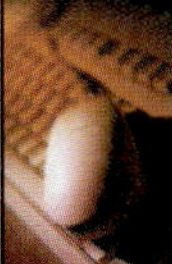

org/trac/nike/announce/clr.html).

In addition, Nike committed to "expanding its current independent monitoring programs to include nongovernmental organizations (NGOs), foundations and educational institutions and making summaries of the findings public" (http://www.corpwatch.org/trac/nike/announce/clr.html).

The Campaign for Labor Rights, a labor NGO, immediately countered that NGOs should not just participate in monitoring; they should lead monitoring. Nike had previously used accounting and consulting firms to audit its labor practices. The NGOs claimed (correctly) that such firms lack the language skills, impartiality, and social sensitivity to objectively monitor workers, work conditions, and progress. NGOs and labor organizations suggested that Nike form an independent monitoring board, consisting of representatives from neutral parties, including government labor officials, NGOs, and labor unions.

The Malaysian factory women described in the text used spirit possession to vent their frustration over working conditions. The Vietnamese Nike workers did something more effective. They employed labor union tactics, including strikes and frequent work stoppages and slowdowns. These practices were in response to disputes about overtime pay, arbitrary firings, and abusive treatment. The Vietnamese workers also enlisted the support of NGOs, international labor organizations, and concerned Vietnamese Americans. Some of their efforts have already paid off.

Compared with nonindustrial states and contemporary peripheral and semiperipheral nations, core industrial nations tend to have more open class systems. Under industrialism, wealth is based to some extent on **income**—earnings from wages and salaries. Economists contrast such a *return on labor* with interest, dividends, rent, and profits, which are *returns on property* or capital.

Even in advanced industrial nations, stratification is more marked in wealth (investments, property, possessions, etc.) than it is in income. In 1997, the bottom fifth of American families got 4.2 percent of total national income, compared with 47.2 percent for the top fifth (*Statistical Abstract of the United States* 1999, p. 479, Table 751). However, if we consider wealth rather than income, the contrast is much more extreme: 1 percent of American families hold one-third of the nation's wealth (Calhoun, Light, and Keller 1997).

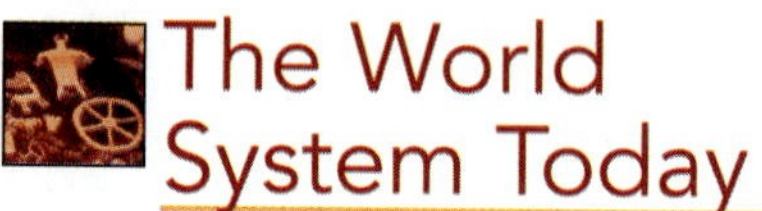

The World System Today

We will see in "Interesting Issues: The American Periphery" (pp. 560–561) that the world economy also can create peripheral regions within core nations, such as rural areas of the American South. World-system theory stresses the existence of a global culture. It emphasizes historical contacts, linkages, and power differentials between local people and international forces. The major forces influencing cultural interaction during the past 500 years have been commercial expansion, industrial capitalism, and the differential power of colonial and core nations (Wallerstein 1982, 2000; Wolf 1982). As state formation had done previously, industrialization accelerated local participation in larger networks. According to Bodley (2000), perpetual expansion (whether in population or consumption) is the distinguishing feature of industrial economic systems. Bands and tribes are small, self-sufficient, subsistence-based systems. Industrial economies, by contrast, are large, highly specialized systems in which local areas don't consume the products they produce and in which market exchanges occur with profit as the primary motive (Bodley 2000).

After 1870, European business initiated a concerted search for more secure markets in Asia, Africa, and other less-developed areas. This process led to European imperialism in Africa, Asia, and Oceania. **Imperialism** (*colonialism* is a near synonym) refers to a policy of extending the rule of a nation or empire, such as the British empire, over foreign nations and of taking and holding foreign colonies. *Colonialism* refers to the political, social, economic, and cultural domination of a territory and its people by a foreign power for an extended time. European imperial expansion was aided by improved transportation, which brought huge new areas within easy reach. Europeans also colonized vast areas of previously unsettled or sparsely settled lands in the interior of North and South America and Australia. The new colonies purchased masses of goods from the industrial centers and shipped back wheat, cotton, wool, mutton, beef, and leather. Thus began the second phase of colonialism (the first had been in the New World after Columbus) as European nations competed for colonies between 1875 and 1914, a process that helped cause World War I.

Industrialization spread to many other nations in a process that continues today (Table 21.1). By

Table 21.1
Ascent and Decline of Nations within the World System

Periphery to Semiperiphery	Semiperiphery to Core	Core to Semiperiphery
United States (1800–1860) Japan (1868–1900) Taiwan (1949–1980) S. Korea (1953–1980)	United States (1860–1900) Japan (1945–1970) Germany (1870–1900)	Spain (1620–1700)

Source: Reprinted by permission of Westview Press from *An Introduction to the World-System Perspective* by Thomas Richard Shannon. Copyright Westview Press 1989, Boulder, Colorado.

Figure 21.1
The World System Today

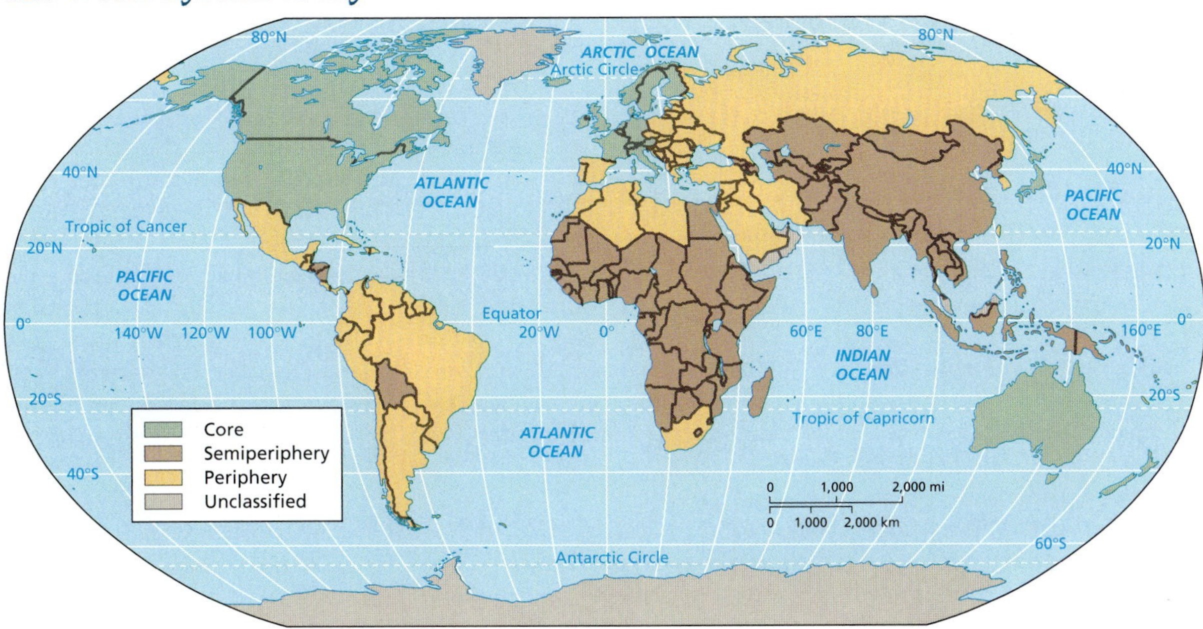

Source: Reprinted by permission of Westview Press from *An Introduction to the World-System Perspective* by Thomas Richard Shannon. Copyright Westview Press 1996, Boulder, Colorado.

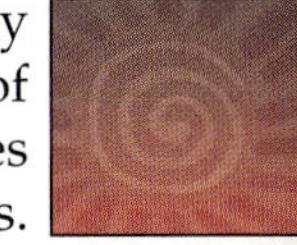

1900, the United States had become a core nation within the world system. It had overtaken Great Britain in iron, coal, and cotton production. In a few decades (1868–1900), Japan changed from a medieval handicraft country to an industrial one, joining the semiperiphery by 1900 and moving to the core between 1945 and 1970. Figure 21.1 is a map showing the modern world system.

Twentieth-century industrialization added hundreds of new industries and millions of new jobs. Production increased, often beyond immediate demand. This spurred strategies such as advertising to sell everything that industry could churn out. Mass production gave rise to a culture of overconsumption, which valued acquisitiveness and conspicuous consumption (Veblen 1934). Bodley defines overconsumption as "consumption in a given area that exceeds the rates at which natural resources are produced by natural processes, to such an extent that the longrun stability of the culture involved is threatened" (1985, p. 39).

Industrialization entailed a shift from reliance on renewable resources to the use of fossil fuels. Fossil fuel energy, stored over millions of years, is being rapidly depleted to support a previously unknown and probably unsustainable level of consumption (Bodley 2000). Table 21.2 compares energy consumption in various types of cultures. Americans are the world's foremost consumers of nonrenewable resources. In energy terms, the average American, drawing on 275,000 calories

Table 21.2
Energy Consumption in Various Contexts

Type of Society	Daily Kilocalories per Person
Bands and tribes	4,000–12,000
Preindustrial states	26,000 (maximum)
Early industrial states	70,000
Americans in 1970	230,000
Americans in 1990	275,000

Source: From John H. Bodley, *Anthropology and Contemporary Human Problems*, 1985. Reprinted by permission of Mayfield Publishing, Mountain View, CA.

interesting issues

The American Periphery

The effects of the world economy also can create peripheral regions within core nations, such as areas of the rural South in the United States. In a comparative study of two counties at opposite ends of Tennessee, Thomas Collins (1989) reviews the effects of industrialization on poverty and unemployment. Hill County, with an Appalachian white population, is on the Cumberland Plateau in eastern Tennessee. Delta County, which is predominantly African-American, is 60 miles from Memphis in western Tennessee's lower Mississippi region. Both counties once had economies based on agriculture and timber, but jobs in those sectors declined sharply with the advent of mechanization. Both counties have unemployment rates more than twice that of Tennessee as a whole. More than a third of the people in each county live below the poverty level. Such poverty pockets represent a slice of the world periphery within modern America. Given very restricted job opportunities, the best-educated local youths have migrated to northern cities for three generations.

To increase jobs, local officials and business leaders have tried to attract industries from outside. Their efforts exemplify a more general rural southern strategy, which began during the 1950s, of courting industry by advertising "a good business climate"—which means low rents, cheap utilities, and a nonunion labor pool. However, few firms are attracted to an impoverished and poorly educated work force. All the industries that have come to such areas have very limited market power and a narrow profit margin. Such firms survive by offering low wages and minimal benefits, with frequent layoffs. These industries tend to emphasize traditional female skills such as sewing and mostly attract women.

The garment industry, which is highly mobile, is Hill County's main employer. The knowledge that a garment plant can be moved to another locale very rapidly tends to reduce employee demands. Management can be as arbitrary and authoritarian as it wishes. The

Rural poverty is part of the American periphery. This Appalachian family represents the bottom fifth of families in terms of income. How much does the top fifth get compared with the bottom fifth? The answer is in the text, but also check out http://www.census.gov/prod/99pubs/99statab/sec14.pdf.

unemployment rate and low educational level ensure that many women will accept sewing jobs for a bit more than the minimum wage.

In neither county has new industry brought many jobs for men, who have a higher unemployment rate than do women (as do blacks, compared with whites). Collins found that many men in Hill County had never been permanently employed; they had just done temporary jobs, always for cash.

The effects of industrialization in Delta County have been similar. That county's recruitment efforts also have drawn only marginal industries. The largest is a bicycle seat and toy manufacturer, which employs 60 percent women. Three other large plants, which make clothing and auto seat covers, employ 95 percent women. Egg production was once significant in Delta County but folded when the market for eggs fell in response to rising national concern over the effects of cholesterol.

In both counties, the men, ignored by industrialization, maintain an informal economy. They sell and trade used goods through personal networks. They take casual jobs, such as operating farm equipment on a daily or seasonal basis. Collins found that maintaining an automobile was the most important and prestigious contribution these men made to their families. Neither county has public transportation; Hill County even lacks school buses. Families need cars to get women to work and kids to school. Men who keep an old car running longest get special respect.

Reduced opportunities for men to do well at work—to which American culture attributes great importance—lead to a feeling of lowered self-worth, which is expressed in physical violence. The rate of domestic violence in Hill County exceeds the state average. Spousal abuse arises from men's demands to control women's paychecks. (Men regard the cash they earn themselves as their own, to spend on male activities.)

One important difference between the two counties involves unionization. In Delta County, organizers have waged successful campaigns for unionization. Attitudes toward workers' rights in Tennessee correlate with race. Rural southern whites usually don't vote for unions when they have a chance to do so, whereas African-Americans are more likely to challenge management about pay and work rules. Local blacks view their work situation in terms of black against white rather than from a position of working-class solidarity. They are attracted to unions because they see only whites in managerial positions and resent differential advancement of white factory workers. One manager expressed to Collins that "once the work force of a plant becomes more than one-third black, you can expect to have union representation within a year" (Collins 1989, p. 10). Responding to this probability of unionization, canny core capitalists from Japan don't build plants in the primarily African-American counties of the lower Mississippi. The state's Japanese factories cluster in eastern and central Tennessee.

Poverty pockets of the rural South (and other regions) represent a slice of the world periphery within modern America. Through mechanization, industrialization, and the other changes promoted by larger systems, local people have been deprived of land and jobs. After years of industrial development, a third of the people of Hill and Delta counties remain below the poverty level. Emigration of educated and talented locals continues as the opportunities shrink. Collins concludes that rural poverty won't be reduced by attracting additional peripheral industries because these firms lack the market power to improve wages and benefits. Different development schemes are needed for these counties and the rural South generally.

beyond the classroom

The Residue of Apartheid in Southern Africa

BACKGROUND INFORMATION

Student:	*Chanelle Mac Nab*
Supervising Professor:	*Les Field*
School:	*University of New Mexico*
Year in School/Major:	*Senior/Anthropology (Ethnology)*
Future Plans:	*Graduate or medical school*
Project Title:	*The Residue of Apartheid in Southern Africa*

Pay attention to the author's use of a personal perspective and personal vignettes in describing an experience abroad. How would you react in the author's situation? Are you surprised that the legacy of apartheid lingers in Southern Africa?

In 1997 I spent six months in Botswana, Africa, on an international youth exchange program. I lived in six different villages and gained insight into the rural life of these pastoral people. During this time, I traveled to South Africa, Namibia, and Zimbabwe and witnessed varying degrees of racism. The color of my skin as a Caucasian allowed me to review both the white and black perspectives on racism.

Apartheid, which is an Afrikaans word that literally means "separateness," was a policy of racial segregation that was implemented in South Africa in 1948 when the Nationalist Party came to power. Apartheid resulted in one of the most unabashed forms of racism in the world.

Prior to going to southern Africa, like most of my American counterparts, I could see little good in the Afrikaners because of all the hate and violence they have bred. However, once I had lived in southern Africa, I realized that I too was passing judgment. In my own personal experience with Afrikaners, I found them to be quite opposite than their stereotypes had described them. To me they were a kindly and humane people, often giving me a ride, a meal, and a free place to stay. It is unfortunate that their view on race has separated them from the world. I had to stop blaming the whites for one moment and realize that the whites, like the blacks, are a product of their own cultural conditioning. They are victims of their own cultural constructions. Yes, the whites are capable of taking a new stance on racism. South Africa must move beyond their issues of race and strive for cohesion if they wish to build an equitable future for both whites and blacks in all of Africa.

Why did the supposed nonracial governments of the neighboring South African countries such as Botswana and Namibia also allow whites to come in and implement their racist laws? This answer lies in the history of Africa.

of energy each day, is about 35 times more expensive than the average forager or tribesperson, averaging just 8,000 daily calories. Since 1900, the United States has tripled its per capita energy use. It also has increased its total energy consumption thirtyfold.

Industrial Degradation

Today's industrialization extends to the Third World. Factory labor now characterizes many countries in Latin America, Africa, the Pacific, and Asia. One effect of the spread of industrialization has been the destruction of indigenous economies, ecologies, and populations.

Two centuries ago, as industrialization was developing, 50 million people still lived beyond the periphery in politically independent bands, tribes, and chiefdoms. Occupying vast areas, those nonstate societies, although not totally isolated, were only marginally affected by nation-states and the world capitalist economy. In 1800, bands, tribes, and chiefdoms controlled half the globe and 20 percent of its population (Bodley

Colonial powers drew lines across the African continent and divided it into pieces. With colonial rule controlling Africa throughout most of the 20th century, I assume that racism was adopted and implemented in all countries where whites were the minority in an effort to maintain power.

The greatest obstacle during my stay in Africa was overcoming the numerous confrontations I had with the whites in regards to race. Every day my own beliefs and cultural norms were being challenged by this unfamiliar culture. I had extensive conversations with whites and blacks about race. Here is a brief description of one of my journal entries.

> August 14—Tonight I went with Rey (the Afrikaner who drove me from Namibia to Botswana) to the opening of the annual Agricultural Trade Fair . . . I am aware that apartheid ended only three years ago, and that, although apartheid is physically gone, it is latently present, but never did those words seem more real than tonight . . . As we drove into the fair grounds, I could see the silhouettes of hundreds of black people dancing against the dimness of the lantern lights. The loud African music was familiar to me . . . [I]nstead of continuing forward to where the blacks were, we took a sharp left turn to the white sector of the fair. The whites were standing around a fire drinking while their black servants stoked the fire and prepared the food. I was stunned to be standing on segregated soil. I could not believe that I was in Botswana and not in South Africa. I could not believe that less than 10 years ago, blacks were not allowed to attend this very same trade fair. Every moment that I was with the whites I felt uncomfortable . . . I could not identify with these people . . . I was furious underneath my skin because they did not know who I was on the inside. Yes, I was white but I was not one of them . . . I felt guilty, as if I were betraying all of my black friends and my black host family . . . As hard as it was, I kept my calm and I told Rey I would never be able to see it the way he does because of my different upbringing. Rey admitted that perhaps his children's children would one day see it the way I do. As Rey and I left the party to go home, I dared him to go with me to the "other side" so that we could dance. He responded with two words: "I cannot." Our conversation ended and we drove home in silence.

Today, the ideology of racism has seeped across borders and across imaginary lines like an oil spill and is ever present throughout the world's social, political, and economic systems. It is important to understand that apartheid is not isolated in South Africa. Apartheid has permeated all of the borders of southern Africa. Hence, racism is not exclusively a South African problem.

This research has attempted to shed light on the serious issue of racism, with its emphasis on the continuing effects of the apartheid regime in southern Africa. I hope that more people will come to understand apartheid and use this knowledge to understand why racism denies and oppresses people all around the world.

1988). Industrialization then tipped the balance in favor of states.

Industrialization is "a global process that has destroyed or transformed all previous cultural adaptations and has given humanity the power not only to bring about its own extinction as a species, but also to speed the extinction of many other species and to alter biological and geological processes as well" (Bodley 1985, p. 4). The negative effects of an expanding industrial world system include genocide, ethnocide, and ecocide. *Genocide* is the physical destruction of ethnic groups by murder, warfare, and introduced diseases. When ethnic groups survive but lose or severely modify their ancestral cultures, we speak of *ethnocide.* The term for the destruction of local ecosystems is *ecocide.*

As industrial states have conquered, annexed, and "developed" nonstates, there has been genocide on a grand scale. Bodley (1988) estimates that an average of 250,000 indigenous people perished annually between 1800 and 1950. The causes included foreign diseases (to which natives had no resistance), warfare, slavery, land grabbing,

Industrial technology is spreading worldwide. In Bangalore, India, young women are taught the principles of electricity using a circuit board. What does this photo say about their participation in the modern world system?

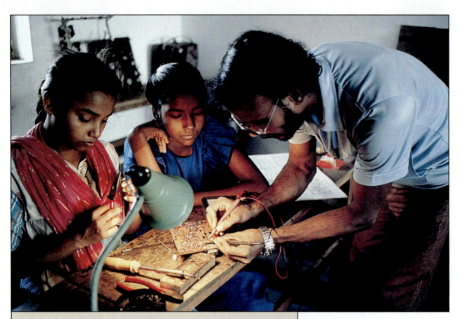

Copsa Mica, Romania, may well be the world's most polluted city. A factory belches out smoke that leaves its mark on these boys' faces, food, and lungs. What's the term for such environmental devastation?

and other forms of dispossession and impoverishment.

Native groups have been incorporated within nation-states, where they have become ethnic minorities. Some such groups have been able to recoup their population. Many indigenous peoples survive and maintain their ethnic identity despite having lost their ancestral cultures to varying degrees (partial ethnocide).

Today's world contains around 200 million tribespeople, most of whom belong to conquered tribes. Only a handful of autonomous tribal nations survive. At the dawn of food production 10,000 years ago, the world's human population is estimated to have been 75 million. Those people belonged to perhaps 150,000 independent bands and tribes (Bodley 1988). Today, many descendants of tribespeople live on as culturally distinct and self-conscious colonized peoples, many of whom aspire to autonomy. As the original inhabitants of their territories, they are called **indigenous peoples.** Bodley (1988) argues that such groups typically resist integration into nation-states. They fear that such integration, which is usually into the impoverished classes, will lead to a decline in their quality of life.

Indigenous peoples have devised various methods to survive and to maintain their ethnic identity. Canada's Nisga'a Indians have used the law to ensure their cultural survival. On August 4, 1998, as shown here, Canada's 5,500 Nisga'a were granted land rights and self-government in their rugged mountain homeland located within British Columbia.

Many contemporary nations are repeating—at an accelerated rate—the process of resource depletion that occurred in Europe and the United States during the Industrial Revolution. Fortunately, however, today's world has some environmental watchdogs that were absent during the first centuries of the Industrial Revolution. Given national and international cooperation and sanctions, the modern world may benefit from the lessons of the past.

summary

1. Local societies increasingly participate in wider systems—regional, national, and global. Columbus's voyages opened the way for a major and continuing exchange between the Old and New Worlds. Seventeenth-century plantation economies in the Caribbean and Brazil were based on sugar. In the 18th century, plantation economies based on cotton arose in the southeastern United States.

2. The capitalist world economy is based on production for sale, with the goal of maximizing profits. World capitalism has political and economic specialization based on three positions. Core, semiperiphery, and periphery have existed since the 16th century, although the particular countries filling these niches have changed.

3. The Industrial Revolution began around 1750. Transoceanic trade and commerce supplied capital for industrial investment. Industrialism began in England rather than in France because French industry could grow through expansion of the domestic system. England, with fewer people, had to industrialize.
4. Industrialization hastened the separation of workers from the means of production. Marx saw stratification as a sharp division between the bourgeoisie (capitalists) and the proletariat (propertyless workers). Class consciousness was a key part of Marx's view of class. Weber believed that social solidarity based on ethnicity, religion, race, or nationality could take priority over class. Today's capitalist world system maintains the contrast between those who own the means of production and those who don't, but the division is now worldwide. Modern stratification systems also include a middle class of skilled and professional workers.
5. Nationalism has prevented global class solidarity. There is a substantial contrast between capitalists and workers in the core nations and workers on the periphery. The extent to which inequalities persist across the generations is a measure of the openness of the class system, the ease of social mobility it permits. Under world capitalism, stratification has taken many forms, including caste, slavery, and class systems.
6. The major forces influencing cultural interaction during the past 500 years have been commercial expansion and industrial capitalism. In the 19th century, industrialization spread to Belgium, France, Germany, and the United States. After 1870, businesses began a concerted search for more secure markets. This process led to European imperialism in Africa, Asia, and Oceania. By 1900 the United States had become a core nation. Mass production gave rise to a culture that valued acquisitiveness and conspicuous consumption. One effect of industrialization has been the destruction of indigenous economies, ecologies, and populations. Two centuries ago, 50 million people lived in independent bands, tribes, and chiefdoms. Industrialization tipped the balance in favor of states.

key terms

bourgeoisie One of Marx's opposed classes; owners of the means of production (factories, mines, large farms, and other sources of subsistence).

capital Wealth or resources invested in business, with the intent of producing a profit.

capitalist world economy The single world system, which emerged in the 16th century, committed to production for sale, with the object of maximizing profits rather than supplying domestic needs.

caste system Closed, hereditary system of stratification, often dictated by religion; hierarchical social status is ascribed at birth, so that people are locked into their parents' social position.

core Dominant structural position in the world system; consists of the strongest and most powerful states with advanced systems of production.

imperialism A policy of extending the rule of a nation or empire over foreign nations or of taking and holding foreign colonies.

income Earnings from wages and salaries.

indigenous peoples The original inhabitants of particular territories; often descendants of tribespeople who live on as culturally distinct colonized peoples, many of whom aspire to autonomy.

Industrial Revolution The historical transformation (in Europe, after 1750) of "traditional" into "modern" societies through industrialization of the economy.

open class system Stratification system that facilitates social mobility, with individual achievement and personal merit determining social rank.

periphery Weakest structural position in the world system.

semiperiphery Structural position in the world system intermediate between core and periphery.

slavery The most extreme, coercive, abusive, and inhumane form of legalized inequality; people are treated as property.

vertical mobility Upward or downward change in a person's social status.

working class Or proletariat; those who must sell their labor to survive; the antithesis of the bourgeoisie in Marx's class analysis.

critical thinking questions

1. According to world-system theory, societies are subsystems of bigger systems, with the world system as the largest. What are the various systems, at different levels, in which you participate?
2. What is the capitalist world economy? Does it have political as well as economic dimensions? What are they?
3. Give two examples each of core, semiperiphery, and periphery nations. Does any nation seem poised to move from one slot to another, such as semiperiphery to core, or vice versa? What's the last nation to make such a move?
4. How has social stratification in industrial societies changed over time? Think of comparing London of the 1850s (the era of Dickens and Marx) and today. Or compare the class structure of the United States in the 1930s with contemporary socioeconomic stratification.
5. Name three causes of the Industrial Revolution. Are they being repeated anywhere today?
6. How did proletarianization change human work? Is any of your work proletarianized?
7. How did the views of Marx and Weber on stratification differ? Which approach makes the most sense to you? Why?
8. How open is the class system of your society? Describe what's open and what's closed about it.
9. How would our class system differ if the Third World didn't exist?
10. Evaluate the positive and negative effects of industrialization, giving five examples of each.

case study

Ju/'hoansi: This chapter has discussed consequences of the spread of the industrial world system. Many foraging societies find their ways of life threatened. Two or three decades ago, the Ju/'hoansi maintained much more traditional lifestyles. They now find themselves fully drawn into a market economy, affected not only by institutions like schools and hospitals, but also by militarization, civil war, sedentism, resettlement, and governmental control. In *Culture Sketches* by Holly Peters-Golden, read the chapter on "Ju/'hoansi: Reciprocity and Sharing." Which effects of the modern world system are demonstrated in contemporary Ju/'hoansi life? The Ju/'hoansi tradition is one of egalitarianism and reciprocity. It is reported that the Dobe Ju/'hoansi still hold those values above all else. Do you think they can integrate their belief that no one should be denied the necessities of life with the demands of their modern situation? Why or why not?

suggested additional readings

Abu-Lughod, J. L.

1989 *Before European Hegemony : The World System A. D. 1250–1350*. New York: Oxford University Press. Regional economies and politics before the age of European exploration and the capitalist world economy.

Arrighi, G.

1994 *The Long Twentieth Century: Money, Power, and the Origins of Our Times*. New York: Verso. How core nations control finance and power in the modern world system.

Braudel, F.

1973 *Capitalism and Material Life: 1400–1800.* London: Fontana. The role of the masses in the history of capitalism.

1982 *Civilization and Capitalism, 15th–18th Century. Volume II: The Wheels of Commerce.* New York: HarperCollins. On the history of capitalism and the role of trade from precapitalist mercantilism to the present.

1992 *Civilization and Capitalism, 15th–18th Century. Volume III: The Perspective of the World.* Berkeley, CA: University of California Press. On the emergence of the world capitalist economy; case histories of European countries and various areas of the rest of the world.

Crosby, A. W., Jr.

1972 *The Columbian Exchange: Biological and Cultural Consequences of 1492.* Westport, CT: Greenwood Press. Describes how Columbus's voyages opened the way for a major exchange of people, resources, and ideas as the Old and New Worlds were forever joined together.

Diamond, J. M.

1997 *Guns, Germs, and Steel: The Fates of Human Societies.* New York: W. W. Norton. An ecological approach to expansion and conquest in world history.

Fagan, B. M.

1998 *Clash of Cultures.* 2nd ed. Walnut Creek, CA: AltaMira. Culture conflicts during European territorial expansion.

Hall, T. D., ed.

1999 *A World-System Reader: New Perspectives on Gender, Urbanism, Cultures, Indigenous Peoples, and Ecology.* Lanham, MD: Rowman and Littlefield. Urbanization, globalization, and indigenous peoples.

Kardulias, P. N.

1999 *World-Systems Theory in Practice: Leadership, Production, and Exchange.* Lanham, MD: Rowman and Littlefield. Social systems, social change, and economic history in the context of world-system theory.

Kearney, M.

1996 *Reconceptualizing the Peasantry: Anthropology in Global Perspective.* Boulder, CO: Westview. The nature of peasant life styles and subsistence patterns within the modern world system.

Mintz, S.

1985 *Sweetness and Power: The Place of Sugar in Modern History.* New York: Viking Penguin. The place of sugar in the formation of the modern world system.

Shannon, T. R.

1996 *An Introduction to the World-System Perspective,* 2nd ed. Boulder, CO: Westview Press. Useful review of world-system theory and developments.

Wallerstein, I. M.

1974 *The Modern World-System: Capitalist Agriculture and the Origins of the European World-Economy in the Sixteenth Century.* New York: Academic Press. The origins of the capitalist world economy; a classic work.

1980 *The Modern World-System II: Mercantilism and the Consolidation of the European World Economy, 1600–1750.* New York: Academic Press. Further development of the world system and the underpinnings of industrialization.

2000 *The Essential Wallerstein.* New York: New Press, W. W. Norton. The father of world-system theory offers the basics of his influential theory.

Wolf, E. R.

1982 *Europe and the People without History.* Berkeley: University of California Press. An anthropologist examines the effects of European expansion on tribal peoples and sets forth a world-system approach to anthropology.

internet exercises

1. *Class and the* Titanic: Go to Eric Klocko and Zero Z. Batzell Dean's page on "Children on the Titanic: Tragedy & Class," **http://www.ume.maine.edu/~mmedia/mdmhty/essays/titanic/titanic.html** and read all the material on the sinking of the *Titanic.*
   a. How were class differences reflected in the layout and construction of the ship?
   b. How was the definition of "child" influenced by class during the disaster?
   c. How did the layout of the ship and the definition of "child" influence the survival rates of children aboard the *Titanic?*
2. Go to the U.S. Census Bureau's Factfinder service at **http://factfinder.census.gov.** Choose to make a map. Under "Show me," choose "Income"; under "for," choose "State by County" and then pick a state in which you are interested. Press Go to view a map of income distributions in your state. Study the map and try to determine the overall patterns. Try to identify the locations with a high income and the locations with low average incomes. Do these patterns make sense? What explains them? Now, go back to the Factfinder, and under "Show me" choose "Education" and view and study that map. Finally make a map of "Poverty."
   a. What are the similarities between the three maps? What are the major differences?
   b. Based on these maps, what is the relationship between poverty, income, and education in a state of your choice?
   c. How do you explain the relationships you see between poverty, education, and income?

See Chapter 21 on your CD-ROM for additional review and interactive exercises. See your McGraw-Hill Online Learning Center for more.

Chapter 22

Colonialism and Development

NYTIMES.COM NEWS BRIEFS

Britain in Africa: Colonialism's Legacy Becomes a Burden

by Alan Cowell
June 10, 2000

LONDON—In recent weeks, Britons have been treated to two conflicting, almost puzzling, sets of images. In Sierra Leone, an African leader pleads with British troops to stay on, after they arrive there to protect the capital from rebel forces who had kidnapped hundreds of United Nations peacekeepers. Across the continent in Zimbabwe, another African president reviles just about everything that smacks of the British and tells them to be gone.

Binding the two images is Britain's colonial past and, with it, a message that has some resonance for the United States in its own new imperial age: Once power is extended, it creates a stubborn, messy and enduring legacy. And even when influence recedes, the tangle of obligation, expectation and resentment survives . . .

In Sierra Leone, a chaotic assemblage of rebel and pro-government forces has turned the nation into a patchwork of armed fiefs competing, essentially, for the country's diamond riches. A United Nations mission to achieve and preserve a peace had collapsed, leaving a dangerous vacuum. This threatened to propel the war-weary nation into further mayhem . . .

In Zimbabwe the fight is different: After 20 unchallenged years in power, [President Robert] Mugabe is facing elections this month that he is afraid of losing. And he has seized on the emotional issue of racial discrimination left over from colonial days—in this case, unfair patterns of land distribution—as a pretext to order a campaign of bloody intimidation of his principal opponents. These include white farmers and workers on the farmers' land.

Hundreds of white-owned farms have been occupied by so-called veterans of Zimbabwe's liberation war in the 1970s, and at least 25 people have died.

In other words, Mr. Mugabe is assailing the very legacy that Britons feel links them to the land. And Britain's choices are circumscribed, illuminating both the ambiguities of its colonial history and the limits on its modern influence.

While Sierra Leone was established in 1787 as a coastal settlement for freed black slaves, white British settlers were encouraged to migrate to Rhodesia—as Zimbabwe was then known—in the late 19th and early 20th centuries, simply seizing vast tracts of land from the indigenous people.

When British officials started to protest Mr. Mugabe's behavior, that inescapable history clouded the moral issue and gave Mr. Mugabe the ammunition to defy the one-time colonial ruler. The collision left Britain's standing in Zimbabwe at its lowest in decades, even as its star rose ever higher in Sierra Leone . . .

The deeper reality in both Zimbabwe and Sierra Leone is that colonialism does not have an easy cut-off point, or a simple close-of-sale date. When the flags are furled, the colonial power maintains a vast array of commercial and other involvements. Just as colonialism itself was propelled by the economics of Europe's industrial revolution with its need for raw materials and markets, so the post-colonial era has been driven by Lord Palmerston's 19th-century dictum that nations do not have eternal allies, but they do have eternal interests.

In Zimbabwe, for instance, by insisting that this month's elections be free and fair and by offering increased financial aid for land redistribution, Britain is signaling its broader interest in the stability of a region that encompasses vast British investment, particularly in South Africa.

Source: http://www.nytimes.com.

overview

Imperialism is the policy of extending the rule of a nation or empire over other nations. Colonialism is the long-term domination of a territory and its people by a foreign power.

European colonialism had two broad phases. The first spanned the period from 1492 to 1825. For Britain, this phase ended with the American revolution. For Spain, it ended with the independence of most of its Latin American colonies. The second, more imperialistic, phase ran from 1850 to just after the end of World War II. The British and French colonial empires reached their height around 1914.

Like colonialism, economic development usually has an intervention philosophy—an ideological justification for outsiders to guide native peoples toward particular goals. Development is often justified by the idea that industrialization and westernization are desirable advances. But many problems faced by Third World peoples reflect their increasing dependence on cash.

Development anthropology focuses on social issues in, and the cultural dimension of, economic development. Culturally compatible development projects tend to be more successful than incompatible ones are. Compatible and successful projects try to change just enough, not too much. Motives to change come from people's traditional culture and the small concerns of everyday life. The most productive strategy for change is to base the social design for innovation on traditional social forms in each affected area.

Colonialism

In the last chapter, we saw that, after 1870, Europe began a concerted search for markets in Asia and Africa. This process led to European imperialism in Africa, Asia, and Oceania. *Imperialism* (*colonialism* is a near synonym) refers to a policy of extending the rule of a nation or empire, such as the British empire, over foreign nations and of taking and holding foreign colonies. **Colonialism** refers to the political, social, economic, and cultural domination of a territory and its people by a foreign power for an extended time.

Imperialism

Imperialism goes back to early states, including Egypt in the Old World and the Incas in the New. A Greek empire was forged by Alexander the Great, and Julius Caesar and his successors spread the Roman empire. The term also has been used for more recent examples, including the British, French, and Soviet empires (Scheinman 1980).

If imperialism is almost as old as the state, colonialism can be traced back to the ancient Phoenicians, who established colonies along the eastern Mediterranean by 3,000 years ago. The ancient Greeks and Romans were avid colonizers, as well as empire builders. Modern colonialism began with the European "Age of Discovery"—of the Americas and of a sea route to the Far East. After 1492, European states started founding colonies abroad. In South America, Portugal gained rule over Brazil. The Spanish, the original conquerors of the Aztecs and the Incas, explored the New World widely. They looked to the Caribbean, Mexico, and the southern portions of what was to become the United States, as well as colonizing in Central and South America. In what is now Latin America, especially in areas that had indigenous chiefdoms (e.g., Colombia and Venezuela) and states (e.g., Mexico, Guatemala, Peru, and Bolivia), native populations were large and dense. Today's Latin American population still reflects the intermingling of peoples and cultures during the first phase of colonialism. North of Mexico, indigenous populations were smaller and sparser. Such intermingling is less marked in the United States and Canada than in Latin America.

Rebellions and wars aimed at independence for American nations ended the first phase of European colonialism by the early 19th century. Brazil's independence from Portugal was declared in 1822. By 1825, most of Spain's colonies were politically independent. Spain held onto Cuba and the Philippines until 1898, but otherwise withdrew from the colonial field.

British Colonialism

The British empire grew through the search for resources and markets. At its peak around 1914, the British empire covered a fifth of the world's land surface and ruled a fourth of its population (see Figure 22.1). Like several other European nations, Britain had two stages of colonialism. The first began with the Elizabethan voyages of the 16th century. During the 17th century, Britain acquired most of the eastern coast of North America, Canada's St. Lawrence basin, islands in the Caribbean, slave stations in Africa, and interests in India. The British shared the exploration of the New World with the Spanish, Portuguese, French, and Dutch. The British by and large left Mexico, along with Central and South America, to the Spanish and the Portuguese. The end of the Seven Years War in 1763 forced a French retreat from most of Canada and India, where France had previously competed with Britain (Cody 1998; Farr 1980).

The American revolution ended the first stage of British colonialism. A second colonial empire, on which the "sun never set," rose from the ashes of the first. Beginning in 1788, but intensifying after 1815, was the British settlement of Australia. Britain had acquired Dutch South Africa by 1815. The establishment of Singapore in 1819 provided a base for a British trade network that extended to much of South Asia and along the coast of China. By this time, the empires of Britain's traditional rivals, particularly Spain, had been severely diminished in size. Britain's position as imperial power and the world's leading industrial nation was unchallenged. Much of the world was dominated by British commercial, financial, and naval power (Cody 1998; Farr 1980).

By the mid-19th century, Britain controlled virtually all of India, which was governed by a British viceroy from 1858. The Dutch exerted

Figure 22.1

Map of the British Empire in 1914

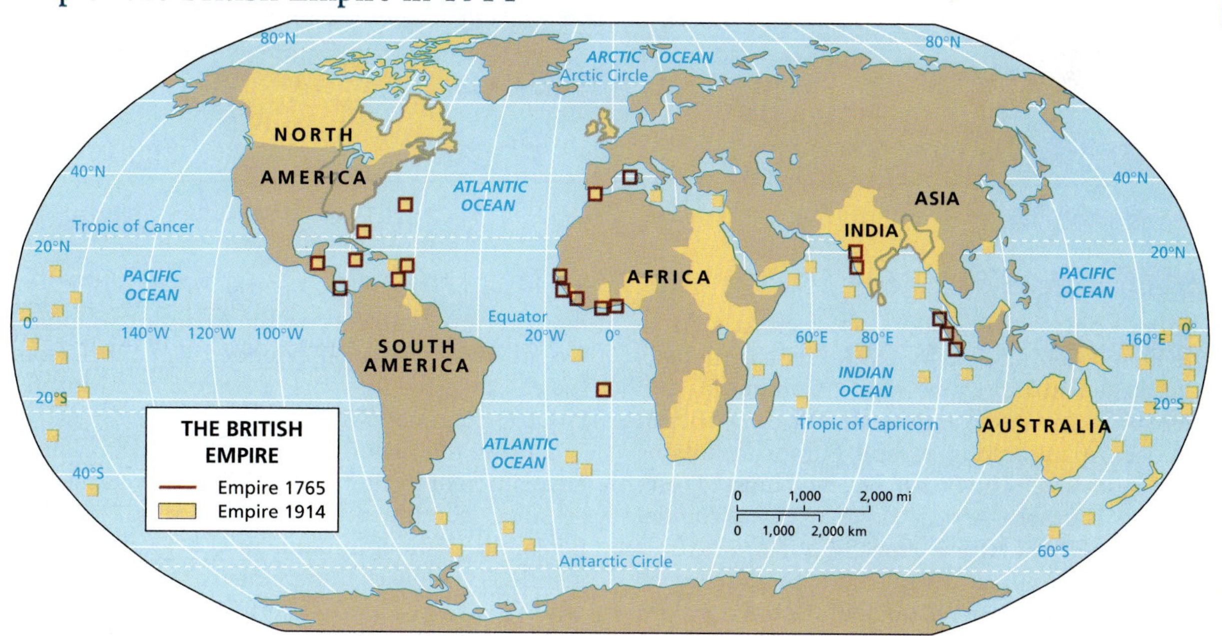

Figure 22.2

Map of Africa Showing Colonial Divisions after Conference of Berlin (1885)

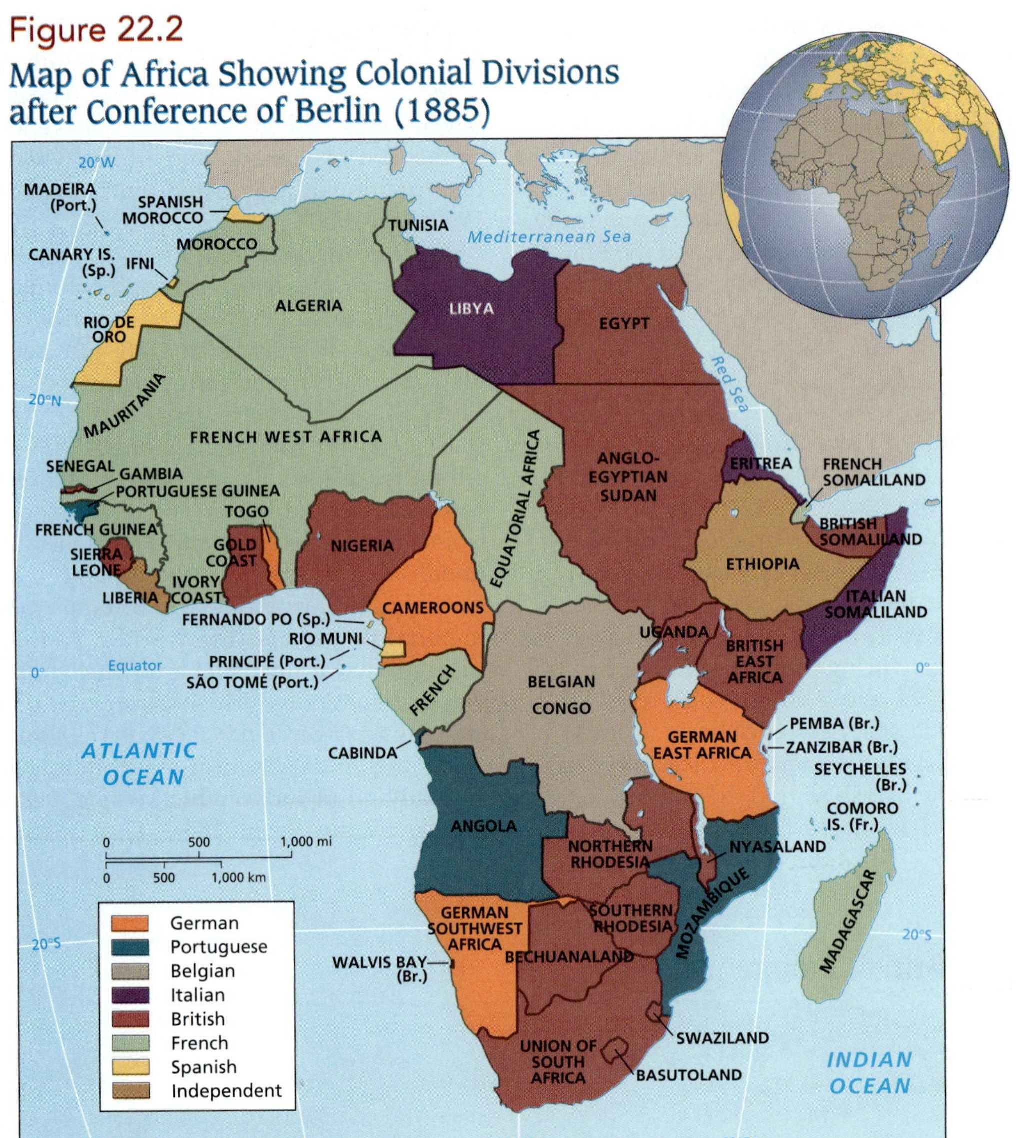

similar control over Indonesia, then known as the Dutch East Indies. By 1893, French rule was established in Indochina (Laos, Cambodia, and Vietnam). In 1885, the Conference of Berlin divided Africa among several European nations (see Figure 22.2). The British received most of eastern and southern Africa, along with substantial portions of West Africa. French Equatorial Africa stretched across the continent, with the French also controlling Madagascar and most of northern Africa. Belgium was awarded the Congo. Germany received territory on the Atlantic and Indian Ocean coasts. Portugal extended its control from the coasts to the interiors of Angola and Mozambique (Scheinman 1980).

During the Victorian Era (1837–1901), Britain's acquisition of territory and of further trading concessions continued. Victoria's Prime Minister Benjamin Disraeli implemented a foreign policy justified by view of imperialism as reflecting "the white man's burden"—a term coined by the poet Rudyard Kipling. People in the empire were seen as unable to govern themselves, so that British guidance was needed to civilize and Christianize them. This paternalistic and racist doctrine served to legitimize Britain's acquisition and control of parts of central Africa and Asia (Cody 1998).

At the height of the British empire in 1914, nationalist movements had already emerged in various colonies. But immediately after World War I (1914–1918), the British empire actually increased in size. Britain became the "trustee" of former German and Turkish territories in Africa and the Middle East. In 1931, Britain, along with its self-governing dominions—Canada, Australia, New Zealand, South Africa, and the Irish Free State—formed the "Commonwealth of Nations." *Dominions* were autonomous units with status equal to Britain's.

After World War II, the British empire fell apart, with nationalist movements for independence. India became independent in 1947, as did Ireland in 1949. Decolonization in Africa and Asia accelerated during the late 1950s. Today, the ties that remain between Britain and its former colonies are mainly linguistic or cultural rather than political (Cody 1998).

Indochina fell fully under French colonial control in 1893. In this historical photo, from the 1920s, a Frenchman sits in a rickshaw (pousse-pousse). What does this mode of transit say to you about colonialism?

French Colonialism

French colonialism also had two phases. The first began in the early 1600s. The second came late in the 19th century. This was the French manifestation of a more general European imperialism that followed the spread of industrialization and the search for new markets, raw materials, and cheap labor. However, compared with Great Britain, where the drive for profit led expansion, French colonialism was spurred more by the state, church, and armed forces than by business interests. Prior to the French revolution, in 1789, missionaries, explorers, and traders had led French expansion. They carved niches for France in Canada, the Louisiana territory, and several Caribbean islands, along with parts of India, which were lost, along with Canada (New France), to Great Britain in 1763. By 1815, only West Indian sugar islands and scattered African and Asian posts remained under French control (Harvey 1980).

The foundations of the second French empire were established between 1830 and 1870. France acquired Algeria and part of what eventually became Indochina. Like Britain, France rode a post-1870 wave of new imperialism. By 1914, the French empire covered 4 million square miles and included some 60 million people (see Figure 22.3). By 1893, French rule had been fully established in Indochina, and Tunisia and Morocco became French protectorates (Harvey 1980).

To be sure, the French, like the British, had substantial business interests in their colonies. But they also sought, again like the British, international glory and prestige. The French promulgated a *mission civilisatrice,* their equivalent of Britain's "white man's burden." The goal was to implant French culture, language, and religion—in the form of Roman Catholicism—throughout the colonies (Harvey 1980).

The French used two forms of colonial rule. They used *indirect rule,* governing through native leaders and established political structures, in

Figure 22.3
Map of the French Empire at Its Height around 1914

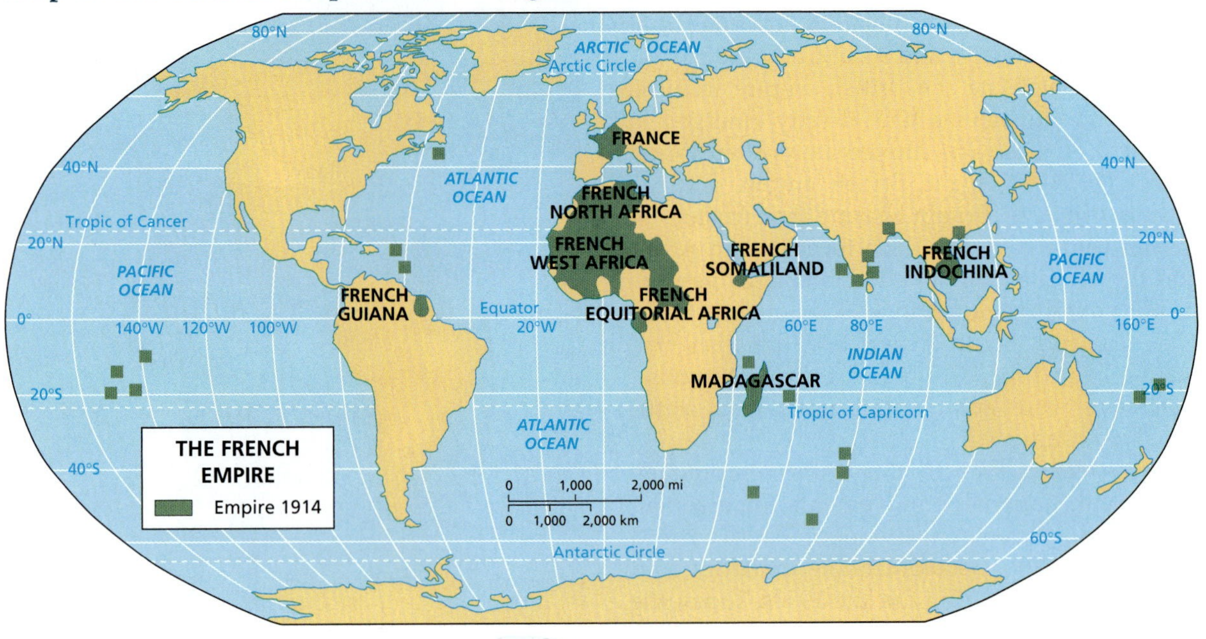

areas with long histories of state organization, such as Morocco and Tunisia. They brought *direct rule* by French officials to many areas of Africa. Here, the French imposed new government structures to control diverse tribes and cultures, many of them previously stateless. Like the British empire, the French empire began to disintegrate after World War II. France fought long—and ultimately futile—wars to keep its empire intact in Indochina and Algeria (Harvey 1980).

Colonialism and Identity

Many political and social labels heard in the news today had no equivalent meaning before colonialism. Whole countries, along with social groups and divisions within them, were colonial inventions. In West Africa, for example, by geographic logic, several adjacent countries could be one (Togo, Ghana, Côte d'Ivoire, Guinea, Guinea-Bissau, Sierra Leone, Liberia). Instead, they are separated by linguistic, political, and economic contrasts promoted under colonialism.

In Madagascar, the French colonial census crystallized a series of ethnic groups (*ethnies*) that had been less distinct previously. Prior to French rule, the indigenous Merina state had conquered most of the island, establishing its own empire. The Merina, too, created ethnic identities where previously they did not exist. Betsileo, which means "too many to be counted," was coined to refer to the large population living south of a certain river. After 1820, reinforced by the census and by official documents, "Betsileo" gradually acquired an ethnic meaning. Similarly, the Mahafaly of southwestern Madagascar have been assumed by the French colonial administration, and more recently by the national government, to be an ethnic group. But, according to Karl Eggert (1988), the people called Mahafaly don't use that term for themselves and have little idea of its origin and meaning.

Hundreds of ethnic groups and "tribes" are colonial constructions (see Ranger 1996). The Sukuma of Tanzania, for instance, were first registered as a single tribe by the colonial administration. Then missionaries standardized a series of dialects into a single Sukuma language as they translated the Bible and other religious texts. Thereafter, those texts were taught in missionary schools, and to European foreigners and other non-Sukuma speakers. Over time, this standardized the Sukuma language and ethnicity (Finnstrom 1997).

As in most of East Africa, in Rwanda and Burundi, farmers and herders live in the same areas and speak the same language. Historically, they have shared the same social world, although their social organization is "extremely hierarchical," almost "castelike" (Malkki 1995:24). There has been a tendency to see the pastoral Tutsis as superior to the agricultural Hutus. Tutsis have been presented as nobles, Hutus as commoners. Yet when distributing identity cards in Rwanda, the Belgian colonizers simply identified all people with more than 10 heads of cattle as Tutsi. Owners of fewer cattle were registered as Hutus (Bjuremalm 1997). Years later, these arbitrary colonial registers were used systematically for "ethnic" identification during the mass killings that took place in Rwanda in 1994.

Postcolonial Studies

In anthropology, history, and literature, the field of postcolonial studies has gained prominence since the 1970s (see Ashcroft, Griffiths, and Tiffin 1989; Cooper and Stoler 1997). **Postcolonial** refers to the study of the interactions between European nations and the societies they colonized (mainly after 1800). In 1914, European empires, which broke up after World War II, ruled more than 85 percent of the world (Petraglia-Bahri 1996). The term "postcolonial" also has been used to describe the second half of the 20th century in general, the period succeeding colonialism. Even more generically, "postcolonial" may be used to signify a position against imperialism and Eurocentrism (Petraglia-Bahri 1996).

The former colonies (*postcolonies*) can be divided into settler, nonsettler, and mixed (Petraglia-Bahri 1996). The settler countries, with large numbers of European colonists and sparser native populations, included Australia and Canada. Examples of nonsettler countries include India, Pakistan, Bangladash, Sri Lanka, Malaysia, Indonesia, Nigeria, Senegal, Madagascar, and Jamaica. All these had substantial native populations and relatively few European settlers. Mixed countries include South Africa, Zimbabwe, Kenya (photo on page 578), and Algeria. Such countries had significant

European settlement despite having sizeable native populations. In what ways would you imagine the issues of race, ethnicity, and language differed in the settler countries, compared with the nonsettler and mixed ones?

What traces of colonialism do you detect in this photo, taken recently at the Jockey Club in Nairobi, Kenya? What story is the photo telling you?

Given the varied experiences of such countries, "postcolonial" has to be a loose term. The United States, for instance, was colonized by Europeans and fought a war for independence from Britain. Is the United States a postcolony? It isn't usually perceived as such, given its current world power position, its treatment of native Americans (sometimes called internal colonization), and its annexation of other parts of the world (Petraglia-Bahri 1996). Research in postcolonial studies is growing, permitting a wide-ranging investigation of power relations in varied contexts. Broad topics in the field include the formation of an empire, the impact of colonization, and the state of the postcolony today (Petraglia-Bahri 1996).

Here are some common questions addressed in postcolonial studies: How did colonization affect colonized people—and their colonizers? How did colonial powers manage to subjugate so much of the world? How did people in the colonies resist colonial control? How have cultures and identities been affected by colonization? How do gender, race, and class function in colonial and postcolonial settings? How have colonial education systems influenced the postcolonies? With regard to literature, should postcolonial writers use a colonial language, like English or French, to reach a wider audience? Or should they write in their native language, to reach others in the postcolony? Finally, are new forms of imperialism, such as development and globalization, replacing old ones? (Petraglia-Bahri 1996).

 Development

During the Industrial Revolution, a strong current of thought viewed industrialization as a beneficial process of organic development and progress. Many economists still assume that industrialization increases production and income. They seek to create in Third World ("developing") countries a process—*economic development*—like the one that first occurred spontaneously in 18th-century Great Britain. Economic development generally aims at getting people to convert from subsistence to cash economies and thus to increase local participation in the world capitalist economy.

We just saw that Great Britain used the "white man's burden" to justify its imperialist expansion. Similarly, France claimed to be involved in a *mission civilisatrice,* a civilizing mission, in its colonies. Both these ideas illustrate an **intervention philosophy,** an ideological justification for outsiders to guide native peoples in specific directions. Economic development plans also have intervention philosophies. John Bodley (1988) argues that the basic belief behind interventions—whether by colonialists, missionaries, governments, or development planners—has been the same for more than 100 years. This belief is that industrialization, modernization, westernization, and individualism are desirable evolutionary advances and that development schemes that promote them will bring long-term benefits to natives. In a more extreme form, intervention philosophy may pit the assumed wisdom of enlightened colonial or other First World planners against the purported conservatism, ignorance, or "obsolescence" of "inferior" natives.

Anthropologists dispute such views. We know that for thousands of years, bands and tribes have done "a reasonable job of taking care of themselves" (Bodley 1988, p. 93). Indeed, because of their low energy needs, they have managed their resources better than we manage our own. Many problems that people face today are due to their position within nation-states and their increasing dependence on the world cash economy.

An anthropological study of an irrigated rice project in Madagascar found several reasons why it failed. If there are no machines to do the work, there have to be people around to do it— like these Betsileo women who are transplanting rice in the traditional manner.

Sometimes when natives are reluctant to change, it isn't because they have unduly conservative attitudes but because powerful interest groups oppose reform. Many Third World governments are reluctant to tamper with existing socioeconomic conditions in their countries (Manners 1956/1973). The attempt to bring the "green revolution" to Java that is analyzed below illustrates this situation. Resistance by elites to land reform is a reality throughout the Third World. Millions of people in colonies and underdeveloped nations have learned from bitter experience that if they increase their incomes, their taxes and rents also rise.

Conflicts between governments and natives often arise when outside interests exploit resources on tribal lands. Driven by deficits and debts, governments seek to wrest as much wealth as possible from the territory they administer. This goal helps explain the worldwide intrusion on indigenous peoples and their local ecosystems by such forms of economic development as highway construction, mining, hydroelectric projects, ranching, lumbering, agribusiness, and planned colonization (Bodley 1988).

Studying people at the local level, ethnographers have a unique view of the impact of national and international development planning on intended "beneficiaries." Local-level research often reveals inadequacies in the measures that economists use to assess development and a nation's economic health. For example, per capita income and gross national product don't measure the distribution of wealth. Because the first is an average and the second is a total, they may rise as the rich get richer and the poor get poorer.

Today, many government agencies, international groups, NGOs, and private foundations encourage attention to local-level social factors and the cultural dimension of economic development. Anthropological expertise in economic development planning is important because social problems can doom even potentially beneficial projects to failure. A study of 50 economic development projects (Lance and McKenna 1975) judged only 21 to be successes. Social and cultural incompatibilities had doomed most of the failed projects.

For example, a 1981 anthropological study of a multimillion-dollar development project in Madagascar uncovered several reasons for its failure. The project had been planned and funded by the World Bank in the late 1960s. The planners (no anthropologists among them) anticipated none of the problems that emerged. The project was aimed at draining and irrigating a large plain to increase rice production. Its goal was to raise production through machinery and double cropping—growing two crops annually on the same plot. However, the planners disregarded several

things, including the unavailability of spare parts and fuel for the machines. The designers also ignored the fact, well-known to anthropologists, that cross-culturally, intensive cultivation is associated with dense populations. If there are no machines to do the work, there have to be people around to do it. However, population densities in the project area (15 per square kilometer) were much too low to support intensive cultivation without modern machinery.

The planners should have known that labor and machinery for the project were unavailable. Furthermore, many local people were understandably hostile toward the project because it gave their ancestral land away to outsiders. (Unfortunately, this is a common occurrence in development projects.) Many land-grant recipients were members of regional and national elites. They used their influence to get fields that were intended for poor farmers. The project also suffered from technical problems. The foreign firm hired to dig the irrigation canals dug them lower than the land they had to irrigate, and so the water couldn't flow up into the fields.

Millions of development dollars could have been spent more wisely if anthropologists, consulting with local farmers, had helped plan, implement, and monitor the project. It stands to reason that experts, such as anthropologists, who are familiar with the language and customs of a country can better evaluate prospects of project success than can those who are not. Accordingly, anthropologists increasingly work in organizations that promote, manage, and assess programs that influence human life in the United States and abroad.

Applied anthropology, examined more fully in a later chapter, refers to the application of anthropological perspectives, theory, methods, and data to identify, assess, and solve social problems. **Development anthropology** is the branch of applied anthropology that focuses on social issues in, and the cultural dimension of, economic development. Development anthropologists do not just carry out development policies planned by others; they also plan and guide policy. (For more detailed discussions of the role of anthropologists in economic development, see Escobar [1995] and Robertson [1995].)

However, ethical dilemmas often confront development anthropologists (Escobar 1991, 1995). Our respect for cultural diversity is often offended because efforts to extend industry and technology may entail profound cultural changes. Foreign aid doesn't usually go where need and suffering are greatest. It is spent on political, economic, and strategic priorities as national leaders and powerful interest groups perceive them. Planners' interests don't always coincide with the best interests of the local people. Although the aim of most development projects is to enhance the quality of life, living standards often decline in the target area (Bodley 1988).

The Brazilian Sisal Scheme

A well-studied case in which development harmed the intended beneficiaries occurred in an arid area of Brazil's northeastern interior called the *sertão.* Here development increased dependence on the world economy, ruined the local subsistence economy, and worsened local health and income distribution. Until the 1950s, the *sertão*'s economy was based on corn, beans, manioc, and other subsistence crops. The *sertão* was also a grazing region for cattle, sheep, and goats. Most years, peasants subsisted on their crops. However, about once every decade, a major drought drastically reduced yields and forced people to migrate to the coast to seek jobs. To develop the northeast and dampen the effects of drought, the Brazilian government began encouraging peasants to plant *sisal,* a fibrous plant used to make rope, as a cash crop.

To ready sisal for export, preparation in the field was necessary. Throughout the *sertão,* there arose local centers with decorticating machines, devices that strip water and residue from sisal leaf, leaving only the fiber. These machines were expensive. Small-scale farmers couldn't afford them and had to use machines owned by the elite.

Small teams of workers were in charge of decorticating. Two jobs were especially hard, both done by adult men. One was that of disfiberer, the person who fed the sisal leaf into the machine. This was a demanding and dangerous job. The machine exerted a strong pull, making it possible for the disfiberers to get their fingers caught in the press. The other job was that of residue man, who shoveled away the residue that fell under the machine and brought new leaves to the disfiberer.

Anthropologist Daniel Gross (1971) studied the effects of sisal on the people of the *sertão.*

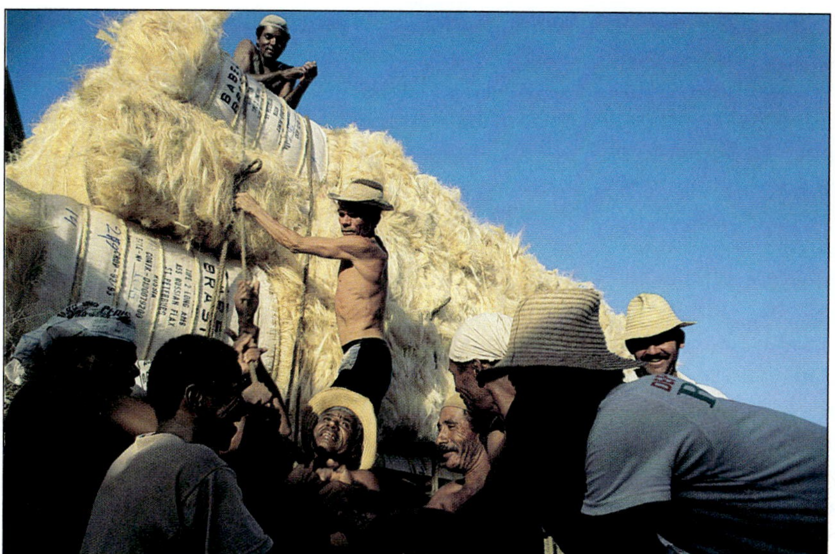

To develop its impoverished northeast and to dampen the effects of drought, the Brazilian government encouraged farmers to plant sisal, a fibrous plant, as a cash crop. Have you ever seen sisal? For what might you use it?

A nutritionist, Barbara Underwood, collaborated with Gross in studying the new economy's effects on nutrition. For people to subsist, they must consume sufficient calories to replace those they expend in daily activity. Gross calculated the energy expended in two of the jobs on the decorticating team: disfiberer and residue man. The former expended an average of 4,400 calories per day; the latter, 3,600 calories.

Gross then examined the diets of the households headed by each man. The disfiberer earned the equivalent of $3.65 per week, whereas the residue man made less—about $3.25. The disfiberer's household included just himself and his wife. The residue man had a pregnant wife and four children, aged three, five, six, and eight. By spending most of his income on food, the disfiberer was getting at least 7,100 calories a day for himself and his wife. This was ample to supply his daily needs of 4,400 calories. It also left his wife a comfortable 2,700 calories.

Most sisal growers were people who had converted most of their land to the cash crop, completely abandoning subsistence cultivation. Because sisal takes four years to mature, peasants had to seek wage work, often as members of a decorticating team, until they could harvest their crop. When they did harvest, they often found that the price of sisal on the world market was less than it had been when they planted the crop. Moreover, once sisal was planted, its strong root system made it almost impossible for the peasants to return to other crops. The land and people of the *sertão* became hooked on sisal.

However, the residue man's household was less fortunate. With more than 95 percent of his tiny income going for food, he could provide himself, his wife, and his four children with only 9,400 calories per day. Of this, he consumed 3,600 calories—enough to go on working. His wife ate 2,200 calories. His children, however, suffered nutritionally. Table 22.1 compares the minimum daily requirements for his children with their actual intake.

Table 22.1

Malnutrition among the Children of a Brazilian Sisal Residue Man

	CALORIES		
Age of Child	Minimum Daily Requirement	Actual Daily Allotment	Percentage of Standard Body Weight
8 (M)	2,100	1,100	62
6 (F)	1,700	900	70
5 (M)	1,700	900	85
3 (M)	1,300	700	90

Source: Gross and Underwood 1971, p. 733.

Long-term malnutrition has results that are reflected in body weight. Table 22.1 shows that the weights of the residue man's malnourished children compared poorly with the standard weights for their ages. The longer malnutrition continues, the greater is the gap between children with poor diets and those with normal diets. The residue man's oldest children had been malnourished longest. They compared least favorably with the standard body weight.

The children of sisal workers were being malnourished to enable their fathers to go on working for wages that were too low to feed them. However, the children of businesspeople and owners of decorticating machines were doing better; malnutrition was much less severe among them. Finally, the nutrition of sisal workers was also worse than that of traditional cultivators in the *sertão*. People who had reached adulthood before sisal cultivation began had more normal weights than did those who grew up after the shift.

This study is important for understanding problems that beset many people today. A shift from a subsistence economy to a cash economy led neither to a better diet nor to more leisure time for most people. The rich merely got richer and the poor got poorer. Badly planned and socially insensitive economic development projects often have such unforeseen consequences.

The Greening of Java

Like Gross in Brazil, anthropologist Richard Franke (1977) conducted an independent study of discrepancies between goals and results in a scheme to promote social and economic change in Java, Indonesia. Experts and planners of the 1960s and 1970s assumed that as small-scale farmers got modern technology and more productive crop varieties, their lives would improve. The media publicized new, high-yielding varieties of wheat, maize, and rice. These new crops, along with chemical fertilizers, pesticides, and new cultivation techniques, were hailed as the basis of a **green revolution.** This "revolution" was expected to increase the world's food supply and thus improve the diets and living conditions of victims of poverty, particularly in land-scarce, overcrowded regions.

The green revolution was an economic success. It did increase the global food supply. New strains of wheat and rice doubled or tripled farm supplies in many Third World countries. Thanks to the green revolution, world food prices declined by more than 20 percent during the 1980s (Stevens 1992). But its social effects were not what its advocates had intended, as we learn from Javanese experience.

Java received a genetic cross between rice strains from Taiwan and Indonesia—a high-yielding "miracle" rice known as IR-8. This hybrid could raise the productivity of a given plot by at least half. Governments throughout southern Asia, including Indonesia, encouraged the cultivation of IR-8, along with the use of chemical fertilizers and pesticides.

The Indonesian island of Java, one of the most densely populated places in the world (over 2000 people per square mile), was a prime target for the green revolution. Java's total crop was insufficient to supply its people with minimal daily requirements of calories (2,150) and protein (55 grams). In 1960, Javanese agriculture supplied 1,950 calories and 38 grams of protein per capita. By 1967, these already inadequate figures had fallen to 1,750 calories and 33 grams. Could miracle rice, by increasing crop yields 50 percent, reverse the trend?

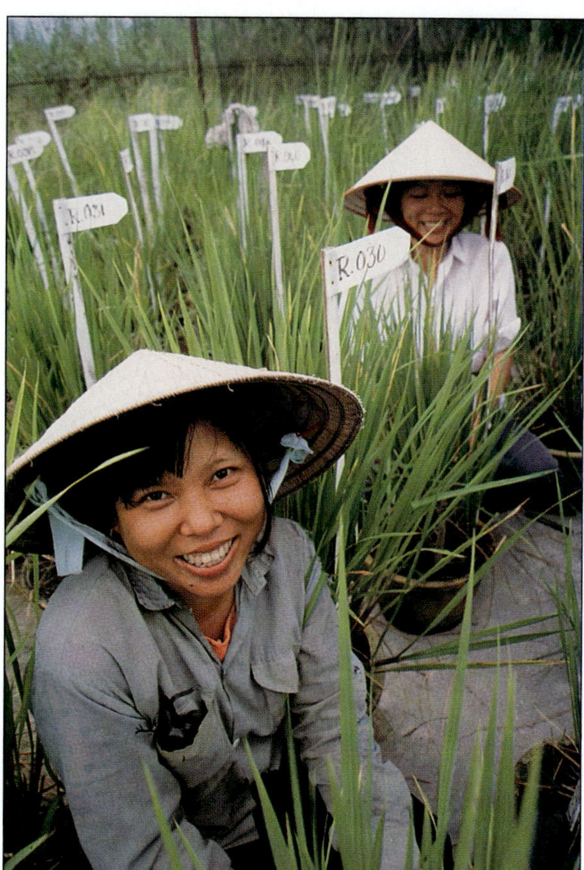

Many Asian governments have promoted the cultivation of new rice varieties, along with the use of chemical fertilizers and pesticides. What costs and benefits may accompany such changes? Shown here is Vietnam's Can Tho Rice Research Institute.

Java shares with many other underdeveloped nations a history of socioeconomic stratification and colonialism. Indigenous contrasts in wealth and power were intensified by Dutch colonialism. Although Indonesia gained political independence from the Netherlands in 1949, internal stratification continued. Today, contrasts between the wealthy (government employees, businesspeople, large landowners) and the poor (small-scale peasants) exist even in small farming communities. Stratification led to problems during Java's green revolution.

In 1963, the University of Indonesia's College of Agriculture launched a program in which students went to live in villages. They worked with peasants in the fields and shared their knowledge of new agricultural techniques while learning from the peasants. The program was a success. Yields in the affected villages increased by half. The program, directed by the Department of Agriculture, was expanded in 1964; nine universities and 400 students joined. These intervention programs succeeded where others had failed because the outside agents recognized that economic development rests not only on technological change but on political change as well. Students could observe firsthand how interest groups resisted attempts by peasants to improve their lot. Once, when local officials stole fertilizer destined for peasant fields, students got it back by threatening in a letter to turn evidence of the crime over to higher-level officials.

The combination of new work patterns and political action was achieving promising results when, in 1965–1966, there was an insurrection against the government. In the eventual military takeover, Indonesia's President Sukarno was ousted and replaced by President Suharto, who ruled Indonesia until 1998. Efforts to increase agricultural production resumed soon after Suharto took control. However, the new government assigned the task to multinational corporations based in Japan, West Germany, and Switzerland rather than to students and peasants. These industrial firms were to supply miracle rice and other high-yielding seeds, fertilizers, and pesticides. Peasants adopting the whole green revolution kit were eligible for loans that would allow them to buy food and other essentials in the lean period just before harvesting.

Java's green revolution soon encountered problems. One pesticide, which had never been tested in Java, killed the fish in the irrigation canals and thus destroyed an important protein resource. One development agency turned out to be a fraud, set up to benefit the military and government officials.

Java's green revolution also encountered problems at the village level because of entrenched interests. Traditionally, peasants had fed their families by taking temporary jobs, or borrowing, from wealthier villagers before the harvest. However, having accepted loans, the peasants were obliged to work for wages lower than those paid on the open market. Low-interest loans would have made peasants less dependent on wealthy villagers, thus depriving local patrons of cheap labor.

Rice cultivation in a densely populated part of Java. What does this photo show you about Java's agricultural economy? Compare it with the discussion of agriculture in the chapter "Making a Living."

Local officials were put in charge of spreading information about how the program worked. Instead, they limited peasant participation by withholding information. Wealthy villagers also discouraged peasant participation more subtly: They raised doubts about the effectiveness of the new techniques and about the wisdom of taking government loans when familiar patrons were nearby. Faced with the thought that starvation might follow if innovation failed, peasants were reluctant to take risks—an understandable reaction.

Production increased, but wealthy villagers rather than small-scale farmers reaped the benefits of the green revolution. Just 20 percent of one village's 151 households participated in the program. However, because they were the wealthiest households, headed by people who owned the most land, 40 percent of the land was being cultivated by means of the new system. Some large-scale landowners used their green revolution profits at the peasants' expense. They bought up peasants' small plots and purchased labor-saving machinery, including rice-milling machines and tractors. As a result, the poorest peasants lost both their means of subsistence—land—and local work opportunities. Their only recourse was to move to cities, where a growing pool of unskilled laborers depressed already low wages.

In a complementary view of the green revolution's social effects, Ann Stoler (1977) focused on gender and stratification. She took issue with Esther Boserup's (1970) contention that colonialism and development inevitably hurt Third World women more than men by favoring commercial agriculture and excluding women from it. Stoler found that the green revolution had permitted some women to gain power over other women and men. Javanese women were not a homogeneous group but varied by class. Stoler found that whether the green revolution helped or harmed Javanese women depended on their position in the class structure. The status of landholding women rose as they gained control over more land and the labor of more poor women. The new economy offered wealthier women higher profits, which they used in trading. However, poor women suffered along with poor men as traditional economic opportunities declined. Nevertheless, the poor women fared better than did the poor men, who had no access at all to off-farm work.

Like Gross's analysis of the Brazilian sisal scheme, these studies of the local effects of the green revolution reveal results different from those foreseen by policy makers, planners, and the media. Again, we see the unintended and undesirable effects of development programs that ignore traditional social, political, and economic divisions. New technology, no matter how promising, does not inevitably help the intended beneficiaries. It may very well hurt them if vested interests interfere. The Javanese student–peasant projects of the 1960s worked because peasants need not just technology but also political clout. Two ambitious development programs in Brazil and Java, although designed to alleviate poverty, actually increased it. Peasants stopped relying on their own subsistence production and started depending on a more volatile pursuit—cash sale of labor. Agricultural production became profit-oriented, machine-based, and chemical-dependent. Local autonomy diminished as linkages with the world system increased. Production rose, as the rich got richer and poverty increased.

A mix of boats harbored at Dai-Lanh fishing village in Vietnam. A boat owner gets a loan to buy a motor. To repay it, he increases the share of the catch he takes from his crew. Later, he uses his rising profits to buy a more expensive boat, and takes even more from his crew. Can a more equitable solution be found?

Equity

A commonly stated goal of development policy today is to promote equity. **Increased equity** means reduced poverty and a more even distribution of wealth. However, if projects are to increase equity, they must have the support of reform-minded governments. Wealthy and powerful people typically resist projects that threaten their vested interests.

Some types of development projects, particularly irrigation schemes, are more likely than others to widen wealth disparities, that is, to have a negative equity impact. An initial uneven distribution of resources (particularly land) often becomes the basis for greater skewing after the project. The social impact of new technology tends to be more severe, contributing negatively to quality of life and to equity, when inputs are channeled to or through the rich, as in Java's green revolution.

Many fisheries projects also have had negative equity results. In Bahia, Brazil (Kottak 1999), sailboat owners (but not nonowners) got loans to buy motors for their boats. To repay the loans, the owners increased the percentage of the catch they took from the men who fished in their boats. Over the years, they used their rising profits to buy larger and more expensive boats. The result was stratification—the creation of a group of wealthy people within a formerly egalitarian community. These events hampered individual initiative and interfered with further development of the fishing industry. With new boats so expensive, ambitious young men who once would have sought careers in fishing no longer had any way to obtain their own boats. They sought wage labor on land instead. To avoid such results, credit-granting agencies must seek out enterprising young fishers rather than giving loans only to owners and established businesspeople.

The Third World Talks Back

In the postcolonial world, anthropologists from industrial nations have heeded criticisms leveled against them by Third World colleagues. For example, the late Mexican anthropologist Guillermo

Batalla (1966) decried certain "conservative and essentially ethnocentric assumptions" of applied anthropology of the 1950s and 1960s in Latin America. He criticized the heavy psychological emphasis of many studies. These studies, he argued, focused too much on attitudes and beliefs about health and nutrition and not enough on the material causes of poor health and malnutrition. Another problem he mentioned was the misuse of cultural relativism by certain anthropologists. Batalla faulted those researchers for refusing to interfere in existing social situations because they considered it inappropriate to judge and to promote change.

Batalla also criticized the multiple causation theory, which assumes that any social event has countless small and diverse causes. Such a theory does not perceive major social and economic inequities as targets for attack. Batalla also faulted certain anthropologists for seeing communities as isolated units, because local-level changes are always accepted or opposed in a larger context. He argued that applied anthropologists should pay more attention to regional, national, and international contexts. Finally, Batalla criticized anthropologists for thinking that diffusion, usually of technical skills and equipment from the First World, is the most significant process involved in change.

Batalla didn't argue that all applied anthropology suffered from these faults. However, many of his criticisms were valid, and other Third World social scientists agreed with him. Those scholars also criticized American anthropology for links between some anthropologists and government agencies that did not promote the best interests of the people.

Partly in response to critics like Batalla, partly out of concern with collaboration by a few anthropologists with the CIA (U.S. Central Intelligence Agency) during the Vietnam War, the American Anthropological Association (AAA) in 1971 adopted a code of ethics entitled "AAA: Principles of Professional Responsibility." In the most recent (1997) revision of that code, the AAA notes that anthropologists have obligations to their scholarly field, to the wider society and culture, and to the human species, other species, and the environment. The code's aim is to offer guidelines and to promote education and discussion of socially responsible anthropology, whether academic or applied.

Strategies for Innovation

Development anthropologists, who are concerned with social issues in, and the cultural dimension of, economic development, must work closely with local people to assess and help realize their own wishes and needs for change. Too many true local needs cry out for a solution to waste money funding development projects that are inappropriate in area A but needed in area B, or unnecessary anywhere. Development anthropology can help sort out the A's and B's and fit projects accordingly. Projects that put people first by consulting with them, and responding to their expressed needs, must be identified (Cernea 1991). Thereafter, development anthropologists can work to ensure socially compatible ways of implementing the project.

In a comparative study of 68 rural development projects from all around the world, I found the *culturally compatible* economic development projects to be twice as successful financially as the incompatible ones (Kottak 1990*b*, 1991). This finding shows that using applied anthropological expertise in planning, to ensure cultural compatibility, is cost-effective. To maximize social and economic benefits, projects must (1) be culturally compatible, (2) respond to locally perceived needs, (3) involve men and women in planning and carrying out the changes that affect them, (4) harness traditional organizations, and (5) be flexible.

Overinnovation

In my comparative study, the compatible and successful projects avoided the fallacy of **overinnovation** (too much change). We would expect people to resist development projects that require major changes in their daily lives, especially ones that interfere with subsistence pursuits. People usually want to change just enough to keep what they have. Motives for modifying behavior come from the traditional culture and the small concerns of ordinary life. Peasants' values are not such abstract ones as "learning a better way," "progressing," "increasing technical know-how," "improving efficiency," or "adopting modern techniques." (Those phrases exemplify intervention philosophy.) Instead, their objectives are

To maximize benefits, development projects should be culturally compatible and respond to locally perceived needs for change. What else should they do? This Zambian farm club, which draws on traditional social organization, plants cabbages.

down-to-earth and specific ones. People want to improve yields in a rice field, amass resources for a ceremony, get a child through school, or have enough cash to pay the tax bill on time. The goals and values of subsistence producers differ from those of people who produce for cash, just as they differ from the intervention philosophies of development planners. Different value systems must be considered during planning.

In the comparative study, the projects that failed were usually both economically and culturally incompatible. For example, one South Asian project promoted the cultivation of onions and peppers, expecting this practice to fit into a preexisting labor-intensive system of rice-growing. Cultivation of these cash crops wasn't traditional in the area. It conflicted with existing crop priorities and other interests of farmers. Also, the labor peaks for pepper and onion production coincided with those for rice, to which the farmers gave priority.

Throughout the world, project problems have arisen from inadequate attention to, and consequent lack of fit with, local culture. Another naive and incompatible project was an overinnovative scheme in Ethiopia. Its major fallacy was to try to convert nomadic herders into sedentary cultivators. It ignored traditional land rights. Outsiders—commercial farmers—were to get much of the herders' territory. The pastoralists were expected to settle down and start farming. This project helped wealthy outsiders instead of the natives. The planners naively expected free-ranging herders to give up a generations-old way of life to work three times harder growing rice and picking cotton. "In the News" describes an extreme—and ongoing—example of a centrally planned, culturally incompatible project. Planning for the world's largest dam involved no consultation with local people and no attention to their needs and wishes. Strong resistance can be expected to continue.

Underdifferentiation

The fallacy of **underdifferentiation** is the tendency to view "the less-developed countries" as more alike than they are. Development agencies often have ignored cultural diversity (e.g., between Brazil and Burundi) and adopted a uniform approach to deal with very different sets of people. Neglecting cultural diversity, many projects also have tried to impose incompatible property notions and social units. Most often, the faulty social design assumes either (1) individualistic productive units that are privately owned by an individual or couple and worked by a nuclear family or (2) cooperatives that are at least partially based on models from the former Eastern bloc and socialist countries.

Often, development aims at generating *individual* cash wealth through exports. This goal contrasts with the tendency of bands and tribes to share resources and to depend on local ecosystems and renewable resources (Bodley 1988). Development planners commonly emphasize benefits that will accrue to individuals. More concern with the effects on communities is needed (Bodley 1988).

One example of faulty Euro-American models (the individual and the nuclear family) was a West African project designed for an area where the extended family was the basic social unit.

People Be Dammed

The relocation of at least 1.2 million people to make way for the Three Gorges Dam in central China is off to a poor start, calling into question the official timetable for filling the dam's reservoir five years from now, a Chinese social scientist who toured five of the most heavily affected counties in January says.

Interviews with local officials and people affected by the giant project to tame the Yangtze River suggested that the resettlement program—said by the Government to have moved about 100,000 people so far—has been plagued by inadequate compensation and a shortage of new jobs and farmland for people being relocated, official corruption and false reports of progress by local officials to national leaders, the researcher's report says.

Last November, to nationalistic fanfare, China diverted the Yangtze around the construction site and began building the dam, which will be the world's largest if completed as planned. The Government has signed contracts with Western companies for turbines and other equipment . . .

Government officials say the dam will provide huge benefits by controlling floods, providing clean energy and opening the interior to shipping. Critics say that the benefits are exaggerated and that the dam will destroy the Yangtze ecosystem, bury priceless cultural relics and cause suffering for hundreds of thousands.

Because of these concerns, the World Bank and United States Export-Import Bank have not lent money to the project, and opponents hope to curb European export credits.

The author of the new report on resettlement, an experienced field researcher, has concealed his identity to protect his career. His report is being distributed this week by the International Rivers Network and Human Rights in China, two American-based groups that oppose the dam on environmental and human rights grounds.

By 2003, when the dam is built and the reservoir of water behind it is filled to its initial level, at least 500,000 people must be moved from cities, towns and villages of Sichuan and Hubei Provinces. By 2009, when the reservoir is filled still higher, the Government says a total of 1.2 million people will have to be moved, mostly to better jobs and farmlands.

But some people are resisting.

"Foot-dragging opposition to resettlement is widespread, presaging a major crisis if the dam project continues as planned," wrote the Chinese researcher, estimating that the number of people moved to date may be little more than half of the official total. Given the slow pace, he wrote, officials in one county said no official would want to be in charge of resettlement as the year 2003 approaches because so many people will have to be moved within such a short time, raising a specter of unrest.

Viewing the construction of China's Three Gorges Dam.

These officials hope that at the least, the Government will decide on a lower final reservoir level, reducing the area to be inundated and thus the number of people who will have to be resettled.

To improve the prospects for displaced people, the Government has offered incentives for companies to locate in the region. But the current effort to shed excess workers in ailing state industries has instead meant rising unemployment. One county official in Sichuan reportedly said, "There is no way to find industrial jobs for rural settlers."

The researcher met with several "model resettlers," families who were happy with their new lives and are showcased by officials as success stories. But the small number who have been officially designated as models have received four times the average compensation for relocation, the report says.

Source: "Relocations for China Dam Are Found to Lag," by Erik Eckholm, March 12, 1998, www.nytimes.com.

The project succeeded despite its faulty social design because the participants used their traditional extended family networks to attract additional settlers. Eventually, twice as many people as planned benefited as extended family members flocked to the project area. Here, settlers modified the project design that had been imposed on them by following the principles of their traditional society.

The second dubious foreign social model that is common in development strategy is the cooperative. In the comparative study of rural development projects, new cooperatives fared badly. Cooperatives succeeded only when they harnessed preexisting local-level communal institutions. This is a corollary of a more general rule: Participants' groups are most effective when they are based on traditional social organization or on a socioeconomic similarity among members.

Deforestation is a worldwide threat. Shown here, Thai Buddhist monks encircle an endangered forest to protect against its destruction. What are other ways of dealing with deforestation?

Neither foreign social model—the nuclear family farm nor the cooperative—has an unblemished record in development. An alternative is needed: greater use of Third World social models for Third World development. These are traditional social units, such as the clans, lineages, and other extended kinship groups of Africa, Oceania, and many other nations, with their communally held estates and resources. The most humane and productive strategy for change is to base the social design for innovation on traditional social forms in each target area.

Third World Models

Many governments are not genuinely, or realistically, committed to improving the lives of their citizens. Interference by major powers also has kept governments from enacting needed reforms. In highly stratified societies, particularly in Latin America, the class structure is very rigid. Movement of individuals into the middle class is difficult. It is equally hard to raise the living standards of the lower class as a whole. These nations have a long history of government control by antidemocratic leaders and powerful interest groups, which tend to oppose reform. (Such governments often have been supported by the United States, especially during the Cold War.)

In some nations, however, the government acts more as an agent of the people. Madagascar provides an example. As in many areas of Africa, precolonial states had developed in Madagascar before its conquest by the French in 1895. The people of Madagascar, the Malagasy, had been organized into descent groups before the origin of the state. The Merina, creators of the major precolonial state of Madagascar, wove descent groups into its structure, making members of important groups advisers to the king and thus giving them authority in government. The Merina state made provisions for the people it ruled. It collected taxes and organized labor for public works projects. In return, it redistributed resources to peasants in need. It also granted them some protection against war and slave raids and allowed them to cultivate their rice fields in peace. The government maintained the water works for rice cultivation. It opened to ambitious peasant boys the chance of becoming, through hard work and study, state bureaucrats.

Throughout the history of the Merina state—and continuing in modern Madagascar—there have been strong relationships between the individual, the descent group, and the state. Local Malagasy communities, where residence is based on descent, are more cohesive and homogeneous than are communities in Java or Latin America. Madagascar gained political independence from France in 1960. Although it was still economically dependent on France when I first did research there in 1966–1967, the new government was committed to a form of economic development designed to increase the ability of the Malagasy to feed themselves. Government policy emphasized increased production of rice, a subsistence crop, rather than cash crops. Furthermore, local communities, with their traditional cooperative patterns and solidarity based on kinship and descent, were treated as partners in, not obstacles to, the development process.

In Bangladesh, women count money at a weekly meeting where loans from the female-run Grameen Credit Bank are repaid. Groups promoting development can be particularly effective when they are based on traditional social organization or on a socioeconomic similarity among members.

In a sense, the descent group is preadapted to equitable national development. In Madagascar, members of local descent groups have customarily pooled their resources to educate their ambitious members. Once educated, these men and women gain economically secure positions in the nation. They then share the advantages of their new positions with their kin. For example, they give room and board to rural cousins attending school and help them find jobs.

Malagasy administrations appear generally to have shared a commitment to democratic economic development. Perhaps this is because government officials are of the peasantry or have strong personal ties to it. By contrast, in Latin American countries, the elites and the lower class typically have different origins and no strong connections through kinship, descent, or marriage.

An effective social design for innovation may incorporate existing groups and institutions, such as descent groups in Africa and Oceania. Here, in Bali, Indonesia, a traditional system of planning and management by Hindu temples and priests has been harnessed for culturally appropriate agricultural development (see Lansing 1991).

Furthermore, societies with descent-group organization contradict an assumption that many social scientists and economists seem to make. It is not inevitable that as nations become more tied to the world capitalist economy, native forms of social organization will break down into nuclear family organization, impersonality, and alienation. Descent groups, with their traditional communalism and corporate solidarity, have important roles to play in economic development.

Realistic development promotes change but not overinnovation. Many changes are possible if the aim is to preserve local systems while making them work better. Successful economic development projects respect, or at least don't attack, local cultural patterns. Effective development draws on indigenous cultural practices and social structures.

summary

1. Imperialism is the policy of extending the rule of a nation or empire over other nations and of taking and holding foreign colonies. Colonialism is the domination of a territory and its people by a foreign power for an extended time. European colonialism has had two main phases. The first started in 1492 and lasted through 1825. For Britain this phase ended with the American revolution. For France it ended when Britain won the Seven Years War, forcing the French to abandon Canada and India. For Spain, it ended with Latin American independence. The second phase of European colonialism extended approximately from 1850 to 1950. The British and French empires were at their height around 1914, when European empires controlled 85 percent of the world. Britain and France had colonies in Africa, Asia, Oceania, and the New World.
2. Political, ethnic, and tribal labels and identities were created under colonialism. Postcolonial studies is a growing academic field. It studies the interactions between European nations and the societies they colonized (mainly after 1800). Its topics include the impact of colonization and the state of postcolonies today.
3. Like colonialism, economic development has an intervention philosophy. This provides a justification for outsiders to guide native peoples toward particular goals. Development is usually justified by the idea that industrialization and modernization are desirable evolutionary advances. Yet many problems faced by Third World peoples have been caused by their incorporation in the world cash economy. Roads, mining, hydroelectric projects, ranching, lumbering, and agribusiness threaten indigenous peoples and their ecosystems.
4. Development anthropology focuses on social issues in, and the cultural dimension of, economic development. Development projects typically promote cash employment and new technology at the expense of subsistence economies. Following a shift to cash cropping in northeastern Brazil, the local diet and poverty worsened. Research in Java found that the green revolution was failing. The reason: It promoted only new technology, rather than a combination of technology and peasant political organization.
5. Not all governments seek to increase equality and end poverty. Resistance by elites to reform is typical—and hard to combat. Local people rarely cooperate with projects requiring major changes in their daily lives, especially ones that interfere with customary subsistence pursuits. Many projects seek to impose inappropriate property notions and incompatible social units on their intended beneficiaries. The best strategy for change is to base the social design for innovation on traditional social forms in each target area.

key terms

colonialism The political, social, economic, and cultural domination of a territory and its people by a foreign power for an extended time.

development anthropology The branch of applied anthropology that focuses on social issues in, and the cultural dimension of, economic development.

equity, increased A reduction in absolute poverty and a fairer (more even) distribution of wealth.

green revolution Agricultural development based on chemical fertilizers, pesticides, 20th-century cultivation techniques, and new crop varieties such as IR-8 ("miracle rice").

intervention philosophy Guiding principle of colonialism, conquest, missionization, or development; an ideological justification for outsiders to guide native peoples in specific directions.

overinnovation Characteristic of projects that require major changes in natives' daily lives, especially ones that interfere with customary subsistence pursuits.

postcolonial Referring to interactions between European nations and the societies they colonized (mainly after 1800); more generally, "postcolonial" may be used to signify a position against imperialism and Eurocentrism.

underdifferentiation Planning fallacy of viewing less-developed countries as an undifferentiated group; ignoring cultural diversity and adopting a uniform approach (often ethnocentric) for very different types of project beneficiaries.

critical thinking questions

1. How is the diversity you see in your classroom related to the colonies and empires discussed in this chapter?
2. Have you read a postcolonial novel? What was the last one you read? What made it postcolonial?
3. Defend the proposition: The United States and Canada are both postcolonies.
4. Think of a recent case in which a core nation, such as the United States, has intervened in the affairs of another nation. What was the intervention philosophy used to justify the action?
5. Broadly describe the equity results of the Brazilian sisal scheme and the green revolution in Java. Do you think that most economic development schemes have similar results? Does this description of Java's green revolution fit what you have previously heard about the green revolution?
6. Devise a plan to equalize the distribution of computers in your public school system. What kind of opposition would you expect? Who would your supporters be?
7. Can you think of some good reasons to get herders to start farming? How would you try to implement such a change? Do you think you'd be successful? Is there an intervention philosophy behind your thinking?
8. Think about ways in which economic development might differently affect men and women.
9. Thinking of your own society and recent history, give an example of a proposal or policy that failed because it was overinnovative.
10. Thinking of your own society and recent history, give an example of a proposal or policy that failed because it did not differentiate sufficiently.
11. Think of a change you'd like to see happen. What groups would you enlist to make it happen? What would their roles be, from start to finish?

case study

Haiti: This chapter has discussed the far-reaching and long-lasting results of colonialism. In *Culture Sketches* by Holly Peters-Golden, read the chapter on "Haiti: A Nation in Turmoil." How do you think Haiti's colonial past has contributed to its contemporary situation? What sorts of problems does Haiti face owing to development, or lack thereof? How does Haiti compare to some other examples mentioned in the text chapter?

suggested additional readings

Arce, A., and N. Long, eds.
1999 *Anthropology, Development, and Modernities: Exploring Discourses, Counter-tendencies, and Violence.* New York: Routledge. Applied anthropology, rural development, social change, violence, and social and economic policy in developing countries.

Barlett, P. F., ed.
1980 *Agricultural Decision Making: Anthropological Contribution to Rural Development.* New York: Academic Press. How farmers choose what to plant and decide how to plant it in various cultures.

Bodley, J. H.
2000 *Anthropology and Contemporary Human Problems,* 4th ed. Mountain View, CA: Mayfield. Overview of major problems of today's industrial world: overconsumption, the environment, resource depletion, hunger, overpopulation, violence, and war.

Bodley, J. H., ed.
1988 *Tribal Peoples and Development Issues: A Global Overview.* Mountain View, CA: Mayfield. An overview of case studies, policies, assessments, and recommendations concerning tribal peoples and development.

Cernea, M., ed.
1991 *Putting People First: Sociological Variables in Rural Development,* 2nd ed. New York: Oxford University Press (published for the World Bank). First collection of articles by social scientists based on World Bank files and project experiences. Examines development successes and failures and the social and cultural reasons for them.

Cooper, F., and A. L. Stoler, eds.
1997 *Tensions of Empire: Colonial Cultures in a Bourgeois World.* Berkeley, CA: University of California Press. The social complexity of colonial encounters is explored in several articles.

Escobar, A.
1995 *Encountering Development: The Making and Unmaking of the Third World.* Princeton, NJ: Princeton University Press. A critique of economic development and development anthropology.

Lansing, J. S.
1991 *Priests and Programmers: Technologies of Power in the Engineered Landscape of Bali.* Princeton, NJ: Princeton University Press. The role of a traditional priesthood in managing irrigation and culturally appropriate economic development in Bali, Indonesia.

Nussbaum, M. C.
2000 *Women and Human Development: The Capabilities Approach.* New York: Cambridge University Press. The untapped power of women in developing countries.

Nussbaum, M., and J. Glover, eds.
1995 *Women, Culture, and Development: A Study of Human Capabilities.* New York: Oxford University Press. How to overcome generalized inequities between men and women in the less-developed countries.

Van Bremen, J., and A. Shimizu, eds.

1999 *Anthropology and Colonialism in Asia and Oceania*. London: Curzon. One in a series on the anthropology of Asia.

Worsley, P.

1984 *The Three Worlds: Culture and World Development*. Chicago: University of Chicago Press. Examines the nature of development processes and critiques existing theories.

internet exercises

1. *Colonialism in California:* Go to the Original Voices website, **http://originalvoices.org/** and read the chapters on Precontact Culture and Economy, **http://originalvoices.org/PreContactOne.htm,** Human Price of Gold Rush, **http://originalvoices.org/PriceOfGoldOne.htm,** and U.S. Government Roles, **http://originalvoices.org/USGovtRolesOne.htm.**
   a. What cultures lived in Northern California before the gold rush? What were their lifestyles like?
   b. What were the gold miners' attitudes toward the indigenous people? What actions did they take that reflected those attitudes? Would you characterize these actions as ethnocide or genocide?
   c. What role did the U.S. government play in the gold rush? Did it just tolerate the actions of the miners or did it encourage them?
   d. Some names of professional sports teams have been in the news recently because some Native Americans consider them offensive (e.g., Washington Redskins, Atlanta Braves, Cleveland Indians). After reading this page, what do you think native groups from Northern California might feel about the name of the San Francisco 49ers (named after the gold rushers of 1849)?

2. *Human Rights:* Read the preamble and skim the articles of the United Nations Universal Declaration of Human Rights, **http://www.un.org/Overview/rights.html.**
   a. What are the central points of the declaration?
   b. Do you agree with them? Do you find them all reasonable? Is anything missing?
   c. How do colonial strategies and development projects threaten human rights as spelled out in this declaration?
   d. How would you suggest the U.N. enforce these rights?

See Chapter 22 on your CD-ROM for additional review and interactive exercises. See your McGraw-Hill Online Learning Center for more.

Chapter 23

Cultural Exchange and Survival

CHAPTER OUTLINE

ARCHAEOLOGY.ORG NEWS BRIEFS

A Museum to Right Past Wrongs

by Ellen Herscher
December 6, 1999

In a vivid and moving ceremony punctuated by whoops and insistent drumming, ancient incantations called upon Mother Earth to lend a small piece of her bosom to hold a new museum, the National Museum of the American Indian. Thus on an overcast day in late September, Native Americans returned in triumph to the National Mall in Washington, D.C., to begin the construction of a living monument to their history and culture. The museum, scheduled to open in 2002 and part of the revered Smithsonian Institution, now rises in the shadow of the U.S.

Capitol, where 170 years ago Congress passed the Indian Removal Act to push tribes westward . . .

The new museum will display the world's finest and largest collection of Native American objects . . . There the 800,000 catalogued items will not simply be stored and conserved, but will be placed according to tribal wishes and readily accessible to native groups . . . Former Smithsonian Secretary Robert Adams, in his remarks at the groundbreaking, succinctly stated the unique perspective of the new institution, that "relics do not float in a timeless void, but have living meaning tied to the past and continually made relevant to the present." . . .

It will be the Smithsonian's sixteenth museum and the tenth located on the prestigious National Mall, where it will fill the last available site. But with its independent board of trustees and largely native staff, it will maintain its unique identity. Even its cafeteria will be different, serving only cuisine of native foods . . . Here the Indians will tell their own story in their own way . . .

A large central rotunda space will be used for performances and demonstrations, as will a planned outdoor space. Three-quarters of the 4.25-acre site will be devoted to reconstructed indigenous natural habitats: hardwood forest, freshwater wetlands, and meadows. Part of the site will be used to grow crops, including ancient corn. . . Collaboration, consultation, and cooperation with the peoples whose history will be celebrated here have marked the gestation of the building and the plans for the programs and exhibits which it will house. The recent groundbreaking ceremony paid homage to the way this new kind of institution came into being and embodied its hopes for the future. Washington suits and traditional native dress mingled in the audience while the blessings from the four cardinal directions were pronounced, invoking the native peoples' ties to the land . . .

The NMAI will not just house objects, but will protect and support the development and continuation of Native culture and community, sustaining the Indian view that cultural objects form a metaphysical chain linking the ancestors with the living people of the tribe.

In the past decade the repatriation issue has engaged the energies of most American museums with Native collections, as they struggled to reconcile the claims of tribes who wished to recover funerary remains with institutions' traditional duty to preserve their collections. The National Museum of the American Indian is pointing a new direction for the future: by honoring the wishes of Native peoples for the care and protection of the collection, it hopes to create a place where Indians will want to leave their traditional artifacts while providing the general public with a new understanding of these ancient cultures.

Source: http://www.archaeology.org/online/features/amindian/index.html. Copyright 1999 by the Archaeological Institute of America.

overview

People travel more than ever. But they also maintain ties with home, thus living multilocally. In this world in flux, new identities and political and ethnic units emerge as others disappear. In worse cases, a culture may collapse or be absorbed (ethnocide). Its people may die off or be exterminated (genocide). Systems of domination have private, "offstage" aspects along with their evident, public dimensions. A critique of power usually goes on out of sight of the power holders. Resistance can be individual and disguised, or collective and defiant.

Cultural imperialism refers to the spread of one culture at the expense of others. A text, such as a media-born image, is interpreted by each person exposed to it. People may accept, resist, or oppose a text's established meaning. People manufacture their own meanings for texts. When outside forces enter new settings, they are typically modified to fit the local culture. Mass media can diffuse the culture of a country within its borders, thus enhancing national identity. The mass media also play a role in preserving ethnic identities among people who lead transnational lives.

Today's global culture is driven by flows of people, technology, finance, and information. Business and the media have stoked a craving for commodities and images worldwide. This has created a global culture of consumption.

This book has examined many aspects of increasing participation by local cultures in wider systems: regional, national, colonial, and global. Since the 1920s, anthropologists have been investigating the changes that arise from contact between industrial and nonindustrial societies. Studies of "social change" and "acculturation" are abundant. British and American ethnographers, respectively, have used these terms to describe the same process. *Acculturation* refers to changes that result when groups come into continuous firsthand contact—changes in the cultural patterns of either or both groups (Redfield, Linton, and Herskovits 1936, p. 149).

Contact and Domination

Acculturation differs from diffusion, or cultural borrowing, which can occur without firsthand contact. For example, most North Americans who eat hot dogs ("frankfurters") have never been to Frankfurt, nor have most North American Toyota owners or sushi eaters ever visited Japan. Although *acculturation* can be applied to any case of cultural contact and change, the term has most often described **westernization**—the influence of Western expansion on native cultures. Thus, natives who wear store-bought clothes, learn Indo-European languages, and otherwise adopt Western customs are called acculturated. Acculturation may be voluntary or forced.

In the chapter "Ethnicity," we saw that sometimes a dominant group may try to destroy the cultures of certain ethnic groups (*ethnocide*) or force them to adopt the dominant culture (*forced assimilation*). Sometimes this involves a ban on, or penalties against, religious practices or use of a minority language.

Different degrees of destruction, domination, resistance, survival, adaptation, and modification of native cultures may follow interethnic contact. In the most destructive encounters, native and subordinate cultures face obliteration. In cases where contact between the indigenous societies and more powerful outsiders leads to destruction—a situation that is particularly char-

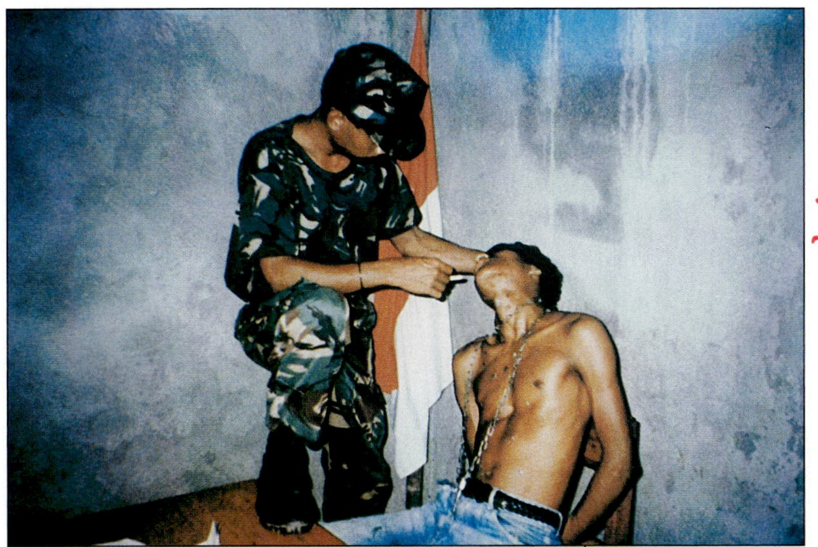

Backed by military force, the Indonesian annexation of East Timor involved civil repression, persecution of Christians, and torture.

acteristic of colonialist and expansionist eras—a "shock phase" often follows the initial encounter (Bodley 1988). Outsiders may attack or exploit the native people. Such exploitation may increase mortality, disrupt subsistence, fragment kin groups, damage social support systems, and inspire new religious movements, such as the cargo cults examined in the chapter "Religion" (Bodley 1988). During the shock phase, there may be civil repression backed by military force. Such factors may lead to the group's cultural collapse (*ethnocide*) or its physical extinction (*genocide*).

Outsiders often attempt to remake native landscapes and cultures in their own image. Political and economic colonialists have tried to redesign conquered and dependent lands, peoples, and cultures, imposing their cultural standards on others. The aim of many agricultural development projects, for example, seems to have been to make the world as much like Iowa as possible, complete with mechanized farming and nuclear family ownership—despite the fact that these models may be inappropriate for settings outside the North American heartland.

Development and Environmentalism

Today it is often multinational corporations, usually based in core nations, rather than the governments of those nations, who are changing the nature of Third World economies. However, nations do tend to support the predatory enterprises that seek cheap labor and raw materials in countries outside the core, such as Brazil, where economic development has contributed to ecological devastation.

Simultaneously, environmentalists from core nations increasingly state their case, promoting conservation, to the rest of the world. The ecological devastation of the Amazon has become a focus of international environmentalist attention. Yet many Brazilians complain that northerners talk about global needs and saving the Amazon after having destroyed their own forests for First World economic growth. Akbar Ahmed (1992) concludes that non-Westerners tend to be cynical about Western ecological morality, seeing it as yet another imperialist message. "The Chinese have cause to snigger at the Western suggestion that they forgo the convenience of the fridge to save the ozone layer" (Ahmed 1992, p. 120).

In the last chapter, we saw that development projects usually fail if they try to replace native forms with culturally alien property concepts and productive units. A strategy that incorporates the native forms is more effective than the fallacies of overinnovation and underdifferentiation. The same caveats would seem to apply to an intervention philosophy that seeks to impose global ecological morality without due attention to cultural variation and autonomy. Countries and cultures may resist interventionist philosophies aimed at either development or globally justified environmentalism.

A clash of cultures related to environmental change may occur when *development threatens indigenous peoples and their environments.* Hundreds of native groups throughout the world, including the Kayapó Indians of Brazil and the

At a mall in Poodong district, China, consumers can shop in one of Asia's biggest supermarkets. What would be the environmental effects if China had a level of consumption paralleling that of the United States?

Kaluli of Papua New Guinea (see "Interesting Issues" on pages 602–603), have been threatened by plans and forces, such as dam construction or commercially driven deforestation, that would *destroy* their homelands.

A second clash of cultures related to environmental change occurs when *external regulation threatens indigenous peoples.* Native groups may actually be threatened by environmental plans that seek to *save* their homelands. Sometimes outsiders expect local people to give up many of their customary economic and cultural activities without clear substitutes, alternatives, or incentives in order to conserve endangered species. The traditional approach to conservation has been to restrict access to protected areas, hire guards, and punish violators.

Problems often arise when external regulation replaces the native system. Like development projects, conservation schemes may ask people to change the way they have been doing things for generations to satisfy planners' goals rather than local goals. Ironically, well-meaning conservation efforts can be as insensitive as development schemes that promote radical changes without involving local people in planning and carrying out the policies that affect them. When people are asked to give up the basis of their livelihood, they usually resist.

Consider the case of a Tanosy man who lives on the edge of the Andohahela forest reserve of southeastern Madagascar. For years he has relied on rice fields and grazing land inside that reserve. Now external agencies are trying to get him to abandon this land for the sake of conservation. This man is a wealthy *ombiasa* (traditional sorcerer-healer). With four wives, a dozen children, and 20 head of cattle, he is an ambitious, hard-working, and productive peasant. With money, social support, and supernatural authority, he is mounting effective resistance against the park ranger who has been trying to get him to abandon his fields. The *ombiasa* claims he has already relinquished some of his land, but he is waiting for compensatory fields. His most effective resistance has been supernatural. The death of the ranger's son was attributed to the *ombiasa*'s magical power. Since then, the ranger has been less vigilant in his enforcement efforts.

Given the threat that deforestation poses to global biodiversity, it is vitally important to devise conservation strategies that will work.

Laws and enforcement may help stem the tide of commercially driven deforestation, which takes the form of burning and clear cutting. However, local people also use and abuse forested lands. A challenge for the environmentally oriented applied anthropologist is to make forest preservation attractive to people like the Tanosy of Madagascar. Like development plans, effective conservation strategies must pay attention to the customs, needs, and incentives of the people living in the affected area. Conservation depends on local cooperation. In the Tanosy case, the guardians of the reserve must do more to satisfy the *ombiasa* and other affected people, through boundary adjustments, negotiation, and compensation. For effective conservation (as for development), the task is to devise culturally appropriate strategies. Neither development agencies nor NGOs (nongovernmental organizations) will succeed if they try to impose their goals without considering the practices, customs, rules, laws, beliefs, and values of the people to be affected.

Religious Change

In the movie *Raiders of the Lost Ark*, Indiana Jones, anthropologist extraordinaire, faces an assassin armed with a scimitar. The Middle Easterner displays an elaborate series of moves showing his skills in traditional weaponry. Impressed by the demonstration, as the audience appreciates the threat, Jones takes out a pistol and shoots the man dead.

This sequence makes a point about dominance and cultural diversity, interethnic encounters, the world system, resistance, and survival. The scimitar-wielding Mid-Easterner can be seen as symbolizing traditional culture against the world system. We should not forget that anthropologists, too, are agents of the world system. A century ago, the anthropologist tended to arrive after the traders (the economic proselytizers), but around the same time, and often competing with, the missionaries (the religious proselytizers). The Christians came to "save souls." The anthropologists were there to salvage cultures. But all were Western presences among the natives.

Religious proselytizing can promote ethnocide, as native beliefs and practices are replaced by Western ones. Sometimes a religion and associated customs are replaced by ideology and behavior more compatible with Western culture. One example is the Handsome Lake religion (as described in the chapter on religion), which led the Iroquois to copy European farming techniques, stressing male rather than female labor. The Iroquois also gave up their communal longhouses and matrilineal descent groups for nuclear family households. The teachings of Handsome Lake led to a new church and religion. This revitalization movement helped the

504

Iroquois survive in a drastically modified environment, but much ethnocide was involved.

Handsome Lake was a native who created a new religion, drawing on Western models. More commonly, missionaries and proselytizers representing the major world religions, especially Christianity and Islam, are the proponents of religious change. Protestant and Catholic missionization continues even in remote corners of the world. Evangelical Protestantism, for example, is advancing in Peru, Brazil, and other parts of Latin America. It challenges an often-jaded Catholicism that has too few priests and that is sometimes seen mainly as women's religion.

Sometimes the political ideology of a nation-state is pitted against traditional religion. Officials of the former Soviet empire discouraged Catholicism, Judaism, and Islam. In Central Asia, Soviet dominators destroyed Muslim mosques and discouraged religious practice. On the other hand,

307–308

governments often use their power to advance a religion, such as Islam in Iran or Sudan.

A military government seized power in Sudan in 1989. It immediately launched a campaign to change that country of more than 35 million people, where one-quarter are not Muslims, into an Islamic nation. Sudan adopted a policy of religious, linguistic, and cultural imperialism. The government sought to extend Islam and the Arabic language to the non-Muslim south. This was an area of Christianity and tribal religions that had resisted the central government for a decade. The new government declared a *jihad* (holy war) against non-Muslims. It persecuted Catholic leaders and purged the military, the civil service, the judiciary, and the educational system of non-Muslims. Students in the south were forced to take their exams in Arabic, for them a foreign language (Hedges 1992*a*).

Voices of the Rainforest

The government of Papua New Guinea has approved oil exploration by American, British, Australian, and Japanese companies in the rainforest habitat of the Kaluli and other indigenous peoples. The forest degradation that usually accompanies logging, ranching, road building, and drilling endangers plants, animals, peoples, and cultures. Lost along with trees are songs, myths, words, ideas, artifacts, and techniques—the cultural knowledge and practices of rainforest people like the Kaluli, whom the anthropologist and ethnomusicologist Steven Feld has been studying for more than 20 years.

Feld teamed up with Mickey Hart of the Grateful Dead in a project designed to promote the cultural survival of the Kaluli through their music. For years, Hart has worked to preserve musical diversity through educational funding, concert promotion, and recording, including a successful series called "The World" on the Rykodisc label. *Voices of the Rainforest* was the first CD completely devoted to indigenous music from Papua New Guinea. In one hour, it encapsulates 24 hours of a day in Kaluli life in Bosavi village. The recording permits a form of cultural survival and diffusion in a high-quality commercial product. Bosavi is presented as a "soundscape" of blended music and natural environmental sounds. Kaluli weave the natural sounds of birds, frogs, rivers, and streams into their texts, melodies, and rhythms. They sing and whistle with birds and waterfalls. They compose instrumental duets with birds and cicadas.

The Kaluli project was launched on Earth Day 1991 at *Star Wars* creator George Lucas's Skywalker Ranch. There, Randy Hayes, the executive director of the Rainforest Action Network, and musician Mickey Hart spoke about the linked issues of rainforest destruction and musical survival. Next came a San Francisco benefit dinner for the Bosavi People's Fund. This is the trust established to receive royalties from the Kaluli recording—a financial prong in Steven Feld's strategy to foster Kaluli cultural survival.

A teacher shows Kaluli children Steven Feld's *Voices of the Rainforest.*

Voices of the Rainforest is being marketed as "world music." This term is intended to point up musical diversity, the fact that musics originate from all world regions and all cultures. "Tribal" music joins Western music as a form of artistic expression worth performing, hearing, and preserving. Hart's series offers musics of non-Western origin as well as those of ethnically dominated groups of the Western world.

Hart's record series aims at preserving "endangered music" against the artistic loss suffered by indigenous peoples. Its intent is to give a "world voice" to people who are being silenced by the dominant world system. In 1993, Hart launched a new series, The Library of Congress Endangered Music Project, which includes digitally remastered field recordings collected by the American Folklife Center. The first of this series, *The Spirit Cries,* concentrated on music from a broad range of cultures in South and Central America and the Caribbean. Proceeds from this project were used to support the performers and their cultural traditions.

In *Voices of the Rainforest,* Feld and Hart excised all "modern" and "dominant" sounds from their recording. Gone are the world system sounds that Kaluli villagers now hear every day. The recording temporarily silences the "machine voices": the tractor that cuts the grass on the local airstrip, the gas generator, the sawmill, the helicopters, and light planes buzzing to and from the oil-drilling areas. Gone, too, are the village church bells, Bible readings, evangelical prayers and hymns, and the voices of teachers and students at an English-only school.

Initially, Feld anticipated criticism for attempting to create an idealized Kaluli "soundscape" insulated from invasive forces and sounds. Among the Kaluli, he expected varied opinions about the value of his project:

> It is a soundscape world that some Kaluli care little about, a world that other Kaluli momentarily choose to forget, a world that some Kaluli are increasingly nostalgic and uneasy about, a world that other Kaluli are still living and creating and listening to. It is a sound world that increasingly fewer Kaluli will actively know about and value, but one that increasingly more Kaluli will only hear on cassette and sentimentally wonder about. (Feld 1991, p. 137)

Despite these concerns, Feld was met with an overwhelmingly positive response when he returned to Papua New Guinea in 1992 armed with a boombox and the recording. The people of Bosavi reacted very favorably. Not only did they appreciate the recording, they also have been able to build a much-needed community school with the *Voices of the Rainforest* royalties that have been donated to the Bosavi People's Fund.

Source: Based on Steven Feld, "Voices of the Rainforest," *Public Culture* 4(1): 131–140 (1991).

Resistance and Survival

Systems of domination—whether political, economic, cultural, or religious—have their more muted aspects along with their public dimensions. In studying systems of domination, we must pay attention to what lies beneath the surface of evident, public behavior. In public, the oppressed may seem to accept their own domination, even as they question it offstage in private. James Scott (1990) uses **"public transcript"** to describe the open, public interactions between dominators and oppressed—the outer shell of power relations. He uses **"hidden transcript"** to describe the critique of power that goes on offstage, where the power holders can't see it.

In public, the elites and the oppressed observe the etiquette of power relations. The dominants act like haughty masters while their subordinates show humility and defer. Antonio Gramsci (1971) developed the concept of **hegemony** for a stratified social order in which subordinates comply with domination by internalizing their rulers' values and accepting the "naturalness" of domination (this is the way things were meant to be). According to Pierre Bourdieu (1977, p. 164), every social order tries to make its own arbitrariness (including its oppression) seem natural. All hegemonic ideologies offer explanations about why the existing order is in everyone's interest. Often promises are made (things will get better if you're patient). Gramsci and others use the idea of hegemony to explain why people conform even without coercion.

Both Bourdieu (1977) and Michel Foucault (1979) argue that it is much easier and more effective to dominate people in their minds than to try to control their bodies. Besides, and often replacing, gross physical violence, industrial societies have devised more insidious forms of social control. These include various techniques of persuading and managing people and of monitoring and recording their beliefs, activities, and contacts. Can you think of some contemporary examples?

Hegemony, the internalization of a dominant ideology, is one way to curb resistance. Another way is to let subordinates know they will eventually gain power—as young people usually foresee when they let their elders dominate them. Another way of curbing resistance is to separate or isolate subordinates while supervising them closely, as in prisons. According to Foucault (1979), describing control over prisoners, solitary confinement is one effective way to get them to submit to authority.

Weapons of the Weak

Often, situations that seem to be hegemonic do have active resistance, but it is individual and disguised rather than collective and defiant. Scott (1985) uses Malay peasants, among whom he did field work, to illustrate small-scale acts of resistance—which he calls "weapons of the weak." The Malay peasants used an indirect strategy to resist an Islamic tithe (religious tax). Peasants were expected to pay the tithe, usually in the form of rice, which was sent to the provincial capital. In theory, the tithe would come back as charity, but it never did. Peasants didn't resist the tithe by rioting, demonstrating, or protesting. Instead they used a "nibbling" strategy, based on small acts of resistance. For example, they failed to declare their land or lied about the amount

Because of its costumed anonymity, *Carnaval* is an excellent arena for expressing normally suppressed speech. This is vividly symbolized by these *Carnaval* headdresses in Trinidad. Is there anything like *Carnaval* in your society?

they farmed. They underpaid or delivered rice paddy contaminated with water, rocks, or mud, to add weight. Because of this resistance, only 15 percent of what was due was actually paid (Scott 1990, p. 89).

Subordinates also use various strategies to resist *publicly,* but, again, usually in disguised form. Discontent may be expressed in public rituals and language, including metaphors, euphemisms, and folk tales. For example, trickster tales (like the Brer Rabbit stories told by slaves in the southern United States) celebrate the wiles of the weak as they triumph over the strong.

Resistance is most likely to be expressed openly when the oppressed are allowed to assemble. The hidden transcript may be publicly revealed on such occasions. People see their dreams and anger shared by others with whom they haven't been in direct contact. The oppressed may draw courage from the crowd, from its visual and emotional impact and its anonymity. Sensing danger, the elites discourage such public gatherings. They try to limit and control holidays, funerals, dances, festivals, and other occasions that might unite the oppressed. Thus, in the pre–Civil War era southern United States, gatherings of five or more slaves were forbidden unless a white person was present.

Factors that interfere with community formation—such as geographic, linguistic, and ethnic separation—also work to curb resistance. Consequently, southern U.S. plantation owners sought slaves with diverse cultural and linguistic backgrounds. Despite the measures used to divide them, the slaves resisted, developing their own popular culture, linguistic codes, and religious vision. The masters taught portions of the Bible that stressed compliance, but the slaves seized on the story of Moses, the promised land, and deliverance. The cornerstone of slave religion became the idea of a reversal in the conditions of whites and blacks. Slaves also resisted directly, through sabotage and flight. In many New World areas, slaves managed to establish free communities in the hills and other isolated areas (Price 1973).

Hidden transcripts tend to be publicly expressed at certain times (festivals and *Carnavals*) and in certain places (for example, markets). Because of its costumed anonymity, *Carnaval* is an excellent arena for expressing normally suppressed speech and aggression—antihegemonic discourse. (*Discourse* includes talk, speeches, gestures, and actions.) *Carnavals* celebrate freedom through immodesty, dancing, gluttony, and sexuality (DaMatta 1991). *Carnaval* may begin as a playful outlet for frustrations built up during the year. Over time, it may evolve into a powerful annual critique of domination and a threat to the established order (Gilmore 1987). (Recognizing that ceremonial license could turn into political defiance, the Spanish dictator Francisco Franco outlawed *Carnaval.*)

In medieval Europe, according to Mikhail Bakhtin (19847), the market was the main place where the dominant ideology was questioned. The anonymity of the crowd and of commerce put people on an equal footing. The rituals and deference used with lords and clergy didn't apply to the marketplace. Later in Europe, the hidden transcript also went public in pubs, taverns, inns, cabarets, beer cellars, and gin mills.

These places fostered a popular culture—in games, songs, gambling, blasphemy, and disorder—that was at odds with the official culture. People met in an atmosphere of freedom encouraged by alcohol. Church and state alike condemned these activities as subversive.

Cultural Imperialism

Cultural imperialism refers to the spread or advance of one culture at the expense of others, or its imposition on other cultures, which it modifies, replaces, or destroys—usually because of differential economic or political influence. The chapter "Ethnicity" described a cultural imperialist campaign waged by the Spanish dictator Francisco Franco, designed to eradicate Basque culture, language, and religion. In this chapter, in the section "Religious Change," we examined Sudan's policy of religious, linguistic, and cultural imperialism against non-Muslims. In both cases, there was armed resistance to cultural imperialism.

305–306

Some forms of cultural imperialism are more subtle, involving long-term indoctrination. Children in the French colonial empire learned French history, language, and culture from standard textbooks also used in France. Tahitians, Malagasy, Vietnamese, and Senegalese learned the French language by reciting from books about "our ancestors the Gauls."

To what extent is modern technology, especially the mass media, an agent of cultural imperialism? Some commentators see modern technology as erasing cultural differences, as homogeneous products reach more people worldwide. But others see a role for modern technology in allowing social groups (local cultures) to express themselves and to survive (Marcus and Fischer 1999) (see "In the News"). Modern radio and TV, for example, constantly bring local happenings (for example, a "chicken festival" in Iowa) to the attention of a larger public. The North American media play a role in stimulating local activities of many sorts. Similarly, in Brazil, local practices, celebrations, and performances are changing in the context of outside forces, including the mass media and tourism.

In the town of Arembepe, TV coverage has stimulated participation in a traditional annual performance, the *Chegança.* This is a fishermen's danceplay that reenacts the Portuguese discovery of Brazil. Arembepeiros have traveled to the state capital to perform the *Chegança* before television cameras, for a TV program featuring traditional performances from many rural communities.

One national Brazilian Sunday-night variety program (*Fantástico*) is especially popular in rural areas because it shows such local events. In several towns along the Amazon River, annual folk ceremonies are now staged more lavishly for TV cameras. In the Amazon town of Parantíns, for example, boatloads of tourists arriving any time of year are shown a videotape of the town's annual Bumba Meu Boi festival. This is a costumed performance mimicking bullfighting, parts of which have been shown on *Fantástico.* This pattern, in which local communities preserve, revive, and intensify the scale of traditional ceremonies to perform for TV and tourists, is expanding.

However, Brazilian television also has played a "topdown" role, by spreading the popularity of holidays like *Carnaval* and Christmas (Kottak 1990*a*). TV has aided the national spread of *Carnaval* beyond its traditional urban centers. Still, local reactions to the nationwide broadcasting of *Carnaval* and its trappings (elaborate parades, costumes, and frenzied dancing) are not simple or uniform responses to external stimuli.

Rather than direct adoption of *Carnaval,* local Brazilians respond in various ways. Often they don't take up *Carnaval* itself but modify their local festivities to fit *Carnaval* images. Others actively spurn *Carnaval.* One example is Arembepe, where *Carnaval* has never been important, probably because of its calendrical closeness to the main local festival, which is held in February to honor Saint Francis of Assisi. In the past, villagers couldn't afford to celebrate both occasions. Now, not only do the people of Arembepe reject *Carnaval,* they are also increasingly hostile to their own main festival. Arembepeiros resent the fact that Saint Francis has become "an outsiders' event," because it draws thousands of tourists to Arembepe each February. The villagers think that commercial interests and outsiders have appropriated Saint Francis.

In opposition to these trends, many Arembepeiros now say they like and participate more

in the news

Using Modern Technology to Preserve Linguistic and Cultural Diversity

Although some see modern technology as a threat to cultural diversity, others see a role for this technology in allowing social groups to express themselves. The anthropologist H. Russell Bernard has been a pioneer in teaching speakers of endangered languages how to write their language using a computer. Bernard's work permits the preservation of languages and cultural memories. Native peoples from Mexico to Cameroon are using their mother tongue to express themselves as individuals and to provide insiders' accounts of different cultures.

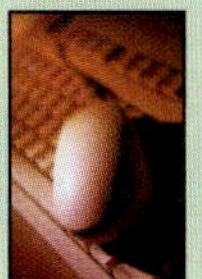

Jesús Salinas Pedraza, a rural schoolteacher in the Mexican state of Hidalgo, sat down to a word processor a few years back and produced a monumental book, a 250,000-word description of his own Indian culture written in the Nähñu language. Nothing seems to be left out: folktales and traditional religious beliefs, the practical uses of plants and minerals and the daily flow of life in field and village . . .

Mr. Salinas is neither a professional anthropologist nor a literary stylist. He is, though, the first person to write a book in Nähñu (NYAW-hnyu), the native tongue of several hundred thousand Indians but a previously unwritten language.

Such a use of microcomputers and desktop publishing for languages with no literary tradition is now being encouraged by anthropologists for recording ethnographies from an insider's perspective. They see this as a means of preserving cultural diversity and a wealth of human knowledge. With even greater urgency, linguists are promoting the techniques as a way of saving some of the world's languages from imminent extinction.

Half of the world's 6,000 languages are considered by linguists to be endangered. These are the languages spoken by small societies that are dwindling with the encroachment of larger, more dynamic cultures. Young people feel economic pressure to learn only the language of the dominant culture, and as the older people die, the non-written language vanishes, unlike languages with a history of writing, like Latin.

Dr. H. Russell Bernard, the anthropologist at the University of Florida at Gainesville who taught Mr. Salinas to read and write his native language, said: "Languages have always come and gone . . . But languages seem to be disappearing faster than ever before.". . .

Dr. Michael E. Krauss, the director of the Alaska Native Language Center at the University of Alaska in Fairbanks, estimates that 300 of the 900 indigenous languages in the Americas are moribund. That is, they are no longer being spoken by children, and so could disappear in a generation or two. Only two of the 20 native languages in Alaska are still being learned by children . . .

In an effort to preserve language diversity in Mexico, Dr. Bernard and Mr. Salinas decided in 1987 on a plan to teach the Indian people to read and write their own language using microcomputers. They established a native literacy center in Oaxaca, Mexico, where others could follow in the footsteps of Mr. Salinas and write books in other Indian languages.

The Oaxaca center goes beyond most bilingual education programs, which concentrate on teaching people to speak and read their native languages. Instead, it operates on the premise that, as Dr. Bernard decided, what most native languages lack is native authors who write books in their own languages . . .

The Oaxaca project's influence is spreading. Impressed by the work of Mr. Salinas and others, Dr. Norman Whitten, an anthropologist at the University of Illinois, arranged for schoolteachers from Ecuador to visit Oaxaca and learn the techniques.

Now Ecuadorian Indians have begun writing about their cultures in the Quechua and Shwara languages. Others from Bolivia and Peru are learning to use the computers to write their languages, including Quecha, the tongue of the ancient Incas, still spoken by about 12 million Andean Indians . . .

Dr. Bernard emphasized that these native literacy programs are not intended to discourage people from learning the dominant language of their country as well. "I see nothing useful or charming about remaining monolingual in any Indian language if that results in being shut out of the national economy," he said.

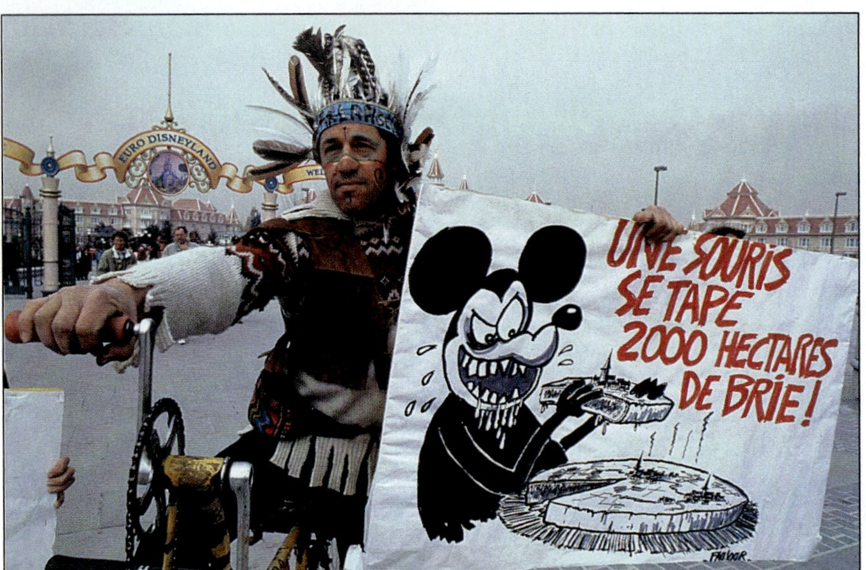

Native children throughout the French colonial empire learned the French language by reciting from books about "our ancestors the Gauls." More recently, French citizens have criticized or resisted what they see as American "cultural imperialism"—one prominent symbol of which has been Euro Disneyland. Has there also been resistance to the expansion of Disney enterprises in the United States?

in the traditional June festivals honoring Saint John, Saint Peter, and Saint Anthony. In the past, these were observed on a much smaller scale than was the festival honoring Saint Francis. Arembepeiros celebrate them now with a new vigor and enthusiasm, as they react to outsiders and their celebrations, real and televised.

Making and Remaking Culture

Any media-borne image, such as that of *Carnaval,* can be analyzed in terms of its nature and effects. It also can be analyzed as a **text.** We usually think of a text as a textbook, like this one. But the term has a more general meaning. Anthropologists use *text* to refer to anything that may be "read," interpreted, and assigned meaning by anyone exposed to it. In this sense, a text doesn't have to be written. The term may refer to a film, an image, or an event, such as *Carnaval.* As Brazilians participate in *Carnaval,* they "read" it as a text. These "readers" derive their own meanings and feelings from *Carnaval* events, images, and activities. Such meanings may be very different from what the creators of the text, such as official sponsors, imagined. (The "reading" or meaning that the creators intended—or the one that the elites consider to be the intended or correct meaning—can be called the *hegemonic reading.*)

"Readers" of media messages constantly produce their own meanings. They may resist or oppose the hegemonic meanings of a text, or they may seize on the antihegemonic aspects of a text. We saw this process when American slaves preferred the biblical story of Moses and deliverance to the hegemonic lessons of acceptance and obedience that their masters taught.

Popular Culture

In his book *Understanding Popular Culture* (1989), John Fiske views each individual's use of popular culture as a creative act (an original "reading" of a text). (For example, Madonna, the Grateful Dead, or *Star Wars* means something different to each of its fans.) As Fiske puts it, "the meanings I make from a text are pleasurable when I feel that they are *my* meanings and that they relate to *my* everyday life in a practical, direct way" (1989,

When products and images enter new settings, they are typically indigenized—modified to fit the local culture. Jeans Street, in Bandung, Indonesia, is a strip of stores, vendors, and restaurants catering to young people interested in Western pop culture. How is the poster of *Batman and Robin* indigenized?

p. 57). All of us can creatively "read" magazines, books, music, television, films, celebrities, and other popular culture products.

Individuals also draw on popular culture to express resistance. Through their use of popular culture, people can symbolically resist the unequal power relations they face each day—in the family, at work, and in the classroom. Popular culture (from rap music to comedy) can be used to express discontent and resistance by groups that are or feel powerless or oppressed.

Indigenizing Popular Culture

To understand culture change, it is important to recognize that meaning may be locally manufactured. People assign their own meanings and value to the texts, messages, and products they receive. Those meanings reflect their cultural backgrounds and experiences. When forces from world centers enter new societies, they are **indigenized**—modified to fit the local culture. This is true of cultural forces as different as fast food, music, housing styles, science, terrorism, celebrations, and political ideas and institutions (Appadurai 1990).

Consider the reception of the movie *Rambo* in Australia as an example of how popular culture may be indigenized. Michaels (1986) found *Rambo* to be very popular among aborigines in the deserts of central Australia, who had manufactured their own meanings from the film. Their "reading" was very different from the one imagined by the movie's creators, and by most North Americans. The Native Australians saw Rambo as a representative of the Third World who was engaged in a battle with the white officer class. This reading expressed their negative feelings about white paternalism and about existing race relations. The Native Australians also imagined that there were tribal ties and kin links between Rambo and the prisoners he was rescuing. All this made sense, based on their experience. Native Australians are disproportionately represented in Australian jails. Their most likely liberator would be someone with a personal link to them. These readings of *Rambo* were relevant meanings produced *from* the text, not *by* it (Fiske 1989).

A World System of Images

All cultures express imagination—in dreams, fantasies, songs, myths, and stories. Today, however, more people in many more places imagine "a wider set of 'possible' lives than they ever did before. One important source of this change is the mass media, which present a rich, ever-changing store of possible lives . . ." (Appadurai 1991, p. 197). The United States as a media center has been joined by Canada, Japan, Western Europe, Brazil, Mexico, Nigeria, Egypt, India, and Hong Kong.

As print has done for centuries (Anderson 1991), the electronic mass media also can spread, even help create, national and ethnic identities. Like print, television and radio can diffuse the cultures of different countries within their own boundaries, thus enhancing national cultural identity. For example, millions of Brazilians who were formerly cut off (by geographic isolation or illiteracy) from urban and national events and information now participate in a national communication system, through TV networks (Kottak 1990*a*).

Cross-cultural studies of television contradict a belief Americans ethnocentrically hold about televiewing in other countries. This misconception is that American programs inevitably triumph over local products. This doesn't happen when there is appealing local competition. In Brazil, for example, the most popular network (TV Globo) relies heavily on native productions. American imports have drawn small audiences. TV Globo's most popular programs are *telenovelas,* locally made serials that are similar to American soap operas. Globo plays each night to the world's largest and most devoted audience (60 to 80 million viewers throughout the nation). The programs that attract this horde are made by Brazilians, for Brazilians. Thus, it is not North American culture but a new pan-Brazilian national culture, that Brazilian TV is propagating. Brazilian productions also compete internationally. They are exported to over 100 countries, spanning Latin America, Europe, Asia, and Africa.

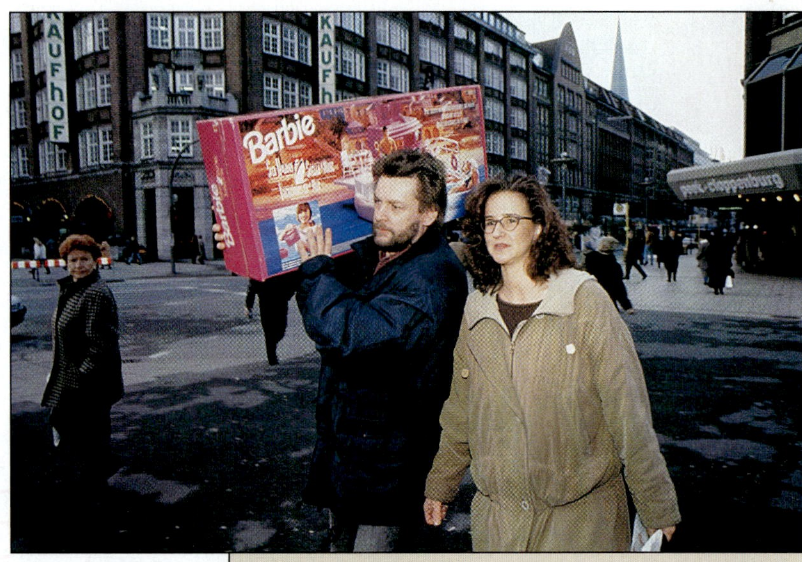

Business and the media have increased the craving for products throughout the world. Here, exiting a shopping mall, a German man takes home a Barbie playset.

We may generalize that programming that is culturally alien won't do very well anywhere when a quality local choice is available. Confirmation comes from many countries. National productions are highly popular in Japan, Mexico, India, Egypt, and Nigeria. In a survey during the mid-1980s, 75 percent of Nigerian viewers preferred local productions. Only 10 percent favored imports, and the remaining 15 percent liked the two options equally. Local productions are successful in Nigeria because "they are filled with everyday moments that audiences can identify with. These shows are locally produced by Nigerians" (Gray 1986). Thirty million people watched one of the most popular series, *The Village Headmaster,* each week. That program brought rural values to the screens of urbanites who had lost touch with their rural roots (Gray 1986).

The mass media also can play a role in maintaining ethnic and national identities among people who lead transnational lives. As groups move, they can stay linked to each other and to their homeland through the media. Diasporas (people who have spread out from an original, ancestral homeland) have enlarged the markets for media, communication, and travel services targeted at specific ethnic, national, or religious audiences. For a fee, a PBS station in Fairfax, Virginia, offers more than 30 hours a week to immigrant groups in the D.C. area, to make programs in their own languages. *Somali Television,* for instance, is a half-hour program with more than 5,000 Somali viewers, who can see their flag and hear their language on TV each week. Starting the program is a reading from the Koran, with clips of mosques from around the world (thus contributing, too, to a transnational Islamic identity). Formerly, an entertainment segment featured folk dances and Somali music. In 1992, as Somalia's civil war dragged on, the entertainment segment was replaced by images of hungry children and parched countryside. *Somali Television* also features obituaries, rallies, and a segment called "Somalia Today," which has interviews with diplomats, immigration lawyers, and travel agents discussing air fares. Guests represent various tribes and subclans. *Somali Television* became a vital link between emigrant Somalis and their homeland (*New York Times,* December 18, 1992).

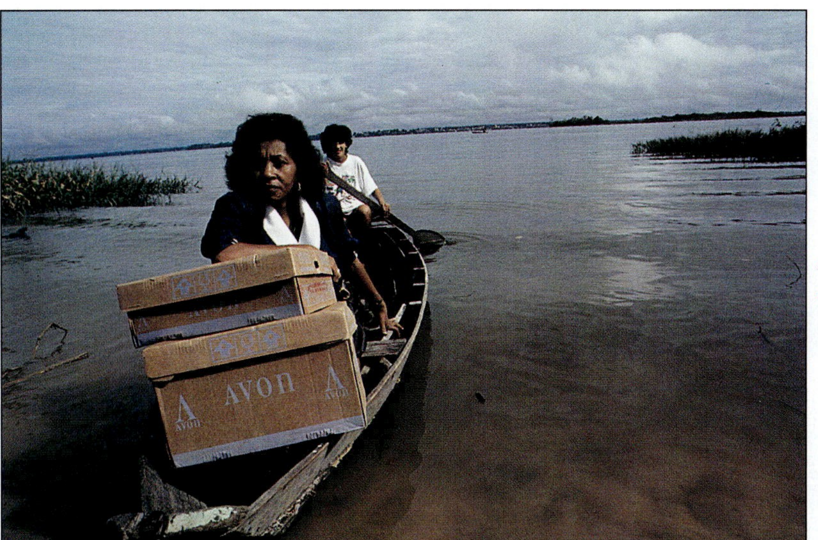

Maria Gomes on Brazil's Tapajos River. Ms. Gomes is the Avon zone manager for 970 representatives in the Amazon rain forest.

A Transnational Culture of Consumption

Besides the electronic media, another key transnational force is finance. Multinational corporations and other business interests look beyond national boundaries for places to invest and draw profits. As Arjun Appadurai (1991, p. 194) puts it, "money, commodities, and persons unendingly chase each other around the world." Residents of many Latin American communities now depend on outside cash, remitted from international labor migration. Also, the economy of the United States is increasingly influenced by foreign investment, especially from Britain, Canada, Germany, the Netherlands, and Japan (Rouse 1991). The American economy also has increased its dependence on foreign labor—through both the immigration of laborers and the export of jobs.

Contemporary global culture is driven by flows of people, technology, finance, information, images, and ideology (Appadurai 1990). Business, technology, and the media have increased the craving for commodities and images throughout the world (Gottdiener 2000). This has forced nation-states, including "Iron Curtains," to open to a global culture of consumption. Almost everyone today participates in this culture. Few people have never seen a T-shirt advertising a Western product. American and English rock stars' recordings blast through the streets of Rio de Janeiro, while taxi drivers from Toronto to Madagascar play Brazilian *lambada* tapes. Peasants and tribal people participate in the modern world system not only because they have been hooked on cash, but also because their products and images are appropriated by world capitalism (Root 1996). They are commercialized by others (like the San in the movie *The Gods Must Be Crazy*). Furthermore, indigenous peoples also market their own images and products, through outlets like Cultural Survival (see Mathews 2000).

Linkages

The linkages in the modern world system have both enlarged and erased old boundaries and distinctions. Arjun Appadurai (1990, p. 1) characterizes today's world as a "translocal" "interactive system" that is "strikingly new." Whether as refugees, migrants, tourists, pilgrims, proselytizers, laborers, businesspeople, development workers, employees of nongovernmental organizations (NGOs), politicians, soldiers, sports figures, or media-borne images, people appear to travel more than ever.

In previous chapters, we saw that foragers and herders are typically semi-nomadic or nomadic. Today, however, the scale of human movement has expanded dramatically. So important is transnational migration that many Mexican villagers find "their most important kin and friends are as likely to be living hundreds or thousands of miles away as immediately around them" (Rouse 1991). Most migrants maintain their ties with their native land (phoning, visiting, sending money, watching "ethnic TV"). In a sense, they live multilocally—in different places at once. Dominicans in New York City, for example, have

With so many people on the move, the unit of anthropological study has expanded from the local community to the diaspora. This refers to the offspring of an area (e.g., Africa) who have spread to many lands, such as these Afro-Caribbean pub owners in West Broomwich, England. Do you belong to a diaspora?

been characterized as living "between two islands": Manhattan and the Dominican Republic (Grasmuck and Pessar 1991). Many Dominicans—like migrants from other countries—migrate to the United States temporarily, seeking cash to transform their life styles when they return to the Caribbean.

People in Motion

With so many people "in motion," the unit of anthropological study expands from the local community to the **diaspora**—the offspring of an area who have spread to many lands. Anthropologists increasingly follow descendants of the villages we have studied as they move from rural to urban areas and across national boundaries. For the 1991 annual meeting of the American Anthropological Association in Chicago, the anthropologist Robert Kemper organized a session of presentations about long-term ethnographic field work. Kemper's own long-time research focus has been the Mexican village of Tzintzuntzan, which, with his mentor George Foster, he has studied for decades. However, their database now includes not just Tzintzuntzan, but its descendants all over the world (one of whom reached Alaska in 1990). Given the Tzintzuntzan diaspora, Kemper was even able to use some of his time in Chicago to visit people from Tzintzuntzan who had established a colony there. In today's world, as people move, they take their traditions and their anthropologists along with them.

Postmodernity describes our time and situation: today's world in flux, these people on the move who have learned to manage multiple identities depending on place and context. In its most general sense, **postmodern** refers to the blurring and breakdown of established canons (rules or standards), categories, distinctions, and boundaries. The word is taken from **postmodernism**—a style and movement in architecture that succeeded modernism, beginning in the 1970s. Postmodern architecture rejected the rules, geometric order, and austerity of modernism. Modernist buildings were expected to have a clear and functional design. Postmodern design is "messier" and more playful. It draws on a diversity of styles

from different times and places—including popular, ethnic, and non-Western cultures. Postmodernism extends "value" well beyond classic, elite, and Western cultural forms. *Postmodern* is now used to describe comparable developments in music, literature, and visual art. From this origin, *postmodernity* describes a world in which traditional standards, contrasts, groups, boundaries, and identities are opening up, reaching out, and breaking down.

Globalization promotes intercultural communication, including travel and migration, which bring people from different societies into direct contact. The world is more integrated than ever. Yet *dis*integration also surrounds us. Nations dissolve (Yugoslavia, the Soviet Union), as do political blocs (the Warsaw Pact nations) and ideologies ("Communism"). The notion of a "Free World" collapses because it existed mainly in opposition to a group of "Captive Nations"—a label once applied by the United States and its allies to the former Soviet empire that has lost much of its meaning today.

Simultaneously, new kinds of political and ethnic units are emerging. In some cases, cultures and ethnic groups have banded together in larger associations. There is a growing Pan-indian identity (Nagel 1996) and an international pantribal movement as well. Thus, in June 1992, the World Conference of Indigenous Peoples met in Rio de Janeiro concurrently with UNCED (the United Nations Conference on the Environment and Development). Along with diplomats, journalists, and environmentalists came 300 representatives of the tribal diversity that survives in the modern world—from Lapland to Mali (Brooke 1992).

Postmodern Moments

Increasingly, anthropologists experience what might be called "postmodern moments in the world system." Some of my own most vivid ones can be traced back to Ambalavao, Madagascar. In 1966–67, my wife and I rented a house in that town in southern Betsileo country. We spent

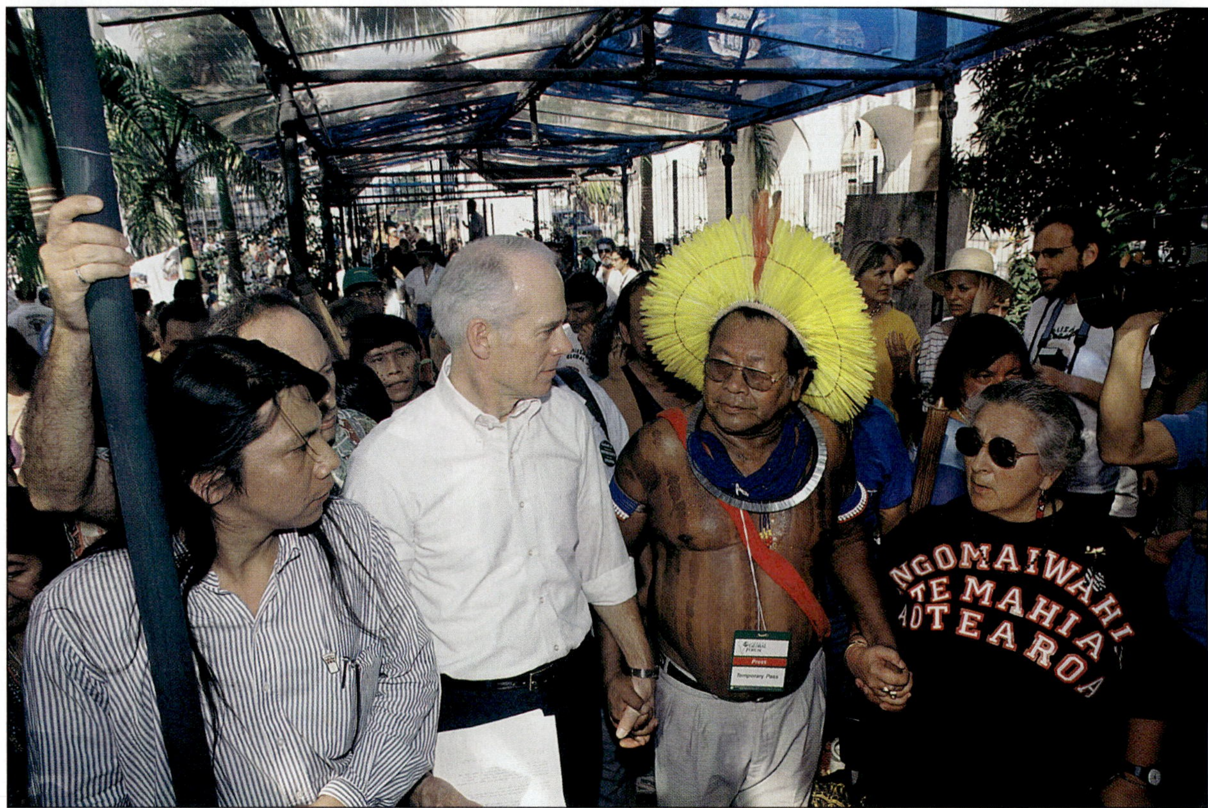

Working to promote cultural survival is a growing international pantribal movement. In June 1992, the World Conference of Indigenous Peoples met in Rio de Janeiro. Along with diplomats, journalists, and environmentalists came 300 representatives of the tribal diversity that survives in the modern world.

weekends there when we came in from the rural villages where our field work was based.

By 1966, Madagascar was independent from France, but its towns still had foreigners to remind them of colonialism. In addition to us, Ambalavao had at least a dozen world system agents, including an Indian cloth merchant, Chinese grocers, and a few French people. A French consultant was there to help develop the tobacco industry. Two young men in the French equivalent of the Peace Corps were there teaching school.

One of them, Noel, served as principal of the junior high school. He lived across the street from a prominent local family (who served as our sponsors in a rural village, their ancestral community, we were studying). Since Noel often spoke disparagingly of the Malagasy, I was surprised to see him courting a young woman from this family. She was Lenore, the sister of Leon, a schoolteacher who became one of my best friends. My wife and I left Ambalavao in December 1967. Noel and the other world system agents stayed on.

Each of my revisits to Madagascar has brought postmodern moments—encounters with people and products on the move, in multilocal and unexpected contexts. After 1967, my next trip to Madagascar was a brief visit in February 1981. I had to spend a few days in Antananarivo, the capital. There I was confined each evening to the newly built Hilton hotel by a curfew imposed after a civil insurrection. I shared the hotel with a group of Russian MIG pilots (and their wives), there to teach the Malagasy to defend their island, strategically placed in the Indian Ocean, against imagined enemies. Later, I went down to Betsileo country to visit Leon, my schoolteacher friend from Ambalavao, who had become a prominent politician. Unfortunately for me, he was in Moscow, participating in a three-month Soviet exchange program.

My next visit to Madagascar was in summer 1990. This time, a postmodern moment occurred when I met Emily, the 22-year-old daughter of Noel and Lenore, whose courtship I had witnessed in 1967. One of her aunts brought Emily to meet me at my hotel in Antananarivo. Emily was about to visit several cities in the United States, where she planned to study marketing. I met her again just a few months later in Gainesville, Florida, where she was taking a course at Santa Fe Community College. As we lunched in a Mexican restaurant, Emily sold me some woodwork she had brought from Madagascar. She asked my wife and me to help her market her Malagasy crafts. Finally, she asked us about her father, whom she had never met. She told us she had sent several letters to France, but Noel had never responded.

Descendants of Ambalavao (and thus of rural Betsileo villages) now live all over the world. Emily, a child of colonialism, has two aunts in France (married to French men) and another in Germany (working as a diplomat). Members of her family, which is not especially wealthy, although regionally prominent, have traveled to Russia, Canada, the United States, France, Germany, and West Africa. How many of your classmates, including perhaps you, yourself, are members of such diasporas?

summary

1. Different degrees of destruction, domination, resistance, survival, and modification of native cultures may follow interethnic contact. This may lead to the tribe's cultural collapse (*ethnocide*) or its physical extinction (*genocide*). Multinational corporations have fueled economic development and ecological devastation. Either development or external regulation may pose a threat to indigenous peoples, their cultures, or their environments. The most effective conservation strategies pay attention to the needs, incentives, and customs of people living in the affected area.

2. "Public transcript" refers to the open, public interactions between the dominators and the oppressed. "Hidden transcript" describes the critique of power that goes on offstage, where the power holders can't see it. Discontent also may be expressed in public rituals and language. *Hegemony* describes a stratified social order in which subordinates comply with domination by internalizing its values and accepting its "naturalness." Often, situations that appear hegemonic have resistance that is individual and disguised rather than collective and defiant.

3. *Cultural imperialism* refers to the spread of one culture and its imposition on other cultures, which it modifies, replaces, or destroys—usually because of differential economic or political influence. Some worry that modern technology, including the mass media, is destroying traditional cultures. But others see an important role for new technology in allowing local cultures to express themselves.

4. The term "text" is used here to describe anything that can be creatively "read," interpreted, and assigned meaning by someone who receives it. People may resist the hegemonic meaning of a text. Or they may seize on its antihegemonic aspects. When forces from world centers enter new societies, they are *indigenized*. Like print, the electronic mass media can help diffuse a national culture within its own boundaries. The media also play a role in preserving ethnic and national identities among people who lead transnational lives. Business, technology, and the media have increased the craving for commodities and images throughout the world, creating a global culture of consumption.

5. People travel more than ever. But migrants also maintain ties with home, so they live multilocally. With so many people "in motion," the unit of anthropological study expands from the local community to the diaspora. *Postmodernity* describes this world in flux, such people on the move who manage multiple social identities depending on place and context. New kinds of political and ethnic units are emerging as others break down or disappear.

key terms

cultural imperialism The rapid spread or advance of one culture at the expense of others, or its imposition on other cultures, which it modifies, replaces, or destroys—usually because of differential economic or political influence.

diaspora The offspring of an area who have spread to many lands.

hegemony As used by Antonio Gramsci, a stratified social order in which subordinates comply with domination by internalizing its values and accepting its "naturalness."

hidden transcript As used by James Scott, the critique of power by the oppressed that goes on offstage—in private—where the power holders can't see it.

indigenized Modified to fit the local culture.

postmodern In its most general sense, describes the blurring and breakdown of established canons (rules, standards), categories, distinctions, and boundaries.

postmodernism A style and movement in architecture that succeeded modernism. Compared with modernism, postmodernism is less geometric, less functional, less austere, more playful, and more willing to include elements from diverse times and cultures; *postmodern* now describes comparable developments in music, literature, visual art, and anthropology.

postmodernity Condition of a world in flux, with people on the move, in which established groups, boundaries, identities, contrasts, and standards are reaching out and breaking down.

public transcript As used by James Scott, the open, public interactions between dominators and oppressed—the outer shell of power relations.

text Something that is creatively "read," interpreted, and assigned meaning by each person who receives it; includes any media-borne image, such as *Carnaval*.

westernization The acculturative influence of Western expansion on native cultures.

critical thinking questions

1. Have you personally observed or experienced a situation involving acculturation?
2. Can you apply some of the observations made in the text about environmentalist strategy to events in your own society?
3. Use your interaction with your parents or teachers to illustrate the difference between hidden and public transcripts.
4. If you were going to resist publicly, how would you choose to do it, and why?
5. Do you consider the mass media to be instruments of cultural imperialism? How about the Internet? How so?
6. How do you participate in a world system of images? Are the images to which you relate mainly national, or foreign/international as well?
7. How do you use the media? Is there a program or group that has special meaning for you? How does that meaning differ from someone else's, with respect to the same program or group? Are you personally irritated when someone questions your meaning?
8. Among the contemporary global flows—people, technology, finance, information, and ideology—which do you consider most important, and why?
9. Name three significant forms of linkages in today's world. How do they apply to you?
10. Do you now live, or have you ever lived, multilocally? How so?
11. What's the difference between postmodernity and postmodernism? Have you had postmodern moments, as discussed in the text?

case study

Yanomamo: This chapter discusses the potentially grave consequences of economic development and environmental degradation. Outside exploitation poses a threat to indigenous peoples. In *Culture Sketches* by Holly Peters-Golden, read the chapter on the Yanomamo: "Challenges in the Rainforest." What are some challenges faced by the Yanomamo (a.k.a. Yanomami)? What is the anthropologist's role in conflicts between indigenous peoples and the governments of the countries in which they live? Should an anthropologist be an objective observer, an advocate, or neither of these? What are some difficulties involved in choosing a position?

suggested additional readings

Ahmed, A. S.

1992 *Postmodernism and Islam: Predicament and Promise.* New York: Routledge. Clear presentation of postmodernism, in relation to the media and to images of Islam.

Balick, M. J., and P. A. Cox

1996 *Plants, People, and Culture: The Science of Ethnobotany.* New York: Scientific American Library. Basics of ethnobotany, the study of plants in their cultural setting.

Balick, M. J., E. Elisabetsky, and S. A. Laird

1995 *Medicinal Resources of the Tropical Forest: Biodiversity and Its Importance to Human Health.* New York: Columbia University Press. The medicinal and health implications of deforestation at the local, regional, national, and global levels.

Bodley, J. H.

1999 *Victims of Progress,* 4th ed. Mountain View, CA: Mayfield. Social change, acculturation, and culture conflict involving indigenous peoples.

2000 *Anthropology and Contemporary Human Problems,* 4th ed. Mountain View, CA: Mayfield. Overview of major problems of today's industrial world: overconsumption, the environment, resource depletion, hunger, overpopulation, violence, and war.

Cultural Survival

1992 *At the Threshold.* Cambridge, MA: Cultural Survival. Originally published as the Spring 1992 issue of *Cultural Survival Quarterly.* Manual for the promotion of the rights of indigenous peoples. Highlights activist successes, gives instructions for affecting policy, working in schools and communities, directly helping native societies, and using the media as a human-rights ally.

DaMatta, R.

1991 *Carnivals, Rogues, and Heroes: An Interpretation of the Brazilian Dilemma.* Translated from the Portuguese by John Drury. Notre Dame, IN: University of Notre Dame Press. Classic study of Brazilian *Carnaval* in relation to Brazilian national culture.

Feld, S.

1990 *Sound and Sentiment: Birds, Weeping, Poetics, and Song in Kaluli Expression,* 2nd ed. Philadelphia: University of Pennsylvania Press. Ethnographic study of sound as a cultural system among the Kaluli people of Papua New Guinea.

Fiske, J.

1989 *Understanding Popular Culture.* Boston: Unwin Hyman. The role of the individual in using popular culture, constructing meaning, and resisting everyday power relations.

Gottdiener, M., ed.
2000 *New Forms of Consumption: Consumers, Culture, and Commodification.* Lanham, MD: Rowman and Littlefield. Cultural consumption, diversity, and market segmentation in today's global economy.

Lutz, C., and J. L. Collins
1993 *Reading National Geographic.* Chicago: University of Chicago Press. How the cultural narratives of the magazine are received and interpreted; the relation between images of other peoples, cultures, and life styles and middle-class North American values.

Marcus, G. E., and M. M. J. Fischer
1999 *Anthropology as Cultural Critique: An Experimental Moment in the Human Sciences,* 2nd ed. Chicago: University of Chicago Press. New edition of an influential book on modern and postmodern anthropology.

Marcus, G. E., and F. R. Myers, eds.
1995 *The Traffic in Culture: Refiguring Art and Anthropology.* Berkeley, CA: University of California Press. Art, society, and the marketing of culture in global perspective.

Mathews, G.
2000 *Global Culture/Individual Identity: Searching for Home in the Cultural Supermarket.* New York: Routledge. National characteristics, relations, identity, and culture under globalization.

Nagel, J.
1996 *American Indian Ethnic Renewal: Red Power and the Resurgence of Identity and Culture.* New York: Oxford University Press. The meaning of activism for Native American individual ethnic identification; the role of federal, tribal, and personal politics in the growth of American Indian identity.

Public Culture
Journal published by the University of Chicago. Articles deal with the anthropology of the modern and postmodern world system.

Root, D.
1996 *Cannibal Culture: Art, Appropriation, and the Commodification of Difference.* Boulder, CO: Westview. How Western art and commerce classify, co-opt, and commodify "native" experiences, creations, and products.

Scott, J. C.
1990 *Domination and the Arts of Resistance.* New Haven, CT: Yale University Press. A study of institutionalized forms of domination, such as colonialism, slavery, serfdom, racism, caste, concentration camps, prisons, and old-age homes—and the forms of resistance that oppose them.
1998 *Seeing Like a State: How Certain Schemes to Improve the Human Condition Have Failed.* New Haven: Yale University Press. Reflections on contemporary lives, social engineering, and authoritarianism.

internet exercises

1. *Peacemaking among the Nuer and Dinka:* Refer back to the discussion of the Nuer in the chapter "Political Systems" to read about the Nuer and their neighbors the Dinka and their segmentary lineage organization. Then read the *Washington Post* article about the recent history of these groups, **http://www.washingtonpost.com/wp-srv/inatl/daily/july99/sudan7.htm.**

   a. Anthropologists in the middle of the 20th century recorded conflict between the Nuer and the Dinka. In this article, they became allies against what opponent? How did conflict re-emerge between the Nuer and the Dinka?

   b. What were the traditional views of warfare and death among the Nuer and the Dinka? How did these change with the introduction of modern machine guns?

   c. What impact did these new views have on the recent Nuer/Dinka conflicts?

   d. Despite the cultural changes brought about by the pressures of modern nations and the introduction of machine guns, the Nuer and the Dinka used traditional cultural symbols to help bring about peace. What are some examples?

   e. Do you think this peace will be short lived? What needs to take place in order to maintain peace?

2. *Ishi, Cultural Survival, and Anthropology:* Read B. Bower's article in *Science News* entitled "Ishi's Long Road Home," **http://www.sciencenews.org/20000108/bob1.asp.**

   a. Who was Ishi? To what tribe did he belong, and what happened to them?

   b. In what way was Ishi successful in preserving native culture and educating people about it?

   c. What attitudes on the part of white Americans led to the demise of Ishi's family? What attitudes on the part of white Americans led to his immense popularity while at the museum in San Francisco? How can you account for the paradox of these seemingly contradictory views of Native Americans among white Americans?

   d. In the past, anthropologists seemed to have cared more about documenting vanishing cultures than about working for the needs of those cultures' living representatives. In what way does the story of Ishi illustrate those conflicts? What role should anthropology play in the future?

See Chapter 23 on your CD-ROM for additional review and interactive exercises. See your McGraw-Hill Online Learning Center for more.

Chapter 24

Applied Anthropology

CHAPTER OUTLINE

NYTIMES.COM NEWS BRIEF

Mystery Factor Is Pondered at AIDS Talk: Circumcision

by Lawrence K. Altman
July 11, 2000

DURBAN, South Africa . . . A potentially important finding about AIDS [is] that circumcised men are much less likely to become infected than uncircumcised men.

The finding was first made in Africa more than a decade ago and has been noted in more than 40 studies since then. Now many scientists . . . have come to suspect that circumcision is an important factor in the vast differences among African countries in rates of infection from HIV, the virus that causes AIDS.

In many countries in southern Africa the rates of HIV infection among adults exceed 20 percent, while among central and west African countries the rates are lower, some below 3 percent.

No one believes that circumcision, which has been widely and traditionally practiced in Africa, could be the sole explanation of such differences. Differing rates could be caused by other cultural or religious practices, or by differences in hygiene or other factors.

Yet compelling evidence from epidemiologic studies has led scientists to debate whether to promote large-scale circumcision programs as a means to help stop the AIDS epidemic . . . In studying the Luo people in Kenya, who do not practice circumcision, Dr. Robert C. Bailey of the University of Illinois at Chicago said he had found that most Luo men and women voiced the opinion that sex would be more pleasurable if the man was circumcised and that most men would prefer to be circumcised.

Dr. Bailey and other experts expressed concern about the safety of the procedure in Africa, because many of those performing it lack medical expertise and do not secure informed consent. Hygiene is a problem, and only one of eight clinics surveyed had all of the instruments needed to perform a circumcision safely, Dr. Bailey said.

Ann Buve of the Institute of Tropical Medicine in Antwerp, Belgium, studied two African cities with high HIV rates and two with low rates. In Yaounde, Cameroon, and Cotonou, Benin, where the prevalence of HIV among sexually active men was 3.8 and 4.4 percent, respectively, 99 percent of the men were circumcised. The practice was less common in Kisumu, Kenya, and Ndola, Zambia, where infection rates were 26.8 percent and 25.9 percent.

Dr. Ronald Gray of the Johns Hopkins University School of Public Health expressed reservations about recommending circumcision, based on his team's studies in Rakai, Uganda. A rigorous type of study, known as a randomized controlled trial, is needed to scientifically determine the degree of protection from circumcising males at birth and as adults, Dr. Gray and others said.

Such trials could determine whether religious, cultural, behavioral, and hygienic factors account for an important part of the protection that seems to be related to circumcision. But the impact of rigorous trials on the epidemic could be limited, because answers might not come until 15 to 20 years after they are started . . .

In providing a possible biological explanation, a paper in a recent issue of the *British Medical Journal* said the inner surface of the foreskin contains so-called langerhans cells that have an area on their surface that allows the entry of HIV . . .

Source: http://www.nytimes.com/library/world/africa/071100safrica-aids.html.

overview

Is anthropology useful? Should it play a public service role? Anthropology can indeed be "applied"—used to identify and solve social problems. Applied anthropologists work for governments, agencies, and businesses. One applied anthropology goal is to identify needs for change that local people perceive. A second is to work with such people to design culturally appropriate change. A third is to protect local people from harmful policies, including destructive development schemes.

Among the domains of applied anthropology are educational, urban, medical, and business anthropology. These domains have theoretical as well as applied dimensions. Educational anthropologists work in classrooms, homes, neighborhoods, and other settings relevant to education. Urban anthropologists study problems and policies involving city life and urbanization. Medical anthropologists study disease and health-care systems cross-culturally. Although modern Western medicine has a scientific basis, it is also a cultural system, with many elements based on custom rather than science.

For business, key aspects of anthropology include ethnography and observation as ways of gathering data, cross-cultural expertise, and a focus on cultural diversity. Anthropology's comparative outlook, long-standing Third World focus, and cultural relativism offer background for overseas work. A focus on culture and diversity is also valuable for work in North America.

Anthropology can reduce ethnocentrism by instilling an appreciation of cultural diversity. This broadening, educational role affects the knowledge, values, and attitudes of people exposed to anthropology. Now we focus on the question: What contributions can anthropology make in identifying and solving problems stirred up by contemporary currents of economic, social, and cultural change?

Anthropologists have held three different positions about applying anthropology—using it to identify and solve social problems. People who hold the **ivory tower view** contend that anthropologists should avoid practical matters and concentrate on research, publication, and teaching. Those who favor what Ralph Piddington (1970) has called the **schizoid view** think that anthropologists should help carry out, but not make or criticize, policy. In this view, personal "value judgments" should be kept strictly separate from scientific investigation. The third view is **advocacy.** Its proponents assert that precisely because anthropologists are experts on human problems and social change and because they study, understand, and respect cultural values, they should make policy affecting people. In this view, proper roles for applied anthropologists include (1) identifying needs for change that local people perceive, (2) working with those people to design culturally appropriate and socially sensitive change, and (3) protecting local people from harmful development schemes.

I join many other anthropologists in favoring advocacy. I share the belief that no one is better qualified to propose and evaluate guidelines for society than are those who study anthropology. To be effective advocates, anthropologists must present their views clearly, thoughtfully, and forcefully to policy makers and the public. Many anthropologists do serve as social commentators and problem solvers, and as policy makers, advisers, and evaluators. We express our policy views in publications and lectures, and through professional associations, such as the Society for Applied Anthropology and the National Association of Practicing Anthropologists.

As was mentioned in Chapter 1, anthropology's foremost professional organization, the American Anthropological Association (AAA), has formally acknowledged a public service role by recognizing that anthropology has two dimensions: (1) theoretical/academic anthropology and

(2) practicing or applied anthropology. **Applied anthropology** refers to the application of anthropological perspectives, theory, methods, and data to identify, assess, and solve social problems. As Erve Chambers (1987, p. 309) states it, applied anthropology is the "field of inquiry concerned with the relationships between anthropological knowledge and the uses of that knowledge in the world beyond anthropology."

As mentioned, there are two important professional groups of applied anthropologists (also called **practicing anthropologists**). The older is the independent Society for Applied Anthropology (SfAA), founded in 1941. The second, the National Association for the Practice of Anthropology (NAPA), was established as a unit of the American Anthropological Association (AAA) in 1983. (Many people belong to both groups.) Practicing anthropologists work (regularly or occasionally, full or part time) for nonacademic clients. These include governments, development agencies, nongovernmental organizations (NGOs), tribal and ethnic associations, interest groups, businesses, and social-service and educational agencies. Applied anthropologists work for groups that promote, manage, and assess programs aimed at influencing human social conditions. The scope of applied anthropology includes change and development abroad and social problems and policies in North America.

580

There was a time—the 1940s in particular—when most anthropologists focused on the application of their knowledge. During World War II, American anthropologists studied Japanese and German "culture at a distance," in an attempt to predict behavior of the enemies of the United States. After the war, Americans did applied anthropology in the Pacific, working to gain native cooperation with American policies in various trust territories.

Modern applied anthropology differs from an earlier version that mainly served the goals of colonial regimes. Application was a central concern of early anthropology in Great Britain (in the context of colonialism) and the United States (in the context of Native American policy). Before turning to the new, we should consider some dangers of the old.

In the context of the British empire, specifically its African colonies, Malinowski (1929*a*) proposed that "practical anthropology" (his term for colonial applied anthropology) should focus on westernization, the diffusion of European culture into tribal societies. He contended that anthropologists should and could avoid politics by concentrating on facts and processes. However, he was actually expressing his own political views, because he questioned neither the legitimacy of colonialism nor the anthropologist's role in making it work. For instance, Malinowski saw nothing wrong with aiding colonial regimes by studying land tenure and land use, to decide how much of their land natives should keep and how much Europeans should get. Malinowski's views exemplify a historical association between anthropology, particularly in Europe, and colonialism (Maquet 1964).

Colonial anthropologists faced, as do some of their modern counterparts (Escobar 1991, 1994), problems posed by their inability to set or influence policy and the difficulty of criticizing programs in which they have participated. Anthropology's professional organizations have addressed some of these problems by establishing codes of ethics and ethics committees. Also, as Tice (1997) notes, attention to such ethical issues is paramount in the teaching of applied anthropology today.

48–49

Academic and Applied Anthropology

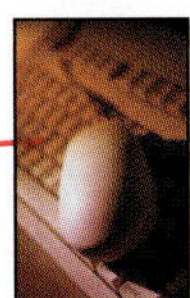

Applied anthropology did not disappear during the 1950s and 1960s, but academic anthropology did most of the growing after World War II. The baby boom, which began in 1946 and peaked in 1957, fueled expansion of the American educational system and thus of academic jobs. New junior, community, and four-year colleges opened. Anthropology became a standard part of the college curriculum. During the 1950s and 1960s, most American anthropologists were college professors, although some still worked in agencies and museums.

This era of academic anthropology continued through the early 1970s. Especially during the Vietnam War, undergraduates flocked to anthropology classes to learn about the cultures of the Third World. Students were especially interested in Southeast Asia, whose cultures were being disrupted by war. Many anthropologists protested the superpowers' blatant disregard for the values, customs, social systems, and lives of Third World peoples.

During the 1970s, and increasing thereafter, although most anthropologists still worked in academia, others found jobs with international organizations, government, business, hospitals, and schools. This shift toward application, though only partial, has benefited the profession. It has forced anthropologists to consider the wider social value and implications of their research.

Theory and Practice

One of the applied anthropologist's most valuable tools is the ethnographic method. Ethnographers study societies firsthand, living with and learning from ordinary people. As we saw in Chapter 2, ethnographers are participant-observers, taking part in the events they study in order to understand native thought and behavior. Ethnographic techniques guide applied anthropologists in both foreign and domestic settings.

Other "expert" participants in social-change programs may be content to converse with officials, read reports, and copy statistics. However, the applied anthropologist's likely early request is some variant of "take me to the local people." We know that people must play an active role in the changes that affect them and that "the people" have information that "the experts" lack.

Anthropological theory—the body of findings and generalizations of the subdisciplines—also guides applied anthropology. Anthropology's holistic perspective—its interest in biology, society, culture, and language—permits the evaluation of many issues that affect people. Anthropology's systemic perspective recognizes that changes don't occur in a vacuum. A project or program always has multiple effects, some unforeseen. For example, dozens of economic development projects intended to increase productivity through irrigation have worsened public health by creating waterways where diseases thrive. In an American example of unintended consequences, a program aimed at enhancing teachers' appreciation of cultural differences led to ethnic stereotyping (Kleinfeld 1975). Specifically, Native American students did not welcome teachers' frequent comments about their Indian heritage. The students felt set apart from their classmates and saw this attention to their ethnicity as patronizing and demeaning.

Theory aids practice, and application fuels theory. As we compare social-change policy and projects, our understanding of cause and effect increases. We add new generalizations about culture change to those discovered in traditional and ancient cultures.

Applied Anthropology and the Subdisciplines

Applied anthropologists come from all four subdisciplines. Biological anthropologists work in public health, nutrition, genetic counseling, substance abuse, epidemiology, aging, and mental illness. They apply their knowledge of human anatomy and physiology to the improvement of automobile safety standards and to the design of airplanes and spacecraft. In forensic work, biological anthropologists help police identify skeletal remains. Similarly, forensic anthropologists, as in the "In the News" account on pages 626–627, reconstruct crimes by analyzing physical evidence. "In the News" describes a massacre in Guatemala whose extent is being documented by forensic biological and archaeological anthropologists.

An important role for applied archaeologists has been created by legislation requiring surveys of prehistoric and historic sites threatened by dams, highways, construction, and other projects supported by federal funds. To save as much as possible of the past when actual sites cannot be preserved is the work of **cultural resource management (CRM).** Applied cultural

anthropologists sometimes work with the applied archaeologists, assessing the human problems generated by the change and determining how they can be reduced.

Cultural anthropologists work with social workers, businesspeople, advertising professionals, factory workers, nurses, physicians, gerontologists, mental-health professionals, school personnel, and economic development experts. Linguistic anthropology, particularly sociolinguistics, aids education. Knowledge of linguistic differences is important in an increasingly multi-

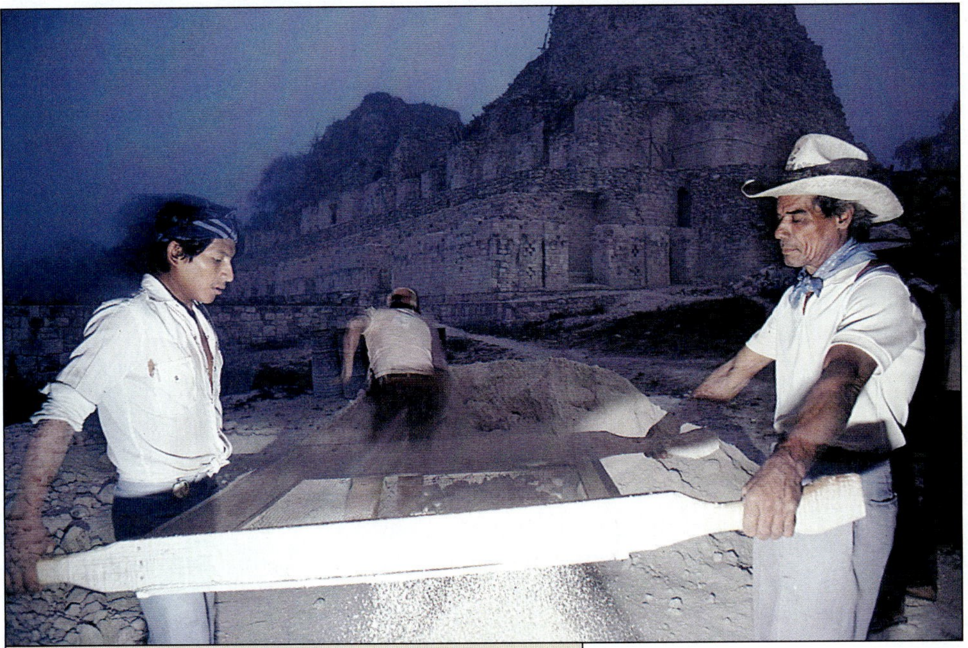

Applied cultural anthropologists may collaborate with archaeologists in cultural resource management and on issues involving tourism at archaeological sites, such as this Mayan site. For more on applied anthropology of tourism, see Chambers (2000).

cultural society whose populace grows up speaking many languages and dialects. Because linguistic differences may affect children's schoolwork and teachers' evaluations, many schools of education now require courses in sociolinguistics.

Anthropology and Education

Anthropology and education refers to anthropological research in classrooms, homes, and neighborhoods (see Spindler 2000). Some of the most interesting research has been done in classrooms, where anthropologists observe interactions among teachers, students, parents, and visitors. Jules Henry's classic account of the American elementary school classroom (1955) shows how students learn to conform to and compete with their peers. Anthropologists also follow students from classrooms into their homes and neighborhoods, viewing children as total cultural creatures whose enculturation and attitudes toward education belong to a context that includes family and peers.

Sociolinguists and cultural anthropologists work side by side in education research, for example, in a study of Puerto Rican seventh-graders in the urban Midwest (Hill-Burnett 1978). In classrooms, neighborhoods, and homes, anthropologists uncovered some misconceptions by teachers. For example, the teachers had mistakenly assumed that Puerto Rican parents valued education less than did non-Hispanics. However, in-depth interviews revealed that the Puerto Rican parents valued it more.

Researchers also found that certain practices were preventing Hispanics from being adequately educated. For example, the teachers' union and the board of education had agreed to teach "English as a foreign language." However, they had not provided bilingual teachers to work with Spanish-speaking students. The school started assigning all students (including non-Hispanics) with low reading scores and behavior problems to the English-as-a-foreign-language classroom.

This educational disaster brought together a teacher who spoke no Spanish, children who

The Anthropology of a Massacre

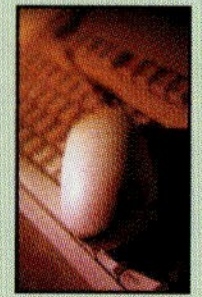

Some of anthropology's applications can be grim. Forensic anthropologists are no strangers to tragedy. This article describes research in Guatemala by biological and archaeological anthropologists, who also have been able to draw on the knowledge of cultural and linguistic anthropologists working in the same area. In 1982, some 376 villagers were massacred in the village of San Francisco de Nenton. Seventeen years later, scientific inquiry began to expose material evidence of the atrocity. This village's fate was common throughout Guatemala in the 1980s, as the government, with the support of the United States, sought to crush rebel guerrilla groups.

SAN FRANCISCO DE NENTON, Guatemala—On the morning of July 17, 1982, a convoy of army trucks made its way up a nearly impassable trail to this remote Mayan Indian hamlet and unloaded a company of troops. Soon afterward a helicopter arrived with the unit's officers . . .

What happened next was a butchery that left all but four of the village's inhabitants dead and all the buildings razed. According to contemporary accounts by people who lived in neighboring communities, many of the women were ordered to disrobe and were raped. Children were torn from mothers' arms and eviscerated by knives or beheaded by machetes. The rampaging troops killed all they found, shooting some villagers, blowing some up with grenades, hacking some to death, burning some or crushing them under the walls of falling buildings.

Relatives and acquaintances of the victims compiled a list of 376 villagers believed to have perished. For 17 years there had been no serious effort to check this list or details of the massacre by independent means, but finally the light of scientific inquiry has begun to expose material evidence of the atrocity . . .

But the tally of dead and missing victims of Guatemala's reign of terror is far from complete, and a band of volunteer forensic anthropologists, acting with the government's blessing, has set out to decipher a few of the massacre sites, gathering evidence from shattered bones, spent bullets and domestic objects including the pitiful remnants of children's clothing.

"We have absolutely no political objectives," said Fredy A. Peccerelli, a forensic anthropologist who heads the Foundation for Forensic Anthropology of Guatemala. "What we're attempting to do is check the accounts of witnesses and wherever possible to apply the techniques of forensic science to set the record straight. We examine massacre sites using many of the same techniques police use at crime scenes.". . .

In the San Francisco project as in dozens of other projects involving massacre sites in Guatemala, the group has had support and guidance from Dr. Clyde Collins Snow, a 71-year-old forensic anthropologist who lives in Norman, Okla. Dr. Snow, virtually a legend among forensic experts, has investigated massacres in 20 countries in Latin America, Africa, the Balkans and Asia . . .

The place where San Francisco de Nenton stood covers a cluster of picturesque hills a few miles south of the Mexican border. Adorned by an ancient Mayan pyramid, the site would make a lovely picnic ground.

But just beneath the grassy surface lies the horror the forensic team is unearthing, as it measures, photographs, and catalogues the grim remnants before transporting them to Mr. Peccerelli's combination home and laboratory in Guatemala City. There, the bones will be X-rayed and further examined.

At one of a half-dozen burial sites discovered at San Francisco de Nenton so far, Renaldo Acevedo, a Guatemalan anthropologist, paused to look into a shallow pit where he and several colleagues had been digging.

"Dos ninos o ninas," he murmured as Dr. Snow arrived. A cluster of little bones covered by the faded but still colorful clothing of an adult Indian woman lay exposed.

Dr. Snow carefully dislodged one of several jawbones in the pit and held it close to his glasses. Speaking carefully in a slow Texas drawl as if addressing a tape recorder in the Oklahoma City morgue where he often works, he said:

"This is the site of a house said to have belonged to one Felipe Sylvestre. We have here a juvenile skull with several fractures, probably post-mortem. Two of the teeth are deciduous but one molar has erupted. This child was between 6 and 7 years old. Sex undetermined, but may be inferred from laboratory measurements and a statistical

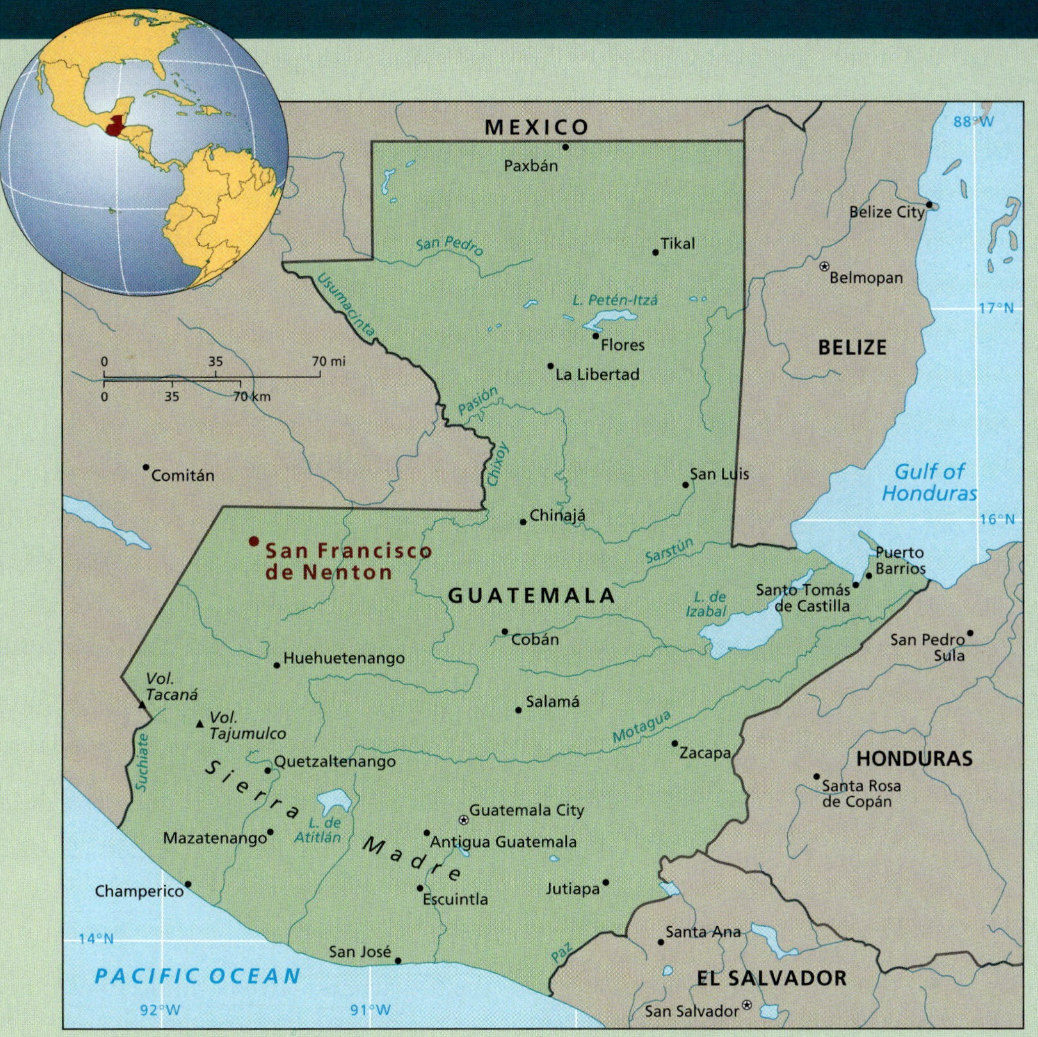

computer program called discriminant function analysis.". . .

A hundred yards away, working with a dental pick and toothbrush, Claudia Rivera and several other Guatemalan archeologists were excavating the village magistrate's office. So far, they had found skull parts and the jaws of 11 bodies.

After a painstaking process of sorting and matching, the first batches of bones and artifacts were packed in plastic bags and cardboard cartons. The team's pickup truck doubles as a hearse, transporting the forensic treasure through the bandit-infested Guatemalan highlands to Mr. Peccerelli's laboratory in Guatemala City. There the skeletons are being laid out on tables for closer scrutiny and measurement.

"It's much the same as excavating an archeological site," Ms. Rivera said. "As the years pass, everything in a site like this decays, and it gets harder to interpret, just as ancient sites are hard to interpret. But for us this is not academic archeology. This place—how shall I say?—it has special meaning for us."

Forensic teams sometimes make as many as 200 skeletal measurements in pursuing identities. For example, slight disparities in the lengths of the radius and ulna arm bones can reveal a person's handedness. Another useful gauge is the degree of fusion between two adjoining pelvic bones (the pubic symphysis), which indicates an adult's age quite accurately.

The ratio of an eye socket's width to its height, the distance between brow ridges, the width of nose bridges and many other facial characteristics can suggest kinships that help in tracing relatives.

In cases where relatives (and money) are available, DNA analysis is a powerful identification tool, Dr. Snow said. Even in badly decayed skeletons, hard shells of dentine usually protect the pulp cavities of teeth, preserving the DNA inside.

Source: "Buried on a Hillside, Clues to Terror," by Malcolm W. Browne, February 23, 1999, www.nytimes.com.

These kids get a basic education in Cite Soleil, a slum of Port-au-Prince, Haiti. What do you see here that differs from classrooms in your country? Do you think these differences would affect how you would do research in Haiti? Assume this classroom would be part of your study.

barely spoke English, and a group of English-speaking students with reading and behavior problems. The Spanish speakers were falling behind not just in reading but in all subjects. They could at least have kept up in the other subjects if a Spanish speaker had been teaching them science, social studies, and math until they were ready for English-language instruction in those areas.

A dramatic illustration of the relevance of applied sociolinguistics to education comes from Ann Arbor, Michigan. In 1979, the parents of several black students at the predominantly white Dr. Martin Luther King Jr. Elementary School sued the Board of Education. They claimed that their children faced linguistic discrimination in the classroom.

332–334

The children, who lived in a neighborhood housing project, spoke Black English Vernacular (BEV, see the chapter on language) at home. At school, most had encountered problems with their classwork. Some had been labeled "learning-impaired" and placed in remedial reading courses. (Consider the embarrassment that children suffer and the effect on self-image of such labeling.)

The African-American parents and their attorney contended that the children had no intrinsic learning disabilities but simply did not understand everything their teachers said. Nor did their teachers always understand them. The lawyer argued that because BEV and Standard English (SE) are so similar, teachers often misinterpreted a child's correct pronunciation (in BEV) of an SE word as a reading error.

The children's attorney recruited several sociolinguists to testify on their behalf. The school board, by contrast, could not find a single qualified linguist to support its argument that there was no linguistic discrimination.

The judge ruled in favor of the children and ordered the following solution: Teachers at the King School had to attend a full-year course designed to improve their knowledge of nonstandard dialects, particularly BEV. The judge did not advocate that the teachers learn to speak BEV or that the children do their assignments in BEV. The school's goal remained to teach the children to use SE, the standard dialect, correctly. Before this could be accomplished, however, teachers and students alike had to learn how to recognize the differences between these similar

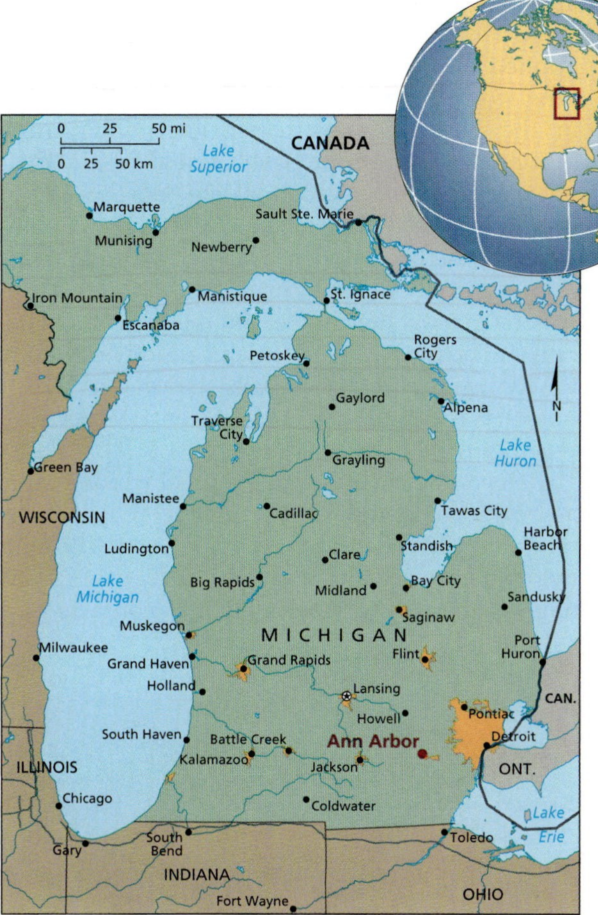

dialects. At the end of the year, most of the teachers interviewed in the local newspaper said the course had helped them.

In a diverse, multicultural populace, teachers should be sensitive to and knowledgeable about linguistic and cultural differences. Children need to be protected so that their ethnic or linguistic background is not used against them. That is what happens when a social variation is regarded as a learning disability.

Urban Anthropology

By 2025, the developing nations will account for 85 percent of the world's population, compared with 77 percent in 1992 (Stevens 1992). Solutions to future problems will depend increasingly on understanding non-Western cultural backgrounds.

The fastest population growth rates are in Third World cities. The world had only 16 cities with more than a million people in 1900, but there are more than 300 such cities today. By 2025, 60 percent of the global population will be urban, compared with 37 percent in 1990 (Stevens 1992). Rural migrants often move to slums, where they live in hovels without utilities and public sanitation facilities. If current trends continue, urban population increase and the concentration of people in slums will be accompanied by rising rates of crime and water, air, and noise pollution. These problems will be most severe in the less-developed countries. Almost all (97 percent) of the projected world population increase will occur in developing countries, 34 percent in Africa alone (Lewis 1992). Global population growth will continue to affect the Northern Hemisphere, especially through international migration.

As industrialization and urbanization spread globally, anthropologists increasingly study these processes and the social problems they create. Urban anthropology, which has theoretical (basic research) and applied dimensions, is the cross-cultural and ethnographic study of global urbanization and life in cities. The United States and Canada also have become popular arenas for urban anthropological research on topics such as ethnicity, poverty, class, and subcultural variations (Mullings 1987).

Urban versus Rural

Recognizing that a city is a social context that is very different from a tribal or peasant village, an early student of Third World urbanization, the anthropologist Robert Redfield, focused on contrasts between rural and urban life. He contrasted rural communities, whose social relations are on a face-to-face basis, with cities, where impersonality characterizes many aspects of life. Redfield (1941) proposed that urbanization be studied along a rural–urban continuum. He described differences in values and social relations in four sites that spanned such a continuum. In Mexico's Yucatán peninsula, Redfield compared an isolated Maya-speaking Indian community, a rural peasant village, a small provincial city, and a large capital. Several studies in Africa (Little 1971) and Asia were influenced by Redfield's view that cities are centers

The world's fastest population growth rates are in Third World cities, such as Kuala Lumpur, Malaysia, where children play in a fountain in front of the Petronas twin towers. Where do you think their parents are?

through which cultural innovations spread to rural and tribal areas.

In any nation, urban and rural represent different social systems. However, cultural diffusion occurs as people, products, and messages move from one to the other. Migrants bring rural practices and beliefs to town and take urban patterns back home. The experiences and social forms of the rural area affect adaptation to city life. For example, principles of tribal organization, including descent, provide migrants to African cities with coping mechanisms that Latin American peasants lack. City folk also develop new institutions to meet specific urban needs (Mitchell 1966).

589–591

The chapter "Colonialism and Development" made the case for the systematic incorporation of native social forms (e.g., descent groups) in programs and policies aimed at change in rural areas. The same strategy applies to urban programs. An applied anthropology approach to urban planning would start by identifying key social groups in the urban context. After identifying those groups, the anthropologist would elicit their wishes for change and translate those needs to funding agencies. The next role would be to work with the agencies and people to ensure that the change is implemented correctly and that it corresponds to what the people said they wanted at the outset. The most humane and productive strategy for change is to base the social design for innovation on traditional social forms in each target area, whether rural or urban.

Relevant African urban groups include ethnic associations, occupational groups, social clubs, religious groups, and burial societies. Through membership in these groups, urban Africans have wide networks of personal contacts and

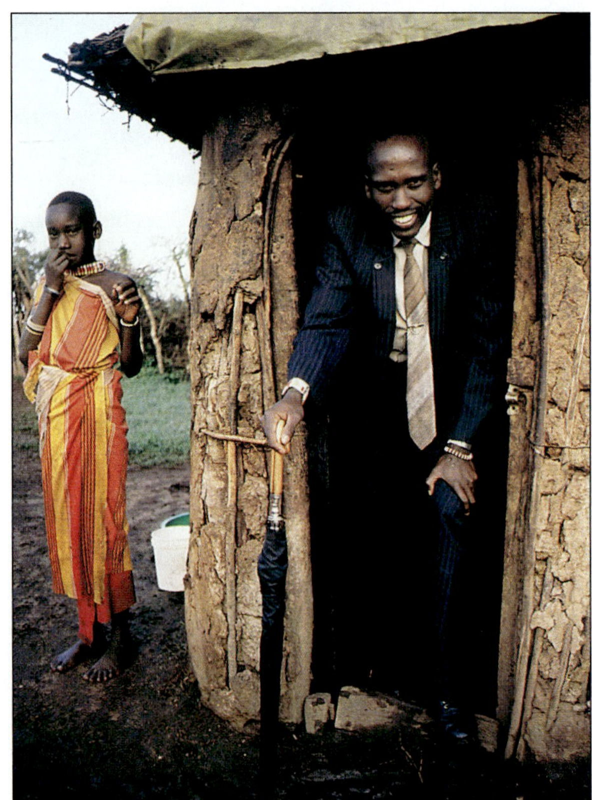

Villagers who "make it" in the city, like this Masai businessman in Kenya, often return home bringing news and gifts to their rural relatives. How else do villagers get information about urban life?

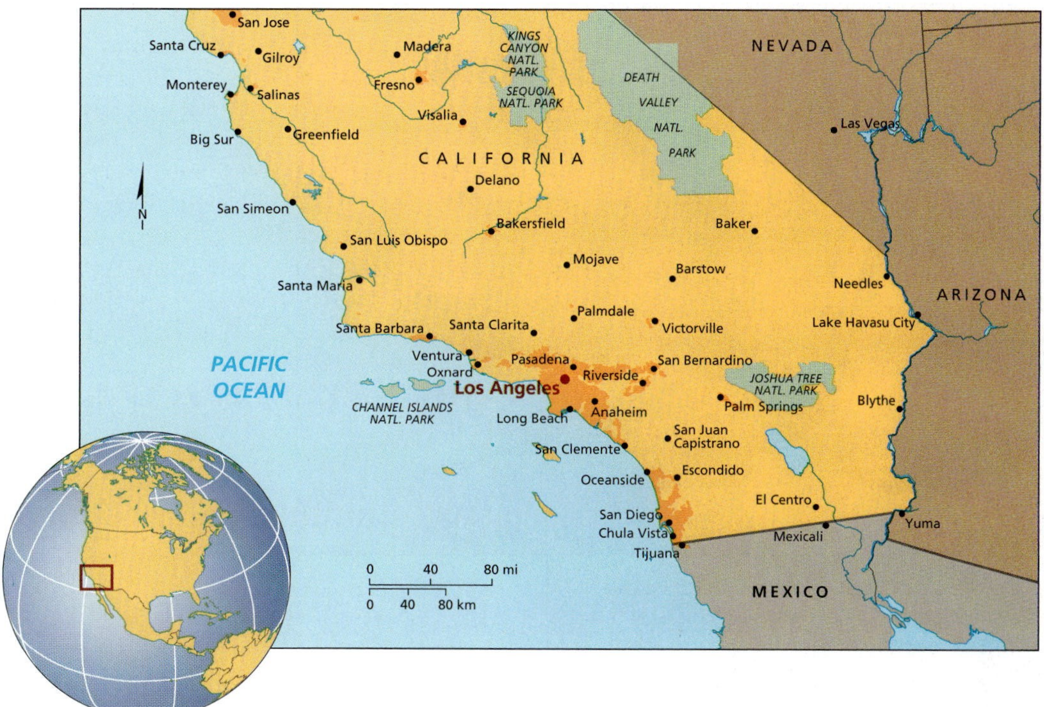

support. Ethnic or "tribal" associations are common both in West and East Africa (Banton 1957; Little 1965). These groups also maintain links with, and provide cash support and urban lodging for, their rural relatives.

The ideology of such associations is that of a gigantic kin group. The members call one another "brother" and "sister." As in an extended family, rich members help their poor relatives. When members fight among themselves, the group acts as judge. A member's improper behavior can lead to expulsion—an unhappy fate for a migrant in a large ethnically heterogeneous city.

Modern North American cities also have kin-based ethnic associations. One example comes from Los Angeles, which has the largest Samoan immigrant community (12,000 people) in the United States. Samoans in Los Angeles draw on their traditional system of *matai* (*matai* means chief; the *matai* system now refers to respect for elders) to deal with modern urban problems. One example: In 1992, a white policeman shot and killed two unarmed Samoan brothers. When a judge dismissed charges against the officer, local leaders used the *matai* system to calm angry youths (who have formed gangs, like other ethnic groups in the Los Angeles area). Clan leaders and elders organized a well-attended community meeting, in which they urged young members to be patient.

Los Angeles Samoans also used the American judicial system. They brought a civil case against the officer in question and pressed the U.S. Justice Department to initiate a civil-rights case in the matter (Mydans 1992*b*). One role for the urban applied anthropologist is to help relevant social groups deal with larger urban institutions, such as legal and social-service agencies with which recent migrants, in particular, may be unfamiliar (see Holtzman 2000).

Medical Anthropology

Medical anthropology is both academic/theoretical and applied/practical. It is a field that includes both biological and sociocultural anthropologists. Medical anthropology is discussed in this chapter because of its many applications. Medical anthropologists examine such questions as: Which diseases affect different populations? How is illness socially constructed? How does

Kin-modeled associations help reduce the stress of urban life on migrants. In Los Angeles, youths of many national backgrounds, like these Cambodians, have formed gangs. If you were an applied anthropologist designing a program for this neighborhood, what role do you think such gangs would play in it?

one treat illness in effective and culturally appropriate ways?

This growing field considers the sociocultural context and implications of disease and illness (Helman 2001; Strathern and Stewart 1999). **Disease** refers to a scientifically identified health threat caused by a bacterium, virus, fungus, parasite, or other pathogen. **Illness** is a condition of poor health perceived or felt by an individual (Inhorn and Brown 1990). Cross-cultural research shows that perceptions of good and bad health, along with health threats and problems, are culturally constructed. Different ethnic groups and cultures recognize different illnesses, symptoms, and causes and have developed different health-care systems and treatment strategies.

Disease also varies among cultures. Traditional and ancient foragers, because of their small numbers, mobility, and relative isolation from other groups, lacked most of the epidemic infectious diseases that affect agrarian and urban societies (Cohen and Armelagos 1984; Inhorn and Brown 1990). Epidemic diseases such as cholera, typhoid, and bubonic plague thrive in dense populations, and thus among farmers and city dwellers. The spread of malaria has been linked to population growth and deforestation associated with food production.

Certain diseases have spread with economic development. *Schistosomiasis* or bilharzia (liver flukes) is probably the fastest-spreading and most dangerous parasitic infection now known (Heyneman 1984). It is propagated by snails that live in ponds, lakes, and waterways, usually ones created by irrigation projects. A study done in a Nile Delta village in Egypt (Farooq 1966) illustrated the role of culture (religion) in the spread of schistosomiasis. The disease was more common among Muslims than among Christians because of an Islamic practice called *wudu,* ritual ablution (bathing) before prayer. The applied anthropology approach to reducing such diseases is to see if natives perceive a connection between the vector (e.g., snails in the water) and the disease, which can take years to develop. If not, such information may be spread by enlisting active local groups and schools. With the worldwide diffusion of the electronic mass media, culturally appropriate public information campaigns have increased awareness and modified behavior that has public health consequences.

In eastern Africa, AIDS and other sexually transmitted diseases (STDs) have spread along highways, via encounters between male truckers and female prostitutes. STDs also are spread through prostitution as young men from rural

Schistosomiasis (liver flukes) is among the fastest spreading and most dangerous parasitic infections now known. It is propagated by snails that live in ponds, lakes, and waterways (often ones created by irrigation projects) such as this one in Luxor, Egypt. As an applied anthropologist, what would you do to cut the rate of infection?

areas seek wage work in cities, labor camps, and mines. When the men return to their natal villages, they infect their wives (Larson 1989; Miller and Rockwell 1988). Cities are also prime sites of STD transmission in Europe, Asia, and North and South America.

The kind and incidence of disease vary among societies, and cultures interpret and treat illness differently. Standards for sick and healthy bodies are cultural constructions that vary in time and space (Martin 1992). Still, all societies have what George Foster and Barbara Anderson (1978) call "disease-theory systems" to identify, classify, and explain illness. According to Foster and Anderson (1978), there are three basic theories about the causes of illness: personalistic, naturalistic, and emotionalistic. **Personalistic disease theories** blame illness on agents (often malicious), such as sorcerers, witches, ghosts, or ancestral spirits. **Naturalistic disease theories** explain illness in impersonal terms. One example is Western medicine or *biomedicine,* which aims to link illness to scientifically demonstrated agents that bear no personal malice toward their victims. Thus, Western medicine attributes illness to organisms (e.g., bacteria, viruses, fungi, or parasites), accidents, or toxic materials. Other naturalistic ethnomedical systems blame poor health on unbalanced body fluids. Many Latin cultures classify food, drink, and environmental conditions as "hot" or "cold." People believe their health suffers when they eat or drink hot or cold substances together or under inappropriate conditions. For example, one shouldn't drink something cold after a hot bath or eat a pineapple (a "cold" fruit) when one is menstruating (a "hot" condition).

Emotionalistic disease theories assume that emotional experiences cause illness. For example, Latin Americans may develop *susto,* or soul loss, an illness caused by anxiety or fright (Bolton 1981; Finkler 1985). Its symptoms include lethargy, vagueness, and distraction. Of course, modern psychoanalysis also focuses on the role of the emotions in physical and psychological well-being.

All societies have **health-care systems.** These consist of beliefs, customs, specialists, and techniques aimed at ensuring health and preventing, diagnosing, and curing illness. A society's illness-causation theory is important for treatment. When illness has a personalistic cause, shamans and other magico-religious specialists may be good curers. They draw on varied techniques (occult and practical) that comprise their special expertise. A shaman may cure soul loss by enticing the spirit back into the body. Shamans may ease difficult childbirths by asking spirits to travel up the birth canal to guide the baby out (Lévi-Strauss 1967). A shaman may cure a cough by counteracting a curse or removing a substance introduced by a sorcerer.

All cultures have health-care specialists. If there is a "world's oldest profession" besides hunter and gatherer, it is **curer,** often a shaman. The curer's role has some universal features (Foster and Anderson 1978). Thus, curers emerge

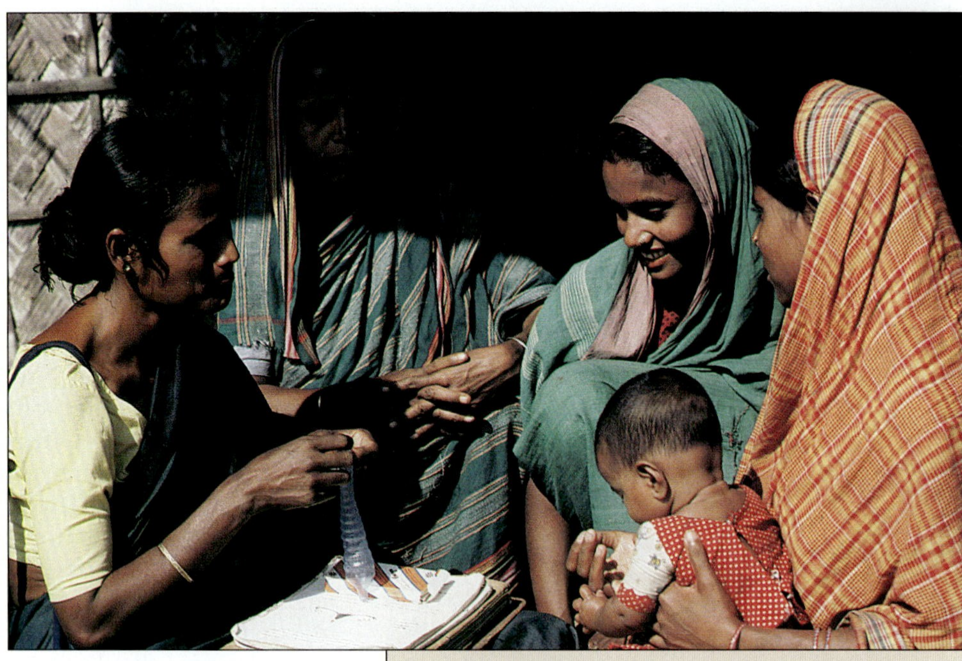

A community health worker illustrates condom basics to two other women in Bangladesh. What would you do to increase condom use in areas with high rates of HIV?

through a culturally defined process of selection (parental prodding, inheritance, visions, dream instructions) and training (apprentice shamanship, medical school). Eventually, the curer is certified by older practitioners and acquires a professional image. Patients believe in the skills of the curer, whom they consult and compensate.

Non-Western systems (traditional medicine) offer some lessons for Western medicine. For example, traditional practitioners may have more success treating certain forms of mental illness than psychotherapists do. Non-Western systems may explain mental illness by causes that are easier to identify and combat. Thus, it may be simpler to rid a body of a spirit possessor than to undo all the damage that a Freudian might attribute to an unresolved Oedipus complex.

Another reason non-Western therapy may succeed is that the mentally ill are diagnosed and treated in cohesive groups with the full support of their kin. Curing may be an intense community ritual in which the shaman heals by temporarily taking on and then rejecting the patient's illness (Lévi-Strauss 1967). In modern mental institutions, by contrast, no prior social ties link patients to each other or to doctors and nurses. Mental illness is viewed as the patient's individual burden. Psychotropic drugs are increasingly used, often effectively, to treat and control psychological disorders. However, for severe mental illness, the context of treatment may be one of isolation and alienation—separation of the afflicted person from society—rather than participation by a group in a common ritual.

We should not lose sight, ethnocentrically, of the difference between **scientific medicine** and Western medicine per se (Lieban 1977). Despite advances in pathology, microbiology, biochemistry, surgery, diagnostic technology, and applications, many Western medical procedures have little justification in logic or fact. Overprescription of tranquilizers and drugs, unnecessary surgery, and the impersonality and inequality of the physician–patient relationship are questionable features of Western medical systems. Also, overuse of antibiotics, not just for people, but also in animal feed, seems to be triggering an explosion of resistant microrganisms, which may pose a long-term global public health hazard.

Still, biomedicine surpasses tribal treatment in many ways. Although medicines like quinine, coca, opium, ephedrine, and rauwolfia were discovered in nonindustrial societies, thousands of effective drugs are available today to treat myriad diseases. Preventive health care improved

A traditional healer at work in Malaysia. What does this remind you of?

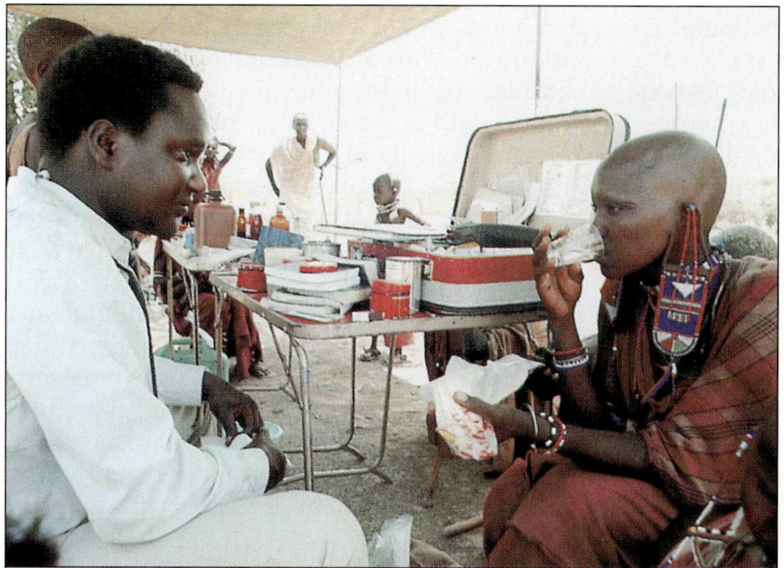

How do Western medicine and scientific medicine differ? Clinics like this one bring antibiotics, minor surgery, and preventive medicine to the Masai of Kenya. What kind of medicine is being shown here? Is it incompatible with the native healing system?

during the 20th century. Today's surgical procedures are safer and more effective than those of traditional societies.

But industrialization has spawned its own health problems. Modern stressors include noise, air, and water pollution; poor nutrition; dangerous machinery; impersonal work; isolation; poverty; homelessness; and substance abuse. Health problems in industrial nations are due as much to economic, social, political, and cultural factors as to pathogens. In modern North America, for example, poverty contributes to many illnesses. These include arthritis, heart conditions, back problems, and hearing and vision impairment. Poverty is also a factor in the differential spread of infectious diseases.

Medical anthropologists have served as cultural interpreters in public health programs, which must pay attention to native theories about the nature, causes, and treatment of illness. Successful health interventions cannot simply be forced on communities. They must fit into local cultures and be accepted by local people. When Western medicine is introduced, people usually retain many of their old methods while also accepting new ones (see Green 1987/1992). Native curers may go on treating certain conditions (like spirit possession), whereas M.D.s may deal with others. If both modern and traditional specialists are consulted and the patient is cured, the native curer may get as much or more credit than the physician.

A more personal treatment of illness that emulates the non-Western curer–patient–community relationship could probably benefit Western systems. Western medicine has tended to draw a rigid line between biological and psychological causation. Non-Western theories usually lack this sharp distinction, recognizing that poor health has intertwined physical, emotional, and social causes. The mind–body opposition is part of Western folk taxonomy, not of science.

Non-Western practitioners often treat symptoms, instead of seeking causes. Their aim—and often their result—is an immediate cure. Traditional curers often succeed with health problems that biomedicine classifies as psychosomatic (not a disease, therefore not an illness) and dismisses as not requiring treatment—despite the feelings of the ill patient. Non-Western medical systems tell us that patients can be treated effectively as whole beings, using any combination of methods that prove beneficial. Indeed there is a growing related field known as *holistic medicine* in contemporary North America.

Anthropology and Business

Carol Taylor (1987) discusses the value of an "anthropologist-in-residence" in a large, complex organization, such as a hospital or a business. A free-ranging ethnographer can be a perceptive oddball when information and decisions usually move through a rigid hierarchy. If allowed to observe and converse freely with all types and levels of personnel, the anthropologist may acquire a unique perspective on organizational conditions and problems. Also, high-tech companies, such as Xerox, IBM, and Apple, have employed anthropologists in various roles. Closely observing how people actually use computer products, anthropologists work with engineers to design products that are more user-friendly.

For many years, anthropologists have used ethnography to study business settings (Arensberg 1987). For example, ethnographic research in an auto factory may view workers, managers, and executives as different social categories participating in a common social system. Each group has characteristic attitudes, values, and behavior patterns. These are transmitted through *microenculturation,* the process by which people learn particular roles in a limited social system. The free-ranging nature of ethnography takes the anthropologist from worker to executive. Each of these people is both an individual with a personal viewpoint and a cultural creature whose perspective is, to some extent, shared with other members of a group. Applied anthropologists have acted as "cultural brokers," translating managers' goals or workers' concerns to the other group.

For business, as we see in "In the News," key features of anthropology include (1) ethnography and observation as ways of gathering data, (2) cross-cultural expertise, and (3) focus on cultural diversity. The cross-cultural perspective enters the picture when businesses seek to know why other nations have higher (or lower) productivity than we do (Ferraro 2001). Reasons for differential productivity are cultural, social, and economic. To find them, anthropologists must focus on key features in the organization of production. Subtle but potentially important differences can emerge from workplace ethnography—close observation of workers and managers in their natural (workplace) setting.

Careers in Anthropology

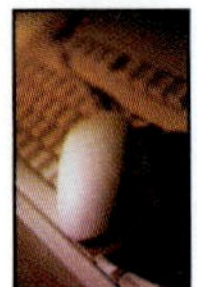

Many college students find anthropology interesting and consider majoring in it. However, their parents or friends may discourage them by asking, "What kind of job are you going to get with an anthropology major?" The purpose of this section (and of the "In the News" box) is to answer that question. The first step in answering "What do you do with an anthropology major?" is to consider the more general question "What do you do with any college major?" The answer is "Not much, without a good bit of effort, thought, and planning." A survey of graduates of the literary college of the University of Michigan showed that few had jobs that were clearly linked to their majors. Medicine, law, and many other professions require advanced degrees. Although many colleges offer bachelor's degrees in engineering, business, accounting, and social work, master's degrees are often needed to get the best jobs in those fields. Anthropologists, too, need an advanced degree, most typically a Ph.D., to find gainful employment in academic, museum, or applied anthropology.

The following discussion is aimed mainly at undergraduates who are thinking of doing an anthropology major—not at students who are considering advanced degrees in anthropology, although there are some comments for them, too. A broad college education, and even a major in anthropology, can be an excellent foundation for success in many fields. A recent survey of women executives showed that most had not majored in business but in the social sciences or humanities. Only after graduating did they study business, obtaining a master's degree in business administration. These executives felt that the breadth of their college educations had contributed to their

in the news

Hot Asset in Corporate: Anthropology Degrees

An important business application of anthropology has to do with knowledge of how consumers use products. Businesses hire anthropologists because of the importance of observation in natural settings and the focus on cultural diversity. Thus, as we see in this article, Hallmark cards has hired anthropologists to observe parties, holidays, and celebrations of ethnic groups to improve its ability to design cards for targeted audiences. Anthropologists go into people's homes to see how they actually use products. This permits better product design and more effective advertising.

Don't throw away the MBA degree yet.

But as companies go global and crave leaders for a diverse workforce, a new hot degree is emerging for aspring executives: anthropology.

The study of man is no longer a degree for museum directors. Citicorp created a vice presidency for anthropologist Steve Barnett, who discovered early warning signs to identify people who don't pay credit card bills.

Not satisfied with consumer surveys, Hallmark is sending anthropologists into the homes of immigrants, attending holidays and birthday parties to design cards they'll want.

No survey can tell engineers what women really want in a razor, so marketing consultant Hauser Design sends anthropologists into bathrooms to watch them shave their legs.

Unlike MBAs, anthropology degrees are rare: one undergraduate degree for every 26 in business and one anthropology Ph.D. for every 235 MBAs.

Textbooks now have chapters on business applications. The University of South Florida has created a course of study for anthropologists headed for commerce.

Motorola corporate lawyer Robert Faulkner got his anthropology degree before going to law school. He says it becomes increasingly valuable as he is promoted into management.

"When you go into business, the only problems you'll have are people problems," was the advice given to teen-ager Michael Koss by his father in the early 1970s.

Koss, now 44, heeded the advice, earned an anthropology degree from Beloit College in 1976, and is today CEO of the Koss headphone manufacturer.

Katherine Burr, CEO of The Hanseatic Group, has masters in both anthropology and business from the University of New Mexico. Hanseatic was among the first money management programs to predict the Asian crisis and last year produced a total return of 315% for investors.

"My competitive edge came completely out of anthropology," she says. "The world is so unknown, changes so rapidly. Preconceptions can kill you."

Companies are starving to know how people use the Internet or why some pickups, even though they are more powerful, are perceived by consumers as less powerful, says Ken Erickson, of the Center for Ethnographic Research.

It takes trained observation, Erickson says. Observation is what anthropologists are trained to do.

Source: Del Jones, "Hot Asset in Corporate: Anthropology Degrees," *USA Today*, February 18, 1991, p. B1.

business careers. Anthropology majors go on to medical, law, and business schools and find success in many professions that often have little explicit connection to anthropology.

Anthropology's breadth provides knowledge and an outlook on the world that are useful in many kinds of work. For example, an anthropology major combined with a master's degree in business is excellent preparation for work in international business. However, job seekers must always convince employers that they have a special and valuable "skillset."

Breadth is anthropology's hallmark. Anthropologists study people biologically, culturally, socially, and linguistically, in time and space, in developed and underdeveloped nations, in simple and complex settings. Most colleges have anthropology courses that compare cultures and others that focus on particular world areas, such as Latin America, Asia, and Native North America. The knowledge of geographic areas acquired in such courses can be useful in many jobs. Anthropology's comparative outlook, its longstanding Third World focus, and its appreciation of diverse life styles combine to provide an excellent foundation for overseas employment.

Even for work in North America, the focus on culture is valuable. Every day we hear about cultural differences and about social problems whose solutions require a multicultural viewpoint—an ability to recognize and reconcile ethnic differences. Government, schools, and private firms constantly deal with people from different social classes, ethnic groups, and tribal backgrounds. Physicians, attorneys, social workers, police officers, judges, teachers, and students can all do a better job if they understand social differences in a part of the world that is one of the most ethnically diverse in history.

What if you want more than an undergraduate degree in anthropology? What if you do decide to pursue an advanced degree? Although some practicing anthropologists find jobs with only the master's degree, the more typical credential for gainful employment in anthropology is the doctorate, the Ph.D. Traditionally, most people with Ph.D.s in anthropology have expected to find employment as college teachers or in museums. Things are changing today. The American Anthropological Association has estimated that at least half of future anthropology Ph.D.s will not find work in academia. One reason for this shift is that academic jobs have become harder to get and are not clearly expanding. Another reason is that the production of Ph.D.s in anthropology has increased faster than the number of academic jobs available. A final reason is that many anthropology Ph.D.s actually prefer applied work to work in academia. Whatever the reason, there is no doubt that more and more anthropologists will be doing applied anthropology.

One place they'll be doing it is business. The cross-cultural perspective and the focus on diversity are two reasons why some North American businesses have become interested in anthropology, as we saw in the "In the News" box. Also, an ethnographic focus on behavior in the daily social setting can help locate problems that plague American businesses, which tend to be overly hierarchical. Attention to the social dimension of business can only gain importance. More and more executives recognize that proper human relations are as important as economic forecasts in maximizing productivity. Contemporary applied anthropologists devise ways to deploy employees more effectively and to increase job satisfaction.

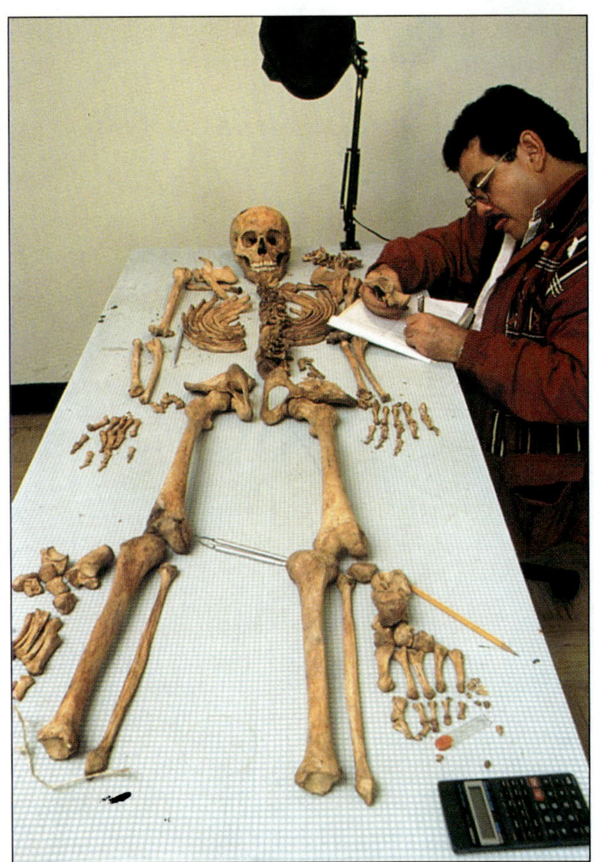

One applied anthropology career is in forensics, as in Guatemala City's Institute for Forensic Anthropology. Identification of war victims proceeds here in 1997, as is described in "In the News" on pages 626–627.

Applied anthropologists also work to help natives threatened by external systems. As highways and power-supply systems cross tribal boundaries, the "modern" world comes into conflict with historic land claims and traditions. An anthropological study is often considered necessary before permission is granted to extend a public works system across native lands.

Because construction, dams, reservoirs, and other public works may threaten archeological sites, fields such as cultural resource management have developed. Government agencies, engineering firms, and construction companies now have jobs for people with an anthropological background because of federal legislation to protect historic and prehistoric sites.

Knowledge about the traditions and beliefs of the many social groups within a modern nation is important in planning and carrying out programs that affect those groups. Attention to social background and cultural categories helps ensure the welfare of affected ethnic groups, communities, and neighborhoods. Experience in planned social change—whether community organization in North America or economic development overseas—shows that a proper social study should be done before a project or policy is implemented. When local people want the change and it fits their lifestyle and traditions, it will be more successful, beneficial, and cost-effective. There will be not only a more humane but a more economical solution to a real social problem.

Some agencies working overseas place particular value on anthropological training. Others seek employees with certain skills without caring much about specific academic backgrounds. Among the government agencies that hire anthropologists are USAID (the United States Agency for International Development) and USDA (the United States Department of Agriculture). These organizations hire anthropologists both full-time and as short-term consultants.

Private voluntary organizations working overseas offer other opportunities. These PVOs (a kind of NGO) include Care, Save the Children, Catholic Relief Services, Foster Parents Plan International, and Oxfam (a hunger relief organization operating out of Boston and Oxford). Some of these groups employ anthropologists full time.

Anthropologists apply their expertise in surprisingly diverse areas. They negotiate business deals, suggest and implement organizational changes, and testify as expert witnesses. Anthropologists also have worked for pharmaceutical firms interested in potential conflicts between traditional and Western medicine, and in culturally appropriate marketing of their products (e.g., Viagra) in new settings. Other anthropologists are working to help native peoples get a share of the profits when their traditional remedies, including medicinal plants, are marketed by drug companies.

People with anthropology backgrounds are doing well in many fields. Furthermore, even if the job has little or nothing to do with anthropology in a formal or obvious sense, anthropology is always useful when we work with fellow human beings. For most of us, this means every day of our lives.

The Continuance of Diversity

Anthropology has a crucial role to play in promoting a more humanistic vision of social change, one that respects the value of cultural diversity. The existence of anthropology is itself a tribute to the continuing need to understand social and cultural similarities and differences. Anthropology teaches us that the adaptive responses of humans can be more flexible than can those of other species because our main adaptive means are sociocultural. However, the cultural forms, institutions, values, and customs of the past always influence subsequent adaptation, producing continued diversity and giving a certain uniqueness to the actions and reactions of different groups. With our knowledge and our awareness of our professional responsibilities, let us work to keep anthropology, the study of humankind, the most humanistic of all the sciences.

A Forensic Anthropology Analysis of Human Skeletal Remains

BACKGROUND INFORMATION

Student:	*Beau J. Goldstein*
Supervising Professor:	*Dr. Curtis W. Wienker*
School:	*University of South Florida*
Year in School/Major:	*Senior/Anthropology*
Future Plans:	*Master's in Bioarchaeology, Ph.D. eventually*
Project Title:	*A Forensic Anthropology Analysis of Human Skeletal Remains from the University of South Florida Department of Anatomy*

How did this student infer and determine the probable geographic origin of the skeletons he studied? To what subfield of anthropology does such forensic anthropology belong?

In beginning my honors thesis, I had many ideas concerning the field of forensic anthropology. However, I wanted to do something to benefit more than just the anthropologist. So, I decided that something that would be appreciated in a more local environment (such as the University of South Florida) would be appropriate. With the aid of my supervisor (Curtis Wienker), I decided to investigate skeletal remains from the department of anatomy.

Although the main purpose was to test and use practical applications of forensic anthropology, another purpose was to show the variation that exists in skeletal remains to those who are not trained in anthropology; in this case, that would include both educators and students from the department of anatomy at USF.

My study in forensic anthropology went quite smoothly. Each skeleton was categorized by sex, height, and population affiliation. The only snag turned out to be quite an interesting one; it had to do with the origin of the skeletons themselves.

When the department acquired the skeletons 20 or 30 years ago, there were no records pertaining to the origin of each individual skeleton. The company that supplied the school with the skeletons had no records but assumed that their place of origin was India. Upon double-checking this "lead," I discovered that their origin was most likely India, but I still have no absolute guarantee of this fact.

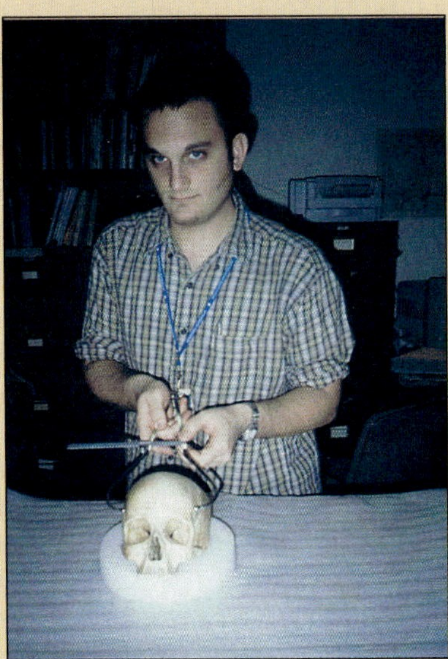

This led to some interesting findings. The results of testing population affiliation by macroscopic means indicated that the skeletons exhibited markers of both European ancestry and Asian ancestry, exactly what would be expected from India, which is a crossroads between East and West. When using the FORDISC 2.0 computer program to determine population affiliation, I encountered a question: These was no classificatory category for "Indians," so how could I expect the program to classify the remains?

I assumed that as long as the program classified all the remains into one category, then we would know that the remains were derived from the same population. Since this is what occurred, we can assume with a good deal of certainty that the remains were derived from India.

In setting out to show others about human variation, I was also able to discover the origin of the skeletal series that I studied. However, this was not the highlight of my work. The actual hands-on investigations taught me more than I could have ever learned otherwise.

summary

1. Applied anthropology uses anthropological perspectives, theory, methods, and data to identify, assess, and solve problems. Applied anthropologists have a range of employers. Examples: development and government agencies; NGOs; tribal, ethnic, and interest groups; businesses; social services and educational agencies. Applied anthropologists come from all four subfields. Ethnography is one of applied anthropology's most valuable research tools. Another is the comparative, cross-cultural perspective. A systemic perspective recognizes that changes have multiple consequences, some unintended.
2. Anthropology and education researchers work in classrooms, homes, and other settings relevant to education. Such studies may lead to policy recommendations. Both academic and applied anthropologists study migration from rural areas to cities and across national boundaries. North America has become a popular arena for urban anthropological research on migration, ethnicity, poverty, and related topics. Although rural and urban are different social systems, there is cultural diffusion from one to the other. Rural and tribal social forms affect adjustment to the city.
3. Medical anthropology is the cross-cultural study of health problems and conditions, disease, illness, disease theories, and health-care systems. Medical anthropology includes biological and cultural anthropologists and has theoretical (academic) and applied dimensions. In a given setting, the characteristic diseases reflect diet, population density, economy, and social complexity. Native theories of illness may be personalistic, naturalistic, or emotionalistic. In applying anthropology to business, the key features are (1) ethnography and observation as ways of gathering data, (2) cross-cultural expertise, and (3) focus on cultural diversity.
4. A broad college education, including anthropology and foreign-area courses, offers excellent background for many fields. Anthropology's comparative outlook and cultural relativism provide an excellent basis for overseas employment. Even for work in North America, a focus on culture and cultural diversity is valuable. Anthropology majors attend medical, law, and business schools and succeed in many fields, some of which have little explicit connection with anthropology.
5. Experience with social-change programs, whether in North America or abroad, offers a common lesson. When local people want a change and when that change fits their life style and traditions, the change is most likely to be successful, beneficial, and cost-effective.

key terms

advocacy view of applied anthropology; the belief that precisely because anthropologists are experts on human problems and social change, and because they study, understand, and respect cultural values, they should make policy affecting people.

anthropology and education Anthropological research in classrooms, homes, and neighborhoods, viewing students as total cultural creatures whose enculturation and attitudes toward education belong to a larger context that includes family, peers, and society.

applied anthropology The application of anthropological data, perspectives, theory, and methods to identify, assess, and solve contemporary social problems.

cultural resource management (CRM) The branch of applied archaeology aimed at preserving sites threatened by dams, highways, and other projects.

curer Specialized role acquired through a culturally appropriate process of selection, training, certification, and acquisition of a professional image; the curer is consulted by patients, who believe in his or her special powers, and receives some form of special consideration; a cultural universal.

disease A scientifically identified health threat caused by a bacterium, virus, fungus, parasite, or other pathogen.

emotionalistic disease theories Theories that assume that illness is caused by intense emotional experiences.

health-care systems Beliefs, customs, and specialists concerned with ensuring health and preventing and curing illness; a cultural universal.

illness A condition of poor health perceived or felt by an individual.

ivory tower view of applied anthropology; the belief that anthropologists should avoid practical matters and concentrate on research, publication, and teaching.

medical anthropology Unites biological and cultural anthropologists in the study of disease, health problems, health-care systems, and theories about illness in different cultures and ethnic groups.

naturalistic disease theories Include scientific medicine; theories that explain illness in impersonal systemic terms.

personalistic disease theories Theories that attribute illness to sorcerers, witches, ghosts, or ancestral spirits.

practicing anthropologists Used as a synonym for *applied anthropology;* anthropologists who practice their profession outside of academia.

schizoid view of applied anthropology; the belief that anthropologists should help carry out, but not make or criticize, policy, and that personal value judgments should be kept strictly separate from scientific investigation in applied anthropology.

scientific medicine As distinguished from Western medicine, a health-care system based on scientific knowledge and procedures, encompassing such fields as pathology, microbiology, biochemistry, surgery, diagnostic technology, and applications.

critical thinking questions

1. What's your position on applied anthropology, given the three views discussed at the beginning of this chapter?
2. What else are you studying this semester? Do those fields have an applied dimension, too? Are they more or less useful than anthropology is?
3. Describe a setting in which you might use ethnography and observation to do applied anthropology. What other research methods might you also use in that setting?
4. Think back to your grade school or high school classroom. Were there any social issues that might have interested an anthropologist? Were there any problems that an applied anthropologist might have been able to solve? How so?
5. What do you see as the costs and benefits of Western medicine compared with tribal medicine? Are there any conditions for which you'd prefer treatment by a tribal curer than a Western curer?
6. Think of a problem in an urban setting that an applied anthropologist might be called on to solve. How do you imagine he or she would go about solving it?
7. Think of a business context you know well. How might applied anthropology help that business function better? How would the applied anthropologist gather the information to suggest improvements?

case study

Ojibwa: Urban anthropology is one applied field presented in this chapter, which discusses differences between rural and urban life, and the process of change through urbanization. In *Culture Sketches* by Holly Peters-Golden, read the chapter on the Ojibwa: "'The People' Endure." What sorts of changes have occurred in Ojibwa life through urbanization? Might the move from reservation to city, for Native Americans, be different from urbanization experienced by other social groups? Why or why not?

suggested additional readings

Anderson, R.

1996 *Magic, Science, and Health: The Aims and Achievements of Medical Anthropology.* Fort Worth: Harcourt Brace. Up-to-date text, focusing on variation associated with race, gender, ethnicity, age, and ableness.

Bailey, E. J.

2000 *Medical Anthropology and African American Health.* Westport, CT: Bergin and Garvey. Medical issues affecting, and anthropological research involving, African-Americans.

Bond, G. C., J. Kreniske, I. Susser, and J. Vincent, eds.

1997 *AIDS in Africa and the Caribbean.* Boulder, CO: Westview. This volume uses detailed ethnographic studies from Africa and the Caribbean to examine AIDS in a global and comparative context.

Brown, P. J.

1998 *Understanding and Applying Medical Anthropology.* Mountain View, CA: Mayfield. Medical anthropology, basic and applied.

Chambers, E.

1985 *Applied Anthropology: A Practical Guide.* Englewood Cliffs, NJ: Prentice Hall. How to do applied anthropology, by a leader in the field.

2000 *Native Tours: The Anthropology of Travel and Tourism.* Prospect Heights, IL: Waveland. How anthropologists study the world's number one business—travel and tourism.

Eddy, E. M., and W. L. Partridge, eds.

1987 *Applied Anthropology in America,* 2nd ed. New York: Columbia University Press. Historical review of applications of anthropological knowledge in the United States.

Ferraro, G. P.

2001 *The Cultural Dimension of International Business,* 4th ed. Upper Saddle River, NJ: Prentice Hall. How the theory and insights of cultural anthropology can influence the conduct of international business.

Helman, C.

2001 *Culture, Health, and Illness: An Introduction for Health Professionals,* 4th ed. Boston: Butterworth-Heinemann. The social context of medical practice.

Holtzman, J.

2000 *Nuer Journeys, Nuer Lives.* Boston: Allyn and Bacon. How immigrants from Sudan adapt to Minnesota's twin cities and to the American social service system.

Human Organization

The quarterly journal of the Society for Applied Anthropology. An excellent source for articles on applied anthropology and development.

Joralemon, D.

1999 *Exploring Medical Anthropology.* Boston: Allyn and Bacon. Recent introduction to a growing field.

McElroy, A., and P. K. Townsend

1996 *Medical Anthropology in Ecological Perspective,* 3rd ed. Boulder, CO: Westview. This established introduction to medical anthropology shows that field's multidisciplinary roots.

Rushing, W. A.

1995 *The AIDS Epidemic: Social Dimensions of an Infectious Disease.* Boulder, CO: Westview. The sociocultural conditions that have contributed to the spread of AIDS.

Sargent, C. F., and C. B. Brettell

1996 *Gender and Health: An International Perspective.* Englewood Cliffs, NJ: Prentice Hall. How culture affects the relation among gender, health-care organization, and health policy.

Sargent, C. F., and T. J. Johnson, eds.

1996 *Medical Anthropology: A Handbook of Theory and Method,* rev. ed. Westport, CT: Praeger Press. Articles cover theoretical perspectives, medical systems, health issues, methods in medical anthropology, and issues of policy and advocacy.

Spindler, G. D., ed.

2000 *Fifty Years of Anthropology and Education, 1950–2000: A Spindler Anthology.* Survey of the field of educational anthropology by two prominent contributors, George and Louise Spindler.

Strathern, A., and P. J. Stewart

1999 *Curing and Healing: Medical Anthropology in Global Perspective.* Durham, NC: Carolina Academic Press. Cross-cultural examples of medical anthropology.

Van Willigen, J.

1993 *Applied Anthropology: An Introduction,* rev. ed. South Hadley, MA: Bergin and Garvey. Excellent review of the growth of applied anthropology and its links to general anthropology.

internet exercises

1. *Forensic Anthropology:* Read Jon Jefferson's article on the American Bar Association's website entitled "Down on the Body Farm," **http://www.abanet.org/journal/sep00/sepfbfarm.html.**
   a. What do forensic anthropologists like Dr. William Bass do? How does this relate to anthropology?
   b. What is the Body Farm? How does it help forensic anthropologists?
   c. The American Board of Forensic Anthropology defines forensic anthropology as "the application of the science of physical anthropology to the legal process" and says that "the identification of skeletal, badly decomposed, or otherwise unidentified human remains is important for both legal and humanitarian reasons." Do you agree with these statements? Do you think forensic anthropology is an example of applied anthropology?

2. Go to the United States Agency for International Development's (USAID) page on "Population and the Environment," **http://www.usaid.gov/pop_health/pop/popenv.htm.**
   a. What are some of the major environmental threats due to population growth the world faces?
   b. What can agencies like USAID do in the face of these threats?
   c. What contributions does anthropology have to offer? Should organizations like USAID employ anthropologists?
   d. What is the role of applied anthropology for environmental issues?

See Chapter 24 on your CD-ROM for additional review and interactive exercises. See your McGraw-Hill Online Learning Center for more.

Appendix

American Popular Culture

APPENDIX OUTLINE

Culture is shared. But all cultures have divisive as well as unifying forces. Tribes are divided by residence in different villages and membership in different descent groups. Nations, though united by government, are divided by class, region, ethnicity, religion, and political party. Unifying forces in tribal cultures include marriage, trade, and segmentary lineage structure. In any society, of course, a common cultural tradition also may provide a basis for uniformity.

Whatever unity contemporary American culture has doesn't rest on a particularly strong central government. Nor is national unity based on segmentary lineage structure or marital exchange networks. In fact, many of the commonalities of experience, belief, behavior, and activity that enable us to speak of "contemporary American culture" are relatively new. Like the globalizing forces discussed in the chapter "Cultural Exchange and Survival," they are founded on and perpetuated by recent developments, particularly in business, transportation, and the mass media.

Anthropologists and American Culture

When anthropologists study urban ethnic groups or relationships between class and household organization, they focus on variation, a very important topic. When we look at the creative use that each individual makes of popular culture, as we did in the chapter "Cultural Exchange and Survival," we are also considering variation. However, anthropology traditionally has been concerned as much with uniformity as with variation. "National character" studies of the 1940s and 1950s foreshadowed anthropology's interest in unifying themes in modern nations. Unfortunately, those studies, of such countries as Japan and Russia, focused too much on the psychological characteristics of individuals.

Contemporary anthropologists interested in national culture realize that culture is an attribute of groups. Despite increasing ethnic diversity, we can still talk about an "American national culture." Through common experiences in their enculturation, especially through the media, most Americans do come to share certain knowledge, beliefs, values, and ways of thinking and acting (as was discussed in the chapter "Culture"). The shared aspects of national culture override differences among individuals, genders, regions, or ethnic groups.

The chapter "Cultural Exchange and Survival" examined the creative use that individuals and cultures make of introduced cultural forces, including media images. That chapter discussed how, through different "readings" of the same media "text," individuals and cultures constantly make and remake popular culture. Here we take a different approach. We focus on some of the "texts" that have diffused most successfully in a given national culture. Such "texts" spread because they are culturally appropriate. For various reasons, they are able to carry some sort of meaning to millions of people. Previous chapters have focused on variation and diversity, but this appendix stresses unifying factors: common experiences, actions, and beliefs in American culture.

Anthropologists *should* study American society and culture. Anthropology, after all, deals with universals, generalities, and uniqueness. A national culture is a particular cultural variant, as interesting as any other. Although survey research is traditionally used to study modern nations, techniques developed to interpret and analyze smaller-scale societies, where sociocultural uniformity is more marked, also can contribute to an understanding of American life.

Native anthropologists are those who study their own cultures—for example, American anthropologists working in the United States, Canadian anthropologists working in Canada, or Nigerians working in Nigeria. Anthropological training and field work abroad provide an anthropologist with a certain degree of detachment and objectivity that most natives lack. However, life experience as a native gives an advantage to anthropologists who wish to study their own cultures. Nevertheless, more than when working abroad, the native anthropologist is both participant and observer, often emotionally and intellectually involved in the events and beliefs being studied. Native anthropologists must be particularly careful to resist their own biases and prejudices as natives. They must strive to be as objective in describing their own cultures as they are in analyzing others.

Natives often see and explain their behavior very differently than anthropologists do. For example, most Americans have probably never considered the possibility that apparently secular, commercial, and recreational institutions such as sports, movies, and fast-food restaurants have things in common with religious beliefs, symbols, and behavior. However, these similarities do exist. Anthropology helps us understand ourselves. By studying other cultures, we learn both to appreciate and to question aspects of our own. Furthermore, the same techniques that anthropologists use in describing and analyzing other cultures can be applied to American culture.

American readers may not find the analyses that follow convincing. In part, this is because you are natives, who know much more about your own culture than you do about any other. Also, as we saw in the chapter "Cultural Exchange and Survival," people in a culture may "read" that culture differently. Furthermore, American culture assigns a high value to differences in individual opinion—and to the belief that one opinion is as good as another. Here I am trying to extract *culture* (widely shared aspects of behavior) from diverse *individual* opinions, actions, and experiences.

The following analyses depart from areas that can be easily quantified, such as demography or economics. We are entering a more impressionistic domain, where cultural analysis sometimes seems much more like literary analysis than like science. You will be right in questioning some of the conclusions that follow. Some are surely debatable; some may be just plain wrong. However, if they illustrate how anthropology can be used to shed light on aspects of your own life and experience and to revise and broaden your understanding of your own culture, they will have served a worthwhile function.

A reminder (from the chapter "Culture") about culture, ethnocentrism, and native anthropologists is needed here. For anthropologists, *culture* means much more than refinement, cultivation, education, and appreciation of "classics" and "fine arts"—its popular usage. Curiously, however, when some anthropologists confront their own culture, they seem to forget this. Like other academics and intellectuals, they may regard American "pop" culture as trivial and unworthy of serious study. In doing so, they demonstrate ethnocentrism and reveal a bias that comes with being members of an academic-intellectual subculture.

In examining American culture, native anthropologists must be careful to overcome the bias associated with the academic subculture. Although some academics discourage their children from watching television, the fact that TVs outnumber toilets in American households is a significant cultural datum that anthropologists can't afford to ignore. My own research on Michigan college students may be generalizable to other young Americans. They visit McDonald's more often than they visit houses of worship. I found that almost all had seen a Walt Disney movie and had attended rock concerts or football games. Such shared experiences are major features of American enculturation patterns. Certainly, any extraterrestrial anthropologist doing field work in the United States would stress them. Within the United States, the mass media and the culture of consumption have created major themes in contemporary national culture. These themes merit study.

From the popular domains of sports, TV, movies, and fast food, I have chosen certain very popular "texts." I could have used other texts (for example, blue jeans, baseball, or pizza) to make the same points: that there are powerful shared aspects of contemporary American national culture and that anthropological techniques can be used to interpret them.

 Football

Football, we say, is only a game, yet it has become a popular spectator sport. On fall Saturdays, millions of people travel to and from college football games. Smaller congregations meet in high school stadiums. Millions of Americans watch televised football. Indeed, nearly half the adult population of the United States watches the Super Bowl. Because football is of general interest to Americans, it is a unifying cultural institution that merits attention. Our most popular sports manage to attract fans of diverse ethnic backgrounds, regions, religions, political parties, jobs, social statuses, levels of wealth, and genders.

The popularity of football, particularly professional football, depends directly on the mass media, especially television. Is football, with its territorial incursion, hard hitting, and violence—occasionally resulting in injury—popular because Americans are violent people? Are football spectators vicariously realizing their own hostile and aggressive tendencies? Anthropologist W. Arens (1981) discounts this interpretation. He points out that football is a peculiarly American pastime. Although a similar game is played in Canada, it is less popular there. Baseball has become a popular sport in the Caribbean, parts of Latin America, and Japan. Basketball and volleyball also are spreading. However, throughout most of the world, soccer is the most popular sport. Arens argues that if football were a particularly effective channel for expressing aggression, it would have spread (like soccer and baseball) to many other countries, where people have as many aggressive tendencies and hostile feelings as Americans do. Furthermore, he suggests that if a sport's popularity rested simply on a bloodthirsty temperament, boxing, a far bloodier sport, would be America's national pastime. Arens concludes that the explanation for the sport's popularity lies elsewhere, and I agree.

He contends that football is popular because it symbolizes certain key features of American life. In particular, it is characterized by teamwork based on specialization and division of labor, which are pervasive features of modern life. Susan Montague and Robert Morais (1981) take the analysis a step further. They argue that Americans appreciate football because it presents a miniaturized and simplified version of modern organizations. People have trouble understanding organizational bureaucracies, whether in business, universities, or government. Football, the anthropologists argue, helps us understand how decisions are made and rewards are allocated in organizations.

Montague and Morais link football's values, particularly teamwork, to those associated with business. Like corporate workers, the ideal players are diligent and dedicated to the team. Within corporations, however, decision making is complicated, and workers aren't always rewarded for their dedication and good job performance. Decisions are simpler and rewards are more consistent in football, these anthropologists contend, and this helps explain its popularity. Even if we can't figure out how Citibank and Microsoft run, any fan can become an expert on football's rules, teams, scores, statistics, and patterns of play. Even more important, football suggests that the values stressed by business really do pay off. Teams whose members work hardest, show the most spirit, and best develop and coordinate their talents can be expected to win more often than other teams do.

Star Trek*

Star Trek, a familiar, powerful, and enduring force in American popular culture, can be used to illustrate the idea that popular media content often is derived from prominent values expressed in many other domains of culture. Americans first encountered the Starship *Enterprise* on NBC in 1966. *Star Trek* was shown in prime time for just three seasons. However, the series not only survives but thrives today in syndication, reruns, books, cassettes, and theatrical films. Revived as a regular weekly series with an entirely new cast in 1987, *Star Trek: The Next Generation* became the third most popular syndicated program in the United States (after *Wheel of Fortune* and *Jeopardy*). *Deep Space Nine* and *Voyager* have been somewhat less popular successors in the *Star Trek* family.

What does the enduring mass appeal of *Star Trek* tell us about American culture? I believe the answer to be this: *Star Trek* is a transformation of a fundamental American origin myth. The same myth shows up in the image and celebration of Thanksgiving, a distinctively American holiday. Thanksgiving sets the myth in the past, and *Star Trek* sets it in the future.

The myths of contemporary America are drawn from a variety of sources, including such popular-culture fantasies as *Star Wars, The Wizard of Oz* (see the chapter on the arts), and *Star Trek.* Our myths also include real people, particularly national ancestors, whose lives have been reinterpreted and endowed with special meaning over the generations. The media, schools, churches, communities, and parents teach the national origin myths to American children. The story of Thanksgiving, for example, continues to be important. It recounts the origin of a national holiday celebrated by Protestants, Catholics, and Jews. All those denominations share a belief in the Old Testament God, and they find it appropriate to thank God for their blessings.

Again and again, Americans have heard idealized retellings of that epochal early harvest. We have learned how Indians taught the Pilgrims to farm in the New World. Grateful Pilgrims then invited the Indians to share their first Thanksgiving. Native American and European labor, techniques, and customs thus blended in that initial biethnic celebration. Annually reenacting the origin myth, the American public schools commemorate "the first Thanksgiving" as children dress up as Pilgrims, Indians, and pumpkins.

More rapidly and pervasively as the mass media grow, each generation of Americans writes its own revisionist history. Our culture constantly reinterprets the origin, nature, and meaning of national holidays. The collective consciousness of contemporary Americans includes TV-saturated memories of "the first Thanksgiving" and "the first Christmas." Our mass culture has instilled the widely shared images of a *Peanuts*-peopled Pilgrim-and-Indian "love-in."

We also conjure up a fictionalized Nativity with Mary, Joseph, Jesus, manger animals, shepherds, three eastern kings, a little drummer boy, and, in some versions, Rudolph the Red-Nosed Reindeer. Note that the interpretation of the Nativity that American culture perpetuates is yet another variation on the same dominant myth. We remember the Nativity as a Thanksgiving involving interethnic contacts (e.g., the three kings) and gift giving. It is set in Bethlehem rather than Massachusetts.

We impose our present on the past as we reinterpret quasi-historic and actual events. For the future, we do it in our science-fiction and fantasy creations. *Star Trek* places in the future what the Thanksgiving story locates in the past: *the myth of the assimilationist, incorporating, melting-pot society.* The myth says that America is distinctive not just because it is assimilationist but because it is *founded* on unity in diversity. (Our *origin* is unity in diversity. After all, we call ourselves "the United States.") Thanksgiving and *Star Trek* illustrate the credo that unity through diversity is essential for survival (whether of a harsh winter or of the perils of outer space). Americans survive by sharing the fruits of specialization.

Star Trek proclaims that the sacred principles that validate American society, because they lie at its foundation, will endure across the generations and even the centuries. The Starship *Enterprise* crew is a melting pot. Captain James Tiberius Kirk is symbolic of real history. His clearest historical prototype is Captain James Cook, whose

*This section is adapted from *Prime-Time Society: An Anthropological Analysis of Television and Culture* by Conrad Phillip Kottak. © 1990 by Wadsworth, Inc. Used by permission of the publisher.

ship, the *Endeavor,* also sought out new life and civilizations. Kirk's infrequently mentioned middle name, from the Roman general and eventual emperor, links the captain to the earth's imperial history. Kirk is also symbolic of the original Anglo-American. He runs the *Enterprise* (America is founded on free enterprise), just as laws, values, and institutions derived from England continue to guide the United States.

McCoy's Irish (or at least Gaelic) name represents the next wave, the established immigrant. Sulu is the successfully assimilated Asian-American. The African-American female character Uhura, "whose name means freedom," indicates that blacks will become full partners with all other Americans. However, Uhura was the only major female character in the original crew. Female extradomestic employment was less characteristic of American society in 1966 than it is now.

One of *Star Trek*'s constant messages is that strangers, even enemies, can become friends. Less obviously, this message is about cultural imperialism, the assumed irresistibility of American culture and institutions. Russian nationals (Chekhov) could be seduced and captured by an expansive American culture. Spock, although from Vulcan, is half human, with human qualities. We learn, therefore, that our assimilationist values will eventually not just rule the earth but extend to other planets as well. By "the next generation," Klingons, even more alien than Vulcans, and personified by Bridge Officer Worf, have joined the melting pot.

Even God is harnessed to serve American culture, in the person of Scotty. His role is that of the ancient Greek *deus ex machina.* He is a stage controller who "beams" people up and down, back and forth, from earth to the heavens. Scotty, who keeps society going, is also a servant-employee who does his engineering for management—illustrating loyalty and technical skill.

The Next Generation contains many analogues of the original characters. Several "partial people" are single-character personifications of particular human qualities represented in more complex form by the original *Star Trek* crew members. Kirk, Spock, and McCoy have all been split into multiple characters. Captain Jean-Luc Picard has the intellectual and managerial attributes of James T. Kirk. With his English accent and French name, Picard, like Kirk, draws his legitimacy from symbolic association with historic Western European empires. First Officer Riker replaces Kirk as a romantic man of action.

Spock, an alien (strange ears) who represents science, reason, and intellect, has been split in two. One half is Worf, a Klingon bridge officer whose cranial protuberances are analogous to Spock's ears. The other is Data, an android whose brain contains the sum of human knowledge. Two female characters, an empath and the ship's doctor, have replaced Dr. McCoy as the repository of healing, emotion, and feeling.

Mirroring contemporary American culture, *The Next Generation* features prominent black, female, and physically challenged characters. An African-American actor plays the Klingon Mr. Worf. Another, LeVar Burton, appears as Geordi La Forge. Although blind, Geordi manages, through a vision-enhancing visor, to see things that other people cannot. His mechanical vision expresses the characteristic American faith in technology. So does the android, Data.

During its first year, *The Next Generation* had three prominent female characters. One was the ship's doctor, a working professional with a teenage son. Another was an empath, the ultimate "helping professional." The third was the ship's security officer.

America had become more specialized, differentiated, and professional than it was in the '60s. The greater role specificity and diversity of *Next Generation* characters reflect this. Nevertheless, both series convey the central *Star Trek* message, one that dominates the culture that created them: Americans are diverse. Individual qualities, talents, and specialties divide us. However, we make our livings and survive as members of cohesive, efficient groups. We explore and advance as members of a crew, a team, an enterprise, or, most generally, a society. Our nation is founded on and endures through assimilation—effective subordination of individual differences within a smoothly functioning multiethnic team. The team is American culture. It worked in the past. It works today. It will go on working across the generations. Orderly and progressive democracy based on mutual respect is best. Inevitably, American culture will triumph over all others—by convincing and assimilating rather than conquering them. Unity in diversity guarantees human survival.

McDonald's

Each day, on the average, a new McDonald's restaurant opens somewhere in the world. The number of McDonald's outlets today far surpasses the total number of all fast-food restaurants in the United States in 1945. McDonald's has grown from a single hamburger stand in San Bernardino, California, into today's international web of thousands of outlets. Have factors less obvious to American natives than relatively low cost, fast service, and taste contributed to McDonald's success? Could it be that natives—in consuming the products and propaganda of McDonald's—are not just eating but experiencing something comparable in certain respects to participation in religious rituals? To answer this question, we must briefly review the nature of ritual.

Rituals, we know from the chapter on religion, are formal—stylized, repetitive, and stereotyped. They are performed in special places at set times. Rituals include liturgical orders—set sequences of words and actions laid down by someone other than the current performers. Rituals also convey information about participants and their cultural traditions. Performed year after year, generation after generation, rituals translate messages, values, and sentiments into action. Rituals are social acts. Inevitably, some participants are more strongly committed than others are to the beliefs on which the rituals are founded. However, just by taking part in a joint public act, people signal that they accept an order that transcends their status as mere individuals.

For many years, like millions of other Americans, I have occasionally eaten at McDonald's. Eventually I began to notice certain ritual-like aspects of Americans' behavior at these fast-food restaurants. Tell your fellow Americans that going to McDonald's is similar in some ways to going to church and their bias as natives will reveal itself in laughter, denial, or questions about your sanity. Just as football is a game and *Star Trek* is "entertainment," McDonald's, for natives, is just a place to eat. However, an analysis of what natives do at McDonald's will reveal a very high degree of formal, uniform behavior by staff members and customers alike. It is particularly interesting that this invariance in word and deed has developed without any theological doctrine. McDonald's ritual aspect is founded on 20th-century technology, particularly automobiles, television, work away from home, and the short lunch break. It is striking, nevertheless, that one commercial organization should be so much more successful than other businesses, the schools, the military, and even many religions in producing behavioral invariance. Factors other than low cost, fast service, and the taste of the food—all of which are approximated by other chains—have contributed to our acceptance of McDonald's and adherence to its rules.

Remarkably, when Americans travel abroad, even in countries noted for good food, many visit the local McDonald's outlet. The same factors that lead us to frequent McDonald's at home are responsible. Because Americans are thoroughly familiar with how to eat and more or less what they will pay at McDonald's, in its outlets overseas, they have a home away from home. In Paris, whose people aren't known for making tourists, particularly Americans, feel at home, McDonald's offers sanctuary (along with relatively clean, free restrooms). It is, after all, an originally American institution, where natives, programmed by years of prior experience, can feel completely at home. Given its international spread, McDonald's is no longer merely an American institution—a fact that McDonald's advertising has not ignored. A TV commercial linked to the 1996 Olympics (of which McDonald's was an "official sponsor") portrayed an Asian athlete finding sanctuary from an alien American culture at a McDonald's restaurant in Atlanta. For her, the ad proclaimed, McDonald's was home-culture turf.

This devotion to McDonald's rests in part on uniformities associated with its outlets: food, setting, architecture, ambience, acts, and utterances. The McDonald's symbol, the golden arches, is an almost universal landmark, as familiar to Americans as Mickey Mouse, Mr. Rogers, and the flag. A McDonald's near my university (now closed) was a brick structure whose stained-glass windows had golden arches as their central theme. Sunlight flooded in through a skylight that was like the clerestory of a church.

Americans enter a McDonald's restaurant for an ordinary, secular act—eating. However, the surroundings tell us that we are somehow apart from the variability of the world outside. We know what we are going to see, what we are going to say, and what will be said to us. We know what we will eat, how it will taste, and how much it will cost. Behind the counter, agents wear similar attire. Permissible utterances by customer and worker are written above the counter. Throughout the United States, with only minor variation, the menu is in the same place, contains the same items, and has the same prices. The food, again with only minor regional variation, is prepared according to plan and varies little in taste. Obviously, customers are limited to what they can choose. Less obviously, they are limited in what they can say. Each item has its appropriate designation: "large fry," "quarter pounder with cheese." The novice who innocently asks, "What kind of hamburgers do you have?" or "What's a Big Mac?" is out of place.

Other ritual phrases are uttered by the person behind the counter. After the customer has completed an order, if no potatoes are requested, the agent ritually asks, "Any fries?" Once food is presented and picked up, the agent conventionally says, "Have a nice day." (McDonald's has surely played a strong role in the diffusion of this cliché into every corner of contemporary American life.) Nonverbal behavior also is programmed. As customers request food, agents look back to see if the desired sandwich item is available. If not, they tell you, "That'll be a few minutes," and prepare your drink. After this, a proper agent will take the order of the next customer in line. McDonald's lore and customs are even taught at a "seminary" called Hamburger University in Illinois. Managers who attend the program pass on what they learn to the people who work in their restaurants.

It isn't simply the formality and regularity of behavior at McDonald's but its total ambience that invites comparison with ritual settings. McDonald's image makers stress "clean living" and refer to a set of values that transcends McDonald's itself. Agents submit to dress codes. Kitchens, grills, and counters should sparkle. Understandably, as the world's number-one fast-food chain, McDonald's also has evoked hostility. In 1975, the Ann Arbor campus McDonald's was the scene of a ritual rebellion—desecration by the Radical Vegetarian League, which held a "puke-in." Standing on the second-story balcony just below the clerestory, a dozen vegetarians gorged themselves on mustard and water and vomited down on the customer waiting area. McDonald's, defiled, lost many customers that day.

The formality and invariance of behavior in a demarcated setting suggest analogies between McDonald's and rituals. Furthermore, as in a ritual, participation in McDonald's occurs at specified times. In American culture, our daily food consumption is supposed to occur as three meals: breakfast, lunch, and dinner. Americans who have traveled abroad are aware that cultures differ in which meal they emphasize. In many countries, the midday meal is primary. Americans are away from home at lunchtime because of their jobs and usually take less than an hour for lunch. They view dinner as the main meal. Lunch is a lighter meal symbolized by the sandwich. McDonald's provides relatively hot and fresh sandwiches and a variety of subsidiary fare that many American palates can tolerate.

The ritual of eating at McDonald's is confined to ordinary, everyday life. Eating at McDonald's and religious feasts are in complementary distribution in American life. That is, when one occurs, the other doesn't. Most Americans would consider it inappropriate to eat at a fast-food restaurant on Christmas, Thanksgiving, Easter, or Passover. Our culture regards these as family days, occasions when relatives and close friends get together. However, although Americans neglect McDonald's on holidays, television reminds us that McDonald's still endures, that it will welcome us back once our holiday is over. The television presence of McDonald's is particularly evident on such occasions—whether through a float in the Macy's Thanksgiving Day parade or through sponsorship of special programs, particularly "family entertainment."

Although Burger King, Wendy's, and Arby's compete with McDonald's for the fast-food business, none has equaled McDonald's success. The explanation may lie in the particularly skillful ways in which McDonald's advertising plays up the features just discussed. For decades, its commercials have been varied to appeal to different audiences. On Saturday morning television, with its steady stream of cartoons, McDonald's has been a ubiquitous sponsor. The McDonald's commercials for children's shows usually differ from the ones adults see in the evening and on sports programs. Children are reminded of McDonald's through fantasy characters, headed by clown

Ronald McDonald. Children can meet "McDonaldland" characters again at outlets. Their pictures appear on cookie boxes and plastic cups. Children also have a chance to meet Ronald McDonald as actors scatter visits throughout the country. One can even rent a Ronald for a birthday party.

Adult advertising has different but equally effective themes. Breakfast at McDonald's has been promoted by a fresh-faced, sincere, happy, clean-cut young woman. Actors gambol on ski slopes or in mountain pastures. The single theme, however, that for years has run through the commercials is personalism. McDonald's, the commercials drone on, is something other than a fast-food restaurant. It's a warm, friendly place where you are graciously welcomed and feel at home, where your children won't get into trouble. McDonald's commercials tell you that you aren't simply an anonymous face in an amorphous crowd. You find respite from a hectic and impersonal society, the break you deserve. Your individuality and dignity are respected at McDonald's.

McDonald's advertising tries to de-emphasize the fact that the chain is a commercial organization. One jingle proclaimed "You, you're the one; we're fixin' breakfast for ya"—not "We're making millions off ya." Commercials make McDonald's seem like a charitable organization by stressing its program of community good works. "Family" television entertainment is often "brought to you by McDonald's." McDonald's commercials regularly tell us that it supports and works to maintain the values of American family life.

I am not at all arguing here that McDonald's has become a religion. I am merely suggesting that specific ways in which Americans participate in McDonald's bear analogies to religious systems involving myth, symbol, and ritual. Just as in rituals, participation in McDonald's requires temporary subordination of individual differences in a social and cultural collectivity. In a land of ethnic, social, economic, and religious diversity, we demonstrate that we share something with millions of others. Furthermore, as in rituals, participation in McDonald's is linked to a cultural system that transcends the chain itself. By eating there, we say something about ourselves as Americans, about our acceptance of certain collective values, customs, and ways of living.

Anthropology and "Pop" Culture

The examples considered in this appendix are shared cultural forms that have appeared and spread rapidly because of major changes in the material conditions of American life—particularly work organization, communication, and transportation. Most contemporary Americans deem at least one automobile a necessity. Televisions outnumber toilets in our households. Through the mass media, institutions such as sports, movies, TV shows, amusement parks, and fast-food restaurants have become powerful elements of national culture. They provide a framework of common expectations, experiences, and behavior overriding differences in region, class, formal religious affiliation, political sentiments, gender, ethnic group, and place of residence. Although some of us may not like these changes, it's difficult to deny their significance.

The rise of these institutions is linked not just to the mass media but also to decreasing participation in traditional religion and the weakening of ties based on kinship, marriage, and community within industrial society. Neither a single church, nor a strong central government, nor segmentary lineage organization unites most Americans.

These dimensions of contemporary culture are dismissed as passing, trivial, or "pop" by some. However, because millions of people share them, they deserve and are receiving scholarly attention. Such studies help fulfill the promise that by studying anthropology, we can learn more about ourselves.

bibliography

Abelmann, N., and J. Lie
1995 *Blue Dreams: Korean Americans and the Los Angeles Riots.* Cambridge, MA: Harvard University Press.

Abiodun, R.
1996 Foreword. In *Art and Religion in Africa,* by R. I. J. Hackett, pp. viii–ix. London: Cassell.

Abu-Lughod, J. L.
1989 *Before European Hegemony: The World System A.D. 1250–1350.* New York: Oxford University Press.

Adams, R. M.
1981 *Heartland of Cities.* Chicago: Aldine.

Adepegba, C. O.
1991 The Yoruba Concept of Art and Its Significance in the Holistic View of Art as Applied to African Art. *African Notes* 15: 1–6.

Agar, M. H.
1980 *The Professional Stranger: An Informal Introduction to Ethnography.* New York: Academic Press.

Ahmed, A. S.
1992 *Postmodernism and Islam: Predicament and Promise.* New York: Routledge.

Akazawa, T.
1980 *The Japanese Paleolithic: A Techno-Typological Study.* Tokyo: Rippo Shobo.

Akazawa, T., and C. M. Aikens, eds.
1986 *Prehistoric Hunter-Gatherers in Japan: New Research Methods.* Tokyo: University of Tokyo Press.

Albert, B.
1989 Yanomami "Violence": Inclusive Fitness or Ethnographer's Representation? *Current Anthropology* 30: 637–640.

Amadiume, I.
1987 *Male Daughters, Female Husbands.* Atlantic Highlands, NJ: Zed.
1997 *Reinventing Africa: Matriarchy, Religion, and Culture.* New York: Zed.

American Almanac 1994–1995
1994 *Statistical Abstract of the United States,* 114th ed. Austin, TX: Reference Press.

American Almanac 1996–1997
1996 *Statistical Abstract of the United States,* 116th ed. Austin, TX: Reference Press.

American Anthropological Association
AAA Guide: A Guide to Departments, a Directory of Members. (Formerly *Guide to Departments of Anthropology.*) Published annually by the American Anthropological Association, Washington, DC.
Anthropology Newsletter. Published 9 times annually by the American Anthropological Association, Washington, DC.
General Anthropology: Bulletin of the Council for General Anthropology.

Amick III, B., S. Levine, A. R. Tarlov, and D. C. Walsh, eds.
1995 *Society and Health.* New York: Oxford University Press.

Anderson, B.
1991 *Imagined Communities: Reflections on the Origin and Spread of Nationalism,* rev. ed. London: Verso.
1998 *The Spectre of Comparisons: Nationalism, Southeast Asia, and the World.* New York: Verso.

Anderson, R.
1989 *Art in Small Scale Societies.* Upper Saddle River, NJ: Prentice Hall.
1990 *Calliope's Sisters: A Comparative Study of Philosophy of Art.* Upper Saddle River, NJ: Prentice Hall.
2000 *American Muse: Anthropological Excursions into Art and Aesthetics.* Upper Saddle River, NJ: Prentice Hall.

Anderson, R., and K. Field, eds.
1993 *Art in Small-Scale Societies: Contemporary Readings.* Upper Saddle River, NJ: Prentice Hall.
1996 *Magic, Science, and Health: The Aims and Achievements of Medical Anthropology.* Fort Worth: Harcourt Brace.

Angier, N.
1998 When Nature Discovers the Same Design Over and Over, Lookalike Creatures Spark Evolutionary Debate. *The New York Times,* December 15, pp. D1, D6.

Annenberg/CPB Exhibits
2000 "Collapse, Why Do Civilizations Fall?" http://www.learner.org/exhibits/collapse/.

Aoki, M. Y., and M. B. Dardess, eds.
1981 *As the Japanese See It: Past and Present.* Honolulu: University Press of Hawaii.

Appadurai, A.
1990 Disjuncture and Difference in the Global Cultural Economy. *Public Culture* 2(2): 1–24.
1991 Global Ethnoscapes: Notes and Queries for a Transnational Anthropology. In *Recapturing Anthropology: Working in the Present,* ed. R. G. Fox, pp. 191–210. Santa Fe: School of American Research Advanced Seminar Series.

Appel, R., and P. Muysken
1987 *Language Contact and Bilingualism.* London: Edward Arnold.

Appell, G. N.
1978 *Ethical Dilemmas in Anthropological Inquiry: A Case Book.* Waltham, MA: Crossroads Press.

Appiah, K. A.
1990 Racisms. In *Anatomy of Racism,* ed. David Theo Goldberg, pp. 3–17. Minneapolis: University of Minnesota Press.

Applebome, P.
1996 English Unique to Blacks Is Officially Recognized. *The New York Times,* December 20, www.nytimes.com.
1997 Dispute over Ebonics Reflects a Volatile Mix. *The New York Times,* March 1, www.nytimes.com.

Arce, A., and N. Long, eds.
2000 *Anthropology, Development, and Modernities: Exploring Discourses, Counter-Tendencies, and Violence.* New York: Routledge.

Archer, M. S.
1996 *Culture and Agency: The Place of Culture in Social Theory,* rev ed. Cambridge: Cambridge University Press.

Arens, W.
1981 Professional Football: An American Symbol and Ritual. In *The American Dimension: Cultural Myths and Social Realities,* 2nd ed., ed. W. Arens and S. P. Montague, pp. 1–10. Sherman Oaks, CA: Alfred.

Arens, W., and S. P. Montague
1981 *The American Dimension: Cultural Myths and Social Realities,* 2nd ed. Sherman Oaks, CA: Alfred.

Arensberg, C.
1987 Theoretical Contributions of Industrial and Development Studies. In *Applied Anthropology in America,* ed. E. M. Eddy and W. L. Partridge. New York: Columbia University Press.

Arnold, B., and B. Gibson, eds.
1995 *Celtic Chiefdom, Celtic State.* New York: Cambridge University Press.

Arrighi, G.
1994 *The Long Twentieth Century: Money, Power, and the Origins of Our Times.* New York: Verso.

Ashcroft, B., G. Griffiths, and H. Tiffin
1989 *The Empire Writes Back: Theory and Practice in Post-colonial Literatures.* New York: Routledge.

Ashmore, W., and R. Sharer
2000 *Discovering Our Past: A Brief Introduction to Archaeology,* 3rd ed. Mountain View, CA: Mayfield.

Bailey, E. J.
2000 *Medical Anthropology and African American Health.* Westport, CT: Bergin and Garvey.

Bailey, R. C.
1990 *The Behavioral Ecology of Efe Pygmy Men in the Ituri Forest, Zaire.* Ann Arbor, MI: Anthropological Papers, Museum of Anthropology, University of Michigan, no. 86.

Bailey, R. C., G. Head, M. Jenike, B. Owen, R. Rechtman, and E. Zechenter
1989 Hunting and Gathering in Tropical Rain Forests: Is It Possible? *American Anthropologist* 91: 59–82.

Baker, P. T.
1978 *The Biology of High Altitude Peoples.* New York: Cambridge University Press.

Baker, P. T., and J. S. Weiner, eds.
1966 *The Biology of Human Adaptability.* Oxford: Oxford University Press.

Bakhtin, M.
1984 *Rabelais and His World.* Translated by Helen Iswolksy. Bloomington: Indiana University Press.

Balick, M. J., and P. A. Cox
1996 *Plants, People, and Culture: The Science of Ethnobotany.* New York: Scientific American Library.

Balick, M. J., E. Elisabetsky, and S. A. Laird
1995 *Medicinal Resources of the Tropical Forest: Biodiversity and Its Importance to Human Health.* New York: Columbia University Press.

Banton, M.
1957 *West African City. A Study in Tribal Life in Freetown.* London: Oxford University Press.

Bar-Yosef, O.
1987 Pleistocene Connections between Africa and Southwest Asia: An Archaeological Perspective. *African Archaeological Review* 5: 29–38.

Barash, D. P.
1982 *Sociobiology and Behavior,* 2nd ed. Amsterdam: Elsevier.

Barlett, P. F., ed.
1980 *Agricultural Decision Making: Anthropological Contribution to Rural Development.* New York: Academic Press.

Barnaby, F., ed.
1984 *Future War: Armed Conflict in the Next Decade.* London: M. Joseph.

Barnard, A.
1979 Kalahari Settlement Patterns. In *Social and Ecological Systems,* ed. P. Burnham and R. Ellen, pp. 131–144. New York: Academic Press.

Barnouw, V.
1985 *Culture and Personality,* 4th ed. Belmont, CA: Wadsworth.

Baron, D.
1986 *Grammar and Gender.* New Haven, CT: Yale University Press.

Barringer, F.
1989 32 Million Lived in Poverty in '88, a Figure Unchanged. *The New York Times,* October 19, p. 18.
1992 New Census Data Show More Children Living in Poverty. *The New York Times,* May 29, pp. A1, A12, A13.

Barry, H., M. K. Bacon, and I. L. Child
1959 Relation of Child Training to Subsistence Economy. *American Anthropologist* 61: 51–63.

Barth, F.
1964 *Nomads of South Persia: The Basseri Tribe of the Khamseh Confederacy.* London: Allen & Unwin.
1968 (orig. 1958). Ecologic Relations of Ethnic Groups in Swat, North Pakistan. In *Man in Adaptation: The Cultural Present,* ed. Yehudi Cohen, pp. 324–331. Chicago: Aldine.
1969 *Ethnic Groups and Boundaries: The Social Organization of Cultural Difference.* London: Allen and Unwin.

Batalla, G. B.
1966 Conservative Thought in Applied Anthropology: A Critique. *Human Organization* 25: 89–92.

Bates, D. G.
2001 *Human Adaptive Strategies: Ecology, Culture, and Politics,* 2nd ed. Boston: Allyn & Bacon.

Bateson, M. C.
1984 *With a Daughter's Eye: A Memoir of Margaret Mead and Gregory Bateson.* New York: William Morrow.

Beeman, W.
1986 *Language, Status, and Power in Iran.* Bloomington: Indiana University Press.

Begun, D. R., C. V. Ward, and M. D. Rose
1997 *Description: Function, Phylogeny, and Fossils: Miocene Hominoid Evolution and Adaptations.* New York: Plenum.

Behar, R.
1993 *Translated Woman: Crossing the Border with Esperanza's Story.* Boston: Beacon.

Behar, R., and D. A. Gordon, eds.
1995 *Women Writing Culture.* Berkeley: University of California Press.

Bell, W.
1981 Neocolonialism. In *Encyclopedia of Sociology,* p. 193. Guilford, CT: DPG Publishing.

Bellah, R. N.
1978 Religious Evolution. In *Reader in Comparative Religion: An Anthropological Approach,* 4th ed., ed. W. A. Lessa and E. Z. Vogt, pp. 36–50. New York: Harper & Row.

Benedict, B.
1970 Pluralism and Stratification. In *Essays in Comparative Social Stratification,* ed. L. Plotnicov and A. Tuden, pp. 29–41. Pittsburgh: University of Pittsburgh Press.

Benedict, R.
1940 *Race, Science and Politics.* New York: Modern Age Books.
1946 *The Chrysanthemum and the Sword.* Boston: Houghton Mifflin.
1959 (orig. 1934). *Patterns of Culture.* New York: New American Library.

Bennett, J. W.
1969 *Northern Plainsmen: Adaptive Strategy and Agrarian Life.* Chicago: Aldine.

Bennett, J. W., and J. R. Bowen, eds.
1988 *Production and Autonomy: Anthropological Studies and Critiques of Development.* Monographs in Economic Anthropology, no. 5, Society for Economic Anthropology. New York: University Press of America.

Berg, B. L.
1997 *Qualitative Research Methods for the Social Sciences,* 3rd ed. Boston: Allyn & Bacon.

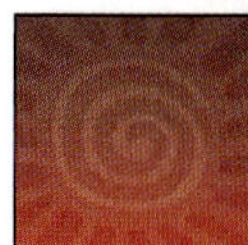

Berlin, B. D., E. Breedlove, and P. H. Raven
1974 *Principles of Tzeltal Plant Classification: An Introduction to the Botanical Ethnography of a Mayan-Speaking People of Highland Chiapas*. New York: Academic Press.

Berlin, B. D., and P. Kay
1969 *Basic Color Terms: Their Universality and Evolution*. Berkeley: University of California Press.
1991 *Basic Color Terms: Their Universality and Evolution*. Berkeley, CA: University of California Press.
1992 *Basic Color Terms: Their Universality and Evolution*, 2nd ed. Berkeley: University of California Press.
1999 *Basic Color Terms: Their Universality and Evolution*. Stanford, CA: Center for the Study of Language and Information.

Bernard, H. R.
1994 *Research Methods in Cultural Anthropology*, 2nd ed. Thousand Oaks, CA: Sage.

Bernard, H. R., ed.
1998 *Handbook of Methods in Cultural Anthropology*. Walnut Creek, CA: Altamira.

Berreman, G. D.
1962 Pahari Polyandry: A Comparison. *American Anthropologist* 64: 60–75.
1975 Himalayan Polyandry and the Domestic Cycle. *American Ethnologist* 2: 127–138.

Bettelheim, B.
1975 *The Uses of Enchantment: The Meaning and Importance of Fairy Tales*. New York: Vintage.

Binford, L. R.
1968 Post-Pleistocene Adaptations. In *New Perspectives in Archeology*, ed. S. R. Binford and L. R. Binford, pp. 313–341. Chicago: Aldine.
1981 *Bones. Ancient Men and Modern Myths*. New York: Academic Press.

Binford, L. R., and S. R. Binford
1979 Stone Tools and Human Behavior. In *Human Ancestors, Readings from Scientific American*, ed. G. L. Isaac and R. E. F. Leakey, pp. 92–101. San Francisco: W. H. Freeman.

Bird-David, N.
1992 Beyond "The Original Affluent Society": A Culturalist Reformulation. *Current Anthropology* 33(1): 25–47.

Birdsell, J. B.
1981 *Human Evolution: An Introduction to the New Physical Anthropology*, 3rd ed. Boston: HarperCollins.

Bjuremalm, H.
1997 Rättvisa kan skipas i Rwanda: Folkmordet 1994 går att förklara och analysera på samma sätt som förintelsen av judarna. *Dagens Nyheter* [06-03-1997, p. B3].

Blackwood, E.
2000 *Webs of Power: Women, Kin, and Community in a Sumatran Village*. Lanham, MD: Rowman and Littlefield.

Blackwood, E., and S. Wieringa, eds.
1999 *Female Desires: Same-Sex Relations and Transgender Practices across Cultures*. New York: Columbia University Press.

Blanton, R. E.
1999 *Ancient Oaxaca: The Monte Alban State*. New York: Cambridge University Press.

Blanton, R. E., S. A. Kowalewski, G. M. Feinman, and L. M. Finsten, eds.
1993 *Ancient Mesoamerica: A Comparison of Change in Three Regions*, 2nd ed. New York: Cambridge University Press.

Bloch, M., ed.
1975 *Political Language and Oratory in Traditional Societies*. London: Academic.

Blum, H. F.
1961 Does the Melanin Pigment of Human Skin Have Adaptive Value? *Quarterly Review of Biology* 36: 50–63.

Boas, F.
1966 (orig. 1940). *Race, Language, and Culture*. New York: Free Press.

Boaz, N. T.
1993 *Quarry: Closing In on the Missing Link*. New York: Free Press.
1997 *Eco Homo: How the Human Being Emerged from the Cataclysmic History of the Earth*. New York: Basic Books.
1999 *Essentials of Biological Anthropology*. Upper Saddle River, N.J.: Prentice Hall.

Bock, P. K.
1980 *Continuities in Psychological Anthropology*. San Francisco: W. H. Freeman.

Bodley, J. H.
1985 *Anthropology and Contemporary Human Problems*, 2nd ed. Mountain View, CA: Mayfield.
1995 *Anthropology and Contemporary Human Problems*, 3rd ed. Mountain View, CA: Mayfield.
1999 *Victims of Progress*, 4th ed. Mountain View, CA: Mayfield.

2000 *Anthropology and Contemporary Human Problems,* 4th ed. Mountain View, CA: Mayfield.

Bodley, J. H., ed.
1988 *Tribal Peoples and Development Issues: A Global Overview.* Mountain View, CA: Mayfield.

Bogin, B.
1999 *Patterns of Human Growth,* 2nd ed. New York: Cambridge University Press.
2001 *The Growth of Humanity.* New York: John Wiley.

Bogoras, W.
1904 The Chukchee. In *The Jesup North Pacific Expedition,* ed. F. Boas. New York: Memoir of the American Museum of Natural History.

Bogucki, P. I.
1988 *Forest Farmers and Stockherders: Early Agriculture and Its Consequences in North-Central Europe.* New York: Cambridge University Press.

Bohannan, P.
1955 Some Principles of Exchange and Investment among the Tiv. *American Anthropologist* 57: 60–70.
1971 Artist and Critic in an African Society. In *Anthropology and Art: Readings in Cross-Cultural Aesthetics,* ed. C. Otten, pp. 172–181. Austin, TX: University of Texas Press.
1995 *How Culture Works.* New York: Free Press.

Bohannan, P., and J. Middleton, eds.
1968 *Marriage, Family, and Residence.* Garden City, NY: Natural History Press.

Bolton, R.
1981 Susto, Hostility, and Hypoglycemia. *Ethnology* 20(4): 227–258.

Bond, G. C., J. Kreniske, I. Susser, and J. Vincent, eds.
1996 *AIDS in Africa and the Caribbean.* Boulder, CO: Westview.

Bonvillain, N.
1997 *Language, Culture, and Communication: The Meaning of Messages,* 2nd ed. Upper Saddle River, NJ: Prentice Hall.
1998 *Women and Men: Cultural Constructions of Gender,* 2nd ed. Upper Saddle River, NJ: Prentice Hall.
2001 *Women and Men: Cultural Constructions of Gender,* 3rd ed. Upper Saddle River, NJ: Prentice Hall.

Borneman, J.
1998 *Subversions of International Order: Studies in the Political Anthropology of Culture.* Albany: State University of New York Press.

Boserup, E.
1965 *The Conditions of Agricultural Growth.* Chicago: Aldine.
1970 *Women's Role in Economic Development.* London: Allen and Unwin.

Bourdieu, P.
1977 *Outline of a Theory of Practice.* Translated by Richard Nice. Cambridge: Cambridge University Press.
1982 *Ce Que Parler Veut Dire.* Paris: Fayard.
1984 *Distinction: A Social Critique of the Judgment of Taste.* Translated by R. Nice. Cambridge, MA: Harvard University Press.

Bourguignon, E.
1979 *Psychological Anthropology: An Introduction to Human Nature and Cultural Differences.* New York: Harcourt Brace Jovanovich.

Bourque, S. C., and K. B. Warren
1981 *Women of the Andes: Patriarchy and Social Change in Two Peruvian Villages.* Ann Arbor: University of Michigan Press.
1987 Technology, Gender and Development. *Daedalus* 116(4): 173–197.

Bower, J., and D. Lubell, eds.
1988 *Prehistoric Cultures and Environments in the Late Quaternary of Africa.* Cambridge Monographs in African Archaeology, 26. Oxford, England: B.A.R.

Brace, C. L.
1964 A Nonracial Approach towards the Understanding of Human Diversity. In *The Concept of Race,* ed. A. Montagu, pp. 103–152. New York: Free Press.
1995 *The Stages of Human Evolution,* 5th ed. Englewood Cliffs, NJ: Prentice Hall.
2000 *Evolution in an Anthropological View.* Walnut Creek, CA: AltaMira.

Brace, C. L., and F. B. Livingstone
1971 On Creeping Jensenism. In *Race and Intelligence,* ed. C. L. Brace, G. R. Gamble, and J. T. Bond, pp. 64–75. Anthropological Studies, no. 8. Washington, DC: American Anthropological Association.

Bradley, C., C. Moore, M. Burton, and D. White
1990 A Cross-Cultural Historical Analysis of Subsistence Change. *American Anthropologist* 92(2): 447–457.

Brady, I., ed.
1983 Special Section: Speaking in the Name of the Real: Freeman and Mead on Samoa. *American Anthropologist* 85: 908–947.

Braidwood, R. J.
1975 *Prehistoric Men*, 8th ed. Glenview, IL: Scott, Foresman.

Braudel, F.
1973 *Capitalism and Material Life: 1400–1800.* Translated by M. Kochan. London: Weidenfeld and Nicolson.
1981 *Civilization and Capitalism, 15th–18th Century.* Volume I: *The Structure of Everyday Life: The Limits.* Translated by S. Reynolds. New York: Harper & Row.
1982 *Civilization and Capitalism, 15th–18th Century.* Volume II: *The Wheels of Commerce.* New York: HarperCollins.
1984 *Civilization and Capitalism, 15th–18th Century.* Volume III: *The Perspective of the World.* New York: HarperCollins.
1992 *Civilization and Capitalism, 15th–18th Century.* Volume III: *The Perspective of the World.* Berkeley, CA: University of California Press.

Brenneis, D.
1988 Language and Disputing. *Annual Review of Anthropology* 17: 221–237.

Brim, J. A., and D. H. Spain
1974 *Research Design in Anthropology.* New York: Harcourt Brace Jovanovich.

Brogger, J.
1992 *Nazaré: Women and Men in a Prebureaucratic Portuguese Fishing Village.* Fort Worth: Harcourt Brace.

Bronfenbrenner, U.
1975 Nature with Nurture: A Reinterpretation of the Evidence. In *Race and IQ*, ed. A. Montagu, pp. 114–144. New York: Oxford University Press.

Brooke, J.
1992 Rio's New Day in Sun Leaves Laplander Limp. *The New York Times,* June 1, p. A7.

Brown, D.
1991 *Human Universals.* New York: McGraw-Hill.

Brown, J. K.
1975 Iroquois Women: An Ethnohistoric Note. In *Toward an Anthropology of Women*, ed. R. Reiter, pp. 235–251. New York: Monthly Review Press.

Brown, K. M.
1991 *Mama Lola: A Vodou Priestess in Brooklyn.* Berkeley: University of California Press.

Brown, P. J.
1998 *Understanding and Applying Medical Anthropology.* Mountain View, CA: Mayfield.

Brown, R. W.
1958 *Words and Things.* Glencoe, IL: Free Press.

Brumfiel, E. M.
1980 Specialization, Market Exchange, and the Aztec State: A View from Huexotla. *Current Anthropology* 21(4): 459–478.

Bryant, B., and P. Mohai
1991 Race, Class, and Environmental Quality in the Detroit Area. In *Environmental Racism: Issues and Dilemmas,* ed. B. P. Bryant and Mohai. Ann Arbor: University of Michigan Office of Minority Affairs.

Bryson, K.
1996 Household and Family Characteristics: March 1995, P20-488, November 26, 1996. United States Department of Commerce, Bureau of Census, Public Information Office, CB96-195.

Buchler, I. R., and H. A. Selby
1968 *Kinship and Social Organization: An Introduction to Theory and Method.* New York: Macmillan.

Burke, P., and R. Porter
1987 *The Social History of Language.* Cambridge: Cambridge University Press.

Burling, R.
1970 *Man's Many Voices: Language in Its Cultural Context.* New York: Harcourt Brace Jovanovich.

Burns, J. F.
1992*a* Bosnian Strife Cuts Old Bridges of Trust. *The New York Times,* May 22, pp. A1, A6.
1992*b* A Serb, Fighting Serbs, Defends Sarajevo. *The New York Times,* July 12, Section 4, p. E3.

Burton, F. D., and M. Eaton
1995*a* *The Multimedia Guide to Non-Human Primates.* Englewood Cliffs, NJ: Prentice Hall. A CD-ROM combining photos, illustrations, video, sound, and text—presenting over 200 species of nonhuman primates.
1995*b* *The Guide to Non-Human Primates.* Englewood Cliffs, NJ: Prentice-Hall. The print version of the above.

Buvinic, M.
1995 The Feminization of Poverty? Research and Policy Needs. In *Reducing Poverty through Labour Market Policies.* Geneva: International Institute for Labour Studies.

Caldeira, T. P. R.
1996 Fortified Enclaves: The New Urban Segregation. *Public Culture* 8(2): 303–328.

Calhoun, C., D. Light, and S. Keller
1997 *Sociology*, 7th ed. New York: McGraw-Hill.

Campbell, B. G.
1998 *Human Evolution: An Introduction to Man's Adaptations*, 4th ed. New York: Aldine de Gruyter.

Campbell, B. G., and J. D. Loy, eds.
2000 *Humankind Emerging*, 8th ed. New York: Longman.

Cann, R. L., M. Stoneking, and A. C. Wilson
1987 Mitochondrial DNA and Human Evolution. *Nature* 325: 31–36.

Carneiro, R. L.
1956 Slash-and-Burn Agriculture: A Closer Look at Its Implications for Settlement Patterns. In *Men and Cultures*, Selected Papers of the Fifth International Congress of Anthropological and Ethnological Sciences, pp. 229–234. Philadelphia: University of Pennsylvania Press.
1968 (orig. 1961). Slash-and-Burn Cultivation among the Kuikuru and Its Implications for Cultural Development in the Amazon Basin. In *Man in Adaptation: The Cultural Present*, ed. Y. A. Cohen, pp. 131–145. Chicago: Aldine.
1970 A Theory of the Origin of the State. *Science* 69: 733–738.
1990 Chiefdom-Level Warfare as Exemplified in Fiji and the Cauca Valley. In *The Anthropology of War*, ed. J. Haas, pp. 190–211. Cambridge: Cambridge University Press.
1991 The Nature of the Chiefdom as Revealed by Evidence from the Cauca Valley of Colombia. In *Profiles in Cultural Evolution;* ed. A. T. Rambo and K. Gillogly, *Anthropological Papers* 85, pp. 167–190. Ann Arbor: University of Michigan Museum of Anthropology.

Carrier, J.
1995 *De Los Otros: Intimacy and Homosexuality among Mexican Men: Hidden in the Blood.* New York: Columbia University Press.

Carter, J.
1988 Freed from Keepers and Cages, Chimps Come of Age on Baboon Island. *Smithsonian*, June, pp. 36–48.

Cartmill, M.
1974 Rethinking Primate Origins. *Science* (April 26): 436–437.
1992 New Views on Primate Origins. *Evolutionary Anthropology* 1: 105–111.

Carver, T.
1996 *Gender Is Not a Synonym for Women.* Boulder, CO: Lynne Reinner.

Casper, L., and K. Bryson
1998 Growth in Single Fathers Outpaces Growth in Single Mothers, Census Bureau Reports. http://www.census.gov/Press-Release/cb98-228.html.

Casson, R.
1983 Schemata in Cognitive Anthropology. *Annual Review of Anthropology* 12: 429–462.

Cavalli-Sforza, L. L.
1977 *Elements of Human Genetics*, 2nd ed. Menlo Park, CA: W. A. Benjamin.

Cavalli-Sforza, L. L., P. Menozzi, and A. Piazza
1994 *The History and Geography of Human Genes.* Princeton, NJ: Princeton University Press.

Cernea, M., ed.
1991 *Putting People First: Sociological Variables in Rural Development*, 2nd ed. New York: Oxford University Press (published for The World Bank).

Chagnon, N. A.
1968 *Yanomamo: The Fierce People*. New York: Holt, Rinehart, and Winston.
1992 (orig. 1983) *Yanomamo: The Fierce People*, 4th ed. New York: Harcourt Brace.
1997 *Yanomamö*, 5th ed. Fort Worth: Harcourt Brace.

Chagnon, N. A., and W. Irons, eds.
1979 *Evolutionary Biology and Human Social Behavior: An Anthropological Perspective.* North Scituate, MA: Duxbury.

Chambers, E.
1985 *Applied Anthropology: A Practical Guide.* Englewood Cliffs, NJ: Prentice Hall.
1987 Applied Anthropology in the Post-Vietnam Era: Anticipations and Ironies. *Annual Review of Anthropology* 16: 309–337.
2000 *Native Tours: The Anthropology of Travel and Tourism*. Prospect Heights, IL: Waveland.

Chambers, E., ed.
1997 *Tourism and Culture: An Applied Perspective.* Albany: State University of New York Press.

Champion, T., and C. Gamble, eds.
1984 *Prehistoric Europe*. New York: Academic Press.

Chang, K. C.
1977 *The Archaeology of Ancient China*. New Haven: Yale University Press.

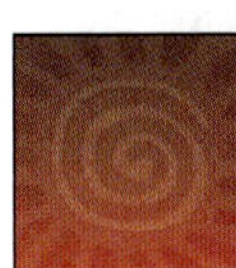

Chatty, D.
1996 *Mobile Pastoralists: Development Planning and Social Change in Oman.* New York: Columbia University Press.

Cheater, A. P., ed.
1999 *The Anthropology of Power: Empowerment and Disempowerment in Changing Structures.* New York: Routledge.

Cheney, D. L., and R. M. Seyfarth
1990 In the Minds of Monkeys: What Do They Know and How Do They Know It? *Natural History,* September, pp. 38–46.

Cheney, D. L., R. M. Seyfarth, B. B. Smuts, and R. W. Wrangham
1987 The Study of Primate Societies. In *Primate Societies,* ed. B. B. Smuts, D. L. Cheney, R. M. Seyfarth, R. W. Wrangham, and T. T. Struhsaker, pp. 1–8. Chicago: University of Chicago Press.

Cherlin, A. J.
1992 *Marriage, Divorce, Remarriage.* Cambridge, MA: Harvard University Press.

Child, A. B., and I. L. Child
1993 *Religion and Magic in the Lives of Traditional Peoples.* Englewood Cliffs, NJ: Prentice Hall.

Childe, V. G.
1951 *Man Makes Himself.* New York: New American Library.

Chiseri-Strater, E., and B. S. Sunstein
1997 *Fieldworking: Reading and Writing Research.* Upper Saddle River, NJ: Prentice Hall.

Chomsky, N.
1955 *Syntactic Structures.* The Hague: Mouton.

Cigno, A.
1994 *Economics of the Family.* New York: Oxford University Press.

Ciochon, R. L.
1983 Hominoid Cladistics and the Ancestry of Modern Apes and Humans. In *New Interpretations of Ape and Human Ancestry,* ed. R. L. Ciochon and R. S. Corruccini, pp. 783–843. New York: Plenum.

Ciochon, R. L., J. Olsen, and J. James
1990 *Other Origins: The Search for the Giant Ape in Human Prehistory.* New York: Bantam Books.

Clammer, J., ed.
1976 *The New Economic Anthropology.* New York: St. Martin's.

Clark, J. D., and S. A. Brandt
1984 *From Hunters to Farmers: The Causes and Consequences of Food Production in Africa.* Berkeley: University of California Press.

Clarke, S. C.
1995 Advance Report of Final Divorce Statistics, 1989 and 1990. *Monthly Vital Statistics Report,* v. 43, nos. 8, 9. Hyattsville, MD: National Center for Health Statistics.

Clifford, J.
1982 *Person and Myth: Maurice Leenhardt in the Melanesian World.* Berkeley: University of California Press.
1988 *The Predicament of Culture: Twentieth-Century Ethnography, Literature, and Art.* Cambridge: Harvard University Press.

Clifton, J. A.
1970 *Applied Anthropology: Readings in the Uses of the Science of Man.* Boston: Houghton Mifflin.

Coates, J.
1986 *Women, Men, and Language.* London: Longman.

Cody, D.
1998 British Empire. http://www.stg.brown.edu/projects/hypertext/landow/victorian/history/Empire.htm1, May 18.

Coe, M. D., and K. Flannery
1964 Microenvironments and Mesoamerican Prehistory. *Science* 143: 650–654.

Cohen, M.
1998 *Culture of Intolerance: Chauvinism, Class, and Racism.* New Haven: Yale University Press.

Cohen, M. N., and G. J. Armelagos, eds.
1984 *Paleopathology at the Origins of Agriculture.* New York: Academic Press.

Cohen, Roger
1995 Serbs Shift Opens a Chance for Peace, a U.S. Envoy Says. *The New York Times,* September 1, pp. A1, A6.

Cohen, Ronald
1967 *The Kanuri of Bornu.* New York: Harcourt Brace Jovanovich.

Cohen, Ronald, and E. R. Service, eds.
1978 *Origins of the State: The Anthropology of Political Evolution.* Philadelphia: Institute for the Study of Human Issues.

Cohen, Y. A.
1974*a* *Man in Adaptation: The Cultural Present,* 2nd ed. Chicago: Aldine.

1974*b* Culture as Adaptation. In *Man in Adaptation: The Cultural Present,* 2nd ed., ed. Y. A. Cohen, pp. 45–68. Chicago: Aldine.

Cole, S.
1975 *Leakey's Luck: The Life of Louis Bazett Leakey, 1903–1972.* New York: Harcourt Brace Jovanovich.

Collier, J. F.
1997 *From Duty to Desire: Remaking Families in a Spanish Village.* Princeton, NJ: Princeton University Press.

Collier, J. F., ed.
1988 *Marriage and Inequality in Classless Societies.* Stanford, CA: Stanford University Press.

Collier, J. F., and S. J. Yanagisako, eds.
1987 *Gender and Kinship: Essays toward a Unified Analysis.* Stanford, CA: Stanford University Press.

Collins, T. W.
1989 Rural Economic Development in Two Tennessee Counties: A Racial Dimension. Paper presented at the annual meetings of the American Anthropological Association, Washington, DC.

Colson, E.
1971 *The Social Consequences of Resettlement: The Impact of the Kariba Resettlement on the Gwembe Tonga.* Manchester: Manchester University Press.

Colson, E., and T. Scudder
1975 New Economic Relationships between the Gwembe Valley and the Line of Rail. In *Town and Country in Central and Eastern Africa,* ed. David Parkin, pp. 190–210. London: Oxford University Press.
1988 *For Prayer and Profit: The Ritual, Economic, and Social Importance of Beer in Gwembe District, Zambia, 1950–1982.* Stanford, CA: Stanford University Press.

Comaroff, J.
1982 Dialectical Systems, History and Anthropology: Units of Study and Questions of Theory. *Journal of Southern African Studies* 8: 143–172.

Combs-Schilling, E.
1989 *Sacred Performances: Islam, Sexuality, and Sacrifice.* New York: Columbia University Press.

Conkey, M., O. Soffer, D. Stratmann, and N. Jablonski
1997 *Beyond Art: Pleistocene Image and Symbol.* San Francisco: Memoirs of the California Academy of Sciences, no. 23.

Conklin, H. C.
1954 *The Relation of Hanunóo Culture to the Plant World.* Unpublished Ph.D. dissertation, Yale University.

Connah, G.
1987 *African Civilizations.* New York: Cambridge University Press.

Connell, R. W.
1995 *Masculinities.* Berkeley: University of California Press.

Connor, W.
1972 Nation-Building or Nation Destroying. *World Politics* 24(3): 319–355.

Cook-Gumperz, J.
1986 *The Social Construction of Literacy.* Cambridge: Cambridge University Press.

Cooper, F., and A. L. Stoler
1989 Introduction, Tensions of Empire: Colonial Control and Visions of Rule. *American Ethnologist* 16: 609–621.

Cooper, F., and A. L. Stoler, eds.
1997 *Tensions of Empire: Colonial Cultures in a Bourgeois World.* Berkeley, CA: University of California Press.

Coote, J., and A. Shelton, eds.
1992 *Anthropology, Art, and Aesthetics.* New York: Oxford University Press.

Crane, J. G., and M. V. Angrosino
1992 *Field Projects in Anthropology: A Student Handbook,* 3rd ed. Prospect Heights, IL: Waveland.

Crick, F. H. C.
1968 (orig. 1962). The Genetic Code. In *The Molecular Basis of Life: An Introduction to Molecular Biology, Readings from Scientific American,* pp. 198–205. San Francisco: W. H. Freeman.

Crosby, A. W., Jr.
1972 *The Columbian Exchange: Biological and Cultural Consequences of 1492.* Westport, CT: Greenwood Press.
1986 *Ecological Imperialism: The Biological Expansion of Europe, 900–1900.* New York: Cambridge University Press.
1994 *Germs, Seeds & Animals: Studies in Ecological History.* Armonk, NY: M.E. Sharpe.

Cultural Survival
1992 *At the Threshold.* Cambridge, MA: Cultural Survival. Originally published as the Spring 1992 issue of *Cultural Survival Quarterly.*

Cultural Survival Quarterly
Quarterly journal. Cambridge, MA: Cultural Survival.

Cunliffe, B., ed.
1998 *Prehistoric Europe: An Illustrated History.* New York: Oxford University Press.

Dahlberg, F., ed.
1981 *Woman the Gatherer.* New Haven: Yale University Press.

Dalton, G., ed.
1967 *Tribal and Peasant Economies.* Garden City, NY: Natural History Press.

DaMatta, R.
1991 *Carnivals, Rogues, and Heroes: An Interpretation of the Brazilian Dilemma.* Translated from the Portuguese by John Drury. Notre Dame, IN: University of Notre Dame Press.

D'Andrade, R.
1984 Cultural Meaning Systems. In *Culture Theory: Essays on Mind, Self, and Emotion,* ed. R. A. Shweder and R. A. Levine, pp. 88–119. Cambridge: Cambridge University Press.
1995 *The Development of Cognitive Anthropology.* New York: Cambridge University Press.

Darwin, C.
1958 (orig. 1859). *On the Origin of Species.* New York: Dutton.

Darwin, E.
1796 (orig. 1794). *Zoonomia, Or the Laws of Organic Life,* 2nd ed. London: J. Johnson.

Das, V.
1995 *Critical Events: An Anthropological Perspective on Contemporary India.* New York: Oxford University Press.

Davis, D. L., and R. G. Whitten
1987 The Cross-Cultural Study of Human Sexuality. *Annual Review of Anthropology* 16: 69–98.

Degler, C.
1970 *Neither Black nor White: Slavery and Race Relations in Brazil and the United States.* New York: Macmillan.

Delamont, S.
1995 *Appetites and Identities: An Introduction to the Social Anthropology of Western Europe.* London: Routledge.

Delson, E., ed.
1985 *Ancestors: The Hard Evidence.* New York: Alan R. Liss.

DeLumley, H.
1976 (orig. 1969). A Paleolithic Camp at Nice. In *Avenues to Antiquity, Readings from Scientific American,* ed. B. M. Fagan, pp. 36–44. San Francisco: W. H. Freeman.

DeMarco, E.
1997 New Dig at 9,000-Year-Old City Is Changing Views on Ancient Life. www.nytimes.com, November 11.

Dentan, R. K.
1979 *The Semai: A Nonviolent People of Malaya.* Fieldwork edition. New York: Harcourt Brace.

Desjarlais, R., L. Eisenberg, B. Good, and A. Kleinman, eds.
1995 *World Mental Health: Problems and Priorities in Low-Income Countries.* New York: Oxford University Press.

Despres, L., ed.
1975 *Ethnicity and Resource Competition.* The Hague: Mouton.

DeVita, P. R., and J. D. Armstrong, eds.
1998 *Distant Mirrors: America as a Foreign Culture.* Belmont, CA: Wadsworth.

De Vos, G. A.
1971 *Japan's Outcastes: The Problem of the Burakumin.* London: Minority Rights Group.

De Vos, G. A., and H. Wagatsuma
1966 *Japan's Invisible Race: Caste in Culture and Personality.* Berkeley: University of California Press.

De Vos, G. A., W. O. Wetherall, and K. Stearman
1983 *Japan's Minorities: Burakumin, Koreans, Ainu and Okinawans.* Report no. 3. London: Minority Rights Group.

De Waal, F. B. M.
1997 *Bonobo: The Forgotten Ape.* Berkeley: University of California Press.
1998 *Chimpanzee Politics: Power and Sex among Apes,* rev. ed. Baltimore: Johns Hopkins University Press.

Diamond, J. M.
1989 Blood, Genes, and Malaria. *Natural History,* February, pp. 8–18.
1990 A Pox upon Our Genes. *Natural History,* February, pp. 26–30.
1997 *Guns, Germs, and Steel: The Fates of Human Societies.* New York: W.W. Norton.

Dibble, H. L., S. P. McPherron, and B. J. Roth
1999 *Virtual Dig: A Simulated Archaeological Excavation of a Middle Paleolithic Site in France.* Mountain View, CA: Mayfield.

di Leonardo, M., ed.
1991 *Gender at the Crossroads of Knowledge: Feminist Anthropology in the Postmodern Era.* Berkeley: University of California Press.

Divale, W. T., and M. Harris
1976 Population, Warfare, and the Male Supremacist Complex. *American Anthropologist* 78: 521–538.

Dobzhansky, T., F. J. Ayala, G. L. Stebbins, and J. W. Valentine
1977 *Evolution*. San Francisco: W. H. Freeman.

Dolhinow, P., and A. Fuentes, eds.
1999 *The Nonhuman Primates*. Mountain View, CA: Mayfield.

Downes, W.
1998 *Language and Society*, 2nd ed. New York: Cambridge University Press.

Draper, P.
1975 !Kung Women: Contrasts in Sexual Egalitarianism in Foraging and Sedentary Contexts. In *Toward an Anthropology of Women*, ed. R. Reiter, pp. 77–109. New York: Monthly Review Press.

Drennan, R. D., and C. A. Uribe, eds.
1987 *Chiefdoms in the Americas*. Landon, MD: University Press of America.

Durkheim, E.
1951 (orig. 1897). *Suicide: A Study in Sociology*. Glencoe, IL: Free Press.
1961 (orig. 1912). *The Elementary Forms of the Religious Life*. New York: Collier Books.

Dwyer, K.
1982 *Moroccan Dialogues: Anthropology in Question*. Baltimore: Johns Hopkins University Press.

Eagleton, T.
1983 *Literary Theory: An Introduction*. Minneapolis: University of Minnesota Press.

Earle, T. K.
1987 Chiefdoms in Archaeological and Ethnohistorical Perspective. *Annual Review of Anthropology* 16: 279–308.
1991 *Chiefdoms: Power, Economy, and Ideology*. New York: Cambridge University Press.
1997 *How Chiefs Come to Power: The Political Economy in Prehistory*. Stanford, CA: Stanford University Press.

Eastman, C. M.
1975 *Aspects of Language and Culture*. San Francisco: Chandler and Sharp.

Eckert, P.
1989 *Jocks and Burnouts: Social Categories and Identity in the High School*. New York: Teachers College Press, Columbia University.
2000 *Linguistic Variation as Social Practice: The Linguistic Construction of Identity in Belten High*. Malden, MA: Blackwell.

Eckert, P., and J. R. Rickford, eds.
2001 *Style and Sociolinguistic Variation*. New York: Cambridge University Press.

Eddy, E. M., and W. L. Partridge, eds.
1987 *Applied Anthropology in America*, 2nd ed. New York: Columbia University Press.

Eder, J.
1987 *On the Road to Tribal Extinction: Depopulation, Deculturation, and Adaptive Well-Being among the Batak of the Philippines*. Berkeley: University of California Press.

Edgerton, R.
1965 "Cultural" versus "Ecological" Factors in the Expression of Values, Attitudes and Personality Characteristics. *American Anthropologist* 67: 442–447.

Eggert, K.
1988 Malafaly as Misnomer. In *Madagascar: Society and History*, ed. C. P. Kottak, J. A. Rakotoarisoa, A. Southall, and P. Verin, pp. 321–336. Durham, NC: Carolina Academic Press.

Eiseley, L.
1961 *Darwin's Century*. Garden City, NY: Doubleday, Anchor Books.

Eldredge, N.
1985 *Time Frames: The Rethinking of Darwinian Evolution and the Theory of Punctuated Equilibria*. New York: Simon & Schuster.
1997 *Fossils: The Evolution and Extinction of Species*. Princeton, NJ: Princeton University Press.

Ember, M., and C. R. Ember
1997 Science in Anthropology. In *The Teaching of Anthropology: Problems, Issues, and Decisions*, eds. C. P. Kottak, J. J. White, R. H. Furlow, and P. C. Rice, pp. 29–33. Mountain View, CA: Mayfield.

Erlanger, S.
1992 An Islamic Awakening in Central Asian Lands. *The New York Times*, June 9, pp. A1, A7.

Errington, F., and D. Gewertz
1987 *Cultural Alternatives and a Feminist Anthropology: An Analysis of Culturally Constructed Gender Interests in Papua New Guinea*. New York: Cambridge University Press.

Escobar, A.
1991 Anthropology and the Development Encounter: The Making and Marketing of Development Anthropology. *American Ethnologist* 18: 658–682.

1994 Welcome to Cyberia: Notes on the Anthropology of Cyberculture. *Current Anthropology* 35(3): 211–231.

1995 *Encountering Development: The Making and Unmaking of the Third World.* Princeton, NJ: Princeton University Press.

Eskridge, W. N., Jr.

1996 *The Case for Same-Sex Marriage: From Sexual Liberty to Civilized Commitment.* New York: Free Press.

Evans-Pritchard, E. E.

1940 *The Nuer: A Description of the Modes of Livelihood and Political Institutions of a Nilotic People.* Oxford: Clarendon Press.

1970 Sexual Inversion among the Azande. *American Anthropologist* 72: 1428–1433.

Ezra, K.

1986 *A Human Ideal in African Art: Bamana Figurative Sculpture.* Washington, DC: Smithsonian Institution Press for the National Museum of African Art.

Fagan, B. M.

1987 *The Great Journey: The Peopling of Ancient America.* London: Thames and Hudson.

1994 *Archeology: A Brief Introduction,* 5th ed. New York: HarperCollins.

1996 *World Prehistory: A Brief Introduction.* New York: HarperCollins.

1997 *Archeology: A Brief Introduction,* 6th ed. New York: Longman.

1998*a* *World Prehistory: A Brief Introduction,* 4th ed. New York: Longman.

1998*b* *People of the Earth: A Brief Introduction to World Prehistory,* 9th ed. New York: Longman.

1998*c* *Clash of Cultures,* 2nd ed. Walnut Creek, CA: AltaMira.

2000 *Ancient Lives: An Introduction to Method and Theory in Archaeology.* Upper Saddle River, NJ: Prentice Hall.

Falk, D.

2000 *Primate Diversity.* New York: W. W. Norton.

Farnsworth, C. H.

1992 Canada to Divide Its Northern Land. *The New York Times,* May 6, p. A7.

Farooq, M.

1966 Importance of Determining Transmission Sites in Planning Bilharziasis Control: Field Observations from the Egypt-49 Project Area. *American Journal of Epidemiology* 83: 603–612.

Farr, D. M. L.

1980 British Empire. *Academic American Encyclopedia,* volume 3, pp. 495–496. Princeton, NJ: Arete.

Fasold, R. W.

1990 *The Sociolinguistics of Language.* Oxford: Basil Blackwell.

Fedigan, L. M.

1992 *Primate Paradigms: Sex Roles and Social Bonds.* Chicago: University of Chicago Press.

Feinman, G. M., and T. D. Price

2001 *Archaeology at the Millennium: A Sourcebook.* New York: Kluwer Academic/Plenum.

Feld, S.

1990 *Sound and Sentiment: Birds, Weeping, Poetics, and Song in Kaluli Expression,* 2nd ed. Philadelphia: University of Pennsylvania Press.

1991 Voices of the Rainforest. *Public Culture* 4(1): 131–140.

Fenlason, L.

1990 Wolpoff Questions "Eve's" Origin Date, Says It Ignores Contradictory Fossil Data. *University Record* (University of Michigan, Ann Arbor) 45(21): 12.

Ferguson, R. B.

1995 *Yanomami Warfare: A Political History.* Santa Fe, NM: School of American Research.

Ferguson, R. B., and N. L. Whitehead

1991 *War in the Tribal Zone: Expanding States and Indigenous Warfare.* Santa Fe: School of American Research Press.

Ferraro, G. P.

1998 *The Cultural Dimension of International Business,* 3rd ed. Upper Saddle River, NJ: Prentice Hall.

2001 *The Cultural Dimension of International Business,* 4th ed. Upper Saddle River, NJ: Prentice Hall.

Finkler, K.

1985 *Spiritualist Healers in Mexico: Successes and Failures of Alternative Therapeutics.* South Hadley, MA: Bergin and Garvey.

2000 *Experiencing the New Genetics: Family and Kinship on the Medical Frontier.* Philadelphia: University of Pennsylvania Press.

Finnstrom, S.

1997 Postcoloniality and the Postcolony: Theories of the Global and the Local. http://www.stg.brown.edu/projects/hypertext/landow/post/poldiscourse/finnstrom/finnstrom1.html.

Fisher, A.
1988*a* The More Things Change. *MOSAIC* 19(1): 22–33.
1988*b* On the Emergence of Humanness. *MOSAIC* 19(1): 34–45.

Fiske, J.
1989 *Understanding Popular Culture.* Boston: Unwin Hyman.

Flannery, K. V.
1969 Origins and Ecological Effects of Early Domestication in Iran and the Near East. In *The Domestication and Exploitation of Plants and Animals,* ed. P. J. Ucko and G. W. Dimbleby, pp. 73–100. Chicago: Aldine.
1972 The Cultural Evolution of Civilizations. *Annual Review of Ecology and Systematics* 3: 399–426.
1973 The Origins of Agriculture. *Annual Review of Anthropology* 2: 271–310.
1995 Prehistoric Social Evolution. In *Research Frontiers in Anthropology,* eds. C. R. Ember and M. Ember, pp. 1–26. Englewood Cliffs, NJ: Prentice Hall.
1999 Chiefdoms in the Early Near East: Why It's So Hard to Identify Them. In *The Iranian World: Essays on Iranian Art and Archaeology,* eds. A. Alizadeh, Y. Majidzadeh, and S. M. Shahmirzadi. Tehran: Iran University Press.

Flannery, K. V., ed.
1986 *Guila Naquitz: Archaic Foraging and Early Agriculture in Oaxaca, Mexico.* Orlando: Academic Press.

Flannery, K. V., J. Marcus, and R. G. Reynolds
1989 *The Flocks of the Wamani: A Study of Llama Herders on the Punas of Ayacucho, Peru.* San Diego: Academic Press.

Fleagle, J. G.
1999 *Primate Adaptation and Evolution,* 2nd ed. San Diego: Academic Press.

Fleagle, J. G., C. H. Janson, and K. E. Reed, eds.
1999 *Primate Communities.* New York: Cambridge University Press.

Fleisher, M. L.
1998 Cattle Raiding and Its Correlates: The Cultural-Ecological Consequences of Market-Oriented Cattle Raiding among the Kuria of Tanzania. *Human Ecology* 26(4): 547–572.
2000 *Kuria Cattle Raiders: Violence and Vigilantism on the Tanzania/Kenya Frontier.* Ann Arbor, MI: University of Michigan Press.

Foley, W. A.
1997 *Anthropological Linguistics: An Introduction.* Cambridge, MA: Blackwell Publishers.

Ford, C. S., and F. A. Beach
1951 *Patterns of Sexual Behavior.* New York: Harper Torchbooks.

Forman, S., ed.
1994 *Diagnosing America: Anthropology and Public Engagement.* Ann Arbor: University of Michigan Press.

Fossey, D.
1981 The Imperiled Mountain Gorilla. *National Geographic* 159: 501–523.
1983 *Gorillas in the Mist.* Boston: Houghton Mifflin.

Foster, G. M.
1965 Peasant Society and the Image of Limited Good. *American Anthropologist* 67: 293–315.

Foster, G. M., and B. G. Anderson
1978 *Medical Anthropology.* New York: McGraw-Hill.

Foucault, M.
1979 *Discipline and Punish: The Birth of the Prison.* Translated by Alan Sheridan. New York: Vintage Books, University Press.

Fouts, R.
1997 *Next of Kin: What Chimpanzees Have Taught Me about Who We Are.* New York: William Morrow.

Fouts, R. S., D. H. Fouts, and T. E. Van Cantfort
1989 The Infant Loulis Learns Signs from Cross-Fostered Chimpanzees. In *Teaching Sign Language to Chimpanzees,* ed. R. A. Gardner, B. T. Gardner, and T. E. Van Cantfort, pp. 280–292. Albany: State University of New York Press.

Fox, J. W.
1987 *Maya Postclassic State Formation.* Cambridge: Cambridge University Press.

Fox, Richard. G., ed.
1990 Nationalist Ideologies and the Production of National Cultures. American Ethnological Society Monograph Series, no. 2. Washington, DC: American Anthropological Association.

Fox, Robin
1985 *Kinship and Marriage.* New York: Viking Penguin.

Frake, C. O.
1961 The Diagnosis of Disease among the Subanun of Mindanao. *American Anthropologist* 63: 113–132.

Franke, R.
1977 Miracle Seeds and Shattered Dreams in Java. In *Readings in Anthropology,* pp. 197–201. Guilford, CT: Dushkin.

Freeman, D.
1983 *Margaret Mead and Samoa: The Making and Unmaking of an Anthropological Myth.* Cambridge, MA: Harvard University Press.

Freilich, M., D. Raybeck, and J. Savishinsky
1991 *Deviance: Anthropological Perspectives.* Westport, CT: Bergin and Garvey.

French, H. W.
1992 Unending Exodus from the Caribbean, with the U.S. a Constant Magnet. *The New York Times,* May 6, pp. A1, A8.

Freud, S.
1950 (orig. 1918). *Totem and Taboo.* Translated by J. Strachey. New York: W. W. Norton.

Fricke, T.
1994 *Himalayan Households: Tamang Demography and Domestic Processes,* 2nd ed. New York: Columbia University Press.

Fried, M. H.
1960 On the Evolution of Social Stratification and the State. In *Culture in History,* ed. S. Diamond, pp. 713–731. New York: Columbia University Press.
1967 *The Evolution of Political Society: An Essay in Political Anthropology.* New York: McGraw-Hill.

Friedan, B.
1963 *The Feminine Mystique.* New York: Norton.

Friedl, E.
1975 *Women and Men: An Anthropologist's View.* New York: Harcourt Brace Jovanovich.

Friedman, J.
1994 *Cultural Identity and Global Process.* Thousand Oaks, CA: Sage.

Friedman, J., and M. J. Rowlands, eds.
1978 *The Evolution of Social Systems.* Pittsburgh: University of Pittsburgh Press.

Frisancho, A. R.
1975 Functional Adaptation to High Altitude Hypoxia. *Science* 187: 313–319.
1993 *Human Adaptation and Accommodation.* Ann Arbor: University of Michigan Press.

Futuyma, D. J.
1995 *Science on Trial,* updated ed. New York: Pantheon.
1998 *Evolutionary Biology.* Sunderland, MA: Sinauer Associates.

Gal, S.
1989 Language and Political Economy. *Annual Review of Anthropology* 18: 345–367.

Gamble, C.
1999 *The Palaeolithic Societies of Europe.* New York: Cambridge University Press.
2000 *Archaeology, the Basics.* New York: Routledge.

Garbarino, M. S., and R. F. Sasso
1994 *Native American Heritage,* 3rd ed. Prospect Heights, IL: Waveland.

Gardner, R. A., B. T. Gardner, and T. E. Van Cantfort, eds.
1989 *Teaching Sign Language to Chimpanzees.* Albany: State University of New York Press.

Gargan, E. A.
1992 A Single-Minded Man Battles to Free Slaves. *The New York Times,* June 4, p. A7.

Geertz, C.
1973 *The Interpretation of Cultures.* New York: Basic Books.
1980 Blurred Genres: The Refiguration of Social Thought. *American Scholar* 29(2): 165–79.
1983 *Local Knowledge.* New York: Basic Books.
1995 *After the Fact: Two Countries, Four Decades, One Anthropologist.* Cambridge, MA: Harvard University Press.

Geis, M. L.
1987 *The Language of Politics.* New York: Springer-Verlag.

Gellner, E.
1983 *Nations and Nationalism.* Ithaca, NY: Cornell University Press.
1997 *Nationalism.* New York: New York University Press.

General Anthropology: Bulletin of the Council for General Anthropology

Gibbs, N.
1989 How America Has Run Out of Time. *Time,* April 24, pp. 59–67.

Giddens, A.
1973 *The Class Structure of the Advanced Societies.* New York: Cambridge University Press.

Gilchrist, R.
1999 *Gender and Archaeology: Contesting the Past.* New York: Routledge.

Gillespie, J. H.
1998 *Population Genetics: A Concise Guide.* Baltimore: The Johns Hopkins University Press.

Gilmore, D.
1987 *Aggression and Community: Paradoxes of Andalusian Culture.* New Haven: Yale University Press.
1991 *Manhood in the Making: Cultural Concepts of Masculinity.* New Haven: Yale University Press.

Gilmore-Lehne, W. J.
2000 Pre-Sumerian Cultures: Natufian through Ubaid Eras: 10,500–3500 B.C.E. http://www.stockton.edu/~gilbmorew/consorti/1bnear.htm.

Glick-Schiller, N., and G. Fouron
1990 "Everywhere We Go, We Are in Danger": Ti Manno and the Emergence of Haitian Transnational Identity. *American Ethnologist* 17(2): 327–347.

Goldberg, D. T.
1997 *Racial Subjects: Writing on Race in America.* New York: Routledge.

Goldberg, D. T., ed.
1990 *Anatomy of Racism.* Minneapolis: University of Minnesota Press.

Golden, T.
1997 Oakland Revamps Plan to Teach Black English. *The New York Times,* January 14, www.nytimes.com.

Goldschmidt, W.
1965 Theory and Strategy in the Study of Cultural Adaptability. *American Anthropologist* 67: 402–407.

Goodale, J., and J. D. Koss
1971 The Cultural Context of Creativity among Tiwi. In *Anthropology and Art: Readings in Cross-Cultural Aesthetics,* ed. C. Otten, pp.182–203. Austin, TX: University of Texas Press.

Goodall, J.
1968*a* A Preliminary Report on Expressive Movements and Communication in Gombe Stream Chimpanzees. In *Primates: Studies in Adaptation and Variability,* ed. P. C. Jay, pp. 313–374. New York: Harcourt Brace Jovanovich.
1968*b* The Behavior of Free Living Chimpanzees in the Gombe Stream Reserve. *Animal Behavior Monographs* 1: 161–311.
1986 *The Chimpanzees of Gombe: Patterns of Behavior.* Cambridge, MA: Belknap Press of Harvard University Press.
1988 *In the Shadow of Man,* rev. ed. Boston: Houghton Mifflin.
1996 *My Life with the Chimpanzees.* New York: Pocket Books.

Goodenough, W. H.
1953 *Native Astronomy in the Central Carolines.* Philadelphia: University of Pennsylvania Press.

Goodman, J., P. E. Lovejoy, and A. Sherratt
1995 *Consuming Habits: Drugs in History and Anthropology.* London: Routledge.

Goodman, M., M. L. Baba, and L. L. Darga
1983 The Bearings of Molecular Data on the Cladograms and Times of Divergence of Hominoid Lineages. In *New Interpretations of Ape and Human Ancestry,* ed. R. L. Ciochon and R. S. Corruccini, pp. 67–87. New York: Plenum.

Goody, J.
1977 *Production and Reproduction: A Comparative Study of the Domestic Domain.* New York: Cambridge University Press.

Goody, J., and S. T. Tambiah
1973 *Bridewealth and Dowry.* Cambridge: Cambridge University Press.

Gordon, A. A.
1996 *Transforming Capitalism and Patriarchy: Gender and Development in Africa.* Boulder, CO: Lynne Reinner.

Gorer, G.
1943 Themes in Japanese Culture. *Transactions of the New York Academy of Sciences* (Series II) 5: 106–124.

Gorman, C. F.
1969 Hoabinhian: A Pebble-Tool Complex with Early Plant Associations in Southeast Asia. *Science* 163: 671–673.

Gottdiener, M., ed.
2000 *New Forms of Consumption: Consumers, Culture, and Commodification.* Lanham, MD: Rowman and Littlefield.

Gough, E. K.
1959 The Nayars and the Definition of Marriage. *Journal of Royal Anthropological Institute* 89: 23–34.

Gould, S. J.
1996 *The Mismeasure of Man.* New York: Norton.
1999 *Rock of Ages: Science and Religion in the Fullness of Life.* New York: Ballantine Books.

Gowlett, J. A. J.
1993 *Ascent to Civilization: The Archaeology of Early Humans.* New York: McGraw-Hill.

Graburn, N.
1976 *Ethnic and Tourist Arts: Cultural Expressions from the Fourth World.* Berkeley: University of California Press.

Graburn, N., ed.
1971 *Readings in Kinship and Social Structure.* New York: Harper & Row.

Gramsci, A.
1971 *Selections from the Prison Notebooks.* Edited and translated by Quenten Hoare and Geoffrey Nowell Smith. London: Wishart.

Grasmuck, S., and P. Pessar
1991 *Between Two Islands: Dominican International Migration.* Berkeley: University of California Press.

Grassmuck, K.
1985 Local Educators Join Push for "a Computer in Every Classroom." *The Ann Arbor News,* February 10, p. A11. (Quotes testimony of Linda Tarr-Whelan of the National Education Association to the House Committee on Science, Research and Technology.)

Gray, J.
1986 With a Few Exceptions, Television in Africa Fails to Educate and Enlighten. *Ann Arbor News,* December 8.

Gray, J. P.
1985 *Primate Sociobiology.* New Haven: HRAF Press.

Greaves, T. C.
1995 Problems Facing Anthropologists: Cultural Rights and Ethnography. *General Anthropology* 1(2): 1, 3–6.

Green, E. C.
1992 (orig. 1987). The Integration of Modern and Traditional Health Sectors in Swaziland. In *Applying Anthropology,* ed. A. Podolefsky and P. J. Brown, pp. 246–251. Mountain View, CA: Mayfield.

Griffin, P. B., and A. Estioko-Griffin, eds.
1985 *The Agta of Northeastern Luzon: Recent Studies.* Cebu City, Philippines: University of San Carlos.

Gross, D.
1971 The Great Sisal Scheme. *Natural History,* March, pp. 49–55.

Gross, D., and B. Underwood
1971 Technological Change and Caloric Costs: Sisal Agriculture in Northeastern Brazil. *American Anthropologist* 73: 725–740.

Gudeman, S., ed.
1999 *Economic Anthropology.* Northhampton, MA: E. Elgar.

Gulliver, P. H.
1974 (orig. 1965). The Jie of Uganda. In *Man in Adaptation: The Cultural Present,* 2nd ed., ed. Y. A. Cohen, pp. 323–345. Chicago: Aldine.

Gumperz, J. J.
1982 *Language and Social Identity.* Cambridge: Cambridge University Press.

Gumperz, J. J., and S. C. Levinson, eds.
1996 *Rethinking Linguistic Relativity.* New York: Cambridge University Press.

Gunther, E.
1971 Northwest Coast Indian Art. In *Anthropology and Art: Readings in Cross-Cultural Aesthetics,* ed. C. Otten, 318–340. Austin, TX: University of Texas Press.

Guthrie, S.
1995 *Faces in the Clouds: A New Theory of Religion.* New York: Oxford University Press.

Haapala, A.
1998 Literature: Invention of the Self. *Canadian Aesthetics Journal* 2, http://tornade.ere.umontreal.ca/~guedon/AE/vol_2/haapala.html.

Hackett, R. I. J.
1996 *Art and Religion in Africa.* London: Cassell.

Hall, E. T.
1990 *Understanding Cultural Differences.* Yarmouth, ME: Intercultural Press.
1992 *An Anthropology of Everyday Life: An Autobiography.* New York: Doubleday.

Hall, T. D., ed.
1999 *A World-System Reader: New Perspectives on Gender, Urbanism, Cultures, Indigenous Peoples, and Ecology.* Lanham, MD: Rowman and Littlefield.

Hamburg, D. A., and E. R. McCown, eds.
1979 *The Great Apes.* Menlo Park, CA: Benjamin Cummings.

Hamilton, M. B.
1995 *The Sociology of Religion: Theoretical and Comparative Perspectives.* London: Routledge.

Hanks, W. F.
1995 *Language and Communicative Practices.* Boulder, CO: Westview.

Hansen, K. V., and A. I. Garey, eds.
1998 *Families in the U.S.: Kinship and Domestic Politics.* Philadelphia: Temple University Press.

Harcourt, A. H., D. Fossey, and J. Sabater-Pi
1981 Demography of *Gorilla gorilla. Journal of Zoology* 195: 215–233.

Harding, S.
1975 Women and Words in a Spanish Village. In *Toward an Anthropology of Women,* ed. R. Reiter, pp. 283–308. New York: Monthly Review Press.

Hargrove, E. C.
1986 *Religion and Environmental Crisis.* Athens, GA: University of Georgia Press.

Harlan, J. R., and D. Zohary
1966 Distribution of Wild Wheats and Barley. *Science* 153: 1074–1080.

Harris, M.
1964 *Patterns of Race in the Americas*. New York: Walker.
1968 *The Rise of Anthropological Theory*. New York: Crowell.
1970 Referential Ambiguity in the Calculus of Brazilian Racial Identity. *Southwestern Journal of Anthropology* 26(1): 1–14.
1974 *Cows, Pigs, Wars, and Witches: The Riddles of Culture*. New York: Random House.
1978 *Cannibals and Kings*. New York: Vintage.
1989 *Our Kind: Who We Are, Where We Came from, Where We Are Going*. New York: Harper & Row.

Harris, M., and C. P. Kottak
1963 The Structural Significance of Brazilian Racial Categories. *Sociologia* 25: 203–209.

Harris, N. M., and G. Hillman
1989 *Foraging and Farming: The Evolution of Plant Exploitation*. London: Unwin Hyman.

Harrison, G. G., W. L. Rathje, and W. W. Hughes
1994 Food Waste Behavior in an Urban Population. In *Applying Anthropology: An Introductory Reader*, 3rd ed., ed. A. Podolefsky and P. J. Brown, pp. 107–112. Mountain View, CA: Mayfield.

Hart, C. W. M., A. R. Pilling, and J. C. Goodale
1988 *The Tiwi of North Australia*, 3rd ed. Fort Worth: Harcourt Brace.

Hartl, D. L.
1997 *Principles of Population Genetics*, 3rd ed. Sunderland, MA: Sinaeur.
2000 *A Primer of Population Genetics*, 3rd ed. Sunderland, MA: Sinauer Associates.

Hartl, D. L., and E. W. Jones
1999 *Essential Genetics*. Sudbury, MA: Jones and Bartlett.

Harvey, D. J.
1980 French Empire. *Academic American Encyclopedia*, volume 8, pp. 309–310. Princeton, NJ: Arete.

Harvey, K.
1996 Online for the Ancestors: The Importance of Anthropological Sensibility in Information Superhighway Design. *Social Science Computing Review* 14(1): 65–68.

Hassig, R.
1985 *Trade, Tribute, and Transportation: The Sixteenth-Century Political Economy of the Valley of Mexico*. Norman, OK: University of Oklahoma Press.

Hastings, A.
1997 *The Construction of Nationhood: Ethnicity, Religion, and Nationalism*. New York: Cambridge University Press.

Hatcher, E. P.
1999 *Art as Culture: An Introduction to the Anthropology of Art*, 2nd ed. Westport, CT: Bergin & Garvey.

Hatfield, E., and R. L. Rapson
1996 *Love and Sex: Cross-Cultural Perspectives*. Needham Heights, MA: Allyn & Bacon.

Hausfater, G., and S. Hrdy, eds.
1984 *Infanticide: Comparative and Evolutionary Perspectives*. Hawthorne, NY: Aldine.

Hawkes, K., J. O'Connell, and K. Hill
1982 Why Hunters Gather: Optimal Foraging and the Aché of Eastern Paraguay. *American Ethnologist* 9: 379–398.

Hawley, J. S,. ed.
1993 *Sati, the Blessing and the Curse: The Burning of Wives in India*. New York: Oxford University Press.

Hayden, B.
1981 Subsistence and Ecological Adaptations of Modern Hunter/Gatherers. In *Omnivorous Primates: Gathering and Hunting in Human Evolution*, ed. R. S. Harding and G. Teleki, pp. 344–421. New York: Columbia University Press.

Headland, T. N., ed.
1992 *The Tasaday Controversy: Assessing the Evidence*. Washington, DC: American Anthropological Association.

Headland, T. N., and L. A. Reid
1989 Hunter-Gatherers and Their Neighbors from Prehistory to the Present. *Current Anthropology* 30: 43–66.

Heath, D. B., ed.
1995 *International Handbook on Alcohol and Culture*. Westport, CT: Greenwood Press.

Hedges, C.
1992*a* Sudan Presses Its Campaign to Impose Islamic Law on Non-Muslims. *The New York Times*, June 1, p. A7.
1992*b* Sudan Gives Its Refugees a Desert to Contemplate. *The New York Times*, June 3, p. A4.

Heider, K. G.
1988 The Rashomon Effect: When Ethnographers Disagree. *American Anthropologist* 90: 73–81.
1991 *Grand Valley Dani: Peaceful Warriors*, 2nd ed. Fort Worth: Harcourt Brace.

Heller, M.

1988 *Codeswitching: Anthropological and Sociolinguistic Perspectives*. Berlin: Mouton de Gruyter.

Helman, C.

2001 *Culture, Health, and Illness: An Introduction for Health Professionals*, 4th ed. Boston: Butterworth-Heinemann.

Henry, D. O.

1989 *From Foraging to Agriculture: The Levant at the End of the Ice Age*. Philadelphia: University of Pennsylvania Press.

1995 *Prehistoric Cultural Ecology and Evolution: Insights from Southern Jordan*. New York: Plenum Press.

Henry, J.

1955 Docility, or Giving Teacher What She Wants. *Journal of Social Issues* 2: 33–41.

Herdt, G.

1981 *Guardians of the Flutes*. New York: McGraw-Hill.

1986 *The Sambia: Ritual and Gender in New Guinea*. Fort Worth: Harcourt Brace.

Herdt, G. H., ed.

1984 *Ritualized Homosexuality in Melanesia*. Berkeley, CA: University of California Press.

Herrnstein, R. J.

1971 I.Q. *Atlantic* 228(3): 43–64.

Herrnstein, R. J., and C. Murray

1994 *The Bell Curve: Intelligence and Class Structure in American Life*. New York: Free Press.

Hess, D. J.

1995 A Democratic Research Agenda in the Social Studies of the National Information Infrastructure. Paper prepared for the National Science Foundation Workshop on Culture, Society, and Advanced Information Technology. Washington, DC: May 31–June 1, 1995.

Hess, D. J., and R. A. DaMatta, eds.

1995 *The Brazilian Puzzle: Culture on the Borderlands of the Western World*. New York: Columbia University Press.

Hewitt, R.

1986 *White Talk, Black Talk*. Cambridge: Cambridge University Press.

Heyerdahl, T.

1971 *The Ra Expeditions*. Translated by P. Crampton. Garden City, NY: Doubleday.

Heyneman, D.

1984 Development and Disease: A Dual Dilemma. *Journal of Parasitology* 70: 3–17.

Hicks, D., ed.

1999 *Ritual and Belief: Readings in the Anthropology of Religion*. New York: McGraw-Hill.

Hill, C. E., ed.

1986 Current Health Policy Issues and Alternatives: An Applied Social Science Perspective. *Southern Anthropological Society Proceedings*. Athens, GA: University of Georgia Press.

Hill, J. H.

1978 Apes and Language. *Annual Review of Anthropology* 7: 89–112.

Hill, K., H. Kaplan, K. Hawkes, and A. Hurtado

1987 Foraging Decisions among Aché Hunter-Gatherers: New Data and Implications for Optimal Foraging Models. *Ethology and Sociobiology* 8: 1–36.

Hill-Burnett, J.

1978 Developing Anthropological Knowledge through Application. In *Applied Anthropology in America*, ed. E. M. Eddy and W. L. Partridge, pp. 112–128. New York: Columbia University Press.

Hinde, R. A.

1983 *Primate Social Relationships: An Integrated Approach*. Sunderland, MA: Sinaeur.

Hobhouse, L. T.

1915 *Morals in Evolution*, rev. ed. New York: Holt.

Hobsbawm, E. J.

1992 *Nations and Nationalism since 1780: Programme, Myth, Reality*, 2nd ed. New York: Cambridge University Press.

Hoebel, E. A.

1954 *The Law of Primitive Man*. Cambridge, MA: Harvard University Press.

1968 (orig. 1954). The Eskimo: Rudimentary Law in a Primitive Anarchy. In *Studies in Social and Cultural Anthropology*, ed. J. Middleton, pp. 93–127. New York: Crowell.

Hole, F., K. V. Flannery, and J. A. Neely

1969 *The Prehistory and Human Ecology of the Deh Luran Plain*. Memoir no. 1. Ann Arbor: University of Michigan Museum of Anthropology.

Holland, D., and N. Quinn, eds.

1987 *Cultural Models in Language and Thought*. Cambridge: Cambridge University Press.

Holloway, R. L.

1975 (orig. 1974). The Casts of Fossil Hominid Brains. In *Biological Anthropology, Readings from Scientific American*, ed. S. H. Katz, pp. 69–78. San Francisco: W. H. Freeman.

Holmes, L. D.
1987 *Quest for the Real Samoa: The Mead/Freeman Controversy and Beyond.* South Hadley, MA: Bergin and Garvey.

Holtzman, J.
2000 *Nuer Journeys, Nuer Lives.* Boston: Allyn & Bacon.

Hopkins, T. K.
1996 *The Age of Transition: Trajectory of the World-System 1945–2025.* Atlantic Highlands, NJ: Zed.

Hopkins, T., and I. Wallerstein
1982 Patterns of Development of the Modern World System. In *World System Analysis: Theory and Methodology,* by T. Hopkins, I. Wallerstein, R. Bach, C. Chase-Dunn, and R. Mukherjee, pp. 121–141. Thousand Oaks, CA: Sage.

Horton, R.
1963 The Kalabari Ekine Society: A Borderland of Religion and Art. *Africa* 33: 94–113.
1993 *Patterns of Thought in Africa and the West: Essays on Magic, Religion, and Science.* New York: Cambridge University Press.

Hostetler, J., and G. E. Huntington
1992 *Amish Children: Education in the Family,* 2nd ed. Fort Worth: Harcourt Brace.
1996 *The Hutterites in North America,* 3rd ed. Fort Worth: Harcourt Brace.

Howells, W. W.
1976 Explaining Modern Man: Evolutionists versus Migrationists. *Journal of Human Evolution* 5: 477–496.

Hughes, R., Jr.
1996 Demographics of Divorce. http://www.hec.ohio-state.edu/famlife/divorce/demo.htm.

Human Organization
Quarterly journal. Oklahoma City: Society for Applied Anthropology.

Hutchinson, S.E.
1996 *Nuer Dilemmas: Coping with Money, War, and the State.* Berkeley: University of California Press.

Ingold, T., D. Riches, and J. Woodburn
1991 *Hunters and Gatherers.* New York: Berg (St. Martin's).

Ingraham, C.
1999 *White Weddings: Romancing Heterosexuality in Popular Culture.* New York: Routledge.

Inhorn, M. C., And P. J. Brown
1990 The Anthropology of Infectious Disease. *Annual Review of Anthropology* 19: 89–117.

Irving, W. N.
1985 Context and Chronology of Early Man in the Americas. *Annual Review of Anthropology* 14: 529–555.

Isaac, G. L.
1972 Early Phases of Human Behavior: Models in Lower Paleolithic Archaeology. In *Models in Archaeology,* ed. D. L. Clarke, pp. 167–199. London: Methuen.
1978 Food Sharing and Human Evolution: Archaeological Evidence from the Plio-Pleistocene of East Africa. *Journal of Anthropological Research* 34: 311–325.

Ives, E. D.
1995 *The Tape-Recorded Interview: A Manual for Fieldworkers in Folklore and Oral History,* 2nd. ed. Knoxville, TN: University of Tennessee Press.

Jackson, B.
1987 *Fieldwork.* Champaign-Urbana: University of Illinois Press.

Jacoby, R., and N. Glauberman, eds.
1995 *The Bell Curve Debate: History, Documents, Opinions.* New York: Free Press. New York: Random House Times Books.

Jameson, F.
1984 Postmodernism, or the Cultural Logic of Late Capitalism. *New Left Review* 146: 53–93.
1988 *The Ideologies of Theory: Essays 1971–1986.* Minneapolis: University of Minnesota Press.

Jankowiak, W. R., and E. F. Fischer
1992 A Cross-Cultural Perspective on Romantic Love. *Ethnology* 31(2): 149–156.

Janson, C. H.
1986 Capuchin Counterpoint: Divergent Mating and Feeding Habits Distinguish Two Closely Related Monkey Species of the Peruvian Forest. *Natural History* 95: 44–52.

Jasim, S. A.
1985 The Ubaid Period in Iraq: Recent Excavations in the Hamrin Region. *BAR International Series* 267 (Oxford).

Jensen, A.
1969 How Much Can We Boost I.Q. and Scholastic Achievement? *Harvard Educational Review* 29: 1–123.

Jodelet, D.
1991 *Madness and Social Representations: Living with the Mad in One French Community.* Translated from the French by Gerard Duveen. Berkeley: University of California Press.

Johanson, D. C., and M. Edey
1981 *Lucy: The Origins of Humankind.* New York: Simon & Schuster.

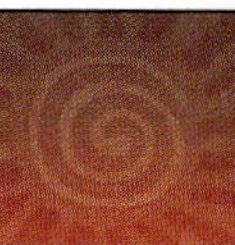

Johanson, D. C., and B. Edgar
1996 *From Lucy to Language*. New York: Simon & Schuster.

Johanson, D. C., and T. D. White
1979 A Systematic Assessment of Early African Hominids. *Science* 203: 321–330.

Johnson, A. W.
1978 *Quantification in Cultural Anthropology: An Introduction to Research Design*. Stanford, CA: Stanford University Press.

Johnson, A. W., and T. Earle, eds.
1987 *The Evolution of Human Societies: From Foraging Group to Agrarian State*. Stanford, CA: Stanford University Press.
2000 *The Evolution of Human Societies: From Foraging Group to Agrarian State*, 2nd ed. Stanford, CA: Stanford University Press.

Johnson, G. A.
1987 The Changing Organization of Uruk Administration in the Susiana Plain. In *The Archaeology of Western Iran*, ed. F. Hole, pp. 107–139. Washington, DC: Smithsonian Institution Press.

Johnson, T. J., and C. F. Sargent, eds.
1990 *Medical Anthropology: A Handbook of Theory and Method.* New York: Greenwood.

Johnston, F. E., and S. Low
1994 *Children of the Urban Poor: The Sociocultural Environment of Growth, Development, and Malnutrition in Guatemala City.* Boulder, CO: Westview.

Jolly, A.
1985 *The Evolution of Primate Behavior*, 2nd ed. New York: Macmillan.

Jolly, C. J., and F. Plog
1986 *Physical Anthropology and Archaeology*, 4th ed. New York: McGraw-Hill.

Jolly, C. J., and R. White
1995 *Physical Anthropology and Archaeology*, 5th ed. New York: McGraw-Hill.

Jones, D.
1999 Hot Asset in Corporate: Anthropology Degrees. *USA Today*, February 18, p. B1.

Jones, G., and R. Krautz
1981 *The Transition to Statehood in the New World.* Cambridge: Cambridge University Press.

Joralemon, D.
1999 *Exploring Medical Anthropology.* Boston: Allyn & Bacon.

Joyce, R. A.
2000 *Gender and Power in Prehispanic Mesoamerica.* Austin, TX: University of Texas Press.

Jurmain, R.
1997 *Introduction to Physical Anthropology*, 7th ed. Belmont, CA: Wadsworth.

Kan, S.
1986 The 19th-Century Tlingit Potlatch: A New Perspective. *American Ethnologist* 13: 191–212.
1989 *Symbolic Immortality: The Tlingit Potlatch of the Nineteenth Century.* Washington, DC: Smithsonian Institution Press.

Kantor, P.
1996 Domestic Violence against Women: A Global Issue. http://metalab.unc.edu/ucis/pubs/Carolina_Papers/Abuse/figure1.html.

Kaplan, R. D.
1994 The Coming Anarchy: How Scarcity, Crime, Overpopulation, and Disease Are Rapidly Destroying the Social Fabric of Our Planet. *Atlantic Monthly*, February, pp. 44–76.

Kardiner, A., ed.
1939 *The Individual and His Society.* New York: Columbia University Press.

Kardulias, P. N.
1999 *World-Systems Theory in Practice: Leadership, Production, and Exchange.* Lanham, MD: Rowman and Littlefield.

Kearney, M.
1996 *Reconceptualizing the Peasantry: Anthropology in Global Perspective*. Boulder, CO: Westview.

Kehoe, A. B.
1989 *The Ghost Dance Religion: Ethnohistory and Revitalization.* Fort Worth: Harcourt Brace.

Keiser, L.
1991 *Friend by Day, Enemy by Night: Organized Vengeance in a Kohistani Community.* Fort Worth: Harcourt Brace.

Kelly, R. C.
1976 Witchcraft and Sexual Relations: An Exploration in the Social and Semantic Implications of the Structure of Belief. In *Man and Woman in the New Guinea Highlands*, ed. P. Brown and G. Buchbinder, pp. 36–53. Special Publication, no. 8. Washington, DC: American Anthropological Association.
1985 *The Nuer Conquest: The Structure and Development of an Expansionist System.* Ann Arbor: University of Michigan Press.

2000 *Warless Societies and the Origin of War.* Ann Arbor: University of Michigan Press.

Kemp, T. S.
1999 *Fossils and Evolution.* New York: Oxford University Press.

Kennedy, R. G.
1994 *Hidden Cities: The Discovery and Loss of Ancient North American Civilization.* New York: Free Press.

Kent, S.
1992 The Current Forager Controversy: Real versus Ideal Views of Hunter-Gatherers. *Man* 27: 45–70.
1996 *Cultural Diversity among Twentieth-Century Foragers: An African Perspective.* New York: Cambridge University Press.
1998 *Gender in African Prehistory.* Walnut Creek, CA: AltaMira Press.

Kent, S., and H. Vierich
1989 The Myth of Ecological Determinism: Anticipated Mobility and Site Organization of Space. In *Farmers as Hunters: The Implications of Sedentism,* ed. S. Kent, pp. 96–130. New York: Cambridge University Press.

Kerr, R. A.
1998 Sea-Floor Dust Shows Drought Felled Akkadian Empire. *Science* 279 (5349— January 16: 325–326.

Kimmel, M. S., and M. A. Messner, eds.
1998 *Men's Lives,* 4th ed. Boston: Allyn & Bacon.

King, B. J., ed.
1994 *The Information Continuum: Evolution of Social Information Transfer in Monkeys, Apes, and Hominids.* Santa Fe: School of American Research Press.

Kinsey, A. C., W. B. Pomeroy, and C. E. Martin
1948 *Sexual Behavior in the Human Male.* Philadelphia: W. B. Saunders.

Kirch, P. V.
1984 *The Evolution of the Polynesian Chiefdoms.* Cambridge: Cambridge University Press.
2000 *On the Road of the Winds: An Archaeological History of the Pacific Islands before European Contact.* Berkeley: University of California Press.

Kirman, P.
1997 An Introduction to Ethnomusicology. http://worldmusic.about.com/musicperform/worldmusic/library/weekly/aa101797.htm and http://worldmusic.about.com/musicperform/worldmusic/library/b11011b.htm.

Klass, M.
1995 *Ordered Universes: Approaches to the Anthropology of Religion.* Boulder, CO: Westview.

Klass, M., and M. Weisgrau, eds.
1999 *Across the Boundaries of Belief: Contemporary Issues in the Anthropology of Religion.* Boulder, CO: Westview.

Klein, R. G.
1999 *The Human Career: Human Biological and Cultural Origins,* 2nd ed. Chicago: University of Chicago Press.

Kleinfeld, J.
1975 Positive Stereotyping: The Cultural Relativist in the Classroom. *Human Organization* 34: 269–274.

Kleymeyer, C. D., ed.
1994 *Cultural Expression and Grassroots Development: Cases from Latin America and the Caribbean.* Boulder, CO: Lynne Rienner.

Klineberg, O.
1951 Race and Psychology. In *The Race Question in Modern Science.* Paris: UNESCO.

Kling, R.
1996 Synergies and Competition between Life in Cyberspace and Face-to-Face Communities. *Social Science Computing Review* 14(1): 50–54.

Kluckhohn, C.
1994 *Mirror for Man: A Survey of Human Behavior and Social Attitudes.* Greenwich, CT: Fawcett.

Kluge, A. G.
1983 Cladistics and the Classification of the Great Apes. In *New Interpretations of Ape and Human Ancestry,* ed. R. L. Ciochon and R. S. Corruccini, pp. 151–177. New York: Plenum.

Knecht, H., A. Pike-Tay, and R. White, eds.
1993 *Before Lascaux: The Complex Record of the Early Upper Paleolithic.* Boca Raton, FL: CRC Press.

Kohler, M., and S. Moya-Sola
1997 Ape-like or Hominid-like? The Positional Behavior of *Oreopithecus bambolii* Reconsidered. *Proceedings of the National Academy of Sciences* 94 (October 14):11, 747.

Korten, D. C.
1980 Community Organization and Rural Development: A Learning Process Approach. *Public Administration Review,* September–October, pp. 480–512.

Kottak, C. P.

1980 *The Past in the Present: History, Ecology, and Social Organization in Highland Madagascar.* Ann Arbor: University of Michigan Press.

1990*a* *Prime-Time Society: An Anthropological Analysis of Television and Culture.* Belmont, CA: Wadsworth.

1990*b* Culture and Economic Development. *American Anthropologist* 92(3): 723–731.

1991 When People Don't Come First: Some Lessons from Completed Projects. In *Putting People First: Sociological Variables in Rural Development*, 2nd ed., ed. M. Cernea, pp. 429–464. New York: Oxford University Press.

1992 *Assault on Paradise: Social Change in a Brazilian Village*, 2nd ed. New York: McGraw-Hill.

1999 *Assault on Paradise: Social Change in a Brazilian Village*, 3rd ed. New York: McGraw-Hill.

Kottak, C. P., ed.

1982 *Researching American Culture: A Guide for Student Anthropologists.* Ann Arbor: University of Michigan Press.

Kottak, C. P., and K. A. Kozaitis

1999 *On Being Different: Diversity and Multiculturalism in the North American Mainstream.* New York: McGraw-Hill.

Kramarae, R., M. Shulz, and M. O'Barr, eds.

1984 *Language and Power.* Thousand Oaks, CA: Sage.

Kretchmer, N.

1975 (orig. 1972). Lactose and Lactase. In *Biological Anthropology, Readings from Scientific American*, ed. S. H. Katz, pp. 310–318. San Francisco: W. H. Freeman.

Kroeber, A. L., and C. Kluckhohn

1963 *Culture: A Critical Review of Concepts and Definitions.* New York: Vintage.

Kulick, D.

1998 *Travesti: Sex, Gender, and Culture among Brazilian Transgendered Prostitutes.* Chicago: University of Chicago Press.

Kunitz, S. J.

1994 *Disease and Social Diversity: The European Impact on the Health of Non-Europeans.* New York: Oxford University Press.

Kurtz, D. V.

2001 *Political Anthropology: Power and Paradigms.* Boulder, CO: Westview.

Kutsche, P.

1998 *Field Ethnography: A Manual for Doing Cultural Anthropology.* Upper Saddle River, NJ: Prentice Hall.

LaBarre, W.

1945 Some Observations of Character Structure in the Orient: The Japanese. *Psychiatry* 8: 326–342.

Labov, W.

1972*a* *Language in the Inner City: Studies in the Black English Vernacular.* Philadelphia: University of Pennsylvania Press.

1972*b* *Sociolinguistic Patterns.* Philadelphia: University of Pennsylvania Press.

Laguerre, M. S.

1984 *American Odyssey: Haitians in New York.* Ithaca, NY: Cornell University Press.

1998 *Diasporic Citizenship: Haitian Americans in Transnational America.* New York: St. Martin's Press.

Lakoff, R. T.

1975 *Language and Woman's Place.* New York: Harper & Row.

2000 *The Language War.* Berkeley: University of California Press.

Lamberg-Karlovsky, C. C., and J. A. Sabloff

1995 *Ancient Civilizations: The Near East and Mesoamerica.* Prospect Heights, IL: Waveland.

Lamphere, L., H. Ragone, and P. Zavella, eds.

1997 *Situated Lives: Gender and Culture in Everyday Life.* New York: Routledge.

Lancaster, R. N., and M. Di Leonardo, eds.

1997 *The Gender/Sexuality Reader: Culture, History, Political Economy.* New York: Routledge.

Lance, L. M., and E. E. McKenna

1975 Analysis of Cases Pertaining to the Impact of Western Technology on the Non-Western World. *Human Organization* 34: 87–94.

Lansing, J. S.

1991 *Priests and Programmers: Technologies of Power in the Engineered Landscape of Bali.* Princeton, NJ: Princeton University Press.

Larson, A.

1989 Social Context of Human Immunodeficiency Virus Transmission in Africa: Historical and Cultural Bases of East and Central African Sexual Relations. *Review of Infectious Diseases* 11: 716–731.

Lassiter, L. E.

1998 *The Power of Kiowa Song: A Collaborative Ethnography.* Tucson: University of Arizona Press.

Layton, R.

1991 *The Anthropology of Art*, 2nd ed. New York: Cambridge University Press.

Leach, E. R.

1955 Polyandry, Inheritance and the Definition of Marriage. *Man* 55: 182–186.

1961 *Rethinking Anthropology.* London: Athlone Press.

1985 *Social Anthropology.* New York: Oxford University Press.

Leakey, R. E., M. G. Leakey, and A. C. Walker

1988 Morphology of *Afropithecus turkanensis* from Kenya. *American Journal of Physical Anthropology* 76: 289–307.

LeClair, E. E., and H. K. Schneider, eds.

1968 (orig. 1961). *Economic Anthropology: Readings in Theory and Analysis.* New York: Holt, Rinehart and Winston.

Lee, R. B.

1974 (orig. 1968). What Hunters Do for a Living, or, How to Make Out on Scarce Resources. In *Man in Adaptation: The Cultural Present,* 2nd ed., ed. Y. A. Cohen, pp. 87–100. Chicago: Aldine.

1979 *The !Kung San: Men, Women, and Work in a Foraging Society.* New York: Cambridge University Press.

1984 *The Dobe !Kung.* New York: Holt, Rinehart and Winston.

1993 *The Dobe Ju/'hoansi,* 2nd ed. Fort Worth: Harcourt Brace.

Lee, R. B., and R. H. Daly

1999 *The Cambridge Encyclopedia of Hunters and Gatherers.* New York: Cambridge University Press.

Lee, R. B., and I. DeVore, eds.

1977 *Kalahari Hunter-Gatherers: Studies of the !Kung San and Their Neighbors.* Cambridge, MA: Harvard University Press.

Lehmann, A. C., and J. E. Meyers, eds.

1997 *Magic, Witchcraft, and Religion: An Anthropological Study of the Supernatural,* 4th ed. Mountain View, CA: Mayfield.

Lemonick, M. D., and A. Dorfman

1999 Up from the Apes: Remarkable New Evidence Is Filling in the Story of How We Became Human. *Time* 154(8): 5–58.

Lenski, G.

1966 *Power and Privilege: A Theory of Social Stratification.* New York: McGraw-Hill.

Lessa, W. A., and E. Z. Vogt, eds.

1978 *Reader in Comparative Religion: An Anthropological Approach,* 4th ed. New York: Harper & Row.

Lévi-Strauss, C.

1963 *Totemism.* Translated by R. Needham. Boston: Beacon Press.

1967 *Structural Anthropology.* New York: Doubleday.

1969 (orig. 1949). *The Elementary Structures of Kinship.* Boston: Beacon Press.

Levine, L., ed.

1995 *Genetics of Natural Populations: The Continuing Importance of Theodosius Dobzhansky.* New York: Columbia University Press.

Levine, N.

1988 *The Dynamics of Polyandry: Kinship, Domesticity, and Population on the Tibetan Border.* Chicago: University of Chicago Press.

Levine, R. A.

1982 *Culture, Behavior, and Personality: An Introduction to the Comparative Study of Psychosocial Adaptation,* 2nd ed. Chicago: Aldine.

Levine, R. A., ed.

1974 *Culture and Personality: Contemporary Readings.* Chicago: Aldine.

Lewin, R.

1998 *Principles of Human Evolution: A Core Textbook.* Malden, MA: Blackwell Science.

1999 *Human Evolution: An Illustrated Introduction,* 4th ed. Malden, MA: Blackwell Science.

Lewis, H. S.

1989 *After the Eagles Landed: The Yemenites of Israel.* Boulder, CO: Westview.

Lewis, O.

1959 *Five Families.* New York: Basic Books.

Lewis, P.

1992 U.N. Sees a Crisis in Overpopulation. *The New York Times,* April 30, p. A6.

Lieban, R. W.

1977 The Field of Medical Anthropology. In *Culture, Disease, and Healing: Studies in Medical Anthropology,* ed. D. Landy, pp. 13–31. New York: Macmillan.

Lieberman, P.

1998 *Eve Spoke: Human Language and Human Evolution.* New York: W. W. Norton.

Light, D., S. Keller, and C. Calhoun

1994 *Sociology,* 6th ed. New York: McGraw-Hill.

Linden, E.

1986 *Silent Partners: The Legacy of the Ape Language Experiments.* New York: Times Books.

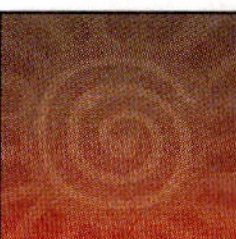

Lindenbaum, S.
1972 Sorcerers, Ghosts, and Polluting Women: An Analysis of Religious Belief and Population Control. *Ethnology 11:* 241–253.

Lindholm, C.
2001 *Culture and Identity: The History, Theory, and Practice of Psychological Anthropology.* Boston: McGraw-Hill.

Linton, R.
1927 Report on Work of Field Museum Expedition in Madagascar. *American Anthropologist* 29: 292–307.
1943 Nativistic Movements. *American Anthropologist* 45: 230–240.

Lipke, D. J.
2000 Dead End Ahead? Income May Be the Real Barrier to the Internet On-Ramp. *American Demographics*, August. http://www.demographics.com/publications/ad/00_ad/ad000805c.htm.

Little, K.
1965 *West African Urbanization: A Study of Voluntary Associations in Social Change.* Cambridge: Cambridge University Press.
1971 *Some Aspects of African Urbanization South of the Sahara. McCaleb Modules in Anthropology.* Reading, MA: Addison-Wesley.

Livingstone, F. B.
1958 Anthropological Implications of Sickle Cell Gene Distribution in West Africa. *American Anthropologist* 60: 533–562.
1969 Gene Frequency Clines of the *b* Hemoglobin Locus in Various Human Populations and Their Similarities by Models Involving Differential Selection. *Human Biology* 41: 223–236.

Lizot, J.
1985 *Tales of the Yanomami: Daily Life in the Venezuelan Forest.* New York: Cambridge University Press.

Lockwood, W. G.
1975 *European Moslems: Economy and Ethnicity in Western Bosnia.* New York: Academic Press.

Loomis, W. F.
1967 Skin-Pigmented Regulation of Vitamin-D Biosynthesis in Man. *Science* 157: 501–506.

Lowie, R. H.
1935 *The Crow Indians.* New York: Farrar and Rinehart.
1961 (orig. 1920). *Primitive Society.* New York: Harper & Brothers.

Lugaila, T.
1998*a* Numbers of Divorced and Never-Married Adults Increasing, Says Census Bureau Report. http://www.census.gov/Press-Release/cb98-56.html.
1998*b* Marital Status and Living Arrangements, March 1998 (Update). http://www.census.gov/prod/99pubs/p20-514.pdf.
1999 Married Adults Still in the Majority, Census Bureau Reports. http://www.census.gov/Press-Release/www/1999/cb99-03.html.

Lutz, C., and J. L. Collins
1993 *Reading National Geographic.* Chicago: University of Chicago Press.

Lyell, C.
1969 (orig. 1830–37). *Principles of Geology.* New York: Johnson.

MacKinnon, J.
1974 *In Search of the Red Ape.* New York: Ballantine.

Maher, J. C., and G. MacDonald, eds.
1995 *Diversity and Language in Japanese Culture.* New York: Columbia University Press.

Mair, L.
1969 *Witchcraft.* New York: McGraw-Hill.

Malinowski, B.
1927 *Sex and Repression in Savage Society.* London and New York: International Library of Psychology, Philosophy and Scientific Method.
1929*a* Practical Anthropology. *Africa* 2: 23–38.
1929*b* *The Sexual Life of Savages in North-Western Melanesia.* New York: Harcourt, Brace, and World.
1961 (orig. 1922). *Argonauts of the Western Pacific.* New York: Dutton.
1978 (orig. 1931). The Role of Magic and Religion. In *Reader in Comparative Religion: An Anthropological Approach*, 4th ed., ed. W. A. Lessa and E. Z. Vogt, pp. 37–46. New York: Harper & Row.
1985 (orig. 1927). *Sex and Repression in Savage Society.* Chicago: University of Chicago Press.

Malkki, L. H.
1995 *Purity and Exile: Violence, Memory, and National Cosmology among Hutu Refugees in Tanzania.* Chicago: University of Chicago Press.

Mann, A.
1975 *Paleodemographic Aspects of the South African Australopithecines.* Publications in Anthropology, no. 1. Philadelphia: University of Pennsylvania.

Manners, R.
1973 (orig. 1956). Functionalism, Realpolitik and Anthropology in Underdeveloped Areas. *America Indigena* 16. Also in *To See Ourselves: Anthropology and Modern Social Issues*, gen. ed. T. Weaver, pp. 113–126. Glenview, IL: Scott, Foresman.

Maquet, J.
1964 Objectivity in Anthropology. *Current Anthropology* 5: 47–55 (also in Clifton, ed., 1970).
1986 *The Aesthetic Experience: An Anthropologist Looks at the Visual Arts.* New Haven, CT: Yale University Press.

Mar, M. E.
1997 Secondary Colors: The Multiracial Option. *Harvard Magazine*, May–June 1997, pp. 19–20.

Marcus, G. E., and D. Cushman
1982 Ethnographies as Texts. *Annual Review of Anthropology* 11: 25–69.

Marcus, G. E., and M. M. J. Fischer
1986 *Anthropology as Cultural Critique: An Experimental Moment in the Human Sciences.* Chicago: University of Chicago Press.
1999 *Anthropology as Cultural Critique: An Experimental Moment in the Human Sciences*, 2nd ed. Chicago: University of Chicago Press.

Marcus, G. E., and F. R. Myers, eds.
1995 *The Traffic in Culture: Refiguring Art and Anthropology.* Berkeley: University of California Press.

Marcus, J.
1992 *Mesoamerican Writing Systems: Propaganda, Myth, and History in Four Ancient Civilizations.* Princeton, NJ: Princeton University Press.

Marcus, J., and K. V. Flannery
1996 *Zapotec Civilization: How Urban Society Evolved in Mexico's Oaxaca Valley.* New York: Thames and Hudson.

Margolis, M.
1984 *Mothers and Such: American Views of Women and How They Changed.* Berkeley: University of California Press.
1994 *Little Brazil: An Ethnography of Brazilian Immigrants in New York City.* Princeton, NJ: Princeton University Press.
2000 *True to Her Nature: Changing Advice to American Women.* Prospect Heights, IL: Waveland.

Marks, J.
1995 *Human Biodiversity: Genes, Race, and History.* New York: Aldine de Gruyter.

Marshack, A.
1972 *Roots of Civilization.* New York: McGraw-Hill.

Martin, E.
1987 *The Woman in the Body: A Cultural Analysis of Reproduction.* Boston: Beacon Press.

Martin, J.
1992 *Cultures in Organizations: Three Perspectives.* New York: Oxford University Press.

Martin, K., and B. Voorhies
1975 *Female of the Species.* New York: Columbia University Press.

Martin, P., and E. Midgley
1994 Immigration to the United States: Journey to an Uncertain Destination. *Population Bulletin* 49(3): 1–47.

Marx, K., and F. Engels
1976 (orig. 1848). *Communist Manifesto.* New York: Pantheon.

Mathews, G.
2000 *Global Culture/Individual Identity: Searching for Home in the Cultural Supermarket.* New York: Routledge.

Mayr, E.
1970 *Population, Species, and Evolution.* Cambridge, MA: Harvard University Press.

McAllester, D. P.
1954 *Enemy Way Music: A Study of Social and Esthetic Values as Seen in Navaho Music.* Cambridge, MA: Peabody Museum of American Archaeology and Ethnology, Papers 41(3).

McCaskie, T. C.
1995 *State and Society in Pre-Colonial Asante.* New York: Cambridge University Press.

McDonald, G.
1984 *Carioca Fletch.* New York: Warner Books.

McElroy, A., and P. K. Townsend
1996 *Medical Anthropology in Ecological Perspective*, 3rd ed. Boulder, CO: Westview.

McGraw, T. K., ed.
1986 *America versus Japan.* Boston: Harvard Business School Press.

McGrew, W. C.
1979 Evolutionary Implications of Sex Differences in Chimpanzee Predation and Tool Use. In D. A. Hamburg and E. R. McCown, eds. *The Great Apes*, pp. 441–463. Menlo Park, CA: Benjamin Cummings.

McGrew, W., L. Marchant, and T. Nishida
1996 *Great Ape Societies.* Cambridge: Cambridge University Press.

McKinley, J.
1996 Board's Decision on Black English Stirs Debate. *The New York Times,* December 21, www.nytimes.com.

McKusick, V.
1966 *Mendelian Inheritance in Man.* Baltimore: Johns Hopkins University Press.
1990 *Mendelian Inheritance in Man: Catalogs of Autosomal Dominant, Autosomal Recessive, and X-Linked Phenotypes,* 9th ed. Baltimore: Johns Hopkins University Press.

Mead, M.
1930 *Growing Up in New Guinea.* New York: Blue Ribbon.
1950 (orig. 1935). *Sex and Temperament in Three Primitive Societies.* New York: New American Library.
1961 (orig. 1928). *Coming of Age in Samoa.* New York: Morrow Quill.
1972 *Blackberry Winter: My Earlier Years.* New York: Simon and Schuster.

Meadow, R., ed.
1991 *Harappa Excavations 1986–1990: A Multidisciplinary Approach to Third Millennium Urbanism.* Monographs in World Archeology, no. 3. Madison, WI: Prehistory Press.

Meadow, R. H., and J. M. Kenoyer
2000 The Indus Valley Mystery: One of the World's First Great Civilizations Is Still a Puzzle. *Discovering Archaeology,* March/April 2000. http://www/discoveringarchaeology.com/0800toc/8feature1-indus.shtml.

Merriam, A.
1971 The Arts and Anthropology. In *Anthropology and Art: Readings in Cross-Cultural Aesthetics,* ed. C. Otten, pp. 93–105. Austin, TX: University of Texas Press.

Michaels, E.
1986 Aboriginal Content. Paper presented at the meeting of the Australian Screen Studies Association, December, Sydney.

Michaelson, K.
1996 Information, Community, and Access. *Social Science Computing Review* 14(1): 57–59.

Michrina, B. P., and C. Richards
1996 *Person to Person: Fieldwork, Dialogue, and the Hermeneutic Method.* Albany, NY: State University of New York Press.

Middleton, J.
1967 *Introduction. In Myth and Cosmos: Readings in Mythology and Symbolism,* ed. John Middleton, pp. ix–xi. Garden City, NY: Natural History Press.
1993 *The Lugbara of Uganda,* 2nd ed. Fort Worth: Harcourt Brace.

Middleton, J., ed.
1967 *Gods and Rituals.* Garden City, NY: Natural History Press.

Miles, H. L.
1983 Apes and Language: The Search for Communicative Competence. In *Language in Primates,* ed. J. de Luce and H. T. Wilder, pp. 43–62. New York: Springer Verlag.

Miller, B. D.
1997 *The Endangered Sex: Neglect of Female Children in Rural North India.* New York: Oxford University Press.

Miller, B. D., ed.
1993 *Sex and Gender Hierarchies.* New York: Cambridge University Press.

Miller, N., and R. C. Rockwell, eds.
1988 *AIDS in Africa: The Social and Policy Impact.* Lewiston: Edwin Mellen.

Mills, G.
1971 Art: An Introduction to Qualitative Anthropology. In *Anthropology and Art: Readings in Cross-Cultural Aesthetics,* ed. C. Otten, pp. 66–92. Austin, TX: University of Texas Press.

Mintz, S.
1985 *Sweetness and Power: The Place of Sugar in Modern History.* New York: Viking Penguin.

Mirzoeff, N.
1999 *An Introduction to Visual Culture.* New York: Routledge.

Mishler, E. G.
1991 *Research Interviewing: Context and Narrative.* Cambridge, MA: Harvard University Press.

Mitani, J. C., and D. P. Watts
1999 Demographic Influences on the Hunting Behavior of Chimpanzees. *American Journal of Physical Anthropology* 109: 439–454.

Mitchell, J. C.
1966 Theoretical Orientations in African Urban Studies. In *The Social Anthropology of Complex Societies,* ed. M. Banton, pp. 37–68. London: Tavistock.

Moerman, M.
1965 Ethnic Identification in a Complex Civilization: Who Are the Lue? *American Anthropologist* 67(5 Part I): 1215–1230.

Molnar, S.
1998 *Human Variation: Races, Types, and Ethnic Groups.* Upper Saddle River, NJ: Prentice Hall.

Montagu, A.
1975 *The Nature of Human Aggression.* New York: Oxford University Press.
1981 *Statement on Race: An Annotated Elaboration and Exposition of the Four Statements on Race Issued by the United Nations Educational, Scientific, and Cultural Organization.* Westport, CT: Greenwood.

Montagu, A., ed.
1996 *Race and IQ,* expanded ed. New York: Oxford University Press.
1997 *Man's Most Dangerous Myth: The Fallacy of Race.* Walnut Creek, CA: AltaMira.

Montague, S., and R. Morais
1981 Football Games and Rock Concerts: The Ritual Enactment. In *The American Dimension: Cultural Myths and Social Realities,* 2nd ed., ed. W. Arens and S. B. Montague, pp. 33–52. Sherman Oaks, CA: Alfred.

Montgomery, S.
1991 *Walking with the Great Apes: Jane Goodall, Dian Fossey, Biruté Galdikas.* Boston: Houghton Mifflin.

Moore, A. D.
1985 *The Development of Neolithic Societies in the Near East. Advances in World Archaeology* 4:1–69.

Moore, S. F.
1986 *Social Facts and Fabrications.* Cambridge: Cambridge University Press.

Moran, E. F.
1982 *Human Adaptability: An Introduction to Ecological Anthropology.* Boulder, CO: Westview.

Morbeck, M. E., A. Galloway, and A. L. Zihlman, eds.
1997 *The Evolving Female: A Life-History Perspective.* Princeton, NJ: Princeton University Press.

Morgan, L. H.
1963 (orig. 1877). *Ancient Society.* Cleveland: World Publishing.

Morgen, S., ed.
1989 *Gender and Anthropology: Critical Reviews for Research and Teaching.* Washington, DC: American Anthropological Association.

Morris, B.
1987 *Anthropological Studies of Religion: An Introductory Text.* New York: Cambridge University Press.

Mowat, F.
1987 *Woman in the Mists: The Story of Dian Fossey and the Mountain Gorillas of Africa.* New York: Warner Books.

Muhlhausler, P.
1986 *Pidgin and Creole Linguistics.* London: Basil Blackwell.

Mukhopadhyay, C., and P. Higgins
1988 Anthropological Studies of Women's Status Revisited: 1977–1987. *Annual Review of Anthropology* 17: 461–495.

Mullings, L., ed.
1987 *Cities of the United States: Studies in Urban Anthropology.* New York: Columbia University Press.

Murdock, G. P.
1934 *Our Primitive Contemporaries.* New York: Macmillan.
1957 World Ethnographic Sample. *American Anthropologist* 59: 664–687.

Murphy, R. F.
1990 *The Body Silent.* New York: W. W. Norton.

Murphy, R. F., and L. Kasdan
1959 The Structure of Parallel Cousin Marriage. *American Anthropologist* 61: 17–29.

Murray, S. O., and W. Roscoe, eds.
1998 *Boy-Wives and Female Husbands: Studies in African Homosexualities.* New York: St. Martin's.

Mydans, S.
1992*a* Criticism Grows over Aliens Seized during Riots. *The New York Times,* May 29, p. A8.
1992*b* Judge Dismisses Case in Shooting by Officer. *The New York Times,* June 4, p. A8.

Nagel, J.
1996 *American Indian Ethnic Renewal: Red Power and the Resurgence of Identity and Culture.* New York: Oxford University Press.

Napier, A. D.
1992 *Foreign Bodies: Performance, Art, and Symbolic Anthropology.* Berkeley: University of California Press.

Napier, J. R., and P. H. Napier
1985 *The Natural History of Primates.* Cambridge, MA: MIT Press.

Narayan, U.
1997 *Dislocating Cultures: Identities, Traditions, and Third World Feminisms.* New York: Routledge.

Nash, D.
1999 *A Little Anthropology,* 3rd ed. Upper Saddle River, NJ: Prentice Hall.

Nash, J., and H. Safa, eds.
1986 *Women and Change in Latin America.* South Hadley, MA: Bergin and Garvey.

National Association for the Practice of Anthropology
1991 *NAPA Directory of Practicing Anthropologists.* Washington, DC: American Anthropological Association.

National Vital Statistics Reports
2000 Births, Marriages, Divorces, and Deaths: Provisional Data for November 1999. October 31, 2000. Hyattsville, MD: U.S. Department of Health and Human Services, Center for Disease Control and Prevention, National Center for Health Statistics.

Naylor, L. L.
1996 *Culture and Change: An Introduction.* Westport, CT: Bergin and Garvey.

Nelson, H., and R. Jurmain
1991 *Introduction to Physical Anthropology,* 5th ed. St. Paul, MN: West.

Netting, R. M. C., R. R. Wilk, and E. J. Arnould, eds.
1984 *Households: Comparative and Historical Studies of the Domestic Group.* Berkeley: University of California Press.

Nevid, J. S., and Rathus, S. A.
1995 *Human Sexuality in a World of Diversity,* 2nd ed. Needham Heights, MA: Allyn & Bacon.

New York Times, The
1990 Tropical Diseases on March, Hitting 1 in 10. March 28, p. A3.
1992*a* Alexandria Journal: TV Program for Somalis Is a Rare Unifying Force. December 18.
1992*b* Married with Children: The Waning Icon. August 23, p. E2.

Newman, M.
1992 Riots Bring Attention to Growing Hispanic Presence in South-Central Area. *The New York Times,* May 11, p. A10.

Nielsson, G. P.
1985 States and Nation-Groups: A Global Taxonomy. In *New Nationalisms of the Developed World,* ed. E. A. Tiryakian and R. Rogowski, pp. 27–56. Boston: Allen and Unwin.

Nowak, R. M.
1999 *Walker's Primates of the World.* Baltimore: Johns Hopkins University Press.

Nussbaum, M. C.
2000 *Women and Human Development: The Capabilities Approach.* New York: Cambridge University Press.

Nussbaum, M., and J. Glover, eds.
1995 *Women, Culture, and Development: A Study of Human Capabilities.* New York: Oxford University Press.

Oakley, K. P.
1976 *Man the Tool-Maker,* 6th ed. Chicago: University of Chicago Press.

Okpewho, I.
1977 Principles of Traditional African Art. *The Journal of Aesthetics and Art Criticism* 35(3): 301–314.

Ong, A.
1987 *Spirits of Resistance and Capitalist Discipline: Factory Women in Malaysia.* Albany: State University of New York Press.
1989 Center, Periphery, and Hierarchy: Gender in Southeast Asia. In *Gender and Anthropology: Critical Reviews for Research and Teaching,* ed. S. Morgen, pp. 294–312. Washington, DC: American Anthropological Association.

Ong, A., and M. G. Peletz, eds.
1995 *Bewitching Women, Pious Men: Gender and Body Politics in Southeast Asia.* Berkeley: University of California Press.

Ontario Consultants on Religious Tolerance
1996 Religious Access Dispute Resolved. Internet Mailing List, April 12, http://www.religious-tolerance.org/news_694.htm.
1997 Swiss Cult Promotes Cloning. http://www.religious-tolerance.org/news_697.htm.

Otten, C. M., ed.
1971 *Anthropology and Art; Readings in Cross-Cultural Aesthetics.* Garden City, NY: American Museum of Natural History.

Otterbein, K. F.
1968 (orig. 1963). Marquesan Polyandry. In *Marriage, Family and Residence,* ed. P. Bohannan and J. Middleton, pp. 287–296. Garden City, NY: Natural History Press.

Park, M. A.
1999 *Biological Anthropology,* 2nd ed. Mountain View, CA: Mayfield.

Parker, S., and R. Kleiner
1970 The Culture of Poverty: An Adjustive Dimension. *American Anthropologist* 72: 516–527.

Parkin, R.
1997 *Kinship: An Introduction to Basic Concepts.* Cambridge, MA: Blackwell.

Parsons, J. R.

1974 The Development of a Prehistoric Complex Society: A Regional Perspective from the Valley of Mexico. *Journal of Field Archaeology* 1: 81–108.

1976 The Role of Chinampa Agriculture in the Food Supply of Aztec Tenochtitlan. In *Cultural Change and Continuity: Essays in Honor of James Bennett Griffin*, ed. C. E. Cleland, pp. 233–262. New York: Academic Press.

Pasternak, B., C. R. Ember, and M. Ember

1997 *Sex, Gender, and Kinship: A Cross-Cultural Perspective*. Upper Saddle River, NJ: Prentice Hall.

Patterson, F.

1978 Conversations with a Gorilla. *National Geographic*, October, pp. 438–465.

Patterson, T. C.

1993 *Archaeology: The Historical Development of Civilizations*, 2nd ed. Englewood Cliffs, NJ: Prentice Hall.

Paul, R.

1989 Psychoanalytic Anthropology. *Annual Review of Anthropology* 18: 177–202.

Pear, R.

1992 Ranks of U.S. Poor Reach 35.7 Million, the Most since '64. *The New York Times*, September 3, pp. A1, A12.

Peletz, M.

1988 *A Share of the Harvest: Kinship, Property, and Social History among the Malays of Rembau*. Berkeley: University of California Press.

Pelto, P.

1973 *The Snowmobile Revolution: Technology and Social Change in the Arctic*. Menlo Park, CA: Cummings.

Pelto, P. J., and G. H. Pelto

1978 *Anthropological Research: The Structure of Inquiry*, 2nd ed. New York: Cambridge University Press.

Peplau, L. A., ed.

1999 *Gender, Culture, and Ethnicity: Current Research about Women and Men*. Mountain View, CA: Mayfield.

Petraglia-Bahri, D.

1996 Introduction to Postcolonial Studies. http://www.emory.edu/ENGLISH/Bahri/.

Pettifor, E.

1995 From the Teeth of the Dragon—*Gigantopithecus blacki*. http://www.wynja.com/arch/gigantopithecus.html.

Pfeiffer, J.

1985 *The Emergence of Humankind*, 4th ed. New York: HarperCollins.

Phillipson, D. W.

1993 *African Archaeology*, 2nd ed. New York: Cambridge University Press.

Piddington, R.

1970 Action Anthropology. In *Applied Anthropology: Readings in the Uses of the Science of Man*, ed. James Clifton, pp. 127–143. Boston: Houghton Mifflin.

Piddocke, S.

1969 The Potlatch System of the Southern Kwakiutl: A New Perspective. In *Environment and Cultural Behavior*, ed. A. P. Vayda, pp. 130–156. Garden City, NY: Natural History Press.

Plattner, S., ed.

1989 *Economic Anthropology*. Stanford, CA: Stanford University Press.

Podolefsky, A.

1992 *Simbu Law: Conflict Management in the New Guinea Highlands*. Fort Worth: Harcourt Brace.

Podolefsky, A., and P. J. Brown, eds.

1992 *Applying Anthropology: An Introductory Reader*, 2nd ed. Mountain View, CA: Mayfield.

1998 *Applying Anthropology: An Introductory Reader*, 5th ed. Mountain View, CA: Mayfield.

Poirier, F. E., and J. K. Mckee

1998 *Understanding Human Evolution*, 4th ed. Upper Saddle River, NJ: Prentice Hall.

Polanyi, K.

1968 *Primitive, Archaic and Modern Economies: Essays of Karl Polanyi*. Edited by G. Dalton. Garden City, NY: Anchor Books.

Pollard, T. M., and S. B. Hyatt

1999 *Sex, Gender, and Health*. New York: Cambridge University Press.

Pollock, S.

1999 *Ancient Mesopotamia: The Eden That Never Was*. Cambridge: Cambridge University Press.

Pospisil, L.

1963 *The Kapauku Papuans of West New Guinea*. New York: Harcourt Brace Jovanovich.

Potash, B., ed.

1986 *Widows in African Societies: Choices and Constraints*. Stanford, CA: Stanford University Press.

Potts, D. T.

1997 *Mesopotamian Civilization: The Material Foundations*. Ithaca, NY: Cornell University Press.

Price, R., ed.
1973 *Maroon Societies*. New York: Anchor Press, Doubleday.

Price, T. D., ed.
2000 *Europe's First Farmers*. New York: Cambridge University Press.

Price, T. D., and G. M. Feinman
1997 *Images of the Past*, 2nd ed. Mountain View, CA: Mayfield.

Price, T. D. and A. B. Gebauer, eds.
1995 *Last Hunters, First Farmers: New Perspectives on the Prehistoric Transition to Agriculture*. Santa Fe, NM: School of American Research Press.

Public Culture
Journal published by the University of Chicago.

Punch, M.
1985 *The Politics and Ethics of Fieldwork*. Beverly Hills, CA: Sage.

Quiatt, D., and V. Reynolds
1995 *Primate Behavior: Information, Social Knowledge, and the Evolution of Culture*. New York: Cambridge University Press.

Quinn, N., and C. Strauss
1989 A Cognitive Cultural Anthropology. Paper presented at the Invited Session "Assessing Developments in Anthropology," American Anthropological Association 88th Annual Meeting, November 15–19, 1989, Washington, DC.
1994 *A Cognitive Cultural Anthropology. In Assessing Cultural Anthropology*, ed. R. Borofsky. New York: McGraw-Hill.

Radcliffe-Brown, A. R.
1965 (orig. 1962). *Structure and Function in Primitive Society*. New York: Free Press.

Radcliffe-Brown, A. R., and D. Forde, eds.
1994 *African Systems of Kinship and Marriage*. New York: Columbia University Press.

Rak, Y.
1986 The Neandertal: A New Look at an Old Face. *Journal of Human Evolution* 15(3): 151–164.

Random House College Dictionary
1982 Revised ed. New York: Random House.

Ranger, T. O.
1996 Postscript. In *Postcolonial Identities*, ed. R. Werbner and T. O. Ranger. London: Zed.

Rappaport, R. A.
1974 Obvious Aspects of Ritual. *Cambridge Anthropology* 2: 2–60.
1979 *Ecology, Meaning, and Religion*. Richmond, CA: North Atlantic Books.
1999 *Holiness and Humanity: Ritual in the Making of Religious Life*. New York: Cambridge University Press.

Rathus, S. A., J. S. Nevid, and J. Fichner-Rathus
1997 *Human Sexuality in a World of Diversity*, 3rd ed. Boston: Allyn & Bacon.
2000 *Human Sexuality in a World of Diversity*, 4th ed. Boston: Allyn & Bacon.

Read-Martin, C. E., and D. W. Read
1975 Australopithecine Scavenging and Human Evolution: An Approach from Faunal Analysis. *Current Anthropology* 16: 359–368.

Reade, J.
1991 *Mesopotamia*. Cambridge, MA: Harvard University Press.

Redfield, R.
1941 *The Folk Culture of Yucatan*. Chicago: University of Chicago Press.

Redfield, R., R. Linton, and M. Herskovits
1936 Memorandum on the Study of Acculturation. *American Anthropologist* 38: 149–152.

Redmond, E. M.
1994 Tribal and Chiefly Warfare in South America. *Museum of Anthropology Memoir* 28, University of Michigan (Ann Arbor).

Redmond, E. M., ed.
1998 *Chiefdoms and Chieftaincy in the Americas*. Gainesville, FL: University Press of Florida Press.

Reiter, R.
1975 Men and Women in the South of France: Public and Private Domains. In *Toward an Anthropology of Women*, ed. R. Reiter, pp. 252–282. New York: Monthly Review Press.

Reiter, R., ed.
1975 *Toward an Anthropology of Women*. New York: Monthly Review Press.

Relethford, J. H.
1997 *The Human Species: An Introduction to Biological Anthropology*, 3rd ed. Mountain View, CA: Mayfield.

Renfrew, C., and P. Bahn
1996 *Archaeology: Theories, Methods, and Practice*, 2nd ed. London: Thames and Hudson.
2000 *Archaeology: Theories, Methods, and Practices*, 3rd ed. New York: Thames and Hudson.

Reynolds, V.
1971 *The Apes*. New York: Harper Colophon.

Richards, D.
1994 *Masks of Difference: Cultural Representations in Literature, Anthropology, and Art.* New York: Cambridge University Press.

Richards, P.
1973 The Tropical Rain Forest. *Scientific American* 229(6): 58–67.

Rickford, J. R.
1997 Suite for Ebony and Phonics. http://www.stanford.edu/~rickford/papers/SuiteForEbonyandPhonics.html (also published in *Discover,* December 1997).
1999 *African American Vernacular English: Features, Evolution, Educational Implications.* Malden, MA: Blackwell.

Rickford, J. R., and Rickford, R. J.
2000 *Spoken Soul: The Story of Black English.* New York: Wiley.

Ricoeur, P.
1971 The Model of the Text: Meaningful Action Considered as a Text. *Social Research* 38: 529–562.

Rightmire, G. P.
1990 *The Evolution of* Homo erectus: *Comparative Anatomical Studies of an Extinct Human Species.* New York: Cambridge University Press.

Roberts, D. F.
1953 Body Weight, Race and Climate. *American Journal of Physical Anthropology* 11: 533–558.
1986 *Genetic Variation and Its Maintenance: With Particular Reference to Tropical Populations.* New York: Cambridge University Press.

Roberts, J. L.
1995 *Dian Fossey.* San Diego, CA: Lucent Books.

Roberts, S.
1979 *Order and Dispute: An Introduction to Legal Anthropology.* New York: Penguin Books.

Robertson, A. F.
1995 *The Big Catch: A Practical Introduction to Development.* Boulder, CO: Westview.

Robertson, J.
1992 Koreans in Japan. Paper presented at the University of Michigan Department of Anthropology, Martin Luther King Jr. Day Panel, January 1992. Ann Arbor: University of Michigan Department of Anthropology (unpublished).

Rodseth, L., R. W. Wrangham, A. M. Harrigan, and B. Smuts
1991 The Human Community as a Primate Society. *Current Anthropology* 32: 221–254.

Romaine, S.
1994 *Language in Society: An Introduction to Sociolinguistics.* New York: Oxford University Press.
1999 *Communicating Gender.* Mahwah, NJ: L. Erlbaum Associates.

Romer, A. S.
1960 *Man and the Vertebrates,* 3rd ed., Vol. 1. Harmondsworth, England: Penguin.

Root, D.
1996 *Cannibal Culture: Art, Appropriation, and the Commodification of Difference.* Boulder, CO: Westview.

Rosaldo, M. Z.
1980*a* *Knowledge and Passion: Notions of Self and Social Life.* Stanford, CA: Stanford University Press.
1980*b* The Use and Abuse of Anthropology: Reflections on Feminism and Cross-Cultural Understanding. *Signs* 5(3): 389–417.

Rosaldo, M. Z., and L. Lamphere, eds.
1974 *Woman, Culture, and Society.* Stanford, CA: Stanford University Press.

Rose, M.
1997 Neandertal DNA. Newsbriefs. *Archaeology* 50 (September/October): 5, http://www.archaeology.org/9709/newsbriefs/dna.html.

Roseberry, W.
1988 Political Economy. *Annual Review of Anthropology* 17: 161–185.

Rouse, R.
1991 Mexican Migration and the Social Space of Postmodernism. *Diaspora* 1(1): 8–23.

Royal Anthropological Institute
1951 *Notes and Queries on Anthropology,* 6th ed. London: Routledge and Kegan Paul.

Rushing, W. A.
1995 *The AIDS Epidemic: Social Dimension of an Infectious Disease.* Boulder, CO: Westview.

Rushing, W. Jackson, ed.
1999 *Native American Art in the Twentieth Century.* New York: Routledge.

Russon, A. E., K. A. Bard, and S. Taylor Parker, eds.
1996 *Reaching into Thought: The Minds of the Great Apes.* New York: Cambridge University Press.

Ryan, S.

1990 *Ethnic Conflict and International Relations.* Brookfield, MA: Dartmouth.

1995 *Ethnic Conflict and International Relations,* 2nd ed. Brookfield, MA: Dartmouth.

Sachs, C. E.

1996 *Gendered Fields: Rural Women, Agriculture, and Environment.* Boulder, CO: Westview.

Sade, D.

1972 A Longitudinal Study of Social Behavior of Rhesus Monkeys. In *The Functional and Evolutionary Biology of Primates,* ed. R. Tuttle, pp. 378–398. Chicago: University of Chicago Press.

Saggs, H.

1989 *Civilization before Greece and Rome.* New Haven: Yale University Press.

Sahlins, M. D.

1961 The Segmentary Lineage: An Organization of Predatory Expansion. *American Anthropologist* 63: 322–345.

1968 *Tribesmen.* Englewood Cliffs, NJ: Prentice Hall.

1972 *Stone Age Economics.* Chicago: Aldine.

1981 *Historical Metaphors and Mythical Realities: Structure in the Early History of the Sandwich Islands Kingdom.* Ann Arbor, MI: University of Michigan Press.

Saitoti, T. O.

1988 *The Worlds of a Maasai Warrior: An Autobiography.* Berkeley: University of California Press.

Saluter, A.

1995 Household and Family Characteristics: March 1994, P20-483, Press release, October 16, CB95-186, Single-Parent Growth Rate Stabilized; 2-parent Family Growth Renewed, Census Bureau Reports. United States Department of Commerce, Bureau of Census, Public Information Office.

1996 Marital Status and Living Arrangements: March 1994, P20-484, U.S. Census Bureau, Press release, March 13, 1996, CB96-33. United States Department of Commerce, Bureau of Census, Public Information Office, http://www.census.gov/prod/www/titles.html #popspec.

Salzman, P. C.

1974 Political Organization among Nomadic Peoples. In *Man in Adaptation: The Cultural Present,* 2nd ed., ed. Y. A. Cohen, pp. 267–284. Chicago: Aldine.

Salzman, P. C., and J. G. Galaty, eds.

1990 *Nomads in a Changing World.* Naples: Istituto Universitario Orientale.

Salzmann, Z.

1993 *Language, Culture, and Society: An Introduction to Linguistic Anthropology.* Boulder, CO: Westview.

Sanday, P. R.

1974 Female Status in the Public Domain. In *Woman, Culture, and Society,* ed. M. Z. Rosaldo and L. Lamphere, pp. 189–206. Stanford, CA: Stanford University Press.

Sanders, W. T.

1972 Population, Agricultural History, and Societal Evolution in Mesoamerica. In *Population Growth: Anthropological Implications,* ed. B. Spooner, pp. 101–153. Cambridge, MA: MIT Press.

1973 The Cultural Ecology of the Lowland Maya: A Reevaluation. In *The Classic Maya Collapse,* ed. T. P. Culbert, pp. 325–366. Albuquerque, NM: University of New Mexico Press.

Sanders, W. T., J. R. Parsons, and R. S. Santley

1979 *The Basin of Mexico: Ecological Processes in the Evolution of a Civilization.* New York: Academic Press.

Sankoff, G.

1980 *The Social Life of Language.* Philadelphia: University of Pennsylvania Press.

Santino, J.

1983 Night of the Wandering Souls. *Natural History* 92(10): 42.

Santley, R. S.

1984 Obsidian Exchange, Economic Stratification, and the Evolution of Complex Society in the Basin of Mexico. In *Trade and Exchange in Early Mesoamerica,* ed. K. G. Hirth, pp. 43–86. Albuquerque, NM: University of New Mexico Press.

1985 The Political Economy of the Aztec Empire. *Journal of Anthropological Research* 41(3): 327–337.

Sapir, E.

1931 Conceptual Categories in Primitive Languages. *Science* 74: 578–584.

Sargent, C. F., and C. B. Brettell

1996 *Gender and Health: An International Perspective.* Englewood Cliffs, NJ: Prentice Hall.

Sargent, C. F., and T. J. Johnson, eds.
1996 *Medical Anthropology: A Handbook of Theory and Method*, rev. ed. Westport, CT: Praeger Press.

Schaefer, R.
1989 *Sociology*, 3rd ed. New York: McGraw-Hill.

Schaefer, R., and R. P. Lamm
1994 *Sociology*. New York: McGraw-Hill.
1997 *Sociology*, 2nd ed. New York: McGraw-Hill.

Schaller, G.
1963 *The Mountain Gorilla: Ecology and Behavior.* Chicago: University of Chicago Press.

Scheffler, H. W.
2000 *Filiation and Affiliation*. Boulder, CO: Westview.

Scheinman, M.
1980 Imperialism. *Academic American Encyclopedia*, volume 11, pp. 61–62. Princeton, NJ: Arete.

Scheper-Hughes, N.
1987 Culture, Scarcity, and Maternal Thinking: Mother Love and Child Death in Northeast Brazil. In *Child Survival*, ed. N. Scheper-Hughes, pp. 187–208. Boston: D. Reidel.
1992 *Death without Weeping: The Violence of Everyday Life in Brazil*. Berkeley: University of California Press.

Schieffelin, E.
1976 *The Sorrow of the Lonely and the Burning of the Dancers*. New York: St. Martin's.

Schildkrout, E., and C. A. Keim
1990 *African Reflections: Art from Northeastern Zaire*. Seattle, WA: University of Washington Press.

Scholte, J. A.
2000 *Globalization: A Critical Introduction*. New York: St. Martin's.

Scott, J. C.
1985 *Weapons of the Weak*. New Haven: Yale University Press.
1990 *Domination and the Arts of Resistance*. New Haven: Yale University Press.
1998 *Seeing Like a State: How Certain Schemes to Improve the Human Condition Have Failed.* New Haven: Yale University Press.

Scudder, T.
1982 The Impact of Big Dam-building on the Zambezi River Basin. In *The Careless Technology: Ecology and International Development*, eds. M. T. Farvar and J. P. Milton, pp. 206–235. New York: Natural History Press.

Scudder, T., and E. Colson
1980 *Secondary Education and the Formation of an Elite: The Impact of Education on Gwembe District, Zambia*. London: Academic Press.

Scudder, T., and J. Habarad
1991 Local Responses to Involuntary Relocation and Development in the Zambian Portion of the Middle Zambezi Valley. In *Migrants in Agricultural Development*, ed. J. A. Mollett, pp. 178–205. New York: New York University Press.

Sebeok, T. A., and J. Umiker-Sebeok, eds.
1980 *Speaking of Apes: A Critical Anthropology of Two-Way Communication with Man*. New York: Plenum.

Seligson, M. A.
1984 *The Gap between Rich and Poor: Contending Perspectives on the Political Economy of Development*. Boulder, CO: Westview.

Sered, S. S.
1996 *Priestess, Mother, Sacred Sister: Religions Dominated by Women*. New York: Oxford University Press.

Service, E. R.
1962 *Primitive Social Organization: An Evolutionary Perspective*. New York: McGraw-Hill.
1966 *The Hunters*. Englewood Cliffs, NJ: Prentice Hall.
1975 *Origins of the State and Civilization: The Process of Cultural Evolution*. New York: W. W. Norton.

Shabecoff, P.
1989*a* Ivory Imports Banned to Aid Elephant. *The New York Times*, June 7, p. 15.
1989*b* New Lobby Is Helping Wildlife of Africa. *The New York Times*, June 9, p. 14.

Shanklin, E.
1995 *Anthropology and Race*. Belmont, CA: Wadsworth.

Shannon, T. R.
1989 *An Introduction to the World-System Perspective*. Boulder, CO: Westview.
1996 *An Introduction to the World-System Perspective*, 2nd ed. Boulder, CO: Westview Press.

Shepher, J.
1983 *Incest, a Biosocial View*. New York: Academic Press.

Shigeru, K.
1994 *Our Land Was a Forest: An Ainu Memoir.* Boulder, CO: Westview.

Shivaram, C.
1996 Where Women Wore the Crown: Kerala's Dissolving Matriarchies Leave a Rich Legacy of Compassionate Family Culture. *Hinduism Today* 96(02), http://www.spiritweb.org/HinduismToday/96-02-Women_Wore_Crown.html.

Shore, B.
1996 *Culture in Mind: Meaning, Construction, and Cultural Cognition.* New York: Oxford University Press.

Shostak, M.
1981 *Nisa, the Life and Words of a !Kung Woman.* New York: Vintage Books.
2000 *Return to Nisa.* Cambridge, MA: Harvard University Press.

Shreeve, J.
1992 The Dating Game: How Old Is the Human Race? *Discover* 13(9): 76–83.

Shweder, R., and H. Levine, eds.
1984 *Culture Theory: Essays on Mind, Self, and Emotion.* Cambridge: Cambridge University Press.

Sibley, C. G., and J. E. Ahlquist
1984 The Phylogeny of the Hominoid Primates, as Indicated by DNA-DNA Hybridization. *Journal of Molecular Evolution* 20: 2–15.

Signo, A.
1994 *Economics of the Family.* New York: Oxford University Press.

Silberbauer, G.
1981 *Hunter and Habitat in the Central Kalahari Desert.* New York: Cambridge University Press.

Silverberg, J., and J. P. Gray, eds.
1992 *Aggression and Peacefulness in Humans and Other Primates.* New York: Oxford University Press.

Simons, A.
1995 *Networks of Dissolution: Somalia Undone.* Boulder, CO: Westview.

Simons, E. L., and P. C. Ettel
1970 *Gigantopithecus. Scientific American,* January, pp. 77–85.

Simpson, B.
1998 *Changing Families: An Ethnographic Approach to Divorce and Separation.* New York: Berg.

Slade, M. F.
1984 Displaying Affection in Public. *The New York Times,* December 17, p. B14.

Small, M., ed.
1984 *Female Primates: Studies by Women Primatologists.* New York: Alan R. Liss.

Small, M. F.
1993 *Female Choices: Sexual Behavior of Female Primates.* Ithaca: Cornell University Press.

Smith, B. D.
1995 *The Emergence of Agriculture.* New York: Scientific American Library, W. H. Freeman.

Smith, C. A.
1990 The Militarization of Civil Society in Guatemala: Economic Reorganization as a Continuation of War. *Latin American Perspectives* 17: 8–41.

Smith, M. E., and M. A. Masson, eds.
2000 *The Ancient Civilizations of Mesoamerica: A Reader.* Malpen, MA: Blackwell.

Smith, M. G.
1965 *The Plural Society in the British West Indies.* Berkeley: University of California Press.

Smitherman, G.
1986 *Talkin and Testifyin: The Language of Black America.* Detroit: Wayne State University Press.

Smuts, B. B.
1985 *Sex and Friendship in Baboons.* New York: Aldine.

Solheim, W. G., II
1976 (orig. 1972). An Earlier Agricultural Revolution. In *Avenues to Antiquity, Readings from Scientific American,* ed. B. M. Fagan, pp. 160–168. San Francisco: W. H. Freeman.

Solway, J., and R. Lee
1990 Foragers, Genuine and Spurious: Situating the Kalahari San in History (with CA treatment). *Current Anthropology* 31(2): 109–146.

Sonneville-Bordes, D. de
1963 Upper Paleolithic Cultures in Western Europe. *Science* 142: 347–355.

Spindler, G. D., ed.
1978 *The Making of Psychological Anthropology.* Berkeley: University of California Press.
1982 *Doing the Ethnography of Schooling: Educational Anthropology in Action.* New York: Holt, Rinehart and Winston.
2000 *Fifty Years of Anthropology and Education, 1950–2000: A Spindler Anthology.* Mahwah, NJ: Erlbaum Associates.

Sponsel, L. E., and T. Gregor, eds.
1994 *The Anthropology of Peace and Nonviolence.* Boulder, CO: Lynne Reinner.

Spradley, J. P.
1979 *The Ethnographic Interview.* New York: Harcourt Brace Jovanovich.

Srivastava, J., N. J. H. Smith, and D. A. Forno
1998 *Integrating Biodiversity in Agricultural Intensification: Toward Sound Practices.* Washington, DC: World Bank.

Stacey, J.
1996 *In the Name of the Family: Rethinking Family Values in the Postmodern Age.* Boston: Beacon Press.
1998 *Brave New Families: Stories of Domestic Upheaval in Late Twentieth Century America.* Berkeley: University of California Press.

Stack, C. B.
1975 *All Our Kin: Strategies for Survival in a Black Community.* New York: Harper Torchbooks.

Staeck, J.
2001 *Back to the Earth: An Introduction to Archaeology.* Mountain View, CA: Mayfield.

Statistical Abstract of the United States
1991 111th ed. Washington, DC: U.S. Bureau of the Census, U.S. Government Printing Office.
1996 116th ed. Washington, DC: U.S. Bureau of the Census, U.S. Government Printing Office.
1999 *Statistical Abstract of the United States, 1999. http://www.census.gov/statab/www/.*

Statistics Canada
1998 1996 Census: Ethnic Origin, Visible Minorities. *The Daily,* February 17. http://www.statcan.ca/Daily/English/980217/d980217.htm.

Staub, S.
1989 *Yemenis in New York City: The Folklore of Ethnicity.* Philadelphia: Balch Institute Press.

Steegman, A. T., Jr.
1975 *Human Adaptation to Cold. In Physiological Anthropology,* ed. A. Damon, pp. 130–166. New York: Oxford University Press.

Steinfels, P.
1997 Beliefs: Cloning, as Seen by Buddhists and Humanists. *The New York Times,* July 12, http://www.nytimes.com.

Stephens, S., ed.
1996 *Children and the Politics of Culture.* Princeton, NJ: Princeton University Press.

Steponaitis, V.
1986 Prehistoric Archaeology in the Southeastern United States. *Annual Review of Anthropology* 15: 363–404.

Stern, A.
2000 Experts Say 138 World Primate Species Endangered. Reuters. http://www.forests.org/archive/general/exsay138.htm.
2000 More Than a Hundred Primate Species Endangered. http://www.foxnews.com/science/051200/primates.sml.

Stevens, W. K.
1992 Humanity Confronts Its Handiwork: An Altered Planet. *The New York Times,* May 5, pp. B5–B7.

Stevenson, R. F.
1968 *Population and Political Systems in Tropical Africa.* New York: Columbia University Press.

Steward, J. H.
1955 *Theory of Culture Change.* Urbana: University of Illinois Press.

Stocking, G. W., ed.
1986 *Malinowski, Rivers, Benedict and Others: Essays on Culture and Personality.* Madison, WI: University of Wisconsin Press.

Stoler, A.
1977 Class Structure and Female Autonomy in Rural Java. *Signs* 3: 74–89.

Stone, L.
2000 *Kinship and Gender: An Introduction,* 2nd ed. Boulder, CO: Westview.
2000 *New Directions in Anthropological Kinship.* Lanham, MD: Rowman and LIttlefield.

Stoneman, B.
1997 Income Is Rising, So Is Poverty. *American Demographics,* Forecast, November 1997, http://www.demographics.com/publications/fc/97_fc/9711_fc/fc97111.htm.

Strathern, A., and P. J. Stewart
1999 *Curing and Healing: Medical Anthropology in Global Perspective.* Durham, NC: Carolina Academic Press.

Strathern, M.
1988 *The Gender of the Gift: Problems with Women and Problems with Society in Melanesia.* Berkeley: University of California Press.

Strum, S. C., and L. M. Fedigan, eds.
2000 *Primate Encounters: Models of Science, Gender, and Society.* Chicago: University of Chicago Press.

Suarez-Orozco, M. M., G. Spindler, and L. Spindler, eds.
1994 *The Making of Psychological Anthropology II.* Fort Worth: Harcourt Brace.

Susman, R. L.
1987 Pygmy Chimpanzees and Common Chimpanzees: Models for the Behavioral Ecology of the Earliest Hominids. In *The Evolution of Human Behavior: Primate Models,* ed. W. G. Kinzey, pp. 72–86. Albany: State University of New York Press.

Susser, I., and T. C. Patterson, eds.
2000 *Cultural Diversity in the United States: A Critical Reader.* Malden, MA: Blackwell.

Suttles, W.
1960 Affinal Ties, Subsistence, and Prestige among the Coast Salish. *American Anthropologist* 62: 296–395.

Swift, M.
1963 Men and Women in Malay Society. In *Women in the New Asia,* ed. B. Ward, pp. 268–286. Paris: UNESCO.

Swindler, D. R.
1998 *Introduction to the Primates.* Seattle: University of Washington Press.

Tague, R. G., and C. O. Lovejoy
1986 The Obstetric Pelvis of A. L. 288-1 (Lucy). *Journal of Human Evolution* 15: 237–255.

Tainter, J.
1987 *The Collapse of Complex Societies.* New York: Cambridge University Press.

Tanaka, J.
1980 *The San Hunter-Gatherers of the Kalahari.* Tokyo: University of Tokyo Press.

Tannen, D.
1990 *You Just Don't Understand: Women and Men in Conversation.* New York: Ballantine.

Tannen, D., ed.
1993 *Gender and Conversational Interaction.* New York: Oxford University Press.

Tanner, N.
1974 Matrifocality in Indonesia and Africa and among Black Americans. In *Women, Culture, and Society,* ed. M. Z. Rosaldo and L. Lamphere, pp. 127–156. Stanford, CA: Stanford University Press.

Tattersall, I.
1995*a* *The Fossil Trail: How We Know What We Think We Know about Human Evolution.* New York: Oxford University Press.
1995*b* *The Last Neanderthal: The Rise, Success, and Mysterious Extinction of Our Closest Human Relatives.* New York: Macmillan.
1998 *Becoming Human: Evolution and Human Uniqueness.* New York: Harcourt Brace.

Taylor, A.
1993 *Women Drug Users: An Ethnography of a Female Injecting Community.* New York: Oxford University Press.

Taylor, C.
1987 Anthropologist-in-Residence. In *Applied Anthropology in America,* 2nd ed., ed. E. M. Eddy and W. L. Partridge. New York: Columbia University Press.
1996 *The Black Churches of Brooklyn.* New York: Columbia University Press.

Teleki, G.
1973 *The Predatory Behavior of Wild Chimpanzees.* Lewisburg, PA: Bucknell University Press.

Terrace, H. S.
1979 *Nim.* New York: Knopf.

Thomas, L.
1999 *Language, Society and Power.* New York: Routledge.

Thomason, S. G., And T. Kaufman
1988 *Language Contact, Creolization and Genetic Linguistics.* Berkeley: University of California Press.

Thompson, W.
1983 Introduction: World System with and without the Hyphen. In *Contending Approaches to World System Analysis,* ed. W. Thompson, pp. 7–26. Thousand Oaks, CA: Sage.

Thomson, A., And L. H. D. Buxton
1923 Man's Nasal Index in Relation to Certain Climatic Conditions. *Journal of the Royal Anthropological Institute* 53: 92–112.

Tice, K.
1997 Reflections on Teaching Anthropology for Use in the Public and Private Sector. In *The Teaching of Anthropology: Problems, Issues, and Decisions,* ed. C. P. Kottak, J. J. White, R. H. Furlow, and P. C. Rice, pp. 273–284. Mountain View, CA: Mayfield.

Tobler, A. J.
1950 *Excavations at Tepe Gawra,* vol. 2. Philadelphia: University of Pennsylvania Museum.

Toner, R.
1992 Los Angeles Riots Are a Warning, Americans Fear. *The New York Times,* May 11, pp. A1, A11.

Toth, N., and Schick, K.
1986 The First Million Years: The Archaeology of Protohuman Culture. *Advances in Archaeological Method and Theory,* pp. 1–96.

Trigger, B. G.
1995 *Early Civilizations: Ancient Egypt in Context.* New York: Columbia University Press.

Trudgill, P.
1983 *Sociolinguistics: An Introduction to Language and Society*, rev. ed. Baltimore: Penguin.
1995 *Sociolinguistics: An Introduction to Language and Society*, 3rd. rev. ed. New York: Penguin.

Turnbull, C.
1965 *Wayward Servants: The Two Worlds of the African Pygmies*. Garden City, NY: Natural History Press.

Turner, B. S.
1998 *Readings in the Anthropology and Sociology of Family and Kinship*. London: Routledge/Thoemmes.

Turner, V. W.
1969 *The Ritual Process*. Chicago: Aldine.
1974 *The Ritual Process*. Harmondsworth, England: Penguin.
1995 (orig. 1969). *The Ritual Process*. Hawthorne, NY: Aldine de Gruyter.

Tylor, E. B.
1889 On a Method of Investigating the Development of Institutions: Applied to Laws of Marriage and Descent. *Journal of the Royal Anthropological Institute* 18: 245–269.
1958 (orig. 1871). *Primitive Culture*. New York: Harper Torchbooks.

Ucko, P. J., and G. W. Dimbleby, eds.
1969 *The Domestication and Exploitation of Plants and Animals*. Chicago: Aldine.

Ucko, P., And A. Rosenfeld
1967 *Paleolithic Cave Art*. London: Weidenfeld and Nicolson.

U.S. Census Bureau
1998 Unpublished Tables—Marital Status and Living Arrangements, March 1998 (Update). http://www.census.gov/prod/99pubs/p20-514u.pdf.
1999 *Statisical Abstract of the United States*. http://www.census.gov/prod/99pubs/99statab/sec01.pdf and http://www.census.gov/prod/99pubs/99statab/sec02.pdf.

Valentine, C.
1968 *Culture and Poverty*. Chicago: University of Chicago Press.

Valladas, H., J. L. Reyss, J. L. Joron, G. Valladas, O. Bar-Joseph, and B. Vandermeersch
1988 Thermoluminescence Dating of Mousterian "Proto-Cro-Magnon" Remains from Israel and the Origin of Modern Man. *Nature* 331: 614–616.

Van Bremen, J., and A. Shimizu, eds.
1999 *Anthropology and Colonialism in Asia and Oceania*. London: Curzon.

Van Cantfort, T. E., and J. B. Rimpau
1982 Sign Language Studies with Children and Chimpanzees. *Sign Language Studies* 34: 15–72.

Van der Elst, D., and P. Bohannan
1999 *Culture as Given, Culture as Choice*. Prospect Heights, IL: Waveland.

van Schaik, C. P., and J. A. R. A. M. van Hooff
1983 On the Ultimate Causes of Primate Social Systems. *Behaviour* 85: 91–117.

Van Willingen, J.
1987 *Becoming a Practicing Anthropologist: A Guide to Careers and Training Programs in Applied Anthropology*. NAPA Bulletin 3. Washington, DC: American Anthropological Association/National Association for the Practice of Anthropology.
1993 *Applied Anthropology: An Introduction*, 2nd ed. South Hadley, MA: Bergin and Garvey.

Vayda, A. P.
1968 (orig. 1961). Economic Systems in Ecological Perspective: The Case of the Northwest Coast. In *Readings in Anthropology*, 2nd ed., vol. 2, ed. M. H. Fried, pp. 172–178. New York: Crowell.

Veblen, T.
1934 *The Theory of the Leisure Class: An Economic Study of Institutions*. New York, The Modern Library.

Verlinden, C.
1980 Colonialism. *Academic American Encyclopedia*, vol. 5, pp. 111–112. Princeton, NJ: Arete.

Viegas, J.
2000 Planet of the Dying Apes: Conference Reveals Steep Decline in Primate Populations. http://abcnews.go.com/sections/science/DailyNews/apeconference000512.html.

Vietnam Labor Watch
1997 Nike Labor Practices in Vietnam, March 20, http://www.saigon.com/~nike/reports/report1.html.

Vincent, J.
1990 *Anthropology and Politics: Visions, Traditions, and Trends*. Tucson: University of Arizona Press.

Viola, H. J., and C. Margolis
1991 *Seeds of Change: Five Hundred Years Since Columbus, a Quincentennial Commemoration*. Washington, DC: Smithsonian Institution Press.

Von Daniken, E.
1971 *Chariots of the Gods: Unsolved Mysteries of the Past*. New York: Bantam.

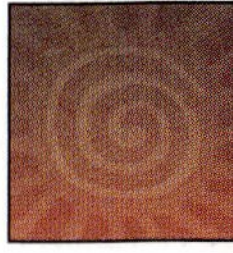

Wade, N.
1997 Testing Genes to Save a Life without Costing You a Job. *The New York Times.* September 14. www.nytimes.com.

Wade, N., ed.
1998 *The Science Times Book of Fossils and Evolution.* New York: Lyons Press.

Wagley, C. W.
1968 (orig. 1959). The Concept of Social Race in the Americas. In *The Latin American Tradition,* ed. C. Wagley, pp. 155–174. New York: Columbia University Press.

Wagner, R.
1981 *The Invention of Culture,* rev. ed. Chicago: University of Chicago Press.

Wallace, A. F. C.
1956 Revitalization Movements. *American Anthropologist* 58: 264–281.
1966 *Religion: An Anthropological View.* New York: McGraw-Hill.
1970 *The Death and Rebirth of the Seneca.* New York: Knopf.

Wallerstein, I. M.
1974 *The Modern World-System: Capitalist Agriculture and the Origins of the European World-Economy in the Sixteenth Century.* New York: Academic Press.
1980 *The Modern World System II: Mercantilism and the Consolidation of the European World-Economy, 1600–1750.* New York: Academic Press.
1982 The Rise and Future Demise of the World Capitalist System: Concepts for Comparative Analysis. In *Introduction to the Sociology of "Developing Societies,"* ed. H. Alavi and T. Shanin, pp. 29–53. New York: Monthly Review Press.
2000 *The Essential Wallerstein.* New York: New Press, W. W. Norton.

Wallman, S., ed.
1977 *Perceptions of Development.* New York: Cambridge University Press.

Ward, M. C.
1996 *A World Full of Women.* Needham Heights, MA: Allyn & Bacon.

Ward, S., B. Brown, A. Hill, J. Kelley, and W. Downs
1999 Equatorius: A New Hominoid Genus from the Middle Miocene of Kenya. *Science EurekAlert!* August 27. http://www.eurekalert.org.

Warren, K. B.
1998 *Indigenous Movements and Their Critics: Pan-Maya Activism in Guatemala.* Princeton, NJ: Princeton University Press.

Washburn, S. L., and R. Moore
1980 *Ape into Human: A Study of Human Evolution,* 2nd ed. Boston: Little, Brown.

Watson, J. D.
1970 *Molecular Biology of the Gene.* New York: Benjamin.

Watson, P.
1972 *Can Racial Discrimination Affect IQ? In Race and Intelligence; The Fallacies behind the Race-IQ Controversy,* ed. K. Richardson and D. Spears, pp. 56–67. Baltimore: Penguin.

Watson, P. J.
1983 The Halafian Culture: A Review and Synthesis. In *The Hilly Flanks and Beyond: Essays on the Prehistory of Southwestern Asia,* ed. T. C. Young Jr., P. E. L. Smith, and P. Mortensen. *Studies in Ancient Oriental Civilization* 36: 231–250. Oriental Institute, University of Chicago.

Weaver, T., gen. ed.
1973 *To See Ourselves: Anthropology and Modern Social Issues.* Glenview, IL: Scott, Foresman.

Weber, M.
1958 (orig. 1904). *The Protestant Ethic and the Spirit of Capitalism.* New York: Scribner's.
1968 (orig. 1922). *Economy and Society.* Translated by E. Fischoff et al. New York: Bedminster Press.

Webster's New World Encyclopedia
1993 College Edition. Englewood Cliffs, NJ: Prentice Hall.

Weiner, J. S.
1954 Nose Shape and Climate. *American Journal of Physical Anthropology* 12: 1–4.

Weiner, J.
1994 *The Beak of the Finch: A Story of Evolution in Our Time.* New York: Alfred A. Knopf.

Weiss, K. M.
1993 *Genetic Variation and Human Disease: Principles and Evolutionary Approaches.* New York: Cambridge University Press.

Weiss, M. L., And A. E. Mann
1990 *Human Biology and Behavior: An Anthropological Perspective,* 5th ed. Glenview, IL: Scott, Foresman.

Wenke, R. J.
1996 *Patterns in Prehistory: Mankind's First Three Million Years,* 4th ed. New York: Oxford University Press.

Westermarck, E.
1894 *The History of Human Marriage.* London: Macmillan.

Weston, K.
1991 *Families We Choose: Lesbians, Gays, Kinship.* New York: Columbia University Press.

White, L. A.
1959 *The Evolution of Culture: The Development of Civilization to the Fall of Rome.* New York: McGraw-Hill.

Whiting, B. E., ed.
1963 *Six Cultures: Studies of Child Rearing.* New York: Wiley.

Whiting, J. M.
1964 Effects of Climate on Certain Cultural Practices. In *Explorations in Cultural Anthropology: Essays in Honor of George Peter Murdock,* ed. W. H. Goodenough, pp. 511–544. New York: McGraw-Hill.

Whorf, B. L.
1956 A Linguistic Consideration of Thinking in Primitive Communities. In *Language, Thought, and Reality: Selected Writings of Benjamin Lee Whorf,* ed. J. B. Carroll, pp. 65–86. Cambridge, MA: MIT Press.

Wilford, J. N.
2000 Ruins Alter Ideas of How Civilization Spread, May 23. www.nytimes.com.

Wilk, R. R.
1996 *Economies and Cultures: An Introduction to Economic Anthropology.* Boulder, CO: Westview.

Williams, B.
1989 A Class Act: Anthropology and the Race to Nation across Ethnic Terrain. *Annual Review of Anthropology* 18: 401–444.

Wilmsen, E. N.
1989 *Land Filled with Flies: A Political Economy of the Kalahari.* Chicago: University of Chicago Press.

Wilmsen, E. N., and P. McAllister, eds.
1996 *The Politics of Difference: Ethnic Premises in a World of Power.* Chicago: University of Chicago Press.

Wilson, C.
1995 *Hidden in the Blood: A Personal Investigation of AIDS in the Yucatan.* New York: Columbia University Press.

Wilson, R., ed.
1996 *Human Rights: Culture and Context: Anthropological Perspectives.* Chicago: Pluto.

Winslow, J. H., and A. Meyer
1983 The Perpetrator at Piltdown. *Science* 83 (September): 33–43.

Winzeler, R. L.
1995 *Latah in Southeast Asia: The Ethnography and History of a Culture-Bound Syndrome.* New York: Cambridge University Press.

Wittfogel, K. A.
1957 *Oriental Despotism: A Comparative Study of Total Power.* New Haven: Yale University Press.

Wolf, E. R.
1966 *Peasants.* Englewood Cliffs, NJ: Prentice Hall.
1982 *Europe and the People without History.* Berkeley: University of California Press.
1999 *Envisioning Power: Ideologies of Dominance and Crisis.* Berkeley: University of California Press.

Wolf, E. R., with S. Silverman
2001 *Pathways of Power: Building an Anthropology of the Modern World.* Berkeley: University of California Press.

Wolpoff, M. H.
1980*a* *Paleoanthropology.* New York: McGraw-Hill.
1980*b* Cranial Remains of Middle Pleistocene Hominids. *Journal of Human Evolution* 9: 339–358.
1999 *Paleoanthropology,* 2nd ed. New York: McGraw-Hill.

Wolpoff, M. H., And R. Caspari
1997 *Race and Human Evolution.* New York: Simon and Schuster.

Woolard, K. A.
1989 *Double Talk: Bilingualism and the Politics of Ethnicity in Catalonia.* Stanford, CA: Stanford University Press.

World Almanac & Book of Facts
Published annually. New York: Newspaper Enterprise Association.

World Health Organization
1995 *World Health Report.* Geneva: World Health Organization.

Worsley, P.
1984 *The Three Worlds: Culture and World Development.* Chicago: University of Chicago Press.
1985 (orig. 1959). Cargo Cults. In *Readings in Anthropology* 85/86. Guilford, CT: Dushkin.

Wrangham, R. W.
1980 An Ecological Model of Female-Bonded Primate Groups. *Behavior* 75: 262–300.
1987 The Significance of African Apes for Reconstructing Human Social Evolution. In *The Evolution of Human Behavior: Primate Models,* ed. W. G. Kinzey, pp. 51–71. Albany: State University of New York Press.

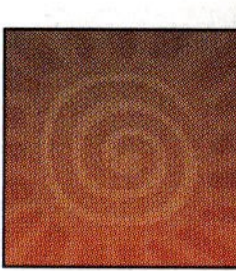

Wrangham, R. W., ed.
1994 *Chimpanzee Cultures.* Cambridge, MA: Harvard University Press.

Wrangham, R., W. McGrew, F. de Waal, and P. Heltne, eds.
1994 *Chimpanzee Cultures.* Cambridge, MA: Harvard University Press.

Wrangham, R. W., and D. Peterson
1996 *Demonic Males: Apes and the Origins of Human Violence.* Boston: Houghton Mifflin.

Wright, H. T., and G. A. Johnson
1975 Population, Exchange, and Early State Formation in Southwestern Iran. *American Anthropologist* 77: 267–289.
1994 Prestate Political Formations. In *Chiefdoms and Early States in the Near East: The Organizational Dynamics of Complexity,* ed. G. Stein and M. S. Rothman, *Monographs in World Archaeology* 18: 67–84. Madison, WI: Prehistory Press.

Wright, S., ed.
1994 *Anthropology of Organizations.* London: Routledge.

Wulff, R. M., and S. J. Fiske, eds.
1987 *Anthropological Praxis: Translating Knowledge into Action.* Boulder, CO: Westview.

Yetman, N., ed.
1991 *Majority and Minority: The Dynamics of Race and Ethnicity in American Life,* 5th ed. Boston: Allyn & Bacon.
1999 *Majority and Minority: The Dynamics of Race and Ethnicity in American Life,* 6th ed. Boston: Allyn & Bacon.

Young, W. C.
1996 *The Rashaayada Bedouin: Arab Pastoralists of Eastern Sudan.* Fort Worth: Harcourt Brace.

glossary

absolute dating Dating techniques that establish dates in numbers or ranges of numbers; examples include the radiometric methods of ^{14}C, K/A, ^{238}U, TL, and ESR dating.

acculturation The exchange of cultural features that results when groups come into continuous firsthand contact; the original cultural patterns of either or both groups may be altered, but the groups remain distinct.

Acheulian Derived from the French village of St. Acheul, where these tools were first identified; Lower Paleolithic tool tradition associated with *H. erectus.*

achieved status Social status that comes through talents, choices, actions, efforts, activities, and accomplishments, rather than ascription.

adapids Early (Eocene) primate family ancestral to lemurs and lorises.

adaptation The process by which organisms cope with environmental stresses.

adaptive Favored by natural selection in a particular environment.

advocacy view of applied anthropology; the belief that precisely because anthropologists are experts on human problems and social change, and because they study, understand, and respect cultural values, they should make policy affecting people.

aesthetics Appreciation of the qualities perceived in works of art; the mind and emotions in relation to a sense of beauty.

affinals Relatives by marriage, whether of lineals (e.g., son's wife) or collaterals (e.g., sister's husband).

age set Group uniting all men or women born during a certain time span; this group controls property and often has political and military functions.

agnates Members of the same patrilineal descent group.

agriculture Nonindustrial systems of plant cultivation characterized by continuous and intensive use of land and labor.

ahimsa Hindu doctrine that prohibits harming life, and thus cattle slaughter.

allele A biochemical difference involving a particular gene.

Allen's rule Rule stating that the relative size of protruding body parts (such as ears, tails, bills, fingers, toes, and limbs) tends to increase in warmer climates.

alluvial Pertaining to rich, fertile soil deposited by rivers and streams.

ambilineal Principle of descent that does not automatically exclude the children of either sons or daughters.

ambilocal Postmarital residence pattern in which the couple may reside with either the husband's or the wife's group.

analogies Similarities arising as a result of similar selective forces; traits produced by convergent evolution.

anatomically modern humans (AMHs) Including the Cro-Magnons of Europe (31,000 B.P.) and the older fossils from Skhūl (100,000) and Qafzeh (92,000); continue through the present; also known as *H. sapiens sapiens.*

animism Belief in souls or doubles.

Anthropoidea One of two suborders of primates; includes monkeys, apes, and humans.

anthropoids Members of Anthropoidea, one of the two suborders of primates; monkeys, apes, and humans are anthropoids.

anthropology The study of the human species and its immediate ancestors.

anthropology and education Anthropological research in classrooms, homes, and neighborhoods, viewing students as total cultural creatures whose enculturation and attitudes toward education belong to a larger context that includes family, peers, and society.

antibody A defending protein that reacts by attacking a foreign substance; see *antigen.*

antigen A chemical substance that triggers the production of an antibody.

apartheid Castelike system in South Africa; blacks, whites, and Asians have separate (and unequal) neighborhoods, schools, laws, and punishments.

apical ancestor In a descent group, the individual who stands at the apex, or top, of the common genealogy.

applied anthropology The application of anthropological data, perspectives, theory, and methods to identify, assess, and solve contemporary social problems.

arboreal Tree-dwelling.

arboreal theory Theory that the primates evolved by adapting to life high up in the trees, where visual abilities would have been favored over the sense of smell, and grasping hands and feet would have been used for movement along branches.

archaeological anthropology (prehistoric archaeology) The study of human behavior and cultural patterns and processes through the culture's material remains.

archaic *Homo sapiens* Early *H. sapiens,* consisting of the Neandertals of Europe and the Middle East, the Neandertal-like hominids of Africa and Asia, and the immediate ancestors of all these hominids; lived from about 300,000 to 30,000 B.P.

archaic state Nonindustrial state.

art An object or event that evokes an aesthetic reaction—a sense of beauty, appreciation, harmony, and/or pleasure; the quality, production, expression, or realm of what is beautiful or of more than ordinary significance; the class of objects subject to aesthetic criteria.

artifacts Material items that humans have manufactured or modified.

arts The arts include the visual arts, literature (written and oral), music, and theater arts.

ascribed status Social status (e.g., race or gender) that people have little or no choice about occupying.

ASL American Sign Language, a medium of communication for deaf and mute humans and apes.

assimilation The process of change that a minority group may experience when it moves to a country where another culture dominates; the minority is incorporated into the dominant culture to the point that it no longer exists as a separate cultural unit.

attitudinal discrimination Discrimination against members of a group because of prejudice toward that group.

Aurignacian Upper Paleolithic tradition, 35,000 to 20,000 B.P.; tools usually found in narrow valleys or near cliff walls, and thick layers suggest long occupation; may have diffused into Europe from elsewhere.

australopithecines Varied group of Pliocene–Pleistocene hominids. The term is derived from their former classification as members of a distinct subfamily, the Australopithecinae; now they are distinguished from *Homo* only at the genus level.

axis Plant part that attaches the grains to the stalk; brittle in wild grains, tough in domesticated ones.

Aztec Last independent state in the Valley of Mexico; capital was Tenochtitlan. Thrived between A.D. 1325 and the Spanish conquest in 1520.

balanced reciprocity See *generalized reciprocity.*

band Basic unit of social organization among foragers. A band includes fewer than 100 people; it often splits up seasonally.

berdaches Among the Crow Indians, members of a third gender, for whom certain ritual duties were reserved.

Bergmann's rule Rule stating that the smaller of two bodies similar in shape has more surface area per unit of weight and can therefore dissipate heat more efficiently; hence, large bodies tend to be found in colder areas and small bodies in warmer ones.

Beringia Area now under the Bering Sea; a dry land mass several hundred miles wide, exposed during the glacial advances.

bifurcate collateral kinship terminology Kinship terminology employing separate terms for M, F, MB, MZ, FB, and FZ.

bifurcate merging kinship terminology Kinship terminology in which M and MZ are called by the same term, F and FB are called by the same term, and MB and FZ are called by different terms.

big man Regional figure often found among tribal horticulturalists and pastoralists. The big man occupies no office but creates his reputation through entrepreneurship and generosity to others. Neither his wealth nor his position passes to his heirs.

bilateral kinship calculation A system in which kinship ties are calculated equally through both sexes: mother and father, sister and brother, daughter and son, and so on.

biochemical genetics Field that studies structure, function, and changes in genetic material.

biological anthropology The study of human biological variation in time and space; includes evolution, genetics, growth and development, and primatology.

biological determinists Those who argue that human behavior and social organization are biologically determined.

biological kin types Actual genealogical relationships, designated by letters and symbols (e.g., FB), as opposed to the kin terms (e.g., *uncle*) used in a particular society.

biomedicine Western medicine, which attributes illness to scientifically demonstrated agents: biological organisms (e.g., bacteria, viruses, fungi, or parasites) or toxic materials.

bipedal Two-footed.

Black English Vernacular (BEV) A rule-governed dialect of American English with roots in southern English. BEV is spoken by African-American youth and by many adults in their casual, intimate speech—sometimes called "ebonics."

blade tool The basic Upper Paleolithic tool type, hammered off a prepared core.

blended family Kin unit formed when parents remarry and bring their children into a new household.

blood feud Feud between families, usually in a nonstate society.

bourgeoisie One of Marx's opposed classes; owners of the means of production (factories, mines, large farms, and other sources of subsistence).

brachiation Under-the-branch swinging; characteristic of gibbons, siamangs, and some New World monkeys.

brideprice See *progeny price.*

bridewealth See *progeny price.*

broad-spectrum revolution Period beginning around 20,000 B.P. in the Middle East and 12,000 B.P. in Europe, during which a wider range, or broader spectrum, of plant and animal life was hunted, gathered, collected, caught, and fished; revolutionary because it led to food production.

bronze An alloy of arsenic and copper or of tin and copper.

bush school Held in a location remote from residential areas; young people go there when they reach puberty to be instructed in knowledge viewed as essential to adult status.

call systems Systems of communication among nonhuman primates, composed of a limited number of sounds that vary in intensity and duration. Tied to environmental stimuli.

caloric staple Major source of dietary carbohydrates—such as wheat, rice, or maize.

candomblé A syncretic "Afro-Brazilian" cult.

capital Wealth or resources invested in business, with the intent of producing a profit.

capitalist world economy The single world system, which emerged in the 16th century, committed to production for sale, with the object of maximizing profits rather than supplying domestic needs.

caprine From *capra,* Latin for "goat"; refers to goats and sheep.

Capsians Mesolithic North African foragers who based much of their subsistence on land snails.

cargo cults Postcolonial, acculturative religious movements, common in Melanesia, that attempt to explain European domination and wealth and to achieve similar success magically by mimicking European behavior.

caste system Closed, hereditary system of stratification, often dictated by religion; hierarchical social status is ascribed at birth, so that people are locked into their parents' social position.

catarrhine Sharp-nosed; anthropoid infraorder that includes Old World monkeys, apes, and humans.

catastrophism View that extinct species were destroyed by fires, floods, and other catastrophes. After each destructive event, God created again, leading to contemporary species.

catharsis Intense emotional release.

Cenozoic Era of recent life—birds and mammals.

ceremonial fund Resources invested in ceremonial or ritual expenses or activity.

ceremonies of increase Rituals held to promote the fertility and reproduction of plants and animals.

chiefdom Form of sociopolitical organization intermediate between the tribe and the state; kin-based with differential access to resources and a permanent political structure. A rank society in which relations among villages as well as among individuals are unequal, with smaller villages under the authority of leaders in larger villages; has a two-level settlement hierarchy.

chromosomes Basic genetic units, occurring in matching (homologous) pairs; lengths of DNA made up of multiple genes.

chronology Time frame, sequence.

civilization A complex society with a government and social classes; synonyms are *nation-state* and *state.*

clan Unilineal descent group based on stipulated descent.

class Zoological: Division of a kingdom; composed of related orders.

class consciousness Recognition of collective interests and personal identification with one's economic group (particularly the proletariat); basic to Marx's view of class.

classic Neandertals Stereotypical Neandertals of Western Europe, considered by some scholars to be too specialized to have evolved into *H. sapiens sapiens.*

cline A gradual shift in gene frequencies between neighboring populations.

Clovis tradition Stone technology based on a projectile point that was fastened to the end of a hunting spear; it flourished between 12,000 and 11,000 B.P. in North America.

collateral household Type of expanded family household including siblings and their spouses and children.

collateral relative A biological relative who is not a lineal; that is, is not in ego's direct line, such as B, Z, FB, or MZ.

colonialism The political, social, economic, and cultural domination of a territory and its people by a foreign power for an extended time.

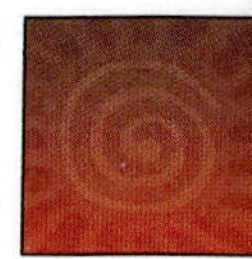

communal religions In Wallace's typology, these religions have, in addition to shamanic cults, communal cults in which people organize community rituals such as harvest ceremonies and rites of passage.

communitas Intense community spirit, a feeling of great social solidarity, equality, and togetherness; characteristic of people experiencing liminality together.

competence What native speakers must (and do) know about their language in order to speak and understand it.

competitive exclusion Ecological principle that if two similar species exploit the same ecological niche, any advantage on the part of one of them, even though minor, eventually will force the other from that niche.

complex societies Nations; large and populous, with social stratification and central governments.

conspecifics Individual members of the same species.

continental shelf Offshore shallow-water zone over which the ocean gradually deepens until the abrupt fall to deep water, which is known as the continental slope.

continental slope See *continental shelf.*

convergent evolution Independent operation of similar selective forces; process by which analogies are produced.

core Dominant structural position in the world system; consists of the strongest and most powerful states with advanced systems of production.

core values Key, basic, or central values that integrate a culture and help distinguish it from others.

correlation An association between two or more variables such that when one changes (varies), the other(s) also change(s) (covaries); for example, temperature and sweating.

cranium Skull.

creationism Explanation for the origin of species given in Genesis: God created the species during the original six days of Creation.

creative opposition Process in which people change their behavior as they consciously and actively avoid or spurn an external image or practice.

cross cousins Children of a brother and a sister.

cultivation continuum A continuum based on the comparative study of nonindustrial cultivating societies in which labor intensity increases and fallowing decreases.

cultural anthropology The study of human society and culture; describes, analyzes, interprets, and explains social and cultural similarities and differences.

cultural colonialism Internal domination—by one group and its culture/ideology over others; for example, Russian domination of the former Soviet Union.

cultural consultants Subjects in ethnographic research; people the ethnographer gets to know in the field, who teach him or her about their culture.

cultural convergence (or convergent cultural evolution) Development of similar traits, institutions, or behavior patterns as a result of adaptation to similar environments; parallel development without contact or mutual influence.

cultural determinists Those who relate behavior and social organization to cultural or environmental factors. This view focuses on variation rather than universals and stresses learning and the role of culture in human adaptation.

cultural ecology The study of ecosystems that include people, focusing on how human use of nature influences and is influenced by social organization and cultural values.

cultural imperialism The rapid spread or advance of one culture at the expense of others, or its imposition on other cultures, which it modifies, replaces, or destroys—usually because of differential economic or political influence.

cultural learning Learning based on the human capacity to think symbolically.

cultural relativism The position that the values and standards of cultures differ and deserve respect. Extreme relativism argues that cultures should be judged solely by their own standards.

cultural resource management (CRM) The branch of applied archaeology aimed at preserving sites threatened by dams, highways, and other projects.

cultural rights Doctrine that certain rights are vested not in individuals but in identifiable groups, such as religious and ethnic minorities and indigenous societies. Cultural rights include a group's ability to preserve its culture, to raise its children in the ways of its forebears, to continue its language, and not to be deprived of its economic base by the nation-state in which it is located.

cultural transmission A basic feature of language; transmission through learning.

culturally compatible economic development projects Projects that harness traditional organizations and locally perceived needs for change and that have a culturally appropriate design and implementation strategy.

culture Distinctly human; transmitted through learning; traditions and customs that govern behavior and beliefs.

culture and personality A subfield of cultural anthropology; examines variation in psychological traits and personality characteristics among cultures.

cuneiform Early Mesopotamian writing that used a stylus (writing implement) to write wedge-shaped impressions on raw clay; from the Latin word for wedge.

curer Specialized role acquired through a culturally appropriate process of selection, training, certification, and acquisition of a professional image; the curer is consulted by patients, who believe in his or her special powers, and receives some form of special consideration; a cultural universal.

cytoplasm The outer area of the cell rather than the nucleus.

daughter languages Languages developing out of the same parent language; for example, French and Spanish are daughter languages of Latin.

demonstrated descent Basis of the lineage; descent-group members cite the names of their forebears in each generation from the apical ancestor through the present.

descent Rule assigning social identity on the basis of some aspect of one's ancestry.

descent group A permanent social unit whose members claim common ancestry; fundamental to tribal society.

development anthropology The branch of applied anthropology that focuses on social issues in, and the cultural dimension of, economic development.

diaspora The offspring of an area who have spread to many lands.

differential access Unequal access to resources; basic attribute of chiefdoms and states. Superordinates have favored access to such resources, while the access of subordinates is limited by superordinates.

diffusion Borrowing of cultural traits between societies, either directly or through intermediaries.

diglossia The existence of "high" (formal) and "low" (informal, familial) dialects of a single language, such as German.

directional selection Long-term selection of the same trait(s); may go on as long as environmental forces remain the same.

discourse Talk, speeches, gestures, and actions.

discrimination Policies and practices that harm a group and its members.

disease A scientifically identified health threat caused by a bacterium, virus, fungus, parasite, or other pathogen.

displacement A basic feature of language; the ability to speak of things and events that are not present.

domestic Within or pertaining to the home.

domestic–public dichotomy Contrast between women's role in the home and men's role in public life, with a corresponding social devaluation of women's work and worth.

domestic system of manufacture, also known as "home handicraft production"; preindustrial manufacturing system in which organizer-entrepreneurs supplied raw materials to people who worked at home and collected finished products from them.

dominant Allele that masks another allele in a heterozygote.

dowry A marital exchange in which the wife's group provides substantial gifts to the husband's family.

dry farming Cultivation that is rainfall-dependent, without irrigation.

dryopithecids Zoological ape family living in Europe during the middle and late Miocene; probably includes the common ancestor of the lesser apes (gibbons and siamangs) and the great apes.

ecocide Destruction of local ecosystems.

ecology The study of interrelationships among living things in an environment.

economic typology Classification of societies based on their adaptive strategies; for example, foraging, horticulture, pastoralism, agriculture.

economizing The rational allocation of scarce means (or resources) to alternative ends (or uses); often considered the subject matter of economics.

economy A population's system of production, distribution, and consumption of resources.

ecosystem A patterned arrangement of energy flows and exchanges; includes organisms sharing a common environment and that environment.

egalitarian society A type of society, most typically found among foragers, that lacks status distinctions except for those based on age, gender, and individual qualities, talents, and achievements.

ego Latin for *I*. In kinship charts, the point from which one views an egocentric genealogy.

elite level Archaeological term for evidence of differential access to strategic resources; found in chiefdoms and states.

emic The research strategy that focuses on native explanations and criteria of significance.

emotionalistic disease theories Theories that assume that illness is caused by intense emotional experiences.

enculturation The social process by which culture is learned and transmitted across the generations.

endogamy Marriage between people of the same social group.

environmental racism The systematic use of institutionally based power by a majority group to make policy decisions that create disproportionate environmental hazards in minority communities.

equity, increased A reduction in absolute poverty and a fairer (more even) distribution of wealth.

estrus Period of maximum sexual receptivity in female baboons, chimpanzees, and other primates, signaled by vaginal area swelling and coloration.

ethnic expulsion A policy aimed at removing groups who are culturally different from a country.

ethnic group Group distinguished by cultural similarities (shared among members of that group) and differences (between that group and others); ethnic group members share beliefs, values, habits, customs, and norms, and a common language, religion, history, geography, kinship, and/or race.

ethnicity Identification with, and feeling part of, an ethnic group, and exclusion from certain other groups because of this affiliation.

ethnocentrism The tendency to view one's own culture as best and to judge the behavior and beliefs of culturally different people by one's own standards.

ethnocide Process in which ethnic groups survive but lose or severely modify their ancestral cultures.

ethnography Field work in a particular culture.

ethnology Cross-cultural comparison; the comparative study of ethnographic data, of society, and of culture.

ethnomusicology The comparative study of the musics of the world and of music as an aspect of culture and society.

ethnoscience See *ethnosemantics.*

ethnosemantics The study of lexical (vocabulary) contrasts and classifications in various languages.

etic The research strategy that emphasizes the observer's rather than the natives' explanations, categories, and criteria of significance.

Etoro Papua New Guinea culture in which males are culturally trained to prefer homosexual behavior.

eugenics Controversial movement aimed at genetic improvement by encouraging the reproduction of individuals with favored features and discouraging that of individuals with features deemed undesirable.

evolution Descent with modification; change in form over generations.

excavation Digging through the layers of deposits that make up an archaeological site.

exogamy Rule requiring people to marry outside their own group.

expanded family household Coresident group that can include siblings and their spouses and children (a *collateral* household) or three generations of kin and their spouses (an *extended family* household).

expressive culture The arts; people express themselves creatively in dance, music, song, painting, sculpture, pottery, cloth, storytelling, verse, prose, drama, and comedy.

extended family Expanded household including three or more generations.

extradomestic Outside the home; within or pertaining to the public domain.

extrasomatic Nonbodily; pertaining to culture, including language, tools, and other cultural means of adaptation.

family, zoological Group of similar genera.

family of orientation Nuclear family in which one is born and grows up.

family of procreation Nuclear family established when one marries and has children.

fictive kinship Personal relationships modeled on kinship, such as that between godparents and godchildren.

First World The "democratic West"—traditionally conceived in opposition to a "Second World" ruled by "communism."

fiscal Pertaining to finances and taxation.

focal vocabulary A set of words and distinctions that are particularly important to certain groups (those with particular foci of experience or activity), such as types of snow to Eskimos or skiers.

folk Of the people; originally coined for European peasants; refers to the art, music, and lore of ordinary people, as contrasted with the "high" art or "classic" art of the European elites.

food production Cultivation of plants and domestication (stockbreeding) of animals; first developed in the Middle East 10,000 to 12,000 years ago.

foramen magnum "Big hole" through which the spinal cord joins the brain; located farther forward in *Australopithecus* and *Homo* than in apes.

forced assimilation Use of force by a dominant group to compel a minority to adopt the dominant culture—for example, penalizing or banning the language and customs of an ethnic group.

fraternal polyandry Marriage of a group of brothers to the same woman or women.

functional explanation Explanation that establishes a correlation or interrelationship between social customs. When customs are functionally interrelated, if one changes, the others also change.

gametes The sex cells: eggs (ova) and sperms.

gender roles The tasks and activities that a culture assigns to each sex.

gender stereotypes Oversimplified but strongly held ideas about the characteristics of males and females.

gender stratification Unequal distribution of rewards (socially valued resources, power, prestige, and personal freedom) between men and women, reflecting their different positions in a social hierarchy.

gene Area in a chromosome pair that determines, wholly or partially, a particular biological trait, such as whether one's blood type is A, B, AB, or O.

gene flow Exchange of genetic material between populations of the same species through direct or indirect interbreeding.

gene pool All the alleles and genotypes within a breeding population—the "pool" of genetic material available.

genealogical method Procedures by which ethnographers discover and record connections of kinship, descent, and marriage, using diagrams and symbols.

general anthropology The field of anthropology as a whole, consisting of cultural, archaeological, biological, and linguistic anthropology.

generality Culture pattern or trait that exists in some but not all societies.

generalized reciprocity Principle that characterizes exchanges between closely related individuals. As social distance increases, reciprocity becomes balanced and finally negative.

generational kinship terminology Kinship terminology with only two terms for the parental generation, one designating M, MZ, and FZ and the other designating F, FB, and MB.

genetic evolution Change in gene frequency within a breeding population.

genitor Biological father of a child.

genocide Physical destruction of ethnic groups by murder, warfare, and introduced diseases.

genotype An organism's hereditary makeup.

genus (plural, genera) Group of similar species.

gibbons The smallest apes, natives of Asia; arboreal and territorial.

glacials The four or five major advances of continental ice sheets in northern Europe and North America.

globalization The accelerating interdependence of nations in a world system linked economically and through mass media and modern transportation systems.

gracile Opposite of robust.

grammar The formal organizing principles that link sound and meaning in a language; the set of abstract rules that make up a language.

green revolution Agricultural development based on chemical fertilizers, pesticides, 20th-century cultivation techniques, and new crop varieties such as IR-8 ("miracle rice").

Halafian An early (7500–6500 B.P.) and widespread pottery style, first found in northern Syria; refers to a delicate ceramic style and to the period when the first chiefdoms emerged.

head, village A local leader in a tribal society who has limited authority, leads by example and persuasion, and must be generous.

health-care systems Beliefs, customs, and specialists concerned with ensuring health and preventing and curing illness; a cultural universal.

hegemonic reading (of a "text") The reading or meaning that the creators intended, or the one the elites consider to be the intended or correct meaning.

hegemony As used by Antonio Gramsci, a stratified social order in which subordinates comply with domination by internalizing its values and accepting its "naturalness."

heterozygous Having dissimilar alleles of a given gene.

hidden transcript As used by James Scott, the critique of power by the oppressed that goes on offstage—in private—where the power holders can't see it.

Hilly Flanks Woodland zone that flanks the Tigris and Euphrates rivers to the north; zone of wild wheat and barley and of sedentism (settled, nonmigratory life) preceding food production.

historical explanation Demonstration that a social institution or practice exists among different populations because they share a period of common history or have been exposed to common sources of information; includes diffusion.

historical linguistics Subdivision of linguistics that studies languages over time.

Hogopans Nickname for the ancestral population of Miocene hominoids that eventually split three ways to give rise to humans, gorillas, and chimps; derived from the genus names *Homo*, *Gorilla*, and *Pan* (chimpanzee).

holistic Interested in the whole of the human condition: past, present, and future; biology, society, language, and culture.

Hominidae Zoological superfamily that includes fossil and living humans; according to some taxonomists, also includes the African apes.

hominids Members of the zoological family (Hominidae) that includes fossil and living humans.

Hominoidea Zoological superfamily that includes fossil and contemporary apes and humans.

hominoids Members of the superfamily including humans and all the apes.

Homo habilis Term coined by L. S. B. and Mary Leakey; immediate ancestor of *H. erectus;* lived from about 2 to 1.7 or 1.6 m.y.a.

Homo sapiens sapiens Anatomically modern humans.

homologies Traits that organisms have jointly inherited from their common ancestor.

homozygous Possessing identical alleles of a particular gene.

horticulture Nonindustrial system of plant cultivation in which plots lie fallow for varying lengths of time.

human rights Doctrine that invokes a realm of justice and morality beyond and superior to particular countries, cultures, and religions. Human rights, usually seen as vested in individuals, would include the right to speak freely, to hold religious beliefs without persecution, and to not be enslaved, or imprisoned without charge.

humanities Academic fields that study languages, texts, philosophies, arts, music, performances, and other forms of creative expression.

hybrid Mixed.

hydraulic systems Systems of water management, including irrigation, drainage, and flood control. Often associated with agricultural societies in arid and river environments.

hypervitaminosis D Condition caused by an excess of vitamin D; calcium deposits build up on the body's soft tissues and the kidneys may fail; symptoms include gallstones and joint and circulation problems; may affect unprotected light-skinned individuals in the tropics.

hypodescent Rule that automatically places the children of a union or mating between members of different socioeconomic groups in the less-privileged group.

hypoxia A body's oxygen deprivation; the difficulty of extracting oxygen from the air increases with altitude because barometric pressure decreases and molecules of air are farther apart.

ideal types Labels that make contrasts seem more extreme than they really are (e.g., big and little). Instead of discrete categories, there is actually a continuum from one type to the next.

identity politics Sociopolitical identities based on the perception of sharing a common culture, language, religion, or "race," rather than citizenship in a nation-state, which may contain diverse social groups.

illness A condition of poor health perceived or felt by an individual.

imperialism A policy of extending the rule of a nation or empire over foreign nations or of taking and holding foreign colonies.

incest Forbidden sexual relations with a close relative.

incest taboo Universal prohibition against marrying or mating with a close relative.

inclusive fitness Reproductive success measured by the representation of genes one shares with other, related individuals.

income Earnings from wages and salaries.

independent assortment Mendel's law of; chromosomes are inherited independently of one another.

independent invention Development of the same cultural trait or pattern in separate cultures as a result of comparable needs and circumstances.

indigenized Modified to fit the local culture.

indigenous peoples The original inhabitants of particular territories; often descendants of tribespeople who live on as culturally distinct colonized peoples, many of whom aspire to autonomy.

individual fitness Reproductive success measured by the number of direct descendants an individual has.

Industrial Revolution The historical transformation (in Europe, after 1750) of "traditional" into "modern" societies through industrialization of the economy.

infanticide Killing a baby; a form of population control in some societies.

institutional discrimination Programs, policies, and arrangements that deny equal rights and opportunities to, or differentially harm, members of particular groups.

interglacials Extended warm periods between such major glacials as Riss and Würm.

international culture Cultural traditions that extend beyond national boundaries.

interstadials Brief warm periods during a glacial; not to be confused with the longer interglacials.

intervention philosophy Guiding principle of colonialism, conquest, missionization, or development; an ideological justification for outsiders to guide native peoples in specific directions.

interview schedule Ethnographic tool for structuring a formal interview. A prepared form (usually printed or mimeographed) that guides interviews with households or individuals being compared systematically. Contrasts with a *questionnaire* because the researcher has personal contact with the local people and records their answers.

IPR Intellectual property rights, consisting of each society's cultural base—its core beliefs and principles. IPR is claimed as a group right—a cultural right, allowing indigenous groups to control who may know and use their collective knowledge and its applications.

Iroquois Confederation of tribes in aboriginal New York; matrilineal with communal longhouses and a prominent political, religious, and economic role for women.

ischial callosities Rough patches of skin of gibbons and Old World monkeys on the buttocks, adapted to sitting on hard rocky ground and rough branches.

ivory tower view of applied anthropology; the belief that anthropologists should avoid practical matters and concentrate on research, publication, and teaching.

Jomon Widespread (30,000 sites known) Japanese Mesolithic culture, dated to 6000 to 5000 B.P.; hunted deer, pigs, bear, and antelope, and also ate fish, shellfish, and plants.

Ju'hoansi Group of San (Bushmen) foragers of southern Africa.

key cultural consultant Person who is an expert on a particular aspect of native life.

kin-based Characteristic of many nonindustrial societies. People spend their lives almost exclusively with their relatives; principles of kinship, descent, and marriage organize social life.

kin terms The words used for different relatives in a particular language, as opposed to actual genealogical relationships (*biological kin types*).

kinesics The study of communication through body movements, stances, gestures, and facial expressions.

kingdom, zoological Group of related classes.

kinship calculation The system by which people in a particular society reckon kin relationships.

knuckle-walking A form of terrestrial locomotion in which long arms and callused knuckles support the trunk; the ape ambles around leaning forward.

Kwakiutl A potlatching society on the North Pacific Coast of North America.

lactase See *lactose*.

lactose A complex sugar in milk; its digestion requires an enzyme called *lactase* in the small intestine. Among most mammals, lactase production ceases after weaning, and the ability to digest milk is lost.

language Human beings' primary means of communication; may be spoken or written; features productivity and displacement and is culturally transmitted.

latent function A custom's underlying function, often unperceived by natives.

law A legal code, including trial and enforcement; characteristic of state-organized societies.

LDC A less-developed country; by contrast with an industrial nation.

leveling mechanisms Customs and social actions that operate to reduce differences in wealth and thus to bring standouts in line with community norms.

levirate Custom by which a widow marries the brother of her deceased husband.

lexicon Vocabulary; a dictionary containing all the morphemes in a language and their meanings.

life history Of a key consultant or narrator; provides a personal cultural portrait of existence or change in a culture.

liminality The critically important marginal or in-between phase of a rite of passage.

lineage Unilineal descent group based on demonstrated descent.

lineal kinship terminology Parental generation kin terminology with four terms: one for M, one for F, one for FB and MB, and one for MZ and FZ.

lineal relative Any of ego's ancestors or descendants (e.g., parents, grandparents, children, grandchildren); on the direct line of descent that leads to and from ego.

linguistic anthropology The descriptive, comparative, and historical study of language and of linguistic similarities and differences in time, space, and society.

linguistic relativity Notion that all languages and dialects are equally effective as systems of communication.

linguistic uniformitarianism Belief that explanations for long-term change in language should be sought in ordinary forces that continue to work today; thus, the forces that have produced linguistic changes over the centuries are observable in linguistic events (variation) taking place today.

linkages Interconnections between small-scale and large-scale units and systems; political, economic, informational, and other cultural links among village, region, nation, and world.

liturgical order A set sequence of words and actions invented prior to the current performance of the ritual in which it occurs.

liturgies Set formal sequences of words and actions; common in political events and rituals or ceremonies.

local descent group All the members of a particular descent group who live in the same place, such as the same village.

longitudinal Long-term; refers to a study carried out over many years.

longitudinal research Long-term study of a community, region, society, culture, or other unit, usually based on repeated visits.

macroband Assembly of foraging bands for intensive collecting or cooperative hunting.

magic Use of supernatural techniques to accomplish specific aims.

maize Corn; domesticated in highland Mexico.

majority groups Superordinate, dominant, or controlling groups in a social-political hierarchy.

maladaptive Harmful; selected against; conferring a disadvantage with respect to survival and reproduction.

mana Sacred impersonal force in Melanesian and Polynesian religions.

manifest function The reasons that natives offer for a custom.

manioc Cassava; a tuber domesticated in the South American lowlands.

market principle Profit-oriented principle of exchange that dominates in states, particularly industrial states. Goods and services are bought and sold, and values are determined by supply and demand.

marriage Socially approved relationship between a socially recognized male (the husband) and a socially recognized female (the wife) such that the children born to the wife are accepted as the offspring of both husband and wife.

mater Socially recognized mother of a child.

matriarchy A society ruled by women; unknown to ethnography.

matrifocal Mother-centered; often refers to a household with no resident husband-father.

matrilateral skewing A preference for relatives on the mother's side.

matrilineal descent Unilineal descent rule in which people join the mother's group automatically at birth and stay members throughout life.

matrilocality Customary residence with the wife's relatives after marriage, so that children grow up in their mother's community.

matrons Senior women, as among the Iroquois.

means (or factors) of production Land, labor, technology, and capital—major productive resources.

medical anthropology Field including biological and cultural, theoretical and applied, anthropologists concerned with the sociocultural context and implications of disease and illness.

meiosis Special process by which sex cells are produced; four cells are produced from one, each with half the genetic material of the original cell.

melanin Substance manufactured in specialized cells in the lower layers of the epidermis (outer skin layer); melanin cells in dark skin produce more melanin than do those in light skin.

Mendelian genetics Studies ways in which chromosomes transmit genes across the generations.

Mesoamerica Middle America, including Mexico, Guatemala, and Belize.

Mesolithic Middle Stone Age, whose characteristic tool type was the microlith; broad-spectrum economy.

Mesopotamia The area between the Tigris and Euphrates rivers in what is now southern Iraq and southwestern Iran; location of the first cities and states.

Mesozoic Era of middle life—reptiles, including the dinosaurs.

metallurgy Knowledge of the properties of metals, including their extraction and processing and the manufacture of metal tools.

microband Small family group of foragers.

microlith Greek for "small stone"; characteristic Mesolithic tool.

Middle Pleistocene The period from the Mindel glacial through the Riss-Würm interglacial.

Mindel The second major glacial advance in Europe.

minimal pairs Words that resemble each other in all but one sound; used to discover phonemes.

minority groups Subordinate groups in a social-political hierarchy, with inferior power and less secure access to resources than majority groups.

mitosis Ordinary cell division; DNA molecules copy themselves, creating two identical cells out of one.

mode of production Way of organizing production—a set of social relations through which labor is deployed to wrest energy from nature by means of tools, skills, and knowledge.

moiety One of two descent groups in a given population; usually moieties intermarry.

monocrop production System of production, often on plantations, based on the cultivation of a single cash crop.

monotheism Worship of an eternal, omniscient, omnipotent, and omnipresent supreme being.

morpheme Minimal linguistic form (usually a word) with meaning.

morphology The study of form; used in linguistics (the study of morphemes and word construction) and for form in general—for example, biomorphology relates to physical form.

Mousterian Middle Paleolithic tool-making tradition associated with Neandertals.

multiculturalism The view of cultural diversity in a country as something good and desirable; a multicultural society socializes individuals not only into the dominant (national) culture but also into an ethnic culture.

multivariate Involving multiple factors, causes, or variables.

mutation Change in the DNA molecules of which genes and chromosomes are built.

m.y.a. Million years ago.

namesakes People who share the same name; a form of fictive kinship among the San, who have a limited number of personal names.

nation Once a synonym for "ethnic group," designating a single culture sharing a language, religion, history, territory, ancestry, and kinship; now usually a synonym for *state* or *nation-state.*

nation-state An autonomous political entity; a country like the United States or Canada.

national culture Cultural experiences, beliefs, learned behavior patterns, and values shared by citizens of the same nation.

nationalities Ethnic groups that once had, or wish to have or regain, autonomous political status (their own country).

native taxonomy Classification system invented and used by natives rather than anthropologists.

Natufians Widespread Middle Eastern culture, dated to between 12,500 and 10,500 B.P.; subsisted on intensive wild cereal collecting and gazelle hunting and had year-round villages.

natural selection Originally formulated by Charles Darwin and Alfred Russell Wallace; the process by which nature selects the forms most fit to survive and reproduce in a given environment, such as the tropics.

naturalistic disease theories Include scientific medicine; theories that explain illness in impersonal systemic terms.

naturists Those who argue that human behavior and social organization are biologically determined.

Neandertals *H. sapiens neanderthalensis*, representing an archaic *H. sapiens* subspecies, lived in Europe and the Middle East between 130,000 and 30,000 B.P.

negative reciprocity See *generalized reciprocity.*

négritude Black association and identity—an idea developed by dark-skinned intellectuals in Francophone (French-speaking) West Africa and the Caribbean.

neocolonialism A revival or new form of colonialism—the political, social, economic, and cultural domination of a territory and its people by a foreign power, often justified by the assertion that foreigners are more enlightened at governing than are natives of the colonial area.

Neolithic "New Stone Age," coined to describe techniques of grinding and polishing stone tools; the first cultural period in a region in which the first signs of domestication are present.

neolocality Postmarital residence pattern in which a couple establishes a new place of residence rather than living with or near either set of parents.

Nilotic populations Populations, including the Nuer, that inhabit the Upper Nile region of eastern Africa.

nomadism, pastoral Movement throughout the year by the whole pastoral group (men, women, and children) with their animals; more generally, such constant movement in pursuit of strategic resources.

nuclear family Kinship group consisting of parents and children.

nurturists Those who relate behavior and social organization to environmental factors. Nurturists focus on variation rather than universals and stress learning and the role of culture in human adaptation.

Oaxaca, Valley of Southern Mexican valley that was an early area of food production and state formation.

office Permanent political position.

Oldowan pebble tools Earliest (2 to 2.5 m.y.a.) stone tools; first discovered in 1931 by L. S. B. and Mary Leakey at Olduvai Gorge.

Olmec Elite-level society on Mexico's Gulf Coast, 3200 to 2500 B.P.

Olympian religions In Wallace's typology, develop with state organization; have full-time religious specialists—professional priesthoods.

omomyids Early (Eocene) primate family found in North America, Europe, and Asia; early omomyids may be ancestral to all anthropoids; later ones may be ancestral to tarsiers.

open class system Stratification system that facilitates social mobility, with individual achievement and personal merit determining social rank.

opposable thumb A thumb that can touch all the other fingers.

order, zoological Division of a zoological class; a group of related suborders, such as the primates.

orthograde posture Straight and upright; the posture among apes and humans.

osteology The study of bones; useful to biological anthropologists studying the fossil record.

overinnovation Characteristic of projects that require major changes in natives' daily lives, especially ones that interfere with customary subsistence pursuits.

paleoanthropology The study of hominid evolution and human life as revealed by the fossil record.

paleoecology The study, often by archaeologists, of ecosystems of the past.

Paleoindians Early North American Indians who hunted horses, camels, bison, elephants, mammoths, and giant sloths.

Paleolithic Old Stone Age (from Greek roots meaning "old" and "stone"); divided into Lower (early), Middle, and Upper (late).

paleontology Study of ancient life through the fossil record.

Paleozoic Era of ancient life—fishes, amphibians, and primitive reptiles.

pantheon A collection of supernatural beings in a particular religion.

pantribal sodality A non-kin-based group that exists throughout a tribe, spanning several villages.

parallel cousins Children of two brothers or two sisters.

participant observation A characteristic ethnographic technique; taking part in the events one is observing, describing, and analyzing.

particularity Distinctive or unique culture trait, pattern, or integration.

pastoralists People who use a food-producing strategy of adaptation based on care of herds of domesticated animals.

pater Socially recognized father of a child; not necessarily the genitor.

patriarchy Political system ruled by men in which women have inferior social and political status, including basic human rights.

patrilineal descent Unilineal descent rule in which people join the father's group automatically at birth and stay members throughout life.

patrilineal-patrilocal complex An interrelated constellation of patrilineality, patrilocality, warfare, and male supremacy.

patrilocality Customary residence with the husband's relatives after marriage, so that children grow up in their father's community.

peasant Small-scale agriculturalist living in a state with rent fund obligations.

performance What people actually say; the use of speech in social situations.

Perigordian Upper Paleolithic tradition that coexisted with the Aurignacian in Europe between 35,000 and 20,000 B.P. Perigordian tools usually are found in thin deposits and are scattered over large areas; evolved in Western Europe out of Mousterian antecedents.

periphery Weakest structural position in the world system.

personalistic disease theories Theories that attribute illness to sorcerers, witches, ghosts, or ancestral spirits.

phenotype An organism's evident traits, its "manifest biology"—anatomy and physiology.

phenotypical adaptation Adaptive biological changes that occur during the individual's lifetime, made possible by biological plasticity.

phone Any speech sound.

phoneme Significant sound contrast in a language that serves to distinguish meaning, as in minimal pairs.

phonemics The study of the sound contrasts (phonemes) of a particular language.

phonetics The study of speech sounds in general; what people actually say in various languages.

phonology The study of sounds used in speech.

phylogeny Genetic relatedness based on common ancestry.

physical anthropology See *biological anthropology.*

pidgin A mixed language that develops to ease communication between members of different cultures in contact, usually in situations of trade or colonial domination.

plasticity The ability to change; notion that biology is affected by environmental forces, such as diet and altitude, experienced during growth.

platyrrhine Flat-nosed; anthropoid infraorder that includes the New World monkeys.

Pleistocene Epoch of *Homo*'s appearance and evolution; began two million years ago; divided into Lower, Middle, and Upper.

plural marriage See *polygamy.*

plural society A society that combines ethnic contrasts and economic interdependence of the ethnic groups.

polity The political order.

polyandry Variety of plural marriage in which a woman has more than one husband.

polygamy Any marriage with more than two spouses.

polygyny Variety of plural marriage in which a man has more than one wife.

Polynesia Triangle of South Pacific islands formed by Hawaii to the north, Easter Island to the east, and New Zealand to the southwest.

polytheism Belief in several deities who control aspects of nature.

polytypic species Species with considerable phenotypic variation.

pongid Zoological family that includes orangutans.

population genetics Field that studies causes of genetic variation, maintenance, and change in breeding populations.

postcolonial Referring to interactions between European nations and the societies they colonized (mainly after 1800); more generally, "postcolonial" may be used to signify a position against imperialism and Eurocentrism.

postcranium The area behind or below the head; the skeleton.

posterior Back; for example, posterior or back dentition—premolars and molars.

postmodern In its most general sense, describes the blurring and breakdown of established canons (rules, standards), categories, distinctions, and boundaries.

postmodernism A style and movement in architecture that succeeded modernism. Compared with modernism, postmodernism is less geometric, less functional, less austere, more playful, and more willing to include elements from diverse times and cultures; *postmodern* now describes comparable developments in music, literature, visual art, and anthropology.

postmodernity Condition of a world in flux, with people on the move, in which established groups, boundaries, identities, contrasts, and standards are reaching out and breaking down.

pot irrigation Simple irrigation technique used in Oaxaca; by means of pots, water close to the surface is dipped and poured on plants.

potlatch Competitive feast among Indians on the North Pacific Coast of North America.

potsherds Fragments of earthenware; pottery studied by archaeologists in interpreting prehistoric life styles.

power The ability to exercise one's will over others—to do what one wants; the basis of political status.

practicing anthropologists Used as a synonym for *applied anthropology;* anthropologists who practice their profession outside of academia.

prehensile Grasping, as in the tail of the New World monkeys.

prehistory The period before the invention of writing (less than 6,000 years ago).

prejudice Devaluing (looking down on) a group because of its assumed behavior, values, capabilities, attitudes, or other attributes.

prestige Esteem, respect, or approval for acts, deeds, or qualities considered exemplary.

primary groups Primate groups composed of a permanently bonded male and female and their preadolescent offspring.

primary states States that arise on their own (through competition among chiefdoms), and not through contact with other state societies.

primates Monkeys, apes, and prosimians; members of the zoological order that includes humans.

primatology The study of the biology, behavior, social life, and evolution of monkeys, apes, and other nonhuman primates.

primogeniture Inheritance rule that makes the oldest child (usually the oldest son) the only heir.

Proconsul Early Miocene genus of the pliopithecoid superfamily; the most abundant and successful anthropoids of the early Miocene; the last common ancestor shared by the Old World monkeys and the apes.

productivity A basic feature of language; the ability to use the rules of one's language to create new expressions comprehensible to other speakers.

progeny price A gift from the husband and his kin to the wife and her kin before, at, or after marriage; legitimizes children born to the woman as members of the husband's descent group.

proletarianization Separation of workers from the means of production through industrialism.

prosimians The primate suborder that includes lemurs, lorises, and tarsiers.

protolanguage Language ancestral to several daughter languages.

psychological anthropology The ethnographic and cross-cultural study of differences and similarities in human psychology.

public transcript As used by James Scott, the open, public interactions between dominators and oppressed—the outer shell of power relations.

punctuated equilibrium Model of evolution; long periods of equilibrium, during which species change little, are interrupted by sudden changes—evolutionary jumps.

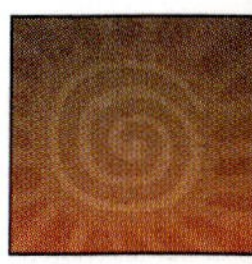

questionnaire Form (usually printed) used by sociologists to obtain comparable information from respondents. Often mailed to and filled in by research subjects rather than by the researcher.

race An ethnic group assumed to have a biological basis.

racism Discrimination against an ethnic group assumed to have a biological basis.

radiometric Dating technique that measures radioactive decay.

random genetic drift Change in gene frequency that results not from natural selection but from chance; most common in small populations.

random sample A sample in which all members of the population have an equal statistical chance of being included.

ranked society A type of society with hereditary inequality but not social stratification; individuals are ranked in terms of their genealogical closeness to the chief, but there is a continuum of status, with many individuals and kin groups ranked about equally.

rapport A good, friendly working relationship between people, for example, ethnographers and their hosts and consultants.

recessive Genetic trait masked by a dominant trait.

reciprocity One of the three principles of exchange; governs exchange between social equals; major exchange mode in band and tribal societies.

recombination Following independent assortment of chromosomes, new arrangements of hereditary units produced through bisexual reproduction.

redistribution Major exchange mode of chiefdoms, many archaic states, and some states with managed economies.

refugees People who have been forced (involuntary refugees) or who have chosen (voluntary refugees) to flee a country, to escape persecution or war.

regulation Management of variables within a system of related and interacting variables. Regulation assures that variables stay within their normal ranges, corrects deviations from the norm, and thus maintains the system's integrity.

relative dating Dating technique, e.g., stratigraphy, that establishes a time frame in relation to other strata or materials, rather than absolute dates in numbers.

relativity Of evolution through natural selection; adaptation and fitness are in relation to specific environments, and traits are not adaptive or maladaptive for all times and places.

religion Belief and ritual concerned with supernatural beings, powers, and forces.

rent fund Scarce resources that a social inferior is required to render to an individual or agency that is superior politically or economically.

replacement fund Scarce resources invested in technology and other items essential to production.

respondents Subjects in sociological research; the people who answer questions in questionnaires and other social surveys.

revitalization movements Movements that occur in times of change, in which religious leaders emerge and undertake to alter or revitalize a society.

rickets Nutritional disease caused by a shortage of vitamin D; interferes with the absorption of calcium and causes softening and deformation of the bones.

Riss The third major glacial advance in Europe.

rites of passage Culturally defined activities associated with the transition from one place or stage of life to another.

ritual Behavior that is formal, stylized, repetitive, and stereotyped, performed earnestly as a social act; rituals are held at set times and places and have liturgical orders.

robust Large, strong, sturdy; said of skull, skeleton, muscle, and teeth; opposite of gracile.

Romer's rule Evolutionary rule stating that an innovation that evolves to maintain an existing system can play a major role in changing that system.

sagittal crest Bony ridge atop the skull that forms as bone grows; develops from the pull of chewing muscles as they meet at the midline of the cranium.

sample A smaller study group chosen to represent a larger population.

San Foragers of southern Africa, also known as Bushmen; speakers of San languages.

Sapir-Whorf hypothesis Theory that different languages produce different ways of thinking.

schistosomiasis Disease caused by liver flukes transmitted by snails inhabiting ponds, lakes, and waterways, often created by irrigation projects.

schizoid view of applied anthropology; the belief that anthropologists should help carry out, but not make or criticize, policy, and that personal value judgments should be kept strictly separate from scientific investigation in applied anthropology.

science A systematic field of study or body of knowledge that aims, through experiment, observation, and deduction, to produce reliable explanations of phenomena, with reference to the material and physical world.

scientific medicine As distinguished from Western medicine, a health-care system based on scientific knowledge and procedures, encompassing such fields as pathology, microbiology, biochemistry, surgery, diagnostic technology, and applications.

Second World The Warsaw Pact nations, including the former Soviet Union, the Socialist and once-Socialist countries of Eastern Europe and Asia.

secret societies Sodalities, usually all-male or all-female, with secret initiation ceremonies.

sectorial fallowing Intensive horticulture; plots are cultivated for two to three years, then fallowed for three to five, with a longer rest after several of these shorter cycles.

sedentism Settled (sedentary) life; preceded food production in the Old World and followed it in the New World.

segmentary lineage organization (SLO) Political organization based on descent, usually patrilineal, with multiple descent segments that form at different genealogical levels and function in different contexts.

semantics A language's meaning system.

semiperiphery Structural position in the world system intermediate between core and periphery.

serial monogamy Marriage of a given individual to several spouses, but not at the same time.

sertão Arid interior of northeastern Brazil; backlands.

settlement hierarchy A ranked series of communities differing in size, function, and type of building; a three-level settlement hierarchy indicates state organization.

sexual dimorphism Marked differences in male and female biology, besides the contrasts in breasts and genitals, and temperament.

sexual orientation A person's habitual sexual attraction to, and activities with: persons of the opposite sex, *heterosexuality;* the same sex, *homosexuality;* or both sexes, *bisexuality.*

shaman A part-time religious practitioner who mediates between ordinary people and supernatural beings and forces.

sickle-cell anemia Usually fatal disease in which the red blood cells are shaped like crescents, or sickles, and increase the heart's burden by clogging the small blood vessels.

sisal Plant adapted to arid areas; its fiber is used to make rope.

Sivapithecus Widespread fossil group first found in Pakistan; includes specimens formerly called "*Ramapithecus*" and fossil apes from Turkey, China, and Kenya; early *Sivapithecus* may contain the common ancestor of the orangutan and the African apes; late *Sivapithecus* is now seen as ancestral to the modern orang.

slash and burn Form of horticulture in which the forest cover of a plot is cut down and burned before planting to allow the ashes to fertilize the soil.

slavery The most extreme, coercive, abusive, and inhumane form of legalized inequality; people are treated as property.

smelting The high-temperature process by which pure metal is produced from an ore.

social fund Scarce resources invested to assist friends, relatives, in-laws, and neighbors.

social race A group assumed to have a biological basis but actually perceived and defined in a social context, by a particular culture rather than by scientific criteria.

society Organized life in groups; typical of humans and other animals.

sociobiology The study of the evolutionary basis of social behavior.

sociolinguistics Study of relationships between social and linguistic variation; study of language (performance) in its social context.

sociopolitical typology Classification scheme based on the scale and complexity of social organization and the effectiveness of political regulation; includes band, tribe, chiefdom, and state.

sodality See *pantribal sodality.*

sororate Custom by which a widower marries the sister of the deceased wife.

speciation Formation of new species; occurs when subgroups of the same species are separated for a sufficient length of time.

species Population whose members can interbreed to produce offspring that can live and reproduce.

state (nation-state) Complex sociopolitical system that administers a territory and populace with substantial contrasts in occupation, wealth, prestige, and power. An independent, centrally organized political unit; a government. A form of social and political organization with a formal, central government and a division of society into classes.

status Any position that determines where someone fits in society; may be ascribed or achieved.

stereoscopic vision Ability to see in depth.

stereotypes Fixed ideas—often unfavorable—about what the members of a group are like.

stipulated descent Basis of the clan; members merely say they descend from their apical ancestor; they don't trace the actual genealogical links between themselves and that ancestor.

strategic resources Those necessary for life, such as food and space.

stratification Characteristic of a system with socioeconomic strata, sharp social divisions based on unequal access to wealth and power; see *stratum.*

stratified Class-structured; stratified societies have marked differences in wealth, prestige, and power between social classes.

stratigraphy Science that examines the ways in which earth sediments are deposited in demarcated layers known as *strata* (singular, *stratum*).

stratum One of two or more groups that contrast in regard to social status and access to strategic resources. Each stratum includes people of both sexes and all ages.

style shifts Variations in speech in different contexts.

subaltern Lower in rank, subordinate, traditionally lacking an influential role in decision making.

subcultures Different cultural traditions associated with subgroups in the same complex society.

subgroups Languages within a taxonomy of related languages that are most closely related.

suborder Group of closely related superfamilies.

subordinate The lower, or underprivileged, group in a stratified system.

subsistence fund Scarce resources invested to provide food in order to replace the calories expended in daily activity.

sumptuary goods Items whose consumption is limited to the elite.

superfamily Group of closely related zoological families.

superordinate The upper, or privileged, group in a stratified system.

supply and demand, law of Economic rule that things cost more the scarcer they are and the more people want them.

survey research Characteristic research procedure among social scientists other than anthropologists. Studies society through sampling, statistical analysis, and impersonal data collection.

symbiosis An obligatory interaction between groups that is beneficial to each.

symbol Something, verbal or nonverbal, that arbitrarily and by convention stands for something else, with which it has no necessary or natural connection.

syncretisms Cultural blends, or mixtures, including religious blends, that emerge from acculturation, particularly under colonialism, such as African, Native American, and Roman Catholic saints and deities in Caribbean vodun, or "voodoo," cults.

syntax The arrangement and order of words in phrases and sentences.

systematic survey Information gathered on patterns of settlement over a large area; provides a regional perspective on the archaeological record.

systemic perspective View that changes have multiple consequences, some unforeseen.

taboo Set apart as sacred and off-limits to ordinary people; prohibition backed by supernatural sanctions.

taphonomy The study of the processes—biological and geological—by which dead animals become fossils; from the Greek *taphos,* which means "tomb."

taxonomy Classification scheme; assignment to categories (*taxa;* singular, *taxon*).

teocentli Or *teosinte,* a wild grass; apparent ancestor of maize.

Teotihuacan A.D. 100 to 700, first state in the Valley of Mexico and earliest major Mesoamerican empire.

terrestrial Ground-dwelling.

text Something that is creatively "read," interpreted, and assigned meaning by each person who receives it; includes any media-borne image, such as *Carnaval.*

theory An explanatory framework, containing a series of statements, that helps us understand *why* (something exists); theories suggest patterns, connections, and relationships that may be confirmed by new research.

Third World The less-developed countries (LDCs).

Thomson's nose rule Rule stating that the average nose tends to be longer in areas with lower mean annual temperatures; based on the geographic distribution of nose length among human populations.

totem An animal or plant apical ancestor of a clan.

traditions, in tool making Coherent patterns of tool manufacture.

transecting groups Networks created through direct communication channels between groups that previously had, or otherwise have, trouble communicating—for example, physicians and patients.

transhumance One of two variants of pastoralism; part of the population moves seasonally with the herds while the other part remains in home villages.

tribe Form of sociopolitical organization usually based on horticulture or pastoralism. Socioeconomic stratification and centralized rule are absent in tribes, and there is no means of enforcing political decisions.

tropics Geographic belt extending about 23 degrees north and south of the equator, between the Tropic of Cancer (north) and the Tropic of Capricorn (south).

tundra Cold, treeless plains.

typology, economic See *economic typology.*

typology, sociopolitical See *sociopolitical typology.*

underdifferentiation Planning fallacy of viewing less-developed countries as an undifferentiated group; ignoring cultural diversity and adopting a uniform approach (often ethnocentric) for very different types of project beneficiaries.

uniformitarianism Belief that explanations for past events should be sought in ordinary forces that continue to work today.

unilineal descent Matrilineal or patrilineal descent.

unilocal Either patrilocal or matrilocal postmarital residence; requires that a married couple reside with the relatives of either the husband or the wife, depending on the society.

universal Something that exists in every culture.

Upper Paleolithic Blade-toolmaking traditions associated with early *H. sapiens sapiens;* named from their location in upper, or more recent, layers of sedimentary deposits.

urban anthropology The anthropological study of cities.

uterine Primate groups made up of mothers, sisters, daughters, and sons that have not emigrated.

variables Attributes (e.g., sex, age, height, weight) that differ from one person or case to the next.

vertical economy Economy based on environmental zones that, although close together in space, contrast in altitude, rainfall, overall climate, and vegetation.

vertical mobility Upward or downward change in a person's social status.

visual predation theory Theory that the primates evolved in lower branches and undergrowth by developing visual and tactile abilities to aid in hunting and snaring insects.

wealth All a person's material assets, including income, land, and other types of property; the basis of economic status.

westernization The acculturative influence of Western expansion on native cultures.

working class Or proletariat; those who must sell their labor to survive; the antithesis of the bourgeoisie in Marx's class analysis.

Würm The last glacial; began around 75,000 B.P. and ended between 17,000 and 12,000 B.P.

zygote Fertilized egg, created by the union of two sex cells, one from each parent.

credits

PHOTO CREDITS

Chapter 1

1: Lawrence Migdale/Photo Researchers. **2:** Eastcott/Momotiuk/Woodfin Camp & Assoc. **3:** Jeff Greenberg/Visuals Unlimited, Inc. **5:** Eric Sampers/Gamma Liaison. **7:** Smithsonian Institution. **8:** Catherine Karnow/Woodfin Camp & Assoc. **8:** Lindsay Hebberd/Woodfin Camp & Assoc. **9:** Barton Silverman/The New York Times. **10:** Tom Kienzle/AP/Wide World Photos. **11:** Roberto Pfeil/AP/Wide World Photos. **13:** Jerald T. Milanich. **15:** J. Kyle Keener. **16:** Kenneth Garrett/National Geographic Society. **17:** Jorgen Schytte/Still Pictures/Peter Arnold, Inc. **18:** Mark Edwards/Still Pictures/Peter Arnold, Inc. **23:** Corbis-Bettmann. **25:** Courtesy Alicia Wilbur. **26:** National Geographic Society.

Chapter 2

32: Wesley Bocxe/Photo Researchers. **33:** Professor Marietta Baba, Wayne State University. **36:** Irven DeVore/Anthro-Photo. **37:** Michael Newman/PhotoEdit. **38:** Peggy &Yoran Kahana/Peter Arnold, Inc. **39:** Lawrence Migdale/Photo Researchers. **40:** Georges Ollen/Corbis Sygma. **41:** British Library of Political & Economic Science, London School of Economics and Political Science. **44:** Christopher M. O'Leary. **45:** Kenneth Garrett/National Geographic Society. **46:** Scott Goldsmith. **50:** Rob Kalman/The Image Works. **51:** John Maier/Still Pictures/Peter Arnold, Inc. **53:** Angela C. Stuesse. **54:** William Campbell/Corbis Sygma.

Chapter 3

59: Pierre Boulat/Woodfin Camp & Assoc. **60:** Joel Satore/National Geographic Society. **61:** Israel Talby/Woodfin Camp & Assoc. **63:** *Noah's Ark* by Edward Hicks, 1846, 261/2 x 301/2, Oil on canvas, Philadelphia Museum of Art, Bequest of Lisa Norris Elkins. **68:** Dr. Gopal Mujrti/Phototake. **69:** Jean-Marc Giboux/Gamma Liaison. **70:** Alfred Pasieka/Peter Arnold, Inc. **72:** Bruce Dale/National Geographic Society. **74:** Peter Menzel/Stock, Boston. **75:** Novosti/Science Photo Library/Photo Researchers. **77:** Vivian Moos/The Stock Market. **79:** Robert Caputo/Stock, Boston. **79:** Dennis Stock/Magnum. **80:** Marcello Bertinetti/Photo Researchers.

Chapter 4

84: Beth A. Keiser/AP/Wide World Photos. **85:** Orangutan Foundation International. **87:** Mike K. Nichols/Magnum. **90:** Kenneth Garrett/National Geographic Society. **91:** O. Langrand/Peter Arnold, Inc. **94:** Peter Weimann/Animals,Animals. **96:** Mack Henley/Visuals Unlimited. **97:** Peter Veit/DRK. **100:** M. Gunther/Peter Arnold, Inc. **101:** Jane Goodall/National Geographic Society. **102:** G.Ziesler/Peter Arnold, Inc. **106:** Courtesy Jennifer Burns. **107:** Peter Johnson/Corbis. **108:** Courtesy Natalie Cummings.

Chapter 5

114: A. Compost/Bios/Peter Arnold, Inc. **115:** Kim Reed-Deemer, Northern Illinois University. **117:** Leonardo L.T. Rhodes/Earth Sciences/Animals Animals. **120:** Y. Arthus/Peter Arnold, Inc. **122:** L. & D. Klein/Photo Researchers. **123:** Denver Museum of Natural History. **123:** Tom McHugh/Photo Researchers. **124:** Tom McHugh/Photo Researchers. **124:** Tom Walker/Stock, Boston. **126:** Cabisco/Visuals Unlimited. **128:** Science VU/Visuals Unlimited. **128:** Manoj Shah/Animals Animals. **129:** Russell Ciochon. **131:** Courtesy Barbara Hewitt. **132:** From *Rhetorica Christiana*, by Didacus Valades, 1579.

Chapter 6

136: Kenneth Garrett. **137:** B.G. Richmond and D.S. Strait. **139:** Fred Mayer/Magnum. **143:** John Reader/Science Photo Library/Photo Researchers. **150:** Maurico Anton/National Geographic Society. **151:** Luba Dmytryk/National Geographic Society. **151:** Des Bartlett/Photo Researchers. **152:** Alan Walker, Johns Hopkins University/National Museums of Kenya, Kalakol Account. **155:** Courtesy Josh Trapani.

Chapter 7

160: Pierre Boulat/Woodfin Camp & Assoc. **161:** Gouram Tsibakhashvili/AP/Wide World Photos. **163:** Richard Schlecht/National Geographic Society. **164–165:** Luba Dmytryk/National Geographic Society. **164:** Kenneth Garrett/National Geographic Society. **167:** Jay Kelley/Anthro-Photo. **170:** E.R. Degginger/Earth Scenes. **170:** Tom McHugh/Photo Researchers. **173:** Kenneth Garrett/National Geographic Society. **173:** Kenneth Garrett/National Geographic Society. **174:** E.R. Degginger/Animals Animals. **174:** Kenneth Garrett/National Geographic Society. **180:** Michael Busselle/Corbis. **181:** Medford Taylor/National Geographic Society. **183:** Jean-Marie Chauvet/Corbis Sygma. **184:** Courtesy Kelsey Foster.

Chapter 8

188: J. Pozarik/Gamma Liaison. **189:** Michelle V. Agins/*The New York Times*. **191:** Paul Grebliunas/Tony Stone Images. **194:** Sabine Vielmo/Peter Arnold, Inc. **194:** Penny Tweedie/Woodfin Camp & Assoc. **195:** Tompix/Peter Arnold, Inc. **195:** Jan Spieczny/Peter Arnold, Inc. **197:** Hartmut Schwarzbach/Peter Arnold, Inc. **198:** Donna Binder/Impact Visuals. **199:** W. Bokelberg/The Image Bank. **200:** Chris O'Meam/AP/World Wide Photos. **202:** P.J. Griffiths/Magnum. **203:** Mark Edwards/Peter Arnold, Inc. **204:** Courtesy Heather Norton.

Chapter 9

210: Jean Paul Kay/Peter Arnold, Inc. **211:** Kenneth Garrett/National Geographic Society. **213:** Erich Lessing/Art Resource, NY. **216:** Nevada Wier/The Image Bank. **218:** Mike Yamashita/Woodfin Camp & Assoc. **221:** Hinterleitner/Gamma Liaison. **222:** Michael Andrews/Earth Scenes. **224:** Janet Foster/Masterfile. **227:** Phil Schermeister/Corbis. **227:** Ron Giling/Peter Arnold, Inc.

228: Schalkwijk/Art Resource, NY. **231:** Photofest. **232:** John Isaac/Peter Arnold. **233:** Courtesy Maxine N. Oland.

Chapter 10

238: Dilip Mehta/Woodfin Camp & Assoc. **239:** Stephen D. Houston, Dept. of Anthropology, BYU. **242:** Ancient Art and Architecture Collection Ltd./Bridgeman Art Library. **244:** Francis Dias/Newspix/Corbis Saba. **245:** Heinz Plenge/Peter Arnold, Inc. **248:** Erich Lessing/Art Resource, NY. **248:** Barry Iverson/Woodfin Camp & Assoc. **249:** Georg Gerster/Photo Researchers. **249:** Ashmolean Museum, Oxford/Bridgeman Art Library. **250:** Khue Bui/AP/Wide World Photos. **250:** Freer Gallery of Art. **253:** Walter H. Hodge/Peter Arnold, Inc. **254:** Jacques Jangoux/Peter Arnold, Inc. **254:** Scala/Art Resource, NY. **255:** Daniel Sheehan/The Image Works. **256:** Mark Edwards/Still Pictures/Peter Arnold, Inc. **259:** Courtesy Jerusha Achterberg. **260:** Kenneth Garrett/National Geographic Society.

Chapter 11

265: Micha Bar'am/Magnum. **266:** Michelle Burgess/The Stock Market. **267:** Hiroshi Harada/Dunq/Photo Researchers. **271:** Jason Homa/The Image Bank. **271:** Ted Spiegel/Corbis. **272:** AFP/Corbis. **273:** John Mechling/FPG. **273:** Terry Ashe/Gamma Liaison. **275:** Kim Newton/Woodfin Camp & Assoc. **277:** D. Halleux/Peter Arnold. **279:** Noboru Komine/Photo Researchers. **279:** Bob Daemmrich/The Image Works. **281:** Courtesy Mark Dennis. **282:** Barry Iverson.

Chapter 12

288: Djenidi/Sidali/Gamma Liaison. **289:** David Longstreath/AP/Wide World Photos. **291:** T. Arruza/The Image Works. **293:** Bill Greenblatt/Gamma Liaison. **295:** Luigi Baldelli/Contrasto/Corbis Saba. **297:** Stephanie Maze/Woodfin Camp & Assoc. **298:** Allan Chin/Corbis Sygma. **300:** Alain Buu/Gamma Liaison. **303:** Henry Hurtak/Corbis Sygma. **304:** Mark Ludak/Impact Visuals. **305:** J. Jones/Corbis Sygma. **307:** Diego Goldberg/Corbis Sygma.

Chapter 13

314: L. Mangino/The Image Works. **315:** CBS Photo Archive. **317:** Michael Nichols/Magnum. **320:** David W. Hamilton/The Image Bank. **324:** Lonny Shavelson/Impact Visuals. **325:** Michael Newman/PhotoEdit. **326:** D.R. Stoecklein/The Stock Market. **328:** Photofest. **329:** Charles Gupton/Stock, Boston. **331:** James Nachtwey/Magnum. **333:** John Ricard/Retna. **337:** Courtesy Jasan DeCaro. **338:** Peter Charlesworth/Corbis Saba.

Chapter 14

344: Steve McCurry/National Geographic Society. **345:** Pallava Bagla, Delhi. **349:** Thand Samuels Abell II/National Geographic Society. **350:** D. Halleux/Bios/Peter Arnold, Inc. **351:** Lineair/Peter Arnold, Inc. **353:** Paul Chesley/Tony Stone Images. **355:** The Image Bank. **355:** H. Schwarzbach/Argus Fotoarchiv/Peter Arnold, Inc. **357:** Victor Englebert. **357:** Bill Gillette/Stock, Boston. **359:** Steve Raymer/National Geographic Society. **363:** John Eastcott/Yva Momatiuk/Woodfin Camp & Assoc. **366:** Elbridge W. Merrill Collection/Alaska State Library and Archives, # PCA57-028. **366:** Lawrence Migdale/Stock, Boston.

Chapter 15

372: Rafael Macia/Photo Researchers. **373:** Carlos Osorio/AP/Wide World Photos. **375:** Mark Edwards/Still Pictures/Peter Arnold, Inc. **376:** James L. Stanfield/National Geographic Society. **377:** Terry E. Eiler/Stock, Boston. **379:** Najlah Feanny/Stock, Boston. **380:** Newsmakers/Gamma Liaison. **383:** Photofest. **385:** D.H. Hessell/Stock, Boston. **385:** John Eastcott/Yva Momatiuk/Stock, Boston. **387:** Richard Olenius/National Geographic Society.

Chapter 16

396: Micha Bar'am/Magnum. **397:** Tyler Hicks/Gamma Liaison. **399:** Donna Binder/Impact Visuals. **401:** Betty Press/Woodfin Camp & Assoc. **403:** Mark Edwards/Peter Arnold, Inc. **405:** DPA/The Images Works. **407:** Pablo Bartholomew/Gamma Liaison. **408:** Cary Wolinsky/Stock, Boston. **409:** Gerard Rancinam/Corbis Sygma. **415:** Mark Edwards/Still Pictures/Peter Arnold, Inc. **416:** Frank Fouriner/Contact Press Images. **418:** Thomas Kelly.

Chapter 17

424: Eraldo Peres/AP/Wide World Photos. **425:** Abbas/Magnum. **427:** Ken Lambert/Gamma Liaison. **431:** Jason Lauré/Woodfin Camp & Assoc. **432:** John Maier/The Image Works. **433:** Burt Glinn/Magnum. **436:** Bloss/Anthro-Photo. **438:** Library of Congress (LC-USZC2-3231). **440:** Douglas Kirkland/The Image Bank. **442:** Mike Schneps/The Image Bank. **443:** Topham/The Image Works. **446:** R. H. Beck Courtesy Department Library Services, American Museum of Natural History. **447:** L. Schwartzwald/Corbis Sygma. **449:** C. Karnow/Woodfin Camp & Associates. **451:** Courtesy Abby Dreibelbis.

Chapter 18

458: Paul S. Howell/Gamma Liaison. **459:** Rick Friedman. **461:** Steve McCurry/Magnum. **463:** Steve McCutcheon/Visuals Unlimited. **464:** Wedny Stone/Gamma Liaison. **465:** Stuart Franklin/Magnum. **466:** Micheal Peletz, Hamilton , NY. **468:** Harvey/Magnum. **469:** George Holton/Photo Researchers. **475:** Bruno Barbey/Magnum. **476:** Bruno Veysset/Corbis Saba. **476:** Martha Cooper/Peter Arnold. Inc. **478:** Norman Rockwell Family Trust Copyright © 1943 the Norman Rockwell Family Trust. **480:** Greg Meadors/Stock, Boston.

Chapter 19

486: Anat Givon/AP/Wide World Photos. **487:** Index Stock. **489:** Erich Lessing/Art Resource, NY. **490:** David Alan Harvey/Woodfin Camp & Assoc. **492:** Peter Essick/Aurora. **493:** Bruno Barbey/Magnum. **494:** Thierry Secretan/Cosmos/ Woodfin Camp & Assoc. **494:** Micheal Minardi/Peter Arnold, Inc. **496:** Michele Burgess/The Stock Market. **499:** Carlos Villalon/Impact Visuals. **500:** Anthro-Photo. **506:** Kal Muller/Woodfin Camp & Associates. **509:** © Disney Enterprises, Inc.

Chapter 20

516: F. Schreider/Photo Researchers. **517:** Carolina Salguero. **520:** P.J.

Griffiths/Magnum Photos. **521:** Thomas Hoepker/Magnum Photos. **526:** James P. Blair/National Geogaphic Society. **526:** Abbas/Magnum. **527:** Bruce Hunter/National Geographic Society. **528:** Robert Frerck/The Stock Market. **529:** Yva Momatiuk & John Eastcott/Woodfin Camp & Assoc. **533:** Cary Wolinsky/Stock, Boston. **533:** Stephanie Maze/Woodfin Camp & Assoc. **535:** James P. Blair/National Geographic Society. **535:** Joan Marcus. **537:** Courtesy Anne Haggerson.

Chapter 21

541: Andres Hernandez/Gamma Liaison. **542:** Bessard/REA/Corbis Saba. **543:** Graham Ashford/International Institute for Sustainable Development, Winnipeg. **545:** Hiroji Kubota/Magnum. **546:** Bruce Dale/National Geographic Society. **546:** David Reed/Material World. **548:** Mercury Archives/The Image Bank. **550:** Hulton Getty/Gamma Liaison. **551:** Hulton Getty/Gamma Liaison. **551:** Culver. **554:** Dilip Mehta/Woodfin Camp & Assoc. **555:** New York Public Library. **561:** Jean-Yves Rabeuf/The Image Works. **564:** J. Schytte/Still Pictures/Peter Arnold, Inc. **564:** V.Leloup/Gamma Liaison. **565:** Nick Procaylo/AP/Wide World Photos.

Chapter 22

570: Mark Edwards/Still Pictures/Peter Arnold, Inc. **571:** Reuters/STR/Archive Photos. **575:** Roger Viollet/Gamma Liaison. **578:** Stuart Franklin/Magnum. **579:** Alexander Low/Woodfin Camp & Assoc. **581:** Ricardo Funari/Impact Visuals. **583:** Jorgen Schytte/Still Pictures/Peter Arnold, Inc. **584:** Bruno Barbey/Magnum. **585:** Lineair/Peter Arnold, Inc. **587:** Marc & Evelyn Bernheim/Woodfin Camp & Assoc. **588:** UNEP/Peter Arnold, Inc. **589:** Photographers Photos Co. Beijing/Gamma Liaison. **590:** Noorani/Still Pictures/Peter Arnold, Inc. **590:** Dr. Steven Lansing.

Chapter 23

596: John Eastcott/Yva Momatiuk/Photo Researchers. **597:** Richard Strauss/Smithsonian Institution/National Museum of the American Indian. **599:** Gamma Liaison. **600:** Gueorgui Pinkhassov/Magnum. **603:** Steven Feld. **605:** Rob Crandall/Stock, Boston. **608:** Buu/Deville/Turpin/Gamma Liaison. **609:** Andres Hernandez/Gamma Liaison. **610:** H. Schwarzbach/Still Pictures/Peter Arnold, Inc. **611:** John Maier/Still Pictures/Peter Arnold, Inc. **612:** Peter Marlow/Magnum. **614:** Ricardo Funari/Impact Visuals.

Chapter 24

620: Mark Edwards/Still Pictures/Peter Arnold, Inc. **621:** Van Etten/PhotoEdit. **625:** Peter Menzel. **628:** Mark Edwards/Still Pictures/Peter Arnold, Inc. **630:** G. Saussier/Lineair/Peter Arnold, Inc. **630:** A. Arbib/Still Pictures/Peter Arnold, Inc. **632:** Alon Reininger/Woodfin Camp & Assoc. **633:** Erich Lessing/Magnum. **634:** Mark Edwards/Still Pictures/ Peter Arnold, Inc. **635:** UNEP/Peter Arnold, Inc. **635:** YoramKahana/Peter Arnold, Inc. **638:** Thomas Hoepker/ Magnum. **640:** Courtesy Beau J. Goldstein.

TEXT AND ILLUSTRATION CREDITS

Front Matter

ii–iii: Map based on Michael Kidron and Ronald Segal, "Addition and Division 50," in *State of the World Atlas*, New Revised Edition, pp. 122 and 123. Copyright © 1995 by Myriad Editions Limited, maps and graphics. Used by permission of Viking Penguin, a division of Penguin Books USA Inc.

Chapter 1

2–3: Reagan Duplisea, "Public Opinion Pollings Finds Great Support for Archaeology, Discover Archaeology, 6/20/00 in www.discoveringarchaeology.com. Copyright © 2000. Reprinted by permission. **12–13:** Excerpt adapted from Assault on Paradise: Social Change in a Brazilian Village, 2nd Edition, by Conrad Phillip Kottak. Copyright © 1992. Reproduced by permission of The McGraw-Hill Companies.

Chapter 2

32–33: Elizabeth Weise, "Anthropologists Adapt Technology to World's Culture," 5/26/99 in www.usatoday.com, Copyright © 1999. USA TODAY. Reprinted with permission.

Chapter 3

60–61: Nicolas Wade, "Y Chromosome Bears Witness to Story of the Jewish Diaspora," *The New York Times*, 5/9/00,on www.nytimes.com. Copyright by The New York Times Company. Reprinted by permission. **71:** Figure 3.5 adapted from Human Evolution by Joseph B. Birdsell. Copyright © 1981, 1975, 1972 HarperCollins Publishers, Inc. Reproduce by permission of HarperCollins Publishers, Inc. **76–77:** Excerpts from Gina Kolata, "Human Cloning: Yesterday's Never is Today's Why Not?" *The New York Times*, 12/2/97, in www.nytimes.com. Copyright © 1997 by The New York Times Company. Reprinted by permission.

Chapter 4

84–85: Claudia Dreifus, "Saving the Orangutan, Preserving Paradise," *The New York Times*, 3/21/00, in www.nytimes.com. Copyright © 2000 by The New York Times Company. Reprinted by permission. **89:** Table 4.2 adapted from R. Martin, "Classification of Primates," in The Cambridge Encyclopedia of Human Evolution, edited by S. Jones, R. Martin, & D. Polbeam, pp. 20–21. Cambridge University Press, 1992. Used by permission. **90:** Figure 4.2 from Human Evolution: An Illustrated Introduction, 3rd Edition, by Roger Lewin. P. 44. Blackwell Scientific Publishers, 1993. Used by permission. **98:** Figure 4.6 from Physical Anthropology and Archaeology, 4th Edition, by Clifford J. Jolly and F. Plog, p. 115. Copyright © 1986. Reproduced by permission of The McGraw-Hill Companies. **99:** Figure 4.7 from Human Evolution: An Illustrated Introduction, 3rd Edition, by Roger Lewin, p. 45. Blackwell Scientific Publication, 1993. Used by permission. **104–105:** Excerpts from Verne G.

Kopoff, "Meat Viewed as Staple of Chimp Diet and Mores," *The New York Times*, 6/27/95, pp. B5-B6. Copyright "1995 by The New York Times Company. Reprinted by permission.

Chapter 5

114–115: John Noble Wilford, "Tiny Fossil Animal May Link Lower Primates with Humans," *The New York Times*, 3/16/00, in www.nytimes.com. Copyright © 2000 by The New York Times Company. Reprinted by permission. **124:** Figure 5.3 from Introduction to Physical Anthropology, 6th Edition, by Robert Jurmain and Harry Nelson, p. 210. Minneapolis West Publishing, 1994. Reprinted by permission. **127:** Figure 5.4 from Introduction to Physical Anthropology, 6th Edition, by Robert Jurmain and Harry Nelson, p. 302. Minneapolis West Publishing, 1994. Reprinted by permission.

Chapter 6

136–137: Kenneth Chang, "Walk Like an Ape," Daily News, 3/22/00, in www.abcnews.com. Copyright © 2000 ABC News Internet Ventures. Reprinted with permission. **144–145:** John Noble Wilford, "The Transforming Leap, from 4 Leg to 2," *The New York Times*, 9/5/95, pp. B5(N)/C1(L). Copyright © 1995 by The New York Times Company. Reprinted by permission.

Chapter 7

160–161: "Hominids in Europe: Skulls Probably Represent First Populations to Migrate from Africa, © Daily News, 5/12/00, in www.abcnews.go.com. Copyright © 2000 Reuters. Reprinted by permission. **163:** Gary Larson, Far Side Cartoon, 4/28/83. © Chronicle Features, 1983. The Far Side cartoon by Gary Larson is reprinted by permission of Chronicle Features, San Francisco, CA. All rights reserved. **168:** Figure 7.1 from Physical Anthropology and Archaeology, 5th Edition, by Clifford J. Jolly and Randall White, p.271. Copyright © 1995. Reproduced with permission of The McGraw-Hill Companies. **169:** Figure 7.2 from Physical Anthropology and Archaeology, 5th Edition, by Clifford J. Jolly and Randall White, p. 68. Copyright © 1995. Reproduced with permission of The McGraw-Hill Companies. **176:** Figure 7.4 from Physical Anthropology and Archaeology, 5th Edition, by Clifford J. Jolly and Randall White, p. 277. Copyright © 1995. Reproduced with permission of The McGraw-Hill Companies. **182–183:** Excerpts from Marlise Simons, "Prehistoric Art Treasure is found in French Cave," *The New York Times*, 1/19/93, pp. A1, A5. Copyright © 1993 by The New York Times Company. Reprinted by permission.

Chapter 8

188–189: Thomas J. Lueck, "No Fare: New York Cabbies Shoe How Multi-Colored Racism Can Be," *The New York Times*, 11/7/99, in www.nytimes.com. Copyright © 1999 by The New York Times Company. Reprinted by permission. **192-193:** American Anthropological Association Statement on "Race," May 1998. Used by permission. **196:** Figure 8.1 adapted from Human Evolution by Joseph B. Birdsell. Copyright © 1981, 1975, 1972 HarperCollins Publishers, Inc. Reproduced by permission of HarperCollins Publishers, Inc.

Chapter 9

210–211: Ron Todt, "Western Hemisphere Inhabited at Least 15,000 Years Ago," Daily News, 4/7/00, in www.abcnes.go.com. Copyright © 2000 The Associated Press. Reprinted by permission. **220–221:** Excerpts from Boyce Rosenberger, "A Man Who Lived 5,300 Years Ago," The Washington Post, 11/26/92, p. E1. © 1992, The Washington Post. Reprinted with permission. **223:** Fgure 9.4 from The Emergence of Agriculture by B.D. Smith. Copyright "1995. Scientific American Library. Reproduced by permission.

Chapter 10

238–239: Rossella Lorenzi, "Mayan Stone TabletDepicts Horror," 6/30/00, in Discovery.com. Copyright © 2000 Discovery.com. Reprinted by permission. **251:** Figure 10.2 based on Map 1-1, Chapter 1, "Birth of Civilization," in The Heritage of World Civilizations, Volume 1 to 1650, 4th Edition, by Albert M. Craig. Copyright © 1997, Prentice Hall Publishing Company. Reprinted by permission. **252:** Figure 10.3 from Physical Anthropology and Archaeology, 5th Edition, by Clifford J. Jolly and Randall White, p. 115. Copyright © 1885. Reproduced with permission of The McGraw-Hill Companies.

Chapter 11

266–267: Howard W. French, "In ModernJapan, Personal Expression Often Frowned Upon," *The New York Times*, 5/22/00, in Seattle-i.nwsource.com. Copyright © 2000, The New York Times. Reprinted by permission.

Chapter 12

288–289: Judith Miller, "Encyclopedia Raises Veil on Ancient Saudi Culture," *The New York Times*, 6/30/00, in www.nytimes.com. Copyright © 2000, *The New York Times*. Reprinted by permission. **292–293:** Excerpts from Bill Dedman, "Sosa v. McGwire: It's a Race, But is it About Race?" *The New York Times*, 9/20/98. Copyright © 1998 by The New York Times Company. Reprinted by permission. **301:** Figure 12.3 from P. Martin and E. Midgley, "Immigration to the United States: Journey to an Uncertain Destination," Population Bulletin 1994, 49(3): 1-47. Reprinted by permission of Population Reference Bureau, Inc.

Chapter 13

314–315: Scott Pelley, "Children without Language, so They Invent One of Their Own," CBS News, in www.cbsnes.cbs.com, 5/14/00. Copyright © 2000, CBS Worldwide, Inc. Reprinted by permission. **318:** Cartoon © 1999 by Sidney Harris. **322:** Figure 13.1 with excerpts from Aspects of Language, Third Edition, by Dwight L. Bolinger and Donald A. Sears. Copyright © 1981 by Harcourt & Company. Reproduced by permission of pubisher. **328:** Table 13.3 from Sociolinguistics: An Introduction to Language and Society by Peter Trudgill, p. 85. Copyright © 1974, 1983. Reproduced by permission of Penguin Books Ltd. **330–331:** Excerpts from

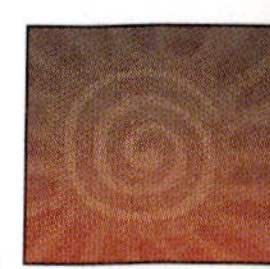

Nicholas D. Kristof, "Japan's Feminine Falsetto Falls Out of Favor," *The New York Times*, 12/13/95, pp. A1, A4. Copyright © 1995 by The New York Times Company, Reprinted by permission. **335:** Figure 13.2 by Thomas C. Moore in "Early History of Indo-European Languages," by Thomas V. Gamkrelidze & V.V. Lanov (with reference to Paul Thieme, "The Indo-European Language," Scientific American, October 1958), Scientific American, March 1990, p. 11. Used with permission. **338:** Table 13.5 base on Lipke 2000.

Chapter 14

344–345: Pallava Bagla, "Tradition Knowledge Brings Bloom Back to India, © National Geographic, in www.ngnews.cbs.com, 5/31/00. Copyright © 2000, National Geographic. Reprinted by permission. **347:** Figure 14.1 by Ray Sim from People of the Stone Age: Hunters and Gatherers & Early Farmers. Illustrated History of Human kind Series. Garan Burenhult, General Editor, Harper-Collins Publishers, Copyright © 1993. Used by permission.

Chapter 15

372–373: Matt Crenson, "Anthropologists Turn to Exotic New Type of Human : The American Middle Class," Fox News, in www.foxnews.com, 7/9/00. Copyright © 2000, Fox News. Reprinted by permission.

Chapter 16

396–397: Ian Fisher, Young Man Decides to Wive it Wealthily in Uganda," *The New York Times*, in www.nytimes.com, 7/5/00. Copyright © 2000, The New York Times Company. Reprinted by permission. **410–411:** Excerpts from Daniel Goleman, "Anthropology Goes Looking in All the Wrong Places," *The New York Times*, 11/24/92, p. B1. copyright © 1995 by The New York Times Company. Reprinted by permission.

Chapter 17

424–425: Ilene R. Prusher, "Chat Rooms, Bedouin Style, National Geographic, in www.ngnews.cbs.com, 4/28/00. Copyright © 2000 The Christian Science Publishing Society. Reprinted by permission.

Chapter 18

458-459: Claudia Dreifus, "A Conversation with Dr. Nawal M. Nour: A Life Devoted to Stopping the Suffering of Mutilation," *The New York Times*, in www.nytimes.com, 7/1/00 Copyright © 2000 The New York Times Company. Reprinted by permission. **473:** Table 18.1 from Kay Martin and Barbara Voorhies, Female of the Species, p. 283. Copyright © 1975 by Columbia University Press. Reprinted with permission of the publisher. **479, 480, 481:** tables 18.2, 18.3, 18.4 from Statistical Abstract of the United States, Edition (Austin, TX: Reference Press, 1996) pp. 416-417, 446, 477.

Chapter 19

486–487: Karen Lincoln Michel, "For Native American Church, Peyote is Sacred," Journal Sentinel, in www.jsonline.com, 12/17/00. copyright © 1999 Journal Sentinel, Inc. Reprinted by permission. **493:** Table 19.1 adapted from The Ritual Process by Victor W. Turner. Copyright © 1969 by Victor W. Turner. By permission of Aldine de Gruyter, New York. **498–499:** Excerpts from John F. Burns, "A Year of Harsh Islamic Rule Weighs Heavily for Afghans," 9/24/97, abridged from www.nytimes.com. Copyright © 1997 The New York Times Company. Used by permission.

Chapter 20

516–517: Matt Crenson, "Is There a Music Gene? Scholars Mull Music's Roots," Fox New, in www.foxnew.com, 7/17/00. Copyright © 2000. Reprinted by permission.

Chapter 21

542–543: Lisa Krause, "Global Warming Melts Inuit's Arctic Lifestyle," National Geographic Society, in www.ngnews.cbs.com, 7/12/00. Copyright © 2000, National Geographic Society. Reprinted by permission. **558–559:** Table 21.1 and Figure 21.1 from Thomas Richard Shannon, An Introduction to the World-System Perspective, 1989, Boulder, Colorado. Reprinted by permission. **559:** Table 21.2 from Anthropology and Contemporary Human Problems by John H. Bodley, 1985. Reprinted by permission of Mayfield Publishing, Mountain View, CA.

Chapter 22

570–571: Alan Cowell, "Britain in Africa: Colonialism's Legacy Becomes a Burden, 6/10/00, from www.nytimes.com. Copyright © 2000 The New York Times Company. Used by permission. **574:** Figure 22.2 from The Times Atlas of World History, 4th Edition, by Geoffrey Parker, Editor, p. 236. Times Books, HarperCollins, London, Reprinted by permission. **581:** table 22.1 from Gross and Underwood, p. 733. 1971. **588:** Excerpts from Erik Eckholm, Foreign Desk, 3/12/98, "Relocations for China Dam Are Found to Lag," *The New York Times* 365-Day Archive, Encyclopedia Britannica Online. Copyright © 1998. Used by permission.

Chapter 23

596–597: Ellen Herscher, "A Museum to Right Pat Wrongs," www.archaeology.org, 12/6/99. Copyright © 1999 by the Archaeological Institute of America. Used by permission. **602–603:** Based on Steven Field, "Voices of the Rainforest," Public Culture, 1991 4(1): 131-140. Reprinted by permission.

Chapter 24

620–621: Lawrence K. Altman, "Mystery Factor is Pondered at AIDS Talk: Circumcision," 7/11/00, from www.nytimes.com. Copyright © 2000 The New York Times Company. Reprinted by permission. **626–627:** Excerpts from Malcom W. Browne, "Buried on a Hillside, Clues to Terror," *The New York Times*, 2/23/99, Copyright © 1999 by The New York Times Company. Reprinted by permission. **637:** Excerpts from Del Jones, "Hot Asset in Corporate: Anthropology Degrees," USA Today, 2/18/91, p.B1. Copyright © 1991. Reprinted by permission.

Appendix

648: Adapted from Prime-Time Society: An Anthropological Analysis of Television and Culture by Conrad Phillip Kottak. Copyright © 1990 by Wadsworth, Inc. Used by permission of the publisher.

name index

subject index